P9-CKA-841

lonely planet

Pacific Northwest

Daniel C Schechter
Jennifer Snarski
Debra Miller
Judy Jewell

LONELY PLANET PUBLICATIONS
Melbourne • Oakland • London • Paris

PACIFIC NORTHWEST

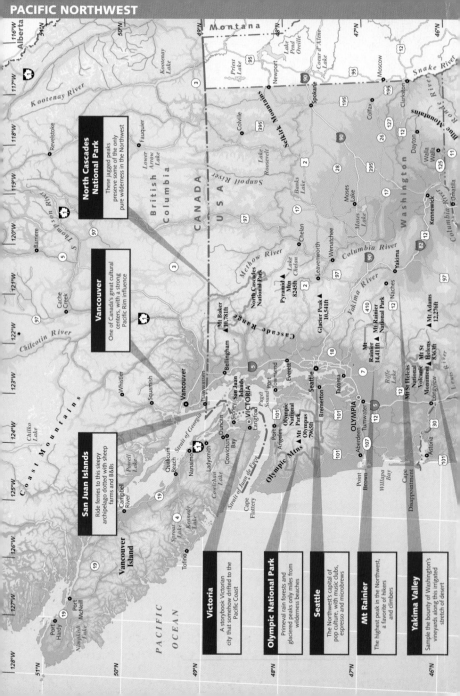

North Cascades National Park
These jagged peaks preserve some of the only pure wilderness in the Northwest

Vancouver
One of Canada's great cultural centers, with a strong Pacific Rim influence

San Juan Islands
Ride ferries to this sleepy archipelago dotted with sheep farms and B&Bs

Victoria
A storybook Victorian city that somehow drifted to the Pacific Coast

Olympic National Park
Primeval rain forests and glaciered peaks only miles from wilderness beaches

Seattle
The Northwest's capital of pop culture, with music clubs, espresso and microbrews

Mt Rainier
The highest peak in the Northwest, a favorite of hikers and climbers

Yakima Valley
Sample the bounty of Washington's vineyards along this irrigated stretch of desert

SOUTHEASTERN WASHINGTON 581

FACTS ABOUT BRITISH COLUMBIA 603

VANCOUVER 617

WHISTLER & THE SUNSHINE COAST 663

VANCOUVER ISLAND 677

THANKS 716

INDEX 718

MAP LEGEND 728

PACIFIC NORTHWEST MAP INDEX

Alberta

British
Columbia

WHISTLER &
THE SUNSHINE COAST
page 663

0   50   100 km
0   30   60 miles

VANCOUVER
ISLAND
page 677

VANCOUVER
page 617

NORTHWESTERN
WASHINGTON &
THE SAN JUAN ISLANDS
page 387

CANADA

USA

NORTH
CASCADES
page 462

NORTHEASTERN
WASHINGTON
page 551

Idaho

OLYMPIC
PENINSULA
page 418

SEATTLE
page 315

SOUTH
SOUND
page 369

CENTRAL
WASHINGTON
page 520

SOUTHEASTERN
WASHINGTON
page 581

SOUTHWESTERN
WASHINGTON
page 444

SOUTH
CASCADES
page 498

PACIFIC

OCEAN

COLUMBIA RIVER
GORGE & MT HOOD
page 124

PORTLAND
page 99

NORTHEASTERN
OREGON
page 283

WILLAMETTE
VALLEY
page 205

CENTRAL
OREGON
page 267

OREGON
COAST
page 150

SOUTHERN
OREGON
page 240

SOUTHEASTERN
OREGON
page 302

OTHER MAPS
Pacific Northwest – after title page
Pacific Northwest Locator – page 13
Historic Trails – page 20
Oregon – page 95
Washington – page 310
Southwestern British Columbia – page 604

California

Nevada

The Authors

Daniel C Schechter

Born in Manhattan, Daniel C Schechter refused to heed his father's helpful advice: 'When you leave New York, you're going nowhere.' Daniel went 'nowhere' fast: his career as teacher of English as a foreign language took him from Bogotá to Lisbon to Barcelona to Mexico City. After earning a teaching degree in Puerto Rico, he promptly left the field for editorial stints at *The News*, Mexico City's English language daily, and the American Chamber of Commerce magazine, *Business Mexico*. As a Lonely Planet author, he's contributed to the *Mexico, Central America on a shoestring*, *Eastern Caribbean* and *USA* guides. Six years in Mexico City left Daniel and his wife, Myra, gasping for air, and they've since transplanted themselves to the moist earth of the Pacific Northwest.

Jennifer Snarski

After spending most of her life in a small timber town on the southern Oregon coast, Jennifer set off for India, Sri Lanka and Thailand during her college years. Upon returning, she put her degree in religious studies to use by writing for a cultural guide to India. The assignments that followed sealed her fate as a travel writer. An avid hiker, Jennifer is most at home roaming the diverse wilderness areas of Oregon and Washington. She is also co-author of Lonely Planet's *Hiking in the USA* and *USA* guides. Jennifer lives in Portland, Oregon, where she works as a writer, desktop publisher and folkdance instructor. When not communing with nature, she's either out dancing jigs and reels at an Irish ceilí or planning her next trip to Ireland.

Debra Miller

Born in Nova Scotia, Deb grew up on the other side of Canada, in North Vancouver. The travel fever hit early, first with her family camping around the USA and Canada, then later with a backpack through Europe and the Middle East. She finally got a writing degree from the University of Victoria and peppered studying with trips around North America and Mexico. After college, she worked as a reporter, covering environmental issues for a variety of publications before joining Lonely Planet as senior editor for Pisces Diving & Snorkeling guides. The magical Pacific Northwest keeps pulling her back to kayak in the Pacific or play in the mountains. In addition to contributing to this book, Deb wrote Lonely Planet's *Seattle* and co-authored *British Columbia* and *Belize*.

Judy Jewell

Judy Jewell researched her home town of Portland, Oregon, on bicycle, bus and light-rail train before heading up Mt Hood, where (a bit off task) she skied off a cliff and broke her ankle. She also covered the Columbia Gorge and central and eastern Oregon. Judy has written and contributed to several other books about the Pacific Northwest, including *Camping! Oregon*. When Judy is not writing about the outdoors and travel, she is lead technical writer at Camp Dusty Technical Services.

FROM THE AUTHORS

Daniel C Schechter These folks deserve mention for their hospitality and/or willingness to share their considerable knowledge of the Pacific Northwest: Surjit Chabra, Greg & Laurie Clayton, Carl Haarstad, Judy Jewell, Paul Levy, Deb Miller and Jennifer Snarski. Appreciation is also merited by Brian Spitek, at Mt St Helens headquarters; Ruth Rhodes, at North Cascades Visitor Center; and the scores of other US Forest Service and National Park Service rangers who generously pitched in suggestions and information. For their editorial savvy and phenomenal patience, Wendy Taylor and Vivek Waglé have earned my deepest gratitude. Special thanks to my wife, Myra Ingmanson, whose spirit is woven into this book, and to her parents, Earl and Margaret Ingmanson, who are intrepid Northwest travelers.

Jennifer Snarski Thanks to tourism officials everywhere for great insights, especially to those who supplied clues to Oregon's elusive bus system. Heather Dawkins showed up in the nick of time to hold down the home front, and Anne Manning held cat duty at least once. Stevyn Travillian and Tricia Sears deserve gratitude for reading the manuscript. Special thanks to the patron saint of old Toyotas and to Irvington neighbors who were always nice when I came to get Jupiter.

Debra Miller I met so many people throughout BC who happily shared their local knowledge, be it in passing or over coffees and pints of beer. Your stories and opinions added uniqueness and energy to this book. Special thanks to everyone at Tourism British Columbia, who offered invaluable logistical and informational support, and to my family and friends throughout the Northwest, whose love and support never wavers. At Lonely Planet, thanks to Tom Downs, Mariah Bear, Wendy Taylor and big kudos to my editor Kanani Kauka. A final burst of gratitude to Julie Fanselow, my cohort and co-author on *British Columbia*, much of whose text was adapted for this book.

Judy Jewell A thousand thanks to my husband, Paul Levy, for driving me around eastern Oregon when my leg was in a cast. Also thanks to my friends who gave me tips, and hiked, dined and skied with me – especially Emily, Sarah, Joel, Dawn and Taylor.

This Book

The 1st edition of *Pacific Northwest* was co-authored by Bill McRae and Judy Jewell, and the 2nd edition was updated by Bill McRae, Judy Jewell and Jennifer Snarski.

In addition to serving as the coordinating author for this 3rd edition, Daniel C Schechter updated the introductory chapters and the Washington chapters. Jennifer Snarski updated the Facts about Oregon, Oregon Coast, Willamette Valley and Southern Oregon chapters. Judy Jewell updated the Portland, Columbia River Gorge & Mt Hood, Central Oregon, Northeastern Oregon and Southeastern Oregon chapters. Deb Miller updated the British Columbia chapters, much of which was adapted from Lonely Planet's *British Columbia* guide, which she co-authored with Julie Fanselow.

FROM THE PUBLISHER

This book was edited by Wendy Taylor, with undeniably indispensable help from Emily Wolman, Kanani 'Damn I'm Good' Kauka, Kevin Anglin, Rachel Bernstein, Rebecca Northen, Tammy 'I Hate Hyphens' Fortin, Vivek 'the Thinker' Waglé and Wade Fox. Rebecca Northen wrote the brief, senior editor Tom Downs got the book's production on its feet and running, and senior editor Suki 'Sourdough' Gear helped it along to the finish line. Managing editor and überwoman Kate Hoffman was always around to keep things on the right path.

The many many maps were created and cultivated by Stephanie Sims, under the guidance of Bart Wright and Alex Guilbert and with the help of Anneka Imkamp, Brad Lodge, Carole Nuttall, David Ryder, Dion Good, Ed Turley, Graham Neale, Herman So, John 'Peabody' Spelman, Kat Smith, Laurie Mikkelsen, Molly Green, Nao Ogawa, Patrick Phelan, Rachel Jereb and Rudie 'Gang Green' Watzig.

The book was laid out by designers Lora Santiago and Candice Jacobus, the color pages were created by Candice Jacobus, and the cover was designed by Beca Lafore and Lora Santiago. All this was governed by senior designer Tracey 'Boom Boom' Croom and art director Susan Rimerman. Illustrations were drawn by Hugh D'Andrade, Hayden Foell and Justin Marler, who also coordinated the illustrations. The index was created by Ken DellaPenta. We'd also like to give special thanks to Donna 'Queen of Grunge' Dresch for pulling out of the fast lane long enough to let us interview her.

Foreword

ABOUT LONELY PLANET GUIDEBOOKS

The story begins with a classic travel adventure: Tony and Maureen Wheeler's 1972 journey across Europe and Asia to Australia. Useful information about the overland trail did not exist at that time, so Tony and Maureen published the first Lonely Planet guidebook to meet a growing need.

From a kitchen table, then from a tiny office in Melbourne (Australia), Lonely Planet has become the largest independent travel publisher in the world, an international company with offices in Melbourne, Oakland (USA), London (UK) and Paris (France).

Today Lonely Planet guidebooks cover the globe. There is an ever-growing list of books, and there's information in a variety of forms and media. Some things haven't changed. The main aim is still to help make it possible for adventurous travelers to get out there – to explore and better understand the world.

At Lonely Planet we believe travelers can make a positive contribution to the countries they visit – if they respect their host communities and spend their money wisely. Since 1986 a percentage of the income from each book has been donated to aid projects and human-rights campaigns.

Updates Lonely Planet thoroughly updates each guidebook as often as possible. This usually means there are around two years between editions, although for more unusual or more stable destinations the gap can be longer. Check the imprint page (usually following the color map at the beginning of the book) for publication dates.

Between editions up-to-date information is available in two free newsletters – the paper *Planet Talk* and email *Comet* (to subscribe, contact any Lonely Planet office) – and on our Web site at www.lonelyplanet.com. The *Upgrades* section of the Web site covers a number of important and volatile destinations and is regularly updated by Lonely Planet authors. *Scoop* covers news and current affairs relevant to travelers. And, lastly, the *Thorn Tree* bulletin board and *Postcards* section of the site carry unverified, but fascinating, reports from travelers.

Correspondence The process of creating new editions begins with the letters, postcards and emails received from travelers. This correspondence often includes suggestions, criticisms and comments about the current editions. Interesting excerpts are immediately passed on via newsletters and the Web site, and everything goes to our authors to be verified when they're researching on the road. We're keen to get more feedback from organizations or individuals who represent communities visited by travelers.

Lonely Planet gathers information for everyone who's curious about the planet – and especially for those who explore it firsthand. Through guidebooks, phrasebooks, activity guides, maps, literature, newsletters, image library, TV series and Web site we act as an information exchange for a worldwide community of travelers.

Research Authors aim to gather sufficient practical information to enable travelers to make informed choices and to make the mechanics of a journey run smoothly. They also research historical and cultural background to help enrich the travel experience and allow travelers to understand and respond appropriately to cultural and environmental issues.

Authors don't stay in every hotel because that would mean spending a couple of months in each medium-size city and, no, they don't eat at every restaurant because that would mean stretching belts beyond capacity. They do visit hotels and restaurants to check standards and prices, but feedback based on readers' direct experiences can be very helpful.

Many of our authors work undercover; others aren't so secretive. None of them accept freebies in exchange for positive write-ups. And none of our guidebooks contain any advertising.

Production Authors submit their manuscripts and maps to offices in Australia, the USA, UK or France. Editors and cartographers – all experienced travelers themselves – then begin the process of assembling the pieces. When the book finally hits the shops, some things are already out of date, we start getting feedback from readers and the process begins again…

WARNING & REQUEST

Things change – prices go up, schedules change, good places go bad and bad places go bankrupt – nothing stays the same. So, if you find things better or worse, recently opened or long since closed, please tell us and help make the next edition even more accurate and useful. We genuinely value all the feedback we receive. A well-traveled team reads and acknowledges every letter, postcard and email and ensures that every morsel of information finds its way to the appropriate authors, editors and cartographers for verification.

Everyone who writes to us will find their name listed in the next edition of the appropriate guidebook. They will also receive the latest issue of *Planet Talk*, our quarterly printed newsletter, or *Comet*, our monthly email newsletter. Subscriptions to both newsletters are free. The very best contributions will be rewarded with a free guidebook.

We may edit, reproduce and incorporate your comments in all Lonely Planet products, such as guidebooks, Web sites and digital products, so let us know if you don't want your comments reproduced or your name acknowledged.

Send all correspondence to the Lonely Planet office closest to you:

Australia: Locked Bag 1, Footscray, Victoria 3011
USA: 150 Linden St, Oakland, CA 94607
UK: 10a Spring Place, London NW5 3BH
France: 1 rue du Dahomey, 75011 Paris

Or email us at: talk2us@lonelyplanet.com.au

For news, views and updates, see our Web site: www.lonelyplanet.com

HOW TO USE A LONELY PLANET GUIDEBOOK

The best way to use a Lonely Planet guidebook is any way you choose. At Lonely Planet, we believe the most memorable travel experiences are often those that are unexpected, and the finest discoveries are those you make yourself. Guidebooks are not intended to be used as if they provided a detailed set of infallible instructions!

Contents All Lonely Planet guidebooks follow roughly the same format. The Facts about the Destination chapters or sections give background information ranging from history to weather. Facts for the Visitor gives practical information on issues like visas and health. Getting There & Away gives a brief starting point for re-searching travel to and from the destination. Getting Around gives an overview of the transport options when you arrive.

The peculiar demands of each destination determine how sub-sequent chapters are broken up, but some things remain constant. We always start with background, then proceed to sights, places to stay, places to eat, entertainment, getting there and away, and getting around information – in that order.

Heading Hierarchy Lonely Planet headings are used in a strict hierarchical structure that can be visualized as a set of Russian dolls. Each heading (and its following text) is encompassed by any preceding heading that is higher on the hierarchical ladder.

Entry Points We do not assume guidebooks will be read from beginning to end, but that people will dip into them. The tradi-tional entry points are the list of contents and the index. In addi-tion, however, some books have a complete list of maps and an index map illustrating map coverage.

There may also be a color map that shows highlights. These highlights are dealt with in greater detail in the Facts for the Visitor chapter, along with planning questions and suggested itin-eraries. Each chapter covering a geographical region usually begins with a locator map and another list of highlights. Once you find something of interest in a list of highlights, turn to the index.

Maps Maps play a crucial role in Lonely Planet guidebooks and include a huge amount of information. A legend is printed on the back page. We seek to have complete consistency between maps and text and to have every important place in the text captured on a map. Map key numbers usually start in the top left corner.

Although inclusion in a guidebook usually implies a recommen-dation, we cannot list every good place. Exclusion does not necessarily imply criticism. In fact there are a number of reasons why we might exclude a place – sometimes it is simply inappropriate to encourage an influx of travelers.

Introduction

The Pacific Northwest contains some of the most diverse and extravagantly scenic landscapes in North America. To the west, the turbulent Pacific Ocean pounds the cliff-hung Oregon coast and swirls among the islands and fjords of the Puget Sound, Vancouver Island and the Georgia Strait. Just inland, massive volcanic peaks – including Mt St Helens, Mt Rainier, Mt Hood and the imploded cone that forms Crater Lake – rise above dense forests. Canyon-cut plateaus and arid mountain ranges stretch for hundreds of desert miles to the east before buckling up to form the foothills of the Rocky Mountains, the spine of the North American continent.

These pristine landscapes aren't just for looking at: In the Northwest, you're expected to get outdoors and enjoy yourself. The forests and coastlines are webbed with hiking trails; rafts and kayaks plunge down white-water rivers; and every peak is fair game for rock climbers and mountaineers. Some of the best skiing in North America is found here. British Columbia's Whistler, Oregon's Mt Bachelor and Washington's Stevens Pass are the most renowned of the region's many downhill resorts. Hood River, in the imposing Columbia River Gorge, is one of the world's most popular and challenging windsurfing spots.

The cities of the Pacific Northwest are noted for their high standards of living and exuberant civic and cultural life. Long known as a slightly stodgy if beautifully situated city, Seattle blossomed toward the end of the 20th century as a vital, trendy hot spot of youth culture and high-tech industry, complete with Microsoft headquarters.

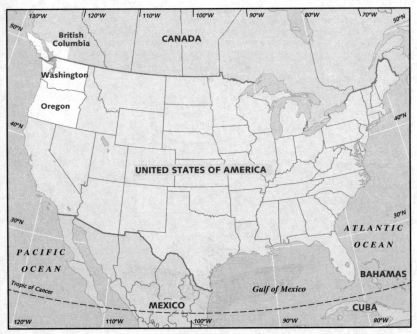

More reserved Portland hides its fun-loving vitality behind an outwardly quiet, gracious facade. Vancouver, the largest city on the Canadian west coast and the second-busiest port in North America, combines worldly savoir-faire, a mosaic of heritages and an open-minded, inquiring spirit. The city of Victoria – with its core of oh-so-English quaintness – seems a world away from other urban centers of the Northwest.

But there's even more to the Pacific Northwest than hip cosmopolitan cities and rugged landscapes: It's a long way from the traditional centers of mainstream culture and power in this quirky corner of the continent, and locals like it that way. Unified by the Cascade Range, the region is defined less by national borders than by spiritual and environmental similarities. The Northwest was born of the Oregon Trail and its resilient pioneers, who were fueled by a determination to push ever farther into the unknown. Though today's settlers are more likely to be fueled by espresso than by the desire to chart new territory, this remains a culture founded on restless idealism, and there is a strong, slightly uneasy sense that there's still more exploring to do.

Facts about the Pacific Northwest

HISTORY

Nearly 20,000 years ago, when the accumulated ice of the great polar glaciers of the Pleistocene epoch (commonly referred to as the Ice Age) lowered sea levels throughout the world, humans migrated from Siberia to Alaska via a then-existing land bridge across what is now the Bering Strait, becoming the ancestors of the Native Americans. Over millennia, subsequent migrations distributed the population throughout the Americas.

Native Peoples

The first inhabitants of North America, some 20,000 years ago, were nomadic hunter-gatherers who lived in small bands. In the West – along the Pacific Ocean, around Puget Sound and in major coastal river valleys – societies based on fishing were developed. While some tribes (such as the Quinault, Quileute, Makah and Nootka) went out to sea in pursuit of whales, others (notably the Chinook, Coos and Tillamook) depended on catching salmon, cod and shellfish. On land, deer and elk were hunted.

Summer and fall were dedicated to harvesting the bounties from the sea and forests. Food was stored in such quantities that the long winter months could be spent on activities unrelated to subsistence. Thus the Northwest Coastal Indians reached a level of artistic, religious and cultural sophistication unmatched by most Native American groups.

The construction of ornately carved cedar canoes led to extensive trading networks among the permanent settlements that stretched up and down the coast and along the river valleys. Extended family groups lived in cedar-sided longhouses, which were constructed over a central, pitlike living area. The social structure in these self-sustaining villages was quite stratified, with the wealth and power held by an aristocratic class of chiefs. Wealth was measured in goods such as blankets, salmon and fish oil. These items were consumed and, to some degree, redistributed in potlatches, or ceremonial feasts, in which great honor accrued for the person who gave away valued items.

Inland, on the arid plateaus between the Cascades and the Rocky Mountains, a culture based on seasonal migration between rivers and temperate uplands developed. These tribes, including the Nez Perce, Cayuse, Spokane, Yakama and Kootenai, displayed cultural features of both the Coastal Indians and Plains Indians east of the Rockies. During salmon runs, the tribes gathered at rapids and waterfalls to net or harpoon fish, which they then dried or smoked. At other times, they would move to upland hunting grounds to gather fruit and pursue deer and elk. Tribal groups returned to traditional winter camps at the end of the year, where they maintained semipermanent pit-type dwellings. Most transportation was overland, with large dogs serving as pack animals until horses arrived on the scene in the 18th century. Authority in tribal units was loosely organized, with responsibility for leading the tribe divided among a number of chiefs, each of whom had specific duties. Great religious importance was attached to 'vision quests,' in which young men sought to recognize the supernatural guardian that guided their individual lives.

In the harsh landscapes of Oregon's southern desert, another culture evolved. Tribes such as the Shoshone, Paiute and Bannock were nomadic peoples who hunted and scavenged in the northern reaches of the Great Basin desert. Berries, roots and small game such as gophers and rabbits constituted their meager diet. Clusters of easily transported, woven-reed shelters made up migratory villages. Religious and cultural life focused on shamans, who could intercede with the spirit world to heal sickness or bring success in hunting. The Shoshone and Paiute became fearsome warriors and hunters after the 18th century, when horses (stolen from Spanish California) gave them easy mobility.

Early Exploration

This distant corner of the world map was one of the last to be explored by Europeans. In fact, exactly 300 years passed between Columbus' discovery of America and the discovery of the Columbia River – one of the continent's largest river systems. The Pacific Northwest was, therefore, one of the last areas up for grabs for European colonialism and economic exploitation.

The rocky and storm-wracked coast of the Pacific Northwest resisted many early seafaring explorers. Probably the first Europeans to see the Oregon countryside were those accompanying Spanish explorer Juan Rodríguez Cabrillo. In 1543, his ship reached the mouth of the Rogue River, but the coastline was too wild and stormy to attempt landing. By the 18th century, the Spanish had colonized the southern parts of California and had begun to explore the northern Pacific Coast, in part seeking to discover the Strait of Anián (the Spanish name for the Northwest Passage, a fabled direct water route from the Pacific Ocean to the Atlantic Ocean around the north coast of North America). The Spanish also sought to explore the land that lay between them and their potential new neighbor to the north, Russia. (The Russians had begun to make claims along the Pacific Coast in the late 18th century, after Peter the Great sent Danish explorer and navigator Vitus Bering on an expedition of the area.) By 1774, Spanish frigates reached as far north as the Queen Charlotte Islands, claiming the Northwest coast for the Spanish crown.

The British also sought to find a Northwest Passage. Fresh from their victory over the French in the French & Indian War (1756–63), they were eager to explore the western shores of British Canada. In 1778, Captain James Cook explored the coast of present-day Oregon, Washington and British Columbia, landing at Nootka Sound on

Vancouver Island. Captain George Vancouver was, in 1792, the first explorer to sail the waters of Puget Sound; thereby, he asserted British sovereignty over the entire region. He was also responsible for the first accurate maps of the region. The British also sought to explore the region by land from its colonies in eastern Canada. The first white man to cross the continent, fur-trader Alexander Mackenzie, followed Native American trails across the Canadian Rockies to arrive at present-day Bella Coola, on the British Columbian coast, in 1793.

The Spanish attempted to build colonies along the Northwest coast – first in 1790 at Neah Bay, on the Olympic Peninsula, and then at Nootka Sound. Cattle and horses were imported from Spanish California, and fields were cleared for cultivation. However, for reasons that had more to do with European politics than the success of these rain-drenched colonies, Spain gave over its claim of the Northwest coast to Britain in 1792.

The Americans also entered the region in 1792, when Captain Robert Gray discovered the Columbia River's mouth, which was obscured by sandbars and hazardous currents. Gray sailed up the great river, traded with the Indians and named his discovery the Columbia (after his ship).

The Lewis and Clark expedition (1803–06) was promoted as an exploration of the USA's newly acquired Louisiana Purchase, which extended from the Mississippi River to the northern Continental Divide of the Rocky Mountains. Somewhat circumspectly, the US explorers also crossed over the Rockies into then-Spanish territory and made their way down the Columbia River to the Pacific Ocean. By doing so, they established a further US claim on the territory (see the boxed text 'Intrepid Travelers: Lewis & Clark's Westward Odyssey').

Although no settlement or even permanent trading post resulted from these pioneering explorations, the British and Americans were discovering the Northwest's bounty of fur-bearing wildlife and the profits to be made in the peltry trade. While in the Northwest in 1778, Captain Cook's crew traded buttons, cloth and trinkets with the

Intrepid Travelers: Lewis & Clark's Westward Odyssey

When President Thomas Jefferson made the decision in 1801 to explore the uncharted western part of North America to find a waterway to the Pacific, he enlisted his young protégé and personal secretary, Meriwether Lewis, to lead an expedition. Lewis, then 27, had no expertise in botany, cartography or Indian languages and was known to have bouts of 'hypochondriac affections' – a euphemism for schizophrenia – but couldn't resist the opportunity. He in turn asked his good friend William Clark, already an experienced frontiersman and army veteran at the age of 33, to join him. In 1803, they left St Louis, Missouri, and headed west with an entourage of 40, including 27 bachelors; Clark's African American servant, York; and a dog.

William Clark & Meriwether Lewis

They traveled some 8000 miles (12,900km) in about two years, documenting everything they came across in their journals with such bad spelling that it must have taken historians a few extra years just to sort out what they wrote. In an almost biblical fashion they named some 120 animals and 170 plants, including the grizzly bear and the prairie dog. While Clark's entries are the more scientific, Lewis was known to explore alone and write pensive, almost romantic accounts of the journey.

The Corps of Discovery – the expedition's official name – fared quite well, in part because of the presence of Sacagawea, a young Shoshone woman who had been sold to and became the wife of Toussaint Charbonneau, a French-Canadian trapper who joined Lewis and Clark on their journey. The presence of Sacagawea and her baby boy prevented many a potential conflict between the explorers and the Native Americans. York also softened tensions between the group and the Indians – his color and stature both fascinated and intimidated the Indians.

Lewis and Clark returned to a heroes' welcome in St Louis in 1806 and were soon appointed to high offices. In 1808, Lewis was appointed governor of the just-purchased Louisiana Territory, but he died a year later, at the age of 35, purportedly during a 'fit' in which he either committed suicide or was murdered. Clark dealt with his new fame a bit better and was appointed governor of the Missouri Territory. He died at the age of 68.

Indians for sea-otter skins. Upon reaching Asian ports, they learned the Chinese were willing to pay a high price for such pelts.

Thus was born the Chinese trade triangle that would dominate British and US economic interests in the northern Pacific for the next 30 years. Ships entered the waters of the Pacific Northwest, traded cloth and trinkets for sea-otter pelts and then set sail for China, where the skins were traded for tea and luxury items. The ships then returned to their port of call – usually London or Boston – where the Asian goods were sold. Vast fortunes were made by profiteers before the sea otters died out and before the War of 1812 (between the USA and Britain) made such trade expeditions dangerous, as ships were often threatened by buccaneers from the warring nations.

The Fur Trade

The region's first trickle of white settlers did not arrive from the coast (which had already seen dozens of exploratory voyages), but from inland. Trappers from two competing British fur-trading companies – the Hudson's Bay Company (HBC) and the North West Company – began to expand from their bases around Hudson's Bay and the Great Lakes. By 1809, both companies had edged over the Rocky Mountains into today's British Columbia, Montana, Idaho and eastern Washington to establish fur-trading forts. These trading posts were quite successful, even though each was linked to eastern markets by an 1800-mile (2900km) overland trail. Each fort was given an assortment of trade goods to induce the local Indians to trap beaver, otter, fox, wolf or whatever fur-bearing animals were present. While blankets, beads and cloth were popular with the Indians, nothing produced the goods as dependably as whiskey. (One historian estimates that 195,000 gallons of alcohol were traded with the Indians for fur during the heyday of the Northwest fur trade.)

As the fur-trading forts edged closer to the Pacific Coast, it became clear that shipment of furs made more and more sense; however, there was no coastal port as of yet. Even though British fur interests controlled the Pacific Northwest's regions inland, it was an American fur magnate, John Jacob Astor, who first established a coastal fur-trading post in 1811 at the mouth of the Columbia River. However, the trading post, called Fort Astoria, was assailed by bad luck from its inception. When British soldiers arrived during the War of 1812 to take possession of the fort, the bedraggled Americans seemed only too glad to sell the operation to British fur-trading companies.

With the Americans out of the way, the HBC moved quickly to establish a network of fur-trading forts and relationships with Indian tribes throughout this region, working its way into the drainages of the Columbia River; the Willamette and Umpqua Rivers, in Oregon; and the Fraser River, in British Columbia. Fort Vancouver – located at the strategically important confluence of the Willamette and Columbia Rivers – was established in 1824 to serve as the HBC headquarters for the entire Columbia region and was placed under the leadership of the capable Dr John McLoughlin, often called the Father of Oregon.

By 1827, significant changes in European and American colonial aspirations in the Northwest had led to treaties and events that served to better define the territory. Spain had withdrawn its claim to the Northwest, establishing the northern border of New Spain at the 47th parallel (the current Oregon-California border). Russian ambitions were limited to the land north of the 54°40' parallel, at the start of the Alaska panhandle, near Prince Rupert, BC. The USA, through the Louisiana Purchase, owned all land south of the 49th parallel but east of the Rocky Mountains, while Britain controlled the territory north of this line. This left a vast territory – all of present-day British Columbia, the states of Oregon, Washington and Idaho and parts of western Montana and Wyoming – open to claims by both Britain and the USA.

The terms of an 1818 codicil to the Treaty of Ghent (which ended the War of 1812) sought to resolve the competing British and US territorial claims in the Northwest by declaring that the region was open to joint occupancy by both nations: Britain and the USA could continue economic development in the area, but neither could establish an official government.

The First White Settlements

Unlike most other early trading posts, which were basically repositories for goods, Fort Vancouver became, under the stewardship of the Canadian-born McLoughlin (see The Fur Trade, earlier), a thriving, nearly self-sufficient agricultural community, complete with mills, a dairy, gardens and fields.

McLoughlin also encouraged settlement beyond the precincts of the fort. Contrary to protocol, he allowed older trappers who were retiring from the HBC to settle along the Willamette River, in an area still called French Prairie (just upriver from Champoeg State Park). By 1828, these French Canadians, with their Native American wives, began to clear the land and build cabins – these were the first true settlers in the Northwest. McLoughlin established a mill and incorporated the first town in the Northwest in 1829, at Oregon City.

American trapping and trading parties began to filter into the Northwest in the 1830s. Sensing that one day the USA and Britain would divide the territory, McLoughlin urged the newcomers to move south along the Willamette River. If US settlement could be limited to the territory south of the Columbia, he reasoned, then Britain would have a stronger claim to the land north of the river.

Accompanying one of these groups were New England Methodists Daniel and Jason Lee, who in 1834 founded a mission north of present-day Salem. They soon discovered that the local Native Americans weren't particularly susceptible to Christianity, although the two did succeed in establishing the first schools in Oregon and in infusing the young territory with their doctrinaire brand of idealism. The Lees' failure, however, didn't deter an increasing number of missionaries from streaming into the Oregon country. Protestant missionaries Marcus and Narcissa Whitman and Henry and Eliza Spalding crossed the North American continent in 1836 (Narcissa and Eliza were the first women to cross what would later be known as the Oregon Trail), establishing missions near Walla Walla, Washington, and Lapwai, Idaho. In 1838, a Catholic mission was established at St Paul, on the Willamette River.

The ranks of the Methodists in the Willamette Valley were greatly bolstered in 1837 and 1840, when missionary 'enforcements' arrived from the eastern USA. However, the overriding mission of these Yankee newcomers was to carve out farmsteads and foment anti-British sentiment.

Despite the limits set by the Treaty of Ghent, the HBC, with its strict code of procedures and conduct for employees, provided the effective legal background for the nascent settlement, particularly as long as the majority of the settlers were retired trappers. Yet even though the HBC's influence in matters was largely benign, the Methodists refused to tolerate any degree of British hegemony. To make matters worse, McLoughlin and most of the French-Canadian settlers were Catholic. With tensions mounting, the HBC established another center of operations:

Fort Victoria, on Vancouver Island, far from the Yankee rabble-rousers.

This was an era when belief in Manifest Destiny – the idea that it was the USA's natural right to expand its territory to the Pacific coast – ran strong, and sentiment to annex the Northwest ran high. However, despite fulminations from Protestant pulpits and fiery oratory in the US Senate, federal troops were not ordered into a military occupation of the lower Columbia River in order to rid the region of the British and the Natives. If the settlers in the Oregon country were to have an independent civil authority, they would have to take the steps themselves.

The Vote at Champoeg

By 1843, the Willamette Valley was home to roughly 700 people – a ragtag mixture of French-Canadian trappers and their half-Indian families, Protestant missionaries, and a group best described as mountain men (who were often married to Indian women).

The Methodists, who were the most anxious to link the young settlement with the USA, held a series of meetings and drew up a framework for a provisional government. The French and British settlers initially balked at the plan, which would replace the authority of the HBC with an independent – but largely American – code of laws. In 1843, an up-or-down vote was called at Champoeg, along the Willamette River about 30 miles (48km) south of Portland. Americans, Canadians and Britons were represented pretty equally. A bare majority voted to organize a provisional government independent of the HBC, thereby casting the settlement's lot with the USA. The land north of the Columbia remained in the control of the HBC. Had the vote gone the other way, today's maps of the Pacific Northwest might look quite different.

The USA–Canada boundary dispute became increasingly antagonistic. The popular slogan of the 1844 presidential campaign was '54/40 or fight,' which urged the USA to occupy all of the Northwest up to the present Alaskan border (at the 54°40' parallel), including all of present-day Washington State and British Columbia. Finally, in 1846, the British and Americans agreed to the present border, along the 49th parallel. The HBC headquarters withdrew from Fort Vancouver to Fort Victoria on Vancouver Island, and many British citizens moved north as well. In order to better protect its interests and citizens, Vancouver Island was designated a crown colony in 1849.

The Oregon Trail

After the Champoeg referendum put Oregon on track for statehood, an overland party of nearly 900 arrived in the Willamette Valley, more than doubling its population. Thus began the great migration along the 2000-mile-long (3200km-long) Oregon Trail, which between 1843 and 1860 brought over 50,000 settlers to the Northwest.

The trail began in Independence, Missouri; traced the North Platte River to South Pass, in Wyoming; cut across the Snake River Plain, in Idaho; and continued up and over the Blue Mountains of eastern Oregon to the Columbia River at The Dalles. Families embarked on the perilous journey with their belongings in canvas-topped wagons, often trailing cattle and livestock. By the time the emigrants reached eastern Oregon, food stores were running low, people and

livestock were exhausted, and fall had arrived in the high mountain passes.

When the parties arrived at the Columbia River in The Dalles, they faced one of the most treacherous parts of their journey: weary travelers had to choose between rafting themselves and all their belongings through the rapids in the Columbia River Gorge or struggling up the flanks of Mt Hood and descending via the precipitous Barlow Trail.

The Oregon Trail ended at Oregon City, in the Willamette Valley. Here, settlers established farms, businesses and towns. Portland, near the Willamette's confluence with the Columbia River, took on an early importance as a trade center. Oregon City, at the falls of the Willamette River, was the early seat of government, while above the falls, in the river's broad agricultural basin, small farming communities sprang up.

After the USA wrested control of Fort Vancouver in 1846, settlers began to spread up the Cowlitz River to the Puget Sound area, initially putting down roots at Tumwater, near Olympia. By 1851, a group of Oregon Trail pioneers led by brothers Arthur and David Denny set sights on

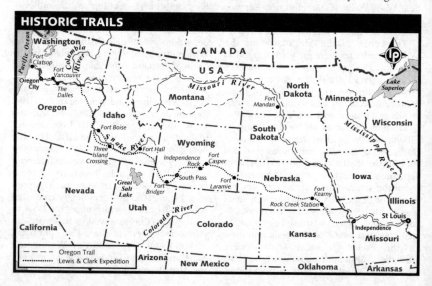

HISTORIC TRAILS

- - - - Oregon Trail
.... Lewis & Clark Expedition

Elliott Bay and founded the port city of Seattle.

The difficulty in passing the Columbia River Gorge from The Dalles motivated a party of pioneers in 1846 to blaze a southern route into the Willamette Valley. The new Applegate Trail cut south from Fort Hall, Idaho, through the deserts of northern Nevada and California before turning north and traversing the valleys of southern Oregon. Immigrants along this route were the first to settle the upper Willamette Valley and towns such as Eugene; they also scouted the land in the Rogue, Umpqua and Klamath river valleys.

By the late 1850s, the western valleys were filling with settlers, and some emigrants began to move east of the Cascades to begin farms and ranches, particularly in the Walla Walla river valley, in Washington, and in the Grande Ronde river valley of Oregon. Settlement of eastern Oregon didn't occur until the discovery of gold, during the 1860s.

Latter-day Oregonians have always made much of the assumed stellar qualities of these early settlers who went West not in search of easy wealth but to start farms, businesses and communities. They were mostly young and remarkably homogeneous in their philosophy, goals and culture.

The pride that Northwesterners take in their early settlers is best illustrated by an apocryphal story: At a fork in the Oregon Trail, a sign indicated the terminus of each route. Pointing south, toward California, the sign pictured a sparkling gold nugget. Pointing north, the sign read 'To Oregon.' Only those who could read made their way to the Northwest.

Decimation of the Indian Nation

By 1860, the coastal valleys and protected harbors of the maritime Pacific Northwest were settled, and most major cities were established. However, the rapid development of the region had come at some cost. The long domination of the Northwest by fur companies meant that trappers and hunters had drained the region's wealth in wildlife, especially in beaver and otter populations.

More deplorable was the effect settlers had on the region's Indian population. Alcohol corrupted Native culture: Indian hunters and gatherers, who once followed a seasonal pattern of fishing salmon and stalking deer, now trapped the streams free of beaver in return for a steady flow of whiskey. The Indians had no natural immunity to diseases brought by the whites, and the mortality rate, particularly along the coast, was devastating. Contemporary observers estimated that nine-tenths of the population of Chinook tribes along the Columbia River died of a mysterious fever during the summer of 1829.

However lamentable the impact of the fur traders on the Indians, the traders made no conscious attempt to change the general culture of the Indians or to move them from their homelands. This didn't occur until the arrival of the missionaries and agricultural settlers, in the 1830s and 1840s. Methodist missionaries among the Calapooia Indians, in Oregon, had little luck converting adult Indians, so they turned their attention to the children, whom they took from their families and placed in Methodist religious schools. Near Walla Walla, the Whitman mission's attempts to bring Christianity to eastern Washington tribes ended in tragedy: Cayuse Indians slew the missionaries in revenge for what they saw as an intentionally spread measles epidemic. Following the Whitman Massacre, as the attack became known, American settlers felt justified and compelled to remove the Indians from their land and incarcerate them on reservations. That this would also make the territory safer for farmers and miners could not be ignored.

In general, the Coastal Indians had been so debilitated by disease that they could mount little resistance to white incursions. These tribes were marched or shipped to reservations in 1855 and 1856, where increased illness, starvation and dislocation led to the complete extinction of many tribal groups. Even on Vancouver Island, where British policies were generally more enlightened regarding Indian culture, most of the arable land was given over to white settlers (the Indians retained only their village sites). Christian missionaries worked to make illegal the traditional potlatches that formed the nucleus of Coastal Indian religion and social life.

The Native Americans east of the Cascades resisted manipulation by the US military and settlers more strenuously than the coastal tribes. A series of fierce battles were fought between the US Army and various Indian tribes from 1855 to 1877. Especially bloody were the Rogue River and the Modoc Wars, in southern Oregon, and the Cayuse War, near Walla Walla. However, in the end, these Native American groups also ended up on reservations, deracinated, alienated from their traditional cultural lives and utterly dependent upon the federal government for subsistence.

The Northwest was now wide open for settlement, and Oregon, Washington and British Columbia quickly grew into economic forces on the national and international stage.

See the introductory chapters to Oregon, Washington and British Columbia for history from this point on.

GEOGRAPHY

By the usual definition, the Pacific Northwest comprises two major geographical regions: the islands, mountains and valleys of the Pacific coastline and the Cascade Range; and the plateaus east of the Cascades to the Rocky Mountain foothills. Linking these two regions is the mighty Columbia River, an intrinsic part of life throughout the Northwest. A long series of dams harnesses the river's strongly flowing waters for hydroelectric power and irrigation.

Two significant geological features are due to the Columbia River's awesome forces: the Grand Coulee, in central Washington, an abandoned ice-age channel of the ancient Columbia that cuts through spectacular lava flows and the Columbia River Gorge, which cuts through the Cascade Range.

Much of the northern Pacific Coast is quite rugged, lined with cliffs and rocky promontories and arrayed with mountainous islands. Sandy beaches dominate only along southwestern Washington's Long Beach

Peninsula; along the central coast at the Oregon Dunes; and at Vancouver Island's Long Beach. Rising from the Pacific shore are coastal mountains – in Oregon, the Coast Range; in Washington, the Olympic Mountains; and in British Columbia, the Coast Mountains. These mountains are covered with some of the last remaining virgin woodlands in North America.

Throughout much of the Northwest, the coastal ranges and the towering volcanic peaks of the Cascades are separated by a low-lying basin officially known as the Willamette-Puget Trough. In Oregon and southern Washington, this basin is drained by the Willamette and Cowlitz Rivers, respectively, while in northern Washington and British Columbia, the ocean has partially invaded the lowlands, forming the Puget Sound, the Hood Canal and the Georgia Strait. These lowlands contain extremely fertile agricultural land, as well as the vast majority of the region's population.

In southern Oregon, two major rivers, the Rogue and the Umpqua, drain from the Cascades directly into the Pacific. In northern Washington, several large rivers, most notably the Skagit, debouch into the Puget Sound, while the Fraser River drains a wide basin of central British Columbia before fanning into a delta and emptying into the Georgia Strait at Vancouver.

The Cascades run like a spine along the western third of Oregon and Washington. These peaks are very recent, geologically. Mt Baker, Mt Rainier, Mt St Helens, Mt Hood and Crater Lake's Mt Mazama, among many others, form a wide barrier that serves to halt the moist, eastward flow of Pacific air, creating the arid plateaus of central and eastern Oregon and Washington.

Underlain by some of the largest lava flows in the world, the steppe-like uplands east of the Cascades are now devoted to dryland farming and ranching. The Deschutes, John Day, Grande Ronde and Yakima Rivers – to say nothing of the massive Columbia – have each furrowed deeply into the underlying basalt of the region. Isolated mountain ranges float above the lava prairies, especially in northeastern Washington and in eastern Oregon, where peaks in the Ochoco, Blue and Wallowa Ranges reach as high as 10,000 feet (3000m). Much of Oregon's eastern border with Idaho is defined by the Snake River, which charges through Hells Canyon, North America's deepest gorge, on its way to meet the Columbia.

South of the Columbia Basin, in southern Oregon, are the arid fault-block mountain ranges of the Great Basin desert, which is scattered with a series of landlocked, usually saline, lakes.

GEOLOGY

A textbook example of plate tectonics, the geology of the Pacific Northwest is largely due to its position at the leading edge of North America's westward movement. About 200 million years ago, the North American continent wrenched loose from Europe and Africa, beginning its inexorable westward journey (an inch or two a year, over millions of years). The coastal plain was buckled by the collision with the Pacific sea floor, forming the mountainous ridges that would grow into the Rocky Mountains. Continuing along its course, the continental landmass would occasionally collide with offshore islands and small continents, adding mountain ranges to British Columbia (the Selkirks), to eastern and southern Oregon (the Klamaths, Wallowas, Ochocos and Blues) and to northern Washington (the Okanogans and the North Cascades). Between these northern and southern highlands was a large shallow bay.

A snapshot of the Pacific Northwest 60 million years ago would show a jumble of offshore islands, low coastal mountains and marine marshes, all invaded by the shallow Pacific. Slowly, sediment filled the channels between the island chains. Plant and animal life thrived in the warm tropical climate. As there was no extensive coastal mountain range, Pacific weather flowed inland unobstructed, resulting in a widespread moist environment.

During the same era, a large chunk of continental crust again docked onto the westward-trending edge of the Northwest. As before, coastal sediments and offshore islands were wedged and jumbled together along the new shoreline to form today's Coast Range and Olympic Mountains.

Volcanoes

Three intense periods of volcanism soon followed, each of which would utterly change the face of the region. First, a line of volcanoes shot up through the newly arrived landmass about 40 million years ago. As the range – called the Old or Western Cascades – grew higher, it isolated the old ocean bay of the interior Northwest, creating an inland sea surrounded by temperate grasslands. Enormous volcanic explosions of ash and mud repeatedly buried the plant and animal life of this area, resulting in the John Day formations; their fossil beds have become national monuments (see the Northeastern Oregon chapter).

Then, about 20 million years ago, the volcanic scene shifted eastward. Extensive faulting of the southern and eastern Oregon and Idaho bedrock allowed vast amounts of lava to rise to the surface. Successive lava flows deposited molten rock into the sea of central Oregon and Washington, submerging all but the highest peaks of Oregon's eastern mountains below a massive basalt plain known as the Columbia Plateau. It would be many millions of years before the barren lava fields would erode into soil.

By this stage, the Northwest had taken on much of its present shape. The region's last great volcanic era began relatively recently, as indicated by the conical, uneroded peaks of the Northwest skyline. Mt Mazama, better known as the caldera of Crater Lake, erupted 6900 years ago, devastating much of central Oregon with its massive explosion. Mt St Helens drew worldwide attention in 1980, when its eruption spread ash through five states and three Canadian provinces. Mt Hood, Mt Rainier, Mt Baker and the region around the Three Sisters have each seen eruptions in the last 500 years and are still considered volcanically active today.

Ice-Age Floods

During the most recent Ice Age, which lasted until 15,000 years ago, glaciers crept over western Montana. This huge wall of ice blocked water from draining out of Montana valleys toward the Pacific Ocean. Lake Missoula – a 3000-sq-mile pool – formed behind the ice dam. However, when the water level of the lake grew high enough, it floated the plug of ice, and the entire lake rushed through the Columbia Basin.

At full flood, swiftly flowing waters lashed 1000 feet above the present site of The Dalles. The intense currents of the flood scoured out the Columbia watercourse and cut away the canyon walls. Columbia Gorge waterfalls were formed when the floods flushed away the stream paths that entered the Columbia River, causing streams to tumble over towering cliffs.

As astonishing as the magnitude of these floods is the fact that, over the course of about 2000 years, they recurred at least 40 times. The ice dam would re-form after each flood and fill with meltwater until the dam lifted with the pressure of the water. Each time the flood coursed through the gorge, the chasm was cut deeper and the canyon walls scoured cleaner.

About 700 years ago, an enormous landslide fell into the gorge, briefly damming the Columbia and forming the mighty rapids that were later called the Cascades. The Native American myth of the 'Bridge of the Gods' – a rock arch that spanned the Columbia – apparently derived from this jumble of rock strewn across the river.

CLIMATE

The Cascades serve as a meteorological division between the Pacific Northwest's two distinct weather patterns. West of the Cascades, the weather is dominated by the marine air of the Pacific Ocean. Winters are moderate, and freezing temperatures are uncommon, except at higher elevations. In Portland, Seattle and Vancouver, winter temperatures range from 30°F to 50°F (-1°C to 10°C). Summer highs occasionally reach into the 90s, though pleasant 80°F (26°C) days are more the rule, and summer evenings are usually cool enough for a jacket. Spring and fall are transitional, with warm but rainy days common in the spring

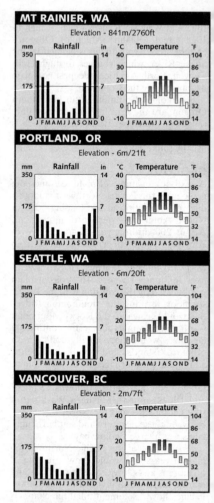

and beautiful Indian summers that sometimes last well into October.

Rain is seasonally abundant, particularly along the coastal areas and the Coast Range, the Olympic Mountains and Vancouver Island, where over 100 inches fall yearly. In the interior Willamette Valley and around the inland waterways of Washington and British Columbia, rainfall is more moderate; Vancouver, Seattle and Portland receive less than 40 inches of rain a year, though marine clouds and fog are prevalent year round, particularly in the winter and early spring. Snowfall is heavy in the coastal ranges and the Cascades, yet infrequent between the two.

The Cascades halt the flow of moist and cloudy Pacific air, allowing a continental weather pattern to prevail east of the mountains. Precipitation is much less abundant, though rainfall patterns vary greatly throughout the region. Sunshine is the norm in both winter and summer. Summer temperatures can be extreme: highs above 100°F (37°C) are common, particularly along the Columbia Plateau and in the deserts of southern Oregon. Humidity is low, however, and evenings are cool. Winter temperatures vary greatly and can drop below 0°F (-18°C) for short periods. Snow is common throughout the area and can make for difficult driving conditions.

ECOLOGY & ENVIRONMENT

Environmental issues dominate politics and civic life in the Pacific Northwest. The region's vast forests, mighty rivers, rocky islands and glaciered volcanic peaks are more than a beautiful backdrop for the tourists: Access to nature is what brought many residents here, and preserving the environment is a deeply felt concern. However, the natural ecosystem for one person is another person's natural-resource bonanza. Thus, the Northwest is home to contentious and difficult environmental issues. The traditional Northwest economy was largely based on logging and other resource-extractive industries, with the changeover to a more modern, service-based economy having tremendous impact, particularly in the rural areas and small towns. Another source of increasing concern is the endangered fish runs, especially for seagoing salmon. Just who is culpable for the species' fast-approaching extinction is one of the region's most hotly contested political issues (see the boxed text 'An Upstream Battle').

Low-cost timber sales, unsustainable harvest levels and devastating cutting practices have made logging one of the region's most heated environmental issues. Much of the logging is done on national forest lands, which are administered by the government under the US Forest Service (USFS). Because the Cascades and coastal mountain ranges are densely covered with national-forest lands, a traveler need not stray too far from the interstate before coming across a clear-cut – a series of hillsides logged flat and stripped of all vegetation. Clear-cutting causes the erosion of hillsides, choking salmon-rich streambeds with silt and destroying wildlife habitats. And although forests are regarded as an agricultural crop that theoretically can be planted and harvested indefinitely, they're being cut down much faster than they can grow back.

Due to successful lawsuits against the USFS by environmental groups seeking to protect wildlife habitats, the late 1980s and early 1990s saw federal forests closed to logging. The endangered northern spotted owl in particular became the object of an emotional skirmish between environmentalists and timber interests. Once old trees were proved to be the birds' primary nesting habitat, courts ordered millions of acres of federal forests that were ripe with old-growth timber to be removed from sale. Mills closed, leaving embittered loggers and mill workers to spend their days screenprinting T-shirts with slogans such as 'I love spotted owl…fried.'

Environmentalists were divided over the Clinton administration's landmark 1993 Northwest Forest plan, a compromise under which 16% of USFS lands remain open to logging, including substantial stands of old-growth forests in the managed reserves of southwestern Washington and Oregon's Willamette and Umpqua valleys. Opponents of logging on federal lands can expect stiff resistance from Mark Rey, who was appointed by President George W Bush to oversee national-forest policy and who is a longtime lobbyist for the timber industry.

FLORA & FAUNA

The Cascades effectively divide the Northwest into two ecosystems. West of the Cascades are mossy, heavily forested valleys,

An Upstream Battle

'Your power is turning our darkness to dawn, so roll on Columbia, roll on...'
                                                    – Woody Guthrie, from *Roll On, Columbia*

When people's poet Woody Guthrie penned these song lyrics as a paean to public power in the Pacific Northwest, he could hardly have envisioned the surge of popular support six decades later for taking down the dams on the Columbia Basin.

Hydroelectric power dams – specifically, the four dams built in the 1960s along the Lower Snake River – are seen by many as the culprit in the alarming loss of wild salmon varieties along the Snake and Columbia Rivers. Young salmon migrating from mountain streams in Idaho face these imposing obstacles on their 800-mile (1300km) journey down to the sea. Environmental groups such as the Sierra Club and Friends of the Earth assert that up to 95% of juvenile salmon are stopped midstream by the spinning blades of the hydroelectric turbines.

To the dissatisfaction of Native American tribes and environmental groups, the Bonneville Power Administration (BPA) has responded to the situation by sucking the fish out of the water, pumping them into special containerized boats and shipping them downriver on barges.

A better way to save the salmon from extinction, the environmentalists say, is to restore the river system to pre-dam conditions by breaching the dams, perforating their sides to create a passageway for the fish. But breaching, which would force the hydroelectric plants to shut down, is stiffly opposed by shipping and irrigation interests that depend on the reservoir network associated with the dams – the waterway is a major shipping corridor for US wheat and other exports to the Pacific Rim. Predictably, opponents claim that salmon depletion has little to do with the dams and that overfishing, competition from other species and the climatic conditions of the ocean are more crucial factors. They see removing the dams as an unnecessarily drastic measure, preferring improved enforcement of existing fishing restrictions and hatchery management as solutions.

Along these lines, federal agencies released a plan for salmon recovery in December 2000. Their 'restoration blueprint' focuses on restoring habitats and restricting the harvesting of endangered salmon varieties, leaving the hot-button option of breaching the dams to be examined in 2003 if these efforts prove unsuccessful.

while arid uplands and high deserts stretch east of the range.

West of the Cascades

Forests on the Pacific side of Washington, Oregon and maritime British Columbia are dense and fast growing. Dominant throughout the western valleys is the Douglas fir, a statuesque conifer that can grow to nearly 300 feet (90m). In coastal forests, you'll also find Sitka spruce, Western hemlock, maples, oaks and (especially along streams) red cedar.

Watch for madrone trees, which have a distinctive red, peeling bark and broad, though evergreen, leaves, and stands of white oak in southern Oregon.

In the understory of old forests grow a number of ferns, rhododendrons and the purple-fruited Oregon grape (Oregon's state flower). Fall brings bright red leaves to vine maples; salmonberries, with their orange fruit; and omnipresent thorny blackberries that grab at clothing but provide welcome sweet snacks. You'll discover the most recently commercialized of the Northwest's riches – wild mushrooms – on the forest floor. Chanterelle, morel, porcini and oyster mushrooms are a few of the mountains' fungal varieties.

Though much of the Northwest still seems wild and unpopulated, a lack of major wildlife reflects its vulnerability to logging and other human activities.

Crested, blue-bodied Steller's jays are noisy and common in forests, as are enormous crows and ravens. Sharp eyes may spot rufous hummingbirds buzzing around flowers. Bird watchers may want to concentrate on the region's many varieties of woodpecker. Notable streamside birds include blue herons, belted kingfishers and many kinds of ducks; watch for handsome, black-necked loons. Along the coast, gulls are ubiquitous, while puffins or cormorants may only be glimpsed through binoculars.

Almost all of the Northwest's sea-flowing rivers and streams produce their own salmon species. Northwestern waters are also trout-rich; notable is the seagoing steelhead trout. Beaver, otter and mink, the abundance of which brought white settlers to the Northwest in the first place, are still found along mountain streams.

Mule deer and elk are the most easily spotted of the forests' large mammals. Black bears inhabit the deep woods, and although not as dangerous as the grizzly (which isn't found here), they deserve respect.

Tide pools provide a window into the ocean. Look for sea anemones, starfish, mussels and hermit crabs. Sea mammals such as seals and sea lions are not uncommon along the coast, especially along quiet, rocky promontories. From these same outcroppings, travelers in the spring can watch for whales migrating up the coast. Those traveling by ferry between the San Juan, Vancouver and Gulf Islands are often treated to views of orcas, also known as killer whales.

East of the Cascades

The forests of the dry eastern uplands are dominated by ponderosa and lodgepole pines. The former are tall, handsome trees with long, bunched needles and cinnamon-colored trunks. Sporadic, low-growing western juniper trees dominate the region's extensive savannas, as does silver sage. Along prairie rivers and irrigation canals, cottonwood and poplar trees abound. In late spring, you'll find spectacular displays of deep-blue lupines sharing eastern Oregon hillsides with golden balsamroot.

In the desert areas of southeastern Oregon, plant life is found along seasonal lakes and intermittent streams. Tule, a rush-like reed, grows in marshy lake bottoms; Native Americans used it to weave house-building mats. In arid steppes, rabbitbrush, with its yellow flowers, brings the late-summer desert to bloom.

The open landscapes of central and eastern Oregon and Washington make bird life more visible. The western meadowlark, Oregon's state bird, trills its lovely song across the region. Spot the male's telltale black 'V' on its yellow breast. Listen at dusk for the swooping whistle of the nighthawk – its sudden dives to seize insects create a sound like a sharp, echoing intake of breath. Raptors are common: watch for falcons, hawks and (especially along the desert lakes) osprey and bald eagles.

The big rivers of central and eastern Oregon are home to salmon and various kinds of trout, while bass and sturgeon lure anglers to the Columbia. Rainbow trout is the most common variety of sport fish; the Deschutes River boasts its own subspecies of rainbow trout, called the red side, with ruby-red flanks.

Campers in any part of eastern Oregon and Washington are likely to be serenaded by coyotes. Abundant mule deer and pronghorn antelope make the area popular with hunters in fall. Bighorn sheep have been reintroduced into the high mountain peaks and river canyons.

The hot, dry conditions in central and eastern Oregon and Washington make for ideal snake territory. If you're scrambling or climbing on rock faces, beware of the rattlers sunning themselves on the ledges.

National & State Parks

The US part of the Pacific Northwest has four national parks: Olympic, North Cascades and Mt Rainier in Washington; and Crater Lake in Oregon. The National Park Service (NPS) also administers a number of historic sites, recreation areas and monuments in the region. British Columbia has six national parks, including Pacific Rim National Park, on Vancouver Island.

The real riches of the Northwest, however, are the many state and provincial parks and wildlife refuges, which often provide more intimate contact with nature or history than the major nationally administered parks.

Day-use parks – designed for picnicking, hiking or other daytime recreation (but not for camping) – are abundant in the Northwest. Because of tax-revenue shortages, however, some Oregon day-use parks charge a $3 parking fee ($25 for an annual pass), and Washington state parks plans to levy a similar fee for daytime visitors.

Wildlife refuges draw bird watchers as well as plant and animal enthusiasts. See the Bird & Wildlife Watching section of the Activities chapter for suggestions on where to go.

GOVERNMENT & POLITICS
The USA
The USA has a federal system with a president and a bicameral Congress, consisting of the 100-member Senate and the 435-member House of Representatives. Each of the 50 states has two senators and a number of representatives in proportion to its population – Oregon has five representatives; Washington has nine.

The president is chosen by the Electoral College, which consists of electors from each state in a number equivalent to the state's sum of senators and representatives, who vote for the electors in accordance with a popular vote within the state. To be elected, the president must obtain a majority of the total 538 electoral votes (at least 270, or half plus one). The president can be elected for no more than two four-year terms.

The federal government has three branches: The legislative branch makes the laws, the executive branch carries them out, and the judicial branch studies and interprets both the Constitution and the laws.

The two main political parties are the Democrats and the Republicans; the Green and Libertarian parties are among the smaller parties. Currently, the presidency is held by Republican scion George W Bush.

The head of state government is the governor, who presides over a bicameral legislature consisting of a senate and a house delegation. Democratic governors John Kitzhaber, of Oregon, and Gary Locke, of Washington, were re-elected to second terms in 1998 and 2000, respectively.

Oregon and Washington share a reputation for progressive, somewhat maverick politics. It's a long way to the traditional centers of American politics on the East Coast, and people tend to look elsewhere for political leadership and innovation.

Canada
Canada is a constitutional monarchy; that is, it is ruled by a parliamentary system, with the monarch of Britain remaining the official head of state. Canada's 10 provinces send representatives to the national House of Commons and Senate in Ottawa, Ontario, but they remain largely autonomous from the federal government.

British Columbia has a parliamentary government, with a 79-member Legislative Assembly that convenes in Victoria. The lieutenant governor is the formal head of state, but the real power goes to the premier, who is usually the head of the majority party. Premier Gordon Campbell, of the BC Liberal Party, assumed his post in 2001. In that year's elections, Liberals (who, despite their name, follow a mostly right-wing agenda) gained the upper hand, taking all of the legislative seats but two, which went to the New Democratic Party (NDP), which was the dominant party in the 1990s.

Indian Reservations
US Indian reservations are recognized by the federal government as independent political units. Tribes run their own schools; regulate transportation and trade; and have their own constitutions, legislative councils and tribal-court and police systems.

Visitors need to be aware that certain state laws do not apply on the 36 reservations within Washington and Oregon's boundaries. State taxes aren't levied on fuel and cigarettes sold by tribal members within reservations. Some local roads on reservation land are maintained by the tribes, and access to some places may be reserved for tribal members. For instance, much of the Yakama Reservation, in Washington, is off-limits to non-Indians. In addition, not all areas are open for recreation. Tribes can issue their own licenses for hunting and fishing and may levy a user fee for hikers and campers. Always check with tribal authorities before crossing onto reservation land.

Canada's native people are grouped into tribal bands, which are collectively administered by tribal councils. Made up of chiefs or other representatives from member bands, the councils provide advisory services to their members, including financial management, economic development and community planning. In British Columbia, 33 tribal councils serve the needs of 197 tribal bands.

ECONOMY

Blessed with abundant natural resources, busy international waterways and a well-educated populace, the Pacific Northwest's economy has outperformed the US and Canadian averages since the 1980s. The traditional economic engines have been resource-extractive industries, but the phenomenal success of high-tech firms and computer-hardware and -software developers has reshaped the region's profile.

The area's economy has historically been tied to forestry products. Oregon leads the USA in lumber production, and British Columbia contains nearly 40% of the marketable timber in Canada. However, most of the easily cut, easily transportable trees were logged long ago, and federal restrictions on logging public land have crippled much of what remains of the established lumber industry.

The fishing industry can also trace its decline to its own excesses. The Columbia and other Northwest rivers were once known as the world's great salmon fisheries until overfishing and habitat degradation brought about the near extinction of the species. Though much diminished, commercial fishing still plays an important role in the regional economy. Sport-fishing remains a viable industry in many small coastal towns, where anglers cast for crab,

cod, shark, tuna, shrimp, bottom fish and salmon.

Also see Economy in the Facts about British Columbia chapter.

High Technology

As timber and fishing have receded, many technology-based industries have to some extent filled the void, becoming major employers and business generators in the region. The Northwest is today home to some of the largest high-tech firms on the planet.

The Seattle area is headquarters for the software giant Microsoft, Nintendo and AT&T Wireless, as well as for numerous other computer-software and telecommunications firms, not to mention biotechnology companies. Real Networks, Amazon.com and go2.net are among the Washington companies that rode the crest of the Internet wave, though many dot-coms folded or downsized as revenues fell short of overblown expectations. Oregon's largest private employer is the semiconductor producer Intel, which maintains eight 'campuses' and construction plants in the suburbs west of Portland. Other major technology firms in the Willamette Valley include Hewlett-Packard (Corvallis), Symantec (Eugene) and the silicon-wafer manufacturer Fujitsu (Salem).

Boeing, the world's number-one aircraft manufacturer, is not the economic engine of western Washington that it used to be, a situation symbolized by the decision in 2001 to move its corporate offices to Chicago. Though it remains responsible for around 12% of Seattle's jobs, Boeing is far from being the corporate heavyweight it was in the 1960s, when at least a third of the city's workers owed their jobs to the aerospace industry. Due to industry cutbacks in the wake of the September 2001 terrorist attacks on the USA, Boeing said that it would cut as many as 20,000 employees from the ranks of its commercial-airline division in the Puget Sound. The slowdown was expected to have a serious ripple effect on the local economy, with suppliers and other related industries being forced to scale down their workload.

USA vs Microsoft

Northwesterners have closely followed the case against Microsoft, a company that directly employs 20,000 people in the Puget Sound area. The US Justice Department kept an eye on the business dealings of the Redmond, Washington–based software monolith for close to a decade; in 2000, the federal government and 18 states brought a landmark lawsuit against the company.

Microsoft was accused of illegally linking its Explorer Internet browser to the Windows 95 operating system through agreements with PC manufacturers, effectively barring competition from other browsers on the market. Justice Thomas Penfield Jackson ruled that the company had violated the Sherman Antitrust Act, an 1890 statute that prohibits monopolistic practices. The penalty: Microsoft would be split into two companies, one for Windows and a second for applications and other business interests. However, Judge Jackson undermined his own ruling by making indiscreet comments to the press in which he likened Microsoft cofounder Bill Gates to Napoleon and the company to a band of drug dealers. Microsoft appealed on the basis that Jackson's comments clearly demonstrated bias. The appeals court threw out the ruling, and Jackson was later dismissed.

Attuned to the less conflictive tone set by the recently installed Bush administration, the Justice Department and half of the plaintiff states reached a settlement with the software developer in October 2001. Generally interpreted as a Microsoft victory, the settlement ensures that computer makers will have the option of contracting with competing software developers, but does not force Microsoft to unhitch its software applications from the Windows operating system (which indeed it continued to do with the release of its new XP version). Some legislators have complained that the settlement does little to curb the Redmond company's anticompetition behavior and fear the deliberately vague terms guarantee litigation for years to come. With the other nine states in the suit contesting the accord and a European investigation under way, it appears Microsoft's day in court isn't over yet.

Fueling the high-tech industry, specialty-coffee entrepreneurs have established a huge niche in the region. Leading the pack, Starbucks, which has its headquarters in Seattle, has over 4500 retail outlets around the world and a reported annual revenue of over $2.2 billion.

International Trade

The ports of Seattle, Tacoma, Portland and Vancouver are among the largest on the West Coast. Practically all of Canada's trade with Pacific Rim countries passes through Vancouver, the second-busiest port on the North American continent. Televisions and other electronic gadgets pour through the port of Seattle, while Japanese and Korean cars arrive in Tacoma and Portland. Situated at the terminus of the Columbia River barge system, Portland is also the principal grain-shipment point for the West Coast.

Agriculture

From the moist valleys of the Rogue, Umpqua, Skagit and Fraser Rivers to the temperate grasslands east of the Cascades, agriculture flourishes. The extraordinarily fertile Willamette Valley yields crops as varied as hops, sod, wheat, berries, Christmas trees and grass seed. Cattle and sheep graze the eastern uplands, and golden wheat fields stretch across volcanic plateaus. Federally funded irrigation projects have made the desert bloom along numerous rivers, notably the Columbia, Yakima and Deschutes. Along the Columbia and Okanogan Rivers, vast orchards of apples, cherries, peaches and pears are harvested for the international market.

The rain-swept valleys along the Pacific Coast are famous for their dairy farms, especially along the Tillamook estuary, the Rogue River and on Vancouver Island. Flower bulbs are grown extensively along the Skagit River, in northern Washington. Mushroom gathering is an increasingly fundamental part of coastal Oregon economies.

Wine grapes in the northern end of the Willamette have achieved great success. The irrigated vineyards of Washington's Columbia, Walla Walla and Yakima Valleys have come into their own, producing world-class chardonnays and merlots and making the state the second-largest wine producer in the USA after California.

POPULATION & PEOPLE

Combined, the current population of Oregon and Washington is about 9.3 million, which amounts to about 3% of the total US population. By far the greatest concentrations of people are in Washington's Puget Sound area and Oregon's Willamette Valley. Oregon and Washington are among the fastest-growing states in the USA, each expanding 20% in the past decade.

With a population of four million, British Columbia is the fastest-growing Canadian province, due both to immigration – largely from China and Southeast Asia – and to movement within Canada.

Most US Northwesterners are white – African Americans comprise only 2.7% of the region's population (compared with a 12% component nationally) – but the 1990s saw an influx of Hispanic and Asian residents. British Columbia, while largely founded by British settlers, has a much more racially mixed population – nearly one-fifth of the people living in the Vancouver metro area are of East Asian origin.

The US government recognizes 36 Pacific Northwestern Native American tribes, for whom reservations or trust lands have been set aside. A number of other Native American groups in the region have no federally recognized status (without which they are ineligible for government assistance to support tribal schools and cultural centers) nor any guaranteed land base. Moreover, without legal recognition, it is difficult for tribes to maintain cultural identity. The total Native American population of Oregon and Washington is around 140,000.

In Canada, tribal bands control small tracts of land called reserves, the parameters of which were determined through treaties with Great Britain prior to independence (though only about a quarter of the country's Native people actually inhabit these lands). Only about one-third of 1% of BC's total area is under the control of the province's 197 tribal bands, who continue to press for a more equitable distribution of territory in negotiations overseen by the British Columbia Treaty Commission. First Nations inhabitants of British Columbia number roughly 140,000 according to the 1996 census, comprising 17.5% of Canada's total indigenous population.

EDUCATION

School attendance in the USA is usually obligatory until the age of 16, and almost everyone graduates from high school. However, local school districts are funded by property taxes, and consequently, there are great disparities in the resources available to schools in affluent suburbs versus those impoverished innercity neighborhoods and depressed rural areas. There are several levels of higher education: junior or community colleges (two-year institutions with advanced career training or introductory university courses), colleges or universities with four-year baccalaureate programs, and research universities with advanced-degree programs.

The largest university in the Pacific Northwest is the University of Washington, in Seattle, which has approximately 35,000 students. Washington's other large public universities include Western Washington University, in Bellingham, and Washington State University, in Pullman. Evergreen State College, in Olympia, is infamous for its unstructured curriculum and politically idealistic students.

Oregon's principal institutes of higher learning are the University of Oregon and Oregon State University, just miles apart in Eugene and Corvallis, respectively. Other notable schools include Portland State University; Southern Oregon University, in Ashland; and Portland's Reed College, a haven of lefty politics, environmentalism and fairly unabashed hedonism.

In British Columbia, about 2000 elementary and secondary schools educate more than 600,000 students. BC children typically attend school through grade 12 (age 18); most then go on to technical-school training or to a university. BC's major universities include the University of British Columbia, in Vancouver; Simon Fraser University, in Burnaby (a suburb of Vancouver); and the University of Victoria.

ARTS
Music
Portland, Vancouver and Seattle each offer a full array of classical-music venues, including well-respected professional symphony and opera companies, while smaller centers – such as Spokane, Victoria and Eugene – have community classical-music companies.

Thanks to the success of several Seattle bands – notably Nirvana and Pearl Jam – who gave birth to the postpunk phenomenon called grunge, the Northwest is well known for its modern music scene. Seattle, Vancouver and Portland are filled with dark and smoky music clubs, each with youthful musicians hoping to make the leap to stardom.

Literature
Portland and Seattle boast some of the largest independent bookstores in the nation, with author readings and signings among the cities' most popular events. Seattle claims to have the most bookstores per capita in the nation, while Portland boasts the busiest public-library system per capita. Vancouver's reading scene is no less rich, with literary cafes and bookstores dotting the streets of residential neighborhoods. The standard saying is that it rains so much in the Northwest that there's little to do but read.

The Northwest isn't just about consumption of reading material, it is also a major producer. Small publishing houses abound, while special-interest newspapers, tabloids and 'zines serve just about every group.

See Books, in the Facts for the Visitor chapter, for recommendations on good history books on Pacific Northwest.

Writers also find the Northwest an accommodating place in which to live and work. For a taste of current local fiction, read *Edge Walking on the Western Rim,* edited by Mayumi Tsutakawa; it's an anthology of modern Northwest writers.

Oregon has produced such literary giants as Ken Kesey, whose *One Flew over the Cuckoo's Nest* became a textbook of 1960s nonconformity – though many readers prefer his second novel, *Sometimes a Great Notion,* a sprawling epic that captures the brio of life in a small logging community. Kesey's death at age 66 in 2001 revived interest in the author, whose LSD-inspired exploits are as much a part of his myth as his books. David James Duncan *(The River Why* and *The Brothers K)* and Tom Spanbauer *(The Man Who Fell in Love with the Moon)* are acclaimed contemporary novelists from the Beaver State. Barry Lopez explores how people relate to their environment in short stories (such as *Desert Notes)* and nonfiction works (such as *Arctic Dreams).* Oregon seems to attract novelists with a bent toward science fiction and fantasy: Ursula LeGuin *(The Left Hand of Darkness)* and Anne McCaffrey *(Dragonquest)* live in the state, as does Jean Auel, whose widely read *Clan of the Cave Bear* series can best be described as 'prehistoric fiction.'

Washington's literary roster is equally impressive. The late Raymond Carver, whose precise use of language has been compared with Hemingway's, resided in his latter years on the Olympic Peninsula with Tess Gallagher, an important figure in the poetry world. Carver's best stories are collected in the volume *Where I'm Calling From.* David Guterson is best known for his award-winning *Snow Falling on Cedars,* a vivid tale of prejudice in a San Juan Island fishing community. Ivan Doig *(Dancing at the Rascal Fair)* has been praised for his powerful writing on the American West. He makes his home in Seattle, as do Sherman Alexie, the Spokane Indian author of *The Lone Ranger and Tonto Fistfight in Heaven,* and Jon Krakauer, the author of the best-seller *Into Thin Air,* a gripping account of a Mt Everest climbing disaster. Popular author Tom Robbins, a La Conner resident, has won numerous devotees for his wacky, countercultural novels *Another Roadside Attraction* and *Even Cowgirls Get the Blues,* among others.

Seattle has become a recognized center for graphic novelists and is the home of Fantagraphics, a major publisher and distributor of independent comics. Peter Bagge *(Hate)* and Daniel Clowes, whose graphic novel *Ghost World* was recently brought to the screen, are among the leading comic-book artists based in Seattle.

British Columbia's ever-active literary scene has cultivated a wide range of talent. Hard-drinking Malcolm Lowry, best known for *Under the Volcano,* was a profoundly influential BC writer. Alberta native WP Kinsella has long lived in BC; his novel *Shoeless Joe* was adapted for the film *Field of Dreams. Generation X* chronicler Douglas Coupland makes his home in Vancouver, as does science-fiction writer William Gibson, who coined the term 'cyberspace' in his 1984 novel *Neuromancer.* Nick Bantock, originally from England but now based in Vancouver, drew acclaim in the early 1990s with his *Griffin & Sabine* trilogy. William Deverell *(Kill All the Lawyers)* and Christopher Hyde *(A Gathering of Saints)* are well-known BC-based writers of thrillers.

Theater

Seattle and Vancouver have two of the most vibrant professional-theater scenes on the West Coast. There are apparently more equity theaters in Seattle than anywhere in the USA except New York City. The city also offers an array of amateur and special-interest troupes. Ashland, in southern Oregon, is famous for its Shakespeare Festival, which puts on open-air and indoor productions of Elizabethan and contemporary drama. See the regional chapters for more information.

Cinema

Seattle hosts a lively community of independent filmmakers, whose works are screened during the spring Seattle International Film Festival.

Maverick director Alan Rudolph, a Bainbridge Island resident, is the creator of *Choose Me, Afterglow* and other unconventional takes on modern romantic angst, as well as the futuristic film-noir *Trouble in Mind,* set in a Seattle-like metropolis called Rain City. Portland resident Gus Van Sant rose to prominence in the 1980s with the films *Mala Noche* and *Drugstore Cowboy,* which used his adopted city as the seedy setting for the exploits of characters on the fringe of society. Van Sant later directed the screen adaptation of Washington novelist Tom Robbins' *Even Cowgirls Get the Blues* – a box-office flop – followed by the smash hit *Good Will Hunting.*

For more about films set in the region, see Films, in Facts for the Visitor.

Visual Arts

The Native American art of the Pacific Coast is the most highly developed of the region's indigenous art. Distinctive painted wood and bone carvings, most often seen in masks, totem poles and canoes, are instantly recognizable by their motifs of stylized sacred animals, geometric shapes and colors. Good places to view such artifacts are the Seattle Art Museum, the University of Washington's Burke Museum (also in Seattle) and the UBC Museum of Anthropology (in Vancouver).

The coastal art tradition lives on through the work of contemporary Native American artists such as Bill Reid, a BC artist who acquired his skills from Mungo Martin, a Kwakiutl master carver of totem poles.

The sophisticated current art scene is well represented at galleries in Portland, Seattle, Vancouver, the Oregon coast, Victoria and the San Juan Islands.

A specialty of the Puget Sound area is glassblowing, led by a group of inventive and influential artisans from the Pilchuk School, whose most famous exponent is Dale Chihuly. Chihuly's works can be seen in a number of Seattle galleries, as well as in his hometown of Tacoma, where a new museum devoted entirely to glass art is scheduled to open in 2002.

Seattle public art abounds, thanks to its '1% for Art' program, which earmarks capital-improvement funds for public artwork.

SOCIETY & CONDUCT

Visitors from other parts of the world are often struck by the informality of Northwesterners: dressing up and putting on airs is not a part of life, even in situations where formal dress is usually expected. So travelers needn't worry much about dress codes at restaurants, concerts or social functions.

In a broad sense, the Northwest shares the general US and Canadian culture, but with a few important twists. In rural parts of eastern Oregon and Washington, the culture of the Old West is still very much alive. Fishing towns along the coast and islands have a distinctive and often gritty sensibility that comes from making a living on the stormy Pacific Ocean. Urban dwellers get out of town on weekends to ski, hike, climb or windsurf. It's fair to say that the natural environment is an overriding and cherished part of life for most people in this region.

The Northwest still puts a lot of emphasis on 'old family' legitimacy and connections. People boast of ancestors who came across the Oregon Trail or who were early Brits in Victoria. While not exactly clubby, there are certainly some longtime Northwesterners who differentiate between newcomers (ie, anyone who moved to the region after WWII) and members of old families.

While most urban Americans and Canadians are tolerant of individual eccentricities, rural Northwesterners in particular may be skeptical of outsiders and may resent what they perceive as an unfair criticism of their country or as interference in local matters. Visitors should show sensitivity over local political issues – don't broadcast your animal-rights convictions in a bar full of hunters or denounce clear-cutting in a mill town, for example.

RELIGION

The US Constitution mandates separation of church and state. However, matters such as prayer in public schools and abortion have brought theological issues onto the secular stage. Nominal allegiance is more widespread than church attendance, but many churchgoers are very devout.

Native American religions have been greatly modified since their contact with Europeans. Some, such as the Native American Church, which uses hallucinatory peyote buttons as a sacrament, are pan-Indian responses to encroachment by the politically dominant culture.

The dominant religion in the USA and Canada is Christianity, with Catholicism and Protestant sects roughly equal in number of adherents. The Mormon Church is prevalent throughout the Northwest. Judaism, Islam and Buddhism are also represented in urban areas. Rural areas, especially in the Willamette Valley, are home to Mennonites and Protestant communes (there's a Russian Old Believer community in the Willamette Valley and a Doukhobor enclave in BC, not too far from the city of Vancouver).

Nature religions also have a strong foothold in the Northwest, perhaps due to the Celtic gloom that presides here much of the year. Wicca (a pagan religion) and myriad other spiritual movements are found in the woods of western Oregon, Washington and British Columbia.

Facts for the Visitor

HIGHLIGHTS

The Pacific Northwest covers a vast area, so those with limited time would do well to organize a journey around a few favorite destinations. Most travelers are drawn to the western edge, with its urban centers and coastal adventures, but anyone who likes to veer off the beaten path should consider exploring the eastern part of the region, which features incredible landscapes.

Portland This sizable city with a small-town feel has a clean and accessible downtown, ample parks and gardens, and plenty of culture.

Oregon Coast Spectacular cliffs drop off into the throbbing surf; wild forested mountains rise into Pacific mists.

Mt Hood Northern Oregon's highest peak provides powdery snowpack year round.

Historic Columbia River Highway The mile-wide river carves a majestic gorge through the Cascade range; this slow road allows visitors to best appreciate the beauty.

Crater Lake The continent's deepest lake is a startlingly blue-green souvenir of an immense volcanic explosion.

Eastern Oregon The often-overlooked but fascinating region features Eocene-era fossil beds and immense fault block vistas.

Seattle The largest and most exciting city in the Northwest is famous for its youthful music scene, good restaurants, lively street life and caffeine culture.

Puget Sound In late spring and early summer, ogle pods of orcas off the shores of the San Juan Islands. Easily reached by ferry, but pleasantly remote, the islands offer travelers an abundance of cozy resorts and B&Bs.

Olympic Peninsula Glacier-hung peaks, rain forest trails, rugged coastline and historic seaports comprise the undeniable appeal of the USA's extreme northwest corner.

Washington's Cascade Peaks The western range is a mecca for outdoor recreationists.

Vancouver The superb setting – below snow-covered peaks on a series of peninsulas – only enhances the pleasure of visiting this cosmopolitan city.

Victoria British Columbia's capital is an open-air museum of late Victorian architecture, but it's not all tea and scones: Hearty recreation and after-hours entertainment also tempt travelers.

SUGGESTED ITINERARIES

Journeys can either be focused on a particular interest or type of landscape, or designed to enhance contrasting altitudes and attitudes.

Any of the major cities – Seattle, Portland, or Vancouver – could serve as a base for recreational or exploratory sojourns, or a combination trip can easily be done with a couple of days each in Vancouver and Seattle, or Seattle and Portland. Seattle provides a jump-off for visits to Mt Rainier and Mt St Helens, a couple of days in the San Juan Islands or parts of the Olympic Peninsula. From Vancouver, it's easy to venture out to Vancouver Island and Victoria, while a few days in Portland can be broken up by a jaunt to the beach or to Mt Hood. From any of these cities, short or long trips east of the mountains highlight the contrast between the densely populated coastal region and the wide-open dry country.

Alternatively consider making Bellingham your base. It's cheaper than the bigger cities and offers easy access for short trips to Mt Baker, Vancouver, the San Juan Islands, Seattle, the North Cascades and the Olympic Peninsula. Consider designing your itinerary as a loop to allow you a taste of the region's variety and make the most of each day. You can see a lot in a few active days, especially if you have a car. But any route could be stretched out to fit the time you have by going a little farther, spending more time exploring the small towns, taking an extra day to enjoy a festival, or packing your gear on your back and tramping the trails of the Cascades or Olympics.

PLANNING
When to Go
When to visit depends largely on what you want to do when you get there. Most travelers prefer the summer and fall, when the weather is pleasant and rainfall less frequent. If your plans include hiking and camping, then it's best to be west of the Cascades after May – the region gets 65% of its precipitation from November to March. Spring reaches eastern Oregon and Washington a little sooner; a trip to the high desert and eastern mountain ranges in May and June will reward travelers with fine weather and wildflower viewing. September and October are often glorious, with warm days and cool nights. Autumn brings a palpable sense of harvest, as apples, pears, wine grapes, nuts and vegetables all ripen at once. After October, the gray Pacific pall moves in and the rains begin.

If your itinerary brings you to the Northwest in winter, there'll still be plenty to do. Many cultural events, such as the symphony, opera and theater, are most active during this time. There's incredible skiing at Whistler, in BC; at Oregon's Mt Bachelor and Mt Hood; and Snoqualmie Pass and Stevens Pass, in Washington. Pacific Coast towns are often busy with 'storm watchers,' who come to experience the spectacular weather changes, high winds and waves that batter the coast.

Maps
Highway Maps The American Automobile Association (AAA; spoken as 'Triple A') issues the most comprehensive and dependable highway maps, which are free with a AAA membership. Membership privileges between the AAA and CAA (the Canadian equivalent) are reciprocal. See Useful Organizations in the Getting Around chapter for more information.

State and provincial transportation departments put out free maps that are widely available from tourist offices. Good town street maps and regional maps are often distributed by local tourist bureaus. US Forest Service maps, available at ranger stations, are good for navigating backcountry roads on USFS lands.

Topographic Maps Green Trails 1:69,500 maps cover Washington's Cascade range and Olympic Peninsula and most of Oregon's northern Cascades. Ideal for hikers, climbers and cross-country skiers, they include campground and information sources on the reverse. US Geological Survey (USGS; ☎ 888-275-8747) 7½-minute series topographic maps give a closer view at 1:24,000, though they're often too cumbersome for trail use. Both kinds of maps cost $4 and are widely available at area outfitters and ranger stations or via the Web (W www.greentrails.com or W mcmcweb.er .usgs.gov/topomaps).

Atlases Benchmark Maps produces useful atlases of Washington and Oregon, containing detailed topographic/highway maps at a scale of 1:200,000, as well as larger-scale maps keyed to park and campground information. Also look for the DeLorme series of atlases and gazetteers, which have useful lists of bike routes, wineries, golf courses and other recreational detours. Both are available in bookstores, department stores and gas stations and cost about $20 each. MapArt produces many sheet maps and atlas books covering BC; see them online at W www.mapart.com.

What to Bring
In all seasons but the height of summer, it's a good idea to bring a rain jacket, or at least an umbrella; don't bring clothing that can't stand up to a little rain.

Summers are usually warm enough for shorts and T-shirts, but evenings can get chilly, even in August, so pack a sweater or windbreaker.

Unless you are planning a sustained mountain trip in winter, heavy winter gear isn't usually necessary. Winters in western Oregon, Washington and BC are usually chilly and wet, but not extremely cold. If you're going to travel in the eastern parts of these areas, take along a wind-proof coat, gloves, hat and scarf.

If camping is on your agenda, make sure that your tent is waterproof: Northwest dews are as heavy as rain showers elsewhere. Nights will be cool, so bring a warm sleeping bag. Hiking trails are often muddy; dedicating a pair of shoes to trail walking and beachcombing is probably a good idea.

When you spot your first sea lion or bighorn sheep, you'll be glad you packed a pair of binoculars. Likewise, consider bringing along a good wildlife or wildflower guide (see Books, later in this chapter).

RESPONSIBLE TOURISM

Many travelers come to this part of North America primarily to get out into the open air and experience the deep forests, expansive deserts and ocean beaches. Unfortunately, the very urge to experience these treasures could end up damaging them.

Some runs of wild salmon – particularly Chinook and coho – are highly endangered, and the continued existence of an entire species may hinge on the survival of individual fish. While sport fishing is just one of a range of factors causing their depletion, you should be sure to follow seasonal restrictions and observe annual catch limits.

Soil erosion is another major problem, mostly due to overzealous logging and agriculture that have clear cut mountainsides and broken down stream banks. But individual hikers can have an impact too – impromptu shortcuts can expose soil and form new water courses. Stay on trails, don't remove vegetation from hillsides, and do your best not to muddy streams. Certain kinds of recreational activities, such as four-wheeling, dirt biking and ORVing, are enor-

mously erosive, and even mountain biking can be destructive. To minimize damage, park and forest services have set up trail networks for such activities, and responsible riders should stick to them.

TOURIST OFFICES

Oregon, Washington and British Columbia have state and provincial tourist bureaus that offer glossy guides, maps and scads of other pertinent travel information. Individual cities and regions also maintain visitor centers, which are often run by the local chamber of commerce; addresses and phone numbers for these are in the regional chapters.

Oregon Tourism Commission (☎ 503-986-0000, out-of-state ☎ 800-547-7842, fax 503-986-0001, W www.traveloregon.com), 775 Summer St NE, Salem, OR 97310 USA

Washington State Tourism Division (☎ 360-725-5052, 800-544-1800, W www.tourism.wa.gov), PO Box 42500, Olympia, WA 98504-2500 USA

Tourism BC (☎ 604-435-5622, 800-435-5622, outside North America ☎ 250-387-1642, W www.hellobc.com), PO Box 9830, Stn Prov Govt, Victoria, BC V8W 9W5

VISAS & DOCUMENTS

All important documents (passport data page, visa, credit cards, travel insurance policy, air/bus/train tickets, driver's license etc) should be photocopied before you leave home. Leave one copy with someone at home and keep another with you, separate from the originals.

It's also a good idea to store details of your vital travel documents in Lonely Planet's free online Travel Vault. Your password-protected Travel Vault is accessible online anywhere in the world – create one at W www.ekno.lonelyplanet.com.

Visas & Passports

The USA To enter the United States, Canadians must have proof of Canadian citizenship, such as a citizenship card with photo ID or a passport. Visitors from other countries need a valid passport and usually a US visa.

However, under a reciprocal visa-waiver program, citizens of about 30 countries may

HIV & Entering the Region

Travelers with HIV (human immunodeficiency virus) should be aware that the Immigration & Naturalization Service (INS) has the authority to bar their entry into the USA. Though being HIV-positive is not grounds for deportation, it is a 'ground of exclusion,' and the INS can invoke it to refuse admission.

Although the INS doesn't test people for HIV at customs, it may try to exclude anyone who answers 'yes' to this question on the nonimmigrant visa application form: 'Have you ever been afflicted with a communicable disease of public-health significance?' INS officials may also stop people if they seem sick, are carrying AIDS/HIV medicine or, sadly, if the officer happens to think the person 'looks gay,' though sexual orientation is not legally grounds for exclusion.

Canadian immigration policy is to not exclude people because they are HIV-positive unless it can be shown that they 'place excessive demand on Canada's health- and social-service systems. This is unlikely to apply to short-term visitors. Nonimmigrant travelers are not tested for HIV, nor can they be denied entry if carrying HIV medication.

Immigrants and visitors who may face exclusion should discuss their rights and options with a trained immigration advocate before applying for a visa. For legal advice in the USA, contact the Immigrant HIV Assistance Project, Bar Association of San Francisco (☎ 415-782-8995), 465 California St, Suite 1100, San Francisco, CA 94104. In Canada, contact the Canadian HIV/AIDS Legal Network (☎ 514-397-6828), 417 Saint-Pierre St, Suite 408, Montréal, Québec H2Y 2M4.

enter the USA for stays of up to 90 days without a visa. Check the US State Department's website (W www.travel.state.gov/vwp.html) for a current listing. Air travelers must have a roundtrip ticket that is nonrefundable in the USA, as well as proof of financial solvency. Visitors arriving by land need not present a roundtrip ticket. Extensions are not allowed under the reciprocity program.

Those who do need a visa can apply via a local US consulate or embassy, usually by mail. There's a nonrefundable fee of $45. Your passport should be valid for at least six months longer than your intended stay, and you'll need to submit a 1½-inch-square (37mm x 37mm) recent photo with the application. Documents of financial stability and/or guarantees from a US resident are sometimes required.

Visa applicants may be required to 'demonstrate binding obligations' that will ensure their return to their countries. Consequently, you're better off applying for a US visa while you are still in your home country rather than attempting it while you're on the road.

The most common visa is the Non-Immigrant Visitors Visa: B1 for business purposes, B2 for tourism or visiting friends and relatives. Visitors visas are good for one or five years, depending on your nationality, and it specifically prohibits the visitor from taking paid employment in the USA. Ultimately, the period of validity is determined by US immigration authorities at the port of entry. Multiple entries are permitted.

Other kinds of visas are required to work or study in the USA, and your potential employer or school should make the arrangements. Allow six months for the processing of the application. For information on work visas and employment in the US, see Work, later in this chapter.

If you want, need, or hope to stay in the USA longer than the date stamped on your passport, go to the local INS office (or call ☎ 800-755-0777) before the stamped date to apply for an extension. After that date, expect an unpleasant conversation with doubting INS officials. If you find yourself in that situation, it's a good idea to bring a US citizen with you to vouch for your character, and to have some verification of sufficient funds.

Also see the Arriving in the USA and Arriving in Canada sections of the Getting There & Away chapter.

Canada Visitors to Canada from major Western countries need no visa, but citizens of more than 130 nations do, including those from countries in Eastern Europe and the former Soviet Union. Visa requirements change frequently, so check before you leave – the most current information can be found at Citizenship and Immigration Canada's website (W www.cic.gc.ca). Visitor visas cost $75 and are valid for a period of six months. Applications for a visa extension must be submitted at least three weeks before the current visa expires, and there is an additional $75 fee. Apply for extensions at a Canadian Immigration Centre (☎ 604-666-2171) for information on how to proceed with your application.

Visitors from nearly all countries need a passport, though a passport and/or visa do not guarantee entry. Admission and duration of stay are at the discretion of the immigration officer at the border. Those under 18 years of age should have a letter from a parent or guardian.

Officially, US citizens don't need a passport or visa to enter Canada, and some proof of citizenship, such as a birth certificate along with state-issued photo identification, will ordinarily suffice. However, since the introduction of tighter border security in the wake of the terrorist attacks of September 2001, border officials recommend that US citizens carry a passport to facilitate entry.

Air travelers from countries other than the USA may be required to have either a return or onward ticket in their possession. These tickets may be 'open,' or undated.

Travel Insurance

It makes good sense to obtain a policy covering in-transit theft, loss and medical problems. Policies come in all shapes and sizes, so read the small print. In the USA, with its exorbitant health-care costs, it's best to spring for a higher medical-expense option. Check that the policy you're con-

sidering covers ambulances or an emergency flight home.

Some policies specifically exclude 'dangerous activities,' which can include scuba diving, motorcycling and even trekking. A locally acquired motorcycle license may invalidate your coverage.

You may prefer a policy that pays doctors or hospitals directly rather than requiring you to pay on the spot and claim later. If you have to claim later, make sure you keep all documentation. Some policies ask you to call back (reverse charges) to a center in your home country, where an immediate assessment of your problem is made.

International Driving Permit

Local traffic police are more likely to accept an International Driving Permit than an unfamiliar foreign license as valid identification. Your national automobile association can provide one for a small fee, and they're usually valid for one year. Canadian and US citizens need not worry about obtaining an IDP to drive in the Pacific Northwest.

Hostel Cards

Most hostels in the USA are members of Hostelling International/American Youth Hostel (HI/AYH), which is affiliated with the International Youth Hostel Federation (IYHF). You can purchase membership before you leave home or on the spot when checking in. Most hostels allow nonmembers to stay but charge them a few dollars more.

US and Canadian citizens can join online (W www.hiayh.org) or by phone (in the US ☎ 202-783-6161, in Canada ☎ 800-663-5777) at the rate of $25/$15/free for adult/senior/youth. Foreign membership cards are valid for HI/AYH hostels; see the International Youth Hostel Federation website (W www.iyhf.org) for contact details of your home country's hostelling organization. To join the US or Canadian affiliates, foreign visitors should obtain a 'welcome card' upon checking in. This card is stamped for the first six nights at hostels for a $3 fee per night, after which it becomes an HI/AYH membership card that's good for the member rate.

Student & Senior Cards

Students and people over the age of 65 are often entitled to discounts on museums and other attractions throughout the USA and Canada, with the appropriate identification.

Students should bring along an international student identification card, or a school or university student identification card. Seniors need only present some proof of age. The American Association of Retired People (see Senior Travelers, later in this chapter) offers membership cards for discounts, and coverage is also available for citizens of other countries.

EMBASSIES & CONSULATES
US & Canadian Diplomatic Offices Abroad

The following are some US and Canadian diplomatic offices abroad:

Australia

US Embassy: (☎ 02-6214-5600) 21 Moonah Place, Yarralumla ACT 2600

US Consulate: (☎ 02-9373-9200) MLC Centre, Level 59, 19-29 Martin Place, Sydney NSW 2000

US Consulate: (☎ 03-9526-5900) 553 St Kilda Rd, Melbourne, Victoria

Canadian High Commission: (☎ 02-6273-3844, W www.canada.org.au) Commonwealth Ave, Canberra ACT 2600

Denmark

US Embassy: (☎ 35 55 31 44) Dag Hammarskjölds Allé 24, 2100 Copenhagen

Canadian Embassy: (☎ 33 48 32 00), Kr Bernikowsgade 1, 1105 Copenhagen

France

US Embassy: (☎ 01 43 12 22 22) 2 Ave Gabriel, 75008 Paris

Canadian Embassy: (☎ 01 44 43 29 00) 35 Ave Montaigne, 75008 Paris

Germany

US Embassy: (☎ 030 238 5174) Neustädtische Kirchstr 4-5, 10117 Berlin

Canadian Embassy: (☎ 030 203 120, W www .kanada-info.de) 12th floor, Friedrichstrasse 95, 10117 Berlin

Ireland

US Embassy: (☎ 01-668-7122) 42 Elgin Rd, Dublin 4

Canadian Embassy: (☎ 01-478-1988) Canada House, 65 St Stephen's Green, Dublin 2

Israel

US Embassy: (☎ 3-510-3822) 1 Ben Yehuda St, Tel Aviv

Canadian Embassy: (☎ 3-636-3300) 3 Nirim St, 4th floor, Tel Aviv 67060

Italy

US Embassy: (☎ 6-46-741) Via Vittorio Veneto 119/A, 00187 Rome

Canadian Embassy: (☎ 6-44-598) Via GB de Rossi 27, 00161 Rome

Japan

US Embassy: (☎ 03-3224-5000) 1-10-5 Akasaka, Minato-ku, Tokyo 107-8420

Canadian Embassy: (☎ 03-5412-6200) 3-38 Akasaka 7-chome, Minato-ku, Tokyo 107-5803

Mexico

US Embassy: (☎ 5-211-0042) Paseo de la Reforma 305, Col Cuauhtémoc, 06500 Mexico City

Canadian Embassy: (☎ 5-257-2479) Calle Schiller 529, Col Bosque de Chapultepec, 11580 Mexico City

Netherlands

US Embassy: (☎ 70-310-9209) Lange Voorhout 102, 2514 EJ, The Hague

US Consulate: (☎ 20-575-5309) Museumplein 19, 1071 DJ Amsterdam

Canadian Embassy: (☎ 70-311-1600) Sophialaan 7, 2500 GV, The Hague

New Zealand

US Embassy: (☎ 04-462-6000) 29 Fitzherbert Terrace, Thorndon, Wellington

Canadian High Commission: (☎ 04-473-9577) 61 Molesworth St, 3rd floor, Thorndon, Wellington

UK

US Embassy: (☎ 20-7499-9000) 24 Grosvenor Square, London W1A 1AE

Canadian High Commission: (☎ 020-258-6600) Canada House, Consular Services, Trafalgar Square, London SW1Y 5BJ

Consulates in the Pacific Northwest

Most nations' principal diplomatic offices are in Washington, DC, and Ottawa. To find out the telephone number of your embassy or consulate in DC, call ☎ 202-555-1212; in Canada, call ☎ 613-555-1212.

Twenty-six nations maintain consular representatives in Seattle, 14 in Portland and 40 in Vancouver. Many of these are not regular offices, but rather individuals who represent their native countries in ceremonial functions. To find addresses and numbers of consular offices that are not listed here, look under 'Consulates' in the local yellow pages.

Australia
In British Columbia: (☎ 604-684-1177) 888 Dunsmuir St, Vancouver

Canada
In Washington: (☎ 206-443-1777) 412 Plaza 600, Sixth and Stewart, Seattle

France
In Oregon: (☎ 503-220-2269) 921 SW 6th Ave, Portland

In Washington: (☎ 206-256-6184) 2200 Alaskan Way, Seattle

In British Columbia: (☎ 604-681-2301) 1130 Pender St, Vancouver

Germany
In Washington: (☎ 206-682-4312) 600 University St No 25, Seattle

In British Columbia: (☎ 604-684-8377) 999 Canada Place, Vancouver

Ireland
In British Columbia: (☎ 604-683-9233) 1385 8th Ave W, Vancouver

Japan
In Oregon: (☎ 503-221-1811) 1300 SW 5th Ave, Suite 2700, Portland

In Washington: (☎ 206-682-9107) 601 Union St, Seattle

In British Columbia: (☎ 604-684-5868) 1177 Hastings St, Vancouver

Netherlands
In Oregon: (☎ 503-222-7957) 1001 SW 5th Ave, Portland

In British Columbia: (☎ 604-684-6448) 475 Howe St, Vancouver

New Zealand
In Washington: (☎ 206-525-0271) calls only

In British Columbia: (☎ 604-684-7388) 888 Dunsmuir St, Vancouver

UK
In Oregon: (☎ 503-227-5669) calls only

In Washington: (☎ 206-622-9255) 900 4th Ave, Seattle

In British Columbia: (☎ 604-683-4421) 1111 Melville St, Vancouver

USA
In British Columbia: (☎ 604-685-4311) 1095 W Pender St, Vancouver

CUSTOMS

US Customs allows each person over the age of 21 to bring 1L of liquor and 200 cigarettes duty-free into the USA. US citizens are allowed to import, duty-free, $400 worth of gifts from abroad; non-US citizens are allowed to bring in $100 worth. Should you happen to be carrying more than $10,000 in US and foreign cash, traveler's checks, money orders or the like, you need to declare the excess amount.

Canadian Customs allows visitors 19 years and older to bring in 1.1L (40 ounces) of liquor or a case of beer (24 beers), as well as 200 cigarettes. You can bring in gifts up to C$60 in value. Sporting goods, cameras and film, can also be brought in without trouble. Registering these items upon arrival might save you some hassle when you leave, especially if you'll be crossing the Canadian/US border a number of times. If you have a dog or cat, you will need proof that it has had a rabies shot in the past 36 months.

MONEY
Currencies

The US dollar is divided into 100 cents (¢). Coins come in denominations of 1¢ (penny),

5¢ (nickel), 10¢ (dime), 25¢ (quarter) and the seldom-seen 50¢ (half dollar). Quarters are the most commonly used coins for vending machines and parking meters, so it's handy to have a stash of them. A recently introduced $1 coin bears the image of Sacagawea; unlike the previous Susan B Anthony version, which was often confused with the quarter, the new, gold-colored coin appears to be catching on. Notes, commonly called 'bills,' come in $1, $2, $5, $10, $20, $50, and $100 denominations – $2 bills are rare but perfectly legal.

The Canadian dollar ($) is divided into 100 cents (¢). Coins come in denominations of 1¢ (penny), 5¢ (nickel), 10¢ (dime), 25¢ (quarter), $1 (loonie) and $2 (twoonie) pieces. There is also a 50¢ coin, but this is seldom seen. Notes come in $5, $10, $20, $50 and $100 denominations.

Exchange Rates

At press time, one US dollar equaled C$1.59, and one Canadian dollar equaled 63¢. Other exchange rates were as follows:

country	unit		US$	C$
Australia	A$1	=	51¢	81¢
European Union	€1	=	86¢	$1.36
Japan	¥100	=	74¢	$1.18
New Zealand	NZ$1	=	42¢	66¢
United Kingdom	UK£1	=	$1.41	$2.24

Exchanging & Obtaining Money

Banks in larger towns usually can exchange cash or traveler's checks in major foreign currencies, but those in outlying areas may take some time to complete the transaction. Additionally, Thomas Cook, American Express and exchange windows in international airports offer exchange (although you'll get a better rate at a bank).

Traveler's Checks Traveler's checks offer protection from theft or loss and in many places can be used as cash. American Express and Thomas Cook are widely accepted and have efficient replacement policies. Though traveling with cash is more risky, it's convenient to pocket some bills for all those tips, and a few out-of-the-way places may not accept credit cards or traveler's checks.

Keep a record of the checks you have used, and store it separately from the checks themselves. This is vital when it comes to replacing lost checks.

You'll save yourself trouble and expense if you buy traveler's checks in US dollars. Restaurants, hotels and most stores accept US-dollar-denominated traveler's checks as if they were cash, so you'll rarely have to use a bank or pay an exchange fee. BC businesses also accept US dollar traveler's checks, but you'll get a better rate by exchanging them at the bank before making purchases.

Credit & Debit Cards Major credit cards are generally accepted at hotels, restaurants, gas stations, shops and car rental agencies throughout the region. In fact, you'll find it hard to perform certain transactions – such as renting a car or purchasing concert tickets – without one. It would be wise to have a Visa or MasterCard in your deck, since other cards aren't as widely accepted.

Places that accept Visa and MasterCard are also likely to accept debit cards; those issued by large commercial banks can often be used worldwide. Unlike a credit card, a debit card deducts payment directly from the user's checking account, as if they were writing a check. Banks generally charge no fee for debit-card purchases, but the merchant may charge a small fee.

Carry copies of your credit-card and debit-card numbers separately from the cards (or store them in your Lonely Planet travel vault; see Visas & Documents, earlier). If your credit cards are lost or stolen, contact the company immediately to stop further charges.

The following toll-free assistance lines are working around the clock. (To invalidate a debit card, you'll have to contact the issuing bank.)

American Express	☎ 800-528-4800
Diners Club	☎ 800-234-6377
Discover	☎ 800-347-2683
MasterCard	☎ 800-826-2181
Visa	☎ 800-336-8472

ATMs Automatic teller machines are a convenient way of obtaining cash from a bank account back home. Even small-town banks in the middle of nowhere have ATMs, which are generally working 24 hours, as do shopping malls and convenience stores throughout the land. Debit cards are usually used at ATMs, but check with your bank to see if your credit card can be set up for cash withdrawals.

Most banks are affiliated with several ATM networks; Exchange, Accel, Plus and Cirrus are the predominant ones. Check with your bank or credit-card company for exact fees, which may be charged by both card-issuing and cash-dispensing banks. Credit cards usually charge a 2% fee for these transactions, and the interest rate on cash advances is often significantly higher than the rate for purchases.

International Transfers You can transfer money by American Express, Thomas Cook or Western Union, or instruct your bank back home to send you a draft. Specify the city, bank and branch to which you want your money directed, or ask your home bank to suggest one, and make sure you get the details right. The procedure is easier if you've authorized someone back home to access your account.

Expect funds via telegraphic transfer to reach you within a week; by mail, allow at least two weeks. The amount will likely be converted into dollars on arrival – you can take cash or buy traveler's checks.

Security
You should be cautious – but not paranoid – about carrying money. If you're not planning to use your cash, plastic or other valuables on a particular outing, leave them at your hotel or hostel, preferably inside a safe. If you must carry large amounts of cash when you're on the move, try not to make it too obvious. A money belt worn under your clothes is a good place to stash excess currency. Avoid carrying your wallet in a back pocket, in handbags or in the outside pockets of day packs and fanny packs (bum bags). See Dangers & Annoyances, later in this chapter.

Costs
Cost for accommodations vary seasonally, between the cities and the countryside, and between resorts and everywhere else. Generally, rates are higher in summer, between Memorial Day and Labor Day, but winter rates at ski resorts can be astronomical. The cheapest motel rates will usually be in the $35 range. Rustic camping can be inexpensive, only about $10 or so per night; amenities such as hot showers boost the price to $15 or $20.

Food can be very reasonable. The occasional splurge at a first-rate restaurant will cost anywhere between $25 and $50, depending on the location, but good restaurant meals can be found for $10 – or even half that for some lunch specials. If you purchase food at markets, you can get by even more cheaply.

City public transportation is relatively inexpensive; buses or subways will cost anywhere from 50¢ to $2.50, depending on distance; some regional bus companies offer free transportation.

Owning or renting a car is much less expensive than in other parts of the world, and fuel is relatively cheap – these are important factors in the Pacific Northwest, where vast areas are not served by public transportation. See the Getting Around chapter for information on purchasing or renting a car.

Tipping
Tipping is expected in restaurants and better hotels, and by taxi drivers, hairdressers and baggage carriers. Restaurant waitstaff are paid minimal wages and rely upon tips for their livelihoods. Tip 15% unless the service is terrible, or 20% for great service. There's no need to tip at fast-food, takeout or buffet-style restaurants.

Taxi drivers expect 10%, and hairdressers get 15% above the tab if their service is satisfactory. Baggage carriers (skycaps in airports, attendants in hotels) get $1 for the first bag and 50¢ for each additional bag.

Discounts
The USA is probably the most promotion-oriented society on earth. Though the

bargaining common in many other countries is generally not accepted, you can work angles to cut costs. For example, at hotels in the off-season, casually and respectfully mentioning a competitor's rate may prompt a manager to lower the quoted rate. Artisans may consider a negotiated price for large purchases. Discount coupons are widely available – check circulars in the Sunday edition of newspapers, at supermarkets and at tourist offices.

Taxes & Refunds

Almost everything you pay for in the USA is taxed, including restaurant meals, drinks and accommodations, but only occasionally are taxes included in the advertised price. Keep this invisible charge in mind to avoid rude surprises when being handed the bill. Unless otherwise stated, the prices given in this book don't reflect local taxes.

One exception to the above general rule is Oregon, which has no sales tax or value-added tax (VAT). Washington's base state sales tax is 6.5%, though counties and cities can assess an additional percentage. This tax is not levied on food in grocery stores; it does, however, apply to prepared takeout meals. British Columbia assesses the national Canadian Goods and Services Tax (GST) of 7% and also a provincial sales tax of 7%. See the Information section of the Vancouver chapter for more information on the GST.

When inquiring about hotel or motel rates, be sure to ask whether taxes are included. The so-called bed tax is added to the cost of accommodations in motels, hotels, lodges and B&Bs in the Northwest (including everything from phone calls to parking fees to room service). These fees normally range from 2% to 8% (though they can be much higher) and vary from community to community. In Seattle, the combined bed and sales tax exceeds 15%, which can be a significant additional cost.

POST & COMMUNICATIONS
Postal Rates

At the time of writing, rates for 1st-class mail within the USA are 34¢ for letters up to 1oz (23¢ for each additional ounce) and 21¢ for postcards.

International airmail rates (except to Canada and Mexico) are 80¢ for a 1oz letter and 75¢ for each additional ounce; postcards and aerogrammes are 70¢.

The cost for packages airmailed anywhere within the USA is $3.45 for 2lb or less, increasing by $1 per pound up to $6 for 5lb. For heavier items, rates differ according to the distance mailed. Books, periodicals and computer disks can be sent by a cheaper parcel-post rate.

In Canada, first-class letters or postcards up to 30g are C$0.47 within Canada and C$0.60 to the USA. To all other destinations, 1st-class letters or postcards are C$1.05 for up to 20g, more for heavier items. See the Canada Post website (W www.canadapost .ca) for a handy rate calculator.

Sending Mail

Drop stamped letters or packages up to 16oz into any public mailbox (they're blue in the USA and red in Canada). Bring larger items to the post office. Larger towns have branch post offices and postal centers in some supermarkets and drugstores. For the address of the nearest office, call the US Postal Service at ☎ 800-275-8777, or check W www.usps.com.

Usually, post offices in main towns are open 8am to 5pm Monday to Friday and 8am to 3pm Saturday (Canada Post is not open Saturdays), but call first.

Receiving Mail

In the US and Canada, you can have mail sent to you care of General Delivery at any post office that has its own zip (postal) code. Mail should be addressed like this:

Lucy Chang
c/o General Delivery
Caballo, NM 87931
USA

Mail is usually held for 10 days before it's returned to the sender; you might request your correspondents to write 'Hold for Arrival' on their envelopes.

Telephone

To make a local call in Oregon and the Vancouver area, you need to dial 10 digits – the three-digit area code + the seven-digit number. Western Washington is also switching to a 10-digit local dialing system, probably in late 2002. At the same time, a new area code, 564, will overlay the current 206, 253, 425 and 360 area codes: the old numbers won't change, but new phone lines in those regions will be assigned the new code. Thus, you might find two phones on the same street, or even in the same home, that have different area codes. Outside of Oregon and Vancouver, just dial the seven-digit number for local calls.

If you're calling long distance, dial ☎ 1 + the three-digit area code + the seven-digit number. The international country code for the USA and Canada is 1.

For local and nationwide directory assistance, dial ☎ 411 (fee charged). To obtain directory assistance for a toll-free number, dial ☎ 800-555-1212.

The 800, 877 and 888 area codes are designated for toll-free numbers within the USA and sometimes in Canada as well. Toll-free 800 numbers can be limited to specific regions (ie, the number may work in Oregon but not in Washington).

Local calls usually cost 50¢ at public phones. Long-distance rates vary, depending on the destination and which telephone company you use; call the operator (☎ 0) for rate information. Don't have your call put through, however, because operator-assisted calls are much more expensive than direct-dial calls. Generally, nights (11pm to 8am), all day Saturday and 8am to 5pm Sunday are the cheapest times to call; evenings (5pm to 11pm Sunday to Friday) are mid-priced; and calls made between 8am and 5pm Monday to Friday are full price.

International Calls To make an international call direct, dial ☎ 011, then the country code, followed by the area code and the phone number. International rates vary depending on the time of day, destination and service provider; check with the operator (☎ 0).

Hotel Phones More expensive hotels add a service charge of 50¢ to $1 for each local call made from a room phone and slap hefty surcharges on long-distance calls. In budget hotels, local calls may be free, while long-distance calls are often blocked – guests are expected to call collect or use a phone card (see below).

Phone Cards These allow you to pay for calls in advance; access your 'account' by dialing a toll-free number followed by a code found under a scratch-off surface on the back of the card. Available from Western Union and Fred Meyer supermarkets among other places, cards may be denominated in $5, $10, $20 or $50 amounts. Both domestic and international versions are sold.

eKno Communication Service Lonely Planet's eKno global communication service provides low-cost international calls – for local calls, you're usually better off with a local phone card. eKno also offers free messaging services, email, travel information and an online travel vault, where you can securely store all your important document information. You can join online at ⓦ www.ekno.lonelyplanet.com, where you will find the local access numbers for the 24-hour customer service center. Once you have joined, check the eKno website for the latest access numbers for each country and for updates on new features.

The access number throughout the USA's lower 48 states is ☎ 800-706-1333; in Canada, dial ☎ 877-635-3575 or ☎ 800-808-5773.

Fax

Fax machines are easy to find in the Northwest – they're at shipping companies (such as Mail Boxes Etc in the USA), photocopy stores and hotel business service centers, but be prepared to pay high prices ($1 a page nationally, $3 internationally).

Email & Internet Access

Despite the rise of email as a method of communication, cybercafes are still relatively scarce throughout most of the Pacific

Northwest, with the exceptions of Seattle and throughout BC. However, most public libraries in Oregon and Washington offer Internet access, usually at no charge. Where cybercafes do exist, you'll find them listed in the text.

To collect your mail through a cybercafe, you have several options. One is to open a free Web-based email account such as Hotmail (ⓦ www.hotmail.com) or Yahoo! Mail (ⓦ mail.yahoo.com). You can then access your mail from any net-connected machine running a standard Web browser. Another alternative is to access your home Internet mail account via a mail program such as Outlook Express. You'll need to provide your incoming (POP or IMAP) mail server name, your account name and your password.

If you plan to carry your laptop or hand-held computer with you and would like to use it to check your email, your most convenient option is to open an account with a global Internet service provider. Major ISPs such as AOL (ⓦ www.aol.com), Compu-Serve (ⓦ www.compuserve.com), Earthlink (ⓦ www.earthlink.net) and IBM Net (ⓦ www.ibm.net) have dial-in nodes throughout the USA and Canada, which means you can access your account by dialing up a local number. Remember that North American power supply voltage (110V) may vary from that at home. Unless your computer can handle variable voltages, you'll need a universal AC adapter. Also check the requirements of your modem and telephone connections.

DIGITAL RESOURCES
The World Wide Web is a rich resource for travelers. You can research your trip, hunt down bargain airfares, book hotels, check on weather conditions or chat with locals and other travelers about the best places to visit (or avoid!).

There's no better place to start your Web explorations than the Lonely Planet website (ⓦ www.lonelyplanet.com). Here, you'll find succinct summaries on traveling to most places on earth; postcards from other travelers; and the Thorn Tree bulletin board,

where you can ask questions or dispense advice. You can also find travel news and updates to many of our most popular guidebooks, and the subWWWay section links you to the most useful travel resources elsewhere on the Web.

Following is a sampling of websites that will help you plan your travels in the Pacific Northwest.

Oregon Tourism Commission The official Oregon Tourism site includes a state map and calendar of events.
ⓦ www.traveloregon.com

National Park Service This site features fast facts on national parks, recreation areas and historic sites in the USA.
ⓦ www.nps.gov/parks.html

Nature of the Northwest This is a helpful virtual visitor center for Oregon and Washington, containing information on USFS campground reservations and Northwest Forest passes, which can be ordered online.
ⓦ www.naturenw.org

Tourism BC The province's official site lists trip ideas, accommodations and activities.
ⓦ www.hellobc.com

Washington State Tourism Division This site covers accommodations, transportation, sights and recreation, including information pages for every town in the state.
ⓦ www.tourism.wa.gov

BOOKS
In addition to the following guides and reference works on the Pacific Northwest, readers would do well to immerse themselves in Northwest fiction (see Literature in the Facts about the Pacific Northwest chapter). A few of the titles in this section may be out of print but can nevertheless be found on the shelves of Portland's Powell's and Seattle's Elliott Bay bookstores, or in local libraries.

Lonely Planet
Lonely Planet's *Seattle* and *Vancouver* city guides, *British Columbia, Rocky Mountains, California & Nevada* and *Canada* are good supplemental guides for travelers heading to North America's western region. *Hiking in the USA* and *Cycling USA – West Coast*

show you some of the best trails and bike routes, with maps and detailed itineraries.

Guidebooks

In this outdoors-oriented region, numerous field guides crowd bookstore shelves. National Audubon Society's *Field Guide to the Pacific Northwest* is a compact, color reference to the ecology of Oregon and Washington. *Plants & Animals of the Pacific Northwest: An Illustrated Guide to the Natural History of Western Oregon, Washington, and British Columbia,* by Eugene N Kozloff, is another good general resource.

Those hitting the trails should look for the 100 Hikes guide series published by The Mountaineers, available at many ranger stations. Washington travelers seeking a historical perspective on the state will appreciate the well-researched *Exploring Washington's Past: A Road Guide to History,* by Ruth Kirk & Carmela Alexander.

History

The daily logs of Lewis and Clark, as presented in Bernard DeVoto's carefully edited *Journals of Lewis and Clark,* are full of wild adventures, misspellings and wonderful candor. For a narrative retelling of the Corps of Discovery's journey, turn to Stephen E Ambrose's *Undaunted Courage: Meriwether Lewis, Thomas Jefferson, and the Opening of the American West.*

Lewis and Clark weren't the only pioneers to set down their observations in journals and memoirs. *Women's Diaries of the Westward Journey,* edited by Lillian Schlissel, provides a revealing look into day-to-day life along the Oregon Trail. In 1888, Arthur A Denny, one of the founders of Seattle, penned *Pioneer Days on Puget Sound.*

About the best volume covering the region as a whole is *The Great Northwest,* by Oscar O Winther. *The Good Rain: Across Time and Terrain in the Pacific Northwest,* by *New York Times* correspondent Timothy Egan, is an insightful discussion of the Northwest and its people.

Other histories focus on individual states. *The Balance So Rare: The Story of Oregon,* by Terence O'Donnell, is a gracefully written

overview of the state's past illustrated with vintage photos. *Skid Road* and *Puget's Sound,* both by Murray Morgan, are richly textured sagas on the growth of Seattle and Tacoma, respectively. For a comprehensive overview of BC's development, read *The West Beyond the West,* by Jean Barman.

Native Peoples

A Guide to the Indian Tribes of the Pacific Northwest and *Indians of the Pacific Northwest: A History,* by Robert H Ruby & John A Brown, are both superlative: The first is a tribe-by-tribe encyclopedia of the region's Native Americans; the second, an overview of Northwest Indian history and culture. *Native People of the Northwest: A Travelers Guide to Land, Art and Culture,* by Jan Halliday & Gail Chehak, directs travelers to significant Native American places, such as galleries, museums and historical sites. *Raven, a Trickster Tale from the Pacific Northwest* retells an indigenous myth in the form of a children's book.

FILMS

The film and TV industries are quite active in the Pacific Northwest, owing to the relatively low production costs and range of scenic locales. Thus, many films produced in the region are set somewhere else: Oregon's Cascades have served as the Colorado Rockies in *The Shining;* Roslyn, Washington doubled as Alaska in the TV series *Northern Exposure;* and the Vancouver area has stood in for everything from Tibet in Martin Scorsese's *Kundun* to New York City in Jackie Chan's *Rumble in the Bronx.*

The Northwest does occasionally appear as itself in motion pictures. Nowadays, Seattle's skyline and quirky lifestyles are recognizable internationally, thanks to such films as *Sleepless in Seattle* and *Singles.* Portland serves as a menacing backdrop for the brooding films of Gus Van Sant (see Cinema, in the Facts about the Pacific Northwest chapter). Noted Canadian director Atom Egoyan first drew wide notice with *The Sweet Hereafter,* which won the Grand Jury prize at the 1997 Cannes Film Festival for its portrayal of a fictional BC town torn apart by a school-bus crash.

The explosive rise (and depressing fall) of Seattle's grunge scene is documented in the film *Hype,* through interviews and concert footage of dozens of seminal bands such as Pearl Jam, Soundgarden, Mudhoney and of course Nirvana, whose first live performance of *Smells Like Teen Spirit* is highlighted.

British Columbia is one of the centers of film in Canada, and many Canadian features are set in Vancouver. Recent movies and TV series shot in BC include *The X-Files* (now relocated to California), the remake of *Get Carter* and *Scary Movie.*

NEWSPAPERS & MAGAZINES

The *Seattle Post-Intelligencer* (usually called the PI) and the *Seattle Times;* Vancouver's the *Province* and *Vancouver Sun;* and Portland's *Oregonian* are the region's principal print news sources. Friday editions of these papers have extended arts and events information.

Travelers will discover that there are dozens of alternative weekly newspapers throughout the Northwest that discuss music, arts and local issues from a hipper, more youthful and political point of view. Look for these usually free publications in coffeehouses, bars, bookstores and music stores. In Portland, there's *Willamette Week,* Seattle has the *Stranger* and the *Seattle Weekly,* and Vancouver puts out the *Georgia Straight. Just Out,* in Portland; *Seattle Gay News;* and *Xtra West,* in Vancouver, cover the gay and lesbian beat.

National newspapers such as the *New York Times, USA Today* and the *Wall Street Journal* are widely available in the cities and larger towns of the Northwest. Canada's nationally distributed paper is the *Globe & Mail* newspaper, published daily in Toronto.

Northwest Travel and *Oregon Coast* are bimonthly magazines with glossy articles on both urban and outdoor destinations, plus seasonal events coverage. Also worth checking is *Northwest Weekend,* a Thursday pullout section of the *Seattle Times,* with weekend getaway suggestions and lists of festivals around the region. Other magazines, such as *Northwest Palate* and *Active Northwest,* focus on specific interests.

RADIO & TV

Scores of radio stations crowd the airwaves in and near major cities, dominated by commercial playlist formats with heavy doses of classic rock and contemporary country. In university towns, college radio stations may offer a more interesting alternative. Noncommercial stations carrying news-oriented National Public Radio (NPR) can be found in the lower numbers of the FM band: In Seattle, NPR is heard on University of Washington's KUOW (94.9 FM); in Portland, on KOPB (91.5 FM). Many public stations also carry the BBC World Service, which is a good source for foreign news. You can pick up the Canadian Broadcasting Corporation (CBC), with its lively mix of arts, news and commentary, at 690 AM in Vancouver and 90.5 FM in Victoria.

All the major TV networks have affiliated stations throughout the USA. These include ABC, CBS, NBC, FOX (all commercial stations) and PBS (non-commercial). Nationwide cable channels include ESPN (sports), HBO (mainly movies) and the Weather Channel; Cable News Network (CNN) and MSNBC provide continuous news coverage. You'll find nonstop local news coverage on Northwest Cable News (Channel 2 in Seattle; 8 in Portland). The major US-based broadcast and cable networks are also carried on many cable systems in BC. The CBC is on TV, too; it's broadcast in Vancouver on CBUT (3) and CBUFT in French (7).

PHOTOGRAPHY & VIDEO
Film & Equipment

Print film is widely available at supermarkets and discount drugstores. Color print film can handle a wider range of light and shadow than slide film. However, slide film, particularly the slower speeds (under 100 ASA), has better resolution than print film. Like B&W film, slide film is rarely sold outside of major cities, and when available, it's expensive.

Film can be damaged by excessive heat, so don't leave your camera in the car on a hot summer day, and avoid placing it on the dashboard while you're driving. Carry a spare battery to avoid disappointment when your camera dies in the middle of nowhere.

Drugstores do inexpensive film processing. If you drop it off by noon, you can usually pick it up the next day. A roll of 100 ASA 35mm color film with 24 exposures will cost about $7 to get processed. Many one-hour photo finishers operate in the larger towns, and a few can be found near tourist attractions.

Video Systems
The USA and Canada use the National Television System Committee (NTSC) color TV standard, which is not compatible with other standards (PAL or SECAM) used in Africa, Europe, Asia and Australia unless converted.

Airport Security
Slow and medium-speed film can withstand being passed through airport X-ray machines used to scan luggage at airports. Higher-speed films are more sensitive, but even 400 ASA film can be X-rayed four or five times without any noticeable effects. If you are carrying film rated 1600 ASA or above, you may want to carry film and cameras separately and ask the security inspector to manually inspect them.

Avoid packing film in your check-in luggage: today's high-intensity scanners may fog undeveloped film after just a single pass.

TIME
All of Washington, most of Oregon and western British Columbia are on Pacific Standard Time (PST), which is eight hours behind Greenwich Mean Time (GMT), three hours behind New York City and 17 hours ahead of Tokyo. A small sliver of easternmost Oregon is on Mountain Standard Time (MST), an hour ahead of PST.

Oregon, Washington and BC observe the switch to daylight saving time, when clocks are moved ahead one hour for a period of time (it begins the first Sunday in April and lasts until the last Sunday in October).

ELECTRICITY
In Canada and the USA, voltage is 110V, and the plugs have two (flat) or three (two flat,

one round) pins. Plugs with three pins don't fit into a two-hole socket, but adapters are easy to buy at hardware stores or drugstores.

WEIGHTS & MEASURES
In the USA, distances are in feet, yards and miles. Three feet equal one yard (.914m); 1760 yards or 5280 feet are 1 mile. Dry weights are in ounces (oz), pounds (lb) and tons (16 ounces are 1 pound; 2000 pounds are 1 ton). Liquid measures are in pints (16 fluid ounces) and quarts (two pints). The latter is a common measure for liquids such as milk, which is also sold in half gallons (two quarts) and gallons (four quarts). In the USA, gasoline is dispensed by the US gallon, which is about 20% less than the imperial gallon; in Canada, it's dispensed by the liter. See the inside back cover of this book for a handy conversion chart.

All measures in Canada are in metric, though many people persist in thinking of distance in miles.

LAUNDRY
You'll find self-service, coin-operated laundry facilities in most towns of any size and in better campgrounds. Washing and drying a load should not cost more than $3. Some laundries have attendants who will wash, dry and fold your clothes for you for an additional charge. This guide lists laundry locations in most towns; otherwise, see 'Laundries' or 'Laundries – Self-Service' in the yellow pages of the local phone directory.

HEALTH
Your health while traveling depends on your pre-departure preparations, your daily health care while traveling and how you handle any medical problem that does develop. While the potential dangers can seem quite frightening, in reality, few travelers experience anything more than a minor upset stomach.

In the Pacific Northwest, there are no unexpected health dangers, and excellent medical attention is readily available. However, a collision with the health-care system can cause severe injuries to your financial condition!

In a serious emergency, call ☎ 911 for an ambulance to take you to the nearest hospital emergency room.

Predeparture Planning

Make sure you're healthy before you start traveling. If you're going on a long trip, have a dental checkup. If you wear glasses, take a spare pair and your prescription.

Those who require a particular medication should take an adequate supply, as it may not be available locally. Take a part of the packaging that shows the generic name rather than the brand. To avoid any problems, it's a good idea to have a legible prescription or letter from your doctor showing that you're required to use the medication.

Make sure that you have adequate medical-insurance coverage. See Travel Insurance, under Visas & Documents, earlier in this chapter, for details.

Medical Problems & Treatment

Self-diagnosis and treatment can be risky, so you should generally seek medical help. An embassy, consulate or hotel can usually recommend a local doctor or clinic. Although we do give drug dosages in this section, they are for emergency use only. Correct diagnosis is vital. In this section, we have used the generic names for medications – check with a pharmacist for brands available locally.

Note that antibiotics are generally not available without a prescription, and in any case should be administered only under medical supervision. Take only the recommended dose at the prescribed intervals, and use the whole course, even if the illness seems to be cured earlier. If you are allergic to commonly prescribed antibiotics such as penicillin, carry this information (eg, on a bracelet) when traveling.

Environmental Hazards

Altitude Sickness Lack of oxygen at high altitudes (over 8200 feet, or 2500m), such as the Cascade peaks, affects most people to some extent. Acute Mountain Sickness (AMS) may develop during the first 24 hours at these heights and may be fatal.

Mild symptoms include headache, lethargy, dizziness, difficulty sleeping and loss of appetite. Severe symptoms include breathlessness, a dry cough, intense headache, lack of coordination and balance, confusion, irrational behavior, vomiting, drowsiness and losing consciousness. There is no hard-and-fast rule as to what is too high: AMS has been fatal at 10,000 feet (3000m), although 11,500 feet to 15,000 feet (3500m to 4500m) is the usual range.

Treat mild symptoms by resting at the same altitude until recovery, usually a day or two. Paracetamol or aspirin can be taken for headaches. If symptoms persist or become worse, however, immediate descent to a lower elevation is necessary.

To help prevent acute mountain sickness, do the following:

- Ascend slowly – have frequent rest days, spending two to three nights at each rise of about 3000 feet (1000m).
- Sleep at a lower altitude than the greatest height reached during the day. Also, once above 10,000 feet (3000m), care should be taken to not increase the sleeping altitude by more than 1000 feet (300m) per day.
- Drink extra fluids. Mountain air is dry and cold, and moisture is lost as you breathe. Evaporation of sweat may occur unnoticed and could result in dehydration.
- Eat light, high-carbohydrate meals for more energy.
- Avoid alcohol, as it may increase the risk of dehydration.
- Avoid sedatives.

Hypothermia Changeable weather at high altitudes can leave you vulnerable to exposure; after dark, temperatures in the mountains can drop from balmy to perilously cold in a surprisingly brief interval. A combination of wind, wet clothing, fatigue and hunger can cause your body to lose heat faster than it can produce it, a condition known as hypothermia. It is best to dress in layers; silk, wool and some of the new artificial fibers are all good insulating materials. Also, a strong, waterproof outer layer is essential; pack a 'space blanket' for emergencies. Carry basic supplies, including food containing simple sugars to generate heat quickly and something to drink.

Symptoms of hypothermia are exhaustion, numb skin (particularly toes and fingers), shivering, slurred speech, irrational or violent behavior, lethargy, stumbling, dizzy spells, muscle cramps and bursts of energy.

To treat mild hypothermia, first get the victim out of the wind and/or rain, then remove wet clothing and dress him or her in something warm and dry. Administer hot liquids – not alcohol – and some high-energy, easily digestible food. Do not rub the victim; allow them to slowly warm themselves.

Jet Lag Jet lag is experienced when a person travels by air across more than three time zones. It occurs because many of the functions of the human body are regulated by internal 24-hour cycles. The stress of adjusting to the new time may cause fatigue, disorientation, insomnia, anxiety, impaired concentration and a loss of appetite. These effects will usually be gone within three days after arrival, but to minimize the impact of jet lag, do the following:

• Rest for a couple of days prior to departure.
• Try to select flight schedules that minimize sleep deprivation; arriving late in the day means you can go to sleep soon after you arrive. For very long flights, try to organize a stopover.
• Avoid excessive eating (which bloats the stomach) and alcohol (which causes dehydration) during the flight. Instead, drink plenty of noncarbonated, nonalcoholic drinks, such as fruit juice or water.
• Make yourself comfortable by wearing loose-fitting clothes and by bringing an eye mask and ear plugs to help you sleep on the plane.
• Try to sleep at the appropriate time for the time zone you are traveling to.

Motion Sickness Eating lightly before and during a trip will reduce the chances of motion sickness. In transit, look for a place that minimizes movement – near the wing on aircraft, close to midships on ferries, near the center on buses. Fresh air usually helps; reading and cigarette smoke don't. Commercial motion-sickness preparations, which can cause drowsiness, have to be taken before the trip commences. Ginger (available in capsule form) and peppermint (including mint-flavored sweets) are natural preventatives.

Poison Oak Poison oak, related to poison ivy, is a tall, thin shrub with shiny, three-part leaves. It grows in shady, moist areas in the western USA, including the Pacific Northwest. Just brushing past this plant while on a hike can cause a blistery and extremely itchy rash on bare skin, which should be washed with a strong soap (Fels Naphtha is a recommended brand) immediately after exposure. Cortisone creams will lessen the itching in minor cases.

Sunburn You can get sunburned surprisingly fast, even through cloud cover. Use sunscreen, a hat, and a barrier cream for your nose and lips. Calamine lotion or a commercial after-sun preparation are good for mild sunburn. Protect your eyes with good-quality sunglasses, particularly if you'll be near water, sand or snow.

Bites & Stings

Bee and wasp stings are usually more painful than dangerous. Calamine lotion or a sting-relief spray should ease the pain, and ice packs will reduce swelling. Black widow spiders, found east of the Cascades, and hobo spiders, recognizable by their funnel-shaped web, have poisonous bites, but incidents are rarely reported.

Devoid of the sort of venomous creatures found in warmer seas, Pacific Northwest waters are considered a benign environment for divers. Injuries may occur when divers inadvertently step on the spikes of sea urchins, which can cause infection, or brush against the stinging spines of rockfish or dogfish.

See Less-Common Diseases, later, for details on rabies, which is passed through bites and scratches from mammals.

Ticks Ticks are parasitic arachnids that may be present in brush, forest and grasslands, where hikers often get them on their legs or in their boots. The adults suck blood from hosts by burying their heads into the skin, but they're often found unattached and can simply be brushed off.

If you have been walking through a tick-infested area, check all over your body, as ticks can cause skin infections and other, more serious, diseases. If a tick is found attached, grab its head with tweezers and gently pull upward. Avoid pulling the rear of the body, as the resulting release of fluid through the skin increases the risk of infection. Also see Lyme Disease, under Less-Common Diseases, later.

Snakes Rattlesnakes are pervasive in much of eastern Oregon, Washington and BC. There's no mistaking this snake for anything else, with its distinctive diamond-back markings and rattle. To minimize your chances of being bitten, always wear boots, socks and long trousers when walking through undergrowth where snakes may be present. Don't put your hands into holes and crevices, and be careful when collecting firewood.

Snakebites do not cause instantaneous death, and antivenins are usually available. If you are bitten or stung by a rattlesnake, wash the wound with soap and water and apply a clean dressing. Immediately wrap the bitten limb tightly, as you would for a sprained ankle, and then attach a splint to immobilize it. Keep the victim still and seek medical help. If possible, bring the dead snake for identification, but don't attempt to catch it if there's a chance of being bitten again. Tourniquets and sucking out the poison are now comprehensively discredited as remedies.

Infectious Diseases

Diarrhea Canadian and American standards of cleanliness in places serving food and drink are very high, and travelers in the Pacific Northwest are not likely to experience more than minor stomach upset resulting from changes in diet. A change of water, food or climate can cause a mild bout of traveler's diarrhea, but a few rushed toilet trips with no other symptoms is not indicative of a major problem.

Dehydration is the main danger with any diarrhea – particularly for children or the elderly, in whom it can occur quite quickly. Under all circumstances, *fluid replacement* (at least equal to the volume being lost) is the most important thing to remember. Soda water, weak black tea with a little sugar, or soft drinks allowed to go flat and diluted 50% with clean water are all good. With severe diarrhea, a rehydrating solution is preferable to replace lost minerals and salts.

Giardiasis Backpacking travelers who drink water from mountain streams risk contracting giardiasis, a cause of persistent diarrhea. This condition is caused by a microscopic parasite that enters streams through the fecal remains of animals – especially beaver. Giardia is prevalent throughout the Northwest – it has even been known to enter the water supply of mountain towns – thus, water should never be drunk straight from streams, springs or lakes.

Symptoms – which can appear several weeks after you have been exposed to the parasite – include stomach cramps, nausea, a bloated stomach, watery and foul-smelling diarrhea, and frequent gas. The symptoms may disappear for a few days and then return; this can go on for several weeks.

If you think you have giardiasis, seek medical advice, but where this is not possible, tinidazole or metronidazole is the recommended drug. Treatment is a 2g single dose of tinidazole or a 250mg dose of metronidazole three times daily for five to 10 days.

Hepatitis Hepatitis is a general term for inflammation of the liver. It is a common disease worldwide. There are several different viruses that cause hepatitis, and they differ in the way that they are transmitted. Hepatitis A is transmitted by contaminated food and drinking water. Hepatitis B is spread through contact with infected blood, blood products or body fluids – for example, through sexual contact, unsterilized needles and blood transfusions – or through contact with blood via small breaks in the skin. Hepatitis C and D are spread in the same way, while hepatitis E is transmitted in the same way as type A. There are vaccines to guard against hepatitis A and B, but currently none against the other types.

The symptoms are similar in all forms of the illness and include fever, chills, headache, fatigue, feelings of weakness, and aches and pains; these are followed by loss of appetite, nausea, vomiting, abdominal pain, dark urine, light-colored feces, jaundiced (yellow) skin and eyes. The symptoms of hepatitis B may be more severe than type A, and the disease can lead to long-term problems, such as chronic liver damage, liver cancer or a long-term carrier state.

HIV & AIDS Infection with the human immunodeficiency virus (HIV) may lead to acquired immune deficiency syndrome (AIDS), which is a fatal disease. Any exposure to contaminated blood, blood products or body fluids may put the individual at risk. The disease is often transmitted through sexual contact or dirty needles. HIV/AIDS can also be spread through infected blood transfusions; however, the blood supply in the USA and Canada is well screened. If you do need an injection, ask to see the syringe unwrapped in front of you, or take a needle and syringe pack with you.

Fear of HIV infection should never preclude treatment for serious medical conditions. See the boxed text in the Visas & Documents section for information on HIV-positive travelers entering the USA & Canada.

Red Tide The Puget Sound area in Washington, parts of the BC coast and some small bays along the Oregon coast are often affected by red tide (also called paralytic shellfish poisoning). The syndrome is caused by the proliferation of toxin-producing algae that contaminate clams, mussels, oysters and the like, making them lethal to ingest. Warning signs will not necessarily be posted at beach access sites, nor is the color of the water an accurate indicator of the condition. To be sure, phone the local Marine Biotoxin Hotline (in Washington, ☎ 800-562-5632; in Oregon, ☎ 503-986-4728; in BC, ☎ 604-666-3169) before attempting to catch shellfish from the Pacific.

Sexually Transmitted Diseases Other than HIV, diseases that can be transmitted through sexual contact include gonorrhea, herpes and syphilis. Sores, blisters or rashes around the genitals and discharges or pain when urinating are common symptoms. In some STDs, such as wart virus or chlamydia, symptoms may be less marked or not observed at all, especially in women. Chlamydia infection can cause infertility in both men and women before any symptoms have been noticed. Syphilis symptoms eventually disappear completely, but the disease continues and can cause severe problems in later years. While abstinence from sexual contact is the only 100% effective prevention, using condoms is also effective. Gonorrhea, syphilis and some other STDs can be treated with antibiotics.

Less-Common Diseases
The following diseases pose a small risk to travelers, and so are only mentioned in passing. Seek medical advice if you think you may have any of these diseases.

Lyme Disease This is a tick-borne infection that may be acquired in some parts of North America, though the risk is considered low in the Pacific Northwest. The illness usually begins with a spreading rash at the site of the tick bite and is accompanied by fever, headache, extreme fatigue, aching joints and muscles, and mild neck stiffness. If untreated, these symptoms usually go away over several weeks, but over subsequent weeks or months, disorders of the nervous system, heart and joints may develop. Medical help should be sought early in the illness when treatment is most effective. According to the US Centers for Disease Control, an effective vaccine is available for prevention of the North American variety of Lyme disease.

Rabies This fatal viral infection may be carried in the saliva of dogs, cats, bats, skunks, squirrels and other mammals. Any bite, scratch or even lick from a rabid animal should be cleaned immediately and thoroughly. Scrub with soap and running water, and then apply alcohol or iodine solution. Medical help should be sought promptly to receive a course of injections to prevent the onset of symptoms and/or death.

Tetanus This potentially fatal disease poses a risk only to unvaccinated travelers. Found all over the world, tetanus is caused by a germ that lives in soil and in the feces of horses and other animals. It enters the body via breaks in the skin. The first symptom may be discomfort in swallowing, or a stiffening of the jaw and neck; this is followed by painful convulsions of the jaw and whole body.

WOMEN TRAVELERS

In the Pacific Northwest, women travelers usually have a wonderful time, unmarred by dangerous encounters. To ensure that this is the case, consider the following suggestions.

Exercise vigilance in large cities. In Vancouver, the Main & Hastings Sts area is best avoided, and Stanley Park is not recommended for after-dark strolls. In Seattle, don't go unaccompanied at night to the Belltown, Pioneer Square or the Central and International Districts.

While there may be less to watch out for in rural areas, men who are unaccustomed to seeing women traveling alone may still harass them. Try to avoid hiking or camping alone, especially in unfamiliar places.

If despite your precautions you are assaulted, call the police (☎ 911). (In some rural areas where 911 is not active, just dial 0 for the operator.) Larger towns usually have rape crisis centers and women's shelters that provide help and support; check the telephone directory for listings or ask the police for referrals.

The following are a couple useful organizations for women:

National Organization for Women (NOW; ☎ 202-331-0066, ⓦ www.now.org) 1000 16th St NW, Suite 700, Washington, DC 20036 USA. An ad-

vocacy group, NOW is a good resource for political and women's rights issues. The national center can refer you to state and local chapters.

Planned Parenthood (☎ 212-541-7800) 810 7th Ave, New York, NY 10019 USA. This organization can refer women to health clinics throughout the country and offer advice on health issues.

GAY & LESBIAN TRAVELERS

As elsewhere in North America, gay life in the Pacific Northwest is most tolerated in urban centers, while attitudes tend to be far less accepting in the hinterlands. In Seattle, Vancouver and Portland, and even some smaller towns, such as Eugene and Victoria, travelers will find everything from gay religious congregations to gay hiking clubs, while in the rural areas, they may want to keep their orientation to themselves.

The following national resource numbers may prove useful: National AIDS/HIV Hotline (☎ 800-342-2437), National Gay/Lesbian Task Force (☎ 202-332-6483 in Washington, DC) and Lambda Legal Defense Fund (☎ 212-809-8585 in New York City, ☎ 213-937-2728 in Los Angeles).

In Oregon, a valuable source of information is Portland's gay newspaper, *Just Out* (or their website: ⓦ www.justout.com). Portland's Gay & Lesbian Community Yellow Pages, published by the Portland Area Business Association (☎ 503-241-2222, ⓦ www.paba.com) lists gay-oriented businesses. Portland-based Cascade AIDS Project is the lead agency for HIV/AIDS services and operates the statewide Oregon AIDS hotline (☎ 800-777-2437); the number doubles as a gay and lesbian resources line.

The Capitol Hill neighborhood is the center of gay life in Seattle. Contact the Lesbian Resource Center (☎ 206-322-3953), at 2214 S Jackson St, for information, or stop by Beyond the Closet bookstore (☎ 206-322-4609), 518 E Pike St at Belmont Ave, to pick up flyers and newspapers and check the bulletin board. Gay Community Social Services (☎ 206-322-2873), at PO Box 22228, Seattle, WA 98122 USA, is another good contact. To get a listing of gay-friendly businesses, get in touch with the Gay/Lesbian Business Association (☎ 206-363-9188).

On Vancouver Island, look for copies of the *Vancouver Island region Pink Pages*, also available online at w www.gayvictoria .com/pinkpages, with links to gay and lesbian companies and activities in Victoria and Vancouver, BC.

DISABLED TRAVELERS

The region is highly developed for disabled travelers. Hotel, restaurants, theaters and other public buildings are required by law to be wheelchair accessible. Larger private and chain hotels offer suites for disabled guests.

Lift-equipped buses are the norm in BC, Washington and Oregon, and many taxi companies have wheelchair-accessible cabs. Some municipal bus networks provide door-to-door service for people with disabilities. Call the local transit systems listed in the guide for information. Disabled travelers using Washington State Ferries can phone ☎ 206-464-6400 to find out which ferries provide elevators or ramps. Most car rental franchises offer hand-controlled models at no extra charge. All major airlines, Greyhound buses and Amtrak trains allow service animals to accompany passengers, and they will frequently sell two-for-one packages when attendants for disabled passengers are required. Airlines will also provide assistance for connecting, boarding and deplaning if requested with your reservation.

Many state and national parks in the Northwest maintain a nature trail or two for use by wheelchair-using travelers. The Golden Access Passport, available free to disabled travelers at NPS and USFS offices, gives free lifetime access to US national parks and wildlife refuges and 50% off campground use. *Washington Accessible Outdoor Recreation Guide,* available from Washington tourist offices, is a useful catalogue of parks and campgrounds with accessible facilities throughout the state.

A number of organizations and tour providers specialize in the needs of disabled travelers:

Access-Able Travel Source (☎ 303-232-2979, fax 239-8486, w www.access-able.com) PO Box 1796, Wheat Ridge, CO 80034 USA

Mobility International USA (for international exchange opportunities; ☎ 541-343-1284, fax 541-343-6812, w miusa.org) PO Box 10767, Eugene, OR 97440 USA

Society for Accessible Travel & Hospitality (SATH; ☎ 212-447-7284, w www.sath.org) 347 Fifth Ave, Suite 610, New York, NY 10016 USA

SENIOR TRAVELERS

Travelers 50 years and up can expect to receive cut rates at many hotels, campgrounds, restaurants, parks and museums; be sure to inquire.

Visitors to national parks and campgrounds can reduce costs by using the Golden Age Passport, a card that allows US citizens aged 62 and over (and those traveling in the same car) free admission nationwide and a 50% reduction on camping fees. You can purchase one ($10) at any national park or regional office of the USFS or NPS. Washington and Oregon State Parks also offer discount camping passes for seniors.

The following groups can help seniors plan their travels:

American Association of Retired Persons (AARP; ☎ 800-424-3410, w www.aarp.org) PO Box 189, Long Beach, CA 90801 USA. This is an advocacy group for Americans 50 years and older and a good resource for travel bargains. Membership, available to all nationalities, is $10 per year.

Elderhostel (☎ 877-426-8056; outside North America, ☎ 978-323-4141, w www.elderhostel .org) 11 Avenue de Lafayette, Boston, MA 02111-1746 USA. This is a nonprofit organization that offers academic-oriented tours for seniors, combining university lectures with field trips throughout North America. It's open to people 55 years and older and their companions; the programs last one to three weeks, and meals and accommodations are included.

TRAVEL WITH CHILDREN

Children receive discounts on many things in the Pacific Northwest, ranging from motel stays to museum admissions. However, the defining age for 'child' varies widely – some places count anyone under 18 eligible for discounts, while others only include children under six.

Many hotels and motels allow children to share a room with their parents for free or for a modest fee, though B&Bs rarely do (some don't allow children at all). More expensive hotels can arrange baby-sitting services. Some restaurants offer kid's menus.

Airlines do discount children's tickets, but these may turn out to be more expensive than the cheapest APEX adult tickets. Most buses and tours have discounted children's prices, though the discounts are not always significant. Car rental companies provide infant seats for their cars on request.

Local tourist offices can suggest where to have fun with children of all ages. Children's museums, loaded with entertaining and educational activities, are found in Seattle, Tacoma, Olympia, Ellensburg, Portland, Salem and elsewhere, while aquariums, zoos, amusement parks and county fairs will keep the kids busy. Vancouver holds its International Children's Festival (☎ 604-687-7697) in Vanier Park each May; it has clowns, puppeteers, jugglers and storytellers.

Lonely Planet's *Travel With Children,* by Cathy Lanigan, is filled with practical suggestions for allowing the kids (and yourself) to get the most out of your trip.

DANGERS & ANNOYANCES

Although street crime is an issue in large urban areas, visitors need not be obsessed with security. Still, always lock cars and put valuables out of sight, whether you are in a town or in the remote backcountry – even if you're leaving the car for just a few minutes. Consider investing in a steering wheel locking device ('the Club') if you intend to park your car on city streets. Aim to use ATM machines in well-trafficked areas. In hotels, don't leave valuables lying around your room; use safe-deposit boxes, or at least place things in a locked bag.

Do be careful in the woods during the fall hunting season: unsuccessful or drunken hunters may be less selective in their targets than one might hope.

Marijuana Farms & Meth Labs

In the USA and Canada, possession and use of marijuana is a federal offense, although in Canada, it is now legal to cultivate and use it for medicinal purposes. Despite legal ramifications, persistent demand for cannabis creates a lively, highly profitable market for the producer. North of the border, cultivation of highly potent 'BC bud' has become a multibillion-dollar industry, rivaling logging and mining for export dollars.

Conditions for growing pot – which calls for both the right climate and near total seclusion – are perfect in remote southern Oregon and elsewhere in the Northwest. Maverick pot growers often hide their plots in isolated pockets of national forests. Travelers who accidentally stumble upon hidden marijuana fields are at risk: Growers are especially protective of their plots and have been known to rig the area with traps set to maim or kill trespassers. If you do wander onto a marijuana field, it is important to leave the area as quickly and quietly as possible.

Surreptitious methamphetamine labs have proliferated on USFS lands, posing another hazard to unsuspecting hikers, not to mention the environmental damage caused by the dumping of chemical ingredients used to cook up the drug. Though you're unlikely to stumble upon one of these outfits, you should be aware of their dangerously explosive potential, which has prompted closures of sections of national forests. Forest service authorities also warn that these sites may be surrounded by

If you walk into a field of marijuana, turn around.

dangerous booby traps and manned by armed individuals.

Ocean Hazards

Coastal beaches are unsupervised, and those who venture into the water to wade or bodysurf should be wary of rip tides and drop-offs. Never turn your back on the ocean when beachcombing in or near the water. Large 'sneaker waves' may catch you unexpectedly during incoming tides. If caught in a rip tide or undertow, it's best to relax and go with the flow of the current until it dissipates (struggling will only exhaust you). Incoming tides have the potential to strand visitors busily exploring tide pools or climbing coastal rocks.

Wildlife

As more and more people spend time in the backcountry, attacks on humans and pets are becoming more common. Black bears and cougars are the most serious hazards, but seemingly innocuous creatures such as mule deer and raccoons are equally capable of inflicting serious injury or even fatal wounds on unsuspecting tourists.

Bears can, and occasionally do, kill people, but most people who enter bear country never have any problem. Black bears are found in mountainous areas throughout the region. They usually weigh about 200lb (90kg) and stand about 3 feet (1m) tall when on all fours. Avoid surprising them: Stay alert and make some noise while hiking. At night, keep food (including toothpaste and other scented products) and smelly clothing inside a car or strung high in a tree. If you do see a bear, give it plenty of room. Try to stay upwind of the animal so it can get your scent. If the bear becomes aggressive, drop something that may absorb its attention and climb the nearest tall tree. If this isn't possible, the next best bet is probably to curl up into a ball, clasp your hands behind your neck and play dead, even if the bear begins to bat you around.

Mountain lions (also called cougars or pumas) are not as dangerous as bears, but as their territory in the mountains gets whittled away by development, these animals increasingly come in contact with humans. Adult travelers aren't much at risk of mountain-lion attack, but unattended children and pets have been attacked and killed. If you come upon a moose (which live in parts of Northeastern Washington and on Vancouver Island), keep your distance – if surprised, they might charge.

EMERGENCIES

Throughout most of the USA and Canada, dial ☎ 911 for emergency service of any sort. This is a free call from any phone. A few rural phones might not have this service, in which case, dial ☎ 0 for the operator and ask for emergency assistance – it's still free. Each state also maintains toll-free numbers for traffic information and emergencies.

In Oregon, call ☎ 503-375-3555 for the state police. For road conditions, call ☎ 800-977-6368 in Oregon, ☎ 503-588-2941 out-of-state.

In Washington, call ☎ 425-649-4370 for the state police. For road conditions, call ☎ 206-368-4499 or 800-695-7623.

In British Columbia, call ☎ 604-717-3535 for the Vancouver police. For road conditions, call ☎ 800-550-4997 (payment by credit card required).

LEGAL MATTERS

If you are stopped by the police for any reason in the USA, bear in mind that there is no system of paying fines on the spot. For traffic offenses, the police officer will explain your options to you. Attempting to pay the fine to the officer is frowned upon at best and may compound your troubles by resulting in a charge of bribery. Should the officer decide that you pay up front, he or she has the authority to take you directly to the magistrate instead of allowing you the usual 30-day period to pay the fine.

If you are arrested for more serious offenses, you're allowed to remain silent. There is no legal reason to speak to a police officer if you don't wish, but never walk away from an officer until given permission. All persons who are arrested are legally allowed (and given) the right to make one phone call. If you don't have a lawyer or family member to help you, call your embassy. The police will give you the number upon request.

Each state and province has its own drinking and drivng laws, and what is legal in one may be illegal in others.

You must be at least 16 years old to drive in Oregon, Washington or British Columbia. Unless otherwise posted, speed limits are 65 mph (100 kph) on interstates and freeways in Oregon and British Columbia, and 70 mph (110 kph) in Washington. You can drive 5 mph over the limit without much likelihood of being pulled over, but if you're doing 10 mph or more over the limit, you'll be caught sooner or later. In small towns, driving over the posted speed by any amount may attract attention. Watch for school zones, which can be as low as 15 mph (25 kph) during school hours – these limits are strictly enforced. Seat belts and motorcycle helmets must be worn.

The drinking age is 21 in Washington and Oregon and 19 in BC, and you need photo identification that proves your age. You could incur stiff fines or jail time if caught driving under the influence of alcohol or other drugs. During festive holidays and special events, road blocks are sometimes set up to check for this.

BUSINESS HOURS

Most businesses stay open from 9am to 5pm, but there are certainly no hard and fast rules. In any large city, a few supermarkets and restaurants are open 24 hours. Shops are usually open from either 9 or 10am to 5 or 6pm (often until 9pm in shopping malls), except Sundays, when hours are usually noon to 5pm.

Many art galleries, museums and theaters are closed on Mondays.

PUBLIC HOLIDAYS & SPECIAL EVENTS

National public holidays are celebrated throughout the USA and Canada. Banks, schools and government offices (including post offices) close on national holidays, and transportation, museums and other services are usually on Sunday's regular schedule. Holidays falling on a weekend are usually observed the following Monday.

Listed below are official US and Canadian national holidays.

New Year's Day – January 1 (USA & Canada)

Martin Luther King Jr Day – third Monday in January (USA)

Presidents' Day – third Monday in February (USA)

Easter – Sunday in late March or early April (USA & Canada)

Victoria Day – Monday preceding May 24 (Canada)

Memorial Day – last Monday in May (USA)

Canada Day – July 1 (Canada)

Independence Day – July 4 (USA)

Labor Day – first Monday in September (USA & Canada)

Columbus Day – second Monday in October (USA)

Thanksgiving Day – second Monday in October (Canada); fourth Thursday in November (USA)

Veterans' Day – November 11 (USA)

Remembrance Day – November 11 (Canada)

Christmas Day – December 25 (USA & Canada)

Boxing Day – December 26 (Canada)

Each region of the Pacific Northwest celebrates unique local festivals, including the following:

Oregon

Sandcastle Day – Cannon Beach, early June

Portland Rose Festival – Portland, early June

Oregon Country Fair – Veneta (near Eugene), weekend after the Fourth of July

Oregon Brewers Festival – Portland, late July

Mt Hood Jazz Festival – Gresham, early August

Pendleton Round-Up – Pendleton, mid-September

Washington

Upper Skagit Bald Eagle Festival – Concrete, Rockport and Marblemount, first weekend in February

Skagit Valley Tulip Festival – Mt Vernon, first two weeks of April

Northwest Folklife Festival – Seattle, Memorial Day weekend

Yakama Nation Cultural Powwow & Rodeo – Toppenish, Fourth of July weekend

Seafair – Seattle, late July

Omak Stampede – Omak, second weekend in August

Bumbershoot – Seattle, Labor Day weekend

British Columbia

Chinese New Year – Vancouver, end of January or beginning of February

Victoria Day Festival – Victoria, fourth week of May

duMaurier International Jazz Festival – late June

First Peoples' Festival – Victoria, mid-August

Molson Indy Vancouver – Vancouver, early September

Vancouver Fringe Festival – Vancouver, mid-September

WORK

Seasonal work is possible in national parks and other tourist sites in the USA, especially ski areas; for information, contact park concessionaires or local chambers of commerce. Casual labor can be found in the Northwest during the harvest seasons, when farmers hire hundreds of laborers to pick fruit and other crops. Cafes and coffee shops are also good bets for quick employment.

If you're not a US citizen, you'll need to apply for a work visa from the US embassy in your home country before you leave. The type of visa varies depending on how long you're staying and the kind of work you plan to do. Generally, you need either a J-1 visa, which you can obtain by joining a visitor-exchange program, or an H-2B visa, which you get when being sponsored by a US employer. The latter is not easy to obtain (since the employer has to prove that no US citizen or permanent resident is available to do the job); the former is issued mostly to students for work in summer camps.

ACCOMMODATIONS
Camping

Camping is the cheapest – and in many ways the most enjoyable – approach to a vacation. Visitors with a car and a tent can take advantage of hundreds of public and private campgrounds and RV parks at prices as low as $10 per night.

Camping is permitted in many public backcountry areas. Backpackers wanting to camp in national parks must obtain a permit (often free) from a designated wilderness information center. In the most heavily used national forests of Oregon and Washington, a Northwest Forest Pass ($5 per day, $30 annual) is required.

Basic campgrounds usually have toilets, fire pits (or charcoal grills), picnic benches and drinking water. Public campgrounds often have length-of-stay limits, with a seven to 10-day maximum the norm in peak season.

Yurts, found at state parks and some private campgrounds, are Mongolian-style domed round houses in a canvas shell. They're usually furnished with a few bunk beds and futons and may have electrical outlets or a wood stove, but campers need to bring sleeping bags and cooking utensils. Another option is to stay in a traditional Native American tepee, a cone-shaped tent, offered by some state parks and a few Indian reservations. Yurts and teepees generally must be reserved.

Reservations for campsites at state parks are both possible and advised during the summer. Washington sponsors a toll-free number (☎ 888-226-7688), or you can reserve online: W www.parks.wa.gov. Either way you're charged a reservation fee of $7, regardless of the length of stay, payable by credit card. To make reservations for Oregon state parks, call ☎ 800-452-5687, TDD 800-858-9659 or go to W www.oregon stateparks.org; the reservation fee is $6. Certain National Forest sites can also be reserved by phone (☎ 877-444-6777, outside USA ☎ 518-885-3639) or online (W www .reserveusa.com). National Park campgrounds in the Pacific Northwest do not generally take reservations, with the exception of Mt Ranier National Park (☎ 800-365-2267, W reservations.nps.gov).

British Columbia Parks manages hundreds of campgrounds. Campsites in about 70 parks can be reserved by calling ☎ 604-689-9025, 800-689-9025, or online at W www .discovercamping.ca. There's a C$6.50 *per night* reservation fee, with a maximum of C$19.50 for the same site.

Usually close to or in a town, private campgrounds tend to be designed with RVs in mind, though tenters can usually camp at some sites. Prices quoted in this guide are for two people per site; there's usually an extra person charge. Facilities can include hot showers, coin laundry, swimming pool, full RV hookups (including cable TV), games area, a playground and a convenience store.

Hostels

Hostels are an excellent option for those trying to travel economically. What they lack in amenities and privacy they more than make up for in providing a readymade travelers' community. Unfortunately, they're relatively sparse in the USA: Washington and Oregon each has only four hostels affiliated with Hostelling International/American Youth Hostels (HI/AYH), including two in Portland and one in Seattle. British Columbia's network is more widespread, with 16 HI/AYH hostels, most in the southern end of the province. Dormitory beds cost $14 to $17 a night for HI/AYH members, $3 more for nonmembers. Many hostels offer a few private rooms for couples or families, priced similarly to a budget hotel.

Some HI/AYH hostels expect you to rent or carry a sheet and towel. Dormitories are usually segregated by sex, and curfews may exist. Kitchen and laundry privileges are usually available in return for light housekeeping duties. Information boards, TV rooms and lounge areas are standard features.

Independent hostels have comparable rates and conditions to HI/AYH hostels. Because they're not bound by HI regulations, these establishments tend to be more marked by the character of their owners. Both HI and independent hostels are listed in *The Hostel Handbook for the USA & Canada,* by Jim Williams, available for $5 payable to the author at 722 St Nicholas Ave, New York, NY 10031 USA; you'll find the same info at W www.hostelhandbook .com. Another great online resource is W www.hostels.com.

Reservations are accepted and advised during the high season, when there may be a three-night limit. Get further information from HI/AYH (☎ 202-783-6161, e hostels@ hiayh.org), 733 15th St NW, Suite 840, Washington, DC 20005 USA, or use their reservation service at ☎ 800-909-4776, which will route your call to the hostel you're interested in. Alternatively, make reservations online at W www.hiayh.org; the site includes descriptions of all the hostels. To reserve a space at BC hostels, phone ☎ 800-663-7884 or visit W www.hihostels.ca.

B&Bs

European visitors should be aware that North American bed-and-breakfast inns differ from their casual, inexpensive counterparts. While they are usually family-run, many B&Bs here require advance reservations, though some will be happy to oblige the occasional drop-in. Most prohibit smoking, and many don't allow children. Substantial breakfasts are often included in the price, but lighter 'continental breakfasts' are not unheard of.

B&Bs may be in historical buildings, quaint country houses or luxurious urban townhouses. The best are distinguished by a friendly attention to detail by owners/hosts who can provide you with local information and contacts.

Most B&Bs fall in the $80 to $100 price range, but quite a few go over $100. Rates listed in this guide are for peak season; travelers will find significant discounts outside this period.

B&Bs abound throughout Oregon and Washington, but are particularly concentrated on the islands of Puget Sound and along the Oregon coast. Ashland, southern Oregon's theater-loving community, is another B&B center, with dozens of inns. Search for B&Bs by region via the websites of the Washington Bed & Breakfast Guild (W www.wbbg.com) and the Oregon B&B Guild (W www .obbg.org). Both associations also publish brochures listing their member inns, which can be ordered online. Another excellent Internet resource is *The Bed & Breakfast Explorer* (W www.bbexplorer.com), covering

Washington, Oregon and several other western states; order a print version ($5) via the site.

The Western Canada B&B Innkeepers Association compiles over 140 member listings in Vancouver and across the province at their website: W www.wcbbia.com.

Motels & Hotels

Prices for these lodgings vary tremendously from season to season. A hotel charging $50 for a double in July may drop to $35 in January and then raise its rates to $70 for a special event when the town is overflowing with visitors. Prices given in this guide are generally for peak season and don't include taxes. Children are often allowed to stay free with their parents, but the age marking the end of childhood can vary from six to 18.

The official prices listed by hotels are called 'rack rates' and are not written in stone. If you simply ask about any specials, you can often save quite a bit of money. Booking through a travel agent or the Internet may save you money as well.

Almost all US and Canadian hotels now designate rooms as smoking or nonsmoking. Some places allow guests to keep a small pet in their room.

Price Categories In this guide, what's considered a 'budget' motel or hotel may vary with the destination. In the major cities and resort areas, the lower end of accommodations can range from $50 to $80 per night, while in less tourist-oriented destinations, $80 will get you the best room available. In general, motels and hotels listed as budget will cost you between $40 and $60 per double room.

Lodgings under $50 are found especially in small towns on major highways and the motel strips of larger towns. Levels of quality and maintenance vary widely in this category, so it's worth inspecting the room before making a choice. Some level of cleanliness is generally maintained. A private shower, toilet and a TV are standard motel amenities, along with heating and usually air-con. Even the cheapest motels may advertise 'kitchenettes,' which can mean anything from a two-ring burner to a spiffy little mini-kitchen with microwave, coffee maker and small fridge. If you plan on doing a lot of kitchenette cooking, carry your own set of utensils.

Throughout this guide, motels and hotels listed as 'mid-range' generally have rooms ranging from $60 to $80, though in cities such as Portland, Seattle and Vancouver, rooms in this category can reach $125. Mid-range lodgings are likely to feature larger rooms with queen beds, and facilities often include a swimming pool, a TV with movie channels and a laundry. Full-service hotels, with bellhops and doormen, restaurants and bars, exercise rooms and saunas, and nightly rates of over $125 are considered 'top end,' though rates can top $250 a night in this category.

Chains Appealing to travelers with a low tolerance for surprise, the USA's myriad motel and hotel chains seek to standardize levels of quality and style. If any particular chain appeals to you, you should look into its frequent-guest program.

Among the cheapest US chains is Motel 6, with no-frills rooms starting in the $40s for a double in smaller towns and in the $50s in big cities (plus a flat $3 for each extra person). At the next price level, with corresponding upgrades in room size, comfort and amenities, are Super 8 Motels, Days Inn and Econo Lodge.

Stepping up to chains with rooms in the $70 to $90 range, you'll find noticeably nicer rooms, restaurants on the premises and indoor swimming pools with spa or workout rooms. Best Western, Comfort Inn, Quality Inn and Red Lion – and in BC, Accent Inn and Coast Hotel – are just a few of the hotel chains in this category.

Booking ahead gives you the peace of mind of a guaranteed room when you arrive. The cheapest places may not accept reservations, but at least phone from the road to see what's available; they'll often hold a room for an hour or two. Chain hotels all take reservations days or months ahead, via toll-free numbers or online. Normally, you have to give a credit-card number to hold the room.

Cancellation policies vary, so find out when you book. Also make sure to let the hotel know if you plan on a late arrival. Some motels will give your room away if you haven't arrived or called by 6pm (unless you've reserved by credit card).

Accent Inns
☎ 800-663-0298, W www.accentinns.com

Best Western
☎ 800-238-7234, W www.bestwestern.com

Coast Hotels
☎ 800-663-0298, W www.coasthotels.com

Comfort Inn
☎ 800-228-5150, W www.comfortinn.com

Days Inn
☎ 800-329-7466, W www.daysinn.com

Econo Lodge
☎ 800-553-2666, W www.econolodge.com

Howard Johnson
☎ 800-446-4656, W www.hojo.com

Motel 6
☎ 800-466-8356, W www.motel6.com

Super 8 Motel
☎ 800-800-8000

Quality Inn
☎ 800-228-5151, W www.qualityinn.com

Travelodge
☎ 800-578-7878, W www.travelodge.com

Red Lion
☎ 800-733-5466, W www.redlion.com

Lodges

The word 'lodge' is used with great latitude in the Northwest. Places like Timberline Lodge on Mt Hood and Paradise Lodge on Mt Rainier are magnificent old log structures with dozens of rooms infused with a sense of the woods and hand-crafted venerability. Most other lodges are more modest. Those on the lakes of the Cascades have cabin accommodations, campsites, boat rentals and at least a small store if not a cafe. Some of these lodges are just fine; others are quite funky and unspectacular. If your standards are exacting, make careful inquiries before heading up long mountain roads to marginal accommodations best suited to hardened anglers.

Lodges in national parks may look rustic but are usually quite comfortable inside.

Restaurants are on the premises, and tour services are often available. Make reservations months in advance for high season, when double rooms with private bath go for over $100 a night.

Resorts

In Oregon and Washington especially, the last 20 years have seen a proliferation of resorts – sprawling recreational complexes alongside mountain lakes and coastal inlets. The more upscale versions, such as Rosario Resort on Orcas Island, boast golf courses, tennis courts, swimming pools and guided outdoor activities. Diverse lodging options may include condominiums, hotel-like lodge rooms, private cottages rented on a short-term basis, rustic cabins, tent sites and RV hookups.

Vacation Rentals

In many coastal areas and in central Oregon and Washington, owners of weekend or vacation homes depend on occasional rentals to help pay the mortgage. Most of these well-maintained, furnished homes have at least three bedrooms. For a family, or for a group of friends, these homes may represent one of the best lodging values in the area.

To rent a private home, contact the local property management companies listed in this guide. Descriptions of their properties can be found in locally distributed newsletters and on the Internet. Some restrictions apply: houses are often occupied by the owners on major holiday and summer weekends, there's usually a minimum stay of two nights, and there may be a housekeeping fee.

FOOD

With a long seacoast, fertile valleys filled with farms and orchards, and miles and miles of grasslands devoted to livestock, the Northwest offers high-quality, locally grown food products to both enterprising home cooks and restaurant chefs. There's little that's unique to Northwest kitchens, but there are a number of items and dishes that are regional specialties.

Master chef and food writer James Beard hails from Portland. His legacy to Northwest regional cuisine is an appreciation of indigenous ingredients prepared with simple elegance, and an attitude that eating great food ought to be great fun.

Served between 6 and 10am, typical North American breakfasts are large and filling, often including eggs or an omelet, bacon or ham, fried potatoes, toast with butter and jam and coffee or tea. Some diners offer a breakfast menu throughout the day. Lunch is usually available between 11am and 2pm. One strategy for enjoying good restaurants on a budget is to frequent them for lunch, when fixed-price specials can go for $6 or $7. Dinner, served between about 5 and 10pm, is more expensive, but portions tend to be huge.

Seafood is a cornerstone of the Northwest table. Coastal restaurants vie to claim the best clam chowder, which is often thick and starchy. Crab, fresh from the boat, is available almost everywhere along the coast. It's usually served in salad, or else simply with drawn butter.

The chill waters of the Pacific produce sweet-tasting, delicately tangy oysters of the highest quality. In good restaurants, discerning diners can choose which Northwest bay their oysters on the half shell hail from. Stop by an oyster farm on Washington's Long Beach Peninsula or on the northern Oregon coast and handpick a dozen tiny komomoto oysters for an impromptu hors d'oeuvre. Clams, usually steamed in broth or in seawater, are a common appetizer; if you have a chance to order razor clams, by all means do. These elongated, delicately flavored clams are the nobility of Northwest shellfish. Mussels, which cover practically every rock along the Pacific Coast, are only lately catching favor.

Locally caught fish include red snapper, flounder and sole, tuna, halibut and cod. Shrimp is another major catch. Salmon, still a menu staple, are as likely to be from Alaska as from the Northwest. Local trout are also found in fish markets and on menus.

The Northwest offers an incredibly rich diversity in fruits and berries. Marionberries, unique to Oregon, are like a cross between raspberries and blackberries, but twice as big and more succulent. Try a slice of marionberry pie, or cobbler with a scoop of local ice cream. Blueberries thrive in the acidic soil of the Northwest and appear in pies, breads, muffins and scones. Mt Hood strawberries are renowned for their spicy, near-wild taste.

The thick forests also provide a bounty of fruit. Blackberry brambles, snagging clothing and grabbing at the legs of hikers, are an annoyance until they produce their heady abundance of purple-black fruit. More delicate salmonberries are a light orange and make a good hiker's snack, or, if you can gather enough, a beautiful pastel jelly. Huckleberries, found high up in mountain meadows, are a favorite of black bears and backpackers. The small, purplish-black fruit are fun to pick and make great pies. Tart, bright-red cranberries have become an important component of the coastal economy and of cutting-edge cooking.

Wild mushrooms indigenous to Northwest forests and shipped worldwide include oyster, morel, porcini and shiitake varieties. Expect these to turn up on your plate indiscriminately as the pedigree of genuine Northwest cuisine.

Along the coast and western valleys, dairies produce abundant milk, which is made into noted cheeses. The center of Oregon's dairy industry is the Tillamook Valley, with its famous namesake cheddar. One Tillamook-area dairy has begun to fashion French-style brie. In BC, dairies in the Fraser Valley and on Vancouver Island produce excellent cheddar cheeses. Washington State University, located in Pullman, Washington, produces sublime ice cream at its creamery.

Oregon is one of the few states to have an official state nut, the hazelnut (also called the filbert). Look for hazelnut gift packs (some are jazzed up in smokehouse or jalapeño-style); they're also served in baked goods or with meat for that special, Northwest touch.

DRINKS
Nonalcoholic Drinks
Tap water in the Northwest is safe and perfectly acceptable to drink. In fact, its purity is

legendary. Bottled water, including local brands from storied glaciers or lakes, are readily available in supermarkets. Water from streams, however, should never be drunk without purifying, as giardia is a problem (see Health, earlier in this chapter).

Bottled fruit juices are widely available. Keep an eye out for juice bars, where you can buy freshly extracted elixirs.

In case you haven't heard, the Pacific Northwest is the hub of a coffee craze that's swept North America.

In centers such as Vancouver, Victoria, Portland, Seattle, Bellingham and Eugene, you can expect to find a coffee shop on almost every downtown block. Even in the hinterlands, you will find drive-through espresso stands serving caramel macchiatos to truckers.

Starbucks, the international chain of cafes from the Seattle area, is by no means the only coffee empire in the region. Now that the company has achieved world hegemony, fickle (and often downright hostile) locals align themselves with the Northwest's many competitors, including Seattle's Best, Tully's, Torrefazione Italia, Batdorf & Bronson, Portland's Coffee People and Vancouver's Blenz.

Alcoholic Drinks

Persons under the age of 21 (minors) are prohibited from consuming alcohol in the USA; the drinking age in Canada is 19. Carry a driver's license or passport as proof of age to enter a bar, order drinks at a restaurant or make purchases at the liquor store. Servers have the right to ask to see your identification and may refuse service without it. Minors are not allowed in bars or pubs, even to order nonalcoholic beverages. Unfortunately, this means that most dance clubs are also off-limits, although a few clubs have solved the underage problem with a segregated drinking area. Minors are, however, welcome in the dining areas of restaurants where alcohol is served.

Northwest wines have an excellent international reputation. Especially noted are wines from an area south and west of Portland called Yamhill County. Conditions are very similar to France's Burgundy region, and chardonnay and pinot noir grapes do very well. Farther south, in the Rogue River drainage, hot-weather grapes such as Cabernet sauvignon and merlot are more the norm. On the slopes of the Columbia River Gorge, Rieslings, pinot gris and Gewürztraminer grapes produce soft, dry white wines.

Washington's principal wine-growing region is east of the Cascade Mountains, in the arid foothills of the Yakima and Walla Walla River valleys. The sturdy, hot-weather grapes of southern France do best out here; Cabernet sauvignon wines from these areas can rival California wines in strength, if not always in subtlety. Merlots and Semillons are also popular, often boasting an herbaceous intensity not found

Microbreweries

The Pacific Northwest is a major center of the US boom in small, specialty beer-making operations called microbreweries. Beers from these independent businesses tend to echo either British or German brewing styles, but they generally conform to the sorts of standards and styles known as British 'real ale' beers. While microbrewed beer is available at many bars and restaurants, for the real microbrew experience, head to the brewery itself, which often features a pub within sight of the brewing tanks. Northwest brewpubs also produce seasonal or specialty beers and ales, often cask-conditioned. You can usually arrange a tour of the brewery if sufficient notice is given.

Portland is a real center for microbrewing; its summer Oregon Brewers Festival brings in microbrewed beers from all over the nation. Many out-of-the-way places now have their own, sometimes *very micro* brewery.

in these varieties elsewhere. BC has a burgeoning wine industry based in the Okanagan Valley. Conditions are similar to Washington's, and the same varietals are cultivated.

Northwest Wine Country, by Kathleen & Gerald Hill, is a good resource for traveling wine lovers. Oenologists can contact the Washington Wine Commission (☎ 206-667-9463, W www.washingtonwine.org) and the Oregon Wine Advisory Board (☎ 503-228-8336, W www.oregonwine.org).

ENTERTAINMENT

Portland, Seattle and Vancouver are cosmopolitan cities offering a wide variety of films, music, theater, sports and nightlife. Eugene, Bellingham and Victoria are all home to large, well-respected universities that draw speakers, concerts, foreign films and art shows. Theater fans visiting the area should try not to miss the renowned Shakespeare festival in Ashland (see the Southern Oregon chapter).

Coffeehouses

Portland and Seattle, particularly, abound with coffeehouses, which often offer unique and inexpensive entertainment, including literary readings, slam poetry contests, acoustic music and discussion groups.

Coffeehouses are also just about the only venue where underage travelers can easily meet their peers.

Festivals

Outdoor music and arts festivals give you the chance, most any summer weekend, to catch high-spirited entertainment under the sun or stars (or umbrella). Port Townsend, on the Olympic Peninsula, hosts back-to-back jazz, blues and folk festivals, with its American Fiddle Tunes event lassoing in violinists from around the country. Seattle's Bumbershoot, held through Labor Day weekend, bursts with film, art, comedy and top-flight rock and blues. Overlooking the Columbia River in central Washington, the Gorge Amphitheater is the Pacific Northwest's most scenic concert venue, hosting over 20 major touring programs per summer, from CreationFest (Christian contemporary) to Ozzfest (heavy metal). The Britt Festivals, in Jacksonville, Oregon, present a similar summer series on a hillside estate amid ponderosa pines and madrones. Other outdoor jams include the Mt Baker Blues Festival, Ellensburg's Jazz in the Valley, the Winthrop Rhythm & Blues Festival, the Portland Waterfront Blues Festival and the Vancouver folk festival.

Taverns & Cocktail Lounges

Oregon and Washington laws retain certain prohibition-era restrictions on what types of drinks may be consumed in a particular establishment. In general, taverns are authorized to sell only beer and wine. Taverns, more often than not, are intensely local places that may be unaccustomed to strangers. Hard liquor can only be served in establishments that prepare meals. Thus, to get a mixed drink or shot of tequila, one must go to a restaurant or 'cocktail lounge' – basically a bar attached to a restaurant, even though the putative restaurant may only occasionally serve food. No such distinctions are made in British Columbia, where pubs, lounges and bars may all serve whatever booze they choose. BC bars and nightclubs, however, serve alcohol a bit later than do pubs, where last call is usually before 1am.

Casinos

Since federal regulations were relaxed in the 1990s to allow gambling on Indian reservations, gaming halls have sprung up throughout the USA. Northwest tribes now operate 26 casinos on their lands, but hundreds more gambling facilities operate by agreement with Indian tribes. These range from small card rooms to full-blown Las Vegas-style palaces, such as the Yakama Nation's Legends Casino, in south central Washington. Games include blackjack, stud poker, roulette and slot machines. 'Pull tabs' are another popular diversion: Grab one from a bin (available in 25¢, 50¢ and $1 denominations) and pull it apart to find a series of numbers, then check the board to see if you've got a winning combination. Casinos often feature inexpensive buffet-style dining and nearly Vegas-caliber entertainment. For a full list of casinos in the Pacific Northwest and elsewhere, see the website Ⓦ us.casinocity.com.

SPECTATOR SPORTS

Universities vie with professional sports franchises for the allegiance of Northwest fans. Football draws enormous crowds in the fall. The Seattle Seahawks – the Northwest's only National Football League team – are very popular. Vancouver is home to the Canadian Football League's BC Lions. Generating at least as much enthusiasm are contests between university teams, most notably the University of Washington Huskies, the Washington State University Cougars, the University of Oregon Ducks and the Oregon State University Beavers. The season runs from the first week in September (when school starts) to the end of January.

The Seattle Mariners – the region's only professional baseball team – posted the best won-lost record in the history of major league baseball in 2001. The season starts the first week of April and ends in October with the World Series. Outside of Seattle, baseball fans can enjoy minor league baseball played by teams such as the Spokane Indians, Yakima Bears, Eugene Emeralds and Portland Beavers, among others.

Basketball season lasts from late October until mid-June. The National Basketball Association's Seattle SuperSonics and Portland Trail Blazers always draw crowds of frenzied fans. If you're in Vancouver during the ice-hockey season (October to April) try to catch a home game of the National Hockey League's Vancouver Canucks.

SHOPPING

Oregon is a good place to shop, because it doesn't have a sales tax or value-added tax.

Seattle is a shopper's paradise, especially the area around Pike Place Market and the downtown core. Many towns along Oregon's coast, particularly Cannon Beach, are full of boutiques, as is Friday Harbor, in the San Juan Islands of Washington. Vancouver's Robson St and Pacific Centre are major downtown shopping areas, while Chinatown offers visitors a chance to experience Hong Kong without leaving the continent.

Probably the most common souvenir of Oregon is something made from myrtle wood. This rare tree grows only in southern Oregon and Lebanon; it's even mentioned in the Bible.

Pendleton Woolen Mills has its headquarters in the Northwest, and its trademark plaid shirts and blankets make nice, although pricey, souvenirs.

Northwest food and wine are good purchases. Oregon grows over 90% of the nation's filberts, and products made from the state's official nut are found all over. Smoked salmon has a long pedigree here, beginning with the Northwest Indian tribes, who smoked the fish to preserve it over long periods. Local cheeses are popular throughout the region. Northwest wine has been accorded international honors, and is worth a try. Most fish markets can pack fresh seafood for overnight delivery. Jams and syrups made from wild and locally grown berries are easily found; as are candies and food products made from cranberries. Seattle's Pike Place Market and Vancouver's Granville Island Market are good places to shop for food and wine gifts.

A number of Northwest cities have 'Saturday Markets,' where local artisans and farmers bring products to sell, with Portland's reputed to be the largest open-air crafts fair in the nation.

Activities

You'll be amazed by the many options available to recreational enthusiasts in the Pacific Northwest, ranging from near universals like hiking, backpacking and skiing to more esoteric, specialized pursuits like clamming and crabbing.

USEFUL ORGANIZATIONS
The following organizations provide information and issue permits.

General
Bureau of Land Management (BLM; ☎ 503-952-6002, W www.or.blm.gov) 1515 SW 5th Ave, Portland, OR 97208. Manages public use of US federal lands for wildlife, recreation and resource extraction, including much of eastern Oregon; provides maps, permits and information through district offices

Nature of the Northwest (☎ 503-872-2750, W www.naturenw.org) 800 NE Oregon St, Suite 177, Portland, OR 97232. Provides recreational information for national forests, state parks and other agencies in both Oregon and Washington

US Fish & Wildlife Service (☎ 503-231-6828, W pacific.fws.gov) 911 NE 11th Ave, Portland, OR 97232. Responsible for conservation of wildlife habitat on federal lands; manages National Wildlife Refuge network

Oregon
Oregon Dept of Fish & Wildlife (☎ 503-872-5268, W www.dfw.state.or.us) 2501 SW 1st Ave, Portland, OR 97207. Maintains wildlife refuges and issues hunting and fishing permits

Oregon Guides & Packers Association (☎ 541-937-3192, W www.ogpa.org) PO Box 324, Lowell, OR 97452. Statewide listings for guided fishing, hunting and river-floating trips

Oregon State Parks & Recreation Dept (☎ 503-378-6305, recorded info line ☎ 800-551-6949, W www.prd.state.or.us/home.html) 1115 Commercial St NE, Salem, OR 97310. Manages network of 171 state parks and 50 campgrounds

Washington
Outdoor Recreation Information Center (☎ 206-470-4060, W www.nps.gov/ccso/oric.htm) 222 Yale Ave N, Seattle, WA 98109 (in the REI building) A shared USFS headquarters and NPS information center

Washington Dept of Fish & Wildlife (☎ 360-902-2700, recorded information ☎ 360-902-2500, W www.wa.gov/wdfw) 600 Capitol Way N, Olympia, WA 98501. Maintains wildlife habitat; issues hunting and fishing licenses

Washington Outfitters & Guides Association (☎ 509-962-4222, 877-275-9642, W www.woga .org) 110 W 6th Ave, PMB 398, Ellensburg, WA 98926. Statewide listings for guided fishing, hunting and river-floating trips

Washington State Audubon Society (☎ 360-786-8020, W wa.audubon.org) PO Box 462, Olympia, WA 98507. Organizes bird-watching field trips for members ($20 annual fee per family); affiliated with South Vancouver Island branch in Victoria

Washington State Parks & Recreation Commission (☎ 360-902-8844, 800-233-0321, W www .parks.wa.gov) PO Box 42650, Olympia, WA 98504-2650. Manages network of 125 parks, most with campgrounds, as well as 41 marine parks with boat moorage, marine trails and cross-country ski trails; detailed listings available online

British Columbia
BC Parks (☎ 250-387-5002, W www.env.gov.bc.ca/ bcparks) 800 Johnson St, Victoria, BC V8W 1X4. Supervises and maintains provincial park system

Cycling BC (☎ 604-737-3034, W www.cycling .bc.ca) 1367 W Broadway, Vancouver. BC's governing body for racing; also offers plenty of resources for recreational and touring cyclists

Ministry of Forests (☎ 250-356-5012, W www.gov .bc.ca/for) PO Box 9529 Stn Prov Govt, Victoria, BC V8W 9C3. Has a downloadable guide to BC forests with map

Ministry of Water, Land & Air Protection, Wildlife Branch (☎ 250-387-9717, W www.elp.gov.bc.ca/ wld) Parliament Buildings, Victoria, BC V8W 1M1. Maintains wildlife refuges and habitat, and issues hunting permits

HIKING & BACKPACKING
For anyone who enjoys getting outdoors and moving around a bit, the Pacific Northwest is an ideal place to do it. Throughout the region, you'll find opportunities for brief

walks, day hikes and multiday backpack trips that lead to views of spectacular glaciated mountains, enlivening waterfalls and rich natural colors. With spring starting in the eastern regions, then gradually working its way up the mountain sides, spring flowers can be seen for months. When they finally stop blooming in the higher elevations, it's time for wild huckleberries and blueberries.

Keep in mind that it's best to attempt mountain trails after mid-July (snowmelt can be a problem otherwise). Lowland trails on the west side of the mountains can be done most any time of the year, as long as you don't mind a little rain. On the eastern side of the mountains, the weather is best in both spring and fall. Summers can be quite hot.

While the possibilities are endless, some all-around favorites are highlighted here. See the regional chapters for additional information.

Information

Permits & Fees Admission to Olympic, Mt Rainier or Crater Lake National Park is $10 per vehicle, $5 for pedestrians or cyclists (over 16 years old), good for re-entry for one week from purchase. Fees are collected upon entry and are payable by cash, traveler's check or credit card. There's no admission fee for North Cascades National Park, but visitors must purchase a Northwest Forest Pass to park at trailheads (see below).

If you're going to several national fee areas (including national parks, monuments, historic sites, recreation areas and wildlife refuges), it pays to get the $65 Golden Eagle Passport, which admits the passholder and any accompanying passengers in a private vehicle. The pass can be purchased on-site or by phone (☎ 530-647-5390) and is valid for one year from the date of purchase. A National Parks Pass ($50) allows annual access to national parks only but can be upgraded to Golden Eagle privileges by purchasing a Golden Eagle Hologram ($15). Get this pass at national parks or by phoning ☎ 888-467-2757.

The Golden Age Passport ($10) gives admission, plus a 50% reduction on camping, parking and other visitor fees to people 62 years or older. The Golden Access Passport is a free lifetime entrance pass for people who are blind or permanently disabled.

Backpackers must obtain and carry a backcountry permit for overnight camping in national parks. This requirement prevents overcrowding in popular areas and helps keep track of visitors who may get lost. The number of permits issued is limited by the number of campsites available. Specific regulations vary; a fee may be charged and hikers may have to follow a specific itinerary. Backcountry permits are issued from designated wilderness information centers and must be reserved ahead for Rainier and Olympic National Parks during the summer.

To use the most popular national forest trails, hikers must pay a trailhead parking fee by purchasing a Northwest Forest Pass ($5/30 daily/annual), good for a year from the month of purchase. Fees from the recently implemented program are supposed to go toward improving recreation facilities in the forests.

Passes are valid for any national forest in the USFS Recreation Fee Demonstration Program, including the following:

Oregon
Columbia Gorge National Scenic Area
Deschutes National Forest
Mt Hood National Forest
Rogue River National Forest
Siskiyou National Forest
Siuslaw National Forest
Umatilla National Forest
Wallowa-Whitman National Forest
Willamette National Forest

Washington
Gifford-Pinchot National Forest
Mt Baker-Snoqualmie National Forest
Okanogan National Forest
Olympic National Forest
Wenatchee National Forest

Not all trails in the above areas require a pass. To find out which ones do, call ☎ 800-270-7504, or see the Nature of the Northwest visitor center website (W www.naturenw .org). Passes are also mandatory for certain trails in North Cascades National Park as well as at various boat launches and picnic sites in national forests.

Ranger stations, information centers and designated businesses all sell Northwest Forest Passes. You'll save time by ordering an annual pass or several day passes in advance via the above phone number or website. Display passes on the driver's-side dashboard of your car. If you're using daily passes on an overnight trip, you'll need to buy one for each day your car is parked at the trailhead.

For certain places, you may need a *special-use permit* (also called a limited-entry permit), which restricts the number of visitors to overused areas. Permits are limited in number and must be obtained from a designated ranger station; there may be a charge. The Obsidian area in Three Sisters Wilderness and the Pamelia area in Mt Jefferson Wilderness are currently the only places in Oregon to require this permit. In Washington, thousands participate in a yearly lottery for special-use permits to the Enchantment Lakes region of Alpine Lakes Wilderness. Such permits should be carried with you when you hike.

Organized Tours Less-experienced hikers, or those who feel more comfortable hiking with people who know the territory well, should consider joining a group outing. You may have to pay an annual membership fee to participate.

The national environmental advocacy group the Sierra Club (☎ 206-523-2147, W www.cascadechapter.org), 8511 15th Ave NE, Suite 201, Seattle, WA 98115, offers an extremely diverse activities program, ranging from beachcombing and botany walks to weekend day-hiking and car-camping trips along the Pacific Crest Trail. Most outings are free and open to the general public. Call ☎ 206-523-2019 for a recording of future events. Oregon's Sierra Club chapter (☎ 503-238-0442, W www.oregon.sierraclub.org) is at 2950 SE Stark, Suite 110, Portland, OR 97214.

The recreational outfitter REI (☎ 206-223-1944, W www.rei.com), 222 Yale Ave N, organizes year-round training and activities focused on climbing, hiking and kayaking. Rates begin at $800 for a six- to eight-day expedition.

The Mountaineers (☎ 206-284-6310, 800-573-8484, W www.mountaineers.org), 300 3rd Ave West, Seattle, WA 98119, is an outdoor activity and conservation club based in Seattle. They offer courses in wilderness travel and lead a variety of hikes of varying difficulty – check their website for a current list. Nonmembers may participate in two guest activities before joining up.

National Parks Washington has three national parks (Olympic, Mt Rainier and North Cascades) while Oregon has one (Crater Lake). Of British Columbia's six national parks, one (Pacific Rim) is on Vancouver Island.

Inexperienced hikers will appreciate the national parks' well-marked, well-maintained trails, often with restroom facilities at either end and interpretive displays along the way. Self-guided nature trails, often no longer than 2 miles (3km), lead to the parks' most accessible features.

Unless you have a few days to get into the backcountry or are visiting off-season (before Memorial Day and after Labor Day), expect hiking in the Northwest's big parks to be crowded. Those seeking more solitude, away from heavy foot traffic, might head for the less-celebrated wilderness areas.

Wilderness Areas In 1964 the US Congress set aside large roadless areas as federally administered wilderness, defined as 'an area where the earth and its community of life are untrammeled by man, where man himself is a visitor who does not remain.' Most of these designated areas are on USFS land; the Bureau of Land Management is a relative latecomer to the concept, though its wilderness areas can be among the best in terms of sheer solitude.

Backcountry areas are composed of fragile environments and cannot support an of human activity. Camping in such a setting

Pacific Crest Trail

A truly amazing thing about the West Coast is you can walk from Mexico to Canada, across the entire expanse of California, Oregon and Washington, almost without ever leaving national park or national forest lands. Simply follow the Pacific Crest Trail (PCT). This 2650-mile (4270km) trail passes through 24 national forests, seven national parks, 33 designated wilderness areas and six state parks, always following as closely as possible the crest of the Sierras in California and the Cascade Range in Oregon and Washington, at an average elevation of 5000 feet.

To hike the trail in its entirety, at a good clip of 15 miles (24km) a day, would take nearly half a year; the Oregon and Washington portions can each feasibly be hiked in one month. But you don't have to undertake such a dramatic, cross-state trek to take advantage of the PCT. Day or weekend hikers can plan short trips along any stretch of the trail.

Many of the West Coast's most spectacular wilderness sites are traversed by the PCT, including Yosemite and Sequoia National Parks in California; Crater Lake National Park, Three Sisters Wilderness and Mt Hood in Oregon; and Mt Rainier and North Cascades National Parks in Washington.

The Pacific Crest Trail Association (☎ 916-349-2109, 888-728-7245, ⓦ www.pcta.org, 5325 Elkhorn Blvd, Suite 256, Sacramento, CA 95842-2526) can provide detailed information on the trail, weather conditions and wilderness permit requirements, as well as addresses for regional USFS and wilderness area offices and tips on long- and short-distance backpacking trips.

presents special concerns. Ensure that the area you choose can comfortably support your presence, and leave no evidence of your stay. The following list of guidelines should help:

- Camp below timberline, since alpine areas are generally more fragile. Good campsites are found, not made. Altering a site shouldn't be necessary.

- Camp at least 200 feet (70 adult steps) away from the nearest lake, river or stream.

- Bury human waste in holes dug 6 to 8 inches deep at least 200 feet from water, camp or trails. Camouflage the hole when finished.

- Use soaps and detergents sparingly or not at all, and never allow these things to enter streams or lakes. Scatter dishwater after removing all food particles. When washing yourself, lather up with biodegradable soap and rinse yourself 200 feet away from your water source.

- Establish a cooking area at least 100 yards away from your tent and designate cooking clothes to leave in the food bag, away from your tent, to avoid attracting critters. Use a lightweight stove for cooking instead of a fire.

- If a fire is allowed and appropriate, dig out the native topsoil and build a fire in the hole. Gather sticks no thicker than 3 inches. Do not snap branches off live, dead or downed trees. Pour wastewater from meals around the perimeter of the campfire to prevent it from spreading, and thoroughly douse the fire before leaving or going to bed.

- Pack out what you pack in, including all trash.

General Guidelines Before embarking on a hiking trip, carefully consider the following points to ensure a safe and enjoyable experience:

- Pay any fees and obtain any permits required by local authorities.

- Be sure you are healthy and feel comfortable walking for a sustained period.

- Be aware of local laws, regulations and etiquette about wildlife and the environment.

- Know your limitations. Know the route you are going to take and pace yourself accordingly. There's nothing wrong with turning back or not going as far as you originally planned.

- Always let someone know where you're going and how long you plan to be gone. Use sign-in registers at trailheads or ranger stations.

- Be prepared for the Northwest's unpredictable weather – you may go to bed under a clear sky and wake up to 2 feet of snow. Carry a rain jacket and light pair of long underwear at all times, even on short afternoon hikes.

- Take extra care when fording rivers and streams, an obstacle often encountered in designated wilderness areas where bridges are taboo. Upon reaching a river, unclip all your pack straps. Avoid crossing barefoot; river cobbles will suck body heat right out of your feet, numbing them and making it impossible to navigate. Wear sturdy sandals or lightweight canvas sneakers to avoid sloshing around in wet boots for the rest of your hike. Don't enter water higher than mid-thigh.

- If you get wet, wring your clothes out immediately. Wipe off excess water on your body as much as possible and put on any dry clothes you have. Synthetic fabrics and wool, unlike cotton, retain heat when they get wet.

Careful preparations for a long-distance backpack hike (long enough that you will need to resupply along the way) are of the utmost importance. Don't think you can jump from a weekend trip into a multiple-week trek without preparation; you've got to train and you've got to lay out a resupply plan in advance. Many established hiking trails have organizations that will supply you with a list of area post offices, stores and ranger stations that can receive your resupply packages in the mail and hold them until you arrive to claim them. Some may charge a holding fee. Preparations for a long-distance trip should include the following:

- Learn first aid suitable to mountaineering situations, backcountry protocol and how to care for the outdoors.

- Practice on weekend trips. Decide how much ground you want to cover per day and make sure you're able to handle it.

- Study guides and maps to the trail or region you plan to cover. Obtain current information about trail conditions from park authorities or local outfitters.

- Buy supplies; pack resupply packages for mailing to resupply points.

- Plan a daily itinerary taking into account resupply points.

Oregon

For hikers, Oregon's varied splendors include abundant waterfalls, mountain meadows ablaze with wildflowers and enor-mous wind-carved sand dunes. The following are some of the highlights.

The historic Eagle Creek Trail on the Oregon side of the Columbia Gorge makes a satisfying day hike or can be extended into a multi-day trip. (See the Cascade Locks Area section of the Columbia River Gorge & Mt Hood chapter.)

Circumnavigating Mt Hood near Portland on the 40-mile (64km) Timberline Trail provides day hikers with easy access to waterfalls, quiet reflecting lakes, wildflower meadows and mountain vistas. (See the Columbia River Gorge & Mt Hood chapter.)

Mountains of sand up to 500 feet tall highlight the hike across restless, shifting dunes to a deserted ocean beach in the Oregon Dunes National Recreation Area, the nation's largest dunes area. (See the Oregon Coast chapter.)

Rich in history, the 40-mile (64km) Rogue River Trail from Illahe to Grave Creek follows a roadless canyon end to end along a wild, twisting river famed for its white water. (See the Wild Rogue Wilderness Area section of the Southern Oregon chapter.)

Washington

Mountaineers love this state, the cradle of the loftiest Cascade peaks. Some of the Northwest's most beloved trails traverse the alpine range, a major portion of which is preserved in a patchwork of parks and wilderness areas. The following are some of the highlights.

In the southeast corner of the Alpine Lakes Wilderness, the 20-mile (32km) Enchantment Lakes Trail is considered by many to be one of the most magnificent backpacking trips in the Northwest. It's an otherworldly realm of granite slabs, jewel-like tarns, lofty spires and mythical names. (See the Around Leavenworth section of the Central Washington chapter.)

The extensive trail system on Mt Rainier features waterfalls, glaciers, wildflower meadows and stately old-growth forests, making it an extremely popular place to hike. At the heart of the network is the 93-mile (150km) Wonderland Trail, which takes hikers for a scenic spin around the entire mountain. (See Mt Rainier National Park Area in the South Cascades chapter.)

Mt Baker is flanked on all sides by trails offering a wide variety of terrain. Short, parklike trails at Heather Meadows are favored for moderate day hikes through high meadowed lakes and hanging glaciers. A number of trailside camps provide memorable backpacking destinations for beginners and families with children. The area makes a beautiful, low-key alternative to crowded alpine trails at Mt Rainier. (See the Mt Baker Area section of the North Cascades chapter.)

In North Cascades National Park, the short overnight or long day hike to Cascade Pass at the west end of the Stehekin Valley offers a spectacular view down the valley and samples a popular route to the isolated village of Stehekin. (See the North Cascades National Park section of the North Cascades chapter.)

Ancient petroglyphs hidden on a rocky coastal headland are the main highlight of the flat, 9.3-mile (15km) Cape Alava-Sand Point Loop through a rain forest to a wilderness beach in Olympic National Park. (See the Olympic Coastal Strip section of the Olympic Peninsula chapter.)

British Columbia

Don't forget BC as a hiking and backpacking destination. One of the Northwest's great coastal treks is within easy reach of Victoria, while a splendid seaside jaunt is steps from downtown Vancouver.

The most southerly section of the Pacific Rim National Park Reserve on Vancouver Island is the 75km (46½-mile) West Coast Trail, one of Canada's best-known and toughest hiking routes. Thousands of hikers trek part or all of the trail each year for its spectacular coastal scenery and old-growth spruce, cedar and hemlock forest. (See the Pacific Rim National Park Reserve section of the Vancouver Island chapter.)

To experience one of the world's great urban walks, try the Seawall Walkway, winding more than 9.5km (6 miles) along the shoreline of Vancouver's Stanley Park.

Hiking, cycling and jogging trails meander through the woods. (See Stanley Park in the Vancouver chapter.)

BICYCLING

Not only is cycling a recreational activity here, in some of the more progressive communities, it's become a mode of commuter transport in its own right. Towns such as Bellingham, Eugene and Corvallis have designated bike lanes sharing roads with auto traffic. Local transit systems often equip their buses with a front rack to transport bikes.

Lonely Planet's *Cycling USA – West Coast* offers details and maps for 29 days of riding in Washington and 26 days in Oregon. The guide describes one-day, weekend and mountain-bike rides, and has all the practical information a cyclist needs, including details of the best bike shops and bike-maintenance tips.

Organized Tours

Bicycle Adventures (☎ 360-786-0989, 800-443-6060, ⓦ www.bicycleadventures.com, PO Box 11219, Olympia, WA 98508), the bike gurus of Washington State, offers numerous bicycle tours of the Pacific Northwest at varying levels of difficulty. Tours in Washington include the Cascades, Olympic Peninsula, Puget Sound and the San Juan Islands. In Oregon you can choose from a tour of the Columbia Gorge or the Oregon coast, and in BC, they'll take you on a cycling tour of the Gulf Islands. You'll cycle 30 to 70 miles (50 to 110km) a day on average. Rates range from around $950 for a five-day camping tour of the San Juans to $2400 for a week-long tour of Crater Lake, including food, lodging and bike rental.

A kind of week-long party on wheels, the Cycle Oregon ride (☎ 503-736-3478, 800-292-5367, ⓦ www.cycleoregon.com, PO Box 15339, Portland, OR 97293-5339) traverses 60 to 80 miles (100 to 130km) a day of Oregon landscape, covering a different route each year. Cyclists from all over the USA vie for one of 2000 spaces in the limited registration, and then take to the road in September in a huge caravan of bikes, supply trucks, portable toilets, mobile snack stands and the like. The fee (about $700) covers camping (bring your own tent), food, gear transport, emergency bike repair and medical care.

Cyclists who really want to see the USA can go all out on the summer-long, coast-to-coast Cycle America ride (☎ 507-263-2665, 800-245-3263, Ⓦ www.cycleamerica.com, PO Box 485, Cannon Falls, MN 55009). The ride is broken down into nine-week-long segments. You can do any or all of them, and the cost depends on how long you're on the road.

Oregon

The Oregon Coast Bike Route follows US 101 from northern to southern state borders. A few side loop routes make passes of scenic areas that are not accessible from the highway. Also popular with bicyclists is the Cascade Lakes Hwy in central Oregon, which passes through the mountainous region south of Mt Bachelor and the Three Sisters Wilderness. Not far away, the Newberry Crater Rim Loop, 14 miles (23km) long, winds around one of the state's most fascinating volcanic features.

Contact the Bicycle & Pedestrian Program Manager (☎ 503-986-3555, fax 503-986-4063, Ⓦ www.odot.state.or.us/techserv/bikewalk/index.htm, Oregon Dept of Transportation, 355 Capitol St NE, 5th Floor, Salem, OR 97310) for the free *Oregon Bicycling Guide,* and a map of the Oregon Coast Bike Route.

Washington

A favorite destination for cyclists, the San Juan Islands are mostly flat, with gently rolling hills and inland lakes and forests just minutes from stunning coastal paths. Bikes can be transported by ferry to the islands for a fee, or rented on the islands.

Throughout Washington, old rail beds have been converted to recreational trails for all-terrain bikes, turning a cycling trip into a historical journey. Seattle's 16½-mile (27km) Burke-Gilman Trail is one of the nation's first such trails. The 110-mile (178km) Iron Horse Trail follows the old 'Milwaukee Road' across the Cascades

from the Cedar Falls east to the upper Columbia River. In summer, cross-country ski trails are taken over by mountain bikes, notably in the Methow Valley on the eastern foothills of the Cascades.

British Columbia

Put your bicycle on a ferry and head to the Gulf Islands, which are specially suited for exploring on two wheels due to their easy-going topography and tranquil back roads. On Vancouver Island, cycle the byroads around Sooke Harbour, or explore the Cowichan Valley vineyard country west of Duncan. Smaller, coast-hugging roads on the eastern side of the island are popular with more-ambitious cyclists. In Vancouver, heavy vehicular traffic makes bicycling less than pleasant on the streets, but Stanley Park, with its miles-long paved cycling and walking path – much of it along a sea wall – makes a great destination for the casual cyclist. The British Columbia Mountain Bike Directory website (Ⓦ www.oroad.com/bcmtbdir) has trail reports, message boards, bike-shop and bike-club links and a lot more.

SKIING

From at least December to April, skiing takes over the slopes of the Cascade Range, as well as the snow-glazed backcountry byways and riverside trails of nonmountainous wilderness areas. Most downhill ski resorts in the region also have areas for snowboarding, notably Washington's Mt Baker.

Downhill

Noted downhill ski areas in Oregon include the five resorts at Mt Hood – the most famous of which, Timberline Lodge, offers nearly year-round conditions – as well as Mt Bachelor and Anthony Lakes, both famous for their powder skiing. In Washington, Crystal Mountain, Stevens Pass, Mt Baker and Snoqualmie Pass are the popular resorts. World-class Whistler Mountain in BC is by far the region's most sophisticated destination. Grouse Mountain, perched above Vancouver, is just minutes from the city center and has night skiing.

Cross-Country

Cross-country skiing is huge in the Northwest. A number of downhill ski resorts offer groomed cross-country trails; private ski groups sometimes offer groomed trails on national forest lands for a small fee. However, cross-country skiing need not be so regimented. The heavy snowfall in the Northwest converts the vast wilderness areas of Washington, Oregon and BC into winter playgrounds. When there's enough snow, any USFS road is a makeshift ski trail; better yet, you'll probably have the road, and the mountainside, to yourself.

In Oregon, the Rim Drive that circles Crater Lake is popular with Nordic skiers. All Mt Hood downhill resorts also offer trails, but a better bet may be the Tea Cup Lake trails maintained by the Oregon Nordic Club, with 18.6 miles (30km) of skiing. Mt Hood National Forest offices can provide a list of other trails in the area.

Some spectacular regions for off-the-beaten-path skiing in Washington are Mt St Helens, Mt Rainier, the Lake Chelan area and Olympic National Park. Hurricane Ridge, near the Olympic's northern entrance, accesses high mountain meadows. In the Methow Valley, a series of ski huts are spaced along the trails for multi-day expeditions; you can even hire outfitters to transport your gear.

Garibaldi Park, in BC, is a popular cross-country destination for Vancouver skiers, as are the provincial parks – Mt Seymour and Cypress – that flank the mountains directly north of the city. Whistler offers 16 miles/26km of groomed Nordic trails.

CLIMBING & MOUNTAINEERING

If you're interested in climbing in the Cascades, the local USFS office is a good place to get information on guided hikes. You'll want to get *Selected Climbs in the Cascades* by Jim Nelson and Peter Potterfield, a Mountaineering title that also covers rock scaling.

Climbing and mountaineering are demanding activities requiring top physical condition, an understanding of the composition of various rock types and their hazards, and familiarity with a variety of equipment, including ropes, chocks, bolts, carabiners and harnesses.

Oregon's Mt Hood claims the distinction of being the world's second-most-climbed peak over 10,000 feet (after Japan's Mt Fuji). The climb is sort of an Oregonian pilgrimage – a trek that must be made at least once in a lifetime. Smith Rock is a world-renowned rock-climbing venue, towering above central Oregon's Crooked River and the Cascades' South Sister. And, at 10,358 feet, it can be conquered without technical equipment.

The highest peak in the Cascades is Mt Rainier at 14,411 feet; it is also the most heavily glaciated summit in the lower 48 states. Emmons Glacier, on the mountain's east side, is a popular and challenging ascent. Mt Adams (12,276 feet), also in the South Cascades, is one of Washington's easiest peak climbs, and the all-too-recently-active volcano, Mt St Helens, is a unique challenge.

The craggy peaks of the North Cascades offer extremely challenging ascents for experienced climbers. Mt Baker, at 10,781 feet, features a number of glacier climbs; Easton Glacier is the easiest ascent, while Coleman and Roosevelt are more technically demanding.

To complete the trio of Washington's national parks, Olympic National Park also contains glaciated mountain peaks for climbers, of which Mt Olympus (at 7965 feet) is the most popular.

In British Columbia, the massive granite faces near Squamish, midway between Vancouver and Whistler, are a noteworthy destination for rock climbers. The second-largest freestanding granite outcropping in the world (the largest is the Rock of Gibraltar), Stawamus Chief has 280 climbing routes on its various faces, walls and slabs. The University Wall is rated as one of the most difficult climbs in Canada. The pullout off Hwy 99 for Shannon Falls is a good place to stop and watch climbers scale these massive cliffs. For information on climbing Stawamus Chief, contact the Federation of Mountain Clubs of British Columbia (☎ 604-878-7007, Ⓦ www.mountainclubs.bc.ca).

RAFTING & KAYAKING

The mighty rivers of the Northwest make it one of the top rafting and kayaking areas in the US. Numerous outfitters guide trips down these waterways, ranging from half-day floats to three- and four-day expeditions through untracked wilderness. Sea kayaking is also popular, with marine trail systems established along the coasts of western Washington and BC.

Those who feel confident enough to paddle without guidance will find kayak and raft rentals, but be aware that many rivers are not for novices. Certain rivers are closely regulated and have rafting seasons; some may require permits, issued by a random draw.

River trips are classified on a scale of one to six according to difficulty. On any given river, classifications can vary over the course of the year, depending on the water level. Higher water levels, usually associated with spring runoff, can make a river trip either easier or more difficult by covering up hazards or increasing the velocity of the river, while lower water levels can expose hazards like rocks and whirlpools, making the river more exciting. Some, if not most, rivers depend on water releases from upstream dams.

Guided white-water trips take place in either large rafts seating a dozen or more people, or smaller six-person rafts, which make for a rougher, more exciting ride. While white-water trips are not without danger, a huge majority of trips are without incident. All participants must wear US Coast Guard–approved life jackets, and all expeditions have at least one river guide trained in lifesaving techniques.

River Rafting

Oregon's Deschutes and Rogue Rivers are rafters' favorites. On the Deschutes, the multi-day trip between Sherar's Falls and the Columbia River features Class IV rapids and no road access for miles and miles. The 84-mile (135km) stretch of the Rogue River within the Wild Rogue Wilderness Area is among the nation's most legendary white-water runs, with abundant Class IV rapids and waterfalls and rustic lodges along the way. The Upper Rogue, where runoff from Crater Lake and the Cascades gives birth to the river, is popular for gentler, more leisurely float trips. The Snake River through Hells Canyon, on the Oregon-Idaho border, also offers some mean rapids along with the striking scenery.

The Skagit, Yakima and Wenatchee Rivers are the principal kayaking and rafting rivers in Washington. Some outfitters on the Skagit River offer eagle-watching float trips in winter. In Olympic National Park, guided runs down the Hoh, Elwha and Queets Rivers glide through some of North America's only rain forests.

Rugged topography and an abundance of snowmelt make BC's rivers great for white-water action. The Fraser, Thompson, Chilliwack and Nahatlatch Rivers are all handy to Vancouver. Wilderness rafting averages about C$200 per day for everything, while half-day trips start at about C$45. Check with the local Visitor Info Centres for details about where to go and which companies to hire.

Sea Kayaking

Sea kayaking in the Puget Sound can be an extraordinary adventure, whether you're just puttering in the shadow of Seattle's skyline or paddling from island to island in the San Juans as orcas play around you. Outfitters offer rentals and guided tours.

Sea kayaks are easy to paddle and amazingly stable, and unlike larger boats, they can hug the shoreline, offering the perfect perch for watching shore birds and other marine life. It's always best to kayak with other people for safety. Someone in the group should know how to plot a course by navigational chart and compass, pilot in fog, read weather patterns, assess water hazards, interpret tide tables, handle boats in adverse conditions and perform group- and self-rescue techniques.

Western Washington's recently completed Cascadia Marine Trail stretches 160 miles (258km) along a protected marine corridor from Olympia to the Canadian border. Along the way, 40 campgrounds at state and county parks make convenient stopovers every few miles, giving paddlers the opportunity to plan limitless itineraries through Puget Sound. Users of the trail carry a daily/annual permit ($7/20), entitling them to stay at designated water trail campsites bearing its official logo. For more information on the trail, contact the Washington Water Trails Association (☎ 206-545-9161, Ⓦ www.wwta.org).

You can kayak just about everywhere along BC's coast, but you'll find the greatest concentration of outfitters on Vancouver Island. For multi-day trips, the best-known destination is the Broken Group Islands, part of Pacific Rim National Park Reserve, on the west coast of Vancouver Island. A great resource that includes launch-area maps and trip information for sea kayaking is Ⓦ www.easykayaker.com.

WINDSURFING

Summer is the time when the big afternoon winds rush up the Columbia River Gorge, creating the kinds of waves that bring 'boardheads' in from around the world. The Gorge is reckoned to be one of the world's foremost windsurfing locales, and the activity has elevated the sleepy orchard town of Hood River to a sports capital. Instruction and rentals ($40 to $65 for a full rig) are easily found in Hood River.

Nitinat Lake on Vancouver Island offers some of the best windsurfing in Canada, but you can also find good places to windsurf just outside Vancouver and Victoria. Check out the website Ⓦ www.coastalbc.com for lots of information on surf sports and other outdoor activities.

BIRD & WILDLIFE WATCHING

Endowed with numerous wildlife refuges and public lands – ranging from the rocky shores of the Pacific to the high desert of the Columbia Basin – the Pacific Northwest makes a great place to observe the local fauna. Bird watching is particularly well rewarded. Local Audubon Society chapters (see Useful Organizations, earlier) often sponsor trips to birding areas.

The National Wildlife Refuge system, managed by the US Fish & Wildlife Service,

sets aside more than 90 million acres nationwide as protected habitat, with 27 refuges in Washington and Oregon alone.

Oregon

The Malheur Wildlife Refuge, located in southeastern Oregon, covers 289 sq miles (749 sq km) of protected lands teeming with coyote, deer and more than 200 species of birds. It is the perfect place to study a high-desert ecosystem; seminars are offered at its facilities.

Southern Oregon's Klamath Basin Wildlife Refuges support more than 400 species. Its Bear Valley section is a major roost site for wintering bald eagles, best spotted between December and February. Herds of thousands of antelope roam the Hart Mountain National Antelope Refuge in southeastern Oregon, also a great place to watch for raptors.

Along the length of the Oregon Coast, all offshore sea stacks and promontories are preserved as wildlife refuges and are inhabited by seals, sea lions and a wide variety of sea birds. A trip to the Sea Lion Caves, south of Yachats, is mandatory.

Washington

The Upper Skagit Bald Eagle Area, in Washington's North Cascades, is best visited in winter, when eagles come to feast on the salmon spawning in the Skagit River. The Turnbull National Wildlife Refuge near Spokane and the Little Pend Oreille Refuge near Colville are stopovers for migratory waterfowl, as is the Potholes Wildlife Area in central Washington, an irrigated wetlands surrounded by sand dunes. Near Ellensburg, a Dept of Wildlife feeding program brings in hundreds of breakfasting elk each day when there's snow on the ground.

The Willapa National Wildlife Refuge, composed of five different areas in and around Willapa Bay on Washington's southern coast, is an excellent spot to glimpse shore birds. On Long Island – part of the refuge accessible only by canoe or kayak – black bear, coyote and elk roam undisturbed by man. Wolves aren't exactly prolific in Washington, but Wolf Haven

America, south of Olympia, offers visitors an educational look at these beautiful animals.

The Washington Dept of Fish & Wildlife's wildlife-viewing page (**W** www.wa.gov/wdfw/viewing/wildview.htm) is a valuable resource featuring heron and bat watch-cams.

British Columbia

BC offers superb bird watching, with more than 500 winged varieties to admire. Some of the best spots include the Brackendale area north of Squamish, where thousands of bald eagles congregate in winter; the Parksville/Qualicum areas on Vancouver Island, where brant geese and other migrating species flock each spring; and the Creston Valley Wildlife Management Area in the Kootenays. BC's extensive bird watching community maintains a helpful website (**W** birding.bc.ca/bc-home.htm).

Ask at any Visitor Info Centre for the free *British Columbia Wildlife Watch* brochure, a concise and handy guide to viewing opportunities across the province.

WHALE WATCHING

The high capes and headlands of the Oregon coast are excellent vantage points for gray whales. There are both spring and fall migrations; the springtime journey (which peaks in March) brings the whales closer to the shore. Favorite whale-watching spots include Cape Sebastian, Cape Blanco, Cape Perpetua, Neahkahnie Mountain and Cape Arago. On weekends, at most of these sites, volunteers from local wildlife groups will answer questions and help locate whales. Although whales can occasionally be seen with the naked eye, it's best to have a good pair of binoculars.

Killer whales (also known as orcas) reside in complex communities in the coastal waters of Vancouver Island. The 90 or so 'southern residents' (as opposed to a distinct community found at the island's northern half) migrate down to Puget Sound in summer, presumably to feast on the salmon runs, and are best spotted around the San Juan Islands. Expeditions can be organized out of Bellingham or the islands themselves.

Guided kayak tours are an adventurous way to cruise the coves and channels of this archipelago. There's even a state park – at San Juan Island's Lime Kiln Point – expressly devoted to whale watching.

Dozens of outfitters offer whale-watching cruises out of Victoria Harbour, often combined with excursions to islands and rocky promontories covered with sea lions, seals and sea-bird colonies. Sometimes you can even see whales from the deck of a BC Ferries vessel or from shore, especially on headlands of the Southern Gulf Islands and on Vancouver Island's west coast.

FISHING

The fishing mainstay of the Northwest for thousands of years has been the salmon. Today, populations of the anadromous species are so threatened that sport-fishing seasons on many rivers are offered only sporadically. Fish with a less ambitious life cycle still abound, however, including various kinds of trout, sturgeon and bass. There's great fishing on the Deschutes River in central Oregon, and on the Rogue and Umpqua Rivers in the southern part of the state. Among the Washington hot spots are the central Yakima and Wenatchee Rivers, the many lakes and rivers of Olympic National Park, the North Cascades' Methow and Stehekin Rivers, Lake Chelan and Lake Roosevelt.

Coastal towns offer charter trips into the Pacific to fish for whatever is in season, including salmon, cod, red snapper or rockfish. Charter boats out of Port Townsend, Washington, prowl the Strait of Juan de Fuca; excursions also depart from Westport in Gray's Harbor. Depoe Bay, Newport and Winchester Bay in Oregon are some of the coast's busiest harbors, offering good ocean fishing.

Anglers are required in all situations to have the appropriate state or provincial licenses and to abide by whatever seasonal or territorial restrictions are in place. For instance, the same stream may have several sections that have quite different restrictions on types of hooks, bait, seasons and what size and type of fish can be kept. Fishing licenses are issued to local and, more expensively, to visiting anglers and can be purchased (at bait shops or hardware stores) on a daily, weekly or annual basis. Obtain a rules brochure from the local Fish & Wildlife departments or at their websites (see Useful Organizations, earlier).

CLAMMING & CRABBING

Clamming and crabbing are fun alternatives to fishing: Rent a boat and crab rings and catch yourself some dinner, or dig a big bucket of clams and have yourself a bake.

Washington authorities charge a $7/20 annual fee (residents/nonresidents) for a license to dig shellfish; no license is required in Oregon. In either state, you must abide by the bag limits stated in the most recent Fish & Wildlife guidelines (in Washington,

call ☎ 360-796-3215). Otherwise all you need is a shovel and a bucket. Be sure that the shellfish is free of red tide (see Health in the Facts for the Visitor chapter).

Much of the harvesting action takes place along Puget Sound shorelines and on Pacific beaches, particularly around southwest Washington's Willapa Bay. Hood Canal, skirting the eastern Olympic Peninsula, is a center for recreational oyster collection. The namesake of the scrumptious Dungeness crab is Washington's Dungeness Spit on the Olympic Peninsula. In Oregon, Netarts, Wheeler and Reedsport are also known for great crabbing. Some Oregon Coast marinas will rent a boat and crab rings at around $50 for two hours' rental, and they'll clean and boil the crabs for you.

Getting There & Away

AIR

The terrorist attacks of September 11, 2001, have had far-reaching effects on the international travel industry, especially airlines. As we go to press, it remains unclear what the long-term restructuring may be. Therefore, information in this chapter should be followed up with thorough research of your own.

Airports & Airlines

Most air travelers to the Pacific Northwest will arrive either at Seattle-Tacoma International (SEA) – the region's largest airport, known locally as Sea-Tac – or Vancouver International Airport (YVR). Both are served by most national and international airlines, with regularly scheduled flights to many points worldwide. Portland International Airport (PDX) has connections to most US domestic destinations, as well as direct flights to Asia.

Some international airlines, their websites and phone numbers within the USA and Canada, and the Northwest airports they serve are listed below:

Aeroflot (☎ 206-464-1005) SEA
W www.aeroflot.org

Air Canada/Air BC (☎ 888-247-2262)
SEA/PDX/YVR
W www.aircanada.ca

Air China (☎ 800-685-0921) YVR
W www.air-china.co.uk

Air New Zealand (☎ 800-663-5494) YVR
W www.airnz.com

American Airlines (☎ 800-433-7300)
SEA/PDX/YVR
W www.aa.com

British Airways (☎ 800-247-9297)
SEA/PDX/YVR
W www.british-airways.com

Cathay Pacific Airways (☎ 800-607-3388) YVR
W www.cathaypacific.com

Continental Airlines (☎ 800-525-0280)
SEA/PDX/YVR
W www.continental.com

Delta Air Lines (☎ 800-221-1212) SEA/PDX
W www.delta.com

Japan Airlines (☎ 800-525-3663) YVR
W www.japanair.com

Lufthansa Airlines (☎ 800-645-3880) YVR
W www.lufthansa.com

Northwest Airlines/KLM (☎ 800-225-2525)
SEA/PDX/YVR
W www.nwa.com

Qantas (☎ 800-227-4500) YVR
W www.qantas.com.au

Scandinavian Airlines (SAS) (☎ 800-221-2350)
SEA/PDX/YVR
W www.scandinavian.net

Singapore Airlines (☎ 800-742-8333) YVR
W www.singaporeair.com

United Airlines (☎ 800-241-6522) SEA/PDX/YVR
W www.ual.com

Domestic US and Canadian airlines include the following:

Alaska Airlines (☎ 800-252-7522)
SEA/PDX/YVR
W www.alaska-air.com

Warning

The information in this chapter is particularly vulnerable to change: Prices for international travel are volatile, routes are introduced and canceled, schedules change, special deals come and go, and rules and visa requirements are amended. Airlines and governments seem to take a perverse pleasure in making price structures and regulations as complicated as possible. You should check directly with the airline or a travel agent to make sure you understand how a fare (and any ticket you may buy) works. In addition, the travel industry is highly competitive, and there are many lurks and perks.

The upshot of this is that you should get opinions, quotes and advice from as many airlines and travel agents as possible before you part with your hard-earned cash. The details given in this chapter should be regarded as pointers and are not a substitute for your own careful, up-to-date research.

America West Airlines (☎ 800-235-9292)
SEA/PDX/YVR
W www.americawest.com

Frontier Airlines (☎ 800-432-1359)
SEA/PDX/YVR
W www.frontierairlines.com

Hawaiian Airlines (☎ 800-367-5320) SEA/PDX
W www.hawaiianair.com

Horizon Air (☎ 800-547-9308) SEA/PDX
W www.horizonair.com

Jet Blue Airways (☎ 800-538-2583) SEA
W www.jetblue.com

Southwest Airlines (☎ 800-435-9792) SEA/PDX
W www.iflyswa.com

United Express (☎ 800-241-6522)
SEA/PDX/YVR
W www.ual.com

US Airways (☎ 800-428-4322) SEA
W www.usairways.com

WestJet (☎ 800-538-5696) YVR
W www.westjet.ca

Buying Tickets

Your plane ticket will probably be the single most expensive item in your budget. It is thus worth putting aside a few hours to research the current state of the market and to shop around. Start shopping for a ticket early – some of the cheapest tickets must be bought months in advance, and some popular flights sell out early.

Talk to other recent travelers and look at the travel sections of magazines and newspapers. The Internet is an increasingly useful resource for checking out airfares. Travelocity (W www.travelocity.com), Cheap Tickets (W www.cheaptickets .com), Expedia (W www.expedia.com) and Hotwire (W www.hotwire.com) are just a few of the many online reservation services now available. However, they're no substitute for a travel agent who knows all about special deals, has strategies for avoiding layovers and can offer advice on everything from which airline offers the best vegetarian meals to which is the best travel insurance to bundle with your ticket.

Generally, there is little to be gained by buying a ticket directly from the airline, since discounted tickets are released to selected travel agents and specialist discount agencies, and these are usually the cheapest deals going. The exception is the Internet, where many airlines offer excellent fares. They may sell seats by auction or simply cut prices to reflect the reduced cost of electronic selling.

Note that high season in the USA is from mid-June to mid-September and the weeks before and after Christmas and Thanksgiving. The best rates for travel to and within the region are generally found November to March. Roundtrip tickets usually work out cheaper than two one-way fares – often much cheaper. The cheapest tickets are often nonrefundable and require an extra fee for changing your flight.

Airlines issue refunds only to the purchaser of a ticket – usually the travel agent who bought the ticket on your behalf. Thus, you'll need to contact the agent to get a refund. Many travelers change their routes halfway through their trips, so think carefully before you buy a ticket that is not easily refunded.

Almost all domestic carriers offer discounted multitrip passes to non-US citizens. Northwest, Continental and American have the Visit USA pass; Delta's is called the Discover America pass; and United has the Skypass. The passes are actually books of coupons – each coupon equals a single flight. Typically, the minimum number of coupons is four and the maximum is 12, and they must be purchased in conjunction with an international airline ticket to the USA from a foreign country other than Canada or Mexico. Coupons cost $100 to $550 apiece, depending on how many you buy and where you're flying from.

Most airlines require you to plan your itinerary in advance and to complete your flights within 60 days of arrival, but rules can vary between individual airlines. A few airlines may allow you to use coupons on standby.

Travelers with Special Needs

If you have special needs of any sort, you should let the airline know as soon as possible so that they can make arrangements accordingly. It may also be worth calling various airlines before you make your booking to find out how they can handle your particular needs.

Most international airports can provide escorts from the check-in desk to the plane, and there should also be wheelchair-accessible phones, ramps, elevators and toilets in the airport. Guide dogs for the blind will often have to travel in a specially pressurized baggage compartment with other animals.

Children under two travel for 10% of the standard fare (or free on some airlines), as long as they don't occupy a seat, in which case they don't get baggage allowance. Children between two and 12 can usually occupy a seat for half to two-thirds of the full fare, and do get a baggage allowance. Strollers can often be taken on as hand luggage. 'Skycots' should be provided by the airline if requested in advance; these can hold a child weighing up to about 22lb (8kg).

Baggage & Other Restrictions

On most domestic and international flights, you are limited to two checked bags, or three if you don't have a carry-on item. There could be a charge if you bring more or if the size of the bag exceeds the airline's limits. It's best to check with the individual airline if you are worried about this.

If your luggage is delayed upon arrival (which is rare), some airlines will give you a cash advance to purchase necessities. Should the luggage be lost, it is important to submit a claim. It may take them anywhere from six weeks to three months to process the claim.

In the wake of the terrorist attacks of 2001, security on US flights has been tightened considerably, though the situation is probably no different from what's already the norm at most European airports. Nothing that could be conceived of as a weapon – including scissors, razors and pocket knives – will be allowed in the cabin. To allow for more thorough scrutiny of passengers and their belongings, airlines ask you to arrive two hours prior to departure, even for domestic flights. As before, it is illegal to check in or take on baggage that contains aerosols, pepper spray, camp stoves with fuel or scuba tanks that are full.

Departure Taxes

There's a $6 airport departure tax charged to all passengers leaving the USA. Taxes are normally included in the cost of tickets bought in the USA, though not necessarily for tickets purchased abroad. Vancouver International Airport charges an Airport Improvement Fee (AIF), which varies according to your destination. The price is C$5 for BC and Yukon destinations, C$10 to all other North American locations including Mexico, and C$15 to everywhere else. It can be paid at a booth or at machines, which accept credit cards or US and Canadian dollars. There is no charge if you are on a connecting flight.

Arriving in the USA

The first US airport that you land in is where you must carry out immigration and customs formalities – even if you are continuing immediately to another city in the USA. For instance, if your luggage is checked from, say, London to Seattle, you will still have to take it through customs if you first land in New York.

If you have a non-US passport, with a visa, you must complete an Arrival/Departure Record (Form I-94) before you go to the immigration desk. It's usually handed out on the plane, along with the customs declaration. Answers should be written *below* the questions.

The staff of the Immigration & Naturalization Service (INS) can be less than welcoming. Since their main concern is to exclude those who are likely to work illegally or overstay, visitors will be asked about their plans, and perhaps about whether they have sufficient funds for their stay in the USA. If the INS official thinks you're OK, a six-month entry is usually approved.

It's a good idea to be able to list an itinerary that will account for the period for which you ask to be admitted, and to be able to show you have $300 or $400 for every week of your intended stay. A couple of major credit cards will go a long way toward establishing 'sufficient funds.' Don't make too much of having friends, relatives or business contacts in the USA – the INS official may decide that this will make you more likely to overstay.

Arriving in Canada

How thoroughly customs will check you out upon arrival at a Canadian entry point depends on a number of things, but primarily, it depends on your point of departure, nationality and appearance. Arriving from countries known as illegal-drug sources or with a history of illegal immigration will add to the scrutiny.

The border between the USA and Canada has tightened up considerably in recent years, with the World Trade Center attacks further intensifying security measures. By law, you are required to carry a passport (or, for US citizens, a birth certificate) and picture identification, even though you may not be asked to produce any of these. Predictably, people of who look to be of Hispanic or Arab origin are more likely to be asked to present identification.

Don't risk carrying drugs across the border in either direction. Customs even advises checking rental cars for items left by previous drivers.

Within the USA

Seattle's Sea-Tac and Portland's PDX are the principal hubs for air travel to the US Pacific Northwest.

Horizon Air and United Express (a subsidiary of United Airlines) sometimes offer direct flights to small Northwest cities from San Francisco or Los Angeles.

US domestic airfares vary tremendously depending on the season you travel, the day of the week you fly, the length of your stay and the flexibility the ticket allows for flight changes and refunds. Still, nothing determines fares more than demand, and when things are slow, regardless of the season, airlines will lower their fares to fill empty seats. America West and Southwest Airlines often outdo the competition with some of the lowest fares for domestic flights.

If you're buying tickets within the USA, the *New York Times, Los Angeles Times,*

Chicago Tribune, San Francisco Examiner and other major newspapers all produce weekly travel sections that run numerous travel agencies' advertisements.

Council Travel (☎ 800-226-8624, W www .counciltravel.com), the largest student-travel organization in America, has around 60 offices in the USA. STA Travel (☎ 800-781-4040, W www.statravel.com) is another well-known agent for cheap fares.

Discount travel agents in the USA are known as consolidators. San Francisco is the ticket consolidator capital of America, although some good deals can be found in Los Angeles, New York and other big cities. Air Brokers International (☎ 415-397-1383, 800-883-3273, W www.airbrokers.com) is a leading US consolidator.

Within Canada

If you want to connect to the Pacific Northwest from the rest of Canada, you'll most likely need to go through Vancouver. A roundtrip ticket to Vancouver with Air Canada will cost you about C$275 from Calgary, C$400 from Winnipeg, C$460 from Toronto and C$480 from Montréal. You may be able to reduce the cost by looking out for seat sales or taking late-night flights, often referred to as red-eye specials.

Travelers flying from Canada's east coast may find it more economical to go to Seattle or Portland, as Canadian airfares tend to be about 10% higher than US fares. Be sure to factor in the cost of connections between Canadian and US airports at either end.

Travel CUTS (☎ 800-667-2887, W www .travelcuts.com), Canada's national student-travel agency, has offices in all major cities. The Toronto *Globe & Mail* and the *Vancouver Sun* carry travel agencies' ads.

Australia & New Zealand

From Australia and New Zealand, there are a number of flight and fare options for travelers to the Pacific Northwest. Shop around, as there are often some good deals. Check travel agents' ads in the yellow pages and newspapers such as the *Sydney Morning Herald* and the *Age.* STA Travel's main Australia office (☎ 03-9349 2411) is at 224 Faraday St,

Carlton, in Melbourne; its New Zealand headquarters (☎ 09-309 0458) is at 10 High St, Auckland. Call ☎ 131 776 Australia-wide for the location of your nearest branch, or visit the website at W www.statravel.com.au. Another leading discounter, Flight Centre (Australia-wide ☎ 131 600, W www.flight centre.com.au) has a central office at 82 Elizabeth St, in Sydney, and in Auckland at National Bank Towers (on the corner of Queen and Darby Sts).

Most of the mainstream airlines, including Qantas, Air New Zealand and Air Canada, travel via Los Angeles, San Francisco or Honolulu. Cheaper flights with an extra stop in Asia – most likely in Seoul, Taipei or Tokyo – are available with Korean Air and Japan Airlines.

High-season roundtrip fares from Australia to Vancouver start at around A$2389 with Air New Zealand. Qantas fares to Seattle start from A$2600; to Portland, A$2745.

From New Zealand, Air New Zealand and United high-season fares to Vancouver start from NZ$2470. Flights to Seattle are more expensive – expect to pay around NZ$2800 for a roundtrip fare.

The UK & Ireland

If you're planning to remain on the Pacific Coast, you can save hours of flight time and airport-dawdling by flying directly from London to Seattle or Vancouver. British Airways offers daily nonstop service from London Heathrow to Seattle, and Air Canada has flights to Vancouver from London. Fares are usually around $600 roundtrip from London to Seattle, $800 to Vancouver.

Look for travel agencies' ads in magazines such as *Time Out,* the *Evening Standard* and *TNT*. Also check out the free magazines widely available in London – start by looking outside the main railway stations.

Most agents are registered with the ABTA (Association of British Travel Agents). Some are bonded under agreements such as the Air Transport Operators License (ATOL); if you buy a ticket from

such an agent, and the agent then goes out of business, ATOL guarantees a refund or an alternative. Unregistered or unbonded 'bucket shops' are riskier but are sometimes cheaper. London is arguably the world's headquarters for bucket shops, which try to sell the seats that would otherwise go empty.

Recommended agents for cheap tickets in the UK are Trailfinders (☎ 020-7938-3939, W www.trailfinder.com), 194 Kensington High St, London, W8 7RG; and STA Travel (☎ 020-7361-6262), W www.statravel .co.uk, 86 Old Brompton Rd, London, SW7 3LQ.

Continental Europe

There are nonstop flights to Seattle from Copenhagen (roundtrip $670) and Amsterdam ($1200) by SAS and Northwest Airlines. Vancouver has direct air links to Frankfurt ($830) and Amsterdam ($1350). You can also fly directly from Paris to San Francisco, where you can easily catch a flight to Portland, Seattle or Vancouver. Quoted prices are standard published fares; watch for promotions.

Council Travel has offices in Paris (☎ 01 44 41 89 80), 1 place de l'Odeon, 75006 Paris, and in Munich (☎ 089-39-50-22), Adalbert Strasse 32, 80799 Munich 40. STA Travel has branches throughout Germany; its Berlin branch (☎ 030-311-0950) is at Goethesttrasse 73.

Asia

Japan Airlines and Air Canada both have direct flights from Tokyo to Vancouver, where you can connect to other Pacific Northwest destinations. Northwest, United and American Airlines have nonstop flights to and from Seattle. Expect to pay around ¥78,400 roundtrip from Tokyo to Vancouver; ¥89,700 to Seattle. From Singapore, fares to Vancouver start from S$2090; to Seattle, S$2846.

Other flights from Japan travel via Los Angeles, San Francisco or Honolulu, where a free stopover may be allowed. Malaysia Airlines flies to Honolulu from Hong Kong, Bangkok, Manila, Seoul and Singapore, with connections to Vancouver and other West Coast cities.

Bangkok and Singapore have replaced Hong Kong as discount airfare capitals of the region, with a number of bucket shops. Ask the advice of other travelers before buying a ticket. STA Travel has branches in Hong Kong, Tokyo, Singapore, Bangkok and Kuala Lumpur.

Central & South America

There are nonstop flights between Seattle and Mexico City on American Airlines for around $500 roundtrip, as well as service from Puerto Vallarta and Cancún. Other flights from Central America and South America go via Miami, Dallas/Fort Worth or Los Angeles. Most countries' international carriers, such as Aerolíneas Argentinas and LanChile, as well as US airlines such as United and American, serve these US destinations, with onward connections to the Pacific Northwest. Continental has flights to the USA from various cities in Central America, including San José, Guatemala City, Cancún and Mérida.

LAND
Border Crossings

The main overland point of entry from Washington to Vancouver, BC, is at Blaine/Douglas, on the northern end of I-5, which continues as Hwy 99 on the Canadian side. This crossing has the longest lines.

Slightly less busy on weekdays is the Pacific crossing, 3 miles (5km) east of Blaine; from I-5, take exit 275 (the one before Blaine). Northbound travelers purchasing duty-free items must use this crossing. Other BC entry points are at Lynden/Aldergrove (Hwy 539 from Bellingham), and Sumas/Huntingdon, 62 miles (100km) east of Blaine. The latter is best for heading into BC's interior. All crossings are open 24 hours except Lynden, which is open 8am to midnight. During the week, expect to wait five to 30 minutes; on weekends, as long as an hour; and on holiday weekends, longer. Wait times and security inspections have increased significantly in the wake of the September 2001 terrorist attacks. Do not use

the nonstop lanes unless your car has a PACE sticker.

Many travelers also cross the border by ferry, principally on journeys from Anacortes to Sidney, BC (near Victoria) and from Port Angeles to Victoria. See the Sea section, later in this chapter, as well as the Ferry section of the Getting Around chapter, for details.

Also see the Visas & Documents section of the Facts for the Visitor chapter.

Bus

Because bus service is infrequent and networks are sparse, schedules are often inconvenient, and fares are relatively high. Therefore, bargain airfares can often undercut bus fares on long-distance routes. In some cases, it can be cheaper to rent a car than to ride the bus, especially on shorter routes. However, very long-distance bus trips are often available at bargain prices if you purchase or reserve tickets three or more days in advance.

Greyhound The only nationwide bus company in the USA and Canada, Greyhound (☎ 800-231-2222, ⓦ www.greyhound.com) runs cross-country buses between New York and Seattle ($136/209 one way/roundtrip). Along the US West Coast, you can travel to Vancouver from Los Angeles ($95/160) via Seattle, Portland and San Francisco. The most direct Greyhound route up and down the West Coast follows I-5, though if you have time, the route from Portland to San Francisco following US 101 along the coast is much more scenic.

Tickets can be purchased by phone or online with a major credit card and mailed to you if purchased 10 days in advance, or picked up at the terminal with proper identification. Currently, tickets cannot be mailed to addresses outside the USA or Canada. Note that all buses are designated as nonsmoking, and that only by purchasing a ticket can you reserve a space.

Special Fares Greyhound's Friendly Fare allows up to 1000 miles of one-way travel for

$49. Each additional 500 miles costs another $10 to a maximum fare of $99, so a journey of over 3000 miles won't exceed $99. It's a bargain if you're looking for a cheap way to cover a long distance (Portland to Chicago, for instance). The ticket must be booked at least seven days in advance, and no stopovers are allowed. As with regular fares, this promotional deal is subject to change.

Greyhound also offers a Companion Fare, which allows two people to travel for the price of one. The ticket must be bought at least three days in advance. It's not available at all locations, and it's not refundable.

Seniors and students should make sure to ask about discounts.

North America Discovery Pass Greyhound's Discovery Pass allows unlimited travel and stopovers within particular regions of the USA and Canada over a certain period. The pass comes in various versions and fares: The Domestic Americapass, aimed at US and Canadian travelers, is good for travel throughout the USA for periods of seven to 60 days ($185-509). A domestic Western/CanAm Pass costs $299/399 for 15/30 days of unlimited travel in the western USA and Canada. Discounts are available for seniors, students and children. Purchase the Discovery Pass at any Greyhound terminal or online.

International Discovery Passes can be purchased only by foreign tourists and foreign students staying in the USA for less than one year. The International West Coast Regional Pass, valid for travel in the western USA and Vancouver, BC, costs $199/299 for 10/21 days. International passes can be bought at overseas travel agencies or in the USA at the Greyhound International Office in New York City (☎ 212-971-0492), at the Port Authority Bus Terminal. It can also be purchased online at least 21 days before travel.

Train

The Pacific Northwest is well served by Amtrak (☎ 800-872-7245, W www.amtrak.com) in the USA and VIA Rail (☎ 888-842-7245, W www.viarail.com) in Canada.

Amtrak's *Coast Starlight* links Los Angeles to Portland and Seattle via Oakland and other West Coast cities. The *Empire Builder* runs from Chicago to the Pacific Northwest via Minneapolis and Spokane, where it separates to reach Portland and Seattle. VIA Rail's *Canadian* runs between Vancouver and Toronto three times a week (C$615 one way), leaving Toronto at 8:45am on Tuesday, Thursday and Saturday and departing Vancouver at 5:30pm on Tuesday, Friday and Sunday. Note that schedules can be very fluid: Arrival and departure times become more tenuous the farther you are from the starting point.

Fares on Amtrak vary greatly, depending on the season and what promotions are going. You can beat the rather stiff full-price fares by purchasing in advance – the sooner made, the better the fare. Roundtrips are the best bargain, but even these are usually as expensive as airfares.

Tickets can be purchased by credit card over the phone or online, from a travel agent or at an Amtrak depot. If the train station is closed 30 minutes prior to boarding, you can purchase the ticket on the train; otherwise, there's a penalty. In many stations, credit card–operated ticket machines are available.

Rail Passes The best value overall is Amtrak and VIA Rail's North America Rail Pass, which allows 30 days of unlimited travel in the USA and Canada. The peak-season fare (June 1 to October 15) is $674/C$1004; off season, it's $471/C$702. Seniors, students and children receive a 10% discount. Reservations for the pass can be made by phone, and tickets can be picked up at staffed stations, or you can purchase the pass online.

For non-US citizens, Amtrak offers three types of USA Rail Passes – national, regional and coastal – which must be purchased outside the USA (check with your travel agent). A 15-/30-day national pass costs $385/$550 in the high season. Regional passes vary in price: a 15-day Far West pass, covering US territory west of the Rockies, runs $245. Sleeping accommodations cost extra. Advanced booking is highly recommended, especially during the peak season.

Amtrak's Air/Rail pass lets you to fly one way on United Airlines, then return by train with three stopovers allowed. Train tickets are for reclining seats; sleeping cars cost extra.

Car & Motorcycle

Drivers need the vehicle's registration papers, liability insurance and an international driver's permit, in addition to their domestic license.

Note that driving regulations, such as speed limits and the permissibility of right turns on red lights, vary somewhat from state to state. Also, Oregon law prohibits you from pumping your own gasoline – all stations are full service.

For information on buying or renting a car, see the Getting Around chapter.

SEA

Chances that you will arrive on a boat and still have time to enjoy being in the Pacific Northwest are slim. There are cruises, such as the *QE2* from England, that make transatlantic voyages, but the cruise itself is usually the vacation. Cities in the Puget Sound and Georgia Strait region of the Pacific Northwest are linked by ferry, and while – strictly speaking – they're international journeys, they are best thought of as commuter ferries. Probably the grand-daddy of all Northwest ferry rides is the Inside Passage trip, which travels between Bellingham, Washington, and Skagway, Alaska. See the Bellingham section of the Northwestern Washington chapter for more information.

ORGANIZED TOURS

Tours of the USA are so numerous that it would be impossible to attempt any kind of comprehensive listing. For overseas visitors, the most reliable sources of information on the constantly changing offerings are major international travel agents such as Thomas Cook and American Express. Probably those of most interest to the general traveler are coach tours that visit the national parks and guest-ranch excursions. For those with limited time, package tours can be an efficient and relatively inexpensive way to go.

The near-mythic Green Tortoise (☎ 415-956-7500, 800-867-8647, W www.green tortoise.com), 494 Broadway, San Francisco, CA 94133, offers alternative bus transportation with stops at places such as hot springs and national parks. Meals are cooperatively cooked, and you either camp or sleep on bunks on the bus. This is not luxury travel, but it is fun. The National Parks Loop takes 16 days and costs $629, plus $191 toward the food fund.

TrekAmerica (☎ 973-983-1144, 800-221-0596, W www.trekamerica.com), PO Box 189, Rockaway, NJ 07866, offers roundtrip camping tours to different areas of the country. These tours last from one to nine weeks and are designed for small, international groups (13 people maximum) of people ranging from 18 to 38 years old. Tours including food and occasional hotel nights will cost you about $600 for a seven-day tour of the West, or $3500 for a nine-week tour of the entire country.

AmeriCan Adventures & Road Runner (☎ 800-873-5872, W www.americanadven tures.com), PO Box 1155, Gardena, CA 90249, organizes regional treks for groups of up to 13 people in conjunction with Hostelling International. Prices range from $480 to $1270 for one to three weeks.

Getting Around

This chapter deals with the intricacies of getting around within the Pacific Northwest; see the Getting There & Away chapter for details on getting to the Northwest. Don't automatically assume that, once arriving in the Northwest, ground travel is going to be the cheapest method of transportation. The west coasts of the USA and Canada are home to a number of inexpensive, no-frills airlines, whose rates rival bus and train fares. Ask a travel agent for information about discount airlines, or have a look at the website Ⓦ www.gonorthwest.com, with links to many regional carriers.

AIR
Domestic Air Services
Portland and Seattle are linked by Horizon Air, Delta and United Express, a subsidiary of United Airlines (see Getting There & Away for contact information), with flights departing every half hour. From either city, frequent flights go to Vancouver on Air Canada, Horizon and United Express, and a roundtrip flight usually costs under $200.

Portland and Seattle are the principal hubs for flights to outlying Northwest communities. United Express and Horizon Air are the most common carriers on these commuter flights. Flights are available from either city to Klamath Falls, Coos Bay, Eugene, Medford, Port Angeles, Yakima, the Tri-Cities, Walla Walla, Spokane, Bellingham and Wenatchee, as well as from Seattle to destinations in the San Juan Islands and Victoria.

These short flights are usually moderately priced if bought seven or 14 days in advance, especially when considering the distance covered and the overland alternatives. Generally, fares can drop substantially if you fly very early in the morning or on specific less-used flights. Ask airlines and travel agents about special-fare flights.

Small floatplanes serve the San Juan Islands from Seattle, and Vancouver Island

and Whistler from Vancouver. See the appropriate chapters for details.

Note that if you are arriving in the Northwest from overseas or another major US airport, it is usually much cheaper to buy a through ticket to small airports as part of your fare rather than separately.

Departure Taxes
Domestic departures in the USA are subject to a series of taxes and surcharges that may not be reflected in published fares. These include a federal tax of 7.5% on all US flights, a local departure tax of $5 or $6, an variably priced airport tax and a fuel-service fee, which depends on the price of fuel at the time the ticket is purchased.

BUS
Since Americans rely so much on their cars, bus transportation is relatively infrequent, especially in more remote areas. Greyhound (☎ 800-231-2222, Ⓦ www.greyhound.com), the main bus line for the Northwest, largely sticks to the interstate freeway system, while regional carriers provide service to outlying areas. In almost all cases, these smaller bus lines share depots and information services with Greyhound.

In many small towns, Greyhound no longer maintains terminals but may instead have a ticket window in a gas station or convenience store. Elsewhere, the bus merely stops at a given location, such as a grocery-store parking lot, and boarding passengers usually pay the driver with exact change.

TRAIN
Amtrak (USA) and VIA Rail (Canada) trains provide an attractive, if costly, alternative to buses for travel between major points. See the Getting There & Away chapter for details on fares, rail passes and purchasing Amtrak tickets.

A branch of Amtrak's daily *Empire Builder* leaves Portland and crosses to Vancouver, Washington, before making its extraordinarily scenic run up the north side of the Columbia Gorge to meet the other eastbound half of the train in Spokane. The Seattle branch of the *Empire Builder* heads north to Everett before winding east to Wenatchee and Spokane. Note that the westbound *Empire Builder* divides in Spokane for Portland and Seattle: Make sure you're sitting in the correct portion of the train!

Three times daily, Amtrak's *Cascades* train links Seattle to Tacoma, Olympia, Portland, Salem, Albany and Eugene. These trains connect with Amtrak Thruway buses (actually a regional bus line under contract with Amtrak) to continue north to Vancouver, BC, with a stop in Bellingham. A morning train makes the same Seattle-Vancouver run, returning in the afternoon, but this doesn't connect with the Portland extension.

Other Thruway buses carry Amtrak passengers out to the Oregon coast from Portland and Albany.

CAR & MOTORCYCLE

When you're traveling around the most car-oriented society on the planet, auto transportation is well worth considering, if only to delve into the national mindset. A car is more flexible than public transportation, and in a country where gas is still a relatively inexpensive commodity, it's likely to be cheaper. Officially, if you're traveling outside of your country, you must have an International Driving Permit (IDP) to supplement your national or state driver's license; note that the IDP is only valid if issued in the same country as your driver's license.

Keep in mind that Oregon law prohibits you from pumping your own gasoline – all stations are full service, so just sit back and enjoy it.

Useful Organizations

The American Automobile Association (AAA) and Canadian Automobile Association (CAA) provide useful information, free maps and routine road services such as tire repair and towing (free within a limited radius) for their members. The same benefits are extended to the members of foreign

Driving Distances

Portland to	distance	hours
Salem	47 miles (76km)	1
Lincoln City	88 miles (142km)	1½
Eugene	110 miles (177km)	2
Bend	160 miles (257km)	3
Pendleton	208 miles (335km)	4
Medford	273 miles (439km)	5
Vancouver, BC	313 miles (504km)	6
Seattle to	**distance**	**hours**
Bellingham	89 miles (143km)	1½
Vancouver, BC	141 miles (227km)	3
Yakima	142 miles (228km)	2½
Portland	172 miles (277km)	3
Tri-Cities	216 miles (348km)	4
Spokane	280 miles (451km)	5
Vancouver to	**distance**	**hours**
Victoria	70 miles (113km)	3½
Whistler	75 miles (121km)	1½
Seattle	141 miles (227km)	3
Portland	313 miles (504km)	6

(Note: driving time to Victoria is approximate due to ferry schedules.)

affiliates, such as the Automobile Association in the UK.

To become a member of AAA, call ☎ 800-562-2582 or visit ⓦ www.aaa.com. The basic membership fee is $49 per year, plus a one-time initiation fee of $10 (still an excellent investment for the maps alone, even for nonmotorists). AAA's nationwide toll-free roadside-assistance number is ☎ 800-222-4357.

For CAA membership, call ☎ 877-325-8888 or visit ⓦ www.caa.ca. The basic CAA plan costs C$76, and the toll-free roadside-assistance phone number is ☎ 800-222-4357.

Safety

Drivers should be aware that much of the Pacific Northwest region is open-range country in which cattle and, less frequently, sheep forage along the highway. A collision with a large animal (including game animals such as deer or elk) can wreck a car and severely injure or kill the driver and passengers, not to mention the animal, so pay attention to the roadside – especially at night. Seat belts are obligatory for the driver and all passengers.

During winter months – especially at the higher elevations – there will be times when tire chains are required on snowy or icy roads. Sometimes such roads will be closed to cars without chains or 4WD, so it's a good idea to keep a set of chains in the trunk. (Note that many car rental companies specifically prohibit the use of chains on their vehicles.) Roadside services might be available to attach chains to your tires for a fee (around $20). Other cold-weather precautions include keeping a wool blanket, a windshield ice scraper, a spade or snow shovel, flares and an extra set of gloves and boots in the trunk for emergencies.

Oregon, Washington and BC all require that anyone (including passengers) riding a motorcycle wear a helmet.

Weather is a serious factor throughout the Pacific Northwest, especially in wintertime. Oregon, Washington and BC all provide road and travel information, as well as state and provincial highway-patrol information, by telephone. For these numbers, see the Emergencies section in the Facts for the Visitor chapter.

Rental

Major international rental agencies – such as Hertz, Avis, Budget and A-1 – have offices throughout the region. To rent a car in the Pacific Northwest, you must have a valid driver's license, be at least 21 years of age and present a major credit card or a large cash deposit. Drivers under 25 are charged an additional $20 per day over the regular rental.

Agencies often have bargain rates for weekend or weeklong rentals, especially outside the peak summer season or in conjunction with airline tickets. Prices vary greatly in relation to region, season and type or size of the car.

Basic liability insurance, also called third-party coverage, covers damage you may cause to another vehicle. It is required by law and comes with the price of renting the car.

Optional collision insurance, also called the Liability Damage Waiver, is optional. It covers the full value of the vehicle in case of an accident, except when caused by acts of nature or fire. For a midsize car, the cost for this extra coverage is around $15 per day. Rental agencies also tack on a daily fee for each additional driver.

Some credit cards will cover collision insurance if you rent for 15 days or less and charge the rental to your card. If you opt to do that, you'll need to sign a waiver declining standard coverage. If you already have collision insurance on your personal policy, the credit card will cover the large deductible. To find out if your credit card offers such a service, contact your card provider.

Be aware that some major rental agencies no longer offer unlimited mileage in noncompetitive markets (which is most of the Pacific Northwest); this greatly increases the cost of renting a car.

A few western Washington companies rent motor homes, also known as recreational vehicles (RVs). In Bellingham, Northwest Campers (☎ 360-733-1982, ⒲ www.northwestcampers.com), at 208 McKenzie Ave, specializes in VW camper rental. Western Motorhome Rentals (☎ 425-774-1414, 800-800-1181), 19303 Hwy 99, in Lynnwood (north of Seattle) is another option.

Purchase

If you're spending several months in the USA and Canada, a car may be a good investment, particularly if you're splitting the expense with others. Keep in mind, however, that it can be complicated and requires plenty of research.

It is possible to purchase a viable used car for about $1500, but don't expect to get too far before you'll need some repair work that could cost several hundred dollars or more. It doesn't hurt to spend more to get a quality vehicle – you can usually sell it for close to what you paid for it. It's also worth spending $50 or so to have a mechanic check the vehicle for defects (some AAA offices have diagnostic centers where they can do this on-the spot for members).

You can check out the official valuation of a used car by looking it up in the *Kelley Blue Book* (W www.kbb.com), which is a listing of cars by make, model and year that gives the average resale price. Local public libraries have copies of the *Blue Book,* as well as back issues of *Consumer Reports,* a magazine that annually tallies the repair records of common makes of cars.

If you want to purchase a car, the first thing to do is contact AAA (☎ 800-222-4357) or CAA (☎ 877-325-8888) for some general information. Then contact the Department of Motor Vehicles (DMV) to find out about registration fees and insurance. As an example, say you are a 30-year-old non-US citizen and you want to buy a 1989 Honda. If this is the first time you have registered a car in the USA, you'll have to fork over about $300 first and then about $100 to $200 more for general registration. In Oregon, you're required to establish residency in the state before you can register a vehicle, while Washington only requires official photo identification from your country of residence.

Inspect the title carefully before purchasing the car; the owner's name on the title must match the identification of the person selling you the car. If you're a foreigner, you may find it useful to obtain a notarized document authorizing your use of the car, since it may take several weeks or more to process the change in title.

Insurance

Auto insurance is obligatory for car owners in the Pacific Northwest. Rates fluctuate widely, depending on where the car is registered; it's usually cheaper if registered at an address in the suburbs or in a rural area, rather than in a central city. Male drivers under the age of 25 will pay astronomical rates. Collision coverage has become very expensive, with high deductibles, and is generally not worthwhile unless the car is somewhat valuable.

Obtaining insurance, however, is not as simple as walking into an agency, filling out a form and paying for it. Many agencies refuse to insure drivers who have no car insurance – a classic Catch-22! Those agencies who will do so often charge much higher rates because they presume a higher risk. The minimum term for a policy is usually six months, but some insurance companies will refund the difference on a prorated basis if the car is sold and the policy voluntarily terminated. It is advisable to shop around. If you're planning to drive in both the USA and Canada, make sure the insurance you negotiate is valid on both sides of the border.

BICYCLE

Cycling is an interesting, inexpensive and increasingly popular way to travel in the USA, especially in the Pacific Northwest. Roads are good, shoulders are usually wide, and there are many decent routes for road bikes, as well as mountain bikes. The changeable weather can be a drawback, especially at high altitudes where thunderstorms are frequent. In some areas, the wind can slow your progress to a crawl (traveling west to east is generally easier than east to west), and water sources are far apart. Spare parts are widely available, and repair shops are numerous, but it's still important to be able to do basic mechanical work, such as fixing a flat, yourself.

Not only is cycling a recreational activity here, but in some of the more progressive communities, it's become a mode of commuter transportation in its own right. Towns like Bellingham, Eugene and Corvallis have designated bike lanes sharing roads with auto traffic. Increasingly, local buses are equipped with a front rack to transport bikes, allowing cyclists to save energy for their enjoying destination rather than getting there. Motorists are generally courteous to cyclists, though you may encounter the occasional arrested-development imbecile who harasses cyclists to show off. Bicycle riders are generally required to wear a helmet in the Northwest, though the rule is seldom enforced.

Bicycles can be transported by air, usually in a bike bag or box, although airlines often charge an additional fee. Check this with the airline in advance, preferably before you pay for your ticket. Be aware that some airlines welcome bicycles, while others treat them as an undesirable nuisance and do everything possible to discourage them.

For more details on cycling in the Pacific Northwest, see Bicycling in the Outdoor Activities chapter.

HITCHHIKING
Hitchhiking is never entirely safe in any country in the world, and we don't recommend it. Travelers who decide to hitchhike should understand that they are taking a small but potentially serious risk. People who do choose to hitchhike will be safer if they travel in pairs and let someone know where they are planning to go.

FERRY
Washington and BC have two of the largest state-owned ferry systems in the world, and you cannot travel extensively in the Pacific Northwest without hopping a ferry. Note that there are both passenger-only and car-and-passenger ferries to popular destinations. Pick up a free copy of *Dan Youra's Ferry Travel Guide* in visitor centers and on the ferries themselves for the most up-to-date schedules and routes.

Washington State Ferries (WSF; ☎ 206-464-6400, in Washington ☎ 800-843-3779) operates most of the ferries that run in the Puget Sound area. Popular routes go to Bremerton and to Bainbridge and Vashon Islands from Seattle. WSF also operates the ferry system through the San Juan Islands and on to Sidney (near Victoria, on Vancouver Island) from Anacortes. The WSF website (W www.wsdot.wa.gov/ferries) contains fares and schedules, route maps and tourist information, plus links to other ferry services.

BC Ferries (☎ 604-277-0277, W www.bcferries.com) operates most of the ferries in that province. Primary links are between Tsawwassen (south of Vancouver) and Swartz Bay (on Vancouver Island), and to Nanaimo from Tsawwassen and Horseshoe Bay. The Gulf Islands are also linked to Tsawwassen by BC Ferries.

Privately operated ferries are also important transportation links in this area. Black Ball's *Coho* ferry (in Washington ☎ 360-457-4491, in BC ☎ 250-386-2202) connects Victoria with Washington's Olympic Peninsula via Port Angeles year round.

Clipper Navigation (☎ 206-448-5000, 800-888-2535) operates the *Victoria Clipper,* a year-round passenger ferry, with stops in the San Juan Islands during the summer.

LOCAL TRANSPORTATION
Bus
Though local bus networks are minimally developed in the hinterlands, the metropolitan areas have extensive service. Particularly in the western, more populated, part of the region, one can usually get wherever one wants to go by bus, though it may take some planning. In general, transit systems are very much aimed at the commuting workforce rather than tourists, so service is sparse or nonexistent outside of peak commuting hours and may be unavailable on weekends.

Seattle in particular has a highly developed public transportation system, with underground bus tunnels, a light rail, a monorail and a vintage trolley car – all interconnected.

Bus fares are usually on a zone system, so you'll pay a base fare within a town's core area, usually 50¢ to $1, and additional increments to outlying zones. Drivers almost never make change, so you'll need to have the exact amount ready.

Taxi & Shuttle
Outside of the big cities, taxis can't be hailed off the street – you have to phone a dispatcher. Check the 'Taxi' listings in the yellow pages for local services. City cabs are metered: A ride in downtown Seattle costs $1.80 per mile. Drivers expect a tip of about 10% of the total fare.

In some hiking destinations, such as Olympic National Park, shuttle services can take you to a trailhead and arrange to pick you up at the other end of the trail.

ORGANIZED TOURS
A number of cruise lines offer trips up the Columbia River from Portland to Lewiston,

Idaho, in spring and fall. The weeklong trip passes through the Columbia Gorge and the lock systems of eight major dams. Fares range from $800 to $4000, depending on the season, type of vessel and cabin category. For information on trips, contact Cruise West (☎ 800-888-9378, W www.cruisewest.com).

Tauck Tours (☎ 800-788-7885, W www .tauck.com), the nation's largest full-service tour operator, offers frequent tours of Oregon, Washington and Canada during the spring and summer. Travel is done mostly on buses, but may also include trips on company-owned trains, cruise ships and helicopters. All expenses are paid, including meals, lodging in upscale hotels and resorts, and fees for activities and attractions. An eight-day tour of Oregon, which takes in the Oregon coast, Crater Lake, Mt Hood and the Columbia Gorge, and also includes theater tickets to Ashland's Shakespeare

Festival, costs $1860 per person. Their two-week tour of the entire Pacific Northwest, from San Francisco to Vancouver, costs around $3500 per person. Tour bookings are made through local travel agents.

Local day tours are available from Seattle to Mt Rainier and the islands of the Puget Sound, and from Portland to the Columbia Gorge, Mt Hood, Oregon's wine country and the northern Oregon coast. See the Organized Tours section in the appropriate chapters for complete details.

Maverick Tours (☎ 604-940-8727, W www .maverickcoachlines.bc.ca) runs organized bus tours in BC and beyond. Some of its offerings include an overnight to Salt Spring Island ($200 per person double occupancy), a four-day trip to the west coast of Vancouver Island ($400) and a five-day trip that takes in the Okanagan Valley, Kootenay National Park, Lake Louise and more ($500).

Facts about Oregon

Few states can boast such a varied landscape as Oregon. Beginning with the distinctively rugged Pacific Coast, then passing over rich valleys to glaciered volcanic peaks and on to rolling expanses of high-desert plains cut by deep river canyons and spiked with errant mountain ranges, the land is epic in its breadth and drama.

But what makes Oregon more than a scenic abstraction is the attitude of its citizens. Oregonians are fiercely proud of their state – its cities, culture and wild areas – and are involved in all its varied aspects, whether it's grand opera in Portland, rock climbing at Smith Rock, biking along the Oregon coast or shooting Widowmaker Rapids on the Owyhee River.

The unique character of Oregonians can be traced to the state's history. While the growth of West Coast neighbors Washington and California derived from the outbreaks of gold fever, Oregon was settled by the greatest human migration in US history. During the 1840s and 1850s, approximately 53,000 sturdy and idealistic farmers, traders and their families came over the 2000-mile-long Oregon Trail, looking not for gold but

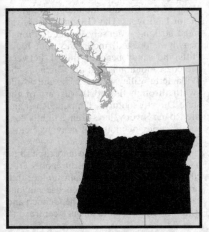

to create enduring settlements. This pioneer purposefulness is still felt in the attitudes that Oregonians bring to land-use legislation, cultural institutions, civic planning and environmental concerns.

The migration is scarcely over. The same vaguely agrarian ideals still lure people to Oregon, which is currently one of the fastest-growing states in the country.

HISTORY

At the pivotal vote at Champoeg in 1843, the citizens of Oregon (who then comprised an ad hoc collection of New England missionaries and French and British trappers) voted to organize a local government on the US model. As a result, the path to territorial status and statehood should have been assured. However, partisan rankling in Washington, DC, delayed the action until 1848, at which time Oregon officially became a US territory.

The years leading up to Oregon's statehood were also the years in which the issues of the Civil War began to play out across the USA. The admission of Oregon to the Union became a political football between advocates and opponents of slavery, with southern senators in the capital blocking consideration of statehood unless Oregon was admitted as a slave state. However, in 1859, when Oregon became the 33rd state to enter the Union, it voted overwhelmingly to do so as a free state. Salem and Oregon City contended for the capital, but Salem eventually prevailed.

The Oregon Trail, a six-month journey filled with hardship and danger, began at Independence, Missouri, and ended at Oregon City, in the Willamette Valley. In the 1850s and 1860s, when the Willamette Valley was experiencing near population saturation, settlement began to spread.

In 1852, gold was discovered near Jacksonville, in southern Oregon. After the gold ran out, settlers filled the steep valleys with orchards and logging camps. In 1861, gold was again struck in the Blue Mountains of eastern Oregon, and the rush was on. However, the frenzy for mineral fortunes was not met without resistance, and violent clashes ensued as the traditional homelands of Native Americans were invaded by new Oregonians. The Rogue River Indians fought against white settlement in southern Oregon, Modocs waged a war against the US Army, the Nez Perce under Chief Joseph fled from the US Army up into Canada, and the Bannock Indians led an uprising of several eastern Oregon tribes. The result for most Native Americans was incarceration on reservations – in some cases, on reservations as far away as Oklahoma.

From the 1880s onward, the grasslands of eastern Oregon were open to settlement. Huge ranches held sway until homesteaders arrived – the early part of the 20th century brought many thousands – breaking the land into 1-sq-mile lots. The high lava plains of central Oregon were tilled and soon blossomed with wheat.

By the end of the century, Portland was a boomtown, acting as the trade conduit for agricultural products of the fertile inland valleys. Portland was also the terminus of the Northern Pacific Railroad, which in 1883 linked the Pacific Northwest to the eastern part of the USA. Three years later, Portland and San Francisco were linked by rail. Grain poured into Portland from the Columbia River basin and from as far away as Montana. By 1890, Portland was one of the world's largest wheat-shipment points.

The world wars brought further economic expansion to Oregon, much of it related to resource exploitation. In the early years of the 20th century, logging of the great forests of the Pacific Northwest began in earnest; by WWII, Oregon had become the nation's largest lumber producer. (The nation's need for lumber products seems to increase exponentially; in the 1980s, nearly all of the state's ancient forests were slated for logging. A series of court battles in the late 1980s and early '90s, most of them involving the bashful spotted owl, turned the Pacific Northwest's forests into a battleground between traditional industry and environmentalism.)

During WWII, the shipyards and light manufacturing of Portland brought the state another flood of immigrants. A large part of this new migration was made up of African Americans, the first influx of nonwhite settlers in the state's history (despite Oregon's anti-slavery position during the Civil War, it was only in 1926 that the state legislature repealed an 1844 law excluding blacks from the state).

From the 1960s, western Oregon saw a new migration of settlers. Educated, idealistic and politically progressive, these newcomers from the eastern USA and California served to tilt the state's political balance toward a liberal and environmental stance during the 1970s and early 1980s. Oregon passed some groundbreakingly conservation-minded legislation (eg, a strict land-use planning law and a bottle-recycling bill), which gained it the reputation of a bellwether state.

However, the 1990s saw Oregon retrenching in the face of economic and social change. A number of heated controversies – from logging to gay rights – have created a political rift between liberal and conservative factions in this normally close-knit state. Oregon enters the 21st century wearily divided.

GEOGRAPHY

West of the Cascade mountains are three major land types. The Oregon coast is the most striking – densely forested (though heavily *de*forested) mountains abut rocky cliffs and sandy beaches. Inland, between the coast mountains and the Cascades, the Willamette Valley cuts a wide and fertile swath through the northern part of the state. Directly south, the Umpqua River and the Rogue River valleys drain a tightly contorted series of mountain canyons before flowing into the Pacific Ocean.

East of the Cascades, the landscape shifts to arid uplands. In central Oregon's Deschutes River valley, sage and juniper-tree savannas drop away into immense canyons carved through lava flows. The Ochoco and Blue Mountains amble through central and

OREGON

OREGON

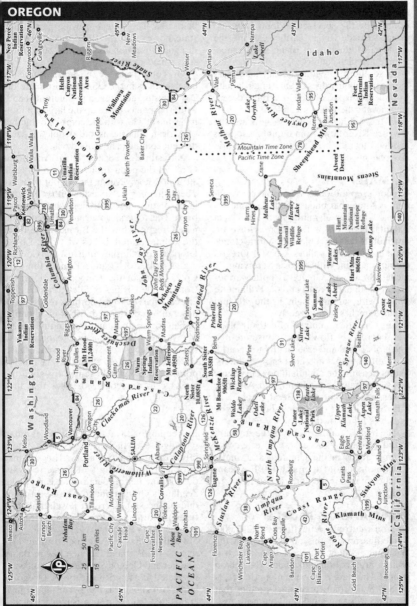

eastern Oregon. These low-slung peaks are drained by the spectacular John Day and Grande Ronde Rivers. Farther east are the Wallowa Mountains, an island of glaciated, Alpine-like high country.

In southern Oregon, the salt lakes and barren mountain ridges of Lake and Klamath Counties form part of the Great Basin desert, whose watersheds find no outlet.

In the southeast corner of the state, the Owyhee River flows from mountain sources in Idaho to trench its way through an arid lava plateau.

CLIMATE

Oregon's reputation as a rain-soaked woodland is somewhat undeserved. Portland receives 37 inches of rain a year – less than Atlanta, Houston or Baltimore. However, much of the year is sunless, as marine clouds blanket the inner valleys. Coastal Oregon gets more rain, with Astoria receiving 77 inches. Southwest Oregon is both warmer and drier than the coast and the Willamette Valley, with summer highs in the 90s and about 20 inches of rain yearly.

The Cascade mountains effectively block wet Pacific air flows, and consequently, much of central and eastern Oregon is arid, with hot summers and cold snowy winters. Skiers treasure the abundant powdery snow of Mt Bachelor, near Bend, and Anthony Lakes, near Baker City. Bend receives as little as 12 inches of precipitation annually (much of it in snowfall).

The highest temperatures in the state are found farther to the east, where average summer highs in the Umatilla and Snake River basin regions approach 100°F. A scant 8 inches of rain is the norm in southeastern Oregon.

POPULATION & PEOPLE

Oregon's current population is 3,243,000. Three-quarters of this number live in the Willamette Valley, and the Portland metropolitan area is home to about 1.4 million people. The state is growing at a rate of 2% a year, and urban forecasters predict that the state will gain a half million more residents in the next 10 years; half of these new

residents are expected to settle in the Portland area. The fastest-growing part of the state, however, is the Bend area, in central Oregon. Migration accounts for 80% of the state's new growth.

Oregon is one of the least ethnically diverse states in the USA. According to the 2000 census, the Oregon population is 85% white. Hispanics make up the largest minority group at 7%, with the combined number of African Americans and people of Asian descent coming in at around 6%.

An estimated 38,500 Native Americans (1.6% of the population) reside in Oregon, 89% of whom live in metropolitan areas. The remaining 11% reside either in rural areas or on one of Oregon's five reservations. The federal government recognizes nine Oregon tribes: the Burns Paiute tribe; the Confederated Tribes of Coos; Lower Umpqua and Siuslaw Indians; the Confederated Tribes of Grande Ronde; the Cow Creek Band of the Umpqua Indians; the Confederated Tribes of Siletz; the Confederated Tribes of Warm Springs; the Klamath tribe; the Confederated Tribes of Umatilla Indian Reservation and the Coquille tribe. Many other tribes reside in Oregon without federally recognized status or a land base. Federally recognized status is very much a political tool which tends to give the message to unrecognized tribes that they simply don't exist.

ARTS

In keeping with a seemingly Oregonian paradigm, even the arts scene in the state is informal and participatory. The summer season brings a bounty of music festivals, outdoor theater productions and art shows. Ashland's Oregon Shakespeare Festival is one of the state's crown jewels and features performances from February to November every year.

Portland has a lively performing arts scene – the Portland Opera, Oregon Ballet Theater and Oregon Symphony are all well-respected Portland institutions. Oregon's larger cities host seasonal performance programs that feature a surprising variety and quality of traveling shows.

JOHN ELK III

Blue pod lupine in the Paradise Area, Mt Rainier National Park

SHANNON NACE

Pronghorn antelope

DOUG MCKINLAY

Great blue heron, Stanley Park

JOHN ELK III

Red-barked madrone glowing in the sunset, San Juan Island

MATT SWINDEN

What a life: Harbor seals catching some rays, San Juan Island

Rogue River rafters bracing for the plunge

Snowshoer fleeing bigfoot family

Hiker taking the path less traveled in Olympic National Par

Skater cruising Vancouver's seawall walkway

Young man and the sea, Vancouver

Kayakers under Burrard St Bridge, Vancouver

In the visual arts arena, Oregon's most distinctive attraction is Mt Hood's Timberline Lodge, which showcases the handiwork of Works Progress Administration (WPA)–era artisans and painters. The ambitious Portland Art Museum pursues traveling exhibits of world-famous artists such as Monet, O'Keeffe and Picasso, while the best regional art awaits quiet contemplation at universities and colleges such as the Schneider Museum, at Ashland's Southern Oregon University, and the University of Oregon Museum of Art (closed through 2003), in Eugene. Portland's Pearl District harbors Oregon's highest concentration of creative professionals and contains highly esteemed galleries, art schools and advertising agencies. The city of Joseph, in northeastern Oregon, is famous for its bronze foundry.

Portland has the state's most vital music club scene. Jazz, Celtic, hip-hop, techno, blues, country music and punk can be found throughout the city in clubs ranging from upscale joints to real dives. Indian gaming casinos double as performance venues in rural areas, drawing national entertainers to the state's unlikeliest corners.

INFORMATION

Oregon has three area codes. Portland, Salem, the northern Willamette Valley and

Is Oregon Conservative or Liberal?

Most people would characterize Oregon's culture in terms of its politics: terms such as 'politically progressive,' 'liberal,' 'environmentally aware' and 'ex-hippie' capture the image that many hold of the state. However, anyone who has followed the state's politics in recent years knows that there's another side to Oregon that is socially conservative and opposed to many forms of environmentalism. Both of these archetypes are true of the state's culture at the same time, and the contradiction is at the heart of what it is to be an Oregonian.

Elements that give the state its progressive reputation are in evidence everywhere. Land-use laws strictly limit urban growth; all Oregon beaches are public property; and bike paths, parks and works of public art are scattered across the state. A live-and-let-live attitude toward minorities and alternative lifestyles typifies the larger cities, and even out-of-the-way towns have thriving artistic and countercultural communities.

However, the same urban centers that are models of tolerance have also witnessed Oregon's most disturbing racial incidents. Conservative tax revolts have resulted in the evisceration of public institutions and educational facilities, and now, even land-use laws face an uncertain fate. In rural communities, acts to halt logging of old-growth forests, protect wildlife habitat or establish new monuments are met with angry protests and acts of civil disobedience. The Oregon Citizens Alliance's campaign against gays and lesbians has succeeded in dividing families and communities by advancing ballot initiatives that offer communities a chance to vote to limit the civil rights of their citizens.

Which of these is the real Oregon? The truth is that both urges – to change Oregon in order to save it, and to save Oregon by halting change – derive from the same impulse. Most Oregonians believe in the intrinsic worth and value of the state, its institutions and its land. Both sides are ready and willing to fight in the public forum to preserve the state that they see threatened. The desire to save Oregon from itself is the one value that unites both sides in this ideological battle.

OREGON

the northern coast are served by ☎ 503; area code 971 is in use with cell phones and pagers in Portland and Salem. The rest of the state is served by 541. Ten-digit dialing is in place throughout Oregon, which means it's necessary to include the area code for all calls, whether local or long distance.

Oregon has no sales tax or value-added tax (VAT). However, most towns allow a local lodging tax of 4% to 9% on rooms in hotels, motels, lodges and B&Bs. Advertised room rates often don't include the tax, so ask to be certain.

If you are driving, you should keep in mind that Oregon state law prohibits you from pumping your own gasoline – all stations are full service, so just sit back and enjoy it.

Portland

Portlanders are justifiably proud of their vibrant city, with its beautiful parks and architecture and its worldly but unfussy comforts. Although nearly 1.8 million people live in the Portland metropolitan area, the city has the friendly feeling of a smaller town.

Portland (population 513,325) is known nationally for its progressive politics, easygoing pace and love of the outdoors and the environment, and it's always near the top of

Highlights

- Hiking or mountain biking Forest Park's trails
- Riding the newfangled streetcar and the light-rail trains
- Strolling through the Rose Gardens, Japanese Gardens and Classical Chinese Gardens
- Playing the hipster on SE Hawthorne Blvd or NE Alberta St
- Savoring downtown's relaxed pace

the list of 'most livable cities in the USA.' A vibrant downtown, interesting neighborhoods and easy access to the coast – as well as to the Willamette Valley, the Columbia Gorge and Mt Hood – make it a great place to spend time.

HISTORY

Portland straddles the Willamette River near its confluence with the Columbia. Here, in 1844, two New Englanders filed a claim for 640 acres of land on the Willamette's west bank. They built a store, platted streets and decided to name the new settlement after one of their hometowns. A coin toss resulted in Portland winning over Boston, and the new town was up and running.

Trade drove the young city's growth. The California gold rush of 1849 and the building of San Francisco demanded Oregon lumber, which was routed through Portland. Around the same time, Oregon Trail settlers began farming the Willamette Valley, and the inland drew miners and ranchers. Each relied upon Portland for shipping and for shopping.

Portland's status solidified when the Northern Pacific Railroad arrived in 1883, linking the Pacific Northwest to the rest of the country. The first bridges were built across the Willamette River in the late 1880s, and the city spread eastward. Portland's population increased fivefold between 1880 and 1900.

During the 20th century, Portland grew steadily. The influx of workers, including many African Americans, to the shipbuilding factories during WWII was so great that an entire new city, called Vanport, was created in 1944 to house them. Unwisely built on a Columbia River flood plain, Vanport was destroyed when a wall of water burst through a dike in 1948, killing 18 people and leaving almost 20,000 homeless.

Portland's economy is now driven by high-tech firms and outdoor-clothing manufacturers, including Nike and Columbia Sportswear.

ORIENTATION

When using the maps in this chapter, remember that the directionals in the street name (NE, NW, SW, SE) may indicate which map to refer to – Downtown (NW and SW), Northwest, Northeast or Southeast.

Neighborhoods

The Willamette River flows through the center of Portland, dividing the city into east and west. Burnside St divides north from south, organizing the city into four quadrants: Northwest, Southwest, Northeast and Southeast.

Downtown Portland is on the edge of Southwest and is surrounded by close-in Northwest neighborhoods, including frontier-era (and still rough-and-tumble) Old Town, the converted warehouses of the upscale Pearl District, and the West Hills, with its exclusive residential areas and wonderful parks. Forest Park, a wild 7-sq-mile haven for songbirds, coyotes, deer, hikers and

Transportation Cheat Sheet

Visit w www.trimet.org or Tri-Met's Customer Service office in Pioneer Courthouse Square for schedules and maps.

Washington Park complex: Take bus No 63 (catch on SW Main St at 4th); alternatively, westbound MAX (SW Morrison St) stops at the zoo.

Northwest Portland: Walk from downtown, or bus No 15 (catch at SW Washington St and SW Broadway) or the streetcar (catch on SW 10th Ave) will ferry you there.

Forest Park: Bus No 15 (catch the one marked Gordon/Thurman on SW Washington St) turns around just downhill from Leif Erikson Dr. Bus No 63 stops at Hoyt Arboretum, quite near the Wildwood Trail.

SE Hawthorne Blvd: Take bus No 14 (catch it on 5th Ave at any shelter with a brown beaver icon).

NE Alberta St: Take bus No 8 (catch it on 6th Ave at a purple raindrop shelter).

Sellwood: Take bus No 40 (catch it on 5th Ave at a green leaf shelter).

mountain bikers, is a short bus ride from downtown.

Inner (that is, by the river) Northeast and Southeast have late-19th-century residential neighborhoods dotted with commercial and civic developments. Conventioneers, basketball fans and mall shoppers visit the Northeast's Lloyd District, where the Oregon Convention Center, the Rose Garden Arena sports stadium and the Lloyd Center shopping complex hold sway.

A little rougher around the edges, but with a lot more spunk, is NE Alberta St, a couple of miles north of the Lloyd District, where emerging artists can get their work exhibited and diners can choose from taquerías and vegan restaurants.

The lively Southeast neighborhood centers on the Hawthorne District, where Portland's ex-hippie lifestyle is still in full bloom. Farther south is Sellwood, a friendly old neighborhood now filled with antique stores.

Street Savvy

I-5 and I-84 intersect across the river from downtown Portland. I-405 loops west off I-5 to provide a shortcut around the downtown core. Farther to the east, I-205 cuts through the Portland suburbs between Oregon City and Vancouver, Washington. Heading west from downtown, US 26 is the main link to the suburbs of Beaverton, Hillsboro and, eventually, to the northern Oregon coast.

In Portland, avenues are numbered and run north to south, whereas streets are named and run east to west. Pay attention to directional prefixes in addresses: For instance, NE Davis St and NW Davis St are on opposite sides of the Willamette River, and NW 6th Ave and SW 6th Ave are on opposite sides of W Burnside St.

Northwest Portland streets proceed northward in alphabetical order. Thus, one block north of W Burnside St is NW Couch St, followed by NW Davis St, NW Everett St and so on.

Because Portland is a river town, important streets tend to be those that turn into a Willamette River bridge. The Broadway Bridge is the main link between downtown and Northeast Portland, with access to both

I-5 and I-84; the Morrison Bridge connects downtown to Southeast Portland and has on-ramps to I-84 and I-5 north.

Naito Parkway (aka SW Front Ave) flanks the Tom McCall Waterfront Park along the Willamette River and is the 'zero' avenue for numbering purposes. Broadway, one block west of 6th Ave, is essentially downtown's main street.

Almost all downtown streets are one way; SW 5th and 6th Aves are primarily bus zones. Also, on the portions of SW Yamhill and SW Morrison Sts where there are MAX (Metropolitan Area Express, the light-rail system) tracks, the streets are open to only one lane of traffic.

INFORMATION
Tourist Offices

Downtown, the Portland/Oregon Visitors Association operates a visitor center (☎ 503-275-8355, 877-678-5263, W www.pova.com) in Pioneer Courthouse Square; it's open Monday to Friday 8:30am to 5:30pm, Saturday 10am to 4pm and Sunday 10am to 4pm. In the same location, a ticketing kiosk has half-price tickets to concerts and plays on the day of the event. This is also the place to

PORTLAND

Fareless Square

1 Pittock Mansion
2 World Forestry Center
3 Children's Museum
4 John's Landing; Water Tower Books
5 Crystal Springs Rhododendron Garden

get information about Tri-Met (☎ 503-238-7433, ⓦ www.trimet.org), the local bus and light-rail systems.

Information about outdoor recreation is better found at the Nature of the Northwest visitor center (☎ 503-872-2750, ⓦ www.naturenw.org), in the State Office Building at 800 NE Oregon (in Northeast); it's open Monday to Friday 9am to 5pm.

Money
The Portland International Airport (PDX) has a foreign-exchange counter in the main lobby; it's open 5:30am to 5pm. Thomas Cook (☎ 503-222-2665), in downtown's Pioneer Courthouse Square, exchanges currency as well; it's open 9am-5:30pm Monday to Friday and in summer, it's also open 10:30am to 2pm Saturday. ATMs are as numerous as coffee shops in downtown Portland. The American Express office (☎ 503-226-2961) is also downtown, at 1100 SW 6th Ave; hours are 8:30am-5:30pm Monday to Friday.

Stock up on US dollars before heading out to small Oregon towns. Even though ATM machines are ubiquitous, very few places in rural Oregon are equipped to exchange foreign currency.

Post
The main post office is at 715 NW Hoyt St. If you're downtown, the Pioneer Post Office, in the historic Pioneer Courthouse at the corner of SW 6th Ave and Yamhill St, is handier.

Email & Internet Access
All Multnomah County (Portland's county) libraries have free Internet access, but the computers are heavily used, and it's rare to be able just waltz in and log on. The Central Library (☎ 503-988-5123) is downtown at 801 SW 10th Ave. Just across the street, it's easy to get online at Internet Arena (☎ 503-224-2718), at 1016 SW Taylor St; the charge is $6 per hour and it's open 10:30am to 7pm Monday to Friday.

Travel Agencies
Council Travel (☎ 503-228-1900, 800-226-8245), near Portland State University at 1430 SW Park Ave, specializes in student and discount travel. In Northwest, Journeys: A World Travel Company (☎ 503-226-7200), at 1536 NW 23rd Ave, offers full-service ticketing, plus adventure- and discount-travel options.

Bookstores
Portland is one of the bookstore capitals of the USA. That people read so much here because it's always raining and dark is a frequently repeated canard. But no amount of flooding could really explain the success and quality of bookstores in Portland.

Megalithic Powell's Books is one of the nation's largest bookstores. Downtown, the flagship store, known as the City of Books (☎ 503-228-4651, 800-878-7323), 1005 W Burnside St, is a full city block of crowded bookshelves with more than 1 million titles for sale. Not all Powell's branches are so imposing. Check out the company's specialty stores, such as Powell's Technical Store (☎ 503-228-3906), at 33 NW Park Ave, only two blocks away from the City of Books. Also nearby is Powell's Travel Store (☎ 503-228-1108), 701 SW 6th Ave, in Pioneer Courthouse Square. Portland's bookstore riches hardly end with Powell's. Less than a block from the City of Books, Reading Frenzy (☎ 503-274-1449), 921 SW Oak St, has an incredible selection of 'zines and small-press books. Looking Glass Books (☎ 503-227-4760), 318 SW Taylor St, is a good general bookstore.

In Southeast are Powell's Books for Cooks (☎ 503-235-3802), 3739 SE Hawthorne Blvd, which shares space with an Italian specialty food shop, and pleasantly funky Powell's on Hawthorne (☎ 503-238-1668), just down the block at 3723 SE Hawthorne Blvd. Laughing Horse Books (☎ 503-236-2893), 3652 SE Division St, is Portland's best leftwing bookstore. In Other Words (☎ 503-232-6003), 3734 SE Hawthorne Blvd, offers a wide variety of books by women writers.

In Northeast Portland, go to Broadway Books (☎ 503-284-1726), 1714 NE Broadway; in Northwest, shop at Twenty-third

Avenue Books (☎ 503-224-5097), 1015 NW 23rd Ave. Water Tower Books (☎ 503-228-0290), 5331 SW Macadam Ave, is south of downtown at John's Landing shopping center (see the Portland map, earlier).

Laundry

In Northeast Portland, go to Washworld (☎ 503-281-6133), 1419 NE Fremont St, near a clutch of coffee shops and a large natural foods store. City Laundry (☎ 503-224-7773), 1414 NW Glisan St, is convenient to downtown and Northwest.

Medical Services & Emergencies

Legacy Good Samaritan Hospital and Medical Center (☎ 503-413-7711), 1015 NW 22nd Ave, is convenient to downtown. Good Samaritan's Convenience Care Center (☎ 503-413-8090), at the same location, handles minor illness and injuries. It's cheaper and quicker than the emergency room and is open 9am to 9pm weekdays, 10am to 9pm weekends.

The police station is downtown at 1111 SW 2nd Ave. Call ☎ 911 for medical, fire or crime emergencies.

THINGS TO SEE & DO
Downtown

Downtown Portland is an urban success story. An activist city government began work in the 1970s to ensure that Portland's business and nightlife did not flee the city center. The effort was successful, and downtown Portland is still vital.

Visitors should be armed with Powell's *Walking Map of Downtown Portland*. Free from any Powell's store and many hotels, the map charts a historical and architectural route through the city's center.

Pioneer Courthouse Square This brick plaza between SW Broadway and 6th Ave and between SW Morrison and Yamhill Sts is the center of downtown Portland. A fountain, a 'weather machine' sculpture, food carts and many levels of open-air seating bring people to the square to play music, eat lunch and gawk. Concerts, festivals and

rallies occur almost daily in summer, especially at lunch hour.

One of Portland's grandest Victorian hotels once stood here; it fell into disrepair and was torn down and replaced by a parking structure. When the city decided to build Pioneer Courthouse Square, downtown business interests feared it would be a gathering place for riffraff and blocked funding. Grassroots support for the square resulted in a program that encouraged citizens to buy and personalize the bricks that eventually built the square.

Across 6th Ave is the **Pioneer Courthouse**. Built in 1875, this was the legal center of 19th-century Portland.

South Park Blocks Two museums flank the South Park Blocks, the 12-block-long greenway between SW Park and 9th Aves that runs through much of the downtown. Just as tempting as the museums are the Park Blocks themselves, a leafy refuge from downtown's bustle.

The **Oregon History Center** *(☎ 503-222-1741, 1200 SW Park Ave; adult/student/child 6-12 years $6/3/1.50, seniors free Thur; open 10am-5pm Tues, Wed & Fri, 10am-8pm Thur, 10am-5pm Sat, noon-5pm Sun)* is the state's largest historical museum. A research library, press and bookstore round out the complex.

Across the park, the **Portland Art Museum** *(☎ 503-226-2811, 1219 SW Park Ave; adult/senior/student 5-18 years $7.50/6/4; open 10am-5pm Tues-Sat, noon-5pm Sun)* has an especially good collection of Northwest Native American carvings. Upstairs galleries contain a small international collection, and blockbuster exhibits are mounted regularly.

At the southern end of the South Park Blocks is **Portland State University**, the city's largest (over 20,000 students).

Portland Building & *Portlandia* No local building has drawn more notoriety than the Portland Building, at SW 5th Ave and SW Main St. It was designed by postmodern architect Michael Graves to house city offices. No one seems indifferent about this blocky, pastel-colored edifice that's decorated like a wedding cake. The Portland Building is

Portland's Public Art

Portland's public art is abundant, thanks to programs that set aside about 1% of the cost of any major construction for public art. Pick up the brochure *Public Art Walking Tour* from the visitor center at Pioneer Courthouse Square. (You'll probably have to ask for it, as it's usually kept behind the counter.) Most public art is found along the 5th and 6th Ave Transit Mall, the South Park Blocks and near the Convention Center.

Traditional commemorative statues dominate the South Park Blocks, though a few more conceptual projects have slipped in over the years. Note the trompe l'oeil mural on the back of the Oregon History Center at SW Park Ave and SW Jefferson St.

The Transit Mall is lined with statues and fountains, including *Portlandia*, crouching above the entry of the Portland Building, at SE 5th Ave and Main St.

Some of the most popular statues are the bronze animals playing in the fountains surrounding the Pioneer Courthouse. The bronze female nude on 5th Ave near Washington St was made famous in the 1980s *Expose Yourself to Art* poster (featuring a former Portland mayor as a flasher).

Ride the MAX west from downtown to see a wide variety of public art. Perhaps the most intriguing piece is at the Washington Park Station, located underground in a tunnel beneath the West Hills. Artists collaborated with the tunnel engineers and geologists to preserve core samples taken from the earth during the tunnel's construction. These core samples are stretched along the platform and are accompanied by a 260-foot timeline starting 16 million years ago, when volcanoes spewed the rocks that form the West Hills. Rather than coming off as some preachy science museum, the effect is playful and stands up to repeated viewings.

---

considered the world's first major postmodern structure.

Towering above the main doors of the Portland Building is *Portlandia*, an immense statue of the (ahem) Goddess of Commerce (Portland's supposed patroness). This crouching female figure is, at 36 feet, the second largest hammered-copper statue in the world (the largest is the Statue of Liberty).

Tom McCall Waterfront Park & RiverPlace Two-mile-long Waterfront Park, which flanks the west bank of the Willamette River, was once a freeway. The freeway was later torn up and replaced with grass and sidewalks. Popular with joggers, inline skaters, strollers and cyclists, the park also hosts a number of summer festivals.

Salmon Springs Fountain, at the base of Salmon St, changes its play of water with the pace of the city; wild displays at rush hour mimic the busy city. North of the Burnside Bridge is the Japanese-American Historical Plaza, a memorial to Japanese Americans who were interned by the US government during WWII. RiverPlace, at the southern end of Waterfront Park, is a hotel, restaurant and apartment complex overlooking a marina.

Old Town & Chinatown The core of 1890s Portland, the tattered-on-the-edges Old Town, resists gentrification. Missions for the homeless coexist with galleries and restaurants. The boundaries of Old Town vary depending upon whom you ask, but the essence of old Portland is captured between SW Pine St and NW Glisan St, east of NW Broadway to the Willamette River.

Portland's Chinatown is a subset of Old Town. The **Chinatown Gates**, at the corner of NW 4th Ave and W Burnside St, announce the Asian businesses that have thrived in this neighborhood since the 1880s. Visit the **Classical Chinese Gardens** (☎ *503-228-8131, NW 3rd Ave & NW Everett St; adult/senior/child $6/5/5; open 9am-6pm Apr-Oct, 10am-5pm Nov-Mar).* The walled garden occupies a full city block and is a quiet, reflective spot.

The Italianate **Union Station** was built in 1890, and its marble walls and high ceilings still seem grand. It's near the corner of NW 6th Ave and NW Irving St.

The Old Town area becomes less savory by night; you might want to avoid walking around alone.

Saturday Market & Skidmore Fountain Victorian-era architecture and the lovely Skidmore Fountain give the area beneath the Burnside Bridge some flair. Try to stop by on a weekend for the Saturday Market (☎ 503-222-6072, SW 1st Ave & SW Ankeny St; open 10am-5pm Sat, 11am-4:30pm Sun, 1st weekend in Mar-Christmas Eve), a giant outdoor crafts fair. Street entertainers and various food carts round out the festivities.

Beside the fountain is the **New Market Theater**, built in 1871 as Portland's first theater for stage productions. It's now home to shops and restaurants.

Burnside Skate Park Tucked under the east end of the Burnside Bridge, this Gaudiesque arena of concrete bowls and quarterpipes attracts the city's best skaters and is definitely worth a visit if you're traveling with a skateboard (W www.oregonskateparks.com/Parks/Burnside). From downtown, head east over the Burnside Bridge and take the first right turn off the bridge, onto SE Martin Luther King Blvd. Go one block and turn right again, onto SE Ankeny St. Follow Ankeny two blocks to SE 2nd Ave, turn right and continue one block until you're under the bridge.

Oregon Maritime Center & Museum This museum (☎ 503-224-7724, 113 Naito Pkwy; adult/senior/student $4/3/2, child under 8 free; open 11am-4pm Wed-Sun May-Aug, 11am-4pm Fri-Sun Sept-Apr) charts Portland's long history as a seaport and shipbuilding center. A tour of the steam sternwheeler Portland, moored in the Willamette just across Waterfront Park, is included in museum admission.

West Hills This area is known for its lovely, elevated abodes.

The **Portland Audubon Society** (☎ 503-292-6855, 5151 NW Cornell Rd; admission free; open 10am-6pm Mon-Sat, 10am-5pm Sun) is nestled in a gulch beside Forest Park. Visit the bookstore and wildlife rehabilitation center, then observe birds and other wildlife in the adjoining sanctuary.

Also in the West Hills is **Pittock Mansion** (☎ 503-823-3624, 3229 NW Pittock Dr; adult/senior/youth 6-18 years $5/4.50/2.50, child under 6 free; open noon-4pm Feb-Dec), which was built in 1914 by the then-editor of the Oregonian newspaper. Guided tours of this grand, 22-room house are available, but it is also worth a visit on a clear day simply for the spectacular views to the east.

Washington Park Perched on the slopes of the West Hills is the enormous Washington Park complex, which includes the city's zoo, rose gardens and an arboretum, as well as hiking access to Forest Park.

The **International Rose Test Gardens** (☎ 503-823-3636, 400 SW Kingston Ave) is the main reason that Portland is called the Rose City. The gardens sprawl across 4½ acres of manicured lawns, fountains and flowerbeds, and on a clear day, you'll be able to enjoy postcard views of downtown and Mt Hood. Over 400 rose varieties grow in the permanent gardens, including many old and rare varieties. From June to September, the scent and colors are intoxicating.

Farther uphill, past the tennis courts, are the tranquil, formal **Japanese Gardens** (☎ 503-223-1321, 611 SW Kingston Ave; adult/senior/student with ID $6/4/3.50, child under 6 years free; open 10am-7pm Tues-Sun, noon-4pm Mon Apr-Sept, 10am-4pm Tues-Sun, noon-4pm Mon Oct-Mar). The grounds encompass 5 acres of tumbling water, pools of koi, flowers, a teahouse and a sand garden. Tours are available at 2:30pm daily from April 15 to October 31.

In summer, ride the Zoo Train from the rose gardens (or follow Kingston Rd up the hill) to the **Oregon Zoo** (☎ 503-226-1561, W www.oregonzoo.org, 4001 SW Canyon Rd;

adult/senior/child 3-11 years $5.50/4/3.50; open 9:30am-5pm Apr 3-May 27, 9:30am-6pm May 28-Sept 5, 9:30am-4pm Sept 6-Apr 2). The zoo specializes in Asian elephants and maintains one of the world's most successful elephant-breeding programs. Inquire about summer concerts on the zoo's lawns. It's just a short MAX ride west from downtown to the zoo; by car, follow US 26 west 1 mile from downtown to the zoo exit.

Just across the parking lot from the zoo is the **Children's Museum** (☎ 503-223-6500, Ⓦ *www.pdxchildrensmuseum.org, 4015 SW Canyon Rd; admission $5; open 9am-5pm Tues-Thur & Sat, 9am-8pm Fri, 11am-5pm Sun)*. This is a good place to spend a rainy afternoon with children under 13.

Next door to the Children's Museum is the **World Forestry Center** (☎ 503-228-1367, *4033 SW Canyon Rd; adult/senior over 61 & youth 6-18 years $4.50/3.50; open 10am-5pm)*, an educational facility supported by the timber industry. Exhibits focus on the world's forests, their ecosystems and forestry industries.

Next to the World Forestry Center, a spiraling path passes **Oregon Vietnam Veter-** ans Living Memorial, which consists of black granite slabs inscribed with details of events related to the war that occurred in both Vietnam and Oregon.

Ten miles of trails (including 2 miles of wheelchair-accessible trails) wind through **Hoyt Arboretum** (☎ 503-228-8733, *4000 Fairview Blvd; admission free; visitor center open 9am-4pm; park open 6am-10pm)*, a ridge-top garden above the zoo and planted with both native and exotic trees. It's a great place for an easy hike any time of year. Pick up a map at the visitor center.

See the Activities section of this chapter for information on hiking on the Wildwood Trail.

To reach Washington Park and associated sites, take Tri-Met bus No 63 from downtown's SW Washington St or catch MAX to the zoo. To reach the park by car, take the zoo exit off US 26, or follow signs for the Rose Gardens off W Burnside St at Tichner Dr.

Northwest

When Portlanders talk about the Northwest, they are referring to the neighborhood bisected by NW 21st and 23rd Aves and north of W Burnside St. The residential heart of late-19th-century Portland, this attractive neighborhood hums with street life.

NW 23rd Ave is lined with clothing stores, home decor shops, and cafes. Restaurants – including some of Portland's finest – stretch along NW 21st Ave. This is a great neighborhood for people watching, browsing and consuming. Northwest Portland also has Oregon's highest population density, so parking can be tough.

Just east of Northwest, the **Pearl District** is an old warehouse and light-industrial precinct that has gone the way of loft development. Once an eyesore, the area between NW 9th and 14th Aves and W Burnside and NW Johnson Sts is now one of Portland's most chic neighborhoods. The Pearl District has Portland's highest concentration of art galleries, and as actual artists are being driven out by skyrocketing rents, an increasing number of shops devoted to furniture and knickknacks are replacing their studios.

Dawn Redwood

What's the wildest, most improbable tree growing in the Hoyt Arboretum? Well, the silk trees are lovely and delicate, and the agaves a surprise to see in Oregon, but for the tree with the best story, it's hard to beat the dawn redwood, a rare deciduous conifer.

Eons ago, the dawn redwood grew in Oregon, but it became extinct. Or so it seemed. In the 1940s, a Chinese forester came across a remote grove of unusual trees that turned out to match the fossilized traces of the dawn redwood. Seeds were sent to the US and planted in the Hoyt Arboretum. The tree bore cones when it was only four years old, making them the first dawn-redwood cones produced in the Western Hemisphere in 50 million years.

Northeast

Across the Willamette River in Northeast Portland, the **Lloyd District** is the neighborhood surrounding the nation's first full-blown shopping mall, the Lloyd Center. Increasingly, this area forms an adjunct to downtown. The Oregon Convention Center and the Rose Garden Arena are also here.

Not too long ago, **NE Alberta St** was a rundown stretch of vacant buildings and dubious bars. Its recent renaissance is absolutely uncorporate. Galleries, vegan restaurants, performance spaces, a yoga studio and a food co-op are thriving between NE 14th and NE 33rd Aves.

Southeast

The **Oregon Museum of Science & Industry** *(OMSI; ☎ 503-797-6674, ⓦ www.omsi.edu, 1945 SE Water St; admission to museum or Omnimax theater adult/senior/child 3-13 years $7/5/5; open 9:30am-7:30pm June 15-Labor Day, 9:30am-5:30pm Tues-Sun Labor Day-June 14)* is a hands-on science museum that draws adults to its Omnimax theater, but it's mostly kids who go for the rotating exhibits, such as *Grossology*.

It's quite all right to dress like a hippie in the **Hawthorne District**; around here, 'alternative' reigns. Along SE Hawthorne Blvd between 30th and 45th Aves, visit bookstores, delis, vintage-clothing stores, brewpubs, head shops, restaurants and coffee shops, where Reed College students, old hippies, gays and lesbians hang out. Street life is dynamic, with flower vendors, friendly dogs and pamphleteers competing for sidewalk space. Portland's largest youth hostel is on Hawthorne (see Places to Stay).

Sellwood, an old working-class neighborhood southeast of downtown, has long been a hub for antique stores. SE 13th Ave, between Tacoma St and Bybee Blvd, buzzes with curio shoppers. Several fine restaurants and a sprawling riverside park combine to make Sellwood a pleasant detour.

Urban greenspaces are tucked into Portland's Eastside neighborhoods. **Oaks Bottom Wildlife Refuge** is a huge wetland laced with trails along the east bank of the Willamette below SE Milwaukie Blvd. It's one of the best spots in the city for bird-watching. **Crystal Springs Rhododendron Garden**, near Reed College at SE 28th Ave and SE Woodstock St, is popular in early spring for the burst of color and fragrance from the garden's more than 2000 full-grown rhododendrons and azaleas.

Laurelhurst Park, near the corner of SE 39th Ave and Oak St, has a small lake, towering conifers and flocks of ducks. Join the local dog-walkers, cyclists and runners at **Mt Tabor Park**, on the slopes of an extinct volcano near the corner of SE 69th Ave and Yamhill St.

ACTIVITIES
Hiking

Hikers can enjoy over 50 miles of trails in **Forest Park**. The **Wildwood Trail** starts at the Hoyt Arboretum and winds through 30 miles of forest. The many spur trails off Wildwood allow for loop hikes. Other trailheads into Forest Park are at the western ends of NW Thurman and NW Upshur Sts. Pick up a map of Forest Park at the Hoyt Arboretum Visitor Center. (Maps are also posted on placards throughout the park.)

Out past Lewis & Clark College, in Southwest Portland, is **Tryon Creek State Park** *(☎ 503-653-3166, 11321 SW Terwilliger Blvd)*, with 8 miles of trails. Streamside wildlife includes beavers and songbirds. In late March, there are wondrous displays of trillium, a wild marsh lily.

Biking

Though it may not be the universal practice, bicycle commuting isn't considered abnormal in Portland, where a visit to most any downtown office will reveal bikes stashed in spare corners. It's common to spot Portland's official bird – the great blue heron – on an early-morning ride along the Willamette (follow the Waterfront Park path and keep going either north or south, or ride east across the Steel or Hawthorne Bridges and cycle the Eastside Esplanade, a splendid riverbank bike path). Mountain bikers should ride uphill to the western end of NW Thurman St,

OREGON

DOWNTOWN PORTLAND

PLACES TO STAY
22 Park Lane Suites
26 Mark Spencer Hotel
28 Clyde Hotel
31 Benson Hotel
40 Mallory Hotel
41 Governor Hotel
46 Hotel Vintage Plaza
47 Imperial Hotel
63 Four Points Sheraton
65 Heathman Hotel;
   Heathman Restaurant
83 4th Ave Motel
87 6th Ave Motel
88 Travelodge

PLACES TO EAT
1 Le Bouchon
2 Little Wing Café
5 Bluehour
8 Cafe Azul
9 Pearl Bakery
14 Dogs Dig Vegetarian Deli
25 Jake's Famous Crawfish
32 Saucebox
34 Bijou Café
42 Pasta Veloce
44 Good Dog/Bad Dog
45 Pizzicato
48 Pazzoria
49 The Pod
51 Al-Amir
53 Mother's Bistro
78 Higgins

ENTERTAINMENT
11 Embers
12 Satyricon
23 Artists Repertory Theatre
27 Scandals
35 Berbati's Pan
50 Huber's
67 Portland Center for the
   Performing Arts
75 Northwest Film Center

OTHER
3 Main Post Office
4 Greyhound Bus Depot
6 Jimmy Mak's
7 Classical Chinese Gardens
10 Dollar Rent-A-Car
13 Hobo's
15 Oregon Mountain
   Community
16 Japanese-American
   Historical Plaza
17 Powell's City of Books;
   Anne Hughes Coffee Shop
18 Powell's Technical Store
19 Chinatown Gates

20 Made in Oregon
21 Saturday Market
24 Crystal Ballroom
29 Reading Frenzy
30 24-Hour Church of Elvis
33 Hertz
36 New Market Theater
37 Skidmore Fountain
38 Oregon Maritime Center &
   Museum
39 Sternwheeler *Portland*
43 Galleria Shopping Center
52 Avis
54 Japanese Gardens
55 International Rose Test
   Gardens
56 Central Library
57 Internet Arena
58 Portland/Oregon Visitors
   Association; Ticketing Kiosk
   & Tri-Met Office
59 Powell's Travel Store;
   Thomas Cook
60 Pioneer Courthouse;
   Pioneer Post Office
61 Pioneer Place
62 Bike Central Co-op
64 Hoyt Arboretum

66 Arlene Schnitzer Concert
   Hall
68 American Express
69 Alaska Airlines; United
   Airlines
70 Portland Building; *Portlandia*
71 Looking Glass Books
72 Police Station
73 Salmon Springs Fountain
74 Portland Spirit
76 Portland Art Museum
77 Oregon History Center
79 Council Travel
80 Ira Keller Memorial Fountain
81 Keller Auditorium
82 Oregon Vietnam Veterns
   Living Memorial
84 Budget Rent-A-Car
85 Portland River Company
86 Oregon Zoo

Washington Park

DOWNTOWN PORTLAND

see Northwest Portland map

Couch Park

Pearl District

Old Town & Chinatown

Union Station (Amtrak)

Steel Bridge

NW-Irving St

NW-Hoyt St

□ 3

NW Flanders St

☐ 4

NW-Glisan St

1 ▼ 2 ▼

NW-19th Ave
NW-18th Ave
NW-17th Ave
NW-16th Ave
NW-15th Ave
NW-14th Ave
NW-13th Ave
NW-12th Ave
NW-11th Ave
NW-10th Ave
NW-9th Ave
NW-8th Ave
NW-Park Ave
NW-Broadway
NW-6th Ave
NW-5th Ave
NW-4th Ave
NW-3rd Ave
NW-2nd Ave
NW-1st Ave

NW Everett St

☼ 7

● 6

▼ 5

NW-Davis St

10

□ 12

NW Couch St

▼ 8
▼ 9

North Park Blocks

11

13
14

● 15

16

17

18

● 19

20
● 21

Burnside Bridge

W Burnside St

● 29

● 30

SW-Ankeny St

☐ 35

● 24   25 ▼

▼ 32

36

SW Ash St

37

PGE Park

23

SW-Morrison St

26

28
27

31 ▪

SW Oak St

SW Pine St

34

33

38

39 ●

Willamette River

40

SW-Yamhill-St

SW Washington St

46 ▪ ● 47

SW Stark St

41 ●

SW Alder St

▼ 45

SW-14th-Ave
SW-13th-Ave

MAX Light Rail

☼ 43

44 ▼

▼ 48

● 49   50 ☐

● 51

MAX Light Rail

42

56 ●

Pioneer Courthouse Square

52 ●

53 ●

57 ☐

58 ●
59 ●

● 60

☼ 61

SW-2nd Ave
SW-1st Ave

SW Front Ave (Naito Pkwy)

Morrison Bridge

SW-12th-Ave
SW-11th-Ave

SW Taylor St

Portland Streetcar

South Park Blocks

65 ●
66 ●

SW-Salmon St

71

● 63

62

67 ☐

SW Main St

Lonsdale Square

Tom McCall Waterfront Park

75 ●
76 ▥

77 ▥

68 ● 69
70 ●

Chapman Square

73

SW-Park Ave
SW-Park Ave

▼ 78

72

74 ●

SW-Broadway

79 ●

SW-6th Ave
SW-5th Ave
SW-4th Ave

SW Madison St

Hawthorne Bridge

SW Jefferson St

SW Columbia St

SW Clay St

80

SW Market St

● 81

Portland State University

SW Mill St

River-Place Hotel

SW-Montgomery St

83 ●

Pettygrove Park

SW Harrison St

SW Hall St

84 ●

SW College St

85

SW-Montgomery St

5

Marquam Bridge

87 ▪

SW-6th Ave

88 ▪

405

SW-Sheridan St

Duniway Park

Fareless Square

and continue past the gate onto Leif Erikson Dr, an old dirt logging road leading 11 miles into Forest Park. (Don't bike on the hiking trails!)

For bicycle rentals, see the Getting Around section at the end of this chapter.

Swimming

A couple of public indoor pools are open year round and are convenient to downtown. **Matt Dishman Community Center** (☎ 503-823-3673, 77 NE Knott St) has a nice, though often crowded, pool; the **Metropolitan Learning Center Pool** (☎ 503-823-3671, 2033 NW Glisan St) is small but near the Northwest Portland International Hostel. In summer, the outdoor pool at **US Grant Park** (☎ 503-823-3674, near cnr NE 33rd Ave & US Grant St), in Northeast Portland, is a great place to cool off. City pools are open 6am-9pm Mon-Fri, 8am-7pm Sat, 10am-6pm Sun; admission is approximately adult/senior/teen/child 5-12 years $4/3/3/2, child under 5 free. There is some variation from pool to pool, so call for details or check the Portland Parks website, at W www.parks.ci.portland.or.us.

ORGANIZED TOURS

A number of individuals offer walking tours of downtown Portland, but it's a changing cast of characters with unpredictable schedules; ask at the Pioneer Courthouse Square visitor center to find out what's current.

Evergreen Trailways Gray Line (☎ 503-285-9845, 1430 N Suttle Rd) Adult/child under 12 years $27/13.50. Gray Line conducts guided bus tours of Portland and also hosts tours to other northwest Oregon sites. Clients are picked up from their hotels.

Ecotours of Oregon (☎ 503-245-1428, W www.ecotours-of-oregon.com, 1906 SW Iowa) $40-60. This outfit specializes in naturalist-led day trips to Mt Hood and the Columbia Gorge but also offers tours of the wine country and of local brewpubs. Call to arrange hotel pickup.

Portland River Company (☎ 503-229-0551, W www.portlandrivercompany.com, 0315

SW Montgomery) $35. This company does tours of the Willamette River in a sea kayak.

Portland Spirit (☎ 503-224-3900, 800-224-3901, W www.portlandspirit.com, 110 SE Caruthers St) Sightseeing tours $15, full-service dining cruises $28-52. Cruises depart from Waterfront Park near the Salmon Springs Fountain or from the RiverPlace marina.

SPECIAL EVENTS

Nearly every summer weekend, there's some sort of festival in Portland. Contact the visitor center for information and a complete

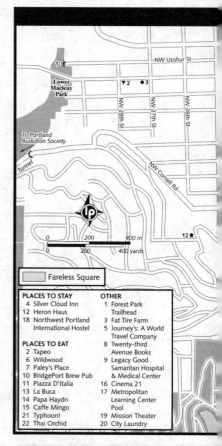

Fareless Square

PLACES TO STAY	OTHER
4 Silver Cloud Inn	1 Forest Park
12 Heron Haus	Trailhead
18 Northwest Portland	3 Fat Tire Farm
International Hostel	5 Journey's: A World
	Travel Company
PLACES TO EAT	8 Twenty-third
2 Tapeo	Avenue Books
6 Wildwood	9 Legacy Good
7 Paley's Place	Samaritan Hospital
10 BridgePort Brew Pub	& Medical Center
11 Piazza D'Italia	16 Cinema 21
13 La Buca	17 Metropolitan
14 Papa Haydn	Learning Center
15 Caffe Mingo	Pool
21 Typhoon!	19 Mission Theater
22 Thai Orchid	20 City Laundry

listings of events. Below are some of the many parties and gatherings that the city throws for itself.

Portland Rose Festival (☎ 503-227-2681, W www.rosefestival.org) Parades, a riverfront carnival, ships full of sailors, a Rose Queen and – oh yeah – lots of blooming roses make this Portland's biggest celebration. Early June.

Gay Pride Parade & Celebration (☎ 503-295-9788) March through downtown with Dykes on Bikes, the chief of police, and 10,000 others. Late June.

Chamber Music Northwest (☎ 503-223-3202, W www.cmnw.org) Exceptionally good summer series of chamber music concerts are held at both Reed College and Catlin Gabel School, at 8825 SW Barnes Rd. Late June-July.

Waterfront Blues Festival (☎ 503-282-0555, W www.waterfrontbluesfest.com) Enjoy full-bore music and partying in Waterfront Park; proceeds go to the Oregon Food Bank. July 4th weekend.

Oregon Brewers Festival (☎ 503-241-7179) Quaff microbrews from near and far in Waterfront Park. Late July.

Mt Hood Jazz Festival (☎ 503-666-3810) Local and national jazz musicians play at Mt Hood Community College, in Gresham, 12 miles east of Portland. Early August.

NORTHWEST PORTLAND

OREGON

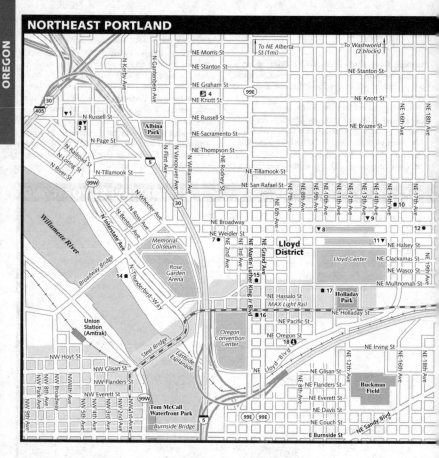

NORTHEAST PORTLAND

PLACES TO STAY

The accommodations listed here are convenient to downtown. Outside the center, chain motels can be found at freeway exits.

The majority of central Portland's hotels are downtown, or in Northeast, near the Oregon Convention Center. Prices noted are for the high summer season, when advance reservations are almost always necessary. A 12% bed tax is added to all lodging prices.

Camping

Oxbow Park (☎ 503-663-4708, 3010 SE Oxbow Pkwy, Gresham) Campsite $13, open year round. This is the best option for camping close to Portland. A woodsy, riverside setting makes Oxbow a pleasant place to pitch a tent or park an RV. No pets are allowed.

Hostels

Northwest Portland International Hostel (☎ 503-241-2783, 1818 NW Glisan St) Nonmember/member $19/16, private room $40-50. Within easy walking distance of downtown, the Pearl District and NW 23rd Ave, this friendly hostel is a good base for urban exploration.

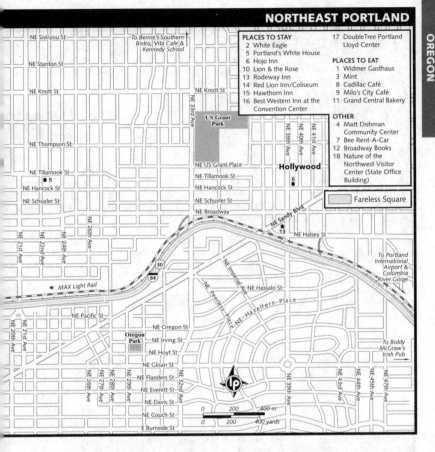

NORTHEAST PORTLAND

PLACES TO STAY
2 White Eagle
5 Portland's White House
6 Hojo Inn
10 Lion & the Rose
13 Rodeway Inn
14 Red Lion Inn/Coliseum
15 Hawthorn Inn
16 Best Western Inn at the Convention Center
17 DoubleTree Portland Lloyd Center

PLACES TO EAT
1 Widmer Gasthaus
3 Mint
8 Cadillac Café
9 Milo's City Café
11 Grand Central Bakery

OTHER
4 Matt Dishman Community Center
7 Bee Rent-A-Car
12 Broadway Books
18 Nature of the Northwest Visitor Center (State Office Building)

Fareless Square

Hostelling International – Portland (☎ 503-236-3380, ⓔ hip@teleport.com, 3031 SE Hawthorne Blvd) Bus No 14 from downtown. Nonmember/member $18/15, private room $36/42. This hostel is in one of the city's most dynamic and youthful neighborhoods.

See B&Bs & Inns for other hostel-like options.

B&Bs & Inns
The following B&Bs are among Portland's finest. All have in-room phones and computer jacks.

Portland's White House (☎ 503-287-7131, ⓦ www.portlandswhitehouse.com, 1914 NE 22nd Ave) $98-179. In Northeast near Lloyd Center, this gay-friendly place looks a lot like the President's house.

Lion & the Rose (☎ 503-287-9245, 800-955-9247, ⓦ www.lionrose.com, 1810 NE 15th Ave) $120-140. This fanciful, turreted Queen Anne mansion is a block off bustling NE Broadway, an easy walk from the MAX line.

Heron Haus (☎ 503-274-1846, ⓦ www.heronhaus.com, 2545 NW Westover Rd) Rooms $95-350. Check out the views from this fabulous Tudor-style home

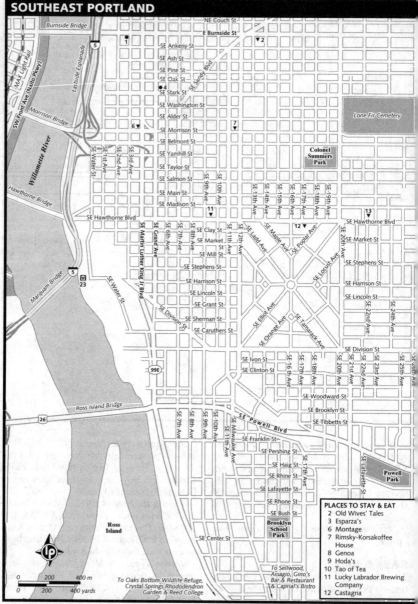

SOUTHEAST PORTLAND

NE Couch St
E Burnside St

Burnside Bridge

SE Ankeny St
SE Ash St
SE Pine St
SE Oak St
SE Stark St
SE Washington St
SE Alder St
SE Morrison St
SE Belmont St
SE Yamhill St
SE Taylor St
SE Salmon St
SE Main St
SE Madison St

Eastside Esplanade
MAX Light Rail
SW Front Ave (Naito Pkwy)
Morrison Bridge

Willamette River

Hawthorne Bridge

SE 1st Ave
SE 2nd Ave
SE 3rd Ave
SE Water St

SE Sandy Blvd

Lone Fir Cemetery

Colonel
Summers
Park

SE Hawthorne Blvd

SE Martin Luther King Jr Blvd
SE Grand Ave
SE 6th Ave
SE 7th Ave
SE 8th Ave
SE 9th Ave
SE 10th Ave
SE 11th Ave
SE 12th Ave
SE 13th Ave
SE 14th Ave
SE 15th Ave
SE 16th Ave
SE 17th Ave
SE 18th Ave
SE 19th Ave
SE 20th Ave
SE 21st Ave
SE 22nd Ave
SE 23rd Ave
SE 24th Ave
SE 25th Ave
SE 26th Ave

SE Clay St
SE Market St
SE Mill St
SE Stephens St
SE Harrison St
SE Lincoln St
SE Grant St
SE Sherman St
SE Caruthers St

SE Ladd Ave
SE Maple Ave
SE Poplar Ave
SE Locust Ave
SE Elliot Ave
SE Orange Ave
SE Tamarack Ave

SE Market St
SE Stephens St
SE Harrison St
SE Lincoln St

Marquam Bridge

SE Water St

SE Division St

SE Ivon St
SE Clinton St

SE Woodward St
SE Brooklyn St
SE Tibbetts St

SE Powell Blvd

SE Franklin St
SE Pershing St
SE Haig St
SE Rhine St
SE Lafayette St
SE Rhone St
SE Bush St

Ross Island Bridge

Ross
Island

SE 7th Ave
SE 9th Ave
SE 10th Ave
SE 11th Ave
SE Milwaukie Ave
SE 17th Ave
SE Lafayette Ave

Brooklyn
School
Park

Powell
Park

SE Center St

To Oaks Bottom Wildlife Refuge,
Crystal Springs Rhododendron
Garden & Reed College

To Sellwood,
Assagio, Gino's
Bar & Restaurant
& Caprial's Bistro

0   200   400 m
0   200   400 yards

PLACES TO STAY & EAT
2 Old Wives' Tales
3 Esparza's
6 Montage
7 Rimsky-Korsakoffee
   House
8 Genoa
9 Hoda's
10 Tao of Tea
11 Lucky Labrador Brewing
   Company
12 Castagna

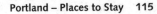

OREGON

perched just above the Northwest's shopping district.

If B&Bs are generally a little too prissy for your taste, check out the inns run by Portland's McMenamin brothers, who have bought up some great old buildings and brought them new life as brewpubs and B&Bs. One website serves all: ☒ www.mc menamins.com.

Kennedy School (☎ *503-249-3983, 888-249-3983, 5736 NE 33rd Ave*) $99-109. This former elementary school is a popular community hangout as well as a B&B. Check out the tiled soaking pool, then decide whether you'll smoke cigars in the Detention Bar or sip port in the Honors Bar.

White Eagle (☎ *503-335-8900, 866-271-3377, 836 N Russell St*) $25-45. If you're not afraid of a little rock 'n' roll coming up through the floorboards, this industrial-section haunt is one of the best deals in town. Rooms are spartan and have shared bathrooms, everyone shares the hallway pay phone, and the downstairs saloon hosts live music every night. (Early risers should request a room in the front of the hotel, which is sheltered from the music but which gets early-morning street noise.)

See the Columbia Gorge & Mt Hood chapter, in the Western Columbia River Highway section, for information on McMenamin's Edgefield, about 18 miles east of downtown Portland.

Hotels – Downtown & Northwest

For all accommodations in this chapter, refer to the Downtown map (except for Silver Cloud Inn, which is placed on the Northwest map).

Budget Downtown hotels tend to be pricey, but there are a couple of budget places at the south end of downtown.

4th Ave Motel (☎ *503-226-7646, fax 503-226-7646, 1889 SW 4th Ave*) Singles/doubles $45/55. This no-frills motel is near Portland State University (PSU), just south of the city center.

6th Ave Motel (☎ *503-226-2979, 800-686-7199, ☒ www.6ave-motel-portland.com, 2221 SW 6th Ave*) Singles/doubles $55/65,

---

13 Café Lena
14 Hostelling International -
   Portland
17 Cup & Saucer
18 Bread & Ink Café
19 BridgePort Ale House

ENTERTAINMENT
5 Starky's
20 Bagdad Theater
22 Do Jump (Echo Theatre)
24 Egyptian Room

OTHER
1 Burnside Skate Park
4 Next Adventure
15 Powell's on Hawthorne
16 Powell's Books for
   Cooks
21 In Other Words
23 Oregon Museum of
   Science & Industry
   (OMSI)
25 Laughing Horse Books

discounts for AAA members, seniors and business travelers are often available. The rooms are tiny and the walls thin, but the price is right. It's also near PSU.

Mid-Range Many of downtown's mid-range hotels are older places with a bit of charm.

Mallory Hotel (☎ 503-223-6311, 800-228-8657, fax 503-223-0522, W *www.mallory hotel.com, 729 SW 15th Ave)* Singles/doubles $90/95. Only blocks away from the city center, the old-fashioned Mallory offers free parking and welcomes dogs. No wonder it's got a cultlike following.

Mark Spencer Hotel (☎ 503-224-3293, 800-548-3934, fax 503-223-7848, W *mark spencer.com, 409 SW 11th Ave)* Rooms $89 and up. This is another good deal in a well-tended hotel. All rooms have full kitchens.

Clyde Hotel (☎ 503-224-8000, fax 503-224-9999, W *www.clydehotel.com, 1022 SW Stark St)* Shared/private bath $60/70 and up. The Clyde is just down the street from the Mark Spencer Hotel and is being restored after years of neglect. Pay phones and an Internet room take the place of in-room amenities. Neighboring businesses include Powell's, Jake's Famous Crawfish and a host of gay bars.

Park Lane Suites (☎ 503-226-6288, 800-532-9543, 809 SW King Ave)* Kitchenette suites $79 and up. A short walk from downtown in a nice residential neighborhood, this inn is just down the hill from Washington Park.

Travelodge (☎ 503-226-1121, 800-992-2401, fax 503-274-2681, 2401 SW 4th Ave)* Singles/doubles $68/72. This rather generic motel is just south of PSU. Runners will appreciate the easy access to the track at the nearby YMCA and running trails starting at the track and heading uphill on Terwilliger Blvd.

Imperial Hotel (☎ 503-228-7221, 800-452-2323, W *www.hotel-imperial.com, 400 SW Broadway)* Singles/doubles $100/110. This face-lifted hotel is convenient to downtown restaurants, shopping and entertainment.

Four Points Sheraton (☎ 503-221-0711, 800-899-0247, W *www.fourpointsportland.com, 50 SW Morrison St)* Singles/doubles $99/109. River-view rooms are the nicest, but all are convenient to a morning stroll in Waterfront Park.

Silver Cloud Inn (☎ 503-242-2400, 800-205-6939, W *www.scinns.com, 2426 NW Vaughn St)* Singles/doubles $99/109. Just off the I-405 freeway and a couple of miles from downtown, this is a good base for exploring Northwest Portland and Forest Park.

Top End It's easy to flinch when you see the prices of Portland's top-end hotels, but special deals abound during the off-season. Check hotel websites or ask about discounts when you call for reservations.

Heathman Hotel (☎ 503-241-4100, 800-551-0011, W *www.heathmanhotel.com, 1001 SW Broadway)* Rooms $209 and up, discounts commonly available. This is one of the city's finest hotels. The Heathman's service is legendary: When Pavarotti stayed here, the hotel had the city stop daytime construction nearby so that the tenor could rest before his performance. Heathman Restaurant is one of Portland's most elegant places to dine, and a lovely bar is downstairs.

Benson Hotel (☎ 503-228-2000, 888-523-6766, W *www.bensonhotel.com, 309 SW Broadway)* Singles or doubles $220. The Benson, featuring a lobby lined with walnut and filled with chandeliers, is where the president stays when in town.

Hotel Vintage Plaza (☎ 503-228-1212, 800-243-0555, W *www.vintageplaza.com, 422 SW Broadway)*. Rooms $145 and up. The Vintage Plaza is a lovely refurbished hotel with amazing suites for those who can afford them.

Governor Hotel (☎ 503-224-3400, 800-554-3456, W *www.govhotel.com, 611 SW 10th Ave)* Rooms $165-240. The art deco Governor is another old hotel that has metamorphosed into a stylish luxury option without losing its period charm.

RiverPlace Hotel (☎ 503-228-3233, 800-227-1333, W *www.riverplacehotel.com, 1510 SW Harbor Way)* Singles/doubles $195/215. The modern RiverPlace is right on the waterfront. Ask for a room overlooking the marina.

Hotels – Northeast

Some of Portland's best hotel bargains are in the conveniently located Hollywood District.

Hojo Inn (☎ *503-288-6891, fax 503-288-1995, 3939 NE Hancock St*) Singles/doubles $55/65. Don't expect elegance, but the Hojo is an easy commute via car or light rail. It's east of downtown off I-84's Hollywood exit, or a few blocks from the Hollywood MAX stop.

Rodeway Inn (☎ *503-460-9000, 3800 NE Sandy Blvd*) Rooms $59. This motel is in the same neighborhood as the Hojo but is perched right above noisy I-84.

Northeast Portland's mid-range hotels are clustered around the convention center and are all a short MAX ride from downtown. These are fairly standard chain hotels; for more luxury, stay at one of downtown's top-end hotels.

Red Lion Inn/Coliseum (☎ *503-235-8311, 800-547-8010, fax 503-872-4278, 1225 N Thunderbird Way*) Rooms $72 and up. The Red Lion is right on the Willamette River.

Hawthorn Inn (☎ *503-233-7933, 800-527-1133,* W *www.hawthorn.com, 431 NE Multnomah St*) Singles/doubles $99/109. Walk from here to the Lloyd Center, the Oregon Convention Center or MAX.

Best Western Inn at the Convention Center (☎ *503-233-6331, 420 NE Holladay St*) Singles/doubles $75/80. This motel has a good location, right on the MAX line.

DoubleTree Portland Lloyd Center (☎ *503-281-6111, 800-996-0510, fax 503-284-8553, 1000 NE Multnomah St*) Rooms $99 and up. Just across the street from the Lloyd Center, this is the Eastside's fanciest hotel.

PLACES TO EAT

Portland has, in recent years, emerged as a minor culinary mecca, and even in the high-end joints a casually dressed traveler can eat cheaply from the bar menu.

Downtown

It's easy to find a good, inexpensive breakfast or lunch downtown. Don't be afraid to eat from sidewalk food carts.

Budget Many downtown corners have food carts offering cheap carryout fare. Office workers flock to the parking lot at SW 5th Ave and SW Stark St, nicknamed *The Pod*, where everybody you ask seems to recommend a different cart. If it's raining and you just want something easy, quick and indoors, head to the basement of the Pioneer Place shopping center, where the *food court* has a wide variety of fast-food options.

Bijou Café (☎ *503-222-3187, 132 SW 3rd Ave*) Breakfast, lunch $5-10. This is Portland's favorite downtown breakfast spot – the snapper hash is on the spendy side but is delicious. The lunch menu changes daily, the food is reliably good, and the customers are slavishly devoted.

Pazzoria (☎ *503-228-1695, 625 SW Washington St*) Lunch $3-7. City bureaucrats, FedEx drivers and musicians all stop by for a midmorning roll or a lunchtime salad sampler. Some of Portland's nicest counter people make this a pleasant place to hang.

Good Dog/Bad Dog (☎ *503-222-3410, 708 SW Alder St*) Under $5. Sausage lovers, go no farther. Big spicy dogs of all descriptions make a quick and hearty meal.

Pizzicato (☎ *503-226-1007, 705 SW Alder St*) Slice/pie $3/8-18. Pizzas range from traditional to quirky. The salads are good, too.

Pasta Veloce (☎ *503-242-0747, 1022 SW Morrison St*) Pasta $6. Big plates of simple pasta come for as little as $4.25; a couple of extra bucks will get you sauces beyond olive oil and garlic.

Anne Hughes Coffee Shop (☎ *503-228-4651, 1005 W Burnside St*) Drinks $1 and up. This cafe in Powell's City of Books serves caffeine to book-lovers, and according to surveys, it's also one of the best singles scenes in the city.

Pearl Bakery (☎ *503-827-0910, 102 NW 9th Ave*) Pastries from $1, sandwiches $2-5. Midmorning, drop by the Pearl for fig panini. Come back at lunch for a Gorgonzola-pear sandwich. Scratch that afternoon chocolate itch with a bouchon. It's all so good!

Little Wing Café (☎ *503-228-3101, 529 NW 13th Ave*) Lunch $6. Stop in for lunch or an afternoon cookie and munch it on the loading dock (the cafe space is a former warehouse).

Dogs Dig Vegetarian Deli *(☎ 503-223-3362, 212 NW Davis St)* Under $5. Grab a tofu-salad sandwich or a cup of really good soup from this takeout cubbyhole, and lunch at a sidewalk table, where you'll soak up the ungentrified, easygoing ambiance of Old Town. (For more of a picnic, take your sandwich to nearby Waterfront Park.)

Mid-Range Business lunches give way to casual evening dining at these diverse restaurants.

Al-Amir *(☎ 503-274-0010, 223 SW Stark St)* Entrees $13. Al-Amir serves delicious Lebanese food in a delightful old building that was once the residence of Portland's Catholic archbishop.

Saucebox *(☎ 503-241-3393, 214 SW Broadway)* Entrees $12. Fusion cuisine dominates the menu at this supertrendy eatery; stay late for cocktails and DJ-spun hits.

Mother's Bistro *(☎ 503-464-1122, 409 SW 2nd Ave)* Entrees $12-16. Homey comfort food has made this place a hit.

Le Bouchon *(☎ 503-248-2193, 517 NW 14th Ave)* Entrees $15. This place offers a little bit of France right beside a body shop. The convivial (often noisy) French atmosphere is as memorable as the food, which is good bistro fare.

Top End Some of Portland's best restaurants are downtown or in the nearby Pearl District.

Jake's Famous Crawfish *(☎ 503-226-1419, 401 SW 12th Ave)* Entrees $17. Portland's most famous restaurant may not be its greatest, but it captures more of the city's charm and esprit than fussier locales. Delicious seafood and a vibrant bar scene make this vintage landmark perennially popular.

Higgins *(☎ 503-222-9070, 1239 SW Broadway)* Entrees $20. Close to the Portland Center for Performing Arts, Higgins offers fresh, often organically grown, ingredients and innovative preparations. Vegetarians will find several options.

Heathman Restaurant *(☎ 503-241-4100, 1001 SW Broadway)* Entrees $18. Don't always mistrust hotel restaurants. The French chef here turns out some of Portland's most elegant dinners. (The Heathman also serves a wonderful afternoon tea.)

Bluehour *(☎ 503-226-3394, 250 NW 13th Ave)* Entrees $25. If you want to make the scene in Portland, this is where you'll be eating dinner. And if you can't afford that, have a drink at the bar just to take in the smoothness of it all. The continental food is really terrific, with fabulously fresh ingredients.

Cafe Azul *(☎ 503-525-4422, 112 NW 9th Ave)* Entrees $12-24. Dinner only. Cafe Azul specializes in cuisine from central and southern Mexico. It'll take willpower to resist any dish served with the toasted green pumpkin-seed mole.

Northwest

Budget These are the places where the folks who live in Northwest Portland's many apartment buildings meet their friends for casual dinners.

Thai Orchid *(☎ 503-226-4542, 2231 W Burnside St)* Entrees $8. It's not fancy, and parking can be a pain, but Thai Orchid is a good neighborhood joint with reliably good food and plenty of vegetarian options. The soups are great, and they do a respectable pad thai.

La Buca *(☎ 503-279-8040, 2309 NW Kearney St)* Average $6. This is a sassy neighborhood pasta joint where the simple menu standards are usually better than the specials. Order cheap; eat happy.

BridgePort Brew Pub *(☎ 503-241-7179, 1313 NW Marshall St)* This earthy, informal brewpub is housed in an old rope factory with outdoor seating on the loading dock. Pizza by the slice and British-style brews are served.

Mid-Range Good Italian and Thai restaurants are easy to find in Northwest.

Caffe Mingo *(☎ 503-226-4646, 807 NW 21st Ave)* Entrees $11-20. There's always a crowd waiting to eat the rustic pastas and melt-in-your-mouth risotto at Caffe Mingo, so come prepared to wait in the doorway. If seats open up at the tiny bar, go for 'em.

Typhoon! (☎ 503-243-7557, 2310 NW Everett St) Entrees $12. This place is a little spendier than the average Thai restaurant, but it's oh so delicious – and pretty darn stylish as well.

Papa Haydn (☎ 503-228-7317, 701 NW 23rd Ave) Brunch around $9. Though most come here for the incredible desserts, the rest of the food is also quite good. The Sunday brunch is very popular.

Piazza D'Italia (☎ 503-478-0619, 1129 NW Johnson St) Pasta $11. This small deli/restaurant is Portland's most exuberantly Italian spot and features good food and a friendly atmosphere.

Tapeo (☎ 503-226-0409, 2764 NW Thurman St) Tapas $2-9. Tasty tapas, smooth sherries and comfy banquette seating make it tempting to order more and more small plates. It's easy to make the leap from moderate to expensive here.

Top End The freshest organic ingredients are featured at these Northwest favorites.

Wildwood (☎ 503-248-9663, 1221 NW 21st Ave) Entrees $18-20. Chef Corey Schreiber has literally written the book on Northwest cuisine. To save a few bucks, order off the cheaper bar menu.

Paley's Place (☎ 503-243-2403, 1204 NW 21st Ave) Entrees $22. Just across the street from Wildwood is another one of Portland's best restaurants. The chef's French training shows up in the meals here.

Northeast
Budget The NE Broadway corridor is home to many good, inexpensive restaurants, and more are cropping up on NE Alberta all the time.

Cadillac Café (☎ 503-287-4750, 914 NE Broadway) Omelets about $7. Good for breakfast and lunch, the Cadillac is not too far from the convention-center hotel cluster.

Milo's City Café (☎ 503-288-6456, 1325 NE Broadway) Breakfast $6-7. This is another good breakfast spot just a couple of blocks from the Cadillac. Try the scrambled eggs with smoked salmon.

Grand Central Bakery (☎ 503-288-1614, 1444 NE Weidler St) Sandwiches $5-6. In addition to the great breads and pastries, soup, pizza and light entrees are available in the cafe.

Vita Cafe (☎ 503-335-8233, 3024 NE Alberta St) Entrees $8. A vegan joint that also serves burgers! The lasagna is delicious, the atmosphere neo-hippie.

Widmer Gasthaus (☎ 503-281-3333, 929 N Russell St) Sausages $7-8, entrees $11. Make your way below the arches of the Fremont Bridge to quaff the wonderful Hefeweizen (unfiltered wheat beer) and to nibble sausage and schnitzel at this bustling pub.

Mid-Range There are a couple of good midrange options.

Bernie's Southern Bistro (☎ 503-282-9864, 2904 NE Alberta St) Entrees $11-19. This joint is classy but casual, with plenty of neighborhood folks in for gumbo, fried chicken, hush puppies and maybe a shot of bourbon. The backyard patio is like its own little world.

Mint (☎ 503-284-5518, 816 N Russell St) Entrees $15. Tucked into an industrial area, this stylish bar and restaurant has Latin America–inspired food.

Southeast
Budget SE Hawthorne and Belmont Sts are flush with hip, inexpensive cafes.

Cup & Saucer (☎ 503-236-6001, 3566 SE Hawthorne Blvd) Breakfast or lunch $6-7. It can take a while to get your omelet here, but it's worth the wait. Tofu scrambles attract vegans, and the people-watching is top notch.

Montage (☎ 503-234-1324, 301 SE Morrison St) Entrees $5-10. Open 6pm-4am. Montage is a popular Creole nightspot with delicious, inexpensive dishes and a broad cross-section of Portland's nightlife.

Hoda's (☎ 503-236-8325, 3401 SE Belmont St) Entrees $7. No money was wasted on fancying up the decor here, so the focus is entirely on the delicious, cheap Middle Eastern food. (No credit cards.)

Café Lena (☎ 503-238-7087, 2239 SE Hawthorne Blvd) 4-course dinner $14. This cafe, near the Hawthorne hostel, has open-mike poetry weekly.

Tao of Tea *(☎ 736-0119, 3430 SE Belmont St)* Pot of tea $3-6. Buck the coffeehouse trend at this Asian countryside tea hut in Southeast Portland. It's a great escape on a rainy afternoon and has good food, too. Visit the Leaf Room to sip rare teas in a ceremonial atmosphere.

Rimsky-Korsakoffee House *(☎ 503-232-2640, 707 SE 12th Ave)* Desserts $4-5. Open at night. Portland's most unusual nightspot is this eccentric coffeehouse, next door to the Plaid Pantry (there's no sign, so act like a regular and barge right in). Be sure to check out the bathroom upstairs.

BridgePort Ale House *(☎ 503-233-6540, 3632 SE Hawthorne Blvd)* Entrees $4-8. This place, BridgePort's Southeast location, features good food (the Ale House salad is huge and delicious) and a friendly welcome.

Lucky Labrador Brewing Company *(☎ 503-236-3555, 915 SE Hawthorne Blvd)* About $5. Just back from a long hike? Plunk down on the back porch of the Lucky Lab and meet all the locals and their dogs.

Mid-Range Good mid-range restaurants are scattered through Southeast Portland, with a particularly high concentration in Sellwood.

Bread & Ink Café *(☎ 503-239-4756, 3610 SE Hawthorne Blvd)* Breakfast or lunch $6-7, dinner $10-12. Come for a leisurely breakfast or lunch at this quintessential Portland cafe. Blintzes are a standby here; the salmon sandwich is also good.

Esparza's *(☎ 503-234-7909, 2715 SE Ankeny St)* Entrees $10-15. Authentic where others are trendy, the meaty Tex-Mex food here has people lined up out the door.

Old Wives' Tales *(☎ 503-238-0470, 1300 E Burnside St)* Dinner $12. Vegetarians, gays, lesbians and children gather here, drawn in by the yummy international comfort food and warm welcome.

Assaggio *(☎ 503-232-6151, 7742 SE 13th Ave)* Entrees $13. Pasta dishes are the stronghold here, but they're not the kind of pasta dinners you're likely to cook up at home. Though most dishes are meatless, the smoked trout will appeal to fish-eaters.

Gino's Restaurant & Bar *(☎ 503-233-4613, 8057 SE 13th Ave)* Entrees $11. Neighborhood hangout with great (and reasonably priced) wine list and down-home Italian dinners.

Top End Some of Portland's best restaurants are in very unassuming locations.

Caprial's Bistro *(☎ 503-236-6457, 7015 SE Milwaukie Ave)* Entrees $20. Asian and European influences mingle in a Northwest way. Caprial, who hosts a PBS cooking show, has many fans who make pilgrimages to this Sellwood restaurant. Along with good food, there's a great wine selection.

Castagna *(☎ 503-231-7373, 1752 SE Hawthorne Blvd)* Entrees $20. Minimalist decor makes the food really jump out at you. The rich, sumptuous meals are inspired by French cooking (with perhaps a side trip to Italy) but are executed in a pleasingly unique way.

Genoa *(☎ 503-238-1464, 2832 SE Belmont St)* 4-course meal $56, 7-course meal $68. Big tax refund? Milestone birthday? Just feel like a splurge? Genoa's location is decidedly unglamorous, but the food is spectacular. Each course is small but perfect and, with the exception of the main course, it's whatever the chef wants to serve you.

ENTERTAINMENT

The best guide to local entertainment is the free *Willamette Week,* which comes out on Wednesdays and contains complete listings of all theater, music, clubs, cinema and events in the metro area. The Friday edition of the *Oregonian* contains the *A&E,* an insert with arts and entertainment information.

Cinemas

Downtown and Lloyd Center are both flush with multiplex theaters. The following are a few of the more obscure cinemas.

Cinema 21 *(☎ 503-223-4515, 616 NW 21st Ave)* Tickets $5-6. This is Portland's art- and foreign-film theater.

Northwest Film Center *(☎ 503-221-1156, 1219 SW Park Ave)* Tickets $6.50. More unusual films make it to this film center, which holds screenings at the Portland Art Museum and at the Guild Theatre (915 SW 9th Ave).

Mission Theater (☎ *503-223-4031, 1624 NW Glisan St)* Tickets $2-3. This picturesque old movie theater is now owned by a brewpub. Order beer and snacks and watch a film.

Bagdad Theater (☎ *503-230-0895, 3702 SE Hawthorne Blvd)* Tickets $2-3. This is another brewpub-theater with bargain flicks.

Performing Arts

Arlene Schnitzer Concert Hall (☎ *503-228-1353, 800-228-7343, 1037 SW Broadway)* The Oregon Symphony performs in this beautiful, if not acoustically brilliant, downtown venue.

Keller Auditorium (☎ *503-248-4335, 222 SW Clay St)* The Portland Opera stages five performances a year here.

Portland Center for the Performing Arts (☎ *503-796-9293,* w *www.pcpa.com, 1111 SW Broadway)* Portland's showcase theatrical stages are here. Call for information on current shows; the recording gives phone numbers for ticket ordering. Portland Center Stage, Tygres Heart Shakespeare Co and several other local theater groups perform here.

Artists Repertory Theatre (☎ *503-241-1278, 1516 SW Alder St)* Some of Portland's best plays, including regional premieres, original works and classics, are performed in this intimate space.

Do Jump (☎ *503-231-1232, 1515 SE 37th Ave)* 'Extremely physical theater' is this company's tag line – don't miss a chance to see the wild and extremely fun productions. Do Jump's home base is the Echo Theatre, just off SE Hawthorne Blvd, in Southeast Portland.

Bars & Clubs

For the most current listings, check the *Willamette Week*.

When in doubt about how to spend an evening out, Portlanders like as not will head to one of the ***McMenamin's***. These brewpubs are found all over the city and offer their own ales and a wide selection of brews from other regional producers. Check the phone book for the McMenamin's

nearest you. (Other local brewpubs are listed as Places to Eat.)

Satyricon (☎ *503-243-2380, 125 NW 6th Ave)* Cover free or up to $10. This downtown locale serves up rough-and-ready punk rock and poetry. Though not quite as lively as it once was, Satyricon still draws an interesting crowd.

Berbati's Pan (☎ *503-248-4579, 10 SW 3rd Ave)* Cover free or up to $15. So is tonight swing night at Berbati's, or is it open-mike poetry night? No, it must be fetish night! Jazz and local and Northwest touring bands round things out.

Jimmy Mak's (☎ *503-295-6542, 300 NW 10th Ave)* Cover $5-15. This downtown venue is Portland's best jazz club.

Crystal Ballroom (☎ *503-778-5625, 1332 W Burnside St)* Cover free or up to $20. All sorts of bands are booked at the Crystal, which is a historic ballroom complete with floating dance floor.

Huber's (☎ *503-228-5686, 411 SW 3rd Ave)* This is Portland's oldest restaurant, but most people know it as a beautiful bar with lethal Spanish coffees. Also on offer are tasty turkey sandwiches and a great old-Portland atmosphere.

Biddy McGraw's Irish Pub (☎ *503-233-1178, 6000 NE Glisan St)* When Gerry Adams came to town, this extra-friendly pub is where he headed for a pint of Guinness.

Gay & Lesbian Venues

Many of Portland's gay bars are on SW Stark St between SW 10th and SW 11th Aves. Hawthorne Blvd is pretty much regarded as 'lesbian central,' and its many cafes and coffee shops are good meeting places.

Scandals (☎ *503-227-5887, 1038 SW Stark St)* This is a friendly, predominantly male place.

Embers (☎ *503-222-3082, 110 NW Broadway)* Cover $2-4. The '70s have never died at this club, which features drag shows in the front and disco in the back. The crowd is mixed – gay, lesbian, and straight – and the DJ is top-notch.

Hobo's (☎ *503-224-3285, 120 NW 3rd Ave)* Gay men hang at this piano bar housed in a historic old storefront. Women go into the back room and shoot pool.

Starky's (☎ *503-230-7980, 2913 SE Stark St*) Gays, lesbians and straights are all welcome at this bar and restaurant.

Egyptian Room (☎ *503-236-8689, 3701 SE Division St*) Dance with the girls at this smoky club.

SPECTATOR SPORTS

Rose Garden Arena (☎ *503-797-9619,* Ⓦ *www .rosequarter.com, 1 Center Court*) Portlanders have an unaccountable obsession with the ***Trail Blazers*** (☎ *503-231-8000*), the local National Basketball Association team, and tickets are tough to come by. It's easier to see the ***Portland Fire*** (☎ *503-233-9622*) women's professional basketball team, which also plays here, as do the ***Winter Hawks*** (☎ *503-238-6366*), Portland's minor-league hockey team.

PGE Park (☎ *503-224-4400,* Ⓦ *www.pge park.com*) The ***Portland Beavers*** (☎ *503-553-5555*), the San Diego Padres' Triple-A team, play baseball here; and the ***Portland Timbers*** (☎ *503-553-5555*) play A-League soccer here.

SHOPPING

Portland's downtown shopping district extends in a two-block radius from Pioneer Courthouse Square. ***Pioneer Place***, an upscale mall, is between SW Morrison and SW Yamhill St, east of the square.

Galleries are clustered in the Pearl District and along NE Alberta St. Ask for the gallery map at the visitor center, or check out the gallery listings in the *Willamette Week*.

On the first Thursday of every month, the First Thursday Art Walk brings out Portland's art lovers. Galleries remain open until 8pm, and the Pearl District street scene explodes with art of all calibres. It's a great way to see both art and the arty set. The NE Alberta St galleries have Last Thursday openings; it's an equally happening scene.

Made in Oregon (☎ *503-273-8354, 10 NW 1st Ave*) Stock up on locally made gifts, food, and wines here. Branch outlets are at the Galleria Shopping Center, at SW 10th Ave and SW Alder St, and at the Portland airport.

Check out local crafts and listen to street music at the Saturday Market, beneath the Burnside Bridge (see Things to See & Do, Downtown).

Oregon Mountain Community (☎ *503-227-1038, 60 NW Davis St*) This is downtown Portland's best outdoor store; they also rent equipment.

Next Adventure (☎ *503-233-0706, 426 SE Grand Ave*) Used and bargain-priced outdoor gear fills this large store.

GETTING THERE & AWAY
Air
Portland International Airport (PDX; Ⓦ www.flypdx.com) is served by over a dozen airlines with connections to major US cities. Commuter flights on Horizon Air and United Airlines connect to cities and towns all over the West. Bargain fares are available from Southwest Airlines. Portland is the West Coast hub of Delta Air Lines. Alaska Airlines (☎ 800-252-7522), 530 SW Madison St, and United Airlines (☎ 800-241-6522), 502 SW Madison St, have downtown offices.

Bus
Buses leave from the Greyhound Depot (☎ 503-243-2357, 800-231-2222), 550 NW 6th Ave, and connect Portland with cities along I-5 and I-84.

Key routes are the following: Bend, Oregon ($23; 4 hours; 2 daily); Chicago via Spokane, Washington ($132; 2 days; 6 daily); Denver via Boise, Idaho ($90; 30 hours; 3 daily); Newport, Oregon ($40; 4 hours; 4 daily); San Francisco ($55; 19 hours; 7 daily); Seattle ($22; 4 hours; 9 daily); Vancouver ($42; 10 hours; 5 daily).

Green Tortoise service to San Francisco and Seattle has been discontinued indefinitely.

Train
Amtrak (☎ 503-241-4290), at Union Station, NW 6th Ave at Irving St, offers service up and down the West Coast. Eastbound *Empire Builder* trains travel up the Columbia River Gorge on their way to Chicago.

Key routes are the following: Chicago via Spokane, Washington ($234; 2 days; 1 daily); Eugene, Oregon ($15; 3 hours; 3 daily); Los Angeles ($135; 31 hours; 1 daily); Seattle ($28; 4 hours; 4 daily).

Car

Most major car rental agencies have outlets both downtown and at Portland International Airport (PDX):

Avis (☎ 503-227-0220, 800-831-2847; PDX ☎ 503-249-4950) 330 SW Washington St

Budget Rent-A-Car (☎ 503-249-6500, 800-527-7000; PDX ☎ 503-249-6500) 2033 SW 4th Ave

Dollar Rent-A-Car (☎ 503-228-3540, 800-800-4000; PDX ☎ 503-249-4792) 132 NW Broadway

Hertz (☎ 503-249-5727, 800-654-3131; PDX ☎ 503-249-8216) 330 SW Pine St

Forgo the latest-model cars and save a few bucks at Bee Rent-A-Car (☎ 503-233-7368), 84 NE Weidler St.

GETTING AROUND
To/From the Airport

PDX is about 10 miles northeast of downtown, along the Columbia River. The Airport MAX takes about 40 minutes to get from downtown to the airport ($1.50).

Gray Line Express (☎ 503-249-1837) offers bus service between PDX and most major downtown hotels. Depending on the number of stops, the $15 trip takes about 30 minutes.

The taxi fare, including tip, between the airport and downtown costs about $25.

If you're driving to the airport from downtown, take I-84 east, follow signs to I-205 north and get off at exit 24A. Traffic can be heavy in the afternoon. From the airport, follow Airport Way past all the parking areas and turn right onto I-205 south. Take I-205 south to I-84 west and continue on I-84 until joins I-5. Follow the signs for City Center, which will put you on I-5 south for just a moment before directing you west across the Morrison Bridge into the heart of downtown Portland.

Bus, Light Rail & Streetcar

Tri-Met (☎ 503-238-7433, Ⓦ www.trimet.org) operates the local buses and light-rail trains (MAX). The independently operated Portland Streetcar links up with Tri-Met's buses and trains. All buses are equipped with bike

racks, and bikes are permitted on MAX trains (call or see website for particulars).

Most downtown buses travel along 5th and 6th Aves, the 'bus mall.'

The MAX links east Portland suburbs, the airport and the Lloyd District to downtown, then continues west to the zoo, Beaverton and Hillsboro.

The streetcar runs from Portland State University north through downtown and the Pearl District, to NW 23rd Ave and NW Northrup St.

All public transportation is free within the downtown core and Lloyd District, an area called Fareless Square. Outside this area, there are three zones in the Tri-Met fare system; tickets for travel within zones 1 and 2, which cover most close destinations (including the zoo and Washington Park), cost $1.25. Bus riders buy tickets from the driver – no change is given. Tickets for MAX must be bought from ticket machines at MAX stations; there is no conductor or ticket-seller on board. Bus, light-rail and streetcar tickets are completely transferable within two hours of the time of purchase. Visitors can buy an unlimited-use three-day pass for $10 from the Tri-Met Customer Assistance Office (☎ 503-231-3198) at Pioneer Courthouse Square.

Taxi

There are taxi stands near most major downtown hotels. If you're not near a hotel, call Broadway Cab (☎ 503-227-1234) or Radio Cab (☎ 503-227-1212).

Bicycle

It's easy to get around Portland on a bicycle. The *Bike There* map, available from bike shops and Powell's Travel Store, details the best routes. Downtown, you can rent a bike from Bike Central Co-op (☎ 503-227-4439), 732 SW 1st Ave, or Fat Tire Farm (☎ 503-222-3276), 2714 NW Thurman St, which is in Northwest, near mountain-bike routes.

Of the city's many bridges, Broadway, Steel and Hawthorne have the best bike paths.

Columbia River Gorge & Mt Hood

Stunning geology and beauty converge in the Columbia River Gorge, where the mile-wide river carves a 3000-foot-deep chasm through the Cascade Range. The gorge is famous for its waterfalls, which tumble hundreds of feet through fern-filled forests to the river.

Immediately south of the Columbia River Gorge rises 11,240-foot Mt Hood, the highest peak in Oregon and a favorite desti-

Highlights

- Skiing year round above historic Timberline Lodge
- Watching waterfalls, including spectacular Multnomah Falls
- Catching sight of a mountainside full of wild pink rhododendrons
- Visiting Stonehenge (yes, really!)
- Windsurfing, parasailing, kite sailing

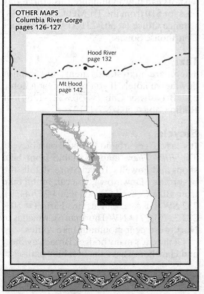

OTHER MAPS
Columbia River Gorge
pages 126-127

Hood River
page 132

Mt Hood
page 142

nation for skiers, hikers, mountain climbers and those who come to pay homage to the WPA (Works Progress Administration)-era Timberline Lodge, built during the Depression by unemployed artisans hired on by the federal government.

The Columbia River divides Washington and Oregon, and both states share the gorge. Information for both states is included in this chapter. Pay attention to telephone area codes: This part of Washington is ☎ 509, while Oregon uses ☎ 503 at the western end of the gorge and ☎ 541 from Hood River east.

The Gorge

Besides being a scenic wonder, the Columbia Gorge is also the Pacific Northwest's only sea-level passage through the Cascades, and it has been a transportation corridor for centuries.

Five hundred years ago, during the fall and spring salmon migrations, many Native American tribes gathered near The Dalles to trade, fish and socialize. This is the place where the migratory hunting-and-gathering tribes of the Columbia Plateau converged with the river- and oceangoing tribes of the coast.

Lewis and Clark floated down the gorge in the fall of 1805, and later, when Oregon Trail travelers reached The Dalles, they could either negotiate the rapids at the Cascade Locks or slog over Mt Hood on the Barlow Rd. Either way was a dangerous end to a 2000-mile journey.

The Columbia River Hwy (also known as US 30), a marvel of modern engineering and a beautiful route, opened the gorge to automobile traffic in the 1910s. Beginning in 1938, a series of dams transformed the Columbia River into a controlled waterway and hydro-electric source; and the once-wild river became a series of slack-water reservoirs allowing barges to head upriver into Idaho. In 1986, the gorge was declared a National

Scenic Area, and further development is now regulated.

Two highways pass through the gorge, one each on the north and south banks of the Columbia River. Busy I-84 traverses the Oregon side and is the quicker route, with easy access to the most popular sites and activities. Washington's slower but scenic Hwy 14 follows the north bank of the river.

The gorge's major cities are Hood River and The Dalles; both are home to many motels and restaurants. Washington-side towns are smaller. Campers will find state parks dotting both sides of the river, though they're often crowded and are plagued by highway and railroad noise. It's 63 miles between Portland and Hood River; 21 miles farther east is The Dalles.

Hikers should pick up the USFS *Trails of the Columbia Gorge* map from the Multnomah Falls gift shop.

WESTERN COLUMBIA RIVER HIGHWAY

Two late-19th-century Oregon business and civic leaders, Sam Hill and Simon Lancaster, designed the Columbia River Hwy (US 30) to fit neatly into the landscape. The Troutdale-to-Warrendale section of the road, which opened in 1915, links some of the most spectacular sights in the gorge – but it can be slow going, both because of traffic and because you'll be tempted to stop often. Don't take a large RV on this road – it's a precarious route, built for Model Ts.

Orientation & Information

There are several ways to get onto the Columbia River Hwy from Portland. If you're in no hurry, head east on I-84 and take exit 17, turning right at the outlet mall, then left at the light up the hill from the outlets onto US 30. This route snakes up the Sandy River and through the towns of Troutdale and Corbett before reaching the gorge's big attractions.

For quicker access to waterfalls and hikes from Portland, take exit 28 from I-84, at Bridal Veil. If you're coming in on I-84 from the east, take exit 35 at Ainsworth State Park.

US Forest Service visitor centers at the Multnomah Falls Lodge (☎ 503-695-2372), at the base of the falls, and Skamania Lodge (☎ 509-427-2528) are the best sources of information; both places are open 9am to 5pm.

Portland Women's Forum Park

Though it's little more than a roadside parking lot, this is one of the best viewpoints onto the Columbia Gorge. Stop here on a misty morning for a photo shoot.

Crown Point

This viewpoint atop a craggy point of basalt marks the western edge of the gorge. The 1916 **Vista House**, an art nouveau–style rotunda, houses an information center (☎ 503-695-2230; admission free; open 8:30am-6pm Apr 15-Oct 15).

To the east, the Columbia River unfurls between green cliffs. From the high ground of the Vista House, the Columbia River Hwy coils downhill in a series of switchbacks and curves.

Latourell Falls

The first major waterfall you encounter coming east on US 30, Latourell Falls drops 249 feet into a rocky pool. A 10-minute hike leads to the base of the falls and back along Latourell Creek to a picnic area in Talbot State Park. It's about 2 miles roundtrip to Upper Latourell Falls, a 100-foot-high chute. Both trails begin at the bridge over Latourell Creek.

Bridal Veil Falls

An easy 1-mile round-trip hike leads to two-tiered Bridal Veil Falls, which first plunges 100 feet in one direction, then turns a right angle for its final 60-foot drop. A separate wheelchair-accessible trail passes through a meadow with great spring wildflowers. It's easy to reach this falls from either I-84 (exit 28) or the Columbia Gorge Highway.

Wahkeena Falls

Lovely, cascading 242-foot Wahkeena Falls serves as a trailhead for some of the most popular hiking trails in the gorge. Hike up the Wahkeena Trail to the side of the falls, then follow the creek to join the Larch Mountain Trail No 441. Follow this trail down to the top of Multnomah Falls; from there, the trail descends to Multnomah Falls Lodge. A roadside trail completes the 5-mile loop.

Multnomah Falls

At 642 feet, Multnomah Falls is the second-highest nonseasonal waterfall in the nation and is one of the Northwest's most spectacular sights. The falls drop twice: the first is a drop of over 560 feet from a notch in an amphitheater of vertical rock, and then there's another 70-foot drop over a ledge of basalt. A short trail leads to an arch bridge directly over the lower falls.

Continue past the bridge up a steep trail (Larch Mountain Trail No 441) to the top of the falls (1 mile). The Larch Mountain Trail continues up Multnomah Creek, leading arduously to the top of Larch Mountain (7 miles).

Drivers on I-84 should note that the exits for Multnomah Falls are from the freeway's left-hand lanes.

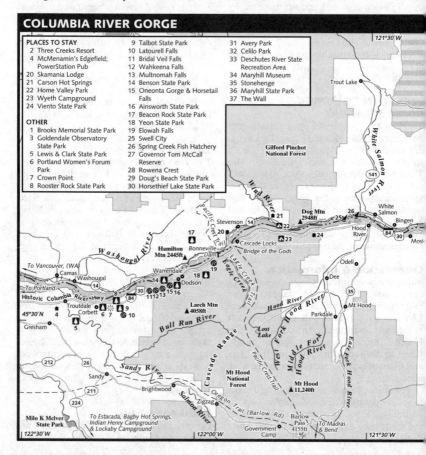

COLUMBIA RIVER GORGE

PLACES TO STAY
2 Three Creeks Resort
4 McMenamin's Edgefield; PowerStation Pub
20 Skamania Lodge
21 Carson Hot Springs
22 Home Valley Park
23 Wyeth Campground
24 Viento State Park

OTHER
1 Brooks Memorial State Park
3 Goldendale Observatory State Park
5 Lewis & Clark State Park
6 Portland Women's Forum Park
7 Crown Point
8 Rooster Rock State Park
9 Talbot State Park
10 Latourell Falls
11 Bridal Veil Falls
12 Wahkeena Falls
13 Multnomah Falls
14 Benson State Park
15 Oneonta Gorge & Horsetail Falls
16 Ainsworth State Park
17 Beacon Rock State Park
18 Yeon State Park
19 Elowah Falls
25 Swell City
26 Spring Creek Fish Hatchery
27 Governor Tom McCall Reserve
28 Rowena Crest
29 Doug's Beach State Park
30 Horsethief Lake State Park
31 Avery Park
32 Celilo Park
33 Deschutes River State Recreation Area
34 Maryhill Museum
35 Stonehenge
36 Maryhill State Park
37 The Wall

Oneonta Gorge & Horsetail Falls

These two nearly adjacent sites are easily accessible from US 30. Oneonta (pronounced oh-nee-**own**-tah) Gorge is a narrow chasm cut into a thick basalt flow by Oneonta Creek. Walls over 100 feet high arch over the stream. This peculiar ecosystem, preserved as Oneonta Gorge Botanical Area, is home to a number of rare, cliff-dwelling plants that thrive in this moist, shadowy chasm. There's no room along the sheer walls of Oneonta Gorge for a trail. However, for those unperturbed by wet sneakers, the shallow stream can be waded in for about half a mile to Oneonta Falls, where Oneonta Creek drops 75 feet into its gorge.

A few hundred feet east of Oneonta Gorge, Horsetail Falls drops out of a notch in the rock to fall 176 feet. The 3-mile **Horsetail-Oneonta Loop Trail** begins at Horsetail Falls and quickly climbs up the side of the gorge wall, then passes behind **Ponytail Falls** (also called Upper Horsetail Falls), which pours out of a tiny crack into a mossy cirque. After dropping down to great views of Oneonta Creek, with its narrow gorge and waterfalls, the trail returns to US 30 about half a mile west of the trailhead.

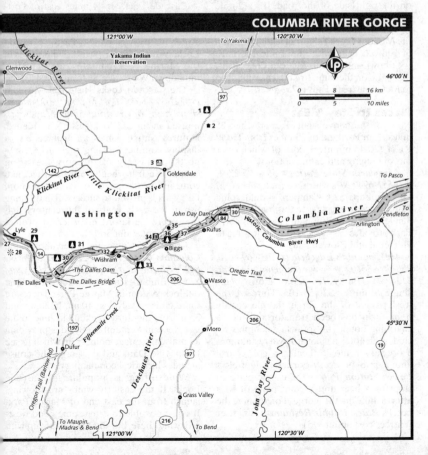

COLUMBIA RIVER GORGE

OREGON

Elowah Falls

Stunning 289-foot Elowah Falls is much less visited than its brethren along the Columbia River, because it's about a mile off the highway. The falls plunge into an enormous rock-walled bowl, where mosses, ferns and wildflowers thrive in the mists and breezes.

To reach Elowah Falls from US 30, continue east past Ainsworth State Park on Frontage Rd toward Dodson. From I-84, take the Ainsworth State Park exit 35, and follow the eastbound Frontage Rd. From this point, continue 2½ miles until, at signs for Yeon State Park, you see a parking area on the right side of the road. It's a 2-mile roundtrip hike to Elowah Falls, with some steep switchbacks. From the same trailhead, the **McCord Creek Falls Trail** leads to the top of Elowah Falls, with views into the falls' rock bowl, and then to **McCord Creek Falls**, higher up on the same stream. The roundtrip to McCord Creek Falls is 2½ miles.

Places to Stay & Eat

None of the above sights is more than 35 miles from Portland or 25 miles from Hood River (30-45 minutes), both of which offer lots of lodging and eating options.

Ainsworth State Park (☎ 503-695-2301, 800-551-6949, Ⓦ www.oregonstateparks.org) Full hookups $20. Campers should come equipped with earplugs to this roadside spot 3 miles east of Multnomah Falls. Ainsworth Park provides easy access to trails leading to Horsetail and Elowah Falls.

McMenamin's Edgefield (☎ 503-669-8610, 888-669-8610, Ⓦ www.mcmenamins.com, 2126 SW Halsey, Troutdale) Dorm beds/singles/doubles $20/50/105. Here at the western end of the gorge, the old county poor farm has been transformed into a charming hotel. The sprawling complex includes the hotel, a vineyard, two restaurants, a brewery, a movie theater, a golf course and a pub in every corner. Edgefield's ***Power Station Pub*** is the classic place to stop for a beer and a giant plate of fries after a hike in the gorge. For dinner, the hotel's ***Black Rabbit Restaurant*** is fancier (entrees cost about $15).

CASCADE LOCKS AREA
Cascade Locks

An early transportation center and present-day summer home to the sternwheeler *Columbia Gorge,* Cascade Locks (population 1130) derives its name from the navigational locks, completed in 1896, that cut through the treacherous rapids here. The town flourished throughout the 1930s, when the area was home to thousands of Bonneville Dam construction workers. (Bonneville Lake – ie, the backed-up dam waters – flooded the rapids in 1938, and they remain submerged.)

Cascade Locks is 44 miles east of Portland on I-84, exit 44. From here, it's 19 miles east to the town of Hood River. The main street in town is Wa-Na-Pa St. Cascade Locks Visitor Center (☎ 541-374-8619) is in the Marine Park complex, about half a mile down Wa-Na-Pa St from exit 44.

The **Cascade Locks Historical Museum** (☎ *541-374-8535, Port Marina Park; admission free; open noon-5pm May-Sept),* housed in an old lockmaster's residence, features Native American artifacts and a display commemorating the early transportation history of the gorge. Also on exhibit is a fish wheel – a waterwheel-like contraption designed to harvest salmon. Fish wheels proved so successful in trapping fish in the early years of this century that they were outlawed in order to protect salmon from extinction.

Cruise the Columbia River aboard the ***Columbia Gorge*** (☎ *503-223-3928, 541-374-8427, Marine Park; adult/child 4-12 years $15/9).* Embark from the eastern end of the old lock system in Marine Park. There are three cruises daily – at 10am, 12:30pm and 3pm, from the third weekend in June to the last week in September. Besides providing an unusual vantage point from which to see Bonneville Dam and the gorge, the cruise includes historical commentary.

Windsurfing is popular in Cascade Locks. If the easterly winds are blowing, launch from the east end of Marine Park. It's also possible to catch some good westerly winds here, but the town lights up with

Unlucky ducks in Chinatown, Portland

Steam train at World Forestry Center, Portland

Farm scene on Sauvie Island, near Portland

Portland skyline from across the Willamette River, which runs right through the center of the city

Mt Hood, known to local Native Americans as Wy'east, is Oregon's highest peak.

Eagle Creek Trail, Columbia River Gorge

Multnomah Falls, Columbia River Gorge

sails on hot summer mornings when the wind blows down the river.

A couple of campgrounds, a few motels and some burger joints offer the basics. Most travelers stay in Hood River, 14 miles to the east, or across the river at elegant Skamania Lodge (see Stevenson, later in this section).

Wyeth Campground (☎ 541-386-2333, W *www.fs.fed.us/r6/columbia)* Sites $10. Take I-84 exit 51; the campsites are set back a ways from the freeway, and so it's a little quieter than the neighboring roadside campgrounds.

Econo Inn (☎ 541-374-8417, fax 541-374-8926, Columbia Gorge Center) Singles/doubles $45/50. Of the several budget motels in town, this one is the nicest.

Char Burger (☎ 541-374-8477, 714 SW Wa-Na-Pa St) Burgers $5-6. Char Burger serves good burgers and onion rings and is a local institution. Local Native Americans sometimes sell salmon in the parking lot.

Bonneville Dam

The Bonneville Dam *(☎ 541-374-8820; admission free; open 9am-5pm)* was one of the largest Depression-era New Deal projects. Completed in 1937, it was the first major dam on the Columbia River. Dam construction brought thousands of jobs, and the cheap electricity produced by the dam promised future industrial employment. Bonneville's two hydroelectric powerhouses back up the Columbia River for 15 miles and together produce over 1 million kilowatts of power.

Reach the Bradford Island Visitor Center from the Oregon side by crossing one of the two powerhouse dams. Fish ladders, which allow migrating fish to negotiate around the dams, circle the visitor center. On the main floor of the visitor center are displays of local Native American culture and the history of the dam. Downstairs, underwater windows allow visitors to watch salmon swim by. From the Washington side of the river, follow signs to the Visitor Orientation Building near the second powerhouse. From there, take a self-guided tour of the hydroelectric generation facilities or inspect another fish ladder.

Eagle Creek Recreation Area

This historic trail on the Oregon side of the Columbia Gorge makes a satisfying day hike or can be extended into a multi-day trip.

The trail passes 11 waterfalls as it meanders up wooded slopes and sheer rock walls through a narrow basalt canyon. Early gorge promoters engineered it in 1910 to coincide with the opening of the Columbia Gorge Hwy, and blasted some segments into cliff walls that hang high above Eagle Creek. These perilous ledges have no guardrails and can be dangerous for children and dogs.

It's a classic 12-mile (down and back) hike to Tunnel Falls, which passes a swimmable pool at the foot of a cliff and crosses a dizzying bridge over a 150-foot chasm before reaching a tunnel carved behind a waterfall. An overnight at 7½ Mile Camp (1½ miles past Tunnel Falls) turns a tiring day hike into an easy two-day trip. Punchbowl Falls (4.2 miles roundtrip) and High Bridge (6½ miles roundtrip) are turning points for shorter hikes.

The trail continues past Tunnel Falls for longer backcountry loops to viewpoints at Wahtum Lake and Benson Plateau,

Roll On, Columbia

In 1937, the Bonneville Power Administration (BPA) hired Woody Guthrie to write folksongs extolling the virtues of hard work and hydropower. After a month of work, he handed over 26 new songs.

Guthrie was paid $266.66 for these songs, which include the classic, *Roll On, Columbia*, now the official folksong of the state of Washington.

In 1987, Rounder Records released the *Columbia River Collection*, a compilation of these songs, most resurrected from the BPA archives and all sung by Guthrie himself.

accessible via connections with the Pacific Crest Trail, Wy'East Trail No 434 and Ruckel Creek Trail No 405.

Summer and fall are the best times to hike. Waterfalls, mossy rocks and shady trees cool the trail on hot days. Holidays and weekends can be very busy.

Just uphill from the Eagle Creek Trailhead parking lot, **Eagle Creek Campground** has views of the Columbia River and sounds of the freeway. Backpackers can find campsites just past High Bridge or near Tunnel Falls.

To reach the trailhead from eastbound I-84, take exit 41. Westbound travelers should take the Bonneville Dam exit 40, then double back for 1 mile.

Stevenson (Washington)

This town was just a windy riverside mill town until developers took a fancy to the views from the hills above town and built a toney resort.

Stevenson (population 1147) is 38 miles east of Vancouver, Washington, on Hwy 14, and 3 miles north of the **Bridge of the Gods** (75¢ toll), with access to Oregon and I-84. For local hiking and recreational information, contact the USFS Visitor Center (☎ 509-427-2528) in the lobby of Skamania Lodge (see below).

Below Skamania Lodge, the **Columbia Gorge Interpretive Center** (☎ 509-427-8211, 800-991-2338, 900 SW Rock Creek Dr; adult/senior/child 6-12 years $6/5/4; open 10am-5pm) attempts to weave together the many threads that form the area's history – Native Americans, early explorers, pioneer settlers, logging, fishing, shipping, power generation and recreation. That said, the center is perhaps most famous for its huge rosary collection.

Stevenson is a small town, with several good places to eat, and a high-end lodge.

Home Valley Park (☎ 509-427-9478, Hwy 14 milepost 50) Sites $7. The campground at this popular windsurfing beach is attractive but subject to railroad noise.

Skamania Lodge (☎ 509-427-7700, 800-221-7117, Ⓦ www.skamanialodge.citysearch .com, 1131 SW Skamania Lodge Way) Rooms $159-229. This is the gorge's biggest

and cushiest resort. Facilities include swimming pools, exercise rooms, horseback riding, hiking trails, tennis courts and an 18-hole golf course. The restaurant has dinners in the $20-30 range and emphasizes high-quality local ingredients prepared with determined eclecticism. Unfortunately, for the prices, the quality is uneven.

Big River Grill (☎ 509-427-4888, 192 SW 2nd Ave) Breakfast/lunch/dinner $6/7/13. This is a comfortable cafe with unfussy but semi-sophisticated food (ie, steelhead sandwiches).

Joe's El Rio (☎ 509-427-4479, 187 SW 2nd Ave) Dinner $10. Just across the street from the Big River Grill, you'll find good Tex-Mex cooking here, with house-smoked meats.

Beacon Rock State Park

Towering Beacon Rock is actually the core of an ancient volcano. The pleasant state park (☎ 509-427-8265, Hwy 14 milepost 35; admission free), about 7 miles west of the Bridge of the Gods, offers hiking, mountain-bike trails, picnicking, camping and river access.

The park's most obvious hike is the ascent up 848-foot Beacon Rock itself, a three-quarter-mile trail with 53 switchbacks.

A short, easygoing hike along the park's nature trail leads through a wetlands meadow to tiny Riddell Lake. For a longer, more strenuous hike, climb 2445-foot Hamilton Mountain. If you're not up to the five-hour roundtrip hike to the top, consider hiking a mile up the trail to Hardy and Rodney Falls. Trailhead parking is in the picnic area lot.

Beacon Rock is one of the few rock-climbing sites in the gorge – the rock comprising this monolith is more stable than other cliffs in the area. The majority of climbs are on the south face of Beacon Rock. The routes are for experienced climbers only.

Old logging roads wind through the state park's 4500 acres. Mountain bikers and horseback riders share these routes to the upper reaches of Hardy Creek and the back side of Hamilton Mountain. Access to the road system begins at a locked gate about half a mile up the Group Camp road.

Beacon Rock State Park's *campsites* (no hookups, $6-13) are across the road from Beacon Rock and the Columbia River in a forested area near a small stream.

Carson Hot Springs Resort

Feeling stiff and sore after days of traveling? This old-fashioned restorative spa (☎ 509-427-8292, 1 St Martin Rd; soak & wrap/massage $12/55, rooms from $35, cabins from $60; open 8am-8pm) might be just what you need. After soaking in 126°F mineral water, you're swaddled in towels to sweat out some toxins, then unrolled and massaged. The whole experience is more old-fashioned therapy than New Age spa. Weekends are busy, so call for reservations. The accommodations here are politely called 'rustic' and have no telephones or televisions. Basic meals are available in the hotel dining room.

The hot-springs complex is about half a mile north of Hwy 14, just east of Carson (3 miles east of Stevenson) on the Wind River.

Dog Mountain

It's a steep 4 miles up 2900-foot Dog Mountain, but it's the best place in the gorge for late-spring wildflowers. Once on top, the views up and down the Columbia River and over the nearby Cascade volcanoes are spectacular. Allow approximately six hours roundtrip.

To reach the trailhead, drive 9 miles east of Stevenson, near Hwy 14 milepost 54.

HOOD RIVER & AROUND

Hood River (population 5315) is the gorge's most dynamic city as well as its recreational hub. A combination of strong river currents, prevailing westerly winds and a vast body of water make the Columbia River around Hood River a windsurfing hot spot. When the conditions are right – and they frequently are in the gorge – hundreds of windsurfers (and a handful of even more daring kitesurfers) will be zipping across the wide Columbia River.

South of town, the Hood River drains a wide valley planted with orchards. During

Native American Legends of the Columbia Gorge

Native Americans living near the Columbia Gorge explained the creation of the gorge's natural features in ways that bring the waterfalls and mountains to life.

Latourell Falls The spirit of the Coyote God's wife was transformed into this beautiful waterfall to prevent her from ever leaving her husband.

Multnomah Falls A maiden princess leaped to her death from these cliffs in order to save her people from pestilence. The Great Spirit thus created the Multnomah Falls in her memory; her face appears in the shifting rainbows of mist floating from the upper falls.

Bridge of the Gods A bridge of rock, called the Bridge of the Gods, allegedly once spanned the Columbia River. It was tended by Loo-Wit, a venerable but old and homely woman. At some point during Loo-Wit's tenure, the spirit of Mt Adams, called Klickitat, and the spirit of Mt Hood, called Wy'east, fell to feuding, as they both loved the female spirit of Squaw Mountain (a lesser Cascade peak). The two volcanic peaks exploded in anger, hurling rock and fire. Finally, so many rocks were thrown between the two peaks that the Bridge of the Gods collapsed. Loo-Wit, the bridge guardian, fell with the bridge. However, the Great Spirit felt sorry for her and granted her wish to be made young and beautiful once more. She moved west from the warring peaks, where she came to rest as Mt St Helens.

Beacon Rock This rock was the final resting place of princess Wahatpolitan and her young son. The princess sought refuge on the rock when her father became angry about her marriage to an unsuitable warrior. Mother and son died atop the rock, and legend has it that you can hear the mother's grief in the howling of the winds.

OREGON

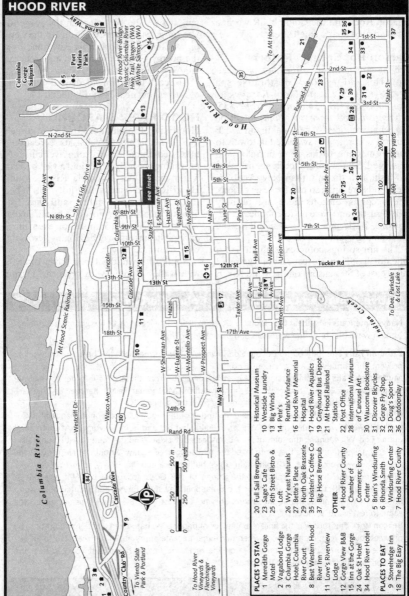

HOOD RIVER

PLACES TO STAY
1   Meredith Gorge Motel
2   Vagabond Lodge
3   Columbia Gorge Hotel; Columbia River Court
8   Best Western Hood River Inn
11 Love's Riverview Lodge
12 Gorge View B&B
15 Inn at the Gorge
24 Oak St Hotel
34 Hood River Hotel

PLACES TO EAT
9   Stonehedge Inn
18 The Big Easy
20 Full Sail Brewpub
23 Sage's Cafe
25 6th Street Bistro & Loft
26 Wy'east Naturals
27 Bette's Place
29 North Oak Brasserie
35 Holstein's Coffee Co
37 Big Horse Brewpub

OTHER
4   Hood River County Chamber of Commerce; Expo Center
5   Brian's Windsurfing
6   Rhonda Smith Windsurfing Center
7   Hood River County Historical Museum
10 Westside Laundry
13 Big Winds
14 Pete's Rentals/Windance
16 Hood River Memorial Hospital
17 Hood River Aquatics
19 Greyhound Bus Depot
21 Mt Hood Railroad Station
22 Post Office
28 International Museum of Carousel Art
30 Waucoma Bookstore
31 Discover Bicycles
32 Gorge Fly Shop
33 Doug's Sports
36 Outdoorplay

spring, the valley fills with the scent and color of pink and white blossoms. Later on, roadside fruit stands sell apples, pears, cherries, berries and vegetables. Hwy 35, which traverses the valley, continues south to Mt Hood.

Orientation & Information

Hood River is 63 miles east of Portland on I-84 and 21 miles west of The Dalles. On Hwy 35, it's 44 miles from Hood River to Government Camp on Mt Hood.

Downtown Hood River faces the Columbia River, along steeply terraced streets cut into the walls of the gorge. I-84 exit 63 puts you onto 2nd St, which crosses the rail lines to intersect with Oak St, the town's lively main street.

The Hood River County Chamber of Commerce (☎ 541-386-2000, 800-366-3530) is adjacent to the Expo Center at 405 Portway Ave.

You'll find the post office on 4th St at Cascade Ave. Waucoma Bookstore (☎ 541-386-5353), 212 Oak St, is a good bookstore with a strong regional travel section. Oregon Public Radio is heard at 94.3 FM.

Westside Laundry (☎ 541-386-5650) is close to downtown at 1911 Cascade Ave. Hood River Memorial Hospital (☎ 541-386-3911) is at the corner of 13th and May Sts.

Things to See & Do

The **Hood River County Historical Museum** (☎ 541-386-6772, Port Marina Park; admission free; open 10am-4pm Mon-Sat, noon-4pm Sun) includes Native American artifacts, pioneer quilts and early logging equipment among its displays.

The **Mt Hood Scenic Railroad** (☎ 541-386-3556, 800-872-4661, ₩ www.mthoodrr.com, 110 Railroad Ave; fare adult/senior/child $23/21/15; schedule varies, but 4-hour excursions depart most days at 10am), built in 1906, once transported fruit and lumber from the upper Hood River valley to the main railhead in Hood River. The vintage trains now operate between the Blossom Festival (late April) and Harvest Fest (fall) as a scenic excursion through the valley, beneath Mt Hood's snowy peak and past fragrant orchards. Trains depart

from the station, right under the viaduct between I-84 exit 63 (2nd St) and downtown Hood River. The train stops in Parkdale, a farm and orchard town south of Hood River with antique stores and a couple of cafes. Saturday evening dinner ($70) and Sunday morning brunch ($56) are served on special train runs. Call ahead for reservations.

Antique carousel animals, a Wurlitzer organ, and steam engines are all on display at the **International Museum of Carousel Art** (☎ 541-387-4622, 304 Oak St; adult/senior/child under 10 years $5/4/2; open noon-5pm Wed-Sun). Besides showcasing the carousel art, the museum staff is always busy restoring old merry-go-rounds.

Some good wines are being made from local grapes. **Hood River Vineyards** (☎ 541-386-3772, 4693 Westwood Dr; admission free; open 11am-5pm Mar-Nov) and **Flerchinger Vineyards** (☎ 541-386-2882, 4200 Post Canyon Dr; admission free; open 11am-5pm) offer wine tasting. Both are found off Country Club Rd, west of Hood River.

The postcard photo of Mt Hood from 240-acre **Lost Lake** – the white mountain peak rising from a deep-blue lake amid a thick green forest – is probably the most famous image of Oregon's most famous volcano. This side trip onto the northern flanks of Mt Hood offers relief when the gorge gets hot. To reach Lost Lake, take Hwy 281 south from Hood River to Dee. Signs will point to Lost Lake Rd; the lake is 25 miles south of Hood River. **Canoe rentals** are available at the resort here.

Go **fishing** for steelhead trout, which run throughout the year in the Hood River; the summer run is especially good. Visit the **Gorge Fly Shop** (☎ 541-386-6977, 201 Oak St; $8 for a 1-day license) for up-to-date information, tackle and licenses.

Head south of town for great **mountain biking**. Most of the area's trails are off Hwy 35 and Forest Rd 44 (which branches off Hwy 35 about 20 miles south of Hood River). The 5-mile East Fork Trail connecting Sherwood and Robinhood Campgrounds is a fairly easy ride. **Discover**

OREGON

Bicycles *(☎ 541-386-4820, 205 Oak St; $30-50 per day)* rents mountain bikes.

Bikers, walkers, runners and skaters share the pavement on the refurbished stretch of the Historic Columbia River Hwy between Hood River and Mosier. No cars are permitted on the 4½-mile road, which passes through two old highway tunnels and is popular with families. To reach the trailhead, head east out of downtown, cross Hwy 35, and continue up the hill to the parking area (there's a $3 parking fee).

For white-water kayaking, head to the White Salmon, Hood, or Klickitat Rivers. It

Windsurfing

Twenty years ago, the wind was just a nuisance. West winds in the summer and east winds in the winter meant messy hair year round. Now, in the windsurfing era, folks read the river and sky for wind and listen for wind reports on the local radio stations.

No matter what the wind reports say, the cardinal rule of windsurfing is 'Never leave wind to find wind.' A fairly reliable way to find wind is to look at the sky and find the place where clouds end and the sun begins – this is usually the windiest spot. Or, get on the computer and check out the excellent Wind Cam reports at W www.windance.com.

In summer, winds tend to shoot up the gorge from the cool coastal west to the hot, dry east. These westerlies, which directly oppose the river's flow, creating optimal surfing conditions, are generally strongest at the eastern end of the gorge. Viento State Park is a good place to stop and check the wind. **Swell City**, the **Spring Creek Fish Hatchery** and **Doug's Beach State Park** are Washington-side sites with reliably strong west winds. Experienced windsurfers head upriver, where there are a couple of heavy-duty sites near Maryhill. **Maryhill State Park** has a fairly unappealing campground, free parking and a spacious beach to complement the strong river current and strong west winds. Just upriver, **The Wall** is a small launch spot that attracts expert windsurfers who can handle huge swells.

Wintertime east winds shift the focus to the western end of the gorge, where **Rooster Rock State Park** and the Cascade Locks marina both provide good river access and strong easterlies.

If you're new to big wind, try setting out from the Hood River marina or Rhonda's, just to the east. The wind's not quite as gusty in these somewhat sheltered spots. Another fairly protected beach is across the river at Home Valley, where the west winds are relatively gentle. A very popular spot for beginners is The Dalles' Riverfront Park, with a long, sandy shoreline, light west winds and a fairly smooth stretch of river.

Many of these sites, especially on the Oregon side, have a $3 parking fee.

If you've never windsurfed, it really helps to take a lesson. **Rhonda Smith Windsurfing Center** *(☎ 541-386-9463, Port Marina Park, Hood River)* has a two-day beginners' class for $125, including equipment. **Brian's Windsurfing** *(☎ 888-386-1121, Port Marina Park, Hood River)* offers three-hour lessons for $60. **Gorge Wind Guide Service** *(☎ 541-490-4401 W www.windguide.com)*, in Hood River, offers advanced windsurfing instruction and transportation to the day's windiest launch sites.

Rent equipment in Hood River from **Big Winds** *(☎ 541-386-6086, 207 Front St)*, **Pete's Rentals** *(☎ 541-387-4455, next to Windance at 108 Hwy 35)* or **Doug's Sports** *(☎ 541-386-5787, 101 Oak St)*. A full rig for a day costs $40-65.

costs $55 for a trip on the White Salmon River with **Phil's White Water Adventure** (☎ 509-493-2641, 800-366-2004, 38 Northwestern Lake, White Salmon). In Hood River, **Outdoorplay** (☎ 541-386-4286, 877-725-2925, 6 Oak St; $35) rents kayaks.

You can go swimming at the **Hood River Aquatics Center** (☎ 541-386-1303, 1601 May St; $2.50).

Special Events
The Hood River valley springs to life the third weekend of April with the Blossom Festival (☎ 541-386-2000). Orchard tours are the highlight, supplemented by food, music, and crafts.

Mid-July brings the Gorge Games (☎ 541-386-7774), a weeklong extravaganza of windsurfing, mountain biking, kayaking and a host of other outdoor sports. Competitions are wide-open, age-group events. There are also instructional clinics, kids' events and concerts.

Held the second weekend of October, the Hood River Harvest Fest (☎ 541-386-2000) celebrates the valley's agricultural bounty with local crafts, food and musical entertainment at the Hood River Expo Center, along the riverfront.

Places to Stay
Camping The closest public campsites are squeezed between the highway and the railroad tracks 8 miles west of Hood River, at **Viento State Park** (☎ 541-374-8811, 800-551-6949, W www.oregonstateparks.org, exit 56 from I-84) Sites $16-18. The closest public campsites are squeezed between the highway and the railroad tracks 8 miles west of Hood River. The park also has good river access for windsurfers.

Hostels There is one hostel option in the area.

Bingen School Inn (☎ 509-493-3363, W www.bsi-cgoc.com, cnr Cedar & Franklin Sts) Dorm beds/doubles $14/35-50. Across the Columbia River in Bingen, Washington, this is the area's best lodging value and has a quirky atmosphere. It's a cross between a hostel and an inn and is housed in an old elementary school built by the Civilian Conservation Corps (CCC) in 1938. Lodgings are in the old classrooms, and there's a large common area with kitchen access, a gym, a weight room and rock-climbing walls.

B&Bs Though there's no formal booking agency in Hood River, local B&B owners take turns answering the phone at Room-Finder (☎ 541-386-6767) and will help you find a B&B that'll suit your needs.

Gorge View B&B (☎ 541-386-5770, e gorgeview@gorge.net, 1009 Columbia St; open May-Oct) Bed $35 in bunkroom, singles/doubles $69/79. Meet up with windsurfers, mountain bikers and snowboarders at this B&B. Everybody mingles at breakfast or in the hot tub.

Inn at the Gorge (☎ 541-386-4429, W www.innatthegorge.com, 1113 Eugene St) Rooms $85-105. This is an attractive 1908 home with wide porches. Three of the four rooms have kitchenettes and separate guest entrances.

Motels Hood River's accommodations run the gamut, from budget motel to elegant resort hotel.

Vagabond Lodge (☎ 541-386-2992, 877-386-2992, W www.vagabondlodge.com, 4070 Westcliff Dr) Singles/doubles $45/55. This motel is between the freeway and the river, next to the swanky Columbia Gorge Hotel. Take an evening stroll through the fancier hotel's gardens.

Meredith Gorge Motel (☎ 541-386-1515, e meredithmotel@gorge.net, 4300 Westcliff Dr) Singles/doubles $59/69. A little farther west on the same road as the Vagabond, this motel has renovated its rooms to their 1950s style.

Hood River Hotel (☎ 541-386-1900, 800-386-1859, W www.hoodriverhotel.com, 102 Oak St) Rooms $50-165. This classy 1913 hotel is right in the heart of downtown.

Oak St Hotel (☎ 541-386-3845, e dsllngr@aol.com, 610 Oak St) Singles/doubles $55/67. This small 1910 hotel is right on the edge of downtown. It's been nicely remodeled, and several rooms have river views.

Love's Riverview Lodge *(☎ 541-386-8719, 800-789-9568,* **W** *www.lovesriverview.com, 1505 Oak St)* Rooms from $65. Within walking distance of downtown, Love's has standard rooms and suites with kitchens.

Best Western Hood River Inn *(☎ 541-386-2200, 800-828-7873,* **W** *www.hoodriverinn.com, 1108 E Marina Way)* Singles/doubles $69/79, $89/99 with river view. This is the only motel in town with its own beach. There's also an outdoor pool.

Columbia Gorge Hotel *(☎ 541-386-5566, 800-345-1921,* **W** *www.columbiagorgehotel.com, 4000 Westcliff Dr)* Rooms $160-280. If you're looking for a classy, romantic place to stay in Hood River, and you don't mind dropping big bucks, try this Spanish-style hotel, built in 1921 by one of the early backers of the Columbia River Hwy. The grounds are as lovely as the building.

Places to Eat
Downtown Hood River is peppered with inexpensive cafes.

Bette's Place *(☎ 541-386-1880, 416 Oak St)* Breakfast $3-6. Windsurfers and old-timers all hunker down over breakfast here. Stop by for a muffin to go if you don't have time for a big meal.

Holstein's Coffee Co *(☎ 541-386-4115, 12 Oak St)* Lunch $6. This is a great place for coffee, pastries and sandwiches.

Sage's Cafe *(☎ 541-386-9404, 202 Cascade Ave)* Breakfast & lunch $3-6. Locals crowd this place at lunchtime to munch on the tasty sandwiches.

Full Sail Brewpub *(☎ 541-386-2281, 506 Columbia St)* Bar food $5. There are nice views and good beer at this fruit-cannery-turned-brewpub but only a mere nod toward food.

Big Horse Brewpub *(☎ 541-386-4411, 115 State St)* Sandwiches $7. Climb the long flight of stairs to this hillside brewpub, then quench your thirst with a microbrew. The food and beer are both good.

The Big Easy *(☎ 541-386-1970, 1302 B St)* Dinners about $12. A little bit of New Orleans in Hood River, this place is relaxed, with really good appetizers and reasonably good dinners.

North Oak Brasserie *(☎ 541-387-2310, 113 3rd St)* Dinner $12-18. Descend the stairs to this cavelike bistro, where you can come for good Italian food, then linger to explore the extensive wine list.

6th Street Bistro & Loft *(☎ 541-386-5737, 509 Cascade Ave)* Entrees $10-12. Eat here when you can't bear to be inside. There's a garden dining area, and the food ranges from burgers and salads to full dinners.

Stonehedge Inn *(☎ 541-386-3940, 3405 Cascade Ave)* Standard/'lite' dinner $20-28/9-15. Head up the long gravel drive to this homey restaurant in a wooded grove. The standard menu is, well, standard. The 'lite' menu is more interesting. The food and wine are both very good.

Columbia River Court *(☎ 541-386-5566, in the Columbia Gorge Hotel, 4000 Westcliff Dr)* Breakfast/dinner $27/25. By far the most famous meal served in this beautiful river-view dining room is the 'Farm Breakfast.' The multicourse extravaganza will leave you wondering what farmer could have conceived of such a bounty (or could afford it). Reservations are a must.

Getting There & Around
Greyhound (☎ 541-386-1212), 1205 B St, runs four direct buses a day to/from Portland ($11, 1¼ hours, 64 miles). Amtrak's *Empire Builder* stops at Bingen ($10, 1¾ hours), on the Washington side of the gorge, daily along its Portland-Spokane leg.

Call Hood River Taxi (☎ 541-386-2255) for a cab.

THE DALLES & AROUND
Though specific translations vary, it seems likely that French Canadian trappers named The Dalles (population 12,175) after the troughlike shape of the Columbia River just upstream from town, which they may have associated with the stones used to pave gutters back home (the name is French for 'flagstones').

With the discovery of gold and the establishment of agriculture in eastern Oregon, white settlers came to view The Dalles in the same way Native Americans long had – as an important trade town and transportation point.

Today, The Dalles continues its legacy as a transportation hub. The area is also the nation's largest producer of sweet cherries. Despite all the nearby recreation, The Dalles remains steadfastly unglamorous and down-to-earth.

Orientation & Information

The Dalles is 84 miles east of Portland along I-84. US 197 cuts south from The Dalles to Bend, 131 miles away. The Dalles Bridge crosses the Columbia River to link up with Hwy 14 in Washington.

The main business district lies along 2nd and 3rd Sts, both of which are one way. Court St divides the town into east and west.

South of downtown, The Dalles is built on a series of steep terraces, with rocky outcroppings jutting up in the middle of streets and in people's backyards. Ask for a walking tour map at the visitor center; it's worth the walk to see the fins and ledges of rock incorporated into streets and gardens.

The Dalles Chamber of Commerce (☎ 541-296-2231, 800-255-3385) is at 404 W 2nd St. The post office is at 100 W 2nd St. Klindt's Bookseller & Stationers (☎ 541-296-3355), 315 E 2nd St, has been in operation since 1870 and still has an old-fashioned atmosphere. Tune in to Oregon Public Radio at 91.5 FM.

The Mid-Columbia Medical Center (☎ 541-296-1111) is at 1700 E 19th St.

Columbia Gorge Discovery Center

This museum (☎ 541-296-8600, 5000 Discovery Dr; adult/senior/child 6-16 years $6.50/ 5.50/3.50; open 10am-6pm mid-Mar–Dec, 10am-4pm Tues-Sat Jan–mid-Mar) combines a striking riverbank setting and dramatic architecture, with indoor and outdoor exhibits that focus on the land and what people have made of it.

In the main foyer, the Columbia River is mapped in granite, inlaid in the tile floor. A large, three-dimensional model of the un-dammed river is filled with rushing water; push a button, and The Dalles Dam rises up, stilling and pooling the water.

The Discovery Center is on the western edge of The Dalles. From the west, take exit 82 off I-84, turn right onto the Historic Columbia River Hwy (US 30) and go 1½ miles, then turn right at the sign onto Discovery Dr. From the east, take exit 84 onto W 2nd St, turn left at the first light onto W 6th St, continue for 3 miles and then turn right at the sign onto Discovery Dr.

Fort Dalles Museum

This museum (☎ 541-296-4547, 500 W 15th St; adult $3, child & student free; open 10:30am-5pm Mon-Fri, 10am-5pm Sat & Sun Mar-Oct; 1pm-4pm Wed-Fri, 10am-4pm Sat & Sun winter) is at the corner of W 15th and Garrison Sts. (From downtown, signs point the way uphill.) Established in 1850, Fort Dalles was meant to protect the incoming Oregon Trail settlers from the local Native Americans. Of the original 10-sq-mile encampment, only a grassy park with the surgeon's quarters remains.

Rock Fort

Lewis and Clark camped at this naturally fortified indentation in the rocky riverbank. The corps must have presented a curious spectacle to the Native Americans who gathered around them. At Celilo Falls, the explorers had become infested with fleas. Lewis wrote the following in his journal:

The fleas are very troublesom and dificuelt to get rid of, perticularly as the men have not a Change of Clothes to put on, they strip off their Clothes and kill the flees, dureing which time they remain nakid.

To reach Rock Fort from downtown, follow US 30 west (it becomes W 6th St). Turn right on Webber St and drive toward the river into an industrial area. Turn right on 1st St and continue half a mile to a sign pointing to a parking area. There's not much interpretive information at Rock Fort, but Lewis-and-Clark buffs will enjoy it.

The Dalles Dam & Lock

The Dalles Dam, built in 1957, produces enough electricity to power a city the size of Seattle. Access to this power came at a price, however. The dam's reservoir, Lake Celilo, flooded the culturally rich area around Celilo Falls, which was for thousands of years a Native American meeting place and fishery.

Dam tours begin at two points. In Seufert Park, east on the frontage road from I-84 exit 87, is **The Dalles Dam Visitor Center** *(☎ 541-296-9778, Clodfelter Way; 9am-5pm June-Labor Day weekend)*. This small museum and information center contains the usual homage to hydroelectricity, along with exhibits on local history. From here, a small train (no charge) leaves every half-hour to visit the dam itself.

To skip the train ride, take I-84 exit 88 directly to The Dalles Dam. The self-guided tour of the turbines and the powerhouse is available 9am to 5pm weekdays year round.

Horsethief Lake State Park

Some of the most famous remaining **pictographs** along the Columbia River are at this Washington state park *(☎ 509-767-1159, Hwy 14 milepost 85; open Apr-Oct)*, just across from The Dalles. *Tsagaglalal,* or 'She Who Watches,' is the most widely known image: an owl-like female presence presiding over the river.

The pictograph area can be visited only on a free guided tour, at 10am Friday and Saturday. Reservations are required; call the park at least a few days in advance.

Rock climbers practice their moves on the basalt walls of **Horsethief Butte**, just east of the park entrance, and this section of the Columbia River is a good place for beginning windsurfers to catch some wind without strong river currents. Horsethief Lake State Park also offers fishing and swimming in the lake, as well as camping (see Places to Stay) and hiking.

Rowena Crest

Between Hood River and The Dalles, the heavy vegetation of the western gorge diminishes, and the basaltic architecture of the gorge appears.

On top of Rowena Crest are spectacular views and vast meadows now preserved as a wildflower sanctuary. Established by the Nature Conservancy, the **Governor Tom McCall Reserve**, on Rowena Plateau, is one of the best places to see native plants. Spring time wildflowers include balsamroot, wild parsley, penstemons and wild lilies. Watch out for poison oak.

To reach this section of the Historic Columbia River Hwy from The Dalles, follow W 6th St westward out of town until it becomes US 30. From the west, take I-84 exit 69 at Mosier, and travel east on US 30.

Windsurfing

Hood River may be the gorge's windsurfing capital, but the wind blows at The Dalles too. Right in town, **Riverfront Park** (exit 85) is a good spot for beginners. **Avery Park**, 4 miles upriver from Horsethief Lake State Park, offers access to the river from the Washington side. A favorite entry point, with strong west winds, is **Celilo Park**, 9 miles east of town.

Special Events

The Dalles' biggest summer event is Fort Dalles Day *(☎ 541-296-6616, 800-255-3385)*, held the second weekend of July. There's a parade and chili cook-off, but the main attraction is the PRCA Rodeo. Call for details and rodeo tickets.

Places to Stay

The closest public campground to The Dalles is *Horsethief Lake State Park* *(☎ 509-767-1159,* Ⓦ *www.parks.wa.gov, Hwy 14 milepost 85; open Apr-Oct)* Sites $13. Expect to hear trains passing in the night and wind gusting in the tent flaps. The park is located across The Dalles Bridge in Washington, 2 miles east on Hwy 14 from the junction with US 197. See Deschutes River Recreation Area, later, for more The Dalles–area campsites.

Not all B&Bs are fussy, frilly places. Take *Columbia Windrider Inn* *(☎ 541-296-2607, 800-635-0051,* Ⓦ *www.windriderinn.com,*

200 W 4th St) Rooms $40-50. It's a casual but tidy inn catering to windsurfers and other sports enthusiasts. Rates include use of the swimming pool, hot tub, pool table and kitchen.

Best Eastern Oregon Motor Motel *(☎ 541-296-9111, 200 W 2nd St)* Singles/doubles $40/46. This rather basic downtown motel does have a pool.

Best Western River City Inn *(☎ 541-296-9107, 800-722-8277,* Ⓦ *www.bestwesternoregon.com, 112 W 2nd St)* Singles/doubles $54/59. This is the nicest lodging downtown. It also has a pool.

Lyle Hotel *(☎ 509-365-5953,* Ⓦ *www.lylehotel.com, 100 7th St, Lyle, WA)* Singles/doubles $49/59. If you'd rather not stay right in The Dalles, cross the river and head 8 miles west on Hwy 14 to the tiny riverside town of Lyle, where this old hotel has been nicely restored. Don't expect televisions, phones or private bathrooms – come instead for the friendly owners, the good dinners (see below) and the relaxing atmosphere.

Places to Eat

Holstein's Coffee Co *(☎ 541-298-2326, 811 E 3rd St)* Sandwiches $6. Here's a good coffee stop at the east end of downtown. Stop in for morning coffee, and you may be back for lunchtime sandwich.

Burgerville USA *(☎ 541-298-5753, 118 W 3rd St)* Meals $5-8. Sometimes only fast food will do. And if that's your eating strategy, stop here. Burgerville is a local chain, and the food is far better than what you get from their larger competitors. When strawberries are in season, order the fresh berry shake.

Baldwin Saloon *(☎ 541-296-5666, 205 Court St)* Dinner $15. In its 120-year history, this place has been a bar, a brothel, a saddlery and a warehouse. Now it's back to its original purpose, serving up good food and strong drinks.

Lyle Hotel *(☎ 509-365-5953,* Ⓦ *www.lylehotel.com, 100 7th St, Lyle, WA; open Wed-Sat 5pm-9pm, Sun 10am-3pm)* Dinner & brunch $14. Head over to the Washington side of the river for some of the area's best

dinners and a fine selection of local wines. (See also Places to Stay.)

Getting There & Around

Greyhound's depot *(☎ 541-296-2421)* is at 201 1st St. Buses travel along I-84 to Portland ($16, 1¾ hours, 98 miles, 4 daily) and along US 97 to Bend ($21, 4 hours, 145 miles). Amtrak stops at Wishram, on the Washington side of the Columbia River, every day on its way to/from Portland ($18, 2¼ hours). There's no bus connection from Wishram to The Dalles – call White Lion Cab *(☎ 541-296-6299)* for taxi service.

For car rentals in The Dalles, contact Brace Bros Rent-a-Car *(☎ 541-296-3761)*, at 1119 W 2nd St.

EASTERN GORGE
Deschutes River State Recreation Area

The Deschutes River, Oregon's second largest, cuts through central Oregon on its way to this state park *(☎ 541-739-2322,* Ⓦ *www.oregonstateparks.org, south of Hwy 206 on the Deschutes River)* Primitive sites/hookups/riverfront/covered wagon $12/17/19/27. Camp riverside at this state park, or play out your Oregon Trail fantasies by sleeping in a covered wagon. This is a popular spot during spring and summer weekends, so make reservations early.

Rafting parties take out here after the four-day ride down the Deschutes from Sherar's Bridge (see Lower Deschutes Canyon, in the Central Oregon chapter). Hikers can explore the east side of the river's desert canyon. Watch for raptors and migrating songbirds. This is a great place to find sage-scented warmth and sun, in spring especially, when western Oregon is wet and dank.

From the south end of the park, riverside **hiking trails** pass old homesteads, springs and groves of willow and locust trees.

A **mountain-biking trail** starts near the park entrance and runs some 25 miles upriver, though after the 11-mile point, there are often big washouts. This path was the rail bed for the Deschutes Railroad

Company, which attempted but failed to build a line to Bend in the early 1900s.

Trails follow the Deschutes for 12 miles from its mouth on the Columbia River, allowing anglers to hike into remote **fishing holes**. Summer steelhead fishing is very good along this stretch. At the mouth of the river, where it meets Lake Celilo, there's good fishing for walleye, steelhead and sturgeon.

Maryhill Museum

Eccentric Sam Hill is responsible for some of the most famous building projects in the gorge, not the least of which is this museum (☎ 509-773-3733, 35 Maryhill Museum Dr, WA; adult/child $5/1.50; open 9am-5pm Mar-Nov). Located on a bluff overlooking the gorge, this place is known for its quirky collections and is the perfect focus for a day trip – or a great break from I-84.

The collections include Native American baskets, carvings, tools and other cultural items. There is also one of the world's largest collections of chess sets. An American dancer with ties to Parisian artists helped Hill obtain a collection of French drawings and sculpture by a then-unheralded artist

named Auguste Rodin – including a cast of *The Thinker.*

Among the museum's curiosities is a collection of French fashion dolls. In 1945, some of Paris's top fashion houses, seeking to revitalize the industry, sewed haute-couture clothing for a traveling display. Artists of the time, including Jean Cocteau, painted backdrops for the dolls, and special music was composed to accompany the viewing.

The museum is 10 miles south of Goldendale, Washington, on US 97, and 22 miles east of The Dalles, along I-84. Cross the US 97 bridge and look up; you can't miss it.

Stonehenge

Not one for small gestures, Sam Hill built a full-scale replica of Salisbury Plain's Stonehenge a few miles from Maryhill on the cliffs above the Columbia River. Dedicated as a memorial to Klickitat County's WWI dead, his Stonehenge was built of poured concrete and was constructed to represent the site as it was when it stood intact (unlike its tumbled-down English cousin).

Hill planned that his Stonehenge would line up for celestial events such as equinoxes, but many local Stonehenge scholars think

What in the Sam Hill...?

In the 1880s, Sam Hill was an impertinent young Minneapolis lawyer whose reputation was made in part by his success in bringing legal suits against the Great Northern Railroad. Great Northern mogul James Hill (no relation at the time) decided to co-opt the young attorney. He brought Sam into the company, and soon into his family: Sam wooed and married James' daughter Mary.

Sam Hill then turned toward a life of good works. His great contribution to the Northwest was the Columbia River Hwy, the region's first paved road and a wonder of engineering and scenic value. Hill worked closely with Oregon businessmen and state officials to promote the road.

At the same time that the highway was being built, Hill began construction of a country home at the top of an 800-foot cliff along the Columbia River. Ever an idealist, Hill hoped that the estate would be home to him and his wife (who refused to live in this godforsaken country) and the center of a utopian Quaker farm community.

The Maryhill Castle, as it was then called, was supposed to resemble a French country chateau. Hill's plans began to fall apart when his wife returned to her beloved Philadelphia and when the imported Belgian Quakers found the desiccated cliff sides unsuitable for agriculture. His enthusiasm for the project flagged, and the building was not completed until 1926, when his friend, Queen Marie of Romania, came to the USA to dedicate Maryhill as a museum. However, the museum did not open to the public until 1940.

the keystone is in the wrong place. At any rate, this is a popular place for odd rites and ceremonies.

To reach Sam Hill's Stonehenge from Maryhill, continue east on Hwy 14 past the US 97 junction. One mile later, follow signs to the right for Stonehenge.

Goldendale (Washington)

Up over the escarpment of the gorge, on a fertile plateau beneath forested hills and distant Mt Adams, lies Goldendale (population 3570). It is 31 miles northeast of The Dalles and about 10 miles north of the Columbia River on US 97. The climb up out of the gorge on US 97 is long and steep; vehicles prone to overheating will surely do so, especially on summer days. You can write the Goldendale Chamber of Commerce (☎ 509-773-3400, ẹ ggcc@gorge .net), PO Box 524, Goldendale, WA 98620. During the summer, there's an informational kiosk near the entrance to Maryhill State Park.

The main reason to come here is the **Goldendale Observatory State Park** (☎ 509-773-3141, 1602 Observatory Dr; admission free; open 2pm-5pm, 8pm-midnight Wed-Sun Apr-Sept; 1pm-5pm Sat & Sun, 7pm-9pm Sat Oct-Mar). Located on an old volcanic cone just north of town, this is home to a 24½-inch reflecting telescope, one of the largest available to the public in the USA. Plan an evening visit, when programs include videos, slide presentations and talks. Depending on what's going on astronomically, there are also views through the telescope to planets, galaxies, stars and comets.

Though there are a couple of inexpensive motels in Goldendale, it's more pleasant to stay just a few miles out of town.

Brooks Memorial State Park (☎ 509-773-4611, ẉ www.parks.wa.gov, 2465 US 97) Standard sites/hookups $13/19. Campers should head 13 miles north of Goldendale on US 97 to this woodsy park on the Little Klickitat River. It's just off the highway, making it convenient, if not absolutely idyllic. Hiking trails start at the park and head up the Little Klickitat.

Three Creeks Resort (☎ 509-773-3325, 2120 US 97) Cabins from $49. This resort in the Simcoe Mountains, 8 miles north of town, has spanking new cabins tucked under the pine trees. The restaurant in the lodge is a good place for a steak dinner, about $15.

But don't go to Goldendale looking for a culinary experience. In fact, it's worth knowing that the resort store near Brooks Memorial State Park has good sandwiches.

Ayutla Mexican Restaurant (☎ 509-773-7188, 630 Simcoe Dr) Entrees $8. This restaurant at the Simcoe St exit off US 97 is convenient, inexpensive and popular with the locals.

Mt Hood

The state's highest peak, Mt Hood (11,240 feet), pops into view over much of northern Oregon whenever there's a sunny day and exerts an almost magnetic tug on skiers, hikers and sightseers. Five downhill ski areas and Timberline Lodge, a well-crafted gem from the 1930s, make up most of the development here...the rest is just the mountain. Cross-country skiing and snowshoeing are popular in the winter, and in summer, hikers head to hidden lakes and wildflower meadows.

Mt Hood rises above the Western Cascades, a ridge of older volcanoes stretching between Mt Rainier and Mt Shasta. These volcanoes erupted between 20 and 40 million years ago, and their peaks have long since eroded. Mt Hood began to erupt toward the end of the last Ice Age, and there have been many more recent eruptions. The peak's conical shape is evidence that new lava flows have repaired whatever damage Pleistocene-era glaciers – which retreated about 10,000 years ago – had done. Geologists reckon that Mt Hood's last major eruption was about 1000 years ago, although Native Americans and early settlers both reported small eruptions in the 1800s.

Mt Hood was known to local Native Americans as Wy'east. In 1792, English Captain William Broughton sailed up the

OREGON

Columbia River as far as Crown Point and sighted the peak, which he named after a British admiral, Lord Samuel Hood.

Orientation

Mt Hood is accessible year round on US 26 from Portland, and from Hood River on Hwy 35. Together with the Columbia River Hwy, these routes comprise the Mt Hood Loop, a popular scenic drive. Government Camp is at the pass over Mt Hood, and – such as it is – constitutes the center of business on the mountain. From Portland, it's 56 miles east to Government Camp; from

Hood River, it's 44 miles south. US 26 continues on to Madras, 40 miles farther on, and Bend.

Most facilities for travelers are on the western side of Mt Hood; these serve Portlanders as they zip back and forth on US 26.

Information

The Mt Hood Area Chamber of Commerce and the USFS office are at the Mt Hood Information Center (☎ 503-622-4822, 888-622-4822, ⓦ www.fs.fed.us/r6/mthood/winter, 65000 E US 26, Welches). This is the place to obtain maps, permits, advice and informa-

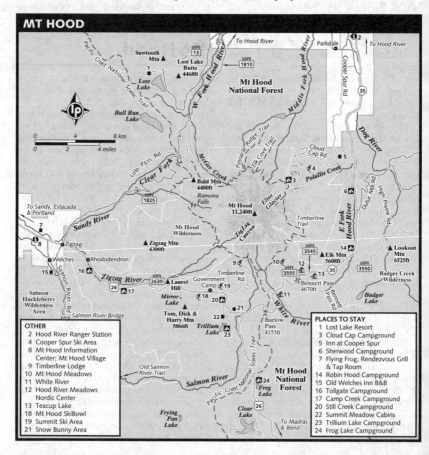

MT HOOD

To Hood River

Parkdale   To Hood River

Sawtooth Mtn ▲
USFS 13
Lost Lake Butte ▲ 4468ft
1 ■

W Fork Hood River   *Middle Fork Hood River*

USFS 1810

Cooper Spur Rd

Mt Hood National Forest

35

Lost Lake

Bull Run Lake

Pacific Crest National Scenic Trail

Lolo Pass Rd

Clear Fork

Pinnacle Ridge Trail   *Elk Cove Trail*

McGee Creek

Cloud Cap Rd

Cloud Cap 4 ▲

3 ▲

Polallie Creek

5 ■

Dog River

6 ▲

Dutch Mill

E Fork Hood River

High Prairie Rd

▲ Bald Mtn 4400ft
Ramona Falls

USFS 1825

Mt Hood 11,240ft
Eliot Glacier

ZigZag Canyon

Timberline Trail

To Sandy, Estacada & Portland

Sandy River

7 ■
8 ●
● Zigzag
● Welches   ● Rhododendron

Mt Hood Wilderness

▲ Zigzag Mtn 4300ft

USFS 3545
14 ▲

▲ Elk Mtn 5608ft

▲ Lookout Mtn 6525ft

USFS 3550

Salmon River Rd

15 ■   16 ●
Zigzag River
USFS 2639 ▲ Laurel Hill

9 ●
10 ●
USFS 3555
12
35

USFS 3555

Bennett Pass 4670ft

Badger Creek Wilderness

Bennett Pass Rd

26 ▲ 17

Timberline Rd
Government Camp
19 ●

18 ●
20 ▲

Mirror Lake

11 ▲

White River

Badger Lake

Salmon Huckleberry Wilderness Area

Salmon River Bridge

Tom, Dick & Harry Mtn 5066ft

22 ■
21 ●
Trillium Lake 23

Barlow Pass 4155ft

OTHER
2 Hood River Ranger Station
4 Cooper Spur Ski Area
8 Mt Hood Information Center; Mt Hood Village
9 Timberline Lodge
10 Mt Hood Meadows
11 White River
12 Hood River Meadows Nordic Center
13 Teacup Lake
18 Mt Hood SkiBowl
19 Summit Ski Area
21 Snow Bunny Area

Old Salmon River Trail

Salmon River

Pacific Crest National Scenic Trail

24 ▲
Frog Lake

Mt Hood National Forest

Clear Lake 26

To Madras & Bend

Frying Pan Lake

PLACES TO STAY
1 Lost Lake Resort
3 Cloud Cap Campground
5 Inn at Cooper Spur
6 Sherwood Campground
7 Flying Frog; Rendezvous Grill & Tap Room
14 Robin Hood Campground
15 Old Welches Inn B&B
16 Tollgate Campground
17 Camp Creek Campground
20 Still Creek Campground
22 Summit Meadow Cabins
23 Trillium Lake Campground
24 Frog Lake Campground

0   4   8 km
0 2   4 miles

LP

tion about ski trails; it is open 7:45am to 4:30pm daily except holidays.

Government Camp has the mountain's most convenient post office (☎ 503-272-3238), 88331 E Government Camp Loop.

The pass at Mt Hood receives a lot of snow, and winter travelers should check on road conditions before starting up the mountain. For up-to-date road conditions, call the Oregon Department of Transportation (☎ 800-977-6368) or look through its online road cameras at W www.tripcheck.com.

The Hood River Ranger Station (☎ 541-352-6002, 6780 Hwy 35, Parkdale) is open 8am to 4:30pm weekdays Labor Day to Memorial Day, same hours and daily the rest of the year.

Skiing & Tubing

Downhill It's easiest to rent downhill skis at ski areas.

Mt Hood Meadows (☎ 503-337-2222, snowphone ☎ 503-227-7669, W www.ski hood.com, Hwy 35, Mt Hood; adult lift tickets day/night $43/20, child 7-12 years $25/20) is the largest ski area on Mt Hood and usually has the best conditions, as it's on the sunnier, drier side of the mountain. It also has Mt Hood's most varied terrain, with 20% of its runs rated 'advanced.' Expert skiers and boarders can head into the steep, wild and utterly beautiful Heather Canyon. Weekend excursions from Portland including lift tickets are $50/40 adult/child; for details, call ☎ 503-287-5438. Facilities include two-day lodges with a handful of snack bars and restaurants; rentals and lessons are easily available.

The legendary **Timberline Lodge** (☎ 503-622-0717, snowphone ☎ 503-222-2211, W www .timberlinelodge.com, Timberline, Mt Hood; lift tickets adult/child $37/21) is renowned for its year-round skiing (lifts shut down for maintenance during September). Ski teams and snowboarders from all over the world flock here for summer training. Timberline has good intermediate skiing and usually has the mountain's deepest snow. Reduced prices for ski lifts are sometimes available during the week, as well as during spring and fall. Timberline Lodge is 6 miles north of US 26 from Government Camp.

Mt Hood SkiBowl (☎ 503-272-3206, W www.skibowl.com; US 26, Government Camp; lift tickets adult weekend/midweek/night $31/25/18, senior & child $18/15/12) is the USA's largest night-ski area and is the closest skiing to Portland. It's smaller than Meadows or Timberline and is most popular with people who buzz out from Portland for an evening of skiing.

Summit Ski Area (☎ 503-272-0256, W www.summitskiarea.com, US 26, Government Camp; lift tickets full day/half day $20/13), next to the Government Camp rest area, has gentle terrain and inexpensive fees. Anybody who's skied more than a couple of times, though, will find Summit incredibly dull.

Cooper Spur Ski Area (☎ 503-352-7803, W www.cooperspur.com, Cloud Cap Rd; lift tickets adult/senior/child $15/10/10), on the northeast slopes of Mt Hood 26 miles south of Hood River, caters to beginning skiers and families. It also offers the cheapest lift tickets on Mt Hood (don't get excited, it's a T-bar lift). There's a 500-foot drop and 10 runs. If skiing is too daunting, rent a snow tube and just slide down the hill.

Cross-Country Just down the road from the Mt Hood Meadows ski area is the **Hood River Meadows Nordic Center** (☎ 503-337-2222 ext 262, Hwy 35; trail-use fees adult/senior/child $9/7/5; open 9am-4pm Tues-Sat), which offers about 9 miles of groomed cross-country trails, ski rentals and lessons. In addition to the groomed trails, several other free (ungroomed) trails start from the same parking area, including an easy mile-long trail to Sahalie Falls; warm up on this, then make the longer, more challenging ski to Elk Meadows.

Across from Hood River Meadows is **Teacup Lake** (W www.teleport.com/~tcup; trail fee $3), which has about 12 miles of groomed trails and is operated by the Oregon Nordic Club; it has a good variety of terrain. Dogs are prohibited on Teacup's trails. A few miles from the US 26 junction on Hwy 35, **White River** (☎ 503-622-4822, Hwy 35; no trail fees) is another cross-country ski area with a big bowl popular

OREGON

with telemark skiers, as well as nice trails up through the trees.

Rent cross-country skis at **Mountain Tracks** (☎ 503-272-3380, 88611 Government Camp Loop), in the Huckleberry Inn. If you're driving up from Portland, stop in Sandy to rent cross-country skis or snowshoes at **Otto's Cross-Country Ski Shop** (☎ 503-668-5947, 38716 Pioneer Blvd; $12 a day). It's easiest to rent downhill skis at ski areas.

Tubing If skiing and snowboarding are not in your repetoire, try **Snow Bunny** (☎ 503-272-0256). Located 1½ miles east of Government Camp on US 26, this is a supervised snow-tubing area. Cooper Spur and Summit ski areas (see Downhill, earlier) also have tubing areas. All these places require you to rent their equipment (about $10) – you can't bring your own.

Hiking

Ask around for some advice on hiking trails, and everybody will offer up a different favorite. The USFS's free pamphlet, *Day Hikes Around Mt Hood,* lists 30 hikes ranging widely in difficulty. Hikers should also have the *Mt Hood National Forest* map or the GeoGraphics *Mt Hood Wilderness* map. Both are available from the Mt Hood Information Center and most outdoor stores.

The following are a few deservedly popular day hikes. On a sunny weekend, these trails won't provide an experience of wilderness solitude, but they are well loved for good reasons.

Ramona Falls A lower and an upper trailhead converge and lead to beautiful Ramona Falls, which tumbles 120 feet down a face of mossy columnar basalt. To reach the trail, turn north at Zigzag onto Lolo Pass Rd for 5 miles; turn right on USFS Rd 1825 for 3 miles. The first trailhead is here. A very rocky road leads to an upper trailhead, 1.4 miles distant. From the lower trailhead, it's a 7½-mile roundtrip hike to the falls.

Mirror Lake Hike 2 miles up from US 26 to Mirror Lake, which serves as a reflecting

pond for Mt Hood. The trail begins at the parking area between mileposts 51 and 52 on US 26, 1½ miles west of Government Camp.

Salmon River Trail Hike alongside the Salmon River through lush old-growth forests. The grade is very gentle, and the trail parallels a USFS road much of the way, so it's easy to arrange a shuttle. To find the trailhead, at Zigzag, turn south on Salmon River Rd and drive 3 miles to a sign for the Old Salmon River Trail. Most day-hikers continue on the trail to the Salmon River Bridge for a 2.6-mile hike. The trail continues along the river for those who want a longer hike.

Laurel Hill Trail On this trail, follow a section of the Barlow Rd that was roundly cursed by the Oregon Trail pioneers who were forced to winch their wagons down the precipitous slopes. Thanks to the CCC, who constructed the present trail in the 1930s, modern hikers have it somewhat easier. The upper trailhead is near milepost 52, 2½ miles west of Government Camp on US 26, just off USFS Rd 552. The lower trailhead is just off US 26 on USFS Rd 2639, called the Kiwanis Camp Rd. The trail is 3.7 miles long, all up or downhill, depending on which trailhead you choose.

Timberline Trail Circumnavigating 11,240-foot Mt Hood near Portland, this 40-mile trail is really a system of trails that provides day hikers with easy access to a scenic wilderness of waterfalls, quiet reflecting lakes, wildflower meadows and mountain vistas. The hike to McNeil Point follows a ridgeline portion of the longer trail to two ponds rimmed with wildflowers and offers the Mt Hood area's most photogenic scenery.

For a shorter hike, it's only a short distance and a moderate climb to the first breathtaking viewpoint at Bald Mountain, from where it's possible to make an abbreviated 2.3-mile loop back to the car.

From Timberline Lodge, Zigzag Canyon Overlook is a 4½-mile roundtrip through meadows of wildflowers to a canyon vista.

From there, a strenuous 10-mile one-way trip drops down into the canyon and back up to Paradise Park.

The short loop to Bald Mountain opens in June, but the trail to the ponds at McNeil Point isn't completely snow-free until mid-July. Bank on wildflowers all summer long. In September and October the valleys flanking Mt Hood are painted in deep veins of yellow and gold. Hiking is pleasant on cloudy days, though if it's too cloudy you may lose the view of the mountain completely.

Climbing

Mt Hood is the second-most-climbed peak over 10,000 feet in the world, after Japan's Mt Fuji, and many Oregonians feel that their lives cannot be complete without climbing it at least once. The first known ascent was made in 1845 or 1857 (nobody's sure). In 1867, the first women made the climb in full-length skirts, and photographs of Victorian ladies roped together on the slopes adorn the walls of the Mazama Lodge (in Government Camp). About 10,000 people climb Mt Hood every year. It's been climbed both by a woman wearing high heels, and by a man without any legs!

This isn't to say Mt Hood does not require both climbing skills and stamina: Nearly every year, a few people die making the ascent. Climbing is best between May and mid-July, and a typical climb from Timberline Lodge on the south side takes 10 to 12 hours. Experienced climbers who wish to organize their own expedition can get information from the Mt Hood Information Center (see Information, earlier).

One well-established guide service and climbing school is **Timberline Mountain Guides** (☎ 541-312-9242, ⓦ www.timberline mtguides.com, PO Box 1167, Bend, OR 97709). This company's basic Mt Hood summit climb starts with a day of instruction; the next day is devoted to a summit attempt. The package costs $375 and is offered from March through July.

Northwest School of Survival (☎ 888-668-8264, ⓦ www.nwsos.com, 2229 NE Burnside No 74, Gresham, OR 97030) also offers mountaineering classes and summit climbs.

Climbs are scheduled from December through August, and it's best to book well in advance. The cost is $400 for training and a climb.

The Mazamas (☎ 503-227-2345, ⓦ www .mazamas.org, 909 NW 19th Ave, Portland, OR 97209), a mountaineering and hiking club founded in 1894, sponsors climbs of many Northwest peaks, including Mt Hood. Club membership isn't necessary to participate, although you should realize that the Mazamas are not a guide service. Trip leaders volunteer, and not all take beginners. Climbs cost nonmembers $15, and climbers are expected to come prepared with their own gear and knowledge of how to use it.

In downtown Portland, **Oregon Mountain Community** (☎ 503-227-1038, 60 NW Davis St) charges $25 to rent crampons, an ice axe, plastic mountaineering boots and a helmet for up to three days.

Mountain Biking

When the snow is gone, **Mt Hood SkiBowl** (☎ 503-272-3206, ⓦ www.skibowl.com; US 26, Government Camp; day pass $15; 11am-6pm Sat & Sun in summer) is transformed into a mountain-bike arena.

Of course, mountain biking at a downhill ski area is a little bit like skiing there, and if you're more the cross-country type, cross US 26 to the free Government Camp recreational trail network. Trail maps are posted at Glacier View (just opposite the west entrance to SkiBowl), at the base of the Skiway Trail in Government Camp, and at the Summit Ski Area (see Skiing & Tubing, earlier). The Crosstown Trail is a fairly easy 3-mile single track between Glacier View and the Summit Ski Area. More challenging trails sprout from it.

Most of the cross-country ski trails in the area are good for summertime mountain biking. Trails shoot uphill from several points around the easy Trillium Lake loop.

Fishing

Fish the Salmon River, a southerly tributary of the Sandy River, for summer steelhead. Reach it from the community of Brightwood, on US 26, via good USFS roads and trails leading to isolated pools and rapids in deep old-growth forest. Many of Mt Hood's lakes are stocked with trout.

In Welches, the **Fly Fishing Shop** (*☎ 503-622-4607, 800-266-3971, US 26*) specializes in guided fly-fishing trips on the upper Sandy River and in other areas of the state. Float trips run $350 (for two people), and four-hour fly-fishing classes are $100; fishing licenses and gear are available here as well.

Hot Springs

At the southern end of Mt Hood National Forest, the remote yet popular **Bagby Hot Springs** is a free hike-in hot springs with rustic hollowed-log tubs and a couple of private bathhouses. Volunteers maintain the facilities here and generally keep things calm – Bagby has ongoing problems with disruptive visitors; car break-ins are unfortunately common, and nighttime visits are best avoided. The mile-long hike in from the parking area is one of the delights of this place – it's through a lovely old-growth forest.

From US 26 at Sandy, take Hwy 211 south to Estacada. From there, drive south on Hwy 224 (which becomes Forest Rd 46) for about 30 miles. Turn right onto Forest Rd 63 and follow it 3½ miles to USFS Rd 70. Turn right and go about 6 miles to the parking area and trailhead. Several signs along the way indicate the route.

Places to Stay

Camping Camping on Mt Hood makes a convenient getaway from Portland, so competition for sites can be fierce. Reservations for some campgrounds can be made by contacting the National Recreation Reservation Service (*☎ 877-444-6777,* **W** *www .reserveusa.com*). An $8.65 reservation charge is tacked onto the camping fee.

Fees for camping at the following campgrounds run about $12 unless otherwise stated. They all have drinking water and vault toilets, but no hookups.

On the west side and at the base of Mt Hood is **Tollgate Campground** (*☎ 503-622-4822*), which was constructed by the Civilian

Conservation Corps (CCC). **Camp Creek Campground**, 3 miles southeast of Rhododendron, has some nice streamside sites. Both of these campgrounds border US 26.

Still Creek Campground (*☎ 503-622-4822*) This popular campground is just half a mile east of Government Camp. From here, all the recreation on Mt Hood is in your backyard.

Trillium Lake Campground (*☎ 503-622-4822*) Even more popular is this campground, on the shores of the lake in a postcard setting, with Mt Hood rising above the lake.

Mt Hood Village (*☎ 503-622-4011, 800-255-3069,* **W** *www.mthoodvillage.com, 65000 E US 26*) Full hookups $32. Near Brightwood, this huge resort complex, which shares a driveway with the Mt Hood Information Center, is the only campground on Mt Hood with RV hookups. Luxuries include showers, an indoor swimming pool, a fitness center and a laundry. You can also rent cabins for $45.

On the north side is **Cloud Cap Campground** (*☎ 541-352-6002*). To get there, turn west off Hwy 35 onto Cooper Spur Rd and head past the Cooper Spur Ski Area 10 miles up the long, rough USFS Rd 3512. Campers here have easy access to the Timberline Trail.

On the east side, on Hwy 35, **Robin Hood Campground** (*☎ 541-352-6002*) is a roadside campground that is 12 miles northeast of Government Camp, on the East Fork of Hood River. **Sherwood Campground** (*☎ 541-352-6002*) is just a few miles farther down the mountain.

On the south side, there are tent sites at **Frog Lake Campground** (*☎ 541-352-6002*), 8 miles south of Government Camp on US 26, on the shores of tiny Frog Lake.

Anglers, rafters, hikers and hot-springs soakers head up the Clackamas River on the southern flanks of Mt Hood. Campgrounds dot the riverbanks, starting from Estacada.

Lockaby (*☎ 503-630-6861*) Perched above a stretch of Clackamas River white water, this forested campground is 15 miles southeast of Estacada on Hwy 224.

Indian Henry (*☎ 503-630-6861*) This large, multilooped campground has good access to a lovely riverside trail. It's 24 miles east of Estacada, just south of Hwy 224.

Hostels Two Government Camp lodges operated by outdoor clubs offer bunk space to nonmembers:

Mazama Lodge (☎ 503-272-9214, e maza malodg@oregontrail.net, Westlake Rd) Beds $16.50 nonmembers. Open Thur-Mon year round. The lodge is often booked up by club members. Bring your own bedding.

Cascade Ski Club Lodge (☎ 503-272-9204, w www.cascadeskiclub.org, Blossom Trail) Beds $22 nonmembers. Call Cascade Ski Club to reserve a bed in this family-friendly place.

B&Bs Just past a sprawling resort complex is this B&B.

Old Welches Inn B&B (☎ 503-622-3754, w www.lodging-mthood.com, 26401 E Welches Rd) Rooms $96-144, cottage $163.

The original Welches Hotel, built in 1890, is now a comfortable B&B. Accommodations are in the main lodge or in the separate one-bedroom cottage.

Motels Also consider staying in Hood River, which has a number of reasonably priced motels.

Oregon Ark Motel (☎ 503-622-3131, 61716 E US 26) Singles/doubles $35/40. It's pretty basic (some cabinlike rooms are heated with wood stoves), and it's right on the highway, but this is the place for budget-minded travelers.

Shamrock Motel (☎ 503-622-4911, 59550 E US 26) Singles/doubles $52/62. This tidy motel, 12 miles east of Sandy, is also a good deal. During the winter, guests can get discounted lift tickets.

Timberline Lodge

One of the masterpieces of the WPA-era building boom, Timberline Lodge is the culmination of a kind of rustic Arts and Crafts design that came to be known as Cascadian. The building of Timberline in 1936 and 1937 was the largest of the federal work creation projects directed by the WPA (Works Progress Administration) in Oregon, employing up to 500 workers to construct the 43,700-sq-foot log-and-stone lodge. For many employed on the project, Timberline was more than a job – it was an expression of a cultural ideal. As stated in a 1937 publication accompanying the dedication:

In Mt Hood's Timberline Lodge the mystic strength that lives in the hills has been captured in wood and stone and, in the hands of laborer and craftsman, has been presented as man's effort at approximating an ideal in which society, through concern for the individual, surpasses the standard it has unconsciously set for itself.

There is hardly an element of the building that was not handcrafted, from the selection of stones in the massive lobby fireplaces to the hand-loomed coverlets on the beds. To emphasize the natural beauty of the area, architects not only quarried local stone and cut local timber, they also designed the six-sided central tower to echo the faceted peak of Mt Hood. The steeply slanted wings leading away from the common rooms are meant both to shed the heavy snowfalls and resemble mountain ridges. Even the exterior paint was mixed to match the color of mountain frost.

The interior of the lodge is where the workmanship is most evident. The central fireplace rises 92 feet through three floors of open lobby. All the furniture was made by hand in WPA carpentry halls, and murals and paintings of stocky, stylized workers, in the best Socialist-Realist tradition, adorn the walls.

Of course, Timberline Lodge is not a museum: it is a hotel, ski resort and restaurant. Don't feel so reverential about this magnificent old building that you don't at least enjoy a hot chocolate on the mezzanine. And don't forget about its quirkier side: The horror movie The Shining was filmed here – pass by room 217 ('redrum redrum') for a quick chill.

Motel lodging in Government Camp is expensive. If you're coming to ski, consider commuting from Hood River, where many motels offer good deals on lift tickets.

Huckleberry Inn (☎ 503-272-3325, 88611 E Government Camp Loop) Standard/ deluxe rooms $60/100. Even the deluxe rooms are by no means luxurious, but they sleep up to 10 people, and the 'downtown' Government Camp location is very handy.

Thunderhead Lodge Condominiums (☎ 503-272-3368, W www.thunderheadlodge .com, 87451 E Government Camp Loop) Studios/suite $95/305. Stay here for easy access to SkiBowl's night skiing, an outdoor heated swimming pool and full kitchens.

Inn at Cooper Spur (☎ 541-352-6037, e cooperspurinn@gorge.net, 10755 Cooper Spur Rd) Lodge rooms $79-199, cabins $149-209. You'll be well off the beaten track here on the northeast side of Mt Hood, 19 miles north of Government Camp on Hwy 35. Facilities include hot tubs, tennis courts and an adjoining restaurant.

Resorts You can find all sorts of resorts on Mt Hood: the rustic, the historic and the predictably comfortable golf resort.

Timberline Lodge (☎ 503-272-3311, in Portland ☎ 503-231-7979, W www.timber linelodge.com) Rooms $75-200. The lodge here oozes rustic charm and is a great place to relax after a day of hiking or skiing. Accommodations range from cramped units with bunk beds to large fireplace chambers.

The Resort at the Mountain (☎ 503-622-3101, W www.theresort.com, 68010 E Fairway Ave) Standard rooms $99-129. This large, manicured property in Welches focuses on its 27-hole golf course in the summer and ski packages in the winter. Facilities include a swimming pool, tennis courts and two restaurants.

Summit Meadow Cabins (☎ 503-272-3494, W www.summitmeadow.com, Summit Meadow) Cabins $125-180. These A-frame cabins, just south of Government Camp in the Trillium Lake basin, make great bases for vigorous wintertime getaways. During winter, it's a 1½-mile cross-country ski in to the cabins. In summer, it's possible to drive

in. Ski and mountain-bike trails surround the cabins.

Lost Lake Resort (☎ 541-386-6366, USFS Rd 1340) Campsites from $15, cabins $45-100. Rent a rustic cabin or pitch a tent on Mt Hood's northern flank, then spend your days canoeing and hiking. There's a small store here but no restaurant.

Places to Eat

Mountain High Espresso (☎ 503-622-6334, 73265 E US 26, Rhododendron) Snacks $3. Do like the locals and stop by this trailer next door to the Rhododendron grocery store. The espresso here is the real goods, and the muffins are tasty too.

Flying Frog (☎ 503-622-7638, Arrah Wanna Rendezvous Center, 67211 E US 26) Breakfast/lunch $5/6. This is a comfortable place for a sit-down meal and also a great place for a delicious pastry and a cup of tea on the fly.

Rendezvous Grill & Tap Room (☎ 503-622-6837, 67149 E US 26) Lunch/dinner $8/16. Head and shoulders above the other dinner restaurants on US 26, the Rendezvous' signature dish is a tasty alder-smoked chicken with cranberries and toasted hazelnuts.

Of the several places to eat around Government Camp, two stand out:

Mt Hood Brewing Company & Brew Pub (☎ 503-272-3724, 87304 E Government Camp Loop) Lunch/dinner $8-10. This is Mt Hood's only brewery, and a pleasant place it is. The English-style beers go well with the tasty pizzas. Substantial sandwiches are also available at the family-friendly brewpub.

Several restaurants operate at the Timberline Lodge (see Places to Stay, earlier). In the day lodge, *Wy'east Kitchen* has cafeteria food for skiers (lunch about $6). In the old lodge, the basement *Blue Ox Bar* is graced by a tiled mosaic of the legendary lumberjack Paul Bunyan and his ox, Babe. Soups, sandwiches and pizza are served ($5 and up). At the *Ram's Head Bar*, hearty sandwiches, salads and fondue are available along with drinks (about $10); this is a great place to stake out a table and watch the sun set. Mt Hood's best food is served in the lodge's log-beamed *Cascade Dining Room* (lunch/dinner $10/16-31). If you're not bankrolled for dinner here, soak up the atmosphere at lunchtime, when skiers' specials are sometimes offered ($8).

Getting There & Away

Bus Greyhound runs one bus a day between Portland and Government Camp ($8, 1¾ hours, 55 miles), but the timing is inconvenient for day-trippers.

On winter weekends and holidays, a bus transports skiers from various pickup points in Portland to Mt Hood Meadows (☎ 503-287-5438). The cost is $50 for combination roundtrip transportation and lift ticket. Call or check W www.skihood.com for route details.

Timberline Lodge (in Portland ☎ 503-231-7979) also operates weekend and holiday bus service from Portland to the lodge from December to March. A combination roundtrip transportation and lift ticket ($45) can be purchased at any GI Joe's store or through TicketMaster (☎ 503-224-4440, W www.ticketmaster.com).

Car For road conditions, dial the 24-hour information line (☎ 503-588-2941, 800-977-6368). State law requires traction devices to be carried in vehicles during winter, and trailers are sometimes banned. For details on weather conditions, see Information, earlier.

In the wintertime, if you park a vehicle at most places on Mt Hood, you will need a Sno-Park permit ($3 daily, $7 for a three-day pass, $15 for a season pass). During the rest of the year, a Northwest Forest Pass is required to park at trailheads. Permits are available at the Mt Hood Information Center, from many Government Camp businesses and at Timberline Lodge.

Oregon Coast

Highlights

- Cruising the Oregon Coast Hwy, with its spectacular scenery and beautiful bridges
- Vaulting off a 500-foot sand dune in the Oregon Dunes National Recreation Area
- Antique-hunting and ship-watching in Maritime Astoria

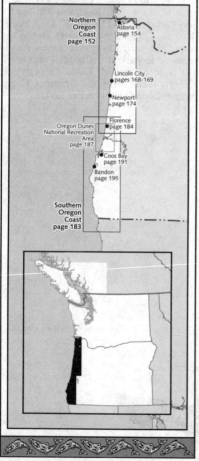

Northern Oregon Coast page 152

Astoria page 154

Lincoln City pages 168-169

Newport page 174

Florence page 184

Oregon Dunes National Recreation Area page 187

Coos Bay page 191

Bandon page 195

Southern Oregon Coast page 183

Forest, mountain, beach, ocean and river all meet through a prism of mist and green translucence along the Oregon coast. Rocky headlands rise hundreds of feet above the ocean, dropping away to the pounding waves below. Craggy spires and columns of volcanic rock march far out to sea and arch up out of sandy beaches. Rising just to the east of the shoreline is the Coast Range, a young mountain range deeply etched by great rivers and shrouded by a patchwork of large forests and recent clear-cuts. The Oregon Dunes, among the largest ocean-fronting sand dunes in the world, drift along the edge of the coast for over 50 miles. Grey whales migrate offshore, to and from Arctic waters.

Thanks to a farsighted state government in the 1910s, Oregon's 362-mile Pacific Coast was entirely set aside as public land, and access is provided by over 70 state parks and natural areas. The north coast has a handful of small resort towns, but most of the coast, especially the central and southern regions, is almost unspoiled by development.

Along the coast, designated off-road-vehicle (ORV) and non-ORV areas are set up to restrict ORVs. Hikers venturing into ORV territory need to remain keen to the direction of ORV traffic. Climbing the crest of a high dune is an especially bad place to be when a dune buggy comes flying over the top. Red (sometimes orange) flags waving above the dunes indicate oncoming ORVs. If one is moving fast in your direction, get out of the way.

History

Civilization developed in Native American villages along the bays of mighty rivers, such as the Columbia, Yaquina, Rogue and Umpqua. Although Lewis and Clark visited the northern coast in 1805–06, and Astoria was founded as a fur-trading fort in 1811, settlement didn't really start until the 1860s, after Native American tribes had been restricted to reservations.

Fishing, logging and agriculture formed the nucleus of the early coast economy, and dairy and tourism took hold along the northern coast. Early south-coast settlements such as Port Orford were established in the 1850s, when gold was discovered in coastal rivers and prospectors seeped in to collect.

That quickly fizzled out, and young coastal communities turned to shipping out the lumber and agricultural products demanded by the California gold rush and booming San Francisco. During WWI and WWII, Oregon became the largest timber producer in the USA, and Coos Bay became the world's largest timber-shipping port.

The depletion of old-growth forests and the export of raw logs for milling overseas have spelled the end of the boom for many lumber-dependent families. Niche industries, such as lily-bulb production, dairy farms, wild-mushroom hunting and tourism, seek to fill the gulf.

US 101, which traverses the Pacific Coast north to south, wasn't completed through Oregon until the 1930s, and forever after has been known as a classic scenic drive with a legacy of beautiful bridges.

Places to Stay

Hotels are expensive all along the coast, with the cheapest rooms going for $60 in the summer. Prices given here are for peak season (July to August), and off-season rooms are typically 40% less. Competition for campsites can be fierce on the north coast, especially in some of the bigger state parks. Many coastal parks feature canvass-walled yurts, which are a cheap alternative to a hotel room. Yurts along the north coast are often noisy with partying youth from urban areas.

Getting There & Away

US 101 stretches the length of the Oregon coast – the Yachats-to-Florence and Port Orford-to-Brookings segments offer the most spectacular scenery. Summer traffic is intense along this route and on the two-lane highways that lead inland.

The Oregon coast is not well served by public transportation. Although there are no trains, rail passes are valid for Amtrak buses to the north coast. Only Coos Bay has scheduled air service, and only Newport and Coos Bay have staffed bus stations. Other towns simply have bus stops in front of grocery stores or gas stations.

Conde McCullough

The strikingly beautiful bridges along US 101 are the work of Conde McCullough, who brought dramatic style to the utilitarian business of bridge-building. McCullough built bridges all over the state, but his most famous are along the Oregon coast, across Coos Bay at North Bend, Alsea Bay at Waldport, Yaquina Bay at Newport and Cape Creek Bridge at Devil's Elbow State Park, near Yachats.

Until the 1930s, the coast was ill served by highways, partly because wide estuaries presented engineering problems, and partly because steel – the bridge-making ingredient of choice – didn't last very long on the salty Pacific Coast. In 1936, McCullough was given teams of WPA workers, and he turned to new engineering and design techniques to span the final links of US 101. From France, he borrowed the Freyssinet method, which pioneered the use of prestressed concrete arches in bridge-building. From the Arts and Crafts movement, he developed a sensitivity for harmony of structures and their natural surroundings. From the Art Deco movement, he borrowed a severe, neo-Gothic formality.

The resulting bridges span wide estuaries and bays in a high-flying, immediately identifiable style; bridges that have almost become metaphors for the coast itself. Once you've seen one, you'll recognize McCullough bridges at many other places throughout the state.

Horizon Air serves the south coast with commuter flights to Portland from Coos Bay's North Bend Airport.

Bus service is disjointed, but you can almost bus the coast end to end, with a gap in service between Cloverdale and Lincoln City. Greyhound's coast route travels from Portland to San Francisco via Lincoln City. Amtrak Thruway buses connect Portland with Astoria, Seaside and Cannon Beach; and Corvallis (or Albany) with Newport. Tillamook Country Transit goes from Portland to Tillamook, and Porter Stages goes from Eugene to Florence. The Pacific Trails bus from Kelso, WA to Astoria is the fastest way to the coast from Washington.

Travel between coastal towns is relatively easy (and cheap) on local transit buses, which often don't run on weekends.

Northern Oregon Coast

Oregon's northern coast begins at the Columbia River and stretches south to Florence. The most famous beach resorts in Oregon – Seaside, Cannon Beach and Lincoln City – are here on long strips of sandy beach. Affable Newport, known since the 1860s for its oysters, is now famed for its aquarium. Astoria is the oldest US settlement west of the Mississippi.

The north coast between Newport and Seaside is the domain of tourism, clogged by weekend visitors from Portland and the Willamette Valley. Some restaurants don't even bother opening on weekdays, and the price of lodging goes up on Friday and Saturday nights. And you'd better have wads of cash handy, since some hotels and restaurants – even well-established ones – won't accept credit cards.

ASTORIA

Astoria (population 10,075), at the mouth of the 5-mile-wide Columbia River, is historically significant as the turning point of the Lewis and Clark expedition and as the first US settlement west of the Mississippi.

NORTHERN OREGON COAST

The city contains a great deal of seafaring history and scruffy charm, not to mention some of the most lovingly restored and precipitously poised Victorian homes outside of San Francisco (only one is regularly open for touring, and others are operated as B&Bs). Along the derelict harbor, low rent and a sense of history have attracted artists, writers and restaurateurs. The downtown maintains a number of antique shops. The 4.1-mile-long **Astoria Bridge**, the world's longest continuous truss bridge, crosses the Columbia River here to Washington state.

History

Lewis and Clark and the Corps of Discovery tolerated the winter of 1805–06 at a crude fort along an inlet of Youngs Bay, just south of present-day Astoria. When they returned to St Louis in 1811, they told all who would listen about the great wealth in pelts in the Pacific Northwest. Within months, John Jacob Astor and his Pacific Fur Trading Company established a small fur-trading fort here at the mouth of the Columbia River.

Trade and fishing made Astoria very powerful and wealthy. By the end of the 19th century, it would be Oregon's second-largest city, settled largely by Finns, Norwegians and Swedes. A salmon cannery opened here in 1866, and sawmills, flour mills, shipping and deep-sea fishing soon took hold. In the 1880s, sea captains and other captains of industry built magnificent Victorian homes overlooking the Columbia River. The city's reputation for affluence and gentility was rivaled only by its reputation for bawdy excess in the bar-and-brothel district near the harbor.

Orientation

Astoria is northwest of Portland, a few miles inland from the ocean on the Columbia River – it can be reached by US 30 or by US 26 and US 101 via Seaside. US 101 enters the city from the southwest, along Youngs Bay Bridge, and almost instantly corkscrews up to cross the Astoria Bridge to Washington. Beaches near the mouth of Columbia are located on Clatsop Spit, accessed from Warrenton, on the west side of Youngs Bay. Seaside is 16 miles south.

Downtown is perched on a narrow slip of land between the river and the steeply sloped residential area, which contains many lovely homes. The best way to explore the area is on foot – pick up a walking guide ($3) to historic homes from the Heritage Museum (see Things to See & Do, later). The **Astoria Riverwalk** follows the trolley route between the west and east mooring basins, passing old canneries along the riverfront between 6th and 12th Sts.

Information

The Astoria Visitors Center (☎ 503-325-6311, 800-875-6807, W www.oldoregon.com) is at 111 W Marine Dr. The post office is at 748 Commercial St.

Godfather's Books & Espresso Bar (☎ 503-325-8143), 1108 Commercial St, has a nice selection of books on local travel and history. Astoria's alternative newsmonthly, *hipfish*, has quite a lot to say about coastal issues and local happenings. Coast Community Radio is heard at 91.9 FM.

Clean Services Coin Laundry (☎ 503-325-2027), 823 W Marine Dr, offers both self-service and drop-off laundry.

Things to See & Do

Astoria's 150-year-old seafaring heritage is well interpreted at the **Columbia River Maritime Museum** (☎ *503-325-2323,* W *www .crmm.org, 1792 Marine Dr; adult/senior/ student/child under 6 years $5/4/2/free; open 9:30am-5pm)*. On display are a number of small boats, harpoons and a US Navy submarine periscope from which you can watch local river traffic. History exhibits highlight the salmon-packing industry, local lighthouses and delicate scrimshaw work. Admission includes boarding a decommissioned lightship.

The highly ornamented **Flavel House** *(☎ 503-325-2203, 441 8th St; adult/senior/ student/youth $5/4/4/2; open 11am-4pm)* was built by Captain George Flavel, one of Astoria's leading citizens during the 1870s and 1880s. It has great views over the harbor – so that Flavel could keep an eye on his ships.

ASTORIA

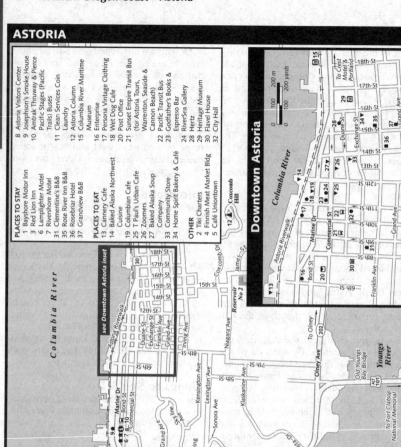

PLACES TO STAY
1 Bayshore Motor Inn
3 Red Lion Inn
6 Lamplighter Motel
7 Rivershore Motel
31 Clementine's B&B
35 Rose River Inn B&B
36 Rosebriar Hotel
37 Grandview B&B

PLACES TO EAT
13 Cannery Cafe
14 Baked Alaska Northwest
    Cuisine
19 Columbian Cafe
25 Paul's Urban Cafe
26 Zoomers
27 Baked Alaska Soup
    Company
33 Community Store
34 Home Spirit Bakery & Cafe

8 Astoria Visitors Center
9 Josephson's Smoke House
10 Amtrak Thruway & Pierce
    Pacific Stages (Pacific
    Trails) Buses
11 Clean Services Coin
    Laundry
12 Astoria Column
15 Columbia River Maritime
    Museum
16 Enterprise
17 Persona Vintage Clothing
18 Wet Dog Cafe
20 Post Office
21 Sunset Empire Transit Bus
    (for Astoria Tours,
    Warrenton, Seaside &
    Cannon Beach)
22 Pacific Transit Bus
23 Godfather's Books &
    Espresso Bar
24 RiverSea Gallery
28 Hertz
29 Heritage Museum
30 Flavel House
32 City Hall

OTHER
2 Tiki Charters
4 Finnish Meat Market Bldg
5 Café Uniontown

Downtown Astoria

The restored house has been repainted with its original colors, and the grounds have been returned to Victorian-era landscaping.

Housed in the former city hall, the **Heritage Museum** *(☎ 503-325-2203, 1618 Exchange St; adult/senior/youth $3/2/1; open 11am-4pm)* commemorates Astoria's seafaring heritage, as well as the various ethnic communities that came together to form the city – note the Tong shrine. Another room is dedicated to the Clatsop Indians and the early days of exploration.

Rising high on Coxcomb Hill, the **Astoria Column** (built in 1926) is a 125-foot tower painted with scenes from the westward sweep of US exploration and settlement. The top of the column offers good views over Astoria, Clatsop Spit and Youngs Bay. To get there from downtown, follow signs up 14th St.

Fort Clatsop National Memorial *(☎ 503-861-2471, W www.nps.gov/focl; adult/family $2/4 or Coast Passport; open 8am-5pm Sept–mid-June, 8am-6pm mid-June–Aug)* is a worthwhile stop, especially for families with children or for anyone interested in pioneer history. Built according to sketches left by Lewis and Clark and named after a local Indian tribe, the fort is a reconstruction of one the Corps of Discovery occupied during the wet and miserable winter of 1805–06. During summer, costumed docents demonstrate common fort pastimes, such as candle-making, leather-tanning, flintlock marksmanship and cedar-canoe building. Expedition history and Clatsop Indian artifacts are exhibited at the well-curated visitor center. The site is 8 miles south of Astoria off US 101.

Located 10 miles west of Astoria on Clatsop Spit, **Fort Stevens State Park** *(☎ 503-861-1671)*, in Hammond (near Warrenton), commemorates the historic military and strategic garrisons here and offers near-endless beach access and camping. Nine miles of bike trails wind through the 6-sq-mile park, including 2 miles of trail along the beach.

Pick up a map at the park headquarters or the **Military Museum** *(☎ 503-861-1470, W www.visitftstevens.com, Pacific Dr and Ridge Rd in Hammond; $3 day-use fee or Coast Passport; open 10am-6pm June-Sept, 10am-4pm Oct-May)*. Here, the military history of Civil War–era Fort Stevens is preserved. Displays capture especially well the mood of the area during WWII. The concrete batteries – grim, warrenlike garrisons dug into sand dunes – are the most interesting remnants of the fort's mostly demolished military buildings. A reconstructed Civil War earthworks, complete with moat, sets the stage for Civil War reenactments over Memorial Day weekend.

Beach access begins a mile past the campground entrance, where on the sands of Fort Stevens the rotting hull of the *Peter Iredale* sits like a beached whale's skeleton. In 1906, this British, four-masted freight ship sailed from Australia to Astoria to pick up a load of wheat. It encountered a dense fog at the Columbia bar and ran aground, but no lives were lost. Over 2000 ships have sunk or wrecked while attempting to enter the Columbia River, earning it the name 'Graveyard of the Pacific.' The best scenery is from the end of Clatsop Spit, where a viewing platform looks out over the South Jetty as it reaches out from the mouth of the Columbia far to sea.

Charter Fishing & Cruises

Tiki Charters *(☎ 503-325-7818, 350 Industry St)*, in Astoria's West Mooring Basin, and **Charlton Deep Sea Charters** *(☎ 503-861-2429, 795 Cedar Ave)*, in nearby Warrenton, both offer charter trips for bottom-fish, sturgeon and salmon fishing ($75-85); they also offer river cruises. **Tackle Time Bait Shop** *(☎ 503-861-3693, 530 E Harbor St)*, in Warrenton, has licenses and tackle.

Special Events

Astoria is one of several cities across the nation gearing up to celebrate the centennial of the Lewis and Clark Expedition in 2003–06. Contact the visitor center or Fort Clatsop National Memorial for details.

Astoria's biggest annual event, the Astoria-Warrenton Crab & Seafood Festival, brings 150 wine and seafood vendors together under one roof the last weekend in April.

Oregon Pacific Coast Passport

If you're traveling the Oregon coast, you may want to purchase the Oregon Pacific Coast Passport. Instead of paying separate fees to visit trails, state parks, natural areas and monuments ($3-5 per visit), you can buy a single pass for $10 that will get you into 16 recreation sites. The pass is good for five days and can be purchased at participating sites. For more information, contact Oregon State Parks (☎ 800-551-6949, W www.prd.state.or.us). The following are included:

Fort Stevens State Park
Fort Clatsop National Memorial
Ecola State Park
Nehalem Bay State Park
Cape Lookout State Park
Yaquina Head Outstanding Natural Area
Marys Peak (Willamette Valley)
Cape Perpetua Scenic Area
Heceta Head Lighthouse
Honeyman State Park
Oregon Dunes National Recreation Area
Shore Acres State Park

The Scandinavian Midsummer Festival honors the area's Swedish, Finnish and Norwegian heritage during the third weekend of June with dance contests, a parade and the crowning of Miss Scandinavia.

Places to Stay

Camping The closest campgrounds are out on Clatsop Spit, near Warrenton.

Fort Stevens State Park (☎ 503-861-1671, reservations 800-452-5687) Yurts/hookups/tents $33/19/17. Ocean beaches are less than a mile away from this campground in Hammond. With over 400 sites, Fort Stevens is the largest in the state-park system.

Astoria-Seaside KOA (☎ 503-861-2606, 800-562-8506, 1100 NW Ridge Rd) Cabins/hookups/tents from $37/24/20. Right across the street from Fort Stevens is this smaller campground, which has an indoor pool.

B&Bs Astoria is a good place to consider staying in a B&B, as there are some gorgeous homes.

Grandview B&B (☎ 503-325-5555, 800-488-3250, W www.moriah.com/grandview, 1574 Grand Ave) Rooms with shared/private bathroom from $49/71. The towering Grandview has stunning views of the river.

Rosebriar Hotel (☎ 503-325-7427, 800-487-0224, W www.astoria-usa.com/rosebriar, 636 14th St) Rooms with breakfast $75-149. Built in 1902, this hotel offers European-style lodging in 11 rooms – all have private bathrooms, wide porches and a brick patio.

Clementine's B&B (☎ 503-325-2005, 800-521-6801, W www.clementines-bb.com, 847 Exchange St) Rooms $70-135. This 1888 Italianate mansion has five guest rooms.

Rose River Inn B&B (☎ 503-325-7175, 888-876-0028, W www.moriah.com/roseriver, 1510 Franklin St) Rooms $85-115. There are four guest rooms at this elegant old home, which is run by Finnish innkeepers.

Officer's Inn B&B (☎ 503-861-0884, 800-377-2524, W www.moriah.com/officersinn, 540 Russell Place, Hammond) Rooms $79-99. Military officers had it pretty nice in 1906, as denoted by the eight lovely guest rooms at these former officer's quarters near Fort Stevens State Park.

Hotels Most hotels are right along US 30 and can be noisy.

Rivershore Motel (☎ 503-325-2921, 888-322-8047, 59 W Marine Dr) Rooms weekday/weekend $50/60. This older style motel is clean and inexpensive.

Lamplighter Motel (☎ 503-325-4051, 800-845-8847, 131 W Marine Dr) Rooms $62. This is another good budget-lodging choice.

Crest Motel (☎ 503-325-3141, 800-421-3141, 5366 Leif Ericson Dr) Nonview/view rooms from $72/82. This pleasant, older motel on the eastern edge of town sits atop a wooded hill overlooking the river.

Bayshore Motor Inn (☎ 503-325-2205, 800-621-0641, 555 Hamburg Ave) Rooms $80. There's an indoor pool at this comfortable mid-range motel, which is located at an industrial site near the Youngs Bay Bridge.

Red Lion Inn (☎ 503-325-7373, 400 Industry St) Rooms with breakfast from $104-124. The Red Lion, at the marina, features balconied rooms with river views.

Places to Eat
Astoria offers great food and an informal atmosphere, with a mix of old-fashioned diners and up-to-date eateries. Astoria's **Community Store** (1389 Duane St) is a good natural-foods store and all-around hippie gathering place. For light snacks, head to tripped-out **Zoomers** (1213 Commercial St) for smoothies, muffins and espresso.

Baked Alaska Soup Company (☎ 503-325-3842, 225 14th St) Breakfast & lunch $3-7. A mound of flaming ice cream is the signature dessert at this downtown hole-in-the-wall, which is the local favorite for breakfast and house-made soup. **Baked Alaska Northwest Cuisine** (☎ 503-325-7414) is a new location at end of 12th St and has upscale river-view dining.

T Paul's Urban Cafe (☎ 503-338-5133, 1119 Commercial St) Lunch & dinner from $7-8. Modish T Paul's features casual bistro fare with sandwiches, pasta and quesadillas.

Home Spirit Bakery & Café (☎ 503-325-8642, 1585 Exchange St) Lunch $4-8, dinner $20-25. Open for lunch Tues-Sat, dinner Wed-Sat. Admire the inside of an old Victorian home with lunch at this cafe, which has notable croissants and gourmet dinners.

Cannery Cafe (☎ 503-325-8642, 1 6th St) Lunch from $7. Big ships float right by this cafe, which overlooks the river.

Columbian Cafe (☎ 503-325-2233, 1114 Marine Dr) Dinner $17-21. Don't let the down-on-its-luck facade put you off – the food here is great, and there's a daily selection of fresh fish.

Entertainment
A number of venues feature local and traveling blues and acoustic groups. Among them is **Café Uniontown** (☎ 503-325-8708, 218 W Marine Dr). On the waterfront is the **Wet Dog Cafe** (☎ 503-325-6975, 144 11th St), a brewpub with live music, DJs, dancing and second-run movies. The latest copy of *hipfish* has listings.

The bad old days of Astoria are portrayed as a spoofy musical comedy, **Shanghaied in Astoria** (☎ 503-325-6104, Finnish Meat Market Bldg; tickets $8-15; runs Thur-Sat & sometimes Sun July-Aug), which is actually kind of fun.

Shopping
Josephson's Smoke House (☎ 503-325-2190, 106 Marine Dr) is the last of the many canneries and smokehouses that once thrived here; it offers a wide range of smoked fish and shellfish.

Cheap storefront rent in the downtown area has made Astoria favorable to art galleries and antique stores. One of the best is the **RiverSea Gallery** (☎ 503-325-1270, 1160 Commercial St). There's a complete list of local galleries in *hipfish*.

Persona Vintage Clothing (☎ 503-325-3837, 100 10th St) is a great secondhand clothing store.

Getting There & Away
Amtrak Thruway buses from Portland ($16 one way) and Seaside ($3), as well as Pacific Trails buses from Kelso, Washington, stop daily at the Mini Mart (☎ 503-325-4162), 95 W Marine Dr.

Local buses leave from Duane St between 9th and 11th Sts downtown: Sunset Empire Transit (☎ 800-776-6406) bus No 101 goes to Seaside ($2.25), Warrenton and Cannon Beach. The Pacific Transit bus (☎ 503-692-4437) goes to Long Beach and Anacortes, in Washington. Pick up schedules at City Hall, at 1095 Duane St.

Rent a car from Hertz (☎ 503-325-7700), 1492 Duane St, or Enterprise (☎ 503-325-6500), 609 Bond St.

Getting Around
Astoria's Riverfront Trolley (☎ 503-325-6311) plies through the old cannery district, between the East and West Mooring Basins, daily in summer and weekends only in winter (fare $1).

Local Sunset Empire Transit (☎ 800-776-6406) buses run daily except Sunday from the main transfer point, at 9th & Duane Sts, downtown. The No 15 bus goes out to Fort

Clatsop and the Astoria-Seaside KOA (also near Fort Stevens).

For a taxi, call Royal Cab (☎ 503-325-5818).

SEASIDE & AROUND

Subtlety is not among the allures of Seaside (population 6220), which is one of Oregon's largest oceanfront resort towns. On summer weekends, the town's central precinct – dominated by bumper-car tracks, fish-and-chips shops, video-game arcades and gift stores – is completely thronged with tourists. Bicycles, 'fun-cycles' and surreys have the run of Seaside's boardwalk, called 'the Prom.' Pedestrians simply serve as the obstacles along the course. The miles of sandy beach are quite pleasant, largely because most visitors are off buying things.

Summer holidays here are a family tradition. At its best, Seaside seems old-fashioned and venerable, but it can also seem garish and crowded. Generally, kids will like it here, while adults may want to seek out calmer surroundings.

Orientation & Information

Seaside is 76 miles northwest of Portland on US 26.

The old town center is several blocks from the beach, along Holladay Dr. Broadway, the main tourist strip, intersects Holladay Dr and leads out to the beach and the Turnaround (Seaside's ground zero), where a statue of Lewis and Clark overlooks the Pacific. The Prom is a 2-mile-long cement boardwalk stretching along the beach. The Seaside Visitors Bureau (☎ 503-738-3097, 888-306-2326, Ⓦ www.seasideor.com) is at 989 Broadway.

Quiet Gearhart (population 1045), north and across the Necanicum River, is a nice alternative to the gaudy Seaside. Turn west off of US 101 onto Pacific Way (the first blinking light).

Saddle Mountain State Park

About 13 miles east of Seaside on US 26, this park (no fee) features a popular 3-mile hiking trail through alpine wildflower meadows to the top of Saddle Mountain (3283 feet). Views of the Columbia River and the Pacific coastline are pretty spectacular, but the trail is steep and grueling. Storms can blow in quickly from the ocean, so be prepared for changeable weather.

Saddle Mountain's barren monolith and curious pillow basalt was formed underwater. As North America rammed into the old Pacific seafloor, the formation was hoisted high above sea level. Erosion eventually wore away the softer sedimentary rock, exposing this gray volcanic plug.

See Places to Stay for information on camping here.

Golf & Surfing

The **Seaside Golf Course** (☎ 503-738-5261, 451 Ave U; green fees $10-12), is a nine-hole course that's popular with tourists and novice players. **Gearhart Golf Links** (☎ 503-738-3538, 10th & N Marion Sts, Gearhart; green fees $35-45), a British links-style course established in 1892, is the second-oldest golf course in western North America.

Rent surfing gear and get advice on where to hit the waves from **Cleanline Surf Company** (☎ 503-738-7888, 710 1st St; $15-35). They also rent in-line skates and body boards.

Special Events

Avoid Seaside when it's convulsed with one of its festivals. Rooms are impossible to find, and you'll spend hours just looking for a place to park. The Miss Oregon Contest is usually held here the weekend after the Fourth of July. The Hood to Coast Relay Marathon, a team endurance race that begins on Mt Hood and follows US 26 all the way to Seaside, not only jams the main road between Portland and Seaside, it also packs out the town, and a huge beach party is thrown for the runners. The relay is usually held the third weekend in August. The Seaside Beach Volleyball Tournament is held on the beach the weekend before Labor Day.

Places to Stay

Seaside is one of those places where room prices fluctuate wildly – make reservations well in advance. The prices below reflect peak-season rates.

Camping Head out of Seaside proper, to the state parks at Saddle Mountain or Fort Stevens (see Astoria, earlier), for more serene campgrounds.

Circle Creek Campground (☎ 503-738-6070, 1 mile south on US 101) Tents/hookups $17/22. Right on the highway, this campground has riverside sites in a grassy meadow.

Saddle Mountain State Park (☎ 503-861-1671, reservations 503-861-1671, 7 miles north of Hwy 26) Tents $14. The campground here has flush toilets and drinking water.

Hostels There is one local hostel option.

Seaside International Hostel (☎ 503-738-7911, 800-909-4776, 930 N Holladay Dr) Dorm beds $15/18 members/nonmembers, private rooms $58. This is a popular riverside place.

B&Bs One nice B&B is only a block from the beach and downtown.

Gilbert House B&B (☎ 503-738-9770, 800-410-9770, W www.gilbertinn.com, 341 Beach Dr) Rooms $106-133. There are 10 guest rooms at this resplendent, 1892 Queen Anne home.

Nonbeachfront Hotels The best lodging deals are a short walk to the beach.

Mariner Motel (☎ 503-738-3690, 429 S Holladay Dr) Singles/doubles from $48/60. It looks dodgy, but it's Seaside's cheapest.

Night Cap Inn (☎ 503-738-7473, 24 Ave U) Rooms from $59. This place is nicer, with basic rooms just blocks from the beach.

Sundowner Motor Inn (☎ 503-738-8301, 800-645-8678, 125 Oceanway) Rooms $69-80. Rooms are a good value at this pleasant motor lodge just one block off the beach.

Hillcrest Inn (☎ 503-738-6273, 800-270-7659, 118 N Columbia) Rooms $36-111. The nearby Hillcrest presents a variety of Cape Cod–style lodging options. Most single and double rooms fall between $67-81 and may include kitchens or Jacuzzi tubs.

Gearhart Ocean Inn (☎ 503-738-7373, 800-352-8034, W www.oregoncoastlodgings.com/

gearhart, 67 N Cottage, Gearhart) Rooms $63-117, 2-night minimum. Some of the cottage-style lodgings at this renovated older motel include a fireplace and a kitchen.

Beachfront Hotels A nonview room at a beachfront hotel is sometimes a better deal than at a nonbeachfront one.

The Tides Resort (☎ 503-738-6317, 800-548-2846, W www.clatsop.com/thetides, 2316 Beach Dr) Nonview/view rooms from $73/97. Located at the south end of the Prom and away from the frenzy of downtown, this resort is one of the best deals in Seaside.

Hi-Tide Motel (☎ 503-738-8414, 800-621-9876, 30 Ave G) Nonview/view rooms $107/128. Kitchenettes and fireplaces are standard at this condo, which has an indoor pool.

Ebb Tide Resort (☎ 503-738-8371, 800-468-6232, 300 N Prom) Nonview/view rooms from $75/123, kitchenettes $139-171. This condo is similar to the Hi-Tide, with fireplaces in every room.

Four Winds Motel (☎ 503-738-9524, 800-818-9524, W www.fourwindsmotel.com, 820 N Prom) Rooms $138-181. This small inn offers the best value in luxury lodging.

Inn at the Shore (☎ 503-738-3113, 800-713-9914, W www.innattheshore.com, 40 Ave U) Nonview/view rooms $127/202, one-/two-bedroom suites $213/266. The spacious luxury suites here feature balconies and fireplaces.

Shilo Inn (☎ 503-738-9571, 800-222-2244, W www.shiloinns.com, 30 N Prom) Nonview/view rooms from $138/266. The Shilo, right at the Turnaround, has all the amenities you'd expect to find at a big convention-style hotel, including room service, a restaurant and an indoor pool; however, the rooms aren't as nice as Seaside's other motels.

Vacation-Home Rentals Nicer vacation homes cost around $200, or upwards of $300 for a house on the Prom. The visitor center has complete listings, or contact *Seaside Vacation Homes* (☎ 888-738-0982, W www.seasidevacationhomes.com).

Places to Eat

There are few hidden secrets to dining in Seaside.

The old-fashioned **Harrison Bakery** *(608 Broadway)* offers coffee and fresh baked goods. **Pacific Bento** *(111 Broadway)* has breakfast burritos, smoothies and pastries. You can also eat cheap at **Morning Star Café** *(846 Ave C)*.

Lil' Bayou *(☎ 503-717-0624, 20 N Holladay Dr)* Entrees $12-17. Open lunch & dinner. It's Mardi Gras everyday at this seafood-focused Cajun restaurant. For under $10, you can easily feast off the large selection of side dishes.

Vista Sea Café *(☎ 503-738-8108, 150 Broadway)* Entrees $6, pizzas $12-22. This is a lively place for good sandwiches, gourmet pizzas and microbrewed beers.

Dooger's *(☎ 503-738-3773, 505 Broadway)* Lunch $5-8, dinner $10-20. Dooger's has a good selection of fresh fish.

Shilo Inn Restaurant *(☎ 503-738-8481, 30 N Prom)* Lunch $7-19, dinner $14-26. The Shilo has good ocean-view dining, with innovative seafood and an extensive regional wine list.

Pacific Way Bakery & Cafe *(☎ 503-738-0245, 601 Pacific Way)* Lunch/dinner $6/15. Breakfast and fresh baked breads have people lined up out the door at this charming old storefront cafe. For lunch, there's homemade soup, and there's seafood and pizza for dinner.

Getting There & Around

Amtrak Thruway buses to Portland ($16 one way), Astoria and Cannon Beach stop daily at Tony's True Value Hardware *(☎ 503-738-5966)*, 34 N Holladay Dr. The Pacific Trails *(☎ 503-692-4437)* bus to Kelso, Washington ($11), stops daily in front of the Seaside Hostel.

Sunset Empire Transit *(☎ 800-776-6406)* buses to Astoria, Cannon Beach and Manzanita depart several times Monday to Saturday from the corner of Holladay Dr and Broadway.

Seaside Yellow Cab *(☎ 503-738-5252)* is the local taxi company.

CANNON BEACH & AROUND

Miles of sandy beaches, broken by immense basalt promontories and rocky tide pools, front Cannon Beach (population 1430). Directly behind, the Coast Range rises in steep parapets.

Charming Cannon Beach is undoubtedly one of the most popular beach towns of northern Oregon. Some of the coast's premier hotels are here, along with interesting boutiques and galleries. In summer, the streets are ablaze with flowers. Unlike Seaside's Coney Island–like atmosphere, Cannon Beach is artsy and a little smug and is apparently reserved for the wealthy – the city council has historically opposed affordable-housing developments. Only 20% of the town's workers actually live here – the rest are bused in from outlying towns around Portland. Lodging is expensive, and the streets are jammed – on a sunny Saturday, you'll spend the better part of an hour just parking.

Orientation & Information

Cannon Beach is 78 miles northwest of Portland and 9 miles south of Seaside.

Cannon Beach Magazine is a helpful tourist publication available from the Cannon Beach Information Center *(☎ 503-436-2623, W www.cannonbeach.org)*, 201 E 2nd St. Pick up beach reading from Cannon Beach Book Company *(☎ 503-436-1301)*, 130 N Hemlock St.

Downtown Cannon Beach

The delightful downtown area around Hemlock and 2nd Sts is filled with little alleys winding around a maze of boutiques and galleries. About a half-mile south is **Icefire Glassworks** *(☎ 503-436-2359, 116 E Gower)*, where you can sometimes see glass artisans at work.

Beaches

Beaches here are some of the most beautiful in Oregon, with **Haystack Rock** and other outcroppings rising out of the surf. There's easy beach access at the end of Harrison St downtown, or at the end of Gower

St, a mile south. **Tolovana Beach Wayside** is 3 miles south along Hemlock St.

Other beach points are accessible at **Hug Point State Park**, which is 5 miles south on US 101.

Ecola State Park

Beaches at this state park (*☎ 503-436-2844, 2 miles north of Cannon Beach on Ecola Beach Rd; $3 day-use fee or Coast Passport*) offer more seclusion and great picnicking. Short paths at Ecola Point lead over the headland to dramatic views of Cannon Beach's 7-mile-long sandy shore, sharply punctuated with stone monoliths and all hunkered beneath the Coast Range.

This area marks the farthest reach of the Lewis and Clark expedition's westward journey; they came here hoping to get the blubber from a beached whale. (The state park here takes its name from the word 'ecola,' which means 'whale' in the Clatsop language.)

Leading north from here, past tremendous vistas, is the Oregon Coast Trail, which follows the same route traversed by the Corps of Discovery in 1806. Follow the trail 1½ miles north around the headland to reach the next sandy cove at **Indian Beach**, which is popular with surfers (who drive here). The trail continues north to **Tillamook Head**, which looms 1200 feet above the crashing Pacific for a view of the **Tillamook Lighthouse**, right offshore on a 100-foot-high sea stack. Now inactive, the lighthouse serves as resting place for cremation ashes. Most turn back here, though the 7-mile trail continues north to wind up in Seaside.

Oswald West State Park

This beautiful preserve (*☎ 800-551-6949, 9 miles south of Cannon Beach on US 101; no*

The Mystery of Neahkahnie Mountain

According to Tillamook and Clatsop legend, a Spanish ship landed long ago at the base of Neahkahnie Mountain. The crew disembarked, dug a deep hole and lowered a chest into the cavity. Crew members placed heavy bags inside the chest and sealed it. The captain of the ship then shot a black sailor, whose body was thrown on top of the chest before it was buried. The Native Americans who had witnessed the scene abandoned the site, fearing the spirits of the murdered man.

A number of circumstances corroborate the tale. By the time explorers reached the Nehalem Bay area, tribes along northern Oregon had gathered a great deal of beeswax, which seems to confirm that Spanish ships had already been there: Beeswax was used in candle-making and was a common article of trade aboard 17th-century Pacific-going Spanish vessels, and old shipping records indicate a number of beeswax-bearing ships were lost in the northern Pacific.

Around 1890, a farmer found a curious rock in a meadow on the southern face of the mountain. Etched in the rock were letters, Christian crosses, arrows and a series of dots. After other rocks were discovered with the same design, the immediate assumption was that the stones contained information that would lead to the buried treasure. Much digging ensued in the early 20th century, and many claim to have solved the mystery of the buried treasure, though no one has ever come forward with it. The carved rocks, called the Neahkahnie Stones, are on display at the Tillamook Pioneer Museum.

fee) of beach, mountain, rocky headland and dense coastal rain forest is named after Governor Oswald West, who championed the state's beach-access bill, putting all oceanfront land into public ownership.

Two major headlands, **Neahkahnie Mountain** and **Cape Falcon**, reach far out into the Pacific, protecting a small bay called Smugglers Cove.

It's a quarter-mile hike from highway parking lots past a tent-only campground to isolated **Short Sands Beach**, one of the coast's most popular surf beaches. The rocky prominences north along Cape Falcon offer expansive views and are good places to watch for sea birds. An easy trail leads 2 miles through old-growth forest to a viewpoint from the salal-covered headland.

A more strenuous hike is the 4-mile climb to the top of 1660-foot Neahkahnie Mountain, which towers above Nehalem Bay. The approach from the campground passes through forests and broad meadows edged by sheer cliffs that drop away to the raging Pacific. Shave off 2 miles by starting the climb from the unsigned turnout a mile south on US 101. Views are amazing – on a clear day, you can see 50 miles out to sea.

Special Events

The **Haystack Summer Program** (☎ *503-725-4027, 800-547-8887, ext 3484,* W *www.haystack.pdx.edu)* is a PSU-sponsored program with six weeks of art, writing and music seminars in Cannon Beach every summer. Nationally recognized artists and writers serve as faculty, and courses may be taken for college credit.

At Cannon Beach's largest festival – **Sandcastle Day**, held on a Saturday in June – teams compete for originality and execution in sand sculpture, many of which go far beyond standard castles. The date changes due to the tides; call the information center (☎ 503-436-2623) for exact dates. The sculptures are very impressive, making the festival one of the coast's most famous. Lodging is booked up and parking is worse than usual around the time of the festival.

Places to Stay

Older motels that would be rundown and cheap anywhere else are quaint and expensive here, with the cheapest rooms starting at $70-80 in summer. Kitchens, fireplaces and suites are available at most motels. A minimum stay may be required.

Camping Wheelbarrows are provided for hauling gear down a short trail to forested tent sites above Smuggler's Cove at *Oswald West State Park* (☎ *503-368-5154, 10 miles south on US 101)* Sites $14. Open Mar-Sept. Sites have flush toilets and are assigned on a first-come, first-served basis. Although it's undeniably lovely, the campground is often rowdy with young surfers.

Cannon Beach RV Resort (☎ *503-436-2231, 800-847-2231, 345 Elk Creek Rd at US 101)* Hookups $33.50. This wooded RV park is pretty nice, with an indoor pool and laundry.

Sea Ranch RV Park (☎ *503-436-2815, Beach Loop & 5th St)* Tents/hookups $19/21. Smaller Sea Ranch, on quiet Ecola Creek, is across from the entrance to Ecola State Park.

Nonbeachfront Hotels Renovated motor lodges and boarding houses offer Cannon Beach's coziest lodgings.

Blue Gull Inn Motel (☎ *503-436-2714, 800-507-2714,* W *www.bluegullinn.net, 487 S Hemlock St)* Rooms $73-126. Cottage-style rooms at this renovated older motel are surprisingly spacious and pleasant.

McBee Motel (☎ *503-436-2569, 866-262-2336,* W *www.mcbeecottages.com, 888 S Hemlock St)* Rooms $73-123. Cottages here are similar to the Blue Gull, only not as fixed up.

Sand Trap Inn (☎ *503-436-0247, 800-400-4106,* W *www.sandtrapinn.com, 539 S Hemlock St)* Rates $85-159. The Sand Trap controls a number of houses and cabins (including the McBee).

Quiet Cannon Lodgings (☎ *503-436-2415, 372 N Spruce St)* Cabins $102. This place has a number of homey cabins close to the beach at the north end of town, off bustling Hemlock St.

Cannon Beach Hotel (☎ 503-436-1392, 800-238-4107, W www.cannonbeachhotel com, 1116 S Hemlock St) Rooms $105-170. Once a boarding house for loggers, this inn is now a thoroughly updated European-style hotel.

Haystack Resort (☎ 503-436-1577, 800-499-2220, W www.haystackresort.com, 3339 S Hemlock St) Rooms/suites from $106/170. Rooms here all have ocean views, but the ocean is across the street and across a parking lot. Standard rooms are small, but not bad, and there's an indoor pool.

Beachfront Hotels Balconies are standard at most beachfront motels here.

Hallmark Resort (☎ 503-436-1566, 800-345-5676, 1400 S Hemlock St) Nonview/view rooms from $106/181. This big luxury resort fronts onto Haystack Rock and has some of the nicest oceanfront rooms around.

The Waves Motel (☎ 503-436-2205, 800-822-2468, 188 W 2nd St) Nonview/view/oceanfront rooms from $106/149/170. Close to downtown, The Waves offers rooms in several upscale buildings.

Webb's Scenic Surf (☎ 503-436-2706, 800-374-9322, 255 N Larch St) Rooms $155-203. Right next door, friendly Webb's is modest but well maintained, with all oceanfront rooms (most with kitchens) right on the beach.

Tolovana Inn (☎ 503-436-2211, 800-333-8890, W www.tolovanainn.com, 3400 S Hemlock St) Nonview/view/oceanfront rooms from $76/149/169. Recent development has made this large condo complex at Tolovana Beach the coast's largest conference facility. Nonview rooms are a bargain, considering that all rooms have kitchens and great beach access.

Major Motel (☎ 503-436-2241, 2863 Pacific St) Rooms $95-170. It's a little rundown, but the rates at this Tolovana Beach motel aren't too bad for an ocean view, and most rooms have kitchens.

Stephanie Inn (☎ 503-436-2221, 800-633-3466, 2740 Pacific St) Nonview/oceanfront rooms with breakfast from $170/245. Gabled and turreted in Queen Anne–revival style,

this 'country inn' is exclusively adult and very upscale, and sort of represents the ultimate special-occasion hotel. Pastimes include an afternoon wine gathering and ocean-view dining in the guests-only restaurant.

Vacation-Home Rentals A beach home can be a good value if you're traveling with a group of friends. For a range of rental options try *Cannon Beach Property Management* (☎ 503-436-2021, 877-386-3402, W www.cbpm .com, 1415 S Hemlock St) Rates $155-400.

Places to Eat
Cannon Beach is a weekenders' kind of place, and many of its best restaurants close midweek.

Sand & Grain Bakery (1064 S Hemlock St). This is a good place to pick up some pastries and spend time browsing art.

Lazy Susan Grill & Scoop (☎ 503-436-9551, 156 N Hemlock St) Sandwiches $5. This standard cafe and bakery is one of the cheapest places for breakfast or lunch.

Pizza à Fetta (☎ 503-436-0333, 231 N Hemlock St) Slices/pies from $2.25/$15. Gourmet pizza at this courtyard pizzeria is served by the slice.

Midtown Cafe (☎ 503-436-1016, 1235 S Hemlock St) Breakfast $7. Omelets and frittatas are the specialty of this kitschy cafe.

Dooger's (☎ 503-436-2225, 1371 S Hemlock St) Lunch/dinner $7/14. Deep-fried seafood is the staple of Dooger's, one of the few establishments open every day.

Be sure to make reservations for the following places.

Kalypso (☎ 503-436-1585, 140 N Hemlock St) Entrees $15-20. Open Thur-Tues. Asian and Mediterranean influences are strong here in seafood dishes such as salmon miso and curried fish; the atmosphere is casual but intimate.

JP's Restaurant (☎ 503-436-0908, Cannon Beach Hotel, 1116 S Hemlock St) Entrees $15-20. Noted for its excellent wine list, JP's serves seafood and pasta in an upscale bistro.

The Bistro (☎ 503-436-2661, 263 N Hemlock St) Open Thur-Mon. Entrees $14-21.

Seafood dishes at this tiny courtyard restaurant feature locally caught fish and shellfish.

Entertainment
Lodge-style *Clark's* brewpub, at the north end of Hemlock St, is the highpoint of Cannon Beach nightlife.

Coaster Theater (☎ 503-436-1242, W *www .coastertheater.com, 108 N Hemlock St)* puts on community stage productions.

Getting There & Around
Amtrak Thruway buses to Portland ($15 one way), Seaside ($3) and Astoria depart daily from the Family Market (☎ 503-436-0515), at 1170 S Hemlock St.

The information center on 2nd St is the stop for daily Pacific Trails (☎ 503-692-4437) buses to Kelso, Washington ($11), as well as for local Sunset Empire Transit (☎ 800-776-6406) buses, which go to Seaside, Astoria and Manzanita (for connections south) several times Monday to Saturday.

The half-hourly Cannon Beach shuttle (fare by donation) runs the length of Hemlock St to the end of Tolovana Beach.

MANZANITA & AROUND
The Nehalem River slows down considerably as it approaches the Pacific, creating both a wide estuarial valley, that's prized by farmers, and narrow Nehalem Bay, protected from the lashings of the Pacific by a 7-mile-long sand spit.

On the ocean side of the spit, Manzanita (population 810), with its lovely white-sand beaches, is the center of tourism. The town verges on upscale, but with far less hype than Cannon Beach. Right on the river, the historic and colorful fishing villages of Nehalem (population 235) and Wheeler (population 385) are becoming centers for antiques and river recreation. Magical Neahkahnie Mountain rises above the Pacific, dropping away in 700-foot-high cliffs to the pounding waves.

Activities
In Manzanita, there's **beach access** along the entire length of Ocean Rd, west of downtown, and south of Manzanita at nearby

Nehalem Bay State Park ($3 day-use or Coast Passport). Rent bicycles from **Manzanita Fun Merchants** (☎ *503-368-6606, 186 Laneda Ave; $14 per day)*, and spend a leisurely day pedaling between beaches. **Pearl Creek Stables** (☎ *503-368-5267, 4th St & Laneda Ave; $35-40 per hour)* offers **horseback** riding.

The quiet waters of Nehalem Bay are good for contemplative **paddling** and **bird watching**, as the estuaries are rich in bird life. Activity centers on the marina in downtown Wheeler. **Kayaking** is possible too – rent equipment from **Wheeler on the Bay Lodge** (☎ *503-368-5858, 800-469-3204, 580 Marine Dr; half-/full-day $22.50/32)*. **Crabbing** and steelhead **fishing** are exceptionally good here too.

Places to Stay
Camping and B&Bs are not so readily available, but there's a decent option of motels in the area.

Nehalem Bay State Park (☎ *800-452-5687, 3 miles south of Manzanita off US 101)* Campsites/yurts $19/33. This big campground on the dunes of Nehalem Spit has showers, equestrian facilities and a boat ramp.

Arbors at Manzanita (☎ *503-368-7566, 888-664-9857, 78 Idaho Ave)* Rooms $107-123. This classic, small, cottage-style B&B has two ocean-view rooms.

Sand Dune Motel (☎ *503-368-5163, 428 Dorcas Lane)* Rooms without/with kitchens $64-75/91. The beach is a few blocks away from this tidy, well-maintained motel.

Sunset Surf Motel (☎ *503-368-5224, 800-243-8035, 248 Ocean Rd)* Rooms $75-128. Straight across from the beach, this motel is family-oriented and a bit outdated.

Ocean Inn (☎ *503-368-7701, 866-368-7701,* W *www.manzanitarentals.com, 32 Laneda Ave)* Rooms $102-155. Rooms at this newly built ocean-view inn are more comfortable.

Inn at Manzanita (☎ *503-368-6754,* W *www.neahkahnie.net, 67 Laneda Ave)* Rooms $128-171. Head to this forested inn for a relaxing retreat, with wood-paneled rooms featuring hot tubs, fireplaces, kitchenettes and ocean views.

OREGON

Places to Eat

Head to *Manzanita News & Espresso (500 Laneda Ave)* for coffee and a newspaper. There's a *cafe* at the Manzanita junction on US 101 that serves breakfast (closed Saturday). A stop for a gourmet breakfast at Wheeler's *Treasure Cafe (☎ 503-368-7740, 92 Rorvik St)*, open Thur-Sun, is on the way for southbound travelers.

Left Coast Siesta (☎ 503-368-7997, 298 Laneda Ave) Lunch $5. Burritos and enchiladas here are satisfying and inexpensive.

Blue Sky Cafe (☎ 503-368-5712, 154 Laneda Ave) Entrees $12.50-27. Dinner only. This eclectic restaurant is noteworthy for pan-Pacific touches, such as soy-tamarind salmon.

Marzano's Pizza Pie (☎ 503-368-3663, 60 Laneda Ave) Medium pies $12-17. Dinner only. The calzones here are good too.

Getting There & Around

Three buses go to Cannon Beach and Seaside on Sunset Empire Transit (☎ 800-776-6406). Four to five buses go to Tillamook ($2) for connections to Oceanside or Pacific City on Tillamook County Transportation (☎ 503-815-8283). Buses pick up Monday to Saturday from 5th St at Laneda Ave.

GARIBALDI

Ten miles north of Tillamook, at the mouth of Tillamook Bay, sits the scrappy village of Garibaldi (population 1000), home to one of Oregon's largest charter-fishing fleets. **Troller Deep Sea Charters** *(☎ 503-332-3666, 800-546-3666)* and **Siggi-G Ocean Charters** *(☎ 503-332-3285)*, at the boat basin, specialize in deep-sea and salmon fishing ($65-150). Outfit your own fishing trip at **Garibaldi Marina** *(☎ 503-322-3312, 302 Mooring Basin Rd)*, which rents boats, crab rings and tackle. Most companies also run **whale-watching trips** upon request.

For no-frills lodging, check along Garibaldi's piers, where modest *motels* provide shelter for charter fishers.

Pirates Cove Restaurant (☎ 503-322-2092, 14170 US 101 N) Lunch/dinner $6.50/17. There's an incredible view of the bay from this steak-and-seafood restaurant north of Garibaldi.

TILLAMOOK & AROUND

The first thing you'll notice when you arrive in Tillamook is the smell – *a lot* of cows live in this area. Five coastal rivers flow into the flat Tillamook Valley, making it perfect for raising dairy cattle. Cheese production began in Tillamook in the 1890s, when an English cheese maker brought his cheddar-making techniques to the fledgling dairies along Tillamook Bay. Thousands stop here annually to visit the famed Tillamook Cheese Factory, which produces 40 million pounds of cheese a year. The Tillamook visitor center (☎ 503-842-7525) is in the parking lot.

South of Tillamook, US 101 loses the beaches and headlands and follows the Nestucca River through pastureland and logged-off mountains. The slower but prettier 30-mile Three Capes Dr begins in Tillamook and follows the coast.

Things to See & Do

Besides visiting the **Tillamook Cheese Factory** *(☎ 503-815-1300, 4175 N US 101; admission free; open 8am-8pm)*, there's the **Tillamook Pioneer Museum** *(☎ 503-842-4553, 2106 2nd St; adult/senior/student $2/1.50/50¢; open 8am-5pm Mon-Sat, 11am-5pm Sun)*, with its curiously carved Neahkahnie stones, meant to point to a legendary buried treasure near Manzanita.

There's a collection of fighter planes in a 7-acre blimp hangar 3 miles south at the **Tillamook Naval Air Museum** *(☎ 503-842-1130, ⓦ www.tillamookair.com, 6030 Hangar Rd; adult/senior/youth/child $9.50/8.50/5.50/2; open 10am-5pm)*.

At Munson Creek State Natural Site, 6 miles south off US 101, an easy half-mile hike through old-growth spruce visits **Munson Creek Falls**, the highest waterfall in the Coast Range at 319 feet.

Places to Eat

There's little reason to stay in Tillamook. Grab lunch at the cheese factory's *cafe*, or at one of the inexpensive *Mexican restaurants* around town. Unwind from a day touring the Three Capes Dr with tea and a plough-man's lunch at *La Tea Da* (☎ *503-842-5447, 904 Main Ave*).

Getting There & Away
Tillamook County Transportation (☎ 503-815-8283) buses depart from 4th & Pacific Sts to Oceanside, Netarts and Pacific City on the capes, as well as to Manzanita and Portland ($10 one way).

THREE CAPES SCENIC ROUTE
Cape Meares, Cape Lookout and Cape Kiwanda are some of the coast's most stunning headlands, strung together on Three Capes Drive, a 30-mile alternative to US 101. Along the way are a handful of isolated beach towns. Facilities are limited; buy groceries in Tillamook if you plan on cooking.

This slow and winding drive begins in Tillamook and emerges near the junction for Pacific City. Side roads at Netarts and Sandlake will return you to US 101.

Tillamook County Transit (☎ 503-815-8283) has bus connections to Oceanside, Netarts and Pacific City from Tillamook (fare $1-2; no Sunday service).

Cape Meares State Park
The forested headland at this state park (☎ 800-551-6949, 10 miles west of Tillamook; no fee) is a welcome relief from the relentless clear-cutting that edges much of the Three Capes Drive. Short trails link the **Cape Meares Lighthouse**, which was built in 1890 and is Oregon's shortest, to the **Octopus Tree**, a massive Sitka spruce that lacks a central trunk. Native American legend holds that the tree was shaped to cradle funeral canoes. A platform offers viewing of offshore bird life and whales.

Oceanside
Once an unheralded beach resort, Oceanside, 9 miles west of Tillamook, has been 'discovered,' and now a massive condominium resort clings to the headland above the town. Rising immediately out to sea are the towering 400-foot-high **Three Arch Rocks**, preserved as a seabird refuge shared by sea lions and seals.

Accomodations with a kitchen are a must if you're planning to stay more than a day or two.

House on the Hill Motel (☎ *503-842-6030, 1816 Maxwell Mt Rd*) Rooms $95-130. Views are grand from this motel on a bluff above Oceanside; some rooms have kitchens.

Oceanside Inn (☎ *503-842-2961, 800-347-2972, 1440 NW Pacific St*) Rooms $55-100. Kitchen-equipped rooms are a plus at this inviting motel near the beach.

For a list of vacation rentals near Three Capes Dr, contact the *Tillamook Visitors Center* (☎ *503-842-7525*, W *www.tillamoo .com/lodging.html*).

Roseanna's Cafe (☎ *503-842-7351, 1490 NW Pacific St*) Entrees $13-19. Roseanna's has a casual maritime atmosphere and is widely noted for good seafood and slow service.

Netarts
Marina-oriented Netarts, 6 miles west of Tillamook, offers few facilities for travelers, and the locals prefer it that way. The area is known for its excellent clamming, crabbing and fishing. Rent a boat at **Bay Shore RV Park & Marina** (☎ *503-842-7774, 1 mile south of Netarts*).

Bay Shore RV Park & Marina (☎ *503-842-7774, 2260 Bilyeu Ave*) Hookups without/with view $18.50/21. Boating is the main pastime at this bayside RV park.

Terimore Motel (☎ *503-842-4623, 800-635-1821, 5105 Crab Ave*) Rooms $45-89. The modest Terimore overlooks the beach and features nice rooms (some with kitchens).

Cape Lookout State Park
Cape Lookout juts out nearly a mile from the mainland, like a finger pointing out to sea. A panoramic vista atop sheer cliffs that rise 800 feet above the pounding Pacific makes this state park (☎ *503-842-4981, 12 miles southwest of Tillamook*) the highpoint of the Three Capes. In the dead of winter, the end of the cape is thronged with whale-watchers. At the base of the cape are wide sandy beaches ($3 day use or Coast Passport) and a popular campground on Netarts Spit, a grassy dune that stretches nearly 4 miles

across Netarts Bay. Clamming is popular along the beach at low tides.

The popular 2.4-mile **Cape Trail**, which leads to views at the end of Cape Lookout, begins from a trailhead (no fee) 2½ miles south of the campground. The **South Trail** also starts here and winds 1.8 miles down to beaches on the south side of the headland. A longer approach to the cape on the **North Trail** spends 2.3 miles climbing the headland from the day-use area near the campground before intercepting the Cape Trail.

Cape Lookout Campground (☎ 800-452-5687) Tents/hookups/yurts $16/19/33. The name implies grand seascapes right out your tent flap, but this big campground is actually down by the beach.

Cape Kiwanda

The third in this route's trilogy of capes is Cape Kiwanda, a squat, sandstone bluff that rises just north of the little town of Pacific City, which is where locals go to take a break from dairy farming. To reach the cape, hike up the spine of the dunes that drape around it; the dunes are popular with hang gliders. Watching the dory fleet launch their craft straight into the surf is the most interesting thing about the beach here, which is otherwise cluttered with pickup trucks. **Bob Straub State Park**, at the south end of the spit, affords access to miles and miles of lonelier beach.

The views of crashing surf that you might expect from Cape Kiwanda are nonexistent at hotels and restaurants here.

Cape Kiwanda RV Park (☎ 503-965-6230, 33005 Kiwanda Rd) Tents/hookups $16/25. There's nothing special about this RV park just opposite the beach.

Inn at Pacific City (☎ 503-965-6366, 800-722-2489, w www.innatpacificcity.com, 35215 Brooten Rd) Rooms $69-75. This Cape Cod–style lodging has nice, moderately priced rooms.

Inn at Cape Kiwanda (☎ 503-965-7001, 888-965-7001, w www.innatcapekiwanda .com, 33105 Cape Kiwanda Dr) Rooms $159-279. This perfectly lovely upscale inn near the beach seems at odds with all the fishing shacks and boat trailers. Take a

break from driving at the inn's ocean-view espresso bar.

Pelican Pub & Brewery (☎ 503-965-7707, 33180 Cape Kiwanda Dr) Entrees $8-17. Pizza and burgers are mainstays at this popular beachside brewpub.

Grateful Bread Bakery (☎ 503-965-7337, 34805 Brooten Rd) Breakfast & lunch $7. In good weather, meals are served on the deck.

The Riverhouse (☎ 503-965-6722, 34450 Brooten Rd) Lunch $8-15, dinner $15-20. The cozy and unpretentious Riverhouse, on the Nestucca River, is a favorite restaurant in these parts.

LINCOLN CITY & AROUND

A 7-mile-long series of commercial strips, motels, snack bars and gift shops that fronting a fairly wide – if lackluster – stretch of sandy beach, Lincoln City (population 7045) is a major family-vacation destination and is also the principal trade center for a large area of the coast.

The town itself isn't very attractive and sprawls uncontrollably across too much of the Oregon coast. It does, however, contain numerous beaches, as well as the only affordable beachfront motels on the Oregon coast, and there are a lot of them – only Portland has more.

Other attractions include a complex of **outlet stores**, and the **Chinook Winds Casino**, operated by the Siletz Indians, at the north end of town.

Orientation & Information

Lincoln City is 25 miles north of Newport on US 101. Portland is 88 miles away via Hwy 18, which joins US 101 just north of town. To the north is one of the coast's major capes, Cascade Head, and 9 miles south is Gleneden Beach, the site of the Westin Salishan, the coast's most upscale resort.

US 101 streams through a number of monotonous commercial districts, with the height of activity centered on the D River Beach State Wayside.

The visitor center (☎ 541-994-3070, 800-452-2151, w www.oregoncoast.org) is at 801 SW US 101. The post office is at 1501 SE Devil's Lake Rd.

OREGON

LINCOLN CITY

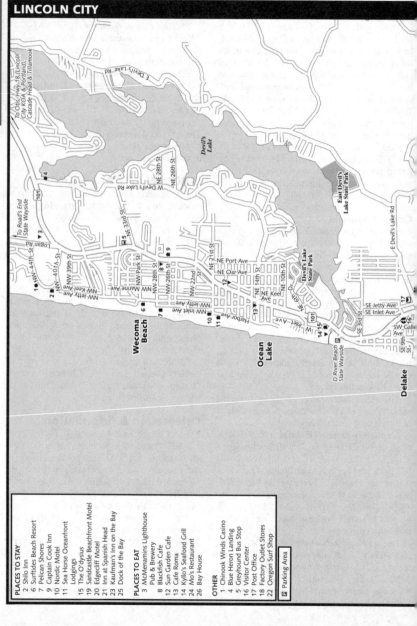

PLACES TO STAY
2   Shilo Inn
6   Surftides Beach Resort
7   Pelican Shores
9   Captain Cook Inn
10 Nordic Motel
11 Sea Horse Oceanfront Lodgings
15 The O'dysius
19 Sandcastle Beachfront Motel
20 Edgecliff Motel
21 Inn at Spanish Head
23 Kaufman's Inn on the Bay
25 Dock of the Bay

PLACES TO EAT
3   McMenamins Lighthouse Pub & Brewery
8   Blackfish Cafe
12 Sun Garden Cafe
13 Cafe Roma
14 Kyllo's Seafood Grill
24 Mo's Restaurant
26 Bay House

OTHER
1   Chinook Winds Casino
4   Blue Heron Landing
5   Greyhound Bus Stop
16 Visitor Center
17 Post Office
18 Factory Outlet Stores
22 Oregon Surf Shop

P Parking Area

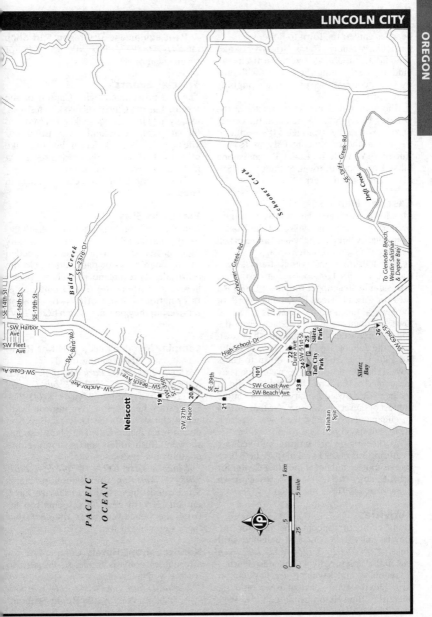

LINCOLN CITY

OREGON

PACIFIC OCEAN

Nelscott

SE 14th St
SE 16th St
SE 19th St
SW Harbor Ave
SW Fleet Ave

Baldy Creek

SE 23rd Dr

SW Bird Rd

SW Coast Ave

SW Anchor Ave

SW Beach Ave

SW 35th St

SW 37th Place

SE 39th St

19
20
21

Schooner Creek

Schooner Creek Rd

High School Dr

101

SW Coast Ave
SW Beach Ave

22
Dune Ave
SW 51st St
24
23
25

Taft City Park

Siletz Park

SE Drift Creek Rd

Drift Creek

To Gleneden Beach,
Westin Salishan
& Depoe Bay

SW 62nd St
26

Siletz Bay

Salishan Spit

1 km
.5 mile

0 .5
0 .25

Beaches

Lincoln City's 7-mile stretch of wide sandy beaches endear the town to holidaymakers, particularly family groups. Brightly colored glass floats, handblown by local artisans, are hidden weekly along the beach for finding by beachcombers as part of an ongoing beach promotion.

The main public access points are at the D River Beach State Wayside, in the center of town where the river meets the Pacific; at the north end of Lincoln City, at Road's End State Wayside, off Logan Rd; and along Siletz Bay, south of town, at the end of SW 51st St, at Taft City Park.

Cascade Head

Meadowed Cascade Head was slated to become a resort in the 1960s, but the Nature Conservancy bought up the land and worked to make it a scenic research area.

Two Nature Conservancy **trails** access Cascade Head's 1200-foot ocean vista. The first is a mile-long upper trail from USFS Rd 1861 (or Cascade Head Rd), 4 miles north of the Hwy 18 junction; the second is a 2.7-mile lower trail that scales the headland from the end of Three Rocks Rd, a mile north of town along the Salmon River. At the end of USFS Rd 1861 is the 2.6-mile trail down to **Harts Cove**, a remote meadow along a cliff-lined bay frequented by sea lions. USFS Rd 1861 and its trailheads are closed January to July 15 in the interest of preserving rare flowers that sustain an endangered butterfly; the lower Cascade Head trail stays open year round.

Workshops on art, writing and ecology (featuring lots of sea kayaking) are held here every summer and fall at the **Sitka Center for Art & Ecology** (☎ 541-994-5485, ⓦ www.sitka center.org), off Three Rocks Rd.

Activities

Many come to Lincoln City just for the famous links-style course at **Salishan Golf Links** (☎ 541-764-3632, 7760 N US 101; green fees $65), 9 miles south at Gleneden Beach.

Canoeing and **kayaking** are popular on both Devil's Lake, east of town, and on Siletz Bay. **Blue Heron Landing** (☎ 541-994-

4708, 4006 W Devil's Lake Rd; $10-60) has rentals.

Rent equipment at **Oregon Surf Shop** (☎ 541-996-3957, 4933 SW US 101) for surfing near Siletz Bay.

Special Events

The self-proclaimed 'Kite Capital of the World,' Lincoln City hosts two kite festivals, usually held the second weekend in May and the last weekend of September. Enormous kites – some over 100 feet in length – take off to twist and dive in the ocean breezes. At night, the kites are illuminated.

There's also a big sand-castle contest in late July.

Places to Stay

Lincoln City's beachfront hotels aren't entirely unaffordable, and they're usually right on the beach, with views unimpeded by any boardwalks or parking lots. On the downside, there are no real cheap places here. The visitor center (see Orientation & Information) doesn't offer a reservation service, but they do track which hotels have vacancies.

Camping You don't need a tent or RV to stay at one of these campgrounds.

Devil's Lake State Park (☎ 541-994-2002, reservations 800-452-5687, NE 6th Dr and US 101) Tents/hookups/yurts $16/19/35. Campsites here are a five-minute walk across the street to the D River Beach in downtown Lincoln City. The place also has showers, flush toilets and swimming and boating on a freshwater lake.

Lincoln City KOA (☎ 541-994-2961, 5298 NE Park Lane) Tents/hookups/cabins $20/23/36. If the east side of Devil's Lake, out on Hwy 18 near Otis, seems too far from the beach, consider the fact that there's no wind or fog.

Nonoceanfront Hotels Competition for affordable rooms is fierce, so be sure to reserve well in advance.

Captain Cook Inn (☎ 541-994-2522, 800-994-2522, 2626 NE US 101) Rooms without/

with kitchens $59/64. This well-maintained motor lodge is Lincoln City's only plausible budget choice.

Kaufman's Inn on the Bay *(☎ 541-996-3996, 800-843-4940, 861 SW 51st St)* Rooms $70-134. There's older, economy-class rooms here on Siletz Bay.

The O'dysius *(☎ 541-994-4121, 800-869-8069,* W *www.odysius.com, 120 NW Inlet Court)* Rooms $159-205. Reproduction antiques fill the halls of this newly built luxury hotel near the D River Beach State Wayside. All rooms have fireplaces, featherbeds and ocean views.

Oceanfront Hotels The best deals are the well-maintained older motels in the midsection of town. Most offer kitchens and fireplaces.

Nordic Motel *(☎ 541-994-8145, 800-452-3558, 2133 NW Inlet Ave)* Rooms $85-112. Stairs lead down the bluff to the beach from this older motel, which has all ocean-view rooms, a pool and a spa.

Sea Horse Oceanfront Lodgings *(☎ 541-994-2101, 800-662-2101,* W *www.seahorsemotel.com, 2039 NW Harbor Ave)* Nonview/view rooms from $82/93. The Sea Horse is nicer and offers low beach access.

Pelican Shores *(☎ 541-994-2134, 800-705-5505,* W *www.pelicanshores.com, 2645 NW Inlet Ave)* Rooms $106-138. Ground-floor rooms at this pleasant motel have outdoor patios, and there's both indoor and outdoor pools.

Surftides Beach Resort *(☎ 541-994-2191, 800-452-2159,* W *www.surftidesbeachresort.com, 2945 NW Jetty Ave)* Nonview/view rooms from $81/100 (weekdays less). Balconied rooms are a plus at this attractive condo, which features an indoor pool and tennis courts.

Shilo Inn *(☎ 541-994-3655, 800-222-2244, 1501 NW 40th St)* Nonview/view rooms from $117/214 (weekdays less). While perfectly nice, this sprawling new business-class development next to the casino is overpriced and best left to convention-goers. You'll get more for your money at the fancier resorts south of town.

There are plenty more motels on the south end of town.

Sandcastle Beachfront Motel *(☎ 541-996-3613,* W *www.sandcastlemotel.net, 3417 SW Anchor Ave)* Rooms $83-127. Down in Nelscott is this older, relatively ignored economy-class motel with balconies and some kitchens.

Edgecliff Motel *(☎ 541-996-2055, 3733 SW US 101)* New/old rooms $83/73. Newly built 'studio' rooms with fireplaces and balconies are a great deal at this motel, which is on the bluff by the Inn at Spanish Head (see Resorts, next). Older studios are cheaper but cramped. Avoid the condos.

Dock of the Bay *(☎ 541-996-3549, 800-362-5229,* W *www.dockofthebay-or.com, 1116 SW 51st St)* One-bedroom condos $127. Balconies and fireplaces are standard at this condo on quieter Siletz Bay; the place features a swimming pool, hot tub and sauna.

Resorts Ask about midweek specials and off-season rates.

Inn at Spanish Head *(☎ 541-996-2161, 800-452-8127,* W *www.spanishhead.com, 4009 SW US 101)* Rooms $166-187. At this beach resort, several stories of balconied rooms have been piled to the top of a steep bluff. Amenities include indoor and outdoor pools, exercise facilities and an ocean-view restaurant; most rooms have kitchens.

The Westin Salishan *(☎ 541-764-2371,* W *www.salishan.com, 7760 N US 101, Gleneden Beach)* Rooms $230-316. *Condé Nast Traveler* recently dubbed this fancy four-star resort one of the best places to stay in the world. The first-rate golf course on the rambling 1000-acre wooded estate is ringed by lavish condominiums.

Vacation-Home Rentals A number of nice beachfront homes are available from ***Horizon Rentals*** *(☎ 541-994-2226, 800-995-2411,* W *www.horizonrentals.com)* Rates $200-300.

Places to Eat

Budget Budget travelers can enjoy a simple breakfast of eggs, cereal and homemade pie at *Cafe Roma* (☎ *541-994-6616, 1437 NW US 101)*, which is inside a used bookstore.

Sun Garden Cafe (☎ *541-557-1800, 1816 NE US 101)* Entrees $7-11. Open Wed-Sun. Order a smoothie and have your palm read from the adjoining crystal shop at this cafe, or relax with a salad or enchilada in the courtyard garden.

McMenamins Lighthouse Pub & Brewery (☎ *541-994-7238, 4157 N US 101)* Entrees $6.50. Burgers are good at this place, located in a shopping center on the north end of town.

Otis Cafe (☎ *541-994-2813, in Otis)* Entrees $5. Breakfast is especially good at this unpretentious but highly touted diner 3 miles northeast on Hwy 18; it's known for its German potatoes, great bread and pies. On weekends, anticipate a wait.

Mid-Range If you order a bowl of clam chowder you can still eat on the cheap at one of the following places.

Blackfish Cafe (☎ *541-996-1007, 2733 NW US 101)* Lunch & dinner $6-19. Open Wed-Mon. Known for chic, cutting-edge cuisine centered on fresh seafood, the Blackfish is possibly the best restaurant on the coast, with inventions such as a seafood cocktail served quite literally in tequila or vermouth. The extensive menu includes lighter plates and traditional seafood meals for $8-11; a bowl of clam chowder is a steal at $4.50.

Kyllo's Seafood Grill (☎ *541-994-3179, 1110 NW 1st Court)* Lunch/dinner $9/17. This casual beachfront steak-and-seafood place has a modern, echoey decor.

Mo's Restaurant (☎ *541-996-2535, 850 SW 51st St)* Lunch/dinner $7/10. Convenient to Siletz Bay, this traditional chowder house has a pretty view of the beach.

Side Door Cafe (☎ *541-764-3825, 6675 Gleneden Beach Loop Rd, Gleneden Beach)* Lunch/dinner $8/20. This cafe would be a great lunch spot if the burgers and quiche weren't so expensive. The quiet atmosphere makes it a pleasant stop for coffee or dessert.

Top End These restaurants are south of town, right outside of Lincoln City.

Bay House (☎ *541-996-3222, 5911 SW US 101)* Dinner $20-32. Seafood, lamb and duck are standards at this elegant restaurant overlooking Siletz Bay.

Westin Salishan Dining Room (☎ *541-764-2371, 7760 N US 101, Gleneden Beach)* Entrees from $34, Cedar Room lunch/dinner $8/16. Game and seafood leads the menu at the Salishan's impressive and slightly ostentatious dining room. Tours of the restaurant's legendary 10,000-bottle wine cellar are available. Meals in the Cedar Room, the casual dining room, are more reasonable.

Chez Jeannette (☎ *541-764-3434, 7150 Gleneden Beach Loop Rd, in Gleneden Beach)* Entrees $20. Across from the Salishan, this eatery offers classic French cuisine in a rustic, European-style dining room.

Entertainment

Famous entertainers are featured monthly at the *Chinook Winds Casino* (☎ *888-624-6228,* Ⓦ *www.chinookwindscasino.com, 1777 NW 44th St)*.

Eden Hall (☎ *541-764-3826,* Ⓦ *www.eden hall.com, 6675 Gleneden Beach Loop Rd, in Gleneden Beach)* Enjoy a play or an acoustic concert with or without a meal at this dinner theater.

Getting There & Around

Greyhound buses to Portland ($14 one way) and Newport stop twice daily at the Wendy's restaurant at 3350 US 101; the visitor center (see Orientation & Information) has tickets and schedules. Local Lincoln City Transit (☎ 541-265-4900) buses to Newport ($2) and Yachats ($5) pick up at various points along US 101 four times on weekdays.

Call Lincoln Cab Company (☎ 541-996-2003) for a taxi.

DEPOE BAY

Pounding waves battered a narrow channel through basalt cliffs, which over time created Depoe Bay (population 900), 10 miles north of Newport. These cliffs are exploding with timeshare condominiums, while the tiny fishing village here is busily occupied with organizing **whale-watching trips** ($20) and charter fishing for visitors. South of the town, US 101 climbs up to Cape Foulweather, which towers 500 feet above the Pacific.

The visitor center (☎ 541-765-2889, W www.depoebaychamber.org) and post office are right downtown on US 101.

Greyhound and local Lincoln County Transit buses reach Depoe Bay from Newport.

Dockside Charters (☎ 541-765-2545, 800-733-8915) and **Tradewinds Charters** (☎ 541-765-2345, 800-445-8730) operate from the boat basin.

The usual condos and gated timeshares cling to cliffs both north and south of town. For information about vacation rentals, contact the visitor center.

Whale Inn (☎ 541-765-2789, 416 N US 101) Rooms from $66. Antiques and collectibles lend charm to this affordable cottage-style motel; one room has a piano ($80).

Trollers Lodge (☎ 541-765-2287, 800-472-9335, 355 SW US 101) Partial-/ocean-view rooms $63/91. This snug older motel has some ocean-view rooms with kitchens.

Channel House Inn (☎ 541-765-2140, 800-447-2140, W www.channelhouse.com, 35 Ellingson St) Rooms without/with hot tub from $96/203. Private, outdoor hot tubs above the pounding surf draw romantic couples to this destination inn at the mouth of the harbor.

Inn at Otter Crest (☎ 541-765-2111, 800-452-2101, W www.ottercrest.com, 8 miles north of Newport off US 101) Rooms/suites from $95/202. Miles of beach and tide pools are at your doorstep at this big ocean-view resort on Cape Foulweather.

Siletz Smokehouse (☎ 541-765-2286, 272 SE US 101) Make a meal out of smoked scallops or salmon at this Siletz-owned fish market.

Lincoln Beach Bagel Company (☎ 503-764-3882, 3930 US 101) Stop here for in expensive breakfast bagels and bagel sandwiches.

Tidal Raves (☎ 541-765-2995, 279 US 101) Dinner $8-20. Affordable menu items are available at this great seafood restaurant overlooking the crashing surf.

NEWPORT & AROUND

Oregon's second-largest commercial port, Newport (population 10,715) was first explored in the 1860s by fishing crews, who found high-quality oyster beds at the upper end of Yaquina Bay. It's been a holiday destination since 1866, and tourism still dominates Newport today. In addition to beaches, the town offers a variety of good marine-based attractions, including the Oregon Coast Aquarium. The old downtown is still a very lively seafront, with seafood markets, the smells of a working port and barking seals.

Orientation

Newport is 53 miles west of Corvallis on US 20. Lincoln City is 25 miles north, and Florence is 50 miles south.

US 101 enters Newport from the south over the Yaquina Bay Bridge to form the main strip through town. West off US 101 is Nye Beach, Newport's historic beach district. Modern high-rise development sprawls along the beach south of here along Elizabeth St. At Newport's old bay district, east of US 101, gray and rather ramshackle fish-processing plants line the water's edge along Bay Blvd, opposite chandlers, restaurants, gift shops and galleries.

Across the bay is the beach and marina area collectively known as South Beach.

Information

There's a visitor center (☎ 541-265-8801, 800-262-7844, W www.newportchamber.org) at 555 SW Coast Hwy. The post office is at 310 SW 2nd St. Canyon Way Books (☎ 541-265-8615), 1216 SW Canyon Way, is in the same place as the Canyon Way Restaurant (see Places to Eat). It's one of the coast's best bookstores – pick up a book-on-tape for the road.

Eileen's Coin Laundry, 1078 N Coast Hwy, has drop-off and self-service facilities. Pacific Communities Hospital (☎ 541-265-2244) is at 930 SW Abbey St.

Beaches

There's beach access from Yaquina Bay State Park and at several points along

OREGON

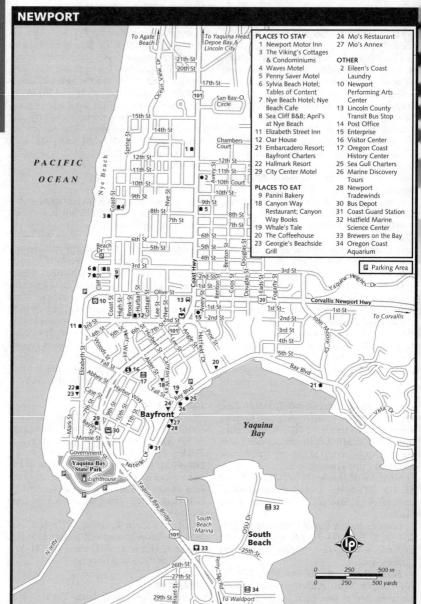

NEWPORT

To Agate Beach
To Yaquina Head, Depoe Bay & Lincoln City

21th St
20th St
17th St
Ocean View Dr
San-Bay-O Circle
101
15th St
14th St
Spring St
Chambers Court
12th St
12th St
11th St
11th St
10th Court
10th St
10th St
Nye St
9th St
9th St
8th St
8th St
7th St
7th St
Avery St
6th St
5th St
5th St
4th St
3rd St
Coast St
Beach Dr
Cliff St
Coast St
High St
Brook St
Hurbart St
Cottage St
Lee St
Nye St
Olive St
Benton St
Coos St
Douglas St
Eads St
Fogarty St
2nd St
1st St
2nd St
1st St
3rd St
1st St
To Corvallis
Corvallis Newport Hwy
Yaquina Heights Dr
2nd St
3rd St
4th St
5th St
Bay Blvd
John Moore Dr
Coast Hwy
101
Elizabeth St
3rd St
4th St
Woods St
Avery St
6th St
Hurbart St
Alder St
Canyon Way
Fall St
Abbey St
Harbor Way
Case St
Angle St
Hatfield St
Pine St
Bay Blvd
Fall St
7th St
9th St
10th St
11th St
Bayley St
Mark St
Minnie St
Government St
Natterlin Dr
Yaquina Bay State Park
Lighthouse
N Jetty
Yaquina Bay Bridge
101
South Beach Marina
OSU Dr
Ferry Slip Rd
Brant St
26th St
27th St
29th St
To Waldport
Vista Dr
Yaquina Bay
South Beach
25th St

PACIFIC OCEAN

Nye Beach

Bayfront

PLACES TO STAY
1 Newport Motor Inn
3 The Viking's Cottages & Condominiums
4 Waves Motel
5 Penny Saver Motel
6 Sylvia Beach Hotel; Tables of Content
7 Nye Beach Hotel; Nye Beach Cafe
8 Sea Cliff B&B; April's at Nye Beach
11 Elizabeth Street Inn
12 Oar House
21 Embarcadero Resort; Bayfront Charters
22 Hallmark Resort
29 City Center Motel

PLACES TO EAT
9 Panini Bakery
18 Canyon Way Restaurant; Canyon Way Books
19 Whale's Tale
20 The Coffeehouse
23 Georgie's Beachside Grill

24 Mo's Restaurant
27 Mo's Annex

OTHER
2 Eileen's Coast Laundry
10 Newport Performing Arts Center
13 Lincoln County Transit Bus Stop
14 Post Office
15 Enterprise
16 Visitor Center
17 Oregon Coast History Center
25 Sea Gull Charters
26 Marine Discovery Tours
28 Newport Tradewinds
30 Bus Depot
31 Coast Guard Station
32 Hatfield Marine Science Center
33 Brewers on the Bay
34 Oregon Coast Aquarium

P Parking Area

0   250   500 m
0   250   500 yards

Elizabeth St. Nye Beach, at the west end of 3rd St, was one of Newport's first beach developments; there's still access along Coast St. There's miles of beaches at South Beach State Park, on the south side of Yaquina Bay, and at Agate Beach State Wayside, 3 miles north.

Oregon Coast Aquarium

The Oregon Coast Aquarium (☎ 541-867-3474, ⓦ www.aquarium.org, 2820 SE Ferry Slip Rd; adult/senior/child $9.25/8.25/4.75; open 9am-6pm May 15-Oct 14; 10am-5pm Oct 15-May 14) is one of Oregon's top attractions. It's known for arresting, roomsized marine exhibits, such as luminous jellyfish floating in cylindrical floor-to-ceiling aquariums. Outside are natural-looking enclosures for seals, sea lions and sea otters; a seabird aviary; and a giant octopus.

The star of the aquarium for many years was Keiko, the orca made famous by the film Free Willy. Keiko was airlifted to Iceland a few years ago in a step toward his eventual release from captivity. Taking his place is a deep-sea exhibit, with a submerged Plexiglas tunnel through a shark-infested tank.

The aquarium is in South Beach, near the Yaquina Bay Bridge.

Hatfield Marine Science Center

Less overwhelming are the exhibits at this Oregon State University–run science center (☎ 541-867-0100, ⓦ www.hmsc.orst.edu/visitor, 2030 Marine Science Dr; admission by donation; open 10am-5pm Memorial Day-Oct 1; 10am-4pm Oct 2-Memorial Day). It too, has a glowering octopus and hands-on tide pools, plus a number of interactive exhibits. Other displays share the center's research endeavors on whales. Although it lacks any big-ticket marine life, the displays here are excellent, and those with an aversion to crowds may find it more enjoyable than the aquarium.

Yaquina Bay State Park

Situated on a brushy bluff above the north entrance of the bay, this day-use park (no fee) is popular for beach access and views over Yaquina Bay. Also here is the unspectacular Yaquina Bay Lighthouse (not to be confused with the Yaquina Head Lighthouse, 3 miles north), built in 1874 and decommissioned three years later. The living quarters are preserved as an informal museum (☎ 541-265-5679; admission by donation; open 11am-5pm summer, noon-4pm rest of year).

Oregon Coast History Center

This museum (☎ 541-265-7509, 545 SW 9th St; admission by donation; open 11am-4pm Tues-Sun), in the Victorian-era Burrows House, contains an excellent collection of Siletz artifacts, including beaded robes, headdresses, baskets and tools – all donated by a woman who ran a trading post on the nearby Siletz reservation.

Yaquina Head Outstanding Natural Area

Stretching a mile out to sea is Yaquina Head ($5 entry or Coast Passport; good for three days), a grassy headland 3 miles north of Newport preserved as a natural site by the Bureau of Land Management (BLM). Short trails visit geology exhibits on the way to viewing areas for shorebirds, harbor seals and whales. An extensive tide-pool area unique for its wheelchair access. The interpretive center (☎ 541-574-3100, 10am-4pm Memorial Day-Labor Day, noon-4pm rest of year) explores different marine environments and relays the history and development of the coast's lighthouses. The coast's tallest, still functioning lighthouse is at the tip of the headland and is open to visitors.

Charter Fishing & Whale Watching

Newport is a noted base for charter fishing ($55-150). Contact Newport Tradewinds (☎ 541-265-2101, 800-676-7819, ⓦ www.newporttradewinds.com, 653 SW Bay Blvd) or Sea Gull Charters (☎ 541-265-7441, 800-865-7441, ⓦ www.seagullcharters.com, 343 SW Bay Blvd).

Chartered crabbing trips cost around $35. Rent rings or traps from Bayfront Charters (☎ 541-265-7558, 890 SE Bay Blvd), near the Embarcadero (charter fishing can be arranged here too).

OREGON

Marine Discovery Tours (☎ 541-265-6200, 800-903-2628, ⓦ www.marinediscovery.com, 345 SW Bay Blvd; Adults/youth/child $22/12/18) specializes in two-hour sea-life cruises to visit whales.

Special Events

One of the coast's premier events, the Newport Wine & Seafood Festival (☎ 541-265-8801) takes place at South Beach Marina in late February, when people hereabouts can usually use something to cheer them up.

The Siletz Powwow (☎ 541-265-8801), held the second weekend of August in Siletz, celebrates the restored federal recognition of the Siletz tribe.

Places to Stay

Camping North and south of Newport are two large state-park campgrounds with about 20 yurts each. Sites fill quickly – make reservations for summer months.

South Beach State Park (☎ 541-867-4715, 800-452-5687, 2 miles south of Newport on US 101) Sites/yurts $19/35. This 248-site campground has great beach access. Amenities include showers, flush toilets and a playground.

Beverly Beach State Park (☎ 541-265-9278, 800-452-5687, 7 miles north of Newport on US 101) Tents/hookups/yurts $16/19/33. Beach access is terrific at Beverly Beach, the mother of all the coast's huge

Whale Watching

Each year, the longest migration known for any mammal takes place in the Pacific Ocean, when approximately 20,000 gray whales make their annual 10,000-mile roundtrip journey between the Arctic Sea and the lagoons of Baja California. Gray-whale migration along the Oregon coast peaks in late December, when southbound whales can be spotted at the rate of about 30 an hour. Whales can also be spotted from March to May as they meander back north.

Whales are air-breathing mammals and frequently surface for oxygen. When they do, they exhale with great force through a blowhole on the top of their head, creating a warm, vaporous cloud of mist (called a blow or spout) 6 to 12 feet high. Blows can be seen with the naked eye, but a pair of binoculars will make seeing them much easier – cast your gaze about halfway between the shore and the horizon, and wait for a burst of white mist.

Once a blow is sighted, watch for glimpses of the whale's head, knuckled back and flukes (tail). A whale's rhythmic breathing and diving usually follows a pattern of three to five short, shallow dives spread a minute or two apart, followed by one deep dive (called a 'sounding') lasting five minutes or more. A tail that breaks the surface usually indicates a sounding – the whale should reappear approximately 300 to 400 yards from where it was last sighted. Whale watching pays off the first time a 30- to 40-ton whale is spotted breaching, which is when a whale propels about half of its body straight out of the water, turns and then splashes onto its side or back.

During the peak migration season, viewpoints are sometimes staffed with volunteers who can help identify and interpret gray-whale behavior. For a close-up view of whales, hire a charter-boat operator for a short trip. These excursions are an especially good activity for children, costing around $20 per person for a two-hour trip.

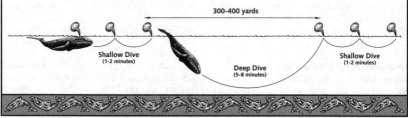

300–400 yards

Shallow Dive
(1-2 minutes)

Deep Dive
(5-8 minutes)

Shallow Dive
(1-2 minutes)

state-park campgrounds, with over 300 campsites and hookups to cable TV!

Hostels Newport is home to the Northwest's most luxurious hostel rooms.

Sylvia Beach Hotel (☎ *541-265-5428*, W *www.sylviabeachhotel.com, 267 NW Cliff St*) Dorm beds with breakfast $26.75. The bathroom is shared and is down the hall, but otherwise, hostel guests of this hotel (see Hotels, later) enjoy the same amenities as other lodgers. Linens are provided.

B&Bs A couple of B&Bs suit the Nye Beach neighborhood perfectly.

Oar House (☎ *541-265-9571, 800-265-9571*, W *www.oarhouse-bed-breakfast.com, 520 SW 2nd St*) Rooms $100-140. There are four guest rooms at this historic Nye Beach home.

Sea Cliff B&B (☎ *541-265-6664, 888-858-6660, 749 NW 3rd St*) Rooms $95-105. Nye Beach is a block from this B&B above April's restaurant (see Places to Eat). There are two guest rooms in the Craftsman house.

Hotels Economy-priced motels line the US 101 strip north of Newport; most allow pets and have kitchens.

Newport Motor Inn (☎ *541-265-8516, 1311 N Coast Hwy*) Singles/doubles $45/50. The clean but undistinguished rooms here have microwaves and coffeemakers.

Penny Saver Motel (☎ *541-265-6631, 877-477-3668, 710 N Coast Hwy*) Singles/doubles $49/56. The truth-in-advertising honor goes to this motel, which has scads of rooms.

Modern, economy-class hotels crowd the highway, while older hotels with more charm lie close to Nye Beach.

City Center Motel (☎ *541-265-7381, 800-687-9099, 538 SW Coast Hwy*) Singles/doubles $59/64. Rooms here are spacious, and some have kitchenettes.

Near Nye Beach are a couple of moderately priced beachfront motels.

The Viking's Cottages & Condominiums (☎ *541-265-2477, 800-480-2477*, W *www.vikingsoregoncoast.com, 729 NW Coast St*) One-/two-bedroom cottages from $86/96, condos $112-278. The intimate 'Crow's Nest'

is the most popular of the Viking's quaint oceanfront cottages.

Waves Motel (☎ *541-265-4661, 800-282-6993, 820 NW Coast St*) Nonview/view rooms $78/88. Behind the Viking's is this motel, which features economy-class lodging across the street from the beach.

Newport's most charming lodging options are two renovated Nye Beach hotels that face the ocean:

Sylvia Beach Hotel (☎ *541-265-5428, 888-795-8422*, W *www.sylviabeachhotel.com, 267 NW Cliff St*) Rooms with breakfast $75-162. At this hotel for book lovers, each room is decorated in the style of a famous author. The 3rd-floor library would be a waste of ocean view if the guests weren't all bibliophiles. It's popular, so reservations are necessary.

Nye Beach Hotel (☎ *541-265-3334*, W *www.nyebeach.com, 219 NW Cliff St*) Rooms $86-161. Next to the Sylvia is this restored hotel (built in the 1910s), where the beachfront rooms all have private hot tubs. On the main floor is a pleasant cafe.

Fireplaces, kitchens, hot tubs and suites are available at all of the following.

Embarcadero Resort (☎ *541-265-8521, 800-547-4779*, W *www.embarcadero-resort.com, 1000 SE Bay Blvd*) Rooms $138-309. Behind the marina, along Yaquina Bay, is Newport's grandest hotel, which offers lodging in bay-view condos.

Elizabeth Street Inn (☎ *541-265-9400, 877-265-9400*, W *www.elizabethstreetinn.com, 232 SW Elizabeth St*) Rooms $117-159. Fireplaces are standard in all the rooms at this lovely new beachfront hotel on Nye Beach.

Hallmark Resort (☎ *541-265-2600, 888-448-4449*, W *www.hallmarkinns.com, 744 SW Elizabeth St*) Rooms $129-239. Views of the ocean from the balconied rooms at this luxury resort are grand, and there's also an indoor pool, a fitness center and room service.

Holiday Inn Newport at Agate Beach (☎ *541-265-9411, 800-547-3310*, W *www.holidayinnnewport.com, 3019 N Coast Hwy*) Nonview/view rooms $127/159. Views of Yaquina Head are outstanding from this well-appointed hotel on quieter Agate Beach.

Vacation-Home Rentals The chamber of commerce has a complete list of agencies that rent beach houses and condos. Contact *Fairhaven Vacation Rentals* (☎ 541-574-0951, 888-523-4179, ⓦ *www.newportnet .com/fairhaven*) to inquire about Cape Cod–style vacation homes at Nye Beach ($165-210).

Places to Eat

Bay Blvd, in the bayfront district, is lined with shabby cafes that dish out chowder and fried fish.

Panini Bakery (☎ 541-265-5033, 232 NW Coast St) Entrees $3-4. Breakfast & lunch. This Nye Beach bakery has homemade soup and pizza by the slice.

Nye Beach Cafe (☎ 541-265-3334, 219 NW Cliff St) Entrees $6-10. The bistro at the Nye Beach Hotel has ethnically inspired meals, and in good weather, there's seating on the verandah above the beach.

The Coffeehouse (☎ 541-265-6263, 156 SW Bay Blvd) Entrees $3-10. Breakfast & lunch. There's outdoor seating on the bay at this unassuming little cafe, which has omelets, pancakes, smoothies and wraps.

Mo's Restaurant (☎ 541-265-2979, 622 SW Bay Blvd) Entrees $8-10. Lunch & dinner. A coast tradition, Mo's seafood restaurants were started decades ago by Mohava Niemi, a local Siletz whose creamy clam chowder and fried fish became the standard of coastal fare. This, the first Mo's, is still here among the crusty bay-front chandlers and bars, and fried seafood is served by the bucket. *Mo's Annex*, on the wharf across the street, has bay-view dining.

Whale's Tale (☎ 541-265-8660, 452 SW Bay Blvd) Lunch/dinner $6/16. Considered another local tradition, this is Newport's most convivial restaurant for favorite seafood dishes, with a great waterfront location and a cozily exaggerated maritime motif.

Tables of Content (☎ 541-265-5428, 267 NW Cliff St) Prix-fixe menu $18. Dinner only. Join other travelers for a delicious family-style dinner at the restaurant in the Sylvia Beach Hotel. Although you don't have to be a hotel guest, reservations are required.

Georgie's Beachside Grill (☎ 541-265-9800, 744 Elizabeth St) Breakfast/lunch/dinner $6/7/15. Seafood is a good value at this busy ocean-view restaurant, with 'light plates' available from $12.

Canyon Way Restaurant (☎ 541-265-8319, 1216 SW Canyon Way) Entrees $15-21. There's an upscale seafood restaurant in the backroom of this bookstore. Up front is a cafe with homemade soups and salads ($6) for lunch.

April's at Nye Beach (☎ 541-265-6855, 749 NW 3rd St) Entree $15. April's, within walking distance of the beach, offers intimate dining across the street from the Sylvia Beach Hotel.

Entertainment

Brewers on the Bay (☎ 541-867-3664, 2320 SW OSU Dr) This brewpub at South Beach Marina has a great view of Yaquina Bay, but to get to it, you'll first have to find your way through the warehouse of the Rogue Ale brewery.

Newport Cinema Center (☎ 541-265-2111, 5837 N Coast Hwy) Head here for first-run films.

Newport Performing Arts Center (☎ 541-265-2787, ⓦ *www.coastarts.org*, 777 W Olive St) This is Newport's main venue for local performance troupes and touring shows.

Getting There & Around

Greyhound buses depart the depot (☎ 541-265-2253), at 956 SW 10th St, twice daily to Florence, and to Portland ($18) via Lincoln City. Rail travelers can get on the Amtrak Thruway bus (two to four daily) from Albany ($16) or Corvallis here. There's also a bus to Bend.

Lincoln City Transit (☎ 541-265-4900) buses make four weekday runs to Lincoln City ($2) and Yachats ($3) from the Naterlin Community Center (US 101 & US 20).

Way to Go! Airport Shuttle (☎ 541-994-9645, 888-743-3847) connects air travelers to the Portland International Airport ($25 one way) once a day on weekdays.

Rent a car from Enterprise (☎ 541-574-1999), 27 S Coast Hwy.

In the summer, ride the Tallyho Trolley (☎ 541-574-4501) to attractions between Nye Beach and South Beach State Park (fare $2).

Call Yaquina Cab Company (☎ 541-265-9552) for a cab.

WALDPORT & AROUND

About 16 miles south of Newport, at the mouth of the Alsea River, Waldport (population 1970) revels in its 'relative obscurity.' The area boasts long stretches of sandy beaches, such as Seal Rock, where a massive hump of rock protects a beach and tide pools. Alsea Bay is also one of the very best **crabbing** areas in the state. Rent crab rings from **Dock of the Bay Marina** (☎ 541-563-2003, 1245 Mill St) for crabbing along the Old Town Wharf.

Slung across the bay is the decommissioned Alsea Bay Bridge, now the subject of the worthwhile **Alsea Bay Bridge Historical Interpretive Center** (☎ 541-563-2002, south end of the bridge on US 101; admission free; open 9am-5pm Memorial Day-Labor Day, 9am-4pm Tues-Sat rest of year). It traces the history of transportation routes along the coast, beginning with trails used by Native Americans.

Hwy 34 to Waldport along the Alsea River from Corvallis is one of the most scenic routes between the Willamette Valley and the coast. The Waldport Visitors Center (☎ 541-563-6086) is at 620 NW Spring St. The post office is at the corner of Hemlock and Johns Sts.

Old Town Gallery, a pizza parlor at the south end of the bridge, is among the few restaurants here.

Beachside State Park (☎ 541-563-3220, reservations 800-452-5687, 4 miles south of Waldport on US 101) Tents/hookups/yurts $16/20/33. If you like the beach, you'll love camping here, where there are 84 sites, 2 yurts, showers and flush toilets.

Tillicum Beach (4 miles south of Waldport on US 101) Sites $12. Just down the road from Beachside State Park is a large USFS campground, right on the beach and best suited to RVs.

Cliffhouse B&B (☎ 541-563-2506, W www.cliffhouseoregon.com, 1450 Ahahi Rd) Rooms $110-225. Guests can watch the Alsea River flow into the ocean from this wood-paneled B&B, which features four cozy guest rooms with ample windows and skylights.

YACHATS & AROUND

The Alsea Indian word 'Yachats' (pronounced ya-**hots**) means 'at the foot of the mountain' – an apt description for this wonderful little community at the base of massive Cape Perpetua. Yachats (population 715) is homey and welcoming, yet rugged and wind-whipped, preserving the illusion that this is a village that the tourist industry hasn't yet discovered.

The Yachats Chamber of Commerce (☎ 541-547-3530, W www.yachats.org) is at 441 US 101.

Seven miles south is a small community called **Tenmile Creek**, with a number of lonely B&Bs and a motel above the beach.

Beginning at Cape Perpetua and continuing south about 20 miles is some of Oregon's most spectacular shoreline. Beautiful and undeveloped, this entire area was once a series of volcanic intrusions, which resisted the pummeling of the Pacific long enough to rise as ocean-side peaks and promontories. Acres of tide pools appear and disappear according to the fancy of the tides and are home to starfish, sea anemones and sea lions. A picturesque lighthouse rises above the surf, and tiny beaches line the cliffs.

Beaches

Beaches around here are small, secluded affairs that share space with tide pools and rocky spires. Among in-town beaches at the mouth of Yachats River is **Yachats State Park**, which has a wheelchair-accessible trail along the surf. A mile north is a beach often called **Smelt Sands Beach** for the run of smelt (sardine-sized fish) that ground themselves here during spawning season.

South of Yachats, **Strawberry Hill Wayside** and **Neptune State Park** offer enjoyable prowling among intertidal rocks and sandy inlets. Sea lions are common here.

Cape Perpetua

First sighted and named by England's Captain James Cook in 1778, this remnant of a volcano is one of the highest points on the Oregon coast. Famous for its dramatic rock formations and crashing surf, this USFS-designated Federal Scenic Area 3 miles south of Yachats contains numerous trails that explore ancient shell middens, tide pools and old-growth forests. Views from the cape are incredible, taking in coastal promontories from Cape Foulweather to Cape Arago. Other attractions include a campground and visitor center.

A Northwest Forest Pass ($5) or Coast Passport is required at all sites.

At the base of the cape is the **visitor center** (☎ 541-547-3289, Ⓦ www.orcoast.com/capeperpetua; open 9am-5pm Memorial Day-Labor Day, seasonal hours rest of year), which relays human and natural histories and has displays on the Alsea tribe, who journeyed here to feast on the abundant shellfish near the tide pools. Middens – centuries-old mounds of shells – attest to their banqueting. Other exhibits discuss intertidal ecology and life cycles of dense spruce, cedar and hemlock forests. The indoor viewing platform is a great place to watch whales in the winter.

From the visitor-center turnoff, turn up Overlook Rd to reach a spectacular ocean view from the **Cape Perpetua Viewpoint**, at the top of the cape.

Deep fractures in the old volcano allow waves to erode narrow channels into the headland, creating effects such as **Devil's Churn**, a mile north of the visitor center. Waves race up this chasm, shooting up the 30-foot inlet to explode against the narrowing sides of the channel. A viewing platform at the parking lot hangs above the end of the channel, or follow the steep stairs to tide pools along the chasm's edge for a closer look. A trail leads from here to the visitor center.

While most sites at Cape Perpetua require only a short stroll, there are longer **day hikes** along the ocean and into forested wilderness areas from the visitor center. A Northwest Forest Pass or Coast Passport is required at all trailheads.

The most popular hike is the 1½-mile climb up Cape Perpetua to a stone CCC shelter used as a lookout for enemy vessels during WWII. The **St Perpetua Trail** gains 640 ft, passing through open meadow and towering Sitka spruce.

For an easier hike, the paved **Captain Cook Trail** (1.2 miles roundtrip) leads down to tide pools and shell middens at Cooks Chasm, where the geyserlike spouting horn blasts water out of a sea cave.

The **Giant Spruce Trail** leads up Cape Creek to the so-called Giant Spruce, a 500-year-old tree with a 9-foot circumference. Six-mile **Cook's Ridge-Gwynn Creek Loop Trail** leads back into the deep old-growth forests along Gwynn Creek. Follow the Oregon Coast Trail south and turn up the Gwynn Creek Trail, which returns via Cook's Ridge.

Heceta Head Lighthouse State Scenic Viewpoint

Heceta Lighthouse (☎ 541-547-3416, 13 miles north of Florence on US 101; $3 day-use or Coast Passport; open daily in summer), which was built in 1894 and is one of the most photographed lighthouses in the US, towers precipitously above the churning ocean at Heceta Head (pronounced huh-**see**-ta). A half-mile trail to the lighthouse begins from the beach at **Devil's Elbow State Park** and winds up the bluff past the whitewashed **Heceta House**, an 1893 lighthouse keeper's house that is now an interpretive center and B&B. At the end of the cape is the lighthouse, which still functions and is open for free tours. It's staffed by volunteers, so hours vary; try early afternoons.

A 3-mile hike (one way) reaches the lighthouse from Carl G Washburne State Park.

Sea Lion Caves

This enormous sea grotto (☎ 541-547-3111, Ⓦ www.sealioncaves.com, 11 miles north of Florence on US 101; adult/child $6.50/4.50; open 8am-7pm July-Aug, 9am-6pm Sept-June), filled with smelly, shrieking sea lions, is a highlight of the central Oregon coast. An elevator descends 208 feet to an observation point 50 feet above the cave, where you can watch almost 200 Steller's sea lions clambering onto rocks, jockeying for position at the top of ledges and letting loose with mighty roars.

Although the caves seem like a real tourist trap, it's definitely worth a stop. Go early or off season to avoid the crowds.

Places to Stay

Most visitors come to Yachats seeking a remote getaway along the undeveloped coastline south of town. A clutch of ocean-front lodgings exists for this purpose at the little community of Tenmile Creek, 7 miles south. Many require a minimum stay.

Camping State-park and USFS campgrounds offer wooded sites and convenient access to beaches and tide pools.

Cape Perpetua Campground (2 miles south of Yachats on US 101) Tents $11. There are 37 campsites at this USFS campground near the turnoff to the visitor center.

Sea Perch Campground (☎ 541-547-3505, 95480 US 101) Sites $28. Seven miles south of Yachats and right on the beach is this RV resort with 75 sites near Tenmile Creek.

Rock Creek Campground (8 miles south of Yachats on US 101) Tents $12. A handful of tent sites with a creek right out back await discovery at this forested USFS campground between Cape Perpetua and Heceta Head. An ocean beach is right across the highway.

Carl G Washburne State Park (☎ 800-452-5687, 14 miles north of Florence on US 101) Tents/hookups/yurts $15/19/33. A 4-mile trail network links this wooded campground to a beach across the highway and to Heceta Head Lighthouse, 3 miles away. The 69 sites include a handful of walk-in spots; reservations are possible only for the two yurts.

B&Bs These B&Bs make the perfect romantic hideaway and include a fabulous ocean view.

Ziggurat B&B (☎ 541-547-3925, W www.new portnet.com/ziggurat, 95330 US 101, 7 miles south of Yachats) Rooms $177. Eye-catching Ziggurat at Tenmile Creek is more like some

fanciful temple (hence the name) than a private home. The two balconied suites are filled with commissioned furniture and art.

Sea Quest B&B (☎ 541-547-3782, 800-341-3782, 95354 US 101, 7 miles south of Yachats) Rooms $161. Also at Tenmile Creek, Sea Quest has five guest rooms, each with private bath, entrance, spa and deck.

Heceta Light Station B&B (☎ 541-547-3696, W www.hecetalighthouse.com, 13 miles north of Florence on US 101) Rooms $135-190. There's a splendid view of the Heceta Lighthouse at night from the original 1894 lighthouse keeper's house, now a B&B. Wake up in the morning to crashing surf and a seven-course breakfast.

Hotels Yachats has everything from funky motor lodges to upscale resorts.

Dublin House (☎ 541-547-3200, US 101 at 7th St) Rooms $73-94. Clean, simple motel rooms (some with kitchens) are the staple of this motor lodge at the north edge of town. There's an indoor pool, and the staff can arrange fly-fishing trips.

Shamrock Lodgettes (☎ 541-547-3312, 800-845-5028, W www.shamrocklodgettes.com, 105 S US 101) Rooms $75-100, cabins $96-100. Lodging is in modern motel units or charming freestanding cabins at this resort, which seems to sit in a large park by the ocean. Rooms have kitchenettes and fireplaces, and views are either of the ocean or the broad sandy bay.

The Adobe Resort (☎ 541-547-3141, 800-522-3623, W www.adoberesort.com, 1555 US 101) Nonview/view rooms from $64/106. Most rooms have ocean views, and some have fireplaces and balconies. There's also an exercise room, a hot tub and a sauna.

Overleaf Lodge (☎ 541-547-4880, 800-338-0507, W www.overleaflodge.com, 280 Overleaf Lodge Lane) Rooms $138-244 with breakfast. The most upscale lodging option is this modern ocean-view resort, with luxury rooms featuring fireplaces, Jacuzzis, and balconies.

There are more options in out-of-the-way pockets south of Cape Perpetua.

The See Vue (☎ 541-547-3227, W www.see vue.com, 95590 US 101, 6 miles south) Rooms $57-75. A real deal, this charming older-style motor lodge has individually decorated theme rooms, all with ocean views and some with kitchens and fireplaces.

Oregon House (☎ 541-547-3329, ⓦ *www* *.oregonhouse.com, 94288 US 101, 8 miles* *south of Cape Perpetua)* Rooms $110-160. This retreat center was once a private estate built in the 1930s and '50s. Its cliffside buildings have been renovated into one-of-a-kind cottages, most with ocean views and kitchens and some with fireplaces.

Vacation-Home Rentals For beach houses, contact the Yachats Chamber of Commerce (☎ 541-547-3530, ⓦ www.yachats.org).

Places to Eat
Yachats' restaurant choices are limited but very pleasant. For breads and pastries, head downtown to **On the Rise Bakery** (☎ *541-547-3440, 281 US 101 S)*, a homespun affair with good scones and slices of pizza. You'll find a home-style breakfast at the nearby **Town Center Cafe.**

The Drift Inn (☎ *541-547-4477, 124 N US 101)* Lunch & dinner $6.25-8.50. A stop at this local watering hole ends a perfect day on the coast. The menu features seafood takes on Mexican food, tea and dessert, as well as Guinness on tap at a handsome bar.

La Serre (☎ *541-547-3420, 2nd & Beach Sts)* Entrees $17.50. Open for dinner Wed-Sat. The cioppino is great here, as is the steak and fresh fish.

Getting There & Away
From Yachats, there are two Greyhound buses daily to Portland and Florence. Lincoln County Transit (☎ 541-265-4900) provides another four buses to Newport ($3) on weekdays. Buses stop across from Clark's IGA grocery store on US 101 at 2nd St.

Southern Oregon Coast

A near continuous succession of dramatic seascapes, the southern coast is far from any major population center and is serviced by a few slow roads. Repeated years of suspended

salmon-fishing seasons and a dried-up wood-products industry have created a recession along this part of the coast, and none of the towns are experiencing the kind of boom evident at resort towns up north. Don't go looking for exquisite sauces for your mesquite-grilled calamari or for a four-star beachfront resort. Chowder and modest older motels are more the norm in this part of the state.

If you enjoy nature and solitude, however, you're in luck. Much of the coastline here is nearly pristine and in many places approaches the condition of wilderness. Find a favorite sandy beach at the end of a hiking trail, and chances are you'll have it to yourself on all but the busiest summer weekends.

FLORENCE
For years, Florence (population 5475) was one of the beach towns you loved to hate: strip commercial development stretched along the highway for miles, the whine of dune buggies navigating sandy bluffs filled the air and the extensive – if characterless – sandy beaches were thronged with idle family groups. Today, life in Florence centers on Old Town along the Siuslaw River, a quaint waterfront district on the Oregon coast's prettiest harbor.

Florence is at the northern end of the Oregon Dunes National Recreation Area, and much of the increasing sophistication of the amenities in Florence has to do with the growing appreciation of the dunes as something other than sandy hills to be dominated by dune buggies and dirt bikes.

Orientation & Information
Florence is 63 miles west of Eugene on Hwy 126. South of Florence is the Oregon Dunes National Recreation Area. North of town, the coast again becomes wild and rocky at Heceta Head. Roughly speaking, Old Town is under the Siuslaw Bridge. Turn west down 9th St for north jetty beaches.

The visitor center (☎ 541-997-3128 ⓦ www .florencechamber.com) is at 270 US 101, just north of the bridge.

The post office is at 770 Maple St. Old Town Books (☎ 541-997-6205), 1340 Bay St, is a small bookstore with a little bit of everything, including coffee.

Do laundry and take a shower while you wait at 37th St Coin Laundry & Showers (☎ 541-997-5111), at N US 101 and 37th St. Peace Harbor Hospital (☎ 541-997-8412) is at 400 9th St.

A floral parade, flower show and slug race are highlights of the Rhododendron Festival (☎ 541-997-3128), which has been celebrated for over 80 years to honor the ubiquitous shrub that erupts into bloom in May. It's held the third weekend in May.

Things to See & Do

Boardwalks, public boat docks and views of the Siuslaw Bridge make **Old Town** a colorful place to explore. The **Siuslaw Pioneer Museum** (☎ 541-997-7884, 85294 S US 101; $1 donation; open 10am-4pm Tues-Sun), on the south side of the bridge, contains the usual mementos of lumbering and a good selection of Siuslaw Indian artifacts.

Five miles north of Florence on US 101 at the **Darlingtonia Wayside**, boardwalks lead out into a bog of *Darlingtonia californica*, an unusual, flesh-eating plant (also called the pitcher plant or cobra lily). Apparently, the plants evolved their meat-eating ways in order to adapt to soils with extremely low nutrients. It's interesting to see these rare plants in their native habitat, though the process of luring insects in and digesting them is quite slow and unspectacular to watch.

South Jetty Beach, off South Jetty Rd, about a mile south of the Siuslaw Bridge provides good beach access; it's within the Oregon Dunes, so expect to pay a fee. There's no charge to visit **Heceta Beach**, about 3 miles north of Florence on Heceta Beach Rd.

One of the most enchanting of all the beaches in Oregon is the little sandy cove at **Devil's Elbow State Park**, about 13 miles north of Florence – the Heceta Head Lighthouse keeps guard, a dense forest bounds the beach, and Conde McCullough bridge arches across placid Cape Creek.

Top-rated **Sandpines Golf Course** (☎ 541-997-1940, 800-917-4653, 1201 35th St; green fees $30-50) offers 18 holes of breathtaking

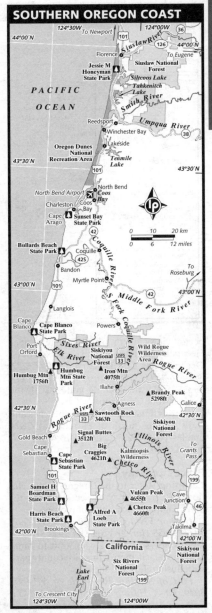

SOUTHERN OREGON COAST

OREGON

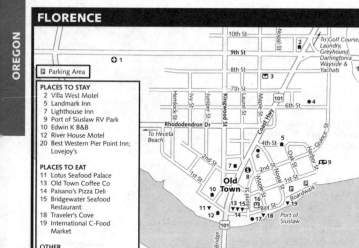

FLORENCE

To Golf Course,
Laundry,
Greyhound,
Darlingtonia
Wayside &
Yachats

Gallagher's
Park

To Mapleton
& Eugene

Munsel Creek

P Parking Area

PLACES TO STAY
2 Villa West Motel
5 Landmark Inn
7 Lighthouse Inn
9 Port of Siuslaw RV Park
10 Edwin K B&B
12 River House Motel
20 Best Western Pier Point Inn;
   Lovejoy's

PLACES TO EAT
11 Lotus Seafood Palace
13 Old Town Coffee Co
14 Paisano's Pizza Deli
15 Bridgewater Seafood
   Restaurant
18 Traveler's Cove
19 International C-Food
   Market

OTHER
1 Peace Harbor Hospital
3 Post Office
4 Florence Events Center
6 Dolphin Property
   Management
8 Porter Stages Bus Stop;
   Visitor Center
16 Harbor Theatre
17 Old Town Books

To Heceta
Beach

Rhododendron Dr

Old
Town

Boardwalk

Port of
Siuslaw

Siuslaw Bridge

Siuslaw River

To Siuslaw Pioneer
Museum & Reedsport

0   250   500 m
0   250   500 yards

ocean views north of town. Right near Heceta Beach, 60-foot sand dunes surround **Ocean Dunes Golf Links** (☎ *541-997-3232, 800-468-4833, 3345 Munsel Lake Rd; green fees $15-35),* threatening golfers with the world's worst sand trap.

There's **horseback riding** on beaches and trails 8 miles north of Florence at **C&M Stables** (☎ *541-997-7540, 90241 N US 101; costs $25-40).*

Places to Stay

Camping Refer to the Oregon Dunes National Recreation Area section, next, for more campgrounds south of Florence.

Harbor Vista Campground (☎ *541-997-5987, 87658 Harbor Vista Dr)* Sites $16. For tent campers or RVers who want to camp near the beach, there's this nice county park with flush toilets and showers.

Port of Siuslaw RV Park (☎ *541-997-3040, 1st & Harbor Sts)* Sites $16-18. Old

Town is a short stroll away at this RV park with views of the harbor.

Edwin K B&B (☎ *541-997-8360, 800-833-9465,* **w** *www.edwink.com, 1155 Bay St)* Rooms $117-196. Along the Siuslaw River are six nicely furnished rooms in this attractive Arts and Crafts–style home, all with luxurious private bathrooms. Backyard, there's a waterfall garden.

Lighthouse Inn (☎ *541-997-3221, 155 US 101)* Rooms from $58. Close to Old Town is this motor lodge, which features plenty of personal touches. The rooms are small but tidy.

Villa West Motel (☎ *541-997-3457, 901 US 101)* Singles/doubles $58/61. This older motel at the junction with Hwy 126 is well maintained.

Landmark Inn (☎ *541-997-9030, 800-822-7811,* **w** *www.landmarkmotel.com, 1551 4th St)* Rooms $63-111. Newly built, this personable hilltop inn offers comfortable mid-range lodging in guest rooms, suites and apartments.

***River House Motel** (☎ 541-997-3933, 877-997-3933, ⓦ www.riverhouseflorence.com, 1202 Bay St)* View rooms $105-111. Stay close to Old Town, right under Siuslaw Bridge, at this motel, which offers hot tubs and views of the river. Rooms in the newly renovated wing are worth the extra money.

***Driftwood Shores** (☎ 541-997-8263, 800-422-5091, 88416 First Ave, Heceta Beach)* Rooms from $95. Florence's beachfront resort offers condo-style rooms, all with a great ocean view. Some rooms have kitchens and fireplaces, and there's an indoor pool.

***Best Western Pier Point Inn** (☎ 541-997-7191, ⓦ www.bestwestern.com/pierpointinn, 85625 US 101)* Rooms $118-171. For views over the harbor, cross the Siuslaw Bridge and climb the hill to this hotel, which has riverfront balconies and a remarkable indoor pool.

You can get a nice vacation home in Florence for around $100. The visitor center has listings, or contact ***Dolphin Property Management** (☎ 541-997-7368, 396 US 101).*

Places to Eat

Start the day here with espresso and pastries from ***Old Town Coffee Co***, at 1269 Bay St.

***Blue Hen Cafe** (☎ 541-997-3907, 1675 US 101)* Breakfast & lunch $3-7. Head here for an incredible omelet.

***Paisano's Pizza Deli** (☎ 541-997-2068, 1285 Bay St)* Dishes $2.50-10. Open lunch & dinner. By-the-slice pizza, calzones and all-you-can-eat pasta are good bargains here.

***Traveler's Cove** (☎ 541-997-6845, 1362 Bay St)* Breakfast, lunch & dinner $7-12. There's a bistro fare at this brewpub, which has a back deck overlooking the river.

***International C-Food Market** (☎ 541-997-9646, 1498 Bay St)* Lunch & dinner $4.50-20. Great views and a lively market atmosphere make this a popular spot for everything from fancy seafood entrees to fish and chips.

***Bridgewater Seafood Restaurant** (☎ 541-997-9405, 1297 Bay St)* Lunch/dinner $9/18. Fresh seafood specialties here make this one

of Florence's better restaurants; it's housed in an old hotel dining room near the waterfront.

***Lotus Seafood Palace** (☎ 541-997-7168, 1150 Bay St)* Dinner $11. Under the bridge and facing the Siuslaw River is this Chinese restaurant.

***Lovejoy's** (☎ 541-902-0502, 85625 US 101)* Lunch/dinner $7/17. Filled with rickety antiques, Lovejoy's is half tea room, half pub, with British fare and a superb bay view.

Entertainment

***Harbor Theatre** (☎ 541-997-3361, 1377 Bay St)* Florence's arts cinema is in Old Town.

***Florence Events Center** (☎ 541-997-1994, 888-968-4086, 715 Quince St)* Florence's performing-arts venue stages everything from symphony concerts to nationally known entertainers.

Getting There & Away

Twice daily, Greyhound buses (☎ 541-902-9076) heading south to Brookings, and to Portland via Lincoln City, stop 2 miles north of downtown at 37th Street Coin Laundry & Showers, at US 101 and 37th St – ignore old signs around town. The one-way fare to Newport is $8. Buses to Eugene ($15) and Coos Bay ($7.50) on Porter Stages leave twice daily on weekdays and once on weekends from the visitor center, downtown.

Call River Cities Taxi (☎ 541-997-8520) for a cab.

OREGON DUNES NATIONAL RECREATION AREA

The Oregon Dunes stretch for 50 miles between Florence and Coos Bay, forming the largest expanse of oceanfront sand dunes in the USA. The National Recreation Area was created in 1972 and takes in 50 sq miles. The dunes undulate inland as far as 3 miles to meet coastal forests, with a succession of curious ecosystems and formations that sustain an abundance of wildlife, especially birds.

The waves that batter the headlands are constantly reducing the coastline to sand, and the south coast's major rivers constantly flush it into the ocean. Oregon's wild and rocky south coast is so steep, and the continental shelf so narrow, that there are few beaches for sand to deposit, and this bounty of sand shifts northward along ocean currents. Between Cape Arago and Heceta Head, there are no cliffs or rock formations to block the flow of sand, which washes ashore to form the dunes, some of them 500 feet high.

Recreation in the area is 'mixed use,' meaning that about half of the area is dominated by dune buggies and dirt bikes (known collectively as off-road vehicles, or ORVs) tearing up and down the dunes, accompanied by the telltale smell and demonic whine of two-stroke engines. Portions preserved for wildlife (closed to ORVs and motorboats) contain hiking trails, bridle paths, canoe trails and swimming areas.

The lower half of the dunes, south of Reedsport, sees the most ORV traffic, while the upper half has the most hiking trails. A map of the area from the visitor center (see Orientation & Information, next) shows designated ORV areas.

Orientation & Information

It's 90 miles from Eugene to Reedsport, which is at the center of the dunes. Florence and Coos Bay are north and south at either end, on US 101.

The Oregon Dunes National Recreation Area is administered by the Siuslaw National Forest, with a few state parks in the mix. Stop by the headquarters (☎ 541-271-3611 w www.fs.fed.us/r6/siuslaw/oregon dunes, 855 Highway Ave, Reedsport; open 8am-4:30pm June-Oct; 8am-4:30pm Mon-Fri, 10am-4pm Sat Nov-May) for hiking information and maps, as well as for interesting exhibits on dune formations and ecosystems.

Except for the Oregon Dunes Overlook, a Northwest Forest Pass ($5) or Coast Passport is required at all USFS sites.

Hiking

Short hikes from trailheads along US 101 lead across the dunes and out to the beach. The free *Hiking Trails in the Oregon Dunes National Recreation Area,* available from the visitor center, has trail descriptions with maps. Most people cross the Oregon Dunes

during the drier summer season, though the dunes may be hiked year round. Sunny summer afternoons sometimes bring strong winds and unpleasant hiking conditions. Wind carves the wet sand into interesting sculptures in the winter.

From the **Stagecoach Trailhead**, down Siltcoos Beach Access Rd, 7 miles south of Florence, three short trails along a river and wetlands afford good wildlife viewing. One of these, the **Waxmyrtle Trail**, winds to the beach for 1½ miles along the Siltcoos River, where herons, deer and waterfowl can be seen. Other trails lead to a freshwater lagoon or up to a forested vista point.

The wheelchair-accessible **Oregon Dunes Overlook**, 10 miles north of Reedsport, also serves as a trailhead for a 1-mile hike to the beach. Guided nature walks leave from here daily in the summer. There's a $1 parking fee.

A longer, 6-mile loop hike starts from Tahkenitch Campground (see Places to Stay, later), 8 miles north of Reedsport. Follow the **Tahkenitch Dunes Trail** west to reach the beach in less than 2 miles. Then walk south along the beach to directional posts for the **Threemile Lake Trail**, which returns hikers to the campground via a freshwater lake and deep forests.

For some of the biggest dunes in the area, take the **Umpqua Dunes Trail** from Eel Creek Campground (see Places to Stay), 10 miles south of Reedsport. The Umpqua Dunes Trail leads out across a wilderness of massive sand peaks before reaching the beach. The hike there and back is 5 miles, involves some dune climbing and can be unpleasant in windy weather.

Swimming & Boating

Jessie M Honeyman State Park (see Places to Stay, later) has two lakes. **Cleawox Lake** is the smaller of the two, and although motorized boats are allowed here, most speedboat drivers prefer **Woahink Lake**, which is deeper and doesn't fill with weeds. Cleawox Lake is especially popular for swimming, and children love skittering down a high dune into the water. Rent canoes and pedal boats at the park concession. A new dive

OREGON

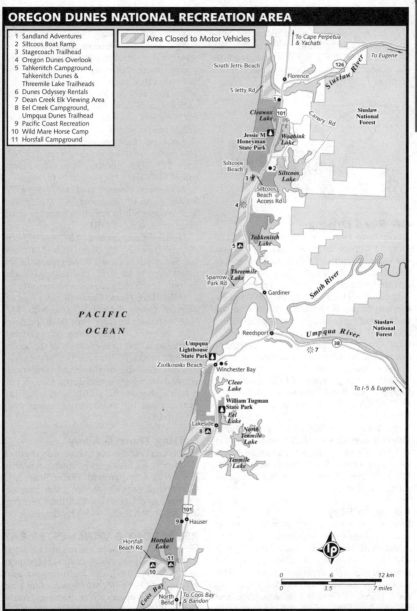

OREGON DUNES NATIONAL RECREATION AREA

1 Sandland Adventures
2 Siltcoos Boat Ramp
3 Stagecoach Trailhead
4 Oregon Dunes Overlook
5 Tahkenitch Campground,
  Tahkenitch Dunes &
  Threemile Lake Trailheads
6 Dunes Odyssey Rentals
7 Dean Creek Elk Viewing Area
8 Eel Creek Campground,
  Umpqua Dunes Trailhead
9 Pacific Coast Recreation
10 Wild Mare Horse Camp
11 Horsfall Campground

Area Closed to Motor Vehicles

To Cape Perpetua & Yachats

To Eugene

Siuslaw River

126

South Jetty Beach

Florence

S Jetty Rd

101

Canary Rd

Siuslaw National Forest

Cleawox Lake

Woahink Lake

Jessie M Honeyman State Park

Siltcoos Beach

Siltcoos Lake

Siltcoos Beach Access Rd

Tahkenitch Lake

Threemile Lake

Sparrow Park Rd

Gardiner

Smith River

Siuslaw National Forest

PACIFIC OCEAN

Reedsport

Umpqua River

38

7

Umpqua Lighthouse State Park

Ziolkouski Beach

Winchester Bay

To I-5 & Eugene

Clear Lake

William Tugman State Park

Eel Lake

Lakeside

North Tenmile Lake

Tenmile Lake

101

Hauser

Horsfall Beach Rd

Horsfall Lake

North Bend

To Coos Bay & Bandon

Coos Bay

0   6   12 km
0   3.5   7 miles

park is planned for Woahink Lake in the future.

Wildlife viewing is good along the **Silt-coos River Canoe Trail**, which travels the Siltcoos River through forest and marsh to the ocean. Put in at Siltcoos Lake, 6 miles south of Florence.

Off-Road Driving

About one-third of the visitors to the Oregon Dunes come to race around on ORVs (also called OHVs, or off-highway vehicles), which include dune buggies, all-terrain vehicles (ATVs), motorcycles, souped-up pickups and jeeps. ORV operators are required to have a driver's license and must observe Oregon's regular speeding and DUI (Driving under the Influence) laws. Operators must also respect quiet hours, and mufflers are required to meet decibel requirements.

ORV rental is around $30 an hour. Near Florence, **Sandland Adventures** (☎ 541-997-8087, 85366 S US 101), south of the Siuslaw Bridge, rents a full line of ORVs and has dune buggy tours. Near Reedsport, go to **Dunes Odyssey Rentals** (☎ 541-271-3863, 75303 US 101, Winchester Bay). Down south by North Bend, try **Pacific Coast Recreation** (☎ 541-756-2322, 2580 Broadway), in the little community of Hauser.

Places to Stay

Florence and Reedsport offer the nearest hotels; see those sections for listings.

Jessie M Honeyman State Park (☎ 800-452-5687 reservations, 3 miles south of Florence on US 101) Tents/hookups/yurts $16/20/35. This forested state park on Cleawox Lake is one of Oregon's most popular and has showers, flush toilets and easy access to

swimming and the dunes. Reservations are a good idea in summer.

USFS campgrounds have the best dune access, and most feature flush toilets and water, but no hookups. Facilities vary, and if you're any sort of naturalist, you'll do well to avoid ORV camps, which are more akin to parking lots. A cluster of three separate campgrounds down *Siltcoos Beach Access Rd*, 7½ miles south of Florence, provides for either type of camper.

Eel Creek Campground (☎ 877-444-6777, 10½ miles south of Reedsport on US 101) Sites $13. These shrubby sites offer refuge from ORVs and a hiking trail to the dunes.

Tahkenitch Campground (☎ 877-444-6777, 7 miles north of Reedsport on US 101) Sites $13. Wooded Tahkenitch is another good place to go to avoid ORVs.

Horsfall Campground (☎ 877-444-6777, on Horsfall Beach Rd off US 101) Sites $13. Horsfall, just north of North Bend, represents the ultimate party for ORV-enthusiasts. It's also the only USFS campground with a shower.

Wild Mare Horse Camp (3 miles west on Horsfall Beach Rd, off US 101) Sites $12. Nearby, but far enough away from the noisy dune buggies, is this horse campground, which has access to horse trails in the southernmost (and ORV-free) section of dunes.

Sand camping or dispersed camping is allowed anywhere in the dunes, though you must register at the visitor center. See the next section for more campgrounds near Reedsport.

Getting There & Away

Hikers can take the bus to Lakeside, south of Reedsport, for hiking and camping at nearby Eel Creek Campground. Porter Stage and Greyhound provide service from Eugene, Florence and Coos Bay. Call the Coos Bay bus depot (☎ 541-267-4436) for details.

REEDSPORT & WINCHESTER BAY

Five miles from where the mighty Umpqua River joins the Pacific Ocean is Reedsport (population 5030), the historic port that ushered out the immense bounty of logs cut in the wide Umpqua River drainage. Neighboring Winchester Bay was once the state's

OREGON

largest sport-fishing port. A herd of about 100 Roosevelt elk live in a roadside wildlife refuge 3 miles east of Reedsport on Hwy 38. Simple, inexpensive lodging and good campgrounds north and south make it an ideal base for exploring the Oregon Dunes.

Chainsaw artists from all over the Northwest come here to compete in the Oregon Chainsaw Sculpture Championships, held the third weekend in June.

Orientation & Information
Reedsport is 22 miles south of Florence and 90 miles southwest of Eugene. There's a rack of tourist brochures in the lobby of the Oregon Dunes National Recreation Area Headquarters (☎ 541-271-3611), at the junction of US 101 and Hwy 38.

The post office is at 301 Fir Ave. Lower Umpqua Hospital (☎ 541-271-2171), 600 Ranch Rd, keeps busy with dune-buggy crashes all summer long.

Things to See & Do
Winchester Bay's **Ziolkouski Beach** is a peaceful, though somewhat windswept, expanse of sand bordering the Oregon Dunes. The first parking area is free, but at others, there's a $5 fee (waived for holders of the Northwest Forest or Coastal Passport). **Umpqua Lighthouse State Park** offers tours of a 1894 lighthouse *(☎ 541-271-4631; admission $1; open 10am-4pm Wed-Sat, 1pm-4pm Sun May-Sept)*, and there is a small museum *(admission free; open 10am-5pm Wed-Sat, 1pm-5pm Sun May-Sept)*. Opposite the lighthouse is a whale-watching platform, and a nearby nature trail rings freshwater Lake Marie, popular for swimming.

The Umpqua River has a bounty of sturgeon, coho salmon and steelhead. For **fishing** advice, licenses and tackle, go to the **Reedsport Outdoor Store** *(☎ 541-271-2311, 2049 Winchester Ave)*.

Places to Stay & Eat
The RV campgrounds that front onto the harbor in Winchester Bay are too exposed and windy for tents. There are more sheltered sites at USFS campgrounds south of town.

Umpqua Lighthouse State Park (☎ 800-452-5687, 1 mile south of Winchester Bay off Hwy 101) Tents/hookups/yurts $13/17/35. Pleasant, wooded campsites here are adjacent to tiny Lake Marie, which warms up quite nicely for swimming. A couple of new, deluxe yurts with TVs, VCRs and refrigerators are still somewhat of a secret.

Hotels in Reedsport tend to be clean and simple and have kitchenettes.

Salty Seagull (☎ 541-271-3729, 1806 US 101) Singles/doubles $45/57. This small motel is a great deal and has three-room units with full kitchens.

Economy Inn (☎ 541-271-3671, 1593 US 101) Rooms $41/45. This inexpensive motel has an outdoor pool and is AAA-rated.

Best Budget Inn (☎ 541-271-3686, 1894 Winchester Ave) Rooms $48, kitchenettes $54. There are more kitchenettes and a pool here.

Salbasgeon Inn of the Umpqua (☎ 541-271-2025, 45209 Hwy 38) Rooms $74-84. Once a rustic angler's resort, this riverfront inn 7 miles east of Reedsport is now more of a romantic hideaway.

Don's Diner (☎ 541-271-2032, 2115 Winchester Ave) Entrees $5. Don's is the longtime local favorite for family dining, with good burgers and homemade soup. Finish up with Umpqua ice cream.

COOS BAY & NORTH BEND
The city of Coos Bay (population 15,995), along with its twin, North Bend (population 10,270), combine to make up the largest urban area on the Oregon coast. Coos Bay, the largest natural harbor between San Francisco and Seattle, has long been a major shipping and manufacturing center, driving the engines of commerce and industry of most of southern Oregon. For many years, Coos Bay was the largest timber port in the world, thronged with foreign vessels waiting to take on board immense mountain-high stacks of timber. Today, most lumber mills have closed, as coastal forests were cleaned of easily harvested timber, and forest-product conglomerates found it cheaper to mill wood overseas or offshore, using foreign labor. Big ships still visit Coos Bay to pick up

wood chips, such as the infamous *New Carrissa*, which wrecked offshore in 1999.

The husk of one prominent mill is now The Mill Casino, its warehouses given over to industrial-sized slot and bingo rooms.

Coos Bay was the traditional home of the Hanis Coos, one of the tribes removed to the Alsea Reservation in the late 1850s. When that reservation was dissolved, the remaining Hanis Coos drifted back to the Coos Bay area without any land. They eventually lost tribal status with the US government, but it was later restored in the 1980s. The Hanis Coos, Siuslaw and the Lower Umpqua tribes are currently confederated and consist of about 500 members.

West of these cities, the Cape Arago Hwy leads 9 miles to Charleston, a fishing village at the end of the bay, and then on to a clutch of beautiful state parks. From North Bend, US 101 sails across the Coos Bay on high-flying McCullough Bridge and into the southern edge of the Oregon Dunes National Recreation Area.

Orientation & Information

Coos Bay is 25 miles south of Reedsport and 24 miles north of Bandon. US 101 enters Coos Bay from the south and passes through downtown before becoming Bayshore Dr. In North Bend, US 101 leaves town as Sherman Ave. Turn west on Central Ave in Coos Bay, or Newark St in North Bend, for parks and beaches around Charleston. Newark St also accesses the airport in North Bend.

Contact the Bay Area Chamber of Commerce (☎ 541-269-0215, 800-824-8486, W www.oregonsbayareachamber.com) at 50 E Central Ave in downtown Coos Bay. The post office is at Golden Ave and S 4th St. There's a limited selection of travel books at Harvest Book Shoppe (☎ 541-267-5824), 307 Central Ave, in Coos Bay's downtown district.

Bay Area Hospital (☎ 541-269-8111) is at 1775 Thompson Rd, in North Bend. The laundry Allen's Wash Tub, at 255 Golden Ave in Coos Bay, is convenient to the highway.

Things to See & Do

The **Coos Art Museum** (☎ 541-267-3901, 235 *Anderson Ave; admission by donation; open 10am-4pm Tues-Fri, 1pm-4pm Sat),* in downtown Coos Bay, is the only civic art gallery on the Oregon coast. Track star Steve Prefontaine, who was born in Coos Bay in 1951, is memorialized in a special exhibit here.

In North Bend, near the bridge, is the **Coos County Historical Museum** (☎ 541-756-6320, 1220 Sherman Ave, North Bend; adult/child $2/1; open 10am-4pm Tues-Sat), which has a good collection of Coos Indian beadwork and basketry, as well as mementos from Coos Bay's big shipping boom. The myrtle-wood coins here were issued as legal tender during the Depression.

Special Events

The Oregon Coast Music Festival (☎ 541-267-0938, W www.coosnet.com/music) happens for two weeks in July in Bandon, Coos Bay and Reedsport, though the festival orchestra concerts are centered at Coos Bay's Marshfield High School Auditorium, at Hall Ave and S 7th St.

The Blackberry Arts Festival is held in downtown Coos Bay in late August, with booths selling crafts and blackberry food items.

Places to Stay

There are oceanside campgrounds near Charleston (see that section, next), only 11 miles west, or north in the Oregon Dunes National Recreation Area (see that section, earlier).

Lucky Loggers RV Park (☎ 541-267-6003, 800-267-6426, 250 Johnson Ave, Coos Bay) Sites $25. Sites at this RV park, on the south end of town, look out across the Coos River to an ugly pulp mill.

Coos Bay Manor B&B (☎ 541-269-1224, 800-269-1224, W www.moriah.com/cbmanor, 955 S 5th St) Rooms without/with bathroom $84/106. Guest rooms are elegant and comfortable at this colonial-style mansion built in 1912, but the views are uninspiring.

Bay Bridge Motel (☎ 541-756-3151, 33 US 101) Nonview/view rooms $52/55.

OREGON

There's quite a view of the bridge from this motel, on the north side of the bay from North Bend.

Bayshore Motel (☎ 541-267-4138, 1685 N Bayshore Dr, Coos Bay) Singles/doubles $34/40. The Bayshore offers cut-rate rooms with queen-size beds.

Motel 6 (☎ 541-267-7171, 1445 Bayshore Dr, Coos Bay) Singles/doubles $51/57. This is a nicer place to stay than the Bayshore.

Edgewater Inn (☎ 541-267-0423, 800-233-0423, 275 E Johnson Ave, Coos Bay) Rooms without/with view $86/94. Rooms here are well-appointed and modern (some with kitchenettes), but don't come for the view. On site is an indoor pool.

The Mill Hotel (☎ 541-756-880, 800-953-4800, ⓦ www.themillcasino.com, 3201 Tremont Ave, Coos Bay) Nonview/view rooms $94/105. Owned and operated by the Coquille Indians, the upscale rooms here are right on par with Oregon's fanciest resorts, and they cost about $30 less in the off season.

Red Lion Inn (☎ 541-267-4141, 800-547-8010, 1313 N Bayshore Dr, Coos Bay) Rooms from $98. This is Coos Bay's finest

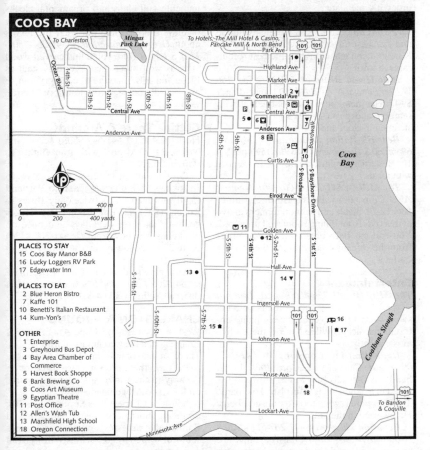

COOS BAY

PLACES TO STAY
15 Coos Bay Manor B&B
16 Lucky Loggers RV Park
17 Edgewater Inn

PLACES TO EAT
2 Blue Heron Bistro
7 Kaffe 101
10 Benetti's Italian Restaurant
14 Kum-Yon's

OTHER
1 Enterprise
3 Greyhound Bus Depot
4 Bay Area Chamber of Commerce
5 Harvest Book Shoppe
6 Bank Brewing Co
8 Coos Art Museum
9 Egyptian Theatre
11 Post Office
12 Allen's Wash Tub
13 Marshfield High School
18 Oregon Connection

business-class hotel, with views over the harbor, courtesy vans to the airport and an outdoor pool.

Places to Eat

Pancake Mill (☎ 541-756-2751, 2390 Tremont, Coos Bay) Head here, in the void between Coos Bay and North Bend, for a good home-style breakfast.

Kaffe 101 (☎ 541-267-4894, 134 S Broadway, Coos Bay) Lunch under $5. Stop here for espresso drinks and muffins, or for a lunch of soup and bagels. On Friday and Saturday, it's open late.

Kum-Yon's (☎ 541-269-2662, 835 S Broadway, Coos Bay) Entrees $8. Familiar Chinese and Japanese favorites and a distinguished Korean menu make this one the best restaurants in town.

Blue Heron Bistro (☎ 541-267-3933, 100 W Commercial Ave, Coos Bay) Lunch/dinner $9/17. The menu here goes continental, with seafood and pasta dishes such as mussels steamed in cider and herbs.

Benetti's Italian Restaurant (☎ 541-267-6066, 260 S Broadway, Coos Bay) Dinner $9-12. Benetti's remains a consistent favorite with locals.

The Mill (☎ 541-756-8800, 3201 Tremont Ave, Coos Bay) Breakfast/lunch/dinner $6/8/12-20. Steak and salmon dinners arrive at this riverfront dining room well prepared. You can eat here under $10 if you order from the cafe, or on days when they have a buffet.

Entertainment

The Mill (☎ 541-756-8800, 3201 Tremont Ave, Coos Bay) Coos Bay's big casino is the south coast's main venue for big-name entertainers such as Willie Nelson; there's live music nightly.

Bank Brewing Company (☎ 541-267-0963, 201 Central Ave, Coos Bay) Local bands occasionally play at this brewpub, situated in a handsomely refurbished old bank. The beer here is good too – try the cranberry Hefeweizen in the fall.

Egyptian Theatre (☎ 541-267-6115, 229 S Broadway, Coos Bay) First-run films are screened in this old-style movie house with a fun Egyptian motif, complete with a concrete-molded mummy.

Little Theater on the Bay (☎ 541-756-4336, 2100 Sherman Ave, North Bend). LTB in North Bend is the most active of the bay area's community theater companies, and puts on several plays a year.

Shopping

Across southern Oregon, wherever tourists have been known to tread, there are **myrtlewood gift shops**. While you may or may not want to buy milled bowls, Christmas tree ornaments, golf clubs and ornamental clocks made out of this rare wood, do go into one of these shops to find out what the fuss is about. **Oregon Connection** (☎ 541-267-7804, 1125 S 1st St) Here you'll find carved-wood gifts, as well other local products such as fudge and jelly. Take the free factory tour to find out all you need to know about myrtle wood.

Getting There & Around

Horizon Air (☎ 541-547-9308) serves the North Bend Airport with four flights to Portland daily.

Greyhound buses link Coos Bay to Brookings ($18 one way), and to Portland ($30) via Lincoln City twice daily. Buses to Eugene ($22) via Florence on Porter Stages go twice daily on weekdays, and once on weekends. The bus depot (☎ 541-267-4436) is at 275 Broadway, in the Tioga Hotel building.

You can rent a car from Enterprise (☎ 541-266-7100), at 455 N Broadway. For a taxi, call Yellow Cab (☎ 541-267-3111).

CHARLESTON & AROUND

West of Coos Bay on Cape Arago Hwy is Charleston, a busy commercial fishing port. There's a kind of maritime hustle and bustle to the town that makes it a nice stopover on the way to the trio of splendid state parks on the Cape Arago headlands.

South of Charleston is Seven Devils Rd, a winding shortcut between Charleston and Bandon that accesses a number of beaches south of Cape Arago, such as Whisky Run and Agate.

The Charleston Visitors Center (☎ 541-888-2311), at the west end of the bridge, is open from May to September.

Parks along the Cape Arago Hwy present many opportunities for hiking, bicycling and surfing. Rent everything you need at **High Tide Rentals & Cafe** *(☎ 541-888-3664, 8073 Cape Arago Hwy)* in Charleston.

Sunset Bay State Park
This state park *(☎ 541-888-4902, 10965 Cape Arago Hwy, 3 miles southwest of Charleston; no fee)* takes in a small, protected bay walled by dramatic cliffs that were once topped by a hotel in the 1910s. It's popular with swimmers, divers and surfers, as well as with hikers and vista-lovers. A 3-mile, cliff-edged stretch of the **Oregon Coast Trail** continues south from here to link all three state parks. The year-round campground is one of the coast's most popular. Cape Arago Lighthouse sits right offshore on a rocky crag.

Shore Acres State Park
The neglected gardens of a vanishing estate were restored to make beautiful Shore Acres State Park *(☎ 541-888-3732, 13030 Cape Arago Hwy; day use $3 or Coast Passport)*, a mile south of Sunset Bay. Louis Simpson, an important shipping and lumber magnate, was exploring for new stands of lumber in 1905 when he discovered this wildly eroded headland. After buying up the 320 acres, he built a three-story mansion here, complete with formal gardens and tennis courts, and called the estate Shore Acres. The original home burned down in 1921. A trail leads out from the gardens to a glass-protected **vista point** on the cliffs where it once stood, and then continues on to the beach.

Cape Arago State Park
Another wild vista point above a pounding sea is Cape Arago State Park, at the termination of Cape Arago Hwy. The cape is a good place to watch migrating whales. A half mile before it is a **sea-lion lookout**, at Simpson's Reef. Trails lead down to the beach and to great tide pools at South Cove, and the

Oregon Coast Trail leads back from here to Shore Acres and Sunset Bay.

South Slough National Estuarine Reserve
Charleston sits on a body of water evocatively called South Slough. South of town it widens from a tidal river basin into a vast, muddy estuary. The **interpretive center** at South Slough National Estuarine Reserve *(☎ 541-888-5558, 4 miles south of Charleston on Seven Devils Rd; admission free; open 8:30am-4:30pm Sept-May, 8:30am-4:30pm, Mon-Fri June-Aug)*, the nation's first estuary preserve, offers exhibits on estuarine ecology and nature trails. There's great **wildlife viewing** for shorebirds, and the estuary is a good spot for **canoeing**. Rent kayaks ($20-40) from **High Tide Rentals** *(☎ 541-888-3664)*, in Charleston.

Charter Fishing & Crabbing
Charleston still has a few charter companies that offer ocean fishing (from $60). Contact **Betty Kay Charters** *(☎ 541-888-9021, 800-752-6303, Ⓦ www.bettykaycharters.com, Charleston Boat Basin)* or **Bob's Sport Fishing** *(☎ 541-888-4241, 800-628-9633, Ⓦ www.bobsportfishing.com, 8013 Albacore Ave)*.

The bay is also popular for crabbing. Rent crab pots ($8) from High Tide Rentals (see above); you can crab right off the docks or rent a boat.

Places to Stay & Eat
A couple small *cafes* offer breakfast and basic meals at the end of the Charleston bridge.

Bastendorff Beach County Park (☎ 541-888-5353, 541-396-3121, ext 354, 4250 Bastendorff Beach Rd) Tents/hookups/cabins $10/14/25. West of Charleston on Cape Arago Hwy, this park has pleasant wooded campsites in a developed campground near the beach.

Sunset Bay State Park (☎ 800-452-5687, 10965 Cape Arago Hwy, 3 miles southwest of Charleston) Tents/hookups/yurts $16/18/35. This sheltered beachside campground is a busy place year round. Expect flush toilets, showers and a playground.

Captain John's Motel (☎ *541-888-4041, 8061 Kingfisher Dr)* Rooms \$48-70. Popular with anglers, Captain John's has a great location right on the boat basin and maintains a crab-cooking facility for guest use.

BANDON
Bandon-by-the-Sea (population 2940), as its promoters have renamed it, sits at the bay of the Coquille River. South of town and not obvious from the highway are miles of sandy beaches, rhythmically broken by outcroppings of towering rocks, which are home to a large number of chattering sea birds. Ledges of stone rise out of the surf to provide shelter for seals, sea lions and myriad forms of life in tide pools.

Whether this little town is one of the crown jewels of the Oregon coast or yet another overrated coastal port is a matter of perspective. Many motels and restaurants fall below the standards expected of most resort towns; however, this lackluster quality seems to be precisely why so many come here. Though not readily apparent, Bandon also has the reputation of being a center of alternative spirituality.

Bandon's commercial center is Old Town, an attractive harborside shopping district that seems vigorous compared to other south-coast communities. A world-class golf resort sits in smug self-containment a few miles north, where it attends to the needs of well-heeled travelers with all the upscale amenities Bandon lacks.

Bandon's most noteworthy industry is cranberry farming, with neighboring bogs yielding a considerable percentage of the cranberry harvest in the US.

Orientation & Information
Bandon's main commercial district is Old Town, a five-block nucleus of restaurants and shops along 1st and 2nd Sts on the harbor. Bandon's most famous beaches are south of town along Beach Loop Dr. Ocean Rd leads there from Old Town, or turn west off of US 101 onto 11th St.

From Bandon, it's 21 miles north to Coos Bay on US 101 and 27 miles south to Port Orford. Hwy 42S leads inland from Bandon to the town of Coquille.

Visit the Bandon Chamber of Commerce (☎ 541-347-9616, [W] www.bandon.com), in Old Town at 2nd St and Chicago Ave. The post office is south of town at 105 12th St. Winter River Books & Gallery (☎ 541-347-4111), 170 2nd St, offers a wide selection of books, with a good local travel section and an odd assortment of country-themed crafts, New Age music, crystals and whatnot.

Danny's Laundromat is on US 101 at 11th St.

Old Town
Bandon's gentrified downtown, long touted as a marketplace for arts and crafts, has digressed into gift stores and T-shirt shops. Still, it's a nice place for a stroll along the harbor's new boardwalk. The largest and most eclectic selection of art is at the **Second Street Gallery** (☎ *541-347-4133, 210 2nd St)*. Closer to the harbor is **CranBerry Sweets** (☎ *541-347-9475, 1st St & Chicago Ave)*, a cranberry-based candy maker with free samples and a video showing the cranberry harvest.

For more on the local cranberry industry, head across the highway from Old Town to the **Coquille River Museum** (☎ *541-347-2164, 270 Fillmore Ave; adults \$2, kids under 13 admitted free; open 10am-4pm Mon-Sat, noon-3pm Sun in summer)*, which also displays artifacts from the Coquille Indians. Just up the street is the **Bandon Cheese Factory** (☎ *541-347-2456, 800-548-8961, 680 2nd St)*, Oregon's second-largest cheese producer. People stop here to sample many varieties of cheddar cheeses and to view the cheese-making process through a glass window.

Beaches
For the best beaches, follow 4th St to Ocean Dr to access points from the bluffs along Beach Loop Dr. There's good whale watching here in the spring and sea-life viewing year round. At **Coquille Point**, at the end of SW 11th St, steps lead down the bluff to a beach interspersed with rocky crags and monoliths. Sea lions and shorebirds such as the tufted puffin inhabit crags like **Table Rock**, which lies just offshore and is protected as the Oregon Islands National Wildlife Refuge.

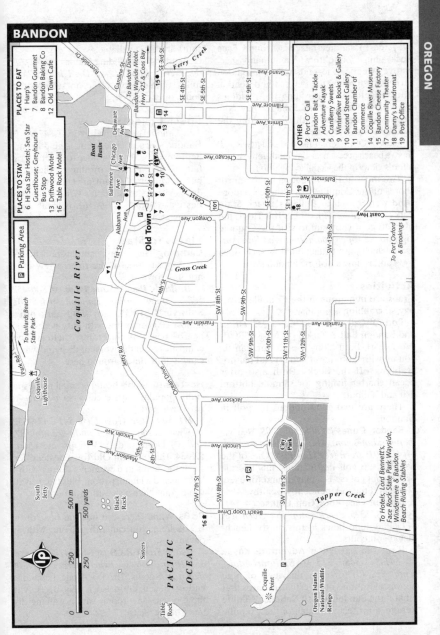

BANDON

PLACES TO STAY
6 HI Sea Star Hostel; Sea Star Guesthouse; Greyhound Bus Stop
13 Driftwood Motel
16 Table Rock Motel

PLACES TO EAT
1 Harp's
7 Bandon Gourmet
8 Bandon Baking Co
12 Old Town Cafe

OTHER
2 Port O' Call
3 Bandon Bait & Tackle
4 Adventure Kayak
5 CranBerry Sweets
9 WinterRiver Books & Gallery
10 Second Street Gallery
11 Bandon Chamber of Commerce
14 Coquille River Museum
15 Bandon Cheese Factory
17 Community Theater
18 Danny's Laundromat
19 Post Office

P Parking Area

Riverside Dr

Caroline St

To Bandon Dunes,
Bandon Wayside Motel,
Hwy 42S & Coos Bay

Ferry Creek

SE 3rd St
SE 4th Ave
SE 5th Ave
SE 9th Ave
Grand Ave

Fillmore Ave

Elmira Ave

Chicago Ave

Baltimore Ave

Alabama Ave

SE 10th St
SE 11th St

Coast Hwy

SW 13th St

To Port Orford
& Brookings

Delaware Ave

Boat Basin

Chicago Ave

Baltimore Ave

SE 2nd St

Oregon Ave

Old Town

Alabama Ave

1st St

Coquille River

To Bullards Beach State Park

Park Rd

Coquille Lighthouse

Jetty Rd

4th St

Gross Creek

Franklin Ave

SW 8th St
SW 9th St

Franklin Ave

SW 9th St
SW 10th St
SW 11th St
SW 12th St

Jackson Ave

Lincoln Ave

Ocean Drive

Lincoln Ave

Madison Ave
5th St
6th St

City Park

SW 7th St
SW 8th St
SW 11th St

Beach Loop Drive

Tupper Creek

To Hotels, Lord Bennett's, Face Rock State Park Wayside, Windermere & Bandon Beach Riding Stables

South Jetty

Black Rock

Sisters

Table Rock

PACIFIC OCEAN

Coquille Point

Oregon Islands National Wildlife Refuge

500 m
500 yards
250
250
0
0

Near the Sunset Motel, a path leads over the headland at **Face Rock State Park Wayside** to sandier beaches around **Face Rock**, a huge monolith with a human visage. Native American legends tell of a maiden turned to stone by the evil sea god Seatka. The vengeful god also flung the maiden's pet kittens far out to sea, where they now rise as sea stacks. A path winds along the headland and to the beach.

West of Old Town at the end of Jetty Road, there's beach access near the **South Jetty**, which affords views of the Coquille Lighthouse.

Two miles north of Bandon on the north shores of the Coquille River, there's a more windswept beach at **Bullards Beach State Park** (☎ 541-347-2209), off US 101. This is the place to go if you want to visit the **Coquille Lighthouse** (open 10am-4pm Wed-Sun Apr-Oct), which hasn't functioned as such since 1939 and is now a historic landmark.

Activities

Crabs are numerous in the Coquille River bay, so **crabbing** is popular.

Port O' Call (☎ 541-347-2875, 155 1st St) and **Bandon Bait & Tackle** (☎ 541-347-3905, 110 1st St), both along the harbor, can fix you up with crab rings ($4/day) and bait for crabbing off the docks. Both also offer ocean **charter fishing** for salmon, bottom fish and halibut.

There are two good options for golf in Bandon.

Bandon Dunes (☎ 888-345-6008, W www.bandondunes.com, 4 miles north of Bandon off US 101; green fees $120-150). One of the nation's top golf destinations, this upscale oceanfront course is a playground for executives and the independently wealthy.

Bandon Face Rock Golf Course (☎ 541-347-3818, 3225 Beach Loop Rd; green fees $11) Play nine holes at this pretty, beach-facing golf course.

Rent sea kayaks at **Adventure Kayak** (☎ 541-347-3480, 315 1st St; hourly/daily rental $12/40) for close-up views of blue herons, egrets and other estuarine birds that inhabit the **Bandon Marsh National Wildlife Refuge**, a protected stretch of the Coquille

River extending north of the harbor. An early start is recommended. Instruction and tours are also available.

Bandon Beach Riding Stables (☎ 541-347-3423, 2640 Beach Loop Dr; 1 hour $25), 3 miles south of town, offers **horseback riding** south of Face Rock.

Special Events

The Cranberry Festival (☎ 541-347-9616), Bandon's largest civic event, is held in early September with a parade, food and craft fair, as well as the crowning of the Cranberry Queen. Memorial Day weekend draws visitors to Bandon's Wine & Seafood Festival (☎ 541-347-9616), a local wine-tasting event.

Places to Stay

Camping The closest campground lies on the opposite side of the river, a few miles north of town.

Bullards Beach State Park (☎ 800-452-5687, 2 miles north of Bandon on US 101) Sites/yurts $19/31. This state park offers almost 200 campsites with easy access to a nearby beach. A thin forest shelters these campsites from the worst of the wind, which can be quite fierce around here.

Hostels Bandon's hostel is small and especially popular with cyclists, so be sure to reserve ahead.

HI Sea Star Hostel (☎ 541-347-9632, W www.seastarbandon.com/hi-sea.htm, 375 2nd St) Dorm beds $13-16, private rooms $28-34. This pleasant Old Town hostel offers separate men's and women's dorms with a kitchen and a laundry room, plus two private rooms that have a shared bathroom.

B&Bs While there are no true beachfront B&Bs here, you can still get one with an oceanview.

Beach Street B&B (☎ 541-347-5124, 888-335-1076, W www.beach-street.com, 200 Beach St) Rooms $107-187. Along the sandier end of Beach Loop Rd is this B&B, with three ocean-view rooms within walking distance of the beach.

Motels & Hotels If you find the beach over-rated, you might prefer a room on the harbor.

***Sea Star Guesthouse** (☎ 541-347-9632,* **W** *www.seastarbandon.com, 370 1st St)* Rooms $69-96. The spacious rooms at this popular harbor-front guesthouse in Old Town have vaulted ceilings and kitchenettes.

For ocean views and beach access, head to one of the motels along the Beach Loop Rd south of town.

***Table Rock Motel** (☎ 541-347-2700, 800-457-9141,* **W** *www.tablerockmotel.com, 840 Beach Loop Rd)* Rooms $48-106. If you don't mind '50s-style decor, this old motor lodge on a bluff near Table Rock has enough homey touches to make it a nice place. Rooms are a good value whether you're looking for economy lodging or an ocean-view apartment with kitchen.

***Sunset Motel** (☎ 541-347-2453, 800-842-2407,* **W** *www.sunsetmotel.com, 1865 Beach Loop Dr)* Oceanfront $95-127, ocean view $70-117. A cluster of old and new buildings offers oceanfront rooms along a cliff, and there are less expensive ocean-view rooms across the street. Amenities vary widely – some rooms have fireplaces and kitchens.

***Windermere** (☎ 541-347-3710,* **W** *www .windermerebythesea.com, 3250 Beach Loop Rd)* Rooms $82-135. Near Face Rock, these older but refurbished chalet-like cottages with kitchens offer Bandon's best deal on oceanfront rooms.

***Best Western Inn at Face Rock** (☎ 541-347-9441, 800-638-3092, 3225 Beach Loop Rd)* Suites $116-243. This sprawling resort-like complex at Face Rock is on the non-ocean side of the road. Luxurious condo-style suites (from $179) feature ocean views and fireplaces. The other rooms are all pretty ordinary. On site is a pool and spa.

If location isn't so important, there are less expensive motels in town along the highway.

***Bandon Wayside Motel** (☎ 541-347-3421, on Hwy 42S)* Rooms $48. Top choice in the budget category is this small motor lodge east of town toward Coquille.

***Driftwood Motel** (☎ 541-347-9022, 888-374-3893, 460 US 101)* Singles/doubles $64/74.

Rooms at this refreshingly modern, mid-range hotel are spacious and well appointed.

Resorts Jet-setting executives who come to exclusive golf resort ***Bandon Dunes** (☎ 888-345-6008,* **W** *www.bandondunes.com, 4 miles north of Bandon off US 101)* are no doubt oblivious to the millions of dollars that environmental agencies have spent trying to eradicate detrimental European beach grass, which has contributed to the demise of the endangered snowy plover. The nesting and breeding habitat for the plover is open sand. European beach grass establishes itself along the foredune and chokes off the supply of sand to the dunes, causing additional vegetation to become established and thereby reducing open sand areas. European beachgrass also provides cover habitat for predators that feed on plover nests and young. Despite the harm it's causing to the plovers, the grass is intentionally planted here as a decorative landscape element. If you hold your love of golf above concerns for local ecology, then at least you'll be in good company at this resort.

Vacation-Home Rentals View private beach homes at the Bandon Chamber of Commerce website (**W** www.bandon.com) or contact ***Coastal Vacation Rentals** (☎ 541-347-3009, 800-336-5693,* **W** *www .coastalvacationrentals.com).*

Places to Eat
In Old Town, ***Bandon Baking Co**,* at 160 2nd St, is the spot for coffee and fresh pastries. There's organic juice, smoothies, tea and toast for breakfast at ***Old Town Cafe**,* across the street from the hostel on 2nd St.

For lunch, fish markets along 1st St dispense fish and chips from shacks along the harbor.

***Bandon Gourmet** (☎ 541-347-3237, 92 2nd St)* This upscale bakery is a good place for a sandwich and a glass of wine.

***Harp's** (☎ 541-347-9057, 480 1st St)* Entrees $12-25, half orders $8-11. Open Tues-Sat. Half orders of seafood or pasta are an affordable way to enjoy a great dinner and a lighthouse view. Meals are made to order, and there's a good regional wine list.

Lord Bennett's (☎ *541-347-3663, 1695 Beach Loop Rd*) Lunch $7-9, dinners $15-20. For ocean-view dining, head here for steak and seafood next to the Sunset Motel. On Sunday there's brunch.

Entertainment

Bandon Playhouse (☎ *541-347-2506*) This ambitious community theater stages musicals, classical drama and contemporary plays at the new community theater at 11th St and Lincoln Ave.

Getting There & Away

Two buses a day on Greyhound to Brookings ($14 one way), and Portland ($32) via Lincoln City, stop in front of the Sea Star Hostel at 375 2nd St. The one-way fare to Coos Bay is $8.

On weekdays, local Curry Public Transit (☎ 541-267-7111) buses travel three times a day to Coos Bay ($2) and Brookings ($8).

LANGLOIS

Unassuming Langlois (population 600), 14 miles south of Bandon, is the closest town to Floras Lake, a covert **windsurfing** spot. Only a thin sand spit separates this spring-water lake from the ocean, which gets enough exposure to make mere spectators feel as if they're right on the Pacific. Summer is the peak season, when the lake is blasted by a steady supply of fierce, Cape Blanco winds, though winter storms help attract boardsailers year round. Put in at Boice-Cope County Park ($2 day-use fee). To reach the park, head 2 miles south of Langlois on US 101 and turn right onto Floras Lake Rd, following the signs all the way to the lake.

Equipment rental and lessons are available on site at **Floras Lake Windsurfing** (☎ *541-348-9912, 92854 Boice Cope Rd; half/ full day rental $15/40, 3-hour lesson with rental from $60*), operated by the owners of Floras Lake House. **Big Air Windsurfing** (☎ *541-348-2213, 48435 US 101; open Sat & Sun Oct-Apr; Sat only rest of year*), in Langlois, sells new and used equipment. Langlois' big blowout is

the Floras Lake Speedcheck, a three-day windsurfing event in late June.

Boice-Cope County Park (*south of Bandon off Hwy 101, at the end of Floras Lake Rd*) Sites $7-8. The campground here has sparsely sheltered sites for RVs (no hookups) and tents (bring lots of stakes). Flush toilets and showers are available.

Floras Lake House B&B (☎ *541-348-2573,* W *www.floraslake.com, 92870 Boice Cope Rd*) Singles/doubles from $95/105. Right outside the park entrance is this B&B, which is popular with boardsailers.

You'll have to either bring groceries or scrounge for food in Langlois. Find meals at **The Greasy Spoon** and deli items at the small **market**; both close by 7pm. There are other motels and restaurants in Bandon (14 miles north) and Port Orford (12 miles south).

PORT ORFORD

On a grassy headland, sleepy Port Orford (population 1025) is one of Oregon's only true ocean harbors (others are situated along the mouths of rivers). In the 1850s, this was the scene of some of Oregon's bloodiest encounters between Native Americans and white settlers. The town has a long history as a fishing and lumber port – Port Orford cedar was an especially important export. During WWII, this area of the coast was repeatedly hit by the Japanese with incendiary balloons aiming to ignite the forests, which they believed were important to the building of US military ships and airplanes.

The town, wedged between two magnificent state parks, is little more than an interruption in one of the most scenic stretches of coast highway. There's a good ocean view with a great **beach** at Battle Rock City Park, a few **art galleries** and not much else.

It's 27 miles north from here to Bandon, and 20 miles south to Gold Beach. There's a visitor center (☎ 541-332-8055, W www.por torfordoregon.com) in the park, and a Duds 'n Suds laundry at the north end of town.

Port Orford Heads State Park

A short drive up 9th St leads to **Point Orford**, which has the best seascape in town. A quick jaunt to a viewpoint on one of the short headland trails here is good consolation if you don't have time for Cape Blanco or Humbug Mountain. Deer and bunnies live on the grassy picnic grounds surrounding the **Point Orford Heads Lifesaving Museum** (open 1pm-4pm Sat & Sun Apr-Oct), which was formerly a Coast Guard Station.

Cape Blanco State Park

First sighted in 1603 by Spanish explorer Martin d'Anguilar, Cape Blanco juts far out into the Pacific, withstanding the lashing winds and fierce winter storms – more than 100 inches of rain falls here a year, and the wind frequently passes the 100-mph mark. One of the westernmost points of the continental USA, this rugged promontory is a fine state park (☎ 541-332-6774, 4 miles north of Port Orford off US 101), with hiking trails spreading out over the headland and exhilarating views in all directions. Visitors can tour the **Cape Blanco Lighthouse** (admission by donation; open 10am-3:30pm Thur-Mon April-Oct 29), which was built in 1870 and is the highest and oldest operational lighthouse in the state. A mile east and open the same hours is the **Hughes House**, a two-story Victorian home built in 1898 by Patrick Hughes, an Irish dairy rancher and gold miner.

Humbug Mountain State Park

Six miles south of Port Orford, mountains edge down to the ocean, and heavily wooded Humbug Mountain rises 1756 feet from the surf. When white settlers first came to the area in 1851, the Tututnis lived in a large village along the beach just north of here. At Humbug Mountain State Park (☎ 541-332-6774, 6 miles south of Port Orford on US 101), a 3-mile trail leads through the coast's largest remaining groves of Port Orford cedar to the top of the mountain for a dramatic view of Cape Sebastian and the Pacific Ocean. The trail begins at turnout across the highway from the campground.

Places to Stay

Cape Blanco State Park (☎ 541-332-6774, 4 miles north of Port Orford off US 101)
Tents/hookups/cabins $13/18/35. The campground on Cape Blanco's high, rocky headland comes with beach access and great views of the lighthouse. Amenities include flush toilets, showers, a boat ramp and hiker-biker sites ($4).

Humbug Mountain State Park (☎ 800-452-5687, 6 miles south of Port Orford on US 101) Tents/hookups $16/18. The wind-weary will find comfortable sites, showers and flush toilets at this lushly forested campground near Humbug Mountain.

Home by the Sea B&B (☎ 541-332-2855, W www.homebythesea.com, 444 Jackson St) Rooms $95-105. This clifftop home has two guest rooms with wonderful views.

Castaway-by-the-Sea Motel (☎ 541-332-4502, 545 W 5th St) Rooms $45-105. Ocean-view rooms here also overlook the harbor; some have fireplaces.

Sea Crest Motel (☎ 541-332-3040, 44 S US 101) Singles/doubles $55/62. There are more views at this older motel, at the south end of town.

Places to Eat

Stock up on natural food items from *Seaweed Grocery & Cafe*, where US 101 turns a corner downtown.

Bartlett's Cafe (☎ 541-332-4175, 831 Oregon St) Breakfast & lunch. Meals at this home-style cafe are tasty and straightforward. Stop here for donuts and pastries.

Spaghetti West (☎ 541-332-9378, 236 US 101) Entrees $14. Lunch & dinner. Food is a real adventure at this funky cafe, with clashing Italian menu and Southwest-meets-coastal-trailer-park decor. Savor a regional wine over dinner or over a round of billiards in the adjoining pool hall.

Port & Starboard (☎ 541-332-4515, US 101 at 436 Madrona Ave) Pizza at the Port & Starboard is your other dinner option.

Getting There & Away

Greyhound stops at 1025 N Oregon St, near the Circle K, with two buses a day going north and south. On weekdays, Port Orford is also served by Curry Public Transit (☎ 541-332-5771) with buses between Coos Bay and Brookings. Call for stops and schedules.

GOLD BEACH

Named for the oceanfront mines that yielded gold in the 1850s, the little settlement of Gold Beach (population 2165) didn't amount to much until the early years of the 20th century, when the salmon-rich waters of the Rogue River caught the fancy of gentleman anglers such as Jack London and Zane Grey (well known for his Western adventure novels) and captured the entrepreneurial zeal of Thomas Hume, who established a salmon cannery here.

Still a place for fishing vacations, the joylessly utilitarian town doesn't offer much charm or esprit. If you're not an angler, the main allure is jet boats that zip up the Rogue River, one of Oregon's wildest and most remote, with access largely limited to hikers and white-water rafters.

Orientation & Information

Gold Beach is 27 miles north of Brookings and 78 miles south of Coos Bay. Ellensburg Ave (US 101) is the main drag through town.

From the south side of the bridge, USFS Rd 33 (called Jerry's Flat Rd in town) leads upriver from Gold Beach to fishing lodges around Agness and Illahe, 35 miles east at the edge of the Wild Rogue Wilderness Area.

The Gold Beach Chamber of Commerce (☎ 541-247-7526, 800-525-2334) shares space with the Gold Beach Ranger Station (☎ 541-247-3600, Ⓦ www.fs.fed.us/r6/siskiyou) at 29279 S Ellensburg Ave. The post office is on 150 W Moore St. Coin-op Laundry is at S 29734 Ellensburg Ave, next to McKay's Market.

Things to See & Do

The Curry County Museum (☎ 541-247-6113, 29410 Ellensburg Ave; open noon-4pm Tues-Sat) preserves Native American artifacts and has displays relating to the beachfront gold rush in the late 1880s.

The drive to Gold Beach is one of the coast's most spectacular. Stop the car at Cape Sebastian State Park, a rocky cliff-hung headland 7 miles south, for a seascape stretching from California to Cape Blanco.

If you'd like to go hiking, the 40-mile Rogue River Trail ends (or begins) east of Gold Beach at Illahe. Day hikers can hike up the canyon 4.3 miles one way up to the waterfall at Flora Dell Creek. (Also see the Wild Rogue Wilderness Area in the Southern Oregon chapter.) For a great hike that won't take all day, head 12 miles up USFS Rd 33 to the Schrader Old Growth Trail, which wanders for 1½ miles through towering Douglas fir, Port Orford cedar and hemlock. There are picnic tables along the way. A Northwest Forest Pass ($5) is required at both trailheads.

Spring Chinook salmon (April to June) and fall and winter steelhead runs keep anglers fishing the Rogue River year round. Guided fishing excursions are popular – a full-day trip costs $150-200. Try Don Pedro (☎ 541-247-7946, Ⓦ www.roguefishingguide.com), Fish Oregon (☎ 541-247-4138, 800-348-4138, Ⓦ www.fishoregon.com) or Terry Kennedy Guide Service (☎ 541-247-9219, Ⓦ www.tkfg.com). Find tackle and fishing information at the Rogue Outdoor Store (☎ 541-247-7142, 29865 Ellensburg Ave).

Jet Boat Tours

Jet boats, which use hydrofoils that can skim over the surface of shallow streams and river rapids, were originally used to deliver mail to far-reaching outposts along the Rogue River. Tours travel up the rugged and barren canyon to the Wild Rogue Wilderness Area. Wildlife viewing is good, with deer, elk, otters, beavers, eagles and osprey seemingly unaffected by the deafening growls of the boat engines.

Jerry's Rogue Jets (☎ 541-247-4571, 800-451-3645, Ⓦ www.roguejets.com) and Rogue River Mail Boats (☎ 541-247-7033, 800-458-3511, Ⓦ www.mailboat.com, Rogue River Rd) both offer similar trips: a six-hour excursion to the little resort community of Agness, 32 miles inland ($30), a slightly longer foray into the roadless Wild Rogue Wilderness ($45), and an eight-hour trip up through narrow canyon and shallow rapids to Blossom Bar ($75). Call for reservations; lunch is not included.

Places to Stay

For a town of few attractions, motels here are inexplicably expensive in the summer. Modern economy rooms start at $65. Luckily, there's plenty of great camping along the river, and rustic cabins are available up in Agness.

Camping There's great riverside camping up USFS Rd 33.

Indian Creek Recreation Park (☎ 541-247-7704, 94680 Jerry's Flat Rd) Tents/ hookups $15/22. This popular RV resort is 5 miles up the river, on the south bank.

Lobster Creek Campground (9 miles east on USFS Rd 33) Tents $5. Established sites are rudimentary, and there's no water. The rocky bar by the river is a popular place for RVs ($3).

Quosantana Campground (14 miles east on USFS Rd 33) Sites $8. This pretty, park-like campground in a myrtle-wood grove is the nicest place to pitch a tent. There are flush toilets and a boat launch.

Agness RV Park (☎ 541-247-2813, 04215 Agness Rd) Hookups $17. Head here for RV camping in Agness.

Illahe Campground (4 miles north of Agness on USFS Rd 33) Tents $6. Pleasant riverside sites here are a popular place for starting and ending journeys through the Wild Rogue Wilderness.

B&Bs Seven miles north of Gold Beach is an imposing Victorian inn that looks straight out onto the ocean.

Inn at Nesika Beach (☎ 541-247-6434, 33026 Nesika Rd, W www.goldbeach lodging.com) Rooms $125-150. The four guest rooms here have whirlpool baths; some have fireplaces.

Hotels & Resorts With the exception of one fancy resort, the hotels here are all straightforward and right along the highway.

City Center Motel (☎ 541-247-6675, 94200 Harlow St) Rooms $40. This place is pretty unappealing, but room prices are rock bottom.

Drift In Motel (☎ 541-247-4547, 800-424-3833, 94250 Port Dr) Rooms $58. Slightly better is the Drift In, near the harbor.

Sand 'n Sea Motel (☎ 541-247-6658, 2932 S US 101) Rooms from $66. Nonview rooms at this oceanfront motel are your best bet for something clean and comfortable.

Gold Beach Resort (☎ 541-247-7066, 800-541-0947, W www.gbresort.com, 29232 Ellensburg Ave) Rooms $99-165. This is one of the nicest oceanfront hotels on the south coast, with condo-style rooms and all the amenities of a fancy business-class hotel, including an indoor pool and spa.

Tu Tu' Tun Lodge (☎ 541-247-6664, 800-864-6357, W www.tututun.com, 96550 N Bank Rogue River Rd) Rooms $160-335. One of Oregon's most exclusive hide-aways is 7 miles upriver on the north bank; it has riverfront rooms (most with fireplaces and private outdoor Jacuzzis) and a fancy dining room reserved for guests.

Jot's Resort (☎ 541-247-6676, 800-367-5687, W www.jotsresort.com, 94360 Weddur-burn Loop) Rooms $110-325. Jot's is one of the original big marina resorts on the south coast, with condos overlooking the harbor.

Lodges Three rustic lodges at Agness serve the needs of anglers, hikers, jet-boat passengers and the occasional stray traveler. All offer buffet-style lunch and dinner.

Lucas Lodge (☎ 541-247-7443, 03904 Cougar Lane) Lodge rooms/cabins $45/65. This lodge was built in the 1910s.

Singing Springs Resort (☎ 541-247-6162, on USFS Rd 33 in Agness) Cabins $50-55. Some of the cabins here have kitchenettes.

Cougar Lane Lodge (☎ 541-247-7233, 04219 Agness Rd) Rooms $45-65. This is the newest of the lodges: Rooms are in motel-like units.

Places to Eat

Grant's (☎ 541-247-7208, 29790 Ellensburg Ave) Breakfast/lunch/dinner $4/6/10. One of the best new things to happen to Gold Beach is this family restaurant, which has especially good breakfasts.

Port Hole Cafe *(☎ 541-247-7411, 29975 Harbor Way)* Lunch $5.50. There are good burgers and pie at this harbor-side chowder house.

Nor'Wester Seafood Restaurant *(☎ 541-247-2333, on Harbor Way)* Dinner $16-40. This steak-and-seafood restaurant, also on the harbor, serves some of the most inspired food around.

Getting There & Away

Greyhound buses (☎ 541-247-7710) to Brookings and Portland via Lincoln City stop at a shack at Colvin and Caughell Sts, across from Grant's restaurant. Additional buses to Coos Bay ($8 one way) and Brookings ($2) on Curry Public Transit (☎ 541-247-7506) stop at the Cannery building on the harbor three times daily on weekdays.

It's a half-mile walk north from the Greyhound stop to the nearest jet-boat dock by the harbor. From here, backpackers can get a jet boat to the Rogue River trailhead at Foster Bar ($22.50); reservations are required (see Jet Boat Tours, earlier).

BROOKINGS

Just 6 miles north of the California-Oregon border on US 101, on the bay of the Chetco River, Brookings (population 5625) is a bustling town – there is lots of traffic crossing the state line from California to avoid sales taxes. The harbor is busy with both commercial and sport fishing. Like so many other coastal towns, the beaches and magnificent state parks are very successful at seducing travelers to spend their vacations here. After the romp, you're likely to look back and wonder what you ever saw in this charmless commercial town.

Brookings leads the nation in Easter lily–bulb production. In July, fields south of town are filled with bright colors and a heavy scent. Roads lead inland from Brookings up the Chetco River to the western edge of the Kalmiopsis Wilderness, the state's largest and one of its most remote. Oregon's only redwood forests are also found up the Chetco River.

Oregonians refer to Brookings as being in 'the banana belt' of the state. Winter temperatures hover around 60°F, which is balmy compared to the stormy climes in the north.

Orientation & Information

Brookings is 27 miles south of Gold Beach on US 101. Getting here from southern Oregon requires a trip down US 199 (the Redwood Hwy) from Grants Pass to Crescent City, California, and then north.

Brookings is in fact two towns: Brookings proper (north of the Chetco River) and Harbor (on the south shore, at the boat basin). US 101 is called Chetco Ave in town.

The Brookings-Harbor Chamber of Commerce (☎ 541-469-3181, 800-535-9469) is at the harbor at 16330 Lower Harbor Rd. For regional information, drop by the Oregon State Welcome Center (☎ 541-469-4117), 1650 US 101, north of town at Harris Beach State Park. The Chetco Ranger Station (☎ 541-469-2196, ⓦ www.fs.fed.us/r6/siskiyou) is at 555 5th St.

The post office is at 711 Spruce St. Economy Laundry is next to the Westward Motel, at 1026 Chetco Ave.

Beaches

There are beaches all along the seafront north of the mouth of the Chetco River. One nice in-town beach is at the end of Wharf St, where **Mill Beach** offers views of promontories off Chetco Point.

North of Brookings on US 101, there are miles of beaches, rocky cliffs and outcroppings, and hiking trails at **Harris Beach State Park**. From the picnic area, you can enjoy views of Goat Island, Oregon's largest offshore island and a bird sanctuary.

WWII Bomb Site

Brookings was the site of one of only two mainland US air attacks during WWII. A seaplane launched from a Japanese submarine in early September 1942 succeeded in bombing Mt Emily, behind the city. The main goal of the attack was to burn the forests, but they failed to ignite. There were no casualties. The bomb site, up S Side Chetco River Rd, is a source of peculiar fascination to the locals – ask for a map at the chamber of commerce.

Chetco Valley Historical Society Museum

Stop by this local museum (☎ 541-469-6651, 15461 Museum Rd; adult/child $1/50¢; open noon-5pm Wed-Sun June-Labor Day; noon-4pm Thur-Sun mid-Mar-Oct) to see an odd iron cast of a face whose resemblance to Queen Elizabeth I is speculative, or check out the cedar canoe used by Native American fishers. Adjacent is the world's largest Monterey cypress, with a girth of 27 feet.

Azalea Park

Hundreds of wild azaleas (some over 200 years old) hold forth in fragrant bloom at this 26-acre park at the south end of town in late May and early June. On Memorial Day weekend, the park becomes the focus of the annual Azalea Festival (☎ 541-469-3181), with a floral parade and craft fair.

Alfred A Loeb State Park

Nature trails at dark and woody Loeb State Park (☎ 541-469-2021, Ⓦ www.prd.state .or.us, 10 miles east on N Bank Chetco Rd) showcase two of Oregon's rarest and most cherished trees – redwood and myrtle. There are also fishing and swimming in the Chetco River, as well as one of the coast's finest public campgrounds.

From the picnic area, the ¾-mile Riverview Nature Trail follows the river through old-growth myrtle. It then continues up the hillside as the 1¼-mile Redwood Nature Trail to loop through a grove of ancient redwoods. One tree with a girth of 33 feet is reckoned to be over 800 years old.

Samuel H Boardman State Park

Four miles north of Brookings, US 101 winds over 11 miles of headlands through Boardman State Park, which contains some of Oregon's most beautiful coastline. Along the highway are a number of roadside turnouts and picnic areas with short trails leading to secluded beaches and dramatic viewpoints. Marching far out to sea are tiny island chains, home to shorebirds and braying sea lions.

The Lone Ranch Picnic Area, the southernmost turnout, is a secluded beach with swimming and tide pools in a sandy cove studded with sea stacks. A mile north, a short path leads to the tip of Cape Ferrelo, a popular spot for spring whale watching. At Whalehead Cove, a patchy but paved road drops steeply down to a fine little beach hemmed in by rocky headlands. Native Americans harvested shellfish at Indian Sands Beach for hundreds of years, leaving high mounds of shells along the dunes. A steep trail leads down the beach, flanked by sandstone cliffs made light red by iron deposits.

Just past the Thomas Creek Bridge, Oregon's highest at 345 feet, is the turnout for Natural Bridge Viewpoint, 2½ miles past Indian Sands. From the viewpoint, a short trail leads to views of rock arches just off the coast. The arches are the remains of sea caves that have been collapsed by pounding waves. Likewise, at Arch Rock Point, 1 mile north, the volcanic headlands have been eroded to leave the arch of a lava tube. Paths down to Whiskey Creek lead to great tidal pools.

There are no campgrounds in the park.

Hiking

Boardman State Park is the southern entry point of the Oregon Coast Trail, a long-distance trail that traverses the entire length of Oregon's Pacific Coast.

While not all sections of the trail are currently complete (hikers have to walk along US 101 for short stretches), Boardman has enough complete segments to offer good day hikes. The down-and-back hike north from Natural Bridge Viewpoint to Arch Rock alternates deep rain forests and grassy headlands for views of coastal fauna, such as puffins, gulls, murres, cormorants and curious seals and sea lions.

Hikers with a high-clearance vehicle can take an hourlong drive to a short hike in the Kalmiopsis Wilderness, Oregon's largest wilderness, with mountains noted for rare botanical specimens. (See the Kalmiopsis Wilderness section, in the Southern Oregon chapter.) Drive up N Bank Chetco River Rd and then onto USFS Rd 1909 for about 13 miles to the Vulcan Lake Trailhead, where a 1.4-mile trail leads to a remote rock cairn lake. A number of long-distance trails lead out from the trailhead as well. A Northwest Forest Pass ($5) is required.

Fishing

The Chetco River is famous for its winter steelhead and fall Chinook salmon. The best fishing is up N Bank Chetco River Rd, above Loeb State Park.

Brookings is the only harbor in the state where ocean sport-fishing for salmon still occasionally opens up. **Tidewind Sportfishing** (☎ *541-469-0337, 800-799-0337,* Ⓦ *www.tide windsportfishing.com, 16368 Lower Harbor Rd*) Salmon/bottom fishing $75/50. This company also offers whale-watching trips.

Places to Stay

Brookings offers a variety of settings for campers, and there's one B&B outside of town. The highway is lined with economy motels that carry business-class rates.

Alfred A Loeb State Park (☎ *800-452-5687,* Ⓦ *www.prd.state.or.us, 10 miles east of Brookings along N Bank Chetco River Rd*) Tents/hookups/cabins $16/16/35. There are four riverfront cabins and 53 campsites situated in a fragrant grove of rare myrtle trees.

Harris Beach State Park (☎ *800-452-5687,* Ⓦ *www.prd.state.or.us, 2 miles north of Brookings on US 101*) Tents/hookups/yurts $16/19/35. Camp beachside at one of 130 sites right on the ocean. Yurts, showers, flush toilets and coin laundry are among the amenities.

Beachfront RV Park (☎ *541-469-5867, 800-441-0856, 16035 Boat Basin Rd*) Hookups $26. RV parks by the harbor like this one are just the thing for campers who want to stay in town.

South Coast Inn B&B (☎ *541-469-5557, 800-525-9273,* Ⓦ *www.southcoastinn.com, 516 Redwood St*) Rooms $94-116. The four guest rooms at this Arts and Crafts–style home offer private bathrooms, a hot tub, sauna and ocean views.

Pacific Sunset Inn (☎ *541-469-2141, 800-469-2141, 1144 Chetco Ave*) Singles/doubles $43/53. This is one of the cheapest places.

Westward Motel (☎ *541-469-7471, 1026 Chetco Ave*) $55/63. This well-kept older motel has kitchenettes and nonsmoking rooms.

Harbor Inn (☎ *541-469-3194, 15991 US 101 S*) Rooms $48/56, $10 more on weekends. Clean, spacious rooms here have refrigerators and offer the best value for midweek travelers.

Best Western Beachfront Inn (☎ *541-469-7779, 800-468-4081, 16008 Boat Basin Rd*) $84/89. The best ocean-view rooms (some with Jacuzzis) are at this hotel on the harbor. There are some suites, private balconies, kitchenettes and a swimming pool.

Places to Eat

Modest market-and-chowder joints on the harbor such as **Chetco Seafood Company** and the **Wharfside Restaurant** serve inexpensive seafood fresh off the docks.

Home Port Bagels & Sandwiches (☎ *541-469-6611, 1011 Chetco Ave*) Homemade bagels are the specialty of this lunch spot.

Smuggler's Cove (☎ *503-469-6006, 160011 Boat Basin Rd*) Entrees $15. The salad is good and the ocean view is excellent at this steak-and-seafood restaurant on the harbor. Breakfast and lunch are affordable, and the bar is nice at sunset.

Chives (☎ *541-469-4121, 1025 Chetco Ave*) Entrees $12-22. Dinner Wed-Sun. There's salmon angel-hair pasta in caper chive beurre blanc at this upmarket restaurant in a strip mall – it all seems too fussy for Brookings.

Getting There & Around

From Brookings, there are two buses daily to Portland ($42 one way) via Lincoln City and San Francisco ($52) on Greyhound. The station (☎ 541-469-3326) is at Fiji Island Tan, 601 Railroad St, near the post office. On weekdays, Curry Public Transit (☎ 541-469-6822) has three buses to Bandon ($8) with connections to Coos Bay. The bus stops at Ray's Market on US 101.

For cyclists, Brookings marks the end of the Oregon Coast Bike Route (most ride north to south). Taking the bus back to your original point of departure will mean packing your bicycle in a cardboard box, available for free from nearby Escape Hatch Sports & Cycles (☎ 541-469-2914), 624 Railroad Ave.

Bob's Taxi (☎ 541-469-7007) provides local taxi service.

Willamette Valley

Between Portland and Eugene stretches the Willamette Valley, the incredibly fertile 60-mile-wide agricultural basin that was the destination of the Oregon Trail pioneers. A hundred and fifty years after the migration, the Willamette Valley is still the center of Oregon, with three-quarters of the state's population living here.

Highlights

- Enjoying a starlit evening on crystal clear Waldo Lake, one of the world's purest
- Cycling the pastoral Willamette Valley countryside
- Admiring snowcapped mountains from the dramatic volcanic landscape at McKenzie Pass
- Letting your hair down at the counter-cultural Oregon Country Fair, in Eugene

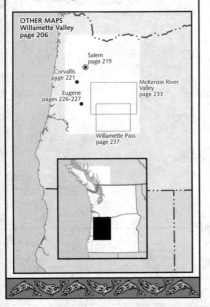

OTHER MAPS
Willamette Valley
page 206

Salem
page 215

Corvallis
page 221

Eugene
pages 226-227

McKenzie River
Valley
page 233

Willamette Pass
page 237

Running down the middle of the valley is I-5, Oregon's main transportation corridor, although Hwys 99E and 99W, on either side of the Willamette River, offer more scenic alternatives. Connected to them are a lacework of country roads. Most travelers zoom up and down the Willamette Valley on I-5. It's a pity, because side roads lead through beautiful farmland to wineries, monasteries, historic settlements and charming old towns whose pedigrees extend back to the 1840s. Because the valley is largely flat and crisscrossed with slow roads, the Willamette is a great place to explore on bicycle.

Historic sites in the northern valley and the Yamhill County vineyards are within easy reach of Portland for day trips, though B&Bs may entice travelers for country weekends. In the mid-valley is Salem, the state capital, bustling with politicians and issues. Corvallis and Eugene, in the southern valley, are dominated by the state's two universities. Both are dynamic and engaging small cities with inexpensive food and lodging.

History

The Chinook and Calapooians were the most numerous of the Native American tribes to inhabit the Willamette Valley. Their numbers were decimated by diseases such as small pox (which was introduced by white settlers), and by the time the Calapooians were gathered onto Grande Ronde Reservation, they numbered only 42 members. There are no speakers of Calapooian today.

The first white settlement was made by French Canadian trappers, who retired from the Hudson's Bay Company in the 1820s to an area east of St Paul called French Prairie. As US pioneers began to arrive and vie for land, the area soon became the scene of British and US rivalries. Oregon was part of an area held in joint occupancy by Britain and the USA. This changed abruptly in 1843, when settlers at Champoeg voted to organize a US-style self-government and declared

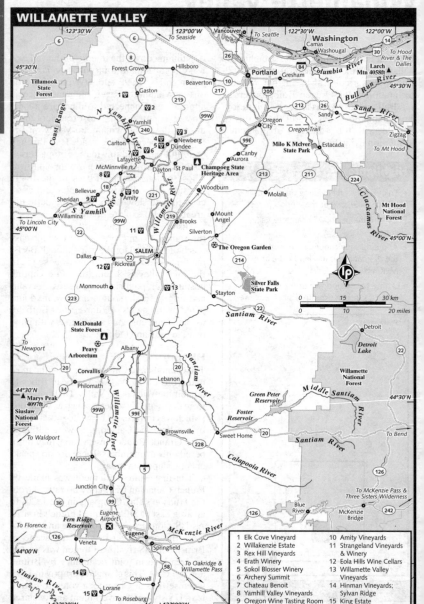

WILLAMETTE VALLEY

1 Elk Cove Vineyard
2 Willakenzie Estate
3 Rex Hill Vineyards
4 Erath Winery
5 Sokol Blosser Winery
6 Archery Summit
7 Chateau Benoit
8 Yamhill Valley Vineyards
9 Oregon Wine Tasting Room
10 Amity Vineyards
11 Strangeland Vineyards & Winery
12 Eola Hills Wine Cellars
13 Willamette Valley Vineyards
14 Hinman Vineyards; Sylvan Ridge
15 King Estate

Oregon City its provisional capital. Thereafter, the British claim to lands in the Pacific Northwest was increasingly insecure. Had the vote gone differently, Oregon and Washington might now be part of Canada.

By 1855, over 50,000 people made the trek to the Northwest along the Oregon Trail, almost all with the goal of settling in the Willamette Valley. Religious doctrine played a large role in the growth of valley communities. Trappers from the Hudson's Bay Company were largely Catholic, while the majority of the earliest US settlers were Methodist. Missionary efforts on the part of both religious groups led to the establishment of various educational and cultural facilities, which have had a long-term impact on the cultural life of the state. The Willamette Valley also provided a haven for other small, sometimes persecuted, sects, such as the Quaker Friends, Russian Old Believers, utopian German communists and Mennonites.

By the 1860s, the Willamette Valley was largely settled. The transportation of agricultural products became increasingly important to the growth of valley communities, and riverside towns such as Albany, Corvallis and Eugene soon thrived as hubs of commerce and light industry. When railroads connected the Willamette Valley to California in the 1860s, industries such as wool, saw and paper mills joined agriculture as the dominant economic foundations of the valley.

OREGON CITY & AROUND

One of the oldest incorporated towns west of the Mississippi, and Oregon's first territorial capital, Oregon City (population 16,810) was founded in 1829, when Fort Vancouver factor John McLoughlin established a lumber mill at Willamette Falls. As the official end point of the Oregon Trail, Oregon City was the goal of almost all the pioneers who ventured across the continent during the 1840s and '50s. In the early days of Oregon, when trade and transportation depended largely upon riverboats, Oregon City grew to be the territory's dominant city and boomed as the Northwest's first industrial center. The Willamette Falls were

also once a center of fishing and trade for many Indians of the northern Willamette Valley.

This once vital frontier town has now been swallowed up by Portland's suburbs, and its famous waterfall is a snaggle of electric generators. However, it abounds with historic sites and museums that preserve everyday items from the homes of early settlers, and it is the place people come to learn about life in early Oregon. You should allow a few hours on a stopover from Portland.

Orientation & Information

Thirteen miles south of Portland on I-205, Oregon City is situated at a natural division point between the upper and lower portions of the Willamette River – the 42-foot Willamette Falls, which can be viewed from Willamette Falls Vista, are along Hwy 99E west of downtown.

A municipal elevator between Railroad and 7th Sts gives free rides between historic homes on the bluff and the river-level commercial district.

The new tourist office will be located at the Oregon Trail Interpretive Center, though signs for the old one are still posted around town. Until the new one opens, contact the Clackamas County Tourism Development Council (☎ 800-647-3843, 𝕎 www.clackamas-oregon.com), at 619 High St. The post office is at 19300 Molalla.

Things to See & Do

The **McLoughlin House** (☎ 503-656-5146, 713 Center St; adult/senior/child $4/3/2; open 10am-4pm Tues-Sat, 1pm-4pm Sun Feb-Dec) was built by John McLoughlin for his family after he moved to Oregon City in 1845. It is now a museum and displays artifacts that belonged to the 'father of Oregon.' At the time it was built, most settlers lived in shanties and log cabins, and this two-story clapboard home with three bedrooms was often referred to as McLoughlin's Mansion. McLoughlin's solid, simple good taste is evident throughout. See the Facts about the Pacific Northwest and Southwestern Washington chapters for more information on McLoughlin.

The Aurora Colony

Aurora Colony founder Dr William Keil, who was born in Prussia in 1811, had many near-fanatical interests, including Protestant communal religion, searching for mystical cures for diseases (his title of 'Doctor' was self-conferred), botany, magnetism and theater. After developing a following in Pittsburgh, Pennsylvania, and Bethel, Missouri, Dr Keil moved his band of followers to the West Coast over the Oregon Trail in 1855. A wagon containing the embalmed body of Keil's son Willie led the way.

The 15,000-acre Aurora Colony, as the commune was called, was for many years prosperous and successful. The town contained a number of shops, flour mills, a tannery, a bakery, a school and a hotel, as well as homes laid out according to an exacting streetless grid (only two houses per block, and only footpaths leading between homes).

Although members of the colony were admonished to live somewhat apart from noncommunists, the community relied on trade for income. Furniture, foodstuffs, leather goods and cloth from Aurora artisans found a ready market, and Aurora sausages were especially prized. The large Aurora Colony Hotel, on the stage line between Portland and California, was favored by travelers of that period.

Particularly mettlesome to the commune members was Keil's reluctance to allow young followers to marry and start families. After Keil's death in 1877, the colony assimilated into the larger rural culture of the Willamette Valley.

History exhibits at the engaging **Museum of the Oregon Territory** (☎ 503-655-5574, *211 Tumwater Dr; adult/senior/child/family $4/3/2/10; open 10am-4pm Mon-Fri, 1pm-5pm Sat & Sun*) offer a good interpretation of the local moonshine trade and of the Willamette Meteor. Other displays include collections of intricately etched military mess kits and Native American basketry. An exhibit of domestic architectural styles is a good study for those interested in historic homes. A tour through the 1907 **Stevens-Crawford House** (☎ 503-655-2866, *603 6th St*) is included with admission.

The **End of the Oregon Trail Interpretive Center** (☎ 503-657-9336, ₩ *www.endofthe oregontrail.org, 1726 Washington St; adult/senior & child $5.50/3; open 9:15am-4:45pm Mon-Sat, 10am-4pm Sun May-Sept; 9:30am-3:30pm Mon-Sat, 11:30am-4pm Sun Oct-Apr)* commemorates the struggle of the Oregon pioneers on their overland journey and the challenges they faced when they arrived in Oregon. The 75-minute living history/multimedia presentation is informative and the collection of artifacts quite good, though the delivery is a bit sluggish.

About 15 miles southwest of Oregon City on Hwy 99E (or 3 miles east of I-5 exit 278), Aurora (population 700) was established in 1856 by Dr William Keil and his followers. The remains of this utopian colony of a small German Protestant sect are a reminder of the many and varied motives of people who came across the Oregon Trail. The **Old Aurora Colony Museum** (☎ 503-678-5754, *2nd & Liberty Sts; adult/senior/child $3.50/3/1.50; open 10am-4pm Tues-Sat, noon-4pm Sun April-mid-Oct; closed Jan & Feb*) tells the story in artifacts and exhibits.

Nowadays, Aurora is famous for its many antique stores.

Special Events

Freakishly huge pumpkins weighing 700lb and more contend for cash prizes in the Great Pumpkin Weigh-Off (☎ 503-266-4703), held in Canby the first weekend in October.

Places to Stay & Eat

Rivershore Hotel (☎ 503-655-7141, 800-443-7777, *1900 Clackamette Dr*) Rooms with breakfast $74. River-view rooms at this hotel near the I-205 exit are a good choice if you want to avoid Portland.

OREGON

The Acoustic Café (☎ 503-723-5255, 502 7th St) Lunch $5.50-7.50. This pleasant coffee shop shares space with an antique mall near the McLoughlin House and serves soup, salad and sandwiches.

McMenamins Oregon City Pub (☎ 503-655-8032, 102 9th St) Entrees $4-8. Portland-based McMenamins is a mellow, family-friendly brewpub with burgers, sandwiches and locally brewed ales.

Getting There & Around

Tri-Met (☎ 503-231-3235) bus No 35 from downtown Portland arrives at the Oregon City Transit Center at 11th and Main Sts. The one-way trip ($1.50) takes 45 minutes.

For a full day of museum-hopping, catch the free Oregon City Trolley, which stops at museums and historic homes between the Oregon Trail Interpretive Center and the Museum of the Oregon Territory.

CHAMPOEG STATE HERITAGE AREA

One of the very first settlements in Oregon, Champoeg (derived from the French *champ* for 'field') was on a flood plain along a bend in the Willamette River. After the historic 1843 vote, the town continued to grow as the era of riverboat travel brought increasing trade to the Willamette Valley. In December 1861, an enormous flood swept through the Willamette drainage, and 27 feet of water rushed over the plain. After the flood subsided, only three buildings remained.

Champoeg was never rebuilt. In 1901, the area was designated a state heritage area. With 107 acres of old-growth woodland and grassy meadows, historic sites and nature trails, beautiful Champoeg State Heritage Area is deservedly well loved.

Champoeg State Heritage Area (☎ 503-678-1251, 8239 Champoeg Rd NE, 🅦 www .oregonstateparks.org; day-use fee $3) is 19 miles southwest of Oregon City and 25 miles southwest of Portland, off I-5 exit 278.

Films and displays at the **Champoeg Visitors Center** (*open 11am-4:30pm Mon-Fri, 9am-4:30pm Sat & Sun*), at the park entrance, explain the events that led up to the

famous vote at Champoeg. There are also exhibits on the Calapooians and the flood patterns of the Willamette River. Nearby is the **Manson Farmstead**, which features a recently restored 1860s barn and garden.

Ten miles of **hiking and biking trails** wind through the park and along the river, leading past the sites of many long-gone buildings, which are noted with plaques. **Interpretive walking and bicycle tours** of historic sites are offered on weekends in summer; check the visitor center for schedules.

Closer to the Willamette and to the location of the old village of Champoeg is the **Pioneer Mothers Memorial Cabin** (☎ 503-633-2237; adult/youth $2/1; open 1pm-5pm Fri-Sun Mar-Oct), a reconstructed log cabin built by the local Daughters of the American Revolution. It's filled with objects brought across the Oregon Trail and other articles of frontier life.

Indian artifacts and inaugural gowns worn by the wives of Oregon governors are housed inside the 1852 **Newell House** (☎ 503-678-5537; youth/adults $1/2; open 1pm-5pm Fri-Sun Mar-Oct), right outside the park entrance.

Grassy **Champoeg Amphitheater** hosts a number of big-name performers throughout the summer.

Champoeg State Heritage Area Campground (☎ 800-452-5687) Tents/hookups/ yurts $17/21/33. Sites here are much sought after, due to the park's verdant setting and proximity to Portland.

YAMHILL COUNTY WINE COUNTRY

The valleys between the rolling oak-forested hills of Yamhill County have been prime agricultural real estate since the days of the Oregon Trail pioneers. But the valley waited until 1965, in the meantime passing through various agricultural stages, for the event that may have revealed the region's true calling: the planting of wine grapes near Dundee.

In just 30 years, the wine industry in Oregon has grown from the crazy notion of a few zealous students of enology to a multimillion-dollar industry. An hour's

OREGON

drive from Portland leads to dozens of vineyards in a landscape of rolling hills, oak forests and lazy streams. In sleepy towns, topnotch restaurants wait to round out a full afternoon of wine touring with an exceptional dinner. The beauty and tranquility of the valley, as well as a number of high-quality B&Bs, make the wine country a favorite weekend destination.

Orientation
Hwys 99W and 18 are the main roads through the wine country; watch for the blue road signs pointing toward wineries. Newberg is 15 miles southwest of Portland on Hwy 99W. McMinnville, on Hwy 18, is another 25 miles.

An alternate route reaches McMinnville by ferry. Take I-5 exit 263 (Brooks), 35 miles south of Portland, and follow signs west to the Wheatland Ferry, which crosses the Willamette River south of McMinnville. You won't gain much time this way, but it's vastly more scenic, and the short ferry ride beats waiting in a traffic jam on Hwy 99W.

Information
The Yamhill County Wineries Association (☎ 503-646-2985, Ⓦ www.yamhillwine.com), PO Box 871, McMinnville, OR 97218, can brief you on the area's wines and vineyards. The association's free map of Yamhill County is an excellent resource and is also available online. *Wine Press Northwest* magazine ($3) lists the newest releases. Visit Ⓦ www.winepressnw.com for winery profiles and links to individual sites.

For tourist information and a complete list of B&Bs, contact the Newberg Area Chamber of Commerce (☎ 503-538-2014), at 115 N Washington St, or the McMinnville Chamber of Commerce (☎ 503-472-6196), at 417 N Adams St.

Wine-Tasting
There are presently over 30 established wineries in Yamhill County, so unless you have a lot of time on your hands – and a designated driver – you'll need to pick and choose to make up your own itinerary. It's difficult to visit more than three or four in one day.

The Wine Country

The state's first grapevine was planted by the Jesuits at St Paul in the 1830s, but it took 150 years for savvy viticulturists to realize Oregon's winemaking potential. Oregon's mild climate and long, although not terribly hot, summers allow some of the world's noblest but fussiest grapes to thrive.

Chardonnay and pinot noir grapes – the grapes of France's Burgundy region – flourish here. Oregon chardonnays are generally light-textured and lemony white wines in the French style, lacking the thick oakiness of Californian and Australian chardonnays. Also much praised are Oregon pinot noir wines, delicate red wines that develop a refined fruitiness from mellow Oregon summers.

Pinot gris, another European grape suited to a cool climate, produces white wines of distinction. Riesling grapes are among the most widely planted grapes in the area, reflecting the sweeter wine tastes of the 1970s, when many of the vineyards were planted. In Oregon, these grapes produce a pleasantly fruity, off-dry wine.

Most vineyards are family-owned and -operated. Nearly all of them welcome visitors to their tasting rooms, which are sometimes grand edifices but just as often homey affairs tucked into the corner of fermentation rooms. Blue signs along the main highways point the way to vineyards and wineries around Newberg, Dundee, Lafayette, Carlton and McMinnville.

If you have time for only one stop, make it the **Oregon Wine Tasting Room** (☎ 503-843-3787, 19700 Hwy 18; open 11am-5:30pm), in Bellevue, 9 miles southwest of McMinnville. It's not a winery, but at least 20 Oregon wines are available for tasting, and hundreds are for sale.

You won't want to miss the following wineries because of their quality wines and appealing locations.

Loved by tourists for its 'vineyard lifestyle' is **Rex Hill Vineyards** (☎ 503-538-0666, 30835 N Hwy 99W; open 10am-5pm in summer, 11am-5pm the rest of the year), just north of Newberg. A display of ceremonial garb explains the recent revival of the ancient Wine Brotherhood.

Hwy 240 leads west from Newberg to reach **Willakenzie Estate** (☎ 503-662-3280, 19143 Laughlin Rd; open noon-5pm Memorial Day-Labor Day), which is tucked in the rolling Chehalem Hills near Yamhill; try the gamay noir. Beautiful **Elk Cove Vineyards** (☎ 503-985-7760, 877-355-2683, 27751 NW Olson Rd; open 11am-5pm), off Hwy 47 near Gaston, has a nice riesling.

In the Dundee area, **Erath Winery** (☎ 503-539-9463, 9409 NE Worden Hill Rd; open 11am-5pm) is a topnotch winery with a good pinot noir. A view of Mt Hood goes nicely with the chardonnay at **Sokol Blosser Winery** (☎ 503-864-2282, 800-582-6668, 5000 Sokol Blosser Lane; open 11am-5pm). **Archery Summit** (☎ 503-864-4300, 18599 NE Archery Summit Rd; tasting fee $10; tours Thur-Sun at 11am, 1pm & 3:30pm) makes Oregon's very best (and priciest) pinot noirs, which are aged in an underground cave; a tour reservation is required to visit.

Chateau Benoit (☎ 503-864-2991, 6580 NE Mineral Springs Rd; open 10am-5pm), north of McMinnville near Lafayette, offers a good sauvignon blanc and a lovely tasting room with great views. Try the pinot gris at **Yamhill Valley Vineyards** (☎ 503-843-3100, 800-825-4845, 16250 NW Oldsville Rd, McMinnville; open 11am-5pm June-Thanksgiving, Sat & Sun only Mar-May).

Southward, near the Eola Hills area around Amity, the low-key and informal **Amity Vineyards** (☎ 503-835-2362, 888-264-8966, 18150 Amity Vineyards Rd SE; open noon-5pm Feb-Dec 23) has good pinot noir and makes sulfite-free wines from organic grapes.

A number of companies offer tours of the vineyards from Portland. **Grape Escape** (☎ 503-282-4262, W www.grapeescapetours .com) specializes in wine-country tours and is adept at providing that behind-the-scenes glimpse ($55-95). **EcoTours** (☎ 503-245-1428, W www.ecotours-of-oregon.com) offers a full-day tour starting at $49.50.

Most wineries have preboxed bottles for sale, which make good gifts for wine-drinking friends. Wineries will also arrange the shipping for case lots of wine.

Lawrence Gallery (☎ 503-843-3633, 19706 Hwy 18), 9 miles south of McMinnville at Bellevue, is a famed gallery that is part of a wine-tasting room and cafe complex featuring local and regional artists. Don't miss the outdoor sculpture garden.

The **Schoolhouse Antique Mall** (☎ 503-864-2720, 748 3rd Ave, Lafayette) is a three-story school that has been turned into Oregon's largest antique market. Over 100 different dealers share the eight original classrooms, dividing it into wild collections of old furniture and whatnot.

Newberg & Around

Newberg (population 14,707) is at the edge of Portland suburbs and the beginnings of the wine country. Founded originally as a Quaker settlement, little of the town's original quiet ways remain – strip malls and shopping centers now lend the town its allure. Dundee, 2 miles west on Hwy 99W, is pretty much just an adjunct to Newberg's sprawl.

George Fox College, founded in 1885 as a Quaker institute of higher education, is a private college with an enrollment of 1200 students.

Things to See & Do The **Hoover-Minthorn House** (☎ 503-538-6629, 115 S River St; adult/senior & student/child $2/1.50/50¢; open 1pm-4pm Wed-Sun) is the boyhood home of Herbert Hoover, the 31st president of the USA. Built in 1881, the restored home is now a museum of period furnishings and early Oregon history. To the south, at the end of S Blane St, is **Chethalem Skate Park**, dubbed the nation's top skate park by *Thrasher* magazine – stop here to watch adolescent skaters sail over concrete bowls and half-pipes.

Get a bird's-eye view of the wine country from **Vista Balloon Adventures** (☎ *503-625-7385, 800-622-2309*, W *www.vistaballoon .com*), which offers hour-long hot-air balloon flights ($179 per person) with a champagne breakfast.

Places to Stay & Eat With choice B&Bs and restaurants in nearby hills, there's little reason to linger in Newberg itself. But in town, you can start the day with espresso and fresh pastries at the *Coffee Cottage* (☎ *503-538-5126, 808 E Hancock St)* or grab a sandwich there on your way out of town.

The wine country's closest camping is at Champoeg State Heritage Area (see that section, earlier), about 7 miles southeast of Newberg.

Newberg's nicest B&Bs are just north of town.

Partridge Farm B&B (☎ *503-538-2050, 4300 E Portland Rd)* Rooms $60-90. There are four guest rooms here in a Victorian farmhouse. Outside are landscaped gardens and pastures filled with llamas and game birds.

Springbrook Hazelnut Farm (☎ *503-538-4606, 800-793-8528*, W *www.nutfarm.com, 30295 N Hwy 99W)* Rooms $95-195. This 60-acre estate has rooms in either an old carriage house or in the guest wing of the large, historic farmhouse. Guests have access to the swimming pool and tennis court.

The best places to eat are in Dundee, 6 miles south of Newberg on Hwy 99W. The following offer vegetarian entrees and wine lists featuring local vintages:

Red Hills Provincial Dining (☎ *503-538-8224, 276 Hwy 99W)* Entrees $18-26. Unassuming Red Hills serves a changing menu with local products transformed into dishes such as pork tenderloin stuffed with prunes and fennel, or beef with wild mushrooms.

Tina's (☎ *503-538-8880, 760 Hwy 99W)* Entrees $18-28. Tina's considers itself a 'French country' restaurant, featuring local duck, lamb, rabbit, vegetables and seafood dishes.

Dundee Bistro (☎ *503-554-1650, 100-A SW 7th St)* Entrees $8-12. The wine country's only foodie lunch spot that's open on weekends is this bistro, in a characterless new development next to the Ponzi tasting room. Choice wines accompany gourmet salads, specialty pizzas, seafood and pastas.

McMinnville & Around

There's no denying that McMinnville (population 22,800) is the center of the local wine industry. Unlike Newberg, the gentrifying effects of the lucrative, upmarket wine trade have finally caught on here, and art galleries, boutiques and fine restaurants lure many sophisticated wine connoisseurs to McMinnville's quaint, red-brick downtown.

Spruce Goose A mile east of McMinnville, the **Evergreen Aviation Museum** (☎ *503-434-4180, 3850 SW Three Mile Lane*, W *www .sprucegoose.com; adult/senior/youth $9/7/5; open 9am-5pm)* showcases the *Hughes Flying Boat*, the world's largest wood-framed airplane. Given the misnomer the *Spruce Goose* (it was made of birch), the aircraft was built by Howard Hughes to carry cargo and troops over submarine-infested waters during WWII. Although the war was over by the time construction was finished in 1947, it was forever after heralded an engineering marvel in the wake of a single trial flight that lasted barely one minute.

Special Events Held at Linfield College in McMinnville the last weekend of July, the International Pinot Noir Celebration (☎ *503-472-8964, 800-775-4762*, W *www.ipnc.org)* is one of the Northwest's largest wine fairs and is an important testing ground for pinot noir wines from all over the world. The three-day festival of tastings and discussions is so popular that registration is awarded by a lottery held early in March – winners shell out $795 per person. Tickets to the public tasting ($125), only on the last Sunday, are distributed the same way.

Anyone can attend the McMinnville Wine & Food Classic (☎ 503-472-4033, W www.macwfc.com), a worthwhile (and affordable) tasting event popular with serious wine buyers. It's held at the aviation museum in mid-March.

Places to Stay Contact the chamber of commerce (see Information, earlier) to locate additional B&Bs in the countryside around McMinnville.

Paragon Motel (☎ 503-472-9493, 800-525-5469, 2065 Hwy 99W) Singles/doubles $45/48. This budget motor lodge has a pool.

Safari Motor Inn (☎ 503-472-5187, 800-321-5543, 345 N Hwy 99W) Singles/doubles $56/60. Rooms here are nicer, and there's a spa and exercise facility.

McMenamins Hotel Oregon (☎ 503-472-8427, 888-472-8427, W www.mcmenamins .com, 310 NE Evans St) Rooms with breakfast $65-115. Rooms at this recently renovated downtown hotel hark back to when it first opened in 1905 (most have shared bathrooms); and it's still just as popular – if not more – as it was then. History and artwork fill the walls, and on-site are three bars and a pub-style restaurant.

Steiger Haus B&B (☎ 503-472-0821, W www.steigerhaus.com, 360 Wilson St) Rooms $70-130. This modern home overlooks a park right in downtown McMinnville. There are five bedrooms with private bathrooms.

Mattey House (☎ 503-434-5058, W www .matteyhouse.com, 10221 NE Mattey Lane) Rooms $100-120. Four rooms are available at this 1869 farmhouse, which is nestled in a vineyard out in the country near Lafayette.

Youngberg Hill Vineyard & Inn (☎ 503-472-2727, 888-657-8668, W www.young berghill.com, 10660 Youngberg Hill Rd) Rooms $99-239. There's a spectacular view from this immense home, which sits atop a 700-foot hill on a working vineyard filled with sheep and deer.

Places to Eat The only question in McMinnville is where to eat lunch. Your best bet is to fix a picnic and head for the vineyards. Pick up salads and deli items from *Harvest Fresh Grocery* (☎ 503-472-5740, 251 E 3rd St). Get wired for a day out in the wine country at *Cornerstone Coffee* (☎ 503-472-6622, 216 E 3rd St). You'll find other cheap eateries downtown along 3rd St.

Wildwood Cafe (☎ 503-435-1454, 319 N Baker St) Breakfast & lunch $5.50-7. Hearty portions of homefries and grinning faces from 1950s American advertising memorabilia make this McMinnville's favorite breakfast joint, despite spotty service.

McMenamins Hotel Oregon (☎ 503-435-3154, 310 NE Evans St) Breakfast, lunch & dinner $4.50-9. Good, inexpensive pub food is served up in the dining room of this historic landmark hotel. Hole up with a drink in the womblike Cellar Bar.

Nick's Italian Cafe (☎ 503-434-4471, 521 E 3rd St) Fixed-price dinner $35. While this handsome oak-trimmed diner has not changed much in decor since the 1930s, the food is the thing – as well as the wine menu, which features over 100 local wines. There's a five-course set menu, or you can order á la carte. Call ahead for reservations or vegetarian meals.

Joel Palmer House (☎ 503-864-2995, 600 Ferry St, Dayton) Lunch/dinner $9/17-25. Wild-mushroom creations featuring regional ingredients are the hallmark of the antique-filled Joel Palmer House, a 1857 plantation-style home in nearby Dayton. Lauded as one of Oregon's best restaurants, dinners are available á la carte or fixed-price ($48) and are matched by a choice wine list. There's lunch on weekdays.

Getting There & Away

Two Greyhound (☎ 503-538-1225) buses from Portland stop in Newberg and McMinnville ($8 one way) en route to Lincoln City. However, in order to visit the wineries, you really need a car (or bike). The bus stops in McMinnville at the Baker Street Market, 523 S Baker St.

A favorite weekend cycling tour is to ride the back roads of the wine country. Neither Newberg nor McMinnville have rental bicycles, so bring one or rent one in Portland.

OREGON

SALEM

The Oregon state capital, Salem (population 131,385) is a sprawling and slightly soulless city filled with gray marble buildings and bureaucrats: It's the sort of place that residents brag about being a good place to raise a family.

For the traveler, there are relics – such as the oldest university west of the Rocky Mountains, and the boxlike state capitol. A couple of mammoth private estates from the 1880s are preserved as public parks and museums. Downtown is pleasant enough, but its unquestioned earnestness makes the city center seem like a museum of the 1950s.

Established in 1840, Salem was the second mission founded by Methodist missionary Jason Lee in the middle Willamette Valley. In 1851, the legislature voted to move the capital from Oregon City to Salem. When disgruntled members of the legislature convened in Salem in 1853, they found only half a dozen families living there, with very little in the way of accommodations or facilities. They voted to move the capital to Corvallis, which they did in 1855. Even less charmed with Corvallis than with Salem, they moved the capital moved back and remained in Salem thereafter.

Orientation & Information

Salem is 47 miles south of Portland and 64 miles north of Eugene on I-5; exits 256 and 253 access the city center.

Salem is a very confusing place to drive in, with Hwys 22, 213, 219, 99E bisecting the city at many angles. Most of the city lies on the east side of the Willamette River. State St divides the city into north and south. The Marion St Bridge spans the river to link west Salem with downtown.

Salem Convention & Visitors Association (☎ 503-581-4325, 800-874-7012, Ⓦ www.scva .org) is at 1313 Mill St SE.

The main post office is at 1050 25th St SE, though the Pringle Park office, 410 Mill St SE, is more convenient to downtown.

Jackson's Books (☎ 503-399-8694) is at 320 Liberty St SE. The Salem *Statesman Journal* is the city's daily paper. Oregon Public Radio can be heard at 91.5 FM.

The State Street Laundromat (☎ 503-371-6130), 2515 State St, offers drop-off service as well as dry cleaning.

Oregon State Capitol

The state's first capitol building was burned down by incendiaries in 1856, and a domed neo-Greek edifice was built to replace it. Then, that building burned down in 1935, and the current capitol (☎ 503-986-1388, *Court & Capitol Sts; admission free; open 7:30am-5:30pm Mon-Fri, 9am-4pm Sat, noon-4pm Sun)*, designed by Francis Keally, was completed in 1939. Bauhaus and art deco influences are apparent, especially in the strident bas-relief in the front statuary and the hatboxlike cupola. The building is faced with gray Vermont marble, and the interior is lined with brown travertine from Montana. The legislative chambers are paneled with Oregon oak and walnut.

The most notable features of the capitol are four Works Progress Administration (WPA)–era **murals** lining the interior of the rotunda, each depicting a turning point in Oregon history. Surmounting the dome is the gleaming *Oregon Pioneer*, a 23-foot-high gilded statue depicting a stylized, early male settler. The grounds are landscaped with native plants.

Free tours are offered daily mid-June to Labor Day and run hourly (except at noon). Tours of the tower – for an up-close look at the gilded pioneer – are offered from mid-March to mid-September and run every half-hour (except at noon). Call ahead to check schedules.

Willamette University

Just south of the capitol, Willamette University (☎ 503-370-6300, 900 State St) is the oldest collegiate institution in North America west of the Missouri. The oldest remaining building on the campus is **Waller Hall**, built between 1864 and 1867. Willamette University, which currently has 2500 students, is well respected for its liberal-arts undergraduate program and its law school. The **Hallie Ford Museum of Art** (☎ 503-370-6855, 700 State St; adult/senior & youth $3/2; open 10am-5pm Tues-Sat), in a bunkerlike

OREGON

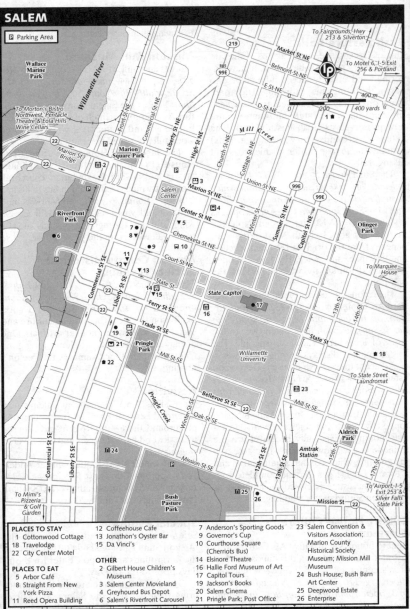

SALEM

⊞ Parking Area

Wallace Marine Park

To Morton's Bistro Northwest, Pentacle Theatre & Eola Hills Wine Cellars

Willamette River

Marion St Bridge

Marion Square Park

Salem Center

Riverfront Park

Front St NE
Commercial St NE
Liberty St NE
High St NE
Church St NE
Cottage St NE

Market St NE
To Fairgrounds, Hwy 213 & Silverton

Belmont St NE

E St NE

D St NE

Mill Creek

To Motel 6, I-5 Exit 256 & Portland

200   400 m
0   200   400 yards

Union St NE

Marion St NE

Center St NE

Chemeketa St NE

Court St NE

State St

Ferry St SE

Trade St SE

Winter St NE
Summer St NE
Capitol St NE

Olinger Park

State Capitol

To Marquee House

Pringle Park

Mill St SE

Willamette University

Pringle Creek

Bellevue St SE

Winter St SE
Oak St SE

Commercial St SE
Liberty St SE

To Mimi's Pizzeria & Golf Garden

Mission St SE

Bush Pasture Park

State St

To State Street Laundromat

Aldrich Park

Amtrak Station

12th St SE
13th St SE
14th St SE
15th St
17th St

Mill St SE

Mission St

To Airport, I-5 Exit 253 & Silver Falls State Park

PLACES TO STAY			
1 Cottonwood Cottage	12 Coffeehouse Cafe	7 Anderson's Sporting Goods	23 Salem Convention &
18 Travelodge	13 Jonathon's Oyster Bar	9 Governor's Cup	Visitors Association;
22 City Center Motel	15 Da Vinci's	10 Courthouse Square	Marion County
		(Cherriots Bus)	Historical Society
PLACES TO EAT	**OTHER**	14 Elsinore Theatre	Museum; Mission Mill
5 Arbor Café	2 Gilbert House Children's	16 Hallie Ford Museum of Art	Museum
8 Straight From New	Museum	17 Capitol Tours	24 Bush House; Bush Barn
York Pizza	3 Salem Center Movieland	19 Jackson's Books	Art Center
11 Reed Opera Building	4 Greyhound Bus Depot	20 Salem Cinema	25 Deepwood Estate
	6 Salem's Riverfront Carousel	21 Pringle Park; Post Office	26 Enterprise

concrete building, houses the work of many famous Northwest artists.

Bush Pasture Park

One of Oregon's leading citizens of the late 19th century was Asahel Bush, a newspaperman and a highly successful banker who began building his rambling Italianate mansion in 1877. Designed to be a self-sufficient farm, the estate and mansion are now preserved as Bush Pasture Park. The extensive grounds (now public gardens) include a large rose garden, picnic areas and hiking trails.

The **Bush House** (☎ 503-363-4714, w www .salemart.org, 600 Mission St SE; adult/senior & student/child $4/3/2; open noon-5pm Tues-Sun May-Sept, 2pm-5pm Oct-Apr) is open as a showplace of Victorian design. Note the marble fireplaces, 10 in all. Most of the wallpaper is from the original 1887 construction and was made in France. The house is open for guided tours only, which leave on the half-hour.

The reconstructed livery stable is the **Bush Barn Art Center** (☎ 503-581-2228; free admission; open 10am-5pm Mon-Fri, noon-5pm Sat & Sun), its main floor given over to the work of local artists and craftspeople. The upstairs gallery displays touring art shows.

Adjacent to the Bush House is **Deepwood Estate** (☎ 503-363-1825, 1116 Mission St SE; adult/senior & student/child $4/3/2; open for tours noon-5pm Sun-Fri May-Sept, Wed-Thur & Sat Oct-Apr), a 1894 Queen Anne mansion topped by turrets and bejeweled with decorative moldings. Especially beautiful are the stained-glass windows. There's free access to the grounds, which contain a nature trail and a formal English tea garden, complete with gazebo. The estate is closed on holidays, as well as on Saturdays for weddings.

Gilbert House Children's Museum

Built to honor Salem native AC Gilbert, who invented the Erector Set, this hands-on children's center (☎ 503-371-3631, w www.ac gilbert.org, 116 Marion St NE; adult/senior $4/3; open 10am-5pm Mon-Sat, noon-5pm Sun) is half technology-and-science museum,

half playroom. There's a wide selection of things to do here – from giant bubble–making to staging alien puppet shows.

Mission Mill Museum

More than a mill, this 5-acre complex (☎ 503-585-7012, w www.missionmill.org, 1313 Mill St SE; adult/senior/youth $6/5/4; open 10am-5pm) houses the Salem Convention & Visitors Association; a clutch of restored pioneer buildings; and a massive, water-powered wool mill preserved as a museum.

The **Jason Lee House**, the **John Boon House** (1847), the **Methodist Parsonage** (1841) and an **old Presbyterian church** all look pretty much as they did in the 1840s and '50s. The **Thomas Kay Woolen Mill** was built in 1889 and was powered by Mill Creek, which still runs through the grounds and still turns waterwheels in the powerhouse.

Marion County Historical Society Museum

This museum (☎ 503-364-2128, 260 12th St SE; adult/senior & child $3/1; open noon-4pm Wed-Fri, 10am-4pm Sat) has a good exhibit on the local Calapooian culture and society, as well as on pioneer artifacts. One display tells the story of Salem's long-gone Chinatown; another examines the region's hop industry.

Activities

Stroll along the Willamette at Salem's new **Riverfront Park**, off Front St. In addition to a playground, there's the Riverfront Carousel, with 41 wood-carved horses and two covered wagons.

Rent winter sports equipment at **Anderson's Sporting Goods** (☎ 503-364-4400, 241 Liberty St NE) before heading off to Santiam Pass, 85 miles east on US 20.

Special Events

Salem's biggest party of the year is the Oregon State Fair (☎ 503-947-3247), held at the fairgrounds and Expo Center for the 12 days prior to Labor Day.

Over 200 artists from around the country bring their work to the Salem Art Fair & Festival (☎ 503-581-2228), the state's largest juried art show, held the third weekend of July at Bush Pasture Park.

Places to Stay

See Around Salem, later in this section, for more camping at Silver Falls State Park.

Salem Campground & RV (☎ 503-581-6736, 800-825-9605, 3700 Hagers Grove Rd SE) Tents/hookups $15/21. Salem's closest campground features 202 campsites with showers, a market and a separate tent area.

The following B&Bs are convenient to the capitol.

Cottonwood Cottage (☎ 503-362-3979, 800 349-3979, W www.cottonwoodcottage.com, 960 E St NE) Rooms $65-71. This English-style country home features two rooms in a quiet neighborhood.

Marquee House (☎ 503-391-0837, 800-949-0837, W www.marqueehouse.com, 333 Wyatt Court NE) Rooms $71-98. Film classics are the theme of the five guest rooms here.

Chain motels are clustered near both freeway exits. You'll pay more to stay close to the capitol.

Motel 6 (☎ 503-371-8024, 1401 Hawthorne Ave NE) Singles/doubles $42/49. This tidy motel at I-5 exit 256 (Market St) is Salem's best budget choice.

City Center Motel (☎ 503-364-0121, 800-289-0121, 510 Liberty St SE) Singles/doubles $44/50. To stay closer to the capitol, try this older motel.

Travelodge (☎ 503-581-2466, 800-578-7878, 1555 State St) Singles/doubles $60/65. Closest to the capitol is this well-maintained motor lodge, with pleasant rooms and an outdoor pool.

Best Western Mill Creek Inn (☎ 503-585-3332, 800-346-9659, 3125 Ryan Dr SE) Singles/doubles with breakfast $71/75. Business travelers will feel right at home at this hotel and conference center near the airport at I-5 exit 253, with breakfast at Denny's.

Places to Eat

Cafes at the intersection of Court and Liberty Sts offer good variety for those on a budget. *Straight from New York Pizza* serves pizza slices from a hole in the wall at 233 Liberty St NE. The *Reed Opera building*, at 189 Liberty

St SE, houses a bento joint and an organic cafe. There's more atmosphere (of the dirty-couch variety) at the street-level *Coffeehouse Cafe*, an all-day organic hangout.

Arbor Café (☎ 503-588-1330, 380 High St NE) Lunch/dinner $5/13. This matronly bakery-cafe is Salem's best lunch spot. Stop by in the morning for pastries and fresh bread.

Jonathon's Oyster Bar (☎ 503-362-7219, 445 State St) Entrees $10-17. Fill up on jambalaya or local oysters ($1.50 each), followed by a bottle from the good selection of wines.

Da Vinci's (☎ 503-399-1413, 180 High St SE) Entrees $14-25. Casual Da Vinci's is popular for Italian food.

Morton's Bistro Northwest (☎ 503-585-1113, 1128 Edgewater St NW) Entrees $14.50-19. On the west side of the river, Morton's offers Northwest fare and intimate dining in a quiet, courtyard setting.

Eola Hills Wine Cellars (☎ 503-623-2405, 800-291-6730, 501 S Pacific Hwy, Rickreall) Brunch $20. On Sundays, this nearby winery's all-you-can-eat wine-and-champagne brunch is an amazing feast. Reservations are required (see the Willamette Valley map for location).

Entertainment

Governor's Cup (☎ 503-581-9675, 471 Court St NE) You'll find live music here three nights a week and a slightly more hushed coffee-house scene at other times.

Mimi's Pizzeria & Golf Garden (☎ 503-365-7225, 1145 Commercial St SE) No ordinary miniature golf, the course at Mimi's features waterfalls and native plants, giving it the air of a pleasant patio garden. Adults will find local microbrews on tap, and kids can get a bottomless supply of crayons.

Salem Cinema (☎ 503-378-7676, 445 High St SE) This is as close to an arts cinema as Salem gets, with foreign and offbeat films.

Salem Center Movieland (☎ 503-588-3456, Marion & High Sts) Head here for first-run films downtown.

Elsinore Theatre (☎ 503-581-8810, 503-485-3048, 170 High St, W www.elsinore theatre.com) Once a silent-movie theater, this dazzling oriental-style landmark is now a

OREGON

venue for big name performers and local talent. Silent movies are shown monthly from October to May, with live accompaniment on a 1644-pipe Wurlitzer organ.

Pentacle Theatre (☎ 503-364-7200, 324 52nd Ave NW) This is Salem's semiprofessional theater company.

LB Day Amphitheater (☎ 503-378-3247, near Lana Ave and Silverton Rd) Salem's local concert venue for touring music groups is at the state fairgrounds, about a mile north of downtown.

Getting There & Away

Horizon Airlines (☎ 800-547-9308) flies between Portland and the Salem Airport, just west of I-5 exit 253 on Hwy 22. Bus No 21 links the airport to downtown.

The Hut Airport Shuttle (☎ 503-363-8059) provides frequent service between Salem and Portland International Airport.

Buses depart the Greyhound depot (☎ 503-362-2407), at 450 Church St NE, seven times daily to Portland ($8 one-way) and eight times to Eugene ($9.50). There's one bus to Bend ($22) every day except Sunday.

Two trains, Amtrak's *Coast Starlight* (Seattle to Los Angeles) and *Cascades* (Eugene to Vancouver, BC) serve the Salem Railway Station (☎ 503-588-1551), 500 13th St SE. Amtrak Thruway buses provide additional service to Portland for connections with other trains.

For car rental, contact Budget (☎ 503-362-0041), 2290 25th St SE, or Enterprise (☎ 503-364-1991), 808 12th St SE.

Getting Around

Cherriots (☎ 503-588-2877, W www.cherriots.org) buses (75¢) serve the city and are free downtown; there's no Sunday service. Get schedules and maps from the main Courthouse Square transit station, at High and Court Sts.

Call Salem-Keizer Yellow Cab Co (☎ 503-362-2411) for a lift.

AROUND SALEM
Iris Gardens

Willamette Valley's most beautiful crops are undoubtedly grown by the many flower and bulb nurseries in the area. Two iris farms near Salem are among the largest in the world and open seasonally to visitors from mid-May to early-June free of charge.

Iris blossoms cover a 250-acre farm at **Cooley's Gardens** *(☎ 503-873-5463, 11553 Silverton Rd NE; open 8am-7pm)*, 11 miles east of Salem on Hwy 213, near Silverton. **Schreiner's Iris Gardens** *(☎ 503-393-3232, 3625 Quinaby Rd; open dawn-dusk)*, about 2 miles north of Salem, opens 10 acres of its grounds for iris-viewing.

Wineries

Oregon's second-largest and only publicly traded winery is **Willamette Valley Vineyards** *(☎ 503-588-9463, 8800 Enchanted Way, Turner; open 11am-6pm)*, on an imposing hilltop south of town. Scenic **Strangeland Vineyards & Winery** *(☎ 503-581-0355, 8500 Hopewell Rd NW; open noon-5pm Sat & Sun May-Dec)*, north of Salem in the Eola Hills, is a smaller winery with good pinot noir.

The Oregon Garden

Come here and you'd better bring your imagination, because it's going to be several years before the 240-acre Oregon Garden *(☎ 503-874-8100, 877-647-2733, W www.oregongarden.org, 15 miles east of Salem off Hwy 213; adults/seniors & youth/children $6/5/3; open 9am-6pm in summer, call for other hours)* grows up to be the botanic showcase it's destined to be. Phase 1 opened in 2001, with much of the 60-acre site covered with fresh bulldozer tracks and bark-o-mulch. However, many world-class plant collections, especially conifers and Northwest perennials, are already well under way.

Mount Angel

The little town of Mount Angel (population 3030), with its Bavarian-style storefronts and lovely Benedictine abbey, is like an Old World holdover in the Oregon countryside. Visit the third weekend of September, during Oktoberfest (☎ 503-845-9440, W www.oktoberfest.org), for maximum effect. It is one of the state's largest harvest festivals, and thousands show up for brass bands, beer and dancers.

Stop by at other times for a stroll at lovely **Mount Angel Abbey** *(☎ 503-845-3030, off College St)*, a Benedictine monastery with quirky museums and ancient manuscripts in the library's rare-book room. Pick up a tour map at the gift shop. Lodging is available to those seeking a spiritual retreat.

Another interesting sideline, the town's old 1910 Catholic church, with mural-covered walls, was badly damaged in an earthquake that was centered near here in 1993.

The town is 18 miles northeast of Salem on Hwy 214.

Silver Falls State Park

Oregon's largest state park, 8700-acre Silver Falls *(☎ 503-873-8681; day-use fee $3)*, 26 miles east of Salem on Hwy 214, is an easy day trip from Portland, Salem and Eugene. What makes these waterfalls so magical is the fact that you can walk behind several of them. North Falls plunges 136 feet over a lava flow, and South Falls drops 177 feet.

The park and the conference center are busy year round. The vast day-use area near **South Falls** is especially popular – almost too much so on summer weekends. Silver Creek is impounded here to form a small lake (a favorite with young waders), and picnic tables are scattered throughout the forest. The WPA built a number of stone shelters and the **South Falls Nature Lodge** during the Depression; they are now on the National Register of Historic Places.

The most famous hike in the park is the **Trail of Ten Falls Loop**, a 7-mile, roundtrip loop that winds up a basalt canyon through thick forests filled with ferns, moss and wildflowers, joining all the major falls in the park. The trail isn't particularly difficult, though the spray from the waterfalls can make it slippery and muddy. Watch for beaver and mule deer, and for displays of colorful butterflies.

The principal point of access is the park's main entrance, at the South Falls day-use area, or at North Falls, near the park's northern boundary on N Fork Silver Creek. Cyclists have their own 4-mile paved trail, which also begins from South Falls.

Avoid camping in the summer unless you don't mind the crowds.

Silver Falls State Park Campground *(☎ 503-873-8681, on Hwy 213)* Tents/hookups/cabins $16/20/35. This popular main campground just opposite the South Falls day-use area has over 100 campsites, half of which are reserved for tent campers. Also on site are cabins, equestrian facilities, a conference center, showers and a playground.

CORVALLIS

Home to Oregon State University (OSU), Corvallis (population 52,215) is a pleasant town at the base of the Coast Range, coursed by the Willamette River and surrounded by miles of farms, orchards and vineyards. The shops and vintage storefronts in the old, tree-lined downtown are busy, filled with bakeries, bookstores and cafes. If this sounds kind of idyllic, well, it *is* kind of idyllic in Corvallis – publications have rated the small city as one of the most livable 'micropolitan' cities, based on safety, environment, housing and education. Over half of the city's population studies or works at the university, and another substantial percentage works at the Hewlett-Packard plant north of town. What's left of the citizenry is seemingly busy making espressos, selling bikes and tending to all the lawns and trees.

Corvallis is an easy place to spend a day drinking coffee, browsing in bookstores, watching students and waiting for dinner at a good restaurant. It's also a good base from which to explore this part of Oregon. As implied in its name, Corvallis is at the 'heart (core) of the valley.'

Orientation

Corvallis is at the junction of US 20 and Hwys 34 and 99W, along the west bank of the Willamette River, 43 miles north of Eugene. It's 13 miles from Corvallis to Albany on US 20.

From the east, Hwy 34 feeds straight into Harrison Blvd and leads to OSU, on the west side of town. The campus, which conforms to a vague quad-and-courtyard design, is bounded on the north by Monroe Ave, which is home to a number of student-oriented businesses.

Western Blvd flanks the campus on the south; the university merges with downtown around 11th St.

Corvallis' downtown district sits near the west bank of the Willamette along 3rd and 4th Sts (Hwy 99W). North Corvallis sprawls with new development along 9th St and Kings Blvd.

Information

The Corvallis Convention & Visitors Bureau (☎ 541-757-1544, 800-334-8118, W www.visit corvallis.com), at 420 NW 2nd St, has the details on the city and the annual festivities. The post office is at 311 SW 2nd St.

The Oregon State University Bookstore (☎ 541-737-4323), at 2301 SW Jefferson Way, in the Memorial Union, has the largest selection of books. For alternative books, magazines and music, go to Grass Roots Bookstore (☎ 541-754-7668), 227 SW 2nd St. The Book Bin (☎ 541-752-0040), 228 SW 3rd St, is the town's best used-book store.

Tune in to Oregon Public Broadcasting at 103.1 FM or 550 AM. The OSU student newspaper, the *Barometer,* is published every weekday during the university term and weekly during summer session.

An espresso bar makes Campbell's Cleaners (☎ 541-752-3794), 1120 NW 9th St, popular for laundry.

Oregon State University

Just west of downtown, this green and leafy campus filled with red-brick buildings was founded in 1852 as Corvallis College, but it didn't take off until 1868, when the college received the federal government's land grant to establish an agricultural college. Today, OSU (☎ 503-737-1000, W *www.osu.orst.edu)* offers a broad range of degrees in the arts and sciences, specializing in computer and technical fields, engineering and pharmacy, as well as in agricultural sciences and veterinarian medicine.

The most notable building on campus is the **Memorial Union**, with its flag-draped vestibule and flights of marble stairs. There's visitor parking at the main campus entrance, at 15th St and Jefferson Way.

There's an information kiosk near the main campus entrance.

Activities

Rent winter sports equipment from **Peak Sports** (☎ *541-754-6444, 129 NW 2nd St; gear $8-25).* They also sell tickets for a Saturday ski bus ($32) to Hoodoo Ski Area (☎ 541-822-3337), 81 miles east at Santiam Pass.

University-owned **Trysting Tree Golf Club** (☎ *541-752-3332, 34028 Electric Rd; green fees $30),* east on Hwy 34, is one of the state's toughest courses. It features 25 sand traps and a number of physics-defying greens and is purposely free of large trees in order to let the capricious weather have its way with your ball.

Special Events

Kinetic sculpture and home-built electric-car races are highlights of da Vinci Days (☎ 800-334-8118, W www.davinci-days.org), a celebration seeking to bridge the gap between high art and big science. It's held the third weekend of July in Central Park.

Costumed players roam an Elizabethan marketplace, engaging visitors in late-16th-century small talk at the Shrewsbury Renaissance Faire (☎ 541-929-4897, W www.shrew faire.com), held the first weekend after Labor Day in nearby Philomath, west of town. With wandering minstrels, bards and jousting knights, this is one of Oregon's top cultural events.

The area's largest event, the Fall Festival, is held mid-September in Central Park with a juried art show featuring the work of nearly 150 artists. Live music fills the streets, and there's a street dance on Saturday night.

Places to Stay

There are two campgrounds nearby.

Willamette Park (☎ *541-757-6918, 541-753-3119, on Goodnight Rd)* Sites $9. Camping feels very transient in the grassy field at this riverside park, a mile south of downtown.

Corvallis/Albany KOA (☎ *541-967-8521, 800-562-8526, 33775 Oakville Rd)* Tent/RV sites $18/23. This RV-oriented

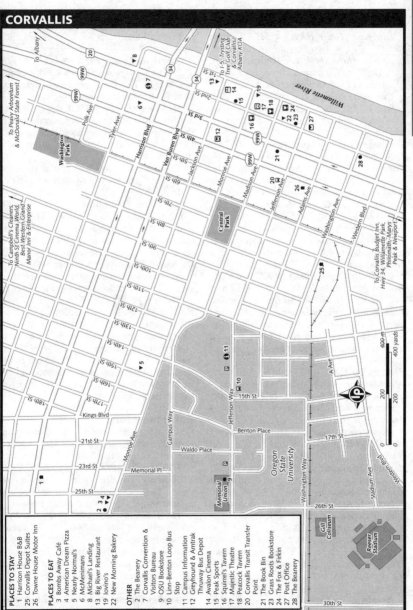

CORVALLIS

To Albany
20
To Albany
99W
99W
34
34
1st St
2nd St
3rd St
Polk Ave
Tyler Ave
Harrison Blvd
Van Buren Blvd
4th St
5th St
Jackson Ave
Monroe Ave
Madison Ave
6th St
7th St
8th St
9th St
10th St
11th St
12th St
13th St
14th St
15th St
16th St
17th St
18th St
Kings Blvd
21st St
23rd St
25th St
Memorial Pl
Monroe Ave
Campus Way
Jefferson Way
Benton Place
Waldo Place
15th St
26th St
30th St
17th St
A Ave
Washington Way
Stadium Ave
Western Blvd
Willamette River
Washington Park
Central Park
Memorial Union
Oregon State University
Gill Coliseum
Reeser Stadium

To Peavy Arboretum & McDonald State Forest
To I-5; Trysting Tree Golf Club & Corvallis/Albany KOA
To Campbell's Cleaners, Ninth St Cinema World, Best Western Grand Manor Inn & Enterprise
To Corvallis Budget Inn, Hwy 34, Willamette Park; Philomath; Marys Peak & Newport

400 m
200
0
400 yards
200
0

PLACES TO STAY
1   Harrison House B&B
25 Corvallis Depot Suites
26 Towne House Motor Inn

PLACES TO EAT
3   Bombs Away Café
4   American Dream Pizza
5   Nearly Normal's
6   McMenimans
8   Michael's Landing
13 Big River Restaurant
19 Iovino's
22 New Morning Bakery

OTHER
2   The Beanery
7   Corvallis Convention &
    Visitors Bureau
9   OSU Bookstore
10 Linn-Benton Loop Bus
    Stop
11 Campus Information
12 Greyhound & Amtrak
    Thruway Bus Depot
14 Avalon Cinema
15 Peak Sports
16 Squirrel's Tavern
17 Majestic Theatre
18 Peacock Tavern
20 Corvallis Transit Transfer
    Point
21 The Book Bin
23 Grass Roots Bookstore
24 The Fox & Firkin
27 Post Office
28 The Beanery

campground is 4½ miles east of Corvallis on Hwy 34.

Harrison House B&B (☎ 541-752-6248, 800-233-6248, W www.corvallis-lodging.com, 2310 NW Harrison Blvd) Rooms $50-80. This B&B near campus offers four guest rooms in a Dutch Colonial residence.

Corvallis Budget Inn (☎ 541-752-8756, 1480 SW 3rd St) Singles/doubles $35/39. This older motel is about the cheapest place around.

Towne House Motor Inn (☎ 541-753-4496, 350 SW 4th St) Singles/doubles $41/48. Corvallis' best budget choice is between the university and downtown. Rooms are a good value, and some have kitchenettes.

Best Western Grand Manor Inn (☎ 541-758-8571, 925 NW Garfield Ave) Singles/doubles $86/93. This is typical of the many new business-class and suite-style hotels cropping up north of downtown. It has a pool and a spa.

Corvallis Depot Suites (☎ 877-754-6506, W www.endex.com/depot, 700 SW Washington Ave) Suites $104, 3-night minimum. Tech-industry execs like the lavish apartments in this converted railway depot. The five-room suites designed for extended stays have kitchens and are fully furnished.

Places to Eat

Warehouses reborn as stylish bars and restaurants are part of Corvallis' blueprint for a vibrant new waterfront district. Head here to discover the city's newest eateries.

Downtown, the **New Morning Bakery** (☎ 541-754-0181, 219 SW 2nd St) is a good place for coffee and freshly baked rolls and muffins. Deli lunch and dinner items ($4.50) are served as well, and there's live music on Friday and Saturday.

Near the university on Monroe Ave are many inexpensive student-oriented restaurants with really good food.

Nearly Normal's (☎ 541-753-0791, 109 NW 15th St) Entrees $6. This is a vegetarian cafe with organic falafel sandwiches, burritos, juice drinks and an exceedingly casual wait staff.

Bombs Away Café (☎ 541-757-7221, 2527 NW Monroe Ave) Lunch & dinner $6.

Mexican dinners at this whimsical cafe are innovative and tasty, and there's a good selection of local beers in the pleasant back room bar.

American Dream Pizza (☎ 541-757-1713, 2525 NW Monroe Ave) Slices $2.50, medium pies $15-16. This funky pizzeria is right next door to the Bombs Away.

McMenamins (☎ 541-758-6044, 420 NW 3rd St) Portland-based McMenamins pours their own excellent brews and a large selection of ales and stouts from other local brewers.

The fanciest restaurants are near the river, though in Corvallis you won't need a suit or tie to get in.

Big River Restaurant (☎ 541-757-0694, 101 NW Jackson Ave) Entrees $17. Local seafood and organic produce are behind the eclectic fare at this lively bistro, which is chock full of young engineers every night of the week. Those with slimmer wallets can make a meal of the designer pizzas or dinner salads. There's patio seating in the summer.

Iovino's (☎ 541-738-9015, 126 SW 1st St) Entrees $10-19. This spartan, upscale Italian restaurant resembles a theater stage – diners share the spotlight with fine wine.

Michael's Landing (☎ 541-754-6141, 603 NW 2nd St) Entrees $15. Prime rib is the specialty of this steak house, housed in Corvallis' old train depot. It's right on the river, with drinks on the patio.

Entertainment

OSU offers a broad spectrum of entertainment, lectures, readings, films and theater – pick up a copy of the *Barometer* for listings.

Majestic Theatre (☎ 541-757-6977, 115 SW 2nd St) Corvallis' main performing-arts venue hosts everything from community theater to the region's top dance troupes.

The Beanery (☎ 541-757-0858, 2541 NW Monroe Ave; ☎ 541-735-7442, 500 SW 2nd St) There's no escaping this Corvallis-based coffeehouse chain. The campus Beanery, on Monroe Ave, is a favorite student hangout; the downtown Beanery is a quieter place for a cup of coffee.

Avalon Cinema (☎ 541-752-4161, W www.avaloncinema.com, 160 NW Jackson Ave)

Follow a nice dinner with an art film at this independently run cinema in the riverfront district.

Ninth St Cinema World (☎ 541-758-7469, 1750 NW 9th) Head to this cinema for first-run releases.

The Fox & Firkin (☎ 541-753-8533, 202 SW 1st St) Nightly live music and outdoor seating are the draws of this nonsmoking, English-style pub.

Peacock Tavern (☎ 541-754-8522, 125 SW 2nd St) This is Corvallis' main venue for live music, with local blues and rock.

Squirrel's Tavern (☎ 541-753-8057, 100 SW 2nd St) Across from the Peacock, an older crowd gathers here for jazz and acoustic music on weekends.

Spectator Sports
OSU's **Beavers** (☎ 800-462-3287, W www.osu beavers.com) are frequent contenders in both college football at **Reeser Stadium** and in basketball at **Gill Coliseum**. Both places are on 26th St off Western Blvd.

Getting There & Away
Greyhound (☎ 541-757-1797) buses link Corvallis with Portland ($13 one way) and Eugene ($7). The Amtrak Thruway bus to Newport ($12) stops here two to four times a day. There's also a bus to Bend ($27) daily except Sunday. Buses depart from the depot, at 153 NW 4th St.

Anthony's Airporter (☎ 541-753-7831, 800-546-6158, W www.portlandairportshuttle .com) connects air travelers with Portland International Airport ($40 one way); there's a stop right on the university campus – call for more information.

Enterprise Rent-A-Car (☎ 541-758-0000) is on the western outskirts of town at 400 NW Walnut Blvd.

Getting Around
Corvallis Transit (☎ 541-766-6998, W www.ci .corvallis.or.us/pw/transport/transit) buses serve the city Monday to Saturday (50¢). Buses rendezvous downtown at 5th St and Jefferson Ave. Linn-Benton Loop buses, which run between Corvallis and Albany, stop at the corner of 15th St and Jefferson Ave.

Call Action Taxi (☎ 541-754-1111) for a cab.

AROUND CORVALLIS
Peavy Arboretum & McDonald State Forest
Both these areas are administered by OSU. At the Peavy Arboretum, two interpretive walks wind through 40 acres of forest. From the arboretum, trails continue into McDonald State Forest, a research forest with 8 miles of hiking and mountain-bike trails. Take Hwy 99W north for 8 miles, then turn west at the signs to get to the forests.

Marys Peak
At 4097 feet, Marys Peak, in the Siuslaw National Forest, is the highest peak in the Coast Range. A favorite with student hikers, the 4.2-mile hike to the top climbs quickly through dense hemlock before finally breaking out into a wildflower meadow. On a clear day, there are views across the valley to the glaciered Central Oregon Cascades.

To reach the trailhead, which is 16 miles from Corvallis, continue on Hwy 20 for 1½ miles past the Hwy 34 junction at Philomath and turn onto graveled USFS Rd 2005 (called Woods Creek Rd). There's alternate access via Hwy 34 on winding USFS Rd 3010 (or Marys Peak Rd), which arrives at a primitive **campground** less than a mile from the top. A Northwest Forest Pass ($5) is required at either trailhead.

Albany
No town in Oregon presents such an ugly face to passing motorists as Albany (population 41,000), 11 miles east of Corvallis. On I-5, an enormous pulp mill surrounded by mountains of wood chips belches out clouds of foul, sulfurous-smelling air. No surprise here that the biggest fete is the **Albany World Timber Carnival** (☎ 541-928-2391), held on Fourth of July weekend at Timber-Linn Memorial Park. Billed as the world's largest logging event, contests include log-rolling, speed-cutting and tree-scaling.

About 350 homes and buildings are registered as National Historic Sites in Albany's city center. Locals come here to shop for antiques. The **Monteith House** (☎ 541-967-8699, 518 2nd Ave SW; admission free; open noon-4pm Wed-Sun Memorial Day-Labor Day; other times by appointment), built in Federal style, is one of Oregon's oldest structures (1849) and is now a museum.

Ask at the Albany Visitors Association (☎ 541-928-0911, 800-526-2256), in the Two Rivers Market, at 300 2nd Ave SW, for maps of the historic districts or of the area's 10 nearby **covered bridges** – a suggested 2½-hour driving tour leads to five.

For rail travelers, Albany is the transfer point for the Amtrak Thruway bus to Newport, on the coast; the station (☎ 541-928-0885) is at 110 10th Ave SW.

EUGENE

In many ways, Eugene (population 136,490) is the prototypic Oregon town, drawing its energy from equal measures of pragmatism and idealism. At the southern end of the wide Willamette Valley, the city maintains its working-class base in timber and manufacturing. Yet the state's largest college campus and some of the state's most unconventional citizens also call Eugene home. During the 1960s, Eugene was rightly famous for its alternative communes, leftist politics and drug culture – in short, its 'hippie lifestyle.' During the Vietnam War, the university became a hotbed of civil disobedience and counterculture.

Eugene's denial that the '60s have passed is gradually fading. Many of the city's successful businesses are owned by former 'radicals' who have found favor in upscale developments around town. Although more prosaic than during the heyday, activism is still de rigueur. Environmental issues especially motivate students, placing them again at odds with the community, whose longtime economic base was in the forest-products industry. As the timber industry gives over to high tech, many of Eugene's radicals are finding new careers as World Trade Organization protesters.

Travelers will find sophisticated yet inexpensive dining; lively shopping districts; and a youthful, relaxing and fun-seeking atmos-phere that almost succeeds in making Eugene seem good for you. Parks flank the Willamette River along much of the length of Eugene, and beautiful public gardens grace the hillsides. Nicknamed 'Tracktown,' Eugene is famous for its track-and-field champions and is also the birthplace of Nike.

Orientation

Eugene is 110 miles south of Portland, at the southern end of the Willamette Valley. Directly east of Eugene is the city's blue-collar suburb of Springfield (population 52,945).

I-5 runs north-south through Eugene, and I-105/Hwy 126 cuts through east-west, depositing motorists on 6th Ave. Willamette St divides Eugene's numbered avenues into east and west.

The University of Oregon has extensive wooded grounds and is roughly girded by Franklin Blvd and E 18th Ave on the north and south, and Alder and Agate Sts on the west and east; the I-5 University exit (192) feeds into Franklin Blvd – which becomes Broadway through downtown – and Hwys 99 and 126 to the east.

Although not large, downtown Eugene can be an infuriating place to drive around. An extensive one-way grid and 12-block pedestrian mall was imposed during the city's urban-renewal heyday; little subsequent growth has justified the tangled mess that it created. The city finally opened those streets back up to cars, leaving the closed stretch of Broadway between Oak and Charnelton Sts as the last holdout of the Eugene Mall. The mall is still not flourishing, but it does contain a number of good restaurants and nightspots.

Information

The Convention & Visitors Association of Lane County (☎ 541-484-5307, 800-547-5445 W www.cvalco.org) is at 115 W 8th Ave, Suite 190. The main post office is at 520 Willamette St.

The U of O Bookstore (☎ 541-346-4331), 895 E 13th Ave, is at the corner of E 13th Ave and Kincaid St. Eugene's premier used-book store is the Smith Family Bookstore, with two locations: near the university

(☎ 541-345-1651), at 768 E 13th Ave, and downtown (☎ 541-343-4717), at 525 Willamette St. The Book Mark (☎ 541-484-0512), 856 Olive St, has Eugene's best selection of maps, as well as books on the outdoors.

Eugene's daily newspaper is the *Register-Guard*. The Friday paper contains an arts-and-events section, as does *Eugene Weekly*, the city's alternative newsweekly. The biweekly *Comic News* brings together political cartoons from around the world.

Expresso Wash, a laundry at 595 E 13th Ave, is convenient to campus.

Sacred Heart Medical Center (☎ 541-686-7300) is at 1255 Hilyard St.

Market

At E 5th Ave, between Pearl and High Sts, is the anchor of a small but lively shopping and cafe district. The **5th St Public Market**, once an old mill, is in fact a boutique mall. Besides the lure of shopping, there's a good bakery and several inexpensive and ethnic places to eat in the building's central atrium.

The **outdoor market** held on Saturdays in the park near E 8th Ave and Oak St is great fun and is a good introduction to Eugene's peculiar vitality. Between Thanksgiving and Christmas, it's renamed the **Holiday Market** and moves indoors to the Lane Sport & Event Center. The market is closed January through March.

University of Oregon

Established in 1872, the University of Oregon (☎ 541-346-1000, ⓦ *www.uoregon.edu*) is the state's foremost institution of higher learning, with a focus on the arts, sciences and law. The forestlike campus is filled with historic ivy-covered buildings. The oldest is **Deady Hall**. Also on campus is **Pioneer Cemetery**, with tombstones that give vivid insight into life and death in the early settlement; note the graves of Civil War veterans. Campus tours are held in the summer.

Housed in a replica of a Native American longhouse, the **University of Oregon Museum of Natural History** (☎ 541-346-3024, ⓦ *natural-history.uoregon.edu, 1680 E 15th Ave; donation $2; open noon-5pm Tues-Sun*) contains the state's best display of fossils, Native American artifacts and geologic curiosities. The renowned **University of Oregon Museum of Art** (☎ 541-346-3027, ⓦ *uoam.uoregon.edu, 1430 Johnson Lane*) is closed for renovation through 2003.

The university sits just south and east of downtown; near the main entrance, at Franklin Blvd and Agate St, there's campus information for visitors.

Lane County Historical Museum

Old logging tools and technology are prominent among the collection of historic artifacts preserved at this local museum (☎ 541-682-4239, 740 W 13th Ave; adult/senior/child $2/1/75¢; open 10am-4pm Wed-Fri, noon-4pm Sat). One exhibit details the experiences of Oregon Trail pioneers who traversed the continent to settle in Lane County.

Skinner Butte

A hike up wooded Skinner Butte, directly north of downtown, provides a good orientation and a little exercise, though there's also a road. Eugene Skinner established the city's first business on the narrow strip of land along the Willamette River below. The grassy waterfront is now **Skinner Butte Park**. A number of beautiful Victorian homes ring the butte, and there's also **rock climbing** along the landmark's western face.

Alton Baker Park

The 5 miles of bike and jogging paths at this popular riverside park connect to other parks via a bikeway that flanks both sides of the Willamette.

The best downtown access is from High St, via the new **DeFazio Bike Bridge**. To visit other parks, follow the path around the north side of Skinner Butte, which hugs the river's edge beneath the Hwy 126 overpass to the **Owens Memorial Rose Garden**, a lovely park with carefully trained climbing roses and an old cherry tree from the 1860s.

The **Autzen Footbridge** spans the Willamette to reach Alton Baker Park from the university.

You can rent bikes from **Paul's Bicycle Way of Life** (☎ 541-344-4105, 152 W 5th Ave; bicycles/tandems $12/15).

OREGON

EUGENE

PLACES TO STAY
1 Valley River Inn
2 The Campbell House
10 Courtesy Inn
18 Downtown Motel
19 Hilton Eugene & Conference Center
29 66 Motel
30 The Oval Door B&B
36 Campus Inn
40 Timbers Motel
46 Best Western New Oregon Motel
54 Excelsior Inn

PLACES TO EAT
3 Hilda's
5 Oregon Electric Station
6 Cafe Navarro
23 West Brothers Bar-B-Que; Eugene City Brewery
27 Full City Coffee; Palace Bakery
28 Café Zenon
33 Adam's Place
34 Ambrosia
37 Ring of Fire
38 The Kiva
45 Mekala's
49 Café Soriah
50 Cozmic Pizza
56 Glenwood Inn

ENTERTAINMENT
4 Sam Bond's Garage
8 Steelhead Brewing Co
9 Jo Federigo's Bar & Cafe
11 The Beanery
20 Hult Center for the Performing Arts; Convention Center
21 WOW Hall
25 Café Paradiso
31 Theo's Jazz Club; Theo's Coffee House
32 Actors Cabaret of Eugene
41 John Henry's
51 McMenamins High St Brewery & Cafe
52 The Bijou
59 MacArthur Court

OTHER
7 Euphoria Chocolate Co
12 Paul's Bicycle Way of Life
13 Down to Earth
14 Main Post Office
15 Smith Family Bookstore
16 Fifth Street Public Market; Nike Eugene Store
17 Enterprise
22 Convention & Visitors Association of Lane County
24 The Book Mark
26 Saturday Market
35 Greyhound Bus Depot
39 LTD Transit Station
42 Sacred Heart Medical Center
43 Deady Hall
44 Campus Information
47 Lane County Historical Museum
48 Berg's Ski Shop
53 Expresso Wash
55 Smith Family Bookstore
57 U of O Bookstore
58 U of O Museum of Art
60 U of O Museum of Natural History

P Parking Area

To Valley River Center

Owens Memorial Rose Garden

Skinner Butte Park

1st Ave W
W-2nd Ave
W-3rd Ave
W 4th Ave
W 5th Ave
W 6th Ave
W 7th Ave
W-8th Ave
W-Broadway
W-10th Ave
W 11th Ave
W-12th Ave
W 13th Ave
W-14th Ave
W-15th Ave
W-16th Ave
W-17th Ave
W 18th Ave
W-19th Ave
W-20th Ave

Van Buren St
Jackson St
Almaden St
Chambers St
Taylor St
Polk St
Tyler St
Adams St
Monroe St
Madison St
Jefferson St
Washington St
Lawrence St
Lincoln St
Charnelton St
Olive St
Blair Blvd

To Airport & Corvallis

To Fern Ridge Reservoir, Veneta & Florence

Amazon Creek

Lane Events Center

Westmoreland Park

0   300   600 m
0   300   600 yards

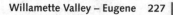

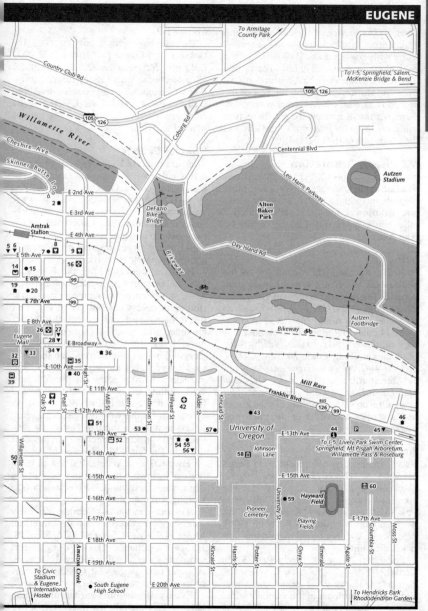

EUGENE

To Armitage
County Park

Country Club Rd

To I-5, Springfield, Salem,
McKenzie Bridge & Bend

Willamette River

105 126

Cheshire Ave

Skinner Butte Loop

Centennial Blvd

Coburg Rd

Leo Harris Parkway

Autzen
Stadium

E 2nd Ave

2

E 3rd Ave

DeFazio
Bike
Bridge

Alton
Baker
Park

Amtrak
Station

E 4th Ave

Day Island Rd

5 6   7   8
E 5th Ave

9

Bikeway

14   15
E 6th Ave

16

19
20
E 7th Ave

99

99

E 8th Ave

Autzen
Footbridge

26   27
28
E Broadway

29

Bikeway

Eugene
Mall

32   33
34

35
E 10th Ave

36

High St

40

Mill Race

Franklin Blvd

BUS
126 99

E 11th Ave

Oak St

Pearl St

Mill St

Ferry St

Patterson St

Hilyard St

Alder St

Kincaid St

42

46

51
E 12th Ave

45

53

57

University of
Oregon

43

44

E 13th Ave

To I-5, Lively Park Swim Center,
Springfield, Mt Pisgah Arboretum,
Willamette Pass & Roseburg

E 13th Ave

52

54 55
56

E 14th Ave

58

Johnson
Lane

Willamette St

50

E 15th Ave

E 15th Ave

60

E 16th Ave

University St

59

Hayward
Field

Pioneer
Cemetery

Playing
Fields

E 17th Ave

E 17th Ave

Columbia St

Moss St

E 18th Ave

Kincaid St

Harris St

Potter St

Onyx St

Emerald St

Agate St

Amazon Creek

E 19th Ave

To Civic
Stadium
& Eugene
International
Hostel

South Eugene
High School

E 20th Ave

To Hendricks Park
Rhododendron Garden

Hendricks Park Rhododendron Garden

Over 5000 varieties of rhododendron and azalea erupt into bloom here in the spring, along with dogwood and daffodils. For the peak bloom season, visit in May. The garden is part of a larger park that features native trees and shrubs, and during the rest of the year, it is a quiet, vernal retreat with lovely views worthy of a picnic. To get there, turn south off Franklin Blvd onto Agate St and then turn east onto Heights Blvd.

Mt Pisgah Arboretum

Nature trails at this 120-acre plant sanctuary wind through a number of Northwest plant habitats, including a marsh, a conifer forest and wildflower meadows. It's located 7 miles south and east of Eugene, off the I-5 30th Ave exit.

Wineries

Nestled in the hills at the southern end of the Willamette Valley are a number of good wineries. Take a picnic to **Hinman Vineyards/ Silvan Ridge** (☎ 541-345-1945, **W** www.silvan ridge.com, 27012 Briggs Hill Rd; open noon-5pm), 11 miles southwest of Eugene, to enjoy their nice facility and grounds. Nearby is the chateauesque **King Estate** (☎ 541-942-9874, 800-884-4441, **W** www.kingestate.com, 80854 Territorial Rd; noon-5pm daily Memorial Day-Labor Day, weekends only the rest of the year), Oregon's largest grower of wine grapes and a serious contender in the pinot noir market.

Activities

Rent winter-sports equipment from **Berg's Ski Shop** (☎ 541-683-1300, **W** www.bergsski shop.com, 367 W 13th Ave; $10-25). The company also runs ski buses to Willamette Pass ($10), out on Hwy 58; Hoodoo ($13), near Santiam Pass; and Mt Bachelor ($20), near Bend. Ask about combination bus-/lift-ticket discounts.

Springfield's indoor **Lively Park Swim Center** (☎ 541-747-9283, 6100 Thurston Rd; cost $4) features wave pools and water slides. Swim outdoors in the summer at the pool at **Amazon Park** (☎ 541-682-5350, 2600 Hilyard St), or in the McKenzie River at **Armitage County Park**, north of Eugene on Coburg Rd.

Eugene has several golf courses. Try **Oakway Golf Course** (☎ 541-484-1927, 2000 Cal Young Rd; green fees $20) for a beautiful 18-hole course with lots of mature trees. One of Eugene's newest courses, **Riveridge Golf Course** (☎ 541-345-9160, 3800 N Delta Hwy; green fees $29) preserves the habitat of local bird life.

Special Events

While the music of Bach – especially the concertos and cantatas – takes center stage at the Hult Center, the Oregon Bach Festival (☎ 541-346-5666, 800-457-1468, **W** www .oregonbachfestival.com) also features workshops and lectures. The festival is held for two weeks in late June and early July, featuring Grammy award–winning performers in about 25 separate concerts.

Held the weekend after the Fourth of July, the Oregon Country Fair (☎ 541-343-4298, **W** www.oregoncountryfair.com) is a riotous three-day celebration of Eugene's folksy, hippie past and present. Booths are crammed with tie-dyed garments, candles, herbs and crafts. Wandering minstrels, jugglers and mimes entertain, and on the festival's many stages are vaudeville acts and musicians. Mostly gone are the old days when clothing was optional and drugs passed freely. But it's still full of infectious high spirits and otherworldly goodwill. Buy tickets in advance through Fastixx (☎ 800-992-8499) – tickets cannot be purchased at the gate. The fair is 13 miles west of Eugene on Hwy 126, near Veneta. It's best to leave the car in town and hop the free fairtime express bus from the LTD bus station (see Getting Around, later).

American music is celebrated in early August with the Oregon Festival of American Music (OFAM; ☎ 541-687-6526, 800-248-1615, **W** www.ofam2.org), a weeklong concert series of jazz and contemporary show tunes. At other times of the year, OFAM produces concerts and traveling shows.

Events at the fun, agricultural Lane County Fair include livestock shows, live music, a carnival and produce displays. It's held the third week of August at the Lane Events Center (☎ 541-682-4292).

On the third weekend of September, the Eugene Celebration (☎ 541-681-4108) takes over downtown with parades and a lively street fair. It's Eugene's usual time-tested mix of artisans, food vendors, political activists and organic farmers – all with students fresh from summer break.

Places to Stay

Camping While most campgrounds here are RV-oriented, they all have tent areas.

Eugene Kamping World (☎ 541-343-4832, 800-343-3008, 90932 S Stuart Way) Tents/ hookups $15/17.50. This campground, 6 miles north of Eugene, is convenient to I-5 exit 199.

KOA Sherwood Forest (☎ 541-895-4110, 298 E Oregon Ave) Tents/hookups/cabins $17/29/33. There's more of the same at this KOA, 9 miles south of Eugene at Creswell (I-5 exit 182).

Richardson Park Campground (☎ 541-935-2005, Richardson Park Rd) Sites $16. Head to this county campground for a spot on Fern Ridge Reservoir, 16 miles west of Eugene.

Hostels Eugene has one hostel.

Eugene International Hostel (☎ 541-349-0589, 2352 Willamette St) Dorm beds $13-16. Closed 11am-4pm. If a mattress on the floor is your kind of place, then this hostel just south of the university should suit you just fine.

B&Bs For a complete list of B&Bs, contact the *Eugene Area B&B Association* (☎ 541-343-3553, 800-507-1357).

The Oval Door B&B (☎ 541-683-3160, 800-882-3160, W www.ovaldoor.com, 988 Lawrence St) Rooms $70-93. There are four guest rooms in this farmhouse in an old neighborhood downtown.

Historic homes refurbished as European-style hotels offer Eugene's most elegant lodgings:

The Campbell House (☎ 541-343-1119, 800-264-2519, W www.campbellhouse.com, 252 Pearl St) Rooms $98-378. This B&B

offers 14 guest rooms within walking distance of parks and downtown.

Excelsior Inn (☎ 541-342-6963, 800-321-6963, W www.excelsiorinn.com, 754 E 13th Ave) Rooms $87-219. Near campus, another 14 guest suites (two with whirlpool tubs) can be found at this stately inn, which shares space with one of Eugene's finest restaurants.

Hotels & Motels Older motels on the fringe of downtown are an easy stroll to shopping, restaurants and parks. Motels west on 6th and 7th Aves become cheaper and grottier the farther you drive. The nicest hotels are downtown and near the Valley River Center mall.

Timbers Motel (☎ 541-343-3345, 800-643-4167, 1015 Pearl St) Singles/doubles $38/40. This centrally located motor lodge near the bus station is a popular budget choice. The cheapest rooms are in the basement ($32) but can't be reserved.

66 Motel (☎ 541-342-5041, 755 E Broadway) Singles/doubles $35/43. Handy to the university, this clean and comfortable motel is remodeled with furniture from the Best Western down the street.

Downtown Motel (☎ 541-345-8739, 800-648-4366, 361 W 7th Ave) Singles/doubles $35/44. These decent rooms are some of the least expensive in town.

Courtesy Inn (☎ 541-345-3391, 345 W 6th Ave) Singles/doubles $44/61. Rooms at this attractive motel are slightly more comfortable that at Downtown Motel.

There are a number of business-class hotels near campus.

Campus Inn (☎ 541-343-3376, 800-888-6313, W www.campus-inn.com, 390 E Broadway) Singles/doubles $50/70. This cheerful business-class motel is convenient to campus and has a fitness center and on-site car rental.

Best Western New Oregon Motel (☎ 541-683-3669, W www.bestwestern.com/new oregonmotel, 1655 Franklin Blvd) Singles/ doubles $71/86. Across from campus is this motel, which is popular with people attending university events. There's an indoor pool, a sauna and an exercise room.

Hilton Eugene & Conference Center (☎ 541-342-2000, 800-937-6660, W www .eugene.hilton.com, 66 E 6th Ave) Rooms

OREGON

$104-131. In the center of downtown, this hotel is part of the convention center and is right next door to the artsy goings-on at the Hult Center.

Valley River Inn (☎ 541-687-0123, 800-543-8266, 1000 Valley River Way, W www.val leyriverinn.com) Rooms $129-400. Balconied rooms at this riverside hotel on the north side of the Willamette have either a courtyard or river view. There are indoor and outdoor pools, a fitness center and bike rental.

Places to Eat

Food in Eugene often surpasses much of what gets flogged as cuisine in cities such as Seattle and Portland, and with so many new, designer restaurants, it's often hard to decide where to start. The best restaurants offer engaging bars and items to fit a student's budget.

Budget Start the day with espresso drinks at *Full City Coffee* (842 Pearl St) and baked goods from the *Palace Bakery* next door. There's organic produce, bulk foods and deli items at *The Kiva* (☎ 541-342-8666, 125 W 11th Ave).

For meals, head for the Fifth Street Market building (on 5th Ave between Pearl and High Sts), where there's a really great *bakery*, plus a number of small *ethnic restaurants*. University-area haunts near W 13th Ave and Alder St also provide inexpensive food.

Glenwood Inn (☎ 541-687-0355, 1340 Alder St) Breakfast $4-5. Head here for a full breakfast with bleary-eyed university students.

Cozmic Pizza (☎ 541-338-9333, 1436 Willamette St) Slices $2.50, whole pies $5-15. This is a uniquely Eugene establishment specializing in almost 100% organic pizzas and free delivery by bike.

Mid-Range See Entertainment, next, for brewpubs, which also serve food.

Mekala's (☎ 541-342-4872, 1769 Franklin Blvd) Entrees $10. Eugene's long-standing favorite for Thai food is this busy place on Franklin Ave.

West Brother's Bar-B-Que (☎ 541-345-8489, 844 Olive St) Lunch/dinner $10/15. House-brewed ales here are teamed with

superior barbecue and Cajun fare; it's also open for lunch.

Ambrosia (☎ 541-342-4141, 174 E Broadway) Pizzas $8.50-10, entrees $14-18. Ambrosia features regional Italian cuisine and wood-fired specialty pizzas in a wonderfully preserved late-19th-century bar.

Cafe Navarro (☎ 541-344-0943, 454 Willamette St) Entrees $6.50-15. Well-seasoned travelers will appreciate this cafe's Caribbean, Latin and African tanginess. The weekend breakfast menu ($6-7) draws quite a crowd.

Ring of Fire (☎ 541-344-6475, 1099 Chambers St) Entrees $9-16.50. The hip bar scene at this pan-Asian restaurant is a flashback to a South Pacific service club out of the 1940s. Thai food dominates the menu.

Hilda's (☎ 541-343-4322, 400 Blair Blvd) Entrees $15. This is Eugene's spiciest restaurant – it features food from Central and South America. If you're on a budget, the tapas ($7-8) are a good value.

Top End The Excelsior Inn (see Places to Stay, earlier) has a great restaurant.

Oregon Electric Station (☎ 541-485-4444, 27 E 5th Ave) Entrees $17-24. For steak and seafood, head for this restaurant (everyone else does) – it's housed in an old railroad station. In the waiting room, settle into an easy chair for a pre-dinner drink.

Café Zenon (☎ 541-343-3005, 898 Pearl St) Entrees $15. Imaginative use of local ingredients is apparent here in regional entrees such as hazelnut-encrusted venison and roast quail in cherry sauce.

Adam's Place (☎ 541-344-6948, 30 E Broadway) Entrees $18-27. Live jazz and an elegant bar are the sophisticated accessories of this classy restaurant.

Café Soriah (☎ 541-342-4410, 384 W 13th Ave) Entrees $15-20. Mediterranean-influenced Soriah is the place for an intimate evening with fine wine.

Entertainment

The *Eugene Weekly* lists the latest happenings. Check the *Daily Emerald* for performances, lectures, films and activities going on at the university.

Hult Center for the Performing Arts *(concert line ☎ 541-682-5746, tickets ☎ 541-687-5000,* W *www.hultcenter.org, 6th Ave & Willamette St)* Eugene's main civic performance space is adjacent to the convention center and the Hilton; the Eugene Opera, Symphony and Ballet each perform here, as do touring groups.

Actors Cabaret of Eugene (☎ 541-683-4368, 996 Willamette St) This is popular for stand-up comedy, musicals and dinner theater.

Coffeehouses Eugene's most popular hangout is *The Beanery (☎ 541-342-3378, 152 W 5th Ave),* which has desserts and light meals.

Café Paradiso (☎ 541-484-9933, 115 W Broadway at Olive St) This quiet coffeehouse is often packed with chess players, except in the evening, when there's live music and events.

Theo's Coffee House (☎ 541-344-6491, 150 W Broadway) Don't be fooled by the chain-smoking teens outside – this is really more sophisticated than you might think.

Brewpubs Eugene has several brewpubs, although locally brewed beers are also served at most restaurants and bars.

Steelhead Brewing Co (☎ 541-485-4444, 199 E 5th Ave) Catercorner to the Fifth Street Market, this brewing outfit serves German-style beers and light meals in an airy old storefront.

Eugene City Brewery (☎ 541-345-8489, 844 Olive St) The strong, dark ales are good here and are well matched to the fiery entrees on the barbecue-restaurant side of the business.

McMenamins High Street Brewery & Cafe (☎ 541-345-4905, 1243 High St) This is a popular spot for a beer near campus.

Cinemas Movie buffs won't have a problem finding a fix in Eugene.

The Bijou (☎ 541-686-2458, 492 E 13th Ave) This is Eugene's art and foreign-movie house.

Cinemark (☎ 541-746-5202, Gateway Mall, I-5 exit 195) The largest selection of first-run films are here in Springfield.

Live Music Eugene's main acoustic venue is the *WOW Hall (☎ 541-687-2746, W 8th Ave & Lincoln St),* an old union hall that hosts eclectic touring groups such as Tuvan throat singers and zydeco bands.

Clubs such as *Sam Bond's Garage (☎ 541-343-2635, 407 Blair Blvd)* and *John Henry's (☎ 541-342-3358, 136 E 11th Ave)* offer alternative and acoustic music.

Jo Federigo's Bar & Cafe (☎ 541-343-8488, 259 E 5th Ave) Head here for live jazz.

Theo's Jazz Club (☎ 541-344-6491, 126 E Broadway) Institute of American Music affiliates play jazz three nights a week at this swank club in the Eugene Mall.

Spectator Sports

The *Eugene Emeralds* are a Class A baseball team who play during the summer at *Civic Stadium (☎ 541-342-5367, 20th Ave & Willamette St).* The *University of Oregon Ducks (☎ 541-346-4461, 800-932-3668,* W *www .goducks.com)* are the much-loved, though not always successful, sports teams of the university. The basketball team plays on campus at *MacArthur Court*; the football team plays at *Autzen Stadium*, off Centennial Blvd, just east of downtown.

Shopping

Down to Earth (☎ 541-342-6820, 532 Olive St) There's nothing more symbolic of Eugene than this shop, which is full of garden and farm supplies, kitchen gear, food-preservation equipment and a plant nursery – everything you need to establish a modern, wholly organic homestead.

Make sure to try the truffles at *Euphoria Chocolate Co (☎ 541-343-9223, 199 E 5th Ave),* a locally famous candy maker.

And let's not forget that Eugene is the birthplace of Nike. You don't have to buy anything, but the *Nike Eugene Store (☎ 541-342-5155, 248 E 5th Ave)* has an interesting corporate-history exhibit, and you can see the waffle iron that stamped out the first Nikes.

Getting There & Around

Horizon and United Express link Eugene Airport (☎ 541-682-5544 W www.eugene airport.com) to Portland, Seattle and San

Francisco. Horizon also flies to Los Angeles, and United goes to Denver. America West flies direct to Phoenix.

At 987 Pearl St, buses depart north to Portland ($13 one way) and south to San Francisco ($48) from the Greyhound depot (☎ 541-344-6265) several times daily. There's one bus to Bend ($22).

Amtrak's *Cascades* and *Coast Starlight* link Eugene to Portland ($24 one way) twice daily; the *Coast Starlight* also goes south to Sacramento or San Francisco ($104). There's additional service to Portland and Ashland on Amtrak Thruway buses. The station (☎ 541-687-1383) is at E 4th Ave and Willamette St.

At the Eugene Airport, you'll find Avis (☎ 541-688-9053), Budget (☎ 541-688-1229) and National Car Rental (☎ 541-688-8161). Enterprise (☎ 541-344-2020), 810 W 6th Ave, is located downtown.

Lane Transit District (LTD; ☎ 541-687-5555, W www.ltd.org) buses arrive and depart from the busy downtown transit station at Olive St between 10th and 11th Aves. Eugene streets also have room for bike lanes. Call Emerald Taxi (☎ 541-686-2010) for a cab.

MCKENZIE RIVER VALLEY

The single name 'McKenzie' identifies a beautiful and mysterious river, a mountain pass, a spectacular historic highway and one of Oregon's most extraordinary and wondrous natural areas. Fantastic fishing, easy hikes and exciting rafting trips make this one of the state's premier recreation areas.

The region is named for Donald McKenzie, who explored the upper Willamette Valley in 1812 as an early fur trapper with JJ Astor's Pacific Fur Company. After gold was discovered in central Oregon in the 1860s, Willamette Valley residents hacked a trail over lava flows near McKenzie Pass (5325 feet). The trail – which carried enough traffic to justify a toll station – was the predecessor to the contorted Old McKenzie Hwy (Hwy 242). This scenic byway follows a tributary of the McKenzie River up a hair-raising escarpment to the pass, where volcanic peaks loom across barren lava flows that are only several hundred years old.

Although the area is an easy day trip from either Eugene or Bend, riverside campgrounds and charming cabins will compel travelers to make it the focus of a longer visit.

The little community of McKenzie Bridge, 50 miles east of Eugene on Hwy 126, offers accommodations and food and is considered the gateway to recreation. Four miles east of McKenzie Bridge, the McKenzie Hwy splits and continues east as Hwy 242 (the Old McKenzie Hwy) over the Cascades toward McKenzie Pass on its way to Sisters, 34 miles distant. Note that this road is closed from November to June.

Hwy 126 continues north along the McKenzie River to US 20, which crosses the Cascades at Santiam Pass (4817 feet), which is open year round.

For travel information, contact the McKenzie River Chamber of Commerce (☎ 541-896-3330, W www.el.com/to/mcken zierivervalley), located in an old fish hatchery on Hwy 126 in Leaburg. In Blue River, there's a rack of brochures and a post office at Myers General Store, at 51748 Cascade St.

The McKenzie Ranger Station (☎ 541-822-3381, W www.fs.fed.us/r6/willamette), 57600 McKenzie Hwy, has information on trails and campgrounds. They also sell Northwest Forest Passes and issue limited-entry permits for the Obsidian Trail, in the Three Sisters Wilderness.

Lane Transit District (☎ 541-687-5555) bus No 91 from Eugene provides service along Hwy 126 to the McKenzie Ranger Station. Across the highway from the station, hikers can pick up the McKenzie River National Recreation Trail (see Hiking, under McKenzie Bridge & Hwy 126, next). The bus trips ($1) take slightly over an hour, and there's no Sunday service.

McKenzie Bridge & Hwy 126

Little more than a general store and a few cabins, the small crossroads of McKenzie Bridge offer the last services on the McKenzie River. Between the junction of Hwys 242 and 20, Hwy 126 follows the main

OREGON

MCKENZIE RIVER VALLEY

Metolius River

Black Butte 6415ft

To Sisters & Bend

Squaw Creek

Broken Top 9173ft

To Bend

Three Fingered Jack 7841ft

Suttle Lake

Old McKenzie Hwy

Black Crater 1451ft

North Sister 10,085ft

Middle Sister 10,047ft

South Sister 10,358ft

Cascade Lakes Hwy

Mt Bachelor Ski Area

Mt Bachelor 9065ft

Deschutes National Forest

Pacific Crest Trail

Santiam Pass 4817ft

20

Mt Washington 7794ft

Belknap Crater 6872ft

242

McKenzie Pass 5325ft

9

8

Cascade Range

Sparks Lake

Elk Lake

To Detroit & Salem

22

Big Lake

Clear Lake

3

Mt Washington Wilderness

7

242

6

24

Three Sisters Wilderness

Separation Creek

Horse Creek

Pacific Crest Trail

1

2

Fish Lake

Sahalie Falls

Koosah Falls

4

126

5

22

23

White Branch

To Oakridge, Westfir & Hwy 58

Tamolitch Pool

21

20

McKenzie Ranger Station

French Pete Creek

Willamette National Forest

19

17

18

16

McKenzie Bridge

14 15

12 13

Rainbow

11

Cougar Reservoir

25

USFS 19

Middle Santiam River

Santiam River

Willamette National Forest

Blue River Reservoir

Blue River

McKenzie River

Willamette National Forest

Green Peter Reservoir

0   16 km

0   10 miles

Cascadia State Park

Calapooia River

McKenzie Hwy

126

10

To Leburg, Eugene & Springfield

Foster Reservoir

20

Sweet Home

228

To I-5 & Albany

0   5   8   16

0   5   10 miles

1 McKenzie River National Recreation Trailhead; Clear Lake Trailhead
2 Clear Lake Trailhead
3 Coldwater Cove Campground
4 Ice Cap Creek Campground; Sahalie Falls Trailhead
5 Olallie Campground
6 Scott Lake Campground; Hand Lake Trailhead
7 Pacific Crest Trailhead to Little Belknap Crater
8 Lava Lake Campground
9 Dee Wright Observatory
10 Featherbed Resort
11 Delta Campground
12 Sleepy Hollow Motel
13 Rustic Skillet
14 Tokatee Golf Club
15 McKenzie Bridge Campground
16 Horse Creek Lodge
17 Caddisfly Resort
18 Log Cabin Inn & Dining Room

19 McKenzie River National Recreation Trail
20 Paradise Campground
21 Belknap Hot Springs Lodge
22 Linton Lake Trailhead; Alder Springs Campground
23 Proxy Falls Trailhead
24 Obsidian Trailhead
25 French Pete Trailhead & Campground

branch of the McKenzie River north through a steep valley to the river's source.

Hiking One of Oregon's showcase 'Wild & Scenic Rivers,' the McKenzie is graced with the 26½-mile **McKenzie River National Recreation Trail**, which follows the here-again, gone-again cascading river from its inception to the hamlet of McKenzie Bridge. Trailheads appear at several places along Hwy 126, so hikers can select whatever distance or segment suits their fancy. Northwest Forest Passes are not required.

From the trailhead near **Fish Lake**, there are nice day hikes downstream to **Clear Lake**. Here the trail divides. To the east, the trail passes the large spring of an underground river, several groves of old-growth forest and an extensive lava flow to arrive at Coldwater Cove Campground. To the west, the path follows the lake past Clear Lake Resort.

Another series of easy hikes begins at the **Sahalie Falls**, where a footbridge crosses the upper falls viewpoint to join the McKenzie River Trail for a 2-mile stroll to Carmen Reservoir past **Koosah Falls**. On the highway side of the river is the more developed and shorter **Waterfall Trail**, which links Sahalie with Koosah Falls. Parts of this trail are wheelchair accessible.

For nearly 4 miles, the McKenzie disappears between Carmen Reservoir and Tamolitch Pool. Long-distance hikers are treated to a lush growth of cedar and fir along the dry riverbed.

Day hikes also reach eerily calm and emerald **Tamolitch Pool** from the south. To reach the trailhead, turn off Hwy 126 at Trail Bridge Reservoir, but follow the gravel road to the right, past the maintenance buildings. The 2-mile trail passes through a mossy lava flow before coming upon the mighty McKenzie River surging up in a cliff-lined bowl of rock (Tamolitch means 'bucket' in Chinookan).

Fishing The McKenzie River is one of the most storied fishing streams in Oregon. The favorite quarry of anglers is the redside trout (a variant of the rainbow), whose sides are flecked with orange spots. The slower water and deep pools west of Blue River offer the best fishing, with access via state and county parks. Summer steelhead fishing is also good here. A summer release of hatchery rainbows means good fishing from trails and campgrounds between Belknap Hot Springs and McKenzie Bridge.

A number of restrictions apply, so check with tackle shops or the Fish & Wildlife office (☎ 541-726-3515) in Springfield for current regulations. For guided fishing trips, instruction or equipment rental, contact **Justus Outfitters** (☎ 541-342-1755). **Jim's Oregon Whitewater** (☎ 541-822-6003, 800-254-5467) also does fishing excursions.

Rafting White-water rafting trips are popular on the McKenzie River's Class I to III rapids from April to October. Jim's Oregon Whitewater (see previous paragraph) and **High Country Expeditions** (☎ 888-461-7238, Ⓦ www .hcexpeditions.com) offer both half-day ($50) and full-day excursions ($70-80).

Golf You wouldn't expect to find a 1st-class golf course in the woods along the McKenzie River, but there is one. **Tokatee Golf Club** (☎ 541-822-3220, 800-452-6376, 54947 McKenzie Hwy; green fees $37), 3 miles west of McKenzie Bridge on Hwy 126, is reckoned to be one of the toughest golf courses in Oregon and has been repeatedly ranked by *Golf Digest* as one of the nation's top 25 public courses.

Places to Stay There are many possibilities for campers, but those looking to be a little pampered will have options as well.

Camping USFS campgrounds appear regularly along the McKenzie. There are water and pit toilets at all of the following.

Paradise Campground (☎ 877-444-6777, 4 miles east of McKenzie Bridge on Hwy 126) Sites $10. This aptly named riverside campground near the Hwy 242 cutoff offers 64 campsites under a canopy of old growth.

McKenzie Bridge Campground (1 mile west of McKenzie Bridge on Hwy 126) Sites

$10. You can reach this roadside campground by taking the No 91 bus from Eugene (see Getting There & Away under Eugene, earlier).

Delta Campground (☎ 877-444-6777, 3 miles east of Blue River on Hwy 126) Sites $12. Near the turnoff to Cougar Reservoir is Delta, which is located in a pleasant stream-side setting with a short nature trail.

Coldwater Cove Campground (☎ 877-444-6777, 18 miles northeast of McKenzie Bridge on Hwy 126) Sites $12. This place offers camping on the quiet side of Clear Lake.

Ice Cap Creek Campground (17 miles northeast of McKenzie Bridge on Hwy 126) Sites $10. This campground is a mile down-river on Carmen Reservoir, where there's good trout fishing. Nearby hiking trails lead to spectacular waterfalls.

Olallie Campground (☎ 877-444-6777, 11 miles northeast of McKenzie Bridge on Hwy 126) Sites $8. This is another nice riverside campground.

Motels The McKenzie River is a classic camping and cabin sort of place; motels are few.

Sleepy Hollow Motel (☎ 541-822-3805, 54791 McKenzie Hwy) Singles/doubles $52/56. This standard motor inn is right next to Tokatee Golf Club; it's open seasonally from April to October.

Featherbed Resort (☎ 541-822-6200, 49733 McKenzie Hwy, ⓦ www.featherbedresort .com) Motel rooms/cabins from $79/120. If an overstuffed featherbed and a cup of hot chocolate sounds like a vacation, then these four pine-paneled motel rooms are for you. Across the highway are four family-sized cabins with balconies overlooking the river. Noisy truck traffic in the morning is the only drawback.

Lodges & Resorts Most lodging around McKenzie Bridge is in freestanding cabins. You should make summer reservations well in advance. Most require a minimum stay.

Caddisfly Resort (☎ 541-822-3556, 56404 McKenzie Hwy) Cabins $70 for two, $7 each additional person. Spacious cabins with decks overlooking the river make this resort one of the most popular. Fireplaces and kitchens are standard, and the cabins sleep four to six.

Log Cabin Inn (☎ 541-822-3432, 800-355-3432, 56483 McKenzie Hwy) Cabins $85-100, teepees $45. For a real cabin, ask for cabin 7 or 8. Other river-view 'cabins' are really cramped motel rooms with porches and fire-places, though the old-fashioned woodsy charm makes them perfectly pleasant.

Horse Creek Lodge (☎ 541-822-3243, 56228 Delta Dr) Cabins $65-85, Delta House $235. Secluded wooded cabins here lack river views, but they're quieter and well off the highway. There's lodging for groups in the four-bedroom Delta House.

Belknap Hot Springs Lodge (☎ 541-822-3512, 59296 Belknap Springs Rd) Campsites $17, cabins $45-175, lodge rooms $70-100. This spa-like mountain resort off Hwy 126 near the Hwy 242 junction offers rooms in the modern lodge or in cabins; campsites are also available. Nonguests can relax in the mineral pool for $4.50. A minimum stay is required on holidays only.

Clear Lake Resort (on Hwy 126, 4 miles south of Hwy 20) Cabins $31-70. These rustic cabins on the shores of 200-foot-deep Clear Lake are lovely – except for the gasoline generators. There are no electric outlets, and older cabins don't have bathrooms. Rowboat rentals and a cafe are pluses. Reservations are recommended and can be made only by writing the Santiam Fish & Game Association, PO Box 500, Lebanon, OR 97355 (no telephone).

Places to Eat There are a couple of decent options for food.

Rustic Skillet (☎ 541-822-3400, 54771 McKenzie Hwy) Entrees $5-12. This family restaurant, 3 miles west of McKenzie Bridge, offers three meals a day and homemade pies.

Log Cabin Inn Dining Room (☎ 541-822-3432, 56483 McKenzie Hwy) Dinner $13-19. Steaks and prime rib lead the menu at this charming and old-fashioned dining room. Gamier dishes involve venison, buffalo or local trout.

OREGON

McKenzie Pass & The Old McKenzie Highway

From its departure off Hwy 126, the historic Old McKenzie Hwy (Hwy 242) climbs 4000 feet on narrow hairpin turns up Lost Creek Valley to the lava fields of 5325-foot-high McKenzie Pass. Here you'll find stunning views of the Cascade Range, intriguing hikes and access to one of the largest and most recent lava flows in the continental USA. Ironically, the most memorable part is likely to be the drive on the Old McKenzie Hwy itself, which, as one local observer mused, was 'seemingly engineered by a madman.'

Trailer travel is not suggested, and the route is closed in the winter. It takes about an hour to reach the pass, 22 miles east.

Dee Wright Observatory Perched on a swell of frozen rock at McKenzie Pass, this fortress of lava built by the Civilian Conservation Corps in the 1930s surveys a desolate volcanic landscape. Its arched windows frame 11 volcanic peaks. From the base, a half-mile interpretive trail winds through the lava.

Hiking A Northwest Forest Pass ($5) is required for all of the following, except Lost Valley Spring.

The **Upper & Lower Proxy Falls** tumble over glacier-carved walls to disappear into lava flows. An easy 1.2-mile loop trail begins directly east of milepost 64, about 12 miles east of McKenzie Bridge.

The easy 2.8-mile **Linton Lake Trailhead** is across from Alder Springs Campground and leads to a close-up view of lava-dammed Linton Lake. In the distance, Linton Falls roars over the valley edge and tumbles to the lake.

Directly east of milepost 59, an informal path leads 100 yards to a lovely spot where the subterranean waters of Lost Valley surface at **Lost Valley Spring**. To find the path, turn north into a large clearing.

The Pacific Crest Trail crosses McKenzie Pass a half mile west of the Dee Wright Observatory. It's 2½ miles across barren lava flows to a spectacular viewpoint atop **Little Belknap Crater**. There's no water or shelter

McKenzie Pass

McKenzie Pass was first traversed by white settlers in 1862, when Felix Scott and a party of 250 men on their way to the Central Oregon gold fields blazed a trail. By 1872, John Craig had scouted a slightly different trail across the lava fields and opened a toll road from McKenzie Bridge to Sisters ($2 per wagon, $1 per horseman and 5¢ per sheep). Craig worked to secure a US mail delivery route for the McKenzie Pass trail, linking Eugene and Prineville. He started across the pass with Christmas mail from McKenzie Bridge in December 1877 but never appeared at Camp Polk (near Sisters). His frozen body was found early in the next year. A monument near the pass commemorates his death.

along the trail – on a hot day, the hike can be oppressive.

Another popular 3-mile day hike leaves from Scott Lake Campground, several miles west of the pass, and winds past several small lakes en route to **Hand Lake**.

Also west of McKenzie Pass is the **Obsidian Trail**, one of the gentlest and most overused entrances into the Three Sisters Wilderness. A special-use permit is required and is available up to 30 days in advance from the McKenzie Ranger Station (☎ 541-822-3381). The full loop to Obsidian Cliffs and back is 13 miles. For a shorter hike, turn around after the first 2½ forested miles, at which point you'll have reached a 50-foot-high lava flow with exhilarating views of the **Three Sisters**.

Places to Stay Primitive tent campgrounds near McKenzie Pass are free but have no water. Fill your jug at Paradise Campground along the way.

Scott Lake Campground (8 miles west of McKenzie Pass on Hwy 242) No fee. This swampy campground has pretty lakeside sites and voracious mosquitoes.

Lava Camp Lake Campground (1 mile east of McKenzie Pass on Hwy 242) No fee.

OREGON

These 10 lakeside sites are convenient to the Pacific Crest Trail.

Three Sisters Wilderness

This 580-sq-mile wilderness area spans the Cascade Range, with access both from the Bend area to the east and the McKenzie River area to the west. The focal points are the glaciered Three Sisters, three recent volcanic peaks, each topping 10,000 feet in height. The west slope of the wilderness is known for dense old-growth forest coursed with strong rivers and streams. Oregon's small population of wolverines live here, as do spotted owl, cougars and black bears. The area is traversed by the **Pacific Crest Trail**, which is easily accessed from Hwy 242 at McKenzie Pass.

USFS Rd 19, also known as the **Aufderheide National Scenic Byway**, edges the westernmost wilderness boundary as it makes the 65-mile connection between Rainbow on Hwy 126 and Westfir (near Oakridge on Hwy 58). From *French Pete Campground*, one popular trail along this route leads up **French Pete Creek** through old growth forest before being halted after 3 miles by a missing bridge.

The Geo-Graphics *Three Sisters Wilderness Map* is the best map and is available from the ranger station. See the Three Sisters Wilderness section in the Central Oregon chapter for more hikes around Bend.

WILLAMETTE PASS

Southeast from Eugene, the Willamette River leaves its wide valley and is immediately impounded into ugly reservoirs. By Oakridge, the Willamette is restored to a rushing mountain river, and Hwy 58 ascends steeply up the Cascades Range's densely forested western slope.

At the Cascade crest, near Willamette Pass, are a number of beautiful lakes and wilderness areas, as well as Oregon's second-highest waterfall, 286-foot **Salt Creek Falls**. There's good hiking here, and in the winter,

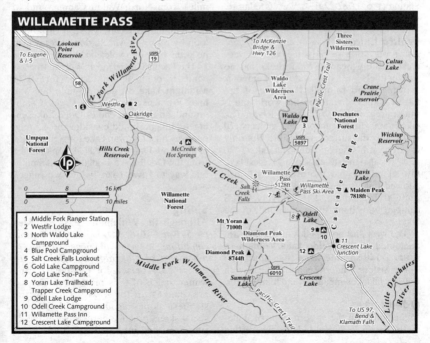

WILLAMETTE PASS

1 Middle Fork Ranger Station
2 Westfir Lodge
3 North Waldo Lake Campground
4 Blue Pool Campground
5 Salt Creek Falls Lookout
6 Gold Lake Campground
7 Gold Lake Sno-Park
8 Yoran Lake Trailhead; Trapper Creek Campground
9 Odell Lake Lodge
10 Odell Creek Campground
11 Willamette Pass Inn
12 Crescent Lake Campground

the area is popular for downhill and cross-country skiing. Along the way, you can let the steaming waters soak away the rigors of driving at undeveloped **McCredie Hot Springs**; it's clothing optional and popular with truckers. The unpaved turnout is just past Blue Pool Campground, 45 miles east of Eugene.

Orientation & Information

Hwy 58 leads southeast from Eugene to reach Willamette Pass in 52 miles; it's 85 miles to the US 97 junction south of Bend. The only town along the way is Oakridge (population 3375), a scruffy logging town with basic services; it's 35 miles east of Eugene.

The pass divides two national forests – most trails and campgrounds lie east, in the Crescent Ranger District of the Deschutes National Forest (☎ 541-433-2539, W www.fs .fed.us/r6/centraloregon). For information on Waldo Lake, in the Willamette National Forest, contact the Middle Fork Ranger Station (☎ 541-782-2291, W www.fs.fed.us/r6/ willamette), at 46375 Hwy 58, in Westfir.

Waldo Lake

At an elevation of 5414 feet on the very crest of the Cascades, Waldo Lake has no stream inlets – the only water that enters is snowmelt and rainfall. It is one of the purest bodies of water in the world and is the source of the Willamette River. The lake is amazingly transparent – objects 120 feet below the surface are visible. Not only is it Oregon's second-deepest lake (420 feet), it's also the state's second-largest lake (10 sq miles). No motorized boats are allowed, but afternoon winds make the lake popular for sailing. Three lovely USFS campgrounds flank the eastern half of the lake.

The west and north sides of the lake are contained in the **Waldo Lake Wilderness Area**, a 148-sq-mile area that abuts the Three Sisters Wilderness and is filled with tiny glacial lakes, meadows and hiking trails.

Odell Lake

Immediately on the eastern slope of Willamette Pass is beautiful Odell Lake, resting in a steep glacial basin. Odell, Crescent and Summit Lakes flank the **Diamond Peak Wilderness Area**, a 126-sq-mile preserve of lakes, craggy mountains and deep forests. Hiking trails lead into this relatively unexplored wilderness from lakeside campgrounds. In the winter, the lake becomes a popular cross-country ski destination.

Crescent & Summit Lakes

A rustic lodge and campgrounds ring Crescent Lake (70 miles east of Eugene), which is popular for snowmobiling and waterskiing. USFS Rd 610 leads west from the end of the lake to reach remote Summit Lake, which is preferred by wilderness purists.

Hiking

A Northwest Forest Pass ($5) is required for all of the following. Trails are snow-free from July to October.

The 20-mile **Waldo Lake Trail** encircles Waldo Lake. A less ambitious hike leads 3.4 miles from North Waldo Campground to sandy swimming beaches at the outlet of the Willamette River. Make it an 8-mile loop by returning via **Rigdon Lakes**, which lie at the base of a volcanic butte.

The Pacific Crest Trail at Willamette Pass winds through old wilderness forests to **Midnight Lake**, an easy 3.3-mile one-way hike. From nearby Trapper Creek Campground, on the west end of Odell Lake, energetic hikers should consider the 4.3-mile one-way hike to **Yoran Lake** for a great view of 8744-foot Diamond Peak. A popular hike from the Odell Lake Lodge leads 3.8 miles one way to **Fawn Lake**, below two rugged peaks.

Skiing

Although the **Willamette Pass Ski Area** (☎ *541-484-5030, 541-345-7669 for snow conditions,* W *www.willamettepass.com, 27 miles east of Oakridge on Hwy 58; lift tickets $31*) gets a lot of snow during winter, much of it is pretty wet. The ski area makes up for it with some of the steepest slopes around – US Olympic speed skiers practice here. Most of the 29 runs are rated intermediate to advanced,

OREGON

with a vertical drop of 1563 feet. It's also a popular night-skiing area. Contact Berg's Ski Shop (☎ 541-683-1300) or Ullr Sport Shop (☎ 541-687-8557) for a ski bus from Eugene.

A trail from the **Gold Lake Sno-Park**, just west of Willamette Pass on Hwy 58, leads to the ski area's Nordic center and 12 miles of groomed cross-country ski trails. **Odell Lake** is another popular spot for cross-country skiing.

Places to Stay & Eat
The lakes offer the closest places to stay for skiers and hikers. Motels in Oakridge, 27 miles west, are all pretty dire. There's a small store and diner at Crescent Lake Junction, a few miles east of Odell Lake.

Camping You'll find pit toilets and running water at all of the following, except Waldo Lake, which has flush toilets (to protect the lake).

North Waldo Lake Campground (11 miles off Hwy 58 at the end of USFS Rd 5898, which is off of USFS Rd 5897) Tents $10-12. Campgrounds don't get much better than this lovely spot on Waldo Lake. Avoid the mosquitoes by camping at the end of the season.

Gold Lake Campground (2 miles north of Hwy 58 on Gold Lake Rd) Sites $10. Near Willamette Pass and convenient to Hwy 58, smaller Gold Lake makes a fine alternative to Waldo Lake.

Odell Creek Campground (east end of Odell Lake, 6 miles east of Willamette Pass off Hwy 58) Sites $10. The wooded lakeshore sites at this small campground next to Odell Lake Lodge are best suited for tents.

Crescent Lake Campground (☎ 877-444-6777, 2.5 miles off Hwy 58 on Crescent Lake Rd) Sites $10. This popular family campground on Crescent Lake is fine if you don't mind lots of boaters.

B&Bs, Motels & Lodges Lodging options at the pass are few, and reservations are advised.

Westfir Lodge (☎ 541-782-3103, 47365 1st St, Westfir) Rooms $50-85. A stone's throw from Oregon's longest covered bridge (the Office Bridge) is this spacious B&B, with four guest rooms (shared bathrooms) and an English-style flower garden.

Willamette Pass Inn (☎ 541-433-2211, 7 miles east of Willamette Pass on Hwy 58) Rooms $72-104. The closest motel to the ski area, rooms here have fireplaces and kitchenettes, and there's a free shuttle to the Willamette Pass.

Odell Lake Lodge (☎ 541-443-2540, ⓦ www.odelllakeresort.com, east end of Odell Lake, 6 miles east of Willamette Pass on Hwy 58, PO Box 72, Crescent Lake, OR 97425) Lodge rooms $48-62, cabins $80-235. Rooms in the lodge are small but have private bathrooms. Scattered along the lakefront are 13 cabins that sleep four to 16; each has a fully equipped kitchen and a wood-burning stove. This is a busy place during ski season, so early reservations are a must; a minimum stay may be required. The lodge rents a full range of winter sports and fishing equipment.

Anyone can dine in the wood-paneled *lodge dining room* ($10-12), though reservations are required and it closes at 8pm; breakfast and lunch hours are seasonal.

Southern Oregon

Some of Oregon's most magical natural sites, including Crater Lake National Park, are found within the valleys of the Rogue and Umpqua Rivers and the Klamath Basin. Magic of another sort takes place in Ashland, the home of the Oregon Shakespeare Festival.

Rugged and remote, the southern Oregon landscape is entwined with a number of designated 'Wild & Scenic' rivers, which are famous for their challenging white-water rafting and excellent fishing. The Siskiyou Mountains expose some of the state's oldest and most puzzling geology. Here, orange-barked madrone, scrub oak and brushy manzanita replace the thick fir forests of the north. Cougars are more common in the south than anywhere else in Oregon, and another rare species is occasionally sighted – the legendary Sasquatch, or bigfoot.

Communities here differ sharply in origin from those of the Willamette Valley. The area was settled largely by displaced southerners and Confederate soldiers migrating westward at the vanguard of the gold rush. Highly autonomous and more socially conservative than the rest of the state, southern Oregon's insularity was broken in the 1960s by young people who set up farms and communes as part of the 'back to the land' movement.

Southern Oregon's social conservatism and homogeneity are today both challenged and triumphant. A new influx of working professionals and retirees from California has brought sprawling new development to Medford and Ashland. Meanwhile, antigovernment sentiment runs stronger than ever in more impoverished areas, as evidenced by recent backlashes over water rights, proposed monuments, and child-welfare rulings.

Siskiyou Pass on I-5 between Oregon and California is known for treacherous winter driving. Call ☎ 800-977-6368 for a state road report.

ASHLAND

Home to the internationally renowned Oregon Shakespeare Festival (OSF), pleasant Ashland (population 20,085) is the cultural center of southern Oregon. B&Bs and food dominate life here – 380,000 people visit annually to attend the productions at three venues, which include a large outdoor theater dedicated to Elizabethan drama.

Even if you don't have a theater ticket, Ashland is still worth a stop. Lovely Lithia

---

Highlights

- Visiting Crater Lake, with its azure-hued waters and fascinating geology
- Angling on the North Umpqua and Upper Rogue Rivers
- Bonding with the Bard at Ashland's Oregon Shakespeare Festival
- Spending the night in a tree on a farm in the foothills of the Siskiyou Mountains

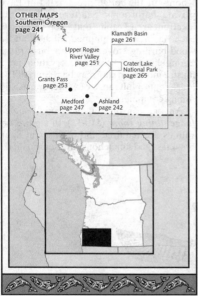

OTHER MAPS
Southern Oregon
page 241

Klamath Basin
page 261

Upper Rogue
River Valley
page 251

Crater Lake
National Park
page 265

Grants Pass
page 253

Medford
page 247

Ashland
page 242

OREGON

SOUTHERN OREGON

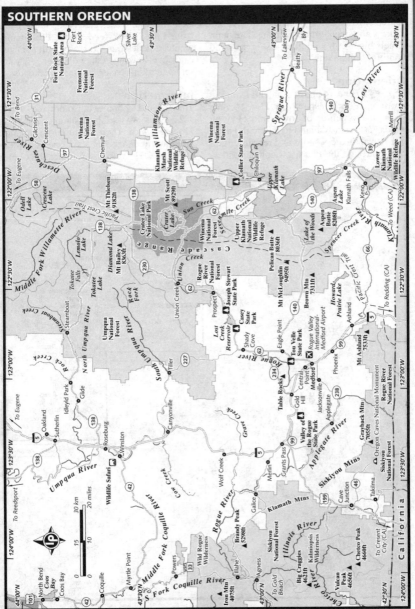

Park winds along Ashland Creek above the center of town and is filled with swans, picnickers and declaiming thespians. The main streets buzz with well-heeled shoppers and youthful bohemians.

Orientation

I-5 exits 19 and 14 access Ashland from the north and south respectively. Hwy 99 runs through the center of town, and Hwy 66 winds east from Ashland to Klamath Falls.

Festival theaters, shops and restaurants all cluster around the Plaza, a triangular pedes-trian zone near the junction of East Main and Oak Sts. On the back side of the Plaza, paths from Lithia Park feed into Calle Guana-juanto, a pedestrian causeway with bars and cafes overlooking Ashland Creek. Artisans set up market here on summer weekends.

Information

The Ashland Chamber of Commerce (☎ 541-482-3486, www.ashlandchamber.com) is at 110 E Main St. There's also an information booth at the Plaza that stays open on weekends. The OSF Welcome & Education Center

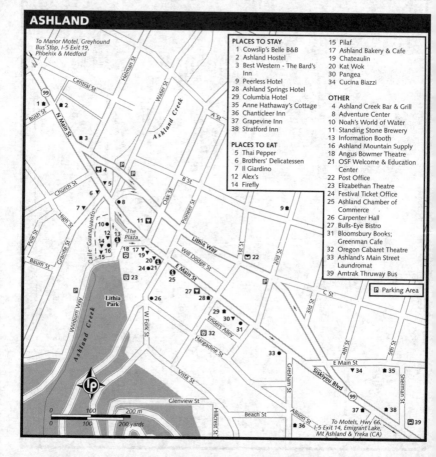

ASHLAND

To Manor Motel, Greyhound
Bus Stop, I-5 Exit 19,
Phoenix & Medford

PLACES TO STAY
1 Cowslip's Belle B&B
2 Ashland Hostel
3 Best Western - The Bard's Inn
9 Peerless Hotel
28 Ashland Springs Hotel
29 Columbia Hotel
35 Anne Hathaway's Cottage
36 Chanticleer Inn
37 Grapevine Inn
38 Stratford Inn

PLACES TO EAT
5 Thai Pepper
6 Brothers' Delicatessen
7 Il Giardino
12 Alex's
14 Firefly
15 Pilaf
17 Ashland Bakery & Cafe
19 Chateaulin
20 Kat Wok
30 Pangea
34 Cucina Biazzi

OTHER
4 Ashland Creek Bar & Grill
8 Adventure Center
10 Noah's World of Water
11 Standing Stone Brewery
13 Information Booth
16 Ashland Mountain Supply
18 Angus Bowmer Theatre
21 OSF Welcome & Education Center
22 Post Office
23 Elizabethan Theatre
24 Festival Ticket Office
25 Ashland Chamber of Commerce
26 Carpenter Hall
27 Bulls-Eye Bistro
31 Bloomsbury Books; Greenman Cafe
32 Oregon Cabaret Theatre
33 Ashland's Main Street Laundromat
39 Amtrak Thruway Bus

P Parking Area

To Motels, Hwy 66,
I-5 Exit 14, Emigrant Lake,
Mt Ashland & Yreka (CA)

W www.osfashland.org), 76 N Main, behind the ticket office on Pioneer & Main Sts, has helpful information on festival productions and events.

The Southern Oregon Reservation Center ☎ 541-488-1011, 800-547-8052, W www.sorc com) is helpful if you don't want to make numerous calls for tickets and lodging.

Open late, Bloomsbury Books (☎ 541-488-0029), 290 E Main St, is a great independent bookstore with a mezzanine coffee shop. The *Ashland Daily Tidings* is distributed six days a week. Jefferson Public Radio is heard at 90.1 FM and 89.1 FM. Ashland's post office is at 120 N 1st and the Main Street Laundromat (☎ 541-482-8042) is at 370 E Main St.

Lithia Park

Swans glide through Lithia Park, which is perfect for a shady picnic or for plowing through that Shakespearean tragedy you avoided reading in college. The park is a venue for concerts and events in the summer, and in the winter, there's an outdoor ice-skating rink.

Schneider Museum of Art

Exhibits at Southern Oregon University's art museum (☎ 541-552-6245, W www.sou .edu/sma, 1250 Siskiyou Blvd; admission free; open Tues-Sat 11am-4pm, first Fri of each month 10am-7pm) are quite impressive and are centered on contemporary American artists.

Oregon Shakespeare Festival

Highly respected and wildly popular, the OSF repertoire is rooted in Shakespearean and Elizabethan drama, but also features revivals and contemporary theater from around the world.

As a young town, Ashland was included in the Methodist Church's cultural education program, called the Chautauqua Series. By the 1930s, one of the venues, Chautauqua Hall, had deteriorated to a dilapidated wooden shell. Angus Bowmer, a drama professor at the local college, noted the resemblance of the roofless structure to drawings of Shakespeare's Globe Theatre.

William Shakespeare

He then convinced the town to sponsor two performances of Shakespeare's plays and a boxing match (the Bard would have approved) as part of its 1935 Fourth of July celebration. The plays proved a great success, and the Oregon Shakespeare Festival was off and running.

Productions run February through October in three theaters near Main and Pioneer Sts: the outdoor **Elizabethan Theatre** (open June to October), the **Angus Bowmer Theatre** and the intimate **New Theatre**. There are no Monday performances.

Performances are sold out months in advance. Often, the only chance for tickets is to wait at the box office (☎ *541-482-4331, 15 S Pioneer St; tickets $28-47; open 9:30am-8pm or 8:30pm Tues-Sun, 9:30am-5pm Mon early Feb-Oct*) for unclaimed tickets, which are released at 9:30am and 6pm (12pm for matinees). You can also wait around for scalpers. Use the computer at the OSF Welcome Center to check availability online at W www.osfashland.org.

Tours of the festival theaters (adult/youth $10/7.50) are booked months in advance and are available only to ticket holders.

The Oregon Shakespeare Festival Institute (☎ *541-488-5406; cost $75-1050*) offers a number of educational seminars for students, educators and everyday theatergoers. Tickets are usually included in the fee, and discount lodging in the dorms at Southern Oregon University is often offered.

Check the OSF Welcome Center for other daily happenings, which may include scholarly lectures and play readings ($6-6.50), concerts ($8.50-10), pre-show performance art and informal park talks with theater-company members. The mid-June opening of the Elizabethan Theatre is the impetus for the Feast of Will, celebrated with a dinner party in Lithia Park ($12). Purchase tickets for all OSF events at the box office.

The Shakespeare courses offered by Southern Oregon University's Elderhostel program (☎ 541-552-6378) are popular with people 55 and older.

Activities

Powdery snow is abundant at **Mt Ashland Ski Resort** (☎ 541-482-2897, 541-482-2754 snow report, **W** www.mtashland.com), 16 miles southwest on 7533-foot Mt Ashland. Rent winter sports equipment from **Ashland Mountain Supply** (☎ 541-488-2749, 31 N Main St). Or, rent a bike ($10) and explore the countryside on the Bear Valley Greenway bike path.

Noah's World of Water (☎ 541-488-2811, 800-858-2811, **W** www.noahsrafting.com, 53 N Main St) and the **Adventure Center** (☎ 541-488-2819, 800-444-2819, **W** www.rafting tours.com, 40 N Main St) both offer rafting trips on the Rogue River ($70-120).

Places to Stay

On summer evenings, thousands converge on Ashland to see the plays, so making reservations is absolutely necessary. For easy room-finding, contact the **Southern Oregon Reservation Center** (☎ 541-488-1011, 800-547-8052, **W** www.sorc.com) or the **Ashland B&B Clearinghouse** (☎ 541-488-0338, 800-944-0329, **W** www.abbnet.com).

Prices below reflect the high season; rates can drop by half in the off season.

Camping The following are the closest campgrounds near boater happy Emigrant Lake.

Glenyan Campground (☎ 541-488-1785, 5310 Hwy 66) Tents/hookups $17.50/22. There are a few tent sites at this shady RV campground 4 miles out of Ashland nea Emigrant Lake. Reservations are advised.

Emigrant Lake RV Park (☎ 541-774-8183, 5 miles east of Ashland, off Hwy 66 Tents/hookups $14/20. Popular for its waterslide, this new RV campground is locate at Jackson County Park.

Hostels This hostel is the cheapest place to stay in town.

Ashland Hostel (☎ 541-482-9217, 150 N Main St) Dorm beds $18. Downtown theaters are just blocks away from this busy place which has 50 dorm beds and not enough bathrooms. Avoid the so-called private rooms, which the staff must walk through to get to their own living spaces.

B&Bs If paying top dollar for an antique-filled room and a fancy breakfast appeals to you, you're in luck. Ashland has about 30 B&Bs, most in fine old homes with two or three rooms. Use a reservation service to shop the options, or try one of the following:

Anne Hathaway's Cottage (☎ 541-488-1050, 800-643-4434, 586 E Main St) Rooms $111-170. Anne Hathaway's is a fancifully named old boarding house with six rooms.

Cowslip's Belle B&B (☎ 541-488-2901, 800-888-6819, **W** www.cowslip.com, 159 N Main) Rooms $127-175. It's a short walk to the Plaza from this 1913 Craftsman bungalow with five lovely guest rooms.

Grape Vine Inn (☎ 541-482-7944, 800-500-8463, **W** www.thegrapevineinn.com, 486 Siskiyou Blvd) Rooms $122-174. Relax in a trellised garden at this distinctive home, which offers three guest rooms south of downtown.

Peerless Hotel (☎ 541-488-1082, 800-460-8758, **W** www.mind.net/peerless, 243 4th St) Rooms $133-223. Claw-foot bathtubs and Jacuzzis are features of this lavish European-style hotel.

Chanticleer Inn (☎ 541-482-1919, 800-898-1950, **W** www.ashland-bed-breakfast.com, 120 Gresham St) Rooms $138-207. Chanticleer is another Craftsman-style home, with six rooms and an outdoor hot tub.

Hotels Inexpensive rooms are hard to come by, but there are a couple.

Ashland Motel (☎ 541-482-2561, 800-460-8858, 1145 Siskiyou Blvd) Singles/doubles $51/53. It's a bit drab, but rooms here are Ashland's cheapest.

Rooms are cheaper in nearby Medford or Phoenix.

Phoenix Motel (☎ 541-535-1555, 510 N Main St) Rooms $40/44. This motel is clean and has a pool.

Prices at the following often dip from mid-range into the budget range during the off-season.

Timbers Motel (☎ 541-482-4242, 1450 Ashland St) Singles/doubles $66/72. Timbers is south of downtown, about a half mile from the theaters.

Columbia Hotel (☎ 541-482-3726, 800-718-2530, W www.columbiahotel.com, 262½ E Main St) Rooms $68-111. The cheapest rooms have shared bathrooms at this European-style hotel, which is just one block from the theaters.

The following two 1940s-style motels have been transformed into quaint cottages that are pleasantly refurbished and landscaped with herbs. Some units have full kitchens:

Manor Motel (☎ 541-488-2246, 476 N Main St) Rooms without/with kitchens $69/84. The Manor offers a peaceful, garden setting.

The Palm (☎ 541-482-2636, 877-482-2635, W www.palmmotel.com, 1065 Siskiyou Blvd) Rooms $84-122. Rooms here are slightly fancier, with antiques and an outdoor pool.

Cedarwood Inn (☎ 541-488-2000, 800-547-4141, 1801 Siskiyou Blvd) Rooms $83. On the south end of town is this comfortable mid-range motel with two pools and a Jacuzzi.

Windmill Inn of Ashland (☎ 541-482-8310, 800-547-4747, W www.windmillinns.com, 2525 Ashland St) Rooms from $96. The resortlike Windmill Inn, by I-5 exit 14, has a pool, exercise facilities and free shuttles to the airport and theaters.

These top-end hotels are all a stone's throw from the Plaza.

Best Western The Bard's Inn (☎ 541-482-0049, 132 N Main St) Singles/doubles $114/129. This hotel takes up several blocks near the Plaza.

Stratford Inn (☎ 541-488-2151, 800-547-4741, 555 Siskiyou Blvd) Singles/doubles $122/127. Stratford Inn is within walking distance of the theaters.

Ashland Springs Hotel (☎ 541-488-1700, W www.ashlandspringshotel.com, 212 E Main St) Rooms $147-169. High tea is the order of the day at this renovated historic landmark.

Places to Eat

Finding a place to eat in Ashland can be overwhelming – the downtown area must have more restaurants than anywhere else in the Pacific Northwest. Ashland is the only place in Oregon to levy a restaurant tax (5%).

Ashland Bakery & Cafe (☎ 541-482-2117, 38 E Main St). Entrees $5. Breakfast is the order of the day. Pizza and gourmet sandwiches are served here as well.

Greenman Cafe (☎ 541-488-0029), 290 E Main St) Entrees under $5. Soup and burritos make cheap eats at this cafe in Bloomsbury Books.

Pilaf (☎ 541-488-7898, 10 Calle Guanajuato) Entrees $5. Inexpensive Mediterranean meals are served here along Ashland Creek.

Pangea (☎ 541-552-1630, 272 E Main St) Lunch $6. Sandwiches and wraps are a good value here.

The Plaza forms the core of Ashland's restaurant scene, with eateries also spilling north and south along Main St.

Brothers' Delicatessen (☎ 541-482-9671, 95 N Main St) Breakfast $7. Breakfast is the thing to order at this New York–style kosher deli.

Il Giardino (☎ 541-488-0816, 5 Granite St) Entrees $10. This place is a bit upmarket, with Italian dining on the deck.

Thai Pepper (☎ 541-482-8058, 84 N Main St) Entrees $11-15. This is Ashland's favorite for fiery Asian cooking, with tables overlooking Ashland Creek.

Kat Wok (☎ 503-482-0787, 62 E Main St) Sushi $3-7, entrees $12-17. Dining is casual at this stylish pan-Asian sushi bar and nightclub.

Alex's (☎ 541-482-8818, 35 N Main St) Entrees $13-25. Alex's lofty 3rd-floor dining room has great views of the Plaza.

Ordering lighter plates and appetizers is a good strategy for enjoying the ambiance of fancier restaurants on the cheap. Call ahead for reservations at the following places.

Chateaulin (☎ *541-482-2264, 50 E Main St*) Entrees $15-28. Topflight French cuisine is served here in an attractive wood-lined dining room.

Firefly (☎ *541-488-3212, 23 N Main St*) Entrees $18-29. Cuisine is bold and adventurous here, with eclectic meals taking the form of abstraction.

Cucina Biazzi (☎ *541-488-3739, 568 E Main St*) Fixed price meals $22-30. Intimate Cucina Biazzi has garden dining and four-course Italian meals.

Entertainment
Obviously, theater's the thing in Ashland, but after a day with the Bard, who can blame an actor or spectator for being thirsty?

Chateaulin (☎ *541-482-2264, 50 E Main St*) The back bar is popular for a quiet drink with the after-theater crowd.

Ashland Creek Bar & Grill (☎ *541-482-4131, 92½ N Main St*) There's a pleasant deck overlooking the creek here.

Standing Stone Brewery (☎ *541-482-2448, 101 Oak St*) There's jazz here three nights a week.

Bulls-Eye Bistro (☎ *541-488-1700, 212 E Main St*) This fun lounge features three nights of jazz, bluegrass and folk.

Kat Wok (☎ *503-482-0787, 62 E Main*) This trendy dance club has a lively bar scene.

The well-respected **Oregon Cabaret Theatre** (☎ *541-488-2902*, W *www.oregon cabaret.com, 1st & Hargadine Sts*) is a worthwhile sideline to Shakespeare Festival performances.

Getting There & Around
For flights, see Medford's Getting There & Around section, later. Cascade Airport Shuttle (☎ 541-488-1998) services the airport from Ashland for $12-16 per person; reservations are required.

Greyhound links Ashland to Portland ($46 one way) and San Francisco ($50) five to six times daily. The stop at Mr C's Market (☎ 541-482-8803, 2073 N Hwy 99) is 3 miles

north by the freeway exit. From there, you can catch the No 10 bus into town or call a taxi for a ride.

Amtrak Thruway buses link Ashland to Eugene ($21) daily for rail connections to Portland and Seattle. The stop is right downtown at Siskiyou Blvd and Sherman St.

RVTD (☎ 541-779-2877) buses run along Siskiyou Blvd (Hwy 99) on weekdays, with the No 10 bus continuing to Medford (fare $1). For a taxi, call Yellow Cab (☎ 541-482-3065).

MEDFORD & AROUND
Famous for fruit trees, especially pears, Medford (population 62,030) is southern Oregon's largest city and is fast-growing with retirees. In April, the valley is bathed in pink and white blossoms. Ashland, Crater Lake, Oregon Caves National Monument and the Rogue River valley are all conveniently located near Medford. Aside from some inexpensive motels and the **Southern Oregon History Center** (☎ *541-773-6536*, W *www.sohs.org, 106 N Central Ave; admission free; open 9am-5pm Mon-Fri)*, which is noted for its collection of period photographs, Medford has few attractions.

Orientation & Information
Medford is 12 miles north of Ashland on I-5. Hwy 62 (Crater Lake Hwy), off I-5 exit 30, heads northeast to Crater Lake National Park. Hwy 99 passes vapidly through downtown on Riverside and Central Aves, connecting Medford's north and south freeway exits.

The Medford Visitors & Convention Bureau (☎ 541-779-4847, 800-469-6307, W www.visitmedford.org) is downtown at 101 E 8th St, but the visitor information center (☎ 541-776-4021) next to Harry & David's Country Village at I-5 exit 27 is more convenient and helpful. The Rogue River National Forest supervisor's office (☎ 541-858-2200, W www.fs.fed.us/r6/rogue) is at 333 W 8th St, as is the post office. Michael's Cleaner & laundry, in the Medford Center strip mall on E Jackson St, is across from Hawthorne Park and convenient to downtown.

OREGON

Activities

Shady **Hawthorne Park**, alongside Bear Creek, has an outdoor pool and is a pleasant place to unwind or escape the heat. In winter, stop by the **Rogue Ski Shop** (☎ 541-772-8047, 309 E Jackson St) to rent cross-country skis on the way to Crater Lake.

Now plant and wildlife preserves, **Table Rocks** are vestiges of the area's volcanic past and figure prominently in local Native American and white-settlement history. Spring is the best time for **hiking** in the grasslands at the top of these 800-foot mesas, 7 miles north of Medford. From downtown, follow Riverside Ave (Hwy 99) north, and turn right onto Table Rock Rd just past the junction for Hwy 62. The road forks after Tou Velle State Park, where you'll need to decide which rock to climb. It's 5.4 miles roundtrip to Lower Table Rock; a steeper path reaches Upper Table Rock in 1.4 miles. Watch for turkey vultures and red-tailed hawks. Rattlesnakes

are also native here. The Medford Bureau of Land Management (BLM; ☎ 541-770-2200, 3040 Biddle Rd) has information.

Tou Velle State Park, on the Rogue River near Table Rocks, is popular for swimming and picnicking.

Medford's most famous fruit growers are brothers Harry and David Holmes. In the early 20th century, their family orchard exported pears to grand European hotels. But when the Depression put an end to that market, the two brothers decided to start a now wildly successful fruit mail-order business. Their produce-and-gift **outlet store** (☎ 541-776-2277, 1314 Center Dr, off I-5 exit 27) is a great place to stock up on Oregon-made food products and fresh fruit. Visitors may tour the nearby fruit-packing operation (☎ 877-322-8000; cost $5; tours Mon-Fri) with advance reservations.

At the corporate headquarters, a half-mile south along a busy highway, is the

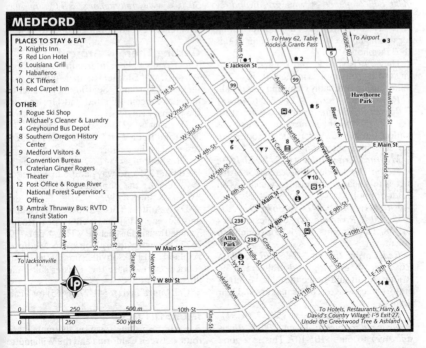

MEDFORD

PLACES TO STAY & EAT
2 Knights Inn
5 Red Lion Hotel
6 Louisiana Grill
7 Habañeros
10 CK Tiffens
14 Red Carpet Inn

OTHER
1 Rogue Ski Shop
3 Michael's Cleaner & Laundry
4 Greyhound Bus Depot
8 Southern Oregon History Center
9 Medford Visitors & Convention Bureau
11 Craterian Ginger Rogers Theater
12 Post Office & Rogue River National Forest Supervisor's Office
13 Amtrak Thruway Bus; RVTD Transit Station

Jackson & Perkins Test & Display Gardens, one of the nation's largest commercial rose growers. There are no facilities, but nobody minds if visitors stop by to smell the roses.

Places to Stay

A number of campgrounds right off I-5 were developed with interstate travelers in mind.

Holiday RV Park (☎ 541-535-2183, 800-452-7970, 201 Fern Valley Rd) and *Pear Tree RV Park* (☎ 541-535-4445, 800-645-7332, 300 Pear Tree Lane) sit on opposite sides of I-5 exit 24, south of Medford (RV sites $23-26).

Valley of the Rogue State Park (☎ 541-582-3128, reservations 800-452-5687, 3792 N River Rd) Tents/hookups/yurts $15/17/33. Handy for interstate travelers, this riverside campground is right off I-5 exit 45B, between Medford and Grants Pass.

Medford's most famous B&B is in the country between Medford and Jacksonville.

Under the Greenwood Tree (☎ 541-776-0000, 800-766-8099, Ⓦ www.greenwoodtree.com, 3045 Bellinger Lane) Rooms $132-170. A 10-acre orchard makes a beautiful setting for five highly acclaimed guest rooms at this 1862 farmhouse.

Hwy 99 (Riverside and Central Aves) is lined with grotty motels in the $40 range. The following are certifiably clean and good deals.

Royal Crest Motel (☎ 541-772-6144, 411 E Barnett Rd) Singles/doubles $46/51. At I-5 exit 27, this motel is next to a busy gas station, but the newly remodeled rooms are perfectly pleasant and a great deal.

Medford Travelodge (☎ 541-773-1579, 954 Alba Dr) Singles/doubles $50/58. Also nice is this nearby Travelodge, which has an outdoor pool.

Knights Inn (☎ 541-773-3676, 800-531-2655, 500 N Riverside Ave) Singles/doubles $45/48. The Knights Inn is convenient to downtown.

Red Carpet Inn (☎ 541-772-6133, 525 S Riverside Ave) Singles/doubles $50/59. Rooms at this mid-range motel have refrigerators, microwaves, coffee makers and hair dryers.

Red Lion Hotel (☎ 541-779-5811, Ⓦ www.redlionmedford.com, 200 N Riverside Ave) Rooms $101-107. This is a good

upscale lodging choice and features a swimming pool and suite-style rooms.

Places to Eat

CK Tiffens (☎ 541-779-0480, 226 E Main St) Entrees under $5. Breakfast & lunch only. House-baked breads make for great sandwiches here.

Habañero's (☎ 541-779-9770, 142 N Front St) Meals $6-12. There's patio seating at this Mexican restaurant near the railroad.

Louisiana Grill (☎ 541-770-1114, 17 W 4th St) Meals $8-15. Fried alligator leads the menu at this Cajun restaurant, which is housed in an old rail depot.

McGrath's Fish House (☎ 541-732-1732, 68 E Stewart Ave) Entrees $10. Seafood and steak dinners here are about as fancy as Medford gets.

Entertainment

Craterian Ginger Rogers Theater (☎ 541-779-3000, Ⓦ www.craterian.org, 23 S Central Ave) The Craterian brings top-notch performances to southern Oregon from October to May.

Getting There & Around

The Rogue Valley International-Medford Airport, off Biddle Rd in Medford, has flights to Portland, Seattle, San Francisco and Los Angeles. United and Horizon are the primary carriers.

Hertz (☎ 541-773-4293), Avis (☎ 541-773-3003) and Budget (☎ 541-773-7023) are represented at the airport.

Greyhound (☎ 541-779-2103) buses to Portland ($31 one way) and San Francisco ($40) depart the depot at 212 Bartlett St five to six times daily.

Daily Amtrak Thruway buses to Ashland and Eugene ($19) – as well as local Rogue Valley Transit District (RVTD; ☎ 541-779-2877, Ⓦ www.rvtd.org) buses to Medford, Ashland and Jacksonville (fare $1, weekday service only) – share the transfer station at 8th and Front Sts.

Call Metro Taxi (☎ 541-773-6665) for a cab.

JACKSONVILLE

A gold-prospecting town on the main stage route between California and the Willamette

Valley, Jacksonville (population 2270), 6 miles west of Medford on Hwy 238, is the oldest settlement in southern Oregon and is a National Historic Landmark town filled with pretty red-bricked buildings dating back to the 1880s. It's also home of the Britt Festival, an outdoor musical experience that attracts world-class performers (see National Historic District, below).

You can visit the Jacksonville Chamber of Commerce (☎ 541-899-8118, W www.jack sonvilleoregon.org) at 185 N Oregon St.

RVTD bus No 30 reaches Jacksonville from Medford on weekdays (fare $1).

National Historic District

The **Jacksonville Museum** (☎ 541-773-6536, *206 N 5th St; adult/senior & child $3/2; open 10am-5pm Wed-Sat, noon-5pm Sun*), in the former county courthouse (1883), is a good place to begin a tour of the town – ask for a walking tour map. The museum contains a tribute to photographer Peter Britt, the first to take pictures of Crater Lake. Adjacent is a **children's museum**, in the old county jail. Peter Britt's mansion once sat in the lovely **gardens** at S 1st and W Pine Sts.

At the 1873 **Beekman House** (*470 E California St; adult/senior & child $3/2; open Wed-Sun 1pm-5pm Memorial Day-Labor Day*), costumed docents portray the lives of the Beekman family. Cornelius Beekman was the founder of Oregon's second bank, which still stands at the corner of California and 3rd Sts.

Another admirable Victorian residence, not open for tours, is the ornate **Nunan House** at 635 N Oregon St, bought from a catalog and assembled here in 1892.

Narrated **trolley tours** provide a good historical overview and run Friday to Sunday from June to September.

In addition to its reputation as an open-air museum, Jacksonville is home to the acclaimed **Britt Festival** (☎ 541-773-6077, 800-882-7488, W *www.brittfest.org; June-Sept*), a summer-long series of outdoor music performances. Tickets go quickly.

Places to Stay & Eat

Jacksonville contains southern Oregon's best restaurants and a number of quaint B&Bs. Reservations are strongly recommended.

Cantrall-Buckley Campground (☎ 541-776-7001, 8 miles west on Hwy 238) Sites

The State of Jefferson

The southern counties of Oregon and the northern counties of California, isolated from the major power and population centers of their respective states, have long been home to strong secessionist movements. While legislation to create a 'State of Shasta' was introduced twice in California in the early 1850s, the most serious attempt at secession occurred in 1854, when a public meeting was held in Jacksonville to gauge support for a separate 'Jackson Territory.' The initiative lost steam after the outbreak of the Rogue River War in 1855. Plans for a new state, this time called Siskiyou, emerged again in 1857 and 1909.

The most memorable secessionist movement occurred in 1941. The State of Jefferson officially seceded from California and Oregon on Thursday, November 27, and it was planned that the territory would secede every Thursday thereafter. In Yreka, residents set up a border patrol on Hwy 99 to interrogate travelers crossing the new state line and to circulate copies of the state's declaration of independence. A newly appointed governor was officially inaugurated at the Yreka Courthouse on December 3. The occasion was celebrated by a torchlight parade, and border patrol stations passed out windshield stickers that read, 'I have visited Jefferson, the 49th State.'

The hoopla captured national attention, and a journalist received a Pulitzer Prize for his reporting of the event. Unfortunately for the State of Jefferson, the nation soon had more pressing news to attend to: the bombing of Pearl Harbor. The State of Jefferson again took a back seat to more serious considerations.

$10. There's riverside camping over the hill in Ruch.

McCully House Inn (☎ 541-899-1942, 800-367-1942, W www.mccullyhouseinn.com, 240 E California St) Singles/doubles $106/132. Dinners $11-17. This is one of Jacksonville's earliest homes, built for the town's first doctor. Upstairs are three guest rooms, and downstairs, there's an intimate, antique-filled dining room.

Jacksonville Inn (☎ 541-899-1900, 800-321-9344, W www.jacksonvilleinn.com, 175 E California St) Rooms $127-238. Entrees $20, bistro menu $8-10. There are eight rooms filled with antiques and modern comforts at this 1863 hotel. The inn's dining room is one of the best in southern Oregon. A five-course dinner with stuffed hazelnut chicken is $27.

Gogi's Restaurant (☎ 541-899-8699, 235 W Main St) Entrees $17-20. Dining is more intimate at Gogi's, near the Britt Festival stage. Call ahead to order picnic boxes for the festival ($6-10).

UPPER ROGUE RIVER VALLEY

From Medford, Hwy 62 (Crater Lake Hwy) follows the Rogue River northeast to its headwaters near Crater Lake. Known for rafting, the Rogue River is also noted for some of the best steelhead and trout fishing in Oregon. Although the real action is far down-river, in the Wild Rogue Wilderness, most people find the gentle bumps and grinds of the section between William L Jess Dam and Shady Cove adventurous enough. In summer, the river is clotted with rafts and kayaks.

Past Shady Cove, about 17 miles north, the valley walls close in, and the silvery river quickens and channels a gorge through thick lava flows. Dense forests robe the steep mountainsides, surrounding sparsely populated Prospect and Union Creek with un-crowded hiking trails, quiet camping and rustic lodging convenient to Crater Lake.

For information, contact the Upper Rogue Regional Tourism Alliance (☎ 541-878-8216, 888-811-3171, W www.upperrogue.org).

Shady Cove & Around

The slightly scrappy-looking town of Shady Cove is a convenient center for raft rentals

($50). Among some of the options are **Raft The Rogue** (☎ 541-878-3623, 800-797-7238, 21171 Hwy 62); **Raging Waters Raft Rental** (☎ 541-878-4000, 21873 Hwy 62); and **Rogue Rafting Company** (☎ 541-878-2585, 888-236-3096, 7725 Rogue River Dr). All offer free shuttles to the launch site.

Upriver from Shady Cove, at the turnoff for William L Jess Dam, is **McGregor Park**, a popular raft put-in and picnic spot. An interpretive center here focuses on the history, wildlife and geology of the Rogue. Up by the dam is the **Cole M Rivers Fish Hatchery**, one of the West's largest.

Fishing is legendary on the Rogue River – Zane Grey, Herbert Hoover, Jack London and Teddy Roosevelt were early champions of the river. Salmon and steelhead fishing is especially good in the stretch of river above Tou Velle State Park to the dam, with frequent parks offering easy river access.

Fishing and boating are the focus of the area's decidedly resort-like campgrounds. Even the hotels here cater primarily to anglers.

Fly Casters RV Park (☎ 541-878-2749, 21655 Hwy 62) RV sites $21-33. One of the best RV parks is right in Shady Cove. River-side sites are available.

Rogue Elk Campground (☎ 541-776-7001, 5 miles east of Shady Cove on Hwy 62) Sites $16-18. Upriver from Shady Cove is this roadside park with showers and a raft-inflating station.

Joseph Stewart State Park (☎ 541-560-3334, 800-452-5687 reservations, 35251 Hwy 62) Tents/hookups $14/15. About 8 miles from both Prospect and Shady Cove is this well-manicured park with several hundred campsites and a busy boat launch on Lost Creek Reservoir.

Royal Coachman Motel (☎ 541-878-2481, 21906 Hwy 62) Singles/doubles $41/46. This perfunctory riverside motel in Shady Cove has some cabins and kitchenettes.

Here are some food options:

Shady Cove Natural Foods (☎ 541-878-7680, 21850 Hwy 62) Entrees $3. Order soups, wraps and smoothies from the deli counter.

Two Pines Smokehouse (☎ 541-878-7463, 21331 Hwy 62) Entrees $6-12. Western artifacts from the late 19th century adorn this touristy Tex-Mex restaurant, which is good for pie.

Bel Di's (☎ *541-878-2010, 21900 Hwy 62*) Entrees $14-16. This is one of the area's best restaurants, with linen-clad tables overlooking the Rogue River.

Prospect & Union Creek

The upper reaches of the river, roughly from Prospect to Union Creek, are in the Rogue River National Forest. From Shady Cove, it's 23 miles to Prospect and another 12 miles to Union Creek, which lies at the junction for Crater Lake. For campground and trail information, contact the Prospect Ranger Station (☎ 541-560-3400, ☒ www .fs.fed.us/r6/rogue), at 47201 Hwy 62 in Prospect.

Hiking A mile south of Prospect on Mill Creek Dr is a short trail to a view of 173-foot **Mill Creek Falls**. A side trail leads beneath the bridge to the **Avenue of Giant Boulders**, where the Rogue River crashes through rocky cataracts.

The **Upper Rogue River Trail** follows the river for 47 miles between Prospect and Crater Lake National Park. A number of trailheads off Hwy 62 easily lend themselves to short day hikes. Upriver from Prospect, it's 3.2 miles down and back from the **Woodruff Bridge picnic area** on USFS Rd 68 to the **Mammoth Pines** old-growth forest and **Takelma Gorge**.

Trails on both sides of the river between Natural Bridge and the Rogue River Gorge, a mile on either side of Union Creek, form two 2½-mile loop hikes. At **Natural Bridge**, the Rogue River borrows a lava tube and goes underground for 200 feet. Upriver is the magical **Rogue River Gorge**, where a narrow, turbulent section of river cuts a sheer-walled cleft into a lava flow. Combine both sites for an 8-mile hike.

Places to Stay & Eat USFS campgrounds line Hwy 62 between Prospect and Union Creek. *Mill Creek* and *River Bridge* campgrounds (sites $5) are upriver from Prospect and have no water. You can get some water

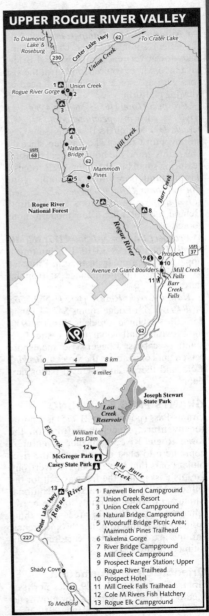

UPPER ROGUE RIVER VALLEY

1 Farewell Bend Campground
2 Union Creek Resort
3 Union Creek Campground
4 Natural Bridge Campground
5 Woodruff Bridge Picnic Area;
  Mammoth Pines Trailhead
6 Takelma Gorge
7 River Bridge Campground
8 Mill Creek Campground
9 Prospect Ranger Station; Upper
  Rogue River Trailhead
10 Prospect Hotel
11 Mill Creek Falls Trailhead
12 Cole M Rivers Fish Hatchery
13 Rogue Elk Campground

OREGON

at *Union Creek* and *Farewell Bend* camp-grounds (sites $10-12), near Union Creek. At *Natural Bridge Campground* (sites $5, no water), south of Union Creek, a short hike downriver reaches the Natural Bridge lava tube, where you can look up at the visitors who are stuck behind the fenced-off viewing platform.

Prospect Hotel (☎ 541-560-3664, 800-944-6490, W www.prospecthotel.com, 391 Mill Creek Dr) Motel/B&B rooms $64/95. A stopover for Crater Lake travelers since the 1890s, this grand old hotel is a real treasure, featuring small but charming B&B rooms, a wraparound porch and a notably good *dining room (dinner entrees $17-28, seasonal hours);* reservations are required. Behind the hotel are a few modern motel rooms.

Prospect Cafe (☎ 541-560-1177, 311 Mill Creek Dr) Entrees $3-10. Elk hunting is apparently a popular pastime in Prospect, as shown by the abundance of trophies here.

Union Creek Resort (☎ 541-560-3565, 56484 Hwy 62) Lodge rooms $42-53, cabins $58-101. At Union Creek is this old 1930s lodge with small rooms and rustic, free-standing cabins. Logger-style meals are served until 6pm across the street at *Beckie's Cafe*, and there's an ice-cream parlor next door.

GRANTS PASS & AROUND

Grants Pass (population 21,775) is a portal to adventure, especially rafting, on the lower Rogue River. Armchair adventurers come here to blast up and down the river on jet boats that leave from the riverfront. Grants Pass is also the freeway exit for the Illinois Valley's Oregon Caves National Monument, which accounts for the prevalent caveman motif in the area – everything from sports teams to philanthropic organizations are named after cartoony, club-toting cave-dwellers.

Orientation & Information

Grant's Pass lies on I-5, 29 miles north of Medford. I-5 exit 58 accesses downtown and the riverfront on 6th St (Hwy 99) before

splitting into US 199 (the Redwood Hwy) and the Rogue River Hwy.

The Grants Pass Visitors & Convention Bureau (☎ 541-476-7717, 800-547-5927, W www.visitgrantspass.org) is right off I-5 exit 58 at 1995 NW Vine St. The Siskiyou National Forest supervisor's office (☎ 541-471-6500, W www.fs.fed.us/r6/siskiyou), at 200 Greenfield Rd, is handy if you're headed for the Kalmiopsis Wilderness.

The main post office is at 132 NW 6th St. Sunshine Laundry (☎ 541-479-9975) is at 870 NE D St. For emergencies, go to Three Rivers Community Hospital (☎ 541-479-7531), at 1505 NW Washington Blvd.

Rafting & Fishing

Grants Pass and the downriver community of Merlin are launch points for rafting, kayaking and fishing trips on the Rogue River. There's a variety of trip options, from shooting rapids on a multi-day excursion through the Wild Rogue Wilderness (see the next section) to an idle afternoon float. The Grants Pass Visitors Center & Convention Bureau has a full list of licensed outfitters. The following conduct half- or full-day float trips from Grants Pass ($50/70). **Orange Torpedo Trips** (☎ 541-479-5061, 800-635-2925) has white-water trips in inflatable kayaks. **Rogue Wilderness, Inc** (☎ 541-479-9554, 800-336-1647, W www.wildrogue.com) offers rafting trips, plus inflatable kayak and raft rentals ($30-60). **Ferron's Fun Trips** (☎ 541-474-2201, 800-404-2201, W www.roguefuntrips.com) provides inflatable kayak and raft rentals ($30-60) as well as trips downriver. Fishing tours are also available here.

If you're interested in fly-fishing instruction and guide service, you can try **Briggs Rogue River Guide Service** (☎ 541-479-1504) or **Geoff's Guide Service** (☎ 541-474-0602).

Special Events

The Josephine County Fair (☎ 541-479-3215) is held the third weekend of August.

The Jedediah Smith Mountain Man Rendezvous brings hatchet-throwing and musket-firing to Merlin's Sportsman Park

I-5 exit 61) over Labor Day weekend and culminates with a buffalo barbecue.

Places to Stay

Camping Southeast of Grants Pass, Hwy 99 leads to campsites at a number of RV resorts along the Rogue River.

Riverpark RV Resort (☎ 541-479-0046, 800-677-8857, 2956 Rogue River Hwy) Sites $22.50. Here, there are pleasant RV-oriented sites along the Rogue River.

There's more riverside camping downriver towards Galice at these Josephine County parks:

Whitehorse Park (☎ 541-474-5285, 6 miles west on Lower River Rd) Sites $12-17. The closest tent sites are at this campground, west on G St.

Indian Mary Park (☎ 541-474-5285, 7 miles west of Merlin on the Merlin-Galice Rd) Sites $12-17. Rafters are fond of this developed, parklike campground near Galice.

B&Bs Outside of Grants Pass are two especially nice B&Bs, both en route to the Rogue River canyon.

Pine Meadow Inn (☎ 541-471-6277, 800-554-0806, ⓦ www.pinemeadowinn.com, 1000 Crow Rd) Rooms $96-128. Extensive gardens and a pastoral setting make this a favorite B&B.

Wolf Creek Inn (☎ 541-866-2474, ⓦ www.wolfcreekinn.com, 20 miles north of Grants Pass at I-5 exit 76) Singles/doubles $59/80. A hotel since its opening in 1883, this historic stagecoach stop 20 miles north of Grants Pass was once the lodging choice of celebrities such as Jack London, Clark Gable and Mary Pickford. The restaurant is open for lunch and dinner.

Hotels The usual chain hotels abound at both freeway exits. Take I-5 exit 58 for the inexpensive motels along 6th & 7th Sts.

Parkway Lodge (☎ 541-476-4260, 1001 NE 6th St) Singles/doubles $34/38. This older motel is cheap and very basic.

Knights Inn (☎ 541-479-5595, 800-826-6835, 104 SE 7th St) Singles/doubles $42/44. The tidy Knights Inn offers a good value close to downtown.

GRANTS PASS

PLACES TO STAY
4 Parkway Lodge
5 Redwood Motel
9 Knights Inn
12 Riverside Inn

PLACES TO EAT
2 Matsukaze
6 Dutch Bros Coffee House
8 The Laughing Clam
10 Wild River Brewing & Pizza
11 River Rock Cafe; Hellgate Jet Boat Excursions

OTHER
1 Three Rivers Community Hospital
3 Enterprise
7 Post Office

To Siskiyou National Forest Supervisor's Office, Visitors & Convention Bureau, Motel 6, I-5 Exit 58, Merlin, Galice & Roseburg

OREGON

Motel 6 (☎ 541-474-1331, 1800 NE 7th St) Singles/doubles $56/63. Cool off in the pool at this comfortable motel at freeway exit 58.

Redwood Motel (☎ 541-476-0878, 815 NE 6th St) Singles/doubles $68/73. The Redwood is the nicest place on this strip.

Riverside Inn (☎ 541-476-6873, 800-334-4567, Ⓦ www.riverside-inn.com, 971 SE 6th St) Rooms without/with river view $77/111. At the end of 6th St is this sprawling conference center with balconied rooms overlooking the jet-boat dock on the Rogue River.

Resorts Fishing trips are offered as part of a package at the following riverside lodges:

Galice Resort (☎ 541-476-3818, Ⓦ www.galice.com, 11744 Galice Rd) Cabins $69, lodge rooms $90. This all-in-one restaurant, store, outfitter and lodging provider comprises the river settlement of Galice, 22 miles west of Grants Pass.

Morrison's Rogue River Lodge (☎ 541-476-3825, 800-826-1963, Ⓦ www.morrisonslodge.com, 8500 Galice Rd) Cabins $111-170 per person, meals included. Lodging is in nine river view cabins at this fancier resort between Galice and Merlin.

Weasku Inn Resort (☎ 541-471-8000, 800-493-2758, 5560 Rogue River Hwy) Lodge rooms $117-291, cabins $207-313. Head here for luxury lodging in a log-hewn fishing lodge along an uninspiring section of river; it's southeast of town on Hwy 99.

Places to Eat

Youthful *Dutch Bros Coffee House* (332 NW 6th St) has espresso, bagels and pastries. Granola, wraps and salads are available at the pleasant *River Rock Cafe* (966 NE 6th St), inside the jet-boat booking office.

Wild River Brewing & Pizza (☎ 541-471-7487, 595 NE E St) Entrees $6-10. Packed with vestiges of rafting culture, this lively brewery features pizza, burgers and calzones.

Matsukaze (☎ 541-479-2961, 1675 NE 7th St) Entrees $9-12. Matsukaze's Japanese favorites are well loved by locals.

The Laughing Clam (☎ 541-479-1110, 121 SW G St) Entrees $7-13. Grilled eggplant sandwiches are the specialty of this red-

bricked bistro. For dinner, there's fish an seafood.

Hamilton River House (☎ 541-479-393? 1936 Rogue River Hwy) Dinner $15. You ca relax at this restaurant, with patio dinin above the river.

Getting Around

Buses leave four times daily for Portlan ($30 one way) on Greyhound and once fo Eugene ($16) on Amtrak from the statio (☎ 541-476-4513), at 460 NE Agness Av near I-5 exit 55.

Rent a car from Budget (☎ 541-471-6311) 825 NE F St, or Enterprise (☎ 541-471 7800), 1325 NE 7th St. For a taxi, call Grant Pass Cab Co (☎ 541-476-6444).

WILD ROGUE WILDERNESS AREA

Famous for its turbulent Class IV rapids, the Rogue River departs civilization at the con fluence of Grave Creek and winds for 4(untamed miles through a remote, roadless canyon preserved within rugged BLM land and the Wild Rogue Wilderness.

From Grants Pass, take the I-5 Merlir exit north of town and follow the Galice Merlin Rd 15 miles to Galice, then continue 7 miles north to the Grave Creek boat ramp and trailhead.

Contact the BLM's Rand Visitors Center (☎ 541-479-3735, Ⓦ www.or.blm.gov/rand) 14335 Galice Rd, in Galice, for all recreation information. They also issue rafting permits, which are required to float the Rogue without an outfitter and are awarded by lottery in December and January. About 50% go unused and are returned to 'the pool,' where they're are available on a first-come, first-served basis by telephone starting in April.

This federally protected 'Wild & Scenic' portion of the Rogue is one of the most legendary white-water rivers in the USA. Not for amateurs, a typical rafting trip takes at least three days and costs upwards of $500. Hiring an outfitter is advised for all but the most experienced. **Rogue River Raft Trips** (☎ 541-476-3825, 800-826-1963, www.rogueriverraft.com), **Rogue Wilderness Inc** (☎ 541-479-9554, 800-336-1647, www.wildrogue.com) and **Sundance River Center** (☎ 888-777-7557, 541-479-8508, www.sundanceriver.com) are all good options.

Fishing-focused white-water trips are the specialty of **River Trips Unlimited** (☎ 541-779-0623, 800-460-3865, www.roguefishing.com).

The oft-neglected 40-mile **Rogue River Trail** parallels the river from Grave Creek to Illahe and is best hiked in spring or fall. Once a pack trail used to transport mail and supplies from Gold Beach, the trail follows a relatively easy grade through scrub oak and laurel past historic homesteads and cabins. The full hike takes five days, assuming you cover about 10 miles a day. Camps and lodges line the way, so it's easy to adjust your itinerary for shorter or longer days. A settlement at Marial divides the trail between Wild Rogue Wilderness and rugged BLM land. Be aware that black bears and poison oak are serious hazards to what is otherwise a relaxing and relatively easy trail.

A 7-mile roundtrip hike to **Whiskey Creek Cabin** from Grave Creek makes a good destination for day hikers.

Rustic lodges that operate along the banks of this roadless region are one of the novelties of the Rogue River. Lodging averages $75 per person and typically includes dinner and the next day's packed lunch; advance reservations are required. The lodges, starting upstream and going down, are: *Black Bar Lodge* (☎ 541-479-6507); *Marial Lodge* (☎ 541-474-4923, ext 7718); *Paradise Lodge* (☎ 541-247-6504); and *Half Moon Lodge* (☎ 541-247-6968).

Primitive campgrounds along the river serve the needs of both rafters and backpackers; the Rand Visitors Center has a map.

ILLINOIS RIVER VALLEY

The Illinois River valley, just shy of California, remains one of Oregon's most remote and neglected corners. While the Oregon Caves National Monument ought to keep the Illinois River valley in the forefront of tourism, the isolation of the area suits various kinds of utopian communes and back-to-the-earth idealists. Remoteness also suits the Kalmiopsis Wilderness, a preserve of rare plants coursed by the Illinois River in the rugged Siskiyou Mountains. The Illinois River, whose roily waters are colored an uncanny green from the outcrops of serpentinite through which it flows, is one of the west's most challenging white-water rivers, suitable only for experienced kayakers.

Cave Junction (population 1440), 28 miles south of Grants Pass on US 199 (Redwood Hwy), exists to serve the needs of tourists bound for the Oregon Caves, which lie 19 miles east on Hwy 46. Some of Oregon's best wineries are found en route to the caves. There's remarkable forest scenery along US 199 as it continues southwest to Crescent City, California.

The interagency Illinois Valley Visitor Information Center (☎ 541-592-2631, 201 Caves Hwy), at the Hwy 46 junction, is well stocked with information on local and regional travel, the Siskiyou National Forest and the Oregon Caves.

Oregon Caves National Monument

The Oregon Caves began as seafloor limestone deposits that were eventually hoisted into the Siskiyou Mountains. Molten rock forced its way up into rock faults to form marble, and acidified groundwater seeped through cracks to carve underground channels. Surface erosion eventually created an opening for air to enter, causing water to mineralize and create a myriad of formations such as cave popcorn, pearls, moonmilk, classic pipe organs, columns and stalactites.

The cave (there's only one) contains about 3 miles of chambers and a fast-moving stream (the River Styx), a handful of short nature trails and a beautiful old lodge – the Oregon Caves Chateau.

Guided **cave tours** (☎ 541-592-2100, www.nps.gov/orca; adult/child $7.50/5; various hours, closed Dec-Mar) run at least hourly and last 90 minutes. Dress warmly and be prepared to get slightly wet. Children

OREGON

Loners & Idealists

There's something about the mountains and valleys of the Illinois River that attracts loners and idealists. Gold prospectors were the first whites to settle in the region, but the thousands of hopefuls who flooded in left just as quickly when the gold ran out early in the 20th century.

Today, the Illinois River valley is known for two seemingly opposing social phenomena. In the 1960s, 'back-to-the-earth' utopians founded Takilma, a then-notorious hippie commune. The community still exists, but only a weathered sign stating 'Nuclear Free Zone' on the outskirts of Takilma gives any indication that this is anything more than an outpost of rural poverty. The other recent emigrants are backwood survivalists, whose compounds are meant to provide safety from Big Brother's many manifestations.

In some sort of fusion of these two social movements, the other activity in the valley is marijuana farming. The right climatic conditions, inaccessible tracts of public forest and underpopulation make this corner of Oregon one of the most noted marijuana-growing areas in the western USA.

under 42 inches tall are generally not allowed, but special (and free) cave tours are sometimes offered.

Would-be spelunkers can explore the cave's undeveloped cataracts on the new **off-trail cave tour** *(cost $25, starts at 10am mid-June-Sept)*. The four-hour tour is physically demanding (participants slither through small spaces and mud) and is not for the claustrophobic or children under 16. Call to confirm details.

Also at the monument is the three-quarter-mile **Cliff Nature Trail** and the 3½ mile **Big Tree Trail**, which loops through old-growth forest to visit a huge Douglas fir reckoned to be at least 1200 years old.

The road to the caves is quite steep and narrow. Leave trailers at the Cave Junction visitor center.

Places to Stay & Eat Sites rarely fill up at the two small, primitive USFS campgrounds on the road to the monument. *Cave Creek Campground (14 miles up Hwy 46)* is closest and has a trail to the caves. A few miles away is *Grayback Campground (11 miles up Hwy 46)*. Sites cost $14.

DeWitt's Town & Country RV Park (☎ *541-592-2656, 28288 Redwood Hwy)* Hookups $16.50. There are pleasant RV sites here, a few miles south of Cave Junction along the Illinois River.

Oregon Caves Chateau (☎ *541-592-3400, Oregon Caves National Monument)* Rooms from $75. Open Memorial Day-mid-October. Huge windows overlook the forest at the Oregon Caves Chateau, an impressive six-story hotel and *dining room* built over a plunging ravine at the cave entrance. Sandwiches are served here at an old-fashioned soda fountain.

Junction Inn (☎ *541-592-3106, 406 S Redwood Hwy)* Singles/doubles $45/55. This is Cave Junction's largest and most comfortable lodging.

Holiday Motel (☎ *541-592-3003, 24810 Redwood Hwy)* Singles/doubles $44/56. There are more rooms here, 2 miles north of town.

Out 'n' About Treesort (☎ *541-592-2208, 800-200-5484,* W *www.treehouses.com, 300 Page Creek Rd)* Treehouses $85-150. Off the beaten path in solitary Takilma, there's lodging in rustic treehouses and cereal for breakfast. It's a little makeshift and not a particularly good value, but it's definitely fun and memorable.

Wild River Brewing & Pizza Co (☎ *541-592-3556, 249 N Redwood Hwy)* Entrees $5-10. This is Cave Junction's pizza joint.

Carols Restaurante (☎ *541-592-4553, 120 N Redwood Hwy)* Entrees $10. If you're hungry for Mexican food, Carols has some tasty dishes.

OREGON

Kalmiopsis Wilderness

Oregon's largest wilderness, the Kalmiopsis is famous for its rare plant life and the state's oldest mountains, comprised of volcanic rock and ancient seafloor. About 200 million years ago, offshore sedimentary beds buckled up into mountains that collided with, but didn't initially adhere to, North America. Between 50 and 100 million years ago, a 60-mile gulf opened between this formation and the continent. Vegetation continued to evolve, so that by the time the mountains were finally fused to the continent, the plant life of the Klamath Mountains was quite different from that of the mainland.

Unusual and unique plant species are showcased on an easy hike to a designated botanical area at deep-green **Babyfoot Lake**. The pink-flowered *Kalmiopsis leachiana* and the rare Port Orford cedar here are found almost nowhere else on earth. Watch meadows for the carnivorous *Darlingtonia* (also called the pitcher plant or cobra lily) that eschews the impoverished soil for nutrition and instead traps and digests insects. To get there, turn onto Eight Dollar Mountain Rd (USFS Rd 4201), 5 miles north of Cave Junction, and follow the signs for 18 winding miles to the trailhead. A Northwest Forest Pass ($5) is required.

Drop by the visitor center in Cave Junction for information, or contact the Siskiyou National Forest supervisor's office (☎ 541-471-6500, W www.fs.fed.us/r6/siskiyou), at 200 NE Greenfield Rd, in Grants Pass. The wilderness is also accessible from the coastal town of Brookings via the Chetco River on USFS Rd 1909.

UMPQUA VALLEY

The Native American word 'Umpqua' means 'thunder water' – an apt description of this mighty river, which is renowned for its secluded beauty and recreation. The North Umpqua River is especially treasured for summer steelhead fishing. Hwy 138 follows the North Umpqua through deep forests, past waterfalls and lakes on a scenic drive to Crater Lake National Park, and eventually meets up with the Upper Rogue River.

At the hub of the valley is Roseburg, known mostly for its logging, but nowadays, the locals are as likely to be discussing the harvest of pinot noir grapes as Douglas firs.

The Umpqua River rises in Maidu Lake, high in the Cascades, and drains over 5500 sq miles of the Cascade and Coast mountains before debouching into the Pacific at Reedsport. Hwys 38 and 138 parallel the main stem Umpqua River and the north fork along most of its length.

I-5 shoots through the Umpqua Valley north to south. Roseburg is about the only town of any consequence.

Roseburg & Around

Sprawling, centerless Roseburg (population 20,955) lies in a valley near the confluence of the South and North Umpqua Rivers. A cheap stopover for travelers bound for Crater Lake or the North Umpqua, Roseburg has been hard hit by changes in the logging industry, and there's a general down-on-its-luck feeling in the air. The town contains a good regional-history museum, and the hills shelter a number of award-winning wineries and a drive-through zoo.

Orientation & Information Take I-5 exit 125 for hotels, restaurants and shopping centers on Garden Valley Blvd; head east along this road for budget lodging along Stephens St (Hwy 99). Continue south along Stephens St to intercept Hwy 138 downtown, which can also be accessed directly off I-5 exit 124.

The Roseburg Visitors & Convention Bureau (☎ 541-672-9731, 800-444-9584, W www.visitroseburg.com) is downtown at 410 SE Spruce St. The Fish & Wildlife office (☎ 541-440-3353) is at 4192 North Umpqua Hwy (Hwy 138).

The post office is at 519 SE Kane St. Speed Queen Laundry is at 161 Garden Valley Center, near I-5 exit 125.

Things to See & Do Exhibits on the local Cow Creek Indians make the **Douglas**

County Museum of History & Natural History (☎ 541-957-7007, W www.co.douglas .or.us/museum, near the fairgrounds at I-5 exit 123; adult/youth $3/1; open 9am-5pm Mon-Fri, 10am-5pm Sat, noon-5pm Sun) a worthwhile stop.

Ten miles southwest near Winston is the overrated Wildlife Safari (☎ 541-679-6761, 800-355-4848, W www.wildlifesafari.org, on Lookingglass Rd; adult/senior/youth $14.50/ 11.50/8.50; summer hours 9am-6pm), one of the nation's largest drive-through zoos, with lions, elephants, giraffes and hippos all lolling around the Oregon countryside.

Break from driving 16 miles north of Roseburg to browse antiques in tiny Oakland, one of the best-preserved frontier towns in Oregon.

Rent skis from the Sport Haus (☎ 541-672-3018, 506 SE Jackson St) before setting out for cross-country skiing around Diamond and Crater Lakes.

Special Events The 'Music on the Half Shell' series brings free concerts to Stewart Park on summer evenings. Contact the visitor center for a schedule.

The Douglas County Fair (☎ 541-440-4505) is held the second week in August.

Places to Stay The following are some lodging options.

Fairgrounds RV Park (☎ 541-440-4505, 2100 Frear St) Sites $15. You can park the RV for the night at the fairgrounds, off I-5 exit 123.

Twin Rivers Vacation Park (☎ 541-673-3811, 433 River Forks Park Rd) Tents/ hookups $15/24. Camping is more pleasant at the confluence of the North and South Umpqua Rivers, 6 miles west of town.

House of Hunter (☎ 541-672-2335, 800-540-7704, W www.wizzards.net/hunter, 813 SE Kane St) Rooms $74-95. This B&B has five guestrooms in a beautiful old home above downtown.

Budget 16 Motel (☎ 541-673-5556, 800-414-1648, 1067 NE Stephens St) Singles/ doubles $34/42. Spacious rooms and a pool make this place the top budget choice on the Stephens St motel strip.

Motel 6 (☎ 541-464-8000, 3100 Aviation Dr) Singles/doubles $48/54. Rooms are also a good value at this newly built motel, off I-5 exit 127.

The following are right at I-5 exit 125:

Best Inn & Suites (☎ 541-673-5561, 427 NW Garden Valley Blvd) Singles/doubles ·$53/58. Friendly staff and an informal lobby dining area make this motel feel just like home; the rooms have refrigerators and microwaves.

Best Western Garden Villa Motel (☎ 541-672-1601, 800-547-3446, 760 NW Garden Valley Blvd) Singles/doubles $73/79. This tidy mid-range motel has a pool, exercise room and hot tub.

Windmill Inn (☎ 541-673-0901, W www .windmillinns.com, 1450 NW Mulholland) Rooms $85. Morning coffee and newspapers are delivered to your room at this business-class motel, which also features a pool.

Places to Eat Travelers won't have any trouble finding food at the Garden Valley freeway exit. However, the best restaurants are hidden in Roseburg's dreary downtown:

Mom's Place (☎ 541-672-8459, 634 SE Cass Ave) Meals under $5. Open 3am-2pm. Mom's opens early for the mill workers. It's not big on ambiance, but breakfasts here are large and tasty.

Village Bistro & Bakery (☎ 541-677-3450, 500 SE Cass Ave) Breakfast & lunch $5-8, dinner $8-17. This cafe near the old train station has hearty meals and fresh bakery items. Stop here to pick up bagels and sandwiches for the trail.

McMenamins Roseburg Station Pub (☎ 541-672-1934, 700 SE Sheridan St) Entrees $6. Eight passenger trains a day once stopped at this old train depot, which is now an inviting pub.

Getting There & Away There are five buses to Eugene ($9 one way) and three to Ashland ($12.50) on Greyhound (☎ 541-673-3348), 835 SE Stephens St. Amtrak Thruway buses stop daily at the Best Western Garden Villa Motel (☎ 541-672-1601), 760 NW Garden Valley Blvd, linking Ashland ($12) with rail connections in Eugene ($8).

Rent a car from Enterprise (☎ 541-440-3030), 1281 NE Stephens St.

North Umpqua River

From Roseburg, Hwy 138 travels east to Crater Lake along the North Umpqua, a designated 'Wild & Scenic' river and one of the best-loved fishing streams in Oregon. The summer steelhead run only partially accounts for the river's fame – its natural beauty makes up the rest. Deep forests crowd the river's boulder-strewn edge, and volcanic crags rise above the trees. This corridor contains one of Oregon's greatest concentrations of waterfalls, and there are short hikes to most of them.

Between Idleyld Park and Diamond Lake are dozens of mostly USFS campgrounds, many right on the river. Plan on pitching a tent unless you've reserved a cabin at one of the resorts. For food, there's either a few resort-run restaurants or your own camp cooking.

For recreation information, stop by Glide's Colliding Rivers Information Center (☎ 541-496-0157), 121 Glide Loop Rd, which is right on the highway and open daily. Adjacent is the North Umpqua Ranger District Station (☎ 541-496-3532, W www.fs.fed.us/r6/umpqua). The USFS-staffed Diamond Lake Information Center (☎ 541-793-3310) is open only in the summer.

Steamboat & Around The area around Steamboat is classic **fly-fishing** water, with steelhead, spring Chinook, coho salmon, rainbow trout and German brown trout. Restrictions limit the season and fishing methods. Contact the Fish & Wildlife office (☎ 541-440-3353) in Roseburg before heading out.

Frothy rapids above Steamboat also make this part of the river good for **rafting** and **kayaking**. Contact **North Umpqua Outfitters** (☎ 541-673-4599, 888-789-7152, W www.nuo rafting.com, half-/full-day trip $75/95) for guided raft trips.

Turn up USFS Rd 38 at Steamboat to glimpse the life cycle of anadromous fish at **Little Falls** and **Steamboat Falls**, where spawning salmon and steelhead struggle up fast-moving Steamboat Creek.

The 79-mile **North Umpqua Trail** begins near Idleyld Park and passes through Steamboat en route to the Pacific Crest Trail near Lemolo Lake. A worthwhile day hike to **Mott Bridge** travels upstream along the south bank through old-growth forest for 5½ miles from the Wright Creek Trailhead, a few miles west of Steamboat on USFS Rd 4711.

Another popular sideline of the North Umpqua Trail is the 0.3-mile jaunt to **Umpqua Hot Springs**, east of Steamboat near Toketee Lake. Follow USFS Rd 34 for 2 miles to Thorn Prairie Rd (USFS Rd 3401) and turn right to the trailhead after 2 more miles (a Northwest Forest Pass is required). Right off the highway at the USFS Rd 34 turnoff is a half-mile stroll to the dramatic, two-tiered **Toketee Falls**, flanked by columnar basalt. Two miles past Toketee Junction on Hwy 138 is **Watson Falls**, which at 272 feet is one of the highest waterfalls in Oregon. The path begins at the picnic area on USFS Rd 37.

West of Steamboat from Susan Creek Campground (13 miles east of Glide on Hwy 138) the 2-mile roundtrip **Indian Mounds Trail** passes Susan Creek Falls before climbing up to a vision-quest site. Four miles east is the 1½-mile hike to double-tiered **Fall Creek Falls**, which leads up a narrow fissure in columnar basalt through Jobs Garden, a natural shade garden of ferns and mosses.

Gorgeous riverside campsites and an exclusive inn are highlights along Hwy 138.

Susan Creek Campground *(13 miles east of Glide on Hwy 138)* Sites $11. There are flush toilets and showers at this lovely BLM campground in a mature Douglas fir forest.

Steamboat Falls Campground *(29 miles east of Glide on USFS Rd 3810, off Hwy 138)* Sites $6, no water. Six miles up from Canton Creek Campground is this prettier site, near Steamboat Falls.

Horseshoe Bend *(☎ 541-496-3532, 30 miles east of Glide off Hwy 138)* Sites $11. The river flows on three sides of this gorgeous campground, which is popular for angling and rafting.

OREGON

Boulder Flat *(36 miles east of Glide on Hwy 138)* Sites $7, no water. This primitive campground, 6 miles east, has views of a spectacular lava formation along the river.

Dogwood Motel *(☎ 541-496-3403, 28866 N Umpqua Hwy)* Singles/doubles $32/58. The rustic Dogwood, 5 miles east of Idleyld Park, is a favorite with anglers. Some rooms have kitchens.

Steamboat Inn *(☎ 541-496-3495, W www .thesteamboatinn.com, 42705 Hwy 138)* Cabins & cottages $157-291. Stay in streamside cottages or in wooded suites at this luxury-level fishing lodge, 38 miles east of Roseburg on the banks of the North Umpqua River. The famed lodge ***restaurant*** *(fixed dinner menu $40-70; open daily in summer, Sat & Sun only Nov-Mar)* is open for breakfast and lunch, but the real treat is the gourmet dinner, which is served family-style to guests and non-guests with reservations.

Lemolo Lake Ten miles north of Diamond Lake is Lemolo Lake, a quieter resort area with views across the reservoir to Mt Thielsen.

The short hike to **Lemolo Falls** is well worth the off-road drive. Turn off Hwy 138 onto USFS Rd 2610 (Lemolo Lake Rd) for 4.3 miles to Lemolo Lake. For the best view, turn left onto USFS Rd 3401 (Thorn Prairie Rd) and then right onto USFS Rd 800 for 2 miles for a mile-long trail to the base of the falls. For a longer hike, continue straight on USFS Rd 2610 over the reservoir's spillway and turn left onto USFS Rd 600 for a half mile to the North Umpqua Trail, which reaches the falls in 1½ miles.

Lakeside sites are a popular feature of USFS-maintained ***Poole Creek Campground*** *(☎ 877-444-6777, USFS Rd 2610)* right next to the resort. Sites $9-14.

Lemolo Lake Resort *(☎ 541-643-0750, USFS Rd 2610)* RV sites $17, lodge rooms $55-69, cabins $99-135. Facilities here include indifferently maintained A-frame cabins, RV campsites, a boat ramp, a small store and a *cafe*.

Diamond Lake Glaciers from the last Ice Age gouged out the basin of 3200-acre Diamond Lake, a beautiful deep-blue lake 76 miles east of Roseburg on Hwy 138, directly north of Crater Lake. Motorboats and RVs throng this family destination in summer, with activity centered on a bustling full-service resort. There's fishing, boating, swimming and a 12-mile paved bike path around the lake. Winter brings lots of cross-country skiers, and the lodge offers **snowcat skiing** (☎ 541-446-4555, W www.mountbailey.com; cost $200) to the top of 8363-foot Mt Bailey and **snowmobile tours** to Crater Lake ($95-135).

Rising to the east of Diamond Lake is pointy **Mt Thielsen**, a 9182-foot basalt spire so often struck by lightning that the rocks at the summit have been recrystalized into fulgurites by electrical fusion. A 5-mile trail (Northwest Forest Pass required) begins a mile north of the junction of Hwys 138 and 230 and stops 80 feet short of the summit, which is attainable only with technical climbing skills.

Snow closes the campgrounds in the winter, but the resort remains a busy place year round.

Diamond Lake Campground *(☎ 877-444-6777, USFS Rd 4795)* Sites $10-15. None of the other campgrounds around here compare to the 238 sites at the north end of the lake, which are packed out solid all summer.

Diamond Lake Resort *(☎ 800-733-7593, W www.diamondlake.net, on Hwy 138)* Motel rooms $71-76, cabins $129-185. This family resort complex offers motel lodging and two-bedroom cabins with fully equipped kitchens and televisions. On-site dining options include a standard *cafe*, a *pizzeria* and the fancier *Mt Thielsen Dining Room*.

KLAMATH BASIN

Oregon's most slighted region, the Klamath Basin is a broad, marshy floodplain extending from the southern base of Mt Mazama into the northernmost part of California. Once one of the world's largest lakes, the Klamath Basin was historically covered with nearly 290 sq miles of shallow water, reeds and rushes, which made it a great place to live – for birds. Roughly 6 million

KLAMATH BASIN

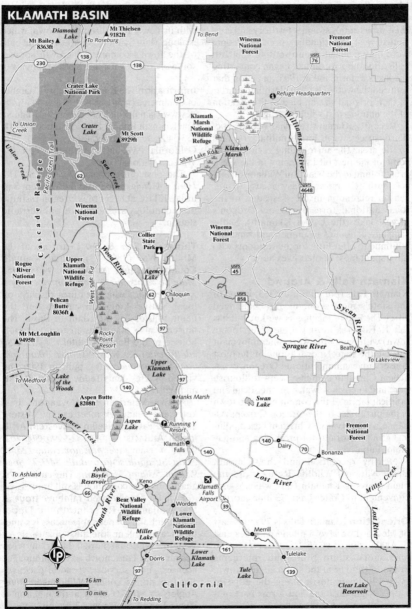

Mt Bailey ▲ 8363ft
Diamond Lake
Mt Thielsen ▲ 9182ft
To Roseburg
To Bend
Winema National Forest
Fremont National Forest
230
138
138
USFS 76
97
Crater Lake National Park
Klamath Marsh National Wildlife Refuge
To Union Creek
Crater Lake
Mt Scott ▲ 8929ft
Klamath Marsh
Silver Lake Rd
Refuge Headquarters
Williamson River
62
Sun Creek
Cascade Range
Pacific Crest Trail
Union Creek
Winema National Forest
USFS 4648
Winema National Forest
Wood River
Collier State Park
Rogue River National Forest
Upper Klamath National Wildlife Refuge
West Side Rd
Agency Lake
USFS 45
Pelican Butte ▲ 8036ft
62
Chiloquin
USFS 858
Mt McLoughlin ▲ 9495ft
Rocky Point Resort
97
Sycan River
To Medford
Lake of the Woods
Sprague River
Beatty
To Lakeview
140
Upper Klamath Lake
Aspen Butte ▲ 8208ft
Hanks Marsh
Swan Lake
Aspen Lake
Spencer Creek
Running Y Resort
Fremont National Forest
Klamath Falls
140
Dairy
70
Bonanza
Miller Creek
John Boyle Reservoir
Keno
140
Lost River
To Ashland
66
Klamath River
Klamath Falls Airport
39
Bear Valley National Wildlife Refuge
Worden
Lower Klamath National Wildlife Refuge
Merrill
Lost River
Miller Lake
97
Dorris
Lower Klamath Lake
161
Tulelake
California
Tule Lake
139
Clear Lake Reservoir
To Redding
0   8   16 km
0   5   10 miles

birds and waterfowl once made their homes here. Pioneers, on the other hand, turned up their noses at this swampy territory and continued west for friendlier prairies. People were only persuaded into settling Klamath Falls after the government began converting the lakes to farmland in 1905, an action that reduced the wetlands to an alarming quarter of their original size and led to the creation of the nation's first wildlife refuge.

Recently, Klamath Falls has been particularly successful in luring military retirees to the area. The surrounding region offers some of the best bird watching in the West; great fishing in the beautiful Williamson and Klamath Rivers; and easy access to all-season recreation in the Cascades, in the local national forests and on Oregon's largest lake (the Upper Klamath). Sadly, sagging economies in timber and ranching continue to offer little for the residents who have spent most of their lives here.

Klamath Falls & Around

Klamath Falls (population 19,365) is one of the state's most economically challenged cities. The end of logging-as-we-knew-it has left K Falls (as most people refer to the town) with one of the worst unemployment rates in the state. Known as one of the most conservative communities in Oregon, evangelical Christian churches seem to flourish here and keep close watch on the social and political fabric of the community. The town is the birthplace of the Oregon Citizens Alliance, a conservative-Christian based political group notorious for producing anti-gay ballot initiatives.

Nearby recreation and the Klamath Basin National Wildlife Refuges are the main draws to Klamath Falls, which is also convenient to Crater Lake, 73 miles north.

Orientation Klamath Falls is 79 miles east of Medford on Hwy 140 and 63 miles east of Ashland on Hwy 66. US 97 serves as the main north-south route and intercepts Hwys 140 and 66 at the south edge of town. Hwy 140 leads north along the edge of Upper Klamath Lake and forms part of a scenic byway to Crater Lake.

Klamath Falls could still use some nice shops, restaurants and galleries to go along with its newly revitalized downtown, which is along Main St and Klamath Ave. The bulk of the town's commercial growth sprawls south of downtown along S 6th St (Hwy 39).

Information The Klamath County Chamber of Commerce (☎ 541-884-5193, 800-445-6728, **W** www.klamathcounty.net), is at 507 Main St. The Klamath Ranger District Station (☎ 541-883-3400, **W** www.fs.fed.us/r6/winema), 1936 California Ave, has information on the Winema National Forest.

The post office is at 317 S 7th St. The *Herald & News* comes out daily except Saturday. KTEC at 89.5 FM is Oregon Institute of Technology's alternative public radio station.

Things to See & Do Learn about the Modoc War (1869–73) at the **Klamath County Museum** (☎ 541-883-4208, *1451 Main St; admission by donation; open 9am-5pm Tues-Sat)*, which features displays on local Native American culture and the natural history of the Klamath Basin. The museum also maintains historic artifacts housed in the **Baldwin Hotel** (*31 Main St; adults/senior & child $2/1; open 10am-4pm Tues-Sat summer only)*, built in 1906 and visited by Presidents Teddy Roosevelt, Taft and Wilson.

Native American tools, weapons, basketry and beadwork meet campy Western art at the **Favell Museum of Western Art & Indian Artifacts** (☎ *541-882-9996, 800-762-9096,* **W** *www.favellmuseum.com, 125 W Main St; adult/senior/youth $4/3/2; open 9:30am-5:30pm Mon-Sat)*. The curation is ghastly, but the collection is still impressive.

Fish for trophy-sized **rainbow trout** at the Williamson River north of Upper Klamath Lake. Dependable access is sometimes a problem; the best access is in Winema National Forest lands or from Collier State Park, north of Chiloquin. For licenses, guide services, vacation packages and fish stories, contact **Williamson River Anglers** (☎ *541-783-2677)*, at the junction of Hwy 62 and US 97, near Chiloquin.

The Ashland-based **Adventure Center** (☎ *541-883-6340, 40 N Main St, Ashland*) offers one-/two-day trips ($110 & $295) down the Upper Klamath River, with enough thrills (several Class IV rapids) for even jaded rafters.

Mountain bikers should inquire about the **OC&E Woods Line State Trail** (☎ *541-783-2471,* W *www.prd.state.or.us*), which follows an old rail bed for 100 miles across ranchland to Bly and beyond.

In winter, there's **cross-country skiing** west on Hwy 140 at Lake of the Woods and north at Crater Lake.

Special Events Every February, the Bald Eagle Conference (☎ 541-884-5193) draws together conservationists, ecologists and bird watchers for lectures, field trips and wildlife art at the Oregon Institute of Technology. The Klamath County Fair & Rodeo (☎ 541-884-5193) is held the first weekend of August at the fairgrounds.

Tribes from all over the west gather in Chiloquin the fourth weekend in August for the Klamath Tribes Restoration Celebration (☎ 541-524-9787, 800-524-9787), which celebrates the Klamath Indians' return to federally recognized tribal status in 1986 with a rodeo and powwow.

Places to Stay There are two private campgrounds right in town.

Klamath Falls KOA (☎ *541-884-4644, 3435 Shasta Way*) Tents/hookups/cabins $17/20/30. Tree-shaded and centrally located, this KOA features an outdoor pool.

Oregon 8 Motel & RV Park (☎ *541-882-0482, 5225 N US 97*) Sites with hookups $18. RV sites behind this motel are right off the highway, on the north edge of town.

For less developed surroundings, try campsites at Rocky Point or Lake of the Woods resorts (see below).

The B&B with the best view is on a hill overlooking Upper Klamath Lake.

Thompson's B&B by the Lake (☎ *541-882-7938, 1420 Wild Plum Court*) Rooms $80. There are four guest rooms here.

Motels are mainly clustered north of town along US 97 and in town along 6th St.

Oregon 8 Motel & RV Park (☎ *541-883-3431, 5225 US 97 N*). Rooms $49. Pleasant and surprisingly quiet, this unassuming motor lodge, 3 miles north of town, features in-room refrigerators, microwaves and handy coffee makers.

Econo Lodge (☎ *541-884-7735, 75 Main St*) Rooms $51. Rooms at this downtown motel are also cheap, but not quite as nice.

Cimarron Motor Inn (☎ *541-882-4601, 800-742-2648, 3060 S 6th St*) Rooms $63. There's an outdoor pool and a continental breakfast at this mid-range motel.

Best Western Olympic Inn (☎ *541-882-9665, 800-600-9665,* W *www.klamathfalls hotelmotel.com*) Rooms $106. One of the nicest places is this new pine-paneled hotel, which features business-class amenities and an outdoor pool.

Nearby lakeshores shelter a handful of recreation-based resorts.

Running Y Resort Lodge (☎ *541-850-5500, 888-850-0275,* W *www.runningy.com, 8 miles north of Klamath Falls off Hwy 140*) Rooms from $121. Luxury hotel rooms at this top-rated golf resort are surrounded by ranchland and a drained lake.

Rocky Point Resort (☎ *541-356-2287, 24 miles north of Klamath Falls off Hwy 140*) Tents/hookups $14/20, guest rooms $58, cabins $94-136. Wooded cabins on the northwest end of the Upper Klamath Lake Wildlife Refuge make this rustic resort perfect for naturalists and anglers. The full-service marina rents canoes, and there's also a tackle shop and restaurant.

Lake of the Woods Resort (☎ *541-949-8300,* W *www.lakowoods.com, 950 Harriman Route, 32 miles west on Hwy 140*) Tents/RV sites $14/20, sleeper/full cabins from $52/106. West of Klamath Falls, there are cooler environs at Lake of the Woods, a family resort area with boating and cross-country skiing. The pine cabins are unbearably cute, and the resort rents boats, bikes and winter sports equipment.

Places to Eat This is one place where you may want to opt for the truck stop. Downtown *looks* promising, but most restaurants there are passing at best.

The Daily Bagel (☎ *541-850-0744, 636 Main St*) Entrees under $5. Open breakfast & lunch Mon-Sat. Good bagels and sandwiches and loose-leaf teas make this bookstore cafe one of the best things about downtown.

Applebee's (☎ *541-850-1080*) Entrees $7. Open lunch & dinner. Believe it or not, this chain restaurant really is the best sit-down place.

Old Town Pizza (☎ *541-884-8858, 722 Main St*) Entrees under $10. This no-frills pizza place is right downtown.

Sergio's (☎ *541-885-6885, 4650 S 6th St*) Lunch/dinner $5/8. Mexican meals at this downtown restaurant aren't too bad.

Schatzie's on the Green (☎ *541-850-5777, 8 miles north of Klamath Falls off Hwy 140, Running Y Resort*). Lunch/dinner $6/16. The clubhouse at the Running Y features fine dining with Northwest and German cuisine, as well as burgers for lunch. There's also inexpensive deli fare at the *Sugar Pine Café*, by the highway.

Entertainment *Ross Ragland Theater* (☎ *541-884-5483, 218 N 7th St*) The community symphony and chorus, country & western celebrities and other traveling acts perform at this art deco theater.

Black Dog Billiards (☎ *541-884-8373, 436 Main St*) If nothing else sounds good, you can shoot pool downtown.

Getting There & Around United Express (☎ 541-884-3331) flies to Portland and Seattle from the Klamath Falls Airport, off Hwy 140 south of town.

The daily Greyhound (☎ 541-882-4616) bus goes to Bend ($23 one way), Portland ($41) and Redding, California ($31), from Molly's Truck Stop, 3817 Hwy 97N. Ask about the daily shuttle to the Medford bus station ($23), which is actually the fastest way to get to points along I-5.

Amtrak's *Coast Starlight* stops twice daily in Klamath Falls between San Francisco and Portland. The station (☎ 541-884-2822) is at S Spring St and Oak Ave.

Contact Hertz (☎ 541-882-0220) at the airport to rent a car. Call AB Taxi (☎ 541-885-5607) for a cab.

Klamath Basin National Wildlife Refuges

Six wildlife refuges totaling more than 263 sq miles string along the old basin of Ice Age Modoc Lake (also known as Lower Klamath Lake), from Upper Klamath Lake, in Oregon, to Tule Lake, in California. The refuges support over 400 species of wildlife and are important stopovers on the Pacific flyway – 45,000 ducks and 26,000 Canadian geese are hatched here annually. Concentrations of up to 2 million birds are possible in spring and fall peak seasons. The basin is also prime winter territory for bald eagles.

Tule rushes fill the northwestern shore of shallow, marshy, Upper Klamath Lake, lending shelter to colonies of cormorants, egrets, herons, cranes, pelicans and many varieties of ducks and geese inhabiting the **Upper Klamath Refuge**. A 9½-mile **canoe trail** starts at Pelican Bay, northwest of Klamath Falls off Hwy 140. Rent canoes ($20-30) from nearby Rocky Point Resort.

West of Worden, the **Bear Valley Refuge** is known mostly as a wintering area for bald eagles; 500 to 1000 gather here between December and February. From Klamath Falls, follow US 97 south to Worden and turn west on the Keno-Worden Rd.

Established in 1908 as the nation's first wildlife refuge, the 83-sq-mile **Lower Klamath Refuge** begins in Oregon but lies mostly in California. This mix of open water, shallow marsh, cropland and grassy upland offers the best year-round viewing and the easiest access for motorists. An **auto tour** begins 5 miles east of the refuge's western entrance on Hwy 161, or State Line Rd.

The Refuge Headquarters (☎ 530-667-2231, W www.klamathnwr.org) is stationed at 4009 Hill Rd in Tulelake, California. Obtain information in Klamath Falls from the Oregon Dept of Fish & Wildlife office (☎ 541-883-5732), 1850 Miller Island Rd West.

CRATER LAKE NATIONAL PARK

Perfectly symmetrical and uncannily blue, Crater Lake is the deepest lake in the USA

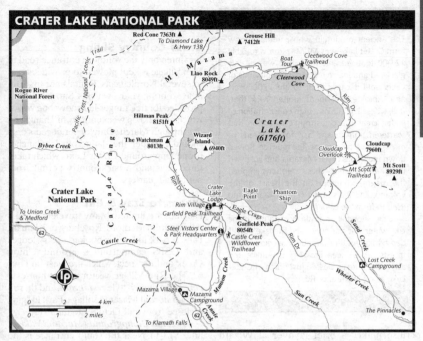

CRATER LAKE NATIONAL PARK

and is Oregon's only national park. Unfortunately, after spending a considerable amount of time getting here, the majority of the park's 500,000 visitors do little more than take the scenic drive around the lip of the crater and hurry on. The park also features hiking and cross-country skiing trails, a boat ride to a rugged island and a lovely landmark lodge.

Orientation & Information

Crater Lake National Park (☎ 541-594-2211, ⓦ www.nps.gov/crla; park admission $10 per vehicle in summer/free during the off season) is 72 miles from Medford and 73 miles from Klamath Falls on Hwy 62. Roseburg is 87 miles on Hwy 138, and it's 90 miles to Bend on US 97.

The popular south entrance is open year round and accesses facilities at Rim Village and Mazama Village, as well as the park headquarters at the Steel Visitors Center. Snow blankets the park from October to June and draws cross-country skiers in the winter. Summer is usually cold and windy, so dress warmly.

Rim Drive

This 33-mile loop road links over 30 viewpoints as it winds around the rim of Crater Lake. The route is usually open by mid-July. A paved side road on the east side of the lake leads to the best views from the crest of Cloudcap, almost 2000 feet above the lake. Another nearby side road leads 10 miles southeast to **The Pinnacles**, a valley of pumice and ash formations carved by erosion into 100-foot spires called hoodoos.

Cleetwood Cove

The popular and steep mile-long Cleetwood Cove Trail, at the north end of the crater, provides the only water access at the cove, the departure point for a 1½ hour narrated **boat tour** (adult/child $19.25/11.50; departures 10am-4:30pm July–mid-Sept). The

OREGON

Explosions at Mt Mazama

The ancient mountain whose remains now form Crater Lake was Mt Mazama, a roughly 12,000-foot volcanic peak that was heavily glaciered and inactive for many thousands of years until it came back to life 7700 years ago. Rhiolite, a kind of molten rock that, unlike basalt, contains a high concentration of water, created a catastrophic explosion that scattered pumice and ash for hundreds of miles. Flows of superheated pumice flowed down the slopes of Mt Mazama and solidified into massive banks. These eruptions emptied the magma chambers at the heart of the volcano, and the summit cone collapsed into itself to form the caldera.

Only snowfall and rain contribute to the lake water. It is this purity and the lake's great depth that give it its famous blue color. Sparse forests can be seen growing in pumice and ash in the Pumice Desert, just north of Crater Lake along N Entrance Rd.

cruise makes a brief layover at **Wizard Island**, a 760-foot cinder cone. Hikers on the morning cruise can climb the short mile to the island's summit or explore icy bays and return on a later boat.

Hiking
High-elevation trails aren't completely clear of snow until late July. From the east edge of the Rim Village parking lot, a 1.7-mile trail leads up 8054-foot **Garfield Peak** to an expansive view of the lake; in July, the slopes are covered with wildflowers. A strenuous, 5-mile roundtrip hike reaches an even better lake vista atop 8929-foot **Mt Scott**, the highest point on Crater Lake. Pick up the trail across from the Cloudcap viewpoint turnoff, on the eastern edge of Rim Dr. Less ambitious is the 0.7-mile trail to **The Watchman**, an old lookout tower on the opposite side of the lake. The park headquarters begins

a 1-mile nature trail through the **Castle Crest Wildflower Garden**.

Cross-Country Skiing
In winter, only the southern entrance road to Rim Village is kept plowed to provide access to several Nordic trails. Rentals are unavailable, so bring your own skis. Snowshoes are provided for free ranger-led **snowshoe walks**, which are held on weekends from Thanksgiving through March. Only experienced skiers should consider the dangerous, avalanche-prone loop around Crater Lake, which takes three days and a backcountry permit from park headquarters.

Places to Stay & Eat
Facilities are limited. Many travelers make a day trip from Medford, Roseburg or Klamath Falls. If park lodging is booked up, try lodges and USFS campgrounds around Union Creek and Prospect, which are west on Hwy 62. The Rim Village visitor center houses a *cafe* and a family-style *restaurant*, and there's a small *store* at Mazama Village. Park lodging is closed from mid-October to mid-May.

Mazama Campground (Mazama Village) Sites $13-14. Near the south entrance is the main park campground, with nearly 200 wooded sites.

Lost Creek Campground (southeast of Rim Village, 7 miles off Rim Dr) Sites $10. There are also 12 dusty campsites on the road to The Pinnacles.

Mazama Village Motor Inn (☎ 541-830-8700, 541-594-2255 same-day reservations, ⓦ www.crater-lake.com, Mazama Village) Rooms $104. There's motel-style lodging here.

Crater Lake Lodge (☎ 541-830-8700, 541-594-2255 same-day reservations, ⓦ www.crater-lake.com, Rim Village) Nonview/lake-view rooms from $124/161. This grand old lodge is booked out six months to a year in advance, though check for cancellations.

Crater Lake Lodge Dining Room (☎ 541-594-1184) Entrees $20. Northwest cuisine is showcased in this formal, lake-view restaurant.

Central Oregon

With its mountain peaks, rushing rivers and clear skies, central Oregon is crystalline in its beauty. And there's so much to *do* here. Fishing, white-water rafting, rock climbing, skiing, hiking and wildlife viewing make it a recreational hotspot.

Volcanoes and erosion both have marked the landscape. Ten million years of volcanic activity in northeastern Oregon covered the land in lava. Rivers then carved through the lava beds, and the Deschutes and Crooked Rivers in particular incised amazing gorges.

Central Oregon's dry, sunny climate and high elevation – between 3000 and 4000 feet – give rise to a high-desert ecosystem, characterized by ponderosa pines, sagebrush and scrub juniper.

This was once the domain of the Wasco Indians, native tribes who were relegated to the Warm Springs Indian Reservation in 1855. Since then, central Oregon has been the provenance of ranchers, farmers and loggers, and the region's beauty and recreational opportunities now lure a new breed of settler – the urban escapee. As a result, real-estate developers have subdivided much of this high-savanna land.

BEND & AROUND

Don't be put off by US 97 (here called 3rd St), which traverses a god-awful commercial strip through Bend (population 53,040) – fast-food restaurants, real-estate offices and nail parlors stretch on for miles. Downtown Bend, just a few blocks west, has riverside parks and good restaurants and is easy to explore on foot. But Bend's main attractions are south of town: Mt Bachelor, arguably the state's best ski mountain, and the Newberry National Volcanic Monument, which includes a collection of geologic sites along the US 97 corridor.

Orientation & Information

The main north-south road through Bend is 3rd St, or US 97. Paralleling 3rd is the newly opened Bend Pkwy, which offers a quick way through town. Downtown Bend is just west of these busy roads; its main streets are Wall and Bond. Century Dr heads southwest to Mt Bachelor and the Cascade Lakes area; from downtown Bend, catch it by going west on Franklin Ave.

Contact the Central Oregon Welcome Center (☎ 541-389-8799, 800-800-8334, W www.covisitors.com), 63085 N US 97, for information and lodging reservations. The Bend-Fort Rock Ranger Station (☎ 541-388-2715) is at 1230 NE 3rd St.

Highlights

- Rafting the Deschutes River
- Rock climbing or hiking at Smith Rock
- Skiing or snowboarding at Mt Bachelor
- Lakeside camping in the Cascades
- Watching Native Americans dip for fish at Sherar's Falls

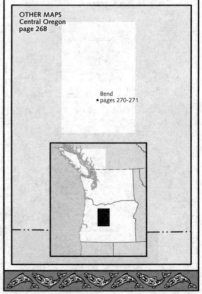

OTHER MAPS
Central Oregon
page 268

Bend
• pages 270-271

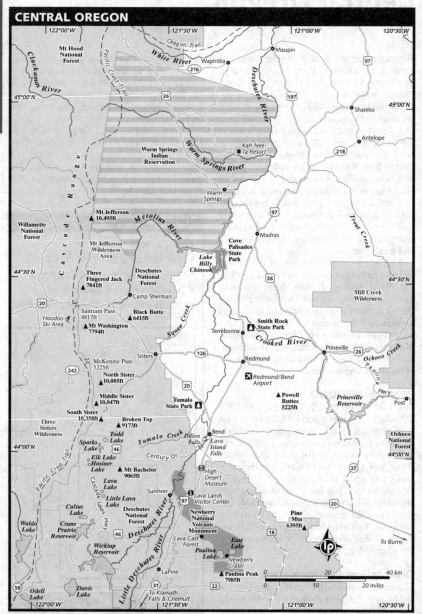

CENTRAL OREGON

The downtown post office is at 47 NW Oregon Ave. Oregon Public Radio is heard at 91.3 FM. You can wash your clothes at Nelson Self-Service Laundry, 407 SE 3rd St. St Charles Medical Center (☎ 541-382-4321) is at 2500 NE Neff Rd, just north of Pilot Butte State Park.

Free Internet access is available at the Bend Public Library (☎ 541-388-6677), 507 NW Wall St; see the librarian about a guest log-on. At Café Internet (☎ 541-318-8802), 133 SW Century Dr, hourly access fees are $8.

Downtown

While the outdoors may be the focus of a visit to Bend, it's easy to spend several hours downtown drinking coffee and poking through shops.

Downtown, storefronts on Wall St back up onto **Drake Park** and a calm stretch of the Deschutes River called **Mirror Pond**. Paths link Drake Park to upstream and downstream parks.

The **Deschutes County Historical Center** (☎ 541-389-1813, 129 NW Idaho Ave; adult/child 7-12 years $2.50/1; open 10am-4:30pm Wed-Sat) houses Native American and pioneer artifacts in the local grade school.

One of Oregon's best museums, the **High Desert Museum** (☎ 541-382-4754, W www .highdesert.org, 59800 S US 97; adult/senior & teen/child 5-12 years $8/7/4; open 9am-5pm), 6 miles south of Bend on US 97, charts the development of central and eastern Oregon. Beginning with Native Americans and proceeding through white settlement, this indoor/outdoor facility provides insights not only into history, but also into nature, wildlife, art and rural society.

Mountain Biking

You wouldn't guess it by driving US 97, but Bend is laced with bike trails. The 6-mile **Deschutes River Trail** runs from Lava Island Falls, just past the Inn of the Seventh Mountain, south to Dillon Falls. It's a lovely riverside route with separate paths for bikers, hikers and horses. To reach the trailhead, drive 7½ miles west of Bend on Hwy 46 (Century Dr) and turn left on Forest Rd 41. Follow the signs to Lava Island Falls.

There's more mountain biking up Hwy 46 at **Swampy Lakes** and **Virginia Meissner Sno-Park** areas. The cross-country ski routes become bike trails once the snow melts and the mud dries up.

Also fun are the mountain-bike routes up Skyliner Rd. Head west out of town on Galveston Ave and keep going straight (rather than turning left for Mt Bachelor) and head up Skyliner Rd 9 miles to the Skyliner's snow-play parking area, the start of the 4½-mile **Tumalo Falls Trail**. A well-marked challenge for novices, the trail rewards mountain bikers with views of rim rock and 90-foot-high Tumalo Falls.

You can rent mountain bikes at **Hutch's Bicycles** (☎ 541-382-9253, 725 NW Columbia St; $20 per day).

Nearby Sunriver is known for its paved bike paths, but mountain bikers can set off on the red dirt roads at the north edge of the resort and pedal to **Benham Falls**. In Sunriver, **Chrome Pony** rents mountain bikes (☎ 541-593-2728, 1 West Mall; hour/day $5/17).

Other Activities

Local fly shops can hook you up with a fishing guide. Check with **Fly & Field** (☎ 541-318-1616, 143 SW Century Dr) or **The Patient Angler** (☎ 541-389-6208, 55 NW Wall St).

Rent canoes, rafts and kayaks from **Alder Creek Kayak & Canoe** (☎ 541-389-0890, 345 SW Century Dr; $30 a day); the company also offers paddling classes. Raft the Deschutes' white water with **Sun Country Tours** (☎ 541-382-6277, 800-770-2161, 531 SW 13th St; $40 & up).

Juniper Aquatic & Fitness Center (☎ 541-389-7665, 800 NE 6th St; $3) has both indoor and outdoor pools.

Contact the welcome center (see Orientation & Information, earlier) for a complete listing of the area's many **golf courses**.

Places to Stay

It's usually easy to find a reasonably priced place to stay in Bend. However, during weekends in July and August, many motels charge whatever they can get – sometimes nearly double regular high-season prices.

BEND

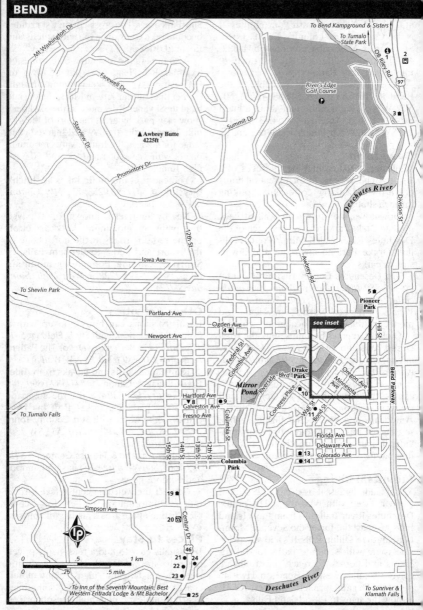

To Bend Kampground & Sisters

To Tumalo
State Park

OB Riley Rd

1
2

97

River's Edge
Golf Course

3

Deschutes River

Division St

Mt Washington Dr

Farewell Dr

Starview Dr

Summit Dr

▲ Awbrey Butte
4225ft

Promintory Dr

12th St

Iowa Ave

Awbrey Rd

To Shevlin Park

5
Pioneer
Park

Portland Ave

Ogden Ave
4

Hill St

Bend Parkway

Newport Ave

Federal St

Columbia Ave

see inset

Drake
Park

Oregon Ave

Minnesota
Ave

Riverside Blvd

Congress Place

10

Mirror
Pond

Hartford Ave
8
Galveston Ave
9

Columbia St

Fresno Ave

Wall St

Bond St

11

To Tumalo Falls

15th St
14th St
13th St
12th St

Florida Ave
Delaware Ave

13

Colorado Ave

14

Columbia
Park

19

Simpson Ave

20

Century Dr

46

21   24
22
23

25

Deschutes River

To Inn of the Seventh Mountain, Best
Western Entrada Lodge & Mt Bachelor

To Sunriver &
Klamath Falls

0   .5   1 km
0   .25   .5 mile

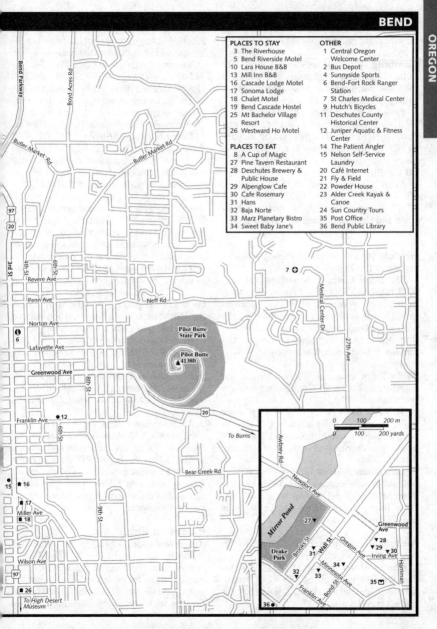

BEND

OREGON

PLACES TO STAY
3 The Riverhouse
5 Bend Riverside Motel
10 Lara House B&B
13 Mill Inn B&B
16 Cascade Lodge Motel
17 Sonoma Lodge
18 Chalet Motel
19 Bend Cascade Hostel
25 Mt Bachelor Village Resort
26 Westward Ho Motel

PLACES TO EAT
8 A Cup of Magic
27 Pine Tavern Restaurant
28 Deschutes Brewery & Public House
29 Alpenglow Cafe
30 Cafe Rosemary
31 Hans
32 Baja Norte
33 Marz Planetary Bistro
34 Sweet Baby Jane's

OTHER
1 Central Oregon Welcome Center
2 Bus Depot
4 Sunnyside Sports
6 Bend-Fort Rock Ranger Station
7 St Charles Medical Center
9 Hutch's Bicycles
11 Deschutes County Historical Center
12 Juniper Aquatic & Fitness Center
14 The Patient Angler
15 Nelson Self-Service Laundry
20 Café Internet
21 Fly & Field
22 Powder House
23 Alder Creek Kayak & Canoe
24 Sun Country Tours
35 Post Office
36 Bend Public Library

Here we've listed the usual high-season rates. Be aware that if Bend is hopping, rates may increase rather capriciously.

Camping A couple of campgrounds are quite convenient to downtown Bend. But there are much more appealing places out of town in the Cascade Lakes area.

Tumalo State Park (☎ 541-382-3586, W *www.oregonstateparks.org, 62976 OB Riley Rd)* Tents/hookups/yurts or teepees $17/21/27. Streamside spots are best at this piney campground 5 miles north of Bend off US 20.

Bend Kampground (☎ 541-382-7738, 800-713-5333, fax 541-388-7332, 63615 N US 97) Tents/hookups $18/24. Just north of town and close to the highway, this is a convenient place to pull over for a night.

Hostels Budget travelers should consider staying at this hostel.

The Bend Cascade Hostel (☎ 541-317-3813, 800-299-3813, 19 SW Century Dr)* Dorm beds/private rooms $15/28. This spacious hostel is just southwest of downtown, on the road to Mt Bachelor. In addition to same-sex dormitories, there are rooms for couples and families. It is wheelchair accessible.

B&Bs There are quite a few B&Bs in the Bend area. The Visitor Center can provide a more extensive list.

Mill Inn B&B (☎ 541-389-9198, W *www.millinn.com, 642 NW Colorado Ave)* Rooms $59-85. This erstwhile hotel and boarding-house near downtown is now a casual, comfortable B&B.

Lara House B&B (☎ 541-388-4064, W *www.moriah.com/larahouse, 640 NW Congress Place)* Rooms $95-150. This large, 1910 historic home across from Drake Park is Bend's most elegant B&B.

Motels Budget motels line busy 3rd St; fancier places are off the main drag.

Chalet Motel (☎ 541-382-6124, 510 SE 3rd St)* Singles/doubles $35/39. A small, simple place, the Chalet is a good bet for budget travelers.

Westward Ho Motel (☎ 541-382-2111, 800-999-8143, 904 SE 3rd St)* Singles/doubles $35/39. The large indoor pool here makes the Westward Ho popular with families.

Sonoma Lodge (☎ 541-382-4891, fax 541-382-4891, 450 SE 3rd St)* Singles/doubles $39/44. This is a particularly pleasant motel, where the owner serves homemade zucchini bread in the morning. Rooms have microwaves and refrigerators; pets are allowed.

Cascade Lodge Motel (☎ 541-382-2612, 800-852-6031, 420 SE 3rd St)* Singles/doubles $39/43. There's an outdoor pool at this nicely remodeled budget motel.

Bend Riverside Motel (☎ 541-389-2363, 800-228-4019, W *www.bendriversidemotel.com, 1565 Hill St)* Standard/condo rooms $52/69, cabins $75. From the basic to the fancy, all the rooms at this well-situated motel have kitchens. Amenities include an indoor pool, a hot tub, a sauna and tennis courts.

The Riverhouse (☎ 541-389-3111, 800-547-3928, W *www.riverhouse.com, 3075 N US 97)* Singles/doubles $69/79, deluxe rooms up to $195. Especially popular with golfers, the Riverhouse has a beautiful location, as well as two pools and a fitness center.

Best Western Entrada Lodge (☎ 541-382-4080, 800-528-1234, W *www.bestwestern.com/entradalodge, 19221 Century Dr)* Singles/doubles $79/89. On the road to Mt Bachelor, this large, comfortable motel has a pool, a hot tub and access to running trails. Pets are OK.

Mt Bachelor Village Resort (☎ 541-389-5900, 800-547-5204, W *www.mtbachelorvillage.com, 19717 Mt Bachelor Dr)* Rooms $190-340. This resort, just off Century Dr, has very nice condos, as well as an outdoor pool, tennis courts and hiking trails. The higher rate is for a three-bedroom condo overlooking the Deschutes.

Places to Eat

Alpenglow Cafe (☎ 541-383-7676, 1040 NW Bond St)* Breakfast/lunch $7. For Bend's best breakfast or a hearty lunch, Alpenglow puts the focus on fresh local ingredients.

Baja Norte (☎ 541-385-0611, 801 Wall St)* Entrees $6-7. This lively Mexican grill rises above the level of gut-bomb burritos. (There's another Baja Norte in Sunriver's mall.)

A Cup of Magic (☎ *541-330-5539, 1304 NW Galveston Ave*) Entrees $5. Coffee, tea and light meals make this a comfortably hip cafe a good place to stop on the way to Mt Bachelor.

Deschutes Brewery & Public House (☎ *541-382-9242, 1044 NW Bond St*) Sandwiches $7. Deschutes serves up microbrewed bitter, ale and porter in a gregarious pub atmosphere. The food is also good.

Sweet Baby Jane's (☎ *541-385-5931, 945 NW Bond St*) Desserts $4. Music, movies, poetry and rich desserts make this a great place to hang out. Light meals and a full bar also available.

Marz Planetary Bistro (☎ *541-389-2025, 163 NW Minnesota Ave*) Entrees $9-13. Join the fun at this Euro-Asian-American restaurant where choices range from noodle bowls to Argentinean skirt steak. Somehow, they manage to pull it all off.

Hans (☎ *541-389-9700, 915 NW Wall St*) Entrees $9-15. The back patio is a perfect place to nibble the tasty grilled pizza here.

Pine Tavern Restaurant (☎ *541-382-5581, 967 NW Brooks St*) Lunch/dinner $9/15. This is probably Bend's best-loved restaurant, with lovely food to match the lovely atmosphere.

Cafe Rosemary (☎ *541-317-0276, 222 NW Irving Ave*) Lunch/dinner $11/30. Splurge on lunch with a superb, intensely flavored salad here.

Getting There & Around

The Redmond/Bend Airport is 18 miles north of Bend. United Express and Horizon Air fly in from Portland, Eugene, Seattle and San Francisco. The one-way airfare to/from Portland is about $70.

CAC Transportation's Redmond Airport Shuttle (☎ 541-389-7469, 800-847-0157) offers door-to-door service to Bend ($19); make reservations at least 24 hours in advance. Call Owl Taxi (☎ 541-382-3311) for a cab.

Greyhound has service to/from Portland ($22, four to five hours, 162 miles, twice daily) and Eugene ($22, 2½ hours, 145 miles, once daily). Another bus travels along US 97

between Bend, Klamath Falls and California. The bus depot (☎ 541-382-2151) is at 63076 N US 97.

CAC Transportation also offers bus service between Portland and Bend ($30, twice daily).

The only central Oregon stop on Amtrak's (☎ 800-872-7245) daily California-Portland run is in Chemult, which is linked to Bend, about 65 miles to the north, by Amtrak Thruway buses. The combination train-bus trip from Oakland, California to Bend takes about 14 hours ($68).

Car rental agencies at the Redmond/Bend Airport include Budget (☎ 541-923-0699), Hertz (☎ 541-923-1411) and National (☎ 541-548-0650).

NEWBERRY NATIONAL VOLCANIC MONUMENT

The Lava Lands Visitor Center (☎ *541-593-2421, 58201 S US 97; admission free; open 9am-5pm daily Memorial Day-Labor Day, Wed-Sun mid-Apr-May & Sept-mid-Oct),* about 11 miles south of Bend, has exhibits on the geology, wildlife and archaeology of the volcanic area south of Bend. A short trail leads to a lava flow.

Adjacent to the visitor center is **Lava Butte**, a perfect cone rising 500 feet above the surrounding lava flows. A road spirals up the side of the butte to an observation deck, where there are spectacular views of the Cascades and nearby volcanic formations. Parking at the top is limited to half an hour; pick up a free parking permit at the visitor center.

Follow signs from the visitor center to **Benham Falls**, on the Deschutes River. More a series of rapids than a waterfall, Benham Falls was formed when lava blocked the river. Watch for otters during the half-mile hike.

Lava River Cave

Lava tubes are formed when the surface of a lava flow solidifies, allowing the still-molten rock below it to flow out. The resulting cave, which often follows the course of a buried streambed, is clean and dry compared to caves caused by water erosion.

OREGON

About 1 mile south of the visitor center, Lava River Cave *(adult/teen $3/2; business hours same as the visitor center)* is one of many such formations in the monument but is the only one that's developed for visitors.

Lava Cast Forest

About 6000 years ago, a wall of molten lava 20 feet deep flowed down from Newberry Crater and engulfed a forest of mature trees. The trees incinerated, but not before cooling and solidifying the lava. The resulting casts of the trees are seen on a mile-long interpretive trail. The Lava Cast Forest is 9 miles east of US 97, on Lava Cast Forest Rd.

Newberry Crater

Newberry Crater was formed by the eruption of what was one of the largest and most active volcanoes in North America. It began erupting about 500,000 years ago, and successive flows built a steep-sided mountain almost a mile above the surrounding plateau. As with Crater Lake, the summit of the volcano collapsed after a large eruption, creating a caldera.

Native Americans collected obsidian for arrowheads from Newberry Crater. Such obsidian was a valuable trade item, and Oregon obsidian has been found in archaeological sites throughout the West.

Initially a single body of water, **Paulina Lake** and **East Lake** are now separated by a lava flow and a pumice cone. Ice Age glaciers carved a niche in the side of the crater, allowing Paulina Creek to drain 250-foot-deep Paulina Lake via a 100-foot-high waterfall. With no visible inflow or outflow, East Lake is fed by snowmelt and springs, and it drains through subterranean passages into Paulina Lake. Due to the lakes' great depths and the constant flow of fresh mineral spring water, stocked trout thrive here. Looming above everything is 7985-foot Paulina Peak, a remnant of the much higher mountain that collapsed during the eruption that formed the 5-mile wide crater.

A short trail halfway between the two lakes leads to the **Big Obsidian Flow**, an enormous deposit on the south flank of

Newberry Crater. The **Newberry Crater Rim Loop Trail** encircles Paulina Lake and is a good place for hiking and mountain biking.

To get there from US 97, take Paulina East Lake Rd to Newberry Crater.

Places to Stay

The eight Newberry Crater campgrounds ($12) usually stay open from late May to October.

LaPine State Recreation Area (☎ 541-536-2071, 800-452-5687, 🌐 www.oregonstateparks .org, State Recreation Rd) Tents/hookups/ cabins $12/17/35. North of LaPine on US 97, the campground at the crater's base has tent sites on the banks of the Deschutes River.

Paulina Lake Lodge (☎ 541-536-2240) Cabins $72-145. Cross-country skiers, snowmobilers, hikers and anglers all stay at this resort, which has cabins, a restaurant, a general store and boat rentals.

East Lake Resort (☎ 541-536-2230, 🌐 www.eastlakeresort.com, 22430 E Lake Rd) Camping rooms/cabins $40/60-115. The camping rooms at this rustic lodging are basic motel rooms without showers (coin-op showers are available).

MT BACHELOR

Slightly east of the main line of Cascade peaks (22 miles southwest of Bend), 9065-foot Mt Bachelor is where central Oregon's cold, continental air meets up with the warm, wet Pacific air. The result is tons of fairly dry snow and ample sunshine.

Skiing & Snowboarding

Lifts go right to Mt Bachelor's perfectly conical peak, and runs shoot down through the trees. The Northwest Express lift provides access to steep, rugged territory on what is, for the most part, a pretty easy mountain to ski or snowboard. With about 350 inches of snow a year, the season begins in November and can last until June. A one-day lift ticket is $43/32/22 per adult/senior/child. Check on ski conditions at ☎ 541-382-7888 or 🌐 www.mtbachelor.com.

Rent skis or snowboards at **Mt Bachelor Ski and Sport Center** (☎ 541-382-2442), at the base of the lifts. In Bend, stop by **Powder House** (☎ *541-389-6234, 311 SW Century Dr; downhill ski equipment packages $14, snowboard packages $29, cross-country packages $10)*, or any one of the several ski shops on Century Dr.

Two lodges offer day-care, food, lessons and shopping. A shuttle bus (☎ 541-382-7888) runs several times a day to Mt Bachelor from Bend ($2) and Sunriver ($2.50).

Mt Bachelor grooms 34 miles of cross-country trails, though the $11 day pass may prompt skiers to check out the free trails at adjacent Dutchman Flat, on public land just past the turnoff for Mt Bachelor on Hwy 46. This is as far as the snowplows maintain the highway during winter. From here on, you'll need skis or snowmobiles.

If there's adequate snow at lower elevations, forget Dutchman Flat and cross-country ski from the Virginia Meissner or Swampy Lakes Sno-Parks, between Bend and Mt Bachelor on Hwy 46.

Be sure to come equipped with a Sno-Park permit, which is required for parking in the mountains in winter and readily available from area businesses ($5).

Places to Stay

There's no lodging right on Mt Bachelor.

Inn of the Seventh Mountain (☎ 541-382-8711, 800-452-6810, W *www.7thmtn.com, 18575 SW Century Dr)* Condo rooms $75-310. The closest accommodations to Mt Bachelor are at this resort, which includes swimming pools, tennis courts, golf, ice-skating, horseback riding and a kids' day camp. It's also near good mountain-bike trails.

Sunriver Lodge (☎ 541-593-1000, 800-547-3922, W *www.sunriver-resort.com, 1 Center Dr, Sunriver)* Rooms $180-400. This resort community, about 25 miles south of Bend, has lodge rooms, condominiums and some private homes available for rent. Sunriver amenities include golf courses, tennis courts, riding stables and 25 miles of paved bike paths. It's an ideal place for families or groups of friends to get together.

Sunriver Realty Vacation Rentals (☎ 800-541-1756, W *www.sr-sunset.com,* *1 Venture Lane, Sunriver)* Condos/houses $80/250-400. Many private houses are available through this agency.

CASCADE LAKES

Long ago, lava from the nearby volcanoes choked this broad basin beneath the rim of the Cascade Range. Lava flows dammed streams, forming lakes. In other areas, streams flowed underground through the porous lava fields to well up as lake-sized springs. Still other lakes formed in the mouths of small, extinct craters.

Hwy 46, usually called the Cascade Lakes Hwy, or Century Dr (the loop road is roughly 100 miles long), leaves Bend to travel west and south between high mountain peaks, and links together alpine lakes known as the Cascade Lakes. Bicyclists pedal the road in summer, while snowmobilers take over during the winter. Beyond Mt Bachelor, the road is closed from November to mid-May.

Tiny **Todd Lake** offers views of Broken Top and relative seclusion, as getting there requires a quarter-mile hike. **Sparks Lake**, in a grassy meadow, is in the process of transforming itself from a body of water to a reedy marsh. It's a good place for bird watching. **Hosmer Lake** is stocked with catch-and-release Atlantic salmon, making it popular with anglers. It's less commercial than nearby lakes and has beautiful views of Mt Bachelor. **Little Lava Lake** is the source of the mighty Deschutes River.

The Deschutes is dammed at **Crane Prairie Reservoir**, where ospreys make use of dead trees for nesting and fish in the shallow lake water.

Both North and South **Twin Lakes** are noted for their good fishing.

There are *public campgrounds* at each of the lakes along the route. Camping fees run $10 and up. A number of the Cascade Lakes have woodsy rustic cabin 'resorts' on their shores, which are usually homey, family-oriented facilities with rudimentary dining, boat rentals and groceries, and usually hookups for RVs. All are open from late spring to early fall; rates run from about $60 to $150 for a cabin.

Among those available are: *Cultus Lake Resort* (☎ *541-389-3230, 800-616-3230,* Ⓦ *www.cultuslakeresort.com); Twin Lakes Resort* (☎ *541-593-6526, PO Box 3550, Sunriver, OR 97777); Elk Lake Resort* (☎ *541-317-2994,* Ⓦ *www.elklakeresort.com; also open mid-Nov-Apr for those who can get there on skis or snowmobiles); and Crane Prairie Resort* (☎ *541-383-3939, PO Box 1171, Bend, OR 97709).*

THREE SISTERS WILDERNESS

Hiking trails depart from the Cascade Lakes Hwy (Hwy 46) into the 580-sq-mile Three Sisters Wilderness, which is dominated by four volcanic peaks. Trails – often snowed in until late June – lead to remote lakes surrounded by wildflower meadows.

One of the most popular hikes is to Green Lake Basin, on a high plateau between 9173-foot Broken Top and 10,358-foot South Sister. These celadon-green lakes are the centerpiece of a tremendous wildflower display in July and August, when the area throngs with crowds (try to avoid the weekends). Park at the Green Lakes Trailhead along Hwy 46, above Sparks Lake, and hike north. The 4.4-mile trail is fairly steep but passes some great waterfalls.

Strong hikers might consider climbing South Sister. It's Oregon's third-highest peak, but during the summer, the southern approach doesn't demand any technical equipment. The steep 5.6-mile trail begins near Devils Lake (just off the Cascade Lakes Hwy) and is passable only in late summer.

For maps and more information, contact the Bend-Fort Rock Ranger District (☎ 541-388-5564), at 1230 NE 3rd St, in Bend. Also see the Three Sisters Wilderness section in the Willamette Valley chapter.

SISTERS

Near a large meadow with stunning views of snowy Cascade peaks, Sisters (population 850) straddles the line where the mountain pine forests mingle with the desert sage and juniper.

Just about the most congested small town in Oregon, Sisters is a victim of its own success. Once a stagecoach stop and trade

town for loggers and ranchers, it was revitalized when the city fathers decided to 'Westernize' it. Now it's a place to spend the afternoon wandering through shops selling antiques, home decor, Christmas ornaments or Western clothing.

Sisters proves its *real* Western character during the second weekend of June, when the Sisters Rodeo (☎ 800-827-7522) comes to town; it's reckoned to be one of the best in the state. Call for tickets.

A month later, in mid-July, is Sisters' other big weekend, the Outdoor Quilt Show (☎ 541-549-6061). Hundreds of quilts and just as many quilters come for the show and classes.

Orientation & Information

US 20 forms Sisters' main street, generally referred to as Cascade St.

Contact the Sisters Area Chamber of Commerce (☎ 541-549-0251), 164 N Elm St, or the local Forest Service office (☎ 541-549-2111), 207 N Pine St, for information. The post office is at 160 Fir St.

Paulina Springs Book Company (☎ 541-549-0866), at 252 W Hood St, is central Oregon's best bookstore.

Places to Stay

Campers are welcome in the *city park*, at the southern end of Sisters.

Indian Ford Campground (☎ *541-549-7700,* Ⓦ *www.fs.fed.us/r6/centraloregon, 5½ miles northwest of Sisters on US 20).* Sites $8 (no hookups). Remember to bring jugs of water to this convenient but basic Forest Service campground.

Sisters KOA (☎ *541-549-3021, fax 541-549-8144, 67667 US 20 W)* Tents/hookups/cabins $26/29/50. Open mid-March to mid-December. This KOA campground is about 4 miles southeast of Sisters on US 20.

Of the handful of motels in Sisters, two are particularly appealing, and Black Butte is one of Oregon's most deluxe resorts.

Sisters Motor Lodge (☎ *541-549-2551,* Ⓔ *sistersml@bendnet.com, 600 W Cascade St)* Singles/doubles $59/65. Convenient and charming, this older motel has been remodeled and has nice kitchenette rooms.

Best Western Ponderosa Lodge *(☎ 541-549-1234, 888-549-4321, fax 541-549-0409, 500 US 20 W)* Singles/doubles $84. This spacious motel in a parklike meadow just north of the town is rather plush.

Black Butte Ranch *(☎ 541-595-6211, 800-452-7455,* W *www.blackbutteranch.com, 13653 Hawks Beard Rd)* Lodge rooms/condos $100/150-350. Eight miles north of Sisters on US 20, the resort fringes a vast meadow and lake, with Mt Washington and the Three Sisters towering over all. With golf, pools, horseback riding and tennis, Black Butte delivers all the amenities you'd expect, but its greatest asset is that it seems integrated into, and not imposed on, the landscape.

Places to Eat

Seasons Café & Wine Shop *(☎ 541-549-8911, 411 E Hood St)* Sandwiches $5. The best lunch in town is one of these sandwiches eaten on a picnic table in the cafe's backyard.

Papandrea's Pizza *(☎ 541-549-6081, 325 E Hood St)* Pizza $18. Locals swear by the pizza here, the pies are thick-crusted and designed for hearty appetites.

The Hotel Sisters Restaurant *(☎ 541-549-7427, 105 W Cascade St)* Steak dinner $20. Hearty local Corriente beef is the specialty here. At night, there's live music in the hotel's old-fashioned bar. Though the restaurant is housed in a refurbished hotel, no rooms are rented.

Black Butte Ranch *(☎ 541-595-1260, 13653 Hawks Beard Rd)* Entrees $20. If you're in the mood for a fancy dinner, head here, where the lodge restaurant puts out very nice dinners.

Getting There & Away

Greyhound buses to/from Eugene ($20, three hours, twice daily) stop at the corner of Elm St and US 20. There's no station here, so call the Bend station (☎ 541-382-2151) for information.

HOODOO SKI AREA

Hoodoo *(☎ 541-822-3799, US 20 at Santiam Pass; lift tickets adult/senior & child $29/22),* Oregon's oldest downhill ski area, is 25 miles west of Sisters at the crest of the Cascades. Though it's small, Hoodoo has a lot of variety in its terrain, with some surprisingly challenging skiing. For snow conditions, call ☎ 541-822-3337.

Hoodoo's north-facing slopes mean good, plentiful snow. There's night skiing Thursday to Saturday. Facilities include two day lodges, rentals and lessons.

Hoodoo also has groomed cross-country ski trails (trail pass $8); free, ungroomed trails start at many of the Sno-Parks near Santiam Pass.

METOLIUS RIVER

The Metolius River bursts fully formed from a ferny hillside. As it flows north through its beautiful pine-filled valley, the Metolius passes beneath rugged Mt Jefferson (10,495 feet), Oregon's second-highest peak. It's heartening that such a magical valley has not been turned into an expensive, golf course–ridden resort. Instead, the valley remains the domain of campers, as the USFS maintains a dozen campgrounds along the river. For information on activities and lodging in the area, contact the Metolius Recreation Association (☎ 541-595-6117, W www.metoliusriver.com).

The spring-fed river keeps a constant temperature – a fact much appreciated by local trout. Fly-fishing on the Metolius is renowned, and special restrictions are in place to keep it that way. Consult the posted fishing regulations before casting your line.

To find the head of the Metolius, turn north from US 20 onto the Camp Sherman Rd (USFS Rd 14), then turn east at the 'Campgrounds' sign and continue about a mile down this road. A short path leads through a forest of ponderosa pines to re-markable **Metolius Springs**, where the river flows out of a hillside.

Hiking

Trails lead from the Metolius Valley up into the **Mt Jefferson Wilderness Area**. While many hikes into these alpine areas are more than day trips, a few shorter hikes access the area's high country. A 4½-mile roundtrip

OREGON

hike climbs up to Canyon Creek Meadows, where summer produces a vibrant wildflower display and great views onto rugged, 7841-foot **Three Fingered Jack**. To reach the trailhead from Sisters, drive 13 miles northwest on US 20. Just south of Suttle Lake, turn north on the 'Jack Lake Rd,' USFS Rd 12. It's about 8 miles to the trailhead, at USFS's Jack Lake Campground.

From the same access road, a shorter hike leads to a trio of mountain lakes. One mile from the turnoff of US 20, take a west-turning fork (USFS Rd 1210) toward **Round Lake**. From the Round Lake Campground, a 2-mile trail leads past tiny Long Lake to **Square Lake**, the highest of the three and nestled in thick forest.

For less-strenuous hiking, follow the trails on either side of the Metolius River, accessed from Camp Sherman or any campground.

Places to Stay & Eat

For information on any of the 12 Metolius campgrounds, check with the *Sisters Ranger Station* (☎ 541-549-7700, W *www.fs.fed.us/r6/centraloregon, 207 N Pine St)*.

Pine Rest (Forest Rd 1419) and *Riverside (Forest Rd 14)*, north and south of Camp Sherman, respectively, are reserved for tent campers only. Campsites cost $12 per night at Pine Rest and $10 at Riverside.

Metolius River Lodges (☎ 541-595-6290, W *www.metoliusriverlodges.com, 12390 Forest Rd 1419-700)* Cabins $80-210. Even the smallest, least expensive of these cozy cabins is right on the river.

Metolius River Resort (☎ 541-595-6281, W *metolius-river-resort.com, 25551 Forest Rd 1419)* Cabins $180. This resort is a bit more upscale, with lodging in well-appointed three-bedroom cabins.

Kokanee Cafe (☎ 541-595-6420, 25545 SW Forest Rd 1419) Entrees $16. Open for dinner May-Oct. Even if it weren't the only restaurant in Camp Sherman, the attractive, log-cabin Kokanee would be a hard act to beat.

REDMOND & AROUND

On a treeless plain between the Cascade Range and Ochoco Mountains, Redmond (population 13,705) lacks the refinement

and charm of Bend or Sisters. But it is close to Smith Rock State Park and thus is a good base for climbers.

Redmond lies at the junction of two major routes. Hwy 126 acts as a shortcut to roads linking eastern Oregon to Eugene and Salem, while US 97 joins I-84 to California. It's a busy town with a lot of traffic.

Find the Redmond Chamber of Commerce (☎ 541-923-6442) at 106 SW 7th St. The post office is at 507 SW 8th St, and the Central Oregon District Hospital (☎ 541-548-8131) is at 1253 N Canal Blvd.

While driving along US 97 north of Redmond, there is no indication you're in the neighborhood of a river, much less one at the bottom of a 400-foot-deep chasm. Stop at **Peter Skene Ogden Scenic Wayside**, a small park area, for a careful look into the Crooked River canyon; walk across the old highway bridge, which was built with much ado in 1911.

The following are recommended places to stay:

Redmond Inn (☎ 541-548-1091, 800-833-3259, W *www.redmondinn.net, 1545 S US 97)* Singles/doubles $43/53. This place is comfortable, with an outdoor pool and rooms equipped with microwaves and refrigerators.

Travelodge New Redmond Hotel (☎ 541-923-7378, 800-578-7878, 521 S 6th St) Singles/doubles $49/59. For a step back in time, there's this renovated historic hotel in the heart of downtown.

Eagle Crest (☎ 541-923-2453, 800-682-4786, W *www.eagle-crest.com, 1522 Cline Falls Rd)* Rooms/suites/condos $97/132/295. This resort, about 6 miles southwest of Redmond off Hwy 126, has golf, tennis, swimming and horseback riding. Lodging is either in a hotel or in three-bedroom condos.

The following are some restaurants that are worth a try:

Harris Wine Cellar (☎ 541-923-9849, 541 SW 7th St) Lunch/dinner $6/12. Great sandwiches are the lunchtime highlight here; at dinner, take advantage of the wine selection.

Mio Pueblito (☎ 541-923-5173, 404 SW 6th St) Lunch special/dinner $5/10. Stop here for a tasty seafood enchilada.

La Siesta (☎ 541-548-4848, 8320 N US 97) Entrees $8. Six miles north of Redmond in

Terrebonne, La Siesta is one of those little restaurants in an out-of-the-way place that somehow manages to command an enormous reputation.

For information on air travel to central Oregon, see Getting There & Around under Bend, earlier in this chapter. Greyhound buses link Redmond to Portland and Bend. The depot (☎ 541-923-1923) is at the McDonald's at 2456 S US 97. There are car rental agencies at the airport. For a cab, call Redmond Taxi (☎ 541-548-1182).

SMITH ROCK STATE PARK

Rock climbers flock to Smith Rock (☎ 541-548-7501, 9241 NE Crooked River Dr; day-use fee $3), where rust-colored 800-foot-high cliffs tower over the river. The area is known primarily for its sport-climbing routes in the 5.6 to 5.10 range.

For technical route descriptions, pick up a copy of Alan Watts' comprehensive *Climber's Guide to Smith Rock* from Portland-area outdoor stores or Smith Rock climbing shops. Rock-climbing classes are available from **First Ascent** (☎ 541-548-5137, 800-325-5462, 1136 SW Deschutes Ave; beginner's class $60).

If you're not a climber, the 7 miles of hiking trails in the state park afford great views of both landscape and climbers, and can involve a little simple rock scrambling.

During climbing season, the park-side **Rock Hard Climbing & Clothing Gear** peddles equipment to climbers, and huckleberry ice cream to everyone else. They also have free maps of the local hiking trails. Another good climbing shop is **Redpoint Climbers' Supply** (☎ 800-923-6207, 975 Smith Rock Way), in Terrebonne, at the Smith Rock turnoff from US 97. A climber's bivouac provides basic walk-in *campsites* in a dusty area.

To visit Smith Rock State Park, drive 6 miles north of Redmond on US 97, turn east at Terrebonne onto Smith Rock Way and continue for another 3 miles.

PRINEVILLE & THE OCHOCO MOUNTAINS

Prineville (population 8208) backs up to the gently sloping Ochoco Mountains – a beautiful, if undramatic, range undulating across much of central Oregon. The region's gentle topography and many USFS roads make it great for mountain bikers (except during the fall hunting season).

Prineville is at the junction of US 26 and Hwy 126; US 26 is the town's main street and is locally called 3rd St. The Prineville Chamber of Commerce (☎ 541-447-6304) is at 390 N Fairview St, and the Prineville Ranger Station (☎ 541-416-6500) is at 3160 NE 3rd St.

Mill Creek Wilderness

Hikes through old-growth forests and curious volcanic formations make for satisfying day outings at Mill Creek, the most accessible of the Ochoco Mountains wilderness areas. Follow US 26 east from Prineville for 9 miles, and then turn north on USFS Rd 33 for 9 miles to Wildcat Campground. From there, a gentle trail winds along the East Fork of Mill Creek through a lovely **pine forest**. For a long day hike, continue along the trail to **Twin Pillars**, two spirelike volcanic crags.

Places to Stay & Eat

Prineville Reservoir State Park (☎ 541-447-4363, W www.oregonstateparks.org, 19300 S Juniper Canyon Rd) Tents/full hookups $18/22. RVs dominate at this busy state park, 17 miles south of town.

The USFS has a number of campgrounds in the Ochoco Mountains. The Prineville Ranger Station (see above) can provide a complete list. Most sites cost $12. **Wildcat Campground**, on Forest Rd 33 northeast of Prineville, is at the edge of the Mill Creek Wilderness.

Ochoco Inn & Motel (☎ 541-447-6231, 888-800-9948, W www.ochocoinn.com, 123 3rd St) Singles/doubles $40/55. Right downtown, the Ochoco Inn & Motel has good prices and an adjacent restaurant.

Best Western of Prineville (☎ 541-447-8080, W www.bestwesternoregon.com, 1475 E 3rd St) Singles/doubles $60/65. For predictable comfort and a pool, try this Best Western on the eastern outskirts of Prineville.

Sandwich Factory (☎ 541-447-4429, 277 NE Court St) Sandwiches $5-6. Fall into line

OREGON

with half of Prineville and order a sandwich to eat on the rooftop patio.

Lantz's B-B-Que (☎ 541-447-1063, 2657 NE 3rd St) Dinner $10. Now don't go looking for a fancy sit-down restaurant. This humble trailer surrounded by picnic tables emits the most wonderful aroma. Follow your nose.

Getting There & Away
Greyhound (☎ 541-416-0533), 498 W 3rd St, runs one bus a day through Prineville, connecting to Bend ($7, one hour, 35 miles) and Portland ($23, four hours, 165 miles). The *People Mover* (☎ 541-575-2370) offers weekday service to Bend ($9.50) and John Day ($15.50), with a stop at the Prineville Greyhound station.

MADRAS & AROUND
Though hardly a travel destination in itself, Madras (population 5230), at the junction of

Rock Collecting

The dusky volcanic mesas of central and eastern Oregon and Washington yield treasures for the rock hound. Sunstones (pale yellow gemstones) are found north of Plush; to find thundereggs (round agatized geodes), go to commercial locations near Prineville or to Succor Creek State Park in far eastern Oregon. The Priday Agate Beds, north of Madras in central Oregon, is a fun thunderegg-hunting site, with a campground and showers on the premises. Agates are also found along the southern Oregon coast, while famous blue agates can be collected near Ellensburg, in central Washington. Concessionaires in old gold-mining areas of eastern Oregon and Idaho offer gold panning.

If you're interested in collecting rocks, check with the local BLM or USFS offices, which can direct you to likely areas. In some cases, you may need a permit to collect specimens. Remember it is a federal felony to remove Native American artifacts from public land.

US 26 and 97, is a useful jumping-off point for Lake Billy Chinook and the Warm Springs Indian Reservation. Find the chamber of commerce (☎ 541-475-2350) at 197 SE 5th St. The post office is at 230 6th St

West of Madras, the three prodigious rivers of central Oregon – the Deschutes, Crooked and Metolius – join at **Lake Billy Chinook**.

From Madras, follow signs to **Cove Palisades State Park**. The west shore of the reservoir (accessible only by boat) belongs to the Warm Springs Reservation. The marina (with boat rentals), a cafe and the boat launch are at the base of the Crooked River canyon. Most other tourist facilities are on **the Island**, an isthmus separating the Crooked and Deschutes river canyons. Hike the **Tam-a-lau Trail** for spring wildflowers and spectacular views.

The following are some places to stay and eat in the area:

Cove Palisades State Park (☎ 541-546-3412, **W** www.oregonstateparks.org, 7300 SW Jordan Rd) Tents/hookups $18/22. For campers, the best choice is this state park at Lake Billy Chinook.

Hoffy's Motel (☎ 541-475-4633, 800-227-6865, 600 N US 26) Singles/doubles $42/52. Well-kept Hoffy's, at the north end of town, has a swimming pool.

Pepe's Mexican Bakery & Restaurant (☎ 541-475-3286, 221 SE 5th St) Lunch/dinner $5/9. In case you were wondering what heaven looks like, it has old Formica tables. The burritos here are insanely good.

Greyhound buses stop at the Madras depot (☎ 541-475-4469), 839 SW US 97, twice daily en route between Portland ($18, three hours, 116 miles) and Bend ($8, 1¼ hours, 46 miles).

WARM SPRINGS INDIAN RESERVATION
Home to three groups – the Wasco, the Tenino and the Northern Paiute (the Confederated Tribes) – Warm Springs stretches from the peaks of the Cascades in the west to the banks of the Deschutes River to the east.

The Wasco, whose culture combined fishing elements of coastal tribes with the hunting and gathering heritage of plateau ndians, are native to this region. The Tenino, originally from the northern bank of the Columbia River, share with the Wasco their reliance on the Columbia salmon runs. In 1855, a treaty between the Tenino, the Wasco and the US government was signed, confining the tribes to a reservation west of the Deschutes River and east of the Cascades. After the Bannock Indian War of 1878, in southeastern Oregon, a part of the Northern Paiute Indian Federation was moved to the reservation. The Paiute are a desert group from eastern Oregon; their removal from that area was largely part of a strategy to divide the tribe into small, indefensible units.

The **Warm Springs Museum** (*☎ 541-553-3331, 2189 US 26; adult/senior/child $6/5/3; open 10am-5pm*), just east of the town of Warm Springs, is a wonderful evocation of traditional Native American life and culture, with artifacts, audio-visual presentations, educational displays, exhibits of cultural art and re-creations of villages. There's a gift shop and art gallery in the facility.

The Pi Ume Sha Treaty Days Celebration is held on the third weekend of June at Warm Springs. Competitive dancing, horse races and a rodeo make this one of the reservation's biggest powwows. Contact the Confederated Tribes of the Warm Springs Reservation (*☎ 541-553-1161, w www.warmsprings.com*), 1233 Veteran St, to find out about this and other events.

The tribe-owned *Kah-Nee-Ta Resort* (*☎ 541-553-1112, 800-554-4786, 100 Main St; lodge rooms/condos/teepees $130/250/70*), 11 miles north of the town of Warm Springs, is popular with families, especially sun-starved Portlanders. Facilities include a casino, golf, horseback riding, tennis, fishing and swimming in a giant hot springs–fed pool. (If you're not staying at the resort, a pool pass is $7, and parking costs $4.) The lodge *restaurant* features Native American specialties.

From US 26, take the Agency-Simnasho Rd, a loop with its southeast terminus by the town of Warm Springs and its northwest end on US 26 about 20 miles north. Kah-Nee-Tah is just off the Agency-Simnasho Rd, along the Warm Springs River.

LOWER DESCHUTES CANYON

Downstream from the little town of Maupin (population 490), the Deschutes River digs its canyon to the Columbia River. Fishing and rafting are popular pastimes on this section of the Deschutes.

From Maupin, river-access roads wind up- and downriver. Below Sherars Bridge, the gravel road is very washboarded. The road ends at Mack's Canyon, 17 miles below Sherars Bridge. From there, the river is accessible only by raft until it reaches the Columbia, 25 miles later.

Find the chamber of commerce (*☎ 541-395-2599*) on US 197 above town.

Sherars Bridge

In 1979, the Warm Springs Reservation bought land around Sherars Bridge. Here, the mighty Deschutes River cuts into a flow of lava and rages through a gorge only 20 feet across. This turbulent series of rapids, called **Sherars Falls**, is a traditional fish-netting location for Warm Springs Indians. Visit the Sherars Bridge area when salmon are running (March to October), and you can watch Native Americans dip nets on long poles into the furious waters to catch salmon.

Fishing

Fly-fishing on the Deschutes River is renowned. The challenge of the river and the beautiful remoteness of the desert canyon make this an anglers' paradise. Certain restrictions are enforced; call the Fish & Wildlife Bureau (*☎ 541-475-2183*) for information.

The **Deschutes Canyon Fly Shop** (*☎ 541-395-2565, 7 N US 197, Maupin*) is a great place to buy tackle and specialized flies and to find out what the fish are thinking.

Rafting

The Deschutes River near Maupin provides one of the Northwest's great white-water trips. Most expeditions leave from Harpham Flat, about 5 miles upstream from Maupin, and end about 15 miles down the river at Sandy Beach, right before unnavigable Sherars Falls. All floaters on the Deschutes River are required to carry a boater pass,

The Railroad Race

As the area east of the Cascades became better explored, it quickly filled up with farmers and ranchers. The Homestead Acts especially lured in thousands of hopeful, but largely inexperienced, settlers. However, for these agricultural producers, there was no ready market for their goods; with only the most rudimentary overland trails for freight roads, and the wild, impassable Deschutes River as the only waterway, there was no transportation corridor into or out of central Oregon.

Two railroad companies – the Oregon Trunk Line and the Deschutes Railroad Company – sized up the opportunities and began to build lines up opposite sides of the Deschutes canyon in 1909. Competition flared between the two crews as they hewed a rail bed out of the rock walls. Railroad owners spurred workers into longer and harder shifts, each seeking to be the first to arrive in the fast-growing agricultural basin of central Oregon. Sabotage and bloody fights erupted, and gunfire frequently disrupted the laying of track.

Finally, the Deschutes Railroad Line, on the east side of the canyon, called it quits after spending millions of dollars to prepare the rail bed. The Oregon Trunk Line, affiliated with Great Northern Railroad's James J Hill, completed its line to Bend in 1911. The grain, cattle and logs of central Oregon suddenly had a market.

The west-side line is still in operation and is run these days by Burlington Northern. The east-side grade of the Deschutes Railroad is used for roads and hiking paths.

which is available from area businesses for $2 per person weekdays and $5 on weekends.

For raft rentals, river gear, shuttle service and guided trips, contact **Deschutes U-Boat** (☎ *541-395-2503, 501 US 197 S; raft rentals $30-180/day*). The storefront is near the Oasis Café, in Maupin. Other local outfitters offering raft rentals ($30 to $100, depending on the size of the raft and the day of the week) and guided trips (about $75 per person) include the following: **Ewing's Whitewater** (☎ *541-395-2697, 800-538-7238, 603 Mill St*); **All Star Rafting** (☎ *800-909-7238, 405 Deschutes Ave*), above the local ice cream store; **Deschutes River Adventures** (☎ *541-395-2238, 800-723-8464, 602 Deschutes Ave*); and **Deschutes Whitewater Service** (☎ *541-395-2232, 301 Bakeoven Rd*).

Places to Stay & Eat

Camping is really the way to go here, but remember to bring plenty of water; few of the public campgrounds have running water.

During the summer, strict fire precautions are in effect, and campfires are forbidden.

Either upstream or downstream from Maupin, a number of BLM campgrounds have minimal facilities and $5 fees. Contact the Prineville BLM office (☎ 541-416-6700 Ⓦ www.or.blm.gov/Prineville), 3050 NE 3rd St, for a list of campgrounds.

Maupin City Park (☎ *541-395-2252, 206 Bakeoven Rd*) Tents/hookups $15/15-20. For running water, showers ($2.50) and RV hookups, go to this park, which is just north of the US 197 bridge.

Oasis (☎ *541-395-2611,* Ⓦ *www.deschutes riveroasis.com, 609 US 97 S*) Cabins $35-65. These tiny cabins are quite well equipped and are a marvel of efficient design.

Imperial River Company (☎ *541-395-2404, 800-395-3903,* Ⓦ *www.deschutesriver .com, 304 Bakeoven Rd*) Singles/doubles from $50/65. This lodge, right on the river, is an old motel transformed into a sort of B&B.

Both the Oasis and the Imperial River Company have ***restaurants***.

Northeastern Oregon

With its remarkable scenery and rich Native American and Oregon Trail history, northeastern Oregon pleasantly surprises many visitors. Rambunctious old cow towns relive their early days with wild rodeos, and the

Highlights

- Horse packing or backpacking in the Eagle Cap Wilderness Area
- Cruising the Western art scene in Joseph
- Checking out the rhino fossils at John Day Fossil Beds
- Reading pioneers' diaries at the Oregon Trail Interpretive Center
- Seeing the Oregon Trail from the Native American perspective at Tamastslikt Cultural Institute

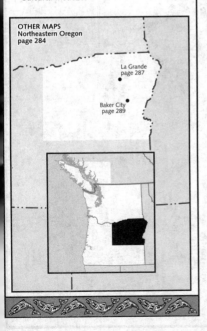

OTHER MAPS
Northeastern Oregon
page 284

La Grande
page 287

Baker City
page 289

Wallowa (wah-**lau**-ah) Mountains rise from wide agricultural valleys and contain 19 of Oregon's 25 highest peaks.

East of the Wallowas, along the Idaho border, the earth suddenly gives way to the mile-deep chasm of Hells Canyon.

Northeastern Oregon is cut diagonally by I-84, which links Boise, Idaho, and Salt Lake City, Utah, to Portland and follows the route of the Oregon Trail throughout the region.

US 395 cuts south from Washington's Tri-Cities to Pendleton and continues southward to John Day and Burns. The area's other major road is Hwy 82, which links La Grande to the Wallowa Mountain towns of Enterprise and Joseph.

History

Oregon's northeastern corner is home to several Native American tribes: the Cayuse, Umatilla, Wallawalla and Nez Perce. Lewis and Clark's Corps of Discovery engaged in friendly trading with them in 1805–06 and were especially impressed with the civility of the Nez Perce.

By the mid-19th century, wagon trains were coming through, and fortune hunters began to focus on eastern Oregon's gold. As settlers encroached on the Wallowa Mountains, the ancestral homeland of the Nez Perce, relations with the tribe quickly deteriorated. A series of tit-for-tat murders began the Nez Perce War in 1877. Chief Joseph and 800 Nez Perce fled Oregon, hoping to reach Canada and freedom from army retribution. Instead, they were defeated in Montana, just shy of the Canadian border, and sent to live on reservations in Oklahoma.

The Union Pacific Railroad opened a transcontinental rail line linking Omaha, Nebraska, with Portland in 1884 via Baker City and La Grande. With the Native Americans incarcerated on reservations, the region quickly filled with farmers and ranchers.

OREGON

NORTHEASTERN OREGON

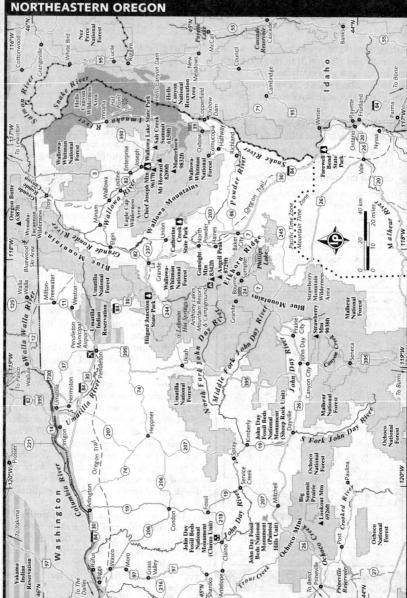

PENDLETON

Synonymous with wool shirts and rodeos, Pendleton (population 17,320) is eastern Oregon's largest city. A handsome old town that's not far removed from its cow-poking past, Pendleton is between steep hills along the Umatilla River and is surrounded by farm- and ranchland.

The Pendleton Round-Up, held the third weekend of September, is one of the USA's most famous and rowdy rodeos.

Orientation & Information

Pendleton is at the western edge of the Blue Mountains. I-84 and US 395 pass through the city, linking Spokane, Washington, and Burns, as does Hwy 11, which leads to Walla Walla, Washington. Pendleton is 208 miles east of Portland; it's 221 miles to Boise, Idaho.

US 30 becomes Court Ave (which is one way, westbound) and Dorion Ave (eastbound) in town. The intersection of Court and Dorion Aves with Main St is the center of downtown.

The Pendleton Chamber of Commerce (☎ 541-276-7411, 800-547-8911) is at 501 S Main St. The post office is at 104 SW Dorion Ave. Regional books and general good reading are available from Armchair Books (☎ 541-276-7323), 39 SW Dorion Ave. Oregon Public Radio is heard at 90.9 FM. For health needs go to St Anthony Hospital (☎ 541-276-5121), 1601 SE Court Ave.

Things to See & Do

The **Pendleton Woolen Mills** (☎ 541-276-6911, 1307 SE Court Place; salesroom open 8am-4:45pm Mon-Fri year round, 8am-2pm Sat May-Sept, 9am-1pm Sat Oct-Apr) was founded here in 1909. Built principally to scour local wool, it also produced blankets to sell on the nearby Umatilla Reservation. Today, its woolen products are known worldwide. Free, short factory tours are given at 9am, 11am, 1:30pm and 3pm Monday to Friday year round. The factory store has some good deals on blankets with minor flaws.

At the end of the 19th century, a network of businesses and establishments boomed beneath Pendleton's old storefronts. Driven underground by prohibition and social ten-

sions, saloons, Chinese laundries, opium dens, card rooms and other businesses found cozy tunnels in which to operate. **Pendleton Underground Tours** (☎ 541-276-0730, 800-226-6398, 37 SW Emigrant Ave; adult/child $10/5) lets you explore the town's subterranean district, as well as an above-ground 1890s brothel. Tours last 1½ hours. Call ahead for reservations and tour times.

The **Umatilla County Historical Museum** (☎ 541-276-0012, 108 SW Frazer Ave; adult/family $2/5; open 10am-4pm Tues-Sat) is housed in Pendleton's old railroad station. Displays include an Oregon Trail commemoration, local Native American artifacts and memorabilia of the region's sheep industry and wool mills.

Take a look at the Oregon Trail from the Native American perspective at the spacious **Tamastslikt Cultural Institute** (☎ 541-996-9748, 72789 Hwy 331; adult/senior & child $6/4; open 9am-5pm), east of Pendleton off I-84 exit 216. Exhibits focus on the history and culture of the Cayuse, Umatilla and Wallawalla tribes – together the Confederated Tribes of the Umatilla Indian Reservation. A mile east of the tribal **Wildhorse Casino**, it's much more rewarding than the slot machines.

Even if it's not Round-Up week (see below), you can go to the **Round-Up Hall of Fame Museum** (☎ 541-278-0815, 1205 SW Court Ave; admission free; open 10am-5pm Mon-Sat in summer) under the grandstands.

Special Events

Promoters call it the USA's best rodeo, and the Pendleton Round-Up, established in 1909, is one of the West's biggest parties. Held Wednesday to Saturday in the second full week of September, the roundup is an all-out Dionysian celebration, featuring cowboy breakfasts, dances and art shows. The rodeo is the main event, but the whole town swells with activity. A Native American powwow is held in conjunction with the roundup.

The rodeo grounds are on Court Ave (US 30), west of downtown. Lodging is scarce at Round-Up time, so plan well in advance. For ticket information and a schedule of events,

OREGON

contact the Pendleton Round-Up (☎ 800-457-6336), 1205 SW Court Ave.

Places to Stay

Emigrant Springs State Park (☎ 541-983-2277, W www.oregonstateparks.org, I-84 exit 234) Tents/hookups/covered wagons/cabins $15/17/27/35. There's a bit of freeway noise here, so consider renting a cabin. The campground is 26 miles east of Pendleton.

Travelodge (☎ 541-276-7531, 800-578-7878, 411 SW Dorion Ave) Singles/doubles $55/65. There are cheaper places to stay in downtown Pendleton, but the Travelodge is a better bet.

Red Lion Hotel (☎ 541-276-6111, W www .redlion.com, 304 SE Nye Ave) Rooms $69. The views out the back of this sprawling hotel are stupendous, and the outdoor pool is a real summertime plus.

Working Girls Old Hotel (☎ 541-276-0730, 21 SW Emigrant Ave) Rooms $50-70. This place, run by Pendleton Underground Tours, offers antique-filled rooms in an old downtown hotel with a shady past.

Parker House B&B (☎ 541-276-8581, 800-700-8581, W www.parkerhousebnb.com, 311 N Main St) Rooms $75-95. Just across the Umatilla and uphill from downtown, this pink stucco mansion shows a more genteel side of Pendleton. It's the nicest place in town and has a very helpful proprietor.

Places to Eat

Como's Italian Eatery (☎ 541-278-9142, 39 SE Court Ave) Entrees $5. Open Mon-Fri. Seating is limited at this bustling Italian deli. It's a good place for lunch or an early dinner of pizza or pasta.

Cimmiyotti's (☎ 541-276-4314, 137 S Main St) Dinner $15. A local favorite, Cimmiyotti's features steak and pasta in a bar/dining room that recalls an Old West speakeasy.

Raphael's Restaurant & Lounge (☎ 541-276-8500, 233 SE 4th St) Full/light dinners $22/10. Pendleton's best food is here. Salmon and smoked prime rib are favorites, and the separate vegetarian menu is a real find in a cow town. Reservations are recommended.

Getting There & Around

Horizon Air (☎ 541-276-9777, 800-547-9308) connects Pendleton Municipal Airport to Portland (from $70, one hour, four flights daily). The airport is about 5 miles west of town on US 30.

Greyhound buses pass regularly between Pendleton and Portland ($32, four hours, 238 miles, three daily). There's also service to Walla Walla and Washington's Tri-Cities. The depot (☎ 541-276-1551) is at 320 SW Court Ave.

If you're driving, the Blue Mountains are notorious for severe winter weather, and Deadman Pass between Pendleton and La Grande can be treacherous. Call ☎ 800-977-6368 for road conditions.

Hertz (☎ 541-276-3783) does business at the airport. For a cab, call Elite Taxis at ☎ 541-276-8294.

LA GRANDE & AROUND

Early French traders, upon seeing the broad, seemingly circular valley, declared it to be *La Grande Ronde*, 'the Big Circle.' Indeed, from the historical marker on US 30 above town, it seems as if the mountain peaks form a giant ring around the valley.

The Oregon Trail crossed this valley, and at La Grande, the pioneers rested and prepared to traverse the Blue Mountains. Some understood the valley's agricultural potential and settled. Today La Grande (population 12,555) is home to Eastern Oregon State College and is a main city for all the rural people in the area.

Orientation & Information

Located on the Grande Ronde River, a confluent of the Snake River, La Grande is at the juncture of I-84 and Hwy 82, the road to the Wallowa Mountains. Adams Ave (US 30) is the main street downtown. Turn from Adams Ave onto Island Ave to reach Hwy 82 and the Wallowas.

The town is 44 miles north of Baker City, 52 miles southeast of Pendleton and 259 miles east of Portland.

Find the La Grande/Union County Chamber of Commerce (☎ 541-963-8588,

OREGON

800-848-9969, W www.visitlagrande.com) at 1912 4th St.

The post office is at 1202 Washington Ave. Sunflower Books (☎ 541-963-5242), 1114 Washington Ave, features good reads and coffee. Oregon Public Broadcasting transmits at 89.9 FM.

Bubbles Laundry (☎ 541-962-7578) is at 2001 Adams Ave, and the Grande Ronde Hospital (☎ 541-963-8421) is at 900 Sunset Dr.

Grande Ronde River

Explore the upper reaches of the Grande Ronde River by taking Hwy 244, 8 miles west of La Grande from I-84 exit 252.

At the site of today's **Hilgard State Park**, just off the freeway exit, Oregon Trail pioneers gathered their strength before climbing up over the Blue Mountains. Information kiosks explain how the pioneers winched their wagons down the steep slopes.

Hwy 244 follows the Grande Ronde Valley, then climbs up to a low pass. **Cross-country skiing** is popular here in winter. Skiers and other explorers can stop to soak at **Lehman Hot Springs** (☎ 541-427-3015; $6), on Hwy 244, 40 miles southwest of La Grande.

The huge pool has three separate areas, with water ranging from warm to sizzling hot. Stop by for an afternoon of swimming or spend the night in the adjacent campground ($9) or cabin ($85).

Blue Mountain Interpretive Center

Better than any other place in the Blue Mountains, this outdoors center (☎ 541-963-7186, I-84 exit 248; $5 Northwest Forest Pass required for parking; open 8am-8pm Memorial Day-Labor Day) gives a visceral feeling of what travel was like for Oregon Trail pioneers. Paths wind through the forest to ruts left by pioneer wagons – still quite visible after 150 years. Steep grades and early snowstorms in the Blue Mountains were a huge concern to the pioneers, who usually made the crossing in early September.

The center is 13 miles west of La Grande and 3 miles on well-marked roads from the freeway exit.

Activities

You can go **fishing** on the Grande Ronde for rainbow trout – try your luck at Red

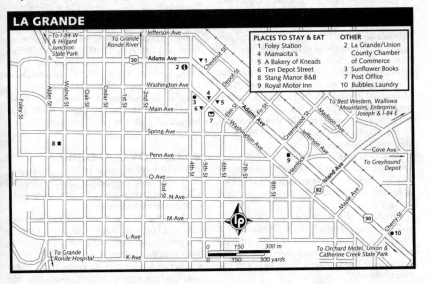

LA GRANDE

PLACES TO STAY & EAT	OTHER
1 Foley Station	2 La Grande/Union
4 Mamacita's	County Chamber
5 A Bakery of Kneads	of Commerce
6 Ten Depot Street	3 Sunflower Books
8 Stang Manor B&B	7 Post Office
9 Royal Motor Inn	10 Bubbles Laundry

To I-84 W & Hilgard Junction State Park
To Grande Ronde River
Jefferson Ave
Adams Ave
Washington Ave
Main Ave
Spring Ave
Penn Ave
O Ave
N Ave
M Ave
L Ave
K Ave
To Grande Ronde Hospital

Alder St, Walnut St, Oak St, Cedar St, 1st St, 2nd St, Chestnut St, Depot St, Elm St, Adams Ave, Fir St, 3rd St, 4th St, 5th St, 6th St, 7th St, 8th St, Foley St

Hemlock, Greenwood St, Jefferson Ave, Madison Ave, Island Ave, Maple Ave, Cherry St

To Best Western, Wallowa Mountains, Enterprise, Joseph & I-84 E
Cove Ave
To Greyhound Depot
To Orchard Motel, Union & Catherine Creek State Park

0   150   300 m
0   150   300 yards

Bridge State Park, west of La Grande on Hwy 244. Fly-fishing for steelhead is popular in winter near the little community of Troy. Contact the Fish & Wildlife office (☎ 541-963-2138, 107 20th St), in La Grande, for current regulations and information.

Float beautiful, remote stretches of the Grande Ronde from Minam to Troy. **Wapiti River Guides** (☎ 800-488-9872, Ⓦ www .wapitiriverguides.com) offers multiday float trips ($400 & up).

Spout Springs Resort (☎ 541-556-2164, Hwy 204 at Tollgate; lift tickets $26) is a tiny, low-key ski area. There are also 13 miles of groomed cross-country ski trails. Rent downhill and cross-country skis at the ski area or from **Blue Mountain Sports** (☎ 541-963-5115, 2212 Island Ave). Rentals are about $18.

Places to Stay

Besides these two sites, look up the Grande Ronde River for less-convenient but more isolated camping spots.

Hilgard Junction State Park (☎ 800-551-6949, I-84 exit 252) Primitive sites $12. Only 8 miles west of La Grande, this park is convenient but right beside the freeway.

Catherine Creek State Park (☎ 541-963-0430, Hwy 203) Sites $10. Camp beside a pretty creek on the back road from La Grande to Baker City.

Of La Grande's several B&Bs, this one has a great location.

Stang Manor B&B (☎ 541-963-2400, 888-286-9463, Ⓦ www.stangmanor.com, 1612 Walnut St) Rooms $85-98. La Grande's nicest accommodations are in this 1920s Georgian mansion once owned by a lumber baron.

It's usually easy to find a room in one of the motels along Adams Ave.

Royal Motor Inn (☎ 541-963-4154, 800-990-7575, 1510 Adams Ave) Singles/doubles $32/39. This downtown motel is comfortable and within walking distance to good restaurants.

Orchard Motel (☎ 541-963-6160, 2206 Adams Ave) Rooms $35-55. Of the cluster of motels east of downtown, this entirely nonsmoking establishment is one of the nicer ones. The Orchard takes pets and has kitchenettes.

Best Western (☎ 541-963-7195, 800-528-1234, 2612 Island Ave) Singles/doubles $66/73. A little fancier than the other La Grande motels, the Best Western has a pool and is convenient to the freeway and shopping, but it is a ways from downtown.

Places to Eat

A Bakery of Kneads (☎ 541-963-5413, 109 Depot St) Pastries $2-3. Really delicious baked goods are served here.

Mamacita's (☎ 541-963-6223, 110 Depot St) Dinner $7. Mamacita's is a fun place with good Mexican food.

Ten Depot Street (☎ 541-963-8766, 10 Depot St) Entrees $14. Kind of fancy, but kind of down home, Ten Depot is a longtime local favorite. The menu is pretty much standard American, but local produce, meats and (in-season) morel mushrooms make it special. Weeknights, the 'Blue Plate Specials' are very good deals.

Foley Station (☎ 541-963-7473, 1011 Adams Ave) Breakfast/lunch/dinner $6/8/19. One breakfast here and you'll be dreaming of when you can return. Lunch and dinner are also good.

Getting There & Around

Buses pass through the Greyhound bus depot (☎ 541-963-5165), 2108 Cove Ave, on their way to/from Portland ($41, 6 hours, 293 miles, three daily). The Wallowa Valley Stage Line (☎ 541-963-5465) offers weekday service to Joseph ($11, two hours, Mon-Sat only) and Enterprise ($10, 2 hours, Mon-Sat only) from the same depot. Call Blue Mountain Cab Co (☎ 541-963-9562) for a lift.

BAKER CITY & AROUND

Baker City (population 10,420), at the head of a wide valley beneath the snowcapped Elkhorn Ridge, is one of eastern Oregon's oldest commercial centers.

Once the largest city between Salt Lake City and Portland, Baker City was a boisterous party town during the late 19th century, with miners, cowboys, sheepherders, shopkeepers and loggers keeping each other company in the city's many saloons, brothels

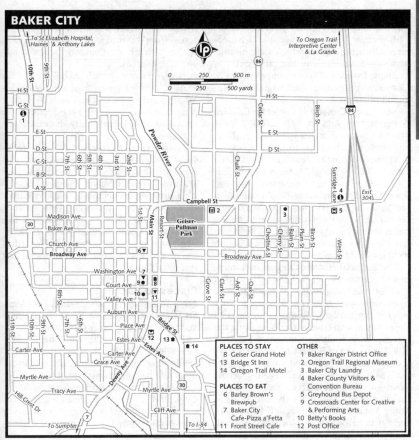

BAKER CITY

To St Elizabeth Hospital,
Haines & Anthony Lakes

To Oregon Trail
Interpretive Center
& La Grande

0   250   500 m
0   250   500 yards

Powder River

Geiser-
Pullman
Park

Campbell St

Madison Ave
Baker Ave
Church Ave
Broadway Ave

Washington Ave
Court Ave
Valley Ave
Auburn Ave
Place Ave
Estes Ave
Carter Ave
Grace Ave
Myrtle Ave
Tracy Ave
Cliff Ave

To Sumpter

To I-84

PLACES TO STAY	OTHER
8 Geiser Grand Hotel	1 Baker Ranger District Office
13 Bridge St Inn	2 Oregon Trail Regional Museum
14 Oregon Trail Motel	3 Baker City Laundry
	4 Baker County Visitors &
PLACES TO EAT	Convention Bureau
6 Barley Brown's	5 Greyhound Bus Depot
Brewpub	9 Crossroads Center for Creative
7 Baker City	& Performing Arts
Cafe-Pizza a'Fetta	10 Betty's Books
11 Front Street Cafe	12 Post Office

and gaming halls. Still an authentic Western town, Baker City's wide streets and gracious architecture recall both the swagger and courtliness of a not-too-distant past.

Orientation & Information

Located where the Powder River leaves the Blue Mountains, Baker City is 44 miles south of La Grande on I-84 at the junction of Hwy 7 (to John Day) and Hwy 86 (to Hells Canyon Wilderness Area). US 30 becomes 10th St in town.

The Baker County Visitors & Convention Bureau (☎ 541-523-3356, 800-523-1235)

is at 490 Campbell St. Visit the Baker Ranger District office (☎ 541-523-4476), 3165 10th St, for information on nearby hiking trails.

The post office is at 1550 Dewey Ave. Betty's Books (☎ 541-523-7551), 1813 Main St, is a good bookstore, with a selection of regional history and touring books. Oregon Public Radio is heard at 91.5 FM.

The Baker City Laundry (☎ 541-523-9817) is at 815 Campbell St.

Baker City's medical center is St Elizabeth Hospital (☎ 541-523-6461), at 3325 Pocahontas Rd.

OREGON

Things to See & Do

The old downtown retains much of its late-19th-century Victorian Italianate architecture. A brochure describing a walking tour of historic buildings in the city center is available from the Baker County Visitors & Convention Bureau or the Oregon Trail Regional Museum.

Stop by the Crossroads Center for Creative & Performing Arts (☎ 541-523-5369, 1901 Main St), where there's a gallery of local arts and crafts, as well as a performance space.

Housed in a natatorium built in 1920, the Oregon Trail Regional Museum (☎ 541-523-9308, 2480 Grove St; $2 donation requested; open 9am-5pm mid-Apr-Oct) contains a jumble of exhibits. The large space that once contained the pool now displays furniture, vehicles and machinery from Baker City's frontier days. An extensive mineral collection includes a wild display of fluorescent rocks.

The National Historic Oregon Trail Interpretive Center (☎ 541-523-1843, Hwy 86 at Flagstaff Hill; adult/senior & youth $5/3.50; open 9am-6pm May-Oct, 9am-4pm Nov-Apr) is the nation's foremost memorial to the pioneers who crossed the West along the Oregon Trail. Built on windswept Flagstaff Hill, 7 miles east of Baker City along Hwy 86, it overlooks well-preserved wagon ruts from the 1840s and '50s. After traveling across deserts and canyon lands for weeks, the pioneers emerged from the aptly named Burnt Water Valley and onto Flagstaff Hill, where the Powder River valley blossomed beneath the forested Blue Mountains. The 23,000-sq-foot exhibition contains interactive displays, artifacts and films that stress the day-to-day realities, choices and predicaments of the pioneers. A trail system explores an old mining claim, the arid sagebrush ecosystem and the ruts of the original Oregon Trail. To get there, take I-84 to exit 302 (onto Hwy 86), just north of Baker City.

Places to Stay

Anthony Lakes Campground (☎ 541-523-4476, Ⓦ www.fs.fed.us/r6/w-w, 47500 Anthony Lakes Hwy) Sites $8. Though it's 30 miles from town, this splendid campground is worth the drive.

Oregon Trail Motel (☎ 541-523-5844, 211 Bridge St) Singles/doubles $35/40. Just across from the Bridge St Inn, this is a good choice, with a heated outdoor pool and adjacent restaurant.

Bridge St Inn (☎ 541-523-6571, 800-932-9220, Ⓦ www.bridgestreetinn.com, 134 Bridge St) Singles/doubles $47/50. This is a friendly place near downtown with a good continental breakfast (free), and many discounts are available.

Geiser Grand Hotel (☎ 541-523-1889, 888-434-7374, Ⓦ www.geisergrand.com, 1996 Main St) Rooms $89-199. It's a treat to stay at Baker City's landmark downtown hotel – it's a stunning, meticulously restored Italian Renaissance Revival building, with a corner cupola and a stained-glass ceiling in the dining area. Locals, including hotel workers, swear that the place is haunted. Nevertheless, the rooms are huge, well decorated and comfortable.

Places to Eat

Front Street Cafe (☎ 541-523-0223, 1840 Main St) Breakfast/lunch $5/7. Sit at the counter and blend into the Baker City milieu.

Baker City Cafe Pizza a'Fetta (☎ 541-523-6099, 1915 Washington Ave) Light meals/pizzas $6/13. This friendly, unpretentious cafe has surprisingly good food.

Barley Brown's Brewpub (☎ 541-523-4266, 2190 Main St) Entrees $11. Downtown's tin-ceilinged good-times joint serves its own microbrews, but it's more of a steak-and-pasta restaurant than a pub.

Geiser Grand Hotel (see Places to Stay) Dinner $8-17. The dining room here is particularly elegant, and on a good day, the food's the best in town.

Haines Steak House (☎ 541-856-3639, Old Hwy 30, Haines) Entrees $19. Dinner only. It's very likely that you'll find Oregon's best steak at this classic Western restaurant 10 miles north of Baker City.

Getting There & Around

Greyhound buses stop at the Truck Corral (☎ 541-523-5011), 515 Campbell St, on their run between Portland ($44, 6½ hours, 334 miles, three times daily) and Boise, Idaho.

For a taxi, call Baker Cab (☎ 541-523-6070).

BLUE MOUNTAINS

Rising to the west from ranchland near Baker City, the Blue Mountains were responsible for the gold strikes that established towns such as Sumpter, Granite and Baker City. Back roads now lead to ghost towns, high mountain lakes, river canyons and hiking trails. Elkhorn Dr, a National Forest Scenic Byway, circles Elkhorn Ridge.

Hwy 7 connects I-84 with US 26 to the south, traversing the Blue Mountains. From Sumpter, USFS Rd 24 leads to Granite and USFS Rd 73 goes to Anthony Lakes.

The Baker Ranger District office (☎ 541-523-4476), 3165 10th St, in Baker City, has information on the scenic byway and the Blue Mountains.

Elkhorn Drive Scenic Byway

It takes all day to properly explore this 106-mile loop drive between Baker City and Granite (along Hwy 7 and US 30, and USFS Rd 73 over the Elkhorn Ridge). The eastern-Oregon gold rush began in these mountains in 1861, when prospectors discovered colors at Griffin Creek, south of Baker City.

By the way, those patches of dead pines between Granite and Gunsight Pass along USFS Rd 73 aren't all due to fires. The byway passes through regions heavily afflicted with mountain-pine beetles.

Phillips Lake

Formed by the dammed Powder River, Phillips Lake offers **fishing** in summer and **ice fishing** in winter. *Union Creek Campground (☎ 541-523-4476, Ⓦ www.fs.fed.us/r6/w-w, Hwy 7 at Phillips Lake)* is a large, pleasant lakeside spot just off the highway.

Sumpter

A relic of the early gold-and-lumber boom days, Sumpter (population 175), 28 miles west of Baker City, now makes a living as a 'ghost town.' In 1862, gold was discovered, but it wasn't until the Sumpter Valley Railroad reached the town site in 1896 that it

---

The Golden Blues

The Blue Mountains were Pacific reefs and islands before the North American continent collided with them about 200 million years ago, wedging them up to mountain heights. Between 160 and 120 million years ago, molten lava shot through the new mountains and hardened into igneous rock.

These new rocks were mostly granite, but they also contained a number of other minerals. As the molten rock cooled, the various component minerals hardened at different rates. Liquid gold, having a very low melting point, squeezed into veins as surrounding rock began to solidify.

In the 1860s, the discovery of gold nuggets in streams in the Blue Mountains led to the unearthing of significant gold veins, or lodes, at several locations in the region. The richest lodes were in an arc between John Day, Baker City and Ukiah.

Ghost-town enthusiasts will find the Blue Mountains dotted with ruined mining camps. Easily reached from Sumpter is Bourne, 7 miles up Cracker Creek. Gold mines are still producing in the area. Granite, 15 miles up Hwy 24, is a ghost town in aspect, but its population is actually growing – it recently reached 25 residents.

---

really began to boom. The town quickly grew to include 4000 residents, an opera house, three newspapers and a hospital.

After the main gold veins were mined, the entire area was dredged for gold, leaving the valley's rocky soil in orderly piles. Today, an abandoned, evil-looking gold dredge is the town's focal point.

From the 1890s to the 1930s, the narrow-gauge **Sumpter Valley Railroad** *(☎ 541-894-2268, Austin St; adult/child/family $9/6.50/$20 roundtrip)* linked Prairie City, on the John Day River, to Baker City. A portion of the wood-fired steam service remains open during summer weekends, linking Sumpter and Phillips Lake. Roundtrip excursions leave Sumpter Depot at 11:30am and 2pm

Saturday and Sunday from Memorial Day to Labor Day.

Anthony Lakes

Right below the impressive crags of Gunsight Mountain (8342 feet) and Angell Peak (8729 feet) is a lake basin offering camping and fishing as well as hikes to alpine meadows. In winter, Oregon's best powder lures skiers and snowboarders.

USFS Rd 73 climbs 19 miles to Anthony Lakes from the town of North Powder (population 560) on I-84; the road is open year round only as far as the ski area. In summer, the road continues over Elkhorn Summit Pass (at 7392 feet, the highest paved road in Oregon) to join the Elkhorn Dr byway.

Activities

Campgrounds along the shores of Grande Ronde, Mud and Anthony Lakes make good base camps for **hiking**. Trails lead out from Anthony Lake to several other small lakes, including a short but steep climb up Parker Creek to tiny Hoffer Lakes. For another short hike, follow the **Elkhorn Crest Trail** east from Anthony Lake and hike up to Black Lake, immediately below impressive 8342-foot Gunsight Mountain.

Anthony Lakes Mountain Resort (☎ 541-856-3277, 47500 Anthony Lakes Hwy; lift tickets $28) has the highest base elevation in Oregon (7100 feet) and 21 runs. The lodge maintains 6 miles of groomed cross-country trails, and nearby are miles of snowy USFS roads to explore. Rentals at the lodge run $15/20/30 for cross-country/downhill/snowboarding.

WALLOWA MOUNTAINS

Rising precipitously from parklike farm-and ranchland in Oregon's far northeastern corner, the Wallowas have 17 peaks over 9000 feet. Ice Age glaciers carved sharp crags and deep canyons into the mountains, and the moraines of one such glacier now impound Wallowa Lake. Much of the high country, including the only remaining glacier (Alpine Glacier) and eastern Oregon's highest peak (the 9832-foot Matterhorn), is part of Eagle Cap Wilderness Area, a 715-sq-mile natural area studded with alpine meadows and lakes.

Pressed up against the Wallowas' north face are two Old West burgs, Enterprise and Joseph. Beauty and isolation draw artists to the area, particularly to Joseph, which has gained a reputation as a center for Western and wildlife art. In fact, it's become Oregon's down-home version of Santa Fe – all glitzy shops with just enough boots-and-jeans street life to keep it from seeming totally fake. Directly behind Joseph is Wallowa Lake, a glacial lake flanked by towering peaks.

Visitors should not be surprised to find crowded trails, campgrounds and fishing holes during the high season. In particular, the lovely state park at Wallowa Lake takes on a carnival atmosphere on weekends in summer.

Some secondary roads over the Wallowa Mountains are closed during winter months. Inquire locally before heading off on side roads between November and May.

South of the Wallowas, the Powder River valley is just as beautiful and isolated as Enterprise and Joseph, and the little town of Halfway is much less hyped and overrun. Additionally, Hwy 86, which follows the Powder River from near Baker City, leads to Oregon's only riverside access to Hells Canyon.

Enterprise

Enterprise (population 2050) both looks and feels the part of a friendly Western town, and it makes an ideal base for exploring northeastern Oregon. Much of the original downtown, built in the 1890s, is still here.

Enterprise is 65 miles east of La Grande on Hwy 82; from here, it's 6 miles to Joseph and 12 miles to Wallowa Lake.

The Wallowa County Chamber of Commerce (☎ 541-426-4622, 800-585-4121), 936 W North St, is open 10am to 3pm on weekdays. The Wallowa Mountains Visitor Center (☎ 541-426-5546), 88401 Hwy 82, is staffed by the US Forest Service and is an excellent resource for outdoor activities. These offices serve Enterprise, Joseph and Wallowa Lake.

The post office is at 201 W North St. The Bookloft (☎ 541-426-3351), 107 E Main St, is one of eastern Oregon's best bookstores, complete with a friendly coffee bar. Wallowa Memorial Hospital (☎ 541-426-3111), 401 E First St, serves the entire Wallowa Valley.

It's far easier to find a motel in Enterprise than in Joseph, but they're often booked up on summer weekends, so it's a good idea to plan ahead.

Country Inn (☎ 541-426-4986, 877-426-4986, 402 W North St) Singles/doubles $42/50. The homey rooms here are some of the best deals in the area.

Wilderness Inn (☎ 541-426-4535, 800-965-1205, fax 541-426-0128, 301 W North St) Singles/doubles $59/64. Rooms at this friendly motel aren't fancy, but they're just fine, and it's an easy stroll to downtown.

Ponderosa Motel (☎ 541-426-3186, fax 541-426-8068, 102 E Greenwood St) Singles/doubles $65/70. The Ponderosa is another good option – it's every bit as friendly as the Wilderness Inn, but it offers a few more amenities.

Best Western Rama Inn (☎ 541-426-2000, 888-726-2466, 1200 Highland Ave) Singles/doubles $99/119. This Best Western, right on the edge of town, has an indoor pool, sauna and fitness room. Since it's a large motel, it often has vacancies when the rest of the valley's full.

Terminal Velocity Brewery (☎ 541-426-0158, 803 School St) Entrees $7. Relax on the front lawn with a tasty IPA and a sausage sandwich and chat with other diners about their recent hikes.

House Cafe (☎ 541-426-9055, 307 W North St) Breakfast/lunch $6/7. If it's not quite time for a brewpub, this is a good choice for breakfast or lunch.

Wallowa Valley Stage Line (☎ 541-963-5465) runs one bus a day (except Sunday) between La Grande and Joseph, stopping in Enterprise at the Mountain Mart Station, at 302 W North St ($10, 2 hours to La Grande).

Joseph

The brick sidewalks of downtown Joseph (population 1280) are adorned with planter boxes and huge bronze statues, including an anatomically compelling bull that men can't seem to resist. Many of the old storefronts now peddle art – everything from nature photos to artsy screen doors to huge, expensive bronzes. Valley Bronze, one of the nation's largest foundries, relocated to Joseph in the 1970s, bringing an artistic focus to this old frontier town.

Orientation & Information Joseph is 6 miles south of Enterprise and 6 miles north of Wallowa Lake State Park. Hwy 350 leaves from Joseph for Imnaha (28 miles northeast), where the Hat Point road climbs up to Hells Canyon vistas. Seasonal USFS Rd 39, part of the Wallowa Mountain Loop Rd, divides off Hwy 350 about 7 miles east of Joseph to wind over the eastern flank of the Wallowas.

Things to See & Do Surely no other town in Oregon can boast more galleries than bars, but Joseph is no ordinary Western town. If Western art is your thing, then you'll find plenty of things to occupy a day in Joseph.

The town is most noted for its cast-bronze sculpture, thanks to the **Valley Bronze Foundry**, which can cast especially large statuary. Call ☎ 541-432-7445 or stop by the Valley Bronze Showroom (☎ 541-432-7551, 18 S Main St; open 10am-5pm) to arrange a foundry tour.

The **Manuel Museum** (☎ 541-432-7235, 400 N Main; admission $6; open 8am-8pm Mon-Sat) is bronze-artist David Manuel's studio and houses a collection of Native American artifacts. Foundry tours are included with museum admission.

The **Wallowa County Museum** (☎ 541-426-6095, 110 S Main; admission by donation; open 10am-5pm Memorial Day-late Sept), housed in an 1888 bank, is notable for its display on Nez Perce history.

Although you can't go **mountain biking** in the Eagle Cap Wilderness Area, the Wallowa-Whitman National Forest and the Hells Canyon National Recreation Area are full of dirt roads and single-tracks. The Wallowa Mountains Visitor Center (see

Enterprise, earlier) has information on bicycle trails.

For starters, try the Wagon Loop Rd, a 10-mile circuit from USFS Rd 39 at the Salt Creek Summit (6150 feet). It's a challenging ride with great scenery. Head east out of town toward Imnaha on Hwy 350. After 8 miles, turn right onto USFS Rd 39, and continue another 8 miles to Salt Creek Summit. When snow falls, this becomes a popular area for **cross-country skiing**.

Special Events Chief Joseph Days, held the last weekend of July, features a rodeo, Native American dancing and other activities. Book your lodging well in advance. Contact the Wallowa County Chamber of Commerce (see Enterprise, earlier) for more information.

Taking its title as the 'Switzerland of America' seriously, Joseph hosts an Alpenfest (☎ 800-585-4121) in late September. Alpenfest features folk music and dancers, German food and local crafts. Be there for the yodeling contest.

Places to Stay & Eat There are a few budget accommodations and dining options.

Hurricane Creek Campground (☎ 541-426-5546, **W** www.fs.fed.us/r6/w-w, Mile 7, Hurricane Creek Rd) Sites free of charge. In season, the real action is at Wallowa Lake, but campers who want to avoid the bustle of the state park should try this primitive campground, 7 miles south of Joseph. Bring your own water.

Indian Lodge Motel (☎ 541-432-2651, **e** gingerdaggett@eoni.com, 201 S Main) Singles/doubles $47/50. Since this is the least expensive motel in town, it fills up quickly. Reserve well in advance.

Wallowa River Camp (☎ 541-426-2039, **W** www.rivercamp.com, 501 Park Dr) Bunkhouse beds/cabins $10/80-250. The bunkhouse (mostly used by groups in the summer, available by-the-bed in the off season) is in a lovely rural setting a short walk from downtown Joseph. Cabins are located in various places around Joseph.

Old Town Cafe (☎ 541-432-9892, 8 S Main St) Entrees $6-7. This is the best place

in town for a leisurely breakfast or lunch, especially if you snare a seat in the garden.

Wildflour Bakery (☎ 541-432-7225, 603 N Main St) Sandwiches $5-6. Better for you than donuts – and much tastier, too – are the Wildflour's berry scones. Lunchtime sandwiches on the deck are equally appealing.

Embers Brewhouse (☎ 541-432-2739, 206 N Main St) Entrees $8. Pizza, calzone and microbrews all go down easy in this relaxed pub.

Getting There & Away Wallowa Valley Stage Line (☎ 541-569-2284) has bus service between La Grande and Joseph ($11, two hours, daily except Sundays); the bus stop is at the Chevron station at the corner of Main and Wallowa Sts.

Wallowa Lake & Around

Wallowa Lake was formed when glaciers plowed down out of the Wallowas, pushing huge piles of displaced rock. These rock moraines eventually stopped the progress of the glacier, which melted, creating a lake basin. Today, the morainal walls of Wallowa Lake rise 900 feet above the plateau at nearby Joseph. On three sides of the lake, Wallowa peaks shoot to the sky; 9617-foot Chief Joseph Mountain rises vertically a mile above the lake.

Old Chief Joseph, the father of Chief Joseph, is buried at a beautiful site at the lake's north end.

Wallowa Lake State Park Reckoned to be one of the most beautiful state parks in the USA, Wallowa Lake State Park (☎ 541-432-4185, 72214 Marina Lane; no day-use fee) is the center of activities at the lake's south end. A swimming beach and a boat launch generate much activity. The best **hiking** is from the end of Wallowa Lake Rd.

Wallowa Lake Tramway The gondola (☎ 541-432-5331, 59919 Wallowa Lake Hwy; adult/child 3-12 years $17/10; 10am-4pm daily June-Sept, open 10am-4pm Sat & Sun May) leaves from Wallowa Lake and climbs 3700 feet to the top of 8200-foot Mt Howard. The ride is thrilling enough, but

The Nez Perce Diaspora

The Wallowa Mountains are at the center of the Nez Perce traditional homeland, which once encompassed adjacent areas of Washington and Idaho. Early treaties effectively divided the Nez Perce into a band that lived in the Wallowa Valley, and another that lived along the Clearwater River in Idaho. In 1863, in a move that demonstrated US diplomatic scheming as well as intertribal rivalries, the Idaho Nez Perce signed a treaty that turned the Oregon reservation lands over to white settlement, while maintaining the Idaho homelands. The Oregon Nez Perce, under Chief Joseph, refused to recognize the treaty and remained in the Wallowas.

Conflicts between settlers and the Nez Perce left several white men dead, and the 1876 Battle of Little Bighorn, in Montana – Custer's defeat at the hands of Sioux and Cheyenne Indians – was fanning distrust of Indians everywhere. Judging that flight to Canada was a wiser choice than awaiting punishment from the army, Chief Joseph and 800 Nez Perce fled eastward. They crossed Idaho and Montana, alternately eluding and fighting the army (most notably at the 1877 Battle of the Big Hole, in western Montana) before being apprehended within miles of the Canadian border. The Wallowa Nez Perce were removed to Indian Territory, now Oklahoma, before being allowed to move to the Colville Reservation, in Washington. The Idaho Nez Perce remain on the Lapwai Reservation, in Idaho.

Chief Joseph

the real rewards are the easy alpine hikes around Mt Howard's summit, with views onto Hells Canyon, the Wallowas and Idaho's Seven Devils. Winter rides for backcountry skiers and summertime mountain-bike access are in the works.

Eagle Cap Wilderness Area Glacier-ripped valleys, high mountain lakes and marble peaks are some of the rewards that long-distance hikers find on overnight treks into Oregon's largest wilderness area. Few hiking destinations readily suit the schedules of day-hikers.

A major trailhead into Eagle Cap Wilderness Area is at the south end of Wallowa Lake Rd. One of the most popular **hiking** routes from here is the 6-mile one-way hike to Aneroid Lake, where the remains of a cabin settlement add to the alpine lake's mystique. Other day hikes from this trailhead require simply hiking up trails until lunch, and then returning. One such option involves taking the **West Fork Trail** to the **Chief Joseph Mountain Trail**, which has good views down to Wallowa Lake. The peak is 7 miles from the trailhead.

From the upper Lostine Valley, or from USFS Rd 39's Sheep Creek Summit, there is easier day-hike access to the Eagle Cap's high country. The Wallowa Mountains Visitor Center (see Enterprise, earlier) has lots of information.

Another option is horse or llama pack trips. **Eagle Cap Wilderness Pack Station** (☎ 541-432-4145, 800-681-6222, 59761 Wallowa Lake Hwy) offers a variety of horseback trips, from hourlong rides ($18) to extended pack trips. For llama excursions, contact **Wallowa Llamas** (☎ 541-742-2961, W www.neoregon.com/wallowallamas, 36678 Allstead Lane, Halfway; $350-700). They run three- to five-day trips into the Eagle Cap. **Hurricane Creek Llama Treks** (☎ 541-432-4455, 800-528-9609, W www.hcltrek.com, 63366 Pine Tree Rd, Enterprise) has five- to seven-day trips, including a five-day women's trip for $700.

Go skiing in the backcountry with **Wing Ridge Ski Tours** (☎ 541-426-4322, 800-646-9050, W www.wingski.com, 65113 Hurricane Creek Rd, Enterprise; $400-500). Their six-day tours feature nights at a wilderness cabin and a tent camp, as well as days of challenging skiing in incredible country (you'll need metal edges and strong thighs). Prices depend on how much you're willing to pitch in doing camp work. Wing Ridge also rents solid, well-equipped ski-in tent shelters (about $30 per person per night).

Places to Stay Wallowa Lake's motels, lodges, and cabin resorts have created a bustling community near the lake's south shore.

Wallowa Lake State Park (☎ 541-432-4185, 72214 Marina Lane) Tents/hookups/yurts $18/22/27. This crowded lakeside state park offers multitudes of campsites complete with flush toilets and showers. Reservations are almost mandatory in summer.

Wallowa Lake Lodge (☎ 541-432-9821, W www.wallowalakelodge.com, 60060 Wallowa Lake Hwy) Rooms/cabins $87/187. This is a fine-looking old lodge on the shores of the lake, with a beautiful fireplace-dominated lobby. Many visitors prefer the lakeside cabins to the lodge rooms.

Eagle Cap Chalets (☎ 541-432-4704, W www.eaglecapchalets.com, 59879 Wallowa Lake Hwy) Rooms $58-125. Choose from motel rooms, cabins or condos, all with at least rudimentary in-room cooking facilities. It's the best deal in the Wallowa Lake neighborhood.

Flying Arrow Resort (☎ 541-432-2951, W www.flyingarrowresort.com, 59782 Wallowa Lake Hwy) Cabins $80-145. The riverside cabins are nicest, unless you want your kids to be close to the nearby arcade and go-cart arena. (They'll also enjoy the heated pool.)

Places to Eat Most food options at Wallowa Lake would be more properly designated as concessions than dining, with the following exceptions.

Wallowa Lake Lodge Dining Room (see Places to Stay) Dinner $15-20. Soak in the ambience of the old-fashioned dining room. The food vaguely aspires to cuisine, with steak, salmon and chicken leading the menu.

Vali's Alpine Deli & Restaurant (☎ 541-432-5691, 59811 Wallowa Lake Hwy) Dinner $10. For Hungarian specialties, eat at this popular restaurant. The menu is very limited but changes from day to day. Call ahead to find out what's cooking and for reservations (which are required).

Wallowa Mountain Loop Road

From Joseph, paved USFS Rd 39 skirts the eastern Wallowas and heads south to Hwy 86, just east of Halfway. While it's a nice enough drive, the real benefit of USFS Rd 39 is that it links the northern and southern halves of the Wallowas. It also provides access to **Hells Canyon Overlook**, 3 miles off USFS Rd 39 on USFS Rd 3965, the only canyon viewpoint you can drive to over a paved surface.

USFS Rd 39 is closed in winter and can stay closed into early summer. Call ahead to the Wallowa Mountains Visitor Center (☎ 541-426-5546) to find out if the road is open. It's 73 miles between Joseph and Halfway along this route. There are no gas stations or other services.

Halfway

Halfway (population 345), on the southern edge of the Wallowas, is every bit as beautiful as Joseph and even more isolated. The beautiful green valley is filled with old barns and hay fields, but, as in the northern Wallowas, the meadows suddenly turn perpendicular and rise to mountain peaks.

Follow USFS Rd 413 for 8 miles up to the ghostly town of Cornucopia for access to recreation in the Eagle Cap Wilderness Area.

The Hells Canyon Chamber of Commerce (☎ 541-742-5772), 160 S Main St, has information on the southern Wallowa region. The Pine Ranger Station (☎ 541-742-7511) is 1 mile south of Halfway.

It's worth spending a night or two in charming Halfway.

Pine Valley Lodge (☎ 541-742-2027, W www.neoregon.net/pinevalleylodge, 163 N Main St) Rooms $75-110. This charmingly quirky collection of restored buildings with lodge rooms and guest houses is run by a colorful, personable couple. The lodge's restaurant, the *Halfway Supper Club*, is open Friday and Saturday evenings and serves the best food for many, many miles.

Halfway Motel (☎ 541-742-5722, 170 S Main St) Rooms $40-70. If you'd rather stay in a traditional motel, this is it for Halfway.

Clear Creek Farm B&B (☎ 541-742-2238, w *www.neoregon.com/ccg, 48212 Clear Creek Rd)* Rooms $60-114, full-ranch option $90-174. At this B&B, 4 miles north of Halfway, you can choose from basic B&B lodgings or full use of the ranch – sort of a holistic, ecofriendly dude ranch – with all meals included.

HELLS CANYON

The Snake River has been flowing through Hells Canyon for only about 13 million years.

Wildflower displays peak in June on the plateaus edging Hells Canyon, where rainfall averages 25 inches a year. Prickly-pear cactus and short-seasoned grasses eke out an existence on the thin soils along the canyon floors 5500 feet down, where the rainfall averages 10 inches a year.

The prehistoric people who dwelled along Hells Canyon left pictographs, petroglyphs and pit dwellings. The Nez Perce and Shoshone battled for dominance along this stretch of the Snake, with the Nez Perce winning out.

Relics of the mining era, from the 1860s to the 1920s, are found throughout the canyon, and tumbledown shacks remain from the unlikely settlement attempts of turn-of-the-century homesteaders.

The roadless **Hells Canyon Wilderness Area** flanks the river from above Hells Canyon Dam to Dug Bar, near the mouth of the Imnaha River. This is where Hells Canyon cuts a trench in the earth nearly 8000 feet deep. Hwy 71 from Cambridge, Idaho, offers the easiest access; just about anyone who fishes, boats or hikes in Hells Canyon comes through here.

The real action is below **Hells Canyon Dam**, 28 miles north (downriver) from Copperfield. The dam briefly pools the Snake in a slack-water reservoir, then releases the river to boil down the mile-deep canyon. Between here and Lewiston, Idaho, 70 miles away, the Snake drops 1300 feet in elevation through wild scenery and equally wild rapids.

Hat Point

High above the Snake River, the Hat Point lookout tower offers great canyon views. Up here, meadows covered in wildflowers give way to steep canyon walls. On each side of the canyon, mountains soar toward 10,000 feet. Across the canyon are the Seven Devils, a cluster of rugged peaks in Idaho. Behind are the towering Wallowas.

From Hat Point, a **hiking trail** edges off the side of the canyon. It's a steep 4 miles to another vista from the top of the river cliffs, then 4 miles down to the river itself.

To reach Hat Point from Joseph, follow Hwy 350 to the little community of Imnaha. From here, a steep and very narrow graveled road (USFS Rd 4240) climbs up the Imnaha River canyon to Hat Point. (Don't even think about taking a trailer here.) Allow at least two hours each way for the 23-mile journey from Imnaha to Hat Point. The road is generally open from late May until snowfall (usually October). Call the Wallowa Mountains Visitor Center (☎ 541-426-5546) for road conditions.

Imnaha River Valley

Just west of Hells Canyon, the Imnaha River digs a parallel canyon that offers good roads, **fishing** access and pastoral scenery in addition to vertical cliff faces.

The Imnaha River Rd (USFS Rd 3955) follows this narrow valley between the hamlet of Imnaha and the junction of USFS Rd 39. The lower valley (the northern end) is very dramatic, as the river cuts more and more deeply through stair-stepped lava formations. The upper valley (going south) is bucolic, with meadows and old farmhouses flanking the river.

North of Imnaha, gravel roads continue for 20 miles to Imnaha Bridge, where several **hiking trails** begin. The Imnaha River Trail follows the churning river to its confluence with the Snake. The Nee-Me-Poo Trail, which traces the path of Chief Joseph and the Nez Perce, begins just north of the bridge, and in 3½ miles climbs to a **viewpoint** over the Snake.

There are public fishing access points along the length of the river.

OREGON

Activities

Long-distance riverside **hiking** trails run along both the Oregon and Idaho shores of the Snake River, but reaching them is a challenge. In some places, it's possible to start from trailheads along the ridges and hike down to the river. Hat Point (see that section, earlier) is a good place to drop onto the **Oregon Snake River Trail**. On the Idaho side, there's road access to the river at Pittsburgh Landing, near White Bird. From here, hikers can walk back up into the wilderness area along the **Idaho Snake River Trail**. It's a good idea to talk to rangers before setting out, as this is extremely remote and challenging wilderness, or phone the Wallowa Mountains Visitor Center (☎ 541-426-5546).

Jet-boat tours of the canyon are popular, but very noisy and disruptive. It's also possible to go **rafting** in Hells Canyon, either as a one-day or multiday trip.

Hells Canyon Adventures (☎ 541-785-3352, 800-422-3568, 4200 Hells Canyon Dam Rd, Oxbow) runs daylong raft trips ($150) regularly from Memorial Day weekend to the end of September. Reservations are required.

See the Clarkston & Lewiston Area section of the Southeastern Washington chapter for boat tours operating from the north end of the canyon.

Places to Stay

There are a few primitive *campsites* at Hat Point; contact the Wallowa Mountains Visitor Center (see Enterprise, earlier) for information. The closest facilities (food, water, gas etc) are in Joseph.

Two USFS campgrounds at the southern end of the canyon, *Ollokot* and *Blackhorse*, are right on USFS Rd 39, about halfway between Halway and Joseph. Contact the Wallowa Mountains Visitor Center (see Enterprise, earlier) for information.

Copperfield Campground (☎ 208-388-2422, 800-422-3143, W www.idahopower.com, Hwy 86 at Oxbow Dam) Tents/hookups $6/10. Just below Oxbow Dam, where Pine Creek joins the Snake River at the beginning of Hells Canyon, is this comfortable, grassy campground.

JOHN DAY COUNTRY

Oregon rivers take erosion seriously. And none more so than the John Day River, a canyon-cutter almost from the get-go. This river gives its name to the enormous swath of land it drains in the center of Oregon, as well as to the John Day Fossil Beds, a trio of national monuments where erosion has exposed spectacular formations rich in the remains of prehistoric life.

This remote region is, undeservedly, one of the least-visited parts of the state. The colorful fossil beds, the dramatic canyons and the river itself make the John Day area a worthwhile trip. The town of John Day, at the eastern edge of the region, provides the most complete tourist amenities and information on the area. Outside of John Day, most towns have only a single motel. Many of the sights associated with the river are farther west, between Dayville and Service Creek.

John Day

The town of John Day (population 2015) strings along a narrow passage of the John Day River valley, at the confluence of gold-rich Canyon Creek. For a community with a long, interesting history, John Day is an oddly colorless and hermetic place to visit. Aside from the Kam Wah Chung Museum and a more standard county historical museum, there's little evidence of the glory days left, and what has replaced it is merely utilitarian.

The largest town in the area, John Day is 264 miles east of Portland on US 26 and 81 miles southwest of Baker City.

The Grant County Chamber of Commerce (☎ 541-575-0547) is at 281 W Main St. The administrative headquarters of the John Day Fossil Beds (☎ 541-575-0721) is also here, at 431 Patterson Bridge Rd, as is the Long Creek & Bear Valley Ranger Station (☎ 541-575-3300).

The tiny stone building housing the **Kam Wah Chung Museum** (☎ 541-575-0028, 250 NW Canton St; adult/senior & student/child under 6 years $3/2.50/1; open 9am-noon, 1pm-5pm Mon-Sat, 1pm-5pm Sun), built in 1866, served primarily as an apothecary for

Ing Hay, a Chinese herbalist and doctor. But it served secondarily as a community center, temple, general store and opium den for the Chinese population that came to John Day to rework mine tailings. Ing Hay's reputation as a healer was widespread, and many white townspeople also used him as their doctor.

The museum gives a look into the day-to-day life of the Chinese in the mining West and commemorates an otherwise ignored facet of frontier history. The museum is south of US 26 at the city park.

Two miles south of downtown John Day, in the center of tiny Canyon City, the **Grant County Historical Museum** (☎ *541-575-0362; 101 S Canyon City Blvd; adult/senior/youth 6-12 $2/1/50¢; open 9:30am-4:30pm Mon-Sat, 1pm-5pm Sun June-Sept*) houses a collection of gold-rush memorabilia and frontier poet Joaquin Miller's cabin.

As long as your tastes aren't fancy, you'll do fine staying in John Day.

Clyde Holliday State Park (☎ *541-575-2773,* W *www.oregonstateparks.org, Hwy 26 milepost 155, Mt Vernon*) Tents/teepees $17/27. Nighttime truck traffic reminds you that this is a convenient, roadside campground. It's also right on the John Day River.

Dreamers Lodge (☎ *541-575-0526, 800-654-2849, fax 541-575-2733, 144 N Canyon Blvd*) Singles/doubles $46/54. This is a pleasant and popular motel with kitchenettes on a downtown side street.

Sunset Inn (☎ *541-575-1462, 800-452-4899, fax 541-575-1471, 390 W Main St*) Singles/doubles $48/51. Sunset Inn has an indoor pool and restaurant in the complex and is set just off the highway.

Grubsteak Mining Co (☎ *541-575-1970, 149 E Main*) Dinner $15. Steak is the specialty here, and it's the best place in town to eat.

The People Mover bus (☎ *541-575-2370*) between Bend and Prairie City stops daily in John Day ($18, 4 hours, 153 miles to Bend).

Strawberry Mountain Wilderness Area

Named for the delicious wild strawberries that thrive on the mountain slopes, the Strawberry Range is covered with ponderosa and lodgepole pines growing on

Who Was John Day?

Named for an early frontiersman, John Day is so common a label in this part of the state as to be all purpose: a river, two towns (John Day and Dayville), a dam and a series of parks were all named for a man who never visited the area.

As a trapper for the Pacific Fur Company, John Day was floating down the Columbia River with a companion when the pair were ambushed, robbed and stripped by hostile Cayuse Indians at the mouth of what was then known as the Mau Hau River. The two survived the ordeal and returned to safety in Astoria. But Day allegedly went crazy a few years later and killed himself. Thereafter, the river was renamed for the ill-starred John Day.

15-million-year-old glacier-chiseled volcanic peaks. The Strawberry Mountains contain deceptively high country: Much of the wilderness is above 6000 feet, and the highest peak – Strawberry Mountain – rises to 9038 feet.

A popular and rewarding 2½-mile round trip hike winds up a steep valley to **Strawberry Lake**. A mile past the lake is **Strawberry Falls**. To reach the trailhead, follow the signs 11 miles south from Prairie City.

Circle around to the south side of the wilderness area on Hwy 14 and paved USFS Rds 65 and 16, past old ponderosa pines and wide meadows, to find more trails. Hike into **High Lake Basin** (2.6-miles roundtrip) from a trailhead high up the mountainside. From USFS Rd 16, turn on USFS Rd 1640 toward Indian Springs Campground. The trailhead is 11 miles up a steep graveled road.

The Strawberry Mountains have a number of good campgrounds (free-$6). Convenient ones include *McNaughton Springs* (☎ *541-820-3311,* W *www.fs.fed.us/r6/malheur, USFS Rd 6001*), 8 miles south of Prairie City on the Strawberry Lake Rd (no fee), and *Trout Farm* (☎ *541-820-3311, USFS Rd 14*), in a lovely streamside spot 15 miles south of Prairie City (sites $6).

Oregon's 'Oasis in the Desert'

In the early 1980s, Bhagwan Shree Rajneesh – an Indian guru whose self-created religion is often described as a mix of Eastern religions and pop psychology – purchased 1000-sq-mile Big Muddy Ranch for $6 million and left Pune, India. His intention (besides avoiding tax-evasion charges at home) was to build an isolationist 'oasis in the desert,' a self-sufficient city with its own fertile valley created by a private lake and dam. Since these plans violated state land-use laws and threatened the water rights of residents, Rajneesh's first move was to take over nearby Antelope, where property was already zoned for city use. Residents of the town watched in disbelief as Rajneeshees (who were primarily disillusioned Westerners) flooded in, voted the city council out of office, changed the town's name to Rajneesh, legalized public nudity and – to top it off – raised taxes. Property abandoned by fleeing locals was promptly snatched up by the Rajneeshees.

Soon enough, stories of the Bhagwan's posh lifestyle circulated in journalistic accounts, and there were endless murmurs of drug use, sexual orgies and a blossoming arsenal of private weapons. When the public outcry became a serious threat, Rajneesh's commander-in-chief, Ma Anand Sheela, announced she would 'paint the bulldozers with blood' before she would witness the collapse of the Bhagwan's empire. But after Sheela suddenly left, Rajneesh declared her a fascist dictator and came forth with her involvement in several serious crimes, including the mass poisoning of The Dalles residents (individual Rajneeshees went from salad bar to salad bar, tainting them with salmonella they carried in glass vials – more than 750 people got sick).

The Bhagwan was apprehended in October 1985. He pleaded guilty to charges of immigration violations and was deported, and members at the commune dispersed. The Bhagwan returned to Pune, where, after taking the new name of Osho, he died in 1990. The ashram at Pune currently functions as the world headquarters for Osho's flock.

Sheela served 29 months in a federal prison. Upon release, she immediately left for Switzerland and married a Swiss citizen. This precluded her from facing extradition for her alleged role in a 1985 plot to assassinate Charles Turner (US Attorney for Oregon). She now works in two small private nursing homes near Basel and claims that her work there is highly acknowledged all over Europe.

John Day Fossil Beds National Monument

Within the soft rocks and crumbly soils of John Day country lies one of the world's greatest fossil collections. Discovered in the 1860s by clergyman and geologist Thomas Condon, these fossil beds were laid down sometime between 25 and 40 million years ago, when this area was a coastal plain with a tropical climate. Roaming the forests at the time were saber-toothed tigers, pint-sized horses, bear-dogs and other early mammals.

The fossils of more than 100 different animal species have been found here. The national monument includes 22 sq miles at three different units: Sheep Rock Unit, Painted Hills Unit and Clarno Unit. Each has hiking trails and interpretive displays. To visit all of the units in one day requires quite a bit of driving, as more than 100 miles separate the fossil beds.

For more information, contact John Day Fossil Beds National Monument Headquarters (☎ 541-575-0721, 431 Patterson Bridge Rd, John Day).

Sheep Rock Unit Some of the monument's fossil findings, including parts of a saber-toothed tiger and a three-toed horse, are on display at the Cant Ranch House Visitors Center, at the Sheep Rock Unit (☎ 541-987-2333, Hwy 19; open 9am-5pm), 10 miles northwest of Dayville on Hwy 19. In the center's lab, you can watch paleontologists clean recent finds. The grounds are good for a riverside picnic.

From the **Blue Basin Trailhead**, 2 miles north of the visitor center off Hwy 19, several hikes lead out to the fossil formations. The **Island in Time Trail** is a well-maintained, mile-long path that climbs up a narrow waterway to a badlands-basin of highly eroded, uncannily green sediments. Along the trail, displays reveal fossils protruding from the soil.

Painted Hills Unit Low-slung, colorfully banded hills northwest of Mitchell (population 205) were formed when red, yellow and ochre-hued ash from a series of eruptions drifted into beds hundreds of feet deep about 30 million years ago. Because no cap rock protects them from erosion, the Painted Hills have slumped into soft mounds, rather like evil-colored, melting ice cream.

The easy **Fossil Leaf Trail** winds over the top of one of the banded hills, with interpretive signs pointing out plant life and geologic history. The **Carroll Rim Trail** winds to the top of a high bluff for great views over the Painted Hills. For a longer hike out into a badlands plant-and-wildlife preserve, take the 3-mile **High Desert Trail** loop.

Clarno Unit The oldest, most remote fossil beds in the area are at the base of the John Day River's canyon. The 40-million-year-old Clarno Unit exposes mud flows that washed over an Eocene-era forest. The Clarno Formation eroded into white cliffs topped with spires and turrets of stone. Short interpretive trails pass through boulder-sized fossils containing logs, seeds and other remains of an ancient forest.

Places to Stay & Eat Several campgrounds provide relatively easy access to the fossil beds. Two nice ones, *Lone Pine* and *Big Bend*, are on the North Fork of John Day River, north of the Sheep Rock Unit and east of Kimberly, on Hwy 402.

Fish House Inn (☎ 541-987-2124, @ fishinn@highdesertnet.com, 110 Franklin St, Dayville) Sites $15, rooms $45-65. This inn has B&B rooms, including two in a free-standing cottage, and an RV/tent area.

Service Creek B&B (☎ 541-468-3331, w www.servicecreekstagestop.com, 38686 Hwy 19) Rooms $60-75. Twenty miles southeast of Fossil, this B&B also has a cafe.

Shaniko Hotel (☎ 541-489-3441, 800-483-3441, 4th & E Sts) Rooms $66. Up the hill from Antelope, on US 97, is the working ghost town of Shaniko (pop 30). This hotel was an imposing landmark when it was built in 1909. It's now noteworthy as a comfortable, completely refurbished B&B. There's a *restaurant* on the main floor of the hotel.

Rafting

From Clarno Bridge (on Hwy 218) to Cottonwood Bridge (on Hwy 206), a distance of 70 miles, the John Day River cuts a deep canyon through basaltic lava flows on its way to the Columbia River. No roads reach the canyon here; along the river are the remains of homesteads, Native American petroglyphs and pristine wildlife habitats.

Plan to float the John Day in spring or early summer, when the toughest rapids are Class III or IV, depending on the water levels. Most float trips take four days through this roadless area, and most rafters float the John Day on their own, without a guide. Shuttle service ($18-100, depending on distance) and raft rentals ($35-90) are available from **Service Creek Stage Stop** (☎ 541-468-3331, Hwy 19 south of Fossil). **Oregon Whitewater Adventures** (☎ 541-746-5422, 800-820-7238; w www.oregon whitewater.com; $345-575 plus shuttle fees) runs three- to five-day trips down the John Day River.

Contact the Prineville Bureau of Land Management office (☎ 541-416-6700, w www.or.blm.gov/Prineville), 3050 NE 3rd St, for maps and more information; they can also provide you with a list of outfitters.

Southeastern Oregon

This vast region of dry alkaline lakebeds, soaring fault-block mountains, remote canyons and bird-filled marshes contains some of Oregon's most unusual and unvisited scenery, as well as a varied and plentiful wildlife population. Malheur National Wildlife Refuge, by Malheur Lake, is a major nesting site and a big migratory stopover along the Pacific Flyway. At the Hart Mountain National Antelope Refuge, watch for glimpses of speeding pronghorns, listen for coyotes and keep an eye peeled for bighorn sheep along rocky escarpments.

Highlights

- Catching the spring migration of waterfowl at Malheur
- Driving the Steens Mountain Loop Rd
- Soaking in one of the region's many hot springs
- Floating the Owyhee River
- Mountain biking on Hart Mountain
- Exploring Leslie Gulch

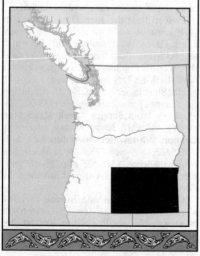

Historically, southeastern Oregon was the home to huge open-range cattle and sheep outfits; most of it is still rangeland.

Distances are great out here, and you can't count on paved roads, luxurious accommodations or many towns with more than a gas station. The towns of Burns and Ontario have the most lodging.

BURNS & AROUND

Named by a wistful early settler for Scottish poet Robert Burns, this town (population 2945) was established in 1883 as the watering hole and social center for incoming settlers and roving cowhands. Today, this isolated high desert town is a useful jumping-off point for expeditions into more remote environs.

US 20 links Burns to Bend and Ontario, and US 395 heads north to John Day. The town of Hines is immediately west of Burns.

You can pick up the detailed Harney County recreation map at the Harney County Chamber of Commerce (☎ 541-573-2636), 18 West D St. The Burns District Bureau of Land Management (BLM) office (☎ 541-573-4400) is at 12533 US 20W, in Hines. You'll find information on the Malheur and Ochoco National Forests (☎ 541-573-4300) in the same building. You can find the post office (☎ 800-275-8777) at 100 S Broadway.

Lots of historical memorabilia and some good early photographs are at the **Harney County Historical Museum** (*☎ 541-573-2636, 18 West D St; donation encouraged; open 9am-5pm Tues-Sat May-mid-Oct),* next to the chamber of commerce.

This rustic resort **Crystal Crane Hot Springs** (*☎ 541-493-2312, Hwy 78 at Crane; pond/hot tub $3 per day/$5 per hour),* 25 miles southeast of Burns, is a perfect stop after a day of bumping around the back roads of southeastern Oregon. The springs flow into a large pond and are also piped into cattle-trough hot tubs in small private bathhouses (go for the pond).

SOUTHEASTERN OREGON

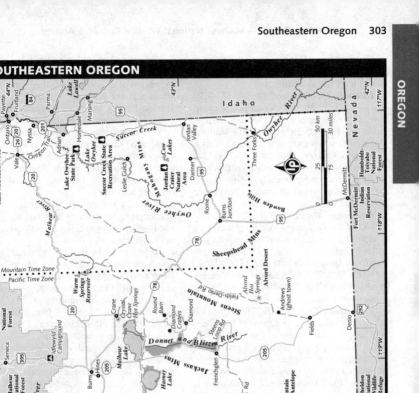

Crystal Crane Hot Springs has a few tiny guest *cabins* ($30) and *campsites* (primitive/hookup $8/12) available.

Idlewild Campground (☎ *541-573-7292, Hwy 395)* Sites $6. The closest public campground to Burns is here, 17 miles north of town on Hwy 395, in the Malheur National Forest. (Yes, there are actual trees here!)

Sage Country Inn (☎ *541-573-7243,* W *www.home.centurytel.net/sagecountryinn, 351½ W Monroe St)* Open Mar-Nov. Rooms $65-80. Burns' most charming (but unpretentious) lodging is at this B&B.

Bontemps Motel (☎ *541-573-2037, 877-229-1394, 74 W Monroe St)* Singles/doubles $30/36. This is a nicely renovated, gay-friendly older motel.

Silver Spur Motel (☎ *541-573-2077, fax 541-573-3921, 789 N Broadway Ave)* Singles/double $40/44. This motel is comfortable and close to downtown.

Pine Room Cafe (☎ *541-573-6631, 543 W Monroe St)* Dinner $15. Opens at 5pm Tues-Sat. Stop here for some of the region's best food, with homemade baked goods and hand-cut steaks. The colorful, friendly Western ambience is no less of an attraction than the food (men should seriously consider wearing some sort of hat).

El Toreo (☎ *541-573-1829, 239 N Broadway Ave)* Lunch $5. If it's too early to dine at the Pine Room, this Mexican restaurant has pretty good food.

Amtrak (☎ 800-872-7245) runs Thruway buses from Portland to Burns ($32, six hours) once a day on Monday, Thursday and Saturday. Make reservations by calling Amtrak or Grayline of Portland (☎ 503-285-9845).

MALHEUR NATIONAL WILDLIFE REFUGE & AROUND

South of Burns, covering 289 sq miles of lake, wetland and prairie, the Malheur National Wildlife Refuge (☎ *541-493-2612, Narrow-Princeton Rd; admission free; open dawn-dusk)* is an important breeding and resting area for birds traveling along the Pacific Flyway. Stop at the refuge headquarters for maps and good bird-watching on Malheur Lake.

The refuge's two big, shallow lakes attract waterfowl, but the best place for wildlife viewing is often south along the Donner und Blitzen River (casually referred to as the Blitzen River), where wide, grassy marshes and ponds shelter many animals.

Waterfowl migration at Malheur peaks in March, shorebirds arrive in April, and songbirds wing in during May. During summer, waterfowl broods skim across the ponds and lakes. In fall, birds come through on their way south.

Between the refuge headquarters and Frenchglen, 35 miles of intersecting gravel roads offer some excellent wildlife-viewing opportunities.

Adjacent to the wildlife refuge, 55 miles south of Burns and east of Hwy 205, is **Diamond Craters**, an area of volcanic craters, cinder cones and other lava formations that were formed about 2500 years ago. Pick up a brochure from the BLM office in Hines to find a map of the area's rather confusing road system.

Twenty miles north of the community of Diamond and off Happy Valley Rd is Pete French's **Round Barn**, an impressive 100-foot-wide structure used to buck out broncos in the glory days of the open range.

There are some places to stay and eat in the area.

Malheur Field Station (☎ *541-493-2629,* e *mfs@burnsnet.com, Narrows-Princeton Rd)* Dorm beds $18, single/double trailers $30/45. This collection of rustic buildings is near the refuge headquarters. Accommodations are in dormitories or trailers; bring your own bedding and a towel. Reasonably priced meals are served in the dining hall, and most housing has cooking facilities. Call ahead for a reservation.

Frenchglen Hotel (☎ *541-493-2825, Hwy 205, Frenchglen)* Rooms with shared bath $60. Open Mar 15-Nov 15. This charming hotel is pretty much unaltered since it was built in the 1910s. Reserve in advance, as it's very popular, especially with birders. Dinners (about $12, reservations required) are family style and are served promptly at 6:30pm. There are eight small, plain guest rooms.

The Pacific Flyway

When birds migrate, they join other members of their species along a migration route. When many migration routes follow the same general path, that broad swath is referred to as a flyway. Since no two species follow exactly the same path from beginning to end, flyways get a bit fuzzy around the edges.

Migration in North America is essentially north-south along four major flyways: Pacific, Central, Mississippi and Atlantic.

The longest and most important strand of the Pacific Flyway originates in Alaska and Yukon Territory, and runs southward through western foothills of the Rocky Mountains. Near the international border, some migration routes head southeastward into the Central and Mississippi flyways, while others traverse northwestern Montana and the Idaho panhandle, then turn southward across eastern Oregon to the interior valleys of California.

Since much of eastern Oregon is very dry, Malheur's lakes and wetlands are important rest stops, providing water, plenty of food and shelter.

Frenchglen Mercantile Guest House (☎ 541-493-2738, Hwy 205, Frenchglen) Rooms $65-85. This place, next to the general store, has three comfortable guest rooms.

STEENS MOUNTAIN

The highest peak in southeastern Oregon, Steens Mountain (9773 feet) is part of a massive, 30-mile-long fault-block range that was formed about 15 million years ago.

On the western slope of the range, ice-age glaciers bulldozed massive U-shaped valleys into the flanks of the mountain; to the east, 'the Steens,' as the range is usually referred to, drop off to the Alvord Desert, 5000 feet below.

Beginning in Frenchglen, the 66-mile **Steens Mountain Loop Road** climbs 4500 feet up the west slope of the Steens and back

down along the side of a gorge, providing access to the BLM's 304-sq-mile **Steens Mountain Recreation Area**.

The drive begins amid sagebrush, then passes through a band of junipers into aspen forests, and finally into fragile rocky tundra. Wild mustangs range along the southern reaches. The rocky faces are also home to many raptors, including golden eagles. The road is open as weather allows, between late June and November.

You can stay the night at the following campground and resort.

Page Springs Campground (☎ 541-573-4400, W *www.or.blm.gov/Burns, N Steens Mountain Loop Rd*) Sites $8. Only 4 miles from Frenchglen is this site along the Blitzen River.

Steens Mountain Resort (☎ 541-493-2415, 800-542-3765; N Steens Mountain Loop Rd) Tents/hookups/cabins $12/20/50-75. Practically next door to Page Springs, this resort has a few more amenities, most notably, showers ($5 for nonguests).

ALVORD DESERT

Once a huge 400-foot-deep lake, the Alvord Basin is now a series of playas. Alternating with irrigated alfalfa fields, sagebrush prairies and old ranches are startlingly white alkali beds, the residue of centuries of lake evaporation. Above everything looms Steens Mountain.

The 75-mile gravel Fields-Denio Rd, between the community of Fields and Hwy 78, is well maintained and open all year.

Directly below the summit of the Steens, a few miles north of the near–ghost town of Andrews and about a hundred yards east of the Fields-Denio Rd, is **Alvord Hot Springs** (look for the small metal shelter – it's hard to miss). As at all free, public hot springs, be respectful of other users and the site.

There's free, de facto *camping* around the edges of the Alvord Desert and beneath the east rim of Steens Mountain. In Fields, the small store and cafe is a good place to stop for a tank of gas and a cold drink.

Even homely Burns Junction, nearly 100 miles by dirt road from Fields, is a welcome

OREGON

sight to anyone needing gasoline or a cold soda. Even though there is a motel attached to the gas station, only car repairs or bad planning can justify spending a night.

ROME

Here, along US 95, is the only bridge to cross the Owyhee River. Both the river and the landscape are misleadingly placid at this old-time ford. A gravel road south of Rome leads to rough country where the Owyhee River leaves its gorge. Three miles north of Rome, along a county road, are the outcroppings for which the town was named. The fancifully named 'Pillars of Rome' are highly eroded cliffs of volcanic tuff several hundred feet high.

There's a tiny *cafe* (☎ 541-586-2294, 3605 Hwy 95 S) in Rome and free, informal *camping* at the Owyhee River launch site, just south of the highway.

JORDAN VALLEY

The closest thing to a town in this enormous desert area is Jordan Valley (population 340). On US 95 only 5 miles from the Idaho border, Jordan Valley is known for its Basque heritage. The *frontón*, a stone ball court used for playing the traditional Basque game of *pelota*, still stands downtown. Other than that, truck stops give the town its identity.

Basque Station Motel (☎ 541-586-9244, 801 Main St) Singles/doubles $39/49. This motel, which is an offshoot of a gas station, is quaint in name only, but as long as you decide not to display an attitude, it's a friendly enough place.

Old Basque Inn (☎ 541-586-2298, 308 Wroten St) Entrees $15. An old Basque hostelry has been converted into this eatery. The steak-dominated menu also features a few Basque dishes.

LESLIE GULCH-SUCCOR CREEK BACK COUNTRY BYWAY

It takes a little doing to get to the wildly eroded Owyhee River country, but this 52-mile gravel route is unforgettable. Running between Adrian and a junction with US 95, 18 miles north of Jordan Valley, it passes

grand landscapes and prime wildlife-viewing areas.

Follow the road south from near Adrian, through sagebrush, thin grass and rolling hills until it drops steeply onto Succor Creek. Here, 100-foot-high vertical walls of volcanic tuff divide to allow the stream and road to wind through. **Succor Creek State Recreation Area** sits at a narrow end of the canyon, with campsites, informal hiking trails and stunning scenery.

The erosion is even more spectacular at **Leslie Gulch**, a 16-mile side road that drops over into the Owyhee River Canyon. This steep, though usually passable, gravel road careens down a narrow creek channel through vividly colored volcanic rock eroded into amazing pinnacle and turreted formations to Lake Owyhee. Bighorn sheep haunt these rock cliffs; watch for them to come down to drink at the creekside.

OWYHEE RIVER

The upper stretch of the Owyhee River, below Three Forks, consists of a number of Class IV rapids. Downstream from Rome the river is less turbulent, but the scenery – highly eroded desert cliffs – is top-notch. Only in spring does the Owyhee contain enough water to be safely rafted – usually from March through May. Call the Burns-area BLM office (☎ 541-573-4400) to check on river levels. There's nothing even approaching a raft rental shop in Rome, so if you plan to raft the Owyhee on your own, you need to bring gear from elsewhere.

Guided trips on the Owyhee ($500-1000) are offered by **Oregon Whitewater Adventures** (☎ 541-746-5422, 800-820-7238, W www .oregonwhitewater.com, 39620 Deerhorn Rd), in Springfield Oregon. Also, you can try **Wapiti River Trips** (☎ 208-628-3523, 800-488-9872, W www.wapitiriverguides.com, 128 Main St), in Riggins, Idaho, or **Steens Mountain Packers** (☎ 541-495-2315, 800-977-3995, W www.steensmountain.com), in Frenchglen.

ONTARIO

Oregon's most easterly city, Ontario (population 11,109) and its environs are often considered to be an extension of Idaho's fertile

Snake River valley. Ontario even shares the same time zone, mountain standard time (MST), with Idaho. Agriculture remains the backbone of the local economy. The Malheur, Payette and Owyhee Rivers join the Snake's wide valley here, with irrigated farms producing varied crops; the region is the nation's largest producer of peppermint.

I-84 and US 20, 26 and 95 intersect near Ontario, putting the city at the hub of eastern Oregon's principal thoroughfares. The Snake River forms Ontario's eastern boundary and the Oregon-Idaho state line. Downtown streets are divided by Oregon St and by Idaho Ave into NE, NW, SE and SW quadrants. Avenues run east-west, while streets run north-south.

The Ontario Visitors & Convention Bureau (☎ 541-889-8012) is at 88 SW 3rd Ave. The central post office (☎ 800-275-8777) is at 88 SW 2nd Ave. Oregon Public Broadcasting is heard at 104.5 FM. Holy Rosary Hospital (☎ 541-889-5331) is at 351 SW 9th Ave.

A far cry from the typical small-town museum, the **Four Rivers Cultural Center** *(☎ 541-889-8191, 888-211-1222, 676 SW 5th Ave; admission $4; open 9am-5pm Mon-Sat)* celebrates the region's diversity, focusing on Paiute Indians, Basque sheepherders, and Japanese- and Mexican-American farm workers.

The following are some lodging and food options.

Farewell Bend State Recreation Area *(☎ 541-869-2365,* W *www.oregonstateparks .org, I-84 exit 353)* Tents/teepees/cabins $16/22/35. While there's nowhere to camp right in Ontario, this large campground is 25 miles north of town, at the Snake River's Brownlee Reservoir.

Carlile Motel *(☎ 541-889-8658, 800-640-8658, 589 N Oregon St)* Singles/doubles $37/48. This family-owned motel is a restored 1940s motor court.

Best Western Inn *(☎ 541-889-2600, 800-828-0364,* W *www.bestwesternoregon.com, 251 Goodfellow St)* Singles/doubles $57/62. This Best Western has an indoor pool and a good free breakfast buffet. It's outside the center between the freeway and the Snake River.

Casa Jaramillo *(☎ 541-889-9258, 157 SE 2nd Ave)* Entrees $8-10. Between the interstate and downtown, this Mexican restaurant is an Ontario institution.

Greyhound (☎ 541-889-5112), 510 NW Oregon St, passes through Ontario on its way from Portland ($44, eight hours, 410 miles, four times daily) to Boise and Salt Lake City. The closest car rentals are in Boise.

LAKEVIEW

There's no longer any lake in view at Lakeview (population 2625), but at an elevation of 4800 feet, it's the highest city in Oregon. Towering, treeless fault-block rims and prevailing westerly winds make Lakeview one of Oregon's centers for hang-gliding.

Lakeview is 96 miles east of Klamath Falls on Hwy 140, and 142 miles south of LaPine on Hwy 31. It's 139 miles between Burns and Lakeview on US 395. It takes a kind of devotion, or *extreme* carelessness, to end up out here.

The Lake County Chamber of Commerce (☎ 541-947-6040) is at 126 North E St. The Lakeview Ranger District of the Fremont National Forest (☎ 541-947-3334) is at 524 North G St. The BLM office (☎ 541-947-2177) is at 1000 9th St S.

The post office is at 18 South G St. Lake District Hospital (☎ 541-947-2114) is at 700 South J St. Diane's Corner, 1103 N 4th St, is the place to do laundry.

The following are some places to stay and eat in the area.

Goose Lake State Park *(☎ 541-947-3111,* W *www.oregonstateparks.org, US 395 at the state line)* Sites $14. This campground is 14 miles south of Lakeview, right on the California border.

Geyser Hot Springs Resort *(☎ 541-947-4142, US 395 N)* Singles/doubles $45/48. This homespun resort just north of town is fun, but the rooms can get cold at night. Nonguests pay $3 for a swim in the hot-springs pool, and it's free to ogle Oregon's only geyser, which erupts every 90 seconds in a pond here.

Lakeview Lodge *(☎ 541-947-2181, 301 N G St)* Singles/doubles $46/52. This comfortable motel is the best place to stay in downtown

OREGON

Lakeview and has in-room microwaves and a fitness room.

Aspen Ridge Resort *(☎ 541-884-8685, 800-393-3323,* **w** *www.aspenrr.com)* Rooms $75-140. This lovely ranch resort, 45 miles west of Lakeview, has wildlife viewing, horseback riding, mountain biking, swimming and fishing. Turn off Hwy 140 about a mile east of Bly, and continue 17 miles south on USFS Rd 3790 (Fishhole Creek Rd).

Plush West *(☎ 541-947-2353, 9 North F St)* Entrees $10-15. Plush West offers good steak, lamb and seafood in a steak-house atmosphere.

El Aguila Real *(☎ 541-947-5655, 406 North G St)* Entrees $8-10. The tasty crab enchiladas here are a nice break from steak.

Red Ball Stage Line operates between Klamath Falls and Lakeview ($17, three hours, twice a day) Monday to Saturday; the bus station (☎ 541-947-2255) is at 619 Center St.

HART MOUNTAIN

Hart Mountain (elevation 7648ft) and Poker Jim Ridge form a near-vertical escarpment 3600 feet above Warner Lakes, about 50 miles northeast of Lakeview.

Rock Creek Rd, which has been designated a BLM Scenic Byway, continues east through the Hart Mountain National Antelope Refuge, and on to Frenchglen. It's a slow, frequently rough road; allow several hours to travel the 50 miles between Plush and Frenchglen. Make sure you have plenty of fuel before setting out, and be prepared for bumpy gravel roads.

Created in 1936, the **Hart Mountain National Antelope Refuge** *(☎ 541-947-3315, 18 S G St, Lakeview)* is home to roughly 1700 pronghorn. Bighorn sheep were reintroduced

to Hart Mountain in the 1970s and live on the steep western side of refuge.

From the tiny town of Plush, the road to the Hart Mountain National Antelope Refuge crosses the Warner Lakes basin (a good place to look for migratory waterfowl), then climbs the face of the Hart Mountain fault block. About 3000 feet later, the road emerges onto the prairie-like expanses of the antelope refuge.

At the refuge field headquarters, 25 miles east of Plush on the road to Frenchglen (Rock Creek Rd), pick up a brochure and information about recent wildlife sightings. The facility is often unstaffed, but this is the only place on the refuge with water and a toilet.

Hart Mountain has an extensive network of Jeep trails and single-tracks, making for great **mountain biking**. After a long drive, test your lungs and legs by making the short hop from the refuge headquarters to **Petroglyph Lake**. For more of a challenge, drive south from the headquarters toward Blue Sky, and park at **Lookout Point**. From there, pedal out to the **Skyline Trail**, which has some steep climbs before hitting a ridge and great views. The refuge's ultimate daylong ride is up Hart Mountain itself. Drive 15 miles south of the refuge headquarters to Blue Sky Hotel, and head uphill from there.

Plush has a small store-cafe-gas station, and there's a campground in the area.

Hot Springs Campground *(☎ 541-947-3315, Hart Mountain Antelope Refuge)* Free. Pitch a tent along a lovely wooded creek about 4 miles south of the refuge headquarters. A plus is the open-air bathhouse that traps a hot spring – just the thing you'll need after a dusty day of hiking the refuge's informal trails.

Facts about Washington

People here like to joke about being in 'the upper left-hand corner,' but Washingtonians take a great deal of pride in their unique geographic position at the northern and western extreme of the continental USA. If there's a virtue to the country's long westering and northering instinct, then it is expressed in the qualities of this progress-oriented state.

Washington likes to keep its distance. Residents have long known that by cloaking the state in tales of rain and gloom, they could keep the rest of the world away from their ruggedly beautiful corner of the country. However, by now there's scarcely a soul who doesn't acknowledge that Seattle is one of the major cultural and trendsetting centers of the USA, and that life in the Evergreen State is as sweet as anywhere in the world.

What's not to like? The western part of the state is about equally divided by glaciered peaks and wilderness, dynamic cities and a seascape of misty islands and harbors. To the east are more arid uplands with 300 days of sunshine, as well as all-season recreation. Does it rain? Sure. But that's the price you pay to live in this well-washed, hospitable and sophisticated state.

HISTORY

See the History section in the Facts about the Pacific Northwest chapter for the historical background prior to white settlement of Washington.

Settlement & Autonomy

Present-day Washington grew out of the old Oregon Territory, which consisted of today's Idaho, Washington, Oregon and western Montana and lay under joint British and American rule. In the early days of settlement, the only towns and centers of population in the Northwest existed in Oregon's Willamette Valley, and Salem became the territorial capital for the entire region.

Although Dr John McLoughlin, a factor of Hudson's Bay Company (HBC), had sought to restrict settlement of the greater Oregon Territory to the region south of the Columbia River, available land along the Willamette began to disappear as pioneers continued to roll into the Pacific Northwest. In the mid-1840s settlers began streaming north, and the first American settlement in Washington was established in 1845 at Tumwater, on the southern edge of Puget Sound. This racially diverse group of 32 Missourians purposely chose to move to British territory because Oregon law forbade the settlement of blacks. Despite the HBC's disapproval, the settlers expected better treatment from the British. The village of Tumwater was soon thriving with mills and trading posts, and Olympia was founded as the town's port in 1846. That same year the British and Americans had agreed on the 49th parallel as the northern limit of the Oregon Country. Following the agreement, the HBC chose to move its operations north to Victoria.

In 1851 both Seattle and Port Townsend were established, and they quickly became logging centers. The forests of the Pacific Northwest began to fall to the saw, and lumber was shipped at great profit to San Francisco, the boomtown of the California gold rush.

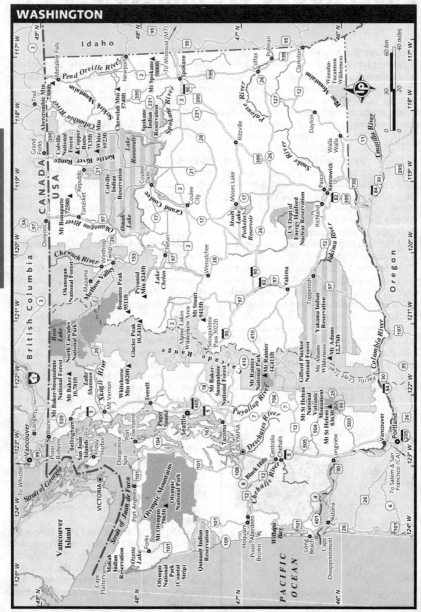

The Oregon-based territorial government tended to focus on the well-established towns of the Willamette Valley. As communities in Washington grew, they found Salem – a couple hundred miles south through deep forest and across the Columbia River – too distant. In 1851 and 1852, representatives from western Washington met and called for the establishment of a separate territory north of the Columbia. The Oregon legislature concurred, and in 1853 the US Congress voted to create Washington Territory. Isaac Ingall Stevens was appointed governor and also Superintendent of Indian Affairs.

The Cavalry & the Indians

One of the most immediate concerns facing the young territory was the quelling of Native American hostilities in the eastern part of the region. The seeds of unrest had been sown in 1847, when a group of Cayuse killed Marcus Whitman, his wife and 12 other white missionaries near Walla Walla. This act both horrified the white settlers of the Northwest and solidified opinion that the Native Americans had to be forced onto reservations. Although the Cayuse responsible for the killings were apprehended, tried and then hanged in Oregon City in 1850, tensions between the Native Americans and white settlers continued to grow. (See the boxed text on the Whitman Massacre in the Southeastern Washington chapter.)

Governor Stevens held a council at Walla Walla in 1855, with representatives of most eastern Indian tribes present. The tribes, which included the Cayuse, Wallawalla, Nez Perce, Yakama and Umatilla, were cajoled into signing various treaties that reduced the land shares open to native peoples for hunting and fishing. However, many of the tribes were not satisfied with their reservations or with Stevens' treatment of them. Nor was the US Congress pleased with Stevens' methods, and it refused to ratify the treaties. The situation rapidly deteriorated.

In 1856, a confederation of Plateau tribes led by the Yakama attacked steamboats on the Columbia River near The Dalles. Over the course of the year the army exchanged hostilities with the Yakama and built Fort Simcoe (in central Washington) to protect the Columbia River from attack. The eastern half of Washington was proclaimed closed to settlement, and Stevens declared martial law in the region.

In 1858, trouble again broke out when a cavalry detachment led by Colonel EJ Steptoe departed from Fort Walla Walla to protect miners in the gold fields along the Okanogan River. Near Rosalia, the soldiers encountered a vastly larger confederated indigenous force led by the Spokane tribe. The cavalry quickly ran through its ammunition and was forced into a humiliating retreat. Four months later, a large army battalion returned for revenge and this time defeated the Native American contingent. By 1859, Congress had finally ratified the eastern-Washington treaties, and the tribes were resettled. With the Indians no longer a threat, the state's eastern section was opened to settlement.

Boom Times

Dairy farming, fishing and logging remained the chief economic underpinnings of settlements in western Washington. Port cities boomed because almost all the transportation to and from Washington was by ship; land transport to the rest of the nation was severely lacking.

Competition between fledgling cities became fierce when railroads began to contemplate lines into the Northwest. In 1883, Portland became the first Northwest city to be linked to the rest of the nation by rail, followed by Tacoma in 1887; Seattle didn't have railroad service until 1893. These rail connections not only created a new, readily accessible national market for products from the Pacific Northwest, but also brought in floods of settlers, many of them newly arrived immigrants to the USA.

Washington was finally admitted to the Union in 1889. Seattle's supremacy as the Northwest's greatest seaport was established in 1897, when gold was discovered in the Canadian Klondike. As the principal port for prospectors and adventurers destined for the Yukon, Seattle boomed. By

1900, Seattle had surpassed Portland as the largest city in the Northwest.

In many ways, the story of Washington State in the 20th century is the story of massive federal works projects and military spending. As early as 1902, the federal government was building dams on the Columbia River. The Bonneville Dam, completed in 1937, was the single largest public works project of Franklin Roosevelt's New Deal. The cheap electrical power it provided proved an enormous boon to Puget Sound's rapid industrial growth during WWII. In 1947, Bonneville was joined by Grand Coulee Dam, the world's largest hydroelectric and irrigation project.

The naval yards at Bremerton were the Northwest's major shipbuilding and repair facility during WWI and WWII, as well as the home of the Northern Fleet. The city's population grew by 235% in the two years following the bombing of Pearl Harbor. William Boeing's bustling commercial airplane factory south of Seattle received the military contracts to build the air force's fleet of 13,000 B-17 and B-29 bombers.

However, not everyone prospered during the war effort. In 1942, the federal government removed 18,000 Japanese Americans from their land and homes and interned them in camps in rural western states such as Idaho, Wyoming and Montana. Japanese immigrants had been moving to the Puget Sound area since the 1880s, and a substantial population also lived in the Yakima Valley, where they operated some of the area's first irrigated farms.

Washington continued to prosper throughout the second half of the 20th century. Seattle and, later, Spokane seemed so certain of their place in the universe that each city threw a world's fair (in 1962 and 1974, respectively), bringing millions of people to the state.

However, all this success has not come without cost. The production of cheap hydroelectricity and the massive irrigation projects along the Columbia have led to the near-irreversible destruction of the Columbia River ecosystem. The dams have all but eliminated most runs of native salmon and

have further disrupted the lives of Native Americans who depended on the river for sustenance and cultural continuity. And while Puget Sound continues to be one of the most rapidly growing areas of the USA, many are finding that the region's much vaunted livability is rapidly disappearing as it becomes one enormous metropolitan area linked by jammed-up freeways.

GEOGRAPHY

The geography of coastal Washington can be described in two words: mountains and water. The mountains in this case are those of the highly glaciated Olympic range on the Olympic Peninsula, which juts out like a thumb into the Pacific Ocean. Moist marine air rolls in off the ocean and hits these nearly 8000-foot peaks, dumping immense amounts of precipitation. North America's only temperate rain forests are the result; much of this unique ecosystem is preserved in Olympic National Park.

The Olympic Mountains are surrounded on the north and east by a low-lying basin fed by the waters of the Pacific Ocean. The Strait of Juan de Fuca, Puget Sound, Hood Canal and many smaller bays and inlets reach like tendrils far inland, isolating hundreds of islands and peninsulas. Except for Spokane, the major population centers of Washington – Seattle, Tacoma, Everett, Bellingham and Olympia – are located along these inlets; all are dependent on deepwater harbors for much of their prosperity.

Marching north and south across the state are the massive volcanoes of the Cascade Range. The southern peaks, including Mt St Helens and Mt Rainier, rise up high from the horizon as isolated, snow-clad cones. The North Cascades are different: More recent volcanoes, such as Mt Baker, have pushed up through an already rugged, mountainous landscape that was formed when an offshore island rammed into the North American continent.

The Cascades block the eastward flow of moist Pacific air. Heavy rains fall on the mountains' western slopes, creating ideal conditions for thick Douglas fir forests. Eastern Washington gets much less rainfall.

Running across the northern boundary of Washington is a series of mountainous highlands (the Okanogans and the Selkirks) and, like the North Cascades, they are the buckled remnants of former Pacific islands that have been jammed onto the leading western edge of the continent. Vegetation is comparatively light on these uplands, with ponderosa pines dominant in the forests.

Encircled by the Columbia River, the desert basin of south-central Washington is given life through the river's many irrigation dams. The eastern edge of the basin, however, is an especially barren piece of real estate: It was denuded of much of its topsoil during massive ice-age floods. In the far eastern flank of the state, the land begins to rise toward the foothills of the Rocky Mountains, alleviating the effects of the Cascade rain shadow.

CLIMATE

The Pacific Ocean and towering Cascade peaks largely determine the climate of Washington. The coast receives the full brunt of moist, marine air, and coastal towns such as Aberdeen get around 85 inches of rain a year. Temperatures are mild, however, with only a 20°F variation between summer and winter averages. Throughout coastal Washington, temperatures rarely rise above 80°F or fall below freezing. Seasonal change is gradual, as both spring and fall are periods of cloud and rain. However, heavy rainfall in the Olympic Mountains serves to insulate other parts of western Washington and the Puget Sound area. Sequim, in the rain shadow of the Olympic peaks, receives only 12 inches of rain a year.

Seattle, while frequently wrapped in gray clouds and mist, actually has much less precipitation than many US cities. However, the pervasive grayness can make the city's otherwise moderate temperatures (winter highs range between 40° and 50°F, summer highs between 75° and 85°F) seem bone-chilling. Summer days can be very pleasant, though cool – a light jacket is often necessary even in the height of summer.

Rain and snowfall are heavy in the western Cascades, with winter coming early, often in October. Trails may not be free of snow until July. Even in midwinter, however, temperatures are also mild – around 20° or 30°F. In summer, highs remain in the 70s.

East of the Cascades, the climate is very different. Summer temperatures on the Columbia Plateau reach highs of over 100°F, sometimes for days on end. Rainfall is scant; Yakima receives only 8 inches yearly. Winters can be harsh, with the average January temperature below 20°F.

POPULATION & PEOPLE

The current population of Washington is nearly 5.9 million, making it the 15th most populous state in the country. According to the 2000 census, the state population grew by about a million between 1990 and 2000, making it the tenth fastest growing state in the nation. The Puget Sound area received over half of the new arrivals, and urban forecasters predict that the population of that region alone will approach five million by the year 2020.

Though the state remains overwhelmingly white (82% in the 2000 census), the number of Hispanics doubled during the 1990s to 441,000. More than half of Seattle's new residents are Asian or Hispanic.

The Puget Sound area was one of the most densely populated areas of prehistoric Native America, and a great many Indians still live here. On the 2000 census, 93,300 people identified themselves as Native American; though that's still only 1.6% of the state's population, the state ranks fifth in the nation for indigenous residents. The federal government recognizes 28 Native American tribes in Washington. Some reservations, particularly along the coast, are very small, consisting basically of just a town and a harbor. The largest are east of the Cascades, where the Yakama and Colville Confederated Tribes each maintain homelands of more than a million acres.

INFORMATION

Western Washington's telephone area-code system is currently being overhauled. With the proliferation of cell phones, the region is running out of phone numbers, so a new area code, ☎ 564, will be overlaid on the already existing array of area codes sometime in 2002. The previous area codes – 206 (Seattle proper), 425 (Bellevue and the Eastside suburbs), 253 (Tacoma) and 360 (Bellingham, Olympia and the rest of Western Washington) – will remain in use, but new phone lines in all of these areas will have the new 564 code.

In addition, 10-digit dialing will be required for local calls in the region. Just as with long-distance calls, you'll have to dial the three-digit area code before the seven-digit number (the difference is that you don't have to dial 1 beforehand). The rest of the state – everything east of the Cascades – will continue to use the 509 area code and will continue to necessitate only seven digits for local calls.

Washington's base state sales tax is 6.5%, but counties and cities can assess an additional percentage. This tax is not levied on food in grocery stores, but it does apply to prepared takeout meals. In Seattle, the combined bed and sales tax exceeds 15%, which can be a significant additional cost.

Seattle

More than any other Pacific Northwest city, Seattle (population 563,374) epitomizes the area's trend from hick to hip. Before the late 1980s and early '90s – when grunge music, coffee and microbrews hit the scene – this city was conservative and tranquil, relatively provincial in comparison with larger cities. Today the Emerald City (Seattle's alias) seems larger than life, more progressive and fashionable than ever before. As a measure of its success, Seattle now finds itself a trend exporter. Musical and fashion tastes evolve and transform in the city's many clubs before leaking out to other pace-setting capitals.

The tallest building on the West Coast casts a long shadow on Seattle's downtown, and overexaggerated sports arenas draw rowdy crowds. But Seattle proper is really quite small; it's the surrounding neighborhoods that bolster its size and create the impression of a city where trees and azaleas outnumber houses.

Seattle's solid success as a trade and manufacturing center, coupled with its beautiful, big-as-all outdoors setting, has made the metropolitan area one of the fastest-growing in the USA. Young people especially have found their way to this seaport in search of a city that offers economic opportunity, easy access to outdoor recreation and forward-looking politics and culture. In short, if you're looking for lifestyle (and who isn't?), Seattle has it in spades.

Highlights

- Watching the skyline views at sunset from Bainbridge Island Ferry
- Wandering through the maze of Pike Place Market
- Scoping out the post-grunge, cutting-edge music scene
- Hanging out and sipping java in alternative Capitol Hill
- Catching Washington Park Arboretum in full springtime bloom
- Dining on delectable dim sum in the International District
- Visiting the Experience Music Project, an amazing museum of rock 'n' roll history

HISTORY

For a major US city, Seattle's civic history begins very late in the chronicle of the nation. When the rest of the country had established firm roots, most of today's Seattle was covered in deep rain-drenched forest.

The Formative Years

The Elliott Bay area was home to the Duwamish, a Salish tribe that fished the bays and rivers of Puget Sound. Generally a peaceable tribe, the Duwamish befriended early white settlers.

In 1851 a New Yorker, David Denny, led a group of settlers across the Oregon Trail with the intention of settling along Puget Sound. Recognizing the seaport possibilities of the sound, Denny and his fellow

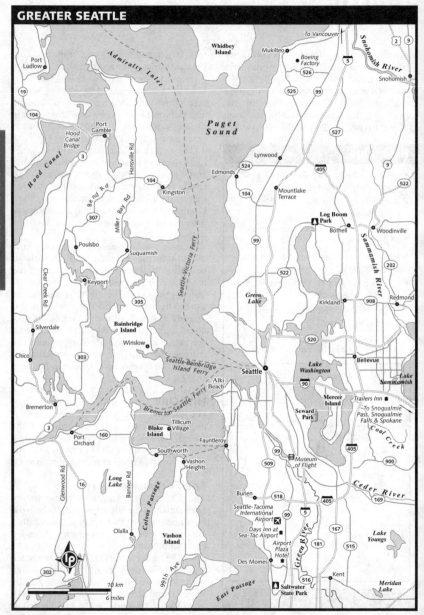

GREATER SEATTLE

WASHINGTON

settlers staked claims on Alki Point, in present-day West Seattle. The group named their encampment Alki–New York (the Chinookan word *alki* means 'by-and-by,' which gives a good sense of Denny's aspirations). After a winter of wind and rain, Denny's group determined that their foundling city needed a deeper harbor and moved the settlement to Elliott Bay. The colony was renamed 'Seattle' after the Duwamish chief, Sealth.

Early Seattle was hardly a boomtown. As a frontier settlement, it was comprised mostly of bachelors. One of the town's founding fathers (and sole professor at the newly founded university), Asa Mercer, went back to the East Coast with the express purpose of inducing young unmarried women to venture to Seattle. On two different trips in the 1860s, a total of 57 women made the cross-continental journey and married into the frontier stock, thereby establishing a more civilized tone for the city.

A spur from the Northern Pacific Railroad's terminus in Portland reached Seattle in 1893, linking it by rail to the rest of the country. Lumber, shipping and general commerce derived from immigration helped the town grow. After the Great Fire of 1889 burned 50 blocks of the old wooden downtown in a single day, Seattle quickly rebounded with a new brick-and-iron city centered on today's Pioneer Square.

Seattle's first boom came when the ship *Portland* docked at the waterfront in 1897 with its now-famous cargo: two tons of gold newly gleaned from Yukon fields. Within weeks, tens of thousands of fortune hunters converged in Seattle on their way north by ship and land.

Since the Canadian government demanded that prospectors bring with them a year's worth of supplies, outfitting them became very big business in Seattle. The city became the banking center for the fortunes made in the Yukon, and the bars, brothels, theaters and honky-tonks of the Pioneer Square area blossomed. Many of the men who made fortunes in Alaska chose to stay in the Northwest, settling in the now-thriving port city on Puget Sound.

The War Years & Beyond

The boom continued through WWI, when Northwest lumber was greatly in demand; the opening of the Panama Canal in 1914 had brought increased trade to Pacific ports, which were free of wartime threats. Shipyards opened along Puget Sound, bringing the shipbuilding industry close to the forests of the Northwest.

In 1916, William Boeing founded the Seattle-based aircraft manufacturing business that remains one of the largest employers in the city (see 'The Boeing Empire' boxed text). The ensuing military boom during WWII propelled Seattle's population to nearly half a million by the war's end. However, WWII also brought less positive change to Seattle: About 6000 Japanese residents were removed from their jobs and homes, and most were sent to internment camps in Idaho and eastern Oregon.

A High-Tech Capital

Thanks in part to Boeing, times were good in Seattle throughout the 1950s. The city increasingly saw itself as the harbinger of all that was new and progressive. The self-assured, forward-ho swagger of Seattle was perfectly captured in the 1962 World's Fair, also known as the 'Century 21 Exposition.' (The Space Needle and the Monorail now evoke a distinctly 1960s notion of tomorrow's world.)

Nonetheless, cuts in defense spending in the 1970s brought a temporary lull to Seattle's forward momentum, as thousands of Boeing employees lost their jobs. The local economy suffered for several years before a reverse in defense spending in the 1980s revived the aircraft industry, helping to bring it to its current position as a dominant force in the economics of Seattle.

The '80s also brought a new wave of high-tech jobs to Puget Sound. Microsoft, the software giant, is headquartered in Redmond, across Lake Washington from Seattle. While Bill Gates' company and other software developers in Seattle's 'Eastside' don't have quite the total control over the Seattle economy that Boeing once had, it has become increasingly hard to find

WASHINGTON

The Boeing Empire

A seminal event in Seattle history occurred in 1916, when William Boeing, a pioneer aviator, laid the foundation for his air-transport empire by designing and producing a pontoon biplane. Boeing went on to establish an airline, Boeing Air Transport, which in 1927 flew the first commercial flight between Chicago and San Francisco. (The company later became United Airlines.) But it was WWII that really started the engines at Boeing, as the factory received contracts to produce the B-17 and B-29 bombers that led the fleet in the US air war against the Axis nations. Huge defense contracts began to flow into Boeing – and by extension into Seattle – fueling rapid growth and prosperity.

Because of Boeing and the shipyards at Bremerton, the Puget Sound became a highly defended area. Military bases brought in thousands of new residents, and at the same time, the boom in aircraft manufacturing and shipbuilding brought tens of thousands of new workers to the area. By the end of the war, Seattle had grown to nearly half a million people.

After the war, Boeing diversified its product line and began to develop civilian aircraft. In 1954, Boeing introduced the 707 and led the revolution in air transportation. By 1960, the metropolitan population of Seattle topped one million people, and Boeing employed one in ten of these; moreover, one in four Seattleites was employed in a job directly affected by Boeing. Boeing was the biggest game in town.

However, the fortunes of Boeing didn't always soar. A combination of overstretched capital (due to cost overruns in the development of the 747) and a cut in defense spending led to a severe financial crisis in the early 1970s. Boeing was forced to cut its workforce by two-thirds; in one year, nearly 60,000 Seattle workers lost their jobs, and the local economy went into a tailspin for a number of years.

Increased defense spending in the 1980s brought vigor back to aircraft production, and expanding trade relations with Pacific Rim nations brought more business. Boeing was already the largest aircraft manufacturer in the world when, in 1997, it merged with once-rival McDonnell Douglas, forming a conglomerate of 200,000 employees with annual revenues of over $50 billion.

In early 2001, just a few weeks after an earthquake shook Seattle, Boeing sent more tremors through the region when it announced its plans to relocate corporate headquarters to Chicago. The news left Seattleites reeling and more than a little anxious about their future. While the company remains an enormous economic force in the Puget Sound and manufacturing of commercial jets continues there, Seattle had to face the fact that after 85 years the Boeing era was ending.

Yet another blow came in the latter part of the year with the horrific terrorist attack on the East Coast in which hijackers steered four Boeing aircraft to their destruction in one unforgettable September morning. Within weeks of the tragedy, Boeing announced plans to cut up to 30,000 workers, two-thirds of them from Seattle's workforce.

someone who isn't a contractor, caterer or car dealer for the Microsoft crowd.

The city kept growing in the 1990s – the 2000 census showed that close to 50,000 new residents had migrated to Seattle during the decade, more than half of them of Asian or Hispanic origin. But as the page turned on a new millennium, the situation took a turn for the worse. The Emerald City was losing its luster, and events seemed calculated to deflate the confidence of even the most upbeat Seattleites. In November 1999, a World Trade Organization summit drew international attention as protests turned violent and police were unable to contain the mayhem. In June 2000, a federal judge ruled that Microsoft would be split up for supposedly monopolistic business practices (the decision was later reversed). The Internet rush of the '90s was fizzling, and as dot-coms tanked in droves, thousands of tech workers found themselves unemployed. Then, on February 28, 2001 a 6.8-magnitude earthquake near the state capital caused billions of dollars in damages (though miraculously little loss of life). Just a few weeks later came the ultimate kick in the teeth: Boeing announced its intention to relocate its headquarters to Chicago.

ORIENTATION

Washington's largest city sits on a slim isthmus between two bodies of water, Puget Sound and Lake Washington; north of Seattle's downtown is Lake Union. All of these bodies of water are now linked by locks and canals. Although Seattle is a major Pacific seaport, the open ocean lies 125 miles away.

Seattle's pioneer settlers liked the fact that their fledgling community, like Rome, was founded on seven hills. While the distinctions between the hills have been obfuscated by developments, and one of the original hills was sluiced into Elliott Bay to make way for the Denny Regrade, pedestrians will discover that a lot of the city's original gradients are still here, especially on Queen Anne Hill and at the south end of downtown.

As the city proper is limited in size by water, most people and many businesses reside in the surrounding suburbs and communities. To the south are Kent, Federal Way and Tacoma. East across Lake Washington are Bellevue and Kirkland and masses of brand new housing developments, and north are Edmonds and Everett. Many of the islands in Puget Sound also serve as suburbs, particularly Bainbridge and Vashon Islands. Commuters from these communities take ferries between home and work in Seattle.

I-5 runs north and south through the center of the city; I-90 joins it just south of downtown, crossing Mercer Island on its way east. Hwy 520 links downtown with Kirkland and Bellevue on the 2-mile-long Evergreen Point Floating Bridge. I-405, known as the 'Eastside Freeway,' cuts north-south through the suburbs east of Lake

Washington. Vancouver, British Columbia, is 141 miles north of Seattle on I-5, Portland is 172 miles south, and Spokane is 280 miles east on I-90.

Neighborhoods

Seattle is a very neighborhood-oriented city. Just north and west of downtown is Queen Anne, one of Seattle's original neighborhoods. To the east of downtown rises Capitol Hill, synonymous with youthful urban culture. The old First Hill section is now largely given over to hospitals (and known as Pill Hill); the Central District, Madison Valley, Madison Park and Madrona are residential neighborhoods on the east side of the Seattle peninsula as it slopes down to Lake Washington. To the west of Seattle, across Elliott Bay, is another peninsula called West Seattle, where settlers originally founded the city.

Lake Union, the Lake Washington Ship Canal and the 'Montlake Cut' divide the city into northern and southern halves. North of the ship canal and Lake Union are the neighborhoods of Ballard (the old mill town), Fremont (now a hip hangout) and Wallingford. Each of these close-in neighborhoods has lively commercial centers filled with restaurants, shops and bars. Just north of Wallingford is Green Lake, the hub of a large park area that also contains the city zoo. Just east of Wallingford, flanking Lake Washington, is the U District, home to the University of Washington.

Four bridges (besides the freeway bridges) cross the shipping canal. The westernmost is the Ballard Bridge, linking Ballard and the neighborhood of Magnolia, west of Queen Anne; the Fremont Bridge crosses from Queen Anne to Fremont; and east of Lake Union, the University and Montlake Bridges both hook the U District to neighborhoods south of the canal.

Street Savvy

Seattle's topographic stew of bays, islands, hills and peninsulas creates a street system that is an amalgam of several separate grids. These grids sometimes overlap, leading to maximum confusion. That said, it's fairly easy to get a working understanding of the numbering system and the way all the areas of the city fit together. Just don't try to understand the system intellectually; it makes little rational sense.

Generally speaking, avenues run north and south, streets run east and west. Address numbers for downtown avenues ascend from Yesler Way near Pioneer Square; address numbers on downtown streets ascend from Western Way, near the Waterfront.

Directional labels give an indication of where streets and avenues are located throughout town. For instance, streets in the Queen Anne neighborhood, northwest of downtown, are labeled 'West' or 'North,' while those on Capitol Hill are 'East.' Fremont streets take a simple 'North' prefix, while those in the U-District have a 'Northeast' attachment. Generally, avenues have a directional suffix ('6th Ave S'), while streets have directional prefixes ('S Charles St'); however, downtown streets and avenues north of Yesler Way have no directional affixes.

In reality, people use neighborhoods to indicate where things are found. For instance, '1st Ave on Queen Anne' distinguishes that 1st Ave from '1st Ave in Wallingford.' Therefore, it's important to garner a working knowledge of Seattle's neighborhoods. With so many numbering systems at odds with each other, it's the only way to easily make sense of the city.

INFORMATION
Tourist Offices
The Visitor Information Bureau (Map 2; ☎ 206-461-5840, W www.seeseattle.org), 800 Convention Place, is at the Washington State Convention & Trade Center, directly above I-5 at 7th Ave and Pike St. You can enter from either Pike St or the Union St underpass. A market information booth just outside the Pike Place Market at 1st Ave and Pike St also dispenses maps and brochures. To write for information, contact the Seattle–King County Convention & Visitors Bureau, 520 Pike St, Suite 1300, Seattle, WA 98101.

Money
There are a number of options for exchanging money. Thomas Cook Foreign Exchange has an office downtown (Map 2; ☎ 206-682-4525) at 1601 5th Ave, Suite 400, in the Westlake Center, and in Bellevue (☎ 425-462-2187) at 10630 NE 8th Ave. The American Express office (Map 2; ☎ 206-441-8622) is at 600 Stewart St.

The main branches of Bank of America (Map 2; ☎ 206-358-7800), 701 5th Ave, and USBank (Map 2; ☎ 206-344-5519), 1301 5th Ave, can exchange foreign currency and traveler's checks. Outside of Seattle it can be difficult to exchange money.

ATMs can be found all around town. Some of them, such as Key Bank, charge hefty service rates in addition to your own bank's fees.

At the airport, two Thomas Cook currency exchange booths are in the main terminal. One, behind the Delta Airlines booth, is open 6am to 8pm; another, behind Alaska Airlines, is open 6am to 6pm. A third branch, in the South Satellite, is open 8am to 6pm. For information, call ☎ 206-248-6960. Should your flight arrive after hours, you can get cash from the ATMs near the booths.

Post & Communications
Seattle's main post office is at 301 Union St (Map 2; zip 98101). If you're staying near the university, use the University station, 4244 NE University Way (Map 8; zip 98105). On Capitol Hill, go to the Broadway station, 101 Broadway E (Map 6; zip 98122).

Email & Internet Access
Most business-class and top-end hotels offer high-speed modem connections, even in standard rooms. For free access, you can stop by any of Seattle's public libraries. Some coffeehouses have Internet terminals for public use. On Capitol Hill, stop by Online Coffee Company (Map 2; ☎ 206-328-3731), 1720 E Olive Way. They're open 8am to midnight daily and charge 12¢ a minute, but you get 20 minutes free when you buy a beverage. Alternatively, try Capitolhill.Net (Map 6; ☎ 206-860-6858), 219 Broadway E, for 10¢ a minute.

[Continued on page 334]

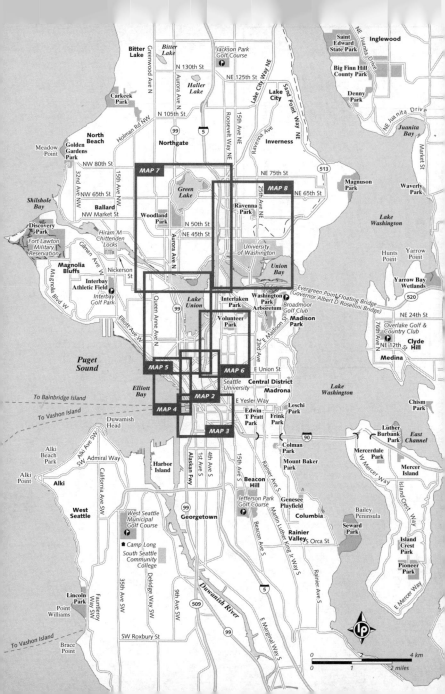

MAP 2 DOWNTOWN SEATTLE

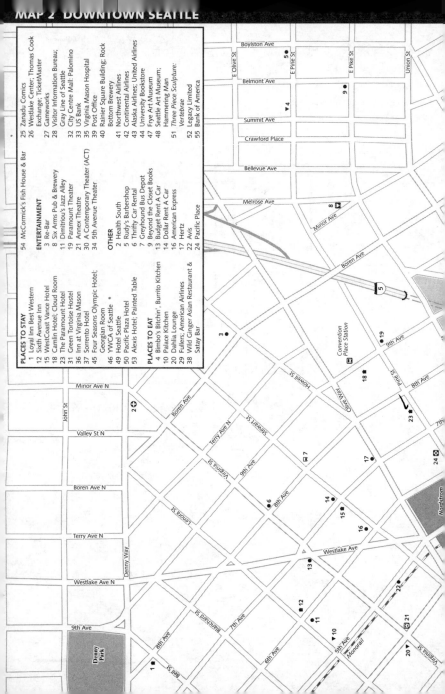

PLACES TO STAY
1 Loyal Inn Best Western
12 Sixth Avenue Inn
15 WestCoast Vance Hotel
18 Camlin Hotel; Cloud Room
23 The Paramount Hotel
31 Green Tortoise Hostel
36 Inn at Virginia Mason
37 Sorrento Hotel
45 Four Seasons Olympic Hotel; Georgian Room
46 YWCA of Seattle
49 Hotel Seattle
50 Pacific Plaza Hotel
53 Alexis Hotel; Painted Table

PLACES TO EAT
4 Bimbo's Bitchin'; Burrito Kitchen
10 Palace Kitchen
20 Dahlia Lounge
29 Fullers; American Airlines
38 Wild Ginger Asian Restaurant & Satay Bar
54 McCormick's Fish House & Bar

ENTERTAINMENT
3 Re-Bar
8 Six Arms Pub & Brewery
11 Dimitriou's Jazz Alley
19 Paramount Theater
21 Annex Theatre
30 A Contemporary Theater (ACT)
34 5th Avenue Theater

OTHER
2 Health South
5 Rudy's Barbershop
6 Thrifty Car Rental
7 Greyhound Bus Depot
9 Beyond the Closet Books
13 Budget Rent A Car
14 Dollar Rent A Car
16 American Express
17 Hertz
22 Avis
24 Pacific Place
25 Zanadu Comics
26 Westlake Center; Thomas Cook Exchange; TicketMaster
27 Gameworks
28 Visitor Information Bureau; Gray Line of Seattle
32 City Centre Mall: Palomino
33 US Bank
35 Virginia Mason Hospital
39 Post Office
40 Rainier Square Building; Rock Bottom Brewery
41 Northwest Airlines
42 Continental Airlines
43 Alaska Airlines; United Airlines
44 University Bookstore
47 Frye Art Museum
48 Seattle Art Museum; Hammering Man
51 *Three Piece Sculpture: Vertebrae*
52 Legacy Limited
55 Bank of America

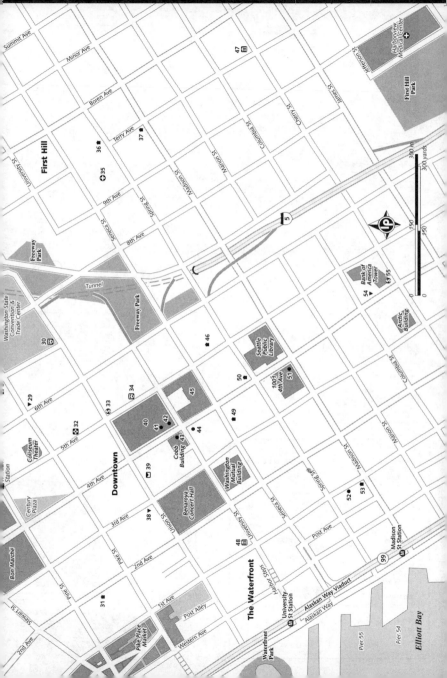

Harborview
Medical Center

First Hill
Park

Summit Ave

Minor Ave

Boren Ave

Terry Ave

36 ☆
35 ✚

First Hill

Jefferson St

James St

Columbia St

Cherry St

47 🏛

Madison St

University St

9th Ave

Spring St

Seneca St

8th Ave

Madison St

37 ■

5

Freeway
Park

Tunnel

Freeway
Park

Washington State
Convention &
Trade Center

30 🅿

Bank of
America
Tower

54 ▶
55 ✚

Arctic
Building

46 ★

Seattle
Public
Library

29 ▼

6th Ave

34 🅿

33 ✚

45

50 ■

51

100
4th Ave

Downtown

32 ✻

5th Ave

40

41
42

Cobb
Building

43

49 ■

44 ●

39 🅿

4th Ave

Coliseum
Theater

Station

Century
Plaza

Benaroya
Concert Hall

Washington
Mutual
Building

38 ▶

3rd Ave

1st Ave

Union St

Seneca St

Spring St

Madison St

52 ●

53 ●

Bon Marché

31 ■

Pike St

2nd Ave

Post Ave

48 🏛

University St

99

Madison
St Station

The Waterfront

Stewart St

2nd Ave

Pike Place
Market

Post Alley

Western Ave

1st Ave

Harbor Steps

University
Ⓜ St Station

Alaskan Way Viaduct

Alaskan Way

Waterfront
Park

Pier 55

Pier 54

Elliott Bay

300 m

300 yards

0   150   300

LP

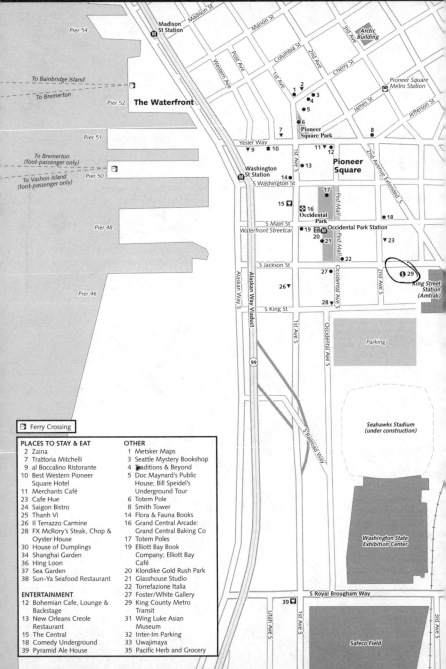

MAP 3 PIONEER SQUARE & INTERNATIONAL DISTRICT

Madison
St Station

Pier 54

To Bainbridge Island

To Bremerton

Pier 52

The Waterfront

Pier 51

To Bremerton
(foot-passenger only)

To Vashon Island
(foot-passenger only)

Pier 50

Pier 48

Pier 46

Madison St

Marion St

Columbia St

3rd Ave

Arctic
Building

Pioneer Square
Metro Station

Western Ave

Post Ave

1st Ave

2nd Ave

Cherry St

James St

Jefferson St

2 ▼
1 ● ● 3
● 4
● 5
● 6
7 ▼

Pioneer
Square Park

8 ●

Yesler Way

Washington
St Station

■ 10

11 ▼ ● 12

● 13

**Pioneer
Square**

2nd Avenue Extended S

14 ●

S Washington St

15 ▣

17 ●

16 ▣
**Occidental
Park**

● 18

Ped Mall

S Main St

Waterfront Streetcar

● 19

20

🚇 Occidental Park Station

▼ 23

21

Ped Mall

● 22

S Jackson St

27 ●

ℹ 29

King Street
Station
(Amtrak)

26 ▼

28 ▼

S King St

Alaskan Way Viaduct

Alaskan Way S

1st Ave S

1st Ave S

Occidental Ave S

2nd Ave S

Parking

S Railroad Way

99

*Seahawks Stadium
(under construction)*

*Washington State
Exhibition Center*

S Royal Brougham Way

39 ▣

Utah Ave S

1st Ave S

3rd Ave S

Safeco Field

🚢 **Ferry Crossing**

PLACES TO STAY & EAT
2 Zaina
7 Trattoria Mitchelli
9 al Boccalino Ristorante
10 Best Western Pioneer
   Square Hotel
11 Merchants Café
23 Cafe Hue
24 Saigon Bistro
25 Thanh Vi
26 Il Terrazzo Carmine
28 FX McRory's Steak, Chop &
   Oyster House
30 House of Dumplings
34 Shanghai Garden
36 Hing Loon
37 Sea Garden
38 Sun-Ya Seafood Restaurant

ENTERTAINMENT
12 Bohemian Cafe, Lounge &
   Backstage
13 New Orleans Creole
   Restaurant
15 The Central
18 Comedy Underground
39 Pyramid Ale House

OTHER
1 Metsker Maps
3 Seattle Mystery Bookshop
4 Traditions & Beyond
5 Doc Maynard's Public
   House; Bill Speidel's
   Underground Tour
6 Totem Pole
8 Smith Tower
14 Flora & Fauna Books
16 Grand Central Arcade:
   Grand Central Baking Co
17 Totem Poles
19 Elliott Bay Book
   Company; Elliott Bay
   Café
20 Klondike Gold Rush Park
21 Glasshouse Studio
22 Torrefazione Italia
27 Foster/White Gallery
29 King County Metro
   Transit
31 Wing Luke Asian
   Museum
32 Inter-Im Parking
33 Uwajimaya
35 Pacific Herb and Grocery

MAP 4 PIKE PLACE MARKET & THE WATERFRONT

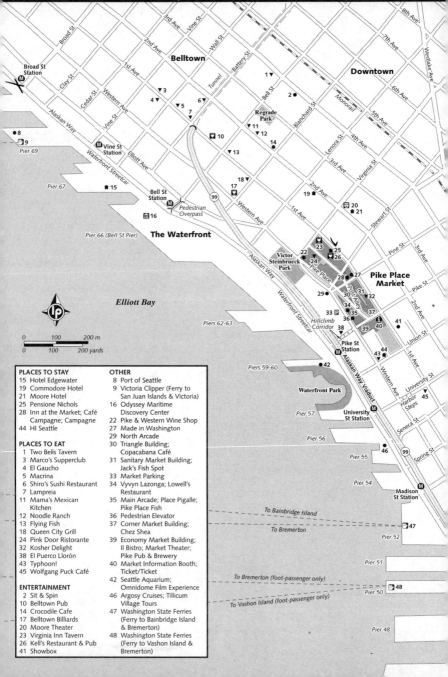

PLACES TO STAY
15 Hotel Edgewater
19 Commodore Hotel
21 Moore Hotel
25 Pensione Nichols
28 Inn at the Market; Café
   Campagne; Campagne
44 HI Seattle

PLACES TO EAT
1 Two Bells Tavern
3 Marco's Supperclub
4 El Gaucho
5 Macrina
6 Shiro's Sushi Restaurant
7 Lampreia
11 Mama's Mexican
   Kitchen
12 Noodle Ranch
13 Flying Fish
18 Queen City Grill
24 Pink Door Ristorante
32 Kosher Delight
38 El Puerco Llorón
43 Typhoon!
45 Wolfgang Puck Café

ENTERTAINMENT
2 Sit & Spin
10 Belltown Pub
14 Crocodile Cafe
17 Belltown Billiards
20 Moore Theater
23 Virginia Inn Tavern
26 Kell's Restaurant & Pub
41 Showbox

OTHER
8 Port of Seattle
9 Victoria Clipper (Ferry to
   San Juan Islands & Victoria)
16 Odyssey Maritime
   Discovery Center
22 Pike & Western Wine Shop
27 Made in Washington
29 North Arcade
30 Triangle Building;
   Copacabana Café
31 Sanitary Market Building;
   Jack's Fish Spot
33 Market Parking
34 Vyvyn Lazonga; Lowell's
   Restaurant
35 Main Arcade; Place Pigalle;
   Pike Place Fish
36 Pedestrian Elevator
37 Corner Market Building;
   Chez Shea
39 Economy Market Building;
   Il Bistro; Market Theater;
   Pike Pub & Brewery
40 Market Information Booth;
   Ticket/Ticket
42 Seattle Aquarium;
   Omnidome Film Experience
46 Argosy Cruises; Tillicum
   Village Tours
47 Washington State Ferries
   (Ferry to Bainbridge Island
   & Bremerton)
48 Washington State Ferries
   (Ferry to Vashon Island &
   Bremerton)

Aurora Bridge (George Washington Memorial Bridge)

Gas Works Park

Rogers Park

Kerry Park

Queen Anne

Lake Union

Bagley Wright Theatre

Seattle Opera House

Seattle Center

International Fountain

Memorial Stadium

Key Arena

Seattle Center House/ Children's Museum

Experience Music Project

Children's Theatre

Space Needle

Pacific Science Center

Belltown

Myrtle Edwards Park

Elliott Bay

Cascade Playground

Denny Park

0   200   400 m
0   200   400 yards

PLACES TO STAY
4 Mildred's B&B
24 Hill House B&B
27 Gaslight Inn B&B

30 The Comet
31 Wildrose
32 Vogue
33 Globe Café

PLACES TO EAT
9 Siam on Broadway
11 Pagliacci Pizza
16 Coastal Kitchen
17 Broadway New
   American Grill
20 Café Septieme

ENTERTAINMENT
5 Cornish College of
   the Arts
7 The Harvard Exit
8 Deluxe Bar & Grill
10 Elite
18 Ileen's Sports Bar
21 B&O Espresso
28 The Egyptian
29 Neighbours

OTHER
1 Volunteer Park
   Conservatory
2 Water Tower
3 Seattle Asian Art
   Museum
6 Marco Polo
12 Council Travel
13 Dilettante Chocolates
14 Broadway Market:
   Gravity Bar;
   Ticket/Ticket; Cinemas
15 Bailey/Coy Books
19 CapitolHill.net
22 Online Coffee Co
23 The Pink Zone
25 Post Office
26 12th Ave Laundry

Capitol Hill

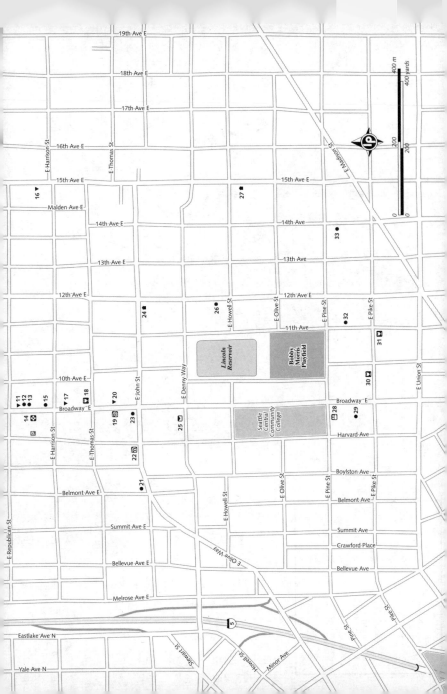

PLACES TO STAY & EAT
6 Bizzarro
9 Julia's of Wallingford
11 Wallingford Pizza
12 Jitterbug Cafe
13 Boulangerie
14 Kabul
16 University Plaza Hotel

ENTERTAINMENT
1 Bathhouse Theatre Company
4 The Latona
10 Teahouse Kuan Yin
17 Trolleyman Pub
18 Redhook Brewery; Fremont Outdoor Movies
20 Triangle Lounge

OTHER
2 Green Lake Boat Rental
3 Gregg's Greenlake Cycle
5 Woodland Park Zoo
7 45th St Clinic
8 Wide World Books & Maps
15 Erotic Bakery
19 Statue of Lenin
21 Fremont Sunday Market
22 Fremont Rocket
23 Fremont Troll
24 Waiting for the Interurban

Roosevelt Way NE

NE 47th St
NE 45th St

University of Washington

University Bridge

Fuhrman Ave E

E Allison St
E Gwinn Pl
E Shelby St
E Hamlin St
E Edgar St

Roanoke Park

Harvard Ave E

5th Ave NE
4th Ave NE
Latona Ave NE
Thackeray Place NE
2nd Ave NE
1st Ave NE
Eastern Ave N

16

NE Northlake Way

Lake Washington Ship Canal Bridge

Fairview Ave E
Eastlake Ave E
Franklin Ave E

Sunnyside Ave N
Corliss Ave N
Bagley Ave N

Wallingford

N 44th St
N 43rd St

15
14

13

N Pacific St

Burke-Gilman Trail

400 m
400 yards

Meridian Ave N

Burke Ave N

Wallingford Ave N

12

11

10

N 42nd St

Meridian Ave N
Burke Ave N
Wallingford Ave N
Densmore Ave N

200

200

9

7
8

Woodlawn Ave N

N 41st St
N 40th St
N 39th St
N 38th St
N 37th St
N 36th St

Woodlawn Ave N
Carr Place N

Gas Works Park

0

0

NE 45th St

N 46th St

6

Interlake Ave N

Stone Way N

N 35th St

N Northlake Way

Lake Union

N 49th St
N 48th St
N 47th St

Green Lake Way N

Midvale Ave N
Woodland Park Ave N
Whitman Ave N
Winslow Place N
Aurora Ave N

N 46 St

N 42nd St
N 41st St
N 40th St

Bridge Way N

N 34th St

Aurora Bridge (George Washington Memorial Bridge)

Westlake Ave N
Dexter Ave N

Linden Ave N

Fremont Way N

23

99

4th Ave N

Fremont Ave N

Fremont Ave N

24

3rd Ave N

Fremont

Evanston Ave N
Dayton Ave N

Steps

Evanston Ave N
Dayton Ave N

19
20
21
22

Fremont Bridge

Mayfair Ave N

Francis Ave N
Phinney Ave N
Greenwood Ave N

Francis Ave N
Phinney Ave N
Greenwood Ave N

17
18

N 34th St

2nd Ave N
Warren Ave N
1st Ave N

N 35th St

N Canal St

Fulton St
Newell St

1st Ave NW

N 36th St

Fremont Canal Park

Nickerson St

2nd Ave NW
Baker Ave NW
3rd Ave NW

NW Bowdoin Place
NW 43rd St
NW 42nd St
NW 41st St
NW 40th St
N 39th St

Lake Washington Ship Canal

Dravus St
Etruria St
W Florentia St

Rogers Park

Seattle Pacific University

Mt Pleasant Cemetery

5th Ave W

MAP 8 U DISTRICT

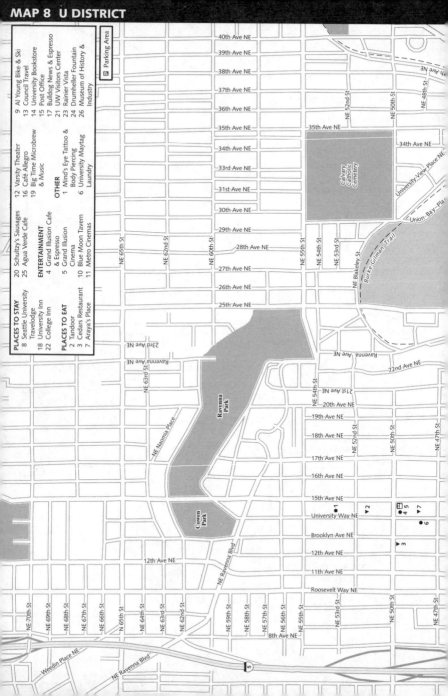

PLACES TO STAY
8 Seattle University Travelodge
18 University Inn
22 College Inn

PLACES TO EAT
2 Tandoor
3 Cedars Restaurant
7 Araya's Place
20 Schultzy's Sausages
25 Agua Verde Cafe

ENTERTAINMENT
4 Grand Illusion Cafe & Espresso
5 Grand Illusion Cinema
10 Blue Moon Tavern
11 Metro Cinemas
12 Varsity Theater
16 Café Allegro
19 Big Time Microbrew & Music

OTHER
1 Mind's Eye Tattoo & Body Piercing
6 University Maytag Laundry
9 Al Young Bike & Ski
13 Council Travel
14 University Bookstore
15 Post Office
17 Bulldog News & Espresso
21 UW Visitors Center
23 Rainier Vista
24 Drumheller Fountain
26 Museum of History & Industry

P Parking Area

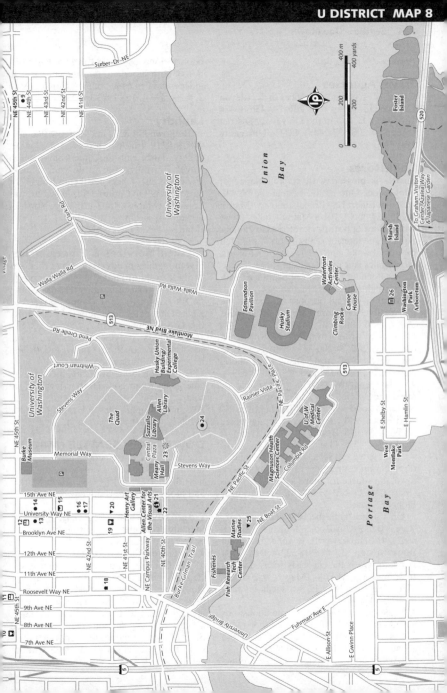

Surber Dr NE

NE 45th St
NE 44th St ● 9
NE 43rd St
NE 42nd St
NE 41st St

University of Washington

Clark Rd

Walla Walla Rd

Union Bay

Foster Island

520

To Graham Visitors Center, Azalea Way & Japanese Garden

400 m
400 yards
200
0

Marsh Island

Washington Park Arboretum

🏛 26

Walla Walla Rd

Pend Oreille Rd

513

Montlake Blvd NE

Waterfront Activities Center

Edmundson Pavilion

Husky Stadium

Climbing Rock

Canoe House

E Shelby St

E Hamlin St

Husky Union Building/ Experimental College

Whitman Court

Stevens Way

University of Washington

The Quad

Allen Library

Suzzallo Library

Central Plaza 23

● 24

Rainier Vista

NE Pacific Pl

NE Pacific St

513

Portage Bay

West Montlake Park

Magnuson Health Sciences Center

U of W Medical Center

Columbia Rd

Burke Museum

Memorial Way

NE 45th St

P

Stevens Way

Meany Hall

Henry Art Gallery

Allen Center for the Visual Arts

15th Ave NE

● 14   📷 15

University Way NE
● 13

12 📷

Brooklyn Ave NE

12th Ave NE

11th Ave NE

Roosevelt Way NE

9th Ave NE

8th Ave NE

7th Ave NE

NE 45th St

● 16
● 17

19 📷   ▼ 20

📷 21
22

NE 42nd St

NE 41st St

▼ 25

Marine Studies

NE Boat St

Fisheries

Fish Research Tech Center

NE Campus Parkway

NE 40th St

Burke-Gilman Trail

■ 18

University Bridge

Fuhrman Ave E

E Allison St

E Gwinn Place

5

5

[Continued from page 320]

Travel Agencies

Council Travel has two offices in Seattle: on Capitol Hill (Map 6; ☎ 206-329-4567), 424 Broadway E, and in the University District (Map 8; ☎ 206-632-2448), 4211½ University Way NE.

Bookstores

Seattle is blessed with an abundance of booksellers. One of the best in the Northwest, the Elliott Bay Book Company (Map 3; ☎ 206-624-6600), 101 S Main St, takes up an entire block of historic storefronts in Pioneer Square. The interior is absolutely stuffed full of new books and browsing customers. Downstairs is a popular cafe. Elliott Bay is the local leader in author appearances, with almost nightly readings or signings.

Another vast all-purpose bookstore, the University Bookstore (Map 8; ☎ 206-634-3400), 4326 University Way NE, serves the University of Washington. A downtown outlet (Map 2; ☎ 206-545-9230) is at 1225 4th Ave. Also in the U District is Bulldog News & Espresso (Map 8; ☎ 206-632-6397), 4208 University Way NE, a great source for magazines, periodicals and newspapers (including a good selection of foreign titles).

Travelers will want to make a pilgrimage to Wide World Books & Maps (Map 7; ☎ 206-634-3453), 4411 Wallingford Ave N. In addition to a great selection of travel guides, this pleasant store offers travel gear. Downtown, the source for maps is Metsker Maps (Map 3; ☎ 206-623-8747), 702 1st Ave, near Pioneer Square.

On Capitol Hill, the best general bookstore is Bailey/Coy Books (Map 6; ☎ 206-323-8842), 414 Broadway E. Beyond the Closet Books (Map 2; ☎ 206-322-4609), 1501 Belmont Ave, is the city's gay-focused bookstore, and Marco Polo (Map 6; ☎ 206-860-3736), 713 Broadway E, is a small, intimate travel bookstore.

Some of Seattle's great theme bookstores include The Seattle Mystery Bookshop (Map 3; ☎ 206-587-5737), 117 Cherry St, and Flora & Fauna Books (Map 3; ☎ 206-623-4727), 121 1st Ave S, both in Pioneer Square. Comic-book aficionados will find an abundant selection of both superhero fare and cutting-edge independent titles at Zanadu Comics (Map 2; ☎ 206-443-1316), 1923 3rd Ave.

Laundry

In Belltown, Sit & Spin (Map 4; ☎ 206-441-9484), 2219 4th Ave, serves as a cafe, art gallery, dance club and laundromat, which leaves you no reason to do your laundry anywhere else. Check local club listings for current acts. On Capitol Hill, go to 12th Ave Laundry (Map 6), 1807 12th Ave. North of downtown is University Maytag Laundry (Map 8), 4733 University Way.

Medical Services & Emergencies

If your medical needs aren't grave, then one of these walk-in clinics should be able to deal with most situations. Health South (☎ 206-682-7418), 1151 Denny Way, at Virginia St, has extended hours. In Wallingford, the 45th St Clinic (Map 7; ☎ 206-633-3350), 1629 N 45th St, provides medical and dental services. Both open at 8am weekdays and have some Saturday hours.

For complete medical care, including an emergency room, go to Harborview Medical Center (Map 2; ☎ 206-731-3000), 325 9th Ave, or to Virginia Mason Hospital (Map 2; ☎ 206-624-1144), 925 Seneca St.

DOWNTOWN SEATTLE (MAP 2)

The area that most people associate with downtown Seattle encompasses the business district as well as Pike Place Market and Pioneer Square (both covered later).

Downtown Walking Tour

Starting from the convention center, the best way to see it all is to walk toward the water down either Pike or Pine Sts.

The first area you will encounter is the classy shopping district that revolves around Nordstrom and the Westlake Center, both between 4th and 5th Aves. Here skateboarders and trench-coat-clad professionals tolerate each others' definition of fun. Right in the heart of the skateboard territory is a 'waterwall' that you can walk through without getting wet. If you're into the latest video games and virtual-reality interactive systems, then make a detour into Gameworks, at 7th and Pike.

The business district is to the south (just look for the looming buildings). There's not much to see there, except the buildings themselves and some sculpture. Most impressive is the Darth Vader–like **Bank of America Tower**, at 5th Ave and Cherry St, the tallest on the West Coast. Ride one of the 46 elevators up to the observation deck on the 73rd floor; tickets cost $5/4 adult/child, and the elevators are open to the public 8:30am to 4:30pm Monday to Friday. Check out the ornamental walruses on the **Arctic Building**, on Cherry St at 3rd Ave. Head up 4th Ave to Madison St to see Henry Moore's *Three Piece Sculpture: Vertebrae*, one of the works funded by Seattle's '1% for art' clause. In the block bordered by 5th Ave and Union St is the **Rainier Square Building**, a top-heavy structure that looks like a beaver started chipping away at its base. Nearby, at University St and 4th Ave, the dour terra-cotta head of a Native American chief peers out from the **Cobb Building**. Sixteen of these 800lb heads once decorated the exterior of the White Henry-Stuart Building, one of the original structures near this site (it was torn down in 1976). The beauty of the Seattle skyline is the blue-and-cream **Washington Mutual Building**, at University St and 2nd Ave, which changes colors with the clouds and sunsets.

The distinctive, white 42-story **Smith Tower (Map 3)**, at the corner of 2nd Ave and Yesler Way near Pioneer Square, was built in 1914 by LC Smith, a man who made his fortune on typewriters. For many years it was the tallest building in the world outside of New York City.

Heading down Pike or Union Sts, you'll notice that the blocks between 3rd and 1st Aves are quite run down. Businesses move out frequently, panhandlers hover around bus stops, and empty lots stand in contrast to the city's prosperity. Unfortunately, this is also where the main post office is and where buses to Capitol Hill and the University District stop (along Pike St). Be careful here. At the end of Pike St is Pike Place Market, directly above the Waterfront.

Seattle Art Museum
Jonathan Borofsky's four-story action sculpture, *Hammering Man,* welcomes visitors to the Seattle Art Museum (☎ 206-654-3100, *100 University St; adult/senior & student $7/5, free 1st Thur of month; open 10am-5pm Tues-Wed & Fri-Sun, 10am-9pm Thur).* Tickets let you into the Seattle Asian Art Museum in Volunteer Park within one week of purchase.

The museum's collection of world art emphasizes Asian, African and Native American folk and tribal artifacts. Especially good are the displays of masks, canoes and totem poles from Northwest Coastal tribes.

Frye Art Museum
This small museum (☎ 206-622-9250, *704 Terry Ave; admission free; open 10am-5pm Tues-Wed & Fri-Sat, 10am-9pm Thur, noon-5pm Sun),* on First Hill, preserves the collection of Charles and Emma Frye. The Fryes collected over 1000 paintings, mostly 19th- and early-20th-century European and American pieces, and a few Alaskan and Russian artworks. With its expansion in 1997, the Frye became a hip place for poetry readings, music performances and interesting rotating exhibits.

PIONEER SQUARE (MAP 3)
The birthplace of Seattle, this red-brick district of historic buildings and totem-pole-lined plazas is still a real crossroads of the modern city. For years this area was in decline, until cheap rents and status on the National Register of Historic Places brought in what are now considered some of the city's very best art galleries and antique shops. A number of restaurants play up the frontier image while serving some of the city's best food.

Pioneer Square is most easily reached by foot or bus (it's in the ride-free zone). For something more touristy-historic, take the Waterfront Streetcar, which will put you smack-dab in the heart of the district.

Right at the corner of Cherry St and 1st Ave you'll come to the original **Pioneer Square Park** – a triangular cobblestone plaza with a totem pole and pergola. The original totem pole, so the story goes, was stolen from the Tlingit Indians in 1890 but subsequently burned down. When asked if they would carve another one, the Tlingit took the money offered, thanking the city for payment of the first totem pole, and waited for a better offer to carve the one now standing.

The pergola may look decorative, but its original purpose was to cover an underground lavatory and to protect people waiting for the cable car that went up and down Yesler Way. Yesler Way, incidentally, is the original Skid Row – timber would 'skid' down the road from a logging camp above town to Henry Yesler's pierside mill. With the decline of the area, the street became a haven for homeless people, and the nickname 'Skid Row' became the standard term for destitute zones in other US cities.

A block southeast of Pioneer Square, **Occidental Park** sports a few more totem poles, all carved by Duane Pasco, a nationally respected Chinookan artist. They depict the welcoming spirit of Kwakiutl, a totem bear, the 35-foot-tall Sun and Raven, and a man riding on the tail of a whale.

The **Grand Central Arcade** (*214 1st Ave S*), with entrances from the park and 1st Ave S, has a good bakery cafe, plenty of tables, a cozy fire and an underground shopping arcade.

Between S Main and S Jackson Sts, the park turns into a tree-lined mall housing galleries, some sculpture art and Torrefazione Italia, where you can drink one of Seattle's best lattes in a real ceramic Italian *tazza*.

Just south of Pioneer Square, at the site of the former Kingdome, is the new Seahawks stadium, slated for completion in late summer 2002. A bit farther south is the new Washington State Exhibition Center and **Safeco Field** (*☎ 206-346-4241; tours adult/ child $7/3; call for schedules*), home to the successful Mariners baseball team.

Seattle's seminal position as the outfitting and transportation hub for the 1897 Alaskan and Yukon gold rush is recognized at **Klondike Gold Rush Park** (*☎ 206-553-7220, 117 S Main St; admission free; open 9am-5pm*), a small national historic park and museum. Exhibits document the abundance of gear and food necessary to stake a claim in the Klondike. Park rangers demonstrate gold panning, and there's a slide presentation.

INTERNATIONAL DISTRICT (MAP 3)

Southeast of Pioneer Square is the International District, Seattle's Chinatown, where Asian groceries and restaurants line the streets. The Chinese, among the early settlers in Seattle, have been followed by Japanese, Filipinos, Vietnamese, Laotians and others.

International District Walking Tour

The district's center is outlined by 5th and 7th Aves and S Weller and S Jackson Sts. From Pioneer Square walk up S Jackson St. You'll pass **King Street Station**, the old Italianate Great Northern Railroad depot, its stately brick tower long an integral (though now dwarfed) piece of the downtown skyline. It's presently in use as the Amtrak station and is benefiting from a slow renovation process.

Weller St is a good road to get a glimpse of it all. Besides the many restaurants, there's **Pacific Herb & Grocery** (*☎ 206-340-6411, 610 S Weller St*), between 6th & Maynard Ave S, where herbal medicine specialists can tell you all about the uses of different roots, bones, flowers and teas. At the shop next door you can watch them make tofu on the premises. Farther east, between 10th and 12th Aves, the Vietnamese influence is more pervasive.

A cornerstone of Seattle's Asian community, **Uwajimaya** (*☎ 206-624-6248, 519 6th Ave S*) is a large Japanese department and grocery store. Within you'll find exotic fruits and vegetables and cooking utensils; you'll also come face to face with those dim sum ingredients you've always wondered about. It's a great place to browse.

Wing Luke Asian Museum

This pan-Asian museum (*☎ 206-623-5124, 407 7th Ave S; adult/senior & student/child 5-12 years $4/3/2; open 11am-4:30pm Tues-Fri, noon-4pm Sat & Sun*) is devoted solely to

Asian and Pacific American culture, history and art. Named after the first Asian elected official in Seattle, the museum examines the often difficult and violent meeting of Asian and Western cultures here. Particularly good are the photos and displays on the Chinese settlement in the 1880s and the recounting of Japanese internment during WWII.

PIKE PLACE MARKET & THE WATERFRONT (MAP 4)

Nearly a century after its beginnings as a farmers' market, Pike Place is one of Seattle's most popular tourist attractions. Heading west, visitors can catch the flavor of a major seaport by walking along the Seattle Waterfront; they can also do a lot of eating and souvenir shopping in the city's tackiest tourist zone.

Pike Place Market

Pike Place is noted as much for its exuberant theatricality and local crafts as for its vastly appealing fish and vegetable market. The market features some of the most boisterous fishmongers in the world; their daredevil antics with salmon merge gymnastics, theater and cuisine.

The best time to enjoy the market is on a weekday morning – summer weekends and Friday mornings the crowds can get overwhelming. Pike Place is made up of several buildings, the most popular of which are the **Main Arcade** and **North Arcades**, with banks of fresh produce arranged in artful displays, and fresh fish, crabs and shellfish piled high with ice.

Over half of the open-air stalls are now devoted to locally made arts and crafts, and the three labyrinthine lower levels are filled with pocket-size shops of all descriptions, from Indian spice stalls to magicians' supply stores to military-button booths. The streets surrounding Pike Place Market continue the warrenlike maze of shops, with ethnic food stalls, plant shops, galleries and gift boutiques.

Once a stable for merchants' horses, the **Economy Market Building**, on the south side of the entrance, has a wonderful Italian grocery store, De Laurenti's, as well as

Tenzing Momo, one of the oldest apothecaries on the West Coast, where you can pick up herbal remedies, incense, oils and books or, occasionally, get a tarot reading.

Across from the Main Arcade is the **Sanitary Market Building** (the first market building to prohibit live animals), a maze of ethnic groceries and great little eateries, including the Three Girls Bakery, which features some of the best breads and sandwiches around. Also, all in a row in the adjacent **Triangle Building** are Mr D's Greek Deli, Mee Sum Pastry (with great pork buns), a juice bar and Cinnamon Works – all great choices for a quick snack.

Most market stalls open around 8am and close at 6pm. The Main Arcade has restrooms. Elevators and stairs lead down to Western Ave and the Waterfront.

The Waterfront

Along the length of the Waterfront – amid horse-drawn carriages, bicycle taxis and cotton-candy vendors – are companies that offer harbor tours and boat excursions (see Organized Tours, later in this chapter).

Ferries depart for Bremerton; Bainbridge Island; the San Juan Islands; and Victoria, British Columbia, from the piers (see Getting There & Away and the Northwestern Washington & the San Juan Islands chapter). The Seattle Aquarium and Omnidome Film Experience (see below) are on Pier 59. Piers 54, 55 and 56 are devoted to shops, restaurants and novelty venues. Pier 57 is now **Waterfront Park**, a small viewing area with benches. Outdoor concerts are held on Pier 62 in the summer.

The **Waterfront Streetcar** (*☎ 206-553-3000; regular/peak fare $1.25/1.50, youth 5-17 years 50¢, valid 1½ hours*) runs along Alaskan Way. These handy little trolleys link the area near Seattle Center (from the base of Broad St) to Pike Place Market, going on to Pioneer Square and the International District.

The elevated Alaskan Way Viaduct runs noisily above the Waterfront, and the parking areas underneath can be a bit scary at night. Luckily, savvy planners have created several walkways down the nearly eight-story descent to the water. The Hill-climb Corridor, flanked by shops, eateries and potted greenery, exits out the back of Pike Place Market's Main Arcade. Alternatively, take the Harbor Steps, a landscaped cascade that sweeps down from below the Seattle Art Museum.

Seattle Aquarium

This well-designed aquarium (☎ 206-386-4320, Pier 59; adult/senior & disabled/youth 6-18 years/child 3-5 years $8.50/7.50/5.75/3.75; open 10am-7pm Memorial Day-Labor Day, 10am-5pm rest of year), in Waterfront Park, offers a view into the underwater world of Puget Sound and the northwestern Pacific coast. Re-creations of bay and ocean ecosystems include tide pools, eelgrass beds, a coral reef and the sea floor. The centerpiece of the aquarium is a glass-domed hall where – on the other side of the glass – sharks, octopuses and other deepwater denizens lurk. Passages eventually lead outdoors to a salmon ladder and a pool where playful sea otters and seals await your attention.

Combination entry tickets with the Omnidome theater are available (see below).

Omnidome Film Experience

Adjacent to the aquarium is this 180-degree surround-screen movie theater (☎ 206-622-1868, Pier 59; adult/senior/youth 6-18 years/child under 6 years $7/6.50/6/free). There are usually two shows available; the ongoing favorite is The Eruption of Mt St Helens, which features a helicopter ride over an exploding volcano. Shows begin at 10am daily; call for times. Most films run 45 minutes.

A combination aquarium-Omnidome ticket is available for $13/11.25 adult/senior, $9.50 youths six to 18 years and $5.50 child three to five years.

Odyssey Maritime Discovery Center

This unique interactive museum (☎ 206-374-4001, Pier 66; adult/senior, student & child $6.50/4; open 10am-5pm Tues-Sat, noon-5pm Sun) includes a simulated kayak trip around Puget Sound, a chance to navigate a virtual ship through Elliott Bay and a visual

journey of the cruise up the Inside Passage to southeast Alaska. You can find out about boat construction and high-tech contributions to boating, learn about oceanography and environmental issues, and hear audio simulations of ocean life.

BELLTOWN (MAP 4)

Long an area of warehouses and office buildings, this neighborhood immediately north of Pike Place Market was home to grunge music and musicians in the glory

---

The Great Fire

In Seattle's early days, the Pioneer Square area was a thrown-together village of wooden storefronts, log homes and lumber mills. Tidewater lapped along 1st Ave, and many of the buildings and the boardwalks that led to them were raised up on stilts. No part of the original downtown was more than 4 feet above the bay at high tide, and the streets were frequently a quagmire.

When the Great Seattle Fire struck in 1889, the boardwalks throughout this district provided an unstoppable conduit for the flames, and most of the original town burned. What might have seemed a catastrophe was in fact a blessing, as the city was rebuilt immediately with handsome structures of brick, steel and stone. This time, however, the streets were regraded, and ravines and inlets filled in. This raised the new city about a dozen feet above the old city; in some areas the regrading was simply built over older ground-level buildings and streets. These are the catacombs explored in the famous Seattle Underground Tour (see Organized Tours, later in this chapter).

The rapid rebuilding of the Pioneer Square area also endowed the district with a rare architectural homogeneity. Most of the buildings around present-day Pioneer Square were built between 1890 and 1905. One architect, Elmer Fisher, was responsible for the plans of 50 buildings erected immediately after the fire.

days. The clubs are still here, but the area has gone seriously upscale. The warehouses are converting to lofts, designer boutiques have moved in, and you're as likely to see professionals in power suits as itinerant artists with multiple nose rings. Today, some of the city's finest restaurants mingle with great cheap eateries (see Places to Eat). Most of the shops and fancy restaurants are along 1st Ave, while 2nd Ave has a string of bars and nightclubs.

SEATTLE CENTER (MAP 5)

In 1962, Seattle was confident and ready for company. And the 1962 World's Fair, also known as the 'Century 21 Exposition,' gave the city the perfect opportunity to display its self-assured, high-tech vision of itself and of the future.

A warehouse area north of downtown was leveled, and a futuristic international enclave of exhibition halls, arenas and public spaces sprang up. Never mind that today the Seattle Center (☎ 206-684-8582, 206-684-7200, W www.seattlecenter.com), as we now term the World's Fair grounds, generates more nostalgia for the Jetsons than thoughts of the future.

Probably no other building in Seattle epitomizes the city as well as the Space Needle, the 605-foot-high futuristic observation station and restaurant. The Monorail, a 1½-mile experiment in mass transit, was another signature element of the 1962 fair. The **Flag Pavilion & Plaza** and **International Fountain** (with jets of water that pulse to the beat of music) point to the cosmopolitan sympathies of the fair. Other Expo landmarks that live on include the Seattle Opera House (home of the opera, symphony and ballet), two playhouses, two sports arenas, the Fun Forest Amusement Park (with carnival rides) and various museums and art spaces. The latest addition to the complex is the **Experience Music Project**, a mind-blowing shrine to rock 'n' roll (see the boxed text under Entertainment, later in this chapter).

A number of fast-food venues, restrooms and other public facilities are located in Center House near the Monorail terminal.

Parking can be tight around the Seattle Center when more than one large event takes place. Parking lots on Mercer St and 5th Ave N charge around $8 a day. There's easy access to the Waterfront Streetcar at Broad St and Western Ave.

Space Needle

Seattle's iconic monument, the Space Needle (☎ 206-905-2100, 219 4th Ave N; elevator for adult/senior/child 5-12 years $11/9/5; open 9am-11pm Sun-Thur, 9am-midnight Fri & Sat), affords 360° views of Seattle and surrounding areas from its 520-foot-high observation deck. Elevators zip you to the top in just 43 seconds. Way back in 1962, the Space Needle surfed the wave of the future with its two revolving restaurants. Today there is only Sky City (see Places to Eat, later).

Pacific Science Center

This museum of science and industry (☎ 206-443-2001, 200 2nd Ave N; adult/senior & child 6-13 years/child 2-5 years $8/5.50/4; open 10am-5pm Mon-Fri, 10am-6pm Sat & Sun) once housed the science pavilion of the World's Fair. Today the center offers virtual-reality exhibits, laser shows, holograms, hands-on demonstrations and other wonders of science. Also on the premises is the vaulted-screen **IMAX Theater** (☎ 206-443-4629) and a planetarium.

Entrance to the IMAX Theater and Laserium, a 'laser theater,' is $3 on top of the general admission price. A ticket for just the IMAX Theater is $6.75 per person; a separate ticket to the laser show is $3.

Children's Museum

This learning center (☎ 206-441-1768; admission $5; open 10am-5pm Tues-Sun, daily in summer) in the basement of Center House offers a number of imaginative activities and displays, many focusing on cross-cultural awareness and hands-on art sessions. The play area includes a child-sized neighborhood and a section dedicated to blowing soap bubbles.

Also for kids is the **Seattle Children's Theatre** (☎ 206-441-3322), in the Charlotte Martin Theater.

Northwest Craft Center

Flanking the International Fountain, this gallery *(☎ 206-728-1555; admission free; open 11am-6pm)* is mostly dedicated to ceramics by regional craftspeople. Exhibits change monthly. A gift shop carries other locally made crafts from the area.

QUEEN ANNE (MAP 5)

Rising above Seattle Center is Queen Anne Hill – a neighborhood of majestic red-brick houses and apartment buildings, sweeping lawns manicured to perfection and gorgeous views of the city and bay. There are two commercial hubs along Queen Anne Ave: at the base of the hill and at the top. Like all Seattle neighborhoods, there's a full array of cafes, trendy music clubs and shops.

The main reason to visit Queen Anne, however, is to check out the view. A **scenic overlook** in Kerry Park on W Highland Dr is the best spot, especially at night or sunset.

From downtown take bus Nos 1, 3 and 4 go up to Queen Anne; No 1 travels on the west side of the hill, while Nos 3 and 4 go up Taylor St on the east side. To reach the Kerry Park vista point, take bus No 2, 13 or 45.

CAPITOL HILL (MAP 6)

Long a counterculture oasis, Capitol Hill distinguishes itself more by its street culture than any particular buildings or landmarks. There are probably more nose rings, tattoos and poetry readings here than anywhere else in the Northwest. Also the principal gay and lesbian neighborhood in Seattle, the area possesses an unmatched vitality and creativity.

From downtown take bus No 7, 10 or 43 and get off at **Broadway** – the main avenue. If the brass-inlaid dance steps along Broadway propel you into a rumba or a tango, you assuredly won't be the most unusual sight around. The best way to enjoy the scene is to buy a cup of coffee, lounge along the street, poke around in the multitudes of shops and watch the crowds.

E John St (the continuation of Olive Way) is the main corner of activity. Between E Harrison and E Republican Sts is the Broadway Market, with two stories of shops, eateries and a cinema featuring art flicks. Across the street, **Dilettante Chocolates** *(☎ 206-329-6463, 416 Broadway E)* is well known for truffles and 'adult' milkshakes. The Broadway strip ends at E Roy St, where the atmosphere changes amid well-maintained houses with manicured lawns. Continue down Broadway until it turns into 10th Ave E and you'll be right by Volunteer Park (see below). Near the corner of 10th Ave E and Galer St is **St Mark's Cathedral** *(1245 10th Ave E)*, where a chorus performs Gregorian chants Sunday nights at 9:30pm.

Seven blocks east of Broadway is **15th Ave E**, another, somewhat tamer, strip. The blocks between E Thomas and E Mercer Sts hold the most interest, with bookstores, wine shops, bakeries and restaurants back to back.

At the south end of Broadway is the hip **Pike/Pine Corridor**, which extends from 12th Ave to about 9th Ave (back near the convention center). If you're looking for late-night action, this is one of Seattle's liveliest scenes. Long considered the city's gay-bar zone, the Corridor has diversified to include all-night coffeehouses, live-music clubs and rowdy, smoke-filled hangouts. It's also the center of the city's tattoo culture.

If you're driving, your best bet is to try parking in the pay lot behind the Broadway Market (under the Fred Meyer store) on Harvard Ave E.

Volunteer Park

This stately 140-acre park, above downtown Seattle on Capitol Hill, began as pioneer Seattle's cemetery. However, as the city grew and the need for water became more pressing (particularly after the Great Seattle Fire), Volunteer Park, with its water tower and reservoir, was created.

Roads and paths wind around the park, with well-kept meadowlike lawns descending to the mansions that flank the area. Keen seekers of views can climb the 1907 **water tower** for wonderful vistas over the city and Elliott Bay.

The **Seattle Asian Art Museum** *(☎ 206-654-3206, 1400 E Prospect St; adult/child $3/*

free; open 10am-5pm Tues-Wed & Fri-Sun, 10am-9pm Thur) houses the extensive collection of Dr Richard Fuller, who donated this severe art moderne–style gallery to the city in 1932.

Nearby is **Volunteer Park Conservatory** *(☎ 206-684-4743, 1400 E Galer St; admission free; open 10am-7pm in summer, 10am-4pm rest of the year)*, a classic Victorian greenhouse built in 1912, filled with palms, cacti and tropical plants.

To reach Volunteer Park, follow 15th Ave E north to E Galer St, then turn west.

FREMONT (MAP 7)

Fremont is located where Lake Union pours into the shipping canal. Probably the most fun-loving of the northern neighborhoods, it's known for its unorthodox public sculpture, junk stores, summer outdoor film festivals and general high spirits. However, it's also an area in transition, as corporate development moves in.

Possibly the most discussed piece of public art in the city, *Waiting for the Interurban* is a recycled aluminum statue of ordinary people (whom locals like to dress up for seasonal events and occasions) waiting for a commuter bus. The *Fremont Troll,* a mammoth cement figure consuming a whole VW bug carcass, lives under the Aurora Bridge. The slightly zany-looking Fremont Rocket stands in the main business district. The latest addition to Fremont's public art scene is a statue of Lenin that made its way here from Slovakia.

Saturday nights from June through September, films are shown at the **Fremont Outdoor Movies** *(☎ 206-781-4230; $5 donation),* in the parking lot behind the Redhook Brewery at 3400 Phinney Ave and N 35th St.

On N 34th St, a block and a half west of Fremont Bridge, the **Fremont Sunday Market** *(☎ 206-781-6776; open 10am-5pm May-Oct, 10am-4pm rest of year)* features fresh fruits and vegetables and an incredible variety of artists, as well as people getting rid of junk.

To get to Fremont from downtown, take Westlake Blvd north along Lake Union to the Fremont Bridge. Fremont Ave N is the focal point of the shops, pubs and restaurants. Bus Nos 26 and 28 go to Fremont.

WALLINGFORD (MAP 7)

Wallingford has blossomed from an old working-class neighborhood into a pleasant district of interesting shops, bookstores and inexpensive eateries, all just across the freeway from the university. The main shopping area focuses on the old Wallingford school, at Wallingford Ave N and N 45th St, which has been remodeled into a boutique and restaurant mall. Just down the street are a couple of art and foreign-film cinemas, amid a clutch of Italian, Greek, Japanese, Thai and Afghani restaurants.

The main hub is along N 45th St approximately between Stone Way N and Easter Ave. There's an incredible mix of stores – including the locally known **Erotic Bakery** *(☎ 206-545-6969, 2323 N 45th St; open 10am-7pm Mon-Sat, noon-5pm Sun),* where phallus-shaped desserts are made to order.

To reach Wallingford from downtown, take I-5 north, exit at N 45th St and turn west. From dowtown take bus No 16 or 26; bus No 44 runs along N 45th St from the university.

Gas Works Park

Urban reclamation has no greater monument in Seattle than Gas Works Park. On a grassy point on the north end of Lake Union, this factory produced heating and lighting gas from 1906 to 1956. The gasworks was thereafter understandably considered an eyesore and environmental menace. Nonetheless, the fine location of the park – with its stellar views of sailboats and yachts to-ing and fro-ing from the shipping canal against a backdrop of downtown Seattle – induced the city government to convert the former industrial site into a public park in 1975. After years of intermittent closures for environmental cleanup projects, Gas Works Park is now one of Seattle's best-loved green areas.

The park is at the southern end of Meridian Ave N. From downtown, take bus No 26.

GREEN LAKE (MAP 7)

Possibly Seattle's busiest outdoor recreation center, Green Lake, just north of Wallingford, is abutted by a couple of pleasant, low-key neighborhoods. If you need to get away from the crowds along the lakefront, the requisite coffee shops and cheap restaurants along NE Ravenna Blvd make a good getaway. Adjacent Woodland Park is home to the civic rose gardens and Seattle's highly acclaimed zoo.

Green Lake Park

A favorite with sunbathers, swimmers and windsurfers, Green Lake Park is incredibly popular in summer. Two paths wind 2¾ miles around the small natural lake, but even these aren't enough to fill the needs of the hundreds of joggers, power walkers, bikers and in-line skaters who throng here daily. In fact, competition for space on the trails has led to altercations between speeding athletes; the city government now regulates traffic on the paths.

Tennis courts, a soccer field, a bowling green and a baseball diamond are some of the other recreational facilities at the park. Rent sailboats, canoes, kayaks, sailboards, paddleboats and rowboats from **Green Lake Boat Rental** *(☎ 206-527-0171, 7351 E Green Lake Dr N; $10-14 per hour; open Mar-Oct).* Two sandy swimming beaches are along the north end of the lake, but on sunny days, the entire shoreline is massed with gleaming pale bodies. (Swimmers should note that the lake's green color is due to algae blooms, which can cause an unpleasant condition called 'swimmer's itch.')

From downtown, take bus No 6, 16 or 26.

Woodland Park

The **Woodland Park Zoo** *(☎ 206-684-4800, 5500 Phinney Ave N; adult/senior/youth 6-17 years/child 3-5 years $9/8.25/6.50/4.25; open 9:30am-6pm in summer, 9:30am-5pm in spring & fall, 9:30am-4pm in winter)* was one of the first in the country to free animals from their restrictive cages in favor of ecosystem enclosures designed to replicate their natural surroundings. Highlights include a tropical rain forest, an Asian elephant forest and an African savanna. Parking is an additional $3.50.

The 2½-acre **Seattle Rose Garden** *(admission free),* near the entrance road to the zoo, contains 5000 plants, including heirloom roses and All-American Rose selections. Take bus No 5 from downtown to reach Woodland Park.

U DISTRICT (MAP 8)

The University of Washington campus sits at the edge of a busy commercial area known as the U District. The main streets here are University Way, also known as **The Ave**, and NE 45th St. On these busy streets are innumerable cheap restaurants and cafes, student-oriented bars, tattoo shops, cinemas and bookstores.

University of Washington

The largest university in the Northwest, with around 35,000 students, the University of Washington *(UW; visitor center ☎ 206-543-9198, 4014 University Way; open 8am-5pm Mon-Fri)* is a lively place and definitely worth touring. It's especially gorgeous in spring, when flowering bulbs and azaleas paint the verdant campus with brilliant colors.

Established in 1861, UW was first built downtown, on the site of the present Four Seasons Olympic Hotel, moving to its present location above Lake Washington in 1895. Today, 'U Dub,' as most people refer to the university, is highly regarded for its law and medical schools.

Campus life revolves around **Central Plaza**, usually referred to as 'Red Square' due to its base of red brick. Maps are available from the visitor center. To the east is **Suzzallo Library**, a fanciful Gothic revival cathedral of books. Beyond the library is the **Quad**, containing many of the original campus buildings. When the ivy turns red in the autumn, the effect is distinctly New Englandesque.

Just below Red Square is a wide promenade leading to lovely **Rainier Vista**, with views across Lake Washington to Mt Rainier. South of the vista is **Drumheller Fountain**, legacy of the 1909 Alaska-Yukon-Pacific Exposition, which took place on this site.

Bus Nos 71, 72 and 73 offer the most direct routes from the downtown bus tunnel to the university.

Burke Museum North Coast Indian artifacts, especially cedar canoes and totem poles, are the principal treasures at the Burke Museum of Natural History & Culture (☎ 206-543-5590, NW cnr of UW campus; adult/senior/student $5.50/4/2.50; open 10am-5pm Fri-Wed, 10am-8pm Thur). Near the junction of 17th Ave NE and NE 45th St, the museum also houses a good collection of dinosaur skeletons and a pleasant ground-level cafe.

Henry Art Gallery Some of the most intelligent exhibits and installations in Seattle are mounted at the university's fine-art gallery, the Henry (☎ 206-543-2280, cnr 15th Ave NE & NE 41st St; adult/senior/student with ID $5/3.50/free; open 11am-5pm Tues-Wed & Fri-Sun, 11am-8pm Thur). The focus is on 20th-century art and artists. There's a small permanent collection, but the changing shows (35 a year) are usually noteworthy. The Burke-Henry Dollar Deal lets you into the Burke Museum, too, for $1 more.

Washington Park Arboretum

This wild and lovely park has a wide variety of gardens, a waterfront nature trail and 200 acres of mature forest threaded by paths. Trail guides to the over 5500 plant species are available at the **Graham Visitors Center** (☎ 206-543-8800, 2300 Arboretum Dr E; open 10am-4pm). Free guided tours of the grounds are available on weekends at 1pm. In the spring, **Azalea Way**, a jogger-free trail that winds through the arboretum is lined with a giddy array of pink- and orange-flowered azaleas and rhododendrons.

At the southern edge of the arboretum is the 3½-acre **Japanese Garden** (☎ 206-684-4725; adult/senior & youth under 20 years $2.50/1.50; open 10am-6pm Mar-Nov), with koi pools, waterfalls, a teahouse and manicured plantings.

At the northwest corner of the arboretum is the **Museum of History & Industry** (Mohai; ☎ 206-324-1126, 2700 24th Ave E;

adult/senior & student $5.50/3; open 10am-5pm). Despite its grand name, Mohai is probably best thought of as a museum of Seattle and Puget Sound history, with a likable collection of old planes, memorabilia from the Great Fire, and artifacts and lore from Seattle's great seafaring era.

A wonderful **wetlands trail** extends from the museum's parking lot across Foster Island in Union Bay and continues on to the visitors center. Along the way, it winds through marshlands and over floating bridges to smaller islands and reedy shoals. Bird watching is popular here, as are canoeing, fishing and swimming.

Access to the arboretum is easiest from the south. Follow Madison St from downtown until it intersects Lake Washington Blvd E. Turn north (left) at the junction and take Arboretum Dr E to the visitor center. The No 11 Madison St bus delivers you to the base of the park at Lake Washington Blvd, but there's still quite a walk (albeit through the park) to the visitor center.

BALLARD & THE CANAL (MAP 1)

Northwest of Seattle, the waters of Lake Washington and Lake Union meet Puget Sound in the 8-mile-long Lake Washington Ship Canal. The idea of linking the freshwater lakes to the sound had been discussed since 1867, but it wasn't until 1911 that the Army Corps of Engineers, under the direction of Hiram Chittenden, began the project. A channel was opened between Lake Washington and Lake Union, lowering the former by 9 feet. The canal was later cut from Salmon Bay south of Ballard to Puget Sound, and two locks were installed in 1917.

Now, 100,000 boats a year pass through the canal. The locks, with their fish ladder and beautiful adjacent park, make a popular destination for families.

Long the brunt of many a local's joke, the traditionally blue-collar Nordic community of Ballard has lately become another hip neighborhood, with several good taverns and some fun budget gourmet restaurants. Activity is centered in the historic district along Ballard Ave NW between 20th and

WASHINGTON

22nd Aves. Bus No 17 from downtown goes to Ballard, as well as to the following sights along the ship canal.

Hiram M Chittenden Locks

Watching boats traverse the locks *(3015 NW 54th St; admission free; open 24 hours)* on the shipping canal offers a strange Zen-like attraction for locals and tourists alike. Walkways alongside the locks allow an intimate look at the workings of these water elevators and the vessels passing through them.

On the southern side of the locks is a **fish ladder**, built in 1976 to assist salmon fighting their way to spawning grounds in the Cascade headwaters of the Sammamish River, which feeds Lake Washington. Visitors can watch the fish through underwater glass-sided tanks or from above. You can also watch sea lions munch on the salmon while the fish thrash around trying to figure out how to negotiate the ladder (just what to do about the salmon-loving sea lions has stymied environmentalists, anglers and the local Fish & Wildlife Department). The best time to see the salmon is during spawning season, from mid-June to September.

At the northern entrance to the lock area is a **visitor center** and small museum documenting the history of the locks *(☎ 206-783-7059; admission free; call for hours and tour schedule)*, as well as the charming **Carl English Jr Botanical Gardens** *(admission free; open 7am-9pm)*.

The Chittenden Locks are northwest of downtown Seattle, about half a mile west of Ballard off NW Market St.

Fishermen's Terminal

Seattle's fishing fleet resides at Fishermen's Terminal at Salmon Bay along the ship canal. About 700 boats dock here, making this the largest halibut and salmon fleet in the world. It's great fun to wander the piers, watching crews unload their catch, clean boats and repair nets. Interpretive displays survey the history of the fleet. A statue of a fisherman at the base of the piers commemorates lost seamen.

In the two shedlike terminal buildings are a couple of good restaurants (including Chinook's at Salmon Bay) specializing in the freshest seafood in Seattle, a tobacconist, a ship chandler and a store devoted to navigational charts and nautical gifts. Stop at the **Wild Salmon Fish Market** *(☎ 206-283-3366, 1900 W Nickerson St; open 10am-6pm)* for the pick of the day's catch.

The Fishermen's Terminal is on the south end of the Ballard Bridge, at 19th Ave and W Nickerson St.

DISCOVERY PARK (MAP 1)

Discovery Park is 534 acres of urban wilderness northwest of downtown. Locals love to come here to wander along the more than 7 miles of hiking trails. The park was originally Fort Lawton, an army base established in 1897 to protect Seattle from unnamed enemies, and significant portions are still used for military housing.

A paved road makes an almost 3-mile loop of the park, with trails branching off to lookout points. One trail skirts the water's edge all the way to the **West Point Lighthouse**, a great scenic spot. For a map of the trail and road system stop by the visitor center *(☎ 206-386-4236, Government Way; open 8:30am-5:30pm)*. Inquire about Saturday nature walks and bird-watching tours.

Bus Nos 19, 24 and 33 leave from downtown and the Seattle Center for the park.

WEST SEATTLE & ALKI BEACH (MAP 1)

At the headland of Alki Point, Seattle's first settlers made their home. Today, this 2-mile stretch of sandy beach is a madhouse in summer, when in emulation of Southern California the volleyball nets go up, mass sunbathing occupies the strand and teens in souped-up cars prowl the streets. Still, it's Seattle's only real beach scene, and the skyline views from Duwamish Head, at the northern end of the beach, are spectacular. You might want to avoid Alki on summer weekends, but good beachside cafes, quaint fish-and-chips joints, the miniature Statue of Liberty on the beach and the Alki Point Lighthouse make it a nice getaway most other times.

Take Hwy 99 or I-5 south to the West Seattle Freeway; get off at Harbor Ave SW, the beach road that skirts the promontory. Bus Nos 37 or 56 will take you there.

ACTIVITIES
Hiking & Biking
In Seattle, it's possible to hike wilderness trails without ever leaving the city. Several miles of paths cross a remnant of the area's old-growth forest at **Seward Park**, set on a promontory that juts into Lake Washington, and even longer trails cut through **Discovery Park**, northwest of downtown (see that section, earlier).

For a long-distance hike or bike ride, try the **Burke-Gilman Trail**, a 16½-mile paved path that runs from Ballard to the suburb of Kenmore on the north end of Lake Washington. The trail follows an old rail line along the shores of the lakes, all at an easy grade. The views are great, though on weekends it can get pretty busy.

A convenient place to rent a bike is **Al Young Bike and Ski** (*Map 8; ☎ 206-524-2642, 3615 NE 45th St; full/half day $30/20*), near both the university and the Burke-Gilman trail. Near Green Lake, you can rent bicycles, in-line skates and just about any other form of recreational conveyance at **Gregg's Greenlake Cycle** (*Map 7; ☎ 206-523-1822, 7007 Woodlawn Ave NE; skates & cruiser bikes $5 per hour*).

Boating & Kayaking
The **Northwest Outdoor Center Inc** (*Map 5; ☎ 206-281-9694, 2100 Westlake Ave N; rentals $15/30 per hour/half day; tours from $25*) rents kayaks on Lake Union and offers instruction in sea and white-water kayaking. Staff also leads sunset tours through the Ballard locks.

UW's **Waterfront Activities Center** (*Map 8; ☎ 206-543-9433; SE corner of Husky Stadium parking lot; rentals $5 per hour*) rents canoes and rowboats for use on Lake Washington. Bring along an ID.

In good weather, Lake Union is brimming with sailboats. Join the fun at **The Center for Wooden Boats** (*Map 5; ☎ 206-382-2628, 1010 Valley St*). Sailboat rentals

run $16 per hour on weekdays, $25 per hour on weekends; rowboats from $12.50 weekdays, $20 weekends. At least one person in your party must demonstrate sailing skills to rent a sailboat.

Windsurfing
Windsurfing is a big sport in Seattle, and Lake Washington is the most popular place to hit the water. It's big enough to accommodate boat traffic and out-of-control windsurfers. The warm waters of Green Lake are good for beginners, but they can be pretty congested in summer. Green Lake Boat Rental (see Boating & Kayaking) offers lessons.

ORGANIZED TOURS
For walking tours, check with the visitors center (see Tourist Offices, earlier).

City Tours
Seattle offers several options for those who want to get to know the city in a planned fashion.

Gray Line of Seattle (*Map 2; ☎ 206-626-5208, 800-426-7505, ⓦ www.graylineofseattle.com, 800 Convention Place*) Adult/child $34/17. Gray Line's six-hour Grand City Tour operates from April to mid-October. Their City Sights Tour ($29) is an abbreviated version that runs year round. They also have a whole catalog of area bus and boat tours.

Bill Speidel's Underground Tour (*Map 3; ☎ 206-682-4646*) Adult/senior & student/child 6-12 years $8/7/4, cash only. These tours start from Doc Maynard's Public House, 610 1st Ave, a restored 1890s saloon. Most of the old subterranean chambers on the tour date from the 1880s, before the Great Fire and the rebuilding of the district above the tide flats. An hourlong three-block hike through a series of rather ordinary-looking basements follows the 20-minute introduction. Guides like to emphasize the underground nature of the tour with whimsical noting of historic bordellos and corrupt politicians. Schedules vary seasonally, and reservations are recommended.

Seattle Trolley Tours (*☎ 206-626-5208; 1500 6th Ave*) Adult/senior & student

$15/10; May 1 to Oct 15. Visitors are encouraged to get on and off these mock streetcars at their leisure. Eleven stops, indicated by bright yellow sandwich boards, are dotted throughout the central area; the narrated ride picks up passengers at each stop every 30 minutes. Tickets, good for the full day, can be purchased either at the information center or upon boarding.

Boat Tours
Argosy Cruises (Map 4; ☎ 206-623-1445, 800-642-7816, W *www.argosycruises.com, Pier 56).* Adult/senior & student/child 5-12 years from $15/14/9. The Seattle Harbor Tour is a one-hour narrated cruise around Elliott Bay that takes in the Waterfront and the Port of Seattle. A two-hour Lake Washington cruise departs from the AGC Marina Dock on Lake Union.

SPECIAL EVENTS
Chinese New Year (☎ 206-382-1197) In January or February, parades, firecrackers, fireworks and lots of food invigorate the International District during this annual event.

Seattle International Film Festival (☎ 206-464-5830) Three weeks in late May and early June, Seattle hosts an extravaganza of cinema from around the world, including many US debuts.

Freedom Day Celebration (☎ 206-323-1229) The last Sunday in June marks Seattle's lesbian- and gay-pride event celebrated on Capitol Hill with a parade, speeches, music and a rally.

Northwest Folklife Festival (☎ 206-684-7300) On Memorial Day weekend, more than 5000 artists from over 100 countries present music, dance, crafts, food and family activities at Seattle Center. Admission is free.

Seafair (☎ 206-728-0123, W www.seafair.com) This civic celebration, held in late July to early August, began as a hydroplane race on Lake Washington. Events include a torchlight parade, an air show, lots of music, a carnival and even the arrival of the naval fleet. Lodging is in short supply in Seattle on Seafair weekends.

Bumbershoot (☎ 206-281-8111, W www.bumbershoot.com) Seattle's biggest arts and cultural event, during Labor Day weekend, includes a crafts fair, performances on 25 stages (featuring an invariably stellar musical lineup), a film festival and fine-arts exhibitions at Seattle Center. It's a bargain at $12 per day.

PLACES TO STAY
Lodging in Seattle can get tight during the popular summer months; at other times of the year, special events can make finding a room difficult, especially in central Seattle. Rates mentioned below are what you can expect to pay in peak season, though beware: They can vary wildly depending on occupancy. November to March, Seattle Visitor and Convention Bureau offers Super Saver Packages – discount coupon books, good for up to 50% off rack rates at downtown hotels. Check the website (W www.seattle supersaver.com) or call the Hotel Hotline.

When Seattle is all booked up, get help from the Seattle Hotel Hotline (☎ 206-461-5882, 800-535-7071), a free reservation service for area hotels.

Another option is the Seattle B&B Association (SBBA; ☎ 206-547-1020), PO Box 31772, Seattle, WA 98103-1772. See the brochure listing their member inns.

Camping
Campers intending to visit downtown Seattle face lengthy commutes.

Camp Long (☎ 206-684-7434, W *www.ci .seattle.wa.us/parks/Environment/camplong .htm, 5200 35th Ave SW)* Cabins with three double bunk beds $35 plus $50 refundable deposit. This city park in West Seattle features 10 1930s-era wood cabins with electricity but no inside cooking facilities. Gates close at 10pm. Take the West Seattle bridge exit from I-5 or Hwy 99 and follow signs to Fauntleroy Way SW. Turn left onto 35th Ave SW and left again onto SW Dawson St, where you'll find Camp Long. Alternatively, take bus No 21 to SW Dawson St.

Trailers Inn (☎ 425-747-9181, 800-659-4684, fax 425-747-0858, 15531 SE 37th St) RV sites $17-30. This property in Bellevue has showers, an indoor pool, a playground and laundry. Take I-90 exit 11, turn south to the frontage road and follow the signs for five blocks.

Saltwater State Park (☎ 800-233-0231) Primitive/standard tent sites $6/14. Tent campers are pretty much limited to this busy but pleasant beachfront park on Puget Sound, about 20 miles south of Seattle. Take

I-5 exit 149 west toward Des Moines. At the junction of Hwy 99 (also called 'Pacific Hwy'), turn south and drive to 240th St. Turn west and follow signs to the park.

Hostels

All of Seattle's hostels cluster in the general downtown area.

HI Seattle (*Map 4;* ☎ *206-622-5443, fax 206-682-2179,* Ⓦ *www.hiseattle.org, 84 Union St*) Dorm beds member/nonmember $17/20, doubles $23/26 per person, child under 11 years $12. This hostel has 199 beds in dormitories, family rooms and double rooms. Kitchen and laundry facilities are provided, as well as a common area with a TV. The hostel is in a good location, central to the Waterfront and to Pike Place Market. Reservations are essential in summer.

Green Tortoise Hostel (*Map 2;* ☎ *206-340-1222, 888-424-6783, fax 206-623-3207,* Ⓔ *info@greentortoise.net, 1525 2nd Ave*) Dorm beds $17, private rooms $40, breakfast included. Green Tortoise shuttle service to San Francisco has been indefinitely halted, but the hostel, a salmon's toss from Pike Place Market, lives on. Free pickup from downtown points can be arranged.

YWCA of Seattle (*Map 2;* ☎ *206-461-4888, 1118 5th Ave*) Singles/doubles with shared bath $33/44, with private bath $50/60. Also central, the YWCA rents rooms to women only.

B&Bs

Several century-old mansions around Capitol Hill make for charming, if somewhat pricey, accommodations.

Mildred's B&B (*Map 6;* ☎ *206-325-6072,* Ⓦ *www.mildredsbnb.com, 1202 15th Ave E*) Doubles $135-150. This is an old Victorian home across the street from Volunteer Park. The four guest rooms have private bath.

Gaslight Inn B&B (*Map 6;* ☎ *206-325-3654,* Ⓦ *www.gaslight-inn.com, 1727 15th Ave E*) Singles/doubles/suites from $78/$118/$148. Gaslight Inn has 15 rooms available in two neighboring homes, some with private bathrooms. There's also a refreshing outdoor pool.

Hill House B&B (*Map 6;* ☎ *206-720-7161, 800-720-7161,* Ⓦ *www.seattlebnb.com, 1113 E John St*) Doubles $95-165. The seven guest rooms in this restored 1903 home all come with down comforters; five have private bathrooms.

Pensione Nichols (*Map 4;* ☎ *206-441-7125, 800-440-7125, 1923 1st Ave*) Singles/doubles $75/95, breakfast included. This charmingly remodeled older hotel is right in the urban thick of things near Pike Place Market. Ten rooms that share four bathrooms come with a full breakfast.

Tugboat Challenger Bunk & Breakfast (*Map 5;* ☎ *206-340-1201, fax 206-332-0303, 1001 Fairview Ave N*) Singles/doubles $55/85, breakfast included. For something really different and special, try this tugboat. Its eight small rooms are perfectly charming, and the fireplace lounge is a good place to meet people. Take Fairview Ave N to the Yale St Landing; it's directly behind the TGI Friday's restaurant.

Hotels

Downtown (Map 2) Most of the following downtown motels offer some kind of parking program with in-and-out privileges, but you'll pay up to $20 a day for it. If you have a car, you'll need to factor in parking fees for accommodations downtown or stay near the Seattle Center, where most lodgings offer free parking.

The following prices are standard midweek rates; at most hotels, weekend packages and off-season deals lower the prices considerably.

Hotel Seattle (☎/*fax 206-623-5110, 800-426-2439, 315 Seneca St*) Singles/doubles $86/96. Accommodations here are basic but cozy.

Pacific Plaza Hotel (☎ *206-623-3900, 800-426-1165, fax 206-623-2059, 400 Spring St*) Doubles $110-135. This is centrally located, just a block from the Four Seasons Olympic. Nicely remodeled rooms come with a big breakfast. Lacking air conditioning, though, it's not the best choice in summer.

Inn at Virginia Mason (☎ *206-583-6453, 800-283-6453, fax 206-223-7545, 1006 Spring St*) Doubles $95-240. This nicely maintained older hotel is on First Hill, just above downtown. It caters to families needing to stay close to the nearby medical facilities, but it also offers quiet rooms to other visitors.

Camlin Hotel (☎ 206-682-0100, fax 206-682-7415, 1619 9th Ave) Doubles $100-110. Long a Seattle landmark, the Camlin has been partially renovated. In winter, it offers reduced rates and a free breakfast.

WestCoast Vance Hotel (☎ 206-441-4200, 800-426-0670, 620 Stewart St) Doubles $120-150. This is another nicely restored older hotel with cheaper winter rates that include breakfast.

Sixth Avenue Inn (☎ 206-441-8300, 800-648-6440, fax 206-441-9903, 2000 6th Ave) Singles/doubles $80-125/110-140. Though the decor here won't win any awards, rooms are clean and convenient to downtown, and there's free parking. Rates vary seasonally.

Loyal Inn Best Western (☎ 206-682-0200, 2301 8th Ave) Doubles $106-149. Amenities here include a sauna, free continental breakfast and parking.

Most large hotel chains have operations in Seattle, offering business travelers and conventioneers modern rooms with a wide range of facilities. For a more distinctly Northwestern experience, stay at one of Seattle's small luxury hotels or various historic grand hotels, many of which have been remodeled.

Alexis Hotel (☎ 206-624-4844, 800-264-8482, fax 206-621-9009, W www.alexishotel.com, 1007 1st Ave) Standard rooms/fireplace suites/two-bedroom suites $250/460/725. Near Madison St, this modern hotel is tucked inside an old architectural exoskeleton. The emphasis is on quiet rooms, high-quality service and amenities rather than dramatic views or ostentatious glamour. You can bring your dog for an extra $25, and the staff will even walk Rover for you.

The Paramount (☎ 206-292-9500, 800-426-0670, fax 206-292-8610, 724 Pine St) Rooms from $159. This is another gem of a hotel offering gracious comforts of another era.

Sorrento Hotel (☎ 206-622-6400, 800-426-1265, W www.hotelsorrento.com, 900 Madison St) Singles/doubles $215-280/235-300. The Sorrento was Seattle's finest hotel

when it was built in 1909. After being substantially refurbished, lined with mahogany and hung with chandeliers, it is back at the top.

Four Seasons Olympic Hotel (☎ 206-621-1700, in Washington ☎ 800-821-8106, elsewhere ☎ 800-332-3442, fax 206-682-9633, 411 University St) Singles/doubles $195-395/255-405. The other doyen of old money and elegance, this hotel could have been a set in an extra-suave Cary Grant movie. Imposing and luxurious, the Olympic was built in 1924, and subsequent remodels have worked to maintain its period glamour.

Pioneer Square (Map 3) If you're looking for plentiful budget options, don't look here.

Best Western Pioneer Square Hotel (☎ 206-340-1234, fax 206-467-0707, W www.pioneersquare.com, 77 Yesler Way) Singles/doubles $160/180. This recently refurbished older hotel, with nicely appointed rooms, is in the historic heart of Seattle. Nightlife, restaurants and shopping are just steps away.

Pike Place Market & the Waterfront (Map 4) Two large but modest older hotels offer inexpensive lodging just a short walk from the market. Rooms are best described as 'no-frills,' but there's nothing scary about staying here, and you can't argue with the rates.

Commodore Hotel (☎ 206-448-8868, 800-714-8868, W www.commodorehotel.com, 2013 2nd Ave) Doubles $59-89. The newly renovated Commodore, near Pike Place Market and Belltown, includes continental breakfast and rooms with or without bath. It also has a coin-op laundry. Parking nearby is extra.

Moore Hotel (☎ 206-448-4851, 800-421-5508, W www.moorehotel.com, 1926 2nd Ave) Singles/doubles $39-67/49-74. This once-grand hotel has 135 rooms with private or shared bathrooms. You can get a suite here for the price of a closet at a remodeled hotel.

Inn at the Market (☎ 206-443-3600, 800-446-4484, fax 206-448-0631, 86 Pine St) Doubles $190-380. This elegant and architecturally interesting hotel is the only lodging in the venerable Pike Place Market. Rooms are large, and most have grand views onto market activity and Puget Sound.

Hotel Edgewater (☎ *206-728-7000, 800-624-0670,* w *www.edgewaterhotel.com, 2411 Alaskan Way, Pier 67)* Doubles $325-450. When Seattle's only hotel actually facing Elliott Bay was first built, people paid a premium for the privilege of being able to fish from the windows of their rooms. Fishing is no longer allowed, but if you came to Seattle to experience the tang of sea air, this might be the hotel for you. Prices range quite a bit depending on the view and season.

Seattle Center & Queen Anne (Map 5)
Near Seattle Center are a cluster of mid-range motels that are only five minutes from downtown by Monorail or bus, yet less costly than downtown lodging. Room prices are usually lower than those downtown. You can also park your vehicle free at your hotel, no small matter in Seattle.

Seattle Inn (☎ *206-728-7666,* w *www.seattleinn.com, fax 206-728-6108, 225 Aurora Ave N)* Doubles $79. An indoor pool, exercise room, spa and play area make this a decent place – if you stay on the west side away from the traffic.

Vagabond Inn by the Space Needle (☎ *206-441-0400, 800-522-1555, fax 206-448-3353, 325 Aurora Ave N)* Singles/doubles $94/105. At the Vagabond, children stay free, which is especially great when you're trying to scrounge enough dough to send your herd up the Space Needle.

Inn at Queen Anne (☎ *206-282-7357, 800-952-5043, fax 206-217-9719, 505 1st Ave N)* Standard/deluxe rooms $99/109. On the west side of Seattle Center, this is an old 1929 apartment building turned hotel. Rooms come with kitchenettes and continental breakfast.

Travelodge by the Space Needle (☎ *206-441-7878, fax 206-448-4825, 200 6th Ave N)* Doubles $119-159. Rooms here are quieter, and amenities include a Jacuzzi, pool and continental breakfast.

Best Western Executive Inn (☎ *206-448-9444,* w *www.bwexec-inn.com, 200 Taylor Ave N)* Singles/doubles $111-149/126-171. Sleep in the shadow of the Space Needle and take the free shuttle downtown.

U District (Map 8) Off I-5 exit 169 are a number of moderately priced motels near the University of Washington; only 3 miles from downtown, these accommodations are also close to eating and drinking spots in the Wallingford and Green Lake area.

College Inn (☎ *206-633-4441, 4000 University Way NE)* Doubles $45-85. This great inexpensive option is a friendly, no-frills place with in-room sinks and shared baths, plus a continental breakfast included. Be warned that rooms are on four stories without an elevator.

University Plaza Hotel (Map 7; ☎ *206-634-0100, 800-343-7040, fax 206-633-2743,* e *university-plaza@travelbase.com, 400 NE 45th St)* Doubles $70-95. This hotel is just across the freeway from campus. Room rates vary seasonally; there's a heated pool and restaurant.

University Inn (☎ *206-632-5055, 800-733-3855, fax 206-547-4937, 4140 Roosevelt Way NE)* Singles/doubles $105-117/115-127. Three blocks from campus, the Inn offers laundry facilities, data ports and an outdoor pool amid a friendly dormlike bustle.

Seattle University Travelodge (☎ *206-525-4612, 800-578-7878, fax 206-524-9106,* w *www.seattleuniversityhotel.com, 4725 25th Ave NE)* Doubles $89. Just east of the university near Husky Stadium, Travelodge has a hot tub and an outdoor pool.

Airport Area For those flying in or out of Sea-Tac, the following hotels all offer complimentary airport shuttles.

Airport Plaza Hotel (☎ *206-433-0400, fax 206-241-2222,* w *www.airportplaza.com, 18601 Pacific Hwy S)* Singles/doubles $50/55. The Airport Plaza has basic, no-frills rooms.

Days Inn at Sea-Tac Airport (☎ *206-244-3600, 800-325-2525, fax 206-439-0277, 19015 International Blvd S)* Singles/doubles $87/91. You'll find more amenities here, such as in-room movies and microwaves.

WASHINGTON

WASHINGTON

PLACES TO EAT

Seattle offers a bewildering array of inexpensive places to eat; it also boasts the most expensive restaurants in the Northwest. In the mid-range restaurants, meals edge toward (and sometimes past) $25 per person. While entrees may not be expensive, you can often rack up quite a bill by the time you add an appetizer, salad, dessert or a few drinks.

Top-end restaurants have entrees or main dishes that usually exceed $20 per person. These places often serve Northwest cuisine, or high-end French or Italian cooking. A leisurely meal with several courses and a bottle of wine can easily top $50 per person (and don't forget the tip). Some restaurants will offer prix-fixe menus that include a number of courses for a set price, usually $40 to $60. If you need to justify such reckless expense, remember that Seattle has one of the hottest restaurant scenes on the West Coast.

Downtown (Map 2)

The majority of the restaurants downtown are designed with business meetings and expense accounts in mind.

Budget If you're on a budget and just want some grub, you'd be much better off finding cheap eats in Pike Place Market, Belltown or Pioneer Square, all within walking distance of the downtown core.

Westlake Center (4th Ave & Pine St) If you're already downtown and just want something cheap and easy, go to this food court. It features several dozen food vendors with pretty good takeout food and a large seating area. Otherwise, head to Pike Place Market (see that section, later).

Rock Bottom Brewery (☎ 206-623-3070, Rainier Square, 5th Ave btw Union & University Sts) $6-10. Open until 2am. This pub brews five of its own beers and serves good, reasonably priced grub. Try the salmon BLT ($9) or veggie enchilada ($8).

Mid-Range The following restaurants are frequented by Seattle's stock brokers and bankers, who pour out of nearby office towers at lunchtime.

McCormick's Fish House & Bar (☎ 206-682-3900, 722 4th Ave) Entrees $15-23. When people think about Northwestern food, images of old-fashioned oyster bars and cavernous chophouses filled with rowdy yeomen spring to mind. The archetype lives on at McCormick's, offering daily fresh fish specials grilled with zesty sauces, as well as a fine selection of local oysters, chops and steaks, all served in wood-lined, brass-outfitted chambers.

Wild Ginger Asian Restaurant and Satay Bar (☎ 206-623-4450, 1403 3rd Ave) Entrees $10-20. This wildly popular restaurant features the fiery cuisine of Indochina. Recently moved from its more intimate location near Pike Place Market, this swanky spot still packs 'em to the rafters.

Palomino (☎ 206-623-1300, 1420 5th Ave) Lunch/dinner entrees $13-15/$16-20. One of downtown's most stylish see-and-be-seen scenes is this bistro, on the top floor of the City Centre Mall. The dining room is saturated with color and always filled with gregarious, well-dressed diners.

Palace Kitchen (☎ 206-448-2001, 2030 5th Ave) Entrees $15-22. Open until 2am. This is by far the best choice for post-bar or après-movie munchies. Daily dinner specials present such wonders as spaetzle stuffed pumpkin ($18) or traditional pork loin ($21).

Top End If Seattle is in fact home to a school of cuisine (as many here fervently presume), then the following restaurants are among the best practitioners.

Dahlia Lounge (☎ 206-682-4142, 2001 4th Ave) Entrees $20-28. Dahlia Lounge usually gets the credit for creating the idea and then the reality of Northwest cuisine.

Fullers (☎ 206-447-5544, 1400 6th Ave) Entrees $22-30. Dinner only. Fullers, inside the Seattle Sheraton, is often considered the city's single best restaurant, with consistently inventive cuisine, impeccable service and an extremely swank dining room.

Georgian Room (☎ 206-621-7889, 411 University Ave) Entrees $16-24. One of the most imposing restaurants in the city can be found at the Four Seasons Olympic Hotel:

The Georgian Room brings stylistic, regionally inspired food to the table.

Pioneer Square (Map 3)

Restaurants occupying this historic district run the gamut from Middle Eastern fast food to Italian formal dining.

Budget A number of Pioneer Square taverns serve inexpensive burgers and sandwiches, but for the same money you can eat good international cuisine.

Zaina (☎ 206-624-5687, 108 Cherry St) $5-10. Stop by here for authentically prepared falafel and hummus, by the pita or platter.

Cafe Hue (☎ 206-625-9833, 312 2nd Ave S) Soups & entrees $5.50-6.50. This is a yummy Vietnamese restaurant with a French-colonial influence.

Grand Central Baking Co (☎ 206-622-3644, 214 1st Ave S) Sandwiches $6. Seattle's best bakery, in the Grand Central Arcade, creates peasant-style loaves and serves lunchtime salads and focaccia sandwiches.

Elliott Bay Café (☎ 206-682-6664, 101 S Main St) Snacks $5-6. Below the bookstore, this literary nook is where bookworms munch on soup, salad, and sandwiches.

Trattoria Mitchelli (☎ 206-623-3883, 84 Yesler Way) Entrees $9. This trattoria serves good pasta, pizza and calzones, though its main attraction is that it stays open until 4am Tuesday to Saturday nights to feed all those prowlers from the local music clubs.

Mid-Range & Top End These well-established restaurants have weathered the trends.

Merchants Cafe (☎ 206-624-1515, 109 Yesler Way) Entrees $10-14. Purportedly the oldest operating restaurant on the West Coast, Merchants serves a wide assortment of salads and hot sandwiches (about $5), as well as steak, seafood and chicken entrees. Omelets are the breakfast specialty. Be sure to check out the historic examples of idiosyncrasy, such as the 30-foot stand-up bar, which came from the East Coast on a schooner.

al Boccalino Ristorante (☎ 206-622-7688, 1 Yesler Way) Entrees $20. More authentic, expensive and dignified, al Boccalino offers excellent pasta dishes but really delivers with innovative grilled fish and seafood dishes.

FX McRory's Steak, Chop & Oyster House (☎ 206-623-4800, 419 Occidental Ave S) Entrees $9-20. This vast Pioneer Square landmark across from the sports stadiums is always full of jocks and can get completely out of hand after home games. At other times, diners can admire the lovely architecture and enjoy well-prepared steak, or relax with less pricey food in the bar.

Il Terrazzo Carmine (☎ 206-467-7797, 411 1st Ave S) Entrees $30-40. Usually mentioned in discussions of Seattle's best restaurants, this is a showcase of European luxury that serves succulent multicourse Italian meals. Plan to spend a leisurely evening and quite a bit of money.

International District (Map 3)

A good neighborhood for cheap eats is the International District. In many of the Vietnamese, Thai and Chinese restaurants clustered along Jackson and Weller Sts east of 5th Ave, you'll have trouble spending over $7 on lunch or $10 at dinner. In this district there are places where the tourists go and places where everyone else goes. The following suggestions emphasize local favorites over those with lines and higher prices.

Hing Loon (☎ 206-682-2828, 628 S Weller St) Entrees $5-10. Cantonese seafood dishes are the specialty here: steamed prawns with garlic, stir-fried scallops and such. You won't need a menu – choose from the handwritten specials posted on the walls.

Sea Garden (☎ 206-623-2100, 509 7th Ave S) Hot pots $9-14, noodle soup $5-9. Open until at least 1am nightly. The bowls of noodle soup are huge. The crab and lobster couldn't be fresher; try *geoduck* (local giant clams).

Shanghai Garden (☎ 206-625-1689, 524 6th Ave S) Entrees $13. This is one of the best Chinese restaurants in the neighborhood, with a selection of dishes that fortunately stray far from the usual sweet-and-sours and *foo yungs*.

Sun-Ya Seafood Restaurant (☎ 206-623-1670, 605 7th Ave S) Entrees $8-10. This is

WASHINGTON

an excellent choice for dim sum (served at lunchtime only).

House of Dumplings (☎ 206-340-0774, 510 S King St) Dishes $4-7. For a cheap snack or meal stop here: A serving of eight very good vegetable dumplings costs $5. It's across from the Asian supermarket, Uwajimaya.

Thanh Vi (☎ 329-0208, 1046 S Jackson St) Entrees $6. In Asian Plaza on the corner of 12th Ave, Thanh Vi offers up authentic Vietnamese cuisine at very reasonable prices. Check out the charbroiled pork chop ($6) or salted fried squid ($6.50) with a bottle of '33' beer.

Saigon Bistro (☎ 206-329-4939, 1032 S Jackson St) Entrees $6. This is a favorite for filling noodle soups and Vietnamese crepes. Their Bún Bistro, topped with beef slices, fresh mussels, tofu and mushrooms, is an outstanding value at $6.

Pike Place Market (Map 4)

Explore the market on an empty stomach and commit to a few hours of snacking; you'll be full by the time you leave and it doesn't have to cost you much.

Budget In addition to its wide selection of fresh produce, bakery products, deli items and takeout ethnic foods, the market contains a number of cafes offering cheap and tasty eats (for other snacking options, see the earlier section on Pike Place Market).

Lowell's Restaurant (☎ 206-622-2036, 1519 Pike Place) Entrees $3-8. Try Lowell's for classic eye-opening breakfasts and cheerful lunches.

Copacabana Cafe (☎ 206-622-6359, Triangle Building, 1502½ Pike Place) Entrees $12-15. This convivial restaurant serves up inexpensive Bolivian dishes such as *pollo salteado* (braised chicken with green peppers and tomatoes). The shrimp or bean soup and appetizer combos ($9.50) are hearty and delicious. An equally compelling reason to come is the great market-view terrace.

El Puerco Llorón (☎ 206-624-0541, Hillclimb Corridor) Lunch $4-5. Worth seeking out is this *típico* Mexican joint en route to

the waterfront, where a plate of tacos, beans and rice is just $5.

Kosher Delight (☎ 206-682-8140, 1509 1st Ave) Lunch $7-9. Nosh on chopped liver or bagels and hummus at this small storefront cafe just above the market.

Mid-Range You'll find more cultural variety at these great market restaurants.

Place Pigalle (☎ 206-624-1756, 81 Pike St) Lunch/dinner entrees $12/20. Place Pigalle offers great views over the sound and inventive Latin- and Asian-influenced dishes.

Pink Door Ristorante (☎ 206-443-3241, 1919 Upper Post Alley) Lunch $8-12, dinner $14-20. A Seattle institution, the Pink Door titillates first-time visitors by posting no sign. Just follow your nose down the alley between Virginia and Stewart Sts to the source of the amazing Italian aromas, and *eccolo!* Lunch is mostly pasta dishes, but there's also a soul-stirring cioppino. Reservations are recommended.

Café Campagne (☎ 206-728-2233, 1600 Post Alley) Entrees $12-16. The quality of the French-style cooking here is on par with its older sibling, the upscale Campagne (see Top End), but the prices are manageable and you don't have to dress up for dinner.

Typhoon! (☎ 262-9797, 1400 Western Ave) Lunch/dinner $8-13. Creative, colorful Thai food fills the menu of Typhoon!, below the market. If you're not up for the full meal, slink on up to the satay bar for a beer and a sampler of grilled lemongrass pork ($2.50).

Wolfgang Puck Café (☎ 206-621-9653, 1225 1st Ave) $10-15. Outside the confines of Pike Place Market, but still part of the scene, is this California food guru's casual, eye-poppingly decorated bistro, which serves pizza, salads and pasta.

Top End If you're looking for serious dining, you can find it here, too; some of Seattle's favorite restaurants are tucked in mysterious corners in the market district.

Il Bistro (☎ 206-682-3049, lower Post Alley) Dinner $18-30. At Il Bistro, the best and freshest of the market is incorporated into daily Italian-influenced specials, and served in an intimate, red-lit gangster-movie atmosphere.

Campagne (☎ 206-728-2800, 86 Pine St) Entrees $25-35. Campagne, in the Inn at the Market, is Seattle's best traditional French restaurant, with an emphasis on the foods of Gascony.

Chez Shea (☎ 206-467-9990, 94 Pike St) Entrees $25, four-course set menu $40. This is a treasure hidden away in the Corner Market Building. Great views over the sound combine with Mediterranean-influenced menus to make this one of the city's most romantic restaurants.

Belltown (Map 4)
This hip neighborhood flanking downtown is the uncontested center of fine dining in Seattle. Yes, you can eat well here, but you don't need to empty your wallet to do it. The beauty of Belltown is that you can spend a little or a lot and still get a fabulous meal.

Budget Thankfully, the starving masses of musicians and students support an abundance of delis, inexpensive pubs and budget hangouts.

Mama's Mexican Kitchen (☎ 206-728-6262, 2234 2nd Ave) $5-8. Mama's is always packed, but that's no surprise for a place that serves $6 burritos, huge combination plates and – from 4pm to 6pm weekdays – $2.75 margaritas, all surrounded with Mexican kitsch artifacts.

Two Bells Tavern (☎ 206-441-3050, 2313 4th Ave) $6-7. The venerable (and non-smoking) Two Bells serves one of Seattle's best burgers and draws a couple of dozen regional beers.

Noodle Ranch (☎ 206-728-0463, 2228 2nd Ave) $10. This is a hip diner with pan-Asian noodle dishes. It's great for vegetarians.

Macrina (☎ 206-448-4032, 2408 1st Ave) $8-14. Macrina is an arty bakery that makes some of the best bread in town. Panini sandwiches are also served.

Mid-Range Those willing to spend a bit more can choose from Japanese, Italian and nouveau Northwest cuisine.

Shiro's Sushi Restaurant (☎ 206-443-9844, 2401 2nd Ave) Entrees $16-20. Sushimaster Shiro Kashiba takes his sushi very seriously, using only the freshest ingredients.

Queen City Grill (☎ 206-443-0975, 2201 1st Ave) Entrees $16-20. The handsomely austere Queen City Grill offers great seafood from its daily menu and a solid and eclectic selection of meats and chicken from its seasonal menu. The goat-cheese appetizer ($9) and the grilled ahi ($22) are divine.

Caffè Minnies (Map 5; ☎ 206-448-6263, 101 Denny Way) Breakfast $7-9, lunch & dinner $10-15. Open 24 hours. At the corner of 1st Ave and Denny Way is this '50s-style diner – a blessing if you've got the munchies at 2am.

Top End Belltown is the uncontested center of fine dining in Seattle.

Flying Fish (☎ 206-728-8595, 2234 1st Ave) Dinner $20. This exciting restaurant makes use of delicate spices and a little *joie de vivre* to transform an ordinary piece of salmon or tuna into pure magic. The dining room is bustling and energetic, the service friendly and top-notch.

El Gaucho (☎ 206-728-1337, 2505 1st Ave) Dinner $28-40. Open Tues-Sat. This is a modern re-creation of a 1950s supper club, complete with massive steaks, a cigar room, dozens of single-malt Scotches and a very stylish clientele. Service is impeccable and an integral part of the show.

Lampreia (☎ 206-443-3301, 2400 1st Ave) Dinner $20-30. A contender for the title of Seattle's best formal Italian restaurant, Lampreia specializes in grilled meat and poultry complemented by a good wine list.

Marco's Supperclub (☎ 206-441-7801, 2510 1st Ave) Entrees $12-18. The multi-ethnic menu makes eating here a bit like traveling around the world. The deep-fried sage leaves ($8) are mandatory.

Seattle Center & Queen Anne (Map 5)
Dining options just west of Seattle Center are geared toward the pre- or postgame crowd attending games at Key Arena. Up on top of the hill, restaurants are a bit more upscale.

WASHINGTON

5 Spot (☎ *206-285-7768, 1502 Queen Anne Ave N)* Entrees $5-8. Everyone's favorite breakfast and hangover diner features good American cooking. Avoid the weekends, when lines snake out the door; it's quieter for lunch or dinner.

Pacific Dessert Company (☎ *206-284-8100, 127 Mercer St)* Dessert $3-7. Famous for its fabulous rich cakes and good coffee, this is a popular after-opera stop for the well dressed.

Queen Anne Café (☎ *206-285-2060, 2121 Queen Anne Ave N)* Entrees $8-12. This ultratrendy neighborhood spot is open for breakfast, lunch and dinner and serves up traditional comfort food.

Kaspar's (☎ *206-298-0123, 19 W Harrison St)* Dinner $20-30. Lower Queen Anne's fine-dining house is where fresh Northwest fish and produce are prepared by one of Seattle's celebrity chefs. The elegantly understated decor adds to the experience.

Sky City (☎ *206-443-2111, 219 4th Ave N)* Dinner $27-$42. While the views are tremendous at the revolving restaurant atop the Space Needle, you pay dearly for it. Appetizers cost almost the price of a meal at a top-end restaurant. The ride up the elevator is free with dinner.

Capitol Hill (Map 6)

As much a destination for the people and vitality as for the food, Capitol Hill features some first-rate restaurants amid the coffeehouses and bars. Broadway, 15th Ave E and the Pike/Pine Corridor are the main centers of activity.

There's no end to good and inexpensive eateries along Broadway, especially if you fancy international food.

Siam on Broadway (☎ *206-324-0892, 616 Broadway Ave E)* Lunch $7, dinner $8-11. This casual, no-nonsense Thai bistro delivers the goods, from prawn satay to *phad phug* (stir-fried vegetables).

Gravity Bar (☎ *206-325-7186, 415 Broadway Ave E)* Entrees $6-12. For vegetarian entrees and fresh juices in a *Jetsons*-like interior, check out Gravity Bar, in the Broadway Market.

Pagliacci Pizza (☎ *206-324-0730, 426 Broadway Ave E)* Medium pizzas from $11.50. A slice of Seattle's favorite pizza ($2) and a pesto salad make a nice light supper for under $5.

Bimbo's Bitchin' Burrito Kitchen (*Map 2;* ☎ *206-329-9978, 506 E Pine St)* Burritos $5. Open until 2am. Near the bottom of the Corridor, Bimbo's has huge burritos that live up to the name. During happy hour, 4pm to 7pm daily, drinks are $2.

Here are some mid-range and top-end options:

Café Septieme (☎ *206-860-8858, 214 Broadway Ave E)* Entrees $8-15. Homemade, deceptively simple fare is the main attraction at this trendy and intensely spare cafe.

Broadway New American Grill (☎ *206-328-7000, 314 Broadway Ave E)* Entrees $8-12. This place mixes a rowdy bar scene with good burgers, ribs and a killer Jamaican jerk chicken ($11).

Coastal Kitchen (☎ *206-322-1145, 429 15th Ave E)* Entrees $12-16. Every few months the menu adopts the tastes of another coast, ranging from Havana to Bombay. A great 'blunch' is served between 8:30am and 3pm weekdays.

Wallingford (Map 7)

In Wallingford, N 45th St stretches past a long strip of inexpensive, mostly internationally themed restaurants.

Julia's of Wallingford (☎ *206-633-1175, 4401 Wallingford Ave N)* Entrees $6-9. If your idea of an eye-opener is a stack of pancakes and gallons of coffee, Julia's is the place. It's equally solid for a simple lunch or dinner.

Jitterbug Cafe (☎ *206-547-6313, 2114 N 45th St)* Entrees $8-10. Try this zippy cafe for a Bloody Mary and a goat cheese and sun-dried tomato frittata.

Boulangerie (☎ *206-634-2211, 2200 N 45th St)* Sandwiches $5. Don't pass up the Boulangerie, as close as Seattle gets to a real French bakery.

Wallingford Pizza (☎ *206-547-3663, 2109 N 45th St)* Entrees $8-15. These guys have a unique way of serving pizza – upside down and in a bowl. It's often packed, but there is a takeout window.

Kabul (☎ 206-545-9000, 2301 N 45th St) Entrees $8-12. Dinner only. You don't find Afghani food on every street corner, but this is a good place to give it a try. The menu includes vegetarian options.

Bizzarro (☎ 206-545-7327, 1307 N 46th St) Entrees $12-15. Despite its bizarre location (inside someone's garage), this Wallingford hotbed is an excellent neighborhood Italian cafe. There's live entertainment some nights.

U District (Map 8)

Along 'The Ave,' as University Way is called, many cheap eateries are geared toward student tastes and budgets.

Agua Verde Cafe (☎ 206-545-8570, 1303 NE Boat St) Entrees $4-7. This little gem, overlooking the bay at the southern end of University Ave NE, serves up mouthwatering *tacos de camarones* (shrimp tacos; $6) and other Mexican favorites.

Schultzy's Sausages (☎ 206-548-9461, 4142 University Way NE) Sausages under $4. Head here for all sorts of grilled sausage sandwiches; it's the 'best of the wurst.'

Tandoor (☎ 206-523-7477, 5024 University Way NE) Entrees $5-8. Tandoor doesn't look like much, but the roasted meats and other Indian dishes are a delight.

Araya's Place (☎ 206-524-4332, 4732 University Way NE) Entrees $7. Vegans and other vegetarians can find good, cheap Thai food here.

Cedars Restaurant (☎ 206-527-5247, 4759 Brooklyn Ave NE) Entrees $9. Cedars serves delicious Middle Eastern and Indian food.

Ballard

Ballard is known for its waterfront restaurants, but recent years have seen a proliferation of hip eateries in its historic district as well.

Ray's Boathouse (☎ 206-789-3770, 6049 Seaview Ave NW) Entrees $20. Ray's offers views over the Olympics, nautical decor and an exhaustive fresh fish menu: It's a tourist's ideal image of Seattle. Ray's is about a mile west of the Ballard locks.

Burk's Café (☎ 206-782-0091, 5411 Ballard Ave NW) Entrees $13-16. Though you won't mistake red-brick Old Ballard for New Orleans, the Cajun and Creole food is good enough to make you say 'oh my!'

Chinook's at Salmon Bay (☎ 206-283-4665, 1900 W Nickerson St) Entrees $17. Fish practically leap out of the water and into the kitchen of this excellent restaurant, across the Ballard Bridge in the Fishermen's Terminal. Picture windows and, in summer, an exterior deck provide fine vantage points from which to watch the incoming fishing fleet.

ENTERTAINMENT

For a listing of live entertainment, consult the *Seattle Weekly*, the *Stranger* or the arts sections of the dailies. Tickets for most events are available at *TicketMaster* (☎ 206-628-0888, ⓦ www.ticket master.com), with agencies in several store chains (including Rite-Aid, Tower Records, The Wherehouse) and at the Key Arena box office. Tickets for certain venues are sold via *TicketWeb* (☎ 866-468-7623, ⓦ www.ticketweb.com).

Ticket/Ticket (☎ 206-324-2744) is a half-price, day-of-show ticket outlet; however, they won't give out ticket availability information over the phone. There are locations at the Pike Place Market Information Booth (open noon to 6pm Tuesday to Sunday) and the Broadway Market (open noon to 7pm Tuesday to Saturday, noon to 6pm Sunday), on Capitol Hill.

Coffeehouses

Seattle's well-recognized coffee fanaticism has served to revitalize the coffeehouse as a social institution and alcohol-free venue for poetry readings, theatrical entertainment and acoustic music.

Sit & Spin (Map 4; ☎ 206-441-9484, 2219 4th Ave) This Belltown original is part coffeehouse, part restaurant, part bar and part laundromat. Live bands play here often, so you can tap your toes while folding your clothes.

Uptown Espresso Bar (Map 5; ☎ 206-285-3757, 525 Queen Anne Ave N) This place is always crowded with refugees from Seattle Center.

B&O Espresso (Map 6; ☎ 206-322-5028, 204 Belmont Ave E) This Capitol Hill location is a pleasant spot to write a postcard.

Globe Café *(Map 6;* ☎ *206-689-8661, 1531 14th Ave)* The Globe features frequent literary events and musical performances.

Café Allegro *(Map 8;* ☎ *206-633-3030, 4214 University Way NE)* This U District favorite launched the Seattle coffee scene.

Grand Illusion Cafe & Espresso *(Map 8;* ☎ *206-525-2755, 1405 NE 50th St)* After screenings at the adjacent cinema, filmgoers linger at this courtyard cafe.

Teahouse Kuan Yin *(Map 7;* ☎ *206-632-2055, 1911 N 45th St)* Open Tues-Sat. Instead of coffee, enjoy a pot of black, oolong, green or herbal tea at this Wallingford salon.

Cinemas

Although suburban multiscreen cinema complexes are common enough, there are still a number of small independent theaters that go out of their way to find the unusual and obscure.

At opposite ends of Capitol Hill are two of the best art cinemas: ***The Egyptian*** *(Map 6;* ☎ *206-323-4978, 805 E Pine St)* and ***The Harvard Exit*** *(Map 6;* ☎ *206-323-8986, 807 E Roy St)* Cineastes will like the offbeat fare at the ***Grand Illusion Cinema*** *(Map 8;* ☎ *206-523-3935, 1403 NE 50th St),* in the U District.

Some first-run houses offer art and foreign films along with the regular mainstream hits, including ***Broadway Market Cinemas*** *(Map 6;* ☎ *206-323-0231, Broadway Market),* between E Harrison and E Republican Sts on Capitol Hill; the ***Varsity Theater*** *(Map 8;* ☎ *206-632-3131, 4329 University Way NE);* and ***Metro Cinemas*** *(Map 8;* ☎ *206-633-0055, cnr 45th St NE & Roosevelt Way NE).*

Performing Arts

Seattle boasts one of the most vibrant theater scenes on the West Coast, as well as a full array of classical-music and dance organizations.

Theater The following equity troupes present a range of classical and modern dramatic theater. Check the newspapers for openings (the 'What's Happening' section of the *Seattle PI* on Fridays has good theater listings). Tickets for most of the following venues are available through TicketMaster (for contact information, see the beginning of the Entertainment section).

A Contemporary Theatre *(Map 2;* ☎ *206-292-7676,* Ⓦ *www.acttheatre.org, 700 Union St at Kreielsheimer Place)* Box office open noon-7pm Tues-Fri. ACT features an excellent year-round performance schedule. Seattle's best thespians join occasional big-name actors.

Seattle Repertory Theatre *(Map 5;* ☎ *206-443-2222,* Ⓦ *www.seattlerep.org, 155 Mercer St)* Performances are in the Bagley Wright Theatre at Seattle Center.

Intiman Theatre Company *(Map 5;* ☎ *206-269-1900,* Ⓦ *www.intiman.org, 201 Mercer St)* Seattle's oldest and largest company performs elaborate dramas at the Intiman Playhouse, also at Seattle Center.

Seattle Children's Theater *(Map 5;* ☎ *206-441-3322, Seattle Center)* This company offers great productions for young theatergoers in the Charlotte Martin and Eve Alvord Theaters.

On the Boards *(Map 5;* ☎ *206-217-9888, 100 W Roy St)* Highly acclaimed original drama and dance are performed in the Behnke Center for Contemporary Performance, in Lower Queen Anne.

5th Avenue Theater *(Map 2;* ☎ *206-625-1418, 1308 5th Ave)* Designed in a Chinese motif in the 1920s, this former vaudeville house has become Seattle's premier theater for Broadway musical revivals.

Bathhouse Theatre Company *(Map 7;* ☎ *206-524-9108, 7312 W Green Lake Dr N)* The Bathhouse takes risks with modern adaptations of classics and original contemporary drama.

Annex Theatre *(Map 2;* ☎ *206-728-0933, 1916 4th Ave)* Alternative productions are also produced by this company.

Both the ***Cornish College of the Arts*** *(Map 6;* ☎ *206-323-1486, 710 E Roy St)* and the ***UW School of Drama*** *(Map 8;* ☎ *206-543-4880, University of Washington)* stage impressive student productions. The School of Drama plays at Meany Hall, on the UW campus, among other venues.

Classical Music & Dance The performance season for the following ensembles generally runs from September to May.

Seattle Symphony (*Map 2;* ☎ *206-215-4747,* W *www.seattlesymphony.org, 200 University St*) Under maestro Gerard Schwartz, the Seattle Symphony has risen to prominence as a major regional orchestra and has released a number of critically acclaimed recordings. The symphony performs at the Benaroya Concert Hall.

Northwest Chamber Orchestra (☎ *206-343-0445,* W *www.nwco.org*) The group performs at the acoustically precise Nordstrom Recital Hall, located in the Benaroya Concert Hall, and at the Seattle Asian Art Museum, located in Volunteer Park.

Seattle Opera (*Map 5;* ☎ *206-389-7676,* W *www.seattleopera.org, Seattle Opera House*) The Seattle Opera has only gotten stronger under the directorship of Speight Jenkins. The company features a program of four or five full-scale operas every season, including a summer rendition of Wagner's *Ring* cycle that draws sellout crowds.

Pacific Northwest Ballet (*Map 5;* ☎ *206-441-9411,* W *www.pnb.org, 301 Mercer St*) Also performing at the Opera House, the PNB is the region's foremost dance company.

Seattle Men's Chorus (☎ *206-323-2992,* W *www.seattlemenschorus.org*) This is one of the nation's most active gay choral groups, with nearly three dozen engagements throughout the year, including their popular Christmas concert. They perform at Benaroya Concert Hall, Paramount Theatre and UW's Meany Hall.

Summer events include the *Seattle International Music Festival* (☎ *206-622-1392*), the *Seattle Chamber Music Festival* (☎ *206-283-8808*) and the *International Chamber Music Series* (☎ *206-543-4880, 800-859-5342*).

Bars & Brewpubs

There's nothing sedate about nightlife in Seattle. While lots of attention is paid to live-music clubs, the microbrew craze has served to establish neighborhood bars as lively and respectable places to while away the hours.

Downtown & Pioneer Square (Maps 2 & 3) Seattle's wage slaves show up here at the end of each business day to put down their briefcases and knock back a few.

Rock Bottom Brewery (☎ *206-623-3070, 1333 5th Ave*) Downtown's only brewpub is an inviting place at the base of the Rainier Square Building.

Cloud Room (☎ *206-682-0100, 1619 9th Ave*) For an elegant cocktail with piano glissandos in the background, take the elevator to the top of the Camlin Hotel.

Six Arms Pub & Brewery (☎ *206-223-1698, 300 E Pike St*) This branch of Portland's McMenamin brewpubs has a real neighborhood feel.

Pyramid Ale House (☎ *206-682-3377, 1201 1st Ave*) This pub near Safeco Field has an expansive bar and terrific beers. Tours and tastings are offered weekdays at 2pm and 4pm daily.

Pike Place Market & Belltown (Map 4) Though the occasional tourist wanders in, these neighborhood haunts generally cater to loyal locals.

Virginia Inn Tavern (☎ *206-728-1937, 1937 1st Ave*) One of Seattle's most likable bars, the Virginia serves folks from every walk of life in a lively, nonsmoking atmosphere. Lots of beers on tap, a nice interior and friendly help make this a great staging area for forays elsewhere.

Pike Pub and Brewery (☎ *206-622-6044, 1415 1st Ave*) This fun-loving place in the Economy Building offers good pub grub in addition to handcrafted ales.

Belltown Pub (☎ *206-728-4311, 2322 1st Ave*) Just up from Pike Place Market is the Belltown, another friendly bar with a stylishly low-key atmosphere.

Belltown Billiards (☎ *206-448-6779, 90 Blanchard St*) The main draw here is playing pool in a swanky location, but if you want a bite, sample from the decent Italian menu.

Seattle Center & Queen Anne (Map 5) Queen Anne's watering holes fill up following arena events.

Five Point Cafe (☎ *206-448-9993, 415 Cedar St*) Open 24 hours. In Tillicum Square, this cafe faces the statue of Chief Seattle. Around since 1929, it's a popular hangout for old-timers as well as bikers and young hipsters. (The urinal in the men's room has a periscope view of the Space Needle.)

Mecca Cafe *(☎ 206-285-9728, 526 Queen Anne Ave N)* This tiny, dark bar-in-a-diner attracts a loyal, late-night crowd.

Sorry Charlies Restaurant & Piano Bar *(☎ 206-283-3245, 529 Queen Anne Ave N)* Here's a fabulous relic of Seattle from before it was hip. The piano man checks in around 8pm, and everybody sings along.

Capitol Hill (Map 6) The main gay-bar district centers along the Pike/Pine Corridor near Broadway, though almost any bar you go into around town is gay-friendly. This area is also home to many arty live music clubs and taverns.

Wildrose *(☎ 206-324-9210, 1201 E Pike St at 11th Ave)* Pool tables, a light menu, Wednesday-night karaoke and occasional live music keep things jumping at this comfortable lesbian bar.

The Comet *(☎ 206-323-9853, 922 E Pike St)* A survivor of the grunge era, this tavern takes no-frills seriously, with cheap pool, cheap beer, bright lights and loyal locals.

Ileen's Sports Bar *(☎ 206-324-0229, 300 Broadway Ave E at E Thomas St)* Ileen's tries really hard to be sporty, but the locals, loyal to its former version as Ernie Steele's, keep coming for the unchanging mix of trendy clientele, alternative music and good, cheap drinks. The smoke, as well as mounted moose and elk heads, reinforce the nonsportiness.

Deluxe Bar & Grill *(☎ 206-324-9697, 625 Broadway Ave E)* Deluxe Bar & Grill, by contrast, maintains a sports-bar atmosphere with vinyl booths, pool tables, constant games on TV and a standard selection of beers and sophisticated diner food. There's a happy hour from 3pm to 7pm, and for those who didn't get enough the first time, there's another from 11pm to 1am.

Fremont & Green Lake (Map 7) Less self-consciously hip than their inner-Seattle brethren, Fremont's pubs are come-as-you-are alternatives.

Trolleyman Pub *(☎ 206-548-8000, 3400 Phinney Ave N)* The pub adjoins Redhook Ale Brewery's main operation. (The name derives from the brewery's original location in the old Fremont trolley-car barn.) There's live music Thursday to Saturday.

Triangle Lounge *(☎ 206-632-0880, 3507 Fremont Place N at 35th St)* This three-sided bar is a fun place, happily lacking in the snobbery to which good bars fall prey when gentrification rolls through.

The Latona *(☎ 206-525-2238, 6423 Latona Ave NE at NE 65th St)* After sunbathing at Green Lake, quench your thirst at this attractive pub. Live jazz is featured on weekends.

U District (Map 8) Drop into these pubs to discuss philosophy or the Huskies game over a few brews.

Big Time Microbrew & Music *(☎ 206-545-4509, 4133 University Way NE)* Watch out for the students on their first drinking binge.

Blue Moon Tavern *(712 NE 45th St)* A legendary dive made famous by the people who drank here, from Kerouac and Ginsberg to Tom Robbins.

Live Music

The Northwest's contribution to the music world, grunge rock, was a short-lived phenomenon, albeit one of epic proportions. Though the cult of grunge is now but a memory, it forced Seattle's club scene into existence. Medium-size clubs sprouted up around town, and suddenly Seattle meant something in the music world. Today, these live-music venues host a spectrum of sounds, giving music fans plenty of alternatives to 'alternative.'

The following places are downtown or in Belltown:

Paramount Theater *(Map 2; ☎ 206-682-1414, 911 E Pine St)* Star attractions play this recently renovated 3000-seat venue, whose hydraulic seats enable the space to morph into a concert hall, Broadway-style theater or banquet facility.

Moore Theater *(Map 4; ☎ 206-443-1744, 1932 2nd Ave)* Bands love playing the

A History of Grunge

During the early 1990s, an unprecedented amount of media attention focused on Seattle's 'grunge rock' music scene.

Actually most Seattle musicians consider the term 'grunge' and all the media coverage of their once-obscure music scene laughable. After all, Seattle has always had a thriving local music scene. Pioneering Northwest rock bands like the Kingsmen and the Sonics – and of course, Seattle's own legendary Jimi Hendrix – helped define rock 'n' roll in the 1960s. Local groups Heart and The Steve Miller Band produced hits in the '70s, and bluesman Robert Cray and saxophonist Kenny G gained notoriety in the '80s. But none of these artists were ever represented or known in the media as 'Seattle musicians' per se. It was not until the city spawned the decade of '90s grunge that the world turned to Seattle as the origin of a unique sound.

Bands like Nirvana, Pearl Jam, Soundgarden, Alice in Chains and Screaming Trees achieved tremendous commercial success and sold millions of records worldwide. Dozens of other bands were offered big-dollar recording contracts just because they were from Seattle or sounded similar to the handful of grunge bands that had the hits. Everyone wanted to sign a Seattle band and cash in on the grunge craze.

But the sound born of the Northwest punk underground was not so easily tamed by corporate America. Most bands that record companies were after had developed their music playing at rowdy house parties and tiny rock clubs, rehearsing in basements and garages in the low-rent districts where they lived. Of the bands that inked major label contracts, most were dropped within a year. Others broke up as a result of the rigors of touring, songwriting demands and constant partying.

Nirvana lived the quintessential rags-to-riches Seattle music story. Working-class kids from Aberdeen, Washington, they started out playing at parties around Olympia and Seattle and saved up enough gig money to record a few songs for a cheap demo tape. The engineer at the studio liked their tape and passed it along to a friend who owned a then-small independent record label in Seattle called SubPop. For an estimated $600, Nirvana recorded and mixed the songs for what was to become their debut album, *Bleach.* Nirvana's second album, *Nevermind,* sold over 10 million copies.

The band's success brought unwelcome celebrity to Nirvana's lead singer, Kurt Cobain, who – disillusioned with rock stardom and addicted to heroin – took his own life in April 1994. The world press converged on Seattle in one final wave to cover the Cobain suicide, and then they withdrew, apparently uninterested in what else Seattle musicians had to offer.

A decade after the hysteria, interest in the grunge era remains strong. A well-publicized biography of Kurt Cobain, *Heavier Than Heaven,* by Charles R Cross, was published in 2001, and Nirvana's influence in rock 'n' roll seems to have outlasted the band's brief existence. The success of grunge spurred flocks of imitators, to be sure, but it also paved the way for the 'alternative' phenomenon of the latter '90s, spurring widespread interest in (and commercial success for) bands following a similar do-it-yourself aesthetic who had previously been admired by a small college-radio audience. Northwest bands that achieved varying measures of national recognition post-Nirvana include the Posies, Presidents of the United States of America, Sleater-Kinney, Modest Mouse and Built to Spill.

In Seattle, a handful of the original venues remain from the grunge era, including the Comet Tavern, Re-Bar (site of Nirvana's release party for their *Nevermind* CD), the Crocodile Cafe and Central Saloon.

– Steve Moriarty, formerly of the Gits,
and Danny Schechter, author

WASHINGTON

Experience Music Project

This much-anticipated and ambitious tribute to rock 'n' roll opened in June 2000. Microsoft co-founder Paul Allen and his sister Jody Patton created the Experience Music Project (*EMP; ☎ 206-367-5483, ⓦ www.emplive.com, 325 5th Ave N; adult/senior & student $20/16; open 9am-11pm daily May-Sept, 10am-6pm Sun-Thur, till 11pm Fri & Sat rest of year*). The $450 million EMP houses some 80,000 artifacts of music memorabilia. Highlights include handwritten lyrics by Nirvana's Kurt Cobain, Jimi Hendrix' signed contract to play at Woodstock, Janis Joplin's pink feather boa and the world's first steel guitar.

Likely to become as much a symbol of Seattle as the Space Needle, the exterior of the Frank O Gehry–designed EMP will have you wiping your eyes and asking to be pinched – is this thing for real? Gehry, most notable for designing the famed Guggenheim Museum in Bilbao, Spain, reportedly went out and bought a bunch of Stratocaster guitars and smashed them up; the resulting pile of guitar bits inspired the building's design.

Upon entering the museum, you'll get your own 'virtual companion,' dubbed 'Meg' (Museum Exhibit Guide), a rather clunky handheld computer that you strap over yourself and lug around, using it to access oral histories and exhibit descriptions.

Not to be missed are the Hendrix Gallery, a major tribute to Jimi, and the Northwest Passage, displaying everything from Seattle native Ray Charles' debut album to Heart's stage apparel, plus a special section on the evolution of grunge. The Artist's Journey is a virtual roller coaster ride through the history of funk, complete with seats that roll as if you were on the real thing. Upstairs is the Sound Lab, a simulated studio that lets you lay down vocal tracks and play guitars, drums and keyboards before a virtual audience. There are also a couple of live-music venues, including the Sky Church theater. Despite criticism of the project's expense and unusual design, the EMP is pretty darn cool.

1500-seat Moore, which makes it an excellent place to see a show.

Crocodile Cafe (Map 4; ☎ 206-441-5611, 2200 2nd Ave) Crocodile Cafe is a springboard for local bands, and a real institution of the alternative-rock scene.

Dimitriou's Jazz Alley (Map 2; ☎ 206-441-9729, 2033 6th Ave) This is Seattle's most prestigious jazz club, with world-class players regularly passing through.

For a good overview of the club scene in Pioneer Square, spring for the $5 joint cover ($10 Fri & Sat) that lets you in to about ten clubs. Pay the cover and pick up a list of participants at any of the following.

The Central (Map 3; ☎ 206-622-0209, 207 1st Ave S) This is one of the city's best and oldest blues clubs.

Bohemian Café, Lounge & Backstage (Map 3; ☎ 206-447-1514, 111 Yesler Way) This spot sports three venues in one: In the Café and Lounge, DJs lay down island grooves, R&B and electronica; the Backstage presents top-flight reggae artists in concert.

New Orleans Creole Restaurant (Map 3; ☎ 206-622-2563, 114 1st Ave S) This nightspot books Basin St–style jazz, blues and zydeco.

There are a few venues at Pike Place Market and the Waterfront:

Showbox (Map 4; ☎ 206-628-3151, 1426 1st Ave) This cavernous hall hosts everything from alternative country to speed metal. When bands aren't playing, DJs take over and the dance party begins.

Kell's Restaurant & Pub (Map 4; ☎ 206-728-1916, 1916 Upper Post Alley) Kell's has live Irish music Wednesday to Saturday evenings.

Summer Nights at the Pier (☎ 206-281-7799, **W** www.summernights.org) Major touring acts perform outdoors on Piers 62 and 63 from June to August.

The *Experience Music Project* (see the boxed text) brought a couple of new venues to town. The entryway to the museum, jazzed up with a video mosaic and great acoustics, doubles as the *Sky Church* concert hall. High-tech decor and a rock 'n' roll vibe make the *Liquid Lounge* a good place to kick back with a psychedelic cocktail. Seattle-area bands from all over the musical map play the mezzanine bar Tuesday to Saturday nights.

Ballard is another music hotbed; the center of things up here are *Tractor Tavern* (☎ 206-789-3599, 5213 Ballard Ave NW) and the *Ballard Firehouse* (☎ 206-784-3516, 5429 Russell Ave NW).

Dance Clubs

Flexibility reigns in Seattle's clubs, so DJ nights transform many live music venues into dance clubs.

Vogue (Map 6; ☎ 206-324-5778, 1516 11th Ave N) Now on Capitol Hill, Vogue varies in tone depending on who's spinning that night.

Some of the hottest dance venues in Seattle are the gay clubs found along the Pike/Pine Corridor. For a mostly gay-male disco scene, head for *Neighbours* (Map 6; ☎ 206-324-5358, 1509 Broadway Ave E) – enter in the alley – or *Elite* (Map 6; ☎ 206-324-4470, 622 Broadway Ave E).

Whether you're gay, lesbian, bi or straight (or if you're still unsure), you'll enjoy the lively theme nights on Thursdays and Saturdays at *Re-Bar* (Map 2; ☎ 206-233-9873, 1114 Howell St at Boren Ave) DJs keep the music going the rest of the week.

Comedy Clubs

Comedy Underground (Map 3; ☎ 206-628-0303, 206-628-0888, **W** www.comedyunder ground.com, 222 S Main St) If you can make a crowd chuckle, stop by Mondays for Open Mic. Comedy shows happen daily at 8pm, with late shows Friday and Saturday at 10pm.

Market Theater (Map 4; ☎ 206-781-9273, 1428 Post Alley below Pike Place Market) If you've never seen theater sports, then plan a wild evening of audience-inspired madness with this combination of improvisation and competition. The popular performances take place on weekends.

SPECTATOR SPORTS

Seattle has a full complement of professional sports teams. The *Seattle Mariners* (☎ 206-628-3555, **W** www.mariners.org), who have risen from obscurity to become one of major league baseball's winningest teams, play in the new open-air *Safeco Field* south of downtown. The *Seattle Seahawks* (☎ 206-827-9777, **W** www.seahawks.com), the Northwest's only NFL franchise, are scheduled to begin use of their new stadium near Pioneer Square in fall 2002. The *Seattle SuperSonics* (☎ 206-283-3865, **W** www.nba .com/sonics) provide plenty of NBA excitement at *Key Arena* in Seattle Center.

The *University of Washington Huskies*, who play football in *Husky Stadium* at the south end of campus, are wildly popular. Call ☎ 206-543-2200 or check **W** www .gohuskies.com for schedule and ticket information.

Tickets to games for all the above teams can be obtained through *Ticket-Master* outlets (☎ 206-628-0888, **W** www .ticketweb.com) or through *Pacific Northwest Ticket Service* (☎ 206-232-0150, **W** www.nwtickets.com).

SHOPPING

The main shopping area in Seattle is downtown between 3rd and 6th Aves and University and Stewart Sts. *Westlake Center* (Map 2; ☎ 206-467-3044, cnr 4th Ave & Pine St), *Rainier Square* (Map 2; ☎ 206-373-7119, 4th Ave btw Union & University Sts), *City Centre Mall* (Map 2; ☎ 206-223-8999, 5th Ave btw Pike & Union Sts) and *Pacific Place* (Map 2; ☎ 206-405-2655, 600 Pine St) each host a plethora of small, interesting boutiques designed to lighten your wallet.

WASHINGTON

Nordstrom *(Map 2; ☎ 206-628-2111, Pine St & 6th Ave)* Nordstrom Downtown is the flagship store of the upscale clothing chain.

Bon Marché *(Map 2; ☎ 206-344-2121, cnr 3rd Ave & Pine St)* This is Seattle's oldest and largest department store.

The streets surrounding Pike Place Market are a maze of food and craft stalls, galleries and small specialty shops. The Pioneer Square area and Capitol Hill are also good neighborhoods for locally owned shops with an idiosyncratic selection of gifts and products.

Also see Bookstores, under Information, earlier in the chapter, for books, periodicals and more.

Local Products & Souvenirs

Shopping for food is great fun at **Pike Place Market** *(Map 4; ☎ 206-467-1600, W www .pikeplacemarket.org, cnr 1st Ave & Pike St);* even if you don't have a kitchen handy, you can channel your shopping urges into buying local jams or syrups, hunting for obscure spices and condiments, or picking out a bottle of local wine for later use.

Northwest food specialties make good gifts. Look for products made from local berries; cranberries especially are likely to turn up in unusual and delicious candies and snacks. Berry syrups and jams also make good gifts. Perhaps the item that says 'I ♥ Seattle' the most is a whole salmon. If you're not up to buying a 15lb chinook, then perhaps a fillet of smoked salmon would make a better souvenir. All of the fish markets will prepare seafood for airplane transportation or arrange overnight shipping. **Jack's Fish Spot** *(Map 4; ☎ 206-467-0514)* and **Pike Place Fish** *(Map 4; ☎ 206-682-7181)* are two of the best.

If a gift of regional wine seems appropriate, check out **Pike & Western Wine Shop** *(Map 4; ☎ 206-441-1307, 1934 Pike Place),* at the northern end of Pike Place Market.

The North Arcade of Pike Place Market is given over to local artists and craftspeople, and you'll be able to find inexpensive jewelry, clothing (watch for hand-knitted, Canadian Native Indian–designed Cowichan sweaters, made on Vancouver Island), wood and bone carvings, and a lot of other things to buy. Most of the fun is in the browsing. For other locally made souvenirs, head to **Made in Washington** *(Map 4; ☎ 206-467-0788, 1530 Post Alley),* in the Post Alley Market Building (another location is in Westlake Center).

Art

Browse Seattle's art galleries to get a feel for Pacific Northwest art. The Seattle area is known for its Pilchuck school of glassblowing art, begun by Dale Chihuly. Both **Glasshouse Studio** *(Map 3; ☎ 206-682-9939, 311 Occidental Ave S)* and the **Foster/White Gallery** *(Map 3; ☎ 206-622-2833, 123 S Jackson St)* feature glassworks, as well as paintings and sculpture from mainstream Northwest artists.

Legacy Limited *(Map 2; ☎ 206-624-6350, 1003 1st Ave)* This is a good gallery for Northwest Native and Inuit art and artifacts.

Traditions & Beyond *(Map 3; ☎ 206-621-0655, 113 Cherry St)* Affordable and authentic Native American crafts are available here; partial proceeds go to native programs and education.

Outdoor Gear

These equipment providers have everything you could possibly need for your next expedition.

REI *(Recreational Equipment Inc; Map 5; ☎ 206-323-8333, 22 Yale Ave N)* The state-of-the-art outfitter is right by I-5, north of downtown. You can scale the store's climbing wall, test out the rainproofing of various brands of gear in a special rainstorm booth, or try out hiking boots on a simulated mountain trail. REI rents all forms of ski packages, climbing gear and camping equipment.

Second Ascent *(☎ 206-545-8810, 5209 Ballard Ave NW)* This unique store sells used gear from boots to backpacks. Look for it in Ballard next to the Tractor Tavern.

Body Art & Accessories

Most shops are located in Capitol Hill, Pike Place Market and the U District. The following list includes those with the best reputation among youthful Seattleites.

Mind's Eye Tattoo & Body Piercing *(Map 8; ☎ 206-522-7954, 5206 University Way NE; open 1pm-10pm Mon-Fri, noon-6pm Sun)*. Co-owner Reverend Eric Eye performs a variety of services from weddings, baptisms and funerals to tattoos. Open since 1992, this was the first tattoo shop in the U District and remains the most reputable.

The Pink Zone *(Map 6; ☎ 206-325-0050, 211 Broadway E; open noon-10pm Mon-Fri, noon-9pm Sat, noon-7pm Sun)* In Capitol Hill's Broadway Market, this shop sells 'visible queer gear' in addition to performing body piercings. The friendly staff prides itself on cleanliness, and the shop attracts a diverse (but generally young) clientele.

Rudy's Barbershop *(Map 2; ☎ 206-329-3008, 614 E Pine St; open 9am-9pm Mon-Sat, 11am-5pm Sun)* Wildly popular with gay men, among others, this stylish haircutter–tattoo parlor chain has other locations in the U-District and Belltown.

Vyvyn Lazonga *(Map 4; ☎ 206-622-1535, 1516 Western Ave; open 11am-7pm)* One of the first modern female tattoo artists, Vyvyn has nationwide name recognition. Her store is just below Pike Place Market.

GETTING THERE & AWAY

Air

Seattle-Tacoma International (☎ 206-431-4444), 13 miles south of Seattle, is one of the nation's busiest airports. 'Sea-Tac,' as it's known, handles service to and from Europe and Asia; it is also a major hub for domestic and regional airlines, with departures to the San Juan Islands, Bellingham, Wenatchee, Yakima and Spokane. Frequent daily flights also link Seattle to Portland and Vancouver, British Columbia.

The following airlines have ticketing desks downtown:

Alaska Airlines (☎ 206-433-3100) 1301 4th Ave

American Airlines (☎ 800-433-7300) 1400 6th Ave (Sheraton Hotel)

Continental Airlines (☎ 206-624-1740, 800-523-3273) 400 University Way

Northwest Airlines/KLM (☎ 800-225-2525) 402 University St

United Airlines (☎ 206-441-3700, 800-241-6522) 1303 4th Ave

Bus

Greyhound buses (Map 2; ☎ 206-628-5561, 800-231-2222, W www.greyhound.com),

811 Stewart St, link Seattle to Portland and Eugene, Oregon, and points in California along I-5 south, as well as to Bellingham and Vancouver, British Columbia, on I-5 north. Buses also service the I-90 corridor from Seattle to Spokane and on through northern Idaho and Montana to Chicago, as well as the route from Seattle to Yakima, the Tri-Cities and points south along Hwy 97.

destination	cost (one-way)	duration	distance	frequency (per day)
Bellingham	$15	2½ hrs	90 miles	6
Vancouver	$23	4 hrs	140 miles	5
Yakima	$25	3½ hrs	145 miles	3
Portland	$24	4 hrs	195 miles	10
Tri-Cities	$36	7 hrs	225 miles	3
Spokane	$30	6 hrs	280 miles	5
Eugene	$29	8 hrs	285 miles	9
San Francisco	$62	20 hrs	805 miles	6
Chicago	$118	48 hrs	2030 miles	4

If you're heading to British Columbia, consider the Quick Shuttle (☎ 206-728-0428, 800-665-2122, W www.quickcoach.com), which makes eight (five in winter) daily runs between Sea-Tac, downtown Seattle and Vancouver. Pickup is at either Sea-Tac airport ($39 one way) or the Travelodge by the Space Needle, 200 6th Ave N ($31 one way).

Train

Amtrak (Map 3; ☎ 800-872-7245, W www.amtrak.com), 303 S Jackson St, in the King St Station, runs train service south to/from Portland, San Francisco, Los Angeles and San Diego. Trains also chug north to Vancouver and east through Spokane, eventually reaching Chicago. Taking the train is somewhat slow, but if you've got the time it can be a comfortable and scenic way to travel.

Fares vary widely, depending on advance purchase, season and availability. One-way fares to Vancouver or Portland range from $21 to $33. To Chicago, the one-way fare averages $240, San Francisco $100 and LA around $110.

WASHINGTON

destination	cost (one-way)	duration	frequency (per day)
Bellingham	$18	2½ hrs	2
Portland	$27	3½ hrs	4
Vancouver	$27	4 hrs	1

Sound Transit (☎ 800-201-4900, W www .soundtransit.org) offers a couple of commuter trains heading to downtown Tacoma between 5pm and 6pm (adult/senior $4/2, one hour). Trains depart from the Amtrak station.

Car
The American Automobile Association (AAA) office (Map 5; ☎ 206-448-5353) is at 330 6th Ave N, near Seattle Center. Before getting on the road, phone for the latest word on traffic (☎ 206-368-4499) or weather (☎ 206-442-2800, ext 2032).

Most national car rental firms have booths at the airport. The following companies also maintain offices in the downtown area:

Avis (☎ 206-448-1700, 800-831-2847) 1919 5th Ave

Budget (☎ 206-448-1940, 800-527-0700) 2001 Westlake Ave N

Dollar Rent A Car (☎ 206-682-1316, 800-800-4000) 710 Stewart St

Enterprise Rent-A-Car (☎ 206-382-1051, 800-736-8222) 2116 Westlake Ave N

EZ Rent-A-Car (☎ 206-770-0199, 800-356-8802) 2402 7th Ave

Hertz (☎ 206-903-6260, 800-654-3131) 720 Olive Way

National Car Rental (☎ 206-448-7368, 800-227-7368) 2300 7th Ave

Rent A Wreck (☎ 800-876-4670) 2701 4th Ave S

Thrifty Car Rental (☎ 206-625-1133, 800-847-4389) 801 Virginia St

Ferry
State-operated car ferries bound for Bainbridge Island and Bremerton depart daily from Pier 52 (Colman Dock); foot-passenger ferries for Vashon Island and Bremerton leave Monday to Friday from Pier 50, just south of the car ferry entrance. For details, see those destinations in the Around Seattle section, later. Vehicles are loaded on a first-come, first-served basis; drivers should show up at least half an hour early to ensure a space. For approximate wait times or other ferry queries, call Washington State Ferries (☎ 206-464-6400, recorded info in Washington ☎ 800-843-3779) or visit W www.wsdot .wa.gov/ferries. Pick up a WSF schedule at any information center in the region.

To/From Victoria & the San Juan Islands Clipper Navigation operates several ferries to/from Victoria, British Columbia, year round. The passenger-only *Victoria Clipper* (☎ 206-448-5000, 800-888-2535, W www.victoriaclipper.com) departs from Pier 69, 2701 Alaskan Way, at 8:30am. Additional boats leave at 7:30am, 8am and 3:30pm in high season (mid-May to mid-September); the earliest departure calls at Friday Harbor on San Juan Island. Adult/senior fare for the two- to three-hour trip is $66-75/$60-69 one way and $109-125/$99-115 roundtrip in high season; children ride for half the adult fare. Travelers should be prepared to go through Canadian customs upon arrival.

GETTING AROUND
No discussion of getting around Seattle can avoid a mention of traffic: It can be heinous. According to a 1999 study, Los Angeles was the only city in the US with worse traffic than Seattle. Unfortunately, unless you know the city intimately, there aren't many ways to avoid the congestion. With only two bridges across Lake Washington, you simply have to wait your turn. Also, because the Boeing shift changes begin at 2:30pm, lunch is about the only time it's not rush hour somewhere in the city. If you have a choice, avoid traveling on freeways after 3pm; chances are that traffic is at a standstill. Also, even when traffic is moving, heavy rains can make driving conditions nightmarish. Use caution and have patience. Seattle traffic will demand both.

To/From the Airport
For information on ground transportation, call ☎ 206-431-5906 or visit the ground

transportation booth on the third level of the parking garage. Gray Line runs an Airport Express (☎ 206-626-6088) every 15 minutes 5am to 11pm between Sea-Tac and downtown Seattle's major hotels ($8.50/14 one way/roundtrip). Shuttle Express (☎ 206-622-1424, 800-487-7433) offers door-to-door service for around $20. One-way taxi fare to/from downtown is around $35, more if traffic is heavy.

Metro Transit public bus Nos 174 and 194 pass by the south end of the baggage claim area ($1.75).

Bus

King County Metro (☎ 206-553-3060, 800-542-7876, TTY 206-684-1739, W www.transit .metrokc.gov) serves the greater Seattle area with over 200 bus routes. Downtown, most buses run through the subterranean 3rd Ave Transit Tunnel, with five street entrances. In the downtown core – between 6th Ave and the Waterfront, and between S Jackson St in Pioneer Square and Battery St – all bus rides are free 6am to 7pm. Note that Seattle Center is outside the ride-free zone.

Regular bus fare is $1.25 during peak hours (6am to 9am and 3pm to 6pm) and $1 at other times. If you are catching a bus that's heading downtown, you purchase your ticket when you get on; however, if you board a bus downtown and head elsewhere, you pay when you get off. Bus drivers do not make change, so you need exact fare. If you're changing buses, ask for a free transfer slip.

Buy tickets in advance, pick up route schedules or purchase a bus map at the King County Metro Transit office, 201 S Jackson St, or at the Westlake Center bus tunnel station.

Waterfront Streetcar

Seattle's old trolley system was dismantled in the 1940s, but the waterfront section has been kept alive. The vintage trolley cars now in use – including two 1927 cars imported from Melbourne – make nine stops. The northern terminus is at the foot of Broad St at Alaskan Way, about a 10-minute walk from Seattle Center; at the southern end, S Main St near Pioneer Square, trolleys turn east and terminate in the International District, across from Union Station. Fares and transfers are the same as for city buses, but the streetcar is not included in the ride-free zone. Buy tickets as you board; they're good for 1½ hours after issuance.

Monorail

The futuristic Monorail (☎ 206-441-6038) provides frequent transportation between downtown's Westlake Center, at Pine St and 4th Ave, and Seattle Center. Cars run the two-minute trip about every 10 minutes from 7:30am to 11pm weekdays, 9am to 11pm weekends. The Monorail passes through a purple slab of the Experience Music Project museum and stops near the base of the Space Needle. Tickets are $1.50/50¢ for adult/child & senior.

Taxi

For a cab, call one of the following companies: Farwest Taxi (☎ 206-622-1717), Graytop Cabs (☎ 206-282-8222), Stita Taxi (☎ 206-246-9980) or Yellow Cabs (☎ 206-622-6500).

Around Seattle

Spend an afternoon in the high-tech mega-burbs of the Eastside, hit the ski slopes of Snoqualmie Pass or take a ferry across Puget Sound to one of the rugged green islands for lunch. Seattle is an excellent launchpad for whatever excursion you plan to make.

IN & ON THE SOUND

Frequent ferries ply Puget Sound on their way to and from these outlying communities, making for easy day trips.

Blake Island

Blake Island is a state park that you can access only by boat; this made it a safe place to host the 1993 APEC conference, where President Clinton met with 14 Asian leaders. The most popular facility on the island is **Tillicum Village**, with its Northwest Coast Indian Cultural Center &

Restaurant. **Tillicum Village Tours** *(Map 2; ☎ 206-933-8600, 800-426-1205, W www .tillicum village.com)* charters boats that depart from Pier 55 in Seattle for a tour of the waterfront and an excursion to Blake Island. The four-hour tours include a traditional salmon bake, native dancing and a film at an old Duwamish Indian village. Tours cost $65/59/25 for adult/senior/child.

Bainbridge Island

A perennially popular ferry trip is between Seattle and Winslow, Bainbridge Island's primary town, with an array of shops and restaurants a short walk from the dock. However, most tourists simply go for the ride and the great views of Seattle as the ferry negotiates Elliott Bay. The **Bainbridge Island Winery** *(☎ 206-842-9463, Hwy 305 just north of Winslow; tastings noon-5pm)* is a good destination for cyclists and wine lovers.

For information on other places to visit and things to do, stop by the **Bainbridge Island Chamber of Commerce** *(☎ 206-842-3700, 590 Winslow Way E)*, near the ferry terminal. Rent a bike at **BI Cycle** *(☎ 206-842-6413, 195 Winslow Way; rentals $5/25 per hour/day)*.

Ferries to Bainbridge Island run around the clock, with at least one departure each hour during the day. They board at Pier 52 for the 35-minute trip; the fare is $4.50 for passengers (seniors half price), $10 for car and driver during peak season (mid-May to mid-October). Passenger fares are collected only on the westbound journey; only those with vehicles pay for the return trip. There's a 90¢ surcharge for taking a bicycle on the ferry, also collected westbound only.

Vashon Island

More rural and countercultural than Bainbridge, Vashon Island has resisted suburbanization – a rare accomplishment in the Puget Sound area. Much of the island is covered with farms and gardens; the little community centers double as commercial hubs and artists' enclaves. Cascade views are great, with unencumbered vistas of Mt Rainier and north to Baker.

Vashon is a good island to explore by bicycle or car, lazily stopping to pick berries or fruit at a 'u-pick' garden or orchard. Alternatively, plan a hike in one of the county parks.

An option for budget travelers is **AYH Ranch Hostel** *(☎ 206-463-2592, W www .vashonhostel.com, 12119 SW Cove St)*. Bunk beds in summer cost $11/14 for HI members/nonmembers, in winter $25 for one person plus $10 for each additional person; private rooms run $45/55 for two HI members/nonmembers.

From Pier 50 in Seattle, a passenger-only ferry leaves eight times each weekday for Vashon Island ($5.50; 25 minutes). However, the ferry deposits you far from the centers of Vashon commerce and culture, so you'll need to bring a bike (90¢ surcharge) or have a lift arranged. From Fauntleroy in West Seattle, a car ferry leaves over 30 times daily for Vashon ($2.90/13 passenger/car & driver; 15 minutes). For either ferry, fares are collected only on the journey to the island.

Travelers from Seattle can make a visit to Vashon into a loop trip by taking the Tahlequah ferry from the southern end of the island to Tacoma, returning via the mainland's I-5.

Bremerton

Seattle's other ferry destination is Bremerton, the largest town on the Kitsap Peninsula and Puget Sound's principal naval base. The main attractions here are the **Naval Museum** *(☎ 360-479-7447, 130 Washington Ave; self-guided tours daily in summer, Thur-Sun in winter)* and the historic destroyer **USS Turner Joy**, right next to the ferry terminal.

The car ferry to Bremerton makes 16 trips daily from the terminal at Pier 52 ($4.50/10 passenger/car & driver; 1 hour). There are also passenger-only ferries weekdays from Pier 50 ($5.50; 30 min). Passengers are charged only on the westbound journey; those with vehicles pay both ways.

NORTH & SOUTH OF SEATTLE

Two airy attractions lie north and south of the city. North on I-5 is the famous Boeing factory. Heading down I-5, you'll hit the Museum of Flight.

Boeing Factory
Near the city of Everett is the facility where most of Boeing's wide-bodied jets – the 747, 767 and 777 – are produced (☎ 206-544-1264, 800-464-1476; adult/senior & child $5/3). Tours of the factory are given 9am to 3pm weekdays; no photography is allowed. Reservations must be made at least 24 hours in advance; call between noon and 3pm to get on the list.

To reach the Boeing factory, follow I-5 north to exit 189; turn west and drive 3 miles on Hwy 526.

Museum of Flight
More than 50 historic aircraft are on display at this vast museum of aviation (☎ 206-764-5720, 9494 E Marginal Way S; adult/senior/youth 5-17 years $9.50/8.50/5, child under 6 years free; open 10am-5pm Fri-Wed, 10am-9pm Thur). The museum presents the entire history of flight, from da Vinci to the Wright Brothers to the NASA space program. Vintage flyers reside on the grounds outside the buildings. The restored 1909 Red Barn – where Boeing had its beginnings – contains more exhibits and displays.

The museum is on Boeing Field, about 10 miles south of downtown. Take I-5 exit 158 south of Seattle; turn west and follow East Marginal Way.

EAST OF SEATTLE
An excursion to the fast-growing suburbs on the east side of Lake Washington may provide a glimpse of high-tech culture, but civic life here can be summed up by a drive to the mall. Toward the Cascades, there's a grand old resort and winter recreation at Snoqualmie Pass.

Eastside
Bellevue was long the suburb that Seattleites loved to disdain. However, mass immigration to the Seattle area has boosted the population of this city on the eastern shores of Lake Washington. Nowadays,

Bellevue is Washington's fifth-largest city, an upscale burg with high-cost housing and attractive parks. Civic and social life centers on Bellevue Square, at Bellevue Way NE and NE 8th St, the shopping mall that sets the tone for downtown and the surrounding communities. Across from the mall is the **Bellevue Art Museum** (☎ 206-454-6021, 510 Bellevue Way NE; adult/student & senior $7/5; open 10am-5pm Tues & Sat, noon-8pm Wed-Fri, noon-5pm Sun), featuring changing exhibits of contemporary Northwest art. To reach Bellevue from downtown Seattle, take I-90 east and exit onto I-405 northbound. By bus, take No 550 from Convention Place or any of the 3rd Ave tunnel stations ($1/1.75 regular/peak).

North of Bellevue on I-405 is **Kirkland**, known for its lakefront business district, marinas and antique shopping malls. Some of the best public access to Lake Washington is along Lake Ave W. Lots of waterfront restaurants are found here, some with docks for their boat-transported customers. East of Kirkland is **Redmond**, a sprawling suburb and the center of Seattle's high-tech industry. Computer giant Microsoft dominates life here. To reach Kirkland and Redmond from downtown Seattle, take Hwy 520 over the Evergreen Point Bridge or catch bus No 251 along 4th Ave.

Snoqualmie Valley
East of the Eastside, the Snoqualmie valley remains a quiet backwater of dairy farms, orchards and produce gardens, still beyond the reach of the advancing suburbs. From North Bend, 31 miles east of Seattle via I-90, follow the Snoqualmie River north on Hwy 202 to the **Salish Lodge and Spa** (☎ 206-888-2556, 800-826-6124, PO Box 1109, Snoqualmie, WA 98065). This beautiful resort sits atop 268-foot Snoqualmie Falls and was the locale for many of the scenes from the TV series Twin Peaks. The drive into the Cascades, views of the waterfall and short hikes in the area, followed by lunch at the lodge, make for a nice day away.

Snoqualmie Pass
Seattle is fortunate to have several ski areas within an easy drive of the city. Closest are

WASHINGTON

the slopes at Stevens Pass, 78 miles east of town on US 2 (see the Central Washington chapter), and Snoqualmie Pass, 53 miles east on I-90.

A popular winter excursion for Seattleites is **Summit at Snoqualmie** (☎ *206-232-8182, snow report* ☎ *206-236-1600;* Ⓦ *www.summit-at-snoqualmie.com).* Its four ski areas, Alpental, Summit Central, Summit West and Summit East, vary greatly in difficulty and conditions. Alpental is generally considered the toughest, with steep slopes and 2200 feet of vertical drop. Summit West boasts superb snowboarding and is good for beginning and intermediate skiers. Summit Central's lower slopes cater to families and beginners, but the upper slopes have treed runs and moguls. Summit East features a Nordic Center, with trails for snowshoers and cross-country skiers. Free buses link the runs.

Lift tickets, valid in all areas, are $40/26/7 for adult/senior & youth/child on weekends & holidays, $32/22/7 midweek. Ski instruction and rental equipment ($25/30 ski/snowboard packages) are available. Night skiing is offered through the week.

If you don't have a vehicle or don't want to face the drive, check with the ski resort about a shuttle bus.

Woodinville

The suburban community of Woodinville, 14 miles north of Bellevue off I-405, is home to two popular wineries and a brewpub.

One of Washington's original wineries, **Chateau Ste Michelle** (☎ *425-415-3300, 14111 NE 145th St; tastings 10am-4:30pm)* pioneered efforts to cultivate vineyards in the Columbia Valley, where most Washington wine production goes on today. The historic 87-acre estate lends itself easily to picnics and concerts in the summer. Noted for its cabernets and merlots, **Columbia Winery** (☎ *425-488-2776, 14030 NE 145th St; tastings 10am-7pm)* offers tours on weekends.

Another beverage trailblazer of sorts, Redhook led Washington's microbrewing wave. Redhook's Woodinville facility showcases its signature ales at the **Forecasters Public House** (☎ *425-483-3232, 14300 NE 145th St)*. Brewery tours are offered at 1pm, 3pm and 5pm weekends, 2pm and 4pm weekdays ($1 per person).

South Sound

Tacoma and Olympia are the two largest cities south of Seattle along Puget Sound, and both can make nice alternatives as places to stay. Though once the principal city on the sound, Tacoma has suffered a bad reputation for years – partly the result of too many pulp mills. But the town has been cleaning up its act, and today it's much nicer than the many jokes about it would lead you to believe. It boasts the largest city park this

side of New York's Central Park, as well as some inexpensive accommodations.

Olympia, the state capital, is a smaller, cozier city that runs on politics but has a surprisingly hip alternative side. In addition to being a pleasant place to visit in and of itself, Olympia makes a good base from which to explore the Olympic Peninsula, Pacific Coast beaches and Mt Rainier National Park.

TACOMA

Long the object of every other northwest city's scorn, Tacoma (population 193,556) has been known for years as a beleaguered mill town with a big-domed stadium and a bombed-out (though architecturally notable) downtown. It didn't take a poet to coin the phrase 'the Tacoma aroma,' but the epitaph stuck: It's a coy euphemism for that certain odor the area's pulp mills lend to the air.

However, Tacoma is turning itself around. People who speak ill of this Puget Sound city probably haven't been here recently, or they didn't bother to look beyond the shopping malls. While nobody was paying attention, artists who found Seattle too expensive moved their studios south. Community activists have renovated old theater buildings and other once-grand downtown structures, including the fabulous Union Station, which has been gussied up and turned into a federal courthouse. Add to this an influx of new residents who've discovered that Tacoma is the only city with affordable housing on Puget Sound, and all of a sudden Tacoma starts looking good.

Students from Tacoma's two universities – University of Puget Sound and Pacific Lutheran University – support the city's nightlife and theater scene. Tacoma boasts an excellent zoo and aquarium in one of the nation's largest city parks, as well as the state historical museum and the Tacoma Dome, a sports and music stadium that is the world's largest wooden-domed structure. And nobody ever complained about the city's

Highlights

- Strolling through the capitol campus and chatting with the eclectic community in Olympia
- Edifying yourself at one of Tacoma's many theaters and museums
- Eating a seafood dinner after a quiet afternoon at Point Defiance Park on Puget Sound

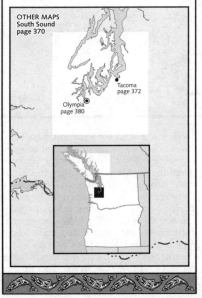

OTHER MAPS
South Sound
page 370

Tacoma
page 372

Olympia
page 380

WASHINGTON

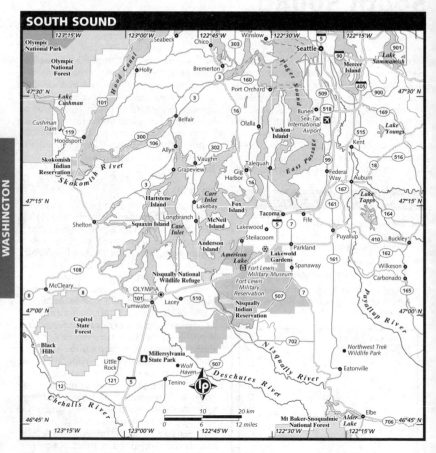

SOUTH SOUND

location, backed up against the foothills of Mt Rainier and facing the fjords of Puget Sound and the jagged peaks of the Olympic Mountains.

History

In 1792, Captain George Vancouver became the first of several early explorers to come to Commencement Bay. The usual settlement pattern of sawmills and farmlands was barely under way when local land speculators began to wager that Tacoma would end up as the Puget Sound rail terminus for the Northern Pacific Railroad, which by the late

1860s was looking for a northwest port city. Tacoma had a real advantage over competing settlements: Commencement Bay was deep and highly protected by the bluffs along Browns Point and Point Defiance.

Tacoma was indeed named the Northern Pacific's western terminus, and trains reached there in 1887; for the next decade, Tacoma was the uncontested trade leader on Puget Sound. Ships from Asia docked at the wharves to unload tea and fabrics, while trains brought metals, grain, coal, lumber and hops to be exported to the Far East and the boomtowns of California. The trains also brought settlers and skilled laborers to the Northwest, and the waterfront became a warren of factories and mills.

This period of prosperity and limitless self-confidence was best expressed in the monumental architecture of the young city's civic and commercial buildings. Even after a century's worth of razing and modification, the city center still boasts one of the finest enclaves of historic buildings in the Northwest.

Tacoma saw its prominence on Puget Sound diminish as Seattle became linked to the rest of the nation by rail in 1893. By the beginning of the 20th century, Seattle had become the financial and cultural center of Washington, while Tacoma became more industrial. The wood-products giant Weyerhaeuser brought its mills – and eventually its corporate headquarters – to Tacoma in the early 1900s, and smelting, especially of aluminum, thrived on cheap hydropower. Tacoma also connected itself closely to the military by donating land in 1917 to build Fort Lewis and McChord Air Force Base just south of the city.

Beginning in the 1960s, Tacoma's industries slipped into Rust Belt–like decline, and the city began to merge into the suburban sprawl of greater Puget Sound. Today, Tacoma seems at the cusp of a second growth period as its architectural beauty and cheap rents lure small industries, artists, musicians and others looking for affordable housing to the boomland of western Washington.

A series of ambitious public works projects should further transform the city's image in coming years. The long-stagnant Thea Foss waterway east of downtown is undergoing a robust redevelopment whose centerpiece is a museum of glass art; the waterway will be spanned by a glass bridge destined to replace the Tacoma Dome as the city's icon. Furthermore, a light-rail line is being installed to conveniently connect downtown with interurban destinations.

Orientation

Tacoma is on Commencement Bay, a deep harbor protected by Point Defiance. The busy Port of Tacoma is immediately north of downtown, on five artificial bays dredged out of the Puyallup River's estuary.

Pacific Ave, Commerce St and Broadway are the main downtown arteries running north-south; the center of Tacoma is largely encompassed between 9th and 15th Sts, which run east-west. Northwest of downtown, centered on N 30th St, is the Old Town district, Tacoma's ancestral core, now an enclave of boutiques and restaurants.

Tacoma is 36 miles south of Seattle via I-5. A branch of the freeway, I-705, departs I-5 at exit 133, skirting the city center on its way north. This becomes Schuster Parkway, and later Ruston Way, a shoreline drive paralleled by a waterfront walking and biking path, and eventually reaches Point Defiance Park at the northern end of the city. From there, a ferry departs for Vashon Island.

Hwy 16 branches west off I-5 at the interstate's southward bend and crosses the impressive Tacoma Narrows Bridge, leading to Gig Harbor and Bremerton on the Kitsap Peninsula.

Information

Look for tourist information at the Tacoma–Pierce County Convention & Visitors Bureau (☎ 800-272-2662, W www .traveltacoma.com), 1001 Pacific Ave, suite 400, open 8:30am to 5pm weekdays; or stop by their branch office at the Washington State History Museum.

The downtown post office is at 1102 A St. For an Internet connection, visit the Tacoma Public Library, 1102 Tacoma Ave S; nonmembers must purchase an access card ($2) for each day of Internet use.

The *Tacoma News Tribune* is the daily paper of record. King's Books (☎ 253-272-8801, 753 St Helens Ave) is a highly browsable secondhand bookstore with a substantial selection of local history and travel books.

For NPR news, along with a steady diet of jazz and blues, tune into 88.5 FM KPLU, the Pacific Lutheran University station.

St Joseph's Medical Center (☎ 253-627-4101) is at 1717 South J St and offers full medical facilities.

TACOMA

PLACES TO STAY
10 Commencement Bay B&B
18 Plum Duff House
33 Travel Inn Motel
53 Sheraton Tacoma Hotel

PLACES TO EAT
6 Anthony's at Point Defiance
8 Antique Sandwich Company
11 Katie Downs
12 Grazie
15 Harbor Lights
22 Engine House No 9
24 Primo Grill
25 Shakabrah Java
30 Harmon Pub & Brewery

34 Freighthouse Square Market
36 Bob's Java Jive
39 Tully's
40 Ravenous Restaurant

OTHER
1 Gig Harbor Viewpoint
2 Fort Nisqually Historic Site
3 Camp 6 Logging Museum
4 Point Defiance Zoo & Aquarium
5 Formal Gardens
7 Point Defiance-Tahlequah Ferry; Boathouse Marina
13 Job Carr's Cabin
14 Spar Tavern; Spar Coffee Bar

16 Stadium High School
17 Tacoma Little Theater
20 Seymour Botanical Conservatory
21 Enterprise Rent-A-Car
23 Jazzbones
26 St Joseph's Medical Center
27 Museum of Glass
28 Courthouse; Union Station
29 The Swiss
31 Washington State History Museum
32 Greyhound Bus Depot
35 Tacoma Dome
37 King's Books
38 Drake's
41 Totem Pole

42 Rialto Theater
43 Pantages Theater
44 Children's Museum of Tacoma
45 Theatre on the Square
46 Olympia Express Bus Stop
47 Farmers Market
48 Destiny's
49 Tacoma-Pierce County Convention & Visitors Bureau
50 Post Office
51 Tacoma Art Museum
52 Tacoma Public Library
54 Budget Rent-A-Car

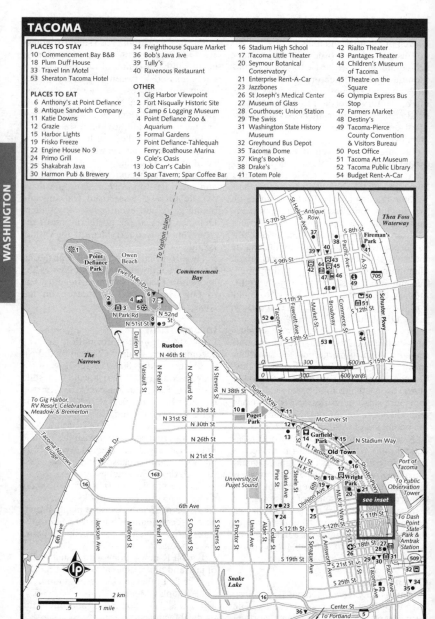

Port of Tacoma

This is the sixth-largest container port in North America, and it's the conduit for 80% of all cargo shipped to Alaska from the lower 48 states. You can view the port at work from the **Public Observation Tower** (☎ 253-383-5841, off E 11th St; admission free; open 24 hours), which features interpretive panels and a video on the port's activities.

Union Station

Start a tour of downtown Tacoma at Union Station (☎ 253-572-9310, 1717 Pacific Ave; open 8am to 5pm Mon-Fri). This enormous copper-domed neoclassical depot was designed by the same architects who built New York's Grand Central Station; it was completed in 1911. By the 1980s it had been boarded up and the surrounding red-brick warehouse neighborhood had begun to decay. The station was renovated in the early '90s and now houses the federal courts.

Step inside the airy Union Station rotunda, which is dominated by several massive installations of glass art by Tacoma native Dale Chihuly. Hanging from the center of the rotunda is a translucent three-story cluster of sensuous, deep-blue grapes; in the north-facing rosette is a collage of poppy-red glass.

To reach Union Station from either the city center or the Greyhound station, take a free Downtown Connector bus.

Washington State History Museum

Located next to Union Station and recently constructed in the same domed style is this top-notch museum (☎ 888-238-4373, W www.wshs.org, 1911 Pacific Ave; adult/senior/student/child under 6 years $7/6.25/5/free; open 10am-5pm Mon-Wed & Fri-Sat, 10am-8pm Thur, 11am-5pm Sun). The primary exhibit, in the ground-floor hall, is a chronological examination of Washington history, starting with Lewis and Clark's encounter with Native Americans and moving through the settlement era up to the present. Particularly well done are the exhibits relating to the Northwest coastal tribes; one interactive module enables you to hear the indigenous dialects of the region. The far end of the hall is dominated by an enormous topographical state map linked to a hands-on computer archive that quizzes visitors on Washingtonia. Behind the map is a multi-screen theater with a presentation on the Columbia River. The lobby bookstore is worth browsing for its excellent selection of Northwest history.

City Center

If you're dying to see more of Dale Chihuly's work after viewing the glass installation at Union Station, visit the **Tacoma Art Museum** (☎ 253-272-4258, 1123 Pacific Ave; adult/student & senior/child under 7 years $5/4/free; open 10am-5pm Tues-Wed & Fri-Sat, 10am-8pm Thur, noon-5pm Sun), which has a permanent display of some of Chihuly's more intimate (smaller) works, as well as a gallery devoted to traveling shows. The museum will be relocated adjacent to Union Station in 2003 and expanded to twice its current size. Admission to the art museum is free from 5pm to 8pm every third Thursday in coordination with Artwalk, a monthly event when a dozen downtown galleries inaugurate new exhibits. For information on participating galleries, phone ☎ 253-284-6678.

The **Children's Museum of Tacoma** (☎ 253-627-6031, 936 Broadway; adult/child 2-12 years $4/3; open 10am-5pm Tues-Sat, noon-5pm Sun) is a hands-on activity center specializing in science and technology exhibits for kids.

Every Thursday from June through mid-October, a **farmers' market** (☎ 253-272-7077) sets up along Broadway between 9th and 11th Sts. There you can find organically grown fruits, veggies and flowers from local farms, and a stage features live music and demonstrations by locally prominent chefs.

Directly north of 9th St on Broadway is **Antique Row**, a two-block-long maze of collectibles shops that lovers of bric-a-brac shouldn't miss. Follow 9th St three blocks east toward the waterfront to reach Fireman's Park – the 105-foot **totem pole** here is claimed to be one of the world's tallest.

Stadium District

Northwest of downtown is this genteel old neighborhood; a walk down N Tacoma Ave from Garfield Park takes in a number of stately Victorian homes. The most amazing structure, however, is the turreted, ivy-wrapped **Stadium High School**, at the corner of N 1st St and Broadway (from downtown, follow Commerce St north until it becomes Stadium Way). Construction began in 1891, when the building was conceived as a monumental luxury hotel, but the depression of 1893 waylaid its completion, and by the turn of the century it was slated for demolition. Fortunately, the Tacoma School District acquired the unfinished chateau-esque structure, which it opened as a much-needed high school in 1906. The result is one of the most architecturally imposing public schools anywhere.

Turn down Division Ave and continue along the east side of Wright Park, where the ornate, domed **Seymour Botanical Conservatory** (☎ 253-591-5330, 316 South G St; admission free; open 10am-4:30pm) is filled with tropical plants in the middle of a park full of native Douglas firs.

Job Carr's Cabin

This is a replica of the one-room home of Tacoma's first inhabitant, who settled here in the 1860s; he would later become the settlement's first mayor. Carr's modest abode sits roughly in its original site, in startling contrast to the bustling port town that grew up around it. Inside the low-key monument (☎ 253-627-5405, 2530 N 30th St; open 1pm-4pm Wed-Sat) are some household objects of the period. Interpretive boards display vintage photos of the early settlement.

Point Defiance Park

A 700-acre expanse of greenery flanked by the waters of Puget Sound, Point Defiance (☎ 253-305-1000, 5400 Pearl St; open dawn-dusk year round) is one Tacoma's preeminent attractions. It features a wealth of gardens, the city zoo and aquarium, and a number of recreational and historic sites.

Nearly 14 miles of hiking trails wind through groves of old-growth forests and lead to sheltered beaches. The main paved road through the park, Five Mile Dr, remains closed to motor vehicles Saturday until 1pm, though it's open to bicycles, joggers and in-line skaters. Popular picnic areas include **Gig Harbor Viewpoint** and **Owen Beach**, a favorite of summer sunbathers.

Abundant **formal gardens**, maintained cooperatively by members of local horticultural clubs, welcome visitors just past the park's main entrance. These include the Japanese Garden, with a Shinto shrine received as a gift from Kitakyushu, Tacoma's sister city in Japan; the Herb Garden; and the Rhododendron Garden, a blaze of color in May. The civic Rose Garden, established in 1895, has over an acre of bushes, many of heirloom varieties. A more recent addition is the Iris Garden, a small circular bed across from the Dahlia Trial Garden. The Northwest Native Garden, near the park's main exit, presents a collection of indigenous plants.

The **Boathouse Marina** (☎ 253-591-5325, 5912 N Waterfront Dr), near the Vashon Island ferry dock, offers boat rentals, moorage and launch facilities, as well as a tackle shop.

To reach Point Defiance from I-5, take exit 132 and follow Hwy 16 just past 6th Ave. Turn right on Pearl St, which leads 3 miles north to the park entrance. If you're on public transportation, take bus No 10 or 11 from Commerce St.

Point Defiance Zoo & Aquarium This award-winning zoo (☎ 253-591-5337; adult/senior/child 4-13 years $7.25/6.25/5.50; open 10am-4pm) is unusual in that it focuses primarily on species from the Pacific Rim, including polar bears, musk oxen and Arctic foxes. No fewer than 50 huge sharks swim among tropical fish and eels in the Discovery Reef Aquarium, while Puget Sound marine life inhabits a second tank. Observe coastline mammals through the underwater windows at Rocky Shores, or gaze at the polar bears and rare waterfowl that populate the Arctic Tundra section.

Fort Nisqually Historic Site In 1833, the Hudson's Bay Company trading post at

Fort Nisqually was established 17 miles south of Tacoma near DuPont. The area has been restored as the Fort Nisqually Historic Site (☎ 253-591-5339; adult/seniors & students/child 5-12 years $3/2/1 June-Aug, free Mon-Fri rest of year; open 11am-6pm June-Aug, 11am-4pm Wed-Sun rest of year). The restoration includes the original factor's house and granary, as well as replicas of a trade store, blacksmith shop, laborers' quarters and corner bastions, all furnished to reflect life on the frontier in the 1850s at the height of the old fort's prominence. Docents in period clothing demonstrate blacksmithing, spinning and beadwork.

Camp 6 Logging Museum An open-air exhibition, Camp 6 (☎ 253-752-0047, adult/senior & child under 13 year $3/1.75; indoor exhibits open 10am-4pm Wed-Sun Apr-Oct, outdoor exhibits open dawn-dusk year round) is a reconstruction of a pioneer logging camp focusing on the steam-powered equipment used from the 1880s to the 1940s. On spring and summer weekends only, take a ride on the logging train.

Places to Stay
For a city of its size, Tacoma offers precious few central accommodations. Most places are along the highways east and south of town.

Camping If you don't mind a short commute, this is the most economical way to go.

Dash Point State Park (☎ 253-593-2206, reservations ☎ 800-452-5687) Tent sites/hookups $13/19. Five miles northeast of downtown Tacoma (off Hwy 509) is this beachfront state park. This is a popular place in summer, when the water warms up enough for swimming.

Gig Harbor RV Resort (☎ 253-858-8138, fax 253-858-8399, 9515 Burnham Dr) Tent sites/hookups $20/38. Across the Hwy 16 Narrows Bridge on the Kitsap Peninsula, this woodsy trailer haven has a pool, playground, showers and a laundry room.

B&Bs Located in some of the older residential districts, Tacoma's B&Bs provide a sense of place that's missing from the highway chains.

Greater Tacoma B&B Reservation Service (☎ 253-759-4088, 800-406-4088, ⓦ www.tacoma-inns.org) maintains comprehensive listings of metropolitan area inns, with most in the $80 to $120 range.

Plum Duff House (☎ 253-627-6916, ⓦ www.narrows.com/plumduff, 619 North K St) Rooms $80-100. A stone's throw from the historic Stadium District, this c.1900 inn shares a tranquil neighborhood with other homes of similar vintage. There are four comfortable guest rooms with private baths, a large living room with a fireplace and a pretty front garden.

Commencement Bay B&B (☎ 253-752-8175, ⓦ www.great-views.com, 3312 N Union Ave) Rooms $110-140. Offering traditional charm and to-die-for bay views, this attractive hilltop inn has three guest rooms, all with private baths, plus a garden hot tub. There's even an office with a modem hookup for business travelers.

Hotels Moderately priced though charmless options are scattered along Pacific Hwy in Fife, an eastern suburb, and south of the center between I-5 exits 128 and 129.

Travel Inn Motel (☎ 253-383-8853, fax 253-572-4582, 2512 Pacific Ave) Single/doubles/triples $39/50/56. In the shadow of the Tacoma Dome, this generic lodging offers easy access to both Greyhound and the city center. Downtown buses stop across the way by the Elephant Car Wash, whose neon mascot is oddly reassuring in this marginal zone.

Econo Lodge North (☎ 253-922-0550, 3518 Pacific Hwy, Fife) Singles/doubles $50/60. A couple of miles east of town off I-5 exit 136, this franchise location offers guest laundry service and modem hookup, and there's a casino next door.

King Oscar Motel (☎ 888-254-5464, ⓦ www.kingoscarmotel.com, 8820 S Hosmer St) Singles/doubles $70/80. An indoor pool, sauna and free morning coffee are features of this nondescript but comfortable local chain, near exit 128.

Sheraton Tacoma Hotel (☎ 800-845-9466, ⓦ www.sheratontacoma.com, 1320

Broadway Plaza) Rooms $139, suites from $189. Just about the only place to stay downtown, the Sheraton is oriented toward expense-account travelers.

Places to Eat

Seafood dinner by the bay and classic Mediterranean fare are some of the tasty morsels on Tacoma's varied plate.

Restaurants Dining well in Tacoma won't break the bank.

Ravenous Restaurant (☎ 253-572-6374, 785 Broadway) Entrees $17-22. A good, central spot for lunch or dinner, Ravenous serves pizza, pasta and urbane Italian dishes.

Grazie (☎ 253-627-0231, 2301 N 30th St) Lunch $9-14, dinner $15-22. This Old Town trattoria offers great views of Commencement Bay from a series of dining nooks. Northern Italian specialties are their forte, but they've been causing a stir with their deli selections, which include a widely revered New York hot pastrami sandwich.

Primo Grill (☎ 253-383-7000, 601 S Pine St) Lunch $9-12, dinner $17-27. This new Italian restaurant has a stylish dining room and an extensive wine list. Their wood-fired pizzas are topped with such earthy ingredients as arugula and goat cheese.

Harbor Lights (☎ 253-752-8600, 2761 Ruston Way) Lunch $9-12, dinner $14-17. A Tacoma original, this bayside venue is a former fishermen's eatery. The clientele has changed, but not the excellent quality, the old-fashioned seafood preparations or the enormous worker's portions.

Antique Sandwich Company (☎ 253-752-4069, 5102 N Pearl St) Lunch $4-7. In Ruston on the way to Point Defiance Park is this landmark luncheonette populated by students, young families and seniors who've been coming for decades.

Anthony's at Point Defiance (☎ 253-752-9700, 5910 N Waterfront Dr) Lunch $9-14. One of a chain of 16 restaurants throughout the Puget Sound area, Anthony's Point Defiance branch offers family-style seafood dining with an emphasis on freshness. Standouts include the alder-plank-roasted salmon ($13) and clam chowder served in a sourdough bread bowl ($9). The restaurant makes the most of its spectacular setting, adjacent to the Vashon Island ferry landing.

Frisko Freeze (☎ 253-272-6843, Division Ave & North L St) Burgers $2-3. Forget McDonald's – follow the neon arrow to this relic of the pre-espresso era. Drive-in standards include tasty burgers, shakes and Frisko fries.

Freighthouse Square Market (S 25th St & East D St) The converted railroad warehouse behind the Tacoma Dome has an assortment of quirky boutiques and a 'food court' with a range of inexpensive ethnic eateries.

Brewpubs & Beer Halls Tacoma offers plenty of spots where you can kick back and enjoy a brew with your meal.

Harmon Pub & Brewery (☎ 253-383-2739, 1938 Pacific Ave S) Entrees $9-14. Housed in a renovated brick warehouse across from the history museum, the handsome (and smoke-free) brewpub draws four trademark homemade ales plus seasonal brews, some of which serve as ingredients for their hearty entrees.

Engine House No 9 (☎ 253-272-3435, 611 N Pine St by 6th St) Snacks $7-9. Open 11am-2am. Yes, it really was a fire engine house, as the array of firefighting paraphernalia will attest. The boisterous brewpub has a great selection of beers and ciders on tap as well as sandwiches, pizzas and salads.

Katie Downs (☎ 253-756-0771, 3211 Ruston Way) Pizzas from $12. Open 11am-midnight. On the waterfront, Katie Downs is a popular place to grab a beer (they have 21 kinds on tap) and a pizza or some steamer clams. There is seating on an outdoor deck with a great view of the sound.

Spar Tavern (☎ 253-627-8215, 2121 N 30th St) If you're in Old Town, check out this classy early-20th-century bar that's now pouring local microbrews. Attached is the Spar Coffee Bar, a cozy corner for cappuccino and fresh croissants.

The Swiss (☎ 253-572-2821, 1904 S Jefferson Ave) Pub fare $6-9. The old Swiss Society Hall has been lovingly converted into this cavernous pub and recreation center, featuring 36 brews on tap, plus six pool tables, darts and live bands or DJs most nights. Check the blackboard for the evening's choice of sandwiches, salads and pastas.

Coffeehouses Coffee isn't as much a part of local culture as in Seattle, but Tacoma offers a few laid-back options.

Tully's (☎ 253-627-5646, 764 Broadway) When the Starbucks-style chain took over this space in the old wedge-shaped Hotel Bostwick, they wisely left the easy chairs and comfy couches that make it such an inviting place to lounge around with a latte. Light fare includes gourmet pastries, biscotti and bagels.

Shakabrah Java (☎ 253-572-4369, 2618 6th Ave) Offering a fine selection of looseleaf teas as well as the full range of coffee concoctions, Shakabrah also serves as a venue for local musical talent.

Bob's Java Jive (☎ 253-475-9843, 2102 S Tacoma Way) A Tacoma institution, the Jive served as a speakeasy, when the entrance was through the ladies' room. Today it's a scream of tacky furniture, pool tables and jukeboxes with a menu of cheap sandwiches, burgers and domestic beer. Look for the pre-fab, larger-than-life coffeepot, built in 1927 by a local veterinarian.

Entertainment

To find out what's happening in Tacoma, pick up the free *Tacoma Reporter*.

Performing Arts Three major venues house most of Tacoma's theater and classical-music productions.

Broadway Center for the Performing Arts (☎ 253-591-5894, Ⓦ www.broadway center.org, 901 Broadway) Comprised of the ornate Pantages Theater, Rialto Theater and Theatre on the Square, all within a three-block stretch of S 9th St, the complex has galvanized the cultural scene in downtown Tacoma since its inception in 1983. Once an elaborate vaudeville hall, the 1100-seat Pantages is today Tacoma's premier performance venue, hosting the Tacoma Opera, the BalleTacoma dance company, the Tacoma Symphony Orchestra and world-class touring artists. The Theatre on the Square,

adjacent to the Pantages, is the home of the Tacoma Actors Guild (☎ 253-272-2145), which performs six shows a season ranging from the classics to contemporary works. A few blocks west, the Rialto is the showcase for the Northwest Sinfonietta chamber ensemble and the Tacoma Youth Symphony. To find out about upcoming events at the Broadway Center, visit the website.

Performance Circle (☎ 253-851-7529) In summer, this Gig Harbor organization stages open-air drama productions at Celebrations Meadow across the Narrows.

Tacoma Little Theater (☎ 253-272-2281, 210 N I St) Established in 1909, this community theater in the Stadium District produces plays for both children and adults.

Clubs As fiercely loyal locals will tell you, you don't have to go to Seattle for a good time.

Drake's (☎ 253-572-4144, 734 Pacific Ave) Cover $5-8. Tacoma's premier dance club delivers live music Thursday to Saturday nights.

Destiny's (☎ 253-627-0987, 754 Pacific Ave) The spacious dance floor at this gay-oriented club next door to Drake's is busiest Thursday to Sunday nights; Sundays there's a drag show.

Cole's Oasis (☎ 253-879-1119, 5811 N 51st St) Cover $2 Fri & Sat. Get to know the local blues scene at this neat little Ruston club.

Jazzbones (☎ 253-396-9169, 2803 6th Ave) Cover $5-10 Fri & Sat. Despite the name, the blues prevails here as well. The stylish supper club has live music nightly plus an array of cocktails.

Tacoma Dome (☎ 253-572-3663, Ⓦ www .tacomadome.org) Though it's home of the West Coast Hockey League's Tacoma Sabercats, the 23,000 capacity dome is more a trade show and mega-concert venue than a sports arena.

Getting There & Away

Fast, frequent public transportation provides easy access to Puget Sound points and the Olympic Peninsula via Olympia.

Bus Greyhound (☎ 253-383-4621) links Tacoma to Seattle ($5/8 one way/roundtrip), Portland ($23/40) and other cities along the

I-5 corridor, arriving at and departing from the Tacoma Dome station, 510 Puyallup Ave. Sound Transit (☎ 800-201-4900) routes 590 and 594 travel between Tacoma and Seattle (one way $2.50/1.25 adult/senior) with frequent service from around 7am to 10pm weekdays, less often on weekends. These use both the Tacoma Dome and downtown (10th & Commerce) stations.

Intercity Transit (☎ 800-287-6348, W www .intercitytransit.com) offers Olympia Express service (one hour, adult/senior $1.50/75¢) daily except Sunday. The bus stop is either 10th & Commerce or the Park & Ride at Hwy 512 (with connections downtown by Pierce Transit).

Train Four Amtrak trains a day link Tacoma to Seattle (1 hour, $14 one way) and Portland (2¾ hours, $28) from the depot at 1001 Puyallup Ave (reservations ☎ 800-872-7245). In addition, Sound Transit (☎ 800-201-4900) runs a pair of rush-hour commuter trains to Seattle between 6am and 7am, returning between 6pm and 7pm (one hour, adult/senior $4/2). Trains use a temporary platform on the north side of Puyallup Ave, at the foot of F St, until late 2002, when a permanent station should be installed on E 25th St beside the Freighthouse Square mall.

Car For a rental vehicle, contact either Enterprise (☎ 253-573-1055), 455 St Helens Ave, or Budget Rent-A-Car (☎ 253-383-4944), 1305 Pacific Ave, both in downtown Tacoma.

Ferry Washington State Ferries (☎ 206-464-6400) between Point Defiance and Vashon Island run from about 6am to 10pm (15 minutes, $13 vehicle and driver, $2.90 additional passenger in peak season).

Getting Around
Capital Aeroporter (☎ 253-927-6179) runs 15 buses daily between Tacoma-area points and Sea-Tac (45 minutes, $20-25 one way). The downtown stop is the Sheraton, 1320 Broadway; they'll stop at your hotel by request. Reservations are required.

Pierce Transit (☎ 800-562-8109, W www .piercetransit.org) has service throughout the Tacoma area. Bus No 11 runs from downtown to Stadium High School, Wright Park and the Vashon Island ferry; No 100 goes to Gig Harbor (regular/senior $1/50¢). The free Downtown Connector service makes a loop between the Tacoma Dome station and the city center every 15 minutes.

For a taxi, call Yellow Cab (☎ 253-472-3303).

AROUND TACOMA
Pierce County holds a great deal of interest for those attuned to history and nature.

Lakewold Gardens
Situated on a 10-acre estate from the early 1900s, Lakewold (☎ 888-858-4106, W www .lakewold.org, 12317 Gravelly Lake Dr; adult/senior & student $5/3, child under 12 years free; open 10am-4pm Thur-Mon Apr-Sept, 10am-3pm Fri-Sun Oct-Mar) is one of the Northwest's finest private gardens. Especially notable are the rhododendrons, which number in the hundreds, and exotic trees chosen for their multicolored and many-shaped foliage.

To get to the gardens, take I-5 south to exit 124, which leads onto Gravelly Lake Dr.

Steilacoom
Founded in 1851 by a New England sea captain, Steilacoom (**shtil**-la-cum) is Washington's oldest incorporated town. After the establishment of a hotel, store and sawmill, Steilacoom was up and running, and for a couple of decades it was an important destination for newly arriving settlers. It didn't take long for nearby Tacoma to overwhelm the little village, especially after the railroad brought galloping development to the area.

The old town center boasts 32 buildings on the National Register of Historic Places, most dating from the late 1800s; many are open for viewing, including the **Steilacoom Historical Museum** (☎ 253-584-4133, 1717 Lafayette St; open 1pm-4pm Tues-Sun May-Oct, Fri-Sun only Nov-Dec and Feb-Apr).

The **Steilacoom Tribal Cultural Center** (☎ 253-584-6308, 1515 Lafayette St; adult/

senior & student $2/1, child under 6 years free; open 10am-4pm Tues-Sun) presents the history of the Steilacoom tribe, whose members numbered 700 at last count. There's a gift shop and a snack bar serving Native American foods.

Steilacoom is 15 miles south of Tacoma on the Puget Sound. From I-5, take exit 129 west, following Steilacoom Blvd.

Fort Lewis Military Museum

Fort Lewis is a large army training camp that was established in 1917 as the USA entered WWI. Pacific Northwest military history from Lewis and Clark onward is retold at the museum *(☎ 253-967-7206; admission free; open noon-4pm Wed-Sun)*.

Perhaps more notable than its contents – mostly old uniforms and equipment – is the museum building itself. The chalet-like structure was built in 1919 by the Salvation Army as a 150-room inn to provide R&R for local military personnel and their guests, and it served as the fort's social center for decades. To get to Fort Lewis and the museum, take I-5 exit 120 west and turn left at the first stoplight.

Northwest Trek Wildlife Park

Northwest native wildlife roams freely at this well-planned facility *(☎ 360-832-6117, ⓦ www.nwtrek.org, 11610 Trek Dr; adult/senior/youth 5-17 years/child 3-4 years $8.75/8.25/6/4; open 9:30am-dusk Apr-Oct; 9:30am-dusk Fri-Sun Nov-Mar)*. Grizzly bears, cougars and wolves live in large natural outdoor enclosures; bison, elk, deer and caribou range pretty much as they see fit in a 435-acre meadow and forest. Trams circle through much of the park, with naturalists leading an hourlong tour.

Northwest Trek is 35 miles south of Tacoma off Hwy 161. Take I-5 south to Hwy 512 east, which leads to Hwy 161 south.

OLYMPIA

Olympia (population 42,514) is a city known to most for its beer and its politics, and as such, it may not initially seem like an obvious magnet for travelers. As Washington's oldest settlement and the state capital, Olympia could easily be just another one of those sleepy, 'insiders-only' towns whose most interesting moments occurred 100 years ago. In fact, Olympia is a vital city – together with sister cities Lacey and Tumwater, the urban area has a population of over 85,000 – with a strong alternative community.

Part of the reason for the vitality of Olympia is its position as the state capital, which keeps political issues in the forefront. But no small part of the equation is Evergreen State College, an innovative public university with 3100 students, which was founded in 1971 as a result of the student movements of the 1960s. Classes, programs and degrees are usually interdisciplinary, multiethnic and relatively unstructured, attracting students and faculty with progressive, out-of-the-mainstream ideas. In fact, Lynda Barry *(Ernie Pook's Comeek)* and Matt Groening (creator of *The Simpsons*) went to school together there. When you find that Olympia offers better music, cinema, coffee and just-under-the-surface hipness than you might expect, thank Evergreen.

Olympia makes a good base for exploring western Washington. Both Mt Rainier and Olympic National Parks are within an hour's drive, and Pacific Coast beaches are just 60 miles away at Ocean Shores.

Olympia made headlines in March 2001 when an earthquake centered just to its north sent tremors through the region, unleashing much of its destructive force on Seattle, 60 miles away. Hundreds of structures,

***The Simpsons* creator, Matt Groening**

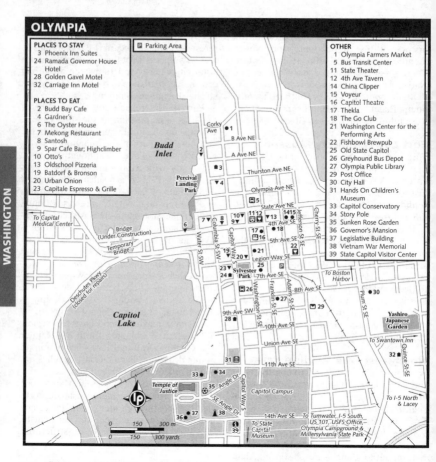

OLYMPIA

□ Parking Area

PLACES TO STAY
3 Phoenix Inn Suites
24 Ramada Governor House Hotel
28 Golden Gavel Motel
32 Carriage Inn Motel

PLACES TO EAT
2 Budd Bay Cafe
4 Gardner's
6 The Oyster House
7 Mekong Restaurant
8 Santosh
9 Spar Cafe Bar; Highclimber
10 Otto's
18 Oldschool Pizzeria
19 Batdorf & Bronson
20 Urban Onion
23 Capitale Espresso & Grille

OTHER
1 Olympia Farmers Market
5 Bus Transit Center
11 State Theater
12 4th Ave Tavern
14 China Clipper
15 Voyeur
16 Capitol Theatre
17 Thekla
18 The Go Club
21 Washington Center for the Performing Arts
22 Fishbowl Brewpub
25 Old State Capitol
26 Greyhound Bus Depot
27 Olympia Public Library
29 Post Office
30 City Hall
31 Hands On Children's Museum
33 Capitol Conservatory
34 Story Pole
35 Sunken Rose Garden
36 Governor's Mansion
37 Legislative Building
38 Vietnam War Memorial
39 State Capitol Visitor Center

including the capitol itself, were damaged, but the human toll was miraculously slight.

History

The lower reaches of Puget Sound were home to the Nisqually, a Salish tribe. Unlike most coastal tribes, the Nisqually maintained large herds of horses, which they pastured in the lowlands of the Nisqually River valley.

The first US settlement in Washington was founded at Tumwater, along the falls of the Deschutes River, when a group of 32 Missourians arrived in 1845. They chose to settle north of the Columbia in British-dominated territory because some of the party's members had African blood – including their leader, George Bush – and Oregon's territorial laws forbade settlement by blacks. Access to waterpower and to the harbor at Budd Inlet propelled the new settlement into industrialization. By 1850, the settlement (then called 'New Market') boasted a gristmill, sawmill, tannery and other small factories. Beer brewing was another early industry.

Olympia was Washington's principal settlement when it was named the territorial capital in 1853. The first legislative sessions met above a bar, then were moved to a local

Masonic lodge. The construction of a permanent capitol was not begun until 1893; due to economic vicissitudes, it was completed only in 1928. During much of this time, the old Thurston County Courthouse served as Washington's state capitol.

Orientation

Olympia is at the southern end of Puget Sound. Immediately south of town is Tumwater, and east on Hwy 510 is Lacey. A number of road systems intersect at Olympia. I-5 passes through, running between Seattle (60 miles away) and Portland (114 miles). Hwy 101 runs northwest, leading to the Hood Canal and Olympic Peninsula; Hwy 8 branches off 101 west to Aberdeen (50 miles).

Olympia is dominated by the Washington state capitol campus, which rises on a bluff above Capitol Lake (formed by damming the Deschutes River). From I-5, exit 105 feeds into 14th Ave, leading directly to the capitol and to Capitol Way, the main north-south street through downtown.

The fingerlike intrusions of Budd Inlet and Capitol Lake serve to divide the city into eastern and western halves, and Olympians often refer to 'westside' and 'eastside' districts of the city. The 4th Ave bridge, which spanned the inlet, was knocked out by the earthquake of 2001. Traffic will use a temporary two-lane bridge during construction of a new 4th Ave bridge, scheduled for completion in late 2003.

Information

The State Capitol Visitor Center (☎ 360-586-3460), right off the freeway at 14th Ave and Capitol Way, offers information on both the capitol campus and the Olympia area. Backcountry permits for wilderness camping in Olympic National Park can be obtained from the USFS office (☎ 360-956-2300), 1835 Black Lake Blvd, west of town.

Olympia's central post office is at 900 Jefferson St, 98507. For medical emergencies, go to Capital Medical Center (☎ 360-754-5858), 3900 Capital Mall Dr. To do laundry, head for Eastside Laundry & Cleaners (☎ 360-352-2575), 122 Turner St, near the Thriftway store

between 4th Ave and State St. Check email at no cost at the Olympia Public Library (☎ 360-352-0595), at Franklin and 8th Ave.

State Capitol Campus

The Washington state capitol sits in a 30-acre, parklike setting above Capitol Lake, with beautiful views of the Olympic Mountains across Budd Inlet. This campus holds the majority of the state's official buildings, including the vast domed **Legislative Building** *(admission free; open 8am-4:30pm)*, completed in 1927. At the time of its construction, the capitol's 287-foot dome was the fourth largest in the world (exceeded only by the US Capitol, St Paul's in London and St Peter's in Rome); the chandelier hanging in the rotunda was made by Louis Tiffany.

Tremors from the 2001 earthquake caused the dome to momentarily bounce off its base, and the supporting columns shifted slightly in the process, causing pieces of their stone segments to come loose. Though most of the damages resulting from the quake have been repaired, the event prompted a major renovation of the building, due to go on from June 2002 till as late as 2006.

Across the plaza from the Legislative Building is the **Temple of Justice** *(admission free; open 8am-5pm Mon-Fri year-round)*, the supreme court building, flanked by sandstone colonnades and lined in the interior by an oppressive quantity of marble. The **Capitol Conservatory** *(admission free; open 8am-4pm Mon-Fri)* is just to the north. On display here is a large collection of tropical and subtropical plants; the flowers for official state occasions are also grown here.

The oldest building on the campus is the **Governor's Mansion**, built in 1908. The home of the governor is open for tours only on Wednesdays; call ☎ 360-586-8687 to reserve a space. Outdoor attractions include the **Vietnam War Memorial**, a sunken rose garden, and various fountains and monumental sculptures. Also located here is a 71-foot **Story Pole**, carved by Snohomish Chief William Shelton during the 1930s on the invitation of the state governor. A free guided tour of these sites is given at 1:30pm from June to August.

WASHINGTON

State Capital Museum

A few blocks south of the campus, this museum (☎ 360-753-2580, 211 W 21st Ave; adult/senior/student $2/1.75/1; open 10am-4pm Tues-Fri, noon-4pm Sat & Sun) is housed in the 1920s Lord Mansion. Exhibits present the general history of Olympia and Washington state, focusing on the move toward statehood. Also included are displays re-creating aspects of the everyday life of the Nisqually Indians, including a longhouse.

Old State Capitol

In 1903, the state government recycled the 1891 Thurston County Courthouse by turning it into the state capitol for nearly 25 years, while the current Legislative Building was very slowly being built. In its heyday, this Romanesque-revival structure (☎ 360-753-6725, 600 S Washington St; admission free; open to visitors 8am-noon, 1-5pm Mon-Fri), across from Sylvester Park, was even more commanding. Its nine-story central tower burned in 1928, and the building's 11 turrets fell off during a 1949 earthquake. The old capitol is now the office for the State Superintendent of Public Instruction. Pick up a brochure for a self-guided tour at the 2nd-floor reception area.

Percival Landing Park

When Olympia was established, its narrow harbor was a mudflat during low tides. After years of dredging, Olympia's harbor is still small potatoes compared to the busy ports of commerce at Tacoma and Seattle, and these days it mostly serves as a marina for pleasure boats. Essentially a boardwalk along the harbor, the park makes a pleasant half-mile stroll, especially when the Olympic Mountains sparkle across the bay. At the north end is an observation tower.

Olympia Farmers Market

One of Olympia's pleasures is this festive market at the north end of town (☎ 360-352-9096, 700 Capitol Way N; open 10am-3pm Thur-Sun Apr-Oct, Sat & Sun Nov-Dec). Browse around for organic herbs and vegetables, flowers, baked goods, toys and crafts, and grab a snack at one of the numerous international-food stalls.

Yashiro Japanese Garden

This small garden (☎ 360-753-8380, 900 Plum St; admission free; open 10am-10pm) is a collaborative effort between Olympia and its Japanese sister city, Yashiro. Highlights include a bamboo grove, pagoda and a pond and waterfall; stone lanterns and other gifts from Yashiro adorn the grounds. The garden is adjacent to Olympia City Hall.

Hands On Children's Museum

Kids will be enthralled by this fun-filled learning center (☎ 360-956-0818, 106 11th Ave; admission $3.50; open 10am-5pm Tues-Sat, noon-5pm Sun), just north of the capitol campus. Creative exhibits on human anatomy and nature include a simulated X-ray machine and a TV studio where children create their own weather reports. There's also an art studio and a special toddlers zone.

Canoeing & Sea Kayaking

Rent a canoe or sea kayak from **Boston Harbor Marina** (☎ 360-357-5670, 312 73rd Ave; from $15/45 per hour/day) and explore the bays of lower Puget Sound. To reach Boston Harbor, follow East Bay Dr from downtown; the marina is about 6 miles north.

Special Events

Olympia's big summer festival is Harbor Days (☎ 800-788-8847, Ⓦ www.harbordays.com), held on Labor Day weekend, when Budd Inlet becomes the scene of tugboat races and the Percival Landing boardwalk is lined with food and craft booths. Arts Walk (☎ 360-709-2678) puts the spotlight on the capital's visual artists with special exhibits at downtown galleries and businesses. The event is held on a Friday evening in April and October. On April 21 (Earth Day), the whole community takes to the streets costumed as their favorite fauna or flora for the Procession of the Species (☎ 360-705-1087), a whimsical and uniquely Olympian celebration.

Places to Stay

If you're planning to spend a night or two in the capital, pack a tent or carry a credit card – or better yet, find some hospitable Evergreen students.

Camping There are two options for campers around Olympia.

Olympia Campground (☎ 360-352-2551, 1441 83rd Ave, off I-5 exit 101) Tent sites/hookups/camper cabins $19/25/39. Open year round. A heated pool (in summer), free showers, a game room and good TV reception are among the amenities at this full-service campground, 4 miles south of downtown.

Millersylvania State Park (☎ 360-753-1519, Tilley Rd off I-5 exit 95) Tent sites/hookups $14/20. Forgo the RV-park scene for this public facility, 6 miles farther south. Activities here include hiking, lake fishing and swimming.

Hotels & B&Bs Room rates tend to be steep if you're not on a lobbyist's expense account. If you're just passing through, try the cluster of motels out at I-5 exit 102 in Tumwater, which includes most of the chains.

Carriage Inn Motel (☎ 360-943-4710, 1211 Quince St) Singles/doubles $50/55. This older motel has pleasant if ordinary units in two shingle-topped buildings plus an outdoor pool. It's within walking distance of Yashiro Japanese Garden.

Golden Gavel Motel (☎ 360-352-8533, W www.goldengavelmotel.com, 909 Capitol Way S) Singles/doubles $50/57. Stay right downtown at this carefully maintained lodging, easily spotted by the sculpted gavel at the entrance.

Swantown Inn (☎ 360-753-9123, W www .olywa.net/swantown, 1431 11th Ave) Singles/doubles $70-105/80-115. In a quiet neighborhood east of downtown, this 1890s home, now a B&B, is listed on the state historic register. The capitol dome can be glimpsed from three of the four elegantly furnished rooms. Innkeeper Lillian speaks German.

Phoenix Inn Suites (☎ 360-570-0555, 877-570-0555, W www.phoenixinnsuites.city search.com, 415 Capitol Way N) Singles/doubles $99/109. This just-unwrapped inn

sits a block from Percival Landing Park. Large units come with leather couches and lounge space, and there's an indoor pool.

Ramada Governor House Hotel (☎ 360-352-7700, e 198@hotel.cendant .com, 621 Capitol Way S) Doubles $160. Dominating Sylvester Park's west side, the eight-story Ramada has an outdoor pool, fitness center, restaurant and convention facilities.

Places to Eat

Dozens of restaurants and cafes crowd the streets of downtown Olympia; even so, you may have to compete for a table in this out-to-eat culture.

Budget Java joints and trendy snack bars cater to an impoverished student population.

Batdorf & Bronson (☎ 360-786-6717, 513 Capitol Way S) The aroma of fresh-roasted java permeates this popular espresso bar, an obligatory stop for coffee connoisseurs.

Otto's (☎ 360-352-8640, 111 N Washington St) Otto's is a big, airy cafe offering excellent fresh bagels, healthful breakfasts and all the espresso variations.

Spar Cafe Bar (☎ 360-357-6444, 114 4th Ave E) Breakfast $4-5, lunch $5-8. There's no better place for a traditional breakfast than this old-fashioned, wood-paneled diner, cigar shop, newsstand and bar combo that hasn't changed since the 1930s.

Urban Onion (☎ 360-943-9242, 116 Legion Way E) Lunch $7. Though the 2001 quake sent a few cracks through its walls, this long-standing vegetarian restaurant in the old Hotel Olympian continues serving up tofu scrambles and vegan burgers.

Oldschool Pizzeria (☎ 360-786-9640, 108 Franklin St) Pizzas $8.50-19. Students gather at this casual place for thick-crust pizza served by the slice.

Mid-Range Worldly palates will find plenty of places for authentic international fare.

Mekong Restaurant (☎ 360-352-9620, 125 N Columbia St) Entrees $7-9. The local favorite for Thai food, Mekong offers an extensive array of meatless options.

Capitale Espresso & Grille (☎ *360-352-8007, 609 Capitol Way S*) Entrees $10-12. Adventurous eaters will go for Capitale's intriguing melange of Asian, Tex-Mex and Mediterranean flavors.

Santosh (☎ *360-943-3442, 116 4th Ave W*) Entrees $8-13. Budget travelers should try Santosh's Indian lunch buffet (under $6).

Top End Not surprisingly, the state capital boasts a number of fine dining establishments – all the better to schmooze in.

Gardner's (☎ *360-786-8466, 111 W Thurston Ave*) Dinner $16-21. Open 5pm-9pm Tues-Sat. Gardner's serves the city's best seafood, pasta and steaks.

Budd Bay Cafe (☎ *360-357-6963, 525 N Columbia St*) Entrees $16-20. For a table with a view, make reservations at this prime-rib and shellfish place right above the marina on Percival Landing. On Sunday there's a popular champagne brunch.

The Oyster House (☎ *360-753-7000, 320 W 4th Ave*) Seafood dinners $15-20. At the edge of the harbor in the old culling house of the Olympia Oyster Company, this family-style restaurant serves its trademark mollusk in stews, pan-fried or straight up.

Entertainment

For a town of such modest proportions, Olympia enjoys a very active nightlife.

Performing Arts & Cinemas There are some good options for theater and film.

Washington Center for the Performing Arts (☎ *360-753-8586, 512 Washington St*) This is Olympia's primary venue for national touring shows and other cultural activities.

State Theater (☎ *360-786-0151, 202 4th Ave E*) Harlequin Productions stages an eclectic lineup of contemporary plays and classics here.

Capitol Theatre (☎ *360-754-6670, 206 E 5th Ave*) This foreign- and independent-film cinema commands the kind of local devotion you'd expect in a small, intellectual community. The theater also hosts the occasional touring rock or rap act, and on Friday evenings backstage is where to catch local bands.

Coffeehouses, Brewpubs & Clubs Saunter down 4th Ave E to find handfuls of trendy nightspots. You're more likely to spot local artists, students and stylishly disenfranchised youth than lobbyists.

Highclimber (☎ *360-357-6444, 114 4th Ave E*) The handsome back room of the Spar Cafe Bar (see Places to Eat) makes a cozy setting for cigar smoking and conversation, or, on Saturday nights, live music.

4th Ave Tavern (☎ *360-786-1444, 210 4th Ave E*) This retrofitted bar is one of the best places to catch local bands Friday and Saturday nights.

China Clipper (☎ *360-943-6300, 402 4th Ave E*) A smoky lounge and throbbing dance floor are the main attractions at this raucous joint patronized by all sorts.

The Go Club (☎ *360-704-7278, 311 4th Ave E*) Appealing to a somewhat more mature crowd, the softly lit Go Club hosts a range of acts, from stand-up comedy to folk and rap.

Voyeur (☎ *360-943-5710, 404 4th Ave E*) This is the place for late-night cups of chai and postfilm discussions. The back room is a performance space for Evergreen's bohemian community.

Fishbowl Brewpub (☎ *360-943-3650, 515 Jefferson St*) Fishbowl serves their own English-style ales, brewed across the way in the merrily painted Fish Tale brewery. The self-proclaimed 'Cascadian Consulate & Cultural Center' presents live music Monday and Saturday evenings and serves fine pub fare – a huge seafood stew is $6.75.

Thekla (☎ *360-352-1855, 425 Franklin St*) Cover $2-5. Open 5pm-10pm Tues-Sun. The music changes nightly at Olympia's premier dance club, but the clientele remains a friendly, gay-straight hodgepodge. Dinner is served 5pm to 10pm nightly.

Getting There & Away

Six Greyhound buses a day link Olympia to Seattle (1¾ hours, $8) and other I-5-corridor cities from its station at 107 7th Ave E (☎ 360-357-5541). Intercity Transit's Olympia Express (☎ 360-786-1881) travels to and from Tacoma (one hour, adult/senior $1.50/75¢), with connections on to Seattle by Sound Transit. These run every half-hour at

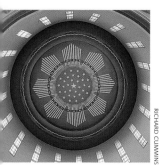

Oregon's lovely coastal dunes (beware of dune buggies!)

Heceta Head Lighthouse (1894)

interior dome of capitol, Salem

Mirror Lake and the Wallowas, northeastern Oregon

A real-life Narnia – Wizard Island at dusk, Crater Lake National Park

RICHARD I'ANSON

Seattle's 1962 Space Needle gives the city a *Jetsons* feel.

RICHARD CUMMINS

Two things Seattle's famous for

TED STRESHINSKY

Stay dry in Pioneer Square, Seattle

RICHARD I'ANSON

Shore of Bainbridge Island, land of the ferry commuter

Grrrl Talk

Tammy Fortin, of the San Francisco band Blue Gum Art, talks about Olympia's riot grrrl scene with Donna Dresch, founder of Chainsaw Records and former member of Team Dresch, Dinosaur Jr and the Screaming Trees.

TF: Seattle, the grunge capital, and Olympia, home of the riot grrrl scene, are only about 45 minutes apart (if you *really* speed). Why the difference?

DD: The difference was more extreme in the '90s. Now that there aren't that many major labels pounding on every band's door, there is less 'urgent grandstanding.' Joe Preston [of the Thrones, formerly of the Melvins] just said that. A big difference is the fact that the rent in Olympia is cheap enough that sometimes you can get away without having a real job. If you live in an expensive city and have to make a lot of money to afford your rent, then you can't be as independent and risky with your music. I think the liberal arts college here, Evergreen, draws in a highly concentrated group of freaky people. And because of Evergreen, there are a lot more women involved in the music scene – especially a lot more feminists, who attract more women to move here...and they tell two friends....

TF: Who are some of the most influential bands to come out of Olympia, and where do they play in town?

DD: Bikini Kill, Beat Happening, Unwound, the Thrones, Tracy & the Plastics, the Need, my really great band [Team Dresch], Sleater-Kinney, Lois, Heavens to Betsy, Bratmobile (sorta). Bands like this play the Capital Theater, the Voyeur...but right now, there is no real solid place. Clubs start up and close quickly.

TF: Olympia's DIY [do-it-yourself] attitude has inspired countless indie labels. Who are the folks behind the music, and how did the movement get started?

DD: Rain. And boredom. Olympia is a small town, and there's not much to do unless you make something up. Being in a band is a great way to escape the rain...especially if you get to tour some- place fancy like Australia for the winter. K Records led the way for the DIY labels – Calvin Johnson started K in his living room, where he dubbed cassette after cassette of local bands, friends' bands – all in his little homemade factory. The idea was conta- gious. In 2001, the Ladyfest [an all women's music-and-arts fes- tival] organizers got on stage and said, 'There. We made a festival, now go do it yourself.' And they did.

peak periods, less frequently at other times, departing from the Olympia Transit Center (see Getting Around). Grays Harbor Transportation Authority (☎ 360-532-2770, 800-562-9730) offers bus service to Aberdeen on the Pacific coast (1½ hours, $2).

Amtrak (☎ 360-923-4602) stops at its station in Lacey at 6600 Yelm Hwy; four trains a day link Olympia with Seattle and Portland. Bus No 64 goes between the station and downtown hourly 6:30am to 7:30pm.

Getting Around
The Capital Aeroporter (☎ 360-754-7113) has frequent service to Sea-Tac, leaving from Phoenix Inn Suites, 415 Capitol Way N (2 hours, $24). Reservations are suggested.

Olympia's public bus system is Intercity Transit (☎ 360-786-1881, 800-287-6348). The downtown transit center is at State Ave and Washington St. Some key routes are No 41 to Evergreen College, No 42 to the capitol campus and No 13 to Tumwater. Standard fare is 60¢; exact change is required. For a cab, call Capitol City Taxi (☎ 360-357-4949).

AROUND OLYMPIA

Within easy reach of the capital are vestiges of the first white settlement on Puget Sound, as well as a pair of unique wildlife preserves.

Tumwater

At the lowest of the three falls on the Deschutes River, **Tumwater Historical Park** *(☎ 360-754-4160; open 8am-6:30pm)* occupies the site of Olympia's original pioneer settlement, the first American community to put down roots north of the Columbia. A nature trail along the river leads down to a wetlands area at the edge of Capitol Lake. Deschutes Falls is the site of a lot of anadromous activity from mid-September to mid-October, when the Deschutes River Chinook salmon run begins. Stand on the viewing platform to watch the fish throw themselves up the falls and climb the fish ladders.

Although the passage of I-5 through this historic corridor obliterated many old homes and buildings, a few remain. Occupying the 1905 home of a German immigrant who prospered off the local brewing industry, the **Henderson House Museum** *(☎ 360-754-4163, 602 Deschutes Way; adult/child $2/1; open 1pm-4pm Thur, Fri & Sun)* contains artifacts and displays of pioneer life and early industry in Tumwater.

Forget regional microbrews for a moment and tour the **Tumwater Brewery** *(☎ 360-754-5217; admission free; open 9am-4:30pm Mon-Sat)*, one of the largest breweries in the West. The former Olympic Brewery has been producing beer since 1896, and it ranks right up there with the state government as the city's largest employer. Miller Brewing, America's second largest brewer, acquired the local institution (from Pabst) in 1999 to produce its popular Lite beer, among other brands. The free 45-minute tour through the fermentation tanks to the tasting room is interesting. The brewery is on Capitol Blvd,

immediately east of I-5 exit 103 in Tumwater; you can't miss it. Take bus No 12 or 13.

Get an eyeful of Deschutes Falls (and the brewery) at *Falls Terrace (☎ 360-943-7830, 106 S Deschutes Way)*. Entrees run around $15, and it's open for lunch and dinner. Offerings include the Northwestern triumvirate of steak, pasta and seafood.

Nisqually National Wildlife Refuge

The estuary of the Nisqually River has been set aside as a preserve for wildlife *(☎ 360-753-9467, 100 Brown Farm Rd; families $3; trails open daylight hours, visitors center open 9am-4pm Wed-Sun)*, particularly for waterfowl and shorebirds. The diverse habitat of the refuge, which includes saltwater and freshwater marshes, mudflats, grasslands and woodlands, is sought out by numerous migratory birds, and great blue herons nest in the conifer forests above the delta.

A number of hikes, ranging from half a mile to over 5 miles, lead out from the parking area. For more information and a wildlife checklist, stop by the visitor center (take I-5 north to exit 114).

Wolf Haven

Wolf Haven *(☎ 360-264-4695, 800-448-9653, 3111 Offut Lake Rd; adult/senior/youth 3-12 years $6/5/4; open 10am-5pm May-Sept; 10am-4pm Wed-Mon Apr & Oct)* is an 80-acre wolf rehabilitation center and permanent home for around 40 wolves no longer able to live in the wild. Associated with the center is the nonprofit Wolf Haven International (Ⓦ www.wolfhaven.org), which offers programs, tours and ecology classes at the interpretive center, all designed to provide a better understanding of the much-maligned wolf. Tours of the grounds are available on the hour. From 6pm to 9pm June through September there are Saturday night Howl Ins (adult/child $10/8), a chance to hear the wolves express themselves, along with music and storytelling.

To reach Wolf Haven from Olympia, take I-5 south to exit 102 and follow signs to Tenino on Capitol Blvd. Continue south (the street becomes Old Hwy 99) about 6 miles and follow the signs.

Northwestern Washington & the San Juan Islands

In the northwestern corner of Washington, the Pacific Ocean washes into Georgia Strait, the Strait of Juan de Fuca and Puget Sound, as well as into a thousand tiny inlets, fjords and channels. Rising above the mist and the

Highlights

- Cycling, hiking and kayaking the San Juans, a chain of serenely rural islands dispersed throughout Puget Sound

- Eavesdropping on orca conversations from a whale-watching cruiser

- Visiting the free-spirited university town of Bellingham at the foot of Mt Baker

- Tiptoeing through the tulips of Skagit Valley

- Sipping loganberry liqueur on Whidbey Island

OTHER MAPS
Northwestern Washington
page 388

Bellingham
pages 390-391

San Juan Islands
pages 404-405

Friday Harbor
page 408

blue-green waves is a mosaic of forested islands and peninsulas along the bay-dented mainland. The primary attraction here is the San Juan Islands, which, together with the Oregon coast, undoubtedly constitute the most beautiful and unique destination in the Pacific Northwest. These remote islands, accessible only by boat or air, range from tightly folded mountain peaks to rolling moors and farmland. Bicycles fill the roads; B&Bs nestle among the trees; and sheep and cattle graze in grassy pastures. And everywhere, the Pacific encroaches.

Across from the islands and on the mainland is the delightful university town of Bellingham, with lively street life, good restaurants and easy access to recreation on Mt Baker and in North Cascades National Park. Along the lower Skagit River, historic La Conner provides a relaxing respite from highway driving, and in spring the fertile flood plains of this valley come alive with acres of tulips and other flowers in a not-to-be-missed display. Whidbey Island contains two of Washington's most popular (read crowded) vacation spots – the beautiful Deception Pass State Park and the quaint, upscale town of Langley.

BELLINGHAM

The handsome old port city of Bellingham (population 67,171) is one of the Northwest's most appealing cultural centers. Perched on hills overlooking a busy harbor, Bellingham faces the southern end of Georgia Strait, which is spangled with forested islands – Lummi, Samish, Orcas and Cypress. Rising immediately behind the city is Mt Baker, crowned with glaciers and hornlike peaks. Bellingham is home to Western Washington University, a busy nightlife scene that favors live bands and local brews and restaurants that are all the more pleasing for their affordability. Like Eugene, Oregon, Bellingham is a collegiate center of left-leaning

NORTHWESTERN WASHINGTON

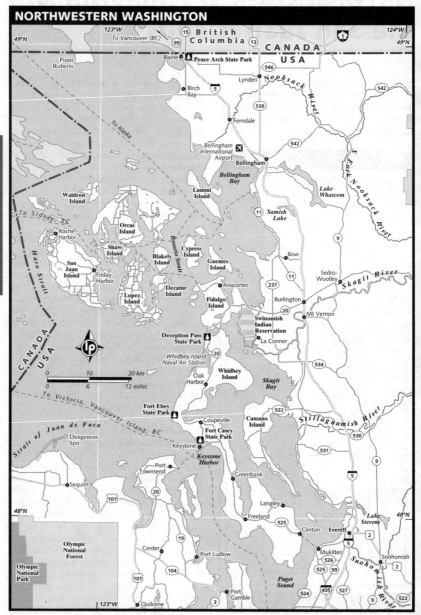

politics and alternative lifestyles. Chosen by *Outside* magazine as one of the USA's top 10 'dream towns,' Bellingham ranks high on the list for outdoorsy folk, with kayaking on three lakes, skiing and snowshoeing on nearby Baker and nearly 30 miles of hiking and biking trails within the city itself.

Bellingham began as three separate communities – Fairhaven, Sehome and Whatcom – each of which developed along deep Bellingham Bay. Fairhaven grew up around speculation that it would be selected as the Great Northern Railroad's Pacific Coast port city, and a core of red-brick storefronts and hotels sprang up in the 1880s. When the Great Northern chose Seattle instead, Fairhaven fell into slumber. Recent renovation has turned the handsome old buildings into a shopping and dining precinct. Whatcom was the county seat, and Sehome was the main business district and site of a coal mine in the 1860s. By 1904 the towns had consolidated into a single civic entity named for the bay.

Orientation

Bellingham is 18 miles south of the Canadian border crossing at Blaine and 54 miles from downtown Vancouver, British Columbia. From Seattle, Bellingham is 89 miles north on I-5.

Because Bellingham is comprised of what were formerly several separate towns, the street systems are pretty confusing. The current city center is west of I-5; exit 253 leads to Holly St, a major downtown artery and one of the few streets to cut through the area without getting caught up in conflicting street grids. Holly St intersects State St, another major artery that runs south to the Fairhaven district and north to I-5 (exit 254). North of the State-Holly intersection is a quadrant of streets with a completely different grid; many city offices and businesses are located here.

It's probably easiest just to park and explore Bellingham on foot. Be sure to stop and get a map from the visitor center.

Information

Tourist Offices For information about the area, contact the Bellingham–Whatcom County Convention & Visitors Bureau (☎ 360-671-3990, 800-487-2032, W www .bellingham.org), 904 Potter St, Bellingham, WA 98229. Just off I-5 exit 253, it's open 9am to 6pm. From Lakeway Dr (following signs for I-5 north), turn north on King St and turn immediately right instead of entering the freeway.

For information about the Canada-US border, contact the US immigration office at Blaine (☎ 360-332-8511) or the Canadian immigration office (☎ 604-666-2171).

Post & Communications The main post office is at 315 Prospect St; a useful branch is at the corner of Cornwall Ave and Magnolia St. Use the Internet free of charge at the Bellingham Public Library, 210 Central Ave. It's open 10am to 9pm Monday to Thursday, 10am to 6pm Friday and Saturday, 1pm to 5pm Sunday.

Bookstores Bellingham is a genuine readers' haven, with a number of great bookstores; it's also a major center for book collectors. A veritable warehouse, Henderson Books (☎ 360-734-6855), 116 Grand Ave, stocks an estimated quarter million titles, both new and used. One could spend the better part of a day browsing the well-organized shelves there. Across the street, Michael's Books, 109 Grand Ave, carries a formidable selection of rare and out-of-print books. In Fairhaven, Village Books (☎ 360-671-2626), 1210 11th St, is a real community resource, with lots of literary activities, to say nothing of being the home of the popular Colophon Cafe (see Places to Eat, later). Another amply stocked Fairhaven locale is Eclipse Bookstore, 915 Harris Ave, above Archer Ale House, with a particularly strong Northwest section.

Newspapers Various free publications profile the local arts and entertainment scene; pick them up at bookstores or cafes around town. The best of these is the *Every Other Weekly*, 'doing what every other weekly does every other week.' Another entertainment guide, *Take Five,* is a supplement to the Thursday edition of the *Bellingham Herald*.

WASHINGTON

Radio For public radio, tune to KZAZ, 91.7 FM. The Western Washington University station is KUGS, 89.3 FM.

Laundry Sunshine Cleaners (☎ 360-733-6610) is in the impossible-to-miss Fred Meyer Shopping Center on Lakeway Dr, immediately east of I-5 exit 253.

Medical Services For health emergencies, go to St Joseph Hospital (☎ 360-734-5400), 2901 Squalicum Parkway, near I-5 exit 255. The hospital's South Campus (same phone number), 809 E Chestnut St, is more convenient to downtown.

Whatcom Museum of History & Art

It's easy enough to spot this excellent regional museum *(☎ 360-676-6981, 121 Prospect St; admission by donation; open noon-5pm Tues-Sun):* The main building is the imposing and fanciful red-brick Whatcom City Hall, dating from 1892. The museum's galleries contain a good collection of artifacts from local native tribes, scenes of early-20th-century Bellingham and a large natural-history section with hundreds of stuffed birds. Other halls are devoted to traveling displays of fine art. Nearby is the **Children's Museum** *(☎ 360-733-8769, 227 Prospect St; admission $2.50; open noon-5pm Sun, Tues & Wed, 10am-5pm Thur-Sat),* with interactive displays for the younger set.

Western Washington University

Founded in 1893 as a teacher training institute, Western served as a regional college before being redesignated as a university in 1977. The campus is just south of downtown Bellingham, nestled between steep hills. With a student body of approximately 12,000, WWU offers a full range of academic programs, though its strengths are in education, business and environmental studies. The staff at the Visitors Information Center (☎ 360-650-3424), open 7am to 5pm weekdays and located at the end of South College Dr, can provide you with information about campus events.

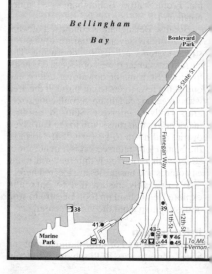

PLACES TO STAY	OTHER
17 Bellingham Inn	1 Base Camp
24 Shangri-La Downtown Motel	2 Post Office
27 North Garden Inn	3 Bellingham Public Library
29 Valu-Inn	4 Whatcom Museum of History & Art; Children's Museum
33 Travelodge	5 Michael's Books
34 Aloha Motel	6 Henderson Books
35 Coachman Inn	11 Post Office
43 Fairhaven Village Inn	16 Whatcom Transport Bus Depot
	25 Bellingham-Whatcom County Convention & Visitors Bureau
PLACES TO EAT	28 St Joseph Hospital, South Campus
8 Old Town Cafe	30 Sunshine Cleaners
13 House of Orient	36 WWU Western Gallery
14 The Bagelry	37 WWU Visitors Center
15 Casa Què Pasa	38 Bellingham Cruise Terminal; Alaska Marine Hwy Ferries; Victoria/San Juan Cruises
18 D'Anna's Cafe Italiano	
19 Boundary Bay Brewery & Bistro	
20 Il Fiamma	
23 Swan Cafe; Community Food Co-op	39 Fairhaven Bike & Mountain Sports
26 Pepper Sisters	40 Amtrak/Greyhound Station
31 Cliff House Restaurant	41 Fairhaven Boatworks
46 Dirty Dan Harris	44 Village Books; Colophon Cafe
ENTERTAINMENT	
7 Mt Baker Theatre	
9 Stuart's Coffee House	
10 Wild Buffalo	
12 Pickford Cinema	
21 Up & Up Tavern	
22 Three Bs Tavern	
32 WWU Performing Arts Center	
42 Archer Ale House	
45 Tony's Coffee & Tea	

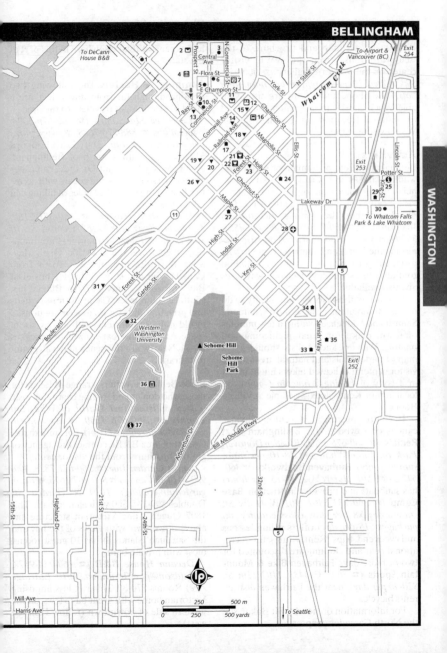

BELLINGHAM

To DeCann House B&B

To Airport & Vancouver (BC)

Exit 254

1

2

3

Central Ave

N Commercial St

Prospect St

4

5

6

Flora St

E Champion St

7

8

9

10

11

12

15

16

13

Bay St

Commercial St

Cornwall Ave

Railroad Ave

Champion St

Magnolia St

York St

N State St

14

18

17

19

20

21

22

Forest St

Holly St

23

24

26

Chestnut St

Maple St

27

28

Lakeway Dr

Ellis St

Whatcom Creek

Exit 253

Potter St

25

King St

29

30

Lincoln St

To Whatcom Falls Park & Lake Whatcom

11

High St

Indian St

Key St

5

34

Samish Way

35

33

Exit 252

31

Forest St

Garden St

Boulevard

32

Western Washington University

Sehome Hill

Sehome Hill Park

36

37

Arboretum Dr

Bill McDonald Pkwy

32nd St

15th St

Highland Dr

21st St

24th St

Mill Ave

Harris Ave

0   250   500 m
0   250   500 yards

To Seattle

Self-guided tours can be made of the two dozen **outdoor sculptures** found on campus. Pick up a free map and brochure of the 'sculpture walk' from the WWU visitor center or the Western Gallery (☎ 360-650-3963; open 10am-4pm Mon-Fri, noon-4pm Sat). Headphone audio tours are also available. When classes are in session you'll need to obtain a free parking permit from the WWU visitor center.

Activities

Bellingham offers a number of scenic and wildlife **cruises** into Georgia Strait and to neighboring islands; pick up brochures at the visitor center or the Bellingham Cruise Terminal and shop the options. **Victoria/San Juan Cruises** (☎ 360-738-8099, 800-443-4552, 355 Harris Ave) offers narrated day trips exploring the San Juan Islands en route to Victoria, British Columbia. Adult/senior/child roundtrip fares are $89/79/45; one-way fares are also available.

Outdoor enthusiasts will find plenty to do in the Bellingham area. Lakes Whatcom, Samish and Padden, all within a few minutes of town, make for great picnicking and boating. Walkers and cyclists should get a map of parks, trails and natural areas at the visitor center. Dedicated hikers might invest in a copy of *Hiking Whatcom County,* by local author Ken Wilcox, available at Village Books.

If you're interested in renting kayaks, canoes or rowboats, try **Bellingham Boat Rentals** (☎ 360-676-1363, Bloedel-Donovan Park on Lake Whatcom; $8-10 per hour, summer only). **Fairhaven Boatworks** (☎ 360-647-2469, 501 Harris Ave, $8-15 per hour) has sailboats and provides instruction. **Base Camp** (☎ 360-733-5461, 901 W Holly St; snowshoes $8 per day, cross-country ski packages $15 per day) offers skiing lessons and weekend trips. Rental rates for recreational gear and clothing are discounted for two or more days. **Fairhaven Bike & Mountain Sports** (☎ 360-733-4433, 1103 11th St; $20-40 per day), near the Fairhaven district, rents bicycles.

For information on nearby Mt Baker, see the North Cascades chapter.

Places to Stay

Accommodations in Bellingham tend to be less expensive than elsewhere in this part of the state.

Camping & Hostels The following two options, though far from downtown, are a good bet for budget travelers to the area.

Larrabee State Park (☎ 360-676-2093, reservations ☎ 888-226-7688, 🅦 www.parks .wa.gov, Chuckanut Dr) Tents/hookups $14/20. Seven miles south of Bellingham, along scenic Chuckanut Dr, these campsites sit among Douglas firs and cedars with access to Chuckanut Bay and 12 miles of hiking and biking trails.

Birch Bay Hostel (☎ 360-371-2180, 🅔 bbhostel@az.com, 7467 Gemini St off Alderson Rd) $14/17 members/nonmembers; sheet/towel rental $1/50¢. Open May-Sept. If you're on your way to or from Canada, you can stay at this HI hostel at Bay Horizon County Park in Blaine, just south of the border. Clean dormitory beds and private rooms for up to four are housed in old military barracks, with a cozy social space. At breakfast, eat your fill of pancakes for $1. Nearby are the beach and waterfront restaurants.

B&Bs Bellingham offers a range of B&Bs for those who don't mind trading charm for cash.

Bed & Breakfast Guild of Whatcom County (☎ 360-676-4560, 🅦 www.north west-bedandbreakfast.com) For an exhaustive list of area B&Bs, contact this agency or get the brochure from the visitor center.

North Garden Inn (☎ 360-671-7828, 800-922-6414, in Canada ☎ 800-367-1676, 🅦 north gardeninn.com/ngi, 1014 N Garden St) Doubles $99-135, $60 with shared bath. This 1897 Queen Anne Victorian structure sits above downtown, with views of the bay and the San Juan Islands. It has 10 guest rooms, most with private bath.

Decann House B&B (☎ 360-734-9172, 🅔 hudson@pacificrim.net, 2610 Eldridge Ave) Rooms $70-80. This is a less imposing Victorian home with great bay views, on the western side of downtown (follow Holly St west).

Hotels The majority of Bellingham's inexpensive motels are along Samish Way off exit 252, not far from WWU. Clean and comfortable, if nondescript, choices here include *Aloha Motel* (☎ 360-733-4900, 315 N Samish Way), *Coachman Inn* (☎ 360-671-9000, 800-962-6641, fax 360-738-1984, 120 Samish Way) and *Travelodge* (☎ 360-676-0332, 800-538-8204, fax 360-676-0899, 116 N Samish Way), all charging $45/55 for singles/doubles. If you want to enjoy downtown Bellingham, stay at one of the motels within walking distance of fine restaurants and entertainment.

Shangri-La Downtown Motel (☎ 360-733-7050, 611 E Holly St) Singles/doubles $41/45. Newly remodeled rooms and pleasant management make this a good deal.

Bellingham Inn (☎ 360-734-1900, fax 360-647-0709, 202 E Holly St) Singles/doubles $42/45. The Bellingham is a trifle modest, but it's right at the lively junction of Holly St and Railroad Ave.

Val-U Inn (☎ 360-671-9600, 800-443-7777, 805 Lakeway Dr) One-/two-bed rooms $54/62. The rooms are quite fine, but convenience is the key: The Airporter Shuttle stops here, and it's close to the freeway and a shopping center.

Fairhaven Village Inn (☎ 360-733-1311, e nwcinns@seanet.com, 1200 10th St) Bayview & park-view rooms $149/129. In another class is this new hotel with a vintage tone in the heart of historic Fairhaven. While the views aren't as fabulous as you'd expect, it is certainly one of the most pleasant places in town and worth the price.

Places to Eat
For a town its size, Bellingham has a wide variety of very good restaurants, at prices well below what you'll find in Seattle.

Downtown None of the downtown spots will put too much of a dent in your wallet.

Old Town Cafe (☎ 360-671-4431, 316 W Holly St) Entrees $5-7. Open till 3pm. Vegetarian dishes are offered at breakfast and lunch, along with fresh pastries and espresso, in a happy-go-lucky hippie atmosphere.

The Bagelry (☎ 360-676-5288, 1319 Railroad Ave) Bagel sandwiches $3.50-5. Open 6:30am-4pm or 5pm. Authentic bagels and bialys and an array of cream cheese spreads will fill your stomach without emptying your pocket at breakfast or lunch.

Swan Cafe (☎ 360-734-0542, 1220 N Forest St) $3-5. The Swan Cafe, inside the Community Food Co-op, serves deli items all day. You can also get organic produce and health foods in the co-op.

House of Orient (☎ 360-738-4009, 209 W Holly St) Entrees $6-8. Spice things up from a wide selection of tasty Thai and Vietnamese vegetarian, meat or seafood dishes accompanied by a little karaoke in the bar.

Casa Qué Pasa (☎ 360-738-8226, 1415 Railroad Ave) $2-8. This is a great informal hangout for tacos, quesadillas and burritos. Vegan and meat-free items are labeled. A dusky bar in back dubbed the 'tequila research institute' offers 80 varieties of the Mexican export.

Il Fiamma (☎ 360-647-0060, 200 E Chestnut St) Medium pizzas $11-13. High-tech styling and wood-fired ovens create a pleasant setting and tasty pizzas topped by local ingredients.

Boundary Bay Brewery & Bistro (☎ 360-647-5593, 1107 Railroad Ave) Entrees $7-11. Perennially popular Boundary Bay crafts its own soulful ales and serves hearty Northwest-influenced fare for lunch and dinner, including pastas, pizzas and salads. The smoked salmon chowder hits the spot on a rainy night.

Pepper Sisters (☎ 360-671-3414, 1055 N State St) Dinners $8-12. Pepper Sisters is the place to go for good Southwestern cooking with a touch of Northwest gourmet.

D'Anna's Cafe Italiano (☎ 360-714-0188, 1317 N State St) Entrees $9-15. Be sure to make dinner reservations to get in on these homemade Sicilian pastas and sausages.

Cliff House Restaurant (☎ 360-734-8660, 331 N State St) Entrees $13-23. Come up here at sunset for achingly beautiful views over Bellingham Bay from the cliff-top deck. While you're gazing, order cocktails and a plate of panfried oysters or a bowl of whiskey crab soup. It's a bit tricky to find – turn south on State St (left off Holly) and stay in the left lane. When you reach a stop

WASHINGTON

sign, continue straight up the hill; you'll see Cliff House on the right.

Fairhaven Earthy cafes mingle with fine restaurants and cute boutiques in this historic village.

Colophon Cafe (☎ 360-647-0092, 1208 11th St) $7-10. Housed inside Village Books in Fairhaven, the Colophon blends the features of a literary cafe with those of a multiethnic eatery. Espresso and pastries (especially the homemade pies) fuel book shoppers, while hearty soups, sandwiches and salads bring people in from the neighborhood for lunch and dinner.

Dirty Dan Harris (☎ 360-676-1011, 1211 11th St) Entrees $16-20. Dirty Dan serves steak, prime rib and seafood in a historic setting.

Entertainment

Bellingham supports a healthy local music scene, and the university ensures a regular dose of visiting talent. Another vital attraction is the bona fide art cinema in the heart of town.

Coffeehouses Java joints play a key social function in this highly conversational culture.

Tony's Coffee & Tea (☎ 360-733-6319, 1101 Harris Ave) Students, unrepentant hippies and housewives come to this Fairhaven favorite for some serious hanging out.

Stuart's Coffee House (☎ 360-752-2024, 1302 Bay St) Stuart's has exhibits, music and readings most nights in a laid-back livingroom ambience. There's a special sunlit romper room for kids.

Theater & Cinemas You'll find Bellingham's first-run movie theaters in outlying shopping malls. Downtown, the marquee-less *Pickford Cinema (☎ 360-738-0735, 1416 Cornwall Ave)* offers alternatives for demanding filmgoers.

Mt Baker Theatre (☎ 360-734-6080, 106 N Commercial St) This grand old historic theater, built in 1925, is now a live-performance stage specializing in national touring acts.

WWU Performing Arts Center (☎ 360-650-6146, W *pacseries.wwu.edu)* WWU's 'PAC' usually features an intriguing lineup of international music and dance figures. See the website for the current program.

Bars & Brewpubs WWU students and faculty sustain a number of worthy watering holes.

Three Bs Tavern (☎ 360-734-1881, 1226 N State St) Downtown, this boisterous student hangout has pool tables, draft beer and several bands on weekends, when there's a $5 cover.

Up & Up Tavern (☎ 360-733-9739, 1234 N State St) Next door to Three Bs, Up & Up is a larger, somewhat more raucous place with similar attractions.

Archer Ale House (☎ 360-647-7002, 1212 10th St) This smoke-free pub, in Fairhaven, has lots of regional microbrews on tap and meal-size snack specials to whet your thirst for another beer.

Wild Buffalo (☎ 360-752-0848, 208 W Holly St) A mostly 30s-and-up crowd gathers at this smoke-free club to dance to live music and quaff microbrew ales.

Getting There & Away

Air Bellingham International Airport is northwest of town off I-5 exit 258. The city is served by Horizon Air (☎ 800-547-9308, W www.horizonair.com) and United Express (☎ 800-241-6522, W www.united.com), with service to Seattle ($160 roundtrip). West Isle Air (☎ 360-671-8463, W www.westisle air.com) flies from Bellingham to the San Juan Islands ($38/76 one way/roundtrip), with both regularly scheduled flights and charters.

Bus Greyhound buses serve Bellingham on the Seattle-Vancouver run, with four heading north to Vancouver ($12.50, 2 hours) and five going south to Seattle ($16.50, 2½ hours). Two additional Seattle-Bellingham buses run on Fridays. The depot (☎ 360-733-5251) is in the same building as the Amtrak station in Fairhaven.

The Airporter Shuttle (☎ 800-235-5247, W www.airporter.com) runs around the clock to Sea-Tac airport ($32/55 one way/roundtrip) and also carries local passengers to Mt Vernon, with links to Anacortes and Oak Harbor. The shuttle stops at the Val-U Inn Motel, just off I-5 exit 253; at Bellingham Airport; and at the ferry terminal. Quick Shuttle (☎ 800-665-2122) runs between downtown Vancouver and Bellingham Airport 6am to 6pm ($13/23 one way/roundtrip).

Train Daily Amtrak trains from Vancouver, British Columbia (from $12, 1½ hours), and twice-daily trains from Seattle (from $18, 2½ hours) stop at the train depot (☎ 360-734-8851) at the end of Harris Ave, near the ferry terminal.

Ferry Bellingham is the terminal for the Alaska Marine Hwy Ferries (☎ 360-676-8445, 800-642-0066, Ⓦ www.ak.gov/ferry), which travel once a week up the Inside Passage to Juneau, Skagway and other southeast Alaskan ports. Passenger fares to Skagway start at $277; add a small car (up to 15 feet), and the fare jumps by $624. Cabins for the three-day trip cost an additional amount and can be hard to come by, so reserve well in advance.

The San Juan Islands Shuttle Express (☎ 888-373-8522, Ⓦ www.orcawhales.com) travels daily, in summer only, from the Fairhaven ferry terminal to San Juan and Orcas Islands ($20/33 one way/roundtrip). Bicycles are welcome on board with a $3/5 surcharge.

Getting Around
Bus service on Whatcom Transportation Authority (☎ 360-676-7433) is modest but functional. The fleet runs weekdays around 6am to 6pm; service is reduced on Saturday. On Sunday one bus route connects Fairhaven, WWU and the Bellis Fair mall to downtown Bellingham. Some WWU routes run only when the university is in session. Bus No 1A goes south to the Bellingham Ferry Terminal at 10 minutes past each hour. Find the main bus terminal downtown on Railroad Ave, between E Champion and Magnolia Sts; the local fare is 50¢.

Yellow Cab (☎ 360-734-8294) has service throughout the area. The fare from downtown to the airport is about $12; to Fairhaven it's about $8.

ANACORTES
Noted principally as the departure point for the San Juan Islands ferries, Anacortes (population 14,370) is actually quite a pleasant town, so all is not lost if you end up spending a night here. In fact, unintended layovers are not uncommon. Ferries can fill up on summer weekends, and once they're full, they're full.

The ferry terminal is 3 miles west of Anacortes, and motels and fast-food franchises line Hwy 20 south of town. However, if you need to spend the night, head downtown, where there are good restaurants and stately old buildings, some decorated with life-size cutouts of early Anacortes residents.

Orientation & Information
Anacortes is itself on Fidalgo Island, separated from the mainland by a narrow channel, 17 miles west of I-5 on Hwy 20. The downtown harbor skirts the edge of the business district, giving the town a real maritime air. Pick up a copy of *Experience Anacortes*, a directory of accommodations and services, at the Visitor Information Center (☎ 360-293-3832, Ⓦ www.anacortes-chamber.com), 819 Commercial Ave, open daily.

Cruises
From June to October, **Mystic Sea Charters** *(☎ 800-308-9387)* offers lunch and dinner cruises ($40-60) through Deception Pass; from late April to October they do whale-watching tours to the San Juan Islands ($69/39 adult/child under 18). Whaling expeditions depart at 10am and 4pm from Dock A of the Cap Sante Marina; brunch is included on weekends. Tours are booked far in advance – make a reservation.

Places to Stay
All sorts of motels and inns are found along Commercial Ave.

Holiday Motel (☎ 360-293-6511, 2903 Commercial Ave) Singles/doubles $50/60.

WASHINGTON

Possibly the best value on the strip, this family-run place next to a bowling alley offers a variation on the usual motel layout, with 10 neatly kept little suites.

Gateway Motel (☎ 360-293-2655, 2019 Commercial Ave) Singles/doubles $44/49. Closer to town, the Gateway is a less expensive if nondescript option, with 13 units squeezed together in low buildings. Bigger units have two bedrooms and kitchenettes.

Cap Sante Inn (☎ 360-293-0602, 800-852-0846, 906 9th St) Singles/doubles $72/81. Downtown and off the main strip, this cozy motor inn is an easy walk to the marina of the same name and some of Anacortes' best restaurants.

San Juan Motel (☎ 360-293-5105, 800-533-8009, 1103 6th St) One-/two-bedroom units $55/65. The generic trilevel structure is near the shopping district and a block east of Causland Park. Rooms seem old if not run down, but they're spacious and some have kitchenettes between a pair of bedrooms.

Ship Harbor Inn (☎ 360-293-5105, W www.shipharborinn.com, 5316 Ferry Terminal Rd) Doubles $75-125. Ship Harbor offers the easiest access to the ferries and features bike rentals for those heading to the San Juans. Rooms have fireplaces and private harbor-view decks or balconies.

Places to Eat

Several stellar restaurants and cafes are clustered along Commercial Ave between 3rd and 6th Sts.

Star Bar & Solé Luna Cafe (☎ 360-299-2120, 416½ Commercial Ave) Breakfast $5-6, lunch $6-7. Healthful eaters appreciate the mostly vegetarian fare at this friendly, funky neighborhood diner. Breakfast and lunch wraps are ethnically themed; fruit and veggie juices are fresh-squeezed; and herbal teas are a soothing alternative to that espresso jolt.

La Vie en Rose (☎ 360-299-9546, 418 Commercial Ave) Open 8am-5:30pm Mon-Sat. Load up on French pastries here.

Gere-A-Deli (☎ 360-293-7383, 502 Commercial Ave) Sandwiches $5-6. Open 7am-4pm Mon-Sat. There's a little of everything at this friendly, boisterous deli, from bowls of granola to eye-popping desserts like marionberry cobbler. Soups, salads and sandwiches are the staples at lunch.

El Jinete (☎ 360-293-2631, 509 Commercial Ave) Combo plates under $9, burritos $5.50-7.50. Decorated in Southwest tones, this cozy cantina brings an authentic touch to classic Tex-Mex fare. Service is remarkably prompt.

Rockfish Grill/Anacortes Brewery (☎ 360-588-1720, 320 Commercial Ave) 10-inch pizzas $7-10. This is a delightful place to sample the local brews and snack on wood-fired pizza. Located in a handsome old bar, the brewery really packs 'em in at night.

Getting There & Away

The Airporter Shuttle (☎ 800-423-4219, W www.airporter.com) offers eight runs a day from Mt Vernon to Anacortes and the San Juan ferries (one way/roundtrip $6.50/11), continuing on to Oak Harbor and Whidbey Island. The shuttle picks up passengers at the Texaco station on 14th St and Commercial Ave (no reservations required). Connections can be made in Mt Vernon to Bellingham and Sea-Tac airport.

Skagit Transit (SKAT; ☎ 360-757-4433) bus No 410 travels hourly between Anacortes (10th St and Commercial Ave) and the San Juan ferry terminal (50¢).

LOWER SKAGIT RIVER VALLEY

The Skagit River originates far to the east in North Cascades National Park and flows west through a low-lying flood plain to meet the Pacific Ocean near the little port town of La Conner. For much of its journey, the road and river travel through a steep-sided glacial valley, a designated 'Wild & Scenic' route that nonetheless is traversed by the undulating power lines of three upper Skagit hydroelectric dams.

As in Holland, early settlers used dikes to channel the Skagit, retrieving rich farmland from the river's seasonal floods. Today, dairy farms and plant nurseries are the norm. In the early spring, lower Skagit Valley fields are a wild display of tulip blooms, as this area is one of the nation's primary sources of spring bulbs. In fact, more acreage is under tulip cultivation here than in Holland.

Sedro Woolley

For travelers, this town isn't of consuming interest. It is, however, a good place to stop before heading into North Cascades National Park (see the North Cascades chapter), as it's the last town of consequence for a couple hundred miles on Hwy 20. Get information about the national park at the Mt Baker–Snoqualmie National Forest Ranger Station (☎ 360-856-5700), on Hwy 20 along the western approach into town. It's open 8am to 4:30pm weekdays (plus weekends in summer). Those spending the night in Sedro Woolley can try *Skagit Motel* (☎ 360-856-6001, 800-582-9121, 1977 Hwy 20), with singles/doubles for $45/55. It's a mile west of the ranger station.

Mt Vernon

This farming center (population 22,059) sits along a wide curve in the Skagit River. The rich soil and abundant water of the river valley make this one of the most productive agricultural areas in the Northwest. The valley is the nation's single largest source of peas and is noted also for its production of strawberries.

The most famous crops of the valley, though, are tulips, daffodils and irises, all of which are the focus of April's annual **Tulip Festival**. While not a festival per se – most travelers simply drive the side roads between Mt Vernon and La Conner armed with a tulip-field map – it does feature an ongoing roster of events: an arts and crafts fair, a salmon bake, a parade, musical concerts and the like. If possible, take in the back roads on a weekday, as weekend afternoons bring long lines of cars, bikes and pedestrians sure to spoil the pace of a leisurely drive. For more information, contact Mt Vernon's chamber of commerce (☎ 360-428-8547, W www .tulipfestival.org), 117 N 1st St.

Among Mt Vernon's rather expensive motels, *West Winds Motel* (☎ 360-424-4224, 2020 Riverside Dr), north of the center, is a modest alternative, with singles/doubles for $46/57. *Skagit River Brewing Company*

(☎ 360-336-2884, 404 S 3rd St), behind the towering Oldtowne Grainery, is a rollicking pub serving its own craft ales, stouts and lagers as well as savory pub fare.

La Conner

At first glance, La Conner is an unlikely little tourist mecca. However, situated just north of the Skagit River's mouth, La Conner's well-maintained and stylish 1880s storefronts and pretty harbor became a magnet for artists and writers during the 1960s and '70s (the likes of Tom Robbins live here). Soon, boutiques, nice restaurants and antique shops took up residence, and not much later, the tour buses began rolling in. La Conner is a charming and relaxing stop for anyone whose nerves are jangled by nearby I-5 traffic or for San Juan–bound travelers early for their ferry. Summer weekends bring hundreds of people to town, however.

The town is 11 miles west of I-5 and 9 miles from Anacortes. Directly across the Swinomish Channel from La Conner is a lobe of Fidalgo Island that is home to the Swinomish Indian Reservation. For tourist information, contact the La Conner Chamber of Commerce (☎ 888-642-9284, W www .laconnerchamber.com), 413A Morris St.

La Conner boasts a trio of worthy museums within a two-block radius. The **Museum of Northwest Art** (☎ 360-466-4446, W www.museumofnwart.org, 121 S 1st St; admission $3; open 10am-5pm Tues-Sun) endeavors to portray the 'special Northwest vision' through the works of representative artists. The ground floor is dedicated to changing shows by regional artisans, and the upstairs space houses pieces from the permanent collection.

Perched atop a hill that affords impressive views of Skagit Bay and the surrounding farmlands, the **Skagit County Historical Museum** (☎ 360-466-3365, 501 S 4th St; adults/seniors & children 6-12 years $2/1; open 11am-5pm Tues-Sun) presents indigenous crafts, dolls, vintage kitchen tools and other paraphernalia used by the region's early inhabitants.

Of more specialized interest is the **La Conner Quilt Museum** (☎ 360-466-4288,

WASHINGTON

703 S 2nd St; admission $3; open 10am-4pm Wed-Sat, noon-4pm Sun), displaying quilt art of several generations. The museum is housed in the old Gaches mansion, which has stood here since 1891.

The reclaimed farmland along the Skagit River delta is home to a number of plant nurseries, and gardeners will enjoy stopping to browse. The oldest of the local nurseries is **Tillinghast Seed Co** *(☎ 360-466-3329, 623 Morris St; open 9am-5:30pm Mon-Sat, 11am-6pm Sun)*, which is still doing business out of its 1885 storefront. Contact the chamber of commerce for a complete list of regional nurseries.

Places to Stay Don't expect any lodging deals in La Conner: Local inns and B&Bs take themselves seriously.

Hotel Planter (☎ 360-466-4710, 800-488-5409, fax 360-466-1320, 715 S 1st St) Doubles $75-129. This refurbished hotel offers a nice blend of c. 1907 charm and modern amenities, including a covered hot tub in the courtyard. Children are allowed on weekdays only.

La Conner Channel Lodge (☎ 360-466-1500, 888-466-4113, 205 N 1st St) Rooms $120-275. Though of recent vintage, this handsome luxury lodge does its best to look in keeping with the rest of old La Conner. Large and airy rooms have fireplaces and decks facing the channel.

La Conner Country Inn (☎ 360-466-3101, 107 S 2nd St) Rooms $98-160. Under the same management as the Channel Lodge, the shingle-sided inn is just steps from the busy waterfront. Comfortable rooms come with gas fireplaces. Attached is Palmer's Restaurant, the local fine-dining establishment.

The White Swan Guest House (☎ 360-445-6805, ⓦ www.thewhiteswan.com, 15872 Moore Rd) Rooms $85. Within biking distance of La Conner, the White Swan consists of three rooms sharing two bathrooms in a Victorian farmhouse on Fir Island, 6 miles from town.

Places to Eat It's easy to work up an appetite gazing at tulips all morning. Some of the most attractive dining options are found alongside Swinomish Channel.

Calico Cupboard (☎ 360-466-4451, 720 S 1st St) Breakfast $4, lunch $6-10. Head to this bakery-cafe for fresh pastries, omelets and light lunches.

Legends (☎ 360-466-5240, 708 1st St) Sample Native American fast food here, and enjoy your snack at the channel-side deck.

Hungry Moon Cafe (☎ 360-466-1602, 110 N 1st St) Sandwiches $4.75-6, salads $3-7.50. Soulful homemade soups and chowders, hefty deli sandwiches and great cookies are available to eat in or take out.

La Conner Brewing Co (☎ 360-466-1415, 117 S 1st St) Pizzas $8-9, sandwiches $7-8. By late afternoon this polished-pine pub is packed with chatty locals savoring wood-fired pizzas, fresh salads and eight home brews on tap.

Kerstin's (☎ 360-466-9111, 505 S 1st St) Lunch $8-12, dinner $17-21. Open noon-9pm Wed-Mon. This is candlelit dining, Northwest style. The daily-designed menu features whatever's in season, from oysters to king salmon to fresh summer veggies. It's worth coming in the early evening for the sunset view from the deck.

WHIDBEY ISLAND

Green, low-lying Whidbey Island snakes 41 miles along the northern Washington mainland from the northern suburbs of Seattle to Deception Pass at Fidalgo Island. The sea is never far away on this long, narrow island, but unlike the San Juan Islands, there is no impression of remoteness here. Weekend visitors from Seattle can make the attractive harbor towns on Whidbey as congested as the mainland suburbs. Langley and Deception Pass State Park are immensely popular vacation spots: the metropolitan sprawl of Puget Sound cities is quite close, and Oak Harbor contains an active naval air base. If you don't have time for a trip to the San Juans but hanker for a ferry ride and island seascape, then a detour across Whidbey is a fine introduction to historic maritime Washington. Don't forget to pick up a bottle of loganberry liqueur near Greenbank and a plate of fresh oysters in Coupeville.

Orientation & Information

'Whid' is threaded by Hwy 525, which links the island's southern end by ferry to the mainland suburb of Mukilteo, and by Hwy 20, the main northern artery, which crosses dramatic Deception Pass via two narrow bridges on its way to Anacortes and the San Juan Island ferries. The two highways join near the center of the island, where Hwy 20 spurs west to Keystone and is connected by ferry to Port Townsend and the Olympic Peninsula.

For more information on Whidbey Island events, activities, accommodations and so on, see W www.whidbey.net/visitor/visitors.html.

Deception Pass State Park

Early explorers of Puget Sound believed that Whidbey Island was a peninsula. It wasn't until 1792 that Captain Joseph Whidbey found the narrow cliff-lined crevasse, churned by rushing water, between Fidalgo and Whidbey Islands. Passage through the channel was nearly impossible in the days of sailing ships, and it remains a challenge today even to motorized boats, as high tides charge through the pass at better than 9 knots.

The bridge linking Whidbey and Fidalgo Islands consists of two steel arches that span Canoe Pass and Deception Pass, with a central support on Pass Island between the two. Visitors to the 5½-sq-mile park (☎ 360-675-2417, 41229 N State Hwy 20) usually introduce themselves to the dramatic land and seascape by parking at the shoulders on either end and walking across the bridge. Built during the 1930s by the Civilian Conservation Corps (CCC), the bridge was considered an engineering feat in its day. The park itself also spans the channel, with facilities – including campgrounds – on both the north and south flanks of the passage.

More than 3.5 million visitors per year visit Deception Pass, which makes it Washington's most popular state park. Besides the dramatic bridge overviews, the park's attractions include over 15 miles of saltwater shoreline and seven nearby islands, three freshwater lakes, boat docks, hundreds of picnic sites and 27 miles of forest trails. Scuba divers and sea kayakers explore the area's reefs and cliff-edge shores. Organized kayak tours (from $30 per person) depart from Bowman Bay; contact the Deception Pass Adventure Center (☎ 360-293-3330) to reserve.

Nearly 250 *campsites* are nestled in the forests beside a lake and a saltwater bay (standard sites $14, hiker/biker sites $6). Facilities include running water, flush toilets, hot showers and snack concessions. Reserve well ahead for summer weekends, as competition can be fierce. Late-arriving cyclists should ride past the disheartening rows of cars and ask about walk-in sites.

Oak Harbor

Boosters of Oak Harbor (population 19,795) have recently gone to a lot of trouble to promote the virtues of this, the largest town on Whidbey Island. However, Oak Harbor remains mostly charmless, dominated by Naval Air Station Whidbey Island. Built during WWII to rearm planes defending the West Coast from attack, the post is largely a flight-training facility for reservists and home to a number of defensive air squadrons.

Oak Harbor is 38 miles from the ferry at Clinton, 9 miles from Deception Pass and 21 miles from Anacortes. Highway 20 is the main drag through the town, although an old downtown area along the harbor is just east of the Pioneer Way junction. The Oak Harbor Visitor Center (☎ 360-675-3755), 32630 State Rte 20, can provide tourist information 10am to 5pm weekdays.

Oak Harbor's most affordable lodging, *Acorn Motor Inn* (☎ 360-675-6646, 800-280-6646, 31530 State Rte 20), is also convenient to downtown. Reasonably comfortable units, some with kitchen facilities, start at $44, including breakfast. *Oak Harbor Pub & Brewery* (☎ 360-675-7408, 32295 State Rte 20) has two dozen brews on tap, including their own handcrafted ales and hard ciders.

Coupeville

One of the oldest towns in Washington, Coupeville (population 1723) has an attractive seafront filled with shops, antique stores and old inns facing Penn Cove, noted for its

WASHINGTON

oyster and mussel production. The town's founder, Captain Thomas Coupe, is the only captain to have sailed a four-rigger through Deception Pass. Although the vintage town remains attractive and is great for a stroll or a weekend getaway, the urban sprawl from Oak Harbor and the influx of refugee Seattleites have begun to take a toll.

The Visitor Information Center (☎ 360-678-5434, W www.centralwhidbeychamber .com), 107 S Main St just south of Hwy 20, is open 10am to 5pm.

The **Island County Historical Society Museum** (☎ 360-678-3310, 908 NW Alexander St; adult/senior & student $2/1.50; open 10am-5pm May-Sept, 10am-4pm Fri-Mon Oct-Apr) tells the story of the community's shipping and farming history. Be sure to pick up a walking-tour map of Coupeville's vintage homes and business district. The museum also serves as the administrative office for the Ebey's Landing National Historical Reserve (see that section, later).

Ten miles south of Coupeville lies **Whidbey's Greenbank Berry Farm** (☎ 360-678-7700, W www.greenbankfarm.com, Hwy 525 off Wonn Rd; open 10am-5pm). The farm is the world's largest producer of loganberries, a sweet, blackish berry rather like a boysenberry or black raspberry. It's most noted for Whidbey's loganberry liqueur, which makes a good gift or souvenir. The winery-style farm is open daily for touring, tasting and picnicking.

Places to Stay A number of original Coupeville homes and inns remain in service as B&Bs.

Inn at Penn Cove (☎ 360-678-8000, 800-688-2683, W www.whidbey.net/penncove, 702 N Main St) Rooms $60-125. Just three blocks from the harbor, the inn is made up of two side-by-side Victorian farmhouses, each containing three rooms.

Anchorage Inn (☎ 360-678-5581, W www .anchorage-inn.com, 807 N Main St) Rooms $80-130. This building is in fact a painstaking reproduction of a Victorian mansion. While history buffs may object to such inauthenticity, at least all seven rooms have

private baths and the floors don't squeak. Children under 14 aren't permitted.

The Coupeville Inn (☎ 360-678-6668, in Washington and British Columbia ☎ 800-247-6162, W www.coupevilleinn.com, 200 Coveland St) Doubles $68-105 with continental breakfast. Convenient to harborfront shopping and strolling, the inn has 24 rooms, most with balconies overlooking Penn Cove.

Captain Whidbey Inn (☎ 800-366-4097, 2072 W Captain Whidbey Inn Rd) Singles/doubles $75/85 to $125/135, cottages $185-225, including full breakfast. This c. 1907 inn, 3 miles west of Coupeville, is a showcase of old-fashioned – almost medieval – charms. Lodging is in 12 low-slung guest rooms in the main lodge (with a bathroom down the hall), as well as wood-heated cottages and a more modern building with verandahs facing a lagoon. Fresh seafood is featured in the inn's noted Northwest-style dining room.

Tyee Motel (☎ 360-678-6616, 405 S Main St) Doubles $44.50. On a more functional level is this modest, standard motel, two blocks south of Hwy 20.

Places to Eat All of the following restaurants face mollusk-strewn Penn Cove.

Knead & Feed (☎ 360-678-5431, 4 Front St, bottom level) Sandwiches & salads $6. Open 10am-3pm Mon-Fri, 9am-4pm Sat & Sun. Fresh bread and pastries, as well as deli-style salads and soups, are served at this charming waterfront eatery.

Toby's Tavern (☎ 360-678-4222, 8 Front St) Chowder $6. For some local flavor, step into this 60-year-old bar, which may very well be the world's leading purveyor of mussels. Try a fabulous bowl of mussel chowder, served with garlic bread.

Captain's Galley (☎ 360-678-0241, 10 Front St) Entrees $9-11. Mussels, oysters and fish and chips (made with beer batter) are served in both the harbor-view dining room and the atmospheric downstairs lounge.

Great Times Waterfront Coffee House (☎ 360-678-5358, 12 Front St) Pizzas from $5. With attractive views of Penn Cove, a few well-worn armchairs and espresso, the setting is right for conversation or journal writing. They also do pizzas.

Ebey's Landing National Historical Reserve

A unique outdoor museum, Ebey's Landing (☎ 360-678-3310; admission free; open 8am-5pm Oct 16-Mar 31, 6:30am-10pm Apr 1-Oct 15) seeks to demonstrate human history on this corner of Whidbey Island. Managed with an eye to preserving the area's past uses, the reserve's 17,400 acres encompass working farms, miles of beaches, two state parks and the town of Coupeville itself. A series of interpretive boards shows visitors how the patterns of croplands, woods (or the lack of them) and even roads reflect the activities of those who have peopled this scenic landscape, from its earliest indigenous inhabitants to 19th-century settlers.

For information on Ebey's Landing, contact the Island County Historical Museum in Coupeville (see that section, earlier), which distributes a brochure on suggested driving and cycling tours through the reserve.

At the reserve's south end is **Fort Casey State Park** (☎ 360-678-4519), with facilities for camping and picnicking. Fort Casey was part of the early 1900s military defense system that once guarded the entrance to Puget Sound. Visitors can investigate the old cement batteries and underground tunnels that line the coast. Other recreational activities here include scuba diving, boating and bird watching, best along Keystone Spit on the southwest tip of Crockett Lake. **Admiralty Head Lighthouse**, built in 1861, houses the park's interpretive center. It's a 4-mile walk north along the beach to **Fort Ebey State Park** (☎ 360-678-4636), arranged around WWII-era defenses, with much the same facilities as Fort Casey.

Fort Casey State Park offers 38 campsites overlooking Keystone Harbor, and **Fort Ebey** has 53 sites ($14) plus four with RV hookups ($20). Facilities include flush toilets and running water. A unique lodging option is **Fort Casey Inn** (☎ 360-678-8792, 866-661-6604, W www.fortcaseyinn.com, 1124 S Engle Rd) The inn consists of a series of five c. 1909 houses that served as WWI officers' quarters and are now rented as overnight accommodations (rooms $135 for up to four guests). Perched on a bluff overlooking the lighthouse at Fort Casey, the houses have restful porches with oak armchairs. Each unit contains two bedrooms (with two or three beds), a kitchen, a bathroom and a fireplace in the sitting room. The comfortable rooms are simply furnished and decorated with patriotic memorabilia and some hand-painted folk art.

Langley

The most popular getaway on Whidbey Island is Langley (population 959), a seaside town that epitomizes the adjectives 'quaint' and 'cute.' Langley *is* an attractive town – its harbor overlooks Saratoga Sound and the distant peaks of the Cascades – and it has a reputation as an artists' colony. But these things merely serve as the bow that wraps Langley's twee commercialism : the upscale boutiques, gift shops and cafes are designed to enchant those whose idea of a rapturous weekend away is not complete without shopping. If you're unencumbered by kids, all the better – few of the expensive B&Bs and inns here allow children.

Langley is 8 miles north of Clinton and the ferry service from Mukilteo, making this the closest of the Whidbey Island communities to the urban areas of northern Seattle.

Places to Stay & Eat Pick up a list of currently available accommodations at the ***Langley Visitor Information Center*** (☎ 360-221-6765, 208 Anthes Ave), which doubles as a lodging referral service. They may be able to find you something for under $100 a night.

Eagles Nest Inn (☎ 360-221-5331, W www.eaglesnestinn.com, 4680 E Saratoga Rd) Rooms $95-$140. Perched on a hill, this contemporary B&B boasts views of Saratoga Passage and Mt Baker. There are four guest rooms and a private cottage.

The Inn at Langley (☎ 360-221-3033, W www.innatlangley.com, 400 1st St) Rooms $189-325, including breakfast. This contemporary, condo-esque inn is the trendsetter in style and expense. The 26 beautifully furnished waterfront rooms have large windows, whirlpool tubs and fireplaces. A full-service spa provides Swedish massage and seaweed body masks.

Cafe Langley (☎ *360-221-3090, 113 1st St*) Lunch under $10, dinner $11-17. This particularly popular place to eat offers Mediterranean cuisine, often given a zip by fresh Northwest seafood.

Village Pizzeria (☎ *360-221-3363, 108 1st St*) Pizzas from $11.25. Head here for classic Neapolitan or thick-crusted Sicilian-style pizza, sold by the pie or slice ($2.35).

Getting There & Around

The Airporter Shuttle (☎ 800-235-5247, Ⓦ www.airporter.com) offers frequent bus service to Oak Harbor from Sea-Tac ($34/60 one way/roundtrip) or from Bellingham ($12/22); transfer at Mt Vernon for the Whidbey-bound connection. Prepaid reservations are required to ensure a seat.

Washington State Ferries run between Clinton and Mukilteo (20 minutes, auto & driver $6.25, passengers $2.70) and between Keystone and Port Townsend (30 minutes, $9.75, $2.70).

Island Transit buses run the length of Whidbey every day except Sunday, from the Clinton ferry dock to Greenbank, Coupeville, Oak Harbor and Deception Pass. Other routes reach the Keystone ferry dock and Langley on weekdays. Service is hourly and free. For more information, call ☎ 360-678-7771 or check out the website Ⓦ www.islandtransit.org.

San Juan Islands

The San Juan archipelago contains 457 islands, all sprawled across 750 sq miles of Pacific waters. They're located in the area where Puget Sound and the Straits of Juan de Fuca and Georgia meet between the US and Canada. Only about 200 of these islands are named, and of these, only a handful are inhabited. Washington State Ferries service the four largest – San Juan, Orcas, Shaw and Lopez Islands – while others are accessible only by private boat or plane.

Long considered an inaccessible backwater of farmers and fisherfolk, the San Juans have been 'discovered' only in the last 25 years. The islands are now a major holiday destination. And yet, despite the inevitable adulteration that commercialization brings, the islands retain their bucolic charm and make for a restful, almost unforgettable retreat.

Situated in a rain shadow created by Vancouver Island, the San Juans receive only 25 inches of annual precipitation and are sunny 250 days a year. Summertime temperatures can reach 85°F; wintertime lows drop into the 30s.

Subtle differences distinguish the four islands linked by the ferry system. Lopez is the most rural island, with fields and pastures stretching across its central plateau. Shaw, with its ferry dock and store run by Franciscan nuns, is the smallest and most remote island, and it has almost no facilities for tourists. San Juan Island boasts the most history, the only incorporated town and a nice mixture of rural landscapes and resort facilities. Orcas Island is the rockiest and most mountainous island, and life is centered almost exclusively on the resorts.

Most motels and inns will pick up registered guests at the ferry, if they are notified in advance, and each of the islands has taxi service. Bicycles, mopeds and cars can be rented on San Juan, Orcas and Lopez Islands. Dozens of smaller islands are accessible by kayak or boat-taxi service; see the harbormaster to contact local boat-taxi operators.

Accommodations

Don't even think about heading out during July and August without reservations, or you may end up having to take the last ferry back to the mainland. Most reservations are filled months ahead, and the most attractive lodging options are often booked even farther in advance. Accommodations are also expensive: You will be pressed to find something for less than $100 a night during the summer (though prices may drop by half in the off-season). During high season, many resorts also demand multiple-day stays. Campsites aren't exactly numerous, either. Happily, there are exceptions to the rule, and with a little planning a trip to the San Juans needn't bust the budget.

If you're having trouble finding rooms, or want someone else to do the hunting, contact All Island Reservations (☎ 360-378-6977).

Those heading to the San Juans expecting to find miles of public beach may be disappointed. In Washington, private landowners control the land down to the tide line, which means that access to beaches, except at state or county parks, is effectively barred. The beach from the tide line to the water *is* public, but you will usually find several 'No Trespassing' signs barring your way.

Information

For information about the San Juans in general, contact the San Juan Islands Visitor Information Center (☎ 360-468-3663, W www .guidetosanjuans.com) from 10am to 2pm weekdays. Their website provides links to numerous San Juan businesses and organizations. In addition, the chambers of commerce of San Juan, Orcas and Lopez Islands maintain their own visitor walk-in information centers – see those sections for details.

You might also invest in *Emily's Guides to the San Juan Islands,* by islander Emily Reed, a useful compendium of accommodations, tour operators, galleries and more. Emily's guides are sold at the Anacortes ferry landing and island bookstores ($5.95 per island). Also pick up the free San Juan Island and Orcas Islands maps by NW Places, with blowups of the principal villages and business listings; you'll find them on the ferries. Alternatively, these maps can be downloaded and printed from W www.nwplaces.com.

Bicycling

These mostly flat islands are immensely popular with cyclists – each is laced with tiny roads that wind through forests and past sheep-filled meadows to remote bays. Though most motorists are courteous to cyclists, these roads are often narrow, winding and overused, so remember to use caution.

Bicycles are transported for a small fee on Washington State Ferries. All the islands except Shaw offer bicycle rentals, so there's no need to bring your own; most companies will meet your ferry if you have reserved a bike.

See Lonely Planet's *Cycling USA – West Coast* for suggested routes. A good map of the islands' cycling trails is sold at Wildlife Cycles, on Orcas Island.

Sea Kayaking & Boating

An increasingly popular means of exploring the shores of the San Juans is by sea kayak. Kayaks are available for rent on Orcas, San Juan and Lopez Islands; most operators provide tours and lessons. Expect a guided half-day trip to cost around $30 to $45. An overnighter might cost as much as $235, and a three- to four-day excursion can run $335 to $425. Kayaks can be transported on ferries, both by vehicles and by accompanying pedestrians.

The calm waters around the San Juans are popular for sailing and yachting. If you're planning on using boats as your primary means of transportation, obtain a copy of *The San Juan Islands, Afoot and Afloat,* by Marge and Ted Mueller, a handbook for the independent boat traveler. Ken Wilcox' recently published *Hiking the San Juan Islands* details 80 walks on 22 different islands, including nearby Fidalgo, Whidbey and Camano.

Marinas on San Juan, Orcas and Lopez Islands offer a wide range of boat rentals, from uncomplicated hourly hires of small rowboats and kayaks to lunch or cocktail cruises to more ambitious multiple-day excursions on yachts and sailboats. Prices range from around $125 a half-day for a self-navigated 'bareboat' charter to several thousand dollars a week for a skippered charter with meals, bedding and other niceties included. See the individual island listings for whom to contact about packages.

Getting There & Away

Two airlines fly from the mainland to the San Juans. Kenmore Air (☎ 800-543-9595, W www.kenmoreair.com) flies to Lopez, Orcas and San Juan Islands on seaplanes from Lake Union and Lake Washington in Seattle. West Isle Air (☎ 800-874-4434) flies from Anacortes, Bellingham and Boeing Field in Seattle. Fares out of Seattle range from $75 to $100 one way, $120 to $180 roundtrip.

By far the majority of people who visit the San Juans arrive on Washington State Ferries (WSF; in Washington ☎ 800-843-3779, elsewhere ☎ 206-464-6400, **w** www.wsdot .wa.gov/ferries). From the mainland, car ferries leave from Anacortes and depart for the four principal islands. At least one Washington State Ferry a day continues on to Sidney, near Victoria, British Columbia, on Vancouver Island. Additionally, in the summer privately owned passenger-only ferries depart from Bellingham, Seattle, Port Townsend and Victoria, bound for the San Juans.

Pick up the small, widely available WSF timetable in advance and take a few minutes to get used to reading the schedules and fares. Generally speaking, there are three different kinds of state-ferry runs here: international, between Anacortes and Sidney; domestic, from Anacortes to some – if not all – of the islands; and interisland. The international run stops at Orcas and/or Friday Harbor, depending on the season. (Note that you will be subject to a customs and immigrations inspection in Anacortes, even if you board this ferry in the San Juans.) On domestic runs from Anacortes, make sure that the ferry stops at your island destination. Interisland ferries travel a circular route exclusively between the four islands, though they may not stop at all of them.

Travel time from Anacortes to the closest island, Lopez, is roughly 45 minutes; to the most distant island port, Friday Harbor on San Juan, it's 1¼ hours; and to Sidney, it's three hours.

From late spring to early autumn, private passenger-only ferries are available from other points of departure. San Juan Shuttle Express (☎ 888-373-8522, **w** www .orcawhales.com) travels from Bellingham to Orcas and Friday Harbor. The *Victoria Clipper* (in Seattle and Victoria ☎ 206-448-5000, elsewhere ☎ 800-888-2535, **w** www .victoriaclipper.com) links Seattle with Friday Harbor on San Juan Island,

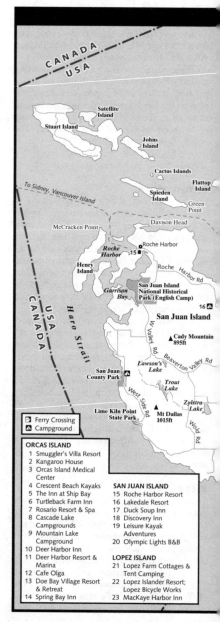

ORCAS ISLAND
1 Smuggler's Villa Resort
2 Kangaroo House
3 Orcas Island Medical Center
4 Crescent Beach Kayaks
5 The Inn at Ship Bay
6 Turtleback Farm Inn
7 Rosario Resort & Spa
8 Cascade Lake Campgrounds
9 Mountain Lake Campground
10 Deer Harbor Inn
11 Deer Harbor Resort & Marina
12 Cafe Olga
13 Doe Bay Village Resort & Retreat
14 Spring Bay Inn

SAN JUAN ISLAND
15 Roche Harbor Resort
16 Lakedale Resort
17 Duck Soup Inn
18 Discovery Inn
19 Leisure Kayak Adventures
20 Olympic Lights B&B

LOPEZ ISLAND
21 Lopez Farm Cottages & Tent Camping
22 Lopez Islander Resort; Lopez Bicycle Works
23 MacKaye Harbor Inn

SAN JUAN ISLANDS

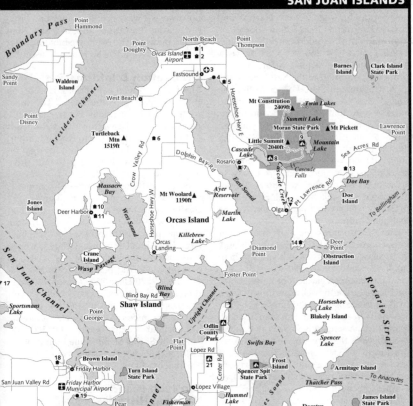

Boundary Pass

Point Hammond

Point Doughty

North Beach

Point Thompson

Orcas Island Airport

■1
■2

Barnes Island

Clark Island State Park

Eastsound

✚3

■4 ■5

Sandy Point

Waldron Island

West Beach

Mt Constitution 2409ft ▲

Twin Lakes

Summit Lake

Point Disney

President Channel

Turtleback Mtn 1519ft ▲

■6

Horseshoe Hwy E

Moran State Park

▲ Mt Pickett

Lawrence Point

Dolphin Bay Rd

Little Summit 2040ft ▲

■9

Mountain Lake

Sea Acres Rd

Cascade Lake

△8

Jones Island

Massacre Bay

Mt Woolard 1190ft ▲

Ayer Reservoir

Rosario

■7

Cascade Creek

Cascade Falls

■13

Doe Bay

Crow Valley Rd

East Sound

Pt Lawrence Rd

Doe Island

Deer Harbor

■10
■11

West Sound

Horseshoe Hwy W

Orcas Island

Martin Lake

To Bellingham

Killebrew Lake

Olga ●

▲12

Crane Island

Orcas Landing

Diamond Point

■14

Deer Point

Obstruction Island

Wasp Passage

Foster Point

San Juan Channel

■17

Blind Bay

Horseshoe Lake

Blakely Island

Rosario Strait

Sportsmans Lake

Blind Bay Rd

Shaw Island

Upright Channel

Point George

Spencer Lake

Flat Point

Odlin County Park

Lopez Rd

Swifts Bay

■18

Brown Island

Friday Harbor

Center Rd

▲21

Spencer Spit State Park

Frost Island

Armitage Island

To Anacortes

San Juan Valley Rd

Friday Harbor Municipal Airport

Turn Island State Park

Lopez Village

Hummel Lake

Lopez Sound

Thatcher Pass

James Island State Park

■19

Pear Point

Fisherman Bay

■22

Decatur Island

Griffin Bay

Bailer Hill Rd

Fisherman Bay Rd

Lopez Island

Trump Island

Center Island

False Bay

False Bay Dr

School Rd

Cattle Point Rd

▲ Lopez Hill 534ft

Mud Bay

■20

San Juan Island National Historical Park (American Camp)

Cape San Juan

Shark Reef Park

Mud Bay Rd

Cape St Mary

Rosario Strait

LP

Mackaye Harbor

■23

Point Colville

0   3   6 km
0   2   4 miles

Iceberg Point

Agate Beach Park

WASHINGTON

with service on to Victoria, British Columbia; an additional ferry, the *San Juan Explorer*, runs between Friday Harbor and Rosario Resort on Orcas Island once a day. From mid-April to mid-September, Puget Sound Express (☎ 360-385-5288, W www .pugetsoundexpress.com) offers service from Port Townsend to the San Juans.

On Washington State Ferries to the San Juans, fares are collected on westbound journeys only; that is, all westbound tickets are considered roundtrip. Hence, if you plan to visit all the islands, it's cheapest to go all the way to westernmost Friday Harbor initially and then work your way back through the other islands, since you won't have to buy another ticket. The exception is the international crossing from Sidney to Anacortes, for which you'll need to pay for the eastbound journey.

High-season fares for a car and driver from Anacortes are $21.25 to Lopez Island, $25 to Shaw and Orcas Islands and $28.25 to San Juan Island, plus $6.80 for each additional passenger (regardless of destination). The charge for motorcyclists, or for stowing a kayak or canoe, is $11.20 to Lopez, $11.90 to Shaw and Orcas, $12.50 to San Juan. The fare for walk-on passengers is $6.80 to all destinations. Bicycles that are wheeled on in Anacortes incur a $3.60 surcharge (no charge if they are attached to a vehicle). Foot passengers and bicyclists ride interisland ferries free in either direction.

The peak season one-way fare for the international ferry between Anacortes and Sidney is $11 for foot passengers, $41 for car and driver.

SAN JUAN ISLAND

Of all the islands, San Juan Island (population 6894) offers the most hospitable blend of sophisticated amenities, rural landscapes and cultural facilities. A large part of the island's draw is Friday Harbor: With a population of about 1990, it's the only sizable town in the archipelago. But follow any of the streets out of town, and you're soon on a central plateau, where small farms, dairies and lakes fill the verdant landscape.

The only other community of any size is Roche Harbor, set on a beautiful bay to the northwest. It was once the center of a lime-processing operation, an early San Juan Island industry. The extensive buildings that remain now form Roche Harbor Resort.

Orientation & Information

The ferry terminal is at Friday Harbor, on the eastern side of the island. The main route south from Friday Harbor is Cattle Point Rd, while Beaverton Valley Rd heads to the west coast. To get to Roche Harbor, take 2nd St to Guard St, then turn right on Tucker Ave; from there it's a 10-mile drive to the resort.

San Juan Island's chamber of commerce (☎ 360-378-5240), inside a small arcade accessible from Front or Spring St, will load you up with brochures. Otherwise, try the national-park visitor center (see San Juan Island National Historical Park), whose staff customarily fields questions outside its park purview. The post office (☎ 360-378-4511) is at 220 Blair Ave. Madelyn's Bagel Bakery (see Places to Eat) will let you check your email on its PC for 10¢ per minute. For medical emergencies, go to the Inter-Island Medical Center (☎ 360-378-2141), 550 Spring St. Sunshine Laundromat, 210B Nichols Ave, has some coin-operated washing machines.

San Juan Island National Historical Park

The so-called Pig War (see the boxed text) between the USA and Britain is the focus of this NPS-administered facility, which consists of two sites on opposite ends of the island. Before heading out, stop by the **visitor center** (☎ 360-378-2240, 125 Spring St; open 8:30am-4pm), featuring an exhibit on the dispute.

At **English Camp**, 9 miles northwest of Friday Harbor off West Valley Rd, are the remains of the British military facilities dating from the 1860s. A path from the parking area leads down to a handful of restored buildings. On a nice day, it's worth the detour just for the views over Garrison Bay. A slide presentation on the history of the site is shown in the old barracks during the summer.

The Pig War

San Juan Island was the scene of an odd battle between the US and Britain, the sole eruption of a mid-19th-century territorial dispute.

In 1846, both nations had agreed to split North America along the 49th parallel, with Britain retaining Vancouver Island. However, ownership of the San Juan Islands was left unresolved, as the treaty had divided the islands through 'the middle of the channel.' The British thought the channel in question was Rosario Strait to the east, while the US believed it was Haro Strait, to the west. The San Juan Islands lay in between.

The misunderstanding wasn't terribly important until American settlement began to take hold. The British Hudson's Bay Company (HBC) had maintained a fishery and various farms on San Juan Island for many years. Then in 1855, a US magistrate attempted to levy import duties on goods from the HBC farms.

Official indignation was expressed by both sides, while US settlers continued to stream onto the islands. Finally, in 1859, shots were fired. A pig from the HBC farms had taken to wandering from its pens and rooting in the potato patch of a US settler. The American shot the pig; the British demanded compensation; and after more mutual indignation, the US sent troops to occupy the island and established Fort Pickett (now known as the American Camp). In retaliation, the British sent warships from Victoria, British Columbia, to the island to protect HBC interests.

Cooler heads prevailed in London and Washington, DC, and a treaty declaring joint military occupation was eventually agreed upon. In 1872, 13 years after the 'Pig War,' Kaiser Wilhelm I of Germany judged in favor of the USA, and the international boundary was established through Haro Strait.

On the southern flank of the island is **American Camp**, 6 miles south of Friday Harbor off Cattle Point Rd, with slightly more developed facilities. The sole remains of the 1859 fort are the officers' quarters and a laundress' house, though a series of interpretive trails lead to earthwork fortifications, a British farm from the dispute era and the beach. Near the trailhead is a small visitor center (☎ 360-378-2902). It's open 8:30am to 4:30pm Thursday to Sunday, daily in summer. The 1¾-mile hike along the ridge of Mt Finlayson is a must; on a clear day, there are splendid views to the Olympic and Cascade ranges.

Lime Kiln Point State Park

Set on the western shore of San Juan Island, off scenic West Side Rd, this is perhaps the only park in the world devoted to whale watching *(open 8am-5pm Oct 16-Mar 31, 6:30am-10pm Apr 1-Oct 15)*. Most sightings are of killer or minke whales, which gather to dine on the June salmon runs through Haro Strait. A trail leads from the parking lot to the main viewing area, equipped with picnic tables and panels explaining the whales' movements and natural history. Bring binoculars (even though whales are frequently spotted quite close to shore) and a little patience.

Friday Harbor

Friday Harbor boasts a lively restaurant scene and more culture than you'd expect in this distant outpost of the USA. There are several unusual museums and plenty of outdoor outfitters to round out your stay. During summer, festivals and events fill the

WASHINGTON

streets. Most notable of these is the Dixieland Jazz Festival, held the last weekend of July.

In an 1890s farmhouse on the outskirts of town, the **San Juan Historical Museum** (☎ *360-378-3949, 405 Price St; adult/child 6-18 years $2/1; open 10am-4pm Thur-Sat, 1pm-4pm Sun May-Sept; 1pm-4pm Sat Mar-Apr & Oct*) commemorates early pioneer life on San Juan Island. While the building itself is interesting for its vernacular architecture, the displays of kitchen and parlor furnishings – like the pump organ and massive wood range – are also worth checking out.

If the San Juan Islands had a mascot, it would surely be the killer whale. Indeed, these 25-foot-long mammals have been given their own natural-history museum, **The Whale Museum** (☎ *360-378-4710, 62 1st St; adult/child 5-18 years $4/2; open 10am-5pm*). It features a number of whale skeletons and life-size models, as well as displays about marine life in general and recordings of ocean mammal songs.

Bicycling

Next to Lopez, San Juan is the flattest of the islands, and it's very popular with the cycling set. While there's great scenery along all the roads on San Juan, the West Side Rd offers some of the best views. Bicycle rentals are available from **Island Bicycles** (☎ *360-378-4941, 380 Argyle St, e islbike@islandbicycles.com*), in Friday Harbor. Rates are $30/20 adults/children per day, for mountain bikes equipped with rear racks, locks and helmets.

Sea Kayaking & Boating

For an educational wildlife tour, take a day-long kayak trip from **Sea Quest Expeditions** (☎ *360-378-5767, W www.sea-quest-kayak .com; $59; open May-Oct*). Both Sea Quest and **San Juan Kayak Expeditions** (☎ *360-378-4436, W www.sanjuankayak.com*) offer fully outfitted, two- to five-day trips with no kayaking experience required. Three-/four-day trips cost $325/420, and they operate

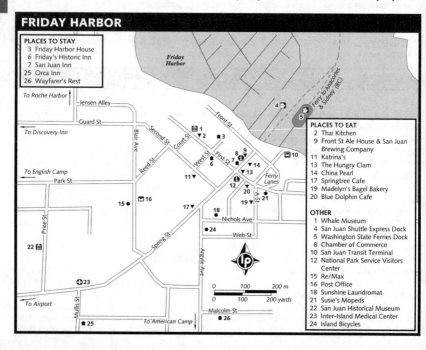

FRIDAY HARBOR

PLACES TO STAY
3 Friday Harbor House
6 Friday's Historic Inn
7 San Juan Inn
25 Orca Inn
26 Wayfarer's Rest

PLACES TO EAT
2 Thai Kitchen
9 Front St Ale House & San Juan Brewing Company
11 Katrina's
13 The Hungry Clam
14 China Pearl
17 Springtree Cafe
19 Madelyn's Bagel Bakery
20 Blue Dolphin Cafe

OTHER
1 Whale Museum
4 San Juan Shuttle Express Dock
5 Washington State Ferries Dock
8 Chamber of Commerce
10 San Juan Transit Terminal
12 National Park Service Visitors Center
15 Re/Max
16 Post Office
18 Sunshine Laundromat
21 Susie's Mopeds
22 San Juan Historical Museum
23 Inter-Island Medical Center
24 Island Bicycles

Friday Harbor

Ferry to Anacortes & Sidney (BC)

To Roche Harbor
Jensen Alley
Guard St
To Discovery Inn
To English Camp
Park St
To Airport

0   100   200 m
0   100   200 yards

To American Camp

June to September. Call for reservations, and they will meet you at the ferry landing. For rentals, contact **Leisure Kayak Adventures** (☎ 800-836-1402, **W** *www.leisurekayak.com; single/double kayak $45/60 per day)*, located at Jackson Beach, south of town.

Most boat-charter companies offer 25- to 55-foot sailboats or powered yachts for scenic day trips, skippered cruises or instruction. Most rent year round, but you'll save heaps if you sail in the off-season. **Trophy Charters** (☎ 360-378-2110) does half-day wildlife-watching cruises at $60 per person and fishing tours at $85-95. **Cap'n Howard's Charters** (☎ 877-346-7245, **e** *capnhoward@ interisland.net)* offers fishing and sightseeing charters, charging $60 per hour for four passengers ($200 minimum) or $400 per day including overnight accommodations. Bareboat charters are available from **Charters Northwest** (☎ 360-378-7196, **e** *boats@ chartersnorthwest.com, 2 Spring St)* at $1100 a week for a 30-foot vessel.

Whale Watching

In summer, **San Juan Boat Tours** (☎ 800-232-6722, **W** *www.whaletour.com; open May-Sept; adult/child 6-12 years $49/39, no children under 6)* operates three- to four-hour whale-watching trips. Board the *Blackfish* Tuesday to Saturday mornings at the Friday Harbor docks. The captain and naturalist have good track records for finding orcas, and visitors can eavesdrop on the whales using the cruiser's underwater hydrophone. Reservations are necessary.

The four-hour wildlife tour offered by **Western Prince Cruises** (☎ 800-757-6722, **W** *www.orcawhalewatch.com)* promises views of eagles, seals and porpoises in addition to the killer whales. Tours on the *Western Prince,* which accommodates up to 33 people, depart daily except Tuesday from June to August (adult/child under 13 years $49/35), less often and less expensively in spring and fall. Reservations are recommended.

Scuba Diving

For scuba gear, instruction and rental, head for **Emerald Sea Diving & Marine Center**

(☎ 800-942-2507, **W** *www.emeraldseas.com)*, at the Spring St landing. Chartered half-day expeditions cost $70, including two dives and tanks.

Places to Stay

To get a feel for island life, stick around after the crowds have taken the last ferry back to the mainland.

Camping & Hostels Budget travelers needn't discard the idea of spending the night on San Juan Island, but summertime stays will take some planning.

Lakedale Resort (☎ 360-378-2350, **W** *www.lakedale.com, 4313 Roche Harbor Rd)* Sites $8-24. Open Mar 15-Oct 15. Four miles outside Friday Harbor on the Roche Harbor road, this sprawling recreation area has 120 tent sites nestled among woods and grassy fields between two trout-stocked lakes, plus 19 RV sites with partial hookups and three tent 'cabins' of four cots each ($45). There are showers, boat rentals and a grocery store.

San Juan County Park Campground (☎ 360-378-2992, *reservations* ☎ 360-378-1842, 380 Westside Rd)* Sites $18, hiker/biker sites $5 per person. Open year round, this small campground on San Juan's west shore offers access to excellent snorkeling and diving as well as views of Victoria, British Columbia. Groceries and tackle are available near the boat launch. Reservations are mandatory during peak season.

Wayfarer's Rest (☎ 360-378-6428, **W** *www .rockisland.com/~wayfarersrest, 35 Malcolm St)* Bunk beds $20, room or cabin for three $45. A short bike ride from the ferry, this backpacker's hostel is a welcome addition to an isle of pricey inns. Sheets and blankets (but no towels) are provided. Guests can avail themselves of a coin-operated hot shower, washing machine, full kitchen and cozy living room.

B&Bs It sometimes seems as if every available farmhouse on the island has been converted to a quaint country inn.

B&B Association of San Juan Island (☎ 360-378-3030, **W** *www.san-juan-island.net,*

PO Box 3016, Friday Harbor, WA, 98250) This association tracks availability status of San Juan's two dozen B&Bs.

Friday's Historic Inn (☎ 360-378-5848, Ⓦ *www.friday-harbor.com, 35 1st St)* Rooms $90-255. In Friday Harbor, two old downtown hotels – this and the San Juan Inn – have been refurbished as B&Bs. Dating from 1891, this one is recently renovated and has rooms with shared or private bath and larger units with a Jacuzzi or outdoor hot tub. Breakfast features homemade scones, fruit and coffee.

San Juan Inn (☎ 360-378-2070, Ⓦ *www .sanjuaninn.com, 50 Spring St)* Rooms $68-190. This refurbished inn has been updated without losing its 1873 Victorian charm. There are nine double rooms with private or shared bath, plus a pair of garden-view suites; all share a 2nd-floor sitting room and dining room.

Olympic Lights B&B (☎ 360-378-3186, Ⓦ *www.olympiclightsbnb.com, 146 Starlight Way)* Rooms $115-135. This restored 1895 farmhouse stands on an open bluff facing south onto the Strait of Juan de Fuca and the Olympic Mountains. Of the four guest rooms, the Ra and Olympic boast the best views.

Hotels & Resorts With one functional exception, the island's inns and resorts cater to guests with deep pockets. Keep in mind, however, that rates can drop by a third in the 'quiet season.'

Orca Inn (☎ 877-541-6722, fax 360-378-1322, 770 Mullis St)*. Doubles $48-52. Friday Harbor's budget alternative has 73 units in a barrackslike compound. Most rooms are small and simple but acceptable; a few larger ones have king-size beds and TVs. All come with air-con and private bath.

Discovery Inn (☎ 800-822-4753, Ⓦ *www .discovery-inn.com, 1016 Guard St)* Rooms $125. Japanese-style gardens and blossoming trees surround this modern motel located at a bend in the road three-quarters of a mile from the ferry landing. Spacious rooms have one or two queen beds, fridge and microwave; there's a cedar sauna and outdoor hot tub that holds 20.

Friday Harbor House (☎ 360-378-8455, Ⓦ *www.fridayharborhouse.com, 130 West St)* Rooms $265-300. The town's most exclusive lodging is a modern boutique hotel with great views over the harbor. All 20 rooms have a fireplace, Jacuzzi and other upscale niceties. The rates include a full breakfast.

Roche Harbor Resort (☎ 800-451-8910, Ⓦ *www.rocheharbor.com, Roche Harbor)* Rooms $79-99, cottages $149-199, condos $125-259. Located on the site of a former lime kiln and country estate, this seaside village is just about the nicest place to stay in all the San Juans. More than 100 years after its initiation as the company hotel by limestone king John McMillin, it's still taking guests, who enjoy its slightly faded gentility. Refurbished workers' cottages fill a grassy meadow above the harbor, and modern condominiums are discreetly tucked behind a stand of trees. Waterfront restaurants, a marina with boat rentals, and an old dockside general store round out the facilities.

Vacation-Home Rentals Visitors contemplating an extended stay or traveling with a large crew should consider renting as an economical alternative.

Re/Max San Juan Island (☎ 360-378-5858, Ⓦ *www.sanjuanrealestate.com, 285 Blair Ave)* From $700/week. This real-estate firm manages 60 year-round vacation homes in the islands, mostly on San Juan. Stop by their office or check their website for a look at currently available cabins and cottages.

Places to Eat

There's no need to stray outside of Friday Harbor for sustenance – the village's many restaurants should appeal to all palates and pocketbooks.

Blue Dolphin Cafe (☎ 360-378-6116, 185 1st St)* Prices $5-9. Popular with morning ferry riders, this local joint has good traditional, egg-rich breakfasts and big plates of hash browns.

Madelyn's Bagel Bakery (☎ 378-4545, 225 A St)* Open 7am-6pm. A takeout or sit-down venue, Madelyn's bakes about 17 kinds of bagels and prepares a slew of tasty spreads to accompany them.

The Hungry Clam (☎ 360-378-3474, 130 1st St) Seafood baskets $5.50-9. It's nothing fancy, but locals line up here at lunchtime for the fish and chips, chowder and cheeseburgers.

Katrina's (☎ 360-378-7290, 135 2nd St) Entrees under $10. Open 11:30am-4pm Mon-Fri. Specializing in vegetarian dishes and bakery items, this cafe has a strong alternative feel.

China Pearl (☎ 360-378-5254, 51 Spring St) Entrees under $10. This is the place for inexpensive Cantonese and Sichuan fare. The upstairs lounge, also known as the Fat Fong Club, features pool tables, plus karaoke (whenever anyone has the nerve).

Thai Kitchen (☎ 378-1917, 42 1st St) Lunch specials $7, dinner entrees $9-13. Those craving more exotic Asian cuisine may prefer this charming locale, overseen by a woman from Laos. Local seafood items dominate the menu – the red-curry mussels are a must.

Front Street Ale House & San Juan Brewing Company (☎ 360-378-2337, 1 Front St) Suppers $10-17. The island's only brewery serves up British-style beers in a real pub atmosphere. The food's good, too: Old-country favorites such as shepherd's pie and bangers and mash keep company with such standbys as oyster stew and chili.

Springtree Cafe (☎ 360-378-4848, 310 Spring St) Lunch $8-11, dinner $15-22. The menu at this casual bistro tends toward seafood and pasta, cooked with Northwest élan. In summer, there's dining in the courtyard.

Friday Harbor House Restaurant (☎ 360-378-8455, 130 West St) Entrees $14-25. Open from 5:30pm Thur-Mon. A fireplace and great views set the mood at the tony inn's intimate dining room. The daily menu sheet emphasizes seasonal cuisine.

Duck Soup Inn (☎ 360-378-4878, 3090 Roche Harbor Rd) Entrees $15-18. Open for dinner Wed-Sun in summer. About 4½ miles northeast of Friday Harbor, this friendly establishment serves local seafood and meats with Continental aplomb set in a handsome, fireplace-dominated dining room.

Getting Around

From May to October, San Juan Transit (☎ 360-378-8887, 800-887-8387) shuttles visitors from the ferry landing to Roche Harbor and points along the west coast, including Lime Kiln Point State Park and the English Camp. Buses run hourly between 9am and 6pm (roundtrip $7, day pass $10). Otherwise, call San Juan Taxi (☎ 360-378-3550).

Susie's Mopeds (☎ 360-378-5244, 800-532-0087), opposite the ferry dock, rents mopeds at $16 an hour, $48 a day. M&W Auto Rentals (☎ 360-378-2886, 800-323-6037, 725 Spring St) offers compact cars from $40 a day, SUVs from $70, and they'll pick you up at the ferry landing.

ORCAS ISLAND

Orcas Island (population 4593) is the largest of the San Juan Islands, and in some ways it is the most exclusive. The mountainous landscape isn't particularly friendly to agriculture, the backbone of local economies on the other islands. However, the rocky promontories and isolated harbors look good in real-estate brochures, so retirement homes, resort communities and weekend manses generally take up the void.

In terms of rugged physical beauty, Orcas is probably the most fetching of the islands. Mt Constitution is the highest point in the San Juans, and from its peak views stretch from Mt Baker to the Olympic Mountains and Vancouver Island. Mt Constitution is only one of several forested peaks on Orcas, around which the rest of the island folds in steep valleys. Along the rocky coast, narrow cliff-lined inlets serve as harbors for small pleasure boats.

Orcas Island offers a wide array of tourist facilities, including the San Juans' largest state park and campground. However, it still retains a palpable sense of being an insider's destination, perhaps because there isn't much of a town on the island. You'll find that lodgings, restaurants and recreation are scattered all over.

Orientation & Information

Orcas Island is shaped like a saddlebag, with two distinct lobes very nearly cleaved

WASHINGTON

Mystery of the Orcas

Every summer a community of orcas migrates down from Vancouver Island to feed in the salmon-flooded waters of Puget Sound. The orcas, also called 'killer whales' (they're actually very large carnivorous dolphins) are a seasonal draw for tourists and cruise operators on the sound. But it appears that this whale community is dwindling, and no one knows why.

Researchers keeping a close watch on the 'southern residents' community (another group resides in the waters around the northern half of Vancouver Island) have noted a steady population decline since 1992. As of 2001 there were 78 whales in the community, 21% fewer than six years earlier. The worrisome reduction could be due to the concurrent drop in salmon stocks, or it could be the result of the high level of toxic PCBs in the waters of the sound, which have been detected in the bloodstreams of the whales. Another possibility is that the numerous whale-watching tours operating around the San Juan Islands are somehow disturbing the orcas' ability to communicate with each other, a requirement for team foraging. Though evidence to support any of these theories remains sparse, it's safe to say that if the orca population continues its recent waning trend, there won't be any left to watch by next century.

by East Sound. The ferry terminal is at the tiny community of Orcas Landing, on the western half of the island. Roads lead north and then west to the village of Deer Harbor and, on the other side of Turtleback Mountain, to West Beach. The island's main population center is Eastsound, at the northern extreme of East Sound, where the two halves of the island meet. Most tourist and commercial facilities are available here, including a post office, laundry, bank, grocery store and gas station. The eastern half of the island is essentially comprised of Moran State Park and of resorts scattered along the coastline, most notably Rosario Resort, whose centerpiece is a mansion and spa built in 1910 by a former mayor of Seattle.

For more information, contact the Orcas Island Chamber of Commerce (☎ 360-376-2273, ⓦ www.orcasisland.org), on North Beach Rd in Eastsound, open 8am to 5:30pm Monday to Friday, 10am to 3pm Saturday. The same office offers public Internet access. Orcas Island Medical Center (☎ 360-376-2561) is off Mt Baker Rd.

Orcas Island Historical Museum

Housed in a series of six log cabins, this museum (☎ 360-376-4849, 181 North Beach Rd, Eastsound; adult/seniors & students $2/1; open 1pm-4pm Tue-Sun, to 7pm Fri, May 26-Sept 30; by appointment rest of year) relates the pioneer and local history of Orcas and the San Juan Islands. Besides the usual collection of household goods, tools, weapons and photographs, there's a good display of Native American artifacts. A curious collection of Chinese 'coolie' hats commemorates the San Juan Islands' role as a passageway for illegal Asian immigrants in the 1880s.

Moran State Park

The fourth-largest state park in Washington, 7-sq-mile Moran State Park (☎ 360-376-2326; open 6:30am-dusk April-Sept, 8am-dusk Oct-Mar) is southeast of Eastsound on Horseshoe Hwy. The park is dominated by 2409-foot **Mt Constitution**. Nearly everyone who visits Orcas Island makes their way up the steep and winding paved road to its summit. The road up the mountain turns off Horseshoe Hwy just past Cascade Lake. This 5-mile ascent is not a road for trailers or large mobile homes, or for the vast majority of cyclists, as the grade is a persistent 7% with frequent hairpin turns. At the top, beside an unfortunately situated microwave receiver, is a three-story stone tower that affords great views over all of northwestern Washington.

The park's two major bodies of water, **Cascade Lake** and **Mountain Lake**, offer campgrounds, good trout fishing, nonmotorized boating (rentals are available), picnic areas and swimming beaches.

Of the more than 30 miles of trails in Moran State Park, about half are open seasonally for mountain biking. Get a trail map from the park headquarters at the south end of Cascade Lake.

Both Cascade and Mountain Lakes are ringed by hiking trails, and a 3-mile trail links the two, passing by the 100-foot **Cascade Falls**. The falls are more easily reached from a trailhead off the Mt Constitution road, about half a mile uphill from the junction with Horseshoe Hwy.

Trails lead from Cascade Lake's North End Campground and climb 4.3 miles up to Mt Constitution; however, it's a lot easier to catch a ride to the summit and take in the views on the way downhill.

Bicycling
For bike rentals, head to **Wildlife Cycles** (☎ 360-376-4708, Ⓦ *www.rockisland.com/ ~wildlifecycles, 350 North Beach Rd, Eastsound; basic mountain bike with helmet $25 per day).* They'll deliver your bike to the ferry landing by prior arrangement. Check out their website, which details nine of the island's most popular cycling routes.

Sea Kayaking
The protected shoreline of East Sound is a good place for beginners to learn the art of sea kayaking or for veterans to view wildlife along the rocky coastline. **Crescent Beach Kayaks** (☎ 360-376-2464, 239 Crescent Beach Dr), directly across the road from Crescent Beach near Eastsound, has a limited number of double and single

kayaks for rent ($10/25 per person per hour/half-day).

Shearwater Adventures (☎ 360-376-4699, Ⓦ *www.shearwaterkayaks.com),* in Eastsound, offers guided half-day trips of East Sound, the Wasp Islands and Deer Harbor (for $45 per person) between April and October. **Orcas Outdoors** (☎ 360-376-4611, Ⓦ *www.orcasoutdoors.com),* at the ferry landing, leads one- to three-hour tours of West Sound Bay from $25 per person. Both outfitters offer overnight expeditions as well.

Boating & Whale Watching
At Deer Harbor Resort, **Deer Harbor Charters** (☎ 800-544-5758, Ⓔ *charter@ rockisland.com)* has various nautical offerings. Take a sailing excursion or lounge around East Sound on a luxury yacht. Wildlife cruises, available May to October, may include sightings of eagles, seals and sea lions, as well as killer whales, minke whales and porpoises (adult/child $45/30).

Orcas Boat Rentals (☎ 360-376-7616,) at Deer Harbor Marina, has powerboats and sailboats from $100 per half-day.

Places to Stay
For those having trouble locating a room, the chamber of commerce offers an accommodations hotline at ☎ 360-376-8888.

Camping Two sites offer camping facilities on Orcas.

Moran State Park (☎ 360-376-2326, reservations ☎ 888-226-7688) Standard sites $13, hiker/biker sites $6. The largest camping area in the San Juans has more than 150 campsites (no hookups) at four lakeside locations: one at Mountain Lake and three at Cascade Lake. Reservations are a must in summer.

Doe Bay Village Resort & Retreat (see Resorts & Vacation-Home Rentals, later) Standard sites $12-20, RV sites $18-22. Campers can set up along a bluff over a picturesque inlet (reserved) or in an open field (first-come, first-served).

B&Bs Dispersed around the island, these offer seclusion and the comforts of home.

Kangaroo House *(☎ 888-371-2175,* W *www.kangaroohouse.com, North Beach Rd)* Rooms $85-135. Just north of Eastsound, this is a 1907 Craftsman-style B&B set on 3 acres. There are five guest rooms, two with private baths.

Turtleback Farm Inn *(☎ 360-376-4914, fax 360-376-5329,* W *www.turtlebackinn .com, 1981 Crow Valley Rd)* Rooms $80-235. Overlooking a wide sheep pasture at the base of Turtleback Mountain, this lovely c. 1900 farmhouse contains seven guest rooms sharing a sitting room and dining room. Recently built in a similar style, the cedar-sided Orchard House contains four larger rooms with view decks.

Spring Bay Inn *(☎ 360-376-5531,* W *www .springbayinn.com, Obstruction Pass Rd)* Rooms $220-260. This unique B&B is run by two former park rangers who include a program of basic kayak instruction and full breakfast in the price of the stay. The inn is set just back from the water, with a beachside hot tub.

Hotels Orcas has a number of attractive inns, from finely renovated historic properties to more contemporary lodgings with all modern conveniences.

Orcas Hotel *(☎ 360-376-4300,* W *www .orcashotel.com, Orcas Landing)* Rooms $79-189. Listed on the National Register of Historic Places, this 1904 building has been completely refurbished and now offers a dozen guest rooms, some with private facilities. Near the ferry landing, the handsome inn features a sun-drenched verandah as well as an espresso bar, restaurant and lounge.

Deer Harbor Inn *(☎ 360-376-4110, fax 360-376-2237,* W *www.deerharborinn.com, Deer Harbor Rd)* Lodge rooms $119-129, cottages $189-325. Just up the road from Deer Harbor Resort (see Resorts & Vacation-Home Rentals), this pleasant inn capitalizes on its harbor-view perch. The old lodge is now a popular tavern; accommodations are in a newer, adjacent log cabin as well as one- and two-bedroom cottages with fireplaces.

Outlook Inn *(☎ 360-376-2200, 888-688-5665,* W *www.outlook-inn.com, Main St,* *Eastsound)* Rooms with shared bath $84, motel rooms $140, suites $245. The bayside complex has at its heart a venerable old hotel from the 1890s. While most rooms in the original hotel share bathrooms, a motel-like wing has modern units with private facilities. The newest addition, set on a nearby bluff, contains luxurious suites with private decks.

Landmark Inn *(☎ 360-376-2423, 800-622-4758,* W *www.landmarkinn.net, 67 Main St, Eastsound)* Rooms $150-165. Next door is this modern lodging, with two-bedroom apartments featuring full kitchens, fireplaces and balconies. Rates depend on the view.

The Inn at Ship Bay *(☎ 360-376-5886, 877-276-7296,* W *www.innatshipbay.com, 326 Olga Rd)*. Doubles $195. Orcas' newest lodging, an addition to the long-standing seafood restaurant, is east of Eastsound. Set beside acres of orchards, the inn's appealingly furnished 11 rooms feature king-size beds, gas log fireplaces and private balconies facing Ship Bay.

Resorts & Vacation-Home Rentals In addition to two sprawling vacation villages, each hugging its own harbor, there's a beachfront spread on the north coast and a remote retreat that's well outside the mainstream.

Deer Harbor Resort & Marina *(☎ 888-376-4480,* W *www.deerharbor.com)* Cottages $189-259, suites $209-399. Nearly every building in this little hamlet, set alongside one of the island's loveliest harbors, is for rent, ranging from motel-style bungalows to cottages, all featuring deck-top hot tubs. Boat and bike rentals, tennis courts, and a small restaurant and market are all on the premises.

Smuggler's Villa Resort *(☎ 360-376-2297, 800-488-2097,* W *www.smuggler.com, N Beach Rd)* 2-bedroom homes $219-275. Well suited for a family or group of friends, this complex comprises 20 small and medium-sized architecturally innovative houses with fireplaces, right on the beach. Facilities include a marina, an outdoor pool, a tennis court and other recreation facilities.

Rosario Resort & Spa *(☎ 360-376-2222, 800-562-8820,* W *www.rosario-resort.com, Rosario Way)* Rooms $188-400. Long the place for upscale Orcas visitors, Rosario was built in the 1910s as the middle-age folly of onetime Seattle mayor Robert Moran. The old mansion is the centerpiece of a resort complex that includes almost 180 modern rooms, tennis courts, swimming pools, a marina and elaborate tiled spa facilities.

Doe Bay Village Resort & Retreat (☎ 360-376-2291, W www.doebay.com) Hostel beds $16; treehouses/yurts from $49; double cabins $67-89, additional person $14. There are resorts, and then there's Doe Bay, 18 miles east of Eastsound on the island's easternmost shore, as lovely a spot as any on Orcas. By far the least expensive resort in the San Juans, Doe Bay has at once the atmosphere of an artists' commune, hippie retreat and New Age center. Accommodations include campsites, a small hostel with dormitory and private rooms, and various levels of cabins and yurts, most with views of the water. There's a natural-foods store and a cafe where healthy meals are served up family-style. The sauna and clothing-optional hot tub are set apart on one side of a creek.

Cherie L Lindholm Real Estate (☎ 360-376-2204, W www.lindholm-realestate.com, North Beach Rd, Eastsound) This agency has over 40 vacation homes for rent with many in the $600-900 a week range. Call for an illustrated brochure with detailed rates or see their website for an electronic version.

Places to Eat
Besides Eastsound, which boasts more good places to eat than its size could possibly justify, only Orcas Landing has any significant dining activity.

The Boardwalk (☎ 360-376-2971, 8292 Orcas Rd, Orcas Landing) Breakfast $3.50-6.50, burgers $5.50. The ferry riders' choice, this Orcas Landing eatery has breakfast, first-rate burgers and Washington wines, which you can enjoy on the adjacent deck.

Orcas Hotel (☎ 360-376-4300, Orcas Rd, Orcas Landing) Dinner entrees $9-24. The old hotel's dining room combines a pub ambience with Northwest cuisine. A small coffee shop is tucked into the west corner of the building for espresso and pastries.

Teezer's (☎ 360-376-2913, North Beach Rd, Eastsound) Fresh-baked scones, croissants, quiches and Starbucks coffee attract locals here Monday to Saturday mornings.

Homegrown Market (☎ 360-376-2009, North Beach Rd, Eastsound) Put together a picnic lunch at this well-stocked natural-foods store; they make sprout-topped sandwiches for around $5.

Chimayo (☎ 360-376-6394, North Beach Rd, Eastsound) Burritos $3.50-5. Open 11am-7pm Mon-Sat. Across the way is this casual cantina doling out well-stuffed burritos and tempting daily specials.

Bilbo's Festivo (☎ 360-376-4728, 310 A St, Eastsound) Dinner entrees from $14. Bilbo's offers a more elegant setting for Mexican and Southwest cuisine, healthily prepared by a Jalisco native – the refried beans are lard-free. There's a wide selection of margaritas.

La Famiglia Ristorante (☎ 360-376-2335, Prune Alley, Eastsound) Entrees $13-20. The family prepares hearty Northern Italian favorites.

The Inn at Ship Bay (☎ 360-376-5886, 326 Olga Rd, Eastsound) Entrees $17-22. Two miles south of Eastsound is this classic seafood restaurant housed in an attractive, 1860s orchard house. More casual fare is served in the adjacent lounge.

Cafe Olga (☎ 360-376-5098, Olga Rd). Entrees $9-11. Open Mar-Dec. Located in the tiny community of the same name, this homey restaurant shares a historic building with Orcas Island Artworks, a gallery presenting the work of local artists. Light meals and bakery goods are served.

Getting Around
Orcas Island Taxi (☎ 360-376-8294) can transport visitors (and their bikes) to and from the ferry and other destinations. For auto rentals, try West Isle Air (☎ 360-376-4176), with rates from $50 per day including 100 free miles.

LOPEZ ISLAND
The most agricultural of the San Juan Islands and the closest to the mainland, Lopez Island (population 2590) is somewhat

WASHINGTON

overlooked in the free-for-all that is tourism in the San Juans. However, if you want quiet, pastoral charm and don't need organized fun, it's hard to beat Lopez.

One of the first things you'll note as you drive around the island is that all the locals wave as you pass – they don't automatically assume you're a stranger. This rather agrarian bonhomie makes the island seem more like a green corner of Iowa than a Pacific Northwest tourist destination. Lopez has also resisted the commercialization of its farmland somewhat better than the other islands. Here, pastures are for grazing sheep or hay making – they aren't merely the aesthetic property of quaint country inns and B&Bs.

Orientation & Information

The ferry terminal is in a purely functional harbor at the extreme north end of the island. The closest thing to a town on Lopez is Lopez Village, no more than a collection of houses and a tiny business district overlooking a shallow bay. Most businesses, including a gas station and bank with ATM, are here. Saturdays and Wednesdays in summer, a farmers market takes over the village. Just to the south of Lopez Village is Fisherman Bay, a hotel and marina complex.

For information about businesses and recreation on Lopez Island, contact the Lopez Island Chamber of Commerce (☎ 360-468-3663, W www.lopezisland.com). For a taxi, call Angie's Cab (☎ 360-468-2227).

Bicycling

Except for the long uphill slope leading from the ferry, Lopez is exceptionally flat, and its few roads have little car traffic. Rent a bike at **Lopez Bicycle Works** *(☎ 360-468-2847, 2847 Fisherman Bay Rd; mountain bikes $5 per hour, $23 per day),* at the marina; you can also rent a sea kayak here. Good cycling destinations are Agate Beach and Shark Reef Park, a fine location for picnicking, whale watching and sea-lion viewing.

Charter Fishing

Skippered day and overnight fishing trips are available from **Harmony Charters** *(☎ 360-468-3310,* e *countess@interisland.net, 973 Shark Reef Rd)* and **Kismet Sailing Charters** *(☎ 360-468-2435),* both of which operate out of Fisherman Bay. Visitors select from a number of organized packages, or they can schedule individualized tours or cruises. A lunch cruise on Harmony Charters' 63-foot yacht costs $60 per person, while an overnight cruise with meals is $200 per person.

Places to Stay

Low-key Lopez has fewer hotels and inns than do its bigger sisters, but there are several fine campgrounds.

Camping These three areas, all at the north end of the island, offer a combined 70 sites, though competition can get heavy in summertime.

Odlin County Park (☎ 360-468-2496, reservations ☎ 360-378-1842, 148 Odlin Rd) Standard sites $15-17, hiker/biker sites $10. Just 1⅓ miles south of the ferry landing is this pleasant waterfront campground, picnic area and public dock. Facilities are minimal – running water, outhouses – but you can't beat the location.

Spencer Spit State Park (☎ 360-468-2251, reservations ☎ 888-226-7688, Bakerview Rd) Standard sites $13, hiker/biker sites $6. Closed Nov-Feb. The campground borders an arrow-shaped sandbar that points to nearby Frost Island. One side is a driftwood-strewn beach popular with clam diggers. There are 32 sites – the seven nearest the water are designated for car-free campers – plus some three-sided cabins with eight bunks ($19).

Lopez Farm Cottages & Tent Camping (☎ 360-468-3555, 800-440-3556, W www.lopez farmcottages.com, Fisherman Bay Rd) Sites $28, cottages $150. Also near the ferry is this peaceful and thoughtfully managed campground, with sites nestled among tall trees slung with hammocks. A camp building is equipped with grills, a fireplace, sheltered picnic tables and hot showers. The cottages are cozily designed with couples in mind. They've got comfy queen-size beds, double-headed showers, kitchenettes and plenty of

Victory Hill totem, Orcas Island

unset at the Lime Kiln Point Lighthouse, San Juan Island

Fresnel lens at the Westport Lighthouse

oats moored in the tranquil bay at Roche Harbor, San Juan Island

The Hoh Rainforest is a lush canvas of greens galore.

A clear day at Olympic National Park's Rialto Beach

Bridge over troubled waters, Sol Duc Falls

Hanging moss and a still, green creek at Staircase Campground, Olympic National Park

polished wood. No kids under 14 or pets are permitted.

B&Bs & Hotels There are a few good options for nicer accomodations.

Edenwild Inn (☎ 360-468-3238, 800-606-0662, ⓦ *www.edenwildinn.com, Lopez Rd, Lopez Village)* Rooms $100-170. With its lovely formal gardens, wide porch and gables, this Victorian-style mansion in Lopez Village is possibly the most eye-catching building on the island. There are eight guest rooms, some with fireplaces, all with private baths.

MacKaye Harbor Inn (☎ 360-468-2253, 888-314-6140, ⓦ *www.mackayeharborinn.com, 949 MacKaye Harbor Rd)* Rooms $99-159. Standing stalwart at the edge of a shallow bay, this early-20th-century farmhouse contains four bedrooms and one harbor-view suite. The popular inn provides kayak rentals and complimentary mountain bikes.

Lopez Islander Resort (☎ 360-468-2233, 800-736-3434, ⓦ *www.lopezislander.com, Fisherman Bay Rd)* Rooms $100-259. This is perhaps the closest to a bona fide motel as you'll find in the San Juans. Most of the 26 spacious units have great bay views; some include kitchenettes. A circular pavilion encloses a hot tub and pool. Across the way

are a fireside dining room and lounge that open onto the marina.

Places to Eat
The following are less than a block apart in Lopez Village (in fact, they practically constitute Lopez Village).

Holly B's Bakery (☎ 360-468-2133, *Lopez Rd)* Open Apr-Nov. This is the early-morning latte and pastry stop.

Isabel's Espresso (☎ 360-468-4114, *Lopez Rd)* The painted cup on the sign lures caffeine fiends into this cheerful village hangout, which prepares all the java variations. All kinds of herbal teas are served, too.

Bucky's Lopez Island Grill (☎ 360-468-2595, *Lopez Rd)* $5.75-6.50. For a microbrew and a burger, head to this popular tavern.

The Bay Cafe (☎ 360-468-3700, 9 Old Post Rd) Dinner entrees $17-23. Inventive, ethnic seafood dishes headline the menu at the most noted restaurant on Lopez, with sunset dining on the bank of the bay.

Vortex Juice Bar (☎ 360-468-4740, *Lopez Rd S)* Lunch $4-6. Fresh juices are Vortex's forte, made with whatever fruits and vegetables are on hand, and hearty salads and wraps are among their other healthful offerings. In case you were wondering, wheatgrass juice is available.

Olympic Peninsula

A remote and rugged area of wild coast-lines, deep old-growth forests and craggy mountains, the Olympic Peninsula sticks out like a massive thumb from the mainland into the Pacific. It's bordered on the north and east by the Strait of Juan de Fuca and Hood Canal, respectively, and by the Chehalis River to the south. This moatlike isolation has allowed the peninsula to develop its own distinct ecological and human history.

One of the least populated parts of Washington, the Olympic Peninsula is home to Olympic National Park, which harbors the continent's only temperate rain forests, as well as genteel Victorian seaports and a number of Native American tribes.

The area has some of the most extreme weather in the USA. Because the towering peaks of the Olympic Mountains trap moist Pacific air, rainfall on the western slopes is massive. However, because the Olympics do such a thorough job of wringing out moisture, the land to the east remains remarkably dry and sunny. Sequim, just a few dozen miles from the rain forests, receives only 16 inches of rain a year, with 300 days of sunshine.

Highlights

- Ambling along loop trails and hiking on transpark treks through Olympic National Park

- Exploring the tide pools of the ruggedly beautiful Olympic Coastal Strip

- Gawking at the primordial, moss-draped Hoh Rain Forest

- Glimpsing treasures of Victorian architecture along Port Townsend's waterfront

History

For thousands of years, Native American communities such as the Makah, Quileute and Quinault lived off the rich bounty of the ocean, forest and rivers of the Olympic Peninsula, attaining a level of cultural sophistication as high as that of any Native American tribe.

European sailors were exploring the Northwest coast as early as 1592, which was when Juan de Fuca, a Greek sailing under the Spanish flag, discovered the strait that now bears his name. However, contact with the local people did not occur until some two centuries later, when the land was claimed by Spain, which planted a colony at Neah Bay but soon moved on to Vancouver Island.

The rugged mountains and inhospitable coast of the Olympic Peninsula didn't initially attract settlers. By 1851, Port Townsend was established, and farmers and fisherfolk began to eke out livings from the coastal verge. Expanses of virgin forest began to fall to the saw in the 1880s as mill towns like Aberdeen and Hoquiam sprang up to the south.

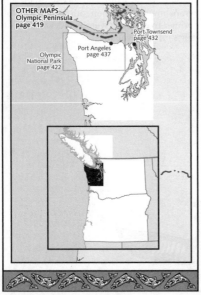

OTHER MAPS
Olympic Peninsula
page 419

Port Townsend
page 432

Port Angeles
page 437

Olympic
National Park
page 422

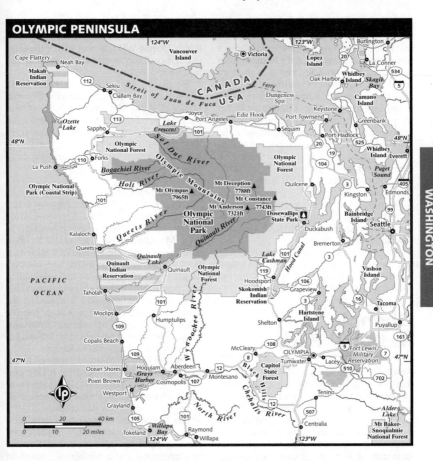

OLYMPIC PENINSULA

From the mid-19th century, efforts were made to explore the interior of the peninsula, but it remained mostly wild and isolated until the 1930s, when US 101 pushed through the deep forests, linking longtime coastal communities by road for the first time. Then, in 1938, after a 40-year struggle among conservationists, industrialists and logging companies, Olympic National Park was established in the heart of the peninsula.

Information

Worth picking up is *Dan Youra's Olympic Peninsula Guide,* usually available from visitor centers; or see the online version at **w** www.OlympicWA.com. The free publication is jammed with information and includes several good maps. The North Olympic Peninsula Visitor & Convention Bureau (☎ 360-452-8552, 800-942-4042, **w** www.olympicpeninsula.org) has a useful website with links to all the communities. Their free *North Olympic Peninsula Visitors Guide* can be ordered online at their website.

Orientation

Only one road, US 101, rings the Olympic Peninsula. Even though it's in excellent condition, distances are immense, and first-time visitors to the peninsula almost always find that it takes longer than expected to get where they're going. It's only 77 miles from Seattle to Port Angeles, but due to ferry schedules and traffic the journey can easily take half a day. The fastest access involves taking either the Seattle–Bainbridge Island ferry or the Edmonds-Kingston ferry and driving from there. You could also take the Whidbey Island ferry from Keystone to Port Townsend and continue on from there. Passenger- and car-ferry service is available from Port Angeles to Victoria, British Columbia.

Bus service along the northern Olympic Peninsula is a bit complicated. Port Angeles is the main hub of transportation (see that section, later, for details).

Horizon Air has service from Portland, Seattle, Whidbey Island and San Juan Island to Fairchild International Airport, on the outskirts of Port Angeles.

Olympic National Park

Noted for its backcountry hiking, dramatic scenery and widely varying ecosystems, Olympic National Park is best thought of as a wilderness preserve. Magnificent waterfalls, wide alpine meadows sparkling with summer wildflowers, eerie moss-bearded forests dripping with fog, and remote lakes shimmering beneath glaciers are among the destinations available to long-distance walkers who venture across the park's interior. Camping is easy, with 17 large, car-accessible campgrounds as well as 95 backcountry campgrounds.

One of the last areas of Washington to be explored, the heavily glaciered Olympic Mountains rise to nearly 8000 feet in only 25 miles from sea level. Calls for the Olympics to be preserved as a national park were made as early as 1897; however, the area was initially declared a forest reserve, and then, in 1909, a national monument by President Theodore Roosevelt. Such designations

didn't save large portions of these federal lands from falling into private and state hands. During WWI, almost half of the original national monument was opened up for mining and logging.

Finally, in 1938, President Franklin D Roosevelt succeeded in establishing Olympic National Park. The original 1012-sq-mile park consisted of only the highest and most rugged peaks in the range, but, in later years the lowland rain forests and coastal strip were added, bringing the total area to nearly 1406 sq miles.

Information

About a mile south of Port Angeles is the Olympic National Park Visitor Center (☎ 360-565-3130, ⓦ www.nps.gov/olym), at 3002 Mt Angeles Rd. The center is open 9am to 4pm and offers children's exhibits, a bookstore and several interactive displays on plant and animal life, as well as a replica of a prehistoric Makah seal-hunting canoe. A lot of free information is available. Be sure to pick up an official park map (yup, it's free), which points out campgrounds and ranger stations, and look for the useful series of self-guided-trail brochures.

Custom Correct Maps, at a scale of 1 inch to 1 mile, are the standard for hiking and climbing on the peninsula. Purchase them ($3 each) at visitor centers or online at ⓦ www.customcorrectmaps.com.

Black bears and other critters have been known to invade campsites in search of food. Animal-resistant food canisters are recommended and available on loan from ranger stations. Backpackers can also hang their food from 'bear wires' installed at certain campgrounds. Pets are not allowed on national-park trails.

For information on the Olympic National Forest, a 630,000-acre area that borders much of the park's perimeter, contact the USFS headquarters outside Olympia (☎ 360-956-2400, ⓦ www.fs.fed.us/r6/olympic), at 1835 Black Lake Blvd SW; office hours are 8am to 4:30pm weekdays. Or you can try the field offices in Hoodsport, Quilcene, Quinault and Forks. These offices distribute free backcountry permits for wilderness camping in the park as well as Northwest Forest Passes ($5), required for parking at trailheads in the forest.

National-park admission fees are $10 per vehicle, $5 per pedestrian/cyclist, and are valid for seven days for park entry and reentry. An annual 'passport' for unlimited entry one year from purchase costs $20. Fees are collected year round at Hoh and Heart o' the Hills entry points, and from May to October at Elwha, Sol Duc and Staircase. (Payment is not mandatory where there is no entrance station or when an entrance station isn't open.)

Backpackers must register for overnight stays in backcountry areas. There's a $5 permit fee for groups of up to 12, valid for two weeks from purchase, plus a $2-per-person nightly fee for anyone over 16 years old. You can get permits from the Wilderness Information Center (☎ 360-565-3100, e olym_wic@nps.gov), at 600 E Park Ave in Port Angeles, behind the visitor center; it's open 8am to 4:30pm April to September. You can also get them from the Hoh visitor center or from ranger stations throughout the park.

Activities

Olympic National Park is approximately 40 miles in diameter, and few roads penetrate more than a relatively few miles into the park proper. This means that the majority of the park's land is the domain of the vehicle-free.

Hiking Most of the park is the province of hikers, especially those who are willing to traverse the wilderness on one of the many long-distance trails. The 57-mile Olympic Coastal Strip, a parcel of the national park that is unconnected to the park proper, is accessible only to hikers, who can marvel at the wildlife, the ancient petroglyphs and the scenery of this rugged coastline. You can arrange to be picked up or dropped off at trailheads by **Olympic Tours & Charters** (☎ 360-452-3500). Packhorses are sometimes used for carrying gear on cross-park expeditions (but are limited to designated stock camps).

Rafting, Kayaking & Fishing A number of outfitters run white-water rafting trips on the park's rivers, including the Hoh, Elwha and Queets. The **Olympic Outdoor Center** (☎ 360-697-6095, W www.kayakproshop.com), in Poulsbo (just north of Bremerton), operates several white-water-rafting and sea-kayaking trips. They also offer equipment sales, rentals and instruction ($250 for a four-session kayaking course). **Olympic Raft & Kayak** (☎ 360-452-1443, 888-452-1443, W www.raftandkayak.com, 123 Lake Aldwell Rd, Port Angeles) offers trips on the Elwha and Hoh Rivers (adult/youth from $49/39) along with rentals and classes.

Rivers and lakes in the park are noted for their trout and salmon fishing. No license is needed, although those fishing for trout or steelhead are required to fill out a Washington state catch record card, and all wild fish must be released. Canoe and kayak rentals are available at many of the larger lakes.

Skiing In winter, the area around Hurricane Ridge has over 20 miles of trails for cross-country skiing, snowboarding and snowshoeing. Downhill skiers will find a 665-foot vertical drop and a couple of rope tow lifts.

Climbing Rugged Mt Olympus (7965 feet) is the most commonly climbed peak. However, don't let its relative lack of stature fool you. Mt Olympus is the first major peak that Pacific storms encounter. A lot of snow – and harsh weather in general – falls here. In the continental USA, only Mt Rainier and Mt Baker have more extensive glacial formations.

Access is from the Hoh Trail, which basically ends at Glacier Meadows, 17 miles from the Hoh visitor center. The campground here is frequently used as a base camp for ascents of the mountain. Much of the remaining climb is on glaciers and along craggy escarpments. Most people make the ascent between June and early September, although adventurous souls begin to climb as early as April.

Each year Mt Olympus claims several lives and causes injuries, usually from falls into glacial crevasses or exposure during storms. Guided climbs and mountaineering

OLYMPIC NATIONAL PARK

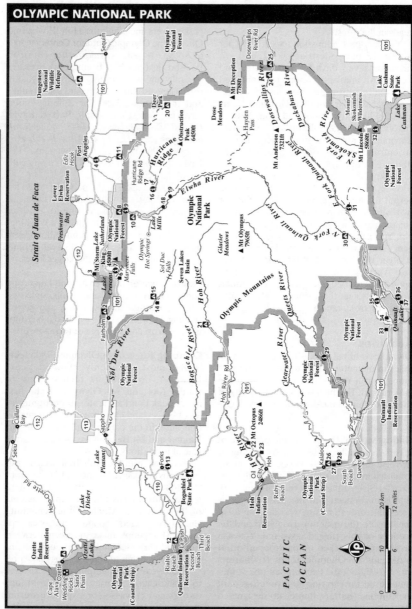

OLYMPIC NATIONAL PARK

PLACES TO STAY
1 Lake Ozette Campground & Ranger Station
2 Fairholm Campground
3 Log Cabin Resort
5 Dungeness Recreation Area
6 Lake Crescent Lodge
8 Elwha Campground
10 Altaire Campground
11 Heart o' the Hills Campground
12 Mora Campground & Ranger Station
14 Sol Duc Hot Springs Resort
15 Sol Duc Campground & Ranger Station
20 Deer Park Campground

21 Hoh Campground; Hoh Rain Forest Visitor Center
22 Hoh Humm Ranch
23 Rain Forest Hostel
24 Dosewallips Campground & Ranger Station
25 Elkhorn Campground
26 Kalaloch Campground
27 Kalaloch Lodge
30 North Fork Campground & Ranger Station
33 Amanda Park Motel
34 Lochaerie Resort
37 Lake Quinault Lodge

OTHER
4 Olympic National Park Visitor Center

7 Storm King Information Station
9 Elwha Ranger Station
13 USFS/NPS Information Station
16 Hurricane Ridge Visitor Center
17 Hurricane Ridge Ski Area
18 Whiskey Bend
19 Humes Ranch
28 Kalaloch Ranger Station
29 Queets Ranger Station; Queets Campground
31 Graves Creek Ranger Station; Graves Creek Campground
32 Staircase Ranger Station; Staircase Campground
35 Quinalt Ranger Station
36 Quinault USFS Office

WASHINGTON

schools for would-be climbers are available and are suggested for novices. **Olympic Mountaineering** (☎ 360-452-0240, W www .olymtn.com, 140 W Front St, Port Angeles; classes $25, guided summit climbs $75-225) is a great clearinghouse for guides, outdoor gear, supplies, classes and lessons in many sports. The store also rents such gear as stoves, packs, tents and skis.

For further reference, get hold of Custom Correct maps for the peak as well as the book *Climber's Guide to the Olympic Mountains,* published by The Mountaineers.

Organized Tours

For ecologically oriented tours of Olympic National Park, contact **Olympic Tours & Charters** (☎ 360-452-3500, W www.tourthe olympics.com, PO Box 2201, Port Angeles, WA 98362). Half-/full-day excursions to Hurricane Ridge are $19/22 for adults, $12/15 for children under 12. They also do a full-day circuit of the peninsula ($52 per person).

The environmentally oriented **Olympic Park Institute** (☎ 360-928-3720, W www.yni .org/opi, 111 Barnes Point Rd, Lake Crescent) offers seminars in a wide variety of fields, including geology, wildflowers, marine mammals, Northwest Native American art and forest ecology. Courses, most given on weekends, involve outdoor field trips and ex-

cursions. Fees range from $150 to $250 and include food and lodging alongside the lake.

Camping

Certain high-use campgrounds may be reserved in season. Reservations are required to camp at Cape Alava and Sand Point beaches on the Olympic Coastal Strip (see that section, later, for details). At other campgrounds, including Seven Lakes Basin and Mink Lake along the Sol Duc Valley, half of the sites may be reserved, while the rest are on a first-come, first-served basis. Make reservations through the Wilderness Information Center in Port Angeles (see Information, earlier).

NORTHERN ENTRANCES

The most popular access to Olympic National Park is from the north. Port Angeles and Sequim are good jumping-off points for valley hikes and for visiting Hurricane Ridge and Deer Park. The park's largest lake, Lake Crescent, is popular with anglers and boaters, and it sports two lodges.

Hurricane Ridge

Beginning at sea level in Port Angeles, the 18-mile Hurricane Ridge Rd climbs up 5300 feet into the Olympic peaks to extensive wildflower meadows and expansive vistas. On a clear day, the rugged peaks and glaciers of Mt Olympus loom across the deep, and frequently cloud-filled, Elwha River valley.

The Hurricane Ridge visitor center (open 9:30am-5pm daily when road is open; Fri-Sun & Mon holidays only in midwinter) has a snack bar, gift shop, toilets, and ski and snowshoe rentals. Call ☎ 360-565-3131 or tune in to 530 AM in Port Angeles for weather and road conditions on the ridge.

Hurricane Ridge is a good base for many activities, though there is no camping. In summer, rangers conduct a number of open-air talks and hikes. During the winter, cross-country and downhill skiing and snowboarding take over; on weekends, rangers lead free guided snowshoe tours.

One of the highest points accessible to vehicles in the park, Hurricane Ridge is the takeoff point for a number of short **hikes** leading through meadows to vista points. **Hurricane Hill Trail**, which begins at the end of the road leading up, and the **Meadow Loop Trails** network, starting at the visitor center, are popular, moderately easy hikes. The first half-mile of these trails is wheelchair-accessible.

From Hurricane Ridge, you can drive a rough and frequently steep 7¾-mile road to **Obstruction Peak**, with even better views of the Olympic peaks. Here, hikers looking for long-distance treks can pick up the **Grand Ridge Trail**, which leads 7½ miles to Deer Park, much of the way above the timberline; or the **Wolf Creek Trail**, an 8-mile downhill jaunt to Whiskey Bend, where it picks up the Elwha Trail.

Hurricane Ridge is a great departure point for **cross-country skiers** to explore pristine high meadows and mountain ridges. The road to the ridge is plowed every weekend and stays open Monday and Thursday, weather permitting. A number of ski trails are indicated in a brochure available from park rangers; alternatively, you can follow trail signs. Avalanche conditions can make some routes dangerous, so check with park rangers before departing on long trails, or phone the Northwest Avalanche Center (☎ 206-526-6677).

The **downhill-skiing** area is open weekends only from mid-December to March.

Although the ski area doesn't offer many challenges for advanced skiers, the gentle 1600-foot slope is a good place for families or beginners. All-day lift tickets are $18. Folks on inner tubes and sleds use a separate area behind the ski hill. For information on rentals, contact the **Hurricane Ridge Winter Sports Club** (*☎ 360-417-1542,* **W** *www.hurricaneridge.net).*

Elwha River Valley

The Elwha, the largest river on the Olympic Peninsula, and Lake Mills (actually a reservoir) are popular for **trout fishing**. Elwha River Rd turns south from US 101 about 8 miles west of Port Angeles. Follow it for 10 miles to the Elwha Ranger Station (☎ 360-452-9191), at 480 Upper Elwha Rd. The road immediately forks. Turn west to reach the Olympic Hot Springs trailhead, or turn east toward Whiskey Bend to reach the Elwha River and other trailheads.

Commercially developed as a resort in the 1930s, the **Olympic Hot Springs** once featured cabins that have long since disappeared. In 1983, park supervisors closed the road out, and the area has largely returned to nature. The 2.2-mile **hike** along the old roadbed is well worth it – what's left of the old pools steam alongside the rushing Boulder Creek, all in a verdant deep-forest grove. (However, authorities warn that the pools do not meet public bathing safety standards and may contain traces of harmful bacteria.) Note that official maps don't even show the hot springs, which are a short hike from Boulder Creek Campground. You'll need a backcountry permit to stay overnight.

From Whiskey Bend, the **Elwha Trail** leads up the main branch of the Elwha River and is one of the primary cross-park trails, leading to the park's eastern entrance at Dosewallips and, over Low Divide, to the North Fork Quinault River entrance. Day hikers may elect to follow the trail for 2 miles to Humes Ranch, the remains of a homestead-era ranch.

Lake Crescent

About 8½ miles long and 624 feet deep, Lake Crescent is among the most popular stops in the park due to its beautiful vistas, its boating and fishing, and Lake Crescent Lodge, one of the park's venerable resorts. For information about the area, contact the Storm King Information Station (☎ 360-928-3380), just east of Lake Crescent Lodge off US 101; it's open only in the summer.

One of the most popular short **hikes** in the park goes to **Marymere Falls**, a 90-foot cascade that drapes down a basalt cliff. This 2-mile roundtrip leads out from the Storm King Ranger Station along the Barnes Creek Trail. The trail is wheelchair-accessible to the Barnes Creek overlook. For a more energetic hike, climb up the side of **Mt Storm King**, the peak that rises to the east of Lake Crescent. The steep, 1.7-mile ascent splits off the Barnes Creek Trail.

Trout fishing is good here, as the lake is very deep with steep shorelines, though only artificial lures are allowed. Boat rentals (rowboats & canoes $9 per hour, kayaks $12 per hour) are available at Lake Crescent Lodge and the Log Cabin Resort (see Places to Stay & Eat, later).

Sol Duc River Valley

Just west of Lake Crescent, the Sol Duc River flows toward the Pacific Coast. Its headwaters fall within the national-park boundaries and offer a developed hot-springs resort and some of the best day-hiking in the Olympics. From US 101, a paved road follows the river for nearly 14 miles, passing the resort and the Sol Duc Ranger Station (☎ 360-327-3534); open summer only.

As Indian legend tells it, the geological phenomenon at Sol Duc is the legacy of a battle between two lightning fish. When neither fish won the contest, each crawled beneath the earth and shed bitter tears, forming the heated mineral springs here. These springs have been diverted into three large tiled pools for health and recreation at **Sol Duc Hot Springs Resort** (☎ 360-327-3583, **w** northolympic.com/solduc; adult/ senior & disabled/child/baby $10/6.75/7.50/3; closed Nov-Apr). There's also a standard swimming pool to cool off in, as well as a restaurant, snack bar, gift shop and overnight accommodations (see Places to

Stay & Eat). In summer, rangers lead programs and activities.

About 1½ miles beyond the resort, the Sol Duc road terminates and **trails** lead into the forest. The most popular hike here is to **Sol Duc Falls**, where the river plummets 40 feet into a narrow gorge. The three-quarter-mile walk follows a gentle grade through a mossy old-growth cedar forest before crossing a bridge above the falls.

For a more strenuous hike, cross the bridge at the falls and climb the **Deer Lake Trail** along Canyon Creek. This sometimes steep, 8-mile (roundtrip) trail reaches the tree-rimmed lake, then joins the **High Divide Trail**. This trail in turn leads to the Seven Lakes Basin, a popular overnight destination. Another good leg-stretcher is the 2½-mile **Mink Lake Trail**, departing from the resort. The marshy lake is noted for its bird and wildlife viewing.

Places to Stay & Eat

In addition to the campgrounds and lodges inside Olympic National Park, there's less-rustic lodging in Port Angeles, within easy reach of the northern entrances.

Camping Nearly all of the national-park campgrounds have running water and toilets and allow pets, but there are no showers or RV hookups. Reservations are not accepted.

Just inside the park along the Elwha River are the ***Elwha Campground*** (☎ 360-452-9191), which has 41 sites, and ***Altaire Campground***, with 30. The fee at either one is $10.

Heart o' the Hills Campground (☎ 360-452-2713, 876 Hurricane Ridge Rd) Sites $10. Five miles south of Port Angeles, this is the closest campground to Hurricane Ridge, with 105 sites.

Deer Park Campground Sites $8. The 14-site campground (no RVs) is the takeoff point for the high-altitude Grand Ridge trail. Access is up a steep gravel road off US 101, 5 miles east of Port Angeles.

Fairholm Campground (☎ 360-928-3380) Sites $10. The only national-park campground on Lake Crescent features 88 sites, a

Roosevelt Elk

The Roosevelt species of elk is found only in the coastal mountains of the Pacific Northwest, and protection of the herds in the Olympic Mountains was one of the initial reasons for establishing the national park. Roosevelt elk – named after Teddy, who assisted in their preservation – are light brown in color, with dark brown underparts. They are larger than the Rocky Mountain wapiti (American elk): Bull elks can weigh upwards of 1000lb and have dark brown manes and antlers up to 5 feet across. They are also more social animals, often running in herds of up to 50. However, Roosevelt elk are notoriously shy animals, and even though an estimated 7000 live on the peninsula, it is unlikely that hikers will sight one.

general store and boat rentals. It's on the lake's west end.

Sol Duc Campground (☎ 360-327-3534) Sites $12. This 82-site facility is immediately upstream from the Sol Duc Hot Springs Resort.

Lodges & Cabins Resorts at Lake Crescent and Sol Duc have lodged visitors since the park's earliest days.

Lake Crescent Lodge (☎ 360-928-3211, 416 Lake Crescent Rd) Lodge rooms with shared bath $69, cabins $105-150 per night. Open May-Oct. Built in 1915 as a fishing resort, this old shake-sided lodge still operates as the main accommodation, restaurant and bar, though a number of lakeside cabins have been added. Make reservations well in advance.

Log Cabin Resort (☎ 360-928-3325, fax 360-928-2088, w www.logcabinresort.net, 3183 E Beach Rd) Accommodations $57-

135. Open April-Oct. On the north bank of Lake Crescent, this resort has cabins, chalets (which sleep six), lodge rooms and RV hookups. The restaurant is favored by anglers and other hungry outdoor types.

Sol Duc Hot Springs Resort (☎ 360-327-3583, fax 360-327-3293, w www.north olympic.com/solduc, Port Angeles) Rooms $104-115, RV sites $16. Open late Apr-Oct. Thirty-two modern, rather unromantic cabins, some with kitchens and all with private baths, provide accommodations for visitors taking to the waters. There is also a restaurant (open in summer only), a grocery store and massage service.

EASTERN ENTRANCES

The eastern entrances to Olympic National Park aren't as developed with lodges and interpretive sites as other access points, but they are the closest to major population centers and serve as access points for long-distance hikers from the Puget Sound area.

Dosewallips River Valley

This narrow valley (**doe**-sey-**wal**-ups) is surrounded by some of the highest mountains in the Olympics, including Mt Anderson and Mt Deception. The gravel Dosewallips River Rd terminates at the ranger station 15 miles from US 101, where trails begin.

Day-hikers won't find many satisfying short loop trails here, but hiking portions of the two long-distance paths – with views of heavily glaciered Mt Anderson – is reason enough to visit. From the Dosewallips Ranger Station, a wide trail leads upriver for 1.4 miles to Dose Forks, where the path divides into two major transpark trails.

The northbound **Dosewallips Trail** climbs up to beautiful Dose Meadows (10 miles from Dose Forks) before crossing Hayden Pass and dropping into the Elwha Valley and the Elwha Trail. The southerly **West Fork Dosewallips Trail** leads to Honeymoon Meadows (9 miles from Dose Forks), a spring-filled basin beneath the glaciers of precipitous 7321-foot Mt Anderson. The trail continues up to Anderson Pass and into the East Fork Quinault River trail system.

Staircase

Staircase is another favorite entrance for hikers, in part because the national-park trail system nearly abuts Lake Cushman State Park, which is immensely popular with families, anglers and boaters from the Tacoma area. The **Staircase Ranger Station** (☎ *360-877-5569*) is just inside the national-park boundary, 16 miles from US 101 and the small town of Hoodsport.

The trail system here follows the drainage of the North Fork Skokomish River, which is flanked by some of the most rugged peaks in the Olympics. The principal long-distance trail is the **North Fork Skokomish Trail**, which leads up this heavily forested valley, eventually crossing into the Duckabush River valley to intercept other transpark trail systems. Ambitious day-hikers might consider following this trail 3.7 miles to the **Flapjack Lakes Trail**, an easy 4-mile climb up to several small lakes that shimmer beneath the crags of the Sawtooth peaks.

A popular short hike follows the south bank of the North Fork Skokomish River through lush old-growth forest along the **Staircase Rapids Loop Trail**. Continue up the trail a short distance to the Rapids Bridge, which crosses over to the North Fork Skokomish Trail and makes for a nice 2-mile loop.

Places to Stay

There are two popular state parks along the east edge of the national park; both have running water, flush toilets and some RV hookups.

Dosewallips State Park (☎ *360-796-4415, reservations* ☎ *888-226-7688*) Tent sites/hookups $13/19. Near Brinnon along US 101 is this 140-site expanse of meadow, close to the mouth of the Dosewallips River and facing Hood Canal.

Lake Cushman State Park (☎ *360-877-5491, reservations* ☎ *888-226-7688, Hwy 119*) Tent sites/hookups $13/19. Eight miles northwest of Hoodsport, this campground is centered on a large reservoir on the Skokomish River, popular with anglers, water-skiers and campers.

Dosewallips Campground (☎ *360-877-5254*) Tent sites $10. At the end of the Dose-

wallips River road (unsuitable for RV travel), just inside the national-park boundary, are 30 primitive sites. Drinking water is available.

Staircase Campground (☎ *360-877-5569*) Tent sites $10. Past Lake Cushman at the end of Forest Rd 24 are these 59 sites, alongside the North Fork Skokomish River.

WESTERN ENTRANCES

The Pacific side of the Olympics is the remotest part of the park and home to the noted temperate rain forests. Three mighty rivers drain this face of the Olympics; their valleys fill with the full force of the Pacific's clouds and moisture, guaranteeing the annual 12 feet of rain necessary for the region's luxuriant plant growth.

US 101 is the only road that accesses this vast, heavily wooded area. By car, it's a long drive to Queets or Hoh from the Puget Sound area.

Hoh Rain Forest

The most famous of the Olympic rain forests, the Hoh River area offers a variety of hikes and an interpretive center. If you have room for only one stop on the western side, this should be it. The following sites are off the paved all-weather Hoh River Rd, which winds through clear-cuts before reaching the national-park boundary, 12 miles from US 101. While driving toward the visitor center, stop at the **giant Sitka spruce tree** just beside the road. This lord of the forest is 270 feet high and over 500 years old.

At the end of Hoh River Rd, the **Hoh Rain Forest Visitor Center** (☎ *360-374-6925; open 9am-4:30pm Sept-June; 9am-6pm July & Aug*) offers displays on the ecology of the rain forest and the plants and animals that inhabit it, as well as a bookstore. Rangers lead guided walks twice a day during summer; call ahead for times.

Leading out from the visitor center are several excellent day **hikes** into virgin rain forest. The most popular is the justly famous **Hall of Moss Trail**, an easy three-quarter-mile loop through some of the shaggiest trees you'll ever see. Epiphytic club moss, ferns and lichens completely overwhelm the massive

WASHINGTON

trunks of maples and Sitka spruces in this misty forest. The 1¼-mile **Spruce Nature Trail** is another short interpreted loop leading out from the visitor center. Just outside the visitor center is a short wheelchair-accessible nature trail through a rain-forest marsh.

The **Hoh River Trail** is the major entry trail into the wide, glacier-channeled Hoh River valley. It is also the principal access to Mt Olympus (see Climbing, under Activities, earlier). The trail follows an easy grade for 12 miles, and day-hikers will find this a very pleasant if undramatic hike; just keep going until you need to turn back. If you are tempted to make this an overnight trip (there are numerous formal and informal campsites along the way), be sure to pick up a backcountry permit from the visitor center.

Queets River Valley

The Queets River valley is the remotest part of Olympic National Park. Part of this isolation is intentional: The park service has made access to the valley rather challenging, and trails don't link up with any other transpark routes. The so-called Queets Corridor was added to the park in 1953 in an attempt to preserve one of the peninsula's river valleys all the way from its glacial beginnings to the coast.

Queets River Rd leaves US 101 and almost immediately drops into the national park. The road then follows the river for 13 miles before ending at **Queets Campground & Ranger Station** (☎ 360-962-2283). From here, there is one popular day hike – the gentle, 3-mile **Queets Campground Loop Trail**.

Experienced or adventurous hikers can elect to ford the Queets River in late summer or fall and explore the **Queets Trail**, which leads up the river for 15 miles before petering out in heavy forest. The trail passes through old-growth rain forest – the trees here are sometimes so large as to be disquieting – and past great fishing holes (the Queets is noted for both salmon and steelhead).

Lake Quinalt

The focus of the Quinault Valley is Lake Quinault, a deep blue glacial lake surrounded by forested peaks. The second-largest lake in Olympic National Park, it offers fishing, boating and swimming for the resorts and homes along the lakeshore (the charming Lake Quinault Lodge is one of the few original Olympic lodges still in business). Upstream from Lake Quinault, the river divides into the North Fork and East Fork Quinault Rivers. Both valleys harbor important transpark trails.

The lake is accessed by two different roads. The South Shore Rd leads to the tiny village of Quinault, with lodges and a **USFS office** (☎ 360-288-2525, 353 S Shore Rd) before climbing up to the trailhead of the famed Enchanted Valley within the East Fork Quinault valley. The North Shore Rd passes the **Quinault Ranger Station** (☎ 360-288-2444) before climbing up to the North Fork Quinault trailhead. (A bridge links the two roads about 13 miles up the valley.)

Lake Quinault is part of the Quinault Indian Reservation, and fishing is regulated by the tribe; check locally for tribal licenses and regulations. Boat rentals are available from Lake Quinault Lodge on South Shore Rd, and boat slips are found at both south-shore public campgrounds.

A number of short **hiking trails** begin just below Lake Quinault Lodge; pick up a free map from the USFS office. The shortest of these is the **Quinault Rain Forest Nature Trail**, a half-mile walk through 500-year-old Douglas firs. This short trail adjoins the 3-mile **Quinault Loop Trail**, which meanders through the rain forests before circling back to the lake. A Northwest Forest Pass is required to park at the trailheads.

Quinault River Valley

Leading to arguably the most famous – and certainly one of the most photographed – parts of the park, the **Enchanted Valley Trail** climbs up to a large meadow (a former glacial lake bed) percolated by streams and springs, and resplendent with wildflowers and copses of alders. To the north are sheer cliff faces and peaks rising 2000 feet from the valley floor; during spring snowmelt, the 3-mile-long precipice is drizzled by thousands of small waterfalls.

The Enchanted Valley is reached after a long hike from the Graves Creek Ranger Station at the end of the South Shore Rd, 19 miles from US 101. (The South Shore Rd was closed indefinitely for flood damage 6 miles from the trailhead – inquire about its condition before setting out.) The first 12 miles of the trail are narrowly walled in by forested ridges. After the Enchanted Valley, the trail is mostly level for 2½ miles, before it arches up to Anderson Pass (19 miles from Graves Creek). Here, long-distance hikers can continue down the **West Fork Dosewallips Trail** to complete a popular transpark trek.

Another cross-park path passes through the North Fork Quinault River valley to join the lengthy Elwha River trail system. The **North Fork Quinault Trail** begins at the end of the North Shore Rd, at the North Fork Campground & Ranger Station, 17 miles from US 101. This major trail is not as picturesque as the East Fork, since much of the lower terrain is heavily forested.

Places to Stay & Eat

Campgrounds abound along the Hoh, Queets and Quinault Valleys, while an HI hostel, a modest motel and several lodges accommodate those who demand a roof over their heads.

Camping & Hostels Sites at the listed NPS campgrounds are available on a first-come, first-served basis; there are no RV hookups.

Hoh Campground (☎ 360-374-6925) Sites $10. Adjacent to the Hoh Rain Forest Visitor Center, the campground features 88 sites, most alongside the Hoh River.

Queets Campground (☎ 360-962-2283) Sites $8. Located at the end of Queets River Rd (not recommended for RVs), these 20 primitive sites are tucked amid temperate rain forest.

North Fork Campground (☎ 360-288-2444) Free. Drinking water is not available at this tents-only facility by the North Fork Quinault trailhead.

Graves Creek Campground (☎ 360-288-2444) Sites $10. There are 30 sites here, plus drinking water and flush toilets, at the point of departure for the Enchanted Valley hike.

Rain Forest Hostel (☎ 360-374-2270, e go2hostel@centurytel.net, 169312 US Hwy 101, Forks) Bunks/private rooms $12/25. Eight miles south of the Hoh Rain Forest road turnoff on US 101 (and 4½ miles from Ruby Beach), this independent hostel feels isolated and has a rather dank interior. Facilities include a full kitchen, common room and fireplace, and Internet access. Guests are asked to do a housekeeping chore.

Hotels & Lodges Of the lodgings in this remote section of the park, only Lake Quinault Lodge includes a restaurant (open to the public).

Hoh Humm Ranch (☎ 360-374-5337, fax 360-374-5344, e hohhumm@olypen.com, 171763 US Hwy 101) Rooms from $40. Seven miles south of the Hoh Rainforest road, this cozy, bright farmhouse has five modest but clean rooms that share a bath and balcony overlooking the Hoh River. A hearty breakfast is included.

Amanda Park Motel (☎ 360-288-2237, 800-410-2237, fax 360-532-1432, Amanda Park) Singles/doubles $60/65. The only motel in the area is just off the highway on the north side of the Lake Quinault. It's aimed at the rod-and-reel crowd, with straightforward wood-paneled rooms and cable TV. There's a Japanese-American restaurant nearby.

Lake Quinault Lodge (☎ 360-288-2900, 800-562-6672, fax 360-288-2901, w www .visitlakequinault.com, 345 S Shore Rd) Lodge rooms $115-140, cabins $150-170. This Northwest landmark was built in 1926, and its classic fireplace lobby has greeted visitors ever since. Rooms are available in the old shake-sided lodge and also in a number of detached cabins. Facilities include a heated pool, gift shop and boat rentals. The lodge's lake-view dining room offers lunches from $7 and dinners, featuring steak and local fish, from $14.

Lochaerie Resort (☎ 360-288-2215, w www.lochaerie.com, 638 N Shore Rd) Cabins $80-95. On the north shore of Lake Quinault, this venerable resort offers lodging in six comfortable cabins, each unique in character.

WASHINGTON

OLYMPIC COASTAL STRIP

Fifty-seven miles of the Olympic Peninsula coast were added to the national park in 1953. This is some of the most rugged and picturesque coastline anywhere: Sea stacks and islands parade out into the pounding surf, often capped by miniature forests (remnants of when these rocks were still part of the headland). There's a wealth of life in tide pools and on rocky aviaries, while gray whales spout offshore. Marine mammals are abundant, and some, such as sea otters and harbor seals, are rarely seen elsewhere in the continental US.

The coastline is accessed by roads at only a few places. Although there are a number of areas where beachcombers can sample the coast's riches, this expanse of rock, sea water and sand belongs largely to hardy trekkers who negotiate the tides, waves and treacherous headlands on foot.

Long-distance hiking along the Pacific Ocean should not be entered into lightly – it's more than just a saunter down a sandy strand. If you are contemplating a trek along the coast, request information from the NPS (see Information under Port Angeles and Forks), buy good maps and learn to read tide tables. Many portions of the coastline can be negotiated only at low tide, while other areas can't be rounded on foot at any time. These promontories require strenuous climbs up and down (often on rope ladders) and cross-country excursions to the next safe beach-walking area. Fast-moving waves can easily isolate hikers on rocky points or headlands. In all but the height of summer, hikers need to be prepared for all kinds of weather.

The most popular long-distance beach hike is the section between Ozette and Rialto Beach, a 20-mile trek that usually requires three or four days. Another favorite three-nighter is the beach hike between Third Beach (near La Push) and Oil City, a 17-mile hike along one of the most rugged stretches of the Olympic Peninsula's coast. Remember that you'll need a backcountry permit to camp overnight along the coast (except at official campgrounds). The brochure *Olympic Coastal Strip,* available from ranger stations,

is useful for those going on coastal loop hikes or overnight treks. Also pick up a copy of The Mountaineers' *Exploring Washington's Wild Olympic Coast,* by David Hooper, which admirably describes the challenges and pleasures of these coastal hikes.

Note that there is no entry fee for this section of Olympic National Park.

Ozette

Noted as the site of an ancient Makah village (see Neah Bay, later in this chapter), the Ozette area is one of the most accessible parts of the Olympic coast. Except on the busiest summer weekends, it's easy to get away from the crowds and experience these beaches as wilderness.

The Hoko-Ozette Rd leaves Hwy 112 about 3 miles west of Sekiu and proceeds 21 miles to **Lake Ozette Ranger Station & Campground** (☎ 360-963-2725; open 8am-4:30pm), on Ozette Lake. The lake, the third largest in Washington, is a popular spot for water-skiers and anglers.

From the ranger station, two boardwalk trails lead out to the beach. The 3.3-mile **Cape Alava Trail** leads north to a section of sandy beach that is the westernmost point of land in the continental US. Just north of Cape Alava is the site of the ancient Makah village of Ozette, unearthed by archaeologists in the 1970s to reveal numerous artifacts that had been preserved under a 500-year-old mudslide. These objects are on display at the Makah Museum in Neah Bay. The southern **Sand Point Trail** from Ozette Ranger Station leads 3 miles to beaches below a low bluff; whale watchers often come here in the migration season.

The two Ozette trails can easily be linked as a long day hike. It's a little over 3 miles between Cape Alava and Sand Point along the beach, making it around 9½ miles for the entire loop. The rather coarse, rocky beach can make this hike strenuous, and it pays to be aware of the tides.

The high point of this hike is the **Wedding Rocks**, the most significant group of petroglyphs on the Olympic Peninsula. Approximately a mile south of Cape Alava, the small outcropping contains carvings of whales, a

European square-rigger and fertility figures. The site was traditionally used for Makah weddings and is still considered sacred.

A $1 parking fee is charged at the trailheads. Lightweight rubber-soled shoes are best for the often slippery boardwalks.

Rialto Beach

One of the few Olympic beaches easily accessed by vehicle, Rialto is a popular place for day excursions. Located at the mouth of the Quillayute River across from La Push, the log-littered, stony beach faces a profusion of flat-topped offshore islands. Hikers with an eye on the tide table can trek up to **Hole-in-the-Wall**, a bluff hollowed out by the pounding surf, about 2 miles north of the parking area. This is a wild place to visit after a storm, when waves barrel up to the edge of the forest, dragging logs out to sea.

Facilities at Rialto Beach include flush toilets and picnic tables. To get there, turn west 1 mile north of Forks off US 101 and follow the La Push road (Hwy 110). In 13 miles the road divides (with Rialto Beach another 4 miles along the northern fork). The **Mora Ranger Station** (☎ 360-374-5460), midway down this road, can issue backcountry permits.

Ruby Beach to South Beach

This southernmost portion of the Olympic Coastal Strip, located between the Hoh and Quinault Indian Reservations, is easily accessed from US 101, though less dramatic than the north. Perhaps the most attractive stretches are found at Ruby Beach, strewn with polished black stones the size of silver dollars, and at Kalaloch (**klay**-lock). Other beachfronts (imaginatively named 'Beach One' through 'Beach Six') are sandy strands popular with beachcombers. At low tide, rangers give talks on tidal-pool life at Beach Four and on the ecosystems of the Olympic Coastal strip. For information about this area, contact the **Kalaloch Ranger Station** (☎ 360-962-2283; open 9am-5pm May-Oct).

Places to Stay & Eat

Between May and September, advance reservations are required to stay at any of the designated campsites along the beach at Cape Alava and Sand Point. To make a reservation, contact the **Wilderness Information Center** (☎ 360-452-0300) or reserve online at [w] www .nps.gov/olym/wic. (Keep in mind that reservations are not assigned to any particular site; early arrivals get the best sites.) In addition, campers must obtain a wilderness permit. Hungry raccoons may invade campsites, so store food in animal-resistant containers, available on loan from ranger stations ($3 donation requested). No reservations are accepted at the listed campgrounds.

Lake Ozette Campground (☎ 360-963-2725) Sites $10. The 13 sites fill every day before noon at this small camp on the lake's north end.

Mora Campground (☎ 360-374-5460) Sites $10. Along the Quillayute River, 2 miles east of Rialto Beach, Mora offers 94 regular sites. Guided nature walks take off from here in summer.

Kalaloch Campground (☎ 360-962-2283) Sites $12. These 175 paved sites are above the beach next to Kalaloch Lodge.

Kalaloch Lodge (☎ 360-962-2271, [w] www.visitkalaloch.com; 157151 US 101) Rooms and cabins $126-241 in peak season. Built in 1953 as an anglers' retreat, this is the only lodging and restaurant between Ruby Beach and Queets. In addition to rooms in the old lodge, there are log cabins and motel-style units, scattered along the headlands above the beach. The restaurant offers family-style meals in a beach-view dining room.

Northeastern Olympic Peninsula

Stretching along the Strait of Juan de Fuca from Port Townsend to Port Angeles, the northeast corner of the Olympic Peninsula is the peninsula's most populated area. Outdoor recreationists love it here for the much vaunted rain shadow: You get the beauty of the Olympics without all of the rain. Sea kayaking, sailing, fishing and golf are all popular pastimes. Port Townsend

WASHINGTON

is an architectural showpiece, with most of its buildings on the National Register of Historic Places. Just a ferry ride from Canada, Port Angeles is on the doorstep to Olympic Mountain high country.

The Port Angeles *Peninsula Daily News* publishes the semiannual *North Olympic Peninsula Newcomers' & Visitors' Guide,* found at visitor centers and on the Web at Ⓦ www.peninsuladailynews.com.

PORT TOWNSEND

Among the best-preserved Victorian-era seaports in the USA, Port Townsend (population 8344) is the only urban must-see in a region otherwise dedicated to the marvels of nature. Block after block of elaborate storefronts line the harbor, and on the hill above the port are ornate mansions built for the merchant kings of the early Washington Territory. On a clear day, views from Port Townsend are stunning: The town looks across Admiralty Inlet, filled with sailboats

and ferries, to Whidbey Island and beyond to the white-glaciered mass of Mt Baker.

Port Townsend was first settled in 1851, the same year that Seattle was established, and for years the two maintained a strident competition for supremacy in Puget Sound trade. Then, in 1888, a subsidiary of Union Pacific announced plans to build rails from Portland to Port Townsend. With the town's dominance now seemingly assured, the citizens of Port Townsend went into a frenzy of commercial development, building a handsome retail core along the harbor and establishing opulent uptown mansions for the elite of trade and industry. But in 1890 the rail link evaporated, and within three years the city was all but deserted.

Today, a new generation of merchant kings has restored historic Port Townsend, turning the downtown district into a shopper's destination for antiques, rare books, upscale clothing and regional art. While Port Townsend hovers at the brink of

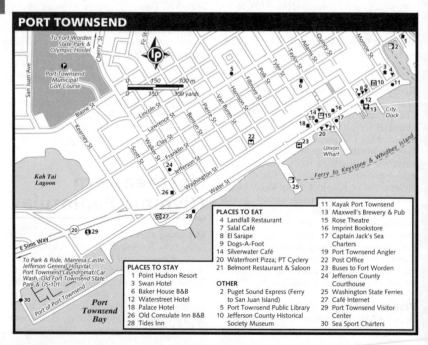

PORT TOWNSEND

PLACES TO EAT
4 Landfall Restaurant
7 Salal Café
8 El Sarape
9 Dogs-A-Foot
14 Silverwater Café
20 Waterfront Pizza; PT Cyclery
21 Belmont Restaurant & Saloon

PLACES TO STAY
1 Point Hudson Resort
3 Swan Hotel
6 Baker House B&B
12 Waterstreet Hotel
18 Palace Hotel
26 Old Consulate Inn B&B
28 Tides Inn

OTHER
2 Puget Sound Express (Ferry to San Juan Island)
5 Port Townsend Public Library
10 Jefferson County Historical Society Museum
11 Kayak Port Townsend
13 Maxwell's Brewery & Pub
15 Rose Theatre
16 Imprint Bookstore
17 Captain Jack's Sea Charters
19 Port Townsend Angler
22 Post Office
23 Buses to Fort Worden
24 Jefferson County Courthouse
25 Washington State Ferries
27 Café Internet
29 Port Townsend Visitor Center
30 Sea Sport Charters

overcommercialization, it remains a great place to spend an afternoon browsing, or to stay a night or two in a vintage hotel.

Orientation & Information

Generally speaking, there are two vintage districts in Port Townsend, both filled with Victorian-era structures. Downtown is the main commercial area, which stretches down Water St along the waterfront. Uptown is atop the bluff, with the main business activity at Lawrence and Tyler Sts. Connections between the two districts are limited: From Water St, the only access is via Quincy and Monroe Sts at the east end. Pedestrians can climb the stairs at Tyler to Washington and continue up on Taylor. The imposing red-brick structure on the west end of Jefferson St is the county courthouse; its 100-foot clock tower makes a convenient landmark.

The Port Townsend Visitor Center (☎ 360-385-2722, 888-365-6978, Ⓦ www .ptchamber.org), 2437 E Sims Way, is open 9am to 5pm weekdays, 10am to 4pm Saturday, 11am to 4pm Sunday. Pick up their useful walking-tour map and guide to the downtown historic district.

The post office, uptown at Washington and Van Buren Sts, is in an amazing stone edifice that once served as the customs house. Port Townsend offers a number of used- and rare-book stores. For travel books, go to Imprint Bookstore (☎ 360-385-3643), 820 Water St. Send email for $10 an hour from Cafe Internet (☎ 360-385-9773), 2021 E Sims Way, or free from the library (☎ 360-385-3181), 1220 Lawrence St.

Do your laundry at the Port Townsend Laundromat/Car Wash (☎ 360-385-5755), 2115 W Sims Way, and wash your car while you wait. Jefferson General Hospital (☎ 360-379-9259) is at 834 Sheridan St.

Fort Worden State Park

Built in 1900, Fort Worden was one of three major fortifications constructed on Puget Sound to defend the area from enemy attack. It has since been converted into a major recreation, lodging and arts center (☎ 360-344-4400, Ⓦ www.olympus.net/ft worden, 200 Battery Way; open 6:30am-dusk daily Apr-Oct, 8am-dusk Nov-Mar). The extensive grounds and array of historic buildings have been refurbished and returned to period spiff (the park served as the backdrop for the filming of An Officer and a Gentleman). The **Commanding Officer's Quarters** ($1; open 10am-5pm daily June-Aug, 1pm-4pm Sat & Sun Mar-May & Sept-Oct), a 12-bedroom mansion, is open for tours, and part of one of the barracks is now the **248th Coast Artillery Museum** (suggested donation $2; open 11am-4pm Tues-Sun June-Labor Day, noon-4pm Apr-May), which tells the story of early Pacific coastal fortifications.

A number of the officers' quarters are available for rent as vacation homes, and HI runs a youth hostel from one of the barracks. In addition, there are 80 campsites, plus boat launches, picnic sites and beach access. Hikes lead along the headland to Point Wilson Lighthouse Station. On the park's fishing pier is the **Port Townsend Marine Science Center** (☎ 360-385-5582, 532 Battery Way; adult/youth under 18 years $3/2; open noon-6pm Tues-Sun June 15-Labor Day, noon-4pm Sat & Sun Apr 1-June 14 & Labor Day-Oct 31), featuring four touch tanks and daily interpretive programs.

Jefferson County Historical Society Museum

The old city-hall building houses the local museum (☎ 360-385-1003, 210 Madison St; adult/youth 12 and under $2/1; open 11am-4pm Mon-Sat, 1pm-4pm Sun, closed Jan-Feb). Part of the charm of visiting is snooping around the old courtrooms and jail cells. Displays detail the pioneer and Native American history of Jefferson County with artifacts and scads of photos. The port's maritime history is well documented with nautical artifacts.

Activities

Port Townsend is the center for **sea kayaking** on Puget Sound – Fort Worden is a stop on the Cascadia Marine Trail. A number of places rent kayaks and gear and teach the fundamentals. **Kayak Port Townsend** (☎ 360-385-6240, fax 360-385-6062, [W] www.kayak pt.com, 435 Water St; rentals from $15/40 per hour/day), at Monroe St on the harbor, leads full- and half-day kayak trips for all experience levels.

Captain Jack's Sea Charters (☎ 360-379-4033, 866-672-2522, [W] www.cpt-jack.com, 118 Taylor St) offers whale-watching tours. Their see-'em-or-get-your-money-back tour is $73. The captain also gives a 1½-hour steamboat cruise of the Port Townsend Harbor ($17) with an emphasis on marine history.

Port Townsend Angler (☎ 360-379-3763, [W] www.ptangler.com, 940 Water St) specializes in catch-and-release tours for fly fishermen.

PT Cyclery (☎ 360-385-6470, 100 Tyler St; rentals $7/25 per hour/day), at the waterfront, has mountain bikes and tandems for rent. They provide local trail maps.

Special Events
Centrum, a nonprofit arts foundation based at Fort Worden State Park, sponsors an endless stream of arts and music festivals and seminars year round, many held at the fort. Among the most popular are the Festival of American Fiddle Tunes and Jazz Port Townsend, both in July. Contact Centrum (☎ 360-385-3102, 800-733-3608, [W] www.centrum.org) for a schedule.

Those enticed by the port's Victorian charm will want to be in town for the Historic Homes Tours in mid-September. Most of the homes on display are private residences that are not normally available for public viewing. For those who want to learn more about the port's early life, Victorian Days (☎ 360-379-0668, 888-898-1116, [W] www.victorianfestival.org) in late March offers an array of exhibits, walking tours and crafts workshops.

Places to Stay
Accenting local history and seaside tableaux, in-town accommodations are very much a part of the Port Townsend experience.

Camping & Hostels The area's old forts provide the best options for budget travelers.

Fort Worden State Park (☎ 360-344-4400, fax 360-385-7248, [W] www.olympus.net/ft worden, 200 Battery Way) Sites $20 plus $6 reservation fee. Of a total 80 RV hookup sites at this popular destination, 50 are between the beachfront and a wooded hillside and 30 are on a field beside the old officers' quarters. Five more hiker/biker sites ($6) are also on this field. Amenities include kitchen shelters, flush toilets and hot showers. Campers can email or fax reservations up to five months in advance.

Old Fort Townsend State Park (☎ 360-385-3595, reservations ☎ 888-226-7688, 1370 Old Fort Townsend Rd) Sites $13. Open mid-April–mid-Sept. Four miles south of Port Townsend on Hwy 20, these sites are lined up on the old parade ground of Fort Townsend. Sporting over 6 miles of hiking trails, the park is a popular spot for crabbing, clamming, fishing and boating (no hookups, though).

Olympic Hostel (☎ 360-385-0655, 800-909-4776, ext 767, [e] olyhost@olympus.net, 272 Battery Way) Member/nonmember $14/17, child $7/10. Open year round. This HI affiliate is in the historic barracks at Fort Worden. Private rooms are available (add $8 to per-person rate), and there's an all-you-can-eat pancake breakfast.

B&Bs Port Townsend boasts many B&Bs, most housed in stately Victorians, but the period charm doesn't come cheap. Contact the chamber of commerce for a full listing.

Baker House B&B (☎ 360-385-6673, 800-240-0725, 905 Franklin St) Doubles with shared/private bath $75/85. This restored 1898 home is relatively affordable and has sweeping bay views from the verandah. There's a two-night minimum stay.

Old Consulate Inn B&B (☎ 360-385-6753, 800-300-6753, fax 360-385-2097, [W] www.old consulateinn.com, 313 Walker St) Doubles $106-210. The former German consul lived in this splendid red-sided Victorian with a wraparound porch and eight rooms, all with private bath.

Hotels & Vacation-Home Rentals Some of the Victorian-era hotels have also been restored.

Waterstreet Hotel (☎ *360-385-5467, 800-735-9810, 635 Water St*) Rooms $55-135. This refurbished hotel above a microbrewery is reminiscent of an old European inn. Each room is uniquely decorated; some have kitchens and private baths. An enormous rear suite features a bedroom loft and plank balcony with a swing from which you can enjoy views of the Cascades.

Palace Hotel (☎ *360-385-0773, 800-962-0741,* w *www.olympus.net/palace, 1004 Water St*) Rooms $60-109. Built in 1889, the former 'Palace of Sweets' has been brought back to its brothel-era elegance, with each of its 16 rooms named for the 'girl' who occupied it. Some rooms have been remodeled into suites with private baths, while others are still authentic (bathroom down the hall).

Manresa Castle (☎ *360-385-5750, 800-732-1281, fax 360-385-5883,* w *www .manresacastle.com, cnr 7th & Sheridan Sts*) Rooms $85-175. The 40-room mansion, built by the first mayor, looks like something out of a fairy tale, sitting high above the town with views on all sides. The most expensive room is in a turret.

Point Hudson Resort (☎ *360-385-2828, 800-826-3854, fax 360-385-7331, 103 Hudson St*) Rooms $49-79, RV sites $22. Set on the tidal flats beside the marina, this former navy barracks has a real portside feeling, from the lap of the waves to the faint scent of creosote. A cozy, modest motel and 56-site RV park constitute the accommodations.

Swan Hotel (☎ *360-385-1718, 800-776-1718, fax 360-379-1010,* e *swan@waypt .com, cnr Monroe & Water Sts*) Cottages/suites $125/135. Newly built but not lacking in charm, the cottages here have a ship's bunk-style beds and maritime furnishings. The suites are huge, with full kitchens.

Tides Inn (☎ *360-385-0595, 800-822-8696, fax 360-379-1115,* w *www.tides-inn.com, 1807 Water St*) Rooms $130-229. These new and remodeled units overlook Admiralty Inlet and Whidbey Island; some feature private decks with Jacuzzis.

Fort Worden State Park (☎ *360-385-4730,* w *www.olympus.net/ftworden, 200 Battery Way*) Houses $104-370. Dating from 1904, the former officers' quarters at Fort Worden retain their period charm with Victorian-era furniture, pressed-tin ceilings and Tiffany lamps. Duplex houses on Officers' Row typically have three or four bedrooms, fireplaces and modern kitchens. Plan to make reservations up to a year in advance if you hope to stay here.

Places to Eat
The center of Port Townsend is packed with trendy cafes and restaurants. You'll have no problem finding someplace to eat, but here are some favorites.

Landfall Restaurant (☎ *360-385-5814, 412 Water St*) Breakfast $3-6, lunch $5-8. Sit down with the local marina folk for a breakfast of homemade corned-beef hash or baked blueberry French toast, and enjoy the sunshine permeating the octagonal room filled with tropical plants.

Salal Café (☎ *360-385-6532, 634 Water St*) Breakfast $7-8, lunch $8-9. Head here for big breakfast omelets and frittatas or a zippy lunch.

Dogs-A-Foot (*cnr Water & Madison Sts*) Hot dogs $2-4. Open summer only. This stand, in an old trailer, wraps a wide variety of juicy sausages and footlongs in a bun.

Waterfront Pizza (☎ *360-385-6629, 951 Water St*) Large pizzas $11-19. Everything here is homemade, from the crust to the artichoke-heart marinade.

El Sarape (☎ *360-379-9343, 628 Water St*) Entrees $6-13. The specialty here is seafood and vegetarian fare with a Mexican flair.

Belmont Restaurant & Saloon (☎ *360-385-3007, 925 Water St*) Entrees $7-12. Dine in a private lace-shaded booth or on a dais overlooking the water, in the lovely dining room of the 1885 Belmont Hotel. Local seafood and produce highlight the wide-ranging international menu.

Silverwater Cafe (☎ *360-385-6448, 237 Taylor St*) Lunch $6-10, dinner $10-17. The Silverwater provides a romantic setting for creatively prepared local dishes such as ahi tuna with lavender or a warm brie and polenta salad, followed up with a slice of blackberry pie.

Entertainment

Between the festivals, several waterfront taverns and a vintage movie theater will keep you busy.

Rose Theatre (☎ *360-385-1089, 235 Taylor St)* Dark for 37 years, this classic movie house was lovingly refurbished and brought back to life in 1995 as an art cinema, replete with balcony and buttered popcorn.

Maxwell's Brewery & Pub (☎ *360-379-6438, 126 Quincy St)* It's OK to smoke, shoot pool and play darts in the nook above the brewing area. Downstairs there's pub food, seafood and steaks.

Getting There & Away

Bus Jefferson Transit (☎ 360-385-4777, W www.jeffersontransit.com), 1615 W Sims Way, serves Port Townsend and outlying areas in Jefferson County. Buses travel as far west as Sequim, where connections can be made to Port Angeles and points west on The Bus, Clallam County's intercity transit system. The fare is 50¢, plus 25¢ for each additional zone. (Another branch of Jefferson Transit's service runs between Lake Quinault and Grays Harbor on the west side of the peninsula).

To reach Port Townsend from Seattle on weekdays, take the ferry from downtown Seattle to Bainbridge Island at 6:20am, 9:25am or 3:50pm ($4.50, 35 minutes). At the ferry dock catch the No 90 Kitsap Transit bus at 7:05am, 10:10am or 4:30pm to Poulsbo ($1, 20 minutes), and transfer to the Jefferson Transit No 7 bus to Port Townsend ($1, 1 hour). Service is less frequent on weekends; phone Jefferson Transit for departure times.

For a more direct journey, Olympic Bus Lines (☎ 360-417-0700, 800-457-4492, W www .olympicbuslines.com) offers connections to and from its Port Angeles-Seattle run, by reservation (see the Getting There & Around section of Port Angeles). Shuttles arrive and depart from the Haines Place Park & Ride on E Sims Way. The fare is $22 to downtown Seattle; $36 to Sea-Tac Airport.

Severe weather can sometimes close down the Hood Canal Bridge. Call ☎ 800-419-9085 for bridge conditions.

Ferry Washington State Ferries (☎ 206-464-6400) operates 15 trips every day to Keystone on Whidbey Island from the downtown terminal ($2 per passenger, $9 car & driver, 30 minutes). Service is occasionally disrupted by severe low tides or by stormy seas.

Puget Sound Express boats (☎ 360-385-5288), at 431 Water St, depart to San Juan Island at 8:30am between April and September (one way/roundtrip adult $30/45, child $22/31, bicycles & kayaks $13 roundtrip, 2½ hours). Whale-watching tours are also available.

Getting Around

Jefferson Transit's Downtown Shuttle (No 3) does a clockwise loop from the ferry dock to the Park & Ride (the terminal for intercity buses) to Lawrence St uptown and back. Bus No 5 runs hourly between Water St and Fort Worden. To rent a car, contact Budget Rent-a-Car (☎ 360-385-7766), 3049 E Sims Way. For a taxi, you can call Key City Transport (☎ 360-385-1872).

DUNGENESS SPIT

Between Port Townsend and Port Angeles is the longest natural sand hook in the nation, Dungeness Spit, extending 5½ miles into the Strait of Juan de Fuca. Now part of the **Dungeness National Wildlife Refuge** (☎ *360-457-8451; $3 per family),* it's a great place to hike and get a closer look at the marine environment of the northern Pacific Coast.

Migrating shorebirds, especially herons, various kinds of ducks and loons, and raptors such as bald eagles comb the tide flats, especially in spring and fall. Harbor seals and their pups crawl up on the sandy beach to sun.

To reach the refuge, head north on Kitchen-Dick Rd off Hwy 101 west of Sequim. Access to the spit, which is possible only on foot or on horseback, is at the Dungeness Recreation Area, a county park. It's a 6-mile hike out to **Dungeness Lighthouse,** built in 1857, at the end of the spit. **Clam digging** is a favorite pastime on the harbor side mid-May to September. You'll need a license to dig, available at local stores; be sure to check with the **Red Tide Hotline** (☎ 800-562-5632).

There is camping adjacent to the refuge at *Dungeness Recreation Area* (☎ 360-417-2291), with 65 sites ($10), showers and flush toilets, but no hookups. Several standard chain motels, all in the $70 to $90 range, are along the stretch of busy US 101 that comprises the town of Sequim. For a romantic retreat, *Domaine Madeleine* (☎ 360-457-4174, fax 360-457-3037, ⓦ *www.domaine madeleine.com, 146 Wildflower Lane*), toward Port Angeles, is a B&B with views of Vancouver Island and a French-inspired garden. Five lavishly decorated guest rooms range from $185 to $225.

Sample Dungeness Harbor's namesake shellfish at *The Three Crabs* (☎ 360-683-4264, 11 Three Crabs Rd), a local institution. From downtown Sequim, follow Sequim-Dungeness Way 4½ miles north; the restaurant is right on the bay.

PORT ANGELES

Although Port Angeles (population 18,397) is known mostly as a place you pass through en route to Canada or Olympic National Park, it's a pleasant enough town with inexpensive motels, good restaurants and a real nautical air, making it a good base for exploring the peninsula.

In the 1860s, President Abraham Lincoln created a Navy and Military Reserve around the natural harbor at Port Angeles as a defense against pesky British installations across the strait in Victoria. However, by the 1890s, the desire to homestead the land outweighed fear of the British, and squatters flooded the military reservation. This influx prompted the federal government to eventually open the area to settlement.

In the 1910s and 1920s, two dams were built on the Elwha River at the base of the Olympic Mountains to generate power for Port Angeles' saw and pulp mills, which still line the waterfront. In recent years,

WASHINGTON

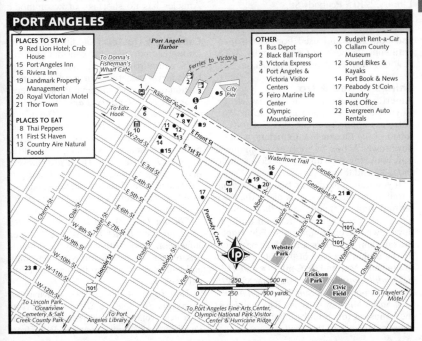

PORT ANGELES

PLACES TO STAY
9 Red Lion Hotel; Crab House
15 Port Angeles Inn
16 Riviera Inn
19 Landmark Property Management
20 Royal Victorian Motel
21 Thor Town

PLACES TO EAT
8 Thai Peppers
11 First St Haven
13 Country Aire Natural Foods

OTHER
1 Bus Depot
2 Black Ball Transport
3 Victoria Express
4 Port Angeles & Victoria Visitor Centers
5 Feiro Marine Life Center
6 Olympic Mountaineering
7 Budget Rent-a-Car
10 Clallam County Museum
12 Sound Bikes & Kayaks
14 Port Book & News
17 Peabody St Coin Laundry
18 Post Office
22 Evergreen Auto Rentals

environmentalists, concerned about the drop in migration of native salmon and steelhead trout to what was formerly the peninsula's greatest spawning grounds, have led a successful campaign to remove the dams and restore the fish to their native habitat. Over the next few years, the Department of the Interior plans to remove both Elwha dams.

Information

Adjacent to the ferry terminal you'll find the Port Angeles Visitor Center (☎ 360-452-2363, 877-456-8372, W www.portangeles.org), 121 E Railroad Ave; it's open 8am to 8pm May 15 to October 15, 10am to 4pm the rest of the year. Sharing the building is a visitor center (☎ 360-998-1224) for Victoria, BC. Olympic National Park's visitor center is 1 mile south of town, off Race St; see the park section earlier in this chapter for details.

The post office is at 424 E 1st St. Internet access is provided free by the Port Angeles Library, 2210 S Peabody St.

Port Book & News (☎ 360-452-6367), 104 E 1st St, offers a vast selection of magazines and both new and used books; it's open until 9pm. Peabody St Coin Laundry, 212 S Peabody St, offers around-the-clock service.

Things to See & Do

American poet and short-story writer Raymond Carver made his home in Port Angeles until his death in 1988. His grave is found in the **Oceanview Cemetery**, west of downtown. A box by the tomb contains a notebook for pilgrims to jot down their thoughts and thanks.

If you want to limber up before taking on a trail in the Olympics, walk along the **Waterfront Trail**, stretching more than 6 miles along the Port Angeles waterfront through downtown and out to the end of **Ediz Hook**, the sand spit that loops around the bay. Pick up the trail at the base of the City Pier, site of the **Feiro Marine Life Center** (☎ 360-417-6254; adult/senior & child 5-12 years $2.50/1; open 10am-6pm Tues-Sun June-Sept; noon-4pm Sat & Sun rest of year). Kids will love the hands-on touch tanks inhabited by the aquatic denizens of the strait.

The **Clallam County Museum** (☎ 360-452-2662, cnr 1st & Oak Sts; admission free; open 8:30am-4pm Mon-Fri, closed holidays), housed in the 1927 Federal Building, retells the story of the community's growth. The **Port Angeles Fine Arts Center** (☎ 360-457-3532, 1203 E Lauridsen St; admission free; open 11am-5pm Tues-Sun) exhibits the work of many of the professional artists who live on the peninsula. The gallery is high above the city amid a 5-acre sculpture garden with views over the strait.

If you'd like to see the area by bicycle, visit **Sound Bikes & Kayaks** (☎ 360-457-1240, 120 Front St; bike rental $9/30 per hour/day). Those endeavoring to scale Mt Olympus will find climbing gear, instruction and guides at Olympic Mountaineering (see the Activities section under Olympic National Park, earlier).

Places to Stay

As a gateway to the national park, Port Angeles has no shortage of accommodations for recreational travelers.

Camping & Hostels In addition to the following, campers may also consider the three NPS campgrounds just inside the park boundary – see the Northern Entrances section of Olympic National Park, earlier.

Salt Creek County Park (☎ 360-928-3441, e ccpsc@olypen.com, 3506 Camp Hayden Rd) Sites $10. Located 16 miles northwest of Port Angeles off Hwy 112, this park has 90 sites with stunning views of the Strait of Juan de Fuca. There are showers, playgrounds, volleyball courts and fire pits. Trails lead to mollusk-strewn kelp beds and WWII-era bunkers, a remnant of the park's former use as an army base.

Lincoln Park (☎ 360-417-4550, Hwy 101 off Lauridsen Blvd) Tent sites $10. Open June-Sept. Next to the county fairgrounds, this recreation area features fishing ponds and ball fields. The campsites are shaded by tall trees.

Thor Town (☎ 360-452-0931, W www.thortown.com, 316 N Race St) $14 per person. This neat, relaxed hostel is in a handsome Dutch colonial home near the Waterfront

Trail. Dormitories and two private rooms accommodate 18. Guests can cook and check their email. Congenial owner Carl Haarstad offers good advice on things to do, rents bikes and provides trailhead transportation.

Hotels & Vacation-Home Rentals Port Angeles sees a lot of travelers due to the ferries, and there are a number of good, reasonably priced motels with rooms starting under $50. Two of the best deals are *Traveler's Motel* (☎ 360-452-2303, fax 360-452-8732, W www.travelersmotel.net, 1133 E 1st St) and *Royal Victorian Motel* (☎ 360-452-2316, 521 E 1st St), both on the main drag eastbound, offering clean, basic rooms with microwaves and minifridges.

Riviera Inn (☎ 360-417-3955, fax 360-452-1726, 535 E Front St) Singles/doubles $65/81. A bit nicer (and pricier) is this unfussy place with remodeled rooms, sauna and spiral ramp for wheelchair access.

Port Angeles Inn (☎ 360-452-9285, 800-421-0706, fax 360-452-7935, W www.port angelesinn.com, 111 E 2nd St) Singles/doubles $80-125/85-140. This clean, friendly motel is perched on the bluff above downtown, with views over the harbor.

Tudor Inn (☎ 360-452-3138, W www .tudorinn.com, 1108 S Oak St) Rooms $85-135. Each of the five bedrooms in this meticulously renovated 1910 home is furnished with fine antiques and private bath. Guests can unwind in the sitting room or library. A full English breakfast is served.

Red Lion Hotel (☎ 360-452-9215, 800-733-5466, fax 360-452-4734, W www.redlion .com, 221 N Lincoln St) Inland/water-view rooms $119/139. This upscale franchise dominates the waterfront. It's a large development with 187 rooms and comforts to match the rates, including a heated pool, data ports, spa and balconies over the harbor.

Landmark Property Management (☎ 360-452-1326, fax 360-457-3212, e property@ olypen.com, 501 E 1st St) This agency rents private homes for short-term stays.

Places to Eat

There's a sly kind of countercultural bent to Port Angeles that's hard to put your finger on. Hang out at some of the local cafes and you begin to get a sense of it.

First St Haven (☎ 360-457-0352, 107 E 1st St) Entrees $6-8. This extra-narrow eatery is the place to go for traditional diner-style breakfasts.

Country Aire Natural Foods (☎ 360-452-7175, 117 E 1st St) Just up the street from First St Haven, this is where to stock up on granola and hiking snacks.

Donna's Fisherman's Wharf Cafe (826 Boathaven Dr) Entrees $5-7. You won't get 'cuisine' sauces at this little local place tucked away over by the sawmill, but the chowder, halibut or oysters and chips are fresh and just plain good.

Thai Peppers (☎ 360-452-4995, 222 N Lincoln St) Entrees $8-10. Spicy complex sauces and lots of vegetarian dishes, along with excellent service, are the highlights here.

Crab House (☎ 360-457-0424, 221 N Lincoln St) Entrees $15-30. Dungeness crabs are the featured item on the menu, but the restaurant at the Red Lion Hotel also serves halibut and salmon, and of course, an array of steaks.

Getting There & Around

Air Horizon Air (☎ 360-547-9308, 800-547-9308, W www.horizonair.com) has six direct flights daily from Seattle to Fairchild International Airport. Other Horizon flights link Port Angeles to Oak Harbor and Portland.

Bus Clallam County's The Bus (☎ 360-452-4511, 800-858-3747, W www.clallamtransit .com) travels as far west as Neah Bay and La Push and as far east as Diamond Point. Bus No 30 travels between Port Angeles and Sequim, where you can connect with Jefferson Transit buses to Port Townsend and points east. To head west, take bus No 14 to Sappho for connections to Neah Bay, or continue to Forks and transfer for La Push. In Port Angeles, the main transfer center is at Oak and Front Sts, conveniently near the ferry dock and visitor center. Fares start at 75¢ for adults, plus 25¢ for additional zones. Call for detailed route and schedule information.

WASHINGTON

Olympic Bus Lines (☎ 360-417-0700, 800-457-4492, ⓦ www.olympicbuslines.com) runs two buses a day to/from Sequim ($5/3 adult/child under 12 years, 30 minutes), the Seattle Greyhound terminal ($29/15 adult/child under 12 years, 2½ hours) and Sea-Tac Airport ($43/22 adult/child, 3½ hours). Buses arrive and depart from the transit terminal at Front and Oak Sts.

Ferry Black Ball Transport's MV *Coho* ferry (☎ 360-457-4491) provides passenger and automobile service to Victoria (one way $30/7.75/3.90 car & driver/adult passenger/child passenger, 1½ hours), with three crossings a day in high season. Service is briefly halted in January for maintenance. The passenger-only *Victoria Express* (☎ 360-452-8088, 800-633-1589) runs two or three times a day from late May through September ($12.50/7 adult/child, 1 hour); there's a $2 fee to transport a bicycle. Reservations are recommended.

Car & Taxi Evergreen Auto Rentals (☎ 360-452-8001, fax 360-452-7051), 808 E Front St, rents cars and minivans and offers 24-hour local pickup service. Budget Rent-A-Car (☎ 360-452-4774), 111 E Front St, is opposite the ferry dock.

If you need a taxi, call Blue Top Cab Co (☎ 360-452-2223).

Northwestern Olympic Peninsula & North Beach Area

In the northwest section of the Olympic Peninsula, US 101 winds through some of the remotest area this side of Puget Sound. The land that's not part of Olympic National Park is heavily logged and mostly unpopulated due to extremes in weather and isolation. Four Indian reservations cling to the western brink of the peninsula, and each welcomes respectful visitors.

If you're traveling in the northwestern peninsula, reservations are a good idea because it's a long way to the next town. Don't let that deter you: The museum in Neah Bay is world-class, and the bay at La Push is beautiful and primordial. Just plan ahead.

The major town in the northwestern peninsula is Forks, with numerous motel rooms and restaurants operating year round. Other smaller towns on the northwest corner essentially shut down outside of tourist season.

NEAH BAY

The center of the Makah Indian Reservation, the old fishing town of Neah Bay (population 794) features one of the best Native American museums in the USA, but otherwise has few amenities for the traveler. Neah Bay sits alongside a wide, wind-frothed harbor overlooked by totem poles, and birds plying the Pacific Flyway touch down en route. There's more than just a sense of history here; in Neah Bay, at the perimeter of the continent, there's also a sense of timelessness.

Hwy 112 links Neah Bay to the rest of the peninsula. From Port Angeles, the long and increasingly winding cliff-side road extends 75 miles west to the village, from which roads press even farther west through forests to Cape Flattery, the most northwesterly point in the continental USA.

For information about the reservation, contact the Makah Tribal Council (☎ 360-645-2201), PO Box 115, Neah Bay, WA 98357.

Makah Cultural & Research Center

On the east end of Neah Bay, one of the USA's greatest collections of Native American archaeology is housed in this transfixing museum and cultural center (☎ 360-645-2711, ⓔ mcrc@olypen.com, Bayview Ave; adult/senior & student $4/$3; open 10am-5pm daily summer, Wed-Sun rest of year).

Exhibits interpret the many objects uncovered at the Ozette site and fit them together into a whole that illustrates the day-to-day life of the ancient Makah. Among the displays are a number of Makah canoes, complete with whaling weapons, and a replica of an Ozette longhouse filled with the tools, baskets and goods of everyday life. The sophistication of ancient Makah life is quite remarkable, and to walk out of the museum and find yourself in the same environment where the ancient Makah lived produces a profound and thoughtful respect.

The film *A Gift from the Past,* shown at 10am and 2pm, recounts the discovery, excavation and importance of the Ozette site.

Cape Flattery
Although no roads go directly to Cape Flattery, the most northwesterly point in the lower 48 states, a three-quarter-mile-long boardwalk through the forest leads to the dramatic promontory. From the four observation decks atop this wild, wind-buffeted point, cliffs fall 60 feet to the raging Pacific. Just offshore is Tatoosh Island, with a lighthouse and Coast Guard station. This is a good place to watch for whales during migration season.

To reach the trailhead, take the main road to the west end of Neah Bay village, where a sign points the way to the Makah Tribal Center. About a quarter-mile past the center, the road turns to gravel; follow this rough road 4 miles to the 'Cape Trail' sign and turn left to a parking lot by the trailhead. The trail splits at the outset; take the left fork.

Users of the trail are required to purchase a permit ($7) issued by the Makah tribe, valid for the remainder of the year of purchase. Get one at the Makah Cultural Center or at the marina in Neah Bay.

Places to Stay & Eat
Most facilities are designed with anglers in mind, who used to come here in droves for the salmon fishing.

Silver Salmon Resort (☎ 360-645-2388, 888-713-6477, W *www.silversalmon resort.com, Neah Bay)* Triples $52-62. Probably the best of the bayside lodgings, the Silver Salmon offers spacious units, most with kitchens. There's also an RV park.

Bay's Best Resort (☎ 360-645-2201, 2 *miles west of Neah Bay, Hwy 112)* Rooms $42-57. Open year round. The Makah have converted the facilities of a former air-force base into this resort, featuring four-bed dormitory-style units. Meals are served at the *Makah Maiden Cafe* (☎ 360-645-2924), on the premises.

Hobuck Beach Park (☎ *360-645-2422)* Tent sites $10. Open June-Aug. This primitive facility, on the beach at Makah Bay, 3 miles west of Neah Bay, offers running water and outhouses.

Beebe's Bayview Cafe (☎ *360-645-2872, Bayview Ave 4)* Entrees $8-16. Open year round. This waterfront joint in Neah Bay specializes in seafood.

FORKS
Forks is unabashedly a lumber town, but it doesn't seem as down on its luck as many other logging communities in the Northwest. Convenient to the Hoh Rain Forest, Neah Bay and the Olympic coastline, the town offers dozens of hotels and places to eat, and it makes a good base for the western half of the peninsula.

The Forks Chamber of Commerce (☎ 360-374-2531, 800-443-6757, W www.forkswa .com) is at 1411 S Forks Ave. Olympic National Park and the USFS share a Recreation Information Station (☎ 360-374-7566), 551 S Forks Ave, along the southern approach to Forks. Staffed by knowledgeable rangers, this is the place to get backcountry permits, maps, tide charts and animal-resistant containers for coastal camping.

Next door, the **Timber Museum** (☎ *360-374-9663; admission by donation; open 10am-4pm mid-Apr–Oct)* commemorates the early settlers and loggers of the region. Included in the museum's collection is a steam donkey – used to transport logs – pioneer farming implements and a fire lookout tower.

Geared toward recreational travelers, Forks makes a convenient pit stop on this side of the peninsula. Everything you could possibly need is along US 101, appropriately called Forks Ave here.

Bogachiel State Park (☎ *360-374-6356, reservations ☎ 888-226-7688, Hwy 101)* Tents/hookups $13/19. The most convenient campground is 6 miles south of Forks, right

WASHINGTON

on the Bogachiel River, with 37 sites, piped water and flush toilets.

Town Motel (☎ *360-374-6231, 800-742-2429, 1080 S Forks Ave)* Singles/doubles/ kitchen units $32/38/42. On the south end of Forks, the Town Motel features a long row of simple, well-kept units, some with kitchens, alongside a pleasant garden. Pets are OK.

Mill Creek Inn (☎ *360-374-5873,* e *grizzly@olypen.com, 1061 South Forks Ave)* Doubles $55-60, cabins $75-100. The cozy, attractive rooms here reflect the personal touch of owners Janice and Mike (the latter offers his services as a fishing guide). They've recently added a couple of log cabins with loft beds and kitchens. A multi-course breakfast is served.

Forks Motel (☎ *360-374-6243, 800-544-3416, fax 360-374-6760, 432 S Forks Ave)* Singles/doubles $65/70. Forks' standard-issue motel is smack in the center of town with 73 straightforward units, a laundry, some kitchenettes and a pool.

South North Garden (☎ *360-374-9779, 140 Sol Duc Way)* Entrees $6-9. A better-than-average selection of Mandarin and Sichuan food is available here.

The In Place (☎ *360-372-6258, 320 S Forks Ave)* Sandwiches $4-7, entrees $9-17. The In Place is the local diner of choice. Try the bumbleberry pie – a luscious blend of blackberries, blueberries, rhubarb and apple.

LA PUSH

La Push is a fishing village at the mouth of the Quillayute River and the principal settlement in the Quileute Indian Reservation. The village looks out onto a jumble of towering, tree-topped islands, which serve to protect its small, busy harbor. It's worth the 17-mile drive down from US 101 just to watch the fishing boats setting out to sea from this rugged bay. The Quileute have made some effort to attract tourism by building a sprawling resort above a magnificent stretch of beach.

For information, contact the Quileute Tribal Council (☎ 360-374-6163, w www .lapushwa.com), PO Box 279, La Push, WA 98350.

Hwy 110, the road down from US 101, divides at the point where the Bogachiel and Sol Duc Rivers join. The northerly road continues to Mora and Rialto Beach on the Olympic Coastal Strip, while the road to the south continues to La Push. Just outside of town are the trailheads to Third and Second Beaches, also part of the park. Both offer a scenic beachfront; however, the coast is too rugged here to walk from one to the other. Third Beach is the starting point for a popular three-day beach hike to Oil City, 17 miles south, at the edge of the Hoh Indian Reservation.

Sitting above one of Washington's most beautiful beaches is the tribally owned and operated ***La Push Ocean Park Resort*** (☎ *360-374-5267, 800-487-1267)*. Tent/RV sites are around $15/25, motel rooms $69 to $78, cabins $62 to $175. Accommodations range from basic A-frame cabins with sleeping-bag loft and WC (no shower) to deluxe ocean-front cottages with stone fireplaces. In between are standard motel rooms in two balconied buildings. No reservations are accepted for camping or RVs.

There's no restaurant in La Push, though there is a small ***market***, and fresh seafood is available from fishing terminals near the harbor. Almost every unit at the resort has some kind of kitchen arrangement, so do your food shopping in Forks if you're going to spend any amount of time at La Push.

NORTH BEACH AREA

South of Queets, at the southern end of the Olympic National Park Coastal Strip, US 101 heads inland to circumvent the Quinault Indian Reservation, then turns south to Hoquiam. There it joins Hwy 109 out to the coast at **Ocean Shores**, what remains of a huge 1960s development that went bust. An alternative route branches off US 101, 7 miles south of Lake Quinault and extends 17 miles southwest over a decent, mostly paved surface to join Hwy 109 at **Moclips**, where the beach is more rugged and picturesque. From there, continue south past modest beachside towns to Ocean Shores, or drive north into Taholah, a fishing village on the Quinault Reservation.

The almost 30 miles of public-access shoreline between Moclips and Point Brown offer beachcombers plenty of opportunity to explore, and in midsummer, temperatures invite sunbathing and dips into the chilly Pacific. These are the closest coastal beaches to Puget Sound population centers, however, and they become quite a playground for family vacationers from the Puget Sound metropolitan area. Vehicles are allowed on the beaches here, so watch out for revved-up pickups careening along the shoreline. Fall brings out the razor-clam diggers, who at low tide hunt the wily and succulent bivalves.

For information, you can contact the Ocean Shores Chamber of Commerce and Ocean Shores–Grays Harbor County Visitor & Conventions Bureau (☎ 360-289-2451, 800-762-3224, Ⓦ www.oceanshores.org), in the Catala Mall, 899 Point Brown Ave.

Places to Stay & Eat

Motels and resorts are scattered along the coast, with the biggest concentration at the southern end. Most places offer specials in the off-season. The following are a couple of dandy choices, but there are dozens of others.

Ocean Shores Reservations Bureau (☎ 360-289-2430, 800-562-8612, Ⓦ www.ocean shoreslodging.com/osrb, 699 Ocean Shores Blvd) Use this service to book any motel, condo or vacation rental along the beach.

Pacific Beach State Park (☎ 360-276-4297, reservations ☎ 888-226-7688, Hwy 109, Pacific Beach) Tent sites/hookups $13/19. Half of the 64 sites at this beachfront campground, 2 miles south of Moclips, have electrical hookups. Vehicle access is restricted, so you'll usually find more people than pickups crossing the sand.

Ocean City State Park (☎ 360-289-3553, reservations ☎ 888-226-7688, 148 Hwy 115)

Tent sites/hookups $14/20. Just north of Ocean Shores, the park offers almost 200 campsites right on the beach.

Discovery Inn (☎ 360-289-3371, 800-882-8821, Ⓦ www.oceanshores.com/discovery, 1031 Discovery Ave SE, Ocean Shores) Rooms $60-139. This pleasant place across from the marina and ferry dock has 22 units and a glass-enclosed hot tub overlooking the Grand Canal.

The Polynesian Resort (☎ 360-289-3361, 800-562-4836, fax 360-289-0294, Ⓦ www.the polynesian.com, 615 Ocean Shores Blvd NW) Motel units $119, studios $139, suites $200-370. Accommodations here range from standard motel rooms to a three-bedroom penthouse, with beach-view balconies standard. An indoor pool and exercise room round out the facilities, and there are a couple of restaurants nearby.

Ocean Crest Resort (☎ 360-276-4465, 800-684-8439, Hwy 109, Sunset Beach) Studios $65-129, suites $110-150. Just south of Moclips, the Ocean Crest is the most attractive option along this stretch of coast, with a heated indoor pool, a sauna and a decent restaurant. The upstairs lounge is a great place for a snug drink while watching for whales. Private beach access is down a winding, wooded path.

Home Port Restaurant (☎ 360-289-2600, 857 Point Brown Ave, Ocean Shores) Entrees $14-16. Open for breakfast, lunch and dinner, Home Port specializes in steak and lobster, and they've got a salad bar, too. Get your pull tabs in the bar, which is open until 10pm.

Mike's Seafood (☎ 360-289-0532, 830 Point Brown Ave, Ocean Shores) If you were farsighted enough to get a kitchen motel unit, then head to Mike's to buy a crab or some razor clams.

WASHINGTON

Southwestern Washington

Separated from the rest of the Pacific Northwest by deep forests, I-5 and the Columbia River, southwestern Washington is an isolated network of mountains, bays and sandy peninsulas that contains some of the state's most popular beaches and most productive dairy farms.

The mouth of the Columbia River is the region's prominent geographical feature, and it's responsible for the local climate as well as for much of the area's history. The great river pours into the Pacific Ocean at Cape Disappointment, its valley forming a trough between Oregon's Coast Range and the Olympic Mountains farther north. Through this gap in the coastal mountains, the clouds, rain and winds of the Pacific flow unhindered, spreading far inland and creating one of the mildest climates in the continental USA.

The first white settlers to the region came down the great navigational thoroughfare, along whose bank arose Longview, today one of the world's major timber ports. The old-growth forests of southwestern Washington once rivaled those of the Olympic Peninsula, but they fell to the logger early because of easy access to the river. Once-prominent salmon-fishing ports at the mouth of the Columbia River and at Grays Harbor have declined along with the salmon, though Westport remains a center for Northwest charter fishing.

In the late 18th century, American and European traders arrived and established long-standing trade relationships with the native Chinook tribes along the river and at Grays Harbor. Lewis and Clark partook of Chinook hospitality during the hard winter of 1805. Access to the Columbia River's trade routes was also important to the Hudson's Bay Company, which established Fort Vancouver across from the confluence of the Willamette River in 1824. This fur-trading outpost was the first real settlement in the Pacific Northwest, and it became the unwitting nucleus of pioneer migration.

The Columbia River is also responsible for the 28 miles of beaches along the Long Beach Peninsula and for those at Grayland, as its abundant sediment flows out into the

Highlights

- Stepping back in time to fur-trading days at Fort Vancouver
- Kite flying and horseback riding on 'the world's longest beach'
- Dining at The Ark, a Northwest classic on the oyster wharf of Willapa Bay
- Hiking to Cape Disappointment's historic lighthouse by the mouth of the Columbia
- Following the trail of Lewis and Clark by canoe down the lower Columbia
- Going for the big one: deep-sea fishing on Westport charters

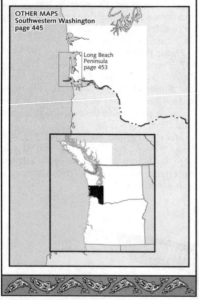

OTHER MAPS
Southwestern Washington
page 445

Long Beach
Peninsula
page 453

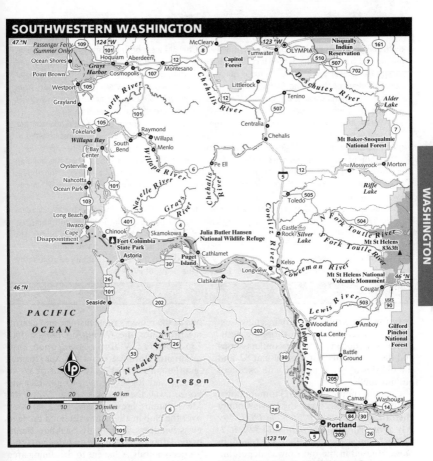

SOUTHWESTERN WASHINGTON

Pacific and is swept northward by currents. Protected by this sandy spit, the shoals and backwaters of Willapa Bay are perfect for raising oysters.

I-5 runs along sections of the Columbia and Cowlitz Rivers on its way from Portland to Seattle. Between this transportation corridor and the Pacific Ocean runs Hwy 4, which continues to parallel the Columbia from Longview, and Hwy 6, which links Chehalis with Raymond. From the south, the quickest access to Long Beach is on Oregon's US 30, crossing the Columbia at Astoria.

CENTRALIA & CHEHALIS

These two old farm and mill communities lodged between logged-off hills on the upper Chehalis River have practically grown together to form a single elongated town. Each boasts a historic red-brick center built alongside the railroad tracks.

Centralia (population 14,742) has the distinction of being the only community in the Northwest founded by an African American. Former slave George Washington moved out west from Missouri and was able to establish a land claim in 1852 near the Chehalis River, which now includes most of

The Centralia Massacre

By the beginning of the 20th century, Centralia and Chehalis were both boomtowns, with logging, mining and farming in the ascendancy. Since both pay and working conditions in the logging and mining camps were poor, several unions quickly took root, including the Chicago-based International Workers of the World (IWW), known as the 'Wobblies.' The IWW enjoyed support from Centralia's working classes; but during WWI, the union's practice of labor slowdowns and strikes angered many who felt that such labor agitations were unpatriotic during wartime.

In 1919, after the return of local soldiers from Europe, the American Legion held an Armistice Day parade to honor the returned veterans. As they had in the past, the Legionnaires boasted of their intent to raid the IWW union hall, but this time the IWW intended to meet fire with fire.

A group of armed veterans assembled in front of the IWW union hall and rushed the building in a raid. Armed IWW supporters then fired into the crowd, killing three Legionnaires; a fourth was killed in a later skirmish. In the melee, most of the IWW assailants escaped, though one, Wesley Everest, was apprehended after a long chase.

Not knowing who had fired the fatal shots, law enforcement officials rounded up the local leaders of the IWW and jailed them. That night, vigilante Legionnaires broke into the jail and abducted Everest. The next day, he was found beaten, castrated and shot, hanging from a railway bridge. His body was brought back to the jail and put on display in front of the remaining IWW members.

Nine IWW members were tried, found guilty of first-degree murder and sentenced to lengthy jail terms. No investigation or charges ever followed the death of Everest.

downtown Centralia. The city has newly established a reputation as a shopping destination, with dozens of factory outlets, shops and discount malls just west of exit 82, and the old downtown is packed with excellent antique malls.

Chehalis (population 7057) is more down on its luck but does boast the **Lewis County Historical Museum** (☎ 360-748-0831, 599 NW Front Way; adult/senior/child $2/1.50/1, family $5; open 9am-5pm Tues-Sat, 1pm-5pm Sun). Housed in the old railway depot, the museum offers a wide perspective on the sometimes violent history of the area. In addition to the usual re-creation of a frontier school room, kitchen and doctor's office, there's a substantial exhibit on the so-called Centralia Massacre (see the boxed text). The museum does a good job of presenting the case from all points of view – plan to spend some time if you hope to absorb the lengthy documents and texts on display.

If that isn't enough to lure you off the freeway for a break (these towns are exactly halfway between Seattle and Portland, 84 miles from either), then consider stopping at one of the region's most historic and charming brewpubs, the **Olympic Club** (☎ 360-736-5164, 112 N Tower Ave), open until midnight. Dating from 1908, the former 'gentleman's resort' catered for years to miners and loggers eager to gamble and booze away their week's wages. When the McMenamins, brewers from Portland, took over the club in 1996, they retained the lead glass windows, mahogany backbar, handmade Tiffany lampshades and skylights, and art deco murals. Adjacent to the dining area is a vintage pool hall. It's a wonderful place for lunch or dinner, with home-brewed ales and stouts serving as additional enticement. Meal-sized sandwiches, pastas and salads are all in the $6 to $8 range.

Two state parks amid stands of old-growth forest are within an easy drive of Chehalis: **Lewis & Clark State Park** (☎ 360-864-2643, Jackson Hwy), 12 miles southeast off Hwy 12, and **Rainbow Falls State Park** (☎ 360-291-3767, Hwy 6), 17 miles west along the Chehalis River. Both charge $13 per site and feature running water, flush toilets, picnic areas and hiking trails. There are a number of reasonably priced motels off I-5 exit 82 in Centralia, convenient to the factory outlet stores.

Greyhound buses stop four times daily at the Texaco Station (☎ 360-736-9811), 1232 Mellen St, near I-5 in Centralia en route between Portland ($20, 2 hours) and Seattle ($15, 2½ hours). Amtrak pulls into the station on Railroad Ave and Magnolia, in downtown Centralia, four times daily ($37 from Seattle or Portland).

For more information about the area, contact Tourism Lewis County (☎ 360-748-8885, 800-525-3323, W www.tourlewis county.com), 500 NW Chamber of Commerce Way, Chehalis, WA 98532.

VANCOUVER

One of the fastest-growing areas in Washington state, Vancouver (population 143,560) is immediately across the Columbia River from Portland and is best thought of as a suburb of Oregon's largest city. As anyone who has tried to get across the bridges during rush hour can testify, a *lot* of people commute between homes in southwest Washington and jobs or shopping in Portland. The reason for this border jumping is partly due to the two states' tax codes: Oregon has no sales tax, and Washington has a marginal property tax. With a little ambition, the savvy local can do a bit more driving and pay a lot less tax.

Vancouver's major appeal to travelers is reconstructed Fort Vancouver, the old Hudson's Bay Company trading post. The adjoining US Army's Officers Row is also a lovely place for a stroll. However, most travelers will find dining, lodging and nightlife options more appealing in nearby Portland.

Orientation

Vancouver sits on the northern bank of the Columbia River, not far from the confluence of the Willamette River. The city is 164 miles from Seattle on I-5 and only 8 miles from downtown Portland across the I-5 Bridge. A second freeway, I-205, branches off I-5 just northeast of town, providing more direct access to Portland International Airport and I-84 eastbound. Highway 14 follows the

north bank of the river, joining the two freeways and continuing east to the Columbia River Gorge. Downtown Vancouver is directly west of I-5. Main St and Broadway, the principal streets, parallel the freeway.

Information

For information about the Vancouver area, contact the Southwest Washington Visitors & Convention Bureau (☎ 360-750-1553, 877-600-0800, W www.southwestwashington .com), which shares an office with the National Park Service (NPS) at OO Howard House, 750 Anderson St, on Officers Row. Hours are 9am to 5pm March to October, 9am to 4pm the rest of the year.

The headquarters for the Gifford-Pinchot National Forest (☎ 360-891-5000, recorded information ☎ 360-891-5009) is at 10699 NE 51st Circle, off I-205 exit 30. This is a good place to pick up maps and get information on hiking and camping at most of the forests in southwestern Washington as well as Mt St Helens National Monument.

Vancouver National Historic Reserve

Administered by the NPS, the US Army, the state of Washington and the city of Vancouver, this reserve encompasses an array of historic buildings that demonstrate the importance of the site throughout Pacific Northwest history. The centerpiece of the complex is the reconstructed Fort Vancouver. Within its stockaded grounds, a living-history program provides insight into life on the Pacific frontier. Even if you're just looking for a place to park the car and stretch your legs, this is a good stop: Between Officers Row and the fort area is an expansive green space that's perfect for picnicking.

The **OO Howard House Visitor Center** *(☎ 360-992-1820, 750 Anderson St; admission free; open 9am-5pm Mar-Oct, 9am-4pm Nov-Feb)* serves as a good introduction to the reserve. Howard, the Civil War general who resided here from 1879 to 1880, was the founder of Howard University in Washington, DC, the country's foremost African American institute of higher learning. The exhibits and a 20-minute video here present an interesting overview of the people and events that contributed to the area's history. Talks on military history are given at 10am and 3pm. This is also the place to join tours of Officers Row.

The first major European operation in the Pacific Northwest, Fort Vancouver served as headquarters for the Hudson's Bay Company from 1825 to 1860. The fur trading post was instrumental in the development of the Oregon Country, with its warehouses and shops supplying settlers newly arrived along the Oregon Trail.

With contemporary drawings and material gleaned from the site, archaeologists in the 1960s began reconstruction of **Fort Vancouver National Historic Site** (☎ 360-696-7655; adult/family $2/4, admission free Nov-Feb; open 9am-5pm Mar-Oct, 9am-4pm Nov-Feb). A 15-foot-high stockade encloses reconstructions of the chief factor's residence, bakery, foundry, trade shop, kitchen and other buildings. The fur warehouse on the south side houses an archaeologist's shop with exhibits on how the fort was rebuilt. Children will enjoy climbing up into the three-story bastion on the northwest corner for views of the fort, the Columbia River and Mt Hood.

Tours depart from the fort entrance at 9am and hourly from noon to 4pm daily. Interpreters in period dress present demonstrations in the fort's forge Thursday to Monday, in the carpenter's shop Tuesday and Wednesday and in the kitchen every day during the summer. The visitor center, 612 E Reserve St, features a gift shop and small museum with exhibits on the fur trade, including a 15-minute film (admission free).

Along the north side of E Evergreen Blvd are the historic homes on **Officers Row**. Built between 1850 and 1906 for US Army officers and their families, they are currently rented out as offices and apartments. Two of the homes are open for self-guided tours. **Grant House** (☎ 360-693-3103, 1101 Officers Row; admission free; open 11am-9pm), built in 1849 from logs and later covered with clapboard, now houses a restaurant. **Marshall House** (open 9am-5pm), home to General George C Marshall

in the 1930s, is a grand Queen Anne–style mansion. Free guided walks of Officers Row depart from OO Howard House at 11am and 1:30pm.

Just east of Fort Vancouver is the new **Pearson Air Museum** (☎ 360-694-7026, 1115 E 5th St; adult/senior/youth 13-18 years/children 6-12 years $5/4/3/2; open 10am-5pm Tues-Sun), devoted to the colorful history of Northwest aviation. The adjacent Pearson Airfield has been in use since 1905, when pilot Lincoln Beachley landed his dirigible Gelatin after making the first aerial crossing of the Columbia River. A number of antique planes are on display in the main hangar, surrounded by exhibits on the golden age of flight.

Places to Stay & Eat

Most people visit Vancouver as a side trip from Portland, but inexpensive lodging can be found north of the Columbia River. Steps from the transit center and convenient to the fort, **Vancouver Lodge** (☎ 360-693-3668, 601 Broadway) has nonsmoking singles/doubles with fridge and microwave for $46/56. If you're looking for something more atmospheric, try **Vintage Inn** (☎ 360-693-6635, 888-693-6635, ⓦ www.vintage-inn.com, 310 W 11th St), a 1903 Craftsman-style home turned B&B. Antique-laden singles/doubles with shared bath are $79/89.

Experience the splendor of old Officers Row at **Grant House Restaurant** (☎ 360-696-1727, 1101 Officers Row). Open for lunch weekdays, dinner Tuesday to Saturday and brunch on Sunday, the restaurant emphasizes classic American regional cuisine, with dinner entrees averaging $15. Otherwise, quaff a handcrafted ale at **Salmon Creek Brewery & Pub** (☎ 360-993-1827, 108 W Evergreen Blvd), serving tasty pub fare and internationally themed entrees ($10).

Shopping

Most of the products from the renowned **Pendleton Woolen Mill** (☎ 360-835-2131, 2 17th St) are made not in Pendleton but in Washougal, 16 miles east of Vancouver on Hwy 14. Free tours of the mill are offered at 9am, 10am, 11am and 1:30pm weekdays.

The outlet store here sells fabric, clothing and blankets at substantial discounts.

Getting There & Away

Portland's Tri-Met Transit (☎ 503-238-7433) offers frequent service between downtown Portland and Vancouver. Bus No 5 runs at least once every half-hour from 6am to 11:30pm daily ($1.50), stopping at E 7th St and Broadway in Vancouver.

LOWER COLUMBIA RIVER

Near Portland, Oregon, the Columbia River picks up the waters of the Willamette and turns north to catch the Lewis and Cowlitz Rivers. Downstream from Longview, the Columbia cuts west again. Islands and shoals slow the current, and the river continually widens until, near Grays Bay, it occupies a channel over 7 miles across.

Chinook villages once stretched along the river's northern banks. Because the lower Columbia was the crossroads for the transportation of goods north and south, as well as east to the Native American trade center at Celilo Falls, the Chinook became one of the most prominent mercantile tribes in the Northwest.

The fast-moving waters of the Columbia meet the roiling surf of the Pacific at the Columbia Bar, a notoriously treacherous crossing for ships. The first of the white explorers to navigate from the Pacific Ocean across the bar and up the Columbia River was the American Robert Gray, in 1792, closely followed by various British explorers. For the next decade, commerce flourished between the Chinook and the white traders. However, European diseases eventually decimated the Indians, leaving the mouth of the Columbia open to settlement.

Ilwaco was the first encampment along the river. Founded in the 1840s, it became the transportation link between the river steamers, oceangoing riggers and newborn communities of Willapa Bay. Later in the century, forts were established at Ilwaco and just upriver at Chinook to defend Columbia River ports. Both sites have been preserved as state parks.

Longview to the Coast

At the westward turn of the Columbia, where it meets the Cowlitz River, are the twin industrial towns of **Longview** and **Kelso**, together making up a metropolitan area of almost 50,000 inhabitants. Founded as a planned community, Longview is where the majority of the logs cut from southwest Washington forests go to be milled and shipped overseas. There's little here to divert the traveler, save convenient lodging and refueling needs.

One of a number of motels around I-5 exit 39, *Best Western Aladdin Motor Inn* (☎ *360-425-9660, 800-764-7378, fax 360-577-9436, 310 Long Ave)* has a pool, a hot tub and good straightforward rooms for $60 (though you can whittle the price down by flashing your AAA membership card). Locals meet at *Country Folks Deli* (☎ *360-425-2837, 1329 Commerce Ave),* in central Longview, for home-baked bread and home-brewed beer; a grilled sandwich served with salad or soup is $7.

Highway 4 clings to the cliffs alongside the Columbia's northern bank from Longview to the Long Beach Peninsula, offering dramatic views of wooded islands and the green, deforested hills of Oregon. The old logging and fishing town of Cathlamet (cath-la-met), 26 miles west of Longview, occupies a position above the Columbia River and **Puget Island**. A bridge leads from Cathlamet to the flat, rural island, the largest on the Columbia and a popular destination for cyclists and kayakers following the Lewis & Clark Trail. *Redfern Farm* (☎ *360-849-4108, 277 Cross Dike Rd),* a gabled home on the Oregon-facing side, offers accommodations at $65 per night, including a country breakfast. Follow Hwy 409 across the island to take a car ferry (☎ 360-795-3301) to Westport, Oregon. Ferries leave from Puget Island on the hour, and from Westport at 15 minutes after the hour between 5am and 10pm (car/cyclist/foot passenger $3/2/1).

Just north of Cathlamet, there's access to the **Julia Butler Hansen National Wildlife Refuge** (☎ *360-795-3915),* a sanctuary for Columbian white-tailed deer. The deer's numbers had dwindled to around 230 when the reserve was set up in 1972. Now there are some 900 deer both on and off the 4400-acre protected area, which straddles the Columbia with its western portion on Oregon's Tenasillahe Island.

Lewis and Clark's Corps of Discovery parked their canoes at **Skamokawa** (skuh-mock-a-way), 6 miles north of Cathlamet, and two centuries later it remains a popular center for paddling on the Columbia. A combined kayak outfitter, B&B and cafe, **Skamokawa Paddle Center** (☎ *360-795-8300, 888-920-2777,* W *www.skamokawapaddle .com, 1391 Hwy 4)* offers a range of day and overnight trips on the Lower Columbia, including a Lewis and Clark historical tour and wildlife adventures. The cost of day tours is $90, while two-day trips cost from $178 per person, including meals, equipment and a night at the B&B. Experienced paddlers will find canoe and kayak rentals and lodging at **Skamokawa Inn B&B**, featuring nine basic doubles ($80 to $90), each with private bath. Rates include breakfast at the cafe. A less pricey alternative is to camp at **Skamokawa Vista Park** (☎ *360-795-8605, 13 School Rd)*, with tent sites/RV hookups for $13/18. The 70-acre park on the west side of the village has coin-op showers and a shoreline trail.

The small town of **Chinook**, 9 miles southeast of Long Beach, is named for the Native American tribe whose villages once lined these shores, but the community might well have been named for the Chinook salmon. By the 1880s, Chinook was one of the region's major fish-canning centers, and the resulting affluence is easily seen in the handsome early-20th-century fishermen's homes and the false-fronted downtown. Chinook is home to one of the Northwest's most notable restaurants, *The Sanctuary* (☎ *360-777-8380, 794 Hwy 101)*. Housed in a c. 1906 Methodist church, the restaurant uses fresh organic ingredients and local seafood in an eclectic multiethnic manner that's always interesting and often excellent. Entrees average $17.

A well-preserved relic of three US wars perches on a rocky bluff above the Columbia River at **Fort Columbia State Park** (☎ *360-*642-3078, Hwy 101, 2 miles south of Chinook; admission free; open 6:30am-9:30pm mid-Apr–early Oct, 8am-5pm Sat, Sun & holidays rest of year)*. Built between 1898 and 1905, during the Spanish-American War, the fort maintained its defensive purpose through the two World Wars. It remains largely unchanged from the glory days of 1900, with the barracks now serving as an **interpretive center** and the commanding officer's residence as a **museum** *(admission free; open 10am-5pm Memorial Day-Sept)*. Trails lead to cement artillery fortifications and batteries, which once housed guns that protected shipping channels on the Columbia.

Ilwaco

The major fishing port on Washington's southern coast, Ilwaco (population 950) still bustles with charter and commercial craft. The early growth of the salmon-canning industry here was aided by the development of salmon traps, a method of catching the fish that was made illegal in the 1930s.

Unlike the flat Long Beach Peninsula, which stretches to the north, Ilwaco is hemmed in by rocky hills. West of town, on a rugged promontory above the mouth of the Columbia River, are the remains of Fort Canby, a Civil War–era bulwark designed to protect river shipping from Confederate interference.

Charter Fishing Ilwaco has plenty of charter-fishing options, with expeditions for salmon, sturgeon, tuna or bottom fish, depending on the season. Charters average $70 per person. Try one of the following outfitters along the harbor, or contact the Ilwaco Charter Association (☎ 360-642-4943) for a full list: Beacon Charters (☎ 360-642-2138, 877-642-6414, W www.beac101charters.com, east end of Howerton Ave), Pacific Salmon Charters (☎ 360-642-3466, 800-831-2695, 191 Howerton Ave), Sea Breeze Charters (☎ 360-642-2300, 185 Howerton Ave).

Ilwaco Heritage Museum The town's maritime past is on display at this museum (☎ *360-642-3446, 115 SE Lake St; adult/ senior/youth 12-17 years/child 6-11 years*

$3/2.50/2/1; open 9am-5pm Mon-Sat, noon-4pm Sun Memorial Day-Labor Day, 10am-4pm Mon-Sat rest of year). Other exhibits present aspects of Chinook culture, as well as the history of the local cranberry and logging industries. The old Clamshell Railway, which ran from Ilwaco to Nahcotta until 1930, still operates here on a 50-foot scale model in the line's old former depot.

Fort Canby State Park Although little remains of the original fort, this state park *(☎ 360-642-3078, Hwy 100, 2 miles southwest of Ilwaco; open dawn-dusk)* is of considerable interest because of its interpretive center, nice beach area and hiking trails to dramatic lighthouses.

Established in 1852, Fort Canby was heavily armed during the Civil War to prevent Confederate gunboats from entering the Columbia. Upgraded dramatically during WWII, the fort stood as the principal defender of the river, whose mouth was webbed with mines. Although no shots were fired from Fort Canby, a Japanese submarine did manage to penetrate close enough to the Oregon side to fire on Fort Stephens in 1942.

Lewis and Clark camped near here in 1805 and climbed up onto the bluff for their first real glimpse of the Pacific Ocean. Their journey is faithfully recounted at the **Lewis & Clark Interpretive Center** *(☎ 360-642-3029, Hwy 100, 3 miles south of Ilwaco; adult/youth/carload suggested donation $2/1/5; open 10am-5pm),* perched atop Cape Disappointment in the state park. Visitors can follow a 'river-line' of the Corps of Discovery expedition – a chronological mural illustrated with diary entries, mementos and engravings. The center also documents the history of navigation on the Columbia, focusing on the dangerous Columbia River Bar, which can be admired from the building's expanse of windows. On display here is a Fresnel lens manufactured in France in 1822, which beamed from atop the North Head Lighthouse till 1937. Look for special events to be held at the center leading up to the Lewis and Clark bicentennial in 2005.

From the interpretive center, a hiking trail leads half a mile to **Cape Disappoint-ment Lighthouse**. Built in 1856, it's the oldest such structure still in use on the West Coast. A second beacon, **North Head Lighthouse**, is off the campground's access road and is reached via a 1.6-mile hiking trail from the parking area. Built 42 years after its sister, the North Head Lighthouse guided ships heading down the coast from the north. Volunteer researchers lead tours of the lighthouse throughout the year; phone the state park (earlier in this section) for departure times.

From the fancifully named **Waikiki Beach** near the park entrance, follow North Jetty Rd to reach the end of the riprap jetty at Benson Beach, affording views of both lighthouses and of migrating whales in season.

To reach Fort Canby State Park from downtown Ilwaco, follow signs to Robert Gray Dr (Hwy 100); an alternate, slightly longer, route (also labeled Hwy 100) reaches the same destination via the North Head lighthouse; follow Spruce St west out of town.

Places to Stay & Eat Ilwaco makes a low-key alternative to Long Beach as a base for the peninsula.

Fort Canby State Park Campground *(☎/fax 360-642-3078, reservations ☎ 888-226-7688, Hwy 100, 2 miles southwest of Ilwaco)* Tent/RV sites $14/20, yurts & cabins $35. There are nearly 250 sites in two zones – by the beach and around a lake near the park entrance. Coin-op hot showers and flush toilets are within easy reach. Yurts and cabins with electric heaters are another option.

Beacon Charters & RV Park *(☎ 360-642-2138, 877-642-6414, ⓦ www.beaconcharters .com, east end of Howerton Ave)* Sites $16-18. This friendly fishing outfit has 60 sites, most with full hookups, plus showers and a tackle shop. Boat owners can sign up for daily bait service.

Inn at Ilwaco *(☎ 360-642-8686, 888-244-2523, fax 360-642-8642, ⓔ bussone@long beachlodging.com, 120 Williams Ave NE)* Singles/doubles $89/99. On a wooded rise just off First St (Hwy 101), Ilwaco's old Presbyterian Church has been redone as a handsome B&B with nine guest rooms in the old parsonage and vestry. The church proper is a community arts center.

Heidi's Inn (☎ *360-642-2387, 800-576-1032, 126 Spruce St*) Singles/doubles/kitchenette units from $48/58/65. Next door to the Inn at Ilwaco, this modest motel offers large, pleasant rooms with fridge; *small* pets are allowed.

Festivals Coffee Net (☎ *360-642-2288, 157 Howerton Ave*) Inside a waterfront shopping arcade, this cafe provides espresso shots and iMac computers with Internet access.

Portside Cafe (☎ *360-642-3477, 303 Main St*) Breakfast from $3.75, lunch $6-8. The coffee is swill, just like it used to be before the coffee craze, but this locally popular dinette in front of the Ilwaco Fruit Packing Company has dandy fruit pies and good home cooking.

LONG BEACH PENINSULA

Long Beach Peninsula, the narrow sand spit north of the Columbia River, claims to have the world's longest beach. And with 28 unbroken miles of it, the boast has to be taken seriously. However, the adjoining 28 miles of rather lackluster development are a disappointment, and the beach itself is overrun with pickup trucks (as Washington state beaches are considered highways). Purists might prefer the Willapa Bay side of the peninsula, with its old towns, oyster beds and wildlife viewing.

The beach resorts here have a long pedigree, dating from the 1880s, when Portland families journeyed down the Columbia River by steamboat to summer at the coast. The 'Clamshell Railway' linked the oyster beds at Nahcotta to boats at Ilwaco in 1888. Besides oysters, the railroad also carried summer vacationers to the sandy beaches on the Pacific side of the spit. Soon the beach towns of Seaview and Long Beach sprang up, and across the bay, beach resorts at Tokeland and North Cove were established.

Willapa Bay is known to oyster lovers around the country for the excellent bivalves that grow in this shallow inlet, which is fed by six rivers. Oyster farming remains the area's major industry.

Long Beach & Seaview

Long Beach and Seaview (combined population 1283) comprise the major population center on the peninsula. Both began as beach resorts in the late 1880s. A few old inns from this era have been beautifully restored, but most visitors will probably find that much of the area's local charm has been overrun by aggressive commercialization. Highway 103, the main drag, is lined with the sorts of T-shirt shops, middlebrow boutiques, fast-food mills and bumper-car arenas that somehow always find their way to beach towns. However, the endless beach is undeniably appealing, if you don't mind sharing it with multitudes of summer vacationers.

Orientation & Information Long Beach is 126 miles from Portland and 146 miles from Seattle. Two main arteries handle peninsula traffic, which can get heavy in the high season. On the west side is Hwy 103 (also known as 'Pacific Hwy'), running from Seaview to Leadbetter Point State Park. On the east (bay) side, Sandridge Rd extends from just east of Seaview to Oysterville. Local access roads cross the peninsula at various points, linking these parallel routes. In Long Beach, streets ascend numerically north and south of Bolstad Ave, though in such a small community, few people pay attention to addresses.

The Long Beach Peninsula Visitors Bureau (☎ 360-642-2400, 800-451-2542, W www.funbeach.com), at the corner of Hwy 101 and Pacific Hwy in Seaview, can help you get reservations for area motels and lodgings. Ask for a free copy of the *Discovery Coast Visitors Guide,* a useful list of peninsula services and activities published by the local *Chinook Observer.* They're open 9am to 5pm Monday to Saturday, 10am to 4pm Sunday.

The peninsula's main health-care facility is Ocean Beach Hospital (☎ 360-642-3181), at 1st and Fir Sts in Ilwaco.

Things to See & Do Primary beach access points in Long Beach are off 10th St SW and Bolstad Ave; an all-abilities, quarter-mile-long boardwalk links the two entryways. In Seaview, take 38th Place, just south

LONG BEACH PENINSULA

PLACES TO STAY
1 Caswell's on the Bay
2 Andersen's on the Ocean RV Park
5 The Breakers
12 Moby Dick Hotel & Oyster Farm
13 Sunset View Resort
14 Boreas B&B
15 Arcadia Court
17 Shaman Motel
18 Boardwalk Cottages
21 Edgewater Inn; Lightship Restaurant
22 Our Place at the Beach
24 Shelburne Country Inn; Shoalwater Restaurant
27 Historic Sou'Wester Lodge

PLACES TO EAT
6 Chuck's
11 The Ark
23 The Crab Pot

OTHER
3 Cranberry Museum
4 Willapa National Wildlife Refuge Headquarters
7 Ocean Beach Hospital
8 North Head Lighthouse
9 Lewis & Clark Interpretive Center
10 Cape Disappointment Lighthouse
16 World Kite Museum & Hall of Fame
19 Skippers Equestrian Center
20 OWW
25 Long Beach Peninsula Visitors Bureau
26 Shell Station

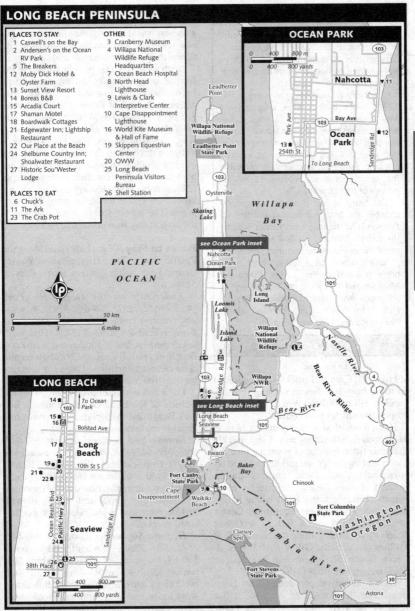

OCEAN PARK

Nahcotta

Ocean Park

PACIFIC OCEAN

Willapa Bay

Long Island

Willapa National Wildlife Refuge

LONG BEACH

Long Beach

Seaview

Ilwaco

Fort Canby State Park

Cape Disappointment

Waikiki Beach

Baker Bay

Chinook

Fort Columbia State Park

Columbia River

Washington
Oregon

Clatsop Spit

Fort Stevens State Park

Astoria

WASHINGTON

Northwest Cranberries

The Long Beach Peninsula is a major producer of cranberries. Many of the roads that crisscross the peninsula pass fields of these low-growing bushes, which are covered with brilliant red, tart berries.

Cranberry production began here in the 1890s, when bushes were shipped from Massachusetts and planted in bogs. Cranberry bushes are very long-lived; some plants in today's farms are originals – over 100 years old. Today there are about 130 cranberry growers in southwestern Washington, which combined produce 15 million pounds of berries yearly.

Cranberry harvest is a colorful time. In October, the fields are flooded and tens of thousands of the bright red berries float to the surface. Workers use floating booms to corral the berries, which are then processed.

Tour cranberry bogs and a historic cranberry research center at the **Cranberry Museum and Gift Shop** (☎ 360-642-5553; admission free; open 10am-5pm daily Apr-Oct, 11am-4pm Fri-Sun Nov-Mar), along Pioneer Rd north of Long Beach.

of Hwy 101. Cars and trucks aren't allowed on these busy beaches in summer, but the beach north of Bolstad Ave to Ocean Park is open to vehicles year round.

Remember that surf swimming here is dangerous due to strong waves and quickly changing tides. Instead of plunging into the water, you might hit the saddle and ride on horseback along these endless dunes. Several Long Beach outfitters offer horseback-riding tours (solo riding is discouraged). Try **Skippers Equestrian Center** (☎ 360-642-3676, cnr S 10th St & Ocean Beach Blvd). Biking along the boardwalk is another fun activity. **OWW** (cnr 10th St & Ocean Beach Blvd) rents out bicycles ($5 per hour) and mopeds ($18).

Thousands of people descend on Long Beach the third week of August for the **Washington State International Kite Festi-val**, billed as the largest such event in the Western Hemisphere. Festival-goers seek to gain new world records: the greatest number of kites in flight at one time, the largest kite flown, the longest time aloft and so on.

With some 150,000 people attending the festival annually, it was just a matter of time before someone opened the **World Kite Museum & Hall of Fame** (☎ 360-642-4020, 3rd St NW near Pacific Way; family/adult/child $4/1.50/1; open 11am-5pm daily June-Aug, Fri-Mon Sep-May). If you think a museum devoted to the history and artistry of kites might be a bore, think again. Kites have been used for scientific research, aerial photography, mail delivery and reconnaissance – as well as for amusement – for centuries. The whole story's here, along with the largest, smallest and wackiest kites.

Places to Stay RV parks abound along the Pacific Hwy. The Historic Sou'Wester Lodge (see below) offers more sites in Seaview.

Andersen's on the Ocean RV Park (☎ 360-642-2231, 800-645-6795, ⓦ www.andersensrv.com, 1400 138th St, Long Beach) Tent/RV sites $18/20. This well-developed facility, 3½ miles north of Long Beach, has 60 full hookups, hot showers and clam-cleaning facilities. There's a separate tenting area nearer the beach.

For a full listing of area B&Bs, visit the website of the Long Beach Peninsula Bed and Breakfast Association (ⓦ www.bedbeachbreakfast.com).

Boreas Bed & Breakfast (☎ 360-642-8069, 888-642-8069, ⓦ www.boreasinn.com, 607 N Ocean Beach Blvd, Long Beach) Suites $130-140. Boreas is a c. 1920 beachview home near the boardwalk. There are five tastefully appointed suites, all with private bath, and a spa housed in a cedarsided gazebo.

Historic Sou'wester Lodge (☎ 360-642-2542, 38th Place, Seaview) Lodge rooms $59-69, lodge suites $71-109, cabins $81, trailers $39-104, tent/RV sites $18/20. Built in 1892 by an Oregon senator, this three-story lodge has a self-amused air of funkiness, eclecticism and nonchalance. It's heavy on irreverence: the owners insist that the establishment is a B&(MYOD)B, or 'bed and make your own damn breakfast.' In the original lodge, there are both simple bedroom units that share a kitchen, bathroom and living area, and also apartment-style suites. Worth investigating (even if you're not staying here) are the 'TCH! TCH!' units, or Trailer Classics Hodgepodge – a collection of 1950s Spartan house trailers, each one renovated and individually decorated à la Sou'wester. There are also sites for tents and RVs with hot showers and laundry.

Shelburne Country Inn (☎ 360-642-2442, 800-466-1896, fax 360-642-8904, **W** *www .theshelburneinn.com, 4415 Pacific Way, Seaview*). Singles/doubles $120-180/130-190. Built in 1896 as a stagecoach inn, the Shelburne is a jewel of late-19th-century artisanship that has been carefully preserved and refurbished with period fixtures. It is also home to one of the top restaurants in the Northwest (see Places to Eat). The 15 elegant guest rooms vary greatly in size, but all include private bath.

Long Beach and Seaview offer quite a mix of old-fashioned inns, resort condos and low-frills motels. The visitor bureau (see Orientation & Information, earlier) keeps track of room availability during the busiest periods. As elsewhere on the peninsula, rates drop as much as 25% outside the summer months.

Arcadia Court (☎ 360-642-2613, 888-642-2613, **W** *www.arcadiacourt.com, 401 Ocean Beach Blvd N, Long Beach*) Doubles $55, $65-95 with kitchen. Steps from the beach, Arcadia Court has eight clean and cozy units, most with kitchen facilities.

Our Place at the Beach (☎ 360-642-3793, 800-538-5107, fax 360-642-3896, **e** *tompson@ aone.com, 1309 S Ocean Beach Blvd, Long Beach*) Singles/doubles $60/65. Although not exactly *at* the beach, this place offers easy access to it via a gravel track through grassy dunes. One of the better deals in the area, the old motel features spacious rooms, a fitness center and a sauna. An upper-deck lounge makes a good spot to savor the sea breezes.

Shaman Motel (☎ 360-642-3714, 800-753-3750, **W** *www.shamanmotel.com, 115 3rd St, Long Beach*) Singles/doubles $74/94. Slightly newer and spiffier than Our Place, the Shaman offers huge rooms, some with ocean views and fireplaces, and a heated pool. Pets are allowed for a $5.50 fee.

Boardwalk Cottages (☎ 360-642-2305, 800-569-3804, **W** *www.boardwalkcottages .com, 800 Ocean Beach Blvd S, Long Beach*) Cottages for two $89, additional person $10 extra; doubles $119. Convenient to both the beach and town center, these restored 1940s cottages feature kitchenettes and porches.

Edgewater Inn (☎ 360-642-2311, 800-561-2456, fax 360-642-8018, 409 10th St SW, Long Beach) Singles/doubles from $64/74. At the head of the boardwalk, the hulking Edgewater is Long Beach's only real beach-front lodging. Its most attractive feature is the rooftop restaurant and lounge.

The Breakers (☎ 360-642-4414, 800-219-9833, **W** *www.breakerslongbeach.com, Hwy 103 at 26th St, Long Beach*) Rooms from $70, with kitchenette from $91; 1-/2-bedroom suites from $130/200. Accommodations at this condominium resort range from ground-level units with patios to luxury two-bedroom suites with fireplaces and ocean-view balconies. An indoor pool and spa are additional attractions.

Sunset View Resort (☎ 360-665-4494, 800-272-9199, **e** *sunsetview@willapabay .org, cnr 256th St & Park Ave, Ocean Park*) Doubles $67-101, quads $77-127. This handsome motel-resort is just south of Ocean Park, a less congested beach community 10 miles north of Long Beach on Hwy 103. Hot tubs, a croquet area and a playground are nestled among the pretty rear garden, which rises up to grassy dunes and the beach. Rates vary with views and kitchen facilities.

Places to Eat There are a number of fast-food restaurants and chowder houses along the Hwy 103 stretch in Long Beach, a few of which stand out from the crowd.

Chuck's (☎ 360-642-2721, N 19th St & Pacific Hwy) Sandwiches $5, entrees $8. Grab a quick burger or sit down for some beer-battered cod, then top it off with a slice of

WASHINGTON

homemade pie. It's not fancy, but Chuck's is the choice of those who live in Long Beach.

The Crab Pot (☎ 360-642-8870, *1917 Pacific Hwy S*) Market prices. This simple Long Beach eatery and adjacent market should satisfy your craving for fresh seafood. Go with a friend and share a platter of chilled crabs' legs or steamed oysters.

Lightship Restaurant (☎ 360-642-3252, *409 SW 10th St*) Lunch/dinner entrees $9/15. Offering great views from the top floor of the Edgewater Inn, the Lightship features fresh local seafood, steaks and prime rib. If you'd just like a beer, try the attractive lounge.

Shoalwater Restaurant (☎ 360-642-4142, *4415 Pacific Way*) Dinner entrees around $20. Open from 5:30pm. Many consider the restaurant at the Shelburne Country Inn one of the showplaces of Northwest cuisine. The dining room, dominated by arched stained-glass windows and old wainscot panels, is certainly one of the most charming you'll find. Local seafood, fish, poultry and lamb are served with a consistently inventive flair. Light meals (from $8) are served in the pub.

Getting There & Around Pacific Transit System (☎ 360-642-9418) runs buses throughout Pacific County, from Aberdeen to towns along the Long Beach Peninsula via South Bend and Raymond, and as far south as Astoria, Oregon. Bus No 20 runs approximately once an hour between Ilwaco and Oysterville from around 6am to 7pm weekdays (35¢, 40 minutes), less often on Saturday and not at all on Sunday.

Oysterville & Nahcotta

The charm of these old communities – the only ones on the bay side of the Long Beach Peninsula – derives not just from their history but also from the absence of the beachfront towns' carnival atmosphere. Here, wildlife viewing, oyster harvesting and gracious dining occupy residents and visitors alike. Oysterville stands largely unchanged since its heyday in the 1870s, when the oyster boom was at its peak.

Held in mid-August, Jazz & Oysters brings live jazz to the grounds of the historic Oysterville Schoolhouse, along with grilled oysters and other seafood to sample. Phone ☎ 360-665-5711 for details.

Historic Sites Just off Hwy 103, Oysterville is filled with well-preserved Victorian homes. The oldest, built in 1863, is the **Red Cottage**, on Territory Rd near Clay St; the building served as the first Pacific County courthouse. The **Big Red House**, the original home of Oysterville cofounder RH Espy, was built in 1871 and stands at Division St and Territory Rd. If you walk down Clay St toward the bay and look back, you can see the house facades that were once the town front: Since no roads led out here, the town was originally oriented toward the bay. Other historic buildings include a one-room schoolhouse and the 1892 **Oysterville Church**, at Clay St and Territory Rd; pick up a walking-tour brochure here. If you have access to a kitchen, a campfire or even just an oyster knife, you'll want to get some oysters for later. The family-owned **Oysterville Sea Farms** (☎ 360-665-6585) harvests the bivalves daily for sale at their dockside outfit, at the end of Oysterville Rd.

Leadbetter Point State Park Natural Area This 807-acre park (☎ 360-642-3078, *Stackpole Rd, 3 miles north of Oysterville*) is a kind of buffer between the straggling developments of Long Beach Peninsula and a section of the Willapa National Wildlife Refuge, a narrowing band of dunes increasingly breached by Pacific waves. Though most people just meander down to the reedy shores of Willapa Bay, two hiking trails lead through forest and marshes to reach these lowering dunes, as good a place as any in the Northwest to watch for shorebirds. Snowy plovers, Lapland longspurs, sooty shearwaters and brown pelicans are just some of the many varieties spotted here. Late summer is the best time to make the 2-mile beach hike, as trails flood from November to mid-May, while part of the dune area is closed from April through August to protect the snowy plovers' nesting sites.

Places to Stay & Eat A handful of hotels in Nahcotta present a peaceful bayside alternative to the Long Beach scene.

Moby Dick Hotel & Oyster Farm (☎ *360-665-4543, fax 360-665-6887,* W *www .nwplace.com/mobydick.html, 25814 Sandridge Rd, Nahcotta)* Doubles $85-110, breakfast included. A 1929 structure that once served as a Coast Guard barracks, this B&B by the bay features eight rooms, most sharing a bath, and a Japanese-style sauna tucked in the woods. Thoughtful decor and warm pastels make it seem more like a genuine home than a museum piece. In addition, the hotel has an excellent restaurant that's made a splash on the peninsula since renowned chef Jeff McMahon took over the kitchen. Innovative dishes incorporate oysters from their own beds and organic produce from the garden, with entrees in the $12 to 16 range.

Caswell's on the Bay (☎ *360-665-6535, 888-553-2319, fax 360-665-6500,* W *www .caswellsinn.com, 25204 Sandridge Rd, Ocean Park)* Rooms $110-160, breakfast included. Just south of Nahcotta, this lovely new home designed with Queen Anne–period decor offers views onto Willapa Bay from its wraparound porches. There are five guest rooms with private baths.

The Ark (☎ *360-665-4133,* W *www.ark restaurant.com, 3310 273rd St)* Entrees $18-22. Open Tues-Sat evenings summer; Wed or Thur-Sat evenings spring & fall, Fri-Sun winter. The Ark, at the oyster wharf in Nahcotta, is celebrated for its sophisticated yet adventurous way with fish. Begun with help from local-boy-made-good James Beard, this Northwest classic combines grilled fish, such as salmon, sturgeon, swordfish (or whatever comes off the fishing boats) with rarefied sauces, fresh wild mushrooms, local vegetables, and nuts. And, of course, oysters, raised within yards of the restaurant.

WILLAPA BAY

The east side of Long Beach Peninsula hems in Willapa Bay, a large estuary that is a haven for wildlife and an economic resource for several small Pacific County communities along its banks. For information on the Willapa Bay area, call ☎ 360-942-9963 or check out W visit.willapabay.org. Alternatively, contact the South Bend Visitor Information Center (☎ 360-875-5224), 1008 W Robert Bush Dr, which shares a building with the **Pacific County Historical Museum**. Both are open 11am to 4pm.

South Bend

This town (population 1807), near the confluence of the Willapa River with the bay, is fond of calling itself the Oyster Capital of the World. As it boasts the world's largest oyster plant and six major oyster companies, it's hard to dispute the title. The town's most notable edifice is the opulent **Pacific County Courthouse**, a Jeffersonian monument exemplifying the region's early-20th-century pride. Not surprisingly, South Bend's big event is the **Oyster Stampede**, held on Memorial Day weekend, with tons of oysters to sample in the large tent along the harbor. At other times of year, get the critters at *Boondocks Restaurant* (☎ *360-875-5155, 1015 W Robert Bush Dr),* where a plate of panfried oysters goes for $13 and creamy oyster stews are $5.

Raymond & Tokeland

Raymond (population 2975), 4 miles up the bay from South Bend, is another historic waterfront town; it holds the distinction of having hosted Nirvana's first performance in front of a paying audience.

The tiny community of Tokeland is on a spit of sand that reaches out into the north end of Willapa Bay. Although the resort community here reached its peak almost a century ago, and has been in gentle decline pretty much ever since, the *Tokeland Hotel* (☎ *360-267-7006, 100 Hotel Rd)* is reason enough to make your way to the village. Notwithstanding a few updates in plumbing, the handsome old resort is still offering the same rooms and hospitality as when it first welcomed guests in 1889. Singles/doubles ($55/65) are small and bathrooms are down the hall, but the charm and authenticity of this well-kept old inn will delight most visitors. Blueberry pancakes, grilled crab and cheddar sandwiches and other homemade

WASHINGTON

treats are served in the dining room, open 7:30am to 8pm. To reach Tokeland, take Hwy 105 from Raymond or Westport, then take the Tokeland exit and continue 2 miles.

Willapa National Wildlife Refuge

A great diversity of wildlife inhabits the shallow bay that is the centerpiece of this refuge (☎ 360-484-3482, headquarters 3888 Hwy 101; admission free; open 7:30am-4pm Mon-Fri). During low tide the salt water retreats, leaving only a few channels filled with water, surrounded by miles of mudflats, salt marshes and reedy estuaries. The nutrient-rich environment attracts shorebirds in migration (over 250 varieties have been sighted and 86 species are known to nest here), as well as birds of prey and songbirds.

Various mammals, such as Roosevelt elk, black bear, beaver and coyote, roam the coastal forest of **Long Island**, at the southern end of the bay. To reach the island, you'll need a canoe or kayak; there's a boat dock across a channel from the refuge headquarters, 8 miles northeast of Seaview. Be sure to inquire about tides before embarking; it's easy to get stranded during low tide. The 8-mile-long island offers five primitive campgrounds as well as a network of hiking trails; ask for a map at headquarters.

Long Island is one of five units that make up the refuge, which includes an area at the mouth of the Bear River and Leadbetter Point, the extreme tip of the Long Beach Peninsula beyond the state park.

GRAYS HARBOR AREA

The large, highly protected bay known as Grays Harbor was a natural for both native and early European settlement. Originally home to the Chehalis tribe, who maintained villages along the bay and the riverbanks, it remained unknown to white explorers until 1788, when American Robert Gray arrived. However, white settlement didn't get under way until 1848.

During these early years of Washington, when most commerce was maritime, the mills, factories and shipping lines of Grays Harbor were among the most important in the Northwest. Now a sleepy backwater, the

area is doing its best to lure in tourism by stressing charter fishing and access to the beaches along the Pacific Coast.

Aberdeen & Hoquiam

In some cities, history looks distinguished; in others, it just looks old. Unfortunately, the faded old mill towns of Aberdeen (population 16,461) and Hoquiam (population 9097) have seen better days. The good news is that beneath the shabby exterior are some inexpensive rooms, a few good restaurants and pleasant, hardworking people.

The industrial engines of Aberdeen were fired in 1877, when a salmon-packing plant opened; Hoquiam's first lumber mill opened in 1882. By 1910, 34 lumber mills ringed Grays Harbor, with dozens of ships docked and waiting to freight the wood to other parts of the nation. Aberdeen and Hoquiam were especially known for their large immigrant populations, who worked the shipyards, fishing boats, forests and mills, as well as for their wealthy captains of industry, whose elaborate homes still watch over Grays Harbor. The boom went bust during the 1930s, and these once-thriving port cities have been in gentle decline ever since. Grunge pioneer Kurt Cobain hailed from Aberdeen – the Wishkah River's muddy banks are referred to in the title of Nirvana's last album, *From the Muddy Banks of the Wishkah* (1996) – though few locals may be aware of the fact.

Aberdeen is at the extreme eastern end of Grays Harbor, on the banks of the Chehalis and Wishkah Rivers. Hoquiam is just to the west, on the banks of the Hoquiam River. A third population center, Cosmopolis (population 1595), sits across the Chehalis River from Aberdeen. Getting around in this thrown-together urban area can be pretty confusing, as each community has a different street grid. Stop and get a free map from the Grays Harbor Chamber of Commerce (☎ 360-532-1924, 800-321-1924, **W** www .graysharbor.org), 506 Duffy St, south of the strip linking Aberdeen and Hoquiam.

Things to See & Do A full-scale replica of the *Lady Washington,* one of the ships piloted by Captain Robert Gray when he first sailed into Grays Harbor, is open for tours when moored at **Grays Harbor Historical Seaport** (☎ 360-532-8611, 800-200-5239, [W] *www.ladywashington.org, 813 E Heron St; adult/student & senior/child under 13 years $3/2/1; open 10am-5pm)*. However, this isn't just a museum piece: The ship is usually on the go and is used for sail training, day excursions and other hands-on sail programs (it has sailed as far as Hawaii). Interested individuals can sign on as crew or as passengers on extended trips. The ship also sails up to Puget Sound during the summer, so be sure to call before heading out to see it.

Other aspects of Grays Harbor's past are found in Hoquiam at the **Arnold Polson Museum** (☎ 360-533-5862, 1611 Riverside Ave; adult/child $2/50¢; open 11am-4pm Wed-Sun June 1-Labor Day weekend, noon-4pm Sat & Sun rest of year). Built in 1924 by one of the timber barons of Hoquiam, the 26-room edifice is filled with period furniture, clothing, a doll collection and logging implements. Next door is the civic rose garden.

Less a museum than a showcase of late-Victorian-era taste, the so-called **Hoquiam's Castle** (☎ 360-533-2005, 515 Chenault Ave; adult/child under 11 years $4/1; open 11am-5pm Wed-Sun in summer, Sat & Sun rest of year) was built in 1897 on a hill above Hoquiam by Robert Lytle, another local lumber tycoon. The lavish cut glass, formal rooms paneled with oak and ornate period furnishings demonstrate the kind of wealth and opulence found along Grays Harbor in its heyday.

Places to Stay & Eat Some of the local lumber barons' private Xanadus have been refurbished as B&Bs.

Cooney Mansion B&B (☎ 360-533-0602, 800-977-7823, [W] www.cooneymansion.com, 1705 5th St, Cosmopolis)* Singles $80-165, doubles $85-185. Industrialist Neil Cooney built this 37-room Craftsman-style home in 1908 as a showpiece for his timber mill's signature spruce. The Cosmopolis mansion features eight guest rooms (five with private bath) furnished with their original antiques.

Rates include a three-course breakfast and use of a hot tub and sauna.

Olympic Inn Motel (☎ 360-533-4200, 800-562-8618, fax 360-533-6223, 616 W Heron St, Aberdeen)* Singles/doubles $56/65. This downtown Aberdeen motel contains 55 standard-issue rooms. Kitchen units and guest laundry are available.

Westwood Inn (☎ 360-532-8161, 800-562 0994, 910 Simpson Ave, Hoquiam)* Singles/doubles $55/69. The best bet over in Hoquiam is this sprawling complex just off Hwy 101 near the center of town.

Billy's Bar & Grill (☎ 360-533-7144, 322 E Heron St, Aberdeen)* Entrees $10. In the rootin' tootin' days of yore, the bars in Aberdeen were haunted by Billy Gohl, a murderous fellow who robbed and killed drunken sailors and loggers. Billy and the era are both commemorated at this handsome old bar and restaurant with good sandwiches, full dinners, and regional microbrews.

Bridges (☎ 360-532-6563, 112 North G St, Aberdeen)* Dinner $15-20. Bridges has the area's best steak and prime rib, along with a good variety of local seafood.

Getting There & Away Grays Harbor Transit (☎ 360-532-2770, 800-562-9730, [W] www.ghtransit.com) offers daily service between Aberdeen and Westport (No 55; 40 minutes), Ocean Shores (No 51; 50 minutes) and Lake Quinault in Olympic National Park (No 60; 1¼ hours), with ongoing connections to North Olympic Peninsula points by Jefferson Transit. The fare to any of the listed destinations is 50¢. In addition, on weekdays bus No 40 makes six trips to/from the Olympia Greyhound station ($2, 1½ hours); on weekends, it makes three. Buses stop in Aberdeen at Wishkah and G Sts, in Hoquiam at 7th and J Sts.

Westport & South Beach

Westport (population 2137) was for years the largest whaling port on the West Coast and the largest charter-fishing center in the Northwest. But whaling ended long ago, and current restrictions on salmon fishing have crippled the economy of this community. A lot of charter fishing still goes on – as there are plenty of other fish in the sea – and boats run whale-watching expeditions during migration. However, without the huge runs of salmon in Grays Harbor, the backbone of the fishing industry seems to have disappeared.

Located at the northern tip of a sandy peninsula, Westport is divided into two centers of activity: the docks area and Uptown Westport, which houses most of the hotels and the primary beach access. The area known as South Beach is the sandy headland from Westport to North Cove – in other words, the thrust of land between Grays Harbor and Willapa Bay. The pace is slower and the atmosphere more tranquil here than at Ocean Shores to the north or on the Long Beach Peninsula. Half a dozen roads access the rather drab 18-mile stretch of flat beach, flanked by scrubby pines and beach grass, with cottages and RV parks inserted here and there.

For more information, contact the Westport-Grayland Chamber of Commerce and Visitors Center (☎ 360-268-9422, W www .westportcam.com), 2985 S Montesano St. Located at the turnoff from Hwy 105, it's open 9am to 5pm weekdays, 10am-3pm weekends.

Things to See & Do For a good look at Grays Harbor and Ocean Shores to the north, head up to the dock area and turn left on Nyhus St, at the end of which you'll find an **observation tower**. Another good vantage point is the observation deck at the far end of the marina, near the Fishermen's Monument. Nearby you can go crabbing off the floats that lead to the boat landings (rent crab rings from the Harbor Resort).

A former Coast Guard station, **Westport Maritime Museum** (☎ 360-268-0078, 2201 Westhaven Dr; adult/child $3/1; open 10am-4pm daily Memorial Day-Labor Day, noon-4pm Thurs-Mon Sept-May) boasts some great period photos and artifacts of seafaring days gone by. The complete skeleton of a gray whale is outside and can be viewed anytime. A separate building houses a first-order Fresnel lens, manufactured in France in 1888, that beamed for over 70 years from

the lighthouse of Destruction Island, 50 miles north of Westport.

Westport's own beacon, the **Grays Harbor Lighthouse**, also used a Fresnel lens until recently, when it was replaced by a simpler electronic device. To reach the lighthouse, the tallest in the state at 107 feet, return to Uptown Westport and head west on Ocean Ave. Tours of this US Coast Guard–operated facility have been indefinitely suspended since the attacks of September 11, 2001; check with the Maritime Museum for the current status. Just beyond the lighthouse, **Westport Light State Park** has windscreened picnic sites and access to a stretch of beach that's closed to motor vehicles in summer. A wheelchair-accessible trail leads over a mile north along the dunes to Westhaven State Park at the South Jetty.

Charter Fishing & Whale Watching
Charter fishing is not what it once was in Westport, but it is still going strong. Though Northwest salmon populations have significantly declined, not all runs of salmon are equally threatened, so fishing is regulated and restricted on a seasonal basis. Nonetheless, charter boats head out regularly in search of bottom fish, tuna, shark, halibut and rockfish – all worthy quarry for the angler, offering much the same thrill and adventure as salmon fishing. Ask about package deals with lodging, or group and weekday discounts, and keep your eyes peeled for discount coupons in local papers.

Most of these charter companies also run whale-watching excursions in the spring. Stroll along the marina and check the offerings usually posted on chalkboard signs near the boats. An hourlong excursion will cost around $25.

For information about charter fishing from Westport, contact one of the following outfitters (or request a full list from the chamber of commerce):

Coho Charters (☎ 360-268-0111, 800-572-0177, W www.westportwa.com/coho) 2501 N Nyhus, Westport; salmon/bottom/halibut fishing $77/73/135

Deep Sea Charters (☎ 360-268-9300, 800-562-0151, **W** www.oceansportfishing.com) PO Box 1115, Westport, WA 98595; halibut/bottom fishing $125/65

Westport Charters (☎ 360-268-0900, 800-562-0157, **W** www.westportcharters.com) PO Box 466, Westport, WA 98595; salmon/bottom fishing $70/68

Places to Stay There are dozens of options in the area, from RV parks to exclusive condos.

The Islander (☎ 360-268-9166, 800-322-1740, fax 360-268-9166, 421 Neddie Rose Dr, Westport) RV sites $18-20. RV campers will find 55 full hookups at this motel, tackle shop and charter operator at the northwest end of the marina. Guests are free to use the motel pool and laundry facilities.

Twin Harbors State Park (☎ 360-268-9717, reservations ☎ 888-226-7688, Hwy 105, 3 miles south of Westport) Tent/RV sites $14/20. About a hundred of the sites at this vast campground are on the beach side of the highway. Facilities include nine restrooms and 16 showers.

Glenacres Inn B&B (☎ 360-268-0958, 222 N Montesano St, Westport) Doubles $80-135. Built in 1898, this recently renovated inn has six top-floor rooms, some with bay windows and all with private baths. A charming gazebo graces the tranquil wooded estate.

McBee's Silver Sands Motel (☎ 360-268-9029, 1001 S Montesano St, Westport) Singles/doubles $48/58. This very friendly establishment has 19 standard units. They don't offer much above the basics, but the price is right.

Ocean Avenue Inn (☎ 360-268-9400, 888-692-5262, **W** westportwa.com/oceaninn, 275 W Ocean Ave) Doubles $59-79. Also a good value is this attractive motel on the way out to the beach, offering well-maintained accommodations that range from single rooms to three-bedroom suites.

Harbor Resort (☎ 360-268-0169, fax 360-268-0338, **W** www.harborresort.com, 871 Neddie Rose Dr) Double rooms/cottages $59/99 plus $8 per extra adult. About the most fun of anything around, the motel rooms and cottages here have a real nautical feel and matchless views of the harbor through picture windows. Best of all are the raised cottages, with full kitchens, stereos and private decks – quite a deal! Located on the far side of the marina, the resort is near the fishing boardwalk; get your crabbing gear and bait at the tackle shop.

Westport by the Sea (☎ 360-268-1119, 800-332-0090, **W** www.westportbythesea.com, 1600 Ocean Ave) 1-/2-bedroom condos $140/190. Exciting new development or crass suburbanization of an otherwise pristine stretch of grassy dunes by the lighthouse? You be the judge…but if the sound of crashing surf drifting up through your private deck window appeals to you, these modern condominium apartments might be just the thing. Rates vary by view.

Places to Eat A string of fish-and-chips shops and other takeout food establishments cover the waterfront, though most are closed off-season.

Coley's Seafood & Sub Shop (☎ 360-268-9000, 2309 Westhaven Dr) Snacks $4-8. The exception to the closing rule is Coley's, opposite Float 6, where you can inexpensively sample local smoked salmon and clams in subs and homemade chowders year round.

Islander Restaurant (☎ 360-268-9166, 421 Neddie Rose Dr) $10-15. The all-purpose vacation complex has both an old-fashioned lunch counter and a harbor-view dining room, the latter serving mostly burgers, steak and local seafood.

Getting There & Away Grays Harbor Transit (☎ 360-532-2770, 800-562-9730) bus No 55 offers service to/from Aberdeen (50¢, 40 minutes), with connections for Olympia and the Long Beach Peninsula. Buses stop at the bottom end of Montesano St, near Twin Harbor State Park, and at the dock area.

A passenger ferry crosses from Westport to Ocean Shores six times daily mid-June to Labor Day, and on weekends only May to mid-June and September ($4.50/8 one way/roundtrip). Purchase tickets at Float 10. Call Westport/Ocean Shores Ferry (☎ 360-268-0047) for information.

WASHINGTON

North Cascades

The Cascade Range starts in Canada and runs as far south as Northern California, but the term 'North Cascades' commonly refers to the rugged, chiseled alpine peaks in northern Washington. Indeed, with their hanging glaciers, valleys, icefalls and cirque-cradled lakes, these particular mountains are so thoroughly alpine in character that it's tempting to call them (as John Muir did) the 'American Alps.'

Rocky, glaciated and wild, the North Cascades are well known to area climbers, hikers, bicyclists, anglers and auto tourists, all of whom tend to give a little sigh of awe before they launch into descriptions of this majestic land. However, don't expect to happen across a motel or lodge, or even much of a cabin resort, on Hwy 20 between Marblemount and Mazama. Due to the lack of facilities, most people merely drive through, but the most dramatic locales are found off-road, by hiking one of the numerous trails or climbing to the crests of the mountains' ridges. Campgrounds, both formal and de facto, abound in the North Cascades, and it's best to come prepared with enough food to see you through your stay, be that a bag of chips to nibble as you drive or a week's worth of camp chow.

Mt Baker, just west of North Cascades National Park, is extremely popular, not only because it offers some of the best hiking, climbing and skiing in the state, but also because there's a little more in the way of accommodations, and there are even a few good restaurants nearby. Farther south, the area around Darrington is another major access point to the North Cascades; it has plenty of hiking, and climbers head for Glacier Peak.

The Cascades are the spine of the Northwest, wringing out Pacific storm fronts like a wet sponge. They divide the land as well as the state, creating wet, forested slopes and valleys to the west, and leaving the eastern plains bone dry. Go prepared for snow, expect rain, and with some luck, the sun will shine long enough for you to see the peaks. If anything, the weather is changeable. Hikers should take this seriously and pack for rain and cold weather – even in summer.

WASHINGTON

Highlights

- Gazing at inspiring vistas of Mt Shuksan and Mt Baker from Artist Point
- Watching bald eagles on the Skagit River
- Hiking Cascade Pass – a wilderness nirvana
- Making it to Stehekin, at the top of Lake Chelan (reachable by boat or overland trek)
- Viewing Washington's dramatic scenery along the North Cascades Hwy
- Skiing in Upper Methow Valley – the nation's second-longest cross-country network

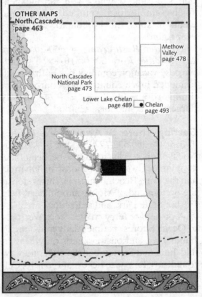

OTHER MAPS
North Cascades
page 463

Methow Valley
page 478

North Cascades National Park
page 473

Lower Lake Chelan
page 489

Chelan
page 493

NORTH CASCADES

East of the Cascades, the Stehekin River flows down out of the mountains and feeds into Lake Chelan, which was carved by glaciers and is 55 miles long and 1500 feet deep – making it the third-deepest lake in the USA after Oregon's Crater Lake and Lake Tahoe, on the California/Nevada border. The lake is central Washington's playground. Anything you can do in or on water – swim, fish, sail, canoe, kayak, water-ski or Jet Ski – is permitted. Windsurfers will have the most luck up near the gustier locales of Stehekin and Lucerne.

Cross-country skiers flock to the Methow Valley in winter – it's got top-notch trails and weather that's generally better than Mt Baker's.

If you want a more in-depth introduction to the area's wilderness, the North Cascades Institute (☎ 360-856-5700, ext 209, w www .ncascades.org, 2105 Hwy 20, Sedro-Woolley, WA 98284) offers a variety of natural-history classes incorporating activities such as backpacking, kayaking, writing and photography. The institute offers programs for both children and adults.

History

The Original Northwesterners, like most folks today, didn't make year-round homes in the North Cascades. Though they migrated to the range in the summer for roots, berries, hunting and fishing, they didn't stick around once the snow began to pile up. Trails first traveled by Native Americans between the Puget Sound and the Columbia Basin are still hiked today; the popular Cascade Pass Trail was one link in what was a traders' route.

When whites arrived, it took them about 70 years to find a way into and through the mountains. Miners kept hoping to strike it rich in the mountains, but few managed to eke out any type of living from the rocky, remote streams.

It took power-thirsty Seattle to put any kind of reins on this rugged country. The abundant water cascading down steep drops caught the attention of engineers, and in the 1920s and '30s, a series of dams were built along the Upper Skagit River, transforming this section of the river into reservoirs. The company towns of Diablo and Newhalem were built to house dam workers.

And all this was done without a road across the North Cascades. A wagon road across Cascade Pass was started in 1896, but construction was halted first by floods and then by changing political pressures. Eventually, road builders decided to extend the road that reached to Diablo over Rainy Pass, and the Cascade Pass route was abandoned. It wasn't until 1968 that a dirt road finally crossed Rainy Pass; during the same year, the North Cascades National Park & Recreation Area was created, shifting the region's economic focus from timber and mining to tourism. And it was in 1972 that the paved North Cascades Hwy officially opened.

Orientation

Only one road, Hwy 20 – the North Cascades Hwy – crosses the North Cascades. What's casually referred to as North Cascades National Park is in fact a jigsaw of different parks, wilderness areas, national forests and recreation areas. The Hwy 20 corridor and Ross Lake constitute the Ross Lake National Recreation Area. To the east of the 781-sq-mile park are the Okanogan National Forest and Pasayten Wilderness; to the west, the Mt Baker-Snoqualmie National Forest. Immediately south is the Lake Chelan National Recreation Area.

To get to the North Cascades from the west, take I-5 to Burlington and follow Hwy 20 east up the Skagit River Valley. From the east, Hwy 20 can be picked up at Omak, Okanogan or Twisp.

There is no public transportation to or through the North Cascades. Cyclists ride alongside automobiles on Hwy 20, which is also the western end of the Bikecentennial Trail, a transcontinental route that crosses the North Cascades on its way to Maine. Don't count on driving between Marblemount and Mazama in winter – this stretch of Hwy 20 usually closes around Thanksgiving (late November) and reopens in early April. Call ☎ 888-766-4636 for road conditions.

North Cascades Volcanoes

Washington's North Cascades began as the southern tip of a volcanic microcontinent that included part of present-day British Columbia. Tropical fossils hint that the erstwhile island had its start in the South Pacific, then drifted north and ran into the western edge of North America. As the two bodies of land joined, rocks crumpled to form long north-south ridges, stretching and faulting along the same axis.

The volcanoes, present before the continental clash, continued to erupt, but not all of the intensely hot rock spewed outward; great pressure crystallized it beneath the earth's surface to form granite. Much of this was ultimately pushed upward into new mountains, the metamorphic forces of pressure and heat creating gneisses (banded or foliated rocks), which form the North Cascades' characteristic spires and horns. These were shaped during several waves of ice ages, beginning about 500,000 years ago. Glaciers carved out long, straight, U-shaped river valleys with exceptionally steep walls, giving the Cascades their distinctive chiseled look. Even today, 318 glaciers continue to work on the rocks. For a good look at the geology, pull off at the Diablo Lake Overlook, Hwy 20 milepost 132, where exhibits describe the various classes of rock found here.

The highest of the North Cascade peaks, Mt Baker, is on the edge of the northern Cascade province. As the Cascade Range began to rise, volcanoes shot up through this older formation. Mt Baker had its first eruption about one million years ago, although its present cone was probably built in the last 20,000 years.

Mt Baker is still an active volcano. A summit cinder cone and a 12-mile-long lava flow down Sulfur Creek are probably only 1000 years old, and eruptions of ash were reported in 1843 and 1859. In 1975, Baker produced significant steam and ash eruptions, leading to speculation that the volcano was building up to a major eruption.

WASHINGTON

MT BAKER AREA

At 10,781 feet, Mt Baker looms over much of northern Washington and provides a craggy, snow-crested backdrop to Bellingham. Retreating Ice Age glaciers incised cirques and deep, notchlike valleys into the surface of the ancient peak. Glaciers are still gnawing away at Mt Baker, and 10,000 acres of permanent snowfields still cling to its flanks. This rugged birthright makes Baker and nearby 9131-foot Mt Shuksan popular destinations for hikers, skiers and climbers, while its far northwestern position (only 15 miles south of the Canadian border) means that precipitation – mostly snow – positively dumps here. Hiking trails may not be free of snowpack until August, but all that snow is good news to skiers – the Mt Baker Ski Area has the deepest base in the state, and informal cross-country trails open up the wilderness to adventurous Nordic skiers.

Ranked as the second-most-active Cascades volcano after Mt St Helens, Baker is occasionally seen emitting a wisp of steam. Lummi Indians called it Kulshan, which translates as 'broken off,' a possible reference to its volcanic nature.

The snowbound territory around Mt Baker wasn't of much interest to either Native Americans or white settlers until rumors of gold brought prospectors swarming into the North Fork Nooksack River in the 1890s and 1900s. Although hard-rock mining did briefly flourish in the area, the difficult climate made transportation and exploration difficult. Logging soon replaced mining as the primary economic force in the area.

Mt Baker was first climbed in 1868, and by 1911, ascents of the mountain were common enough for the Bellingham Chamber of Commerce to sponsor a marathon race that included a climb up and down the peak. However, the annual race was canceled two years later, when a contestant fell into a glacial crevasse. The tradition was revived in the 1970s with the late May Ski-to-Sea event, a multimode relay race down the mountain to Bellingham Bay, culminating in a festival at Fairhaven, on Bellingham Bay.

Orientation

The peak itself, and 184 sq miles of surrounding public land, are enclosed in the Mt Baker Wilderness; wedged into its southern edge is the 8600-acre Mt Baker National Recreation Area (designated as such to allow snowmobiling). Paved Hwy 542 climbs 5100 feet to a breathtaking vista called Artist Point; the road's upper stretch has been designated a National Forest Scenic Byway. Glacier (population 90) is the last community you'll encounter before the final ascent. Although it has a smattering of motels and restaurants designed to service skiers, it has no gas station, so tank up at either Kendall or Maple Falls.

Information

Jointly run by the national forest and park services, Glacier Public Service Center (☎ 360-599-2714), 1094 Mt Baker Hwy, just east of Glacier, is open 8:30am to 4:30pm Memorial Day to October. At this handsome stone lodge built by the Civilian Conservation Corps is a small bookstore, interpretive displays on the park and a ranger to answer questions. Green Trails topographic maps and Northwest Forest Passes are available here. In summer, there's also a staffed visitor center at Heather Meadows.

For more information about the wilderness, contact the Mt Baker Ranger Station (☎ 360-856-5700), located at the junction of Hwy 9 and Hwy 20 in Sedro-Woolley. This office is open year round. Up-to-date information on trail conditions is posted at the Mt Baker-Snoqualmie Forest website: ⓦ www.fs.fed.us/r6/mbs.

Mt Baker Hwy Scenic Byway

Even if you're a travel purist and spurn popular vista points, you'll probably want to join the parade of RVs on Hwy 542 and drive up to **Artist Point**. It's a great introduction to this magnificent area, and hiking trails split off from the highway and lead to less-thronged lookouts and hidden lakes. This route is open all winter as far as Mt Baker Ski Area; the remaining 4 miles to Artist Point are open from mid-July to late October, or until snowfall. Bear in mind that the final 10 miles climb 3200 feet via a series of steep switchbacks. If you're pulling a trailer, it's best to leave it at the base of the mountain.

From Glacier, the first 14 miles climb through old-growth fir forests along the North Fork Nooksack River. One stop you make along this stretch of road ought to be **Nooksack Falls**, which drop 175 feet into a deep gorge. After Silver Fir Campground, the road begins to climb in earnest. Mt Shuksan looms to the east, its glaciers seemingly held back by hornlike peaks. At **Heather Meadows**, the upward climb slows for a moment. The Mt Baker Ski Area is here, and just up the road is **Austin Pass**, a picnic area and the beginning point of several hiking trails. .

The road ends at Artist Point, 24 miles from Glacier, with views onto the face of both Mt Baker and Mt Shuksan. To the north rear the rugged Canadian peaks. This is a magical spot; it's like being at the top of the world.

Hiking

Many hiking trails around Mt Baker require fairly strenuous climbs up glacier-carved valleys to vista points . and wildflower meadows; however, several hikes leave from trailheads at the end of lengthy backroad drives and reach the high country in relatively short order. Green Trails map Nos 13 (Mt Baker) and 14 (Mt Shuksan) show the trails described in this section.

A Northwest Forest Pass is required to park at all of the following trailheads. Purchase a pass at the Public Service Center in Glacier, which has a full list of participating sites. A self-service machine dispenses the pass at Heather Meadows for those on their way up to Artist Point.

Heliotrope Ridge Most climbers ascend to the top of Mt Baker from Heliotrope Ridge and onto Coleman Glacier. The 3-mile, one-way trail to the edge of the glacier is also popular with day-hikers in August, when the meadows, at 6200 feet, are ablaze with wildflowers.

To reach this trail, designated as No 677, turn south onto USFS Rd 39, 1 mile east of Glacier. This unpaved road climbs up the side of Mt Baker for 8 miles to the trailhead. After a 2-mile hike through forest, the trail reaches timberline and then crosses several glacial streams and wildflower meadows. The trail then climbs up onto a moraine and suddenly overlooks Coleman Glacier. The views onto the face of Mt Baker and the massive, deeply riven glacier are incredible. You'll need climbing gear to go any higher along the frequently snow-packed morainal ridge.

Excelsior Peak From this 5700-foot peak, hikers and Mt Baker view each other eye-to-eye across the narrow North Fork Nooksack valley. Several steep trails lead to this vantage point from Hwy 542. The following route lets your vehicle do most of the climbing: drive 2 miles east of Glacier, and turn at the Douglas Fir Campground onto USFS Rd 31, also called Canyon Creek Rd. Follow this road for almost 15 miles around to the back of Excelsior Mountain. Park at the head of trail No 625 and hike 2½ miles past Damfino Lake to Excelsior Pass. A quarter-mile to the east, at the end of an easy path, is Excelsior Peak.

Lake Ann One of the most popular hikes in the area is the 9-mile roundtrip hike to and from Lake Ann, shimmering beneath the massive hanging glaciers of Mt Shuksan. The trail, No 600, leaves from Austin Pass Picnic Area.

Chain Lakes Loop Beginning at Heather Meadows and circling a high plateau, this beautiful 6½-mile loop trail passes a half-dozen icy lakes surrounded by huckleberry meadows. From the visitor center at Heather Meadows, head up the Wild Goose Trail (marked by gray-and-white goose symbols), which makes a steep ascent up stair steps to Austin Pass before pushing on

to Artist Point. The trail continues at the west end of the Artist Point parking lot, where it is sometimes covered by snow; take the trail that drops into the forest, not the one that climbs the plateau. (To avoid the climbs but get the best of the views, go out and back from Artist Point to the vista point where the Chain Lakes Trail meets the Ptarmigan Ridge Trail.)

The trail passes Mazama, Iceberg and Hayes Lakes, then climbs a ridge to drop onto the first of the two Bagley Lakes. Between the two lakes, a trail cuts south, climbs up and returns to the visitor center. Hikers can also continue on the loop trail past the second Bagley Lake, shortly arriving at Mt Baker Ski Area.

Skiing

Boasting the greatest annual snowfall of any ski area in North America, Mt Baker is revered by downhill and cross-country skiers alike for its quality powder and fine mountain scenery. It's also the site of the world's premier snowboarding event – the Legendary Banked Slalom, held in late January.

On the dry, eastern side of the mountain, **Mt Baker Ski Area** (☎ 360-734-6771, snow report ☎ 360-671-0211, W www.mtbaker skiarea.com; lift tickets $34/26 adult/senior & child 7-15 years on Sat, Sun & holidays; $26/21 midweek) has alpine ski runs with a vertical rise of 1500 feet. An exciting variety of chutes, half-pipes, cliffs and excellent powder has gained Mt Baker national distinction among snowboarders, though it's still more or less undiscovered by the masses. The lodge offers complete rental and instruction facilities. Snowboard rentals from the **Mt Baker Snowboard Shop** (☎ 360-599-2008, 9996 Forest St), behind Milano's Restaurant, in Glacier, are less expensive. Better hit the slopes early, as the ski area shuts down at 3:30pm.

The heavy falls of fine, dry snow also make Mt Baker a popular cross-country ski destination. Groomed trails emanate from Salmon Ridge Sno-Park, about 13 miles east of Glacier on Hwy 542, running along the North Fork Nooksack River. The easiest trails extend east along Razorhone Rd, over flat or gently rolling terrain. Farther up the highway, at 3500 feet, White Salmon Rd, below White Salmon Day Lodge, has a longer snow season and great vistas of Mt Shuksan, though it's not machine groomed. (The entrance to the White Salmon Rd is sometimes plowed for parking.) These ski areas are free of charge, but a state Sno-Park permit, available at local businesses ($8/20 per day/season), is mandatory to park at Salmon Ridge.

Cross-country ski rentals are available from the Mt Baker Ski Area lodges (see above), or in Bellingham from the **Base Camp** (☎ 360-733-5461, **W** www.basecamp .com, 901 W Holly St; basic ski package per day/week $15/35; open 10am-6pm Mon-Sat, 11am-5pm Sun).

Climbing

The two principal routes up Mt Baker ascend **Coleman Glacier**, on the northwest side of the mountain, and **Easton Glacier**, on the south side. Both require two days, with a night spent camping at the base of the glaciered peak.

The easiest route is from the south, up Easton Glacier from the Shreiber Meadow trailhead. Although technical equipment is highly recommended, snowmobiles have been known to ascend Mt Baker along this route. The northern ascent begins at the Heliotrope Ridge trailhead (see Hiking, earlier) and continues across Coleman and Roosevelt Glaciers for a final steep and icy climb up the North Ridge to the summit.

In addition to the usual dangers from altitude sickness and glacial crevasses, Mt Baker carries the threat of extremely changeable weather. As the peak is only 35 miles from sea level in Puget Sound, moist air can belt across the hills and shroud the peak in clouds and storms in minutes. Take navigational tools along on any high-elevation hike, and know how to use them.

Novice climbers should consider classes and guided climbs. Highly regarded is the **American Alpine Institute** (☎ 360-671-1505, **W** www.aai.cc, 1515 12th St, Bellingham, WA 98225). Considered one of the nation's top climbing schools, they lead a six-day alpine mountaineering program that culminates with an ascent of Mt Baker for $990. Courses

are taught weekly during the climbing season (mid-May to September).

White-Water Rafting

Rafters put in just above the Douglas Fir Campground and ride down the North Fork Nooksack, a Class III river, to Maple Falls, a total of 10 miles. For a guided raft trip, contact **River Riders** (☎ 800-448-7238, **W** www.riverrider.com).

Places to Stay & Eat

Douglas Fir Campground and **Silver Fir Campground** (☎ 360-599-2714, reservations ☎ 877-444-6777, Mt Baker Hwy) Tents $12. These two attractive USFS campgrounds are positioned along Hwy 542 and the North Fork Nooksack River, which are 3 and 13 miles east of Glacier, respectively. Both have drinking water and pit toilets.

Yogi Bear's Jellystone Park at Mt Baker (☎ 360-599-1908, 888-250-7077, **e** mtbakerrv@gocampingamerica.com, 10443 Mt Baker Hwy) Tents/hookups $17/22, cabins from $65. RV campers will find 30 full-hookup sites at Jellystone, which is just past the Glacier Creek Rd turnoff. Five camper cabins with bathrooms were added in 2001.

Glacier Creek Lodge (☎ 360-599-2991, 800-719-1414, fax 360-599-1048, 10036 Mt Baker Hwy) Rooms $44, cabins $70-115. This Glacier property offers motel rooms and creek-side cabins for two to four people, most with kitchenettes.

The Inn at Mt Baker (☎ 360-599-1359, 877-567-5526, fax 360-599-3000, **W** www.the innatmtbaker.com, 8174 Mt Baker Hwy) Rooms $100. It would be difficult to find a finer view of Mt Baker than from the rooms and deck of this attractive, well-run B&B. Great breakfasts are served on the deck, weather permitting.

Snowline Inn (☎ 360-599-2788, 800-228-0119, **W** www.snowlineinn.com, 10433 Mt Baker Hwy) Studios/loft units from $65/85. These condominiums, a mile east of Glacier, all have satellite TV and kitchen facilities.

The food in Glacier is surprisingly good.

Milano's Restaurant & Deli (☎ 360-599-2863, 9990 Mt Baker Hwy) Dinner $10.

Milano's offers fresh pasta – no surprise – in an attractive bistro atmosphere. The portions are huge, and there's usually a line out the door, but hang in there – it's well worth the wait. It's open for breakfast on weekends.

Seven Loaves Restaurant & Bakery (☎ 360-599-2290, 9393 Mt Baker Hwy) Burgers & tacos $9-10, dinner specials $15-20. Open Thur-Sun July-Oct & Dec-Apr. 'Local' and 'organically grown' best describe the offerings here, and that includes the wine list. Dinner specials highlight veggies and fish – usually halibut, Washington black cod or salmon – and the burgers are 100% American buffalo.

Alpenglow Farms (☎ 360-599-2927, 8040 Mt Baker Hwy) Open July-Sept. Stop at this roadside stand east of Maple Falls for exquisite berry milkshakes and muffins.

Getting There & Away

The most popular road to Mt Baker is Hwy 542 (Mt Baker Hwy), which travels east from Bellingham via Kendall; it's 56 miles from Bellingham to the Mt Baker Ski Area. This road is open year round and offers the highest-altitude access point. From downtown Bellingham, Broadway leads northeast and becomes Sunset Dr before continuing on as Hwy 542.

A second access road, Baker Lake Rd, off Hwy 20 west of Concrete, dead-ends at the northern end of Baker Lake. This is the route used by those staging a climb via the mountain's southern glacier.

From Christmas to February, the Bellair Baker Shuttle (☎ 360-380-8800, **W** www.enjoy theride.com/baker.html) carries skiers to and from the White Salmon Day Lodge (roundtrip $14, two hours). Shuttles depart from Western Washington University's Viking Union at 6:40am Wednesday, Saturday, Sunday and holidays. Reservations are advised; check the website for additional pick-up and drop-off points in Bellingham and Glacier.

MOUNTAIN LOOP HIGHWAY

Strewn with trailheads and peppered with the dregs of old mines, the Mountain Loop Hwy is a woodsy corridor that encloses the

Boulder River Wilderness, a western section of the Mt Baker-Snoqualmie National Forest. It makes a good alternate approach to North Cascades National Park and is also a popular way into the **Glacier Peak Wilderness** and to 10,541-foot Glacier Peak itself.

To reach this route, get off I-5 at Arlington (Hwy 530), then head south on Jordan Rd to Granite Falls. From there, the Mountain Loop Hwy heads east along the Stillaguamish River, turning north at the Sauk River. The first 12 miles of this eastern arc (as far as the White Chuck River) are gravel-surfaced; the road rejoins Hwy 530 at Darrington, 19 miles south of the North Cascades Hwy (Hwy 20).

For hiking information, stop by the Darrington Ranger Station (☎ 360-436-1155), 1405 Emmons St, which is open 8am to 4:30pm Monday to Friday year round (and weekends in summer), or the Verlot Public Service Center (☎ 360-691-7791), 33515 Mountain Loop Hwy, which is open 8am to 4:30pm May to August.

One deservedly popular local hike is to **Kennedy Hot Springs**, in the Glacier Peak Wilderness Area. Eight miles south of Darrington, at the White Chuck Campground, turn onto USFS Rd 23 and continue to the road's end. Park and start hiking along the White Chuck River Trail (No 643). The 96°F hot springs are 5 miles in from the trailhead.

To climb **Glacier Peak**, follow the White Chuck Trail another 1½ miles past the hot springs to the Pacific Crest Trail. Turn north and hike about a half-mile to the Glacier Trail and Sitkum Ridge and the timberline base camp. It's a long approach – about 10 miles all told – before you get onto the Sitkum Glacier, a relatively nontechnical but steep route to the 10,541-foot summit.

There are about a dozen *USFS campgrounds* along the Mountain Loop Hwy, with several clustered around Verlot on the south fork of the Stillaguamish. Expect pit toilets, running water and a $12 camping fee.

UPPER SKAGIT RIVER VALLEY

From Sedro-Woolley, Hwy 20 makes its subtle ascent along this pretty Cascade river valley en route to North Cascades National Park. It's Bible camps, logging outfits and counterculturalist homesteads for most of the way, much like any other forest corridor in this part of the state. Concrete (population 790), 23 miles east of Sedro-Woolley, is the Upper Skagit Valley's largest town and serves as a base for people headed up to Baker Lake or Mt Baker's southern glaciers. Rockport (population 102), at the junction of Hwys 20 and 530, sits where the Sauk River joins the Skagit River and has become known as one of the Northwest's best bald-eagle viewing sites. It's also popular with river rafters and anglers.

Stop and fill the car with gas and snack food at Marblemount, 40 miles east of Sedro-Woolley. It's the last real town on Hwy 20 for 69 miles. The stretch between Marblemount and Mazama is usually snowed under between mid-November and early April. The highway turns north just past Marblemount, and Cascade River Rd heads east across the Skagit River, past a fish hatchery and some campgrounds, to the Cascade Pass Trailhead, some 25 miles from Marblemount.

Baker Lake & Lake Shannon

Just north of Concrete are these two reservoirs, which were formed by a pair of dams on Baker River. Washington's largest colony of nesting osprey is found at Lake Shannon. Baker Lake is a popular place to launch a boat and go fishing for Kokanee salmon or rainbow trout. There are also several hiking trails.

Baker Lake Rd runs along the west side of the lake, passing several campgrounds and the **Shadow of the Sentinels**, a wheelchair-accessible trail through old-growth Douglas firs. Beyond the end of the road, the relatively flat **Baker River Trail** makes a good family hike, running 3 miles up the jade river past huge old cedars and beaver ponds.

The trail to **Baker Hot Springs** is about 3 miles west of the Park Creek Campground, on Baker Lake's north end. Take USFS Rd 1144 (just past the campground) for 3.2 miles to a large parking area. A short trail from the north end of the parking lot leads to the 109°F natural pool. Don't expect bathing suits.

To reach the lakes, turn north off Hwy 20 onto Baker Lake Rd, which is 6 miles west of Concrete.

Upper Skagit Bald Eagle Area

The bald-eagle area is essentially the 10-mile stretch of the Skagit River between Rockport and Marblemount. After salmon spawn, their spent carcasses become meals for the more than 600 eagles who winter here. January is the best time to view the eagles, which are present from November through early March.

Those who want to learn more about these illustrious raptors should visit the **Bald Eagle Interpretive Center** (☎ *360-853-7614,* ⓦ *www.skagiteagle.org, Alfred St, 1 block south of Hwy 20 in Rockport; open 10am-4pm Sat, Sun & holidays late Dec–mid-Feb).* Guided walks of the eagle sanctuary leave from here at 1:30pm weekends and holidays.

The Upper Skagit Bald Eagle Festival (☎ 360-853-7009) is held the first weekend in February in Concrete, Rockport and Marblemount.

Climbing

North Cascades climbers get to choose from glaciers, rock and ice. Many climbs, including **Mt Shuksan**, a 9131-foot peak north of Baker Lake, contain a mix of all three. Shuksan is an exception among the local peaks in that its approach is easy. Reach the Sulfide Glacier route by driving almost all the way up Baker Lake Rd, turning onto Shannon Creek Rd (USFS Rd 1152) at the campground and, after 3 miles, taking the high road until it ends (4½ miles). Hike the **Shannon Ridge Trail** to the timberline. This route is best climbed during the summer, and it's a favorite with ski mountaineers.

Rafting

The upper part of the Skagit River is an easy float. Reach the standard put-in spot by taking Cascade River Rd out of Marblemount and turning left just after the bridge over the Skagit River. Take out at Howard Miller Steelhead Park, in Rockport. Several outfitters run eagle-watching float trips from December to February ($60 per person). Try **Chinook Expeditions** (☎ *800-241-3451, PO Box 324, Index, WA 98256*).

Places to Stay

Cabins and campsites – the main options in these parts – are found at Baker Lake and along a 10-mile stretch of the Skagit.

Camping Baker Lake has seven campgrounds, mostly on the lake's west bank. Campgrounds are smaller and quieter as you go farther up Baker Lake Rd.

Horseshoe Cove Campground (☎ *360-856-5700, reservations ☎ 877-444-6777, Baker Lake Rd, 13 miles north of Concrete*) Sites $12. The spacious wooded sites here are quickly packed with large extended-family groups. Glacier-fed Baker Lake warms up enough for swimming in the summer. Running water and mostly pit toilets are available.

Howard Miller Steelhead Park (☎ *360-853-8808, 52804 Hwy 530*) Tent/RV sites & Adirondaks $12/16. In Rockport, this county-owned campground near the confluence of the Sauk and Skagit Rivers makes a good base for wintertime eagle viewing. Not exactly wilderness, the park features a grassy expanse for RV and tent sites, plus some eight-bunk Adirondak shelters. Even passersby should stop and take a look at the 30-foot-long cedar dugout canoe on display here.

Rockport State Park (☎ *360-853-8461, Hwy 20, 1 mile west of Hwy 530*) Tents/hookups $14/20. Open Apr-Oct. Set in a lush old-growth forest at the base of 5400-foot Sauk Mountain, this popular park has well-developed facilities, including showers and flush toilets. Backpackers and cyclists will find a few secluded walk-in sites.

Cabins The following woodsy retreats are located west of Marblemount.

A Cab-in the Woods (☎ *360-873-4106, W www.cabinwoods.com, Hwy 20 milepost 103.3*) Cabins $85/515 daily/weekly. A bright yellow taxi flags travelers with an appreciation for puns to stop for the night. Five non-smoking cedar log cabins sleep four and come with equipped kitchens.

Clark's Skagit River Resort (☎ *360-873-2250, 800-273-2606, fax 360-873-4077, W www.northcascades.com, 58468 Clark Cabin Rd*) Cabins $79-129, tent/RV sites $15/20. The varied accommodations here share the wooded grounds with a warren of bunnies. Choose from cabins that housed mill workers in the 1940s, vintage trailer homes and B&B lodging, or pitch a tent by the Skagit. Turn off at the funky Eatery between mileposts 103 and 104.

Baker Lake Resort (☎ *360-757-2262, 888-711-3033, Baker Lake Rd, 24 miles north of Hwy 20*) Campsites $15-20, cabins $45-75. Open year round. All of the cabins here include kitchenettes, and the pricier ones have bathrooms; guests are expected to bring their own linens and towels. Rod-and-reelers will find boat rentals and a small store.

Motels Despite the flow of recreational travelers, the area remains relatively motel-free.

North Cascade Inn (☎ *360-853-8870, 800-251-3054, fax 360-853-7123, 44618 Hwy 20*) Singles/doubles/triples $60/70/80. If you're in need of a shag-carpeted bedroom with TV and access to meals, this overpriced motel in Concrete should fit the bill. The popular restaurant next door has a celebrated selection of pies.

Places to Eat

Stock up or chow down in Concrete and Marblemount.

Baker Street Grill (☎ *360-853-7002, 92 Baker St, Concrete*) Lunch $7-9, dinner $13-20. Housed in an attractive century-old building, the Grill brings microbrew ales and tasty, trendy food to Concrete's main drag.

Annie's Pizza Station (☎ *360-853-7227, 44568 Hwy 20, Concrete*) Medium pizzas $13-15. Closed Mon. This renovated gas station fills you up on regular or premium pizza, along with espresso shots and microbrews.

Marblemount Drive-In (☎ *360-873-9309, 59924 Hwy 20*) Snacks $5-8. Open until 8pm. Good food served with a smile – what

WASHINGTON

a concept! Picnic tables in back face the Skagit River.

Cascadian Farms (☎ *360-853-8173, Hwy 20 milepost 100, 3 miles east of Rockport*) Shakes $2. Open May-Oct. Have a shake made of organic blueberries at this roadside stand, then take a self-guided tour of the farm where they're grown.

Buffalo Run Restaurant (☎ *360-873-2461, 60084 Hwy 20, Marblemount*) Entrees $15-40. Perhaps realizing that venison, buffalo, ostrich and elk burgers ($7) won't appeal to everyone, Buffalo Run also offers a selection of vegetarian items, from vegetable linguini to tempeh on a bun.

NORTH CASCADES NATIONAL PARK

For the backcountry hiker and adventurer, North Cascades National Park is paradise. The North Cascades Hwy (Hwy 20) is really the only road, and facilities are few. Though there are plenty of scenic pull-offs along the highway and easily accessible, short interpretive hikes, a whole new world of craggy, rugged mountains awaits those who venture a few miles off the road to the first pass. Come with a backpack, pick up a map and backcountry permit at one of the visitor centers or ranger stations, and strike out into some of the most dramatic scenery Washington has to offer.

The Hwy 20 corridor and Diablo and Ross Lakes are actually in the Ross Lake National Recreation Area, which divides the north and south units of the national park. Newhalem, a utilitarian dam-workers' town, is the jumping-off point for recreation in the area, and the visitor center near there (see Information, below) is definitely worth a stop.

On the east side of the park, the North Cascades Hwy crests two passes, the 4860-foot Rainy Pass and, 5 miles to the east, 5477-foot Washington Pass. A big hairpin loop in the highway at Washington Pass marks the striking climatic contrast between west and east. Two geological landmarks of the North Cascades – Early Winters Spires and Liberty Bell Mountain (a favorite of rock climbers) – are visible from the overlook here.

The relatively large expanse of wilderness and the alpine character of the North Cascades make it hospitable to a variety of wildlife. Small populations of gray wolves and grizzly bears keep a foothold in the remote backcountry. Black bears are more common, as are mountain lions. Marmots laze around on sunny rocks, occasionally standing up to give a shrill yell at intruders. The large rodents spend most of the summer eating, and by the time they enter their winter burrows, 50% of their body weight may be fat. Mountain goats, which are actually members of the antelope family (with pliable split hooves and muscular forelegs), live on rugged mountain slopes, where they can climb amazingly steep rock walls.

Information

Information on trails and camping, an excellent bookstore, and a panoramic vista point all warrant a visit to the North Cascades Visitor Center (☎ 206-386-4495), 502 Newhalem St, near Newhalem. It's open 9am to 4:30pm daily mid-April to October, Saturday and Sunday November to March, with extended hours mid-June to Labor Day. A walk-through exhibit mixes informative placards about the park's different ecosystems with nature videos. And the New Agey slide show, meant to send viewers into a meditative trance, is better than it sounds. In back of the building, a short, wheelchair-accessible boardwalk leads to views of the Picket Range. Park rangers give interpretive talks or lead nature walks from here at 2pm in summer.

Pick up backcountry permits and get briefed on the current trail conditions at the Wilderness Information Center (☎ 360-873-4500, ext 39), 7280 Ranger Station Rd, Marblemount. It's open 8am to 4:30pm daily Memorial Day to September, Saturday and Sunday late April to May and October, with extended hours late June to Labor Day.

Call ☎ 888-766-4636 for road information if you want to travel past Marblemount on either side of winter.

Check the national-park publication *North Cascades Challenger* for current information on ranger-led hikes, campground fees and other park-related news. Another

NORTH CASCADES NATIONAL PARK

PLACES TO STAY
1 Hozomeen Campground
2 Ross Lake Resort
3 Goodell Creek Campground
8 Newhalem Creek Campground
9 Colonial Creek Campground; Thunder Creek Trailhead
16 Marble Creek Campground
18 Cottonwood Campground
19 Bridge Creek Campground
20 High Bridge Campground; Agnes Gorge Trailhead

21 Courtneys' Stehekin Valley Ranch
22 Harlequin Campground; Stehekin River Trailhead
24 Rainbow's End Cabin; Rainbow Loop Trailhead
25 Stehekin Log Cabins
26 Weaver Point Campground
27 Purple Point Campground & Information Center
29 Flick Creek House

OTHER
3 Ross Dam Trailhead
4 East Bank Trailhead
6 Ladder Creek Falls
7 North Cascades Visitor Center
10 Lake Ann Trailhead
11 Blue Lake Trailhead
12 Howard Miller Steelhead Park
13 Sutter Creek Rest Area (Hwy 20 milepost 100)

14 Marblemount Information Center
15 Marblemount Fish Hatchery
17 Cascade Pass Trailhead
23 Rainbow Falls
28 Purple Creek Trailhead; Lakeshore Trailhead; Golden West Visitor Center (under renovation)

WASHINGTON

good source for trail conditions is the North Cascades website: W www.nps.gov/noca.

Though there is no admission fee to North Cascades National Park, a Northwest Forest Pass is required to park at many trailheads, including those along the Cascade River Rd and within the Ross Lake National Recreation Area.

The area code for Newhalem and Diablo is ☎ 206, since Seattle City Light, which operates the dams, is based in Seattle.

Ladder Creek Falls

A splendid garden and a waterfall hide behind Newhalem's old-fashioned hydroelectric dam. Ignore the buzzing power lines, cross the footbridge over the creek, and follow Ladder Creek Loop Trail through terraced gardens of mostly Northwestern plants. Along the way, you'll find several good picnic spots. Mist from Ladder Creek Falls – which cut deep into a rock chasm – sprays hikers. At night, the falls are illuminated, a legacy of engineer and dam builder James Ross' commitment to hydroelectric power. The **light show** is free and pretty much constitutes the high point of local nightlife. There is a small visitor's gallery at the **Gorge Powerhouse** *(open 8am-4pm in summer),* where you can peer down at the turbines.

Ross & Diablo Lakes

Ross Lake stretches out for 24 miles – all the way across the Canadian border – but is accessible only by trail or water from the south. To get to Ross Lake Resort or lakeside trailheads, you must either take the resort-run water taxi (see Places to Stay & Eat, later) or hike one of the trails off Hwy 20. Boats for **fishing** the trout-filled lake can be rented at the resort.

Just below Ross Lake, Diablo Lake is held back by the 389-foot-high **Diablo Dam**. A pullout off Hwy 20 provides stunning views of the blue-green lake framed by glacier-capped peaks. Diablo was the world's highest arch-type dam at the time of its completion in 1930, but is perhaps more notable for the extraordinary efforts it took James Ross and the city of Seattle to build it. Since there was still no road here in the '20s, a narrow-gauge railroad

ferried workers and their supplies from Rockport through the rocky Skagit River Canyon to Diablo, where, one by one, the railroad cars were hoisted 560 feet up the steep hillside to the dam by an incline lift, which consisted of two parallel sets of tracks and a counterweight. At the top of the hill, a locomotive carried the railroad cars a few hundred yards to Diablo Lake, which they crossed on a barge to the Ross Dam construction site.

In another bit of area history, Jack Kerouac spent the summer of 1956 as a fire lookout on Desolation Peak north of here – he hated it. He was bored and lonely, and in his novel *Desolation Angels,* he described Hozomeen Mountain, which loomed large in his field of vision, as 'The Void.'

Organized Tours A popular, three-hour tour of Diablo and the vicinity is offered by *Skagit Tours (☎ 206-684-3030, W www.city ofseattle.net/light/tours/skagit.asp; adult/ senior/child 6-11 years $20/15/10, plus $15 dinner; departs 11am Thur-Mon mid-June–Aug, Sat & Sun Sept, reservations required).* After an introductory slide show at the Diablo auditorium, visitors are hauled up Sourdough Mountain on the Incline Railroad, shown around the hilltop hydroelectric project, ferried across Diablo Lake for a walk through the turbines of Ross Dam and returned to Diablo for a big chicken dinner (there's spaghetti for vegetarians). The tour provides a good insight into local history and geography.

Alternatively, catch one of the twice-daily *supply ferries (departures at 8:30am & 3pm mid-June–Oct; adult/youth 4-11 years $5/4)* from the fisherfolk's ferry dock at Diablo village. The ferries are reached by driving across the top of Diablo Dam, and they ply the lake to the Ross powerhouse dock. Visitors can hike back to the Diablo Dam via the 4½-mile Diablo Lake Trail or hop back on the ferry for the return trip. Reservations are not required, and the boats return half an hour after arrival.

Hiking The North Cascades are a wonder of riches, and the hikes listed in this section are only a smattering of what's available; stop by

Bigfoot Territory

The creatures known as bigfoots (or Sasquatches) are legendary residents of the Pacific Northwest. While sightings have been reported all over North America, this area seems to be their favorite stomping ground. Tales of bigfoots abound, especially among loggers and hunters, but several Native American legends also contain a 'Sasquatch' or 'Omah' – a similar 'wild man of the woods.' The creature is sought by some scientists and wildlife biologists who take bigfoot research seriously.

Commonly described as looking like large apes, bigfoots allegedly stand about 7½ feet tall and walk upright while swinging their arms. Researchers believe that they weigh 400lb to 500lb, are covered in hair (from gray to reddish-brown or black), and have dark brown or yellow eyes and a foul, overpowering odor. Photos and plaster casts of their tracks show humanlike, five-toed footprints averaging 16 inches in length (approximately a shoe-size 21; think Shaquille O'Neal).

According to most reports, bigfoots are nonaggressive and usually flee when sighted, but they have also been said to occasionally throw rocks, shake cars or chase people. In general, bigfoots seem to stick to the woods, but they have been spotted crossing highways and wandering through campgrounds, backyards and other unlikely places.

Despite a variety of 'evidence' – blurred photos and video footage, hair samples, plaster casts of footprints and audio recordings of the bigfoot call (a loud roaring or growling) – their existence has never been confirmed. To catch a virtual glimpse (and hear an audio file), check out the Washington State Sasquatch Search Group website: W www.angelfire.com/wa/sasquatchsearch.

the visitor center (see Information, earlier) for a full listing. The essential reference guide for hikers is *100 Hikes in Washington's North Cascades National Park Region,* by Ira Spring & Harvey Manning. Free permits are required for backcountry camping in the park and must be obtained in person from the Marblemount Wilderness Information Center or at ranger stations in Sedro-Woolley, Hozomeen, Stehekin and Winthrop. Keep in mind that the number of permits issued is dependent upon the number of campsites available, and demand exceeds supply on summer weekends. Reservations are not available.

Cascade Pass Trail The 3½-mile hike to 5384-ft Cascade Pass is perhaps the best loved in these mountains, and for good reason. Close-up views of a glacier greet hikers as soon as they hit the trail, avalanches thunder down nearby **Johannesburg Mountain**, and the relatively easy trail up forested switchbacks pops out at a huge **wildflower meadow** at the pass. Most hikers turn around at Cascade Pass (due to overuse, no camping is allowed here), but the trail continues to the **Stehekin Valley**. In fact, this is the most popular land route into Stehekin, a town of about 76 people accessible only by foot or by a 50-mile boat trip across central Washington's Lake Chelan.

Another option from the pass is to hike an additional two steep miles up the **Sahale Arm** for more wildflowers and some of the North Cascades' best views of peaks and spires. Expect to find plenty of other hikers on this trail.

The Cascade Pass trailhead is at the end of Cascade River Rd, a 23-mile drive east of

Marblemount over a rough gravel surface that's prone to washouts (check on the road's condition at the Marblemount Information Center before setting out). The trail is open late July to October.

Pacific Crest Trail At Rainy Pass, the Pacific Crest Trail crosses Hwy 20. To sample the trail, strike out north from here for 6800-foot **Cutthroat Pass** (4 miles). Heading in the other direction down the PCT will bring you to Bridge Creek Campground, 12 miles away, where you can pick up the road to Stehekin. Several more leisurely hikes also start from Rainy Pass. Try the easy 2-mile walk to cirque-cradled **Lake Ann**, from which it's another 2 miles to 6600-foot **Maple Pass**.

Thunder Creek Trail From the south end of the Colonial Creek Campground (4 miles east of Diablo Dam), the long Thunder Creek Trail leads to a number of interesting sights. It's only a 1.3-mile jaunt from the campground to Thunder Creek, where a surprising number of **wildflowers** flourish in the dank, creek-bottom forest. Just before a footbridge crosses over the creek, a short nature trail branches off the main trail and loops through the woods.

Around 0.7 miles from the bridge, there's a junction for 3501-foot **Fourth of July Pass**. A moderately steep 3.2 miles to the southeast, the pass rewards climbers with views of **Colonial and Snowfield Peaks**. From here, **Panther Creek Trail** continues for 5 miles back to Hwy 20, east of Ross Lake.

Other Trails About 20 miles from the Thunder Creek trailhead, the **Park Creek Trail** offers views and a passageway to the Stehekin River.

From its Hwy 20 trailhead (milepost 134, Northwest Forest Pass required), the **Ross Dam Trail** descends 1 mile, crosses over the dam and follows the west bank of Ross Lake to Ross Lake Resort (1½ miles). The resort's water taxi shuttles hikers to lakeside trailheads at Big and Little Beaver Creeks on the west bank ($25 and $60), Lightning Creek on the east ($50) and Ho-

zomeen Campground ($70) at the north end. Rates are for the whole boat; call ☎ 206-386-4437 for reservations.

After a quick descent from the highway (milepost 138) to Ruby Creek, the **East Bank Trail** cruises alongside the lake north to the Pasayten Wilderness. There are no big expansive views, but if you're in the mood for a dark forest hike, this is the ticket. It's also one way to get to Hozomeen, a remote lakeside campground near the Canadian border.

Just to the west of Washington Pass, between mileposts 161 and 162, the **Blue Lake Trail** is an ambling 2-mile climb through subalpine meadows to Blue Lake, at 6250 feet. Snow blocks the trail's upper reaches until at least July, and once it melts, there can be lots of bugs and almost as many hikers. Nevertheless, the views onto Whistler Mountain (no, not the one in BC), Cutthroat Peak and Liberty Bell Mountain make a hiker willing to put up with a few minor inconveniences.

Rafting Though the dam-controlled water levels make the Skagit River runnable year round, outfitters tend to concentrate on summer white-water trips. Rafters usually put in at Goodell Creek Campground and float to Bacon Creek or Copper Creek, about 10 miles downriver. Conditions depend on what's going on at the dams upriver, but it's usually a Class II or III trip. The waters are a little quieter downriver from Marblemount.

Alpine Adventures (☎ 800-926-7238, W www.alpineadventures.com, PO Box 253, Leavenworth WA 98826) and **Osprey River Adventures** (☎ 800-997-4116, W www.methow .com/~osprey, PO Box 1305, Twisp WA 98856) are among the outfitters that run rafting trips on the Skagit. Expect to pay around $75 for a day on the river.

Places to Stay & Eat Keep in mind that sites at National Park Service (NPS) campgrounds in the North Cascades are snapped up on a first-come first-served basis; reservations aren't accepted.

Newhalem Creek Campground (☎ 206-386-4495, Hwy 20 milepost 120) Sites $12.

Open May-Oct. This sprawling National Park Service (NPS) campground with 111 sites, flush toilets and potable water is near the North Cascades Visitor Center. Slide shows with ranger commentary are presented on Friday and Saturday evenings in summer.

Goodell Creek Campground (☎ 206-386-4495, Hwy 20 milepost 119) Sites $10. Open year round. West of Newhalem, this 21-site campground is used as a launch site by Skagit River rafters. Also run by the NPS, it's smaller and less developed, with pit toilets. Drinking water is available in summer only.

Colonial Creek Campground (☎ 206-386-4495, Hwy 20 milepost 130) Sites $12. Open year round. These 167 sites skirt the Thunder Arm of Diablo Lake on either side of the highway. On the south side, several walk-in sites among dense woods offer a chance to get away from the cars; the lakeside spots are the most coveted and the most crowded. In summer, naturalist programs are given nightly in the amphitheater.

Ross Lake Resort (☎ 206-386-4437, Ⓦ www.rosslakeresort.com, Rockport, WA 98285) Open mid-June–Oct. Double/quad cabins $68-102/181. The floating cabins at this secluded resort, on the west side of the lake just north of Ross Dam, were built in the 1930s for loggers working in the valley soon to be flooded by Ross Dam. There's no road in – guests can either hike the 2-mile trail from Hwy 20 or take the resort's tugboat-taxi-and-truck shuttle from the parking area near Diablo Dam. Cabins vary in size and facilities, but all feature electricity, plumbing and kitchenettes. Bunkhouse cabins can accommodate 10 people ($130 for up to six, plus $8 per each additional person). Bedding and kitchen supplies are provided, but guests should bring food. The resort rents canoes ($22/day), kayaks ($30) and motorboats ($67), and operates a water-taxi service for hikers destined for trailheads around the lake (see Hiking, earlier).

Those who want an early start on the Cascade Pass Trail can camp for $8 at **Marble Creek Campground**, 12 miles down from Marblemount on Cascade River Rd;

the dark and foreboding sites have toilets but no drinking water.

If you need to pick up some food, stop by the **Skagit General Store** in Newhalem, which has sandwiches, fudge and hot coffee.

METHOW VALLEY

East of Washington Pass, the land dries up a bit and the sky is typically less choked with clouds. The Methow (**met**-how) River valley is the land of cross-country skiing, where the snow is more powdery than the 'cement' that falls west of the Cascades. Recreationally, the Methow comes into its own in the winter, but summer's no let-down. When the snow melts, the valley becomes spectacularly green, and there's plenty of hiking, mountain biking, rafting and fishing.

Native Americans have lived along the Methow, Twisp and Chewuch Rivers some 9000 years. In 1811, David Thompson, a North West Company trader and geographer, visited the Salish-speaking Methows and observed tribal members fishing for salmon at the mouth of their namesake river. A small tribe, the Methow were more or less swallowed up when they were sent to the Colville Reservation in 1883.

That year marked the beginning of white settlement in the Methow Valley. Gold was the original lure, commerce proved more permanent, but nothing really boomed until Hwy 20 opened in 1972, bringing a steady stream of visitors.

Major wildfires swept through the region in the summer of 2001, destroying some 14,000 acres of forest around Twisp and Winthrop and reaching as far north as the Pasayten Wilderness. A blaze that tore through the Chewuch River canyon claimed the lives of four firefighters.

Orientation & Information

The upper Methow River flows through a straight, steep-walled valley cut by a glacier during the most recent ice age. The valley begins to widen around Mazama and becomes fairly open by the time it hits Winthrop and Twisp. The Methow eventually flows into the Columbia at Pateros, 40 miles southeast of Winthrop.

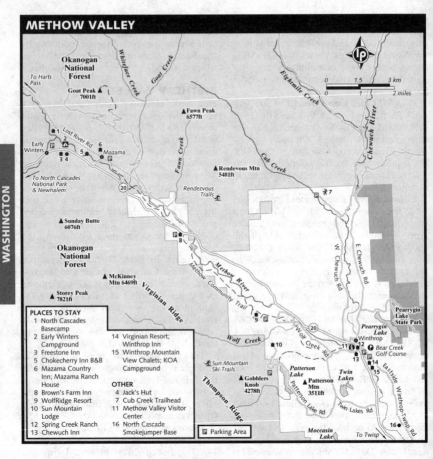

METHOW VALLEY

PLACES TO STAY
1 North Cascades Basecamp
2 Early Winters Campground
3 Freestone Inn
5 Chokecherry Inn B&B
6 Mazama Country Inn; Mazama Ranch House
8 Brown's Farm Inn
9 WolfRidge Resort
10 Sun Mountain Lodge
12 Spring Creek Ranch
13 Chewuch Inn
14 Virginian Resort; Winthrop Inn
15 Winthrop Mountain View Chalets; KOA Campground

OTHER
4 Jack's Hut
7 Cub Creek Trailhead
11 Methow Valley Visitor Center
16 North Cascade Smokejumper Base

P Parking Area

Winter snows block the highest stretch of Hwy 20, between Marblemount and Mazama, from late November to early April (call ☎ 800-695-7623 for road conditions). During that time, Methow-bound skiers make their approach from western Washington by taking US 2 to Wenatchee, then heading north on US 97 past Lake Chelan to Pateros, where Hwy 153 traces the Methow River northwest to Twisp and Hwy 20.

The US Forest Service maintains the Methow Valley Visitor Center (☎ 509-996-4000), 24 West Chewuch Rd, on Hwy 20 at the west end of Winthrop; it's open 8am to 5pm May to October.

While ☎ 911 will summon police or an ambulance, call ☎ 800-832-8408 to report a forest fire.

Harts Pass

Near the end of what may be the state's most terrifying road – a steep one-laner with long, deadly drop-offs and no guard rails – is Harts Pass (6197 feet). Suck in your breath and drive, for the views from the top are outstanding. Catch the road to Harts Pass by heading northwest on Lost River Rd (also known as Mazama Rd) past the Mazama Country Inn to USFS Rd 5400. The road is paved for the first 12 miles, and the last dozen miles are gravel. At Harts Pass, there's still more of a climb for the intrepid driver; head another 3 miles up to **Slate Peak**, where – after a short hike from the road's end – the view from an abandoned fire lookout is a true panorama. At its 7450-foot terminus, this is the state's highest roadside spot. Slate Peak is also the site of the northernmost road access to the Pacific Crest Trail in the USA; north of the road's end, the Pasayten Wilderness reaches to Canada.

Activities
Good, dry snow and plenty of trails make Methow Valley famous for its cross-country skiing. In summer, some of the same trails become routes for hikers, mountain bikers and horseback riders.

Early Winters Outfitting (☎ 509-996-2659, 800-737-8750, ⓦ www.earlywinters outfitting.com, HCR 74 Box B6, Mazama, WA 98833), based in Mazama, offers horsepacking trips, cattle drives and fishing and hunting trips into the Pasayten Wilderness Area. Full-day rides cost $80 to $125, but you can saddle up for an hour for $18.

Jack's Hut (☎ 509-996-2752, 17798 Hwy 20), at the Freestone Inn (see Places to Stay & Eat, later), rents all types of Nordic equipment ($16/12 adult/child per day for full ski set) and mountain bikes ($8/35 hour/day). They can provide guides for whitewater rafting ($70/60 adult/child), fly-fishing ($60/105 one/two people) and cross-country skiing ($140 per day).

Mountain Transporter (☎ 509-996-8294) is a local shuttle service offering trailhead drop-off and pickup for mountain bikers, skiers and hikers ($5).

Cross-Country Skiing The **Methow Valley Sports Trails Association** (MVSTA; ☎ 509-996-3287, snow report ☎ 800-682-5787, ⓦ www.mvsta.com) has built and maintains an extensive network of more than 110 miles of cross-country ski trails. When there's no snow, these trails double as mountain-biking and hiking routes. One- and three-day trail

passes cost $15/30 and are not required for hikers and mountain bikers; maps are available at most local businesses.

There are two main ski hubs for the **Mazama Trails**: one off Hwy 20 near the Mazama Country Inn (see Places to Stay & Eat, later), the other at Early Winters (see above), near the end of the plowed stretch of Hwy 20. Where the highway is left unplowed, cross-country skiers are joined by dogsledders and snowmobilers.

From a trailhead on Lost River Rd just southeast of Mazama, the **Rendezvous Trails** skirt east around the base of Rendezvous Mountain about 21 miles to Cub Creek. The trails here are dotted with ski huts (see Places to Stay & Eat, later), and many loops can be fashioned from either end. There's also ample opportunity to practice telemark skiing. Skiers can pick up the Rendezvous Trails from Winthrop by heading 5 miles north up the Chewuch River Rd to the Cub Creek Trailhead.

The largest and most challenging component of the trail network is at **Sun Mountain** (see Winthrop & Around, later, for details).

The three ski areas are linked by the 15-mile **Methow Community Trail**, which runs along the Methow River between Mazama and Winthrop. You can also pick it up 6 miles south of Mazama, from a trailhead near Brown's Farm Inn.

Passes, maps, and ski rentals are available from The **Mazama Country Inn** (see Places to Stay & Eat), or from **Jack's Hut** (see introduction to this section).

Hiking Many cross-country trails become hiking and mountain-biking trails in the summer. The Methow Community Trail follows the meanders of the Methow River between Mazama and Winthrop.

Several trails start on Harts Pass Rd (USFS Rd 5400). For a lowlands amble and perhaps some fishing along the Methow River, turn off at the River Bend Campground. About a mile past the campground, catch the **West Fork Methow Trail**. The trail follows the river for 6 miles, then climbs 2 more miles to meet the **Pacific**

Accessible Trails

The North Cascades offer plenty of short, beautiful trails that are accessible to wheelchair users. At the back of the North Cascades National Park Visitor Center in Newhalem, for instance, a short boardwalk leads to views of the Picket Range, which features some of the most spectacular peaks in the North Cascades.

To get a feel for the frequently drippy west-side forests, try the half-mile **To Know a Tree Trail**, which skirts Newhalem Campground. The self-guided nature walk is graded and graveled for wheelchair use.

At the end of Main St in Newhalem, the **Trail of the Cedars** is a half-mile loop across a suspension bridge to the Skagit River's forested south shore. The **Happy Creek Forest Walk** makes a 0.3-mile loop through old-growth forests off Hwy 20, milepost 134, right between Diablo and Ross Lakes (about 8 miles east of Diablo). Interpretive signs enhance this boardwalk trail.

At Rainy Pass (Hwy 20 milepost 161), there is the **Rainy Lake Trail**, a mile-long paved trail through the woods to the lake and glacier views. Yet another accessible pathway, Baker Lake's Shadow of the Sentinels, meanders through a grove of century-old Douglas firs. Signs along the trail focus on the interdependence among flora and fauna in the forest.

Crest Trail (no bikes), where a turn to the south will lead to the highly scenic Methow Pass.

Places to Stay & Eat

Several small resorts are in and around Mazama (population 60). There isn't much to the town – just a couple of gas pumps, a tackle shop and a general store with one of the state's busiest pay phones in front.

Methow Valley Central Reservations (☎ 509-996-2148, 800-422-3048, Ⓦ www.methow.com/lodging) 'Central Res' books accommodations in the region's inns, lodges, B&Bs and cabins, in addition to handling vacation-home rentals.

Camping & Ski Huts Three USFS campgrounds are just off Hwy 20 on Early Winters Creek.

Lone Fir Campground (☎ 509-996-4000, 27 miles northwest of Winthrop on Hwy 20) Sites $6. This lovely wooded camp makes a good base for hiking, with a nearby nature loop that connects to trails for Cutthroat Lake and the Pacific Crest Trail. The basic facilities include pit toilets and running water.

Early Winters Campground (☎ 509-996-4000, 16 miles northwest of Winthrop on Hwy 20) Sites $8. At a lower elevation, Early Winters offers camping on the river, with good views of Goat Peak.

Klipchuck Campground, 3 miles farther west, doesn't always have water (check with the forest service).

A series of four ski huts, accessible only by trail, dot the Rendezvous area outside Winthrop. To book a hut, call *Rendezvous Outfitters (☎ 509-996-8100, 800-422-3048, Ⓦ www.methow.com/huts, Box 728, Winthrop, WA 98862)*. $25 per bunk, $100/150 summer/winter for entire 8-person hut. If you're not up to skiing with a pack, freight haul is available for $70 a leg.

B&Bs & Lodges The upper valley's only B&B establishment offers easy access to the Mazama trails.

Chokecherry Inn B&B (☎ 509-996-2049, 17871 Hwy 20, Mazama, WA 98833) Rooms $75. This amiably managed B&B is right on the Methow River about three-quarters of a mile east of the Early Winters campground. Each of the two rooms has a private bath, and there's a hot tub on the river-view deck.

Each of the lodges listed below has its own unique appeal, but all offer seclusion and opportunities for year-round recreation.

Mazama Country Inn (☎ 509-996-2681, 800-843-7951, fax 509-996-2646, Ⓦ www.mazamacountryinn.com, 42 Lost River Rd, Mazama) Lodge rooms from $80/150 summer/winter, cabins $125-225. Ski trails radiate out from this venerable lodge in the Upper Methow Valley. Cozy rooms have one or two quilted queen beds; some feature a loft or a private deck. The restaurant serves the best food for miles around, and in winter, all meals are included in room rates. Linens and kitchen implements are provided for the nine secluded cabins (a two-night minimum stay is required), most of which have a wood-burning stove. Ski packages and mountain-bike rentals are available.

Mazama Ranch House (☎ *509-996-2040,* W *www.mazamaranchhouse.com, HRC 74, Box A-6, Mazama, WA 98833)* Doubles $89. Catering to horse riders, this pleasant place opposite the Mazama Country Inn has stables and a corral. Eight simple, comfortable units have kitchenettes and front and back porches. No pets are allowed – unless they weigh 1000 pounds or so and say 'neigh.'

Freestone Inn (☎ *509-996-3906, 800-639-3809, fax 509-996-3907,* W *www.freestone inn.com, 17798 Hwy 20)* Rooms/suites from $140/175, cabins from $135. Freestone Inn is a beautifully designed luxury lodge at Wilson Ranch, in Early Winters. Hotel rooms all feature stone fireplaces (with an easy, push-button ignition) and have private, wood-slated balconies fronting onto a quiet lake. A trail from the cross-country ski area at Early Winters leads right up to the doorstep, and nonguests are welcome to warm up in the hotel lobby or dine at the gourmet restaurant (reservations are required). The woodsy, creek-front cabins pretend to be rustic but are a far cry from the old horse-packer huts they used to be.

North Cascades Basecamp (☎ *509-996-2334, 866-996-2334,* W *www.ncbasecamp .com, 255 Lost River Rd)* Double rooms from $74 with breakfast, cabin $140. This is a small inn with six lodge rooms (all with shared bathrooms), a cabin (which sleeps up to six), a hot tub, trails and a pond suitable for trout fishing or ice skating. It's a good place to bring kids, as several of the rooms have bunk beds or twin beds in addition to a double or queen, and there's a playroom in the lodge. Full board with lodge rooms is available for an additional $20/12 per adult/child.

Brown's Farm Inn (☎ *509-996-2571,* W *www.methownet.com/brownsfarm, 887* *Wolf Creek Rd)* Studio $80, cabins $90-130. Fresh eggs come with a cabin rental at Brown's Farm, which is located alongside the Methow Community Trail 5 miles from the Mazama Junction, which links Hwy 20 with Mazama. Vintage one- and three-bedroom cabins have complete kitchens.

WINTHROP & AROUND

Winthrop (population 349) has been done over as an upscale Western town, where espresso is sold from false-fronted shops and flower baskets line the streets. As with its sister theme-town, Leavenworth, it's easy to curl a lip or roll the eyes when describing Winthrop, but the fact is, it works. What was once a struggling east-slope town is now a thriving part of the new Old West.

The town was first settled in 1891 by Harvard-educated Guy Waring, who built a trading post at the confluence of the Chewuch (**chee**-wok) and Methow Rivers. After a couple of visits to Winthrop, Waring's Harvard classmate Owen Wister settled down and wrote the best-selling book *The Virginian,* whose characters are supposedly based on Winthropians.

When the North Cascades Hwy opened in 1972, Winthrop was ready and waiting, with many of its frontier-era buildings spiffed up for the tourist trade. You know the routine: stroll the wood-plank sidewalk downtown and browse the gift shops. Be sure to stop and watch the blacksmith if he's at work forging wrought-iron hooks and trivets.

Refer to the Methow Valley map for this section.

Orientation & Information

Winthrop is 13 miles southeast of Mazama on Hwy 20. After crossing the Methow, the highway makes a 90-degree turn as it comes into town and becomes the main drag, sometimes referred to as Riverside Ave. Twisp is 8 miles farther southwest, and it's 38 miles to Omak.

The Winthrop Chamber of Commerce (☎ 509-996-2125, 888-463-8469, W www .winthropwashington.com), 202 Riverside Ave, is at the corner where Hwy 20 enters downtown.

WASHINGTON

The post office (☎ 509-996-2282) is just east of town on Hwy 20. The Medicine Wheel Website (☎ 509-996-2022), 315 Riverside Ave, has a couple of computers for Internet access at $10 per hour. It's open 9am to 4:30pm Monday to Friday.

Things to See & Do

Guy Waring built the log house that is now the centerpiece of the **Shafer Museum** (☎ 509-996-2712, 285 Castle Ave; admission by donation; open 10am-5pm Memorial Day-Labor Day), up the hill from Riverside. Known to Winthropians since its construction in 1897 as 'The Castle,' the home was Waring's reward to his wife for moving west.

Before a local cobbler teamed up with the USFS to make padded, multipocketed jumpsuits, nobody had ever jumped from a plane to extinguish a forest fire. Now that 'smokejumpers' have been elevated to heroes of modern Western mythology, tours can be made of the **North Cascade Smokejumper Base** (☎ 509-997-2031, 23 Intercity Airport Rd; admission free; usually open 8am-5pm June-Oct). It's halfway between Winthrop and Twisp, on Eastside Winthrop-Twisp Rd, which runs parallel to Hwy 20 along the east bank of the river.

West of Winthrop, there's a network of **cross-country ski trails** near the **Sun Mountain Lodge** (☎ 509-996-2211, ext 800, 800-572-0493, fax 509-996-3133, W www.sun mountainlodge.com, PO Box 1000, Winthrop, WA 98862). If you aren't a lodge guest, park at the Chickadee parking lot, just above Patterson Lake. The elevation here is 2600 feet, and the trails climb another 1000 feet on the challenging **Thompson Ridge Rd**. As with other trails maintained by the Methow Valley Sports Trail Association, you'll need to purchase a pass (see Cross-Country Skiing under Methow Valley, earlier). Winthrop is also the southeast terminus of the 15-mile **Methow Community Trail**, which follows the river up to Mazama. Pick up trailheads at the Spring Creek Ranch or at the WolfRidge Resort, about 5½ miles north of town off of Twin Lakes Rd.

You can rent skis and purchase trail passes from **Winthrop Mountain Sports**

(☎ 509-996-2886, W www.winthropmountain sports.com, 257 Riverside Ave; adult package $16/9 first/additional day).

While cross-country skiing is the area's main draw, summer visitors still find plenty to do around here. The ski trails are given over to **mountain biking** once the snow clears. Sun Mountain alone offers 30-odd miles of trail riding. One popular ride from Winthrop is a not-too-strenuous 12-mile loop to **Pearrygin Lake**. Start by following the well-marked road to Pearrygin (**peh**-ri-jin) Lake State Park. After 4 miles of paved-road cycling, continue straight up the dirt Pearrygin Lake Rd rather than turning right onto the paved entrance to the state park. The road climbs gently for 2 miles, affording good views of the valley and surrounding mountains. At the 'T' intersection, turn right and coast, hitting pavement again at the Bear Creek Golf Course. At the valley floor, turn right and pedal 3 miles back to town.

You can rent mountain bikes at Winthrop Mountain Sports (see earlier reference) from $20 per day. Pick up a booklet here describing all the best local mountain-biking routes.

Fishing for steelhead trout and chinook salmon is popular in the Methow River, but anglers are required to use catch-and-release techniques for these endangered species. **Moccasin Lake**, a mile-long hike from Patterson Lake Rd, has very good fly-fishing, with rainbows averaging 3lb to 5lb.

If golf is more your speed, **Bear Creek Golf Course** (☎ 509-996-2284, W www.bear creekgolfcourse.com, Eastside County Rd; weekday greens fees 9/18 holes $13/20), 3 miles southeast of Winthrop, is noted for its lovely surroundings.

Special Events

Winthrop's Memorial Day weekend Rodeo Days (☎ 509-996-2435) makes you remember that this is not just a made-up Western town. The summer season is highlighted by the Winthrop Rhythm & Blues Festival (☎ 509-996-2148), with national acts coming to town for three days in late July. Call the MVSTA (☎ 509-996-3287) for details on their early October Methow Valley Mountain Bike

Festival. And, if you're in town over President's Day weekend, be prepared for the big Snowshoe Softball Tournament.

Places to Stay

Camping If the run of hotels in the Winthrop area seem a bit steep, there are a couple of camping options close to town.

Pearrygin Lake State Park (☎ 509-996-2370, reservations ☎ 888-226-7688, *Pearrygin Lake Rd*) Tents/hookups $11/16. Five miles northeast of town, pretty Pearrygin Lake is actually warm enough to swim in during the summer. Showers, a boat launch, swimming and trout fishing make this a popular and usually crowded spot. During the winter, snowmobilers come here to get away from the cross-country skiers, and in spring, hungry yellow marmots graze the grounds. Reservations are essential on holidays; there's a $6 reservation fee.

KOA (☎ 509-996-2258, reservations ☎ 800-562-2158, W *www.methownet.com/koa, 1114 Hwy 20*) Tents/RV sites $20/26, cabins $40. This busy, family-oriented campground is just east of town on the Methow River. Cute little log cabins have been added; bring your own bedding and cooking utensils. A courtesy shuttle takes guests into town.

Hotels While the Winthrop experience is best savored staying in its downtown lodgings, several reasonably priced options are clustered along Hwy 20 just south of town.

Trail's End Motel (☎ 509-996-2303, 877-996-2339, e *trails-end@methow.com, 130 Riverside Ave*) Singles/doubles from $63/71. The broad facade fronts a fairly modest but comfortable motel with a dose of frontier flavor. Downstairs rooms have showers, while the newer upper units come with full bath. A good bookstore shares space with the office.

Duck Brand Hotel (☎ 509-996-2192, fax 509-996-2001, W *www.methownet.com/duck, 248 Riverside Ave*) Singles/doubles $56/66. This is a handsome hotel on the uphill side of the street with balconies overlooking what there is of local activity. All rooms have private baths with tubs and air conditioning. The saloon-style restaurant is a popular gathering place.

Hotel Rio Vista (☎ 509-996-3535, 800-398-0911, W *www.methow.com/~riovista, 285 Riverside Ave*) Doubles $90. Behind the typically Winthropian false-front, wildlife-themed rooms show off locally crafted furniture, and a rear deck overlooks the meeting of the Methow and Chewuch Rivers.

Farmhouse Inn (☎ 509-996-2191, 888-996-2525, W *www.farmhouse-inn.com, 709 Hwy 20*) Rooms $45-65, 2-bedroom unit $85, including continental breakfast. The cheapest place to stay in Winthrop is also one of the coziest – the Old West gets a touch of Scandinavian design here. Three of the six guest rooms have private bathrooms. The hot tub out back is great for starlight soaking, and guests share a living room with a wood-burning stove and kitchenette.

Winthrop Mountain View Chalets (☎ 509-996-3113, 800-527-3113, W *www.methownet.com/mtnview, 1120 Hwy 20*) Cabins $65. Next door to the KOA, these cute two-person pine cabins feature microwave ovens and nice decks. No 5 has a fireplace.

Lodges & Resorts Winthrop's recreational retreats deliver log-hewn country charm and a luxuriant setting without sacrificing suburban comforts or convenience to town.

Spring Creek Ranch (☎ 509-996-2495, 509-996-2510, 491 Twin Lakes Rd) Doubles from $70. Across the Methow River from downtown is this elegantly renovated 1929 dairy farmhouse with kitchen facilities, a washer and dryer and a big, old willow tree out back. Skiers and walkers will appreciate the Methow Community Trail running right past the front door. To get there, bear right onto Twin Lakes Rd after crossing the bridge on the south end of town.

Chewuch Inn (☎ 509-996-3107, 800-747-3107, W *www.chewuchinn.com, 223 White Ave*) Standard/kitchenette rooms $65/90, cabins $90-115. A bit farther down Twin Lakes Rd, you'll find this attractive lodge, where rooms and cabins are hand-painted by the artist-owner and decorated with such outdoorsy objects as snowshoes. Balconies look out over the meadows and mountains. A breakfast spread is included.

WASHINGTON

Rivers' Edge Resort (☎ 509-996-8000, 800-937-6621, W *www.methow.com/~riveredg, 115 Riverside Ave)* Cabins/chalets $120/175. These custom-built, fully furnished cabins on the Chewuch are just a short walk from the center of town. There are five one-bedroom cabins with kitchenettes and six two-story chalets with full kitchens and matchless views of the river.

Virginian Resort (☎ 509-996-2535, 800-854-2834, W *www.virginianresort.com, 808 Hwy 20)* Rooms from $85, cabins $95. On the outskirts of town but thematically related, the Virginian offers comfortable pseudorustic motel rooms, kitchenette cabins and a heated outdoor pool. The more expensive riverside rooms have rear decks. The adjoining restaurant serves reasonably good trout and steak ($14-16).

WolfRidge Resort (☎ 509-996-2828, 800-237-2388, W *www.wolfridgeresort.com, 412-B Wolf Creek Rd)* Rooms/suites/townhouse $74/108/159. WolfRidge has a wide variety of accommodations, ranging from hotel rooms to log townhouse suites, along with a heated outdoor pool and direct access to the Methow Community Trail. The resort is 5½ miles northwest of town via Twin Lakes Rd.

Sun Mountain Lodge (☎ 509-996-2211, 800-572-0493, fax 509-996-3133, W *www.sun mountain lodge.com, Box 1000, Winthrop, WA 98862)* Lodge rooms $160-620; cabins $160-345. The region's premier resort is 9 miles southwest of town via Twin Lakes and Patterson Lake Rds. The high-gloss rustic lodge has very comfortable rooms and cabins with expansive views of the Methow Valley. Cross-country ski and snowshoe trails lead out from the lodge, and in the summer, there's horseback riding, canoeing and sailing, as well as access to tennis courts and a pool. The restaurant focuses on Northwest cuisine; the Sunday brunch draws hungry hikers and skiers from all over the Methow Valley. Despite the elegance, the dress code is casual. Rates drop by half in spring and fall.

Places to Eat

Like any real Western town, the sidewalks roll up early, so you will be hard pressed to find food after 8pm.

Java Man (☎ 509-996-2182, 94 Bridge St)* Burritos $5.50. A great take-along option is one of the well-filled burritos from this little place. Be sure to grab some espresso, too.

Boulder Creek Deli (☎ 509-996-3990, 94 Bridge St)* Sandwiches $5.50. If you can't decide on a sandwich from the large selection here, you might try an artichoke-heart-and-mushroom calzone ($4.25) or an antipasto salad. Or take a break with a triple ginger cookie and a latte as you gaze at the dancing heifers mural.

Two Rivers Cafe (☎ 509-996-8179, 253 Riverside Ave)* Breakfast & lunch $5-7, dinner $14-17. The rear deck of this low-key eatery across from the Duck Brand is perhaps the best perch in town from which to glimpse the confluence of the Chewuch and Methow Rivers. A dozen varieties of omelets ($7.50) are served all day, and in the evening the chicken and chops are nicely prepared.

Winthrop Brewing Company (☎ 509-996-3183, 155 Riverside Ave)* Entrees $7-13. Occupying a little red schoolhouse on the main street, Winthrop's microbrewery produces an impressive range of handcrafted ales. You can also get things such as chili, barbecued chicken and pizza. The kitchen closes at 8pm, but on Friday there's often live music until 1am.

Duck Brand Cantina (☎ 509-996-2192, 248 Riverside Ave)* Entrees $5-10. The lively, faux-Western cantina in the hotel of the same name serves up everything from Mexican food to yummy apple and rhubarb pie.

TWISP

In the past, Native Americans set up fish-drying camps at the junction of the Methow and Twisp Rivers, and the women who prepared the salmon were often plagued by yellow jackets, or *twips,* setting the stage for one of Washington's most charming town names. Twisp (population 938) isn't loaded with prepackaged entertainment, but if small and unpretentious strikes your fancy, spend a night here, a more genuine version of the West than its false-front-filled neighbor to the north.

Orientation & Information

South of Twisp, Hwy 153 splits off Hwy 20 and follows the Methow River south, joining US 97 and the Columbia River at Pateros. Hwy 20 continues east through the Okanogan and Loup Loup forests for 29 miles to the Okanogan Valley.

The Twisp Visitor Info Center (☎ 509-997-2926, fax 509-997-2164, W www.twispinfo.com), 201 S Methow Way, operates out of the Methow Valley Community Center. Twisp Ranger Station (☎ 509-997-2131), 502 Glover St (Twisp's main street), has information on trails and campgrounds in the Okanogan National Forest, as well as Green Trails hiking maps. It's open 7:45am to 4:30pm Monday to Friday.

Things to See & Do

For a small town, Twisp has a pretty lively cultural scene, anchored in large part by the **Confluence Gallery & Art Center** (☎ 509-997-2787, 104 Glover St; admission free; open 10:30am-3pm Tues-Fri, 9am-3pm Sat). The gallery mounts a new exhibit every six weeks or so, with a focus on work by regional artists.

All along the Twisp River, **hiking** trails abound. A Northwest Forest Pass is required to park at most trailheads; pick one up at the USFS ranger station.

Follow Twisp River Rd west of town for about 11 miles, and veer left onto USFS Rd 4420 (W Buttermilk Creek Rd) to reach a trail up Eagle Creek, which sprouts a branch along Oval Creek 1½ miles from the trailhead. The 7-mile **Eagle Creek Trail** is fairly level (there's more uphill on the Oval Creek route), but it does have the reward of three high mountain lakes starting about 6 miles in. These and other trails in the area can be the first leg of a backpacking trip into the **Lake Chelan-Sawtooth Wilderness Area**. If, at the end of the Twisp River Rd, you follow USFS Rd 4440 along the north bank, you'll pass several campgrounds, each with hiking trails nearby (see Places to Stay, later).

For **rafting**, the Methow River is divided into two floatable stretches. The upper stretch, from the town of Carlton to McFarland Creek (3 miles north of Methow

village) provides an easygoing float; the lower Methow, from McFarland Creek to Pateros, runs through the Black Canyon, with more challenging white-water. From May to July, **Osprey River Adventures** (☎ 509-997-4116, 800-997-4116, W www .methow.com/osprey) runs expeditions here (from $70).

If you don't mind a few snowmobiles, **cross-country skiing** is easy along the flat Twisp River Rd. Nearer to downtown, trails start at the Idle-A-While Motel (see Places to Stay) and tool around Twisp and along the Methow River.

North Cascade Outfitters (☎ 509-997-1015, 888-291-4097, W www.cowboypoet .com) offers **horseback riding** (1½-hour ride $20), including customized pack trips. Or for something a little different, the **Malamute Express** (☎ 509-997-6402, 141A Poorman Creek Rd, Twisp) runs one-/two-person dogsledding trips for $125/200.

Places to Stay

As with most of the recreation around Twisp, the Twisp River is the place to look for campsites. Five *USFS campgrounds* (☎ 509-997-2131) are found along Twisp River Rd, all close to trailheads for the Lake Chelan-Sawtooth Wilderness Area. War Creek and Poplar Flat, the only campgrounds with running water, have a $6 site fee; the rest are $3. The last of the chain is peaceful Road's End campground, 25 miles northwest of Twisp, with four sites.

Black Pine Lake Campground (☎ 509-997-2131, Poorman Creek Rd, 18 miles southwest of Twisp) Sites $8. Campers at this pleasant lakeside spot will appreciate the mountain views. A paved interpretive trail surrounds the lake. From Hwy 20, follow the Twisp River Rd west 11 miles to USFS Rd 300, which reaches the lake after 6½ miles.

Riverbend RV Park (☎ 509-997-3500, 800-686-4498, W www.riverbendrv.com, 19961 Hwy 20) Tents/hookups $15/20. Alongside the swiftly flowing Methow, this roadside RV park are more inviting than most. Grassy sites are shaded by cottonwood trees, and there's a secluded tent-camping area, plus laundry and fire pits.

WASHINGTON

You won't find any place particularly fancy or upscale to stay in Twisp, but there are several reasonably priced, basic motels.

Sportsman Motel (☎ 509-997-2911, 11010 E Hwy 20) Singles/doubles $39/44. The Sportsman has perfectly good knotty-pine rooms, some with kitchens. You can pitch a tent here for $8 and take a shower for $2 more.

Idle-A-While Motel (☎ 509-997-3222, e idle-a-while@methow.com, 505 N Hwy 20) One-/two-bed rooms from $52/56, cottages from $60. Not a bad place to while away a quiet Twisp evening, the motel has a hot tub and sauna. A row of barracks-like cottages with kitchenettes face a lawn equipped with barbecue grills. Dogs (but not cats) are welcome.

Log House Inn B&B (☎ 509-997-5001, e garydian@methow.com, 894 Twisp River Rd) Doubles $62, $10 per child. Ten miles up the Twisp River, this old structure has a real backwoods feel and is convenient to recreation in the Lake Chelan-Sawtooth Wilderness Area. A hearty breakfast is included.

Methow Valley Inn (☎ 509-997-2253, w www.methowvalleyinn.com, 234 2nd St) Rooms with shared/private bath $89/99. This superbly restored 1912 mansion positively brims with Old World charm. The seven guest rooms, grand sitting room with stone fireplace and enormous kitchen all reflect longtime nurturing. Canned fruits and jams from the rear garden's 28 fruit trees are one component of the multicourse breakfast served here.

Places to Eat

Cinnamon Twisp Bakery (☎ 509-997-5030, 116 Glover St) Pastries $2. This is a mandatory stop for wonderful cinnamon twists, awesome cookies and organic coffee.

Glover Street Market (124 Glover St) Next door to the bakery, you can pick up organic produce, juices and granola to take along on hikes.

Fiddlehead Bistro (☎ 509-997-0343, Glover St) Entrees $10-16. Open 5pm-9pm Thur-Sat. Across the street from the Confluence Gallery is this toney bistro specializing in nouveau Northwest cuisine. After a

dinner of braised lamb shank in burgundy-rosemary sauce or pasta tossed with roasted pears and gorgonzola, sit back on the couch for an after-dinner drink.

Methow Valley Brewing Co (☎ 509-997-6822, 209 E 2nd Ave) Entrees $8-14. The MVBC turns fresh local ingredients into soups, sandwiches and other delectable treats, best accompanied by a house-made beer or soda. Live music draws people into the arty environment some weekends.

Mick & Miki's Red Cedars Bar (☎ 997-6425, 110 Glover St) Snacks $3-6. Until 10pm, you can grab a snack here while you play a game of pool or groove to local blues talent.

STEHEKIN

Of all the wonderful spots in the North Cascades, Stehekin (steh-**hee**-kin) is especially charmed. Part of the charm comes from its remoteness, as the tiny community (population 100) is only accessible by boat, plane or a long hike, most often across Cascade Pass. An equal amount of charm accrues from the beauty of its location at the head of Lake Chelan and on the southern edge of North Cascades National Park. Plenty of trails lead into the mountains.

'Stehekin' is roughly translated as 'the way through,' and though Native Americans had no settlement at the north end of Lake Chelan, they did use nearby Cascade Pass as a route across the Cascades.

Miners after North Cascades gold figured a boat ride up Lake Chelan was easier than foot travel across the mountains, and prospectors began tramping through the area in the 1850s. Even Clara Barton, founder of the American Red Cross, visited Stehekin on a wood-fired steamboat in 1891 and filed a mining claim. However, Barton's visit was far upstaged when, in 1944, young Elizabeth Taylor filmed *The Courage of Lassie* here.

Subsistence farmers began putting down roots in the 1880s. Seasonal tourism followed, and a hotel was built in 1892 to accommodate steamboat arrivals. Later enlarged to house 100 guests, the Hotel Field met its demise in 1927, when a dam at the lake's foot raised the water level by 21 feet. Parts of the hotel were salvaged for the construction of the Golden West Lodge, currently being renovated for use as the visitor center and ranger station.

If possible, stay in Stehekin for a day or two rather than making a quick up-and-back tour-boat excursion. Virtually all the tours, activities, places to eat and accommodations are limited to the summer season, which runs from mid-June to mid-September. In the winter, the North Cascades Stehekin Lodge has a few kitchenette units available, but visitors should bring their own food from Chelan.

Orientation
Stehekin is 55 miles north of Chelan, at the tip of Lake Chelan. See the North Cascades National Park map, earlier in this chapter, for sites in and around Stehekin.

Stehekin Valley Rd (the town's only road) is referred to most often as just 'the road.' From the boat landing, it continues to the northwest for 23 miles, only 4 miles of which are paved. The road is clear of snow from High Bridge Campground (11 miles up) to the end from around late June, though severe flooding in past years has been known to close the road for an entire season. Be sure to check the road status with the NPS before making plans.

East of Stehekin, the road dead-ends after 4 miles. Destinations at the landing are all within walking distance, and it's easy to rent a bike or catch a bus to travel up the road.

Information
The Courtney Log Office, 150 yards past the post office, has information about the valley and serves as a sort of activities center and booking office. Write to Stehekin Heritage, PO Box 1, Stehekin, WA 98852, to obtain a copy of *The Stehekin Guidebook,* a useful tourist publication. Information can also be found at w www.stehekinvalley.com.

The Purple Point Information Center (☎ 360-856-5700, ext 340, then ext 14, w www.nps.gov/noca/, Lake Chelan National Recreation Area, PO Box 7, Stehekin,

WA 98852) is temporarily housing the NPS Information Center and the Golden West art gallery. It's open 8:30am to 5pm mid-May to September, 10am to 2pm mid-March to mid-May and in early October. The NPS ranger station next to the North Cascades Stehekin Lodge, above the post office, serves as the off-season information center. (In March 2003, the renovated Golden West Visitor Center is due to re-open and will house both the information center and ranger station.)

On weekends in July and August, the NPS gives evening presentations on natural-history topics at Purple Point. Local residents sometimes supplement the programs with talks on local cultural history. Ask at the information center for a schedule.

The post office is in the lower level of the ranger station.

Telephone service in Stehekin is via expensive radio-telephone, so most business listings are for answering services or voice mailboxes in Chelan. There's a regular credit-card phone for outgoing calls in front of the public laundry and shower house, about 50 yards beyond the post office. Other telephone arrangements can be made at the Courtney Log Office, or the North Cascades Stehekin Lodge.

The nearest hospital is in Chelan. The valley has its own network of individuals and NPS personnel who are certified in first aid, so ask locals for a reference. Contact the ranger station in an emergency; most businesses and NPS employees carry radios for this purpose.

Hiking
Backpackers planning an overnight stay will need a backcountry camping permit, which can be obtained at Purple Point or from the Chelan Ranger Station. A limited number of permits are issued free, on a first-come, first-served basis, up to a day before departure.

If you're not staying overnight, it's hard to get very far on a hike with a layover of only a few hours. **Buckner Orchard**, near Rainbow Falls, is one of the Stehekin area's oldest settlements and makes for a nice walk. Once there, you'll find a homestead cabin built in 1889, plenty of old farm equipment and trees that keep on bearing apples. Head 3.4 miles up Stehekin Valley Rd, turn left at the far end of the Rainbow Creek bridge and look for a sign about 20 yards off the road, marking the Buckner Orchard Walk, an easy 1-mile roundtrip to the apple orchards. From just past the bridge, there's also a short path leading to the 312-foot **Rainbow Falls**.

The easy **Lakeshore Trail** starts at the Golden West Visitor Center (under renovation until March 2003) and heads south near Lake Chelan's shore. It's 6 miles to views of the lake and valley at Hunts Bluff. It's also possible to make this into a backpacking trip; Moore Point is 7 miles from the trailhead, while Prince Creek, the trail's endpoint, is 17 miles. Watch out for rattlesnakes along the way.

The relatively flat **Stehekin River Trail** starts at Harlequin Campground (4½ miles up-valley from the landing) and heads upriver through the forest, past many fishing holes. It's a cool, shady walk – perfect for a hot day.

A steady uphill hike from the **Rainbow Loop** trailhead, 2½ miles from the landing, leads to great lake and valley views. There's a campground 2 miles from the trailhead, at Rainbow Bridge. Take the left fork past the campground for a fairly quick return to the valley above Harlequin Bridge to complete the 5-mile Rainbow Loop. Take the right fork (the Rainbow Creek Trail) 1 mile to reach an incredible vista point of the lake and the Cascades; this trail continues for another 10 miles to McAlester Pass.

Head east from the Golden West Center and immediately begin climbing the **Purple Creek Trail** toward 6884-foot Purple Pass, 7½ miles away. Since it starts at the landing, hikers who are looking for a short, vigorous hike with good views of the lake and mountains can grunt uphill for an hour or so and then return for the afternoon boat to Chelan. The forest yields to views after about 3½ miles.

Just past the turnoff for High Bridge Campground (11 miles from the landing), pick up the **Agnes Gorge Trail** for an easy 2½-mile hike to a 210-foot gorge, past views of 8115-foot Agnes Mountain.

Other Activities

You can rent bikes from the store at the **North Cascades Stehekin Lodge** (☎ 509-682-4494, Box 457, Chelan, WA 98816) or from **Discovery Bikes** (☎ 509-682-4677) at the Courtney Log Office (see Information, earlier). Mountain bikes (for road riding only) rent for $3.50 an hour or $20 a day. Discovery Bikes can also shuttle cyclists and their bikes up the road to the Stehekin Valley Ranch, which is just far enough to bike back down the valley in time to catch the 2pm boat back to Chelan.

The lower Stehekin River is open for catch-and-release fishing from March 1 to June 30, with the regular fishing season running from July 1 to October 31. Both cutthroat and rainbow trout live in the upper river and the creeks feeding into it. Kokanee (landlocked sockeye) salmon begin the run from Lake Chelan up the Stehekin in late August and continue through September. Stop by **McGregor Mountain Outdoor Supply** (e mcgregormountain@starband.net, PO Box 68, Stehekin, WA 98852) at the landing for fishing advice, supplies and regulation updates, and camping gear.

Be sure to check at the Purple Point Information Center for the current listing of interpretive **nature walks** and hikes led by the NPS.

Organized Tours

The **North Cascades Stehekin Lodge** (☎ 509-682-4494, W www.stehekin.com, Box 457, Chelan, WA 98816) leads a daily 45-minute bus trip to Rainbow Falls ($7/4 adult/youth). Buses leave upon arrival of the Lady Express (around 10:45am) and the Lady of the Lake II (12:30pm). They also offer a lunch tour to High Bridge ($20/10/5 adult/youth/child).

The **Stehekin Adventure Company** offers raft trips on the Stehekin River in the spring and summer (day trips $45/35 adult/child). Stehekin Valley Ranch's **Cascade Corrals** leads three-hour horseback rides to Coon Lake ($38 per person), as well as guided

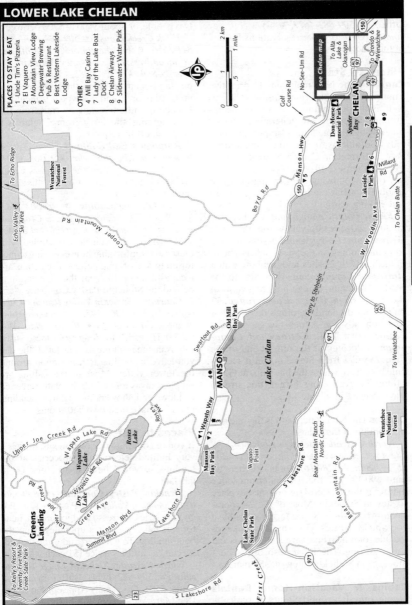

LOWER LAKE CHELAN

PLACES TO STAY & EAT
1 Uncle Tim's Pizzeria
2 El Vaquero
3 Mountain View Lodge
4 Deepwater Brewing
  Pub & Restaurant
6 Best Western Lakeside
  Lodge

OTHER
4 Mill Bay Casino
7 Lady of the Lake Boat
  Dock
8 Chelan Airways
9 Slidewaters Water Park

2 km
1 mile

To Alta
Lake &
Okanogan

see Chelan map

To Orondo &
Wenatchee

No-See-Um Rd

Golf
Course Rd

CHELAN

Don Morse
Memorial Park

Spader
Bay

Manson Hwy

Boyd Rd

Echo Valley
Ski Area

To Echo Ridge

Wenatchee
National
Forest

Cooper Mountain Rd

Millard
Rd

Lakeside
Park

To Chelan Butte

W Woodin Ave

ALT
97

Ferry to Stehekin

To Wenatchee

971

Swartout Rd

Old Mill
Bay Park

MANSON

Wapato Way

Lake Chelan

Wenatchee
National
Forest

Bear Mountain Ranch
Nordic Center

S Lakeshore Rd

Bear Mountain Rd

Upper Joe Creek Rd

E Wapato Lake Rd

Wapato Lake Rd

Wapato
Lake

Roses
Lake

Dry
Lake

Joe Creek

Lower Joe Creek Rd

Green Ave

Manson Blvd

Summit Blvd

Lakeshore Dr

Manson
Bay Park

Wapato
Point

Greens
Landing

To Kelly's Resort &
Twenty-Five Mile
Creek State Park

Lake Chelan
State Park

First Creek

S Lakeshore Rd

23

971

WASHINGTON

hikes into the mountains with gear carried on horseback. Contact the **Courtney Log Office** (☎ 509-682-4677, **w** *www.courtney country.com*) to make reservations for any of these activities.

Places to Stay

Camping The NPS maintains 11 primitive campsites along the road up the valley, as well as a good number of hike-in camp-grounds. Pit toilets are generally available, but only the Purple Point Campground provides potable water. Contact the Purple Point Information Center (☎ 360-856-5700, ext 340, then ext 14) to check the status of any of the following NPS campgrounds or to obtain a backcountry-camping permit (see Hiking, earlier).

Purple Point Campground is right at the landing, 200 yards up-valley from the dock. *Weaver Point Campground*, across the lake from the landing on the west bank, is a boat-in facility, with 22 sites and drinking water. *Harlequin Campground*, 4½ miles up the road at Harlequin Bridge, has great views of the river. *High Bridge Campground*, 11 miles from the landing, offers direct access to trailheads for Agnes Gorge and the Pacific Crest Trail. *Cottonwood Campground* is located at the official end of the road, 23 miles from Stehekin, but it's a 2.7-mile hike from where the bus stops at Glory Mountain. And don't forget, this stretch stays snowed-in till late June.

Lodges The NPS concession is the one and only option in the village.

North Cascades Stehekin Lodge (☎ 509-682-4494, **w** *www.stehekin.com, PO Box 457, Chelan, WA 98816*) Rooms/kitchenette units $90-123/117-133. The lakefront lodge in town is the 'modern' (ie, non-rustic) place to stay in Stehekin. Most of the 28 rooms sleep two or three; seven larger units have cooking facilities. Two-night packages include roundtrip boat fare, some meals and some touring. The lodge also offers boat moorage in Stehekin's new 30-slip marina.

Cabins & Vacation-Home Rentals

Home rentals around Stehekin typically require a minimum stay of at least two nights and rent for around $100 per night for two people, or about $500 to $700 per week.

Flick Creek House (☎ 509-884-1730, 888-841-3556, **e** *barnhartphoto@earthlink.net, postal address: Mike & Nancy Barnhart, PO Box 25, Stehekin, WA 98852*) This two-story, post-and-beam cabin on the lake can sleep up to 10 people, and a rowboat is included. It's about an hour's walk by trail from the boat landing; the ferry from Chelan will drop you off by request.

Rainbow's End Cabin (☎ 509-682-3014, **w** *www.stehekinvalley.com, PO Box 8, Stehekin, WA 98852*) Near the Rainbow Creek Trailhead and Buckner Orchard, this sleeps three to four.

Stehekin Log Cabins (☎ 509-682-7742, 509-682-4677, postal address: Cragg & Roberta Courtney, PO Box 67, Stehekin, WA 98852*) A private vehicle is included with these two comfortable housekeeping cabins for up to five or nine people. The cabins are located 2 miles up from the boat landing, behind the Stehekin Pastry Company.

Courtneys' Stehekin Valley Ranch (☎ 509-682-4677, 800-536-0745, **w** *www.courtney country.com, PO Box 36, Stehekin, WA 98852*) The price for lodging in these rustic cabins includes all meals, plus lunch the day you leave, as well as transportation around the lower valley. Most of the cabins are simple, canvas-topped affairs, with screened windows and showers in a nearby building, but a few have their own bathrooms.

Places to Eat

If you're cooking your own meals, there's a very limited selection of groceries at the landing, so you'd be wise to stock up in Chelan.

Stehekin Pastry Company (☎ 800-536-0745, Stehekin Valley Rd*) Pastries $2-6. For good pastries, espresso and ice cream, head for this bakery, 2 miles up-valley from the boat landing. To get there, take the 'bakery special,' a shuttle service ($1 each way).

North Cascades Stehekin Lodge Restaurant (☎ 509-682-4494) Buffet breakfast/dinner $7/16. Open daily Apr-Sept, Sat & Sun Dec-Mar. Aside from the buffet breakfast and dinner, the lodge restaurant serves sandwiches, vegetarian lasagna and other light meals. They're open for lunch year round to serve the midday ferry arrivals.

Stehekin Valley Ranch (☎ 509-682-4677) Breakfast & lunch $5-8, dinner $13-18. Open for breakfast 7am-9am, lunch noon-1pm, dinner 5:30pm-7pm. Reservations are required here for the daily set dinner menu (there's $3 shuttle service from the dock to the lodge at 5:15pm). Grill items are also available, such as burgers (beef and veggie) and fish.

Getting There & Away

Chelan Airways (☎ 509-682-5555, W www .chelanairways.com) provides seaplane service between Stehekin and Chelan. Flights cost $80/120 one way/roundtrip. Combo plane-boat tours are also available. Inquire at the Lady of the Lake boat dock, in Chelan.

The Lake Chelan Boat Company (☎ 509-682-4584, schedule info ☎ 509-682-2224, W www.ladyofthelake.com), PO Box 186, Chelan, WA 98816, operates a ferry service up and down the lake. A ride on the *Lady of the Lake II* is the most common way to reach Stehekin and Lucerne, and is popular with tourists who simply want to cruise the lake with a 90-minute stop in Stehekin. Another option is the *Lady Express,* which cuts the four-hour (one-way) boat trip down to just over two hours, or the high-speed *Lady Cat,* which makes the run twice a day in a little over an hour (summer only). From mid-June to mid-September, boats leave Chelan every morning at 7:45am and 8:30am, and the last boat leaves Stehekin at 2pm, returning to Chelan by 6pm. If your destination is Lucerne or one of the lakeside campgrounds, check with the tour company as to which boat best suits your needs.

High-season roundtrip fares are $25/44/89 for the *Lady of the Lake II/Lady Express/ Lady Cat;* children under age 11 pay half price. The boats do not transport cars.

The Pacific Crest Trail passes through the Stehekin Valley, making it possible to hike 12 miles from Rainy Pass on Hwy 20 to the Bridge Creek Campground on the Stehekin Valley Rd, where you could then (depending upon the time of the year) be picked up by the NPS shuttle van (see Getting Around, next) or hike the 16 miles down the road into town. Alternatively, hike the 8-mile Cascade Pass Trail from the northwest to the Cottonwood Campground at the end of the road, which is the most popular overland route to Stehekin (see Cascade Pass Trail, under North Cascades National Park, earlier). Until the last stretch of the road is fixed, you'll have to hike another 3 miles down the road to Glory Mountain in order to catch the NPS shuttle.

Getting Around

Although there are roads and cars in Stehekin, there are no roads *to* Stehekin. Courtesy transportation to and from the boat landing is included in most lodging prices. The North Cascades Stehekin Lodge (☎ 509-682-4494/682-4584) has transportation to snow trails in the winter.

Bicycles are the easiest way to get around. See Other Activities, earlier, for rental options. If you'd prefer to bring your own, the Lake Chelan Boat Company charges $13 roundtrip for bike transport.

From late May to September, the NPS runs a shuttle van up and down Stehekin Valley Rd four or five times a day, from the boat landing to High Bridge ($6/3 per adult/ child each way, 45 minutes). In early June, it may only run if there are enough passengers. The bus accommodates both bikes ($3) and backpacks, and passengers get a narrated tour. Additional NPS bus service from High Bridge to Glory Mountain, 20 miles from the landing, runs three or four times daily from July to September ($6/3, one hour). The Early Bird Express, which departs at 7am Friday to Sunday in mid-summer, gets you from Stehekin to Glory Mountain without a change.

Backpackers and campers should make their reservations for the NPS shuttle at the same time they pick up their backcountry permits from the ranger stations in Stehekin, Chelan, Marblemount, the North Cascades Visitor Center (in Newhalem) or the Sedro-Woolley Information Station. Reservations

WASHINGTON

can also be made in person or by phone at the Purple Point Information Center (☎ 360-856-5700, ext 340, then ext 14).

CHELAN & AROUND

At the southeastern tip of the lake, Chelan (population 3522) serves as the primary base for transportation, accommodations, restaurants, recreational services and entertainment in the area. Farther up the lake, mountains rise and trees fill in the shore all the way north to Stehekin (see that section, earlier).

Flush with lakeside condos and views of the North Cascades, Chelan is the hub of commercial and resort traffic on the lake. The town is flanked by dry hills with scattered pines, lots of scrabble and scree, yellow balsamroot in spring and apple trees galore. The apples grown here are supposedly the state's finest, and no one who stops by a roadside fruit stand in late October is apt to argue the point.

The rural community of **Manson** (population 1800), 8 miles west of Chelan on the lake's north shore, makes a scenic drive or bike ride past apple orchards. Manson Bay Park is a popular swimming and picnic area. There's also a boat ramp and a casino, at Old Mill Bay Park, 2 miles east of town on Hwy 150.

Orientation

Chelan is 37 miles northeast of Wenatchee and 54 miles southwest of Omak. From Seattle, it's 166 miles via Stevens Pass on Hwy 2 and 173 miles via Snoqualmie Pass on I-90.

Woodin Ave (US 97) is the main drag into, and out of, town. From Wenatchee, Alt US 97 intercepts US 971 on the west side of town and travels east along the lake's south shore to the city center. S Lakeshore Rd, as US 971 is named, follows Lake Chelan's western shore up as far as Twenty-Five Mile Creek State Park; on the opposite side of the lake, Hwy 150 stops at Greens Landing, a few miles past Manson.

Information

If it's tourist information you seek, don't miss the Lake Chelan Visitor Center (☎ 509-682-3503, W www.lakechelan.com), 102 E Johnson Ave.

The Chelan USFS/NPS Ranger Station (☎ 509-682-2576), 428 W Woodin Ave, provides abundant information on Wenatchee National Forest, Lake Chelan State Park, the Lake Chelan National Recreation Area and North Cascades National Park, as well as Northwest Forest Passes for upper-lake camping. It's open 7:30am to 4:30pm Monday to Friday. Call ☎ 509-682-2549 to reach the NPS desk directly.

The post office (☎ 509-682-2625) is at 144 E Johnson Ave. Internet access is available at Electrik Dreams (☎ 509-682-8889, 246 W Manson Hwy), in Chelan Plaza, for 15¢ a minute.

Riverwalk Books (☎ 509-682-8901), downtown at 116 E Woodin Ave, is a nice place to browse for beach reading.

The Lake Chelan Community Hospital (☎ 509-682-2531) is at 503 E Highland Ave. For coin-operated washing machines, try Town Tub Laundry, at 612 E Woodin Ave.

Water Recreation

This is what Lake Chelan is all about. The lake is open to all manner of watercraft, though speedboats and Jet Skis predominate at this end of the lake. There are scads of power-craft providers, but due to the intolerable impact these activities have on the physical and human environments, we can hardly recommend that you contribute to the noise.

Kayaking is a less disruptive alternative, though you'll want to put in farther up the lake to avoid a high-speed collision. **Uncle Tim's Toys** (☎ 509-670-8467, Lakeshore Marina & Park) has tandem kayaks for rent, including a popular pedal-paddle version ($12/45 per hour/day).

There are public beaches at **Lakeside Park**, near the west side of town and at **Lake Chelan State Park**, 9 miles west on S Lakeshore Rd. Continuing west till the end of the road, you'll find boat launches at **Twenty-Five Mile Creek State Park**. Up the lake, beyond the reach of roads, are another 11 boat docks, most of which are associated with campgrounds.

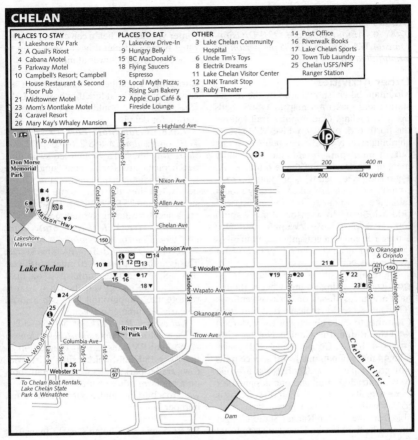

CHELAN

PLACES TO STAY
1 Lakeshore RV Park
2 A Quail's Roost
4 Cabana Motel
5 Parkway Motel
10 Campbell's Resort; Campbell House Restaurant & Second Floor Pub
21 Midtowner Motel
23 Mom's Montlake Motel
24 Caravel Resort
26 Mary Kay's Whaley Mansion

PLACES TO EAT
7 Lakeview Drive-In
9 Hungry Belly
15 BC MacDonald's
18 Flying Saucers Espresso
19 Local Myth Pizza; Rising Sun Bakery
22 Apple Cup Café & Fireside Lounge

OTHER
3 Lake Chelan Community Hospital
6 Uncle Tim's Toys
8 Electrik Dreams
11 Lake Chelan Visitor Center
12 LINK Transit Stop
13 Ruby Theater

14 Post Office
16 Riverwalk Books
17 Lake Chelan Sports
20 Town Tub Laundry
25 Chelan USFS/NPS Ranger Station

On the north shore, **Don Morse Memorial Park** is an in-town water funland, with a beach, boat launch, bumper boats and go-carts.

The swimming area at **Manson Bay Park** (☎ 509-687-9635) features several floating docks, and there's a four-lane boat launch at **Old Mill Bay Park** (☎ 509-687-9635), 2 miles east of Manson.

If you have kids, don't even think they'll let you sneak past **Slidewaters Water Park** (☎ 509-682-5751, 102 Waterslide Dr off W Woodin Ave; day pass $13/10 per adult/child 4-7 years; $10/7 after 4pm; open from 10am May-Sept). It's on a hill above the *Lady of the Lake* boat dock.

In Lake Chelan, you can go **fishing** for lake trout, Kokanee salmon, ling cod and smallmouth bass. Just north of Manson, **Wapato Lake** has good early summer fly-fishing for rainbow trout and a fair number of bluegill and largemouth bass. Nearby **Roses Lake** is open from December 1 to March 31 for rainbow trout, brown trout and catfish. **Antilon Lake**, 3 miles north of Wapato Lake, is popular with families, as the resident bluegills, pumpkinseed and crappies are fairly easy to hook.

For guided fishing excursions, try **Darrell & Dad's Family Guide Service** (☎ 509-687-0709, ⓔ Antonj@aol.com, 231 Division, Manson, WA 98831; $100/135 per person for a half/full day).

Other Activities

Mountain bikers should stop by the ranger station and pick up a map of USFS roads open to **cycling**. One popular trail follows the north fork of Twenty-Five Mile Creek, climbing steeply for 3 miles before leveling out through pine forest and eventually meeting the **Devil's Backbone** trailhead. At Echo Ridge (see below) near Manson, cross-country ski trails are taken over by mountain bikes in summer. Touring cyclists can ride a loop up to Manson along Wapato Lake Rd, past Roses, Wapato, and Dry Lakes. You can rent cruising/mountain bikes ($5/6 hour) at Uncle Tim's Toys (see Water Recreation, earlier).

There are plenty of good places to go **cross-country skiing** around Chelan, though most are run as off-season business ventures. (Chelan's ski season typically runs only from Christmas to mid-February or early March.) At **Echo Ridge**, the Chelan Nordic Club (☎ 800-424-3526, Cooper Gulch Rd) maintains 14 miles of national forest service trails with great valley views. There is also a 7-mile backcountry loop trail and one designed for those who like to ski with their dogs. Skiing is $5/day with a Northwest Forest Pass, available from the Chelan Ranger Station. To get there, take the Manson Hwy 2 miles to Boyd Rd, turn right and go 7 miles to Cooper Mountain Rd, which reaches Echo Ridge 2 miles past the Echo Valley Ski Area.

For **downhill skiing** and **snowmobiling**, check out the aforementioned **Echo Valley Ski Area** (☎ 509-682-4002, 509-687-3167, Cooper Mountain Rd; open Sat & Sun), featuring three tow-ropes and one Poma lift. For rentals, head to **Lake Chelan Sports** (☎ 509-682-2629, ⓦ www.lakechelansports.com, 132 E Woodin Ave; skis & snowshoes $25/day).

Places to Stay

The tourist season peaks in the summer, and in most places, off-season rates drop at least a little bit. Prices in the listings below reflect the midweek high-season summer months; winter visitors to Chelan can count on room rates being considerably cheaper – up to 40% or even 50% lower at motels.

Camping A number of campgrounds accessible only by boat line the shores of Lake Chelan. Boaters should check at the ranger station for details.

Lake Chelan State Park (☎ 509-687-3710, reservations ☎ 888-226-7688, S Lakeshore Rd) Sites $12. A guarded swimming beach, picnic areas and a boat launch make this a busy summertime destination. Of the nearly 150 sites, there are some nice lakeside spots and 35 RV hookups. Reservations are a necessity during the summer.

Twenty-Five Mile Creek State Park (☎ 509-687-3610, reservations ☎ 888-226-7688, S Lakeshore Rd) Tent/RV sites $14/20. This is at the road's end, 20 miles northwest of Chelan, and the emphasis is on boat access to the lake. Even though it's fairly remote, the campground here can also fill up early on summer weekends.

Lakeshore RV Park (☎ 509-682-8023, ⓦ www.chelancityparks.com, 619 W Manson Hwy) Tent/RV sites $25/31. In addition to the over 150 full-hookup sites at this in-town trailer park, there are a few tent spots on a big lawn dotted with trees. It's a short walk to a burger stand, a putting course and bumper boats.

B&Bs Some of Chelan's early mansions have been made over as charming country inns.

A Quail's Roost (☎ 509-682-2892, 800-681-2892, ⓦ www.aquailsroostinn.com, 121 E Highland Ave) Rooms with hall/in-room bath $95/125. Located on a bluff at Chelan's north end, this 1902 Victorian home promises good views from its wraparound verandah. The breakfasts have been warmly recommended.

Mary Kay's Whaley Mansion (☎ 509-682-5735, 800-729-2408, fax 509-682-5385, ⓔ whaleymans@aol.com, 415 3rd St) Rooms from $115. Quaint collectibles, big mirrors and pink carpeting decorate this pricey inn, which could easily function as Chelan's historical museum. All rooms have private baths and get lots of personal attention from Mary Kay, a Chelan aficionado and good information source for the area.

Holden Village B&B (☎ *509-687-9695, fax 509-687-9695,* W *www.holdenvillage.org/bandb.html, 21081 S Lakeshore Rd*) Dorm beds $20, rooms $30/18/10 adult/teen/child per person. Adjacent to Twenty-Five Mile Creek State Park, this B&B offers five no-frills bedrooms plus a three-bunk dorm. Many of the guests are headed to Holden Village, a Lutheran church–based retreat up the lake, but the B&B is open to anyone who's willing to change their own bed linens in the morning. A big pancake breakfast is included.

Hotels Kitchen facilities are an option at all of the following list of family-oriented accommodations.

Parkway Motel (☎ *509-682-2822,* W *www.chelanparkway.com, 402 Manson Hwy*) Rooms without/with kitchenette $40/68. Across from Lakeshore Marina, these wood-paneled rooms that open out to a patio and lawn are a very good deal.

Mom's Montlake Motel (☎ *509-682-5715, 823 Wapato Ave*) One/two beds $49/60. One block off the main drag at the east end of town, this is a quiet, inexpensive place with clean rooms and one small cottage. Discounts are sometimes available.

Midtowner Motel (☎ *509-682-4051, 800-572-0943,* W *www.midtowner.com, 721 E Woodin Ave*) One/two beds $75/85. Despite the dull location, this is a well-rounded place, with an indoor/outdoor pool (a dividing wall goes up in winter); a hot tub; laundry facilities; and spacious, superclean kitchenette rooms.

The Cabana Motel (☎ *509-682-2233, 800-799-2332,* W *www.cabanamotel.com, 420 Manson Rd*) Doubles/quads from $84/126. This family-oriented lodging across from the marina has poolside and larger lake-view units with kitchenettes. Pets are welcomed by the friendly staff.

Mountain View Lodge (☎ *509-687-9505, 800-967-8105,* W *www.mountainviewlake chelan.com, 25 Wapato Pt Parkway, Manson*) Rooms $91-115/96-120 weekdays/weekends. Up the road in Manson, this two-story motel-style property does have a nice mountain view, along with a heated pool, hot tub and picnic area. Early each morning you'll find coffee, tea, apples and fresh chocolate-chip cookies in the lobby. Gambling guests will appreciate the lodge's proximity to the Mill Bay Casino (see Entertainment, later).

Resorts Though they're not quite full-fledged destination resorts, all of the following offer more than the average motel. They're all on the lake, they all have pools and private beaches with boat moorage, and they all are equipped to deal with small conventions or large families.

Caravel Resort (☎ *509-682-2582, 800-962-8723, fax 509-682-3551,* W *www.caravel resort.com, 332 W Woodin Ave*) Rooms $64-150. The main attraction is the waterfront pool deck, which offers sunset views over Lake Chelan. The rooms seem a bit sterile, but those in the new wing have private balconies.

Best Western Lakeside Lodge (☎ *509-682-4396, reservations* ☎ *800-468-2781,* W *www.lakesidelodge.net, 2312 W Woodin Ave*) Doubles $99-179. On the outskirts of town by Lakeside Park, the new and improved Best Western offers barbecue grills and balconies off the upper-level rooms.

Campbell's Resort (☎ *509-682-2561, 800-553-8225,* W *www.campbellsresort.com, 104 W Woodin Ave*) Rooms $160-244, suites $246-360. Chelan's premier resort is a sprawling lakeside complex that has swallowed up the historic Campbell Hotel. The 170 guest rooms in five buildings vary widely, but all have lake-view balconies or patios. A couple of pools, a long sandy beach, several restaurants and impeccable service await those who can afford to stay here.

Kelly's Resort (☎ *509-687-3220, 800-561-8978, fax 509-687-3320,* W *www.kellys resort.com, 12801 S Lakeshore Rd*) Hillside/lakeside cottages $130-190/170-230. About 5 miles past Lake Chelan State Park, this family-run resort has woodsy cottages across the road from the lake and a few at the water's edge. Rowboats, canoes, kayaks and sailboats are available, but Jet Skis are not welcome.

Vacation-Home Rentals Those planning a long-term stay or vacationing with a large crew should consider a lakeside dwelling.

Chelan Vacation Rentals (☎ 509-682-9782, 888-977-1748, Ⓦ www.lakechelanrentals.com, 2323 W Woodin Ave) Sample prices $800-$3000/week. This agency handles a huge selection of homes and condos in the area.

Places to Eat

Flying Saucers Espresso (☎ 509-682-5129, 116 S Emerson St) Snacks $2-5. Open Mon-Sat. Come here early in the morning to engage in local gossip and swill espresso. There's an astounding variety of homemade muffins, as well as cookies and pastries for later in the day.

Hungry Belly (☎ 509-682-8630, 246 W Manson Hwy) Entrees $3-7. Open 11am-7pm Mon-Fri, daily in summer. In Chelan Plaza, you can satisfy everyone's craving here, where there's an eclectic menu of Thai food, stir-fries, salads, sandwiches and barbecued beef brisket.

Apple Cup Café & Fireside Lounge (☎ 509-682-2933, 804 E Woodin Ave) Entrees $4-10. Inside the building with the beautiful apple mural is a solid local diner with big breakfasts, homestyle dinners and all the neighbors.

Local Myth Pizza (☎ 509-682-2914, 514 E Woodin Ave) Medium pizzas $10. Open from 4pm. The pizzas here are a vegetarian's fantasy, though the Canadian bacon and salmon calzones are pretty tempting, too, all dressed up with sauces such as creamy leek.

Rising Sun Bakery (☎ 509-682-8938, 514 E Woodin Ave) Breads $2-5. Next door to Local Myth, artisan bread-makers bake organic sourdough loaves and squeeze wheatgrass juice.

BC MacDonald's (☎ 509-682-1334, 104 E Woodin Ave) Entrees $8-16. Open until 2am. Burgers, steaks, pastas and a few local brews are served in a slick sports-bar ambience. Even if you're not up for dinner,

stop in for a drink and a look at the cherrywood bar, which was brought around Cape Horn from Europe in the late 19th century and was previously installed in a Montana bar.

Campbell House Restaurant & Second Floor Pub (☎ 509-682-4250, 104 W Woodin Ave) Entrees $14. This is the fanciest dining spot in town, and though the meals aren't generally what you'd call innovative, vegetarians will have to give the place credit for serving a couscous-stuffed portobello entree. The upstairs pub serves pricey snacks and fancy vodka cocktails.

Lakeview Drive-In (☎ 509-682-5322, 323 Manson Rd) Entrees $2-5. This little stand by the marina serves up better-than-average burgers and fries, as well as milkshakes of a dozen flavors. There's even a low-fat menu.

Deepwater Brewing Pub & Restaurant (☎ 509-682-2720, 225 Hwy 150) Lunch/dinner $8/16. At this new microbrewery with picture-window lake views, there's a variety of pastas, salads and pub grub. Nightly specials emphasize coastal treats. Besides their own ales and stouts, there's a good selection of regional wines; some weekends, you might catch live entertainment.

There are a couple of decent places to eat in Manson.

Uncle Tim's Pizzeria (☎ 509-687-3035, 76 W Wapato Way) Medium pizzas $14-18. Uncle Tim's serves huge, meaty pizzas and several pasta dishes (with prices topping out at $13.95 for seafood tortellini).

El Vaquero (☎ 509-687-3179, 75 W Wapato Way) Meals under $10. El Vaquero is tastier than the other nacho joints in the area, and it's easy to eat your fill for less than $10.

Entertainment

On busy weekends, bands perform at BC MacDonald's and Deepwater Brewing Pub, and in Manson at Uncle Tim's Pizzeria (See Places to Eat).

Ruby Theatre (☎ 509-682-5016, 135 E Woodin Ave) Dating from 1913, the downtown cinema is named for the original owner's daughter.

Mill Bay Casino (☎ *800-648-2946, Hwy 150)* Open 24 hours. Though not as big an attraction as when it opened in 1989, the Manson casino, which is run by the Colville Tribe, still pulls them in, and it's one of the few that still has coin-operated slots. TJ's Shuttle (☎ 509-679-8961) provides free rides between several local hotels and the casino; it runs hourly from 2pm to 11pm Sunday to Thursday and noon to 2am Friday & Saturday.

Getting There & Away
The nearest airport, Pangborn Memorial, is 38 miles south at Wenatchee and is serviced by Horizon Air from Seattle. Chelan Airways operates daily seaplane service to Stehekin from the airfield, 1 mile west of town on Alt US 97 (see Stehekin, earlier, for details).

The *Lady of the Lake II, Lady Express* and *Lady Cat* board at least one boat daily for trips across Lake Chelan to Lucerne and Stehekin. The dock (☎ 509-682-4584, schedule info ☎ 509-682-2224, ⓦ www.ladyofthe lake.com) is located on the south shore, a mile west of downtown on Alt US 97. See Getting There & Away in the Stehekin section for more details.

Getting Around
Wenatchee-based Link (☎ 509-662-2183, 800-851-5465) provides bus service between Manson and Wenatchee ($1, 1½ hours) via Chelan (50¢, 15 minutes) on route No 21. In Chelan, buses stop on the south side of Johnson Ave, next to the visitor center.

Taxis are available 24 hours a day from Lake Chelan Cab Co (☎ 509-687-8294).

WASHINGTON

South Cascades

The mightiest and most explosive of the Pacific Northwest peaks are found in southern Washington. Mt Rainier (ruh-**neer**), one of the highest peaks in the USA, towers above Tacoma and the Puget Sound. One of the first national parks, this massive peak is extremely popular with hikers, climbers, skiers and onlookers, who wind along the

Highlights

- Visiting deep forests, glaciers and meadows brush-stroked with wildflowers at Mt Rainier
- Exploring the post-eruption moonscape of Mt St Helens, 20 years after the blast
- Huckleberry picking on Mt Adams, the neglected sister of the South Cascade peaks
- Downhill skiing at Crystal Mountain, a major resort at Rainier's northeast corner

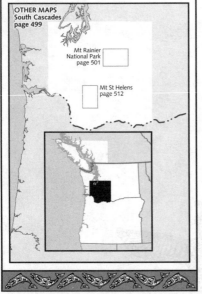

OTHER MAPS
South Cascades
page 499

Mt Rainier
National Park
page 501

Mt St Helens
page 512

area's roads in summer and fall, exultant with the majestic surroundings.

A mountain experience of a completely different sort comes at Mt St Helens, the sawed-off peak whose 1980 eruption showed the world what tremendous forces lay hidden in Northwest landscapes. Three viewpoints and four interpretive centers provide a look at the devastation wrought by the explosion of this volcanic peak.

Tucked into a little-visited corner of southern Washington is Mt Adams, in many ways the neglected sibling in this family of peaks. Fans of this mountain's many marvels hope it stays that way. An easy summit climb, wildflower meadows, berry fields and – most uniquely – relative solitude recommend Mt Adams to the explorers who like a little wilderness in their outdoor experience.

Mt Rainier is big enough, it is often said, to create its own weather, which basically means bad weather. At times it seems to snare any passing cloud and make a storm out of it. In fact, weather is very changeable on and near all the Cascade peaks. Lovely summer days can turn blustery in an instant, so pack a warm sweater and rain gear. Summer temperatures average in the mid-70s; in the winter, temperatures run toward the mid-20s, and snowstorms are common.

Summer comes late in the year to the South Cascades, but it comes with a bang, as high-elevation meadows explode with wildflowers. By mid-August, the huckleberries are plump, sweet and ready for picking, and it's almost worth a special trip – the Mt Adams area has huckleberry fields that are designated especially for harvesters. And while most visitors never come across the black bears and cougars that live in the backcountry, day hikers actually have a fairly good chance of spotting smaller critters, such as hoary marmots, pine martens and mountain goats.

Mt Rainier National Park Area

Mt Rainier, at 14,411 feet, is the Cascades' highest peak, and it is imbued with more myth than any other mountain in the Northwest. Seattleites simply call it 'the Mountain' and judge the weather by its visibility. If you can see the peak for a few days running, the weather is good. But the flat, flying-saucer shaped, lenticular clouds that hover around the summit often herald fierce mountain storms – even on days when hikers at the lower elevations of Paradise or Sunrise are enjoying good weather. With its 26 glaciers, Mt Rainier is the most heavily glaciated peak in the USA outside of Alaska.

The Nisquallies, Yakamas, Puyallups and other local native people knew this volcanic peak as Tahoma. They made regular trips to its foothills to hunt, fish and pick huckleberries, but they were generally uneasy about climbing the mountain. When British captain George Vancouver spotted the peak from the Puget Sound in 1792, he named it for his friend Rear Admiral Peter Rainier.

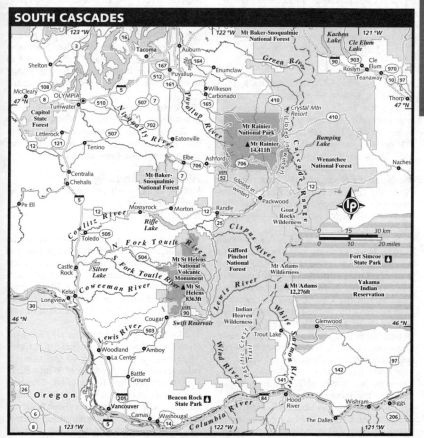

SOUTH CASCADES

When Mt Rainier was declared a national park in 1899, some of the land was obtained through a swap with the Northern Pacific Railroad, which subsequently sold its acquisitions to timber companies. During the 1930s, Depression-era CCC workers built many of the still-existing park structures and trails.

Still a fairly potent volcano, Mt Rainier was created by repeated episodes of lava and mudflow and many eruptions of ash and rock. Before blasting its top some 5800 years ago, Mt Rainier reached as high as 16,000 feet. The 2-mile crater from that eruption was joined by another large crater after a blast 2500 years ago; these two craters mark Mt Rainier's summit now, where gas from mountaintop steam vents creates toasty-warm fern caves.

Orientation

Mt Rainier – so visible from the windows of Seattle – is actually 95 miles southeast of the city. There is no ring road encircling the park, and the four entrances by and large mark separate roads. The main entrance road, Hwy 706 (also known as the Nisqually-Longmire Rd), comes in through the town of Ashford, near the park's southwest corner, and follows the Nisqually River into the park. Past the Nisqually entrance is Longmire, which contains the only hotel open year-round, and Paradise, where the park's other hotel operates during the summer.

East of Paradise, near the park's southeast corner, Hwy 706 runs into Hwy 123; drive south and you'll arrive at the Ohanapecosh entrance. Drive north and Hwy 123 becomes Hwy 410 about halfway up the eastern park boundary at the Cayuse Pass. Just north of that junction, the White River entrance road cuts west off Hwy 410, running along the White River and ending at Sunrise, known for its great views. Hwy 410 bends around and becomes an east-west road across the northern outskirts of the park, passing through the town of Enumclaw before reaching the Tacoma suburbs.

The most remote entrance to Mt Rainier National Park is the Carbon River entrance, south of Hwy 410 in the northwest corner.

Another road near the Carbon River entrance leads to Mowich Lake but is not an official entrance road.

Information

For information on the park, call or write the superintendent's office (☎ 360-569-2211), Mt Rainier National Park, Ashford, WA 98304, or see the National Park Service website at Ⓦ www.nps.gov/mora, which includes downloadable maps and descriptions of 50 park trails.

Park entrance fees are $10 per car and $5 for pedestrians and cyclists (those under 17 admitted free) and are valid for seven days from purchase. An Annual Pass ($20) admits the pass holder and accompanying passengers for 12 months from date of purchase.

All roads but the Hwy 706 Nisqually entrance road to Paradise close down in the winter. For highway pass reports, phone ☎ 800-695-7623. Gas is not available in the park.

Mt Rainier National Park publishes a newspaper, *The Tahoma News,* which is available at visitors centers. This has current information on naturalist walks, evening campground programs and park news.

Hiking & Climbing

Hiking opportunities range from short walks on interpretive nature trails to extended backcountry jaunts. Once hikers have had a taste of Rainier's trails, many pine to circumnavigate the mountain on the **Wonderland Trail**, a 93-mile loop. The trail changes elevation at nearly every turn, passing through lowland forests and subalpine meadows. It's a good 10-day trek, with campgrounds spaced about every 10 miles. See below for information on backcountry permits.

Most climbing expeditions take off from Paradise, making an overnight stop at Camp Muir before pushing on to the summit; other climbs are staged from White River (see those sections for details). Climbing conditions are most favorable in early summer. Climbers must register with the NPS and pay $15 for a climbing permit, which doubles as a wilderness camping

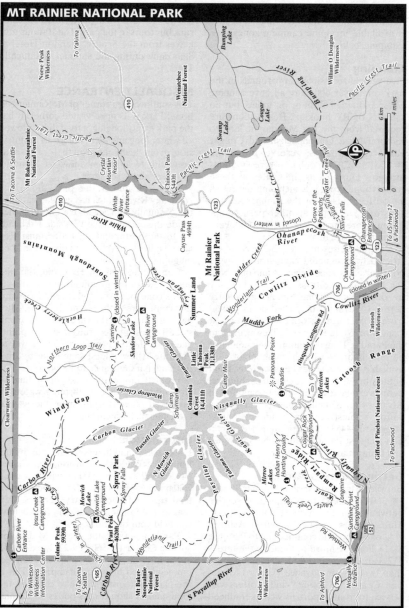

MT RAINIER NATIONAL PARK

Nurse Peak
Wilderness

To Yakima

Bumping
Lake

William O Douglas
Wilderness

Wenatchee
National Forest

410

Bumping River

Pacific Crest Trail

Swamp
Lake

Cougar
Lake

Pacific Crest Trail

Mt Baker-Snoqualmie
National Forest

Crystal
Mountain Resort

Chinook Pass
5440ft

Pacific Crest Trail

6 km

4 miles

To Tacoma & Seattle

410

White River
Entrance

White River

123

Panther Creek

Cayuse Pass
4694ft

(closed in winter)

Mt Rainier
National Park

Grove of the
Patriarchs

Ohanapecosh Falls

Stevens Canyon Rd

Silver Falls

Ohanapecosh
River

Ohanapecosh
Entrance

123

To US Hwy 12
& Packwood

Sourdough Mountains

Huckleberry Creek

Fryingpan Creek

Summer Land

Boulder Creek

Wonderland Trail

Cowlitz Divide

Ohanapecosh
Campground

706

(closed in winter)

Northern Loop Trail

Sunrise

(closed in winter)

Shadow Lake

White River
Campground

Muddy Fork

Cowlitz River

Tatoosh
Wilderness

Clearwater
Wilderness

Little
Tahoma
Peak
11,138ft

Camp Muir

Nisqually Longmire Rd

Winthrop Glacier

Emmons Glacier

Panorama Point

Windy Gap

Columbia
Crest
14,411ft

Camp
Schurman

Paradise

Tatoosh Range

Carbon Glacier

Russell Glacier

Nisqually Glacier

Reflection
Lakes

Carbon River

N Mowich
Glacier

Kautz Glacier

Cougar Rock
Campground

Gifford Pinchot National Forest

Ipsut Creek
Campground

Spray Park

Spray Falls

Puyallup Glacier

Tahoma Glacier

Indian Henry's
Hunting Ground

Mirror
Lakes

Rampart Ridge

Nisqually River

To Packwood

Carbon River
Entrance

Mowich Lake
Campground

Mowich
Lake

Paul Peak
4620ft

Kautz Creek Trail

Longmire

Sunshine Point
Campground

52

To Willeson
Wilderness Information Center

Tolmie Peak
5939ft

Carbon River

(closed in winter)

Wonderland Trail

Westside Rd

706

Nisqually
Entrance

Mt Baker-
Snoqualmie
National Forest

165

To Tacoma
& Seattle

Glacier View
Wilderness

S Puyallup River

To Ashford

706

permit. Reservations are advised for weekend climbs, as a limited number of sites is available in alpine camping zones (see Camping, below).

Camping

Five vehicle-accessible campgrounds in the park offer over 600 sites; all have running water and either flush or pit toilets, but no showers or RV hookups. Reservations are required from the last Monday in June to Labor Day at Ohanapecosh and Cougar Rock campgrounds; reserve by phone (☎ 800-365-2267) or online at W reservations .nps.gov. During this time, sites at these campgrounds cost $15, including the reservation fee; outside of the summer season, sites are $12. Sites at other park campgrounds are first-come first-served year round and cost $10.

Camping elsewhere in the park is restricted to designated campgrounds – the NPS website is a good place to find out about the current conditions at these. For any overnight backpacking trip, a backcountry permit (free) must be picked up in person from Wilderness Information Centers at Longmire, White River or Wilkeson, or from the Paradise Ranger Station. The number of permits is limited by the number of sites available. For weekends between May 1 and September 30, when demand is highest, permits can be reserved up to two months in advance for a $20 nonrefundable fee. Reservation requests can be made by phone (☎ 360-569-4453) or by printing a Reservation Request Form (from the NPS website) and faxing it to fax 360-569-3131.

Getting There & Around

Between May and October, Rainier Shuttle (☎ 360-569-2331) runs scheduled service between Sea-Tac Airport and the park. Three shuttles travel daily to/from Ashford ($42 one-way); one continues on to Paradise ($51). From Ashford to Paradise the fare is $12. Fares are reduced $5 if reserved more than two days in advance. Ashford Mountain Center (☎ 360-569-2604) offers van service to/from airport, as well as trailhead drop-off and pick up throughout the park.

Gray Line of Seattle (☎ 206-626-5208, 800-426-7532, W www.graylineofseattle.com) runs bus tours of the park. The 10-hour tour leaves from the Seattle Sheraton Hotel at 8am daily during the summer (adult/child $54/27).

NISQUALLY ENTRANCE

This southwestern corner of Mt Rainier National Park is its most visited corner. It has the park's only lodging, a road that's plowed all winter long and plenty of lovely countryside, from lush old-growth forests near Longmire to alpine meadows at Paradise, 5400 feet above sea level.

Hwy 706 enters the park along the Nisqually River, which has its headwaters in the Nisqually Glacier above Paradise. Just inside the entrance, the Westside Rd heads off to the north, and car traffic must stop after 3 miles but cyclists and hikers can keep on going.

Continuing east on Hwy 706, the first good views of the mountain come at Kautz Creek, one of several glacier-fed streams that contribute to the Nisqually River. After passing Longmire, the road begins to climb steadily, passing several good viewpoints and some sharp hairpin turns on the way to Paradise. Allow at least 45 minutes to drive from the park entrance to Paradise.

From Paradise, the road (open June to November) heads east through waterfall-bedecked Stevens Canyon on the way to the Ohanapecosh entrance.

Information

Backpackers and hikers should stop by the Longmire Wilderness Information Center (☎ 360-569-2211, ext 3317), which is open 7:30am to 6:30pm daily May to October for trail tips and backcountry permits. Off season, the Longmire Museum (see below) can field your questions.

Park rangers at the Henry M Jackson Visitor Center (☎ 360-569-2211, ext 2328), at Paradise, dispense trail maps and can recommend good hikes and campsites. This is the place to register if you're climbing the mountain. A shop carries books on Rainier and the Cascades, and movies and slide shows about the mountain are shown throughout the day. It's open open 9am to 7pm daily May to September, 10am to 5pm weekends October to April.

There's a post office in the lobby of the adjacent Paradise Inn.

Park naturalists lead interpretive hikes from the Jackson Visitor Center daily in summer, and snowshoe walks on winter weekends. Children ages six to 11 can join a park ranger for 'Junior Ranger' hikes and nature activities at the Cougar Rock. Check the campground bulletin board for the schedule of events.

Longmire

During an 1883 climbing trip, James Longmire noticed mineral hot springs and a lovely meadow near the base of Mt Rainier. He and his family returned the following year and established Longmire's Medical Springs, and in 1890, he built the Longmire Springs Hotel. When Mt Rainier became a national park in 1899, the Longmire area was the hub of activity and the original park headquarters.

The **Longmire Museum** (☎ 360-569-2211, ext 3314; admission free; open 9am-6pm June-Sept, 9am-5pm Oct-May) has exhibits on natural history, Native American culture and early white exploration of the area. To stretch your legs from the long drive in, wander the **Trail of the Shadows**, a ¾-mile loop trail that begins across the road from the museum. Accessible by wheelchair part of the way, the annotated path passes the mineral springs from whence the resort originated and a cabin built in 1888 by Longmire's son.

Paradise

Late-summer visitors to Paradise can expect dazzling wildflowers. The first to bloom, even before the snow has completely melted, are avalanche lilies, glacier lilies and western anemones. They're followed by lupine, mountain bog gentian and paintbrush, creating broad washes of blue and red across the slopes. The Nisqually Glacier dips down toward Paradise. Follow the 1.2-mile **Nisqually Vista Trail** for a good look at it.

Even if you're not staying at the **Paradise Inn** (see Places to Stay, later), the lobby of this classic lodge is worth a visit. Huge fireplaces anchor each end of the lobby, massive timbers support the ceiling, and comfortable leather sofas make relaxing with a good mystery novel as alluring as hiking Paradise's trails.

Hiking

A couple of trails lead to **Indian Henry's Hunting Ground**, a magnificent flower-lit meadow with (on the right days) perfect views of Mt Rainier reflected in Mirror Lake. It's a 5½-mile hike in through meadow after meadow from the Kautz Creek Trailhead, which is about halfway between the entrance and Longmire. Another route to the meadows starts near Longmire and follows the **Wonderland Trail** over Rampart Ridge. This 6½-mile hike is not easy, as the 2400-foot elevation gain is accomplished with lots of ups and downs.

Paradise is laced with trails, many of them paved for the first mile or so, and it's easy enough to wander out from the parking lot and make up an impromptu loop just by following the trail markers. But for a decent leg-stretch and a close-up look at wildflowers, marmots and the Nisqually Glacier, hike the 5-mile **Skyline Trail**, starting at the Paradise Inn and climbing about 1600 feet to **Panorama Point**, with good views of Rainier and the neighboring Tatoosh Range. For a steep shortcut on the return part of the loop, hike down **Golden Gate Trail**.

Ambitious day hikers can continue up the mountain from Panorama Point and follow **Pebble Creek Trail** to the snow-field track leading to **Camp Muir**. Camp Muir is the main overnight bivouac spot for climbing parties, and it has stupendous views south to Mt Adams, Mt St Helens and Mt Hood. However, at 10,000 feet, it's not a hike to be taken lightly, and it requires sufficient clothing for all sorts of weather and a good supply of food and water.

The lower elevation **Lakes Trail**, starts at Paradise and heads a little way down the mountain, making a 5-mile loop through subalpine meadows and passing Reflection

Lakes, with views of the Tatoosh Range. In the fall, trailside huckleberry bushes redden, making this a lovely, not overly strenuous hike.

During the winter, the road is plowed as far as Paradise, and people take to the trails on cross-country skis and snowshoes. There is also a designated 'snowplay' area, which is groomed for inner-tube riders. You'll need tire chains for the drive up. If you'd rather stick to lower elevations, ski the Westside Road, just inside the Nisqually entrance.

The **Longmire Ski Touring Center** (☎ 360-569-2411, e estrauss@mashell.com; open 8am-6pm Sat & Sun Thanksgiving-Apr), in the Longmire General Store, has trail information, lessons and cross-country ski and snowshoe rentals (adult/child ski packages $15/9 per day, snowshoes $12/8).

Climbing
The most popular route to the summit of Mt Rainier starts at Paradise. It involves a brief night's rest at Camp Muir before rising between midnight and 2am to don crampons, rope up, climb over Disappointment Cleaver and ascend the Ingraham Glacier to the summit. All climbers going higher than Camp Muir must register at the Paradise Ranger Station (see Camping, in the beginning of this chapter). Inexperienced climbers should not attempt this rigorous ascent independently: Climb instead with the guide service.

Rainier Mountaineering (☎ 360-569-2227, w www.rmiguides.com, 30027 SR 706 East, Ashford) offers guided climbs to Mt Rainier's summit in late summer and fall, as well as a variety of specialized seminars. Unless you are an expert mountain climber, it is prudent to participate in their three-day summit package ($700), which includes a full-day climbing school. Rent ice axes, crampons, boots and other climbing gear at Summit Haus (☎ 360-569-2142) downstairs from the main office in Ashford.

Places to Stay
Within the park proper, choose between sleeping in a splendid old lodge or pitching a tent.

Sunshine Point Campground (☎ 360-569-2211, 1/4 mile past Nisqually entrance) Sites $10. Open year-round. Just inside the main entrance are these 18 sites alongside the rushing Nisqually River.

Cougar Rock Campground (☎ 360-569-2211, reservations ☎ 800-365-2267, 2.3 miles north of Longmire) Sites $15/12 late June–Labor Day/rest of season. Open late May–mid-Oct. Cougar Rock, on the way to Paradise, has 173 individual sites and flush toilets. Rangers lead campfire talks on summer evenings. See Camping, above, for reservation information.

The park has two lodges (☎ 360-569-2275); it's best to call for reservations far in advance.

Paradise Inn (☎ 360-569-2413, w www.guestservices.com/rainier) Single with shared/private bath $75/112, double $129. Open mid-May–Sept. Planted at the foot of a glacier, this grand, historic lodge offers an unparalleled setting and a handsome lobby warmed by opposing stone fireplaces.

National Park Inn (☎ 360-569-2411, w www.guestservices.com/rainier) 1-bed room $74/104 with shared/private bath, 2-room unit $142. Open year-round. On the site of the old Longmire Springs Hotel, the inn is cozier than Paradise, and offers special winter packages, which include breakfast and afternoon tea.

If the park lodges are full, the closest accommodations are along Hwy 706, from Ashford to the Nisqually Entrance. The following places are found driving west to east.

Whittaker's Bunkhouse (☎ 360-569-2439, fax 360-569-2436, e bunkhouse@mashell.com, 30205 SR 706 E) Bunkroom bed $25, singles & doubles $65. Originally used as a logger's bunkhouse, the building has simple rooms with private bath. Mountain climbers often go for a bunk in the 12-person bunkroom. Guests may run into the owner, renowned mountaineer and raconteur-extraordinaire Lou Whittaker, at the espresso bar in the morning.

Nisqually Lodge (☎ 360-569-8804, 888-674-3554, w www.escapetothemountains.com, 31609 SR 706 E) Singles/doubles $76/80. This is about the only motel in

Ashford where you'll find TVs and telephones in the rooms, and there's also an outdoor hot tub.

Wellspring (☎ 360-569-2514, 54922 Kernahan Rd) Treehouse/tent cabins/log cabins/cottages $79/89/99/119 double occupancy; $10 less for single. In addition to being a spa, Wellspring is a tranquil and hospitable resort. A-frame log cabins and tent cabins feature traditional comforts like woodstoves and feather beds; there's also a treehouse for two. Climbers and hikers can soak their sore bones in the hot tubs here ($5/10 per hour with/without lodging).

Stormking Spa & B&B (☎ 360-569-2964, W stormkingspa.com, 37311 SR 706 E) Rooms with shared/private bath $70-90/110. Set back in the woods, this handsomely renovated pioneer home contains three comfortable guest rooms. The hot tub is set on a deck beside rushing Goat Creek. A self-serve vegetarian breakfast is included, and guests get reduced rates on massages and herbal body wraps.

Stone Creek Lodge (☎ 360-569-2355, 800-678-3942, W www.destination-rainier.com/stone, 38624 SR 706 E) 2-/4-person cabins $105/115. Stone Creek offers cedar cabins for couples and families in a remarkably peaceful setting a short distance from the park entrance. All cabins feature private bath, propane fireplace and small fridge. Deer customarily graze the premises.

Places to Eat

A **snack bar** at the Paradise Inn and a **cafeteria** (open daily May-Sept, Sat & Sun Oct-Apr) in the Jackson Visitor Center offer the most basic sustenance, but even cafeteria chili is welcome after a winter snowshoe expedition. The visitors center **cafeteria** is open daily from May to September and on weekends and holidays the rest of the year.

Paradise Inn Dining Room (☎ 360-569-2413) Lunch $6-9, dinner entrees $15-17. Open mid-May–Sept. People eat here as much for the view as for the concessionaire-prepared food, though the bourbon buffalo meatloaf may appeal to you. Sunday brunch is served from 11:30am to 2pm.

National Park Inn (☎ 360-569-2411) Lunch $6-9, dinner entrees $15-17. Open year-round. The Longmire concession serves three meals a day that are essentially the same as those at the Paradise Inn.

Copper Creek Inn (☎ 360-569-2326, 35707 SR 706 E) Breakfast $5-8, sandwiches & burgers $5.50-8. Open 7am-9pm year-round. Comfort food with a dash of urban soul is the specialty at this Ashford kitchen, near the Storm King Inn. Abundant country breakfasts and espresso set up hikers for the day; homemade chowders and stews and wild blackberry pie await them on the way back down.

OHANAPECOSH ENTRANCE

Ohanapecosh (o-**ha**-nuh-peh-**kosh**), translated as 'standing at the edge,' derives from the name of a Taidnapam (Upper Cowlitz) settlement that edged the rushing river running by this southeastern entry. A few popular trails delve into the dense forests here.

Packwood, 12 miles southwest of Ohanapecosh on US 12, is a convenient base for exploring the east side of Mt Rainier and for launching a trip into the Goat Rocks Wilderness Area to the south. It's on the well-traveled route between Mt Rainier and Mt St Helens, with the less-visited Mt Adams in the neighborhood as well. Note that Packwood is most conveniently linked to Ashford by USFS Road 52, a 25-mile journey through the Gifford Pinchot National Forest, though the road is closed in winter.

Information

The Ohanapecosh Visitor Center (☎ 360-494-2229) is at the park's southeastern corner on Hwy 123; it's open 9am to 5pm May to mid-October. The displays here focus on tree identification and the local old-growth forest. Rangers also offer information on hiking trails.

The Packwood Information Center (☎ 360-494-0600), at 13068 US Hwy 12 near the north end of town, is open 8am to 4:30pm weekdays year round, plus Saturday June to September, and is a good source of information on the Goat Rocks Wilderness Area.

Hiking

The 1½-mile trail into the **Grove of the Patriarchs** is one of Mt Rainier's most popular hikes, and it's worth the walk for a look at some truly large trees. The mostly level trail crosses the Ohanapecosh River to a small island where thousand-year-old Douglas firs and cedars grow. The trailhead is just north of the Ohanapecosh Visitor Center.

Just outside the visitor center, the half-mile **Hot Springs Nature Trail** winds through the forest and visits a small natural hot spring. It's more of a seep than a wallow, but there is a tiny trailside bench that allows weary hikers to soak their sore feet in a six-inch-deep pool. If this trail seems like just a starting point for a hike, follow the signpost just past the hot springs for the **Silver Falls Loop Trail**, an easy 2-mile circuit. Beyond the falls, you can hook up with the trail to the Grove of the Patriarchs.

The **Pacific Crest Trail** runs along the eastern edge of Mt Rainier National Park, and trailheads at Ohanapecosh and Chinook Pass, on Hwy 123 a few miles south of the park's White River entrance, provide local access. It's best to make this fine 19-mile stretch into a two-day, north-to-south hike, starting at Chinook Pass. Plan for cool weather; the trail runs at 5000 feet and above, with peeks at Mt Rainier and plenty of wildlife and late-season huckleberries.

Places to Stay

Both the park service and forest service maintain campgrounds in the area, and there's RV camping in nearby Packwood.

Ohanapecosh Campground (☎ *360-494-2229, reservations* ☎ *800-365-2267, Hwy 123)* Sites $15/12 late June-Labor Day/May-June, Sept-Oct. Near the visitor center, this NPS facility has 188 individual sites and flush toilets. Rangers lead campfire talks on summer evenings. See Camping, earlier, for information on reservations.

La Wis Wis Campground (☎ *360-497-1100, reservations* ☎ *877-444-6777, US Hwy 12)* Standard/riverside sites $12.50/14.50. Open mid-May–Sept. If Ohanapecosh is full, head out of the park and go south about 7 miles to this Gifford Pinchot National Forest campground with running water and flush toilets. Some of the 118 sites are alongside the Cowlitz River.

Packwood RV Park & Campground (☎ *360-494-5145, W Main St & Tatoosh N)* Tent sites/RV hookups $11/22. Right in the heart of Packwood, this pleasant facility has sites amidst lots of tall trees, plus showers ($3).

The nearest lodgings are in Packwood (W www.destinationpackwood.com). The following places are listed west to east along Hwy 12.

Tatoosh Motel (☎ *360-494-6710, fax 360-494-6736,* W *www.tatoosh.net, 12880 Hwy 12)* Rooms $45-75. This family-run place on the west side of town consists of homey duplex cabins; several units have kitchenettes. A hot tub is adjacent to a common room at the rear of the compound.

Hotel Packwood (☎ *360-494-5431, fax 360-494-4884, 104 Main St)* Single/bunks/doubles $20/25/35, double with bath $38. A renovated frontier hotel with a wraparound verandah, the Packwood is an affordable hostel-style alternative. Seven comfortable little rooms with TVs share two bathrooms. Relax in the sheltered hot tub or by the big brick fireplace in the lobby.

Inn of Packwood (☎ *360-494-5500, 877-496-9666, fax 360-494-5505,* W *www.innof packwood.com, 13032 Hwy 12)* Singles/doubles $55/70. This is a large chalet-style building in the center of town with comfortable wood-paneled rooms, an indoor pool and an outdoor tub.

Cowlitz River Lodge (☎ *360-494-4444, 888-305-2185,* W *www.escapetothemountains .com; Hwy 12 at Skate Creek Rd)* Singles/doubles $57/67 with breakfast. The companion to Ashford's Nisqually Lodge offers 32 spacious motel rooms and the obligatory hot tub.

Mountain View Lodge (☎ *360-494-5555, 13163 Hwy 12)* Singles/doubles/triples from $37/55/70. An affordable option on the east end of town, this peaceful lodge has modest accommodations in the main house and larger kitchen units for up to six people in assorted annexes, some with fireplaces. Midweek specials and weekly rates are available.

Places to Eat

There are no food services at Ohanapecosh, but Packwood is home to a number of drive-ins and unprepossessing diners.

Club Cafe (☎ 360-494-5977, Hwy 12 near Main St E) Breakfast $4-7, sandwiches & burgers $6-7, meals from $10. Good pancakes and omelets are served from 6am; later on, chicken fried steaks and burgers hit the grill.

Peters Inn (☎ 360-494-4000, Hwy 12 near Skate Creek Rd) Lunch specials $8, entrees $11-15. The local steak house features a lunch counter, a cozy dining area and a good salad bar. All meals are served.

Blue Spruce Saloon & Diner (☎ 360-494-5605, 13019 Hwy 12) Snacks $5-7, dinner $8-11. This is a friendly tavern with decent grub, and it's the only place to eat after 9pm.

WHITE RIVER ENTRANCE

Some of the best views of Mt Rainier – with Emmons Glacier sliding down its face, Little Tahoma Peak in the foreground, and the craggy Goat Rocks Wilderness Area off to the southeast – are from Sunrise. Sunrise's 6400-foot-high open meadows are scattered with trees and laced with hiking trails. Since it's on the mountain's east side, the whole White River-Sunrise area benefits from Mt Rainier's 'rain shadow' and receives less precipitation than the damp west side.

Basic visitor facilities, including meals and restrooms, are available at the Sunrise Lodge.

Orientation & Information

The White River entrance road, off Hwy 410, follows the river valley to the White River Campground on a spur off the main road about 10 miles from the park entrance. The main road leaves the river and ascends another 2400 feet in the 10-mile stretch to Sunrise.

The Wilderness Information Center (☎ 360-663-2273) at the White River entrance dispenses backcountry permits and hiking information. It's open 8am to 5pm daily late May to September, with extended hours Thursday to Saturday July to Labor Day. You can also get info at the Sunrise Visitor Center (☎ 360-569-2425),

open 9am to 6pm daily from late June to mid-September.

Weekend afternoons in summer, rangers are on hand to answer questions at the Mt Fremont lookout. From Sunrise, it's a hike of almost 3 miles through **mountain goat habitat** to the 7181-foot perch. Find the trailhead at the picnic area behind the visitors center and head up to Sourdough Ridge. Pick up the trail to Mt Fremont just beyond Frozen Lake, a mile west along the ridge.

Hiking

It doesn't take long for hikers to become enraptured with the White River-Sunrise area. The only glitch may be the crowds. Try to hike on a weekday, and hit the trail early in the morning.

A trailhead directly across the parking lot from the Sunrise Lodge provides access to several short walks and a plethora of longer hikes. It's an easy stroll to the **Emmons Vista**, with good views of Mt Rainier, Little Tahoma and the Emmons Glacier (the largest glacier in the lower 48 states). For a longer – but level – walk, turn right just before the Emmons Vista onto the **Sunrise Rim Trail**, which takes about 1½ miles to reach **Shadow Lake** and Sunrise Camp, a backcountry campground. From here, an old service road provides a short route back to the lodge parking lot.

Three miles from the White River entrance, the trail to **Summer Land** takes off along Fryingpan Creek. The 4.3-mile hike along a piece of the Wonderland Trail climbs gradually through forest, then through brush, before reaching Summer Land's open subalpine meadows with views of Mt Rainier and pointy, glacier-chiseled Little Tahoma peak. Mountain goats and elk are often visible from this extremely popular trail.

To get to **Emmons Glacier**, a less-spectacular, but perfectly pleasant trail starts from the far end of the White River Campground and follows a fork of the White River for 3½ miles to Glacier Basin, a meadow surrounded by slopes that are home to mountain goats and form a corridor for mountain climbers. For a close-up

Stalking the Wild Huckleberry

Admired for its tangy flavor, the blue huckleberry can be eaten fresh, made into pies, jams and any number of ice-cream and chocolate confections. The huckleberry was an integral part of the Native American diet. Tribes made summer excursions to the high mountain meadows, where the low, bushy plants flourish; the berries were often dried for winter use.

Southwest of Mt Adams (see that section, at the end of this chapter) are some of the largest and most productive wild huckleberry meadows in the Northwest. The elevation is high – usually above 4000 feet – but quite flat. This land of marsh and lake is perfect for huckleberries (as it is for mosquitoes).

Huckleberry season is usually August through September, and a number of USFS-administered areas are open for berry picking. Free USFS permits are necessary, and rangers will also offer advice and maps indicating where the harvest is most productive. Traditionally, the best berry picking is in the Sawtooth Berryfields, an area immediately north of the Indian Heaven Wilderness Area. Follow signs for the Surprise Lakes or Cold Springs campgrounds, off USFS Rd 24, about 21 miles west of Trout Lake.

look at the glacier, turn off the **Glacier Basin Trail** after 1 mile and hike another half-mile along the glacier's lateral moraine to the overlook. (Actually, the official viewpoint doesn't have much over the many informal tracks up to the moraine's crest that precede it.)

Climbing

From the White River Campground, climbers follow the Glacier Basin Trail to the Inter Glacier, then rope up into teams and continue to the 9500-foot bivouac at Camp Schurman, where rocky Steamboat Prow juts up and separates the Emmons and Winthrop Glaciers. Most climbers follow Emmons' crevasse-free 'corridor' as far as possible, then skirt crevasses, including the gaping bergschrund where the top of the glacier pulls away from the mountain's ice cap to reach the summit.

Places to Stay & Eat

White River Campground (☎ 360-663-2273) Sites $10. Open late June-Sept. This 112-site campground is 10 road miles or 3½ steep trail miles downhill from Sunrise. Facilities include flush toilets, drinking water and crowded, though not unpleasant, camping spaces.

Sunrise Camp (☎ 360-663-2273) Free, backcountry permit required. For campers who are willing to dispense with such amenities as running water and pack in their gear 1½ miles, Sunrise Camp is just down the Sunrise Rim Trail from the lodge parking lot.

There is no indoor lodging at Sunrise. The closest motel rooms are at Crystal Mountain Resort (see that section, later), or in Enumclaw or Packwood.

Sunrise Lodge Cafeteria (☎ 360-569-2425) Snacks $5-7. Open 10am-7pm daily June 30-Sept 16. Don't expect anything fancy here – it's a hamburger and hot dog sort of place.

CARBON RIVER ENTRANCE

This remote northwest corner of Mt Rainier National Park is a dense green pocket, made all the more striking by the intensive clear-cutting that has gone on in the Carbon River valley outside the park boundaries. There's lots of water, mushrooms, moss and several hikes to waterfalls. There's also the park's lowest-reaching glacier, a river cloudy with glacial till, and a remarkable inland rain forest. The Carbon River area has very few glimpses of Mt Rainier; for big mountain views, head to Mowich Lake.

To get to Carbon River and Mowich Lake from the I-5 corridor, it's easiest to take Hwy 167 south to Puyallup where you'll pick up Hwy 410 east to Buckley. From there take Hwy 165 south past the small towns of Wilkeson and Carbonado. The road forks a few miles past Carbonado. The left fork follows the Carbon River and is paved to just inside the park entrance. The right fork is paved for a couple of miles, and then becomes a well-graded gravel road, which climbs above the Carbon River valley and terminates at Mowich Lake, 17 miles from the fork. Neither road is plowed in the winter, though the lower-elevation Carbon River Rd rarely sees much snow. However, it is subject to washouts – it's best to use a high clearance vehicle.

Pick up permits for backcountry camping and north side climbs at the Wilkeson Wilderness Information Center (☎ 360-829-5127), open 8:30am to 4pm daily May to November (7:30am to 7:30pm June to August), 21 miles from the Carbon River entrance. Ten miles farther north in Enumclaw, the USFS-administered Snoqualmie Ranger Station (☎ 360-825-6585) provides information on trails in Mt Rainier National Park and the surrounding national and state forest lands. It's open 8am to 4:15pm Monday to Friday year-round.

Carbon River Rain Forest

Though there are plenty of times when all of Mt Rainier seems like a rain forest, the short **Rain Forest Loop Trail**, just inside the park entrance, loops through the only true inland rain forest in the park – indeed, in all of North America. Huge-leafed plants grow alongside the boardwalk that elevates the trail from the frequently steaming ground below, and the moist air condenses into droplets hanging from big Douglas firs and cedars. Pick up a brochure for a self-guided tour at the trailhead.

Hiking

At 3520 feet, the **Carbon Glacier** reaches a lower elevation than any other glacier on Mt Rainier. A trail starting at the Ipsut Creek Campground passes the glacier's leading

edge 3½ miles to the southeast. Hikers are warned not to approach the glacier too closely, as rockfall from its surface is unpredictable and dangerous. The same trailhead also provides access to the Wonderland Trail (see Hiking & Climbing, at the beginning of this chapter), that crosses Ipsut Pass on the way to Mowich Lake (a 5.3-mile hike from Ipsut Creek).

A 35-mile, three- or four-day trip, the **Northern Loop Trail** passes through some of the park's least-traveled areas. The loop starts at Ipsut Creek and follows the Carbon River Glacier Trail for a couple of miles before taking off to the east and passing through Windy Gap on its steep, up-and-down path toward Sunrise. Just west of Sunrise, the Northern Loop Trail joins up with the Wonderland Trail, which returns hikers to Ipsut Creek or continues around the mountain.

To reach **Summit Lake**, just outside the park's Carbon River entrance, turn north onto USFS Rd 7810 and follow it to the end. The 2½-mile trail is in the Clearwater Wilderness. Mt Rainier's north face – including the practically unclimbable Willis Wall – comes into good view at Summit Lake.

From Mowich Lake, one extremely popular trail heads south and passes **Spray Falls** on its way to **Spray Park**, flush with wildflowers late in the summer. It's just under 3 miles to Spray Park. As popular as this trail is, it's not all that easy. A dizzying run of switchbacks just past the falls pulls the trail out of the forest to the Spray Park meadows.

For views of Mt Rainier, try going to **Tolmie Peak lookout**. Head north on the Wonderland Trail from Mowich Lake, then turn off at Ipsut Pass and climb to the lookout at 5939 feet. If the final chug up Tolmie Peak seems too daunting, Eunice Lake at its base is a perfectly good place to relax.

Places to Stay & Eat

Ipsut Creek Campground (☎ 360-829-5127) Sites $9 late May-Labor Day, no fee rest of year. Open year-round, weather permitting. The campground, at the end of the Carbon River Rd, has 31 sites but no drinking water.

The road up is not recommended for trailers.

Mowich Lake Campground (☎ *360-829-5127*) Free. Open July–mid-Oct. Just past the Mowich Lake parking lot, this walk-in campground is far less inviting than its surroundings. There are vault toilets but no drinking water and fires aren't allowed.

Mountain View Inn (☎ *360-829-1100,* ☎ *800-582-4411,* W *www.mtviewinn.com, 29405 Hwy 410 E*) Singles/doubles $65/75. This is the closest motel, at the junction of Hwys 165 and 410 in Buckley, and it's a fairly luxurious spread with a heated pool.

Wilkeson and Enumclaw are the nearest places to stock up on supplies before getting to the remote northern areas of the park.

CRYSTAL MOUNTAIN RESORT

Just outside the northeast corner of Mt Rainier National Park is one of the largest and most popular ski areas in Washington, Crystal Mountain Resort (☎ *360-663-2265,* W *www.skicrystal.com, 33914 Crystal Mountain Blvd; lift tickets adult/youth 11-17 years/ senior $43/38/12; open 9am-4pm Mon-Fri, 8:30am-8pm Fri-Sun mid-Nov–mid-Apr*). Downhill skiers give Crystal Mountain high marks for its variety of terrain, which includes some very steep chutes and remote, unpatrolled backcountry trails. Its summit (Silver King) tops out at 7012 feet; the vertical drop is 3120 feet. Crystal has 2300 acres of skiable terrain and 50 named runs, more than 50% of which are rated intermediate. The slopes are served by 10 lifts, including four high-speed chairs. There's night skiing Friday through Sunday till 8pm. Snowboarding in the deep bowls is also popular here. For a report on slope conditions, phone ☎ *888-754-6199.*

Rental packages include telemark skis ($25), performance skis ($33) and snowboards ($32). Ski instruction is available at $35/45 for two/four-hour group sessions.

Crystal Mountain is 39 miles east of Enumclaw off Hwy 410. On weekends and holidays, shuttles transport skiers from Seattle and Tacoma for $25 roundtrip, or $58 including a full-day lift ticket. Call ☎ *800-665-2122* for schedules and points of departure.

As you might expect, accommodations are all managed by the resort and there are a bewildering array of package deals, with cut-rate prices during the off-season. Contact Crystal Mountain Hotels (☎ *360-663-2262, 888-754-6400,* W *www.crystal hotels.com*) to find out about promotions at the following three places.

Alpine Inn Doubles from $90. The most atmospheric (and affordable) of the lodgings here is this Bavarian-style inn, within skiing distance of the slopes. A restaurant, rathskeller, deli and ski/snowboard shop are all on the premises.

Village Inn Doubles from $105. More of a standard hotel, the Village Inn offers modern rooms with VCRs, refrigerators and balconies.

Quicksilver Lodge Doubles/triples $115/150. Rooms here are a touch fancier, and some feature a sleeping loft. A huge lobby/lounge with stone fireplace provides the requisite apres-ski ambience.

Silver Skis Chalet & Crystal Chalets (☎ *360-663-2558, 888-668-4368,* W *www .crystal mtlodging-wa.com*) 1-bdrm apts $185 for up to 4, plus $5 for each additional guest. Groups of four or more should look into renting a condominium at one of these chalets, near the lower lifts.

There's also an RV parking area with electrical hookups at $20 per night. A full range of cafes, restaurants and bars caters to skiers.

Alpine Inn (☎ *360-663-2262*) Entrees $15-22. The restaurant at the inn specializes in German and Austrian fare, with a decent wine selection. Breakfast and dinner are served.

Summit House (☎ *360-663-2265*) Lunch $5-10. Take the Rainier Express lift to the top for lunch with a view. Pizzas, pastas and salads highlight the self-serve menu.

GOAT ROCKS WILDERNESS AREA

This wonderful preserve has over 100,000-acres of high country, with great craggy rocks, mountain goats and views of the surrounding Cascade peaks. Goat Rocks was originally a 12,000-foot-high volcano. Long extinct, it has eroded into several peaks averaging 8000 feet. Since it's largely above the timberline, hiking season starts late (July) and ends early (late September). A Northwest Forest Pass is required to park at some of the trailheads; get one from the Cowlitz Valley Ranger District USFS office in Randle (☎ 360-497-1100), 10024 US Hwy 12.

The **Pacific Crest Trail** (PCT) passes through the most spectacular section of the wilderness area. It's a huge hike from one side to the other, 25 to 30 miles total, with the best parts coming about halfway in, making for no easy in-and-out trip. However, for experienced hikers, there is a shorter way to get to the heart of the Goat Rocks. From Packwood, drive a few miles west on US 12, then turn south on USFS Rd 21. Take a left just past Hugo Lake onto USFS Rd 2150, which goes to the trailhead at Chambers Lake, some 21 miles from Packwood. Begin hiking at Chambers Lake to Snowgrass Flat (trail No 96), then cut over on a side trail to the PCT. It's about 5 miles from the trailhead to the PCT, and at that point you're within a mile of good camping spots near some glaciers. The Goat Rocks themselves are stunning, and another 3 miles up to **Elks Pass** on the PCT leads to magnificent mountain vistas.

Mt St Helens

Where were you when Mt St Helens blew? For most people in the Pacific Northwest, the events of May 18, 1980, are as welded into memory as the dates of the bombing of Pearl Harbor and the assassination of John F Kennedy. Mt St Helens erupted with the force of 21,000 atomic bombs, leveling hundreds of square miles of forest and spreading volcanic ash across the Pacific Northwest and as far northeast as Saskatchewan.

After the smoke cleared, Mt St Helens – once a symmetrical 9677-foot mountain covered with glaciers – had blown 1300 feet off its peak, and a mile-wide crater yawned on its north side. Spirit Lake, once a resort destination below the peak, was clogged with fallen timber and debris, and the rivers that flowed off the mountain were flooded with mud and ash. In 1982, 172 sq miles around the mountain were included in the **Mt St Helens National Volcanic Monument**. Two decades later, nature has restored much life to the mountain.

Native American legends depicted Mt St Helens as the youngest of the fire mountains of Oregon and Washington, and it likely is. Much of the volcano is less than 2000 years old. The mountain was known to have erupted several times in the 19th century, significantly in 1857. Radiocarbon studies of trees in nearby forests suggest that there is a pattern to the volcano's eruption. After several centuries of quiescence, it explodes several times in decade-spaced intervals, and again falls into a (geologically) short slumber.

The devastation wrought by the eruption is an incredible sight, and one that will haunt your thoughts for days. A trip to either the east- or westside crater viewpoints is strongly recommended; if you can, take the time to hike and explore this unique area.

Orientation

Mt St Helens is directly east of Castle Rock in a remote part of the Gifford Pinchot National Forest. There are two principal entry routes. The Windy Ridge viewpoint, on the northeast side of the mountain, is accessed by long drives on winding USFS roads. Viewpoints at Coldwater Ridge Visitor Center and Johnston Ridge Observatory, on the northwest side of the mountain, are easily accessed from I-5 off Hwy 504 and are open year-round.

Mt St Helens can be visited as a day-trip from either Portland or Seattle. The town of Castle Rock is about one hour's drive north of Portland, or a little over two hours south of Seattle. On I-5; it's another hour from Castle Rock east to Coldwater Ridge. To reach the Windy Ridge area from I-5 requires another two hours via US 12.

Information

The confusing admission fee system has been streamlined but it remains somewhat

MT ST HELENS

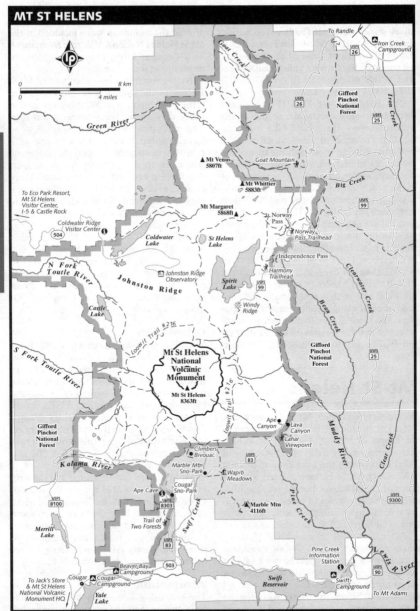

To Randle

USFS 26

Iron Creek Campground

Goat Creek

Gifford Pinchot National Forest

USFS 26

Iron Creek

USFS 25

Green River

Mt Venus 5807ft

Goat Mountain

Big Creek

Mt Whittier 5883ft

USFS 99

To Eco Park Resort, Mt St Helens Visitor Center, I-5 & Castle Rock

Mt Margaret 5868ft

Norway Pass

Coldwater Ridge Visitor Center

504

Norway Pass Trailhead

Coldwater Lake

St Helens Lake

Independence Pass

Clearwater Creek

N Fork Toutle River

Johnston Ridge Observatory

Harmony Trailhead

Spirit Lake

USFS 99

Johnston Ridge

Windy Ridge

Bean Creek

Castle Lake

Loowit Trail #216

Gifford Pinchot National Forest

USFS 25

S Fork Toutle River

Mt St Helens National Volcanic Monument

Mt St Helens 8363ft

Loowit Trail #216

Ape Canyon

Lava Canyon

Muddy River

Gifford Pinchot National Forest

Lahar Viewpoint

Clear Creek

Kalama River

Climbers Bivouac

Marble Mtn Sno-Park

Cougar Sno-Park

USFS 83

Wapiti Meadows

USFS 8100

Ape Cave

USFS 8303

Swift Creek

Marble Mtn 4116ft

USFS 9300

Merrill Lake

Trail of Two Forests

USFS 83

Pine Creek

Pine Creek Information Station

USFS 90

Beaver Bay Campground

503

Swift Campground

To Jack's Store & Mt St Helens National Volcanic Monument HQ

Cougar

Cougar Campground

Yale Lake

Swift Reservoir

Lewis River

To Mt Adams

0   4   8 km
0   2   4 miles

WASHINGTON

complicated – the rangers will be happy to explain it all to you. Visitors have several options depending on what they want to do. A multi-site Monument Pass (adult/youth 5-15 years/4 years & under $6/2/free) allows each pass-holder entry to the two visitors centers, the Johnston Ridge Observatory, and Ape Cave. A single-site pass ($3/1/free) is good for any one of the above sites. Purchase either pass at any monument visitors center or at Apes' Headquarters at Ape Cave. The Northwest Forest Pass ($5/30 daily/annual) validates parking at National Forest trailheads throughout the park (with the exception of those along Hwy 504, for which you'll need the Monument Pass), including those at Windy Ridge viewpoint and Lava Canyon, both of which have self-service pay stations. This pass also lets the pass-holder into the visitor centers, but accompanying passengers will still have to purchase their own Monument passes.

Five miles east of Castle Rock (I-5 exit 49) along Hwy 504 is the Mt St Helens Visitor Center (☎ 360-274-2100), at 3029 Spirit Lake Hwy. This facility, operated by the Washington State Parks Commission, offers lots of free information on the mountain, as well as films and exhibits on the history of the eruption that serve as an excellent introduction to the monument. There's also a good bookstore. It's open 9am to 5pm.

The forest service puts out the info-loaded *Volcano Review,* free at visitor centers. Essentially the same information is found at the Mt St Helens website: **W** www.fs.fed.us/gpnf/mshnvm/.

A couple of other visitors centers are spaced along Hwy 504 on the way to Coldwater Ridge. The Cowlitz County-run Hoffstadt Bluffs Visitor Center (☎ 360-274-7750), at 15000 Spirit Lake Hwy is open 9am to 6pm daily May to September, 10am to 4pm Wednesday to Sunday October to April. It's 27 miles from Castle Rock, and has a restaurant and a panoramic view of the Toutle River Valley. Helicopter tours of the mountain depart every 30 minutes from here in summer. Six miles farther up is the Charles W Bingham Forest Learning Center (☎ 360-414-

3439), at 17000 Spirit Lake Memorial Hwy; admission is free, and it's open 10am to 6pm mid-May to October. The Weyerhauser Corp museum has innovative exhibits designed to show that nature clear cuts forests too (but they grow back eventually).

If you are heading to the Windy Ridge area from the south on Hwy 503, get information and passes at the Mt St Helens Volcanic Monument Headquarters (☎ 360-247-3900, 24-Hr Info 360-247-3903), at 42218 NE Yale Bridge Rd, Amboy, WA; it's open 8am to 5pm weekdays year round, plus Saturday in summer.

Many people also time their visits to take in the 70mm film *The Eruption of Mt St Helens* at the **Cinedome Theater** *(☎ 360-274-8000, 1239 Mt St Helens Way; adult/child & senior $6/5; every 45 minutes from 9am daily May-Oct),* in Castle Rock, just off I-5.

Coldwater Ridge & Around

Coldwater Ridge, a 3200-foot-high spur with views directly into the mouth of Mt St Helens' north-facing crater, is the site of the Coldwater Ridge Visitor Center (☎ 360-274-2131). It's 43 miles east of Castle Rock, and is open 10am to 6pm daily May to October, 9am to 5pm November to April. The interpretive center is a modern lodge overlooking Coldwater Lake, a 3-mile-long body of water created by a massive landslide during the 1980 eruption that blocked the flow of Coldwater Creek. An observation deck and a glassed-in viewing area provide glimpses of the lake. Interactive displays focus on the cycles of nature, and a dozen video screens replay the explosion of Mt St Helens. There's also a bookstore and a cafeteria. The quarter-mile **Winds of Change Trail** demonstrates the re-growth of vegetation in the area. Interpretive talks and hikes are offered year round; call ahead for the schedule.

From Coldwater Ridge, Hwy 504 continues down 2¼ miles to the lake, where it's worth stopping for the **Birth of a Lake Trail**. The boardwalk path skirts the lakeshore (and at some points extends into the lake) and signs illustrate how plant and aquatic life re-established itself here after the catastrophic blast. The road then climbs another

When Mt St Helens Blew Her Stack

The most recent Mt St Helens eruption was first anticipated in March 1980, when small steam clouds began to build above the mountain and earthquakes rocked the area. Initially, geologists thought that the pyrotechnics were simply the result of ground water reaching the molten core of the mountain, and not of rising lava. In fact, it wasn't until late in the game that scientists realized a major eruption was imminent.

Even though the state police worked to evacuate the Mt St Helens area prior to the eruption, some people who had always lived near the mountain simply chose to stay and take their chances, while others ignored the warnings and sneaked in to watch the volcano. The most prominent of those who stayed behind was Harry Truman – not the former US president, but the proprietor of a resort on Spirit Lake. He was among the 59 people killed on the mountain when the blast took place.

The 1980 eruption was one of steam, not lava. The molten rock that rose to the surface of the volcano was heavily infused with water, which at temperatures of 750°F is capable of enormous explosive power. As this piston of lava pushed closer and closer to the surface, it created a bulge on the north side of the peak that grew larger and more unstable with each passing day.

On May 18, the rock finally gave way; the entire north face of Mt St Helens slid down the mountain in what geologist believe was the largest landslide in recorded history. The landslide carried mud, snow, ice and rock at speeds of 200 mph, dumping them into Spirit Lake and 17 miles down the North Fork Toutle River valley. At over 800°F, the mudflows turned Spirit Lake into a boiling cauldron that instantly killed all fish and animal life.

Without the rock cover to hold them back, super-heated steam and gases finally broke through to the surface of the volcano, blasting a 15-mile-high cloud of ash and rock into the air at speeds of 500 mph. The blast, carrying scorching temperatures and poisonous gases, hurtled through the forests north of the crater at speeds of 200 mph, leveling 150 sq miles of forest in an instant.

While Mt St Helens has remained calm since 1980, geologists concur that another explosion is only a matter of time.

1000 feet to **Johnston Ridge Observatory** (☎ *360-274-2140; open 10am-6pm daily May-Oct)*, which looks directly into the mouth of the crater. Exhibits here depict the geologic events surrounding the 1980 blast and how they advanced the science of volcano forecasting and monitoring. Guides lead hikes along the half-mile **Eruption Trail** with views of the crater, the pumice plain, and Spirit Lake off to the east.

Windy Ridge Viewpoint

A somewhat more remote vantage point is on the northeastern side of the mountain, along Windy Ridge. Partisans often hold that this angle is more impressive than that of Coldwater Ridge; while this is probably true, you will also spend more time on winding roads to get there.

Windy Ridge is at the terminus of USFS Rd 99, at a parking lot overlooking log-jammed Spirit Lake and along the line of sight to the lava dome in the mouth of the crater. The reality of the volcano's power and destruction is everywhere apparent. The road passes by entire forests that were blown down by the tremendous blast of the eruption, and boulders and ash are strewn about the mountainside. Trails lead to other viewpoints and down to Spirit Lake.

Rangers offer interpretive talks every half hour Friday to Monday in summer (less often Tuesday to Thursday). There are toilets and a snack bar at the viewpoint.

To reach Windy Ridge from the north, turn onto USFS Rd 25 at Randle on US 12 (48 miles east of I-5 exit 68). Travel 20 miles to the junction of USFS Rd 99. Follow this frequently winding, and – in summer – heavily traveled road for another 17 miles to the viewpoint. From the southwest, turn east off I-5 at Woodland (exit 21) onto Hwy 503. This leads to USFS Rd 90 and the Pine Creek Information Station at the intersection with USFS Rd 25, which heads north for the Windy Ridge turnoff. Allow at least 1¼ hours for the drive from either Randle or Pine Creek.

Ape Cave

A lava tube that runs 12,810 feet, Ape Cave is one of the longest underground hiking trails in the entire USFS trail system. Lava tubes are formed when the exterior of a deep lava flow hardens while the interior continues to flow. Eventually the liquid lava empties out of the crust, leaving a hollow tube with lava walls. In the case of the Ape Cave, the lava from an ancient eruption flowed down a deep watercourse; the top of the ravine sealed, but the lava continued to flow underground.

Hikers can walk and scramble the length of the Ape Cave on two trails, both beginning at an informational kiosk just off USFS Rd 8303. The three-quarter-mile **Lower Ape Cave Trail** follows the cave downstream from the main entrance. This part of the cave has a dry sandy bottom and nearly 20-foot-high ceilings, and it is by far the easier walk. There is no exit at this end of the cave, so you need to retrace your steps to get out. The 1½-mile **Upper Ape Cave Trail** requires a lot of scrambling over rock piles and narrower passages. The trail eventually exits at the upper entrance. Hikers can rent lanterns for $2 at Apes' Headquarters, at the entrance to the caves *(open 10am-5:30pm daily late June-Labor Day, Sat & Sun Memorial Day-late June)*. Free ranger-led explorations of the Ape Cave are offered several times daily from late June through Labor Day; check with the visitors center for schedules. Note that visitors must purchase a Monument Pass to hike the cave trails in summer only; the rest of the year, a Northwest Forest Pass is required to park at the trailhead.

Also in the Ape Cave area is the wheelchair-accessible **Trail of Two Forests**, a quarter-mile boardwalk along a stream and a lava cast forest. Interpretive displays explain the process of reforestation at this ancient lava flow.

By the way, the reference to 'ape' in the name of this cave and a nearby canyon has little to do with primates. A group of boy-scout adventurers took to calling themselves the Mt St Helens Apes after a purported sighting of a bigfoot in Ape Canyon in 1924. Members of this group discovered the cave in 1946, hence the name.

Hiking

A number of short interpretive hikes leave from Coldwater Ridge and the lake, though to reach the principal Mt St Helens trail network from here requires a long slog across desolate pumice fields and mudflows. Hikers are better advised to start from Windy Ridge or the south side of the mountain. In either case, take along plenty of water, as it is scarce along these barren, dry trails. Pick up a *Mount St Helens National Volcanic Monument Trail Guide* ($8) at any of the visitor centers.

Named after the female spirit that inhabits Mt St Helens in Native American myth, the **Loowit Trail** (No 216) is a 27-mile trail system that circles the mountain. Because of the extremely rugged terrain, be sure to check with rangers before setting out for an extended hike, as washouts and landslides are common. The most popular portion of the trail crosses the face of the crater on the mountain's north side. The easiest access to the Loowit Trail is from Windy Ridge viewpoint.

The **Lahar Viewpoint** in Ape Canyon, at the end of USFS Rd 83, provides access to a number of different hikes into wild volcanic landscapes, including the 1.7-mile **Lava Canyon Trail**, a barrier-free path along a recent mudflow to a waterfall vista. This starts out as an all-abilities trail, then after the first half-mile drops down into a steep canyon scoured out by the Mt St Helens eruption. The trail is for the intrepid, but it's great fun. Also beginning at Lahar, the **Ape Canyon Trail** ascends along a wooded ridge top before reaching a deep and narrow chasm cut in the flanks of the mountain. At 4½ miles, it ties into the Loowit Trail.

The long access roads leading into Spirit Lake and Windy Ridge have several trailheads, some of which access the following day hikes. The popular **Harmony Trail** (No 224) leads down past scorched tree stumps to the shores of Spirit Lake. Although just over a mile in length, it is fairly steep going. The trailhead is about 2 miles north of Windy Ridge viewpoint on USFS Rd 99.

The views from **Norway Pass** are among the best in the monument, with Mt St Helens and its open-jawed crater rising directly above the timber-cluttered Spirit Lake. To reach this overview, take the 2½-mile **Boundary Trail** (No 1) from the trailhead off USFS Rd 26, 1 mile north of the junction with USFS Rd 99. Hikers with a shuttle can make a loop by returning along the 3½-mile **Independence Pass Trail**, ending up on USFS Rd 99, 2½ miles south of its junction with USFS Rd 26.

Cross-Country Skiing

Several winter recreation areas attract skiers to the southern part of the monument. Cougar Sno-Park, off USFS Rd 83, accesses a number of snowed-in forest roads near the Ape Cave; Marble Mountain Sno-Park offers access to more snowbound roads and to Wapiti Meadows, with many miles of groomed trails. (The NPS does not rent cross-country skis in this area, but Jack's Restaurant does; see Climbing, below.)

Climbing

Because Mt St Helens is a very delicate and sometimes dangerous mountain, climbers must obtain a permit to ascend the peak. From April to October, there's a $15 per person charge for the permit, which is valid for 24 hours. Between May 15 and October 31, the number of permits issued is limited to 100 people per day. Half of these may be reserved in advance, a recommended procedure on summer weekends when competition is fierce. To make a reservation, contact the monument headquarters in Amboy (see the preceding Information section). Reservation forms are available via Internet by clicking on the Mountain Climbing link at the Mt St Helens website (W www.fs.fed.us/gpnf/mshnvm). The website also shows which days are already booked up. Pick up and pay for permits at **Jack's Restaurant & Store** (☎ 360-231-4276, 13411 Lewis River Rd) on USFS Rd 90, 23 miles east of I-5 exit 23. Jack's also serves as the climber's registry for Mt St Helens, and all climbers must sign in there before and after the ascent.

The other 50 permits are available on a first-come, first-served basis at Jack's, which issues the permits at 6pm the day before the climb. Should the demand exceed availability, a lottery is held to distribute the permits. Each person drawn may purchase up to four permits. Try to show up before 6pm to enter the lottery.

Many people camp by the trailhead at Climber's Bivouac the night before climbing; there are composting toilets (but no running water). It's 14 miles northeast of Cougar at the end of USFS Rd 830, a narrow gravel road that spurs off USFS Rd 83 at Cougar Sno-Park. Your permit serves to validate parking here.

No technical climbing abilities are needed, but it's not fun and games either. From Climber's Bivouac, the Monitor Ridge trail (No 216A) ascends 1100 feet in 2¼ miles to reach timberline at 4800 feet. From there, most of the steep ascent involves scrambling over lava chunks and struggling up loose pumice fields. The 5-mile trail ends at the summit cliffs, with astonishing views down onto the smoking lava dome and the incinerated viscera of the mountain. Be very careful of the lip of the crater, as the rock here is unstable. Allow at least eight hours to make the roundtrip. Weather and climbing conditions are subject to volatile change. For up-to-the-minute information on conditions, call the Climbers Information Line (☎ 360-247-3961).

Places to Stay & Eat

Though facilities are limited and most people will choose to make it a day-trip from a larger center, there are campgrounds scattered around the mountain and a couple of diners and motels in Castle Rock and Randle.

Campsites are most abundant on the south side of the monument, away from the main force of the explosion. Along Hwy 503, Yale Lake and Swift Reservoir, on the Lewis River, are both just south of the mountain and offer three large lakeside campgrounds popular with motor boaters, *Cougar Campground*, *Beaver Bay Campground* and *Swift Campground* (☎ 503-813-6666). Sites cost $15, but since the slopes along the Lewis River have recently been clear-cut, this is a fairly unenthralling place to get away from it all.

Iron Creek Campground (☎ 360-497-1100, reservations ☎ 877-444-6777, USFS Rd 25) Sites from $12. To the north of Mt St Helens, near the junction with USFS Rd 26, is this forest service camp on the banks of the Cispus River. The sites, of which there are nearly 100, go quickly in summer. Facilities include running water and pit toilets.

Seaquest State Park (☎ 206-274-8633, reservations ☎ 888-226-7688, Hwy 504) Tent sites/RV hookups $13/19. Open year-round. Directly across from the entrance to the Mt St Helens Visitor Center, Seaquest has nearly 100 campsites, including a separate hiker/bike camp area, with flush toilets and showers. Set alongside Silver Lake, the campground features over 5 miles of hiking trails.

Eco Park Resort (☎ 360-274-6542, W www.ecoparkresort.com, 14000 Spirit Lake Hwy) Tent & RV sites/yurts/cabins $15/58/60-85. In the heart of the blast zone, along the North Fork Toutle River valley, this 'tent & breakfast' has rustic log cabins and a couple of yurts in addition to the campsites. Home-cooked meals like Logger Stew are served in the Backwoods Café by the road. The owner, whose family owned

the Spirit Lake Lodge swept away by the 1980 eruption, runs off-road van tours of the volcano in summer.

Mt St Helens Motel (☎ 360-274-7721, W www.mtsthelensmotel.com, 1340 Mt St Helens Way NE) Singles/doubles $55/72. The nicest place to stay in Castle Rock is within walking distance of a number of family restaurants, including the adjacent *Rose Tree Restaurant & Lounge*.

Randle, a crossroads town between Mt Rainier and Mt St Helens, doesn't pretend to be anything fancy or upscale. Stay here if 'convenient' and 'cheap' are important words in your vocabulary.

Tall Timber Motel (☎ 360-497-2991, 10023 US 12) Singles/doubles/triples $30/35/40. Rooms here are basic but well-kept, and some include kitchens. A coffee shop and car wash are attached.

Medici Motel & Campgrounds (☎ 360-497-7700, 800-697-7750, 471 Cispus Rd) Double/family $50/85, partial/full RV hookups $17/20. White peacocks wander the tranquil grounds of this out-of-the-way lodging, 3 miles south of US 12 off Hwy 23. Four of the five modestly furnished rooms have full kitchens.

Big Bottom Bar & Grill (☎ 360-497-9982, Hwy 12) Entrees $10-15. Never mind the big pickups in the parking lot – Randle's Big Bottom is *the* place to get a decent steak in town, and they are used to serving people who are just passing through. There's a full list of snacks & sandwiches ($4-8).

Mt Adams

Mt Adams, at 12,276 feet, is the state's second-highest peak, and it towers over the beautiful and mostly undeveloped meadows and valleys of south-central Washington. Although it is one of the most beautiful of the Cascades, with some enchanting hikes and an easily ascended summit, Adams has the distinction of being one of the least-visited and under-utilized mountain areas in the Northwest. Contributing to its isolation is the fact that the entire eastern slope of Mt Adams is enclosed in the Yakama Indian Reservation, and with a few specific exceptions, the land is not open to nontribal members.

What this means is that hikers and campers will find Mt Adams relatively secluded compared with its famous siblings. During the winter, snowed-in logging roads yield miles of cross-country ski trails near Trout Lake. Routes are well-signed and trail maps are available at the ranger station.

The **Mt Adams Wilderness**, a 66-sq-mile preserve, includes the mountain's summit and the western half of the mountain. A unique activity in the area is huckleberry picking; the high meadows around the mountain are famed for their late summer crop of this wild blueberry.

Mt Adams was known to early native tribes as Klickitat or Pah-to. Many myths and legends pit the spirit of Mt Adams against that of Mt Hood, directly south in Oregon. Inevitably, their conflicts ended with each shooting fire and smoke at the other. Adams is considered a sacred site to the Yakama tribe.

Geologically unique among Cascade peaks, Mt Adams is composed of a number of separate volcanic cones, each from a different eruption. These multiple cones lend the mountain its distinctive broadly domed appearance. Though it first began erupting about 450,000 years ago, the peak we see today was largely formed about 15,000 years ago, toward the end of the most recent ice age. Ten major glaciers still cling to the mountain.

Orientation & Information

The easiest access to Mt Adams is from the Columbia River Gorge. From Hood River or White Salmon, take Hwy 141 north (about 25 miles) to the tiny community of Trout Lake. In summer, the mostly paved USFS Rd 23 is open between Randle, south of Mt Rainier on US 12, and Trout Lake (a 1¾-hour drive).

For information on hiking or climbing, or to get permits to pick huckleberries or mushrooms in the national forest, consult the Mt Adams Ranger District USFS office in Trout Lake (☎ 509-395-3400) at 2455 Hwy 141; it's open 8am to 4:30pm Monday to Saturday, plus Sunday in summer. Maps

of the Mt Adams Wilderness and the Indian Heaven Wilderness can be picked up for $4.25 each. Information can also be obtained online at **w** www.fs.fed.us/gpnf.

Hiking

Two famous trails capture the beauty and vastness of Mt Adams. The slightly misnamed **Round-the-Mountain Trail**, also known as Trail 9, skirts the southern base of the peak for 8.3 miles between the Bird Creek area, at the trailhead off USFS Rd 8290, and the **Pacific Crest Trail** (PCT), which enters the wilderness from the southwest. The PCT continues around to the north side of Mt Adams and branches north to skirt the Yakama Indian Reservation's western edge. These two trails manage to traverse about half of the mountain's girth, mostly at timberline and at a gentle grade. The views of surrounding Cascade peaks are incredible. It's about 25 miles from the Bird Creek Trailhead to the northern border of the wilderness area (via the PCT).

To those who know it, the **Bird Creek Meadow Trail** is one of the best-loved hikes in the Northwest. The 3-mile loop trail leads from the Bird Creek Trailhead and gently climbs to an alpine meadow showered by waterfalls and ablaze with wildflowers. Looming above are the cliffs and glaciers of Mt Adams' summit. After ascending to a ridge-top viewpoint, the trail loops back beside tiny lakes and yet more wildflowers. The best time to hike the trail is in July, when blooms are at their peak and most of the trails will be free of ice.

Both of the above trails begin in a small, western portion of the Yakama Indian Reservation that is open to non-Yakamas. However, to hike or camp in this area requires paying a $10-per-vehicle fee to the tribe. The Around the Mountain Trail can also be accessed from the Morrison Creek or Cold Springs Campground trailheads, outside the reservation.

Climbing

Mt Adams is known as one of the easiest Cascade peaks to climb, and it's often used as a trial peak for beginners. While most climbs on Mt Adams are nontechnical slogs up a glacier, even these require basic climbing gear. Altitude sickness and severe weather changes are the biggest threats to novice climbers.

The easiest approaches (Grade II) are from the south, via Cold Springs Campground, and up the South Spur to the summit. These approaches are good between May and August. There's a more difficult route (Grade III) from the north over Adams Glacier via Takhlakh Lake Campground. Climbers should sign in and out at the USFS ranger station at either Trout Lake or Randle.

Places to Stay

Near Bird Creek Meadows are three lakeside *campgrounds* (☎ 509-865-2405) in the Yakama Indian Reservation, all with running water and pit toilets. *Bird Lake Campground* and *Mirror Lake Campground* are about 16 miles northeast of Trout Lake on USFS Rd 8290. Two miles farther down this rough road is *Bench Lake*

Campground, with 41 sites and great views of Mt Adams. Be prepared for insect pests during the summer. Sites are $10, payable at Bird Lake.

There's another cluster of *campgrounds* about 25 miles north along USFS Rd 23. The nicest of these forest service facilities is *Takhlakh Lake Campground* (☎ 509-395-3400) with 62 sites, running water and pit toilets. It costs $11 a night.

Serenity's (☎ 509-395-2500, 800-276-7993, fax 509-395-2500,  w3.gorge.net/serenitys, 2291 Hwy 141) Cabins $90-150. A mile south of Trout Lake on Hwy 141, Serenity's offers four luxury cabins in the woods, each with kitchen, bathroom and faux fireplace.

Flying L Ranch (☎ 509-364-3488, 888-682-3287, fax 364-3634,  www.mt adams.com/index.shtml, 25 Flying L Lane) Lodge rooms $70-110, cabins $120-140, including breakfast. The ranch is in Glenwood, 18 miles east of Trout Lake. Midweek, get a discount of 20 percent if you 'fix your own darned breakfast' in the common kitchen.

WASHINGTON

Central Washington

If there are any defining images of central Washington, they may well be an apple tree and an irrigation ditch. There wouldn't be much out here it if weren't for the dams on the Columbia and Yakima Rivers. The resulting irrigation projects have turned this once-barren desert into one of the nation's greatest agricultural areas. There is still plenty of outback country here too, where farmers get by with dry-land wheat farms and a next-year mentality.

Central Washington's geography is dominated by the Columbia River and its dams. This chapter covers the region that the river cuts through, from the eastern slopes of the Cascade Mountains to the steppes of the central plateau.

The long rain shadow cast by the Cascades over the entire area makes for a dry climate and warm summer temperatures. This lack of Pacific-slope gloom has changed a number of communities from agricultural trading centers or mining ghost towns into retirement and recreational communities. The city of Yakima has grown in stature and sophistication as retirees have settled here, and the local wine-making industry now attracts national attention. The Yakima Valley is home to the Yakama Indian Reservation and more apple orchards than you ever imagined possible.

Despite – or perhaps because of – the general aridity of the region, lakes are some of the prime destinations for travelers. The Bavarian village of Leavenworth makes its mark as a replica of an Alpine burg (the concept may be hokey, but the setting is lovely); it's a hub for lots of cross-country skiing, summer hiking and rock climbing, and water sports on nearby Lake Wenatchee. The Potholes is a curious area south of Moses Lake created when irrigation dams flooded desert sand dunes, which remained as islands above the water. Birds flock here, as do canoeists and anglers.

Two highways cross the Cascades from the west side into central Washington. US 2 heads east from Everett and crosses Stevens Pass to Leavenworth, then heads on to Spokane. From Seattle, I-90 cuts across Snoqualmie Pass and leads to Ellensburg, where I-82 splits off and heads south to Yakima, while I-90 continues west to Moses Lake and Spokane.

Highlights

- Rafting the Wenatchee and gobbling down Wiener schnitzel in Leavenworth

- Finishing the long hard climb to Enchantment Lakes

- Sampling chardonnays and cabernets among the vineyards of the Yakima Valley

- Tuning into the voice of Native America at the Yakama Nation's Cultural Center

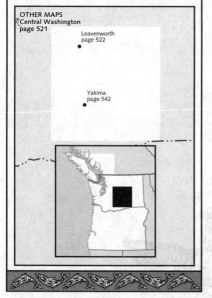

OTHER MAPS
Central Washington page 521

Leavenworth page 522

Yakima page 542

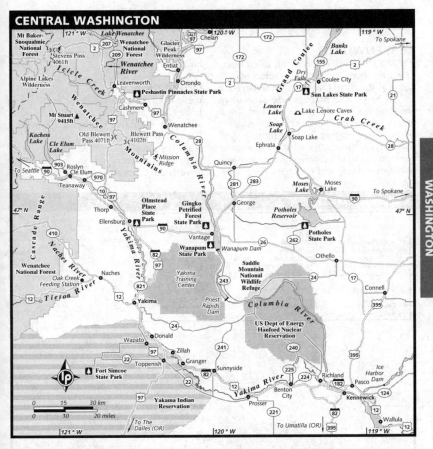

CENTRAL WASHINGTON

Wenatchee River Valley

As the Wenatchee River makes its way east from Lake Wenatchee to the Columbia River, there are remarkable changes in the valley's geography and culture. The area around Lake Wenatchee and Leavenworth is absolutely alpine, craggy and wild. The odd, faux-Bavarian town of Leavenworth itself was remodeled to fit into its landscape and attract visitors for whom the great

mountain and river recreation were not enough of a lure.

Halfway between Leavenworth and Wenatchee is Cashmere, a quiet riverside town, known mostly for its candy factory – Aplets & Cotlets – which produces sugary confections with some fame in the Northwest (every office must get a box of them at Christmas). By the time the Wenatchee River pours into the Columbia River at Wenatchee, the scenery is dominated by apple trees. Wenatchee is the area's urban hub, with an easygoing sort of bustle and lodging that's slightly less expensive than up the road in touristy Leavenworth.

LEAVENWORTH
There are two ways of thinking about Leavenworth (population 2074). Some people see it as the town that went Bavarian back in the '60s – the place where downtown shopkeepers pull on lederhosen and dirndl skirts every morning. Others visualize white-water rafting, rock climbing, and hiking trails. No matter what your point of view, there's so much going on here that just about everybody will find *something* of in-

terest. Leavenworth's spectacular mountain setting – perched 1164 feet above sea level on the east slope of the Cascades, with the Wenatchee River rushing through town – is bound to appeal.

Orientation
Icicle Rd, on the west side of town, traces Icicle Creek south to an assortment of recreational possibilities bordering the Alpine Lakes Wilderness. Another good road to cruise in search of random trailheads, de facto cross-country ski areas or a pretty drive, is the Chumstick Hwy at the east end

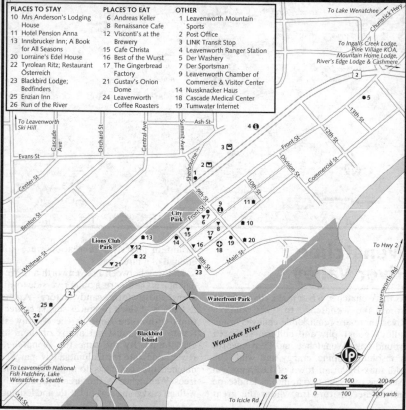

LEAVENWORTH

PLACES TO STAY
10 Mrs Anderson's Lodging House
11 Hotel Pension Anna
13 Innsbrucker Inn; A Book for All Seasons
20 Lorraine's Edel House
22 Tyrolean Ritz; Restaurant Österreich
23 Blackbird Lodge; Bedfinders
25 Enzian Inn
26 Run of the River

PLACES TO EAT
6 Andreas Keller
8 Renaissance Cafe
12 Visconti's at the Brewery
15 Cafe Christa
16 Best of the Wurst
17 The Gingerbread Factory
21 Gustav's Onion Dome
24 Leavenworth Coffee Roasters

OTHER
1 Leavenworth Mountain Sports
2 Post Office
3 LINK Transit Stop
4 Leavenworth Ranger Station
5 Der Washery
7 Der Sportsman
9 Leavenworth Chamber of Commerce & Visitor Center
14 Nussknacker Haus
18 Cascade Medical Center
19 Tumwater Internet

To Lake Wenatchee

To Ingalls Creek Lodge, Pine Village KOA, Mountain Home Lodge, River's Edge Lodge & Cashmere

To Leavenworth Ski Hill

To Hwy 2

To Leavenworth National Fish Hatchery, Lake Wenatchee & Seattle

Waterfront Park

Blackbird Island

Wenatchee River

To Icicle Rd

of town, which heads north along Chumstick Creek, eventually reaching Lake Wenatchee. Blewett Pass is yet another recreation gateway, with plenty of trails and campgrounds to discover off of US 97, south of the junction with US 2.

Information

Drop by the Leavenworth Chamber of Commerce & Visitor Center (☎ 509-548-5807, 220 9th St, ⓦ www.leavenworth.org), in the Obertal Mall. It's open 8am to 5pm Monday to Thursday, until 6pm Friday and Saturday, and 10am to 4pm Sunday. Write them at PO Box 327, Leavenworth, WA 98826. The Leavenworth Ranger Station (☎ 509-548-6977), 600 Sherbourne, off US 2 at the east end of town, provides a wealth of information on recreational opportunities in the Wenatchee National Forest, and issues various types of use permits. It's open 7:30am to 4:30pm daily from June 15 to October 15, and 7:45am to 4:30pm Monday to Friday the rest of the year.

The post office (☎ 509-548-7212) is at 960 Hwy 2, west of the ranger station. A wide selection of regional titles and natural history guides crowd the shelves of A Book for All Seasons (☎ 509-548-1451), 703 Hwy 2. A Starbucks is attached.

Check email at Tumwater Internet, 321 9th St, in the Sonnenhaus Building, open 8am to 8pm Monday to Friday. They charge $2.50 for 15 minutes of access. There's a laundromat, Der Washery, on Front St behind Dan's Market.

Cascade Medical Center (☎ 509-548-5815), 817 Commercial St, is downtown near Waterfront Park.

Bavarian Village

Discover the heart of Leavenworth by cutting south from US 2 onto Front St, which leads into the Bavarian Village. A wander through this ersatz alpine community, with its steeply pitched roofs, painted flower boxes and endless gift shops can be enjoyable and amusing. (Cynics may say otherwise, but we'll let a generous spirit prevail.) If you're inspired to buy a Bavarian souvenir, stop by the *Nussknacker Haus* (☎ 509-548-4708, 735 Front St), which spe-

cializes in nutcracker dolls. Upstairs is a museum displaying hundreds of handmade nutcrackers, many created by European craftsmen. The *Gingerbread Factory (☎ 509-548-6592, 828 Commercial St)* is worth a stop for a snack and an earful of local gossip.

If you'd rather stroll than shop, pocket an extra gingerbread muffin and head down 9th St to **Waterfront Park**. Paths trace the riverside and a footbridge crosses over to Blackbird Island, at the park's west end, where Icicle Creek meets the Wenatchee River. On a clear day, there are great views of Sleeping Lady Mountain, up Icicle Canyon southwest of town. To finish off a walking tour, return to town via 8th St for more food and gifts.

Leavenworth National Fish Hatchery

When the construction of the Grand Coulee Dam blocked salmon from migrating to their upstream spawning grounds, the government tried to ameliorate the loss of these populations by building hatcheries downstream from the dam. Of three such complexes set on tributaries of the Columbia, the largest is at Leavenworth (☎ 509-548-7641, 12790 Fish Hatchery Rd; donation; self-guided tours 8am-4pm). Some 1.6 million spring Chinook salmon are reared each year at the Leavenworth hatchery, off Icicle Rd. The young smolt are released into Icicle Creek and migrate to the Pacific in late spring, when the rivers are running full force. Between May and July, adult Chinook return to the hatchery to spawn, which they're ready to do in late August (see Special Events, later, for details on the Salmon Festival).

From the hatchery, hike the mile-long **Icicle Creek Interpretive Trail** and learn about the local ecology and history.

Hiking

Wildfires struck Icicle Ridge during the summer of 2001, near the same area that had begun to recover from a major 1994 burn. Trails have since reopened, but barren stands of charred forest still remain along the Icicle drainage.

Be sure to pick up a Northwest Forest Pass at the Leavenworth Ranger Station or

Going Bavarian

Leavenworth grew up as a railroad town, and when the Great Northern re-routed its tracks in the 1920s, bypassing the town, Leavenworth foundered. It wasn't long before the other substantial local business, the sawmill, closed, leaving the town badly equipped to handle the Great Depression. Downtown was pretty much boarded up for a few decades.

A local tourism committee, seeking to rejuvenate their town, noted that the California town of Solvang had done well by emphasizing its Danish heritage. A fair number of Russian Germans had pioneered much of eastern Washington, and the mountain setting seemed alpine enough to support a little Bavaria.

Though it took considerable boosterism to get the community to go along with the scheme, economics won out, and in the 1960s Leavenworth's downtown began to lay on the frills. Who would've guessed that busloads of tourists would one day jam the streets of this unlikely milltown, just for a day of eating sausages and snapping photos of accordion players?

Leavenworth Mountain Sports (see Skiing, later) if you intend to park at any of the trailheads.

Walk up Icicle Creek, past waterfalls, pools and little beaches on the easy 3½ mile **Icicle Gorge Loop Trail**. Catch the trail at the Chatter Creek Guard Station, 16 miles up Icicle Rd. Another easy trail along the creek begins at the end of Icicle Rd and follows the valley bottom through an old-growth forest. The trail continues deep into the Alpine Lakes Wilderness (see Around Leavenworth, below), but you can turn around at French Creek, 1½ miles from the trailhead, for an easy day hike.

In the Blewett Pass area off US 97, Ingalls Creek is strewn with big boulders and swimming holes. A trail follows the valley bottom for miles, with half a dozen tributary trails feeding into it. Pick up the Ingalls Creek trailhead at the end of Ingalls Creek Rd, about 7 miles south of US 2.

Skiing

Rent cross-country skis, snowboards and anything else you may need on your way to the slopes from **Leavenworth Mountain Sports** (☎ 509-548-7864, Ⓦ www.leavenworthmtnsports.com, 940 Hwy 2; packages

adult/child $15/11 per day), or **Der Sportsman** (☎ 509-548-5623, 800-548-4145, 837 Front St). Both outfitters also offer ski instruction at $25 per hour for two people.

A mile north of town, **Leavenworth Ski Hill** (☎ 509-548-6975; open Wed, Fri-Sun late Dec-Feb; lift tickets $9) has downhill skiing on two groomed hills equipped with rope tows. Food and drink are available at the Ski Hill Lodge.

The **Leavenworth Winter Sports Club** (☎ 509-548-5477, Nordic conditions ☎ 509-548-5115, Ⓦ www.skileavenworth.com) maintains 15 miles of groomed cross-country ski trails in three areas in and around Leavenworth. There are 5 miles of mostly level trails at Icicle River. Another trail starts downtown at Waterfront Park and continues along the Wenatchee River to a pair of loops around the public golf course. East of the alpine ski area, the Ski Hill Trail offers views and a 3-mile stretch that's lit for night skiing. An $8 daily pass lets you use any of the trails in the system; children under 13 and seniors over 69 ski free.

The state's second-largest downhill venue is 37 miles west of town on US 2 at **Stevens Pass** (☎ 206-812-4510, snow report ☎ 509-782-5516, Ⓦ www.stevenspass.com; Summit

Stevens Pass US Hwy 2; adult/youth/senior lift tickets $43/27/30). The resort features 37 runs, 11 lifts and a vertical drop of 1800 feet. When conditions permit, several lifts are open for night skiing until 10pm. Rentals and classes are readily available.

Stevens Pass also maintains 25 miles of groomed cross-country ski trails (daily pass $12/8 adult/child & senior). Rentals and snacks are available at the **Nordic Center** *(☎ 206-812-4510; open 9am-4pm Fri-Sun & holidays),* which is 5 miles east of the downhill ski area.

Rafting

Leavenworth's close proximity to the Wenatchee River makes it a popular destination for adventure-deprived urbanites. The uppermost stretch of the river, from Lake Wenatchee to Tumwater Campground, is an easy 19-mile, day-long float in a kayak or raft. The water is highest in May and June, when snowmelt contributes generously, but there is more wildlife (including salmon) in and around the river in September and October. All but expert kayakers should be sure to pull out at Tumwater Campground, as the next stretch of the Wenatchee to Leavenworth roils with rapids, big drops and sucking holes.

The following outfitters offer day trips on the river's third and most popular stretch – the 18½ miles from Leavenworth to Monitor. This section of the Wenatchee is typically run April to July, and its waves and holes earn it a Class III rating. Prices range from $50 to $75.

All Rivers Adventures (☎ 509-782-2254, 800-743-5628, **w** www.allrivers.com) PO Box 12, Cashmere, WA 98815

Leavenworth Outfitters Outdoor Center (☎ 509-763-3733, 800-347-7934, **w** www.thrillmakers .com) 21312 Hwy 207, Leavenworth, WA 98826

Osprey Rafting Co (☎ 509-548-6800, 800-743-6269, **w** www.shoottherapids.com) 4342 Icicle Rd, PO Box 668, Leavenworth, WA 98826

Climbing

In Tumwater Canyon, **Castle Rock** is a popular rock-climbing area, partly because of its easy access – it's only about 3 miles

northwest of town off US 2. A nice day will find rock climbers creeping up a cluster of 200-foot sandstone spires at **Peshastin Pinnacles State Park** *(☎ 509-664-6373, North Dryden Rd, 2 miles west of Cashmere; open 6:30am-dusk mid-Apr–mid-Oct).* Link bus No 22, between Leavenworth and Wenatchee, stops near the park.

Serious climbers will no doubt focus on the Alpine Lakes Wilderness, where challenging rock climbing requires a USFS permit (for details, see the Alpine Lakes Wilderness section, later). To reach climbs on the **Snow Creek Wall**, including Orbit (rated 5.8) and Outer Space (rated 5.9), follow the Snow Lakes Trail around 2½ miles through a dismal burn into the Enchantment Lakes area. Rather than climbing all the way to the lakes, you should turn off onto the climbers' path where the trail and Snow Creek approach the steep wall.

Leavenworth Mountain Sports (see Skiing, earlier) rents rock shoes, harnesses and other climbing gear.

Bicycling

Road bikers can decide if they're up to the 50-mile Leavenworth-Lake Wenatchee Loop. The hilly ride goes up Chumstick Hwy to the lake, then returns to town via Hwy 207 and US 2. It's not for the easily fatigued. When there's no snow on Ski Hill, this area just northwest of town becomes 'mountain bike hill.' Two loop trails, used for cross-country skiing in the winter, are open to bikers and hikers in the summer.

Several roads in the Icicle Creek area, off Icicle Rd, have become popular mountain-biking destinations. The USFS ranger station has information on suggested loops and routes in this area, as well as trips through the Chumstick, Blewett Pass and Mission Creek/Devil's Gulch areas. **Leavenworth Outfitters Outdoor Center** *(☎ 509-763-3733, 800-347-7934, 21312 Hwy 207),* near Lake Wenatchee, rents bikes and has a shuttle service (rental & shuttle $45).

Other Activities

North of Leavenworth, both Lake Wenatchee and nearby Fish Lake are popular

fishing spots, notably for Kokanee salmon and rainbow and cutthroat trout. Of the rivers and streams in the area, only Icicle Creek, up to Leland Creek, remains open to fishing (anglers must use a single barbless hook and no bait). Check with Der Sportsman (see Skiing, earlier) to find out current restrictions or to hire a guide.

Capitalizing on the Bavarian theme, **Red-Tail Canyon Farm** (☎ 509-548-4512, 800-678-4512, 11780 Freund Canyon Rd), about 2½ miles up the Chumstick Hwy, gives rides in old-fashioned sleighs drawn by Belgian draft horses during the winter months, and **hay rides** at all other times of the year (adult/child $12/6).

The **Eagle Creek Ranch** (☎ 509-548-7798, 800-221-7433, W www.eaglecreek.ws, 7951 Eagle Creek Rd) has **horseback riding** with trail rides ranging from 1½ hours to six hours ($26-80). **Icicle Outfitters & Guides Inc** (☎ 800-497-3912, cell phone 509-669-1518) offers more extensive four- to seven-day pack trips.

Special Events

Whenever there's a festival, lodgings fill up, so don't count on rolling into town without a reservation.

Spring comes late to Leavenworth, but by mid-May it's time to dance around a May pole, listen to 'oompah' music and flirt with strolling accordion players. During the Maifest there's a parade and a Saturday night street dance, both of which jam the streets of the Bavarian Village. Though some locals call the Maifest 'snooty,' plenty of people make annual oompah pilgrimages.

Leavenworth heralds the arrival of summer with the International Accordion Celebration (☎ 509-548-5807) in late June. Look for squeezebox competitions, workshops and jam sessions. The Leavenworth Fish Hatchery is the site of the Wenatchee River Salmon Festival in late September, which celebrates the return of thousands of salmon to the Wenatchee River. Field trips, including wetlands ecology tours and fishing clinics, are part of the festival.

Leavenworth looks great at Christmas time, and makes the most of the season by holding Christmas tree-lighting festivals during the first three weekends of December. There's usually a good bit of snow on the ground, and plenty of opportunity for organized snowman-building contests and sleigh rides.

Places to Stay

The tourist season peaks in the summer and picks up again around Christmas. At most places, off-season rates drop at least a little bit. If Leavenworth is all booked up or seems too expensive, try Wenatchee, where there are plenty of motel rooms in the $50-60 range. Cheap public transportation links the two towns (see Getting There & Away, later).

Camping There are scads of campgrounds around Leavenworth, making it easy to avoid expensive in-town accommodations. Of course, winter is hard and long hereabouts, so don't plan on camping from November to April. Icicle Rd and Blewett Pass (on US 97 south of US 2) are the main camping corridors. There's more camping north at Lake Wenatchee.

Tumwater Campground (☎ 509-548-6977, reservations ☎ 800-274-6104, Hwy 2, 10 miles northwest of Leavenworth) Sites $12. This is a convenient spot between Leavenworth and Lake Wenatchee. It's about what you'd expect from a busy roadside spot: flush toilets, running water and crowds.

Up Icicle Road there are seven *USFS campgrounds* (☎ 509-548-6977), all with hand-pumped well water, pit toilets, firewood for sale and fees of $8 to $10. *Eightmile Campground* (reservations ☎ 800-274-6104) is the closest to Leavenworth with 45 sites and access to the Enchantment Lakes area. *Johnny Creek Campground*, 12½ miles up, is in a beautiful forested spot with sites right on Icicle Creek. *Blackpine Campground*, 19 miles from US 2 at the end of Icicle Rd, has facilities for horse packers.

Pine Village KOA Kampground (☎ 509-548-7709, 800-562-5709, 11401 River Bend Rd) Tent/RV sites/cabins $26/33/49. Pine Village is a mile east of Leavenworth, just north of US 2. RV and tent sites and camping cabins are spread among pine trees and come with various extras: hay rides, shuttle to Leavenworth, coffee and firewood.

Blu-Shastin RV Resort (☎ 509-548-4184, 888-548-4184, ⓦ www.blushastin.com, 3300 US 97) Tent/RV sites $20/25. Open year-round. More rustic than the KOA, Blu-Shastin is a tranquil creekside spot with 86 hookups, a pool and a horseshoe pitch. It's on the way down to Blewett Pass, 7 miles south of US 2.

B&Bs There are a few B&Bs in the area.

Mrs Anderson's Lodging House (☎ 509-548-6173, 800-253-8990, ⓦ www.quilters heaven.com, 917 Commercial St) Rooms with shared/private bath $47-52/58-73. Right downtown above a quilters shop, this charming longtime inn has some of the least expensive accommodations you'll find. Rooms are decorated with antique furniture and vintage clothing and named for the quilt pattern on display. A light breakfast (muffins, granola, juice) is included.

Lorraine's Edel House Inn (☎ 509-548-4412, 800-487-3335, ⓦ lorrainesedelhouse .com, 320 9th St) Rooms/cottage suite $60/85. This attractive century-old inn is just across from Waterfront Park. Though it's not technically a B&B (no breakfast is served), you do get a 50% discount on dinner at the inn's restaurant – which is, incidentally, one of the best in town.

Innsbrucker Inn (☎ 509-548-5401, fax 548-2062, ⓦ home.earthlink.net/~abookfor, 703 Hwy 2) Room/suite $75/105. Upstairs from the bookstore, the Innsbrucker is also known as the Inn of the Six Authors: each of the six rooms reflects the character of a different literary figure.

Run of the River (☎ 509-548-7171, 800-288-6491, fax 509-548-7547, ⓦ www.runofthe river.com, 9308 E Leavenworth Rd) This out-doorsy inn forgoes Bavarian style in favor of traditional Northwest hewn-log decor. It's on the other side of the Icicle River from Leavenworth – take Hwy 2 south, turn right at East Leavenworth Road and drive 1 mile. The recently remodeled suites have jacuzzis and river rock fireplaces; private decks are equipped with binoculars for bird and

wildlife viewing. Mountain bikes and snow-shoes are provided for guests' use. Terrifically friendly hosts Monty and Karen share their knowledge of the valley.

Hotels Budget lodgings are hard to come by in Leavenworth.

River's Edge Lodge (☎ 509-548-7612, 800-451-5285, 8401 US 2) Doubles $62-77. Somewhat removed from the Bavarian milieu, River's Edge is 3½ miles east of town on the road to Wenatchee. Some of the standard motel rooms here have kitchens and all have balconies facing the wide and rushing Wenatchee River.

Tyrolean Ritz (☎ 509-548-5455, 800-854-6365, 633 Front St) Doubles $70-95, suites $85-150. If you want to get into the thick of things, stay at the Tyrolean Ritz, a 1903 inn with old-world romantic furnishings in the heart of the Bavarian village, though perhaps its most attractive feature is the rear sundeck. Downstairs is the classy Restaurant Österreich.

Hotel Pension Anna (☎ 509-548-6273, 800-509-2662, fax 509-548-4656, ⓦ www.pen sionanna.com, 926 Commercial St) Rooms $99-109, suites $189-199. A particularly charming variation on the alpine theme, this chalet-style inn is elegantly furnished with Austrian antiques. An old renovated chapel now holds two luxury suites. Rates include a traditional breakfast.

Blackbird Lodge (☎ 509-548-5800, 800-446-0240, ⓦ www.blackbirdlodge.com, 305 8th St) Rooms $99-119, suites $145-189. Spacious rooms have fireplaces and balconies overlooking Blackbird Island at this tasteful, non-kitschy European-style lodge. Breakfast is discreetly delivered to your room.

Enzian Inn (☎ 509-548-5269, 800-223-8511, ⓦ www.enzianinn.com, 590 Hwy 2) Singles/doubles $90/100. This motel puts a Bavarian spin on standard business hotel amenities. Along with the exercise room, indoor/outdoor pools and hot tubs, you get an Alphorn concert with the breakfast buffet and cross country skis at no charge.

Ingalls Creek Lodge (☎ 509-548-6281, 3003 US 97) Rooms $45. On the road to Blewett Pass, a mile from the Ingalls Creek

Trailhead, this makes a convenient base for hiking and hunting. Good, comfy rooms have cable TV, and home-cooked food is served Thursday to Monday in the attached restaurant.

Resorts Here's a place for a splurge.

Mountain Home Lodge (☎ 509-548-7077, 800-414-2378, fax 509-548-5008, **W** www.mt home.com, 8201 Mountain Home Rd) Rooms $270-360, cabins $455. The lodge, 3 miles east of and 1000 feet above Leavenworth, enjoys a truly awesome perch, looking over a 20-acre meadow to the Cascades' Stuart range. Handsome accommodations are done up in rugged Northwest splendor with handmade quilts and locally crafted furniture. Since it's snowbound in winter, rates include Snowcat transport from Leavenworth and gourmet meals (two nights minimum), as well as cross-country skis and snowshoes for the miles of trails in the vicinity. In the summer, rates are about $150 less but sack lunch multi-course dinner are extra.

Vacation-Home Rentals Booking services offer a bevy of vacation-home and condominium referrals. Try *Bedfinders* (☎ 509-548-4410, 800-323-2920, **W** www.bedfinders.com, c/o Blackbird Lodge, 305 8th St) or *Destination Leavenworth* (☎ 509-548-4230, 866-904-7368, fax 509-548-4801, **W** www.destination leavenworth.com, 940 Hwy 2, Suite A-1).

Places to Eat

No trip to Leavenworth is complete without a plate of schnitzel or sauerbraten at one of the village's gemütliche eateries.

Best of the Wurst (☎ 509-548-7580, 220 8th St) Sausages under $5. Authentic bratwurst, bockwurst and other grilled sausages are prepared at this sidewalk food stall.

Gustav's Onion Dome (☎ 509-548-4509, 617 US 2) Sausages & sandwiches $5-6. Gustav's has a rooftop beer garden and lots of Northwest brews on tap (including their own Icicle Ale) to complement the sausages and deli sandwiches.

Andreas Keller (☎ 509-548-6000, 829 Front St) Sausages $8, average entrees $13. This basement rathskeller achieves a genuine Oktoberfest atmosphere, complete with a lederhosen-clad accordionist leading a rousing medley of drinking songs. Bring an appetite to best appreciate the array of wieners, sauerkraut and spätzle (noodles) served here.

Cafe Christa (☎ 509-548-5074, upstairs 801 Front St) Lunch $7-9, dinner $14-18. Good service, Mitteleuropa decor and balcony seating complement the schweinebraten (sliced pork roast) and bratwurst for a pleasant sunset dinner. Order a stein of Munich lager for the full effect.

Restaurant Österreich (☎ 509-548-4031, 633A Front St) Entrees $18-30. Dinner Wed-Sun. Below the Tyrolean Ritz Hotel, the most elegant of the Bavarian specialty establishments emphasizes delicate combinations of herbs and seasonings rather than sausages and meats. Specials include regional fish and game.

It's not all sauerkraut and strudel – plenty of restaurants offer a counterpoint to the overriding theme.

Homefires Bakery (☎ 509-548-7362, 13013 Bayne Rd) Cookies 85¢, breads $2-3. Open 9am-5pm Thur-Mon. After the fish hatchery tour, cross the road and pick up whole grain breads, cinnamon rolls and sticky buns here.

Leavenworth Coffee Roasters (☎ 509-548-1428, 220 W Hwy 2) Coffee $2-3. The beans are blended, roasted and served at this cheery cafe on the west end of town.

Renaissance Café (☎ 509-548-6725, 217 8th St) Entrees $5-7. Tofu scrambles, granola and wraps are the specialties here. Or you can design your own omelet from a list of 21 ingredients. The Renaissance also packages lunch to go for hikers, kayakers, skiers or horseback riders.

Lorraine's Edel House (☎ 509-548-4412, 320 9th St) Entrees $12-18. Open daily from 5pm. Lorraine's features Northwest-influenced international cuisine, including nightly salmon variations ($16), in a candlelit ambiance.

Visconti's at the Brewery (☎ 509-548-1213, 636 Front St) Dinners $9-13. This classic Italian restaurant has joined forces with Leavenworth's brewery to create a multi-level food and drink complex. Order up a Dirtyface Stout, Escape Altbier or Blind Pig Dunkelweizen at the casual pub (no theme attached) or enjoy a range of pastas and antipasti in the more formal upper-level dining room. Free brewery tours start at 2pm daily.

Entertainment

Leavenworth Summer Theater (☎ 509-548-2000 box office, Hwy 2 & Icicle Rd) Shows July-Aug. Tickets $12-20. No trip to Washington's little Bavaria is quite complete without attending a full-length production of *The Sound of Music,* performed against an alpine backdrop at the Ski Hill Amphitheater. Other Broadway standards are staged at the fish hatchery.

Getting There & Around

Northwestern Trailways buses stop in Leavenworth twice daily on their way between Seattle ($24, three hours) and Wenatchee ($7, 40 minutes). The bus stop is on Hwy 2 by the post office. Call ☎ 800-366-3830 (in Washington only) for schedules.

Link Transit (☎ 509-662-1155, W www.link transit.com) bus No 22 passes up US 2 between Leavenworth and Wenatchee ($1, 50 minutes), via Peshastin and Cashmere, 18 times daily Monday to Friday (no weekend service). In Leavenworth, the bus stops on Hwy 2, just east of the post office. These buses are equipped with bike racks in summer. Pick up a schedule from the visitor center.

AROUND LEAVENWORTH
Alpine Lakes Wilderness

The Alpine Lakes Wilderness, 614 sq miles of pieced-together lands, got its patchwork shape from a history of mining and railroad land grants. It is best known for its Enchantment Lakes area, an especially compelling region with glacier-carved cirques and reflective alpine pools accessible from Icicle Canyon. Though more than 100,000 people visit the Alpine Lakes Wilderness each year, its most magical destinations are much farther than a casual day-hike. Steep climbs and scrabbly trails demand intermediate-level backpacking skills and top physical condition. October brings fabulous displays of fall color, when the coniferous subalpine larch turns bright yellow and loses its needles like leaf-bearing trees.

You can reach one of the **Enchantment Lakes Trailheads** by heading out of Leavenworth on Icicle Rd (USFS Rd 7600) to Snow Creek, just a couple of miles past the fish hatchery. Hike in (it's an arduous ascent) past Nada and Snow Lakes (5½ and 6¾ miles, respectively), and continue to climb to the basins dotted with the high Enchantment Lakes (10 miles from and 4200 feet above the trailhead).

Another entrance to the Alpine Lakes Wilderness begins on a dirt road just north of Tumwater Campground on US 2. Turn west from the highway to the **Chiwaukum Creek Trailhead** and hike the road for 1½ miles until you hit the wilderness boundary. Once you're on the trail, a pine and Douglas-fir forest shades the creek as far as a trail junction, 5½ miles in. The right-hand fork (trail No 1591) continues up Chiwaukum Creek through increasingly patchy forest, giving way to meadows and, ultimately, to Chiwaukum and other alpine lakes. The hike to the trail's fork is a reasonable day hike; allow at least two days for a roundtrip hike to the lakes.

Due to heavy use of this fragile area, the USFS levies a nonrefundable fee of $3 per day for overnight trips to the Enchantment Lakes between June 15 and October 15. Reservations for permits may be made by mail beginning March 1, and you'll definitely want to make one as there's lots of competition. (The chance of getting a permit is better with a midweek departure.) Pick up a reservation application at the Leavenworth Ranger Station (see Information in the Leavenworth section, earlier) or go to the website (W www.fs.fed.us/r6/wenatchee) to print out a copy. (Applications must be postmarked no earlier than February 21.) Not all is lost if you're beaten out of the reservation pool, since 25% of the permits are reserved for same-day use and are distributed in a daily lottery.

Lake Wenatchee

Swimming, boating and fishing await summertime visitors to Lake Wenatchee, 23 miles north of the city of Wenatchee and actually much closer to Leavenworth. You can also hike the 4½-mile trail up Dirtyface Peak, cycle around the lake, or sign on with one of the rafting companies on Hwy 207 for a float trip.

Once there's snow on the ground, Lake Wenatchee becomes a great cross-country ski area, with 20 miles of marked and groomed trails, though skiers may have to dodge weekend snowmobilers. More trails crisscross the Lower Chiwawa River area off the Chumstick Highway, including a 5-mile scenic loop trail (closed to snowmobiles) that follows the Wenatchee River. Roadside signs indicate Sno-Parks – buy a Sno-Park pass for parking in recreational areas ($8/20 day/season) at any local grocery or sporting goods store.

There are two good routes to the lake: either head north on Chumstick Hwy or take US 2 west of town, then turn north onto Hwy 207. Get maps and details at the Lake Wenatchee Ranger Station (☎ 509-763-3103) at 22976 Hwy 207, open 8am to 4:30pm Monday to Friday, plus Saturday in summer).

Aside from the campgrounds listed here, you'll find several primitive no-fee camps along the White and Little Wenatchee rivers to the west, and others requiring a Northwest Forest Pass along the Chiwawa Valley north of the lake.

Lake Wenatchee State Park (☎ *509-763-3101, 888-226-7688, Cedar Brae Rd & Hwy 207*) Sites $14. Open year-round. The Wenatchee River runs through the campground, dividing it into two 100-site sections (no hookups). The more wooded north campground has trail access to the lake and river, while the south campground offers a lovely swimming beach right on the mountain-fringed lake and a busy day-use area. There's a boat launch, a bathhouse and camp store, along with evening ranger talks on Saturdays in the summer, and a concession for renting horses.

Glacier View Campground (☎ *509-763-3103, Cedar Brae Rd*) Sites $10. If you want more serenity, head around to the lake's south shore to this smaller, lakeside USFS campground with pit toilets and running water.

A handful of secluded resorts along Hwy 207 make great hideaways for ski vacations.

Pine River Ranch (☎ *509-763-3959, 800-669-3877,* W *www.prranch.com, 19668 Hwy 207*) Suites $160-170. Luxury suites with river rock fireplaces, whirlpool baths and VCRs occupy a lovely old farmhouse and a couple of duplex cottages. Guests are loaned snowshoes and skis for the private groomed trails that traverse the 32-acre ranch.

Mountain Springs Lodge (☎ *509-763-2713, 800-858-2276,* W *www.mtsprings.com, 19115 Chiwawa Loop Rd*) Rooms $99, cabins & suites $175-225. These similarly upscale rooms and lodges (they don't call them cabins here) occupy a secluded meadow not far from Lake Wenatchee. Hot tubs, snowmobile tours, barbecues and horseback riding await lodge guests.

Henry M Jackson Wilderness

Named after the Washington senator responsible for designating much of the state's wilderness area, the Henry M Jackson Wilderness straddles the Cascades Crest, north of US 2 and south of the Glacier Peak Wilderness Area. Head up the headwaters of the Little Wenatchee River for some great hiking. From Leavenworth, trailheads are best reached via Lake Wenatchee; continue on Hwy 207 past the head of the lake to USFS Rd 6500. Follow this road up the Little Wenatchee, take the right fork at Riverside Campground and continue to Little Wenatchee Ford Campground at road's end, where there are four trails to choose from.

Three of the four trails here – **Cady Pass, Cady Ridge** and **Little Wenatchee River** trails – eventually hook up with the **Pacific**

Crest Trail, making good loops for a two- or three-day backpacking trip. Day-hikers should choose the **Little Wenatchee Trail**, which follows the river for about 5 miles before climbing to a wildflower meadow. After about a quarter of a mile down this trail, a fourth trail branches off and heads up to great views at the top of **Poe Mountain**. Keep an eye peeled along the roadside for soapstone deposits; if you want to pocket more than a rock or two, get a mineral permit from the Lake Wenatchee Ranger Station.

WENATCHEE

All over the Northwest, folks who hear 'Wenatchee' will predictably free-associate the name with 'apples.' That's the way it's been since central Washington's semi-arid lands were reclaimed for apple orchards between 1890 and 1900, and that's the way it's likely to stay. As if to prove it, the Washington Apple Commission Visitors Center is right there as you roll into town, ready to toast you with swigs of cider.

Although the Wenatchee River valley has a history of Native American settlement stretching back at least 11,000 years, the area's development as an agricultural center began quite recently. A Father De-Grassi, who taught farming to the Wenatchee tribe, is credited as being the first person to irrigate the valley. More small-scale irrigation projects started before the beginning of the 20th century, when farmers began to divert river water through ditches in their fields. In 1903 the Highline Canal carried water from west of Cashmere all the way to East Wenatchee. Within a few years, young fruit trees were growing everywhere that ditch water could reach. Once the trees matured, Wenatchee (population 27,856) became the certified center of the apple world, and today nearly half the state's apple crop is produced in the Wenatchee Valley.

Orientation & Information

Wenatchee is in almost the exact center of Washington. The Wenatchee River comes in from the northwest, the Columbia River from the north, and the confluence of the two rivers is at the north end of town. To the east and west are hills topped with the remains of ancient volcanoes (Saddle Rock, Black Rock and Castle Rock). Hwys 97 and US 2 follow the Wenatchee River from Leavenworth, 22 miles to the west, bypassing the city to the north and continuing up the east side of the Columbia to Chelan, 38 miles north. Alt US 97 goes up the west side of the Columbia to Lake Chelan. At the confluence, Hwy 285 spurs off Hwy 2 and runs southeast as Wenatchee Ave through a strip-malled zone to the center of town. Two vehicle bridges and a pedestrian bridge over the Columbia connect Wenatchee with its sister city of East Wenatchee.

Stop by the Wenatchee Valley Convention & Visitors Bureau (☎ 509-663-3723, 800-572-7753, **w** www.wenatcheevalley.org), at 116 N Wenatchee Ave, for information and walking tour maps of Wenatchee's historic buildings and public art. Wenatchee National Forest Headquarters (☎ 509-662-4335), 215 Melody Lane, is north of town at the junction of Hwy 285 and US 2.

The *Wenatchee World* newspaper is published daily except Sunday. KNWR broadcasts Northwest Public Radio at 90.7 FM. For medical emergencies go to Central Washington Hospital (☎ 509-662-1511), 1300 Fuller St.

The downtown post office is at 301 Yakima St. Internet access is at Computer Park Café (☎ 509-667-9337), 518 N Wenatchee Ave. Browse the shelves for eastern Washington history and nature titles at The Book Store (☎ 509-667-9809), 120 N Wenatchee Ave.

Things to See & Do

Downtown, the **Wenatchee Valley Museum & Cultural Center** *(☎ 509-664-3340, 127 S Mission St; adult/child $3/1; open 10am-4pm Mon-Sat; closed major holidays)* distinguishes itself from other historical museums by its apple heritage exhibits, model trains and good visiting shows.

Go for a taste of apple culture and maybe a nibble of the valley's latest crop at the **Washington Apple Commission Visitors Center** *(☎ 509-662-3090, 2900 Euclid Ave; admission free; open 8am-5pm Mon-Fri,*

WASHINGTON

9am-5pm Sat, 10am-4pm Sun May-Dec), near the Wenatchee Confluence State Park at the northern edge of town. It's obviously an industry effort, but this is a good place to learn how apples are grown, picked and processed.

As clear a testament to irrigation as the valley's apple trees are the **Ohme Gardens** *(☎ 509-662-5785,* w *www.ohmegardens.com, 3327 Ohme Rd; adult/child $6/3; open 9am-6pm spring & fall, 9am-7pm summer).* Carved into a bluff high above the confluence of the Wenatchee and Columbia Rivers, these 9 acres of terraced alpine gardens were coaxed out of the barren rock by a locally prominent family as a getaway. It's easy to spend a couple of peaceful hours in this cool oasis, wandering through the gardens and peering down at the Columbia River. It's 3 miles north of town via Alt US 97.

The Columbia widens into flat and glassy Lake Entiat above **Rocky Reach Dam**. The public power facility has been developed for recreation, with 38 acres of landscaped grounds, a playground and large picnic area. Migrating salmon swimming up fish ladders can be observed from a viewing room inside the visitor center *(☎ 509-667-4206, 7 miles N of Wenatchee on Alt US 97; admission free; open 8am-4pm mid-Feb–Nov, till 6pm Apr-Oct).* However, the thing the kids will remember most is chasing the resident rabbits across the lawn. (As a security measure, the history and electricity museums inside the powerhouse will remain indefinitely closed to the public.)

Riverfront Park stretches along the Columbia River on the edge of downtown Wenatchee – don't be surprised to hear machinery clanking as you **stroll, cycle** or **rollerblade** along this rather industrial stretch of the river. Any number of downtown streets lead to the park: head down 5th St to come out by the skating rink, or go down Orondo Ave to reach the boat launch. Once on the trail, head north to Wenatchee Confluence State Park, or south to reach a footbridge across to East Wenatchee, where the trail continues along the Columbia's somewhat more pastoral east bank to form a 10-mile recreation loop. Rent bikes or in-line skates at **Arlberg Sports** *(☎ 509-663-7401, 25 N Wenatchee Ave),* next to the Convention Center (half-day/overnight bikes $8/10; skates $10/12).

If you feel like **ice skating**, go to the **Riverfront Park Ice Arena** *(☎ 509-664-3396, 2 5th St; $4; open daily Oct-Mar).*

Downhill skiers covet the dry powder covering the slopes of **Mission Ridge** *(☎ 509-663-6543, 888-757-4343, snow report ☎ 509-663-3200,* w *www.missionridge.com; full-day lift tickets adult/student & senior $37/22; open 9am-4pm Wed-Sun Dec-early Apr).* Located 12 miles southwest of Wenatchee, the relatively uncrowded resort features a vertical drop of 2200 feet and 35 runs with four lifts and two rope-tows. SkiLINK buses run between Wenatchee and the ski area weekends and holidays, departing from Columbia Station at 8:15am and 9:45am (roundtrip/one-way $3/2).

Golfers will find a particularly challenging championship 18-hole course at **Desert Canyon** *(☎ 509-784-1111, Hwy 97 & Brays Rd; green fees $55-75),* 12 miles north of East Wenatchee in Orondo.

Special Events

Wenatchee's big hoopla is the Washington State Apple Blossom Festival (☎ 509-662-3616). Parades, a crafts show, a carnival, concerts, dances, a swim meet, a 10K run and the crowning of the Apple Queen make the first week of May a busy time in Wenatchee. The other big event is the Ridge-to-River Relay (☎ 509-662-8799), a 35-mile foot, ski, bike, canoe and kayak race from Mission Ridge to Wenatchee. It's held just before the Apple Blossom Festival, around the third weekend in April.

Places to Stay

A number of campgrounds on the Columbia River are well-developed to meet the needs (and lifestyles) of boaters, and feature flush toilets, showers, RV hookups and boat launches.

Wenatchee Confluence State Park *(☎ 509-664-6373, reservations ☎ 888-226-7688, 333 Olds Station Rd)* Tent/RV sites $14/20. The park is divided in two by the Wenatchee

River where it flows into the Columbia. The campground, with 51 hookups and eight standard sites, is on the north bank. It's an ideal spot for active travelers: besides the swimming beach, there are athletic fields, tennis and basketball courts and 4½ miles of trails. Follow signs from US 2 or US 97 at the north end of town to reach the park in a well-marked but roundabout way.

Lincoln Rock State Park (☎ 509-884-8702, reservations ☎ 888-226-7688, 13253 US 2) Tent/RV sites $14/20. Overlooking Lake Entiat, just above the Rocky Reach Dam, this park is named for a craggy formation across the lake that sort of looks like Honest Abe if you use your imagination. In addition to the 67 hookups and 27 standard sites, there's a popular day use area with basketball courts, a horseshoe pitch and swimming beach. Summer reservations are a must.

If ever there was a motel strip, N Wenatchee Ave is it. Some of the city's best motels are here, cheek-by-jowl with no-frills budget places. Wenatchee does bake in the summer, so even the cheapest motels have swimming pools. The following are listed from downtown up, along Wenatchee Ave.

WestCoast Wenatchee Center Hotel (☎ 509-662-1234, 800-426-0670, fax 509-662-0782, ☒ www.westcoasthotels.com/wenatchee, 201 N Wenatchee Ave) Rooms $89-94. Wenatchee's premier franchise is connected to the Convention Center by sky-bridge. A good rooftop restaurant and fitness center are among the usual conventioneer-oriented amenities.

Welcome Inn (☎ 509-663-7121, 800-561-8856, fax 509-664-3799, 232 N Wenatchee Ave) Singles/doubles $40/50. Opposite the convention center, Wenatchee's cheapest place is also one of the friendliest, with microwaves and mini-fridges in its recently remodeled rooms.

Holiday Lodge (☎ 509-663-8167, 800-722-0852, 610 N Wenatchee Ave) Singles/doubles $40/50 including breakfast. Though well maintained, the rooms at this older motel could use an upgrade. There's a sauna, fitness room and small pool.

Avenue Motel (☎ 509-663-7161, 800-733-8981, 720 N Wenatchee Ave) Singles/doubles $50/60. This is the best of the motel cluster that's across from the Ice Arena. Neat and spacious rooms and a kidney-shaped pool are thoughtfully set back from the road. Add $6 for a kitchenette unit.

Travelodge (☎/fax 509-662-8165, 800-578-7878, 1004 N Wenatchee Ave) Singles/doubles $49/69. This nicer-than-average franchise offers a year-round swimming pool, video rentals and air-con quiet enough for (mascot) Sleepy Bear.

Red Lion Hotel (☎ 509-663-0711, 800-733-5466, fax 509-662-8175, 1225 N Wenatchee Ave) Rooms $89/99. Another businessperson's hotel, the Red Lion offers an office center and large rooms with balconies facing a large pool and patio.

Places to Eat

Budget-conscious street-food connoisseurs will look for Mexican food trucks to appear downtown at lunchtime – try the south end of Mission St. Count on being able to get a couple of beef tacos with fresh toppings for $2.

Owl Drug Co (☎ 509-662-7133, 39 S Wenatchee Ave) Open until 5pm. If you're in the mood for a decent milkshake, stop by the old-fashioned soda fountain at this downtown institution.

Moon River Coffee Cabin (☎ 509-662-3662, 414 N Miller Ave) This attractive cafe has the feel of a mountain lodge and front deck seating for sunny afternoons. Charge up on all manner of espresso drinks, plus scones and a few other pastries.

Coffee Sensations (☎ 509-662-5808, 26 N Wenatchee Ave) Sandwiches $5.50-6.25. Closed Sun. A mural of old Europe graces this bohemian coffee house/delicatessen in the heart of Wenatchee. Besides the cappuccinos and spiced teas, they serve built-to-fill sandwiches and, that old European favorite, spuds smothered in sour cream and chives.

Lemolo Cafe & Deli (☎ 509-664-6576, 114 N Wenatchee Ave) Prices around $6. Closed Sunday. This laid-back luncheonette serves espresso drinks, healthful snacks, homemade soups and salads with a bit of exotica.

Cuc Tran Cafe (☎ 509-663-6281, 7 N Wenatchee Ave) Entrees $4.50-7. Closed Sunday.

Cuc Tran offers authentic Vietnamese food and is easy on the pocketbook – daily specials, including rice and soup, go for $5.50.

Wenatchee Roaster & Ale House (☎ *509-662-1234, 201 N Wenatchee Ave*) Entrees $8. Rotisseried turkey, barbecued pork and 24 beers on tap are the headliners at this classy pub atop the Wenatchee Center Hotel.

Dusty's In-N-Out (☎ *509-662-7805, 1427 N Wenatchee Ave*) Snacks under $3. Open until 10pm. On the way out of town, grab a Dusty Burger or Dusty Dog at this classic drive-through joint.

The Windmill (☎ *509-665-9529, 1501 N Wenatchee Ave*) Average entrees $23. Open 5pm-9pm Mon-Sat. You may have to compete with the locals for a table at this well-established steak house on Wenatchee's north end. Worth the splurge is the New York strip steak flamed with a whisky and mushroom demi-glace.

Getting There & Around

Horizon Air serves the Pangborn Memorial Airport (☎ 509-884-2494, W www.pangborn airport.com) in East Wenatchee, with four or five flights daily to/from Seattle (from $67 one-way).

All bus and rail transit services are centralized at Columbia Station, 300 S Columbia Ave, at the foot of Kittitas St. Northwestern Trailways (☎ 509-662-2183, 800-366-3830) runs two daily buses west to Leavenworth and Seattle ($25, 3½ hours), and one east to Moses Lake and Spokane ($25, 3½ hours). There's also a Monday to Friday departure for Ellensburg at 10:30am ($15, 1½ hours).

You can get to the nearby towns of Leavenworth via Cashmere (Bus No 22, $1, 50 minutes) and Chelan via Entiat (Bus No 21, $1, one hour) on frequent Link Transit buses (☎ 509-662-1155, W www.link transit.com). Buses run until 5pm or 6pm Monday to Friday and are equipped with bike racks. Skiers can use the SkiLINK service to Mission Ridge on buses with specially mounted ski racks (see Things to See & Do, earlier, for details).

Amtrak's *Empire Builder* stops daily in Wenatchee on its way between Seattle and Chicago, westbound at 5:43am, and eastbound at 8:42pm.

Car rentals are available at Pangborn Airport from Budget (☎ 509-663-2626) and Hertz (☎ 509-884-6900), or downtown from U-Save Auto Rental (☎ 509-663-0587), 908 S Wenatchee Ave.

If you need a taxi, call Courtesy Cab (☎ 509-662-2126) or Woody's Cab (☎ 509-884-0358).

GLACIER PEAK WILDERNESS

The small town of Entiat, 19 miles north of Wenatchee via Alt US 97, is the eastern access point for the Glacier Peak Wilderness (Darrington is the western entrance). For a Northwest Forest Pass and trail information before setting off, visit the Entiat Ranger Station (☎ 509-784-1511) at 2108 Entiat Rd; open 7:45am to 4:30pm Monday to Friday.

To reach trails, follow the Entiat River Rd (which becomes USFS Rd 51) 38 miles northeast to road's end at Cottonwood Campground. Glacier views await at the end of a 10½-mile hike up the **Entiat River Trail** (Northwest Forest Pass required), which alpine passes through dense forest and alpine meadows before terminating on a cliff facing Mount Maude and Seven Fingered Jack. Day-hikers should explore **Cow Creek Meadows**, on a wildflower-laden loop hike past Fifth of July Mt and Larch Lakes.

Five USFS campgrounds up the Entiat River appear beyond the first 25 miles of USFS Rd 51: *Fox Creek*, *Lake Creek*, *Silver Falls*, *North Fork* and *Cottonwood*. All have pit toilets and hand-operated well pumps, and cost $8 per vehicle ($9 at Silver Falls), payable on-site. The road (and access to campgrounds) is closed in winter.

MOSES LAKE

An ancient product of the flooded Columbia Basin, sinuous 17-mile-long Moses Lake draws loads of boaters and jet-skiers. The natural lake was augmented by water from the Columbia Basin Irrigation Project, which also feeds the Potholes Reservoir to the south.

The town of Moses Lake (population 14,953) sprawls and is not burdened with an excess of charm. Most travelers know it as a stop on I-90 between Seattle (178 miles west) and Spokane (105 miles east). The main downtown area lies at the upper end of a peninsula that juts into the lake, squeezed between Parker and Pelican Horns, as the lake's eastern extremities are called. Broadway Ave (Rte 171) spurs northeast off I-90 exit 176 to head through town alongside Parker Horn, then loops back as Pioneer Way to I-90 at Exit 179.

The Moses Lake Chamber of Commerce (☎ 509-765-7888, 800-992-6234), 324 S Pioneer Way, is open 8am to 4pm Monday to Friday. Check their visitor website, W www.moses-lake.com, for a complete list of lodgings.

Things to See & Do
Moses Lake itself is appealing mostly to motorboaters, but there are also a number of swimming beaches. Most of the activity is centered on **Moses Lake Community Park** (☎ 509-766-9240), a pleasant, tree-shaded day-use area west of town off I-90 exit 175.

More subtly interesting are the Pothole Lakes southwest of town (see below), and more blatantly fun for hot, car-weary kids is the giant **aquatic center** (☎ 509-766-9246) in downtown Moses Lake at McCosh Park (Dogwood St and 4th Ave). Free summertime concerts and other events are held in the park's open-air **Centennial Theater** (☎ 509-766-9240).

Even if you've stopped just to get gas, don't miss the **Moses Lake Museum & Art Center** (☎ 509-766-9395, 122 W 3rd Ave; admission free; open 11am-5pm Tues-Sat). In addition to its large collection of Native American artifacts, the museum includes a major exhibit on the natural history of the shrub-steppe environment.

If you like odd geography, or yearn to see ruddy ducks swimming past sand-dune islands, spend a morning knocking around the **Potholes Wildlife Area** that surrounds Potholes Reservoir, which is just south of Moses Lake on Hwy 262.

The name 'potholes' derives from the numerous depressions that dot the landscape here, carved out by retreating glaciers. The land is surprisingly lush and green, with lots of water and wetlands surrounded by sand dunes, which sometimes pop up through the streams as islands. The Columbia Basin Irrigation Project is responsible for this weird ecology – O'Sullivan Dam and various irrigation schemes have filled any shallow spot with irrigation water, which courses through the native desert. Bird watchers figure this to be a real oasis and most Northwest birders have made springtime pilgrimages here; come prepared to spot shorebirds, sandpipers, avocets, herons, egrets, burrowing owls and curlews. Canoeists can put in at **Potholes State Park** (☎ 509-346-2759, Hwy 262, 17 miles southwest of Moses Lake) and paddle the waterways.

Lots of the **hiking** here is on causeways running alongside water ditches. Hike beside the Frenchman Hills Wasteway, reached from the end of a gravel road west of the state park. Be aware that summer hiking can be rough going in this desert landscape.

The easiest access to Potholes Reservoir is from the south. From Moses Lake take Hwy 17 southeast 10 miles to Hwy 262. Turn west on Hwy 262, which runs along the foot of the reservoir past O'Sullivan Dam, Potholes State Park and other informal access points. Birders recommend entering from the north side by getting off at I-90 exit 169 (Hiawatha Rd) and driving east 2½ miles along the frontage road. Just before the Highline towers, take the dirt road to the right. This leads onto a dike; park where the dike road makes its first left turn. The abundance of bird life on the reservoir's north shore makes this a worthwhile detour.

Places to Stay & Eat
As a boaters' destination, the area features several lakefront trailer parks where you can pitch a tent.

Big Sun Resort (☎ 509-765-8294, 2300 W Marina Dr) Tent/RV sites $13.50/22. Sixty shaded RV sites, most with full hookups, and a half-dozen tent sites comprise this lakeshore park with boat docks. Campers can access Moses Lake Park via a footbridge across the freeway.

Potholes State Park (☎ *509-346-2759, reservations* ☎ *888-226-7688, 670 O'Sullivan Dam Rd)* Tent/RV sites $8/20. Open year-round. This marina-type campground, 17 miles southwest of Moses Lake, makes a good base for bird watchers or canoeists bent on exploring the Potholes. It can get crowded but sites are amply spaced and edged by poplars.

Most of Moses Lake's motels are clustered around the freeway exits, though there are also a few places to stay downtown.

Maples Motel (☎ *509-765-5665, 1006 W 3rd Ave)* Rooms $35. This friendly older place on downtown's west end has clean rooms, a pool and picnic area. Discounts are available for three nights or more.

Travelodge (☎ *509-765-8631, 316 S Pioneer Way at 3rd St)* Singles/doubles $46/55. This franchise couldn't be more central, right by Civic Center Park, and it's got a pool.

Lakeshore Resort Motel (☎ *509-765-9201, 3206 W Lakeshore Drive)* Singles/doubles $55/65. A popular boaters' haven, the Lakeshore adjoins the marina on the south side of the freeway (exit 176) and has barbecue grills for cooking up your catch.

Though not exactly a culinary capital, Moses Lake does have dozens of places to eat.

Barbecue Depot (☎ *509-764-8247, 805 W Broadway)* Sandwiches $6, entrees $12. Closed Mon. This local favorite serves hickory-smoked ribs and tender steaks out of a vintage railroad car. It's also good for a breakfast of homemade hash browns.

El Abuelo (☎ *509-765-0606, 1075 W Broadway)* Snacks $6, entrees $10-13. Grandpa's burritos and quesadillas make a nice alternative to the usual burgers and fried chicken, and you can order your beans lard-free.

Michael's on the Lake (☎ *509-765-1611, 910 W Broadway)* Entrees $13. Trying its darndest to be Moses Lake's fancy steak-and-seafood place, Michael's features dining on a deck overlooking the lake.

Getting There & Away
Both Greyhound buses pull into Ernie's Truck Stop (☎ *509-765-4470)*, on Kittleson Rd near I-90 exit 179, three times daily on their way between Seattle ($24, 3½ hours) and Spokane ($18, 2 hours).

SOAP LAKE
Soap Lake marks the southern endpoint of the Grand Coulee, where the dramatic river-cut geology of the north gives way to a vast flat region. The lake contains 17 minerals and – according to the lakeside sign – an 'ichthyological (fish)-like' oil, similar in content to that of Germany's Baden-Baden. It became something of a medical resort early in the 1900s. The water is funny-smelling and mildly slippery, and white foam gathers at the shoreline.

The lakeside town of Soap Lake is an odd assortment of dilapidation, antiques and upscale lodgings. It lies 22 miles north of Moses Lake, near the crossroads of Hwys 17 and 28. The Soap Lake Chamber of Commerce (☎ *509-246-1821*, Ⓦ www.soap lakecoc.org), 300 Beach St E, near the foot of the lake, is a good source of information.

Other than taking a dip in the pungent lake, there's not much to do in these parts. Soap Lake's big summer event is the Great Canoe Race, which is held the second Saturday in July.

Water from Soap Lake is piped into the bathtubs of the two lakefront lodges here.

Notaras Lodge (☎ *509-246-0462, fax 509-246-1064*, Ⓦ *www.notaraslodge.com, 13 Canna St)* Rooms $65, whirlpool suites $98. Four log cabins have replaced the original two-story lodge, which burned down in 1998. Decorated theme rooms with kitchenettes maintain a fine line between eccentricity and dopiness.

Inn at Soap Lake (☎ *509-246-1132*, Ⓦ *www.innsoaplake.com, 226 Main Ave E)* Singles/doubles from $58/65, whirlpool suites from $100, cottages $85-110. Dating from 1905, this large brick structure contains surprisingly elegant Euro-style rooms with kitchenettes. A few newly built cottages have fireplaces. Co-owner Sandra Garnett hails from Holland.

Yakima Valley

The Yakima River arises from the slopes of Snoqualmie Pass, far to the west. By the time the river gets to Yakima, most of its mountain freshness is gone and dams have slowed it down, diverting its waters into immense irrigation projects. When viewed on a sweltering hot day (of which there are many), the Yakima seems as life-giving as the Nile. The river flows through scorched ochre-colored hills, but where its water touches the soil, a bounty of life springs forth.

The Yakima Valley is the single largest producer of apples in the world, though hops, cherries, peaches and other tree fruits – as well as vegetables – are also found in abundance. In the last 20 years, wine grapes have taken their place on the hillsides, making this one of the Northwest's major wine areas. The lower Yakima Valley in particular is filled with irrigated fields and little towns dedicated to serving the needs of farmers.

There's no getting around the fact that it's hot and dry here – only eight inches of rain fall a year, summer highs hover around 100°F and there are over 300 days of sunshine annually. These climatic extremes make this area a mecca for sun-lovers. Yakima is noted as a retirement center, especially for the career military, while the sunny weather and access to skiing and fishing serve to attract younger recreation enthusiasts.

The preponderance of orchard work has also brought in a large Hispanic population from Mexico and Latin America; the 2000 census showed close to 80,000 Hispanics living in Yakima County, nearly 40% of the county's population. The vast Yakama Indian Reservation to the southwest adds a strong Native American presence to the population mix.

ELLENSBURG

Even if you're not going to stop in Ellensburg (population 15,414), at least slow down for it – it's the site of the state police training academy. Students like to practice catching speeding motorists and writing up tickets.

The other college in Ellensburg, Central Washington University (CWU), is large enough to give a relaxed collegiate feel to this agricultural hub town. Ellensburg's well-preserved downtown was built after a fire burned nine blocks and more than 200 homes in 1889. The reborn town then thought itself on the way to becoming both the 'Pittsburgh of the West' (because of nearby iron ore and coal deposits) and the capital city of Washington. For better or worse, the iron and coal proved to be very low grade, and Olympia got the state capitol building, leaving Ellensburg the state normal school as a consolation prize.

Today, Ellensburg is a pleasant enough place to while away an afternoon or spend a night, with the old brick downtown and a couple of good restaurants, not to mention the signing chimps at the university's primate center. Ellensburg's cowboy-poetry brand of sophistication lapses just long enough each year for it to become a rowdy cowtown during the Ellensburg Rodeo, one of the nation's largest.

Orientation & Information

The Yakima River runs down the west side of Ellensburg. I-90 sticks close to the river; south of town it turns westward toward Spokane, while I-82 continues south to Yakima, 36 miles south; an alternate route, scenic 821, borders Yakima Canyon (see below). Hop off I-90 either northwest (exit 106) or south (exit 109) of Ellensburg, and let the flow of traffic take you to Main St, which bisects numbered avenues into west and east. Take 8th Ave east off Main to reach the university.

For maps and information, drop by the Ellensburg Chamber of Commerce (☎ 509-925-2002, Ⓦ www.ellensburg-chamber .com), 609 N Main St, open 8am to 5pm Monday to Friday, 10am to 2pm Saturday.

The building is shared by the US Forest Service and Ellensburg Rodeo offices. You'll find the main post office at Pearl St and E 3rd Ave, and a free Internet connection at Ellenburg Public Library, 3rd Ave & Ruby. Catch the *Daily Record* for local news.

Things to See & Do

The chamber of commerce has maps of the downtown **historic district**, which is roughly contained between 6th and 3rd Aves in the few blocks east of Main. Peppered with antique shops, galleries and cafes, it makes a tempting place to while away an afternoon. Also worth a look is **Dick & Jane's Spot**, out front at 101 N Pearl St, a funkified folk garden, crammed with bizarre lawn ornaments made from bicycle reflectors and other found objects.

The **Kittitas County Museum** (☎ 509-925-3778, 114 E 3rd Ave; admission free; open 10am-4pm Mon-Sat June-Sept; noon-4pm Tues-Sat Oct-May), in the 1889 Cadwell Building, is known mostly for its gemstone and petrified wood collections, as well as its horseshoe-arched windows. The paintings of native son John Clymer, whose all-American subjects graced *Saturday Evening Post* covers during the 1950s and '60s, are on display at the **Clymer Museum** (☎ 509-962-6416, 416 N Pearl St; admission free; open 10am-5pm Mon-Thur & Sat, 10am-8pm Fri, noon-5pm Sun). The **Children's Activity Museum** (☎ 509-925-6789, 400 N Main St; admission $3.50; open 10am-3pm Wed-Fri, 6:30pm-8:30pm Fri, 1pm-4pm Sun, 10am-4pm Sat) has a miniature cowboy ranch to play in, a science lab and other engaging hands-on exhibits.

A family farm is preserved at **Olmstead Place State Park Heritage Area** (☎ 509-925-1943; 921 N Ferguson Rd; admission free; open 8am-5pm daily), 4½ miles southeast of Ellensburg off I-90. A log cabin, pioneer barns and other farm buildings dating from 1875 to 1890 depict early homestead life in the Kititas Valley.

Another view of frontier agriculture is on display at the **Thorp Grist Mill** (☎ 509-964-9640; admission free; open 1-4pm Wed-Sun June-Sept), northwest of Ellensburg.

Once a de facto meeting place for local farmers, it is now a rural museum with a multimedia presentation shown in a grain storage bin. Take I-90 exit 101 and travel west 2 miles through Thorp to reach the mill and Ice Pond park.

Once the snow covers the natural forage, the Department of Wildlife (☎ 509-925-6746) takes it upon itself to feed around a thousand elk each day at Joe Watt Canyon, 15 miles north of Ellensburg near Thorp. To watch this spectacle, put on some warm clothes and show up first thing in the morning at the feeding station. Take I-90 exit 101, cross left (over the freeway) and at the top of the hill turn right onto Old Thorp Cemetery Rd. Continue 3 miles to Watt Canyon Rd and turn left. The feeding station is at the end of the road, about 1 mile away.

As with most small-town college campuses, **Central Washington University** is a good place for a student-watching stroll, but there are a couple of other attractions here as well. Formal Japanese dry-landscape gardens, off the Walnut St pedestrian mall, make for a restful wander.

CWU has gained some renown for its studies of chimpanzee-human communication. Yes, this is the home of the chimps who communicate using American Sign Language. On weekends the **Chimpanzee and Human Communication Institute** (☎ 509-963-2244, W *www.cwu.edu/~cwuchci, cnr Nicholson Blvd & D St; adult/student $10/7.50)* presents an informative, hour-long 'Chimposium' workshop that includes an audience with the chimps (9:15am and 10:45am Saturday, 12:30pm and 2pm Sunday). The discussions on linguistics and primate behavior are interesting, but don't expect to have any elaborate conversations with the chimps – chimpanzee-human communication typically takes a lot of time and patience. Reservations are recommended.

Special Events

Ellensburg's ultimate festival, the Ellensburg Rodeo (☎ 509-962-7831, 800-637-2444, W www.ellensburgrodeo.com) takes place Labor Day weekend in tandem with the Kittitas County Fair. It's ranked among the top

10 rodeos in the nation and is one of central Washington's biggest events. Come prepared to see some hard riding and roping – participants take this rodeo very seriously, as there is big money at stake.

Places to Stay

KOA Kampground (☎ 509-925-9319, 32 Thorp Hwy South, W koa.com) Tent/RV sites $19/23. This facility, off I-90 exit 106, has the only camping around Ellensburg. Wedged between the freeway and the Yakima River, it's oriented toward RV travelers with a few patches of grass for tents. KOA extras include a laundromat, pool, playground and showers.

Harold's Motel (☎ 509-925-4141, fax 509-925-4143, 601 N Water St) Singles/doubles $36/40. Harold's offers good value and location, just a block from the historic downtown at 6th Ave, though the small cinderblock-walled rooms are strictly functional.

Travelers Regalodge (☎ 509-925-2547, 800-523-4972, 300 W 6th Ave) Singles/doubles $49/56. Right across the street from Harold's, this is more comfortably furnished and you get a heated indoor pool.

I-90 Inn Motel (☎ 509-925-9844, 1390 Dollarway Rd) Singles/doubles $52/62. The aptly named I-90 Inn is practically on the exit 106 ramp. What it lacks in charm it makes up for in convenience and comfort.

Nites Inn (☎ 509-962-9600, 1200 S Ruby St) Singles & doubles $51. This is one of a plethora of motels at the southern freeway exit (109). Standard-issue rooms come with fridge and microwave, and there are barbecue grills and picnic tables on the landscaped grounds.

Places to Eat

In addition to all the usual fast-food restaurants, any college town in Washington is bound to have a few hip coffee joints.

D&M Coffee (☎ 509-925-5313, 408 S Main St) Coffee drinks $2-3. An old gas station turned drive-through espresso shop with brightly-painted pumps and a deck out back, D&M roasts their own. Other branches are closer to downtown at 416 N Main and at 301 N Pine, opposite the museum; the latter has the most elbow room.

Courtyard Coffee House (☎ 509-933-3333, 211 E 8th Ave) Open 7am-2pm Mon-Fri. Students and faculty meet for coffee and doughnuts at this cozy cafe near the CWU campus.

Billy Mac's Juice Bar & Gallery (☎ 509-962-6620, 115 W 4th Ave) Juices $3.25, sandwiches $3.50. All kinds of fruit and veggie concoctions are squeezed here, and enhanced on request with things like wheatgrass and echinacea.

Valley Cafe (☎ 509-925-3050, 105 W 3rd Ave) Lunch $7.50, dinner entrees $8.50-25. This is a striking art-deco cafe that turns out remarkably good food and offers an excellent selection of Washington wines. At lunch a bowl of cioppino goes for $9.50 and a spinach salad is $7; dinner highlights include Ellensburg lamb and seared ahi tuna. Order a huge boxed lunch and a bottle of Chardonnay from their take-out shop next door.

Café Eden (☎ 509-925-3337, 311 N Main St) Breakfast $2-6, lunch $5-7.50. Another good-looking restaurant in the historic district, this inviting breakfast-and-lunch place has brick walls, bird cages and a big, old-fashioned coffee machine. Their menu is strong on salads, pastas and wraps.

The Palace Café (☎ 509-925-2327, 323 N Main St) Lunch $7, dinner $11-15. A popular saloon-like place housed in the 1908 Pearson building, the Palace has been grilling steaks and baking pies to local acclaim for over 50 years.

Getting There & Around

Ellensburg is a busy crossroads for regional buses, though there's no real bus station – Greyhound and Northwestern Trailways buses stop at the Pilot gas station at I-90 exit 106. The ticket window (☎ 509-925-1177) is in the Subway sandwich shop. Here are some of the most common destinations: Seattle ($18; 2½ hrs; 110 miles; 6 to 7 daily), Spokane (via Moses Lake; $28; 4 hrs; 174 miles; 3 to 4 daily), Wenatchee ($15; 1½ hrs; 75 miles, 1 bus Mon-Fri), Yakima ($7; 1 hr; 36 miles; 3 daily). Some Yakima buses continue on to Walla Walla, the Tri-Cities and Bend, Oregon.

WASHINGTON

From the bus station, Rodeo Town Taxi (☎ 509-929-4222) can get you downtown for $5.

AROUND ELLENSBURG
Roslyn

A tiny town on Hwy 903, about 25 miles northwest of Ellensburg, Roslyn (population 1017) is where the TV show *Northern Exposure* was filmed; on TV, it's supposed to be a small town in the Alaskan bush. Many of the show's scenes were shot in the Brick Tavern (see below). The Cle Elum/Roslyn Chamber of Commerce (☎ 509-674-5958, W www.cleelumroslyn.org), 401 W 1st, in Cle Elum, has visitor information.

Roslyn is yet another gateway to the popular **Alpine Lakes Wilderness Area.** Hwy 903 leads northwest of Roslyn and becomes Salmon la Sac Rd, passing by resort-rimmed Cle Elum Lake and ending some 25 miles later in the heart of the wilderness, just south of Deception Pass. This area gets less use than Snoqualmie Pass or Leavenworth, but don't expect solitude – over 100,000 people visit the Alpine Lakes every year. From the end of USFS Rd 4330 it's a hearty 4½-mile hike to the **Pacific Crest Trail** and 6724-foot **Cathedral Rock.** Hikers should fill out a permit, available at the trailhead, before heading into the wilderness. Contact the Cle Elum Ranger Station (☎ 509-674-4411), 803 W 2nd St, for more information; it's open 7:45am to 5pm Monday to Friday, 8am to 2pm Saturday.

Area accommodations serve hikers, anglers and others on their way into the wilderness.

Salmon La Sac Campground (☎ 509-674-4411, reservations 877-444-6777, Salmon La Sac Rd, 17 miles northwest of Roslyn) Sites $13. Between two rivers, this is a pleasant place to pitch a tent for Alpine Lakes Wilderness treks. Flush toilets and firewood are available. Reservations are recommended on summer weekends, when there's a two-night minimum stay.

Huckleberry House (☎ 649-2900, W www .huckleberryhouse.com, 301 Pennsylvania Ave) Rooms $85-95. This charming hillside B&B in Roslyn has four sunny rooms, an-

tiquely decorated with quilted beds and claw-footed tubs. The wraparound porch makes a nice perch from which to admire the village. A breakfast of scones and organic coffee is served and guests have kitchen access.

Cle Elum Traveler's Inn (☎ 509-674-5535, fax 509-674-5535, 1001 E 1st St) Singles/doubles $34/46. This motel is one of several lodgings in Cle Elum, an otherwise quiet logging town on the way to Roslyn.

Roslyn Cafe (☎ 509-649-2763, 201 W Pennsylvania Ave) Meals $5-8. Stop in here for good old-fashioned comfort food, served seven days a week.

Brick Tavern (☎ 509-649-2643, 1 Pennsylvania Ave) Meals $7-10. This *Northern Exposure* locale claims to be Washington's oldest saloon. Ask for a glass of Roslyn Beer, brewed ultra-locally at the Roslyn Brewing Company.

Cle Elum Bakery (☎ 509-674-2233, 501 E 1st St) Sandwiches $4. A ritual stop for many I-90 travelers, this bakery does good sandwiches and soups.

Yakima Canyon

South of Ellensburg, Hwy 821 follows the Yakima River through Yakima Canyon. The 27-mile backroad is a winding scenic route to Yakima and, unless you hit it on a busy weekend, it's quiet enough for a bike ride.

Floating may be the ideal way to see the Yakima Canyon. Some people put their inflatable rafts in along Hwy 821 south of Ellensburg, and spend three to four hours on a float to the Roza Dam. There's another public put-in north on Hwy 10, below Cle Elum, for a lazy 15-mile, five- to six-hour float to the diversion dam near Thorp. To rent a raft, contact **Rill Adventures** (☎ 509-964-2520, 888-281-1561, 10471 Thorp Hwy), in Thorp (four to eight-person raft $60-80).

There are **hiking trails** around and above the Yakima River. At the Umtanum Creek Recreation Area, about 12 miles south of Ellensburg, a suspension footbridge crosses the river to trails leading up to a ridge-top viewpoint. The bridge, incidentally, is a good vantage point for cliff-nesting swallow colonies.

The stretch of the river between Ellensburg and Roza Dam is also a fine place to fly-fish for rainbow trout. Prime time for angling on the Yakima is in spring but autumn can also reap rewards. **Fishing** here is all catch-and-release, and artificial lures and barbless hooks are required. In Ellensburg, **Coopers Fly Shop** (☎ *509-962-5259, 413 N Main St)* has tackle and gear and can arrange guide service.

Gingko Petrified Forest State Park

This forest of stone gives fascinating evidence of the zone's volcanic nature. Branches and logs that once lay on the bottom of a prehistoric lake were covered in lava that welled up through cracks in the earth's surface. Instead of decomposing, these logs were preserved in a basalt overcoat, their organic material replaced by silicate compounds from the cooling lava. These fossilized trees and leaves dot the trails at the **Ginkgo Petrified Forest State Park & Interpretive Center** (☎ *509-856-2700, Vantage Hwy, 1 mile north of Vantage; $1 donation; interpretive center open 10am-6pm daily mid-June–mid-Sept, Fri-Sun May & Oct)*, on the west bank of the Columbia River about 30 miles east of Ellensburg. A three-quarter-mile interpretive trail and a 2½-mile hiking trail pass not only gingkos but Douglas fir, spruce, maple, elm and gum

trees, all safely preserved behind steel grates. The trailheads are a couple of miles west of I-90 exit 136 along the Vantage Hwy.

The interpretive center has polished samples of petrified wood on display. Take a moment to walk around here – several pictographs have been salvaged from the Wanapum Dam's backwaters, and are displayed on the river side of the visitor center.

There's camping nearby at **Wanapum State Park** (☎ *509-856-2700, Wanapum Hwy, 3 miles south of I-90)*. Closer to the petrified forest is the **Vantage Riverstone Resort & Motel** (☎ *509-856-2230, 551 Main St)*, just north of freeway exit 136, with tent sites ($19), RV sites ($23) and motel rooms ($59-89). This also happens to be the closest lodging for people attending concerts at the Gorge Amphitheater in nearby George.

YAKIMA

Yakima (population 71,845) is the main city of central Washington, and the trading center of an immense agricultural area. The city reflects this prosperity with a converted downtown-cum-mall development, massive commercial strips and some very conspicuous golf courses. Yakima likes to boast that it is the 'Palm Springs of the North.'

Yakima is the seat of local government, and many of the prominent older buildings in the downtown core are courthouses and

Grandfather Cuts Loose the Ponies

Stop by the Wild Horse Monument, off I-90 near the Vantage Bridge, to see a sculpture of wild horses careening recklessly toward the edge of a cliff. The work of Northwest sculptor David Govedare, entitled *Grandfather Cuts Loose the Ponies,* represents a Native American creation story. Inspiring views overlooking the Columbia River make the monument a good place to pause from driving, and the story that accompanies Govedare's powerful image makes it hard not to reflect.

The monument's legend reads:

Creatures of the planet, behold a Great Basket! I send this basket, bearing the gift of life, to all corners of the universe. Now take these ponies, I am cutting them loose. They will inspire a spirit of free will. They will be a companion for work and play on this planet... From the center of my Basket burns the fire of our collective souls. Humans you are responsible. You have the power of reasoning and the gift of free will. Use them wisely. Always be aware of the limitless nature of this ever-expanding universe. Let us live to inspire each other.

such. One particularly attractive structure is the **Larson Building**, at E Yakima Ave and S 2nd St, an art-deco marvel with 13 different shades of brick in its facade; check out the lobby.

The grand, Italianate **Capitol Theatre**, at 19 S 3rd St, is yet another landmark of Yakima's boom years. Built in 1920 as a movie house, it now functions as the city's premier performing arts center.

A single block makes up Yakima's much-touted historic district. North Front St contains several good restaurants and boutiques on its east side, while most of the old North-ern Pacific Depot across the street has been converted into the brewpub of the Northwest's oldest microbrewery, Grant's, established in the early 1980s.

Yakima does offer a few noteworthy restaurants, and an abundance of cheap motel rooms. The riverside greenway, arboretum and adjacent parks make a good place to unload hot passengers and stretch weary muscles.

Orientation

Yakima lies 145 miles east of Seattle, and 76 miles west of Richland. I-82 runs along the

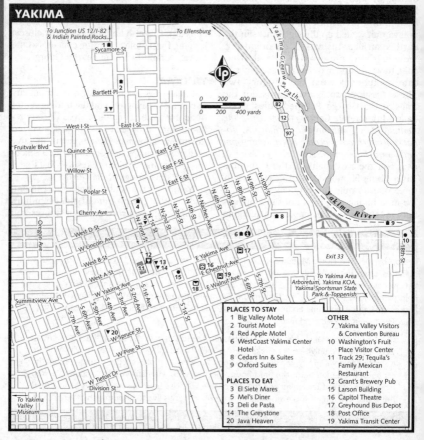

YAKIMA

To Junction US 12/I-82
& Indian Painted Rocks
To Ellensburg
To Yakima Valley Museum

0   200   400 m
0   200   400 yards

PLACES TO STAY
1 Big Valley Motel
2 Tourist Motel
4 Red Apple Motel
6 WestCoast Yakima Center Hotel
8 Cedars Inn & Suites
9 Oxford Suites

PLACES TO EAT
3 El Siete Mares
5 Mel's Diner
13 Deli de Pasta
14 The Greystone
20 Java Heaven

OTHER
7 Yakima Valley Visitors & Convention Bureau
10 Washington's Fruit Place Visitor Center
11 Track 29; Tequila's Family Mexican Restaurant
12 Grant's Brewery Pub
15 Larson Building
16 Capitol Theatre
17 Greyhound Bus Depot
18 Post Office
19 Yakima Transit Center

Yakima River, east of Yakima's main downtown area; exit 33 leads to East Yakima Ave, the quickest route to downtown. The main north-south strip running through town is 1st St, which can be accessed from exit 31. Yakima Ave and Front St (essentially the train tracks) divide the city into directional quadrants.

There are both numbered streets and avenues in Yakima, so pay attention when people give addresses – numbered streets are east of the tracks and numbered avenues are west.

Information

The Yakima Valley Visitors & Convention Bureau (☎ 509-575-3010, 800-221-0751, w www.visityakima.com) is at 10 N 8th St. The main post office is at 205 W Washington Ave, though the station at 112 S 3rd St is more convenient to downtown. The daily paper is the *Yakima Herald-Republic*.

Yakima Valley Memorial Hospital (☎ 509-575-8000) is at 2811 Tieton Dr.

Yakima Greenway

The Yakima Greenway is a scraggly string of parks and recreation areas that stretches the length of the Yakima River throughout the city, passing through natural wetlands and native vegetation. **Sarg Hubbard Park**, at I-82 exit 33, is a popular place to pick up the walking, hiking and biking path that follows the river for 10 miles. It's next to **Washington's Fruit Place Visitor Center** (☎ *509-576-3090, 105 S 18th St; admission free; open 10am-4pm Mon-Fri, plus Sat May-Dec)*, another apple industry showcase. The hands-on displays will appeal to the kids. Stop at the shop for apple-shaped gifts and souvenirs and a very small free can of apple juice.

South along the Greenway, just east of exit 34, is the **Yakima Area Arboretum**, a collection of over 2000 species of trees and shrubs spread out over 46 acres of landscaped gardens. Stop at the **Jewett Interpretive Center** (☎ *509-248-7337, 1401 Arboretum Dr; admission free; open 9am-5pm Tues-Sat)* for a walking-tour brochure. At the north end, near the Japanese garden, is the start of a ⅓-mile interpretive loop trail through a wetlands area.

Yakima Valley Museum

Definitely worth the trip across town is this excellent regional museum (☎ *509-248-0747, 2105 Tieton Drive; adult/senior & student/ family $3/1.50/7; open 10am-5pm Mon-Fri, noon-5pm Sat & Sun)*. Besides the centerpiece collection of horse-drawn conveyances and early motor vehicles, you'll find artifacts and exhibits about native Yakama culture and a replica of the office of late US Supreme Court Justice William O Douglas. Native son Douglas was appointed to the high court by Franklin D Roosevelt in 1939 and served until 1975, making him the longest-serving justice in the court's history. Although he's honored here and elsewhere around town with plaques and commemoratives, during his tenure on the court, Douglas' progressive politics usually rankled his hometown neighbors.

In yet another section, the **Children's Underground** (*open 1pm-5pm Wed-Sun)* does a good job of incorporating Yakima's human and natural history into a number of hands-on exhibits for kids. Afterwards, they'll be ready for a scoop of Tillamook ice cream at the faux Depression-era **Soda Fountain** behind the building.

Adjacent to the museum is **Franklin Park**, a broad lawn planted with evergreens that features a playground, picnic tables, and – an important feature in sun-baked Yakima – a swimming pool.

Other Attractions

For the Native Americans who lived here in prehistoric times, the valley's cliff-lined ravines were natural avenues of transportation, as they are today. A large number of pictographs at **Indian Painted Rocks** remain as evidence of their passage. Found along an old foot trail northwest of Yakima, these stylized images of humans with fantastic headdresses may have conveyed a warning or a mark of territory to those who passed through this narrow gap. To see the rock paintings, take the 40th Ave exit off of US 12, cross Fruitvale Blvd, and turn right onto old US 12, now called Powerhouse Rd. In about a mile, watch for a plaque on the left-hand side of the road, just past Ackley Rd, and park on the shoulder. Concrete steps lead up to the edge of the cliffs.

As many as 3000 Rocky Mountain elk may descend on Oak Creek near Naches on any given winter day to feed on bales of hay provided by the state Fish & Wildlife Dept. Feeding starts at 1:30pm daily between late November and early January at the **Oak Creek Feeding Station** (☎ 509-653-2390, *Hwy 12, 20 miles west of Yakima*), just west of the junction of Hwys 12 and 410. Bighorn sheep are fed at another spot, on Old Naches Hwy east of the junction. A small visitor center, 1 mile west of the feeding station, has exhibits and a slide show from 9am to 4pm. It's open daily during feeding season.

Activities

The nearest downhill skiing is on the southeast side of Mt Rainier at **White Pass Ski Area** (☎ 509-672-3101, *Snowline* ☎ 509-672-3100, ⓦ *www.skiwhitepass.com; lift tickets adult/youth & senior $25/16 Mon-Fri, $36/22 Sat & Sun; open 8:45am-4pm daily*). Located 50 miles west of Yakima on US 12, this popular ski resort offers five lifts and 14 runs with a total vertical drop of 1500 feet. There are also 11 miles of groomed cross-country trails.

The **Apple Tree Golf Course** (☎ 509-966-5877, *8804 Occidental Rd; greens fees 9/18 holes $22/53*) offers 18 holes nestled in an apple orchard (what else?). The signature 17th hole is an apple-shaped island.

See the Yakima Canyon section, earlier, for details on rafting and fishing on the Yakima River.

Special Events

The Central Washington State Fair (☎ 509-248-7160) runs from the end of September to the first week in October and is known as one of the Northwest's best agricultural exhibitions. If you've passed them up everywhere else, this would be the place to give in and try one out. The fairgrounds are at Nob Hill Blvd and Fair Ave.

There's a large Mexican population in the valley, and the Cinco de Mayo Fiesta is understandably a big celebration hereabouts. Usually held on the first weekend of May, the largest celebrations are in nearby Sunnyside.

For something completely different, try the Country Christmas Lighted Farm Implement Parade, also in Sunnyside, held the first Saturday in December. Farmers dress their combines and threshers with festive lights and drive through town; watch for Rudolph and his nose so bright as he mingles with the mower blades, a favorite holiday jest. For more information contact the Sunnyside Chamber of Commerce at ☎ 509-837-5939.

Places to Stay

Camping The two nearest campgrounds are both along the river's east bank with access to Greenway trails.

Yakima Sportsman State Park (☎ 509-575-2774, *reservations* ☎ 888-226-7688, *904 Keys Rd*) Tent/RV sites $14/20. About half the 64 sites at this beautifully landscaped park have RV hookups, and there are coin-operated hot showers, flush toilets, a riverside picnic area and stocked fishing ponds (limited to youth under 15 years). An interpretive trail leads to a swamp lookout, an excellent bird-watching post. Take I-82 exit 34 and follow Hwy 24 east, turning left onto Keys Rd.

Yakima KOA (☎ 509-248-5882, *reservations* ☎ 800-562-5773, ⓦ *koa.com, 1500 Keys Rd*) Tent/RV sites/cabins $22/25-28/39-46. En route to the above state park, you'll pass this KOA facility, with 100 shaded hookup and tent sites by the river. Basketball courts, video games and a pond with paddleboats will keep the kids busy.

B&Bs Travelers can choose from downtown homes or country estates; the Visitors Bureau can suggest more options.

Tree House B&B (☎ 509-469-1704, 877-469-1704, ⓦ *www.treehouse-bedandbreakfast.com, 15 Hall Avenue*) Rooms with exterior/interior bath $65/95. This in-town inn, off W Yakima Ave past 11th Ave, derives its name from the pine tree growing right up through the front porch (an extension was built around it). Three homey guest rooms share a large living room with kitchenette, library and board games. Choose from bacon and eggs or homemade cinnamon rolls for breakfast.

Birchfield Manor (☎ 509-452-1960, 800-375-3420, W www.birchfieldmanor.com, 2018 Birchfield Rd) Manor rooms $99-139, cottage rooms $129-199. Set on park-like grounds east of Yakima off Hwy 24, this stately home contains five guest rooms, most with double whirlpool tub. It's also one of the best places to eat in the area.

Hotels & Motels North 1st St is *the* motel strip, with a major concentration of franchise inns and fast-food outlets. Competition is fierce – look for posted discount rates off-season, when single rooms can be had for under $30. Swimming pools, air-con and morning coffee and pastries are standard.

Big Valley Motel (☎ 509-248-3393, 800-248-3360, fax 509-457-2422, 1504 N 1st St) Singles/doubles $29/42. Though quite a ways out, this is probably the best deal on the strip. Sure, the furniture's old, but the large rooms here are sturdily built and sufficiently quiet.

Tourist Motel (☎ 509-452-6551, fax 509-457-9668, 1223 N 1st St) Singles/doubles $31/40. This family-run operation has a row of small ordinary units with fridge and microwave. They claim to be better than Motel 6, and it's hard to argue the point.

Red Apple Motel (☎ 509-248-7150, fax 509-248-3155, W www.redapplemotel.com, 416 N 1st St) Singles/doubles $33/43. This larger place has a bit more character and a pool shaped like an apple, sort of. A guest laundry and video rentals are available, and pets are welcome.

Cedars Inn & Suites (☎ 509-452-8101, 800-982-7714, fax 509-452-8635, 1010 East A St) Singles/doubles $54/64. If you'd rather be downtown, this mid-range businessperson's option is a block east of the convention center, with modern rooms and amenities.

WestCoast Yakima Center Hotel (☎ 509-248-5900, 800-325-4000, fax 509-575-8975,

607 E Yakima Ave) Singles/doubles $85/95. Attached to the convention center, the West-Coast caters to conventioneers with a pair of pools, a lounge, and Internet connections.

Oxford Suites (☎ 509-457-9000, 800-404-7848, fax 509-576-9757, W www.oxfordsuites .com, 1701 Terrace Heights Dr) Singles/doubles $85/95. Just off I-82 exit 33, this is another expense-account accommodation. All rooms have views of the Yakima River and easy access to the Greenway. Rates include a full breakfast buffet and evening hors d'oeuvres.

Places to Eat
Mel's Diner (☎ 509-248-5382, 314 N 1st St) Breakfast $4-7, lunch & dinner $7-10. Breakfast is served anytime at this 24-hour hash house (they use 100% soy bean oil in their hash browns).

Java Heaven (☎ 509-248-5282, 212 W Walnut St) Closed Sun. This drive-through espresso place does a mean latte.

The Mexican influence in the valley is apparent by the spate of restaurants serving authentic *comida mexicana*.

El Siete Mares (☎ 509-453-2808, 1010 N 1st St) Lunch/dinner $6.50/9. Eating here is a lot like eating in Michoacán, the restaurant owners' place of origin. Spanish is the predominant tongue and mariachis serenade patrons nightly. Seafood dishes highlight the menu; the meal-sized *sopa de mariscos* is a must.

Tequila's Family Mexican Restaurant (☎ 509-457-3296, 1 W Yakima Ave) Lunch/dinner $6/9. Here too the emphasis is on seafood, but this is more like being on the Jalisco coast, including the Corona umbrellas shading the boardwalk deck. A *torta* (overstuffed sandwich with refried bean spread) makes a hearty lunch. The restaurant occupies three vintage railroad cars at the rear end of Track 29 shopping mall.

Several restaurants offer the kind of cuisine (and prices) that you might not expect to find east of the Cascades.

Deli de Pasta (☎ 509-453-0571, 7 N Front St) Lunch/dinner $7/15-20. Closed Sun. Diners can match a variety of fresh pasta with the sauce of their choice – try the creamy lemon linguini. Choose from a list of 85 local wines.

The Greystone *(☎ 509-248-9801, 5 N Front St)* 3-course dinner around $25. Open from 6pm Mon-Sat. Housed in one of the city's original saloons at the base of the century-old Lund building, the Greystone has become Yakima's premier venue for fine Northwest cuisine. The excellent rack of lamb goes for $32.

Birchfield Manor *(☎ 509-452-1960, 2018 Birchfield Rd)* Dinner $35. Thur-Sat only. French-influenced cuisine and an extensive local wine list make this country inn (see Places to Stay) a favorite with serious eaters. Reservations are required.

Shopping
Track 29 *(1 W Yakima Ave)* The old train platform has been given over to a string of false-fronted eateries and quirky boutiques, some housed in old railroad cars, making for a pleasant boardwalk stroll. You'll find antiques and collectibles, gemstones, essential oils and herbs. In summer, a Saturday market is held on the boardwalk with local produce and crafts vendors.

Entertainment
Grant's Brewery Pub *(☎ 509-575-2922, 32 N Front St)* The Northwest boom in microbreweries began in Yakima in 1982, when this brewery pub first released its British-style ales. Since that day, Grant's has remained in the forefront of regional brewing, and has expanded from the former brewery into the old train station across the street. Grant's ales are among the very best of Northwest beers: try the Scottish Ale and the IPA (India Pale Ale). There's also a light menu with sandwiches and homemade soups.

Getting There & Away
Horizon Air flies to/from Seattle ($99 one-way, 6 times daily), Portland and Vancouver, BC. Flights arrive at and depart from Yakima Air Terminal (☎ 509-575-6149), 2400 W Washington Ave.

The Greyhound bus station (☎ 509-457-5131) is at 602 E Yakima Ave at the corner of 6th St. There are three departures daily to/from Seattle via Ellensburg (one-way $23/25 weekday/weekend, 3½ hours) and three to Spokane via Ellensburg or Pasco (one-way $35, 7 to 8 hours). Other buses continue on to Portland, Bend, The Tri-Cities, Walla Walla and Spokane.

Car rentals are available from Enterprise (☎ 509-248-2170), 312 W Nob Hill Blvd, or U-Save Auto Rental (☎ 509-452-5555) at 1117 W Lincoln Ave.

Getting Around
Yakima Transit (☎ 509-575-6175) runs Monday to Saturday, from 6:30am until around 6:30pm. The transit center is on the corner of S 4th St and E Chestnut Ave. Adult fare is 50¢, exact change required. Bus No 9 runs down S 1st St on its way to the airport, with half-hourly departures during rush hour, hourly the rest of the day. Weekdays, the Yakima Valley Express Shuttle (☎ 509-457-1111) has service to/from Wapato, Toppenish and Sunnyside (free, 3 buses daily).

If you're after a taxi, call Black & White Cab (☎ 509-248-2221) or Aces Taxi (☎ 509-249-8303).

YAKIMA VALLEY WINE COUNTRY
Directly south of Yakima, the Yakima River passes through a narrow gap in the hills before coursing out into the wide, amazingly fertile lower Yakima Valley. Apples, hops, vegetables and grapes are everywhere. Stop by roadside stands or wineries to sample the local bounty.

I-82 stretches southeast from Yakima to the Tri-Cities to connect a number of small wine-making communities, including Zillah, Sunnyside and Prosser, 49 miles east of Yakima and 25 miles west of Richland. The Yakima Valley Hwy (old US 12), also called Wine Country Rd, parallels the freeway for most of the way, providing a pastoral alternative to I-82. For a free map and guide to all the wineries in the valley, send a stamped, self-addressed envelope to the Yakima Valley Wine Growers Association, PO Box 39, Grandview, WA 98930. Information is also available online at **w** www.yakimavalley wine.com.

More than 25 established wineries are dispersed between Yakima and Benton City. Most have tasting rooms with a full array of local wines and gift packages.

Bonair Winery (☎ 509-829-6027) 500 S Bonair Rd, Zillah. Tastings 10am-5pm daily spring to fall; 10am-4:30pm Sat & Sun winter. Bonair has notable cabernets and a signature camerlot (a cabernet/merlot hybrid). You can picnic in the gazebo by the koi pond.

Chinook Wines (☎ 509-786-2725) Wine Country Rd, Prosser. Tastings noon-5pm Sat-Sun May-Dec. This is a small-scale winery known for producing the state's finest sauvignon blanc.

Hinzerling Winery (☎ 509-786-2163) 1520 Sheridan Rd, Prosser. Tastings 11am-5pm Mon-Sat, 11am-4pm Sun Mar-Dec 25. The cabernet from Hinzerling is about as good as Washington red wine gets.

Hogue Cellars (☎ 509-786-4557) Wine Country Rd, Prosser. Admission free; tastings 10am-5pm daily. Hogue Cellars is one of the most noted Washington wineries, especially for its cabernet. It also makes one of the best chardonnays east of the Cascades.

Silver Lake Winery at Roza Hills (☎ 509-829-6235) 1500 Vintage Rd, Zillah. Tastings 10am-5pm daily. Silver Lake Winery has a lovely tasting room and picnic tables overlooking the vineyards. As far as the wine goes, stick with the merlot.

Yakima River Winery (☎ 509-786-2805) 143302 N River Rd, Prosser. Tastings 9am-5pm daily. Ask to try John's Port and the Lemberger, an otherwise obscure red varietal that likes the heat of central Washington.

YAKAMA INDIAN RESERVATION

The Yakima Valley is home to the Yakama Indian Reservation, Washington state's largest. Sixteen miles southeast of Yakima at Toppenish, the primary town on the reservation, the Yakamas have built a cultural center that seeks to explain and demonstrate the tribe's ancient traditions. At Fort Simcoe stand the remains of an

army outpost constructed in 1856 to quash Yakama Indian resistance to life on the reservation.

Yakama Indian Nation Cultural Center

Displays, dioramas and audio-visual exhibits explain the traditions and culture of the Yakama people at this 12,000-sq-foot interpretive center and museum (☎ 509-865-2800, 280 Buster Rd; adult/senior/child $4/2/1; open 8am-5pm). The museum focuses on the challenge of Spilyay, the trickster coyote whose legends taught the Yakama how to understand and interact harmoniously with nature. Most of the displays detail the seasonal and daily life of the tribe, from fishing at Celilo Falls to a recreation of a tule mat longhouse. The usual collections of arrowheads and tools aren't much in evidence here. Instead, the dioramas and exhibits, with their accompanying music and sound effects, are meant to evoke a mood or impression of traditional life and spirituality.

The center also houses a gift shop, a public library, an espresso bar, restaurant and cinema showing Hollywood hits. The cultural center is immediately north of Toppenish on US 97; it is designed to look like a traditional teepee, so you probably won't miss it.

Toppenish

Toppenish (population 8946) is doing its best to make itself a tourist destination on the basis of its historic **murals**. The walls of most downtown buildings are now covered with these paintings depicting events from Yakama or Northwest history.

Clearing the Land, the very first mural to be painted back in 1989, graces the building at Washington and Toppenish Aves. No 60, *El Sarape,* was finished in 2001. An evocative tableau of the first Mexican agricultural workers in the valley, it's found at the corner of Bolin Dr and W 2nd St.

On the first weekend of June is the Mural-in-a-Day Festival, during which a group of painters work together to

Yakama Indians

The Yakama Indians were one of the most populous and powerful of the inland plateau tribes. Their subsistence depended on the Yakima River, a major salmon fishery. Although the Yakamas were among the first Native Americans in the Northwest to have horses, they didn't use them extensively for hunting, and preferred fishing to hunting big game.

The Yakamas were among the natives that met Lewis and Clark at Celilo Falls in 1805, and were also among the 14 tribes that signed an 1855 treaty creating the Yakama Reservations. These tribes, which also included Klickatats and Wenatchees, went on to form the Yakama Nation.

However, the treaty was not ratified by the US Congress, and white settlers and miners continued to stream across the Yakama homelands. Conflicts between the Yakamas and the army escalated. In late 1855, the so-called Yakima War began, which involved Yakama attacks on settlements in the Columbia River Gorge and reprisals by Federal troops and Willamette Valley volunteers. The Yakamas were consigned to US Federal control after the army defeated a war party in a key battle at Union Gap in 1856. Fort Simcoe was established to maintain control over the reservation.

The Indian agent responsible for the Yakamas throughout much of the later 19th century was a Methodist preacher and a strong advocate of turning the Yakamas from fishers into farmers. Thus, a major fishing area on the Yakima River was sold out from the reservation and the money used to establish the reservation's first irrigation canal. After the reservation was allotted to individual Yakamas in homestead-sized units, according to the Dawes Act, much of the most fertile and easily irrigated land passed into the hands of white farmers.

complete a mural in an eight-hour period. However, given that the city appears dedicated to covering every available surface with a mural, visitors on *any* day during the summer months can usually find a painter in action. Get information on murals in progress, as well as a guide to the existing murals, from the Toppenish Mural Society's visitor center (☎ 509-865-6516, W www.toppenish.org, 5A S Toppenish Ave; open 10am-4pm Mon-Sat). Or get serious and take a mural tour, conducted by horse-drawn covered wagon and offered by the Double J Ranch (☎ 509-697-8995, 1550 Gibson Rd, Selah; adult/senior/child $10/8/3).

Not only does the Yakima Valley have the distinction of being the state's leading wine producer, it is also a major grower of hops, with over 75% of the US crop harvested in the valley. This underplayed but essential beer ingredient is given its due at the **American Hop Museum** (☎ 509-865-4677, 22 S B St; admission by donation; open 11am-4pm May-Sept). Housed in the restored Hop Growers Supply building, the museum focuses on the history of hop-growing in America.

Fort Simcoe State Park

The site of Fort Simcoe long served as a camp for the Yakamas, who stopped at the natural springs here on their way to their fishing camps at Celilo Falls. After the Yakama War, the army built this fort at the springs in order to keep the peace and to settle ongoing treaty violations. After the treaty creating the Yakama Reservation was ratified in 1859, Fort Simcoe was decommissioned and used as a boarding school for Native American children until 1923.

Today, 200 acres of the old fort grounds are preserved as Fort Simcoe State Park (☎ 509-874-2372, 5150 Fort Simcoe Rd; interpretive center open 9am-4:30pm Wed-Sun Apr-Oct, Sat & Sun Nov-Mar). The blockhouse and barracks have been rebuilt, and the original white clapboard officers' quarters have been restored and opened for tours. The old Indian Agency building is now an interpretive center that retells the story of the fort and the wars.

Almost as striking as the old fort buildings is the surprising midsummer green of the grounds and the ample shade from old oak trees. It's no wonder that both the Yakamas and the army coveted this oasis in the midst of scorched desert hills. The state park is understandably a popular place for summer picnics. Fort Simcoe is 30 miles west of Toppenish along Fort Rd.

Special Events

The Yakama Nation Cultural Powwow & Rodeo is held in Toppenish around the Fourth of July, and is the Yakama tribe's largest celebration. The four-day festival includes dancing, a parade and an 'Indian Village' with teepees, Indian food booths and stick games. For rodeo tickets call ☎ 509-865-5566.

The third Saturday in October, microbrewers descend on Toppenish for Hoptoberfest, a local spin on the traditional Bavarian event. Contact the American Hop Museum (see above) for details.

Places to Stay & Eat

Yakama Nation Resort RV Park (☎ 509-865-2000, 800-874-3087, w www.yakamanation.com, 280 Buster Rd) Tent/RV sites $12/20, teepees $30. The Yakama Tribes operate this large campground on a sun-baked field behind the cultural center. In addition to RV hookups, there is a shaded tent area. The 14 group-sized teepees around the park's perimeter are another option, but you'll need bedding to sleep on the concrete slab they shelter, or rent cots ($2). Facilities include a swimming pool, laundry, showers, saunas and playground.

You'll find the following two motels side by side near the junction of US 97 and Hwy 22.

Oxbow Motor Inn (☎ 509-865-5800, 888-865-5855, fax 509-865-3623, 511 S Elm St) Singles/doubles $40/44. The cheaper choice

offers adequate accommodations with cable TV. If you do stay here, check out the mural next door, which depicts how the Yakamas fished at Celilo Falls before the Dalles Dam ruined things.

Best Western Lincoln Inn (☎ 509-865-7444, 877-509-7444, fax 509-865-7719, 515 S Elm St) Singles/doubles $80/90. The fancy option has nicely furnished units with sleek king-size beds and an indoor pool. The steep rate includes a light breakfast.

If you find yourself hungry in this part of the valley, do as the locals do and eat Mexican.

El Ranchito (☎ 509-829-5880, 1319 E 1st Ave) Entrees $6. Fill up on tacos and enchiladas (under $2 apiece) at this tortilla factory/bakery/cafeteria off I-82 exit 54 in Zillah.

Villaseñor (☎ 509-865-4707, 225 S Toppenish Ave) Entrees $8-10. If you lived in Toppenish, this is where you and your friends would meet for Mexican food.

Pioneer Kitchen (☎ 509-865-3201, 227 S Toppenish Ave) Dishes $4-8. This is the local greasy spoon, serving high-cholesterol home-cooked breakfasts and tasty huckleberry shakes.

Legends Casino (☎ 877-726-6311, 580 Fort Rd) Lunch $6-10, dinner $8-17. People line up for the daily lunch and dinner buffets here, especially on Friday when you get a platter of breaded shrimp, mussels, baked salmon, Dungeness crab *and* a slab of roast sirloin for 8 bucks.

Entertainment

Legends Casino (☎ 877-726-6311, 580 Fort Rd) Near tribal headquarters, Yakama Nation's Vegas-style gambling hall has been a major attraction in the valley since it opened in 1998. Humming with activity at all hours, the 45,000-sq-foot facility features approximately 30 blackjack tables ($3 to $10 minimum), stud poker, hundreds of slot machines and a 600-seat Bingo hall, which also functions as a venue for boxing and concerts. There's a popular buffet (see above) but no alcohol is served on the premises.

WASHINGTON

Getting There & Away

Four Greyhound buses a day link Yakima to Toppenish ($7, 30 minutes), two of which continue to the Tri-Cities ($14, 2 hours) via the valley villages of Sunnyside, Granger and Prosser. In Toppenish the bus stops at Branding Iron Restaurant (☎ 509-865-6100)

at 61311 US 97. A cheaper alternative (it' also one that's free of charge) is to take Yakima Transit's Valley Express Shuttle with weekday service between Yakima and the towns of Wapato, Toppenish and Sun nyside (see Getting There & Around in the Yakima section, earlier in this chapter).

Northeastern Washington

Northeastern Washington's mountains – the Kettle River and Selkirk Ranges – are the far western foothills of the Rockies. Ground down by several successive waves of glaciers, these forested slopes are now more rolling hills than jagged peaks. The Columbia River winds south through these mountains, widening into Lake Roosevelt as it turns west and backs up behind the Grand Coulee Dam. The river here marks the northern boundary of the central Washington steppe.

During the Ice Age, glaciers crept down from the north and overtook the Columbia River's channel, forcing its contents to cut a new southerly path. When the glaciers receded, the river went back to its original streambed, leaving the big, dry river channel known today as the Grand Coulee.

Northeastern Washington lacks the developed recreation that's abundant in the western part of the state, but there are many good places to hike, fish and cross-country ski, especially in the Okanogan and Colville National Forests. The rugged, dramatic landscape of the Columbia Basin provides a suitably dramatic setting for the towering Grand Coulee Dam, one of the world's largest producers of hydroelectric power. Lake Roosevelt is a popular vacation spot for boating and fishing. Spokane is the best place to begin exploring these regions – it's the largest city for many a dry mile and a shopping mecca for the smaller communities of the Inland Northwest. It is also the only place where you have a chance of seeing the opera or eating a good Thai meal.

The Cascades take the brunt of Pacific storms, which is why the land to the east receives so little rainfall. But at the state's northeastern edge, the Selkirks catch storms anew, receiving up to 80 inches of precipitation a year and creating an undeniable winter. Spokane misses the heavy rain and snow that fall in the nearby mountains, but it still gets its fair share.

From the western side of the state, the area can be reached by any of three major routes – I-90, US 2 or Hwy 20 – the last being the western extremity of a coast-to-coast bicycle route. Whether by air, train or bus, most transportation heads to Spokane; local bus service tends to be sparse throughout this region.

Highlights

- Exploring Spokane, the vibrant capital of the inland Northwest
- Feeling the electricity at Grand Coulee Dam
- Visiting Dry Falls – once the world's greatest waterfall
- Fishing in the lake-speckled plateaus of the remote Okanogan National Forest
- Watching wildlife in the Salmo-Priest Wilderness Area

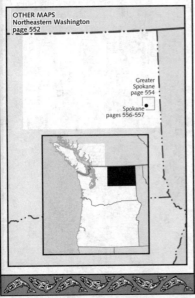

OTHER MAPS
Northeastern Washington
page 552

Greater
Spokane
page 554

Spokane
pages 556-557

NORTHEASTERN WASHINGTON

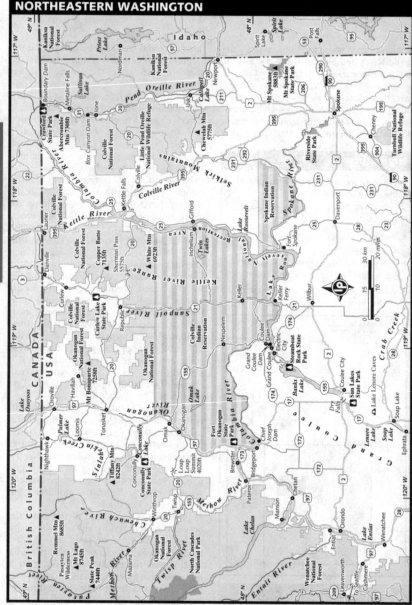

History

Originally, Native Americans lived mainly around the Columbia River and its tributaries. Places like Kettle Falls and Spokane Falls were especially good spots for salmon fishing, and communities grew up around them. David Thompson, a Canadian explorer and fur trader, was the first white person to navigate the entire length of the Columbia River, and his reports and maps of the Inland Northwest laid the way for more fur traders.

Eventually, the Native American tribes were confined to the Colville and Spokane reservations. Disease severely reduced their numbers, and European settlers further appropriated their lands as mineral resources – especially gold – were found in the remote hills to the north. Life was pretty rugged, even after the Northern Pacific Railroad came through in 1881, spurring Spokane's growth. Not until the Columbia Basin Irrigation Project of the 1930s, whose centerpiece was the Grand Coulee Dam, did life begin to change significantly. The project turned the nearby desert into wheat fields, and the electricity these dams produced helped support Washington's post-WWII industrial boom.

SPOKANE

Spokane (population 195,629), the largest city between Seattle and Minneapolis, is the trade center for the Inland Northwest, an area comprising eastern Washington, northern Idaho, western Montana and parts of Oregon, British Columbia and Alberta.

Spokane Indians, whose name is thought to mean 'children of the sun,' originally inhabited the region around the Spokane River, living off the abundant fish, berries and game of the area. Skilled in fishing, they made salmon a key component of their economy. With the other Salish-speaking tribes of the region, the Kalispels, Flatheads and Coeur d'Alenes, they would cross the Rockies to hunt buffalo.

Though Spokane (spo-**can**) was the location of Washington's first trading post in 1810, it was eventually replaced by Fort Colvile, which was more conveniently located on the Columbia River. Indian wars slowed the region's development; it wasn't until 1879 that white settlers staked claims near the falls. After the discovery of gold and other precious metals around Coeur d'Alene, Idaho, in the 1880s, Spokane flourished as a gold capital.

By 1883 it had become a major rail center of the West, served by several transcontinental lines, which brought thousands of new immigrants eager for fresh opportunities in trade and manufacturing. After the burgeoning business district was destroyed by fire in 1889, the downtown area was rebuilt, this time in brick rather than wood.

Spokane grew up to be a market center, and today the city is inordinately proud of its skywalk, an above-ground, covered walkway between a number of downtown buildings and department stores. Gigantic shopping malls and strip developments govern activities on the north side of town. Aside from shopping, Spokane offers a few popular golf courses, several large city parks and a healthy dose of nightlife. While Spokane doesn't offer the bustle and vibrancy of western Washington's cities, there's a little bit of everything in Spokane, and most people who live there are glad it's not too big.

Orientation

Spokane is just 18 miles from the Idaho border and is 110 miles south of Canada. I-90 is the main east-west route through town. The main downtown area, including the skywalk, is between I-90 and Riverfront Park. In general, avenues run east-west, streets north-south. Sprague Ave, just north of the freeway, divides north addresses from south, while Division St, the main north-south drag, divides east from west. It becomes US 2 north of town.

Information

Stop by the Spokane Area Visitor Information Center (☎ 509-747-3230, 800-248-3230, ⓦ www.visitspokane.com), 201 W Main Ave at Browne St, for a raft of information.

Washington Trust Bank (☎ 509-353-3878), downtown at 717 W Sprague, can

WASHINGTON

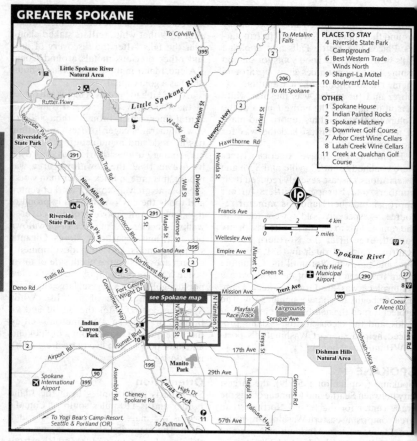

GREATER SPOKANE

To Colville

To Metaline Falls

395

2

Little Spokane River Natural Area

206

To Mt Spokane

Little Spokane River

Rutter Pkwy

Riverside Park Dr

Waikiki Rd

Newport Hwy

Division St

Market St

Hawthorne Rd

Riverside State Park

291

Indian Trail Rd

Nevada St

Nine Mile Rd

Wall St

Francis Ave

Aubrey White Pkwy

A St

Monroe St

Maple St

291

Wellesley Ave

Riverside State Park

Driscol Blvd

Garland Ave

395

Empire Ave

2

Market St

Green St

Spokane River

Trails Rd

Northwest Blvd

Fort George Wright Dr

Felts Field Municipal Airport

290

27

Deno Rd

Government Way

Mission Ave

8

To Coeur d'Alene (ID)

see Spokane map

N Monroe St

N Hamilton St

Playfair Race Track

Fairgrounds

Sprague Ave

90

Indian Canyon Park

2

Sunset Blvd

17th Ave

Freya St

Dishman Hills Natural Area

Dishman-Mica Rd

Pines Rd

Airport Rd

195

Manito Park

29th Ave

Regal St

Glenrose Rd

Spokane International Airport

90

395

Assembly Rd

Latah Creek

High Dr

Cheney-Spokane Rd

Palouse Hwy

To Yogi Bear's Camp-Resort, Seattle & Portland (OR)

To Pullman

57th Ave

11

0   2   4 km
0   1   2 miles

PLACES TO STAY
4 Riverside State Park Campground
6 Best Western Trade Winds North
9 Shangri-La Motel
10 Boulevard Motel

OTHER
1 Spokane House
2 Indian Painted Rocks
3 Spokane Hatchery
5 Downriver Golf Course
7 Arbor Crest Wine Cellars
8 Latah Creek Wine Cellars
11 Creek at Qualchan Golf Course

WASHINGTON

---

exchange foreign currency up to $200 but charges a hefty $10 fee.

The main post office is at 904 W Riverside Ave downtown. Check email, free of charge, at Spokane Public Library (☎ 509-444-5336), 906 W Main Ave at Lincoln.

The *Spokesman-Review* is the local daily newspaper. KPBX, 91.1 FM, broadcasts National Public Radio programming.

Monroe St Laundry (☎ 509-327-1769), 2407 N Monroe St, is open daily until 10pm, as is the Hamilton St Wash & Dry (☎ 509-487-6184), 1725 N Hamilton St, north of Gonzaga University.

Recommended health care facilities include Sacred Heart Medical Center (☎ 509-455-3131), W 101 8th Ave, and Deaconess Medical Center (☎ 509-458-5800), 800 W 5th Ave.

Auntie's Bookstore (☎ 509-838-0206), 402 W Main Ave, is northeastern Washington's best, with a good mix of regional titles. Readings and other events are scheduled several times a week. The adjacent Liberty Café has salads, sandwiches and coffee.

For a great selection of national park maps and travel books, NW Map & Travel

Book Center (☎ 509-455-6981), 525 W Sprague Ave, is the place to go.

Riverfront Park

Once a blot on Spokane's landscape, the downtown area around the Spokane River was spruced up in 1974 in anticipation of the World's Fair & Exposition and converted into the now-attractive Riverfront Park (☎ 509-456-4386, 800-336-7275, W www .spokaneriverfrontpark.com). The 100-acre campus of gardens, playgrounds, amusement rides and activity centers adjoins the convention center.

Spokane Falls is a good place to relax or start exploring. As Native American legend has it, the multitiered falls were created by Coyote, who in a fit of rage smashed the river bottom with his paw. He wanted to exact revenge against the Spokane tribe for refusing to let him marry one of their women. The Coyote legend is engraved into a marble spiral in a circular promenade located between the library and the **Monroe St Bridge**. Built in 1911 and still the largest concrete arch in the USA, the bridge provides views of the falls, and a **gondola** (admission $4.75; open 11am-6pm Sun-Thur year-round, till 10pm Fri-Sat Apr-Sept) takes you directly over them.

In the center of the park is the **Pavilion**, with a small amusement park, open in summer. Wintertime activity centers on the **Ice Palace** (open noon-8pm Mon-Thur, noon-5pm & 7pm-10pm Fri & Sat, noon-5pm Sun Nov-Mar), a skating rink. The **IMAX Theater** (☎ 509-625-6686; adult/senior/child $7/6/5; shows hourly noon-7pm daily summer; Fri-Sun & holidays winter) next door shows eye-popping, large-screen films.

Less of a thrill but still fun at any age are rides on the 1909, hand-carved **carousel** (open noon-5pm weekends & holidays), near the southern edge of the park on Spokane Falls Blvd. Kids will surely want to clamber up on the gigantic reproduction of a Radio Flyer wagon just to the east – the wagon handle is a slide. Pavilion rides and other activities are all charged separately, or you can get a comprehensive day pass for $15. Rent bicycle surreys and 'hotshots' (re-

cumbent bicycles) in the park from **Serendipity Cycles** (☎ 509-893-2880; from $8 per hour) on a pedestrian bridge west of the carousel.

Gonzaga University

Founded in 1887 by the Jesuit Order, Gonzaga University (☎ 509-323-6398) has a reputation as one of the West Coast's top liberal arts institutions. Gonzaga's most famous alumnus, Bing Crosby, donated a comprehensive collection of his recordings and paraphernalia, which are on display in the **Bing Crosby Memorabilia Room** (☎ 509-328-4220, ext 4097, 502 E Boone Ave; open 8am-midnight daily during school year; summer hours vary), at the Crosby Student Center. A bronze statue of the crooner stands out front, with golf clubs in tow.

In the university art center at the end of Pearl St is the **Jundt Art Museum** (☎ 509-323-6611, 202 E Cataldo Ave; open 10am-4pm Mon-Thur, 10am-9pm Fri, noon-4pm Sat, summer hours vary). The museum houses a good collection of classical sculpture and painting, as well as an 18-foot chandelier by glass artist Dale Chihuly.

Gonzaga sits on the north bank of the Spokane River and is easily reached by turning east onto Boone Ave from either Division or Ruby St. Take bus No 26 or 91 from downtown.

Northwest Museum of Arts & Culture

One of the largest collections of indigenous artifacts in the Northwest is on display at this brand new museum in the Browne's Addition district (☎ 509-456-3931, W www .northwestmuseum.org, 2316 W 1st Ave; adult/senior & student/child $7/5/free; open 11am-5pm Tues-Sun, till 8pm Wed & Fri). Incorporating the old Cheney Cowles Museum, the NW MAC also features exhibits on Northwest history and contemporary art. Five galleries are entered via a unique glass foyer overlooking the Spokane River; an outdoor amphitheater hosts plays and lectures. Admission includes a tour of the 1898 **Campbell House** (see the boxed text 'Spokane's Age of Elegance').

WASHINGTON

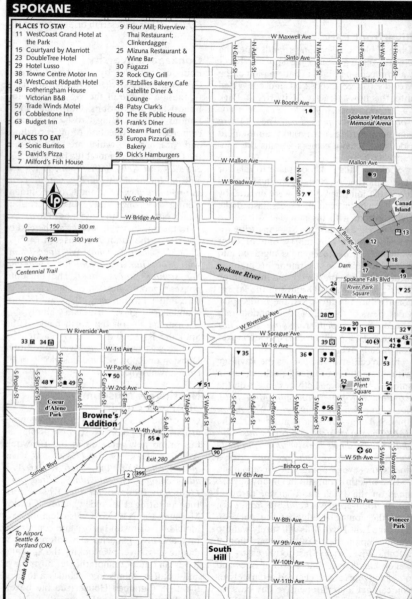

SPOKANE

PLACES TO STAY
11 WestCoast Grand Hotel at the Park
15 Courtyard by Marriott
23 DoubleTree Hotel
29 Hotel Lusso
38 Towne Centre Motor Inn
43 WestCoast Ridpath Hotel
49 Fotheringham House Victorian B&B
57 Trade Winds Motel
61 Cobblestone Inn
63 Budget Inn

PLACES TO EAT
4 Sonic Burritos
5 David's Pizza
7 Milford's Fish House
9 Flour Mill; Riverview Thai Restaurant; Clinkerdagger
25 Mizuna Restaurant & Wine Bar
30 Fugazzi
32 Rock City Grill
35 Fitzbillies Bakery Cafe
44 Satellite Diner & Lounge
48 Patsy Clark's
50 The Elk Public House
51 Frank's Diner
52 Steam Plant Grill
53 Europa Pizzaria & Bakery
59 Dick's Hamburgers

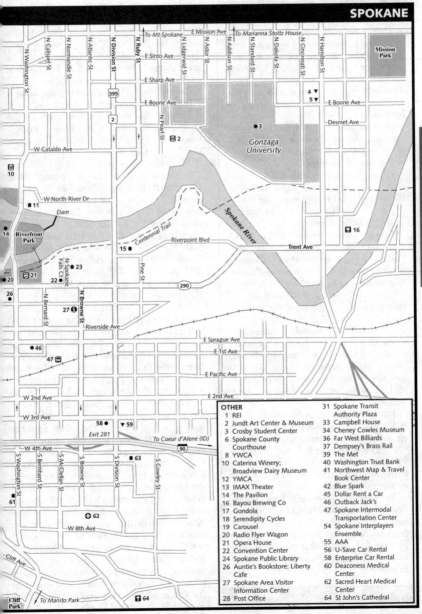

SPOKANE

WASHINGTON

OTHER
1 REI
2 Jundt Art Center & Museum
3 Crosby Student Center
6 Spokane County Courthouse
8 YWCA
10 Caterina Winery; Broadview Dairy Museum
12 YMCA
13 IMAX Theater
14 The Pavilion
16 Bayou Brewing Co
17 Gondola
18 Serendipity Cycles
19 Carousel
20 Radio Flyer Wagon
21 Opera House
22 Convention Center
24 Spokane Public Library
26 Auntie's Bookstore; Liberty Cafe
27 Spokane Area Visitor Information Center
28 Post Office
31 Spokane Transit Authority Plaza
33 Campbell House
34 Cheney Cowles Museum
36 Far West Billiards
37 Dempsey's Brass Rail
39 The Met
40 Washington Trust Bank
41 Northwest Map & Travel Book Center
42 Blue Spark
45 Dollar Rent a Car
46 Outback Jack's
47 Spokane Intermodal Transportation Center
54 Spokane Interplayers Ensemble
55 AAA
56 U-Save Car Rental
58 Enterprise Car Rental
60 Deaconess Medical Center
62 Sacred Heart Medical Center
64 St John's Cathedral

Spokane's Age of Elegance

In 1889, a fire gutted Spokane's burgeoning downtown business core. Having spent a relatively subdued decade as a booming gold capital and trade center, the city catapulted itself out of the ashes with new architectural aspirations, launching into a building frenzy. Mining tycoons spared no expense, hiring the region's best architect, Kirkland K Cutter, to build their stately mansions. Cutter designed many such houses for Browne's Addition, a now historic neighborhood of showplace homes west of downtown.

Gothic, Renaissance, Arts & Crafts, neo-classical and art deco are just a few of the styles represented around town. The following are the most prominent examples of Spokane's architectural legacy.

Spokane's most famous mansion, **Patrick Clark Mansion**, at 2208 W 2nd Ave, was built for mining magnate Patrick D Clark and is now Patsy Clark's, a fancy restaurant. Anyone can stop by to admire the Moorish-influenced exterior, but you'll need a dinner reservation to get a glimpse of the onyx fireplaces inside.

The Tudor-style **Campbell House**, the estate of mining tycoon Amasa Campbell, was built in Browne's Addition in 1898. Admission to the Campbell House, 2316 W First Ave, is included in the price of a ticket to the adjacent Northwest Museum of Arts & Culture.

North of downtown, at W Broadway and N Madison St, the **Spokane County Court House** is almost an apparition. Built in the 1890s by a self-trained architect, the French Renaissance structure was inspired by the chateaus at Chambord and Azay-le-Rideau in France's Loire Valley.

The stunning and ornate **St John's Cathedral** (☎ 509-838-4277), 127 E 12th Ave, built in 1927, is a classic example of English Gothic architecture. Tours are given from noon to 3pm daily except Wednesday and Friday. Follow Stevens St south of downtown to get there.

Riverside State Park

Covering over 10,000 acres along the Spokane River northwest of town, Riverside State Park (☎ 509-456-3964, **w** www.riversidestatepark.org) offers a variety of recreational opportunities and geological phenomena along with a bit of history.

One of the park's highlights is the **Bowl & Pitcher**, a deep gorge with huge boulders at a bend in the river 2 miles north of the southern entrance. A suspension bridge, built in the 1930s by the Civilian Conservation Corps (CCC), crosses the river here.

Stretching through the park is the northwest extremity of the paved **Spokane River Centennial Trail** (☎ 509-624-7188), which extends 37 miles to the Idaho state line and beyond to Coeur d'Alene. Designated portions are open for mountain biking and horseback riding. Contact **Trail Town Riding Stables** (☎ 509-456-8249, 3402 N Aubrey White Parkway) for riding appointments ($15 per hour). Maps are available at the park office, near the Bowl & Pitcher, and at REI (see Activities, later).

Fur trader David Thompson of the North West Company built a trading post in 1810 just north of Nine Mile Falls, beyond the trail's northern endpoint. The site is commemorated by the **Spokane House Interpretive Center** (admission free; open 10am-6pm Thur-Mon June-Aug), where several modest exhibits tell the story with photos and dioramas. Nearby, you can explore one of Thompson's trapping routes, much as it may have looked in his time, at the **Little Spokane River Natural Area**. A hiking/cross-country skiing trail through the protected wetland begins about half a mile beyond Spokane House along Hwy 291, near the point where the Little Spokane River flows into its bigger counterpart, and meanders 3.6 miles to the east as far as Rutter Parkway. Great blue herons nest in the cottonwoods near the trail's midway point. Toward the east end, you'll find Native American **pictographs** at Indian Painted Rocks. The exceptionally peaceful area is perhaps best appreciated by paddling – canoe put-in sites are found by the fish hatchery at the end of Waikiki Rd, and at Indian Painted Rocks.

To reach Riverside State Park from downtown, take Monroe St north over the bridge. Turn left at Maxwell St and follow it west until it turns onto Pettet Dr, which leads past the Downriver Golf Course to the park's southern entrance. You can continue up through the park along Downriver Dr. Otherwise, take bus No 20 from the Plaza downtown.

Wineries
Sample locally crafted merlots and cabernets at the half dozen wineries in and around the city.

A giant checkerboard, fountains, pools and formal gardens impart a fairyland feel to the grounds at **Arbor Crest Wine Cellars** (☎ 509-927-9894, 4705 N Fruithill Rd; tastings noon-5pm daily). The tasting room is housed in a cliff-side mansion overlooking the Spokane River. Only adults are allowed to visit the winery and grounds.

The **Caterina Winery** (☎ 509-328-5069, 905 N Washington; tastings noon-5pm daily), on the northern outskirts of Riverfront Park, is one winery you *can* bring the kids to – it's housed on the bottom floor of the Broadview Dairy Museum. Their Cabernet Sauvignon has received attention in recent years.

Riesling and chardonnay are good wines to try at the **Latah Creek Wine Cellars** (☎ 509-926-0164, 13030 E Indiana Ave; open 9am-5pm daily), east of the city off I-90 exit 289.

Activities
Spokane is known in golf circles for its profusion of courses and its enthusiastic golfers. **The Creek at Qualchan** (☎ 509-448-9317, 301 E Meadow Lane Rd – I-90 exit 279; green fees $22.50), south of town in a bird and wildlife sanctuary, is a challenging 18-hole course that has been a stop on the PGA golf tour.

Indoor swimming pools can be found at the **YMCA** (☎ 509-838-3577, 507 N Howard St, adult/senior $7/5), in Riverfront Park, and the **YWCA** (☎ 509-326-1190, 829 W Broadway, adult/child $5/3), just across the river.

There's downhill skiing sans resort hype at the **Mount Spokane Ski & Snowboard Park** (☎ 509-238-2220, daily snow report ☎ 509-238-4025, W www.mtspokane.com), with a lodge and rental shop. Located 31 miles northeast of Spokane at the end of Hwy 206, it features a 2100-foot vertical drop, and there are several trails for **cross-country skiing** in and just past nearby Mt Spokane State Park.

To outfit yourself for more intense outdoor recreation, go to **REI** (☎ 509-328-9900, 1125 N Monroe St) or **Mountain Gear** (☎ 509-325-9000, 2002 N Division St).

Special Events
If Spokane is famous for any one thing, it's the Bloomsday Run. Held the first Sunday in May, the world's biggest timed road race attracts up to 50,000 runners, walkers and wheelchair racers to trace the 7.2-mile (12km) course. Contact the Bloomsday Lilac Association (☎ 509-838-1579) to register.

Shortly following Bloomsday, the lilacs start blooming and Lilac Festival activities commence with a carnival and big torchlit parade on the third Saturday in May. To see the lilacs, visit Manito Park's Lilac Garden.

Hoopfest (☎ 509-624-2414, W www.spokanehoopfest.net) is an enormous outdoor basketball tournament held at Riverfront Park and in the downtown streets. Held in late June, it's open to all ages and abilities and is accompanied by carnival rides, food, music and contests.

In August, Inland Northwest tribes celebrate their heritage with dancing, drumming and crafts at the Spokane Falls Northwest Native American Encampment and Powwow (☎ 509-534-7120) held at Riverfront Park.

Shopping
Twin smokestacks tower over *Steam Plant Square* (☎ 509-777-3900, 159 S Lincoln), an upgrade of a 1915 power facility where shops, cafes and restaurants now mingle with the former boilers and pipes. Another historic building-cum-mall, the *Flour Mill* (621 W Mallon Ave) was built in 1890 as the region's major wheat-grinding facility. Remodeled for the Expo, the mill now houses more restaurants, pricey boutiques and galleries. From Riverfront Park, it can be reached via a footbridge across the river.

Places to Stay

As a weekend shopping destination for the region, Spokane offers plenty of inexpensive and moderately priced lodgings, mainly in three districts: downtown, north along Division St (US 2) and west along Sunset Blvd toward the airport.

Camping Campgrounds are found on the city's western outskirts.

Riverside State Park (☎ 509-456-3964, fax 509-456-2902) Sites $14. The campground at the park's southern end has 101 sites, most renovated in 2001, and hot showers. Reservations are not accepted.

Yogi Bear's Camp-Resort (☎ 509-747-9415, 800-494-7275, W www.jellystonewa .com, 7520 S Thomas Mallen Rd) Tent/RV Sites $21/33, cabins $40-85. Spokane's premier RV park, at I-90 exit 272, has wooded sites and full hookups, including phone lines. Family-oriented amenities include an indoor pool, mini-golf course and hayrides.

B&Bs These stately inns serve as reminders of Spokane's gilded age.

Fotheringham House Victorian B&B (☎ 509-838-1891, 2128 W 2nd Ave) Rooms with shared/private bath $90/105. This turreted structure in Browne's Addition dates from 1891 and retains many period touches and furnishings.

Cobblestone Inn (☎/fax 509-624-9735, 620 S Washington St) Rooms $85/105 with shared/private bath. Close to downtown, this pretty, arched-roof home contains two guest rooms. The rate includes a pastry-intensive breakfast at the downstairs bakery.

Hotels & Motels In addition to those listed below, you'll also find a collection of decent, similarly priced motels along Division and Houston on the northern approach to town.

Trade Winds Motel (☎ 509-838-2091, 800-586-5397, fax 509-838-2094, 907 W 3rd Ave) Singles/doubles $43/48. There's a kind of tacky grandeur about this curved monument to 1960s design located a block south of Steam Plant Square. All rooms have terraces overlooking the pool.

Towne Centre Motor Inn (☎ 509-747-1041, 800-747-1041, fax 509-624-6674, 901 W 1st Ave) Singles/doubles $43/45. Although the neighboring disco might be a nuisance on the weekend, it's hard to beat the price for a decent downtown place.

Budget Inn (☎ 509-838-6101, fax 509-624-0733, 110 E 4th Ave, off exit 281) Singles/doubles $50/55 with continental breakfast. Convenient to downtown, this is a hulking freeway-side motel with a big pool. Rooms facing I-90 are $10 less.

Boulevard Motel (☎ 509-747-1060, W 2905 Sunset Blvd) Singles/doubles $32/45. The rooms in this newly remodeled motel are clean and fresh-smelling. Larger kitchenette units are available, and there's an outdoor pool.

Shangri-La Motel (☎ 509-747-2066, 800-234-4941, fax 509-456-8696, 2922 W Government Way) Singles/doubles $45/50. The main advantage of the Shangri-La (aside from the heated pool) is that it's off the main drag, Sunset Blvd. Some one- and two-bedroom apartments with kitchens are available.

There are plenty of mid-priced chain motels on the north end of town along Division St, near the malls.

Best Western Trade Winds North (☎ 509-326-5500, 800-528-1234, fax 509-328-1357, 3033 N Division St) Rooms $59. Near Euclid Ave, this standard business travelers' place has an indoor pool and sauna.

WestCoast Ridpath Hotel (☎ 509-838-2711, 800-325-4000, fax 509-747-6970, 515 W Sprague Ave) Rooms $99. Downtown, this huge old hotel has an outdoor pool (open year-round) and a penthouse lounge. A skywalk connects the newer wing with the remodeled former Spokane Hotel.

Courtyard by Marriott (☎ 509-456-7600, 800-321-2211, fax 509-456-0969, W www .courtyard .com, 401 N Riverpoint Blvd) Rooms/suites $94/124. The Courtyard has an indoor pool and exercise room, plus the *Wall St Journal* with your morning coffee.

WestCoast Grand Hotel at the Park (☎ 509-326-8000, 800-325-4000, 303 W North River Dr) Rooms $85-149. For some of the nicest digs in town, go for the Grand, located on the north bank of the Spokane River near

Riverfront Park, with indoor and outdoor pools, kitchen units and an airport shuttle.

DoubleTree Hotel (☎ 509-455-9600, 800-222-8733, fax 509-455-6285, N 322 Spokane Falls Court) Standard/executive rooms $99/129. The DoubleTree is right next to the convention center and offers every amenity an expense-account traveler could desire. Those staying in executive rooms get a full breakfast and evening cocktails in the lobby lounge.

Hotel Lusso (☎ 509-747-9750, fax 509-747-9751, W www.hotellusso.com, N One Post St) Rooms $155-$295. From the fountains in the lobby to the Italian marble floors in the bathrooms, this downtown boutique hotel offers a rare touch of class. Extras include a complimentary breakfast and afternoon beverage, not to mention impeccable service.

Places to Eat

Enjoy the range of ethnic cuisines while you're here – Spokane is as cosmopolitan as it gets in this part of the Northwest.

Budget Eating cheap isn't a problem. Some of the city's more appealing options come under this category.

Dicks Hamburgers (☎ 509-747-2481, 10 E 3rd Ave) Burgers $1. Where else will a cheeseburger and milkshake get you change back from $2?

The Elk Public House (☎ 509-363-1973, 1931 W Pacific Ave) Prices $7-9. West of the downtown area, this old drugstore turned pub is a sunny, friendly spot with homemade soups, sandwiches and a variety of brews on tap.

Fitzbillies Bakery Cafe (☎ 509-747-1834, 1325 W 1st Ave) Sandwiches $5-6. Head here for authentic New York bagels or homegrown 'billie bars' (a twist on the bagel, they're holeless and loaded with whole wheat, apples, raisins and nuts).

Riverview Thai Restaurant (☎ 509-325-8370, 621 W Mallon Ave) Entrees $10. One of several eateries in the Flour Mill, this one offers well-seasoned entrees and a front deck with a glimpse of the falls. Eat well and save money on the lunch buffet for $7.

Frank's Diner (☎ 509-747-8798, 1516 W 2nd Ave) Breakfast $5-8. Nestled in a vintage railway car, this classic diner churns out extraordinarily good eggs, biscuits and gravy to an endlessly full house. Frank's operated as a Seattle diner from 1931 until it was moved to Spokane in 1991. Lunch and dinner are also served.

David's Pizza (☎ 509-483-7460, 829 E Boone) Pizzas $13-18. Gonzaga students know that this is the place for traditional New York–style pizzas with gourmet toppings like feta cheese and sun-dried tomatoes. Next door is **Sonic Burritos** (☎ 509-484-4158, 1209 N Hamilton), another student hangout, where you can custom build your own burrito.

Satellite Diner & Lounge (☎ 509-624-3952, W 425 Sprague) Sandwiches & burgers $6-7. Open 7am-4am weekdays, 6pm-4am Sat & Sun. Here's a greasy spoon with panache. A wide spectrum of humanity sits down at the busy lunch counter to fill up on breakfast (served all day) or a tasty soup and sandwich combo. Thursday and Sunday nights the smoky lounge next door becomes a live music venue.

Mid-Range & Top End The upmarket restaurants in Spokane pack plenty of panache.

Rock City Grill (☎ 509-455-4400, 505 W Riverside Ave) Lunch $6-10, Dinner $12-19. New-wave Italian crops up here. A one-person artichoke heart and Dungeness crab pizza goes for $13.25.

Steam Plant Grill (☎ 509-777-3900, 159 S Lincoln) Wraps & sandwiches $7-9, entrees $15-23. Eclectic international cuisine is abundantly served here, in a neo-industrial setting: Try a Thai chicken wrap or a plate of New Zealand lamb chops, followed up with a Kahlúa mousse–filled pastry. A range of local brews are available.

Europa Pizzaria & Bakery (☎ 509-455-4051, 125 S Wall St) Pizzas & pastas $7-15. Open 11am till at least midnight. There's a cozy after-show ambience at this Spokane salon filled with tapestried furniture. Stay around for live acoustic sets on Sunday and Monday evenings.

Mizuna Restaurant & Wine Bar (☎ 509-747-2004, 214 N Howard St) Lunch $6-8, dinner $15. Gourmet vegetarian (and a few seafood) dishes are the attraction at this casually formal downtown restaurant, which takes on a candlelit ambience at dinner. Weekend brunch might include a portobello benedict or an egg tofu scramble.

Fugazzi (☎ 509-624-1133, 1 N Post St) Lunch $7-9, dinner $15-27. Open from 6am for breakfast. Trendy lunch and dinner food (tortilla crusted halibut, tofu stir-fry with shiitake mushrooms) can be had at Fugazzi, one of Spokane's most stylish restaurants.

Milford's Fish House (☎ 509-326-7251, 719 N Monroe St) Dinner $19-25. This is Spokane's best seafood restaurant, where it's easy to spend a bit of money.

Clinkerdagger (☎ 509-328-5965, 621 W Mallon Ave) Entrees $20. An elegant but relaxed place in the Flour Mill, with wraparound windows and a dining deck jutting over the river. Grilled king salmon and rock-salt roasted prime ribs are typical of the savory fare on the menu.

Patsy Clark's (☎ 509-838-8300, 2208 W 2nd Ave) Dinner entrees $28. Named for the Irish miner who built the mansion in the 1890s, this is as formal a place as you'll find in Spokane. People throng to the Sunday brunch.

Entertainment

For a full listing of what's happening in Spokane and Coeur d'Alene, pick up an *Inlander* or *Local Planet,* both free weeklies, or the Friday edition of the *Spokesman-Review.* A mega movie complex, *AMC 20* (☎ 509-747-3456), is in the River Park Square mall at Main and Post.

Performing Arts For tickets to local events, contact TicketsWest (☎ 509-325-7469, 800-325-7328, Ⓦ www.ticketswest.com).

Opera House (☎ 509-353-6500, Ⓦ www .spokanecenter.com, 334 W Spokane Falls Blvd) Part of the Spokane Convention Center at Riverfront Park, the Opera House hosts touring companies and the Spokane Symphony (☎ 509-624-1200) but not the Spokane Opera.

Metropolitan Performing Arts Center (☎ 509-455-6500, 901 W Sprague Ave, Ⓦ www.metmtg.com/themet) The Met presents concerts, plays, film festivals and the Spokane Opera (☎ 509-533-1150) in a fairly intimate setting.

Spokane Interplayers Ensemble (☎ 509-455-7529, Ⓦ www.interplayers.com, 174 S Howard St) Spokane's local theater offers Broadway-style entertainment from September to June.

Spokane Veterans Memorial Arena (☎ 509-324-7000, 720 W Mallon Ave) Catch major touring acts at this 12,500-seat hall opposite the Flour Mill.

Live Music & Clubs Seattle it ain't, but Spokane boasts a respectable club scene. And unlike many American cities of its size, downtown doesn't shut down after five.

Bayou Brewing Company (☎ 509-484-4818, 1003 E Trent) Near Gonzaga University, this Mardi Gras–themed microbrewery/Cajun kitchen typically draws a college crowd for live music and dancing in three separate venues, Fat Tuesday's, Rendezvous and the Voodoo Lounge. The airplane hangar–sized recreational space has plenty of games.

Outback Jack's (☎ 509-624-4549, 321 W Sprague Ave) $3 cover Mon, Wed, Fri & Sun nights. DJs work the mega dance floor four nights a week at this cavernous downtown bar.

Far West Billiards (☎ 509-455-3429, 1001 W 1st Ave) A pool hall/gallery space that serves about two dozen beers to accompany your game. If you need a snack, they've got falafel and fajitas.

Dempsey's Brass Rail (☎ 509-747-5362, 909 W 1st) Dempsey's offers alternative entertainment with drag cabaret shows and a dance floor, all against a crimson background. It's definitely gay-friendly, but fun-loving straights venture in as well.

Blue Spark (☎ 509-838-5787, 15 S Howard St) Spokane's coolest hangout is this downtown corner tavern with a rock 'n' roll attitude. The place starts to heat up after midnight with a soundtrack provided by local bands or the alt-heavy jukebox.

Getting There & Away

Air From Spokane International Airport (☎ 509-455-6455), 8 miles southeast of downtown off Hwy 2, Alaska, Horizon, Southwest and United all offer daily service to/from Seattle and Portland.

Southwest Airlines often runs special e-fares from Seattle to Spokane for as little as $30 one way; check out its website at [W] www.iflysouthwest.com. Delta and Northwest serve Salt Lake City and Minneapolis, respectively.

Bus All buses arrive at and depart from the Spokane Intermodal Transportation Center at 221 W 1st Ave, a combination bus and train station. Both Greyhound (☎ 509-624-5252, [W] www.greyhound.com) and Northwestern Trailways (☎ 800-366-3830, [W] www.nwadv .com/northw) serve Seattle, the latter via Moses Lake, Wenatchee and Leavenworth. In addition, there's daily shuttle service to Colville ($30, 70 miles); call ☎ 509-680-2801 for reservations.

destination	cost (one-way)	duration	distance	frequency (daily)
Coeur d'Alene, ID	$9	45 min	28 miles	3
Pullman, WA	$15	1½ hrs	75 miles	2
Wenatchee, WA	$25	3½ hrs	170 miles	1
Seattle, WA	$28	6 hrs	323 miles	4
Portland, OR	$38	9 hrs	355 miles	2
Boise, ID	$36	10 hrs	425 miles	1

Train Amtrak's passenger station (☎ 509-624-5144, 800-872-7245, [W] www.amtrak .com) is in the Spokane Intermodal Transportation Center (see Bus, earlier). The westbound *Empire Builder* departs for Seattle ($38, 8 hours) at 2:15am, for Portland ($38, 7½ hours) at 2:45am; the eastbound train to Chicago ($282, 39 hours) leaves at 1:15am. The ticket counter is open 10pm to 5:30am daily and 10am to 5:30pm weekdays.

Car The American Automobile Association (AAA; ☎ 509-358-6900) is downtown at 1717 W 4th Ave.

The following car rental companies have airport outlets:

Avis (☎ 509-747-8081, 800-331-1212)
Budget (☎ 509-623-9710, 800-527-0700)
National (☎ 509-624-8995, 800-227-7368)
Thrifty (☎ 509-838-8223, 800-367-2277)

Those with downtown offices include the following:

Dollar (☎ 509-456-3007) 430 W 1st Ave
Enterprise (☎ 509-458-3340, 800-736-8222) 3 W 3rd Ave
U-Save (☎ 509-455-8018, 800-272-8728) 918 W 3rd Ave

Getting Around

Spokane Transit (☎ 509-328-7433, [W] www .spokanetransit.com) buses depart from streets bordering the Plaza, a huge indoor transit station at Sprague Ave and Wall St. Bus fare is 75¢. Route maps are available free from the Bus Shop on the Plaza's upper level.

Visitors can get to all of the sites surrounding Riverfront Park on the Spokane Falls Streetcar. Streetcars pick up from the east side of the Plaza and loop clockwise around the park, stopping at the Spokane Veteran's Memorial Arena, the Flour Mill and Caterina Winery.

Bus No 64 runs hourly on weekdays between the Plaza and Spokane International Airport, from 6:20am to 5:50pm.

For a taxi, call Spokane Cab (☎ 509-535-2535) or Yellow Cab (☎ 509-624-4321).

AROUND SPOKANE
Turnbull National Wildlife Refuge

Pothole lakes dot the 17,000-acre migratory waterfowl refuge (☎ 509-235-4723, 26010 S Smith Rd; $3; headquarters open 7:30am-4pm, Mon-Fri, refuge open daylight hours) 15 minutes southwest of Spokane near Cheney. Although Turnbull is known for its teeming bird life, especially abundant during the spring and fall, it is also home to threatened water howellia, which grows in clay-bottomed ponds. There's a 6-mile auto

WASHINGTON

tour around the refuge and a couple of hiking trails. Free maps are available at the fee station and headquarters.

From Cheney, turn south off the main drag (Hwy 904) onto the Cheney-Plaza Rd and head another 4½ miles south to the refuge.

Grand Coulee Dam Area

The Grand Coulee Dam, with its three powerhouses, is the country's largest hydroelectric project and the third-largest hydropower producer in the world (after Guri Dam in Venezuela and Itaipu Dam between Paraguay and Brazil). Grand Coulee is the linchpin of the Columbia River's 11 dams, producing 6809 megawatts, about a quarter of hydropower generated along the river. One of the world's largest concrete structures, it was built in the Depression era (beginning in 1933) by the US Bureau of Reclamation to irrigate Columbia Basin farmlands and provide reliable sources of water and electricity.

It was built without fish ladders, a decision that led to the extinction of salmon and other anadromous fish (that is, fish that ascend rivers from the sea for breeding) upriver from the dam. But when you're here, it's easy to see why this was done. The 550-foot dam wall is just too big and steep for conventional fish ladders.

While many people come here to marvel at this engineering feat, an equal number are drawn by the fishing, hunting, swimming and sheer physical beauty of the area. The dam is at the center of a vast recreation area consisting of lakes that were created with the building of the dam. Lake Roosevelt extends 150 miles east and north of the dam. To the southwest is Banks Lake, a holding reservoir for the Columbia Basin Irrigation Project. The diverted waters of the Columbia River fill the upper part of the Grand Coulee, a dramatic canyon bordered by basalt columns sculpted by glacial action.

Orientation

Hwys 155 and 174 intersect at the Grand Coulee Dam, which is 90 miles from either Spokane or Wenatchee and 225 miles from Seattle. Omak is 50 miles north via Hwy 155 and Coulee City, at the end of Banks Lake in the Grand Coulee, is 30 miles south.

Three small, rather drab towns cluster around the dam, and it's easy to get a little disoriented. Grand Coulee (population 897) and Electric City (population 922) are just above the dam, and directly below is Coulee Dam (population 1044), the most interesting of the three.

Information

Information can be found at the Grand Coulee Dam Area Chamber of Commerce (☎ 509-633-3074, 800-268-5332, W www.grand couleedam.org), 306 Midway in Coulee Dam.

Coulee Community Hospital (☎ 509-633-1753), 411 Fortuyn Rd is just northwest of the main business district of Grand Coulee.

Laundry facilities are available in Grand Coulee at King's Court RV Park (☎ 509-633-3655), 212 E Grand Coulee Ave.

Check email for $5 per hour at Terra Byte (☎ 509-633-0493), 531 E Grand Coulee Ave, open noon to 6pm Monday to Friday and occasionally on weekends.

GRAND COULEE DAM

The Grand Coulee Visitor Arrival Center (☎ 509-633-9265), the pie pan–shaped building on Hwy 155, on the west side of the river, has historical exhibits of the dam construction and lots of great WPA-era photos. Three films are shown in rotation: a documentary on the construction of the dam, another on the formation of the Grand Coulee by Ice Age floods and a vaguely propagandistic film about hydropower. If you're lucky, someone who worked on the dam will be visiting at the same time and will be regaling people with stories, a not uncommon occurrence. It's open 9am to 5pm.

Guided **tours** of the dam involve taking a glass-walled elevator 465 feet down an incline into the Third Power Plant, where you can view the tops of the generators from an observation deck. The 35-minute tour is given hourly, from May to September, less often the rest of the year. However, tours were suspended indefinitely in fall 2001 due to the terrorist attacks.

It would be hard to visit Coulee Dam without seeing the nightly **laser show**, which illustrates the history of the Columbia River and its dams. Shows begin after dark from May to September. The best views are from the visitor arrival center or the park below it. Get there early to find parking.

Places to Stay

In addition to these in the vicinity of the dam, there are plenty of other campgrounds around Lake Roosevelt and along the Grand Coulee.

Spring Canyon Campground (☎ 509-633-9188) Sites $10/5 summer/winter. This popular NPS campground and boat launch is on Lake Roosevelt, 3 miles east of Grand Coulee on Hwy 174. The sites have views across the lake. Activities abound, with a swimming beach, volleyball court, and a nature trail that explores the prairie ecosystem.

Coulee Playland Resort (☎ 509-633-2671, fax 509-633-2133, W www.coulee playland.com, Hwy 155 No 1, Electric City) Sites $17.50-20. A mile south of Hwy 174, this fisher-friendly resort has space for RVs and tents on Banks Lake, along with hot showers and a laundry. There's a boat launch and rentals (motorboat/canoe & rowboat $50/15 for four hours, paddleboat $7/hour).

The area's only B&B is within walking distance of the dam.

Four Winds B&B (☎ 509-633-3146, 800-786-3146, e fourwind@televar.com, 301 Lincoln Ave, Coulee Dam) Rooms from $62/79 shared/private bath. This former WPA workers' dorm has simple, attractive rooms, some accommodating up to four people, with quilted beds and period furniture. Breakfast is included. On the porch, a wheelchair used by Franklin D Roosevelt commemorates the president's visit here in 1937.

Of the three towns near the dam, Coulee Dam is the best bet for a motel room.

Columbia River Inn (☎ 509-633-2100, 800-633-6421, fax 509-633-2633, W www .columbiariverinn.com, 10 Lincoln St, Coulee Dam) Rooms $75-85. Opposite the Visitor Arrival Center, the inn features pleasant nonsmoking rooms, each with a dam-view balcony; pine wainscoting creates a country lodge effect. Cool off in the pool.

Coulee House Motel (☎ 509-633-1101, 800-715-7767, fax 509-633-1416, 110 Roosevelt Way) Rooms from $66. Just across the bridge, this motel also overlooks the dam, with excellent seats for the nightly light show. However, of the standard units here, only room 210 affords direct views. Extras include a sauna, spa and small pool.

Grand Coulee Motel (☎ 509-633-2860, 877-633-2860, W www.grandcouleemotel .com, 404 Spokane Way, Grand Coulee) Singles/doubles $37/55. At this newly renovated motel in Grand Coulee, all rooms come with a porch and table, some with a kitchen.

Skydeck Motel (☎ 509-633-0292, 800-708-3014, Hwy 155) Singles/doubles $65/75. In Electric City, the Sky Deck has modern rooms fronting onto Banks Lake, each equipped with fridge and microwave, and a hot tub with sunset views of the lake.

Places to Eat

Don't expect a wide spectrum of culinary choices in the area.

Siam Palace (☎ 509-633-2921, 213 Main St) Entrees $7. Closed Sunday & Monday. This is the only place in Grand Coulee to satisfy a craving for Chinese or Thai food.

Melody Restaurant (☎ 509-633-1151, 512 River Dr) Entrees $6-10. Adjacent to the Coulee House Motel, this no-nonsense cafe offers an exterior deck for laser show viewing. The large nachos make an inexpensive meal for two. The Melody shares a building with a bowling alley and movie theater.

COLVILLE INDIAN RESERVATION

Covering an area bigger than the state of Delaware, the Colville Indian Reservation has its southern boundary in Coulee Dam and extends northward past Omak. It is bordered by US 97 on the west, the Columbia River and Lake Roosevelt to the south and east and the Okanogan National Forest on the north.

WASHINGTON

Colville Confederated Tribes

Twelve different bands make up the Colville Confederated Tribes: the Chelan, Colville, Entiat, Lake, Methow, Moses Columbia, Nespelem, Nez Perce, southern Okanogan, Palus, San Poil and Wenatchi. Up until the mid-19th-century, the ancestors of the Colville Confederated Tribes were nomadic, and many tribes fished and traded around the Kettle Falls area. When white fur traders began working the Northwest, it didn't take long before a fur-trading post, Fort Colvile, was established at Kettle Falls. Trading was active from 1826 to 1887, and as the years passed, whites began referring to all local Native Americans as 'Colvilles.' In 1872, the Colville Indian Reservation was formed.

The reservation covers 2100 sq miles, about half the size of the original reservation, and there are more than 8700 tribal members. The tribal headquarters is near Nespelem, north of Grand Coulee Dam. Tribal industries revolve around timber, and there is a fish hatchery that stocks all of north-central Washington's lakes and streams.

Though the reservation isn't set up for tourists, respectful visitors are welcome. Amenities are limited and there are no real restaurants, but it's easy to make a day trip from the dam area or Omak. Visitors should stick to the roads and not wander off on unauthorized hikes.

The tribal headquarters (☎ 509-634-4711) is just south of Nespelem on Hwy 155. Most of the reservation's sites and towns are located along Hwy 155, which passes from Omak to the Grand Coulee Dam. Buffalo and McGinnis Lakes are open to public fishing; get permits at the Tribal Fish and Wildlife Office (☎ 509-634-8845), at tribal headquarters.

The **Fourth of July Powwow** in Nespelem is a 10-day celebration that draws participants from across the Northwest.

Dioramas of traditional fishing and village life, along with collections of baskets, spears and other art and artifacts can be seen at the **Colville Confederated Tribes Museum** (☎ 509-633-0751, 512 Mead Way; open 10am-6pm daily Apr-Sept, other times by appointment), in Coulee Dam. A gift shop sells books, beadwork and other crafts.

Nez Perce leader Chief Joseph is buried in the tribal cemetery of Nespelem. Joseph and his band were sent to the Colville Reservation in 1884, several years after their long march across eastern Oregon, Idaho and Montana was halted by the Army (see the 'Nez Perce Diaspora' boxed text, in the Northeastern Oregon chapter). Though his gravesite is not open to the general public, visitors can stop at the roadside marker in Nespelem which serves as his memorial; it is the last of 38 separate sites along the Nez Perce National Historic Trail, which begins near Joseph, Oregon.

LAKE ROOSEVELT NATIONAL RECREATION AREA

A 150-mile-long reservoir held back by the Grand Coulee Dam, Lake Roosevelt is a major recreation area along 660 miles of Columbia River shoreline. Popular with anglers, the lake is stocked with prize white sturgeon, which average 100lb to 300lb, as well as walleye, rainbow trout and kokanee salmon landlocked by the dam.

Dry, sunny weather prevails near the southern leg of the lake, drawing people to camp and play on the white sand beaches. As Lake Roosevelt inches its way north to Canada, the desert cliffs and high coulee walls give way to rolling hills and orchards, becoming dense forests of ponderosa pine around Kettle Falls.

As recreation areas go, Lake Roosevelt remains refreshingly undeveloped, partly because its shores abut the 2100-sq-mile Colville Indian Reservation, but also because the lake offers little shoreline access for motorists. Most roads cut straight across the lake or dead-end once they've reached it. To explore Lake Roosevelt at any great length is to do so by boat – about two-thirds of the shoreline campgrounds are accessible only to boaters.

Recreation on the lake is comanaged by three federal agencies – the National Parks Service, Bureau of Reclamation and Bureau of Indian Affairs – and the Colville Confederated Tribes and Spokane tribe, which are responsible for all the shoreline area that borders their lands.

Orientation

US 2 runs west from Spokane to the main turnoff points for recreation areas on Lake Roosevelt at Fort Spokane, Keller Ferry and the Grand Coulee Dam. Fort Spokane, the closest access point to Spokane, lies 58 miles northwest via Davenport on Hwy 25 and is the beginning point for a winding lakeshore drive that continues north another 57 miles to Kettle Falls.

The Keller Ferry (free; open 6am to 11pm) crosses Lake Roosevelt and provides access to the scenic north-south Hwy 21, which passes through the Colville Indian Reservation along the Sanpoil River to the town of Republic on Hwy 20. Catch the ferry by heading north on Hwy 21 from Wilbur, which is 29 miles west of Davenport on US 2.

Information

To find out more, contact the Lake Roosevelt National Recreation Area headquarters (☎ 509-633-9441, fax 509-633-9332, W www.nps.gov/laro), 1008 Crest Dr, Coulee Dam, WA 99116, in Coulee Dam. Park admission is free, and the office is open 8am to 4pm.

Visitor centers can also be found in Kettle Falls (☎ 509-738-6266, fax 509-633-9332), 1368 S Kettle Park Rd, and at Spring Canyon campground near Coulee Dam. The Kettle Falls center is open Wednesday to Sunday mid-June to Labor Day.

Fort Spokane

The army built Fort Spokane in 1880, at the confluence of the Spokane and Columbia Rivers, east of where the dam now sits, to quell any disturbances that might arise between white settlers and local Native Americans recently confined to reservations. Both sides were supposed to stay clear

of each other, and during the fort's tenure, which ended in 1898, there were no hostilities. Later the facility became a boarding school run by the Bureau of Indian Affairs.

A trail runs alongside four of the fort's original buildings, and trailside displays tell the story of the fort, though many visitors come here just to camp, swim at the beach or boat on Lake Roosevelt. The Fort Spokane Visitor Center (☎ 509-725-2715; admission free; open 10am-5pm daily May 26-Oct 10) hosts a living history program Sunday mornings from late June through Labor Day.

Activities

The recreation area offers plenty to do, though fishing is the biggest draw. Lake Roosevelt and Banks Lake are the most popular, but Lake Rufus Woods, below Grand Coulee Dam, also attracts anglers (launch a boat from the Elmer City Lower Road launch, a few miles north of Coulee Dam). A Washington state fishing license is needed to cast a line at any of the three.

Boat launches are located at Coulee Playland near Electric City and at Spring Canyon, east of Grand Coulee. Launch fees are $6 for seven days, or $40 for a year. Call the headquarters for information on receiving permits by mail.

Spring Canyon is also the meeting place on Thursday and Friday evenings for ranger-led canoe trips to nearby Crescent Bay Lake; there is no cost and all equipment is provided. Stop by the visitor center at Spring Canyon campground for a schedule.

The Sanpoil River drains into the lake at Keller Ferry, creating good conditions for water-skiing. Water-ski equipment and inner tubes can be rented at the Keller Ferry Campground, which has a popular marina, playground and swimming beach.

An easy 6½-mile biking trail, the Downriver Trail, follows the Columbia River north from Grand Coulee Dam. Catch the trail at Mason City Park, across from the Coulee Dam Shopping Center.

Places to Stay

There are 35 campgrounds on Lake Roosevelt, 28 of which are managed by the

National Park Service – of those, 18 are accessible by land, 10 by boat. Management of the other campgrounds is handled by the Colville Confederated Tribes and the Spokane tribe. Be sure to obtain a tribal permit when camping on reservation property.

Camping fees at NPS sites are $10 May 1 to September 30 and $5 off-season. There's no fee for boat-in only campgrounds. Most of those with vehicle access have running water and flush toilets, though water availability can be subject to lake levels. There are no hookups, but campsites are paved and RV dump stations are available. Most of the developed campgrounds are accessible for those with disabilities.

If the NPS campgrounds are full, there are a number of other nice facilities north along the highway in the Fort Spokane area.

Fort Spokane Campground (☎ *509-725-2715*) Sites $10/5 summer/winter. The NPS-run campground offers 67 tent and RV sites, with a swimming beach and boat launch just north of the historic site on the mouth of the Spokane River.

Seven Bays Campground & Marina (☎ *509-725-1676, 1250 Marina Dr*) Tent sites/RV hookups $10/15. Seven miles south of Fort Spokane, this lakefront spot has a family-style restaurant, marina, laundry and store (open summers only).

Make camp by the lake or venture up along the Sanpoil River for an even remoter setting.

Keller Ferry Campground (☎ *509-633-9188*) Sites $10/5 summer/winter. Near the ferry landing, this facility offers showers and campsites on a grassy field. Rangers give campfire talks in summer.

Keller Park Campground (☎ *509-634-3142*) Tent sites $10. Eight miles north of Keller Ferry on the Colville Indian Reservation is this small roadside campground with cliffside views of the Sanpoil River where it suddenly broadens into a gorge.

For something completely different, consider renting a houseboat.

Roosevelt Recreation Enterprises (☎ *509-647-5755, 800-648-5253, 45751 SR21 N, Wilbur, WA 99185*) Weekend/midweek/full week $1135/1350/$2060 for a 52-foot

houseboat in peak season, not including fuel and sales tax. This Colville Confederated Tribes–run business rents houseboats at the Keller Ferry marina. The boats vary in features and capacity but can usually accommodate 10 to 13 people. Rates are as much as 40% lower in the off season.

GRAND COULEE

One of northeastern Washington's most spectacular geological events occurred about 10,000 years ago, when glaciers filled the Pend Oreille River valley and much of northern Idaho, creating a huge ice dam that held back a glacial lake so large it covered most of western Montana. This barrier of ice also blocked the Columbia River, forcing it into a new channel. When the dam finally gave way, torrents of water rushed over eastern Washington, scouring topsoil and enlarging river channels. The glaciers eventually receded, and the Columbia returned to its original channel, leaving a network of dry riverbeds called 'coulees,' of which Grand Coulee is the largest.

A vast basalt canyon carved into rocky islands and spires reflecting onto small, shallow lakes, the Grand Coulee extends 53 miles southwest from its namesake dam till it peters out somewhere north of Soap Lake. Hwy 155 skirts the east side of the coulee along its reservoir-dominated upper half, intercepting US 2 at the small town of Coulee City.

Banks Lake

Highly regarded by anglers for its abundant bass, perch and walleye, the 31-mile-long Banks Lake is a reservoir filled with water shuttled over from the Columbia River via Grand Coulee Dam. At the southern end of the lake, near Coulee City, Dry Falls Dam controls the flow of water into the Main Canal, which in turn funnels the water for irrigation of Columbia Basin farms and orchards.

Twelve miles south of the dam along Hwy 155, a basalt butte rises 700 feet above the lake at **Steamboat Rock State Park** (☎ *509-633-1304; open 6:30am-dusk*), with camping, a boat launch and a sandy beach.

A sometimes steep **hiking** trail, which bursts with wildflowers in the spring, leads from the campground to the top of the butte, providing a wonderful view down the Grand Coulee (watch out for rattlesnakes here). Another trail begins in Northrup Canyon, across the road from the state park, and passes through Grand County's only forest. Northrup Lake, at the top of the canyon, is stocked with trout. Check in at the Steamboat Rock Ranger Station before hiking this trail.

Dry Falls

These scalloped cliffs are the remnants of what was once the world's largest waterfall – ten times the size of Niagara by some estimates. Formed by the catastrophic Ice Age floods that washed over northeastern Washington, the falls were originally located 20 miles farther south, where they rushed over an 800-foot cliff. Erosion caused them to recede upstream as the underlying bedrock crumbled. The retreat of the falls formed the 3½-mile-wide canyon that remains just south of Coulee City. Exhibits depicting the region's geologic history are on display at the Dry Falls Visitor Center (☎ 509-632-5214, Hwy 17, 2 miles south of US 2; donation $1; open daily 10am-6pm May-Sept), which is also an excellent vantage point for the canyon.

The coulee at the bottom of the falls is dotted with lakes, which are stocked with trout and popular with fly casters. Reach these lakes via **Sun Lakes State Park** (☎ 509-632-5583, open 6:30am-dusk year round), off Hwy 17, 4 miles south of US 2. It has a boat launch, boat rentals ($20 per day) and tackle shop.

Lake Lenore Caves State Park

Ten miles south of Dry Falls, these caves were formed as the force of water from melting glaciers tore chunks of basalt from the coulee walls. Prehistoric hunters used them as shelters, and Native Americans left pictographs, many of which are still visible near the caves' entrances. A marked trail from the north end of Lenore Lake leads to the caves. Information is available at Sun Lakes State Park and the Dry Falls Visitor Center.

Places to Stay & Eat

Steamboat Rock State Park (☎ 509-633-1304, reservations ☎ 888-226-7688, Hwy 155) Tent/RV sites $14/20. Bordered by a row of poplars, the campground sits on a grassy beach wedged between the namesake rock and the lake. There are over 120 full hookups, a handful of standard tent sites and a dozen boat-in sites, plus a modern bathhouse with hot showers. On summer weekends, it's wise to reserve a spot.

Sun Lakes State Park (☎ 509-632-5583, fax 509-632-5971, 34875 Park Lake Rd NE) Tents/hookups $14/20. Open year round. Located 1½ miles south of Dry Falls Visitor Center, this superbly situated state park has 180 shaded sites with access to nine lakes for swimming or fishing.

Ala Cozy Motel (☎ 509-632-5703, e landerson@odessaoffice.com, 9988 Hwy 2 E) Singles/doubles $52/57. There's no reason to stay in Coulee City, but if you just don't want to drive anymore, then this motel at the north end of town is quite decent, with an outdoor pool.

Dry Falls Cafe (☎ 509-632-5634, junction of Hwys 2 & 17) Prices $6-8. If you're staying at nearby Sun Lakes State Park and get tired of camp cooking, have breakfast (served till 11am) or a salad at this locally popular diner.

Okanogan River Valley

The Okanogan River courses south from the British Columbia Rockies and joins the Columbia near the tiny orchard town of Brewster, a few miles downstream from Chief Joseph Dam. The Okanogan is a slow-moving river, and the surrounding valley is dry and fairly lightly settled, functioning mostly as a transportation corridor. The Colville Indian Reservation lies to the east, with its northern border just north of Omak. On either side of the valley, hills rise

WASHINGTON

into various scattered parts of the Okanogan National Forest, where grasslands and cultivated orchards give way to ponderosa pine and Douglas fir.

Okanogan is Salish for 'rendezvous,' and Native Americans gathered here for thousands of years before a succession of white explorers, prospectors, miners, trappers, loggers, missionaries and fruit growers displaced them.

For a quick roadside history, stop by the interpretive center at **Fort Okanogan State Park** (☎ *509-923-2473, junction of US 97 & Hwy 17, 4 miles northeast of Brewster; admission free; open 10am-5pm Wed-Sun June-Aug)*, which sits on a bluff overlooking the confluence of the Okanogan and Columbia Rivers. The exhibit tells the story of the valley's original inhabitants and of the three fur-trading companies that successively occupied the site of the old fort in the early 19th century. Picnic facilities are available on the grounds.

OKANOGAN & OMAK

Okanogan (population 2484) and Omak (population 4721) have very nearly merged to become one town, but they have very distinct characters. Okanogan is the county seat, and its relatively dignified town center befits this role. Omak is the bustling retail center of the valley, best known for its annual rodeo, the Omak Stampede. To the west, lakes and apple orchards dot the foothills of the Cascade Range, while the hillsides east of here are generally dry and grassy.

There's little to detain travelers here, but it's a good place to gas up or find a bed before moving on. Some interesting exhibits, including frontier photographer Frank Matsura's glass-plate photo collection and a quilt display, are on view at the **Okanogan County Historical Museum** (☎ *509-422-4272, 1410 N 2nd St; admission $2; open 10am-4pm Memorial Day to Labor Day)*.

Orientation & Information

Two roads, US 97 and Hwy 215 (which is the commercial strip), connect Omak and Okanogan. Twisp lies 29 miles to the west of

Omak on Hwy 20, and Hwy 155 cuts southeast across the Colville Indian Reservation 54 miles to Coulee Dam.

The Omak Visitor Information office (☎ 509-826-1880, 800-225-6625, e omakvic@ northcascades.net), 401 Omak Ave, is next to the stampede grounds on Hwy 155 just east of downtown. They offer loads of printed matter on the whole region as well as Internet access, and they'd love to show you a video on the notorious Omak Stampede.

Mid-Valley Hospital (☎ 509-826-1760), 810 Valley Way Rd, is at the south end of Omak, which is also where you'll find the Log Cabin Public Coin-Op Laundromat (☎ 509-826-4462), 531 Okoma Dr (Hwy 215). Call Omak Cab (☎ 509-826-4123) should you need a lift.

Activities

There is some pleasant **hiking** in the national forest to the west, between Okanogan and Twisp. USFS headquarters (☎ 509-826-3275), 1240 S 2nd St, in Okanogan dispenses trail information. Biking is also popular, as Hwy 20 is a long-distance bike-touring route, and there are plenty of back roads up into the Okanogan hills worth exploring. Rent a bike at **The Bike Shop** (☎ *509-422-0710, w www.theokbikeshop.com, 137 S 2nd Ave; $15/day)* in Okanogan.

The **Loup Loup Ski Bowl** (☎ *509-826-2720, w www.skitheloup.com; open Dec-Mar)*, just off Hwy 20, 18 miles west of Okanogan, features a 1240-foot vertical drop, two lifts (adult/youth/child $28/23/16) and a rope tow, as well as 18.6 miles of groomed cross-country ski trails. Ski ($12-16 per day) and snowboard ($25) packages are available for rent.

Omak Stampede

Omak's big rodeo (☎ 509-826-1002, 800-933-6625) has been the subject of controversy for its signature Suicide Race, in which 20 horses and their riders pitch down a steep hillside and across the Okanogan River. The horses sometimes die attempting this feat, which has led to protests from animal-rights activists.

At the adjacent Indian Encampment, Native Americans dance, drum and play stick games. There's also country music, a parade and a barbecue. The Stampede is always held the second weekend of August. Tickets for the Stampede cost $10-12.

Places to Stay & Eat

Cariboo Inn (☎ 509-422-6109, 233 Queen St, Okanogan) Rooms $38-50. Rooms at this older downtown hotel are simple but clean, without the gussied-up fuss of some of the more touristy places. The busy coffee shop here has 'healthy' specials, such as stir-fried veggies, in addition to the meatier standard items.

U & I Motel (☎ 509-422-2920, 838 2nd St, Okanogan) Rooms $37-48. This humble and cheerfully run lodging offers a nice riverside setting with a spruced-up picnic area, and the rooms, though minimally maintained, have kitchenettes and carports. Noise from the main drag can be bothersome.

Motel Nicholas (☎ 509-826-4611, 527 E Grape Ave, Omak) Singles/doubles $38/42. North of Omak's center, the Nicolas has spacious, comfortable units with refrigerators and microwaves.

Omak Inn (☎ 509-826-3822, 800-204-4800, fax 509-826-2980, 912 Koala Dr) Rooms $65-80. Classier than the competition, Omak Inn offers mini-suites in a modern conference-style motel; there's also an indoor pool, spa and fitness center, and an adjacent restaurant and lounge. It's off US 97 on the north end of town.

Breadline Cafe (☎ 509-826-5836, 102 S Ash, Omak) Lunch $5-8, dinner $8-15. Open Mon-Sat. Without a single doubt, the best restaurant in the area is Omak's Breadline Cafe, where you can get great stuff – fresh baked goods, pastas, salads, grilled sandwiches, and fish and meat dishes with European and Cajun accents. The cafe occasionally hosts some alternative, folksy entertainment.

Food Depot (☎ 509-422-2801, 3rd and Rose St, Okanogan) If you want to stock up on food and supplies before heading into the mountains, this supermarket has a little of everything.

CONCONULLY LAKE

The lakeside hamlet of Conconully (population 185), in the eastern foothills of the North Cascades 18 miles northwest of Omak, is a good place to go for a respite from scorching summer days in the Okanogan Valley. Salish for 'money hole,' the name Conconully refers to a creek full of beaver whose pelts were used as money at the local trading post.

Most visitors come for **Conconully State Park** (☎ 509-826-7408, park entrance Hwy 97; open 6:30am-10pm summer, 8am-5pm winter, tent/RV sites $13/19), with campsites on a grassy field alongside the lower of two reservoirs. The resorts around Conconully aren't fancy, but they're certainly more pleasant than Omak's offerings. If you happen to be around here in January, be sure to catch the annual **outhouse races**.

From Omak, take Kernel Rd to the west and follow signs to Conconully.

A couple of **hiking** trails, the Tiffany Lake Trail (8½ miles) and the Clark Ridge Trail (4½ miles), start just past the Salmon Meadows Campground, 8 miles northwest of Conconully on USFS Rd 38. The trails can be hiked in a loop to make a nice overnight trip. Conconully Lake is a popular place in the winter for snowmobiling and **cross-country skiing**.

TONASKET & AROUND

Tonasket (population 994), 24 miles north of Omak, doesn't hold much interest in and of itself, but there's great lake-speckled country to both the east and west in and around the Okanogan National Forest.

For general information, the Tonasket Visitors & Business Resource Center (☎ 509-486-4543) is at 215 S Whitcomb Ave, next to the police station. The Tonasket Ranger Station (☎ 509-486-2186), 1 W Winesap, open Monday to Friday, can guide you to camping and recreation in the area. There's laundry and public showers at the Junction Motel & Laundromat (☎ 509-486-4421), at the junction of Hwy 20 and US 97.

Many Lakes Recreation Area

The area is known for its excellent fishing – the season begins some time in March and

WASHINGTON

lasts through the end of July. Some of the many lakes are on the road to Loomis, which is about 17 miles west of Tonasket. A number of resorts on this road cater to anglers, with boat rentals. **Whitestone Lake**, 5½ miles north of Tonasket, has good warm-water fishing for largemouth bass and crappie. **Spectacle Lake**, just past Whitestone, has rainbow trout. Past Loomis is **Palmer Lake**, where bass are a big attraction, along with rainbow and brown trout and Kokanee salmon. **Chopaka Lake**, 6.3 miles north of Loomis, is open to fly fishing only. Fishing licenses and tackle are available from Loomis Grocery and Sporting Goods.

Mt Bonaparte & Bonaparte Lake

East of Tonasket, the Okanogan National Forest contains Mt Bonaparte and Bonaparte Lake, where there are several campgrounds, a resort, and some beautiful hikes in the scenic Okanogan highlands. Bonaparte Lake has good trout fishing in summer, and during the winter there are 11 miles of groomed **cross-country skiing** trails near the western base of Mt Bonaparte.

One easy, mile-long hike starts at the Lost Lake Campground, north of Bonaparte Lake, and ends up at the **Big Tree Botanical Area**, home to a few 600-year-old Western larch trees. Another short trail from the campground goes to **Strawberry Mountain**, featuring views of the surrounding area and Canada.

One of the most popular hikes near Bonaparte Lake is the 3-mile **Virginia Lilly Old-Growth Trail**, flush with birds and old-growth trees that yield in many places to incredible views. To reach the trail, take USFS Rd 20, which forks off Bonaparte Lake Rd less than a mile past the lake, and turn onto USFS Rd 3240.

For a more challenging, 8-mile roundtrip hike, drive 6 miles west from Lost Lake on USFS Rd 33, then turn south onto USFS Rd 300, which ends a little over a mile later at the trailhead for **Mt Bonaparte**. The trail ascends through forested slopes to the 7258-foot summit and a fire lookout with great views. Another trail up Mt Bonaparte starts at the Bonaparte Lake campground.

To reach Bonaparte Lake head 24 miles east of Tonasket on Hwy 20 and turn north onto Bonaparte Lake Rd (USFS Rd 32). Skiers should pick up the Tonasket-Havillah Rd from downtown Tonasket and follow it 16 miles northeast to the Highlands Sno-Park near Havillah.

Places to Stay

Camping The majority of visitors head for the lakes, but there's also camping in Tonasket.

Tonasket RV Park (☎ 509-486-4429, 7 N Western Ave) Sites summer/winter $12/7. Located at the north end of town, this roadside facility offers hookups year-round. Tent camping is not allowed, but in summer, *Shannon's Ice Cream Parlor (☎ 509-486-2259, junction of US 97 and Hwy 20)*, at the south end of town, opens up its pine tree–shaded yard to tenters, charging $2 per person. Showers are available at the Texaco station across the road.

Most of the resorts in the Many Lakes Recreation Area have places to park an RV or pitch a tent for around $20. There are primitive public campgrounds without running water at Palmer and Chopaka Lakes.

The Bonaparte Lake area contains three excellent lakeside campgrounds, all with running water, pit toilets and sites for $6 to $8. *Bonaparte Campground (☎ 509-486-2186)*, on Bonaparte Lake, has wheelchair accessible facilities. *Lost Lake Campground* isn't that hard to find: Four miles past Bonaparte Lake, the road forks. Take the left fork (USFS 33) and drive 5 miles to a four-corner junction. Then turn left on forest road 3200-050 and drive ¼ mile to reach Lost Lake. Northeast of Bonaparte Lake is *Beth Lake Campground* on the tiny lake of the same name. To reach it, turn northwest off Bonaparte Lake Rd at Beaver Lake and head less than 2 miles up County Rd 9480.

Motels & Lodges Be sure to call ahead if you're planning to stay in this area outside the main fishing season, as some of the businesses close up shop as early as August. The Many Lakes area has several small resorts. Don't expect anything fancy: Rustic kitchenette cabins are the standard.

Bunkhouse Motel at the Junction (☎ 509-486-4500, fax 509-486-1200, 509 S Whitcomb) Rooms $44-66. Where Hwy 97 meets Hwy 20, the Bunkhouse has a variety of rooms that sleep up to five; one room is handicapped accessible. The helpful management run a small store and deli with espresso.

Hidden Hills Guest Ranch (☎ 509-486-1895, 800-468-1890, W www.hidden-hills.net, 144 Fish Lake Rd) Rooms $85-105. About 10 miles south of Tonasket, Hidden Hills attempts to re-create an 1890s atmosphere. The restaurant serves satisfying home-cooked meals. It can be reached by turning west off US 97 onto Pine Creek Rd (which becomes Fish Lake Rd).

Chopaka Lodge (☎ 509-223-3131, e chopaka@nvinet.com, 1995 Loomis Oroville Hwy) Cabins around $50; campsites $10. One of the most scenic places in the area, the lodge offers cute cabins with fireplaces, just steps from Palmer Lake. Kitchen and bath are included, as well as dishes and sheets, but bring your own towels. Campsites have electrical hookups, but no water or showers. Rowboats can be rented for $6 a day.

Sun Cove Resort & Guest Ranch (☎ 509-476-2223, e suncove@nvinet.com, 93 E Wannacut Lane) Campsites/rooms $18/62. Rooms here have kitchens, bath, and linens. Two and three-bedroom cottages are also available by the week. There's a pool and a restaurant, and you can rent a kayak ($6/25 per hour/day) or motorboat ($9/36). Reach Wannacut Lake by turning north off Loomis-Oroville Rd at Enterprise.

Bonaparte Lake Resort (☎ 509-486-2828, fax 509-486-1987 e bonapart@nvinet.com, 615 Bonaparte Lake Rd) Tent/RV Sites $8-12/$12-14, cabins $30-45. The resort offers campsites, cabins and a pretty good restaurant with dinners from $8 to $15. The wood-heated cabins are often booked a year in advance.

Places to Eat
Okanogan River Natural Foods Co-Op (☎ 509-486-4188, 21 W 4th St) Tonasket's

food co-op, one block west of US 97, is a good place for campers to stock up or sit a while with the soup of the day. It's also a de facto community center – ask about the barter fair that's held around here every summer.

Al's IGA (☎ 509-486-2183, 212 N Hwy 97) Another good place to get groceries, baked goods and deli items is at Al's in Tonasket.

Don's Drive Inn (☎ 509-486-2122, 101 N US 97) Burgers $5. Don's pleases crowds with burgers and fries on pleasant summer nights.

OROVILLE
Just 4 miles south of the Canadian border, Oroville (population 1553) sits on the south shore of **Osoyoos Lake**, the town's main attraction. It's popular with Canadian visitors, who come down here for the picnicking, swimming and camping at Osoyoos Lake State Park. The apple orchards here are a legacy of Hiram 'Okanogan' Smith, an early settler who carried down seedlings from Fort Hope, BC, in his backpack.

The Washington State Visitor Information Center (☎ 509-476-2739, W www.orovillewashington.com, 1730 Main St) on US 97 north of Oroville is open daily in summer, on weekends in winter.

The border crossing is open 24 hours. For information, call the US Customs and Immigration office at ☎ 509-476-2955; for the Canadian side, call ☎ 604-495-6531.

If you have a little extra time, stop by **Molson**, 15 miles east, an early-20th-century mining boomtown that's been preserved as an open-air museum (☎ 509-485-3292; open daily Apr-Nov). Some of the pioneer settlement's original buildings are on display, including a 1914 schoolhouse that contains historical exhibits.

Here are some food and lodging options:

Osoyoos Lake State Veteran's Memorial Park (☎ 509-476-3321) Tent/RV Sites $14/20. Open daily mid-march–Oct, weekends only rest of year. When the weather's nice, this the best place in town, with a sandy shore and shade trees. Ice-skating is popular in winter.

Camaray Motel (☎ 509-476-3684, 1320 Main St) Singles/doubles $38/44. Convenient to restaurants, the newly remodeled Camaray includes family-size rooms ($70) and a pool.

Hometown Pizza & Bakery (☎ 509-476-2410, 1315 Main St) Pizzas $7-12. If you pull into Oroville hungry, head here for homemade pizzas and calzones.

Alpine Brewing Co (☎ 509-476-9662, 821 14th Ave) Entrees $5-13. Open daily in summer, Wed-Sat rest of year. Along with locally crafted German-style brews, you'll find smoked and barbecued meats here – try the baby back ribs.

Colville National Forest

The Colville National Forest spans two mountain ranges in the northeastern corner of Washington – the Kettle River and the Selkirk – with the Columbia River slowing and widening into Lake Roosevelt between them. Most of the activity in the Kettle River Range, also known as the Okanogan Highlands, centers around Republic and Curlew Lake State Park.

The Pend Oreille (**pon**-de-**ray**) River flows north through the Selkirk Mountains into Canada, where it joins the Columbia. Lake fishing is the main draw. The Salmo-Priest Wilderness Area is some of the state's wildest country; it's crossed by hiking trails but has little in the way of facilities. Colville and Metaline Falls make good bases for exploring the Selkirks and the Pend Oreille River area, while Kettle Falls, on Lake Roosevelt, is replete with Columbia River history.

REPUBLIC

Republic (population 954) is an attractive western town and a comfortable place to spend the night. Downtown is largely false-fronted, and even though some of these building facades are recently built, there are enough old ones to keep the effect from being phony. Poke around the old-fashioned drugstore and load up on bulk groceries and

local news at the food co-op before setting out the next day.

A gold rush started things up here in 1896, and to this day, two mining companies are still the biggest industries in the county. Several timber companies are also nearby, supplied by trees from the Colville National Forest.

The Sanpoil River runs north-south through Republic (followed by Hwy 21) from Curlew Lake to the Keller Ferry crossing at Lake Roosevelt (see the Grand Coulee Dam section, earlier). The state's highest paved-road pass, Sherman Pass (5575 feet) is on Hwy 20 between Republic and Kettle Falls. Be sure to carry chains if you're driving this stretch between October and April – snowfall can be heavy.

Tourist information (☎ 509-775-3387, Ⓦ www.ferry-county.com/tourism.htm) is available from the Stonerose Interpretive Center, 15 N Kean St. The Republic Ranger Station (☎ 509-775-3305), 180 N Jefferson, has information on hiking trails in the nearby Colville National Forest.

The Ferry County Memorial Hospital (☎ 509-775-3333) is at 36 N Klondike Rd, and there's a laundromat on Keller St, a block east of Clark.

There are two USA/Canada border crossings in this area: Danville, north of Curlew on Hwy 21, is open 8am to midnight. Northwest of Curlew, the Midway/Port of Ferry crossing is open 9am to 5pm.

Stonerose Interpretive Center

The area around Republic contains a good selection of plant fossils from the Eocene Epoch some 50 million years ago. For a good introduction to local fossil finds, visit the Stonerose Interpretive Center *(☎ 509-775-2295, Ⓦ www.stonerosefossil.org, 15 N Kean St; adult/youth & senior $3/2; center & fossil site open 10am-5pm Tues-Sat May-Oct; also 10am-4pm Sun summer)*. The name derives from a nearby site where the oldest known ancestors of the rose family were discovered. The center is on the west side of town at 6th and N Kean Sts, across from the town park.

Visitors are welcome to dig their own fossils (up to three) with a permit from the interpretive center. Maps and directions are provided, and hammers can be rented for $3.

Curlew Lake State Park

The scenic lake, off Hwy 21 approximately 9 miles north of Republic, makes for good canoeing and boating, some pleasant swimming and good fishing for trout and bass. During the winter, you can do a little ice fishing, and cross-country skiers enjoy the open hills around the lake.

Hiking

By far the most interesting hike in the area is the **Kettle Crest Trail**, which crosses Hwy 20 at Sherman Pass some 20 miles east of Republic. North of the highway, the trail passes through thick forest, with plenty of spur trails leading through wildflowers in the spring. South of the highway, the trail passes through part of the huge 1988 White Mountain burn, which charred 20,000 acres. For several miles, hikers can witness a dramatic stage of forest succession, and interpretive road signs explain the rejuvenating effects of fire. Well into spring, snow lingers on the high ridges of the Kettle Crest Trail, making it popular with cross-country skiers. There is also a primitive campground here.

Places to Stay

Near Sherman Pass, about 20 miles east of Republic, the *Kettle Range Campground (free)* is a small Forest Service site that makes a good base for day hikes along the Kettle Ridge Trail.

Triangle J Ranch (☎ 509-775-3933, 31 Old Kettle Falls Rd) Dorm beds $12. During the summer, this hostel-style lodging north of Hwy 20 fills up with bicycle tourists; in the fall, hunters bed down here. There's a four-bed dormitory and a bunkhouse, or you can pitch a tent on the lawn for $8. Use of a big hot tub and an outdoor swimming pool are included in the overnight rate.

All of the following sites are around Curlew Lake.

Curlew Lake State Park (☎ 509-775-3592, 974 Curlew Park Rd) Tent/RV sites $14/20. Open Apr–Oct. An old Indian camp-

Curlew Lake is a pleasant place for fishing.

ground, the 123-acre park features a nature trail and two boat ramps. There are a handful of secluded walk-in sites.

Pine Point Resort (☎ 509-775-3643, W www.pinepointresort.com, 38 Pine Point Resort Rd) Cabins $56-118, tents/RVs $15/19. Open mid-Apr–Oct. On the east side of Curlew Lake, Pine Point is a particularly charming spot with campsites and kitchenette cabins. Cabins for the summer months can be booked five years in advance, so don't plan on showing up without a reservation. The resort is 10 miles north of Republic off Hwy 21.

Fisherman's Cove Resort (☎ 509-775-3641, 888-775-3641, 15 Fisherman's Cove Rd) Cabins from $55. Open Apr–Oct. This resort, just north of Pine Point on Hwy 21 has remodeled cabins with private baths and kitchens. Boats are available for guest use.

Black Beach Resort & RV Park (☎ 509-775-3989, 80 Black Beach Rd) Cabins $76, motel rooms $62-69, tent sites & hookups $14. Open Apr–Oct. Accommodations here consist of two-bedroom cabins, a few motel rooms and the largest RV park on Curlew Lake; tent sites are separate and have showers. Black Beach is on the west side of the lake, 8 miles north of Republic.

Tiffany's Resort (☎ 509-775-3152, W www.tiffanysresort.com, 58 Tiffany Rd) Tents/hookups $18/19, Cabins $45-120. Open Apr–Oct. About 4 miles farther north, Tiffany's has a range of cabins from studio-style to four-bedroom, all set on a point extending into the lake. Bedding is provided, but bring your own towel.

WASHINGTON

Places to Eat

Republic has a few uninspiring places to grab a bite. Besides the standard Mexican, pizza and burgers, these are probably your best options.

Kettle Crust Bakery (☎ 509-775-3754, 34 N Clark Ave) Lunch $3-7. The bakery of the Ferry County Co-op has a light lunch menu of vegetarian salads and soups in addition to organically grown staples.

Loose Blue Moose (☎ 509-775-0441, 1015 S Clark Ave) Chill out on the deck with coffee and pastries.

KETTLE FALLS

Kettle Falls (population 1527) is set in an attractive valley, but there isn't much to keep a traveler here besides an interest in Columbia River history, of which there are several noteworthy examples. The Kettle Falls Campground has a popular swimming beach and marina on Lake Roosevelt.

For at least 9000 years, Kettle Falls was one of the Columbia River's richest fisheries. Native Americans from several different tribes came here each summer to fish and eat salmon, taking as many as 3000 fish a day. The Hudson's Bay Company took note of all the people gathering at the falls and reckoned it would be a good spot for a fur-trading post. Fort Colvile started operations in 1825 and became a hub of activity until it closed in 1871. Catholic missionaries opened St Paul's Mission just up the hill from the trading post in 1848.

Many historic sites – including the original town of Kettle Falls and Fort Colvile – were flooded by Lake Roosevelt when the Columbia River was stopped up by the Grand Coulee Dam in 1939. The town's present site was called Myers Falls until all the transplants from Kettle Falls inundated it.

There are lots of fruit orchards and fruit stands around Kettle Falls, primarily south of town on Peachcrest Rd. Stop by for a bag of peaches, cherries, raspberries, pears or apples.

Orientation & Information

The Columbia River's Lake Roosevelt is just west of town, and Hwy 20 and US 395

meet at the river's west bank. The nearest Canadian border crossing, at Laurier/Cascade, is 31 miles north on US 395, and the Paterson crossing is west of the Columbia River at the end of Hwy 25. Both crossings are open 8am to midnight.

The free Inchelium-Gifford ferry crosses Lake Roosevelt 23 miles south of Kettle Falls. It runs from 6am to 9:30pm daily.

Contact the Lake Roosevelt National Recreation Area office (☎ 509-738-6266), 1368 S Kettle Park Rd, from 6:30am to 4pm weekdays. A visitor information center adjacent to this office is open summer weekends. Between 7:30am and 4pm weekdays, the Kettle Falls USFS Ranger Station (☎ 509-738-6111), 255 W 11th Ave, can tell you about recreation in the Colville National Forest. The Kettle Falls Area Chamber of Commerce (☎ 509-738-2300, W www.kettlefalls.org), 265 E 3rd Ave, dispenses general tourist information.

Things to See & Do

Drop by the Kettle Falls Interpretive Center (☎ 509-738-6964), just north of US 395 on the east side of the Columbia River, to see a giant photo mural showing the pre-dam Columbia as it crashed through Kettle Falls, in marked contrast to the flat lake that has taken its place. It's open 11am to 5pm Wednesday to Saturday in the summer.

Active until 1869, **St Paul's Mission** has been totally restored and is an example of tidy French-Canadian-style log architecture. It's behind the interpretive center, down a dirt road that was once the trail used to portage around the actual falls.

The **Log Flume Heritage Site** (☎ 509-738-6111) is in the middle of ponderosa pine forests 11 miles west of Kettle Falls on Hwy 20 (at Canyon Creek, milepost 335). It's a nice drive, and the site provides a snapshot of logging history. In the 1920s, as Washington timber was being shipped worldwide, one traditional logging technique, the low-tech waterpower-and-horse method, was being challenged by a new technique using steam locomotives and trucks. There are several interpretive displays along a mile-long winding, wheelchair-accessible trail.

Sunbeam Creek, Mt Rainier National Park

Lady of the Lake II at dock on Lake Chelan

RICHARD CUMMINS

DONALD C & PRISCILLA ALEXANDER EASTMAN

The massive, snowcapped Mt Rainier – the largest mountain in the Cascades – is an active volcano.

BRENT WINEBRENNER

Petroglyphs at Gingko Petrified Forest

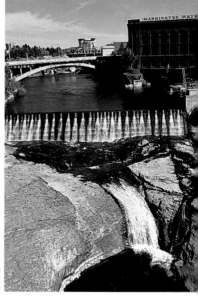

The unique Teapot Dome service station, Zillah

Spokane Falls: A salmon challenge

Lake Roosevelt is home to 300lb sturgeon (anglers, bring a crane).

Places to Stay & Eat

Kettle Falls Campground (☎ *509-738-6266, Boise Rd)* Sites \$10/5 summer/winter. Open year-round. This NPS site, 2 miles south of the bridge, has flush toilets, running water and a boat launch. Rangers lead talks and activities during the summer months.

Canyon Creek Campground (☎ *509-738-6111, Hwy 20 Milepost 335)* Free. Eleven miles west of Kettle Falls on Hwy 20, this USFS-managed campground has pit toilets and running water.

My Parents' Estate B&B (☎ *509-738-6220, 719 US 395)* Rooms \$85-125. Prior to its incarnation as a B&B, this place also happened to be a Catholic mission, convent, school and a boys' home. Rooms are decorated with lace and antiques. The 47-acre estate is located a mile east of Kettle Falls.

Grandview Inn Motel & RV Park (☎ *509-738-6733, 978 US 395 N at junction with Hwy 25)* Singles/doubles \$40/42. The Grandview has a nice grassy lawn overlooking Lake Roosevelt.

Kettle Falls Best Value Inn (☎/fax 509-738-6514, 205 E 3rd St)* Singles/doubles \$50/55. Each room at this friendly franchise downtown comes with microwave oven, refrigerator and data-port phone. Pets are allowed for a fee.

Lake Roosevelt Resort & Marina (☎ *509-738-6121, 800-635-7585, fax 509-738-6122, PO Box 340, Kettle Falls 99141,* **w** *www.lakeroosevelt.com)* Houseboats \$2495/4095 weekend/week July-Aug. Seventeen luxury houseboats are rented from the marina adjacent to the campground. Rates are lower in the off months, higher if you want a hot tub.

Hudson Bay (☎ *509-738-6164, 3986 Hwy 20 E)* Entrees \$7-15. This is the spot for a fancy dinner, with a wide menu selection that includes junior portions.

Little Gallea Restaurant (☎ *509-738-6776, US 395)* Under \$6. Open 5am-2pm Mon-Sat. The prompt and friendly Little Gallea, downtown, has hearty breakfasts, sandwiches and burgers, as well as a reputation for good cheesecake.

COLVILLE

Colville (population 4988) is a town of some substance, with a Wal-Mart and a string of fast food franchises beckoning along the highway. Indeed, it is northeastern Washington's largest town after Spokane and the seat of Stevens County. Colville's gracious older homes and gardens date from 1883, when locals appropriated the buildings from the then-defunct Fort Colvile, carting everything a few miles away to a site along the Colville River. Nowadays, it's a major shopping destination for ranchers from the surrounding area, though most travelers will probably only stop here as a base before exploring Colville National Forest.

The Okanogan Highlands rise to the west of town, and the Kalispell Mountains are to the northeast. Downtown Colville is built on a bench just east of the Colville River. Hwy 20 runs east-west through town; a two-block strip of boutiques centered around Astor St makes up the downtown.

For local information, contact the Colville Chamber of Commerce (☎ 509-684-5973, **w** www.colville.com), 121 E Astor St. The Colville National Forest Ranger Station (☎ 509-684-7000), 765 S Main St, has the lowdown on hiking and camping.

Coin-Op Laundry (☎ 509-684-2137), 156 E Dominion St is on the main drag. Mt Carmel Hospital (☎ 509-684-2561), 982 E Columbia Ave, provides 24-hour emergency care.

Things to See & Do

The only real attraction is the **Keller Heritage Center** (☎ *509-684-5968, 700 N Wynne St; donation adult/child \$2/50¢; open 1pm-4pm daily May; 10am-4pm Mon-Sat, 1pm-4pm Sun June-Sept)*. Its centerpiece is Keller House, a rather large bungalow with nice Craftsman details, built in 1910. Dispersed around the house are reconstructed versions of a pioneer blacksmith's shop, schoolhouse, trapper's cabin, sawmill and fire lookout tower.

Bird watchers should swing down to the **Little Pend Oreille National Wildlife Refuge**, where McDowell Lake attracts waterfowl. White-tailed deer winter here, and the refuge is a haven for such rarely encountered

WASHINGTON

species as gray wolves, peregrine falcons and great gray owls. To reach the refuge headquarters (☎ 509-684-8384, 1310 Bear Creek Rd; open 7:30am-4pm year round), take Hwy 20 for about 8 miles east of Colville, then turn south on Narcisse Creek Rd. There are several rudimentary campsites around the 63-sq-mile wildlife area; a stop at the headquarters will set you up with seasonally appropriate camping, hiking and wildlife viewing information.

Eastern Washington's downhill skiers head to **49 Degrees North** (☎ 509-935-6649, snow report ☎ 509-880-9208, W www.ski 49n.com, 3311 Flowery Trail Road, Chewelah; ski area closed Wed & Thur except holidays). Located about 30 miles southeast of Colville near Chewelah, it's a small ski area with four chairlifts and an 1851-foot vertical drop. Prime-time lift tickets are $32/25 adult/youth & senior, but they're much cheaper on weekdays. There are also 9.3 miles of cross-country trails. Skis/snowboards can be rented for $22/25 a full day.

Cross-country skiers can find miles of informal trails in the national forest and the Little Pend Oreille Wildlife Refuge. Contact the USFS ranger station (☎ 509-684-7000) for an update on groomed trails.

Places to Stay & Eat

Douglas Falls Campground (☎ 509-684-7474, Douglas Falls Rd) Free. Open summer & fall only. Camp alongside Mill Creek at this scenic site, 7 miles north of town. Pit toilets and a water pump are available.

Pend Oreille Wildlife Refuge (☎ 509-684-8384, 1310 Bear Creek Rd) Free. Open late spring to first snow. Campsites here are decidedly primitive, with pit toilets and no water. Stop by refuge headquarters for a map of site locations.

Centsible Inn (☎ 509-684-2565, fax 509-684-8341, 369 S Main St) Singles/doubles $37/43. Remodeled units come with coffee makers, microwave and refrigerator at this in-town place.

Beaver Lodge Resort & Campground (☎ 509-684-5657, 2430 Hwy 20 E) Sites $14, cabins $45. About 25 miles east of Colville on Lake Gillette is this resort near the Pend

Oreille National Wildlife Refuge, with campsites and half a dozen wood-heated cabins (bring your own bedding). Rounding out the amenities are a cafe and canoe, cross-country ski and snowshoe rentals.

It's no culinary mecca, but Colville is not a bad place to stop for a meal. Campers can stock up at the **North County Co-op** (☎ 509-684-6132, 282 W Astor St), open to nonmembers.

Talk 'n Coffee (☎ 509-684-2373, 119 E Astor St) Dishes $3-6. For morning espresso and pastries drop by here.

Cookie's Cafe (☎ 509-684-8660, 157 N Oak St) Dishes $4-10. Within the Pinkney City Mall, Cookie's is a good breakfast or lunch spot if you're willing to burrow through a load of Americana to get into it.

Cafe al Mundo & Espresso (☎ 509-684-8092, 117 W Astor St) Entrees $5-8. Colville's coolest place is Cafe al Mundo, a youthful eatery and brewpub done up in psychedelic southwest decor. Inexpensive tamales, curries and burritos form the backbone of the eclectic menu. Espresso, microbrews and occasional live music are the main draws in the evening.

METALINE FALLS

Metaline (population 162) and Metaline Falls (population 223), small towns separated by the Pend Oreille River, are in the very northeast corner of the state. This is remote, lovely country, with access to the Salmo-Priest Wilderness Area, which is home to a few grizzly bears and rare woodland caribou. Metaline Falls is an exceptionally pretty town that used to house a cement factory, which for years covered pretty much everything in a thin layer of dust. The town was an unlikely setting for the Kevin Costner futuristic epic *The Postman*.

Like so many falls in the area, Metaline Falls was flooded by a dam. The Boundary Dam, up near the Canadian border, was built in the 1960s and is worth a visit. Keep your eyes peeled for mountain goats, bighorn sheep and moose on the road to the Boundary Dam. There's a viewing site at Flume Creek about 3 miles up Boundary Dam Rd from Metaline.

Metaline Falls is 10 miles south of the Canadian border. From Hwy 20, take Hwy 31 north, which reaches Metaline first and then, across the river, Metaline Falls. The border station (☎ 509-446-4421) is open 8am to midnight.

A visitor center has been set up in an old railroad car in the town park, across from Katie's Oven Bakery. To learn more about the area, contact the Metalines Chamber of Commerce *(☎ 509-446-3683)*. The Sullivan Lake Ranger Station *(☎ 509-446-7500, 12641 Sullivan Lake Rd, Metaline Falls; open 8am-4pm)* has information about all of the hiking and campsites in this part of the Colville National Forest.

Boundary Dam

The 340-foot-high Boundary Dam *(☎ 509-446-3083, County Rd 62)*, just south of the US/Canada border, spans two huge rocky cliffs. Its inner workings are pocketed in caverns and connected by tunnels hewn from the limestone. The dam has traditionally been open for tours in summer. However, in the wake of terrorist acts in September 2001, access has been suspended indefinitely. The same goes for the Boundary Dam Vista House on the river's east bank.

Hiking

Anglers know **Sullivan Lake** for its brown trout – the 22lb state-record catch came from here – but it also makes a wonderful hiking destination. Southeast of Metaline Falls, the lake can also be reached by crossing the Pend Oreille River at Ione and heading northeast. Campgrounds at the north and south ends are connected by a 3-mile hiking trail that runs along the lake's east shore.

The 22-mile-long **Shedroof Divide National Recreation Trail** goes through the Salmo-Priest Wilderness Area; it starts east of Sullivan Lake on USFS Rd 22, just beyond Pass Creek Pass. From here, it's a fairly rugged trail north with lots of good views and wildlife. The last woodland caribou herd in the USA is in this area, along with some grizzly bears. Several other trails in the area offer the opportunity to

make a loop hike, lasting either a day or overnight. Otherwise, most backpackers hike the trail one way. To reach the northern end of the Shedroof Divide Trail, cut north from USFS Rd 22 onto USFS Rd 2200 about 6 miles east of Sullivan Lake. Follow this good gravel road 12 miles to the Shedroof Cutoff Trailhead (trail No 535).

The trailhead for the **Hall Mountain** hike is also east of Sullivan Lake on USFS Rd 22; turn south on Johns Creek Rd and take this rough road to the end. The 2½-mile hike to the summit sometimes rewards hikers with visions of bighorn sheep.

Abercrombie Mountain, at 7308 feet, is the highest peak in the Washington Selkirks. From the top, there are views into both the Pend Oreille and Columbia River drainages. It's a 4-mile hike up the mountain along the Flume Creek drainage, with over 2000 feet in elevation gain. Reach the trailhead by turning off Boundary Rd at Flume Creek north of Metaline; take USFS Rd 350 and continue about 7 miles to the end of the dirt road.

Places to Stay & Eat

A pair of USFS campgrounds at the north end of Sullivan Lake, *West Sullivan* and *East Sullivan*, offer a total of 45 sites with fire pits and picnic tables but no hookups. Drinking water and vault toilets are available. Similar facilities are found at *Noisy Creek* at the lake's south end. Rates at all three campgrounds are $10/14 for single/ double family sites. Phone reservations are accepted for Noisy Creek only (☎ 877-444-6777), for a charge of $8.65.

Washington Hotel (☎ 509-446-4415, e *nola@potc.net, 225 5th St)* Rooms from $35. This is a classic, old small-town hotel built in 1910. It has simple rooms with hardwood floors, handmade quilts, bathrooms down the hall and an artist's studio at the foot of the steps.

Circle Motel (☎ 509-446-4343, Hwy 31) Rooms $32-38. Just north of Metaline Falls, the Circle has variably sized units with microwave and refrigerator, and there's a hot tub.

Katie's Oven Bakery (☎ 509-446-4806, 225 E 5th St) Lunch $7. Open Wed-Sat summer, variable rest of year. In a town not noted for culinary extravagance, Katie's at the Washington Hotel stands out. While it may mean a diet heavy on cinnamon rolls, it'll be worth it. The lunch menu changes daily and usually includes something vegetarian – expect to find a few good soups, Mediterranean salads and sandwiches.

Entertainment

Cutter Theatre (☎ 509-446-4108, W www .povn.com/byway, 302 Park St) Housed in a restored school built around 1910 by noted Spokane architect Kirkland Cutter, the theater has shows ranging from goofy melodramas to oboe and horn duets. As with everything else in Metaline Falls, it's easy on the wallet.

IONE

A logging town from the early 1900s, Ione (population 479) freighted its timber down the Pend Oreille via steamer ferry until the arrival of the railroads in 1909. Several weekends a year, a train runs along the Pend Oreille River between Ione's historic rail depot and Metaline Falls. The scenic two-hour trip allows passengers the chance to come to grips with their fear of heights and of the dark – the tracks cross Box Canyon on a 156-foot-high trestle and pass through an 810-foot-long tunnel. The trips are usually scheduled on Father's Day weekend (mid-June), the last weekend in July, Labor Day weekend (early September) and a couple of 'autumn colors' weekends in late September and early October (fare $7 per person). Contact Lions Excursion Train (☎ 509-442-5466, W www .povn.com/byway) for exact scheduling; two weeks' advance reservations are required.

Though less impressive than Boundary Dam to the north, **Box Canyon Dam** (☎ 509-447-6700, open 9am-4pm weekdays) does have a visitors center and a riverside park. People also fish for trout in the reservoir behind the dam.

Here are some lodging and food options:

Edgewater Campground (County Rd 2669) Sites $10. Located on the east bank of the Pend Oreille, 2 miles north of Ione, this USFS facility has recently been upgraded with a paved road in and boat launch for river access. Drinking water and vault toilets are available.

Riverview Inn (☎ 509-442-3990, Hwy 31 & Riverside Ave, Ione) Singles/doubles from $43/47. This in-town motel has a couple of balcony rooms with views across the river. *Del's Restaurant* (☎ 509-442-3990) next door, is the main place to eat in town.

Box Canyon Resort (☎ 509-442-3728, 800-676-8883, 8612 Hwy 31) Singles/doubles $45/60. The riverside rooms are a remarkable value at this small, roadside motel, 5 miles north of Ione.

Southeastern Washington

Southeastern Washington is the state's loneliest corner. Dominated by the big wheat farms of the Palouse, stark desert of the Columbia Plateau and the asparagus and onion fields around Walla Walla, it's no tourism center, and many of the small towns consist of little more than a grain elevator and (if you're lucky) a gas station/cafe. On the other hand, people are generally rather pleased and surprised when someone makes a point of visiting.

The Cascade rain shadow looms over this part of Washington, as moist air from the coast is blocked by the western range; less than 10 inches of rain fall annually on the barren landscape. The land is underlain by enormous foundations of lava that flooded here over the millennia from volcanic ruptures near the Wallowa Mountains in Oregon. Under Pasco, the lava fills a 1½-mile-deep basin. The thin soils that managed to form on this volcanic plateau were swept away during the Spokane Floods, when ice dams in Montana gave way at the end of the last ice age and swept across the Columbia Plateau. It's still easy to see the path of the floods in the area north and south of Ritzville, where the denuded lava flows and gouged-out ponds form a curious geologic zone called the Channeled Scablands. Floodwaters diverted the Palouse River's course to create dramatic Palouse Falls. In contrast is the Palouse region, on Washington's eastern edge, an extremely fertile area defined by rolling hills planted in wheat and legumes.

History

The Yakima, Columbia, Snake and Walla Walla River valleys were all important to prehistoric Native Americans, and the area of their confluence was an ancient crossroads of culture, transportation and trade. Palouse Indians lived along the lower Snake River, where they fished for salmon.

Lewis and Clark were the first white explorers to make their way through this region, in 1805, when they floated down the Snake River to join the Columbia River near Pasco. French-Canadian trappers began working the area soon after, and the Hudson's Bay Company built its first fort at the mouth of the Walla Walla River in 1818. Walla Walla's first settlement, the ill-fated Whitman Mission, was aborted after a bloody confrontation with the indigenous

---

Highlights

- Riding down the Snake River straight to Hells Canyon, North America's deepest river gorge
- Viewing Palouse Falls, a remnant of ice age floods, dropping 200 feet off the desolate Columbia Plateau
- Exploring Walla Walla, a genteel enclave of historic homes and wine-tasting salons amid the wheat fields of the southeast

OTHER MAPS
Southeastern Washington
page 582

Walla Walla
pages 588-589

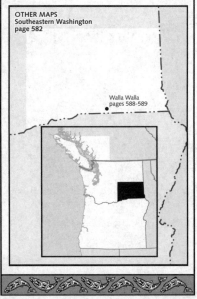

SOUTHEASTERN WASHINGTON

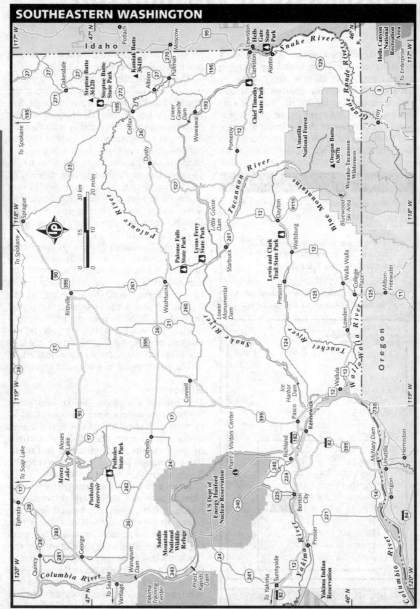

population in 1847, which sparked the Cayuse War. Further settlement awaited treaties with the Indians.

To the north, the Palouse did not easily submit to treaties, and after they defeated army troops at Steptoe Butte in 1858, US militias went after them with a vengeance. Most Palouse refused to go to reservations, and as whites moved in, the Palouse lived under increasingly marginal circumstances.

In 1862, gold was discovered in Idaho and Montana, and the tiny outpost of Walla Walla found itself along the main transportation line between Portland and the gold fields. As the steamboat terminus of the upper Columbia River, the town boomed almost immediately, with merchants and provisioners setting up highly profitable businesses. By 1870, Walla Walla was the largest town in Washington Territory, and its importance was assured with the installation in 1875 of a narrow-gauge rail link to the steamboats at Wallula on the Columbia River.

As the Rocky Mountain gold rush played out, agriculture took over as the mainstay of the local economies. Miners who had swarmed through Pullman during the gold rush gave way to homesteaders, who began farming and ranching in the area around Pullman and Moscow, Idaho, by the 1870s. Irrigation projects in the 20th century established the Tri-Cities.

TRI-CITIES

Pasco, Kennewick and Richland – the Tri-Cities – sprawl along the arid banks of the Columbia River between the confluence of the Yakima and Snake Rivers, constituting Washington's fifth-largest population center.

Early settlement of the region awaited the railroads, which pushed across the Columbia Plateau in 1880. Kennewick grew up around the region's first Columbia River irrigation projects in the early 20th century. However, what really put these cities on the map was the Hanford Nuclear Reservation, which was built north of Richland in the 1940s. Hanford was a plutonium-refining plant for the Manhattan Project, and after WWII it also researched the development of nuclear energy. The facility was shut down in the 1980s due to radiation leaks and the bank-breaking costs of environmental cleanup. Turn off the strip developments that predominate in these 1950s boomtowns to glimpse the vestiges of an era when things nuclear were in the vanguard. You'll begin to see the little whirling nuclear symbol everywhere – on houses of worship, laundromats and high schools (the local team is called the Bombers; their mascot is a mushroom cloud).

Today, the Tri-Cities are the center of a large irrigated farming region, and even in town the summer air is heavy with the peculiar humid odor of sprinkler irrigation. Prior to irrigation, this was the driest part of the desert, as Richland receives only 7 inches of rain a year.

The Tri-Cities offer little in the way of charm or sophistication (odd, considering that Richland has the highest per-capita income in Washington and the greatest concentration of PhDs in the USA). But chances are pretty good that if you're traveling through this part of the state, you'll end up stopping to eat or sleep here, as it's at the intersection of several long, usually hot roads. Of the three cities, Richland offers travelers the most in the way of amenities. Pasco is largely a Latino community, home to most of the area's agricultural workers.

Orientation & Information

Several major Northwest routes intersect at the Tri-Cities. US 395 is the main north-south link between I-90 at Ritzville and I-84 in Oregon. I-82 runs from Ellensburg and Yakima through the Tri-Cities, joining US 395 down to I-84; US 12 splits off I-82, continuing east to Walla Walla and Idaho. From Yakima to Richland on I-82 it's 76 miles; from Pasco to Spokane on US 395 it's 136 miles; and from Pasco to Walla Walla on US 12, it's 47 miles.

Only Richland has a gathering of buildings (along George Washington Way and Jadwin Ave) that could be considered a town center. Pasco and Kennewick are amorphous and centerless; they are best thought of as a series of commercial strips and suburbs. The airport, bus station and rail station are all in Pasco. The main arterial between Richland and Kennewick is Hwy 240, also called Columbia Dr. Freeway spur I-182 (exit 102 off I-82) runs east to west between Pasco and Richland.

For information, contact the Tri-Cities Visitor & Convention Bureau (☎ 509-735-8486, 800-254-5824, W www.visittri-cities .com), 6951 W Grandridge Blvd, in Kennewick, or write to PO Box 2241, Tri-Cities, WA 99302. The most convenient post office

is in Richland, at 815 Jadwin Ave. The *Tri-City Herald* is the daily paper of record.

Things to See & Do

Much of the land between US 240 and the Columbia is interspersed with parks, marinas and golf courses. **Columbia Park**, in Kennewick, is a vast greenway complete with a golf course, play fields, campground and boat moorage, as well as picnic and swimming areas. Richland's **Howard Amon Park** (named after an early irrigation entrepreneur), off George Washington Way,

Kennewick Man

Southeastern Washington's most controversial public figure is an anonymous dead guy believed to be more than 9300 years old.

In the summer of 1996, two college students found a nearly complete skeleton on the banks of the Columbia River near Kennewick. The county coroner examined the skeleton and then called in a forensic anthropologist to help determine if this was a murder victim or the remains of an ancient Indian, in which case the bones would be turned over to local tribes for repatriation (meaning burial on tribal lands).

However, when anthropologist James Chatters examined the skeleton, he made some astonishing discoveries. The skeleton was that of a Caucasian male, between 40 and 45 years of age, who stood about 5 feet 9 inches. Most startling, when Chatters was cleaning the pelvic structure, he noticed a gray object embedded in the bone. Further examination revealed it to be a stone projectile point, of a sort usually associated with the Archaic Indian period about 9000 years ago. If the man whose skeleton was found along the Columbia River was Caucasian, what was he doing in western North America at a time when, according to most historical sources, the American Indians had just arrived via the Bering land bridge from Asia? Radiocarbon dating fixed the skeleton's age at between 9300 and 9600 years.

Just who was the Kennewick Man?

Almost immediately, the story found its way into the press. As the skeleton was discovered on federal land supervised by the US Army Corps of Engineers, this government agency immediately ordered Chatters to stop his investigation and sent a representative to collect the bones; the Corps then declared that the skeleton would be returned to local tribes. Under the terms of the 1990 federal Native American Graves Protection and Repatriation Act (Nagpra), any Native American remains found on public land had to be returned to local tribes. The Umatilla Indians, leading a coalition of Columbia Basin tribes, formally claimed the bones under the act, vowing that they would rebury the skeleton.

includes a riverfront walkway, a grassy beach and a children's museum.

Visitors wanting to learn more about southeastern Washington's unlikely metropolis would do well to stop at the **Columbia River Exhibition of History, Science & Technology** (☎ 509-943-9000, 95 Lee Blvd; adult/senior/student $3.50/2.95/2.50; open 10am-5pm Mon-Sat, noon-5pm Sun), also in Howard Amon Park. Exhibits focus on the Tri-Cities' natural and human histories, while impressive local finds, such as a 13,000-year-old woolly mammoth tusk, chronicle the region's rich prehistoric past. Unsurprisingly, the museum's technology section gives over to a preoccupation with the history and continuing debacle of Hanford. Even if nuclear energy and bomb production give you the creeps, there's a lot to learn here about all things atomic. It's also eye-opening to learn about the US government's policy presumptions during the Cold War years. And if you've ever wanted to operate those robot pincers used to pick up radioactive materials, you can do it here.

Kennewick Man

Upset at the prospect of losing a chance to study this rare discovery, eight anthropologists objected that the skeleton wasn't covered by Nagpra because the remains were not of an American Indian. They initiated a lawsuit against the Army Corps of Engineers in hopes of stalling the reburial and of preserving the skeleton for further study. Eight other groups, including the Asatru Folk Assembly, a Northern California–based religious group with beliefs in ancient Norse gods, came forward a few months later to stake their own claims to the skeleton.

The federal court issued a restraining order against the Army Corps of Engineers, and the Kennewick Man was safely locked in a wooden box inside a vault, away from public view – or so it was thought. Miffed by news that Native Americans had been allowed to perform religious rituals over the skeleton, Asatru leaders threatened a discrimination lawsuit if they weren't allowed to perform their own ceremonies. The Army Corps of Engineers relented, and 10 members of the group, clad in Viking garb, traveled to venerate the skeleton with prayer and a ceremonial toast. (Asatru members had to drink fruit juice out of their cow horn cups, as the traditional toast of mead was prohibited by the Corps' anti-alcohol rules.)

The Kennewick Man skeleton is of vast interest to scientists, Native Americans and the general public for many reasons. If the skeleton proves to be Caucasian, the presence of Europeans in North America nearly 10,000 years ago utterly upsets the standard theory of human migration to North America. Perhaps when the ancestors of today's Native Americans arrived via the Bering land bridge, they encountered a preexisting Stone Age culture made up of Europeans. Other scientists speculate that the skeleton is related to neither the ancestors of Native American tribes nor early Europeans, but rather to an unrelated Caucasoid race from Southeast Asia. The discovery of the Kennewick Man also brings up the interesting, but thorny, question of just who or what is a 'Native American.'

Who will get to do what with the skeleton? Its identity will first need to be established. In September 2000, the US Department of the Interior recommended the remains should be returned to the five Native American tribes who claim ancestral linkage, saying evidence to the contrary has been inconclusive. However, that recommendation has been challenged by scientists who continue to dispute that the term 'Native American' applies to the uncovered bones since no tribes now referred to as Native American existed when the Kennewick Man lived. Meanwhile, the bones remain locked up in the basement of Seattle's Burke Museum pending a definitive decision by the courts.

WASHINGTON

While the mothballed bomb-making facilities at the Hanford Nuclear Reservation proper are closed to the public, visitors are permitted to drive onto the site for a close-up view of a nuclear power plant still in use for commercial purposes. The **Columbia Generating Station**, the state's only nuclear power plant, produces 1150 megawatts of electric power, enough to power a city the size of Seattle. Before you drive out, you may want to know that its fuel core contains 153 tons of uranium dioxide.

Public power consortium Energy Northwest, which owns and operates the plant, explains the difference between fusion and fission and demonstrates the virtues of nuclear energy at its **Washington Public Power Supply System (Plant 2) Visitors Center** (☎ 509-372-5860; admission free; open 11am-4pm Thur & Fri, noon-5pm Sat & Sun).

More fun than the center itself is the eerie drive across the desolate landscape, an ominous nuclear facility appearing on the horizon every few miles. From Richland, follow George Washington Way or Stevens Dr onto Route 4, the entrance road into the site. Turn right at the flashing light, then left after crossing the railroad tracks. Plant 2 is about 10 miles north of Richland, beside a sinister-looking containment tank and cooling towers.

Places to Stay

Most of the national motel chains show up on the major arterials, with some of the cheaper options along the unsightly US 395 strip in Kennewick.

Tapadera Inn (☎ 509-783-6191, 800-722-8277, fax 509-735-3854, 300A N Ely St, Kennewick) Singles/doubles $40/50. Near the busy intersection of US 395 and Clearwater Ave and next door to a decent restaurant, the Tapadera offers pleasant, well-kept rooms and a pool.

Nendels Inn (☎ 509-943-4611, 800-547-0106, 2811 W 2nd Ave, Kennewick) Singles/doubles $43/51. A block off the main drag, this is a bit quieter. Attractions include a complimentary breakfast, swimming pool, friendly staff and spacious, renovated rooms.

Ramada Inn Clover Island (☎ 509-586-0541, fax 509-586-6956, 435 Clover Island Rd, Kennewick) Singles/doubles $55/65. Spend a bit more for a much nicer location – on an island in the Columbia that's linked to shore by a short bridge. The rear pool and patio face the river, which can also be admired from the top-floor restaurant.

Bali Hi Motel (☎ 509-943-3101, 1201 George Washington Way, Richland) Singles/doubles $44/50. Near Howard Amon Park, this tiki-themed lodging is one of Richland's better values, with a pool, hot tub and sundeck.

Places to Eat

Above-average local restaurants are worth seeking out amid the fast-food fodder of Kennewick's 5-mile commercial strip.

Country Gentleman (☎ 509-783-0128, 300 N Ely St) Breakfast $5, dinner $8. Travelers along US 395 swear by the breakfasts here.

Casa Chapala (☎ 509-586-4224, 107 E Columbia Dr) Lunch $7, dinner $10. A large and popular dining hall by the river, Casa Chapala offers Tex-Mex favorites and such authentic fare as *mole poblano* and *carne tampiqueña*. Its all-you-can-eat taco buffet is just $7.

Some of the area's more interesting eateries are tucked into Richland's 1960s shopping centers.

Some Bagels (☎ 509-946-3185, 1317 George Washington Way) Bagels $1.25. Not just any bagels, these come in pesto, blueberry and 21 other variations. You can also score lattes here.

Atomic Ale Brewpub & Eatery (☎ 509-946-5465, 1015 Lee Blvd) Pizzas $9-12, sandwiches $6. Closed Sunday. Nuclear families gather at this attractive brewpub for the wood-fired specialty pizzas; a Half-Life Hefeweizen or Plutonium Porter leaves that warm afterglow.

Monterosso's Italian Restaurant (☎ 509-946-4525, 1026 Lee Blvd) Entrees $15. Open 5pm-9pm Mon-Sat. Across the street from Atomic Ale is this trattoria in an elegantly refurbished Pullman dining car.

Don't overlook Pasco for *típico* Mexican food. Taco stands and cantinas are concentrated in the barrio along 4th St.

Hanford: Of Atomic Bombs & Nuclear Waste

In 1942, the US government established the Hanford Engineering Works as part of the Manhattan Project, the top-secret WWII program designed to develop the first atomic bomb. This remote site was considered ideal because of its distance from population centers and its proximity to the Columbia River's water and hydroelectric power. Richland was founded as an 'Atomic City' at the same time. The plutonium reactors built at Hanford were the world's first, and they produced the payload for the atomic bomb dropped on Nagasaki in 1945.

During the cold war, the Departments of Defense and Energy pumped billions of dollars into plutonium production and the development of nuclear energy at Hanford, and the Tri-Cities boomed. In the early 1960s, when Hanford was working at full capacity, it had nine atomic reactors, employed some 45,000 workers and produced almost 800 tons of plutonium a month – almost single-handedly fueling the massive US nuclear arms buildup in the race with the Soviet Union. Comforted by official reassurances that every precaution was being taken with safety, residents and workers felt quite proud of their patriotic efforts.

However, despite the government's zealous commitment, safety oversights and poor planning eventually doomed their efforts. Billions of gallons of radioactive waste were simply buried in underground storage tanks, many of which are now leaking. Until Hanford was closed as a reactor site in the 1980s, the Columbia was considered the most radioactive river in the world. In 1986, the Department of Energy revealed that, in addition to more than a hundred accidental radiation releases over the years, in 1949 there was one deliberate release, called the Green Run, which was done to test radiation-monitoring equipment.

As might be expected, severe health problems are rampant in the area, and though many lawsuits have been filed against the plant, few expect to win their cases. The deactivation and environmental cleanup has been extremely difficult and costly, attracting billions of dollars in federal tax money, but officials admit that almost nothing has been cleaned up so far. Ironically, the cleanup now employs more people than Hanford ever did as an active nuclear facility. Bechtel, the company that has managed the effort so far, won a bid in 2001 to build a $4 billion facility that would turn the remaining 53 million gallons of radioactive waste into glass. Some 3000 people will work on the construction of two plants, slated to go on line in 2007.

Another odd twist in the Hanford saga is that the reservation also contains some of the most pristine wilderness in Washington, a result of the secrecy and security surrounding the plant. Since Hanford's operations use only 6% of the land, the government is now divesting itself of some of the rest, and the western side has been included in the Arid Lands Ecology Reserve: 120 sq miles of native sagebrush grasslands, a rarity in intensely irrigated central Washington. Plant life here includes bluebunch wheat grass, lupine and balsamroot, and the reserve is home to Swainson's and ferruginous hawks, golden eagles, sage sparrows, sagebrush voles and a large and unusual population of desert elk. Though it's currently a de facto national park, the land's ultimate fate will be decided by contentious debates among environmentalists, the Yakama Nation, land developers and the federal government.

WASHINGTON

Getting There & Around

The Tri-Cities Airport (☎ 509-547-6352), 3601 N 20th Ave, is just north of Pasco off I-182. Horizon Air (☎ 800-547-9308) has flights to Seattle, Portland and Vancouver.

Greyhound (☎ 509-547-3151) and Amtrak (☎ 509-545-1554) share a new terminal at 535 N 1st Ave in Pasco. Greyhound passes through Pasco twice a day on its run between Portland ($37, 5 hours) and Spokane ($24, 2½ hours). Other twice-daily buses go to Seattle via Yakima and Ellensburg ($34, 6½ hours) and to Walla Walla ($9, 1 hour), continuing to Pendleton, Oregon. Amtrak's *Empire Builder* stops here en route to Portland at 5:35am (4½ hours); eastbound, it passes through at 8:57pm on the way to Spokane (3 hours) and Chicago.

Ben Franklin Transit (☎ 509-735-5100, ⓦ www.bft.org) buses run until around 7pm Monday to Saturday. From Greyhound/Amtrak, bus No 62 heads for the Pasco Transit Center at 22nd and Sylvester Sts, where you can pick up connections for Kennewick (No 120), Richland or the airport (No 225). Call Trans Plus Night Service (☎ 509-582-5555) for share-taxi pickup from 7pm to 10:30pm; the fare is an unbeatable $1. For a cab, phone A-1 Tri-City Cab Co (☎ 509-547-7777).

WALLA WALLA

Perhaps it's the awkward, unlikely redundancy of the name itself, or the fact that the state penitentiary is located here (inmates crank out more than 2½ million license plates a year), but Walla Walla (population 29,686) undeservedly suffers a reputation as Washington's town on the backside of beyond. For Puget Sound urbanites, Walla Walla is shorthand for all that's rural and out-of-the-way in eastern Washington.

However, the reality is quite different. Walla Walla's Main St possesses one of the most significant enclaves of historic architecture in eastern Washington, with an ambitious redevelopment highlighting its architectural gems. It boasts plenty of sophistication for a town of its size, with good restaurants, wine-tasting salons, galleries, parks and an academic character, lent by

PLACES TO STAY	PLACES TO EAT
2 Capri Motel	11 Jacobi's Cafe
3 Green Gables Inn	14 Clarette's Restaurant
8 City Center Motel;	18 Backstage Bistro
Enterprise Car Rental	20 Whitehouse-Crawford
13 Travelodge	Restaurant; Seven Hills
17 Walla Walla Residential	Winery
Suites; Coffee	25 Merchants Ltd Delicatessen
Connection Café	& French Bakery
23 Marcus Whitman Hotel	34 Coffee Perk
& Conference Center	36 The Pastime Cafe

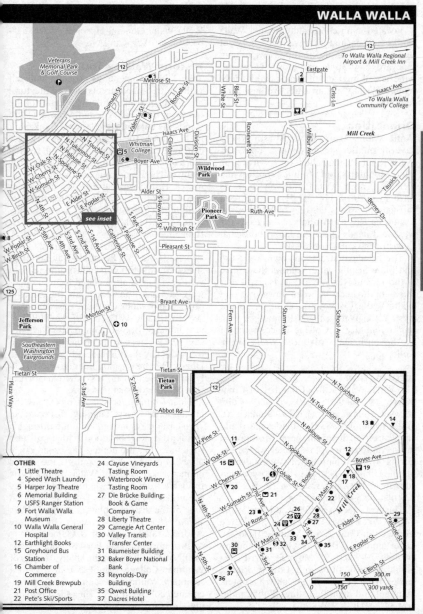

WALLA WALLA

Veterans Memorial Park & Golf Course

Melrose St

To Walla Walla Regional
Airport & Mill Creek Inn

Eastgate

To Walla Walla
Community College

Isaacs Ave

Mill Creek

Whitman College

Boyer Ave

Wildwood Park

Alder St

Pioneer Park

Ruth Ave

see inset

Whitman St

Pleasant St

Bryant Ave

Jefferson Park

Southeastern Washington Fairgrounds

Morton St

Tietan St

Tietan St

Tietan Park

Abbot Rd

WASHINGTON

OTHER

1   Little Theatre
4   Speed Wash Laundry
5   Harper Joy Theatre
6   Memorial Building
7   USFS Ranger Station
9   Fort Walla Walla
    Museum
10 Walla Walla General
    Hospital
12 Earthlight Books
15 Greyhound Bus
    Station
16 Chamber of
    Commerce
19 Mill Creek Brewpub
21 Post Office
22 Pete's Ski/Sports

24 Cayuse Vineyards
    Tasting Room
26 Waterbrook Winery
    Tasting Room
27 Die Brücke Building;
    Book & Game
    Company
28 Liberty Theatre
29 Carnegie Art Center
30 Valley Transit
    Transfer Center
31 Baumeister Building
32 Baker Boyer National
    Bank
33 Reynolds-Day
    Building
35 Qwest Building
37 Dacres Hotel

Boyer Ave

Mill Creek

0   150   300 m
0   150   300 yards

two small but noted colleges. It's also the financial center for this part of the state.

Located in a rich agricultural area, Walla Walla has earned renown for its sweet onions, but you'll also find peas, asparagus, vineyards and apple orchards. Nearby are wineries, skiing and a major wilderness, making Walla Walla an attractive base for a few days.

Orientation

Walla Walla is in a fertile basin where several smaller streams meet the Walla Walla River. Rising behind the town are the Blue Mountains; only 6 miles south is the Oregon border, with Pendleton 35 miles farther south on Hwy 11. The main road through the area is US 12, which leaves the Columbia River at Wallula, 29 miles to the west, and heads up to the Idaho border at Lewiston, 99 miles northeast.

The principal streets in town are Rose and Main Sts; the latter follows the course of the ancient Nez Perce Trail. Isaacs Ave is the main drag east between downtown and Walla Walla Community College. To the west, Walla Walla practically merges with the community of College Place, home of the Seventh Day Adventist Walla Walla College.

Information

The Walla Walla Valley Chamber of Commerce (☎ 509-525-0850, 877-998-4748, w www.wallawalla.org), 29 E Sumach St, Walla Walla, WA 98362, provides maps and suggestions 8:30am to 5pm Monday to Friday and 9am to 4pm summer weekends. For information on the Walla Walla district of the Umatilla National Forest, you can stop in at the ranger station (☎ 509-522-6290) at 1415 W Rose St.

The post office is at 128 N 2nd Ave, Walla Walla, WA 98362. Get online at Coffee Connection Café, 226 E Main St (also see Entertainment). Book & Game Company (☎ 509-529-9963), 38 Main St, carries regional history titles and Lonely Planet guides. *What's Up?*, a free weekly, has entertainment and nightlife listings. Public radio is at 89.7 MHz, KWWS-FM.

Wash your clothes at Speed Wash Laundry (☎ 509-525-9856), 2023 Isaacs Ave. Walla Walla General Hospital (☎ 509-525-0480) is at 1025 S 2nd Ave.

Historic Walking Tour

Take a few moments to acquaint yourself with the tree-lined streets and architectural highlights of Walla Walla. The center of the old town is at 2nd Ave and Main St. Here stands the **Baker Boyer National Bank**, built in 1910 and still doing business nearly a century later. In either direction stretch blocks of 1890s-era commercial buildings; many still house prominent downtown businesses. To the west, at 3rd Ave and Main, you'll find the restored 1889 **Baumeister Building**, with its delicately chiseled bay windows. A block farther west, admire the Italianate facade of the 1899 **Dacres Hotel**.

To the east is one of the city's oldest structures, the 1874 **Reynolds-Day Building**, site of Washington's first constitutional convention. It's best appreciated from the sidewalk tables of the Merchants cafe, on the other side of Main. Continue east across 1st Ave to see the 1903 **Die Brücke Building**, now home of Book & Game. The Germanized name refers to its bridgelike position over Mill Creek. In the next block east, the **Liberty Theatre** is a monument to early Hollywood Orientalism; it's now part of the Bon Marche department store.

Head south on 1st Ave one block, past the art moderne **Qwest Building**, to Poplar St. Turn east on Poplar and continue through a residential neighborhood with large and sometimes fanciful homes. The broad range of styles displayed here reflects the varied ethnic backgrounds of Walla Walla's early residents, from an era when the city actively promoted immigration. For a self-guided tour of the district, obtain a copy of *Walla Walla: Her Historic Homes,* by Penny Andres, available at Book & Game.

Turn north (left) at Park St, which leads over Mill Creek and to the shady campus of **Whitman College**. Established in 1859 as a seminary, Whitman became a four-year accredited college in 1882. The oldest remaining structure on campus is the **Memorial**

Building, 345 Boyer Ave, a Romanesque-revival landmark built in 1899. On the other side of Boyer Ave stand some of the state's tallest bur oak, silver maple and American elm trees. Walking west along Boyer will bring you back to Main St and downtown.

Fort Walla Walla Park

Built in 1856 as an army installation, this site is now a large park and nature preserve with an assortment of playing fields, recreation and picnic areas and the **Fort Walla Walla Museum** (*☎ 509-525-7703, 755 Myra Rd; adult/senior & student/child $5/4/1; open 10am-5pm Tues-Sun Apr-Oct*), south of W Poplar St. Definitely worth a stop, the museum consists of lower and upper sections. The pioneer village is a collection of 16 historic buildings, including a blacksmith shop, schoolhouse (1867), log cabins and a railway depot, arranged around a central meadow. On a hill above the village, the fort's old cavalry stables house the museum proper, with collections of farm implements, ranching tools, Native American artifacts and what could be the world's largest plastic replica of a mule team. Sundays at 2pm (and Saturdays June to August), volunteers don period dress for living history demonstrations.

Wineries

While hardly the center of the Northwest wine industry, the fertile, well-drained volcanic soils of the Walla Walla Valley produce some of Washington's most respected red wines.

The best of the local wineries are found around Lowden, roughly 12 miles west of Walla Walla on US 12. **L'Ecole No 41** (*☎ 509-525-0940, 41 Lowden School Rd; open 11am-4pm, by appointment in winter*) has a tasting room in an old schoolhouse. Try the Semillon and Merlot. **Woodward Canyon Winery** (*☎ 509-525-4129, 11920 US 12; open 10am-5pm Mon-Sat, noon-5pm Sun, to 4pm fall & winter*) has one of the best chardonnays in Washington.

If you can't make it out to the vineyards, stop by one of the tasting rooms recently opened in downtown Walla Walla. The salon of **Waterbrook Winery** (*☎ 509-522-1262, 31 E Main St; open 10:30am-4:30pm*) doubles as a gallery, so you can admire paintings and pottery while sipping its signature chardonnay. Nearby is **Cayuse Vineyards** (*☎ 509-526-0686, 17 E Main St; open 11am-4pm Fri & Sat*), with a full-bodied syrah. **Seven Hills Winery** (*☎ 509-529-7198, 212 N 3rd Ave*), which shares the old Whitehouse-Crawford planing mill with a fine restaurant, is best known for its merlots and cabernets, but has also received praise for its Bordeaux varieties.

Special Events

The Walla Walla Sweet Onion Blues Fest (*☎ 509-525-1031*), held in mid-July at Fort Walla Walla, celebrates the valley's renowned crop with food booths and recipe contests, as well as live music provided by touring blues acts.

One of Walla Walla's biggest events is the Balloon Stampede, held for three days in mid-May at the county fairgrounds. Dozens of competitors launch their hot-air-filled craft at 6am, weather permitting. Besides the balloon gathering, there's also a carnival, pari-mutuel racing and a fun run/walk. Lodging may be scarce during this event.

Places to Stay

Walla Walla's B&Bs generally cater to adults, but arrangements can be made if you're traveling with offspring.

Green Gables Inn (*☎ 509-525-5501, 888-525-5501, [W] www.greengablesinn.com, 922 Bonsella St*) Rooms $105-135. This is a handsome 1909 Craftsman home with nice gardens on two lots. It's on a tree-canopied street opposite Whitman College's North hall.

Mill Creek Inn (*☎ 509-522-1234, [W] www.millcreekbb.com, 2014 Mill Creek Rd*) Rooms $135-155. Eight acres of vineyards surround this former farmstead in the Blue Mountain foothills east of Walla Walla – in fact, it's a working winery. The old chicken house, bunkhouse and dairy barn have been superbly converted into cozy guest cottages with vaulted ceilings, private verandas and skylit bathrooms. To get there, head east on Hwy 12, take the Rooks Park exit and drive about 2 miles up Mill Creek Rd.

WASHINGTON

There are plenty of hotels to choose from along 2nd Ave, but head out along Isaacs Ave for cheaper digs.

Capri Motel *(☎ 509-525-1130, 800-451-1139, fax 509-525-1465, 2003 Melrose St)* Singles/doubles $36/50. Located on the northeast edge of town, the Capri isn't luxurious, but it has a number of clean, spacious units and a pool.

City Center Motel *(☎ 509-529-2660, 800-453-3160, 627 W Main St)* Singles/doubles $43/47. Out toward Fort Walla Walla is this well-maintained (but not quite aptly named) motel.

Travelodge *(☎ 509-529-4940, 800-578-7878, fax 509-529-4943, 421 E Main St)* Singles/doubles $50/60. This efficiently managed franchise is just a block from Whitman College. There's a heated pool and hot tub; rates include breakfast and the morning paper.

Walla Walla Residential Suites *(☎ 509-529-9824, 214 E Main St)* Studios/one-bedroom apartments $75/95. These amply furnished apartments upstairs in the old Walla Walla Hotel offer much better value than similarly priced franchise operations. Each unit includes a large, fully stocked kitchen, Jacuzzi tub, washer/dryer and DSL Internet connection. The broad back deck is equipped with barbecue grills.

Marcus Whitman Hotel & Conference Center *(☎ 509-525-2200, 866-826-9422,* W *www.marcuswhitmanhotel.com, 6 W Rose St)* Rooms/suites $99-119/$229-279. Dating from 1928, this elegantly renovated highrise hotel is a cornerstone in Walla Walla's downtown renaissance. All the details have been carefully restored, down to the frosted chandeliers in the ground-floor restaurant. Luxurious suites feature Italian-crafted furniture and DVD players. Freewheeling owner Kyle Mussman plans to add a motorcycle museum to the premises.

Places to Eat

Vegetarians and others with alternative appetites will have no trouble finding a satisfying meal in this university enclave.

Coffee Perk *(☎ 509-526-0636, 4 1st St)* Sandwiches $6. Tourists frequent the Starbucks at the corner; students prefer to get their lattes (and pastries and sandwiches) here.

Merchants Ltd Delicatessen & French Bakery *(☎ 509-525-0900, 21 E Main St)* Breakfast & sandwiches $5. Closed Sun. For breakfast head to this great deli, coffeehouse and bakery inside the 1885 Barrett Building. With its selection of cheeses and salads, it's also a good place for picnic provisions.

Clarette's Restaurant *(☎ 509-529-3430, 15 S Touchet St)* Breakfast $4, dinner $8. This long-standing eatery near Whitman College serves traditional breakfasts, including all kinds of omelets, and home-style dinners like meatloaf and pork chops. It's often very busy.

Jacobi's Cafe *(☎ 509-525-2677, 416 N 2nd Ave)* Light meals $8, dinner entrees $14-20. The popular Jacobi's is in the converted old train depot, a nice setting whether you dine inside or out. Seafood, steaks and pasta highlight their daily fresh sheet; less pricey options include vegetarian stir-fries, salads and pizza. There are also a number of regional microbrews on tap.

Backstage Bistro *(☎ 509-526-0690, 230 E Main St)* Dinner entrees $18. The specialty at this artistically outfitted ex-gallery is barbecued brisket and ribs, marinated overnight in a spicy sauce. There's live jazz weekend evenings.

Pastime Café *(☎ 509-525-0873, 215 W Main St)* Entrees $10. Closed Sun. A relic of an earlier era, this neon-lit Italian restaurant is no slave to fashion, but you won't go away hungry – or broke. A big plate of ravioli or spaghetti with meatballs is under $10. The adjacent lounge is a good place to get incoherent with the locals.

Whitehouse-Crawford Restaurant *(☎ 509-525-2222, 55 W Cherry St)* Entrees $20. Open from 5pm Wed-Sun. The city's newest fine-dining establishment is housed in an impressively renovated woodworking mill dating from 1905. Great local seafood and produce highlight its seasonally varying menu – try the sweet onion torte in springtime. It's an excellent place to sample the bounty of Walla Walla's vineyards, with more than 60 local vintages in the cellars.

Entertainment

Walla Walla's entertainment scene runs the gamut from coffeehouses to the high arts.

Coffee Connection Café (☎ *509-529-9999, 226 E Main St*) More than just a cybercafe, the Coffee Connection functions as a sort of community social center, with lots of fun stuff to do. There are games, both virtual (networked computer arcade games) and nonvirtual (billiards and chess), a TV lounge, a grand piano for anyone who feels like playing, and coffee, of course.

Mill Creek Brewpub (☎ *509-522-2440, 11 S Palouse St*) Walla Walla's only brewpub pours seven of its own ales; have a Penitentiary Porter or a Walla Walla Wheat. The cavernous beer hall features a patio for open-air quaffing. The food is just functional.

Walla Walla Symphony (☎ *509-529-8020,* ⓦ *www.wwsymphony.com*) Under the direction of maestro Yaacov Bergman, the orchestra includes the works of some new composers in its seven-concert season. Performances are at Whitman College's Cordiner Hall.

Harper Joy Theatre (☎ *509-527-5180, N Park St & Boyer Ave*) Adult/senior $8/5. Whitman College's theater department stages an ambitious series, including premiere works by playwrights-in-residence.

Little Theatre (☎ *509-529-3683,* ⓦ *www .ltww.org, 1130 E Sumach St*) Adult/child $9/8. This well-established community troupe presents four productions a year, ranging from familiar crowd-pleasers to more adventurous plays.

Getting There & Around

Horizon Air (☎ 800-547-9308) has flights to Seattle and Portland from the Walla Walla Regional Airport, which is northeast of town off US 12.

Two daily buses stop at Walla Walla's Greyhound station (☎ 509-525-9313), 315 N 2nd Ave, en route between Pendleton, Oregon ($11, 1 hour), and Pasco ($9, 1 hour), with connections for Portland, Seattle and Spokane.

Budget Rent-A-Car (☎ 509-525-8811) and Hertz (☎ 509-522-3321) are at the airport. In town, Enterprise (☎ 509-529-

1988) maintains an agency at 629 W Main St, next to the City Center Motel.

Local bus service is operated 6:30am to 5:30pm weekdays by Valley Transit (☎ 509-525-9140, ⓦ www.valleytransit.com). Maps and schedules are posted at the Transfer Center, at N 4th and W Main Sts; or pick up a free map at the chamber of commerce. Bus No 1 travels across town every half-hour, from Walla Walla Community College to College Place; No 5 goes to the fairgrounds. Fare is 50¢; there's no Sunday service.

Call ABC Taxi (☎ 509-529-7726) or A-1 Taxi (☎ 509-529-2525) for a lift.

AROUND WALLA WALLA
Whitman Mission
National Historic Site

The site commemorates the tragic demise of the Whitman Mission in 1847 (see the boxed text 'The Whitman Massacre'). A tall obelisk, erected 50 years after the incident as a monument to the 14 slain missionaries, sits atop a bluff overlooking the original mission grounds, which are preserved in a parklike grove of trees. Foundations indicate where the buildings once stood. An interpretive trail passes the graves of Narcissa and Marcus Whitman on the way up to the monument.

Maps of the grounds can be picked up at the visitor center (☎ *509-529-2761; adult $2, family $4; open 8am-4:30pm year round; closed major holidays)*, located 7 miles west of Walla Walla off US 12. Inside, thoughtful exhibits and a short film detail the story of the Whitmans, the local Native Americans, the Oregon Trail pioneers and the events that led up to the deaths of the missionaries.

Dayton

Dayton (population 2655) is an attractive older town on the southern edge of the Palouse region, 31 miles northeast of Walla Walla along Lewis and Clark's return route. Though the sun bakes the farmland on the surrounding plateaus, down in the shady, well-watered valley things are gardenlike and hospitable.

As a result of the town's early agricultural prosperity, local farmers and businesspeople built their dream homes here in a range of

The Whitman Massacre

Walla Walla is the site of one of the seminal confrontations between early white settlers and Native Americans. In 1836, Marcus and Narcissa Whitman established a church mission and farm at Waiilatpu (just west of present-day Walla Walla) in order to minister to local Indians. Relations between the two groups were initially friendly, but tensions mounted with the arrival of increasing numbers of Oregon Trail emigrants. After the difficult Blue Mountain crossing, these white settlers often made a detour north to Waiilatpu to replenish supplies, moving across traditional Native American hunting grounds en route.

In 1847, an outbreak of measles ran through a Cayuse Indian village, killing many Native children but sparing those of the settlers. When Whitman, a doctor, was unable to halt the advance of the epidemic, the Cayuse blamed him for spreading it. In late fall, a group of Cayuse braves entered the mission, asking to speak to Whitman. After Whitman welcomed the Indians into his kitchen, they drew their weapons, killing the missionary and his wife. As the attack spread throughout the mission grounds, 12 other settlers were murdered and 53 more, mostly women and children, were taken captive.

The Whitman Massacre, as the killings were known, set in motion the Cayuse War, the first of many conflicts between Native Americans and US settlers in the Oregon Territory. It also hastened the approval of territorial status for Oregon. By 1848, Oregon had become a US territory, which enabled federal troops to be dispatched to apprehend the killers and to protect the settlers from further violence. After two years of skirmishes, four Cayuse braves surrendered and were tried and hanged for the killings.

The Whitman Mission was abandoned, and the region was soon closed to settlement by Washington's governor, Isaac Stevens. Treaties between the US government and the eastern Washington tribes were signed in 1855, and in 1856 the US Army built Fort Walla Walla to enforce their terms.

architectural styles; 63 of these are on the National Register of Historic Places. The handsome Dayton **train depot** (☎ 509-382-2026, 222 E Commercial St; $2; open 10am-5pm Tues-Sat in summer), a gingerbread structure built in 1881, has been restored along with its original ticket office and stationmaster's quarters. Pick up a walking-tour map of Dayton's historic homes on your way out. Also noteworthy is the old **county courthouse**, built in 1887 and still in use. The chamber of commerce (☎ 509-382-4825, Ⓦ www.historicdayton.com), 166 E Main St, has information for visitors.

Built in 1890 by brewer Henry Weinhard's nephew to house the saloon and lodge hall, the **Weinhard Hotel** (☎ 509-382-4032, fax 509-382-2640, Ⓦ www.weinhard .com, 235 E Main St) now offers 15 elegantly appointed rooms for $70 to $125. On the ground floor, the **Weinhard Cafe** does espresso and innovative pasta and seafood dishes, with dinners costing around $20.

Patit Creek Restaurant (☎ 509-382-2625, 725 E Dayton Ave), an unassuming place just northeast of town, turns out some of the region's best French-inspired cuisine. It's open for lunch ($9) Tuesday to Friday, for dinner (around $24) Tuesday to Saturday. Call ahead for reservations.

Bluewood Ski Area

This heavily forested ski area (☎ 509-382-4725, snow conditions ☎ 509-382-2877, Ⓦ www.bluewood.com, PO Box 88, Dayton, WA 99328; full-day lift tickets adult/student/child & senior $28/23/20; open 9am-4pm Wed-Sun & holidays), in the Blue Mountains, is 21 miles southeast of Dayton (turn down 4th St, also known as N Touchet Rd). Though not a big resort, Bluewood has the state's second-highest base elevation (4545 feet) and remains uncrowded despite its reputation for good weather and powdery snow. It has 22 runs and a vertical drop of 1125 feet, equipment rentals, a cafeteria and a ski school.

Wenaha-Tucannon Wilderness

Part of the Umatilla (yu-ma-**til**-a) National Forest, this wilderness is home to elk, black bears, bighorn sheep, cougars and bobcats. Rivers and streams here have cut deep canyons into the basalt lava flow, forming broad tablelands with narrow-valleyed bottomlands.

To reach the Wenaha-Tucannon, follow US 12 northeast from Dayton for 10 miles and turn east onto the Tucannon River Rd. The wilderness can otherwise be accessed by Hwy 9115 (the road to the Bluewood Ski Area), or from the south along the Wenaha River via Troy, Oregon.

Keep on this road until its end (bear left at the junction 2 miles past Camp Wooten State Park). From here, there's a hiking trail along the Tucannon River, another up Panjab Creek, and many opportunities for days-long backpacking trips or shorter loop hikes. Contact the ranger stations in Pomeroy (☎ 509-843-1891), at 71 W Main St, or Walla Walla (☎ 509-522-6290), at 1415 W Rose St, for details on trails.

CLARKSTON & LEWISTON AREA

The bustling twin cities of Clarkston (population 7337), and Lewiston, Idaho (population 32,000), sprawl across the floodplains where the mighty Snake and Clearwater Rivers meet. These towns are centers of a vast agricultural area whose products include peas, lentils, wheat and livestock. Lewiston is often referred to as the 'Inland Port,' as the Columbia and Snake Rivers' dam-and-lock systems have created hundreds of miles of slack-water reservoirs that allow barges to travel all the way from Lewiston to Portland.

While Clarkston and Lewiston are hardly tourist towns, there is a good reason for Northwest travelers to make the detour here: About 30 miles upriver between Oregon and Idaho on the Snake River is the white water and wilderness of Hells Canyon, reached by a number of jet-boat tours and rafting trips based in Clarkston and Lewiston.

History

The towns' namesakes, Meriwether Lewis and William Clark, passed through here on both legs of their early-19th-century expedition, though there was no settlement in the area until 1860, at the beginning of the Idaho gold rush. The confluence of the Snake and Clearwater Rivers was the head of steamboat navigation from Portland, and the area boomed as a transportation and trade center.

Lewiston and Clarkston continued to grow as trade and transportation hubs, especially as federal irrigation projects brought orchards to flower along the protected and temperate canyon bottoms. However, the biggest advance for the area came in 1955, when the Army Corps of Engineers began to build the four Snake River dams that, in 1975, brought slack water to the port of Lewiston. Lewiston is the USA's most inland port: Vessels drawing less than 14 feet and weighing less than 12,000 tons can journey all the way from the mouth of the Columbia River to the grain-loading docks at Lewiston, 470 miles from the Pacific Ocean.

Information

To find out about events and services on either side of the Snake River, contact the Clarkston Chamber of Commerce (☎ 509-758-7712, 800-933-2128, W www.clarkston chamber.org), 502 Bridge St, Clarkston, WA, 99403, or the Lewiston Chamber of Commerce (☎ 208-743-3531, W www.lewiston chamber.org), 111 Main St, Lewiston, ID 83501.

The USFS headquarters for the Hells Canyon National Recreation Area (☎ 509-758-0616) is at 2535 Riverside Dr in Clarkston. For river-permit reservations and information, call ☎ 509-758-1957.

Lewiston's post office is at 1613 Idaho St. St Joseph Regional Medical Center (☎ 208-799-5210) is at 415 6th St.

WASHINGTON

Lewis & Clark Center for Arts & History

Several galleries of regional artwork, a gift shop/bookstore and a small museum are housed at this cultural center (☎ 208-799-2243, 415 Main St; $1; open 11am-4pm Mon-Fri) in Lewiston's historic downtown. Of particular interest is a permanent exhibit on the Chinese community who settled here after the discovery of gold in the 1860s. Dominoes, opium pipes and other household objects, in addition to a reconstructed Buddhist temple dating from 1888, offer an intriguing look at this little-known chapter in Idaho history.

Hells Gate State Park

The antidote to the often scorching-hot days at the bottom of the Snake River canyon, this 960-acre state park (☎ 208-799-5015, W www.idahoparks.org, 3620 Snake River Ave; day-use fee $3 per vehicle) offers a swimming beach, full-service marina, campground, picnic area and ample room to relax along the river. Located 4 miles south of downtown Lewiston, Hells Gate also has a series of mountain-biking, hiking and horse-riding trails; it's the southern access point for the Levee Parkway Trail.

On a hill above the campground is the **Lewis & Clark Interpretive Center** (admission free; open 8am-4pm daily June-Sept, Wed-Sat rest of year), scheduled for completion in 2003 to coincide with the Lewis & Clark bicentennial. Exhibits focus on the plants and wildlife found by the Corps of Discovery during their travels. A three-dimensional mural depicts the meeting of the explorers and the Nez Perce Indians, who showed the white men how to make dugout canoes; a replica of one of these vessels is incorporated into the tableau.

The park marina (☎ 208-799-5015) is the departure point for most jet-boat tours up the Snake River; charter fishing trips leave from here as well.

Jet-Boat Tours

Although the Hells Canyon of the Snake River begins 50 miles south of Lewiston, the city is the center for upstream jet-boat tours of the deepest river gorge in North America. Operators offer a wide variety of day/overnight trips ($50-100/200-300) and dinner cruises ($50); most offer fishing expeditions on the side.

Expect a day trip to cover anywhere from 90 to 200 miles. Buffalo Eddy Pictographs (see that section, next), the Kirkland Historical Ranch, swimming holes and bighorn sheep herds are typical destinations. Lunch and beverages are provided, though you'll want to take along a small cooler of your own on some of the longer summer trips.

For a complete list of outfitters, contact either of the two chambers of commerce. See the Hells Canyon section of the Northeastern Oregon chapter for details on excursions from the southern end.

Beamers Hells Canyon Tours (☎ 509 758-4800, 800-522-6966, W www.hellscanyontours.com, 1451 Bridge St, Clarkston) This operation is famous for its overnight mail trip to outlying ranches ($230), departing 9am Wed year round.

Northwest Voyageurs (☎ 800-727-9977, W www .voyageurs.com, PO Box 370, Lucille, ID 83542) Northwest offers multiday white-water rafting trips starting at $779 for three days on the Snake River.

OARS Dories (☎ 208-743-4201, 800-346-6277, W www.oars.com, 1127B Airway Ave, Lewiston, ID 83501) Purists who scorn noisy jet boats can ride the river in a dory – a small, wooden craft resembling a drift boat – on multiday tours (from $798/730 adult/youth).

River Quest Excursions (☎ 208-746-8060, 800-589-1129, W www.riverquestexcursions.com, 3665A Snake River Ave, Lewiston)

Snake Dancer Excursions (☎ 509-758-8927, 800-234-1941, W www.snakedancerexcursions.com, PO Box 318, Clarkston, WA 99403)

Snake River Adventures (☎ 208-746-6276, 800-262-8874, W www.snakeriveradventures.com, 227 Snake River Ave, Lewiston) This is the only company that goes all the way to Hells Canyon Dam, 120 miles upriver in Idaho ($170).

Buffalo Eddy Pictographs

Twelve miles south of Asotin on Snake River Rd is a jumble of rocks that constricts the Snake River into a fast-moving channel. On the rocks are a number of well-preserved petroglyphs of warriors brandishing weapons; it's easy to imagine that these images once warned of a prehistoric territorial boundary.

There's no sign for the petroglyphs, but they're easy to find. From Asotin, continue on 1st St until it becomes graveled Snake River Rd. The road winds through an increasingly sheer canyon until it passes through a narrow crevice between two rock faces. Pull off the road and explore the rocks near the river for the petroglyphs.

If you want to have more of a look at the Hells Canyon country but don't fancy a jet-boat excursion, continue on Snake River Rd, which follows the river to the mouth of the Grande Ronde River. The canyon walls get higher and higher, and increasingly striated by basalt lava flows; the landscape is stark and otherworldly. The road eventually joins Hwy 3 in Oregon, a fairly bumpy 31 miles from Buffalo Eddy.

Places to Stay

Camping The following are the main camping spots.

Hells Gate State Park (☎ 208-799-5015, **W** www.idahoparks.org, 3620 Snake River Ave) Tent/RV sites $12/16, reservations $6. The campground's 93 sites flank the Snake River and are within easy reach of a swimming beach, boat launch and trails. Facilities include flush toilets, hot showers, a laundromat and a store with fishing supplies.

Chief Timothy State Park (☎ 509-758-9580, reservations ☎ 888-226-7688, US 12, 8 miles west of Clarkston) Tent/RV sites $14/20. Located on a landscaped island in Lower Granite Lake (a section of the Snake flooded by the Lower Granite Dam in 1975), the park has more than 11,000 feet of freshwater shoreline. Campers are invited to use the boat ramps and moorage docks, making this a popular place for water-skiing weekends. There's a store selling snacks and tackle, and an interpretive center telling the story of the Nez Perce village that once stood here.

B&Bs There are a few B&Bs in the area.

Highland House (☎/fax 509-758-3126, 707 Highland Ave) Rooms $55-85. Eight

blocks south of US 12, this Clarkston establishment is an 1890s Victorian home done up English-style. Rates include a full English breakfast.

Cliff House B&B (☎ 509-758-1267, 1227 Westlake Dr) Rooms $80-85. The contemporary Cliff House B&B, 8 miles west of Clarkston, hangs over the Snake River just above Chief Timothy State Park.

Hotels The following places, listed west to east, are but a few of the lodgings found along (or just off) the US 12 strip.

Best Western RiverTree Inn (☎ 509-758-9551, 800-597-3621, 1257 Bridge St) Rooms $69. Opposite the Little Reno Casino, this franchise features a courtyard swimming pool, sauna and complimentary breakfast. Highway-view balconies are standard, and a few family suites include a sleeping loft. Ask about discounts when checking in.

Sunset Motel (☎ 509-758-2517, 1200 Bridge St) Singles/doubles $30/40. Most of the units in this friendly angler-oriented motel have front porches, and unlike other budget options, they've wisely left the hardwood floors uncarpeted. It's under the same management as the somewhat more secluded Astor Motel across the way.

Quality Inn & Suites (☎ 509-758-9500, 800-228-5151, 700 Port Dr) Singles/doubles $72-92/79-99. Attractively spread along the Snake River, this conference center complex has all the extras you'd expect, like a river-view restaurant and pool, and some you wouldn't, like an 18-hole putting course and private dock for jet-boat excursions. Children and youth under 18 stay free.

Travel Motor Inn (☎ 208-743-4501, 1021 Main St) Singles/doubles $35/45. Across the bridge in Lewiston, this is the closest lodging to the historic downtown, with a helpful staff and well-worn rooms.

Riverview Inn (☎ 208-746-3311, 800-806-7666, 1325 Main St) Singles/doubles $40/49. Probably Lewiston's best value, this large, older hotel offers spacious, well-kept rooms, some with river views, and complimentary breakfast. There's a kidney-shaped pool and smoky lounge. Pets are welcome.

WASHINGTON

WASHINGTON

Sacajawea Motor Inn (☎ 208-746-1393, 800-333-1393, fax 208-743-3620, 1824 Main St) Singles/doubles $46/56. About 2 miles from the bridge, this efficiently run lodging has 90 comfortable units, as well as a pool, fitness room and locally popular restaurant, The Helm.

Hillary Motel (☎ 208-743-8514, 2030 North-South Hwy) Singles/doubles $23/31. If you're on a tight budget, head north across the Clearwater River to the Hillary, an exceptional deal for air-conditioned units with kitchenettes. There are several other inexpensive places in the vicinity.

Places to Eat
The twin towns offer a variety of culinary delights.

Roosters Waterfront Restaurant (☎ 509-751-0155, 1550 Port Dr, Clarkston) Entrees $12. Roosters has deck dining by the Hells Canyon Resort marina and a nautically themed bar. Fresh seafood, salads and sandwiches highlight a healthful menu.

Tomato Bros (☎ 509-758-7902, 200 Bridge St, Clarkston) Entrees $11. Wood-fired pizzas and pastas are typical fare at this slick, pseudo-Italian restaurant near the bridge.

In Lewiston, various restaurants and boutiques occupy Morgan's Alley, a group of four restored 19th-century buildings connected by a series of brick arches and cheerfully cluttered with antiques.

The Dill Pickle (☎ 208-746-8000, 301 Main St, Lewiston) Sandwiches $6. Closed Sun. This popular deli adds a gourmet touch to soups, salads and deluxe sandwiches. Get your espresso drinks here.

Bojack's Broiler Pit (☎ 208-743-9817, 301 Main St, Lewiston) Entrees $14. This subterranean steakhouse is recommended for its bite-size steaks (breaded and deep-fried). Upstairs is a friendly local tavern.

Jonathan's (☎ 208-746-3438, 1516 Main St, Lewiston) Lunch/dinner entrees $8/20. Tucked into Lewiston's motel row, Jonathan's is a classy place for lunch or dinner in a pleasant rock-garden setting. Fresh ingredients liven up the usual salads, sandwiches and burgers, while an eclectic array of international and American regional dishes will appeal to more adventurous eaters.

Getting There & Around
Horizon Air (☎ 208-743-9293) provides frequent service to Sea-Tac (via Pullman) and Boise from the Lewiston-Nez Perce County Regional Airport (☎ 208-746-7962), south of town.

Northwestern Trailways (☎ 208-746-8108, 800-366-3830 in Idaho) operates two buses a day to Spokane ($20, 3 hours) via Pullman, and one a day to Boise at 12:10pm ($35, 7½ hours). The bus stops at the Sportsman Inn, 3001 N & S Hwy, east of town along the north bank of the Clearwater River.

Hertz (☎ 208-746-0411, 800-654-3131), Budget (☎ 208-746-0488, 800-527-0700) and National Car Rental (☎ 208-743-0176, 800-328-4567) are all at the Lewiston-Nez Perce Airport.

For a local taxi, call AAA Ride Cab (☎ 208-743-3222) in Lewiston.

PULLMAN & THE PALOUSE REGION
The Palouse Hills are an extremely fertile region, and it is said that for every 10 miles you travel east, an additional inch of rain falls. Acre after acre, the soft, sensuous Palouse Hills are planted with wheat and legumes. While the richness of the loess soil and the climate are great for agriculture, and it's fascinating country to pass through, there's not much to do here.

Pullman (population 24,675) is the largest and most interesting town, and it's pretty much defined by Washington State University (WSU), Washington's major agricultural school, with more than 22,000 students and faculty.

The Palouse is worth a drive or bicycle tour in the spring, when the fields are amazing shades of green, or at harvest time, when wheat is shipped down the Snake River on barges. Farming methods now aim at conserving the soil, and the rolling, seemingly endless green hills are girded by swaths of stubble wheat to keep it from blowing away.

Orientation

Pullman, 7 miles west of the Idaho state line and 80 miles south of Spokane, spreads out from the south fork of the Palouse River. Hwy 27, known in town as Grand Ave, cuts through Pullman on its north-south route; Hwy 270, the east-west road, follows Davis Way at the west end of town, Main St to the east. WSU's campus, bisected by Stadium Way, takes up a big chunk of town. Downtown proper is just west of the campus, near the intersection of Main St and Grand Ave.

Southwest of Pullman, the Palouse plateau drops off dramatically to the Snake River, about 10 miles away.

Information

The Pullman Chamber of Commerce (☎ 509-334-3565, 800-365-6948, w www.pullman-wa .com), 415 N Grand Ave, is happy to dispense information and coupons.

The WSU Visitor Center (☎ 509-335-8633, w www.wsu.edu/visitor), 225 N Grand Ave at Hwy 270, provides information and directions to visitors from its off-campus site. Stop here to pick up a campus map and parking permit or to buy tickets to WSU games and events. It's open 7am to 4pm weekdays and on football Saturdays.

The main post office is at 1135 S Grand Ave, just south of Crestview St. Students Book Corporation (☎ 509-332-2537), the university bookstore, is on campus at 700 NE Thatuna St. The *Daily News* publishes in both Moscow and Pullman; read the *Evergreen Daily* for campus news. Public radio comes in at 1250 AM or 91.7 FM. Tune in KZUU, the university station, at 90.7 FM.

Drag your dirty clothes over to Betty's Bright & White, 1235 N Grand Ave, at Stadium Way. Pullman Memorial Hospital (☎ 509-332-2541) is at 1125 NE Washington Ave.

Washington State University

In the late 19th century, local business leaders took advantage of the area's rich agricultural and ranching background to get this state land-grant university. WSU, originally the Washington Agricultural College, opened in 1892 with 29 students. Still largely known for its agriculture department, the university features a top veterinary teaching hospital that treats 12,000 animals a year, as well as its own creamery and cheese research facility.

WSU's **Museum of Art** (☎ 509-335-1910; admission free; open 10am-4pm Mon-Fri, 1pm-5pm Sat & Sun, Tues 10am-10pm), in the Fine Arts Center at Stadium Way and Wilson Rd, mounts some lively, well-curated shows featuring Northwest artists, traveling exhibits and work by students and faculty. For those not interested in college sports, it can be one of the most exciting spots in Pullman. Park for free in the garage beneath the center on evenings and weekends.

Other WSU museums are much smaller and more narrowly defined. The **Jacklin Collection** (☎ 509-335-3009; admission free; open 8am-5pm Mon-Fri), in room 124 of the Webster Physical Sciences Building, consists of more than 2000 specimens of petrified wood, some dinosaur bones and fluorescent minerals. Fossils documenting stages of human evolution are on display at the **Museum of Anthropology** (☎ 509-335-3936, 110 College Hall; admission free; open 9am-4pm Mon-Thur, 9am-3pm Fri).

On a campus where athletics plays such an important role, it's not surprising to learn that $39 million went toward the new state-of-the-art **Student Recreation Center** (☎ 509-335-8732, N Fairway Dr; open 6am-11pm Mon-Fri, 10am-11pm Sat & Sun mid-Aug to mid-May, shorter hours in summer). Opened in 2001, the 160,000-sq-foot facility has seven basketball courts, four racquetball courts, a raised track and upper-level gym for indoor hockey and soccer, two pools and a 53-person hot tub. Some 3000 people come here every day to work out on treadmills, rowing machines and Stairmasters, and to pump more than 24,000lbs of iron. There's also a bistro with espresso. A visitor day pass ($7) lets you use any of the facilities.

Free **walking tours** of the campus depart at 1pm weekdays from the Lighty Student Services Building, room 370.

If you want to park on campus, be sure to pick up a parking permit ($2.75) from the WSU Visitor Center (see Information, earlier) or on campus at the Public Safety Building, on Wilson Rd next to the Fine Arts Center. You don't need a permit for a quick trip to places like the bookstore, which has short-term metered parking.

Steptoe Butte State Park

The park (☎ 509-549-3551) is just about the only public land in the Palouse, and it's a good place to get a bird's-eye view of the country. From Pullman, it's a 27-mile drive north on US 195, via Colfax. A side road off Hume Rd spirals 3 miles to the top of the 3618-foot-high butte, where hawks hover and the Rockies are visible off to the east and the Blue Mountains to the south. To the west, the Columbia Plateau appears to extend forever.

Steptoe Butte is an outcropping of Precambrian rock, once an island just off the western edge of the North American continent. Lava flows covered all the lower ground around the butte 10 to 30 million years ago. Loess then blanketed the land, creating the Palouse Hills, none of which comes close to the height of the rocky butte. In more recent history, Palouse Indians defeated Lieutenant Colonel Edward Steptoe and his troops here in 1858.

Special Events

A major event dedicated to an otherwise obscure legume, the National Lentil Festival comes to Pullman for a weekend in late August, with a parade, entertainment, crafts, a quilt show and a myriad of lentil-oriented food booths. Stop by Reaney Park for lentil pancakes, lentil lasagna or lentil ice cream. Contact the Pullman Chamber of Commerce for details, or see W www.lentilfest.com.

Places to Stay

The following are camping options.

Pullman RV Park (☎ 509-334-4555, *South & Riverview Sts)* Tent/RV sites $6/12. Closed Dec-Mar. Camp in town at the City Playfield, right where South St runs into the south fork of the Palouse River. Facilities include 24 full hookups and 10 tent sites, as well as some portable toilets, grills and picnic tables.

Kamiak Butte County Park (☎ 509-397-6238, *Hwy 27, 10 miles north of Pullman)* Campsites $10. Set at the base of 3641-foot-high Kamiak Butte, the campground here has running water, flush toilets and shaded picnic areas. Hike the 3½-mile Pine Ridge Trail through mixed-conifer forest to the top of the butte for grand views of the Palouse.

Hotels in the area include the following.

Compton Union Building (☎ 509-335-9444, *Wilson Rd)* Singles/doubles $48/60, $115/150 per event weekend (two nights). Available Aug 23-May 11. The 'Cub Hotel' offers Howard Johnson–style accommodations on the WSU campus. In summer, temporary dorm housing is an option; phone ☎ 509-335-7732.

Cougarland Motel (☎ 509-334-3535, 800-334-3574, fax 509-332-7815, *W 120 Main St)* Singles/doubles $40/51. Just west of Grand, this is Pullman's best value – quiet and central, with large, well-kept rooms and a pool.

Manor Lodge Motel (☎ 509-334-2511, *455 SE Paradise St)* Singles/doubles $40/50. Rooms at this friendly, modest lodging are a bit smaller but have terraces. Paradise St is one way going east; turn east off Grand a block south of Main.

Nendels Inn (☎ 509-332-2646, 888-619-1202, fax 509-332-2525, W www.palouse .net/nendels/localinfo.htm, *915 SE Main St)* Singles/doubles $49/54. On the southwest edge of the WSU campus, Nendels has generic carpeted units with microwaves, and airport pickup is available.

Quality Inn Paradise Creek (☎ 509-332-0500, 800-669-3212, fax 509-334-4271, *1050 SE Bishop Blvd)* Singles/doubles $65/75. One of several fancier places south of the center, this franchise has a pool and hot tub. Rates include a light breakfast in the lobby and milk and cookies at bedtime. Complimentary airport and WSU shuttle service are offered.

Places to Eat

Most local cuisine is hardly memorable, but a few stops are notable for value or uniqueness.

Ferdinand's (☎ 509-335-2141, *101 Food Quality Bldg at the WSU Creamery)*

Milkshakes $3. Open 9:30am-4:30pm Mon-Fri. Besides Cougar Gold cheese (white sharp cheddar, sold by the can) and tasty milkshakes, the on-campus WSU Creamery serves decent espresso. This is one place that Pullman is famous for; don't miss it.

Daily Grind Coffee House (☎ 509-334-3380, 230 E Main St) Snacks $2-3. For a quick latte, stop by this casual cafe downtown.

Swilly's (☎ 509-334-3395, NE 200 Kamiaken St) Lunch items $6-7, dinner entrees $16. Closed Sun. An easygoing spot with a passably trendy atmosphere, Swilly's does a variety of healthful snacks – from veggie burgers (made with Palouse lentils) to chicken fajitas – and international dishes.

Old European (☎ 509-334-6381, 455 S Grand Ave) Entrees $6-7. Open for breakfast and lunch. This quaint salon serves up German potato pancakes, Belgian waffles, cinnamon rolls and other such delights, and everything's made from scratch.

Azia (☎ 509-332-3163, 1515 NE Merman Dr) Soups $6. This is where the locals go for authentic Vietnamese *pho* (beef noodle soup); portions are ridiculously abundant. The nightclub here offers 'loud music' and more than 13,000 karaoke selections. It's north of WSU; take Valley Rd north off Stadium Way.

Entertainment

Though the main attraction here is college sports, the university community supports a lively arts calendar as well.

Beasley Performing Arts Coliseum (☎ 509-335-3525, 800-325-7328, W www.wsu.edu/BPAC, Stadium Way & Orchard Dr) This 12,000-seat on-campus venue brings in some big names, including rock shows to appease the student population. The coliseum also has a smaller theater for more intimate performances.

WSU Theatre (☎ 509-335-7236, W libarts.wsu.edu/musicandtheatre, Daggy Hall, College Ave) Tickets adult/senior/youth $8/6/4. The university's theater department stages eight productions per academic year, including original plays by WSU students, plus an eight-week summer repertory

season referred to as the Summer Palace. Performances are at Jones and Wadleigh Theaters in Daggy Hall.

Rico's Smokehouse Tavern (☎ 509-332-6566, 200 E Main St at Davis St) Wednesday to Saturday there's live jazz at this nicely preserved brick-walled student hangout.

Spectator Sports

To get the pulse of student life, join the throngs of fans at WSU sporting events. The football season runs from late August to mid-November, with the WSU Cougars meeting their Pac-10 conference opponents five or six Saturdays at the 36,000-capacity Martin Stadium. Tickets for general admission/reserved seating go for around $15/25; sellouts are rare. The Cougars men's and women's basketball teams play at Beasley Coliseum (see Entertainment, above), with Pac-10 conference games from late December to February. For tickets to these and other events, contact the Cougar Ticket Office (☎ 509-335-9626, 800-462-6847, W www.wsucougars.com), at 225 N Grand Ave.

Getting There & Around

Pullman-Moscow Regional Airport is east off Old Farm Way. Horizon (☎ 800-547-9308) flies in from Sea-Tac four times daily. There are more frequent flights from Spokane International Airport, 76 miles north.

Northwestern Trailways (☎ 509-334-1412, 800-366-3830) picks up passengers bound for Spokane ($16, 1½ hours) and Lewiston ($20, 1 hour). The earlier southbound bus continues to Boise ($36, 9 hours) from the bus station at NW 1002 Nye St, behind the Dissmore supermarket. (There's no bus to Walla Walla.)

Link Transportation (☎ 208-882-1223, 800-359-4541, W www.linktrans.com) has shuttle service to/from Spokane International Airport, and they'll pick you up or drop you off at your motel. A one-way fare costs an exorbitant $45.

Pullman Transit (☎ 509-332-6535, W www.pullmantransit.com) runs buses around town and campus from around 7am to 8pm weekdays; adult fare is 50¢. Catch bus No 1 to

WASHINGTON

campus from the corner of Olsen and Grand. The Wheatland Express (☎ 509-334-2200, W www.wheatlandexpress.com), SE 300 Fairmount Rd, has service to Moscow, Idaho ($2), and the airport ($5; tell the driver).

SNAKE RIVER COUNTRY

Somewhere between Dusty and Washtucna (population 260), the Palouse leaves off and the Channeled Scablands begin; just west of Washtucna, Hwy 26 climbs up on top of the Columbia Plateau. This is pretty desolate country, and since it's not on the way to anything, it's easy to miss one of eastern Washington's geological highlights, **Palouse Falls**.

From an arid landscape punctuated with basalt spires, these dramatic falls drop 198 spectacular feet into a rock gorge. The native Palouse referred to this geographical feature as 'the hole in the ground,' and that's indeed what it looks like. It's especially impressive in the spring and early summer, when stream flow is high.

A number of trails wind around the plateau and down to the river gorge. Scan the canyon for prairie falcons, golden eagles, Swainson's hawks and other raptors who nest here. It's a fun place to hike, but watch out for rattlesnakes.

The 10 campsites at ***Palouse Falls State Park*** *(☎ 509-646-3252, Palouse Falls Rd, 2 miles east of Hwy 261)* are one of Washington's best-kept secrets ($8). Camping is permitted from mid-March to late September, though the park itself is open year round.

To get to Palouse Falls State Park from US 395 and points north, follow Hwy 261 to Washtucna, then turn southwest on Hwy 260 and, after about 6 miles, southeast on Hwy 261; from Colfax, Washtucna is 52 miles west on Hwy 26. If you're approaching from the south, turn off US 12 onto Hwy 261 toward Starbuck and follow that road across the Snake River to the falls, 21 miles northwest.

From the foot of the falls, the Palouse River cuts a channel 5 miles to the south to its confluence with the Snake River, beneath the dramatic, trestled span of the **Lyons Ferry Bridge**. Lewis and Clark, David Thompson and a plethora of missionaries passed by this river junction, but they were hardly the first. Palouse Indians, whose fish-drying scaffolds the Corps of Discovery noted, were also relative latecomers.

The **Marmes Rock Shelter**, a small, now-flooded cave about a mile up the Palouse River from its confluence with the Snake, has yielded evidence of the earliest-known North American settlement. Pieces of charred human bone (from a cremation hearth), tools and jewelry date back 10,000 years, almost to the last ice age. Get a glimpse of the site either from the river or from the paved road behind the park caretakers' houses.

Construction of Lower Monumental Dam flooded the Marmes site and a sacred Palouse Indian site, but it created a recreational hot spot. There's a boat launch and swimming area at the **Lyons Ferry State Park** *(☎ 509-646-3252, Hwy 261, 8 miles northwest of Starbuck),* and plenty of people take their speedboats out here. The old Lyons Ferry, used for years to cross the Snake, is now a fishing pier. The campground, with 49 standard sites ($13), attracts mostly boaters with RVs. There's a little marina across the river with a grocery and boat rentals.

Facts about British Columbia

HISTORY
See History in the Facts about the Pacific Northwest chapter for more on the whole region.

Early Inhabitants
The ancestors of British Columbia's modern First Nations peoples showed up in North America at least 10,000 years ago. It's likely that, after the last ice age, they crossed to Alaska on a land bridge over what is now the Bering Strait. Some settled along the Pacific coast, while others found their way into the Province's interior.

The Native Indians that inhabited the Pacific coast included the Nuxalk (Bella Coola), Cowichan, Gitksan, Haida, Kwakwaka'wakw (Kwakiutl), Nisga'a, Nuu-chahnulth (Nootka), Salish, Sechelt and Tsimshian groups. Living off the land and the sea, they staked out hunting and fishing grounds and good places to collect berries, bark and roots. With plenty of animal, marine and plant life available, they were able to evolve a highly sophisticated, structured culture and an intricate trade network.

Inland, where climate extremes are greater than on the coast, the people led a nomadic, subsistence-level life. They followed migratory herds of animals such as caribou, moose and bison.

BC's aboriginal peoples are known for a ceremony called a potlatch, a celebratory feast held to help Native communities mark special occasions, honor elders, or establish ranks and privileges. Often many days long, potlatches still take place today. They involve dancing and elaborate gift-giving from the chief to his people.

European Settlement
During the 18th century, European explorers in search of new sources of wealth appeared off the West Coast. Alexsey Chirikov was probably first, exploring for Russia in 1741, though his travels were mainly along what is now the Alaskan coast. Spaniards were next: Juan Pérez Hernández sailed from Mexico to BC's Queen Charlotte Islands and Nootka Sound in 1774, followed by Juan Francisco de la Bodega y Quadra in 1775.

Britain's Captain James Cook arrived in 1778, looking for a water route across North America from the Pacific to the Atlantic – the legendary Northwest Passage. He was unable to find it, but his account of the riches to be had from furs brought traders eager to cash in. The most famous of these were Alexander Mackenzie, Simon Fraser and David Thompson, who explored overland routes from the east. By the 1820s the Hudson's Bay Company had established trading posts throughout BC. (The HBC, known as The Bay, remains one of Canada's largest department stores.)

In the meantime, initially to counter the Spanish presence, Captain George Vancouver had circumnavigated and claimed Vancouver Island for Britain from 1792 to 1794. (First Nations groups have long resented Vancouver's implication that no one was around before he got there.) Vancouver also explored far up BC's north coast. By the

SOUTHWESTERN BRITISH COLUMBIA

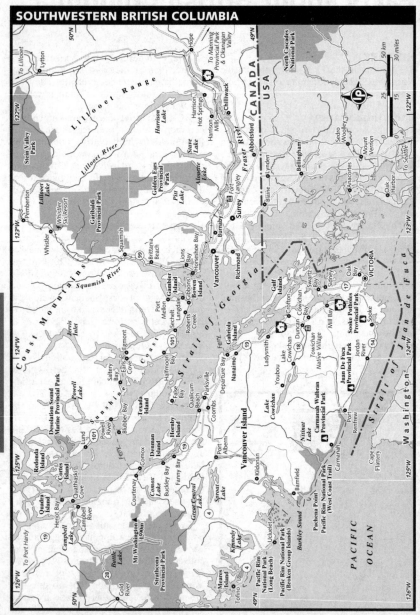

BRITISH COLUMBIA

1840s, the Hudson's Bay Company was warily watching the USA make an increasingly indisputable claim to the Oregon country, which was anchored by HBC's Fort Vancouver on the Columbia River near present-day Portland. In 1843, the HBC dispatched James Douglas to Vancouver Island, where he established Fort Victoria. Vancouver Island became a crown colony in 1849.

The discovery of gold along the Fraser River in 1858 brought a flood of people seeking their fortunes and led to mainland BC also being declared a crown colony, with New Westminster its capital. A second wave of fortune hunters arrived during a short-lived gold rush farther north in BC's interior Cariboo region.

Mainland BC and Vancouver Island were united in 1866, with Victoria named capital in 1868. Meanwhile, in 1867, the British government passed the British North American Act, creating the Dominion of Canada, a confederation that maintained British ties but conferred many powers to a central Canadian government and to the individual provinces. The eastern provinces of Canada united under the confederation, and BC decided to join in 1871 on the condition that a transcontinental railroad be extended to the West Coast. This was finally achieved in 1885; the settlement of Canada's prairie provinces (Alberta, Saskatchewan and Manitoba) around this same time created demand for the BC's resources, particularly timber.

The late 19th century proved a difficult time for BC's First Nations people. The gold rush displaced many tribes from their traditional lands, which led to violence among both Natives and whites. Moreover, the Canadian government, heeding complaints from missionaries and others about pagan Native practices, outlawed the potlatch – the cornerstone of First Nations celebration – in the 1880s with legislation that was not repealed until 1951.

Early 20th Century

The building of the Panama Canal, which was completed in 1914, meant easier access for BC to markets in Europe and along North America's east coast. The province's interior profited, too, with the completion of the Grand Trunk Railway from Edmonton, Alberta, to Prince Rupert on BC's north coast. As big business grew, so did big unions. Workers in great numbers organized into labor unions in the 1910s, protesting working conditions and pay rates. A number of strikes targeted key industries like lumber mills and shipping; and in several instances, BC saw armed confrontations between union members and soldiers. However, one issue where the unions, the government and business were in accord was with nonwhite workers – all felt the growing Chinese and Japanese population was a problem that only punitive legislation and violence could solve.

Large numbers of Chinese had moved to the province and were instrumental in building the Canadian Pacific Railway. Japanese settlers came slightly later, establishing farms and becoming the area's principal commercial fishermen. That these were hard-working people seeking opportunity, like the Europeans who were also flooding the province, seemingly didn't matter to whites. On several occasions in the province's early history, Vancouver's Chinatown and Little Tokyo saw ugly scenes of white mob violence.

Following WWI, Canada experienced an economic downturn that led to industrial unrest and unemployment. The Wall Street crash of 1929 brought more severe depression and hardship. Prosperity only returned with the advent of WWII and was sustained after the war with the discovery of new resources and the development of a manufacturing base.

The war years were hard times for immigrants. During WWI, anti-German riots took hold of the streets of Vancouver and many German-owned businesses were burned. In 1941, more than 20,000 Japanese Canadians were forced from their farms and fishing boats and were herded into animal stalls at Vancouver's Hastings Park. From there, they were transported to remote internment camps in inland BC and throughout the prairies.

First Nations people remained under siege, too. In 1921, Kwakwaka'wakw chief

Dan Cranmer defied the ban on potlatches by staging what may have been the largest gathering of that type ever. Chiefs gathered at Alert Bay to celebrate and exchange gifts, but local whites called the authorities to report the then-illegal activity. Chiefs who agreed to surrender their potlatch possessions were freed, but those who refused – including Cranmer – were sent to jail. Many of the potlatch artifacts wound up at the National Museum of Canada in Ottawa, which finally agreed to return them to the Natives in the 1980s. They now can be seen at museums at Alert Bay and on Quadra Island.

Post-War Prosperity

BC's natural resources-based economy enjoyed periods of great prosperity in the mid-20th century, following WWII, as transportation networks extended farther into the resource-rich interior. Forestry led the way, as BC's mills worked to meet ever-growing demands for pulp, paper and plywood. At the time, small operations dominated logging, but this is no longer true; today, a handful of companies dominate the industry.

Throughout the 20th century, BC's population growth continued, with many people from elsewhere in Canada moving west to call the province home. At the beginning of the 1990s, BC experienced another economic upsurge, led by Vancouver, which enjoyed its links to then-booming Asia. The area also experienced a large influx of moneyed immigrants fleeing Hong Kong ahead of the handover to China. However, what goes up must come down, and these economic ties to Asia were both a blessing and a curse. The crash of the Asian economies in the late 1990s sent a chill through the province. This, coupled with the collapse of fishing stocks, resulted in a recession stretching from the metropolitan southwest to the rural towns of the far north. But BC seemed to be on the rebound at the start of the 21st century, its economy buoyed by a national financial growth spurt, a healthier Asian economy,

leaping gains in high technology and surging tourism.

GEOGRAPHY

BC is Canada's most westerly province and its third largest, after Quebec and Ontario. Its 948,596 sq km make up about 9.5% of Canada's surface area. BC is bordered to the north by the Yukon and the Northwest Territories; to the east by Alberta; to the south by the three US states of Montana, Idaho and Washington; to the northwest by Alaska; and to the west by the Pacific Ocean. With its many inlets, the West Coast is more than 7000km (4340 miles) long; alongside it are hundreds of islands ranging from large (Vancouver Island, the Queen Charlotte Islands) to tiny.

Victoria, BC's provincial capital, is at the southern tip of Vancouver Island, which lies southwest of the mainland. Vancouver, the province's business center and by far its largest city, sits alongside the Georgia Strait near the mouth of the Fraser River.

The bulk of BC lies within the Canadian Cordillera, a system of mountain ranges running roughly northwest to southeast. Within the cordillera are several major mountain ranges – the Rocky Mountains to the east, the Cassiar Mountains in the north and the Columbia Mountains in the south. The glaciated Coast Mountains (the snowy peaks you see in Vancouver) loom over the Pacific almost to water's edge from Vancouver north to the Alaskan panhandle. The province's high point is 4663m (15,295-foot) Mt Fairweather, part of the St Elias Range on the BC-Alaska border.

The province has scores of freshwater lakes and fast-flowing rivers. The Fraser River is BC's longest, stretching from the Rocky Mountains to the Pacific Ocean near Vancouver. Roughly 60% of BC is covered by mainly coniferous forest. More than 90% of BC's landmass is 'Crown Land,' that is, owned by the provincial government.

GEOLOGY

An Ice Age starting about a million years ago was the primary force shaping BC's geology. Huge ice sheets repeatedly scraped over the province's lofty mountain ranges, creating great valleys between the peaks. This continued until about 7000 years ago, when the last ice melted, giving rise to the province's lakes and rivers (which remain fed by annual snowmelt today). Since the end of the Pleistocene epoch, glacial, wind and water erosion have continued to alter BC's landscape in more subtle ways.

BC's mineral wealth spurred Europeans to settle here in the 19th century, and the industry remains important today. Major mineral deposits include coal on the coastal islands and throughout the Rocky Mountains; gold in the Coast Mountains; copper, lead, silver and zinc in BC's interior Kootenay region; and natural gas-containing sandstone and shale in the northeast region of the province. Jade is the official mineral of British Columbia and is widely used in jewelry and sculptures.

CLIMATE

British Columbia has a varied climate, influenced by latitude, mountainous terrain and distance from the moderating effects of the Pacific Ocean. On the coast it is mild, with warm, mostly dry summers (June through September) and cool, very wet winters (December through March). The BC interior is much drier. In the mountains and in the province's northern reaches, summers are short, with warm days and cool nights. Vancouver and Victoria see few snowy days, but elsewhere in the province, winter snowfalls are heavy.

Unless you're coming for winter activities like skiing, the best time to visit is from early June to early October. During this period, you'll get less rain, warmer temperatures, long days and easier transportation. But even if you come in a colder, wetter season, take a cue from BC residents, who rarely seem to let the weather keep them inside or get their spirits down. With good rain gear, you too can have a good time no matter what the skies have in store. Note, however, that when the sun shines, people's spirits visibly lift. It's these periods of sublime weather that help

British Columbians endure the long spells of gray skies.

ECOLOGY & ENVIRONMENT

British Columbia is a schizophrenic place when it comes to the environment. Most urbanites see the province's vast wild lands and coastal environments as places to protect and enjoy, while people living in geographically far-flung, resource-dependent regions tend to view the environment as their meal ticket. Then there are areas like Tofino on Vancouver Island's West Coast, where a sometimes uneasy truce holds between people employed by extractive industries and those sworn to defend the planet from plunder.

In any case, BC has a long history of environmental activism, and even casual visitors are likely to encounter debates and perhaps protests over such issues as forestry practices and large-scale fish farming. Key groups include Greenpeace (founded in Vancouver more than 20 years ago – see the boxed text 'Greenpeace: Making Waves'); the Western Canada Wilderness Committee; and the Tofino-based Friends of Clayoquot Sound.

The provincial government has taken some action, too. In the 1990s, encouraged by the United Nations, BC Parks adopted the 'legacy strategy,' a plan aimed at protecting 12% of the province as parklands – about double the 1993 amount. By 2000, BC Parks had added or expanded several hundred areas and was nearing the 12% goal. Yet the 'legacy strategy' has drawn criticism from environmentalists, who say the plan leaves too many critical areas unprotected. Though BC's Ministry of Forests controls most of the province's public, or Crown, lands (a total of 59 million hectares, or 146 million acres), many environmentalists believe the forest industry remains the ministry's first master.

FLORA & FAUNA

With all its geographical and climatic diversity, it's no surprise BC has a wide range of plants and animals. With 14 distinct ecological

BRITISH COLUMBIA

Greenpeace: Making Waves

The modern Canadian environmental movement can be traced to a Vancouver living room, where a group of concerned people met in 1969 to discuss their outrage at the one-megaton nuclear bomb dropped as quietly as a raindrop on Amchitka, an ecologically diverse island near the tip of Alaska. It was the first bomb in a series of US atmospheric nuclear tests, which were scheduled to continue over the following few years.

The meeting marked the birth of the Don't Make a Wave Committee, which planned to disrupt the nuclear testing on Amchitka. They hit many roadblocks along the way, but eventually the group, now renamed Greenpeace, successfully garnered enough public support. By 1972, all atomic bombing on Amchitka ceased.

In the three decades since, Greenpeace has remained a leader in the international environmental movement. From confronting Russian whalers to convincing the *New York Times* to cancel all contracts with logging giant MacMillan Bloedel, Greenpeace has combined creative protest with determination to attract high-profile media and public attention on issues surrounding hydroelectric industries, forestry, commercial fishing and nuclear and chemical testing.

Greenpeace's opponents argue that the organization's renegade environmentalism and impromptu confrontations cause more harm than good. Like a pesky mosquito that just won't go away, Greenpeace emits an incessant, irritating buzz in the ears of many corporations, creating sleepless nights and public relations nightmares.

However annoying and aggressive, the buzz has made a difference: By forcing companies to wake up to global problems and catastrophes, Greenpeace's eco-warfare has raised the standard for corporate accountability, or at least brought environmental concerns out of the cold and into public concern and corporate boardrooms.

In 1979, national Greenpeace organizations formed Greenpeace International, which is now headquartered in Amsterdam. There are now Greenpeace organizations in more than 30 countries.

From its humble beginning in a Vancouver home, Greenpeace has protected everything from rain forests and whales to drinking water. As for Amchitka, the island is now a flourishing bird sanctuary.

zones, nature flourishes everywhere, from the large urban parks of Vancouver and Victoria to the tops of the Rockies to tiny coastal tide pools. For a selection of field guides to the province's natural history, see Books in the Facts for the Visitor chapter.

Flora

British Columbia has always been a lush place, with species varying widely depending on location, climate and human impacts. The province's official symbol is the white flower of the Pacific Dogwood, a tree known for springtime blossoms and red berries in autumn. BC's summertime wildflower displays are among the best in North America, with showy blooms of every hue scattered along trails and roadways. But BC is probably best known for its trees, which rank among the world's tallest and most majestic.

Western red cedar, Sitka spruce, hemlock and Douglas fir are prevalent trees in the moist coastal regions. Red cedar, the official provincial tree, was of special importance to indigenous coastal peoples, who used it to make everything from canoes and clothing to totem poles and medicines. The tallest tree in Canada, a Sitka spruce known as the Carmanah Giant, stands 95m (312 feet) in the Carmanah Valley of western Vancouver Island.

Coastal BC is well known for the arbutus (are-**byoo**-tus) tree, a distinctive species with twisted branches, reddish peeling bark and shiny dark green leaves. The only broadleafed

The first timid hints of autumn at Vancouver's Stanley Park

Totem in Stanley Park

Native American drummers

Coast Guard station at Tofino, Vancouver Island

The Vancouver Art Gallery features the work of Emily Carr.

Quirky house on Clayoqout Sound

Victoria's Empress Hotel – *the* place for high tea

The daunting Capilano Bridge, near Vancouver

View of downtown Vancouver across tranquil waters from Stanley Park

evergreen tree in Canada, it's similar to the madrona trees found elsewhere in North America. Southern Vancouver Island and the Gulf Islands also are home to Garry oak, though unfortunately, many of these once-prolific, low-growing trees have been wiped out by human development.

Ponderosa pine, Englemann and white spruce, Douglas fir, birch, aspen, cottonwood and larch trees are among the species growing along the river valleys and mountains of BC's interior.

Fauna

BC provides habitat for 143 mammal species, 467 bird species, 453 fish species, 18 reptile species and 20 types of amphibians. About 100 species (including the burrowing owl and Vancouver Island marmot) are on the province's endangered species list; another 100 or so are considered at risk. Ecosystems are at their most diverse in southern BC, but that's also where threats from human pressures are at their strongest.

The province has more mountain goats than anywhere else in North America; in fact, 60% of all the world's mountain goats live here, though you're only likely to see them in the province's northern and interior reaches. Bears are another prominent mammal, with an estimated 150,000 black bears and an unknown but much smaller number of grizzlies. Black bears can show up in parks and forests throughout the province; if you spend any time outside of the cities, your chances of seeing one are good. Grizzly sightings, however, are rare. Kermode bears, sometimes called spirit bears, are whitish in color and unique to BC. They're found mostly near Prince Rupert and Terrace on BC's north coast. Another unusual species, the Columbia black-tailed deer, is a small subspecies native to Vancouver Island and BC's West Coast. Other large mammals include bighorn sheep, mountain lions (also called cougars), moose, Roosevelt elk, Dall and Stone sheep, mule deer, white-tailed deer, coyotes and wolves.

Whales are among the best-known and most beloved of BC's mammal species.

About 20,000 Pacific gray whales migrate along BC's coast twice each year: southbound to Mexico October through December and northbound to the Bering and Chukchi Seas February through May. Less numerous and even more striking are the black-and-white orca, or killer whales. Some groups (called pods) of orca live permanently off the coast of southern Vancouver Island; others range more widely in waters to the north. Other commonly sighted sea mammals include porpoises, dolphins, sea lions, seals and otters.

Salmon rank among the most important fish in BC. Sacred to many First Nations bands and a mainstay of the province's fishing industry, seagoing salmon come in five species: chinook (also called king), coho, chum, sockeye and pink. Salmon life cycles are among the most amazing in the animal world: at adulthood, they leave the ocean to swim upriver to the same spawning grounds where they were born. Once there, they take their turns at reproducing, and then they die. Another species of salmon in BC is the Kokanee, the only salmon species that stays in fresh water lakes and streams and that doesn't migrate to sea. (See the boxed text 'Saluting the Sockeye.') Other fascinating BC sea life include the world's largest species of octopus, playful wolf eels and colorful sea stars (also called starfish), easily seen clinging to rocks and dock pilings all along the coast.

Of the province's nearly 500 bird species, the black-and-blue Steller's jay is among the most famous; it was named the province's official bird after a government-sponsored contest. Prominent birds of prey include bald eagles, golden eagles, great horned owls and peregrine falcons. A variety of seabirds and waterfowl nest on the shores of BC's coastal areas; others migrate through the province, including Canada and snow geese, trumpeter swans, harlequin ducks, sandhill cranes, brant and sandpipers. Blue herons are abundant in riparian areas. Tiny hummingbirds are seen all over southern BC, endlessly flitting to welcoming feeders in many backyards and even at a BC Ferries dock or two.

BRITISH COLUMBIA

Saluting the Sockeye

Sockeye salmon are some of the most hard-core travelers around. These wily fish travel from the Adam's River in the Shuswap area of BC, to the Pacific Ocean and back again in what is one of nature's most miraculous and complete cycles of life. Ever since glaciers carved out river valleys, pairs of male and female sockeye have fought starvation, currents and grueling rapids to return from the ocean to the place of their birth, only to lay eggs and die.

Each spawning female lays about 4000 eggs, many of which do not survive; either they're unsuccessfully fertilized or eaten by rainbow trout and other predators. The ones that do survive spend the winter tucked into the gravel on the riverbed, waiting out frost and weather while slowly growing in the soft, jellylike casing of the eggshell. In spring, the eggs hatch and tiny salmon fry – measuring about 2.5cm (1 inch) in length – emerge and float downriver to spend their first year in a freshwater lake. Though the calm lake water keeps the fry safe from the rushing currents of the river, only one out of four fry eludes the hungry jaws of predators. Survivors of that ordeal grow in the lake, becoming smolt. These hardy fish, up to 10cm (4 inches) long, begin the long journey down the Fraser River to the Pacific Ocean. Once in the salty water, the salmon grow up to 3kg (6.6 pounds), needing size and agility to escape more ravenous predators like killer whales, seals and commercial fishermen. Once they've reached maturity, about four years after their birth, a biological signal as sharp as intuition takes hold and the salmon know it's time to make the great journey back home.

Of every 4000 eggs produced, only two fish survive long enough to make the long, grueling journey home to spawn. When the internal alarm rings, the sleek, silvery ocean sockeye stop eating when they reach the mouth of the Fraser River and leave saltwater. From here on, for about 21 days, the fish rely on body fat and protein to energize their 29km-a-day (18-mile-a-day) swim over rocks and raging rapids.

Scraped, beaten and torn, the fish slowly turn a bright crimson red, a color they'll carry like cloaks until they reach the spawning grounds. There, the red heads turn a deep green, the male's snout elongates and his teeth get sharper, ready to fend off intruders as he and the female, now heavy with eggs, search for a place to nest. But good real estate on the shallow riverbed is hard to come by, and the pairs of fish fight to find a sheltered spot to nest. The female digs her nest by furiously flopping her tail while simultaneously laying eggs. The male quickly swims by, dropping a shower of milt to fertilize the eggs. The female then covers the nest with gravel. Upon completion of this exhausting ordeal, the hardy couple quietly dies, leaving their eggs to follow in this incredible journey.

GOVERNMENT & POLITICS

British Columbia has a parliamentary government, with a 75-member unicameral legislature that convenes in Victoria. The lieutenant governor is the formal head of state, but real power goes to the premier, who is usually the head of the majority party. The current premier, Liberal party head Gordon Campbell, won the post in 2001. Campbell's predecessor, Ujjal Dosanjh of the New Democrat Party (NDP), was the first BC leader of non-European descent.

BC also sends representatives to the national House of Commons and Senate in Ottawa. But, since Canadian power is concentrated on the provincial level, most people in BC pay little heed to what's happening in the national capital. The Social Credit Party (Socreds), ostensibly the party of small business, came to power in BC in the 1950s and governed into the 1970s. During the 1960s the NDP emerged, advocating a form of limited socialism. Beset by scandal, the Socreds fell out of favor by 1990, when the NDP took over. But the NDP has gained its share of scandal, too, and BC NDPers watched their party all but crumble in the 2001 provincial election when the Liberals won government positions throughout the province. The Liberals (who, despite their name, actually take mostly right-wing to moderate stands), have traditionally come out as a viable opposition to the Socreds and NDP. To the farthest right of the political spectrum, the Alliance Party advocates minimal government involvement and ultra-conservative morals.

Not that much of this matters to average BC residents, most of whom feel they have little power to change anything through the political process. Most BC voters are happy to have Canada's strong social services (including universal health care and welfare and an excellent public transportation network), but they're disgusted by scandal and bureaucracy and are fed up that pervasive and unpredictable government regulations seem to affect almost every area of their lives. When people get involved, it tends to be on the local level, often through nongovernmental, community-based activism aimed at bringing about societal or environmental change.

The ongoing effort to resolve aboriginal land claims is a major issue in BC politics. In 1993, the provincial government established the BC Treaty Commission, intended to create a framework by which land claims can be worked out, but little headway has been made since then. In 2000, the province and federal government reached the first modern-day treaty agreement, a pact which would give the Nisga'a Nation in northwestern BC's Nass River valley extensive self-rule rights and about C$190 million in cash. But the treaty was immediately challenged in court by Liberal party leadership, who called it unconstitutional; meanwhile, many of the 100 or so other treaty negotiations have broken down due to various disagreements between the government and aboriginal bands.

ECONOMY

Perhaps more so than the rest of Canada, BC's economy is driven by factors outside its control. The province's fortunes are closely tied to Asian economies, for example – when the East prospers, BC's timber and forestry exports boom. Also, the Lower Mainland sits in the shadow of nearby Seattle, the headquarters of such thriving companies as

Microsoft and Amazon.com and one of the principal areas driving the US-based high-technology boom. Finally, due to its location on the main north-south transportation corridors of western North America, BC was strongly affected by implementation of the North American Free Trade Agreement (NAFTA), which liberalized trade among Canada, the USA and Mexico.

When NAFTA took effect, many Canadians feared a loss of sovereignty to the USA. Certainly, US business interests wasted no time in beefing up their Canadian presence (witness GM Place in Vancouver). Today, 85% of Canada's exports go to the USA, prompting many to worry that Canada is now too reliant on the its southern neighbor for trade. Others voice concerns that, although the USA has invested heavily in Canada, most profits flow to shareholders and corporate headquarters in the States. Concerns that Canada has become a giant storage locker for US goods and a major dumping ground for the USA's hazardous waste keep Canadians wary of US investment. BC's labor pool also gets perpetually weakened by the 'brain drain' to the USA, where educated or experienced British Columbians are lured to US technology firms by the promise of US dollars and better job opportunities.

Canada's weak dollar has also meant mixed blessings for BC. The Canadian dollar has consistently been worth only about two-thirds the value of the US dollar, which has spurred great increases in tourism from the USA (up 12% in 1999) and investment. But prices and taxes in BC tend to be high, and BC residents saw an average 10% drop in real income during the 1990s. Though most BC residents would rather stay in Canada, increasing numbers head south to the USA in search of greater opportunities and better earnings. Those who remain in Canada are often reluctant to change jobs or take entrepreneurial risks because, as one Canadian put it, 'they fear they can't get any better than what they've already got.'

POPULATION & PEOPLE

British Columbia's population was estimated in 1999 at just fewer than four million

BRITISH COLUMBIA

people – about 12% of the entire population of Canada. Nearly two million people live in Greater Vancouver, and another half-million reside on Vancouver Island, most in the Victoria area. About 80% of the population live in areas defined as urban. About 170,000 people are members of First Nations bands.

BC was built by wave upon wave of immigrants, and the province has many people of British, Irish, German, Italian, Japanese, Chinese, Russian and East Indian descent. Immigration isn't a phenomenon of the past, either; during the 1990s, more than a quarter-million people immigrated to BC. Many came from Asia, especially Hong Kong; most settled in the Vancouver area, though pockets of immigrants can be found province-wide.

EDUCATION

The Hudson's Bay Company started the first schools in what is now BC in the 1850s on Vancouver Island. The Public School Act of 1872 provided the framework for the present-day school system. Today, about 2000 elementary and secondary schools educate more than 600,000 students. In the urban areas especially, English is a second language for many students. Though Francophones are much more prevalent in Eastern Canada, students throughout the country need to take French language classes in elementary and high school.

BC children typically attend school through Grade 12 (age 18); most then go on to technical-school training or university. Major universities include the University of British Columbia in Vancouver, Simon Fraser University in Burnaby (a suburb of Vancouver) and the University of Victoria.

ARTS

British Columbia has a strong arts community that bravely forges ahead despite government funding cuts and the always heavy-handed influence of the nearby USA. The following sections mention a mere sampling of BC-based artists, musicians, filmmakers, writers and others who make the province a vibrant arena for the arts.

Music

Vancouver and Victoria have strong music scenes that have produced many major talents known far beyond BC. The province's biggest pop success stories belong to Bryan Adams and Sarah McLachlan. Adams had a string of hits in the 1980s and early 1990s, including 'Cuts Like a Knife,' 'Summer of '69' and 'Everything I Do (I Do It For You).' Ontario-born, he settled in North Vancouver with his family in 1974, shortly before he started waking up the neighborhood with his catchy guitar-driven rock. Sarah McLachlan is among the most successful Canadian singer-songwriters of recent years; her hits include 'Sweet Surrender,' 'I Will Remember You' and 'Building A Mystery.' She's also well known as founder of the Lilith Fair tours that showcased women musicians during the mid- to late 1990s. The Vancouver-based Matthew Good ranks among BC's current stars, selling out concerts across Canada. Burnaby-born singer Michael Buble is another rising talent to watch.

Alternative rock has always done well in BC, even before the Seattle scene gave the world grunge and riot grrrls. Notable BC alternative acts from the 1980s and 1990s include Skinny Puppy, a major industrial rock act through the mid-1990s; Bif Naked (sometimes called Canada's answer to Courtney Love); Nomeansno, a Victoria-based outfit whose music blends punk, funk and jazz; Vancouver's 54-40, compared favorably with REM; and Spirit of the West, which combined Celtic music with rock 'n' roll. Vancouver-based headbangers Superconductor found fame by having as many as nine guitarists. Neko Case is a major alt-country figure on the Northwest scene.

Groups that helped put BC on the map in the '70s include Doug and the Slugs, Chilliwack, Loverboy, Terry Jacks and the Poppy Family (most notably for 'Seasons in the Sun'), Bachman-Turner Overdrive (BTO), Heart (although originally from Seattle) and punk rockers DOA.

Pianist-vocalist Diana Krall, who grew up in Nanaimo, is a major jazz star known for her sophisticated renderings of such standards as 'Peel Me a Grape' and 'I've Got

You Under My Skin.' In Vancouver, key jazz figures include Tony Wilson, who pieces together quintets, sextets, septets and other ensembles from among the city's hottest jazz musicians. Blues guitarist Colin James, a Saskatchewan native, found fame after moving to Vancouver, though he is still better known in Canada than elsewhere.

Literature

British Columbia's ever-active literary scene has cultivated a wide range of literary talent, from fringe 'zine publishers to best-selling authors who were either born here or decided later in life to call the province home. This is a land of readers, too: in the five years after the Vancouver Public Library opened its new downtown facility in 1995, patrons checked out nearly 10 million items. Readers and writers alike devour the quarterly publication *BC Bookworld,* widely available at bookstores or by writing to 3516 W 13th Ave, Vancouver, BC V6R 2S3. The Association of Book Publishers of British Columbia maintains a website at W www.books.bc.ca.

BC writers have a knack for coining terms that become part of the culture. West Vancouver native Douglas Coupland did it in 1992 with his popular novel *Generation X,* and North Carolina transplant William Gibson introduced the word 'cyberspace' way back in 1984's *Neuromancer.* Both continue to write important works that mirror and frequently anticipate modern culture; see Coupland's *Microserfs* or Gibson's *Idoru.*

Both an illustrator and author, Nick Bantock ranks among BC's most adventurous figures. Bantock, originally from England, first drew acclaim with his *Griffin & Sabine* trilogy from the early 1990s. More recent works include his autobiographical *The Artful Dodger: Images & Reflections* and *The Museum at Purgatory.* Lynn Johnston, whose cartoon strip *For Better or For Worse* is published in 1400 newspapers worldwide, grew up and studied art in BC's Vancouver.

Hard-drinking Malcolm Lowry, best known for *Under the Volcano,* was a profoundly influential BC writer. Gordon Bowker's *Pursued by Furies: A Life of Malcolm Lowry* is a fine biography of the enigmatic writer. Roderick Haig-Brown *(The Seasons of a Fisherman)* was an avid angler devoted to conservation, especially of the Adams River sockeye salmon. A provincial park is named in his honor. Jack Hodgins is an influential BC fiction writer whose works capture BC's spirit. His works include *Spit Delaney's Island* and *The Invention of the World.*

A two-time recipient of the Governor-General's Award for poetry and fiction, George Bowering has more than 40 titles to his name, including the novels *Burning Water,* about Captain George Vancouver, and *Caprice.* Alberta native WP Kinsella has long lived in BC; he's best known for his novel *Shoeless Joe,* which was adapted for the film *Field of Dreams.* Denise Chong is author of *The Girl in the Picture: The Story of Kim Phuc, the Photographer and the Vietnam War* and *The Concubine's Children.* Joy Kogawa has written two novels about the internment of Japanese Canadians: *Obasan* and *Itsuka.*

William Deverell *(Kill all the Lawyers)* and Christopher Hyde *(A Gathering of Saints)* are well-known BC-based writers of thrillers. Lee Maracle writes about the struggles of Native Indians, particularly from a woman's perspective, in such books as *Ravensong.* Another Native author, Eden Robinson, is a Haisla (Kwakiutl) woman from Kitimaat on BC's north coast, who has gained notice for her short stories *(Traplines)* and novel *(Monkey Beach).*

George Woodcock, the author of about 150 books and one of BC's most respected writers, was, among other things, a poet *(Tolstoy at Yasnaya Polyana* and *The Cherry Tree on Cherry Street),* a historian, a literary scholar, a biographer and a travel writer. Another influential Canadian poet, Al Purdy, died in 2000 after a long and colorful career, much of which was penned from his home in Sidney on Vancouver Island. Susan Musgrave, a *Vancouver Sun* writer and poet, is still going strong with such collections as *Things That Keep and Do Not Change.* Victoria poet Lorna Crozier has written a fistful of poetry books, most notably *Inventing the Hawk* and *Everything Arrives at the Light.* Patrick Lane, also from Victoria, is well represented in his collection *Too Spare, Too Fierce.* Other writers who have spent time in BC include Evelyn Lau, Margaret Atwood, Simon Gray, Alice Munro and Margaret Laurence.

Cinema

Vancouver is North America's third-largest film and TV production center, ranking behind only Los Angeles and New York, but filmmaking happens all over the province. Recent movies and TV series shot in BC include *The X-Files* (now relocated to California), *Stargate SG-1, The Outer Limits, The Pledge,* the remake of *Get Carter, Scary Movie, The Guilty, Mission to Mars, Millennium* and *The New Addams Family.*

BC was discovered as a film location in the early 1970s, when Robert Altman directed Warren Beatty and Julie Christie in *McCabe and Mrs Miller,* shot in Vancouver. The 1980s brought two BC film classics: *First Blood,* filmed in and around Hope and best known for Sylvester Stallone's first appearance as the character John Rambo; and the delightful *Cyrano de Bergerac* update, *Roxanne,* set in Nelson and starring Steve Martin and Daryl Hannah. Today, the BC film industry generates a billion dollars annually in economic activity.

Many film productions are US-based projects that have headed north of the border to take advantage of lower production costs and BC's wide array of scenic locales. (The Vancouver area has stood in for everything from Tibet in Martin Scorsese's *Kundun* to New York City in Jackie Chan's *Rumble in the Bronx.*) But the province also has a home-grown film industry rich in directing, acting and technical talent. BC-based directors include Lynne Stopkewich *(Suspicious River),* Anne Wheeler *(Bye Bye Blues),* Mina Shum *(Double Happiness)* and Bruce Sweeney *(Hard Core Logo).* Notable BC-bred actors include Hayden Christensen (who will star as the future Darth Vader in Episodes Two and Three of George Lucas' *Star Wars* films), Michael J Fox *(Spin City, Back to the Future),* Jason Priestly *(Beverly Hills 90210),* Cynthia Stevenson *(The Player),* Bruce Greenwood *(St Elsewhere),*

Fairuza Balk *(Gas Food Lodging)* and Joshua Jackson *(The Mighty Ducks).*

The BC Film Commission supports and promotes the province's film industry. Its website is at W www.bcfilmcommission .com. British Columbia Film is a nonprofit society established by the provincial government to expand and diversify independent film and video production in BC; its website is at W www.bcfilm.bc.ca.

Reel West (W www.reelwest.com) is an excellent source for what's going on in BC's film scene, including contact information for upcoming productions.

Vancouver Film School, established in 1997, has 750 full-time and 2000 part-time students training for a variety of careers in the film industry. For information, contact Vancouver Film School (☎ 604-685-5808, 800-661-4101), 400 W Hastings St, Vancouver BC V6B 1L2, or see the school's website at W www.vfs.com.

Visual Arts

The best-known artist in BC history is Emily Carr (1871–1945), beloved for her vibrant visions of the West Coast and its Native people. (See the boxed text 'The Life & Work of Emily Carr,' in the Vancouver Island chapter.) Frederick Horsman Varley (1881–1969) and Lawren Harris (1885–1970) were two members of the Group of Seven, Canadians who most strongly influenced the nation's early 20th-century art scene. WP Weston (1879–1967) did for the mountains in his paintings what Carr had done for the coastal forests in hers. A commercial artist and landscape painter, Paul Rand (1896–1970) was interested in making painting accessible to everyone, while Charles H Scott (1886–1964) was more interested in finding new ways of depicting the landscape. Charles Marega (1871–1939) is best known for his public sculptures, including the lions on the south side of Lions Gate Bridge.

Two exceptional Native Indian carvers in British Columbia did wonders preserving the past while contributing to a new generation of Native artists. Charles Edenshaw (1839–1920), the first professional Haida artist, worked in argillite, gold and silver.

Mungo Martin (1881–1962) was a Kwakiutl master carver of totem poles. Martin passed on his skills to Bill Reid (1920–1988), the outstanding Haida artist of his generation and the first Haida artist to have a retrospective exhibition at the Vancouver Art Gallery.

Charles Edenshaw's great-grandson Robert Davidson explored innovative ways to transform Haida art, while his great-great-grandson Jim Hart is best known for his large carvings, including a newly erected totem in front of the University of British Columbia Museum of Anthropology in Vancouver. Both artists apprenticed under Bill Reid. Another family connection comes by way of Henry Hunt and his son Tony Hunt, the son-in-law and the grandson of Mungo Martin, who continued the carving tradition and the totem preservation work at the Royal British Columbia Museum in Victoria. Roy Henry Vickers is another Native artist who has found new ways to express traditional themes, often through wildlife paintings. Susan Point, a Coast Salish artist, has combined a distinctive personal style with traditional themes in a variety of mediums.

Jack Shadbolt is one of the better-known artists in Vancouver whose experimental work is often abstract, as are the paintings of Gordon Smith. Toni Onley has a distinctive style that imparts the feeling of the West Coast landscape through abstract elements, while EJ Hughes paints more realistic landscapes. Julie Duschenes paints still lifes and landscapes using abstract forms, while the landscapes, cityscapes and still lifes of Vicki Marshall are more traditional. Robin Ward is an illustrator whose drawings focus on Vancouver's heritage buildings.

Richard Prince is a sculptor who specializes in machines that often move with the wind, while Alan Storey also likes to create moving machines, such as *Pendulum* in the Hongkong Bank building on W Georgia St in Vancouver. Video art is best represented by the works of Paul Wong. Chilliwack-based painter Chris Woods recently made the *Macleans* magazine list of '100 Young Canadians to Watch.'

SOCIETY & CONDUCT

Canadians from the eastern and prairie provinces sometimes refer to British Columbia as 'Lotus Land' or 'the California of Canada.' But BC, more than twice as big as California, cannot be so easily contained.

The southwestern parts of the province – Vancouver, Victoria, the southern part of Vancouver Island as well as the Lower Mainland – do share many traits with the US West Coast. People, fashion standards and schedules are all generally more casual than in Eastern Canada. Technological advances have had the same impact here as they've had elsewhere; everyone in Vancouver and Victoria seems to have a cell phone and email address. Yet one senses that these things don't define their users here. Instead, people place higher priority on time to play outdoors, enjoy the arts and simply relax with friends and family. It's a trait that makes even the most urbanized areas in BC feel friendly to both frequent and first-time visitors.

Americans especially sometimes wonder if Canadians are cold, or perhaps shy. Most BC residents simply aren't as gregarious as their American counterparts, but if asked for directions or information, British Columbians are typically more than happy to help. Politeness goes a long way in laid-back BC, where people don't take kindly to loud, boorish behavior.

First Nations culture is evident throughout southwestern BC but it is much more pronounced in BC's north, where aboriginal peoples comprise a substantial percentage of the population. But throughout BC, the First Nations influence can be felt in one important way: widespread – though not universal – respect for the environment and its riches.

LANGUAGE

British Columbia, like the rest of Canada, has two official languages, English and French. English is far and away the language of the majority, though most BC residents speak at least a bit of French, and all government literature and signs use both. But many other tongues are routinely spoken in BC, especially in the Lower Mainland, where Chinese

BRITISH COLUMBIA

has unquestionably surpassed French as a primary language.

BC's aboriginal people are noted for their linguistic diversity. Scholars estimate that when the Europeans arrived, the region's Natives were speaking as many as 30 dialects of seven different languages. Today's First Nations bands do what they can to keep this linguistic heritage alive, although English is now the predominant language spoken among BC's Native people.

The one expression you're sure to hear in BC is 'eh?' (pronounced 'ay'). Canadians use 'eh?' much the way Americans employ 'huh?' – as a friendly interjection that means 'Don't you agree?' or 'What do you think?' Not everyone in BC says it, but you'll hear it enough to start using it yourself if you spend more than a week or so here.

INFORMATION

The Greater Vancouver area has two area codes: the old ☎ 604 and the new ☎ 778 area code. This means if you're calling locally in Greater Vancouver (including the suburbs as far east as Abbotsford and Mission), you'll need to dial 10 digits: the area code plus the seven-digit number. The 778 code is an overlay assigned to newer numbers, so you may find businesses on the same street with two different area codes.

The 604 code covers the Fraser Valley (as far north as Boston Bar), Sunshine Coast and Whistler/Squamish regions. The rest of the province, including Vancouver Island, has the 250 area code.

BC assesses the national Canadian Goods and Services Tax (GST) of 7% and also a provincial sales tax of 7%.

Vancouver

Vancouver enjoys a spectacular setting, surrounded by water on three sides and framed by the backdrop of the lofty Coast Range. Parks pop up everywhere and range from the enormous Stanley Park (which equals the size of the downtown business core) to dozens of small neighborhood green spaces. And, no matter where you are in town, you're never far from a beach.

Vancouver is a young city, both historically and demographically. Its ever-changing face went through yet another transformation in the 1990s, with the arrival of tens of thousands of Hong Kong Chinese. A steady influx of young people from other parts of Canada adds spice to the cultural mix, too; although Vancouver (population 536,000) ranks third among Canada's major cities in population (behind Toronto and Montreal), the city has the lowest median age of any Canadian urban center, with more than a third of its residents between ages 25 and 45.

Vancouver is politically progressive, environmentally conscious and readily accepting of diversity (as proven by its large gay and lesbian population). Yet for all its diversity and celebration of the unconventional, Vancouver retains an old-fashioned cultural refinement – some might say conservatism – that reflects the city's British heritage. It's a dynamic city, full of energy and change, but it's also a city that knows, respects and preserves both its environment and its past.

HISTORY

Salish Indians first inhabited the Vancouver area. Spanish explorers arrived in 1791, but the British – who followed a year later, led by Captain George Vancouver – were the first Europeans to colonize the area.

In 1870, as a condition of confederation with the rest of Canada, Ottawa (Canada's capital) promised British Columbia that it would build a transcontinental railroad. However, if the Canadian Pacific Railway (CPR) was to link east and west, then BC would need a mainland coastal terminus, since the new province's population center and capital, Victoria, sat on an island. Railroad engineers set their sights on the sheltered Burrard Inlet and its ragtag collection of saloons, forests, lumber mills and farms. The first train arrived from Montreal in 1886, stopping at a thrown-together, brand-new settlement called Vancouver.

On June 13, 1886, a fire almost completely destroyed the city, killing 21 people. Reconstruction began immediately and by 1890, just four years after it was officially

BRITISH COLUMBIA

Highlights

- Exploring Stanley Park, Vancouver's world-class green space
- People-watching on Robson St, Davie St or Commercial Dr
- Walking on air at Capilano or Lynn Canyon Suspension Bridges
- Strolling through the public markets at Granville Island or Lonsdale Quay
- Eating your way around the world via Vancouver's restaurants

founded, Vancouver had already outpaced Victoria in population. By 1911, 120,000 people lived in Vancouver.

For West Coast Canadians, the building of the Panama Canal (completed in 1914) promised easier access to markets in Europe and along North America's East Coast. This triggered a boom for the BC economy until World War I and the Wall Street crash of 1929 brought severe economic depression and hardship to Canada. Vancouver, with its comparatively mild climate, became a kind of magnet for young Canadian men who were hungry, desperate and out of work. But Vancouver had no work to offer and could give no easy answers to the problems of mass unemployment. Angry demonstrators soon filled the streets of the city, occupied public buildings and rioted.

World War II catapulted the city into the modern era, and from then on it changed rapidly. The western end of downtown became the high-rise apartment center it remains today. In 1974, portions of Granville St became a pedestrians-only mall; Granville Island's redevelopment took place at about the same time. In 1986, the city hosted Expo '86, a very successful world's fair, the grounds of which are now the site of another urban renaissance.

In advance of China's takeover of Hong Kong in 1997, many wealthy Hong Kong Chinese emigrated to the Vancouver area, boosting its permanent Asian population by about 85%. (The area now boasts the largest Asian population in North America.) Unlike previous, poorer waves of emigrants, the new Chinese came from the Hong Kong business classes. Vancouver real estate prices shot through the roof, with cost-of-living figures suddenly rivaling those of Paris, London and Tokyo. Many of the new arrivals shunned Vancouver in favor of the suburbs, especially Richmond. In the late 1990s, problems with Asian economies slowed the meteoric economic development seen earlier in the decade. But globalization and technological growth have buffered Greater Vancouver's fortunes, and the city entered the 21st century among the economic and cultural capitals of the Pacific Rim.

ORIENTATION

Greater Vancouver (Map 2) is built on a series of peninsulas bounded on the north by Burrard Inlet and on the south by the Fraser River and Boundary Bay. The Coast Mountains rise directly behind the city to the north, while to the west the Georgia Strait is strewn with islands. Much of the city's recent growth has pushed suburbs far up the Fraser River to the east. All told, Greater Vancouver includes 18 municipalities that cover 2930 sq km (1143 sq miles).

Downtown Vancouver lies just 40km (25 miles) north of the Canada-US border. Hwy 99, the continuation of I-5 from Washington State, enters the city on Oak St. But since Oak St doesn't lead directly downtown, motorists usually detour west to Granville St to get downtown. The Trans-Canada Hwy (Hwy 1) bypasses Vancouver proper to the east; Hastings St, off Hwy 1, leads downtown.

The downtown area sits on a peninsula, cut off from the rest of the city by False Creek to the south and from the northern suburbs by Burrard Inlet. Stanley Park takes up the tip of the peninsula. Pacific Centre, a three-block complex of offices, restaurants, shops and theaters, pretty much marks the center of downtown. Robson St and Georgia St, one or two blocks north (depending where you are), are the two principal arteries. Only Georgia St, which becomes the Stanley Park Causeway, continues through Stanley Park to Lions Gate Bridge.

The high-density area to the west of downtown's shopping district is known as the West End – not to be confused with West Vancouver on the North Shore, or the West *Side,* which is actually south and west of downtown across the Burrard and Granville bridges (though locals rarely use this term).

Formerly a seedy warehouse district, Yaletown, in the southeast corner of downtown, has evolved into a hip destination. Warehouses now house bars, restaurants and loft apartments. Gastown, along Water St on the north side of downtown, is the historic center of old Vancouver, a neighborhood full of restored Victorian buildings. Chinatown is just to the southeast. East of Chinatown, East Vancouver revolves around Commercial Dr, a multicultural and vibrant neighborhood that manages to be both trendy and, well, *non*-commercial.

Granville Island, immediately south of downtown across False Creek, is a lively area full of shops and entertainment. Heading west after crossing Burrard Bridge or Granville Bridge, you'll enter Kitsilano, filled with students, young professionals and ex-hippies. To its west, you'll find the residential area of Point Grey, Pacific Spirit Regional Park and the University of British Columbia (UBC), at the tip of the peninsula. To Kitsilano's east are the busy commercial districts of South Granville St and Broadway.

If you head farther east, you'll come to the large suburb of Burnaby; southeast of Burnaby is the city of New Westminster, once the capital of BC and now an industrial area along the Fraser River. Across the Fraser, the suburbs of Delta and Surrey sprawl; White Rock, to their south, contains the most heavily used US border crossing.

Closer to the city, immediately south of Kitsilano, are residential areas like Shaughnessy, Oakridge, Kerrisdale and Cambie. Farther south lie Vancouver International Airport, fast-growing Richmond, the fishing village of Steveston and the BC Ferries terminal at Tsawwassen.

To the north of the city, over Lions Gate Bridge and Second Narrows Bridge, lie West Vancouver and North Vancouver – both essentially upper middle-class residential areas – which comprise the North Shore. If you continue farther west and north, you'll reach the Sea to Sky Hwy to Whistler, Horseshoe Bay (where you can catch a ferry to Nanaimo on Vancouver Island) and the Sunshine Coast (also reached by ferry from Horseshoe Bay). See the Whistler & the Sunshine Coast chapter for more information.

Maps

Tourism Vancouver distributes a nifty free map that's widely available at hotels, tourist sights and Visitor Info Centres. It has a detailed downtown section on one side and a good metropolitan overview on the other. AAA/CAA (☎ 604-268-5000, 293-2222 for 24-hour emergency road service) produces a good street map that's free to members. For even more detail, MapArt offers a selection of sheet maps and atlas books covering the Vancouver metro area; you can order one online at **w** www.mapart.com.

INFORMATION
Tourist Offices

At the Visitor Info Centre (Map 3; ☎ 604-683-2000, fax 682-6839, **w** www.tourismvancouver.com), 200 Burrard St on the Plaza Level of the Waterfront Centre, the friendly staff can help with bookings for accommodations, tours, transport and activities. On busy days, you'll need to take a number, but while you wait, pick up a free copy of *Discover Vancouver on Transit,* an excellent booklet that outlines bus, SkyTrain and SeaBus routes to all area attractions. Other useful publications include *The Vancouver Book* and the monthly mini-magazines *Where Vancouver* and *Visitor's Choice.* The Visitor Info Centre is open 8am to 6pm, late May through early September; 8:30am to 5pm weekdays and 9am to 5pm Saturday the rest of the year.

You'll also find two tourist information desks at Vancouver International Airport: one in the middle of the domestic terminal's baggage carousel area and the other in the international terminal's reception area, after you leave the Canadian Customs hall. The desks can arrange transportation and accommodations.

The Gay & Lesbian Centre (Map 3; ☎ 604-684-5307, help line ☎ 684-6869), 1170 Bute St near Davie St, provides information for gay and lesbian travelers. More information is available from the center's website at **w** www.ltgbcentrevancouver.com.

Money

ATM machines are widely available in the city's shopping and business districts. At the airport, you'll find three kinds of ATMs: cash machines dispensing Canadian dollars, machines dispensing US currency and foreign exchange machines that can accept 10 different currencies and issue some foreign currency.

The major national banks, including TD, Canada Trust, Bank of Montreal, Royal

Bank and CBIC, all have numerous branches throughout the city.

The Vancouver offices of Thomas Cook, which exchange currency, have a branch in the Pan Pacific Hotel (Map 3; ☎ 604-641-1229) at Canada Place and another in the Pacific Centre shopping mall (Map 3; ☎ 604-687-6111), 777 Dunsmuir St. Money Mart (Map 3; ☎ 604-606-9555), 1195 Davie St, offers round-the-clock currency exchange, check-cashing and telegraph services.

Taxes & Refunds

The Goods & Services Tax (GST), also known as the Gouge & Screw Tax, adds 7% to just about every product, service and transaction. The provincial sales tax adds another 7% to the bill and is applied to most items, except groceries, books and magazines. The BC provincial sales tax is nonrefundable; however, items shipped out of BC directly by the seller are exempt. Keep in mind that when you are looking at the price of a product in a store, or the price of a hotel room, be sure to add on another 14%.

Some guesthouses and B&Bs don't charge GST for rooms, and foreign visitors should try asking for an exemption from the GST on their hotel bills when making payments. If paid, however, the GST added to all accommodations (except some campsites) is refundable.

Foreign visitors also get a GST refund on nonconsumable goods bought for use outside Canada, provided the goods are removed from the country within 60 days. To apply for a refund, your purchase amounts (before taxes) of eligible accommodations and goods on which you paid GST must total at least C$200, and each individual receipt for your eligible goods must show a minimum purchase amount of C$50 before taxes. You must have original receipts. Credit-card slips and photocopies are not accepted as proof of purchase.

Most 'tourist' or duty-free shops, hotels and tourist offices have GST rebate booklets and mailing forms, or you can contact Canada Customs and Revenue Agency, Visitor Rebate Program, Summerside Tax Centre, 275 Pope Road, Suite 104, Summerside, PE

C1N 6C6. The website is at W www.ccra-adrc.gc.ca/visitors. Expect to wait four to six weeks for your refund check, which is paid in Canadian dollars, unless issued to a US address, in which case it will be in US dollars. The receipts are not returned.

For those driving to the USA, you can claim an immediate cash rebate to a maximum of C$500 of tax paid, at West Coast Duty Free (☎ 604-538-3222), 111 176th St, Surrey. It's located at the truck crossing. To get there follow the signs just before you get to the main Peace Arch crossing on Hwy 99. Be sure to have the original receipts and proof of residence (picture identification such as a passport or driver's license). The rebate can be claimed from the shop 24 hours a day, even though duty-free sales in the shop are only available 6am to 9pm daily.

Post & Communications

The main post office (Map 3; ☎ 604-662-5725), 349 W Georgia St between Homer and Hamilton Sts, is open 8am to 5:30pm weekdays. General delivery mail should be addressed to 349 W Georgia St, Vancouver, BC, Canada V6B 3P7. The many postal outlets throughout the city include the Shoppers Drug Mart (Map 3; ☎ 604-685-0246), 1125 Davie St, and Commercial Drug Mart (Map 4; ☎ 604-253-3266), 1850 Commercial Dr.

Internet-access terminals abound; access costs C$5 to C$8 per hour. Try the Vancouver Public Library's central branch (see Libraries, below), where the use of the public computer lab on the library's seventh floor costs C$2.50 per 30 minutes; Internet Coffee (Map 3; ☎ 604-682-6668), 1104 Davie St, offering access for C$0.95 for the first 15 minutes and C$0.07 a minute after that; Kitsilano's Cyber-Café (Map 6; ☎ 604-737-0595), 3514 W 4th Ave; the Mail Room (Map 3; ☎ 604-681-6562), 1755 Robson St; or Kinko's (Map 3; ☎ 604-685-3338), 789 W Pender St.

Travel Agencies

Travel CUTS (☎ 604-659-2887), the student and budget travel organization, has several offices in Vancouver, including its main office at 120 W Broadway (Map 5). There are two downtown, at 567 Seymour St and at the HI hostel, 1114 Burnaby St. You'll find other branches on Granville Island, at the University of British Columbia and at Simon Fraser University in Burnaby. American Express (Map 3; ☎ 604-669-2813), 666 Burrard St, is open 8am to 5:30pm Monday to Friday and 10am to 4pm Saturday.

Bookstores

Vancouver's classic independent bookstore, Duthie Books (Map 6; ☎ 604-732-5344) has closed all of its city locations save one: 2239 W 4th Ave in Kitsilano. Blackberry Books (Map 5; ☎ 604-685-6188), 1663 Duranleau St on Granville Island, is another good independent shop.

For travel literature, guidebooks and maps, head to International Travel Maps & Books, at 552 Seymour St (Map 3; ☎ 604-687-3320) and 530 W Broadway (Map 5; ☎ 604-879-3621). The Travel Bug (Map 6; ☎ 604-737-1122), 2667 W Broadway in Kitsilano, is a good bet for language tapes and travel accessories, as is Wanderlust (Map 6; ☎ 604-739-2182), 1929 W 4th Ave. For hiking guidebooks and maps, try the Western Canada Wilderness Committee store (Map 4; ☎ 604-687-2567), 227 Abbott St. Magpie Magazine Gallery (Map 4; ☎ 604-253-6666), 1319 Commercial Dr, is one of the best newsstands in town.

Banyen Books & Sound (Map 6; ☎ 604-732-7912), 2671 W Broadway, offers the city's best selection of New Age and metaphysical books and music. Women in Print (Map 6; ☎ 604-732-4128), 3566 W 4th Ave, sells books about women, for women and by women. Little Sister's Book and Art Emporium (Map 3; ☎ 604-669-1753), 1238 Davie St, specializes in gay and lesbian literature, music, videos and gift items.

Libraries

Reminiscent of the Roman Coliseum, the central branch of the Vancouver Public Library (Map 3; ☎ 604-331-3603), 350 W Georgia St, is a destination in itself. Its airy entrance plaza features food stands, an ATM and several gift shops. The library is open 10am to 8pm Monday to Thursday and 10am to 5pm Friday and Saturday (as well as 1pm to 5pm Sunday, September through June). Visit the website at W www.vpl.vancouver.bc.ca.

The University of British Columbia's libraries (Map 2; ☎ 604-822-3871), 1958 Main Mall, boast nearly 80 miles of books. In addition to the main library, there are specialty libraries, including one dedicated to one of Canada's largest collections of maps, atlases and other geographical materials.

Laundry

Convenient places include the Davie Laundromat (Map 3; ☎ 604-682-2717), 1061 Davie St, and the Great West Coin Laundromat (Map 6; ☎ 604-734-7993), 2955 W 4th Ave in Kitsilano. East Vancouver's Vicious Cycle Laundro & Leisurama (Map 4; ☎ 604-255-7629), 2062 Commercial Dr, includes a cafe that's open until midnight.

Medical Services & Emergencies

St Paul's Hospital (Map 3; ☎ 604-682-2344), 1081 Burrard St, is the closest emergency room to downtown. For non-emergencies, try the Care Point Medical Centre's walk-in clinics, open 9am to 9pm. Locations include 1175 Denman St in the West End (Map 3; ☎ 604-681-5338) and another at 1623 Commercial Dr (Map 4; ☎ 604-254-5554). In emergencies, call ☎ 911.

Dangers & Annoyances

Car break-ins and bike thefts are among the most widespread crimes in Vancouver. Vehicles with out-of-province plates are often targeted. Park in a secure lot if you can, and never leave valuables in sight. Cyclists should use a U-shaped lock (not a simple chain lock) and remove a wheel if possible.

Although safer than many cities of its size, Vancouver has serious problems with drugs. The area around Hastings and Main Sts at the edge of Chinatown can be dodgy day and night, though Vancouverites say that if you play it smart, you'll be safe. Keep your distance from suspicious-looking people or activities. You're likely to encounter panhandlers throughout downtown, Gastown and Chinatown.

[Continued on page 632]

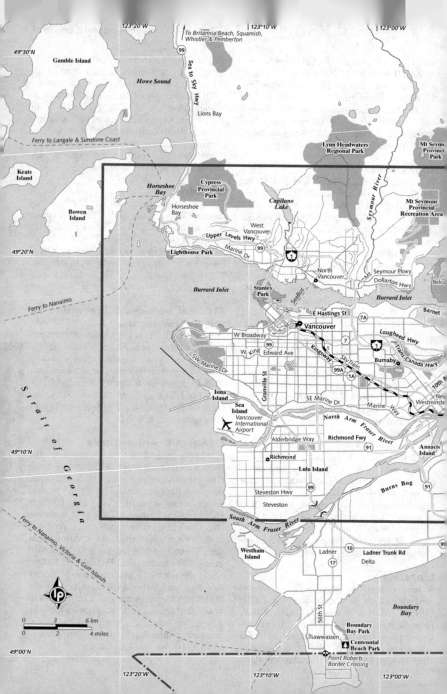

PLACES TO STAY
6 Capilano RV Park
7 Park Royal Hotel
8 The Grouse Inn
12 Globetrotter's Inn
26 Inn at Westminster Quay;
   Westminster Quay Public
   Market & Esplanade
28 Delta Vancouver Airport
   Hotel & Marina
29 Holiday Inn Express
30 Accent Inn
32 Richmond RV Park
35 Steveston Hotel

PLACES TO EAT
2 Salmon House on the Hill
5 Beach House at Dundarave
   Pier
10 Lonsdale Quay Market &
   Hotel; Q Café
11 Sailor Hagar's Brew Pub
17 Seasons in the Park
21 All India Sweets &
   Restaurant
22 Zeenaz Restaurant
37 Dave's Fish & Chips

OTHER
1 Capilano Salmon Hatchery
3 Capilano Suspension Bridge
4 Lynn Canyon Ecology
   Centre
13 UBC Main Library
14 UBC Museum of
   Anthropology
15 UBC Aquatic Centre
16 UBC Botanical Gardens
18 Bloedel Conservatory

19 Nat Bailey Stadium
20 Burnaby Village Museum
23 Swanguard Stadium
24 Metrotown; Holiday Inn
   Metrotown
25 Seaplane Terminal
27 Fraser River Discovery
   Centre; Visitor Information
   Centre; Royal City Star
   Riverboat Casino
31 Seaplane Terminal
33 Parker Place
34 Buddhist Temple
36 Gulf of Georgia Cannery
   National Historic Site

MAP 3 DOWNTOWN VANCOUVER & WEST END

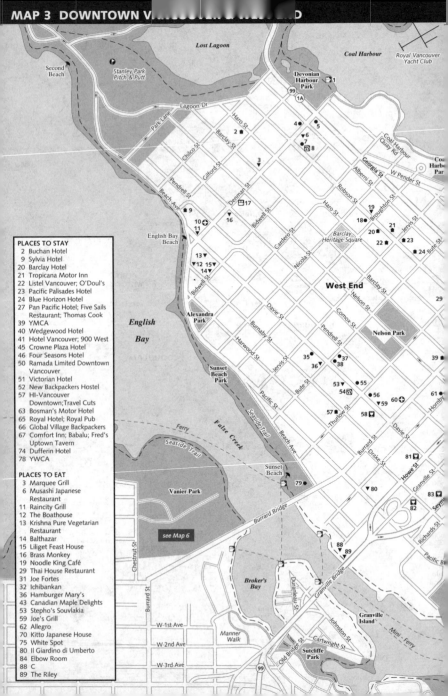

Lost Lagoon

Coal Harbour

Royal Vancouver
Yacht Club

Second
Beach

Stanley Park
Pitch & Putt

Devonian
Harbour
Park

Lagoon Dr

Park Lane

Chilco St

Gilford St

Barclay St

Haro St

Denman St

Bidwell St

Cardero St

Coal
Harbour
Quay Rd

Georgia St

Alberni St

W Pender St

Coal
Harbour
Par

Robson St

Haro St

Broughton St

Jervis St

Bute St

Barclay
Heritage Square

West End

Beach Ave

English Bay
Beach

Pendrell St

Nicola St

Barclay St

Nelson St

Comox St

Nelson Park

**English
Bay**

Alexandra
Park

Burnaby St

Davie St

Pendrell St

Harwood St

Jervis St

Bute St

**Sunset
Beach
Park**

Pacific St

Thurlow St

Burrard St

Davie St

Drake St

Howe St

Granville St

Seymour St

Richards St

Pacific Bl

Seaside Trail

Beach Ave

Ferry

False Creek

Seaside Trail

**Sunset
Beach**

Vanier Park

Chestnut St

Burrard St

see Map 6

Burrard Bridge

**Broker's
Bay**

Granville Bridge

Duranleau St

**Granville
Island**

Mini-Ferry

W 1st Ave

Manner
Walk

W 2nd Ave

Cartwright St

W 3rd Ave

Old Bridge St

Johnston St

**Sutcliffe
Park**

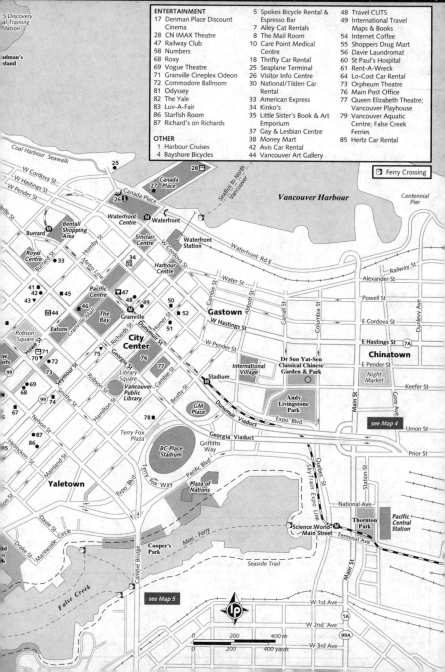

ENTERTAINMENT
17 Denman Place Discount Cinema
28 CN IMAX Theatre
47 Railway Club
58 Numbers
68 Roxy
69 Vogue Theatre
71 Granville Cineplex Odeon
72 Commodore Ballroom
81 Odyssey
82 The Yale
83 Luv-A-Fair
86 Starfish Room
87 Richard's on Richards

OTHER
1 Harbour Cruises
4 Bayshore Bicycles
5 Spokes Bicycle Rental & Espresso Bar
7 Alley Cat Rentals
8 The Mail Room
10 Care Point Medical Centre
18 Thrifty Car Rental
25 Seaplane Terminal
26 Visitor Info Centre
30 National/Tilden Car Rental
33 American Express
34 Kinko's
35 Little Sister's Book & Art Emporium
37 Gay & Lesbian Centre
38 Money Mart
42 Avis Car Rental
44 Vancouver Art Gallery
48 Travel CUTS
49 International Travel Maps & Books
54 Internet Coffee
55 Shoppers Drug Mart
56 Davie Laundromat
60 St Paul's Hospital
61 Rent-A-Wreck
64 Lo-Cost Car Rental
73 Orpheum Theatre
76 Main Post Office
77 Queen Elizabeth Theatre; Vancouver Playhouse
79 Vancouver Aquatic Centre; False Creek Ferries
85 Hertz Car Rental

Ferry Crossing

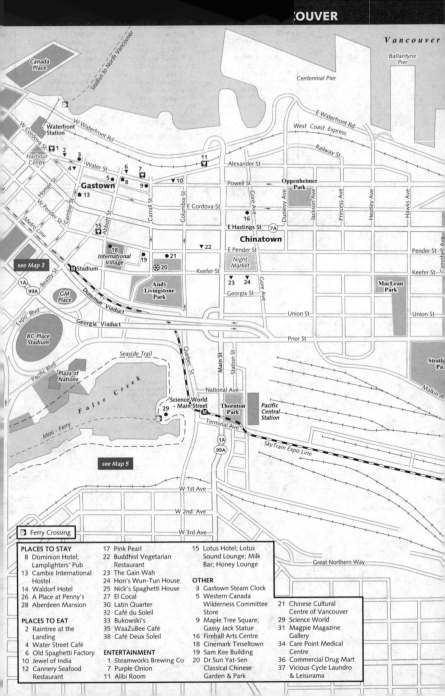

OUVER

☐ Ferry Crossing

PLACES TO STAY
8 Dominion Hotel;
   Lamplighters' Pub
13 Cambie International
   Hostel
14 Waldorf Hotel
26 A Place at Penny's
28 Aberdeen Mansion

PLACES TO EAT
2 Raintree at the
   Landing
4 Water Street Café
6 Old Spaghetti Factory
10 Jewel of India
12 Cannery Seafood
   Restaurant

17 Pink Pearl
22 Buddhist Vegetarian
   Restaurant
23 The Gain Wah
24 Hon's Wun-Tun House
25 Nick's Spaghetti House
27 El Cocal
30 Latin Quarter
32 Café du Soleil
33 Bukowski's
35 WaaZuBee Café
38 Café Deux Soleil

ENTERTAINMENT
1 Steamworks Brewing Co
7 Purple Onion
11 Alibi Room

15 Lotus Hotel; Lotus
   Sound Lounge; Milk
   Bar; Honey Lounge

OTHER
3 Gastown Steam Clock
5 Western Canada
   Wilderness Committee
   Store
9 Maple Tree Square;
   Gassy Jack Statue
16 Firehall Arts Centre
18 Cinemark Tinseltown
19 Sam Kee Building
20 Dr Sun Yat-Sen
   Classical Chinese
   Garden & Park

21 Chinese Cultural
   Centre of Vancouver
29 Science World
31 Magpie Magazine
   Gallery
34 Care Point Medical
   Centre
36 Commercial Drug Mart
37 Vicious Cycle Laundro
   & Leisurama

Harbour

Trinity St
McGill St
McGill St
Eton St
Cambridge St
Oxford St
Dundas St
Triumph St
Pandora St

12 ▼

Commissioner St
Wall St
Nanaimo St
Kamloops St

Stewart St
West Coast Express

Powell St

Franklin St

Rogers St

14 ■
E Hastings St

▼ 17

Glen Dr
Vernon Dr
Clark Dr
McLean Dr
Woodland Dr
Commercial Dr
Salsbury Dr

E Pender St

Frances St

Georgia St   Woodland
                    Park
Adanac St

Venables St

Pandora Park
To Hastings Park,
Second Narrows Bridge, Hwy 1,
Playland & Simon Fraser University
7A   E Hastings St

Ferndale St
Turner St
Templeton
Park

Garden Dr

25 ▼

■ 26

27 ▼

Commercial Dr
Salsbury Dr
Victoria Dr
Semlin Dr
Lakewood Dr
Templeton Dr

Venables St
Parker St
Napier St

■ 28

William St

Odlum Dr
McLean Dr

Grandview
Park

30 ▼
31 ●
32 ▼

33 ▼   Victoria
              Park

Charles St
Kitchener St
Grant St
Graveley St

Il Mercato
Mall
34 ✛   ▼ 35

E 1st Ave

Grandview Viaduct

Vernon Dr
Clark Dr
McLean Dr
Woodland Dr
Cotton Dr

E 2nd Ave
Garden
Park
E 3rd Ave

Nanaimo St
Kamloops St

✉ 36

E 4th Ave

● 37
              McSpadden
              Park
▼ 38
E 5th Ave

E 4th Ave

E 5th Ave

E 6th Ave

SkyTrain Expo Line
Grandview Hwy N

E 7th Ave

E 8th Ave

a
r
k

Glen Dr
Keith Dr

Vancouver
Community
College

VCC Ⓜ

Ⓜ Commercial

To Burnaby,
Metrotown &
New Westminster

Ⓜ Broadway

E Broadway

7

MAP 5 GRANVILLE ISL

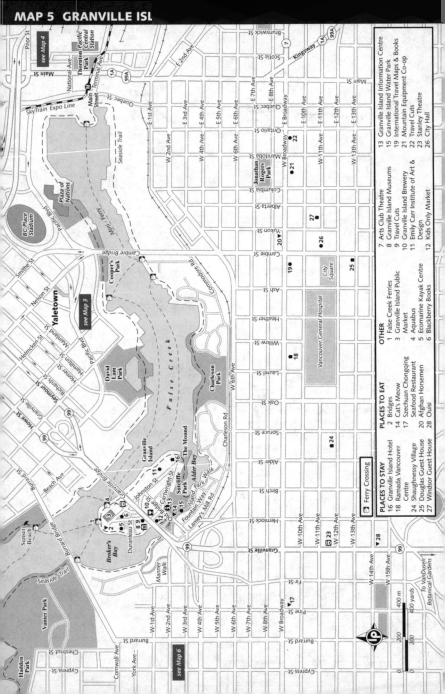

PLACES TO STAY
16 Granville Island Hotel
18 Ramada Vancouver Centre
24 Shaughnessy Village
25 Douglas Guest House
27 Windsor Guest House

PLACES TO EAT
2 Bridges
14 Cat's Meow
17 Szechuan Chongqing Seafood Restaurant
20 Afghan Horsemen
28 Ouisi

OTHER
1 False Creek Ferries
3 Granville Island Public Market
4 Aquabus
5 Ecomarine Kayak Centre
6 Blackberry Books
7 Arts Club Theatre
8 Granville Island Museums
9 Travel Cuts
10 Granville Island Brewery
11 Emily Carr Institute of Art & Design
12 Kids Only Market
13 Granville Island Information Centre
15 Granville Island Water Park
19 International Travel Maps & Books
21 Mountain Equipment Co-op
22 Travel Cuts
23 Stanley Theatre
26 City Hall

Ferry Crossing
▼ Ferry Crossing

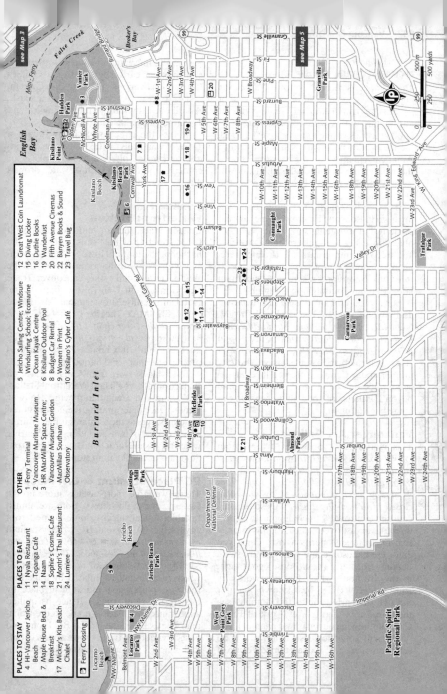

PLACES TO STAY
4 HI-Vancouver Jericho
   Beach
7 Maple House Bed &
   Breakfast
17 Mickey's Kits Beach
   Chalet

PLACES TO EAT
11 Nyala Restaurant
13 Topanga Café
14 Naam
18 Sophie's Cosmic Cafe
21 Montri's Thai Restaurant
24 Lumiere

OTHER
1 Ferry Terminal
2 Vancouver Maritime Museum
3 HR MacMillan Space Centre;
   Vancouver Museum; Gordon
   MacMillan Southam
   Observatory
5 Jericho Sailing Centre; Windsure
   Windsurfing School; Ecomarine
   Ocean Kayak Centre
6 Kitsilano Outdoor Pool
8 Budget Car Rental
9 Women in Print
10 Kitsilano's Cyber Café

12 Great West Coin Laundromat
15 Diving Locker
16 Duthie Books
19 Wanderlust
20 Fifth Avenue Cinemas
22 Banyen Books & Sound
23 Travel Bug

see Map 3

see Map 5

English Bay

False Creek

Broker's Bay

Burrard Inlet

Ferry Crossing

[Continued from page 621]

DOWNTOWN (MAP 3)

The compact size of downtown Vancouver makes it easy to get around on foot. A *lot* of people live right downtown, creating vibrant mini-communities with colorful neighborhood groceries, coffeehouses and drug stores. Unlike the downtown areas in a lot of North American cities (where the energy dies once the workers go home for the night), downtown Vancouver stays lively well into the evening hours.

If you're looking for the center of downtown, go to **Robson St**, a crowded pedestrian scene full of intriguing shops and plenty of places to eat. Locals, international tourists and recent immigrants all throng here, giving a good example of Vancouver's cultural mix. Shops and restaurants stay open late, often until midnight in summer.

For a good bird's-eye view of downtown and beyond, stop by **The Lookout!** *(☎ 604-689-0421, 555 W Hastings St; adult/senior/ student C$9/8/6, family pass C$25; open 8:30am-10:30pm May-Oct, 9am-9pm Nov-Apr),* set 169m (554 feet) above the city atop Harbour Centre. Here you'll get an excellent 360-degree view of Vancouver and beyond. Tickets are good all day, so you can come back at night.

Vancouver Art Gallery

This is the city's principal art museum *(☎ 604-662-4719, 750 Hornby St; adult/senior/ student C$11/8/6.5, children under 12 free; open daily 10am-5:30pm, and until 9pm Thursday when admission is by donation, closed Mon mid-Oct–Easter).* Despite near-constant controversy (including six executive directors in just over a decade), this impressive museum still merits a visit. Once you enter the handsome late 19th-century stone building (formerly a courthouse), go straight to the 4th floor, which features works by Emily Carr, BC's best-known painter through the early to mid-20th century (see the boxed text 'The Life & Work of Emily Carr,' in the Vancouver Island chapter). The permanent collection also features a good selection of art by Canada's famed Group of

Seven. The museum gift shop sells plenty of cool posters, cards and gifts. The Gallery Café, which overlooks the Sculpture Garden, makes a great spot for coffee and a snack. Ask about exhibition tours (in English and Japanese), available daily in summer.

Across the street on **Robson Square**, a series of waterfalls on the wall of the provincial courthouse offers a tranquil place for contemplation as the rush of water drowns out the city's din.

Canada Place & Waterfront Station

Canada Place, the convention center with the distinctive white 'sails,' juts into the harbor at the foot of Howe St. Built to coincide with Expo '86, the complex contains the World Trade Centre, the Vancouver Trade and Convention Centre, the Pan Pacific Hotel and a cruise-ship terminal. Also inside is the **CN IMAX Theatre** *(☎ 604-682-4629; tickets adult/senior/child C$10.50/9.50/8.50; movies shown at various times daily).* The northern end of Canada Place features promenade shops and a food court.

Just a block away from Canada Place on Waterfront Rd, you'll find **Waterfront Station**, the grand old Canadian Pacific Railway station. Once deteriorating, the now-restored building serves as the terminus for an entirely different kind of transportation – the SeaBus, which travels to North Vancouver. Waterfront Station is also a SkyTrain stop.

BC Place Stadium & GM Place

These two large sports arenas shore up the eastern edge of downtown. Both are unmistakable. A translucent dome-shaped roof covers the 60,000-seat BC Place Stadium *(general information ☎ 604-669-2300, events information ☎ 604-444-3663, 777 Pacific Blvd S).* The thin Teflon roof is 'air-supported,' which means that it's inflated by huge fans (no, not sports fans) and kept in place by crisscrossed steel wires – hence its quilted appearance. BC Place is home to the Canadian Football League (CFL) BC Lions, and hosts a variety of trade shows, sports events and concerts (though acoustics in the giant dome are notoriously bad). Hour-long stadium tours start at 11am and 1pm Tuesday and Friday, June through August. Meet at Gate H; the cost is C$6/5/4 adult/senior and student/child.

Adjacent GM Place (☎ 604-899-7889, 800 Griffiths Way), is the city's major venue for professional sports; both the Vancouver Canucks of the National Hockey League (NHL) and the Vancouver Grizzlies of the National Basketball Association (NBA) play here. Many big-name concerts are held here (the acoustics are much better). Bus Nos 2, 5, 15 and 17 access BC Place, while Nos 2, 5 and 17 stop at GM Place. SkyTrain's Stadium station serves both arenas.

STANLEY PARK

Vancouver's largest and much-beloved green space, Stanley Park (☎ 604-257-8400) is a 404-hectare (998-acre) cedar forest flanked by beaches that extend north and west of downtown. The park began as a military reserve in 1863, after Canadians became nervous about US occupation of the San Juan Islands in 1859. When these fears subsided, the lands were rededicated as parkland. And what a park it is. Hiking, cycling and jogging trails meander through the woods. To experience one of the world's great urban walks, try the seawall walkway, winding more than 9.5km (6 miles) along the park's shoreline. The three park beaches – Second Beach, Third Beach and English Bay Beach – attract lots of sunbathers and swimmers in summer; families also frolic in the outdoor swimming pool at Second Beach and in the Variety Kids Water Park at Lumbermen's Arch. Vista points afford stunning views of downtown Vancouver, the North Shore and the strait.

A well-known collection of **totem poles** sits on the east side of the park near Brockton Point. Also near here, the **Nine O'Clock Gun** has fired faithfully each evening for more than 100 years. Off the southern side near the Royal Vancouver Yacht Club looms **Deadman's Island**; it's said that a northern First Nations tribe once used the island as a camp for women captured in raids. Later a

burial ground for aboriginal and Chinese people and Native Indians, it now serves as a naval reserve. Kids enjoy the **Variety Kids Farmyard** and the **miniature railway**.

Lions Gate Bridge extends from the northern tip of the park. Just to its west sits **Prospect Point**, a popular spot for views of the First Narrows and passing ships. On the park's west side, the **National Geographic Tree**, a red cedar almost 30m (98 feet) around, is among the largest of its kind in the world – though it's not as well known as the nearby **Hollow Tree**.

Stanley Park is an easy walk from downtown; you can also take Bus No 23, 35, 56, 123 or 135. The free Stanley Park Shuttle runs through the park 9:30am to 6pm, June through mid-September, with stops near many major sights. Stanley Park Horse-Drawn Tours (☎ 604-681-5115) offers narrated one-hour tours that depart every 20 to 30 minutes from 9:40am to 5pm, mid-March through October, from the information booth on Stanley Park Dr, east of the Vancouver Rowing Club. The tours for adult/senior/student and child are $18.65/16.80/11.20.

Vancouver Aquarium

The Vancouver Aquarium (☎ 604-659-3474, Ⓦ www.vanaqua.org; admission adult/senior/teen & child C$13.85/11.70/9.15; open 9:30am-7pm July-Sept, 10am-5:30pm Oct-June) is Canada's largest. It holds more than 8000 marine creatures and ranks as the country's biggest marine-mammal rescue and rehabilitation center. Though the Vancouver Aquarium's programs are highly regarded by marine biologists and other scientists, the aquarium gets its share of controversy, brought on by conservation groups that object to aquariums raising marine mammals in captivity. For 20 years the aquarium was home to Bjossa, a female orca who was relocated to SeaWorld in San Diego in 2000. Vancouverites were devastated in 2001, when Bjossa died of a lung infection at SeaWorld.

But plenty of big creatures still live here, including beluga whales, Pacific white-sided dolphins, seals, otters and octopuses. Other exhibits include crocodiles, eels, piranhas and a wide variety of local sea life and freshwater fish.

From downtown, take Georgia St into Stanley Park and follow the signs, or take bus No 135 (daytime Monday to Saturday), 23 or 35 (evenings, Sundays and holidays). Bring money for parking (C$1/hour or C$5/day) if you drive.

GASTOWN (MAP 4)

Vancouver's Victorian-era district takes its name from 'Gassy' Jack Deighton, a onetime English sailor who set up a saloon on the Burrard Inlet waterfront in 1867. When a village sprang up around his establishment, people started calling the area Gassy's Town. (Today, a statue of Gassy Jack stands at Maple Tree Square, where Cordova and Water Sts meet.)

After the center of Vancouver moved elsewhere, Gastown gradually became a skid row, but in the 1970s the district's restoration pushed Vancouver's seedier characters a little farther south to Hastings St. The old Victorian buildings now house restaurants, boutiques, galleries and nightclubs. The old-fashioned lampposts, street

Gassy Jack

In the mid-19th century, the hardworking men laboring in the sawmills along the shores of Burrard Inlet weren't allowed to drink alcohol on mill property. The thirsty workers had to travel all the way to the town at New Westminster to find somewhere to imbibe.

Before long, an enterprising former riverboat captain, John Deighton, recognized a golden opportunity. Along with his wife, a few animals and a barrel of booze, Deighton docked his canoe close to the mills and began selling whiskey. He was a huge success and later opened a saloon. His customers called him 'Gassy Jack' because he talked so much; the community that developed around his saloon became known as Gassy's Town, and eventually Gastown.

vendors and entertainers add to the holiday feel of the area.

Possibly the most photographed object in Vancouver, the **Gastown Steam Clock** on Water St toots every 15 minutes, powered by the same system used to steam-heat many nearby office buildings. Although the clock looks old, it dates from the not-so-way-back days of 1977.

Free Gastown walking tours take place at 2pm daily, mid-June through August; meet at Maple Tree Square. Gastown itself is an easy walk from downtown or the SkyTrain Waterfront Station.

CHINATOWN (MAP 4)

About 36,000 people of Chinese descent live in the area around W Pender St, roughly bordered by Abbott St and Gore Ave; thousands of others come here to shop, making this the third-largest Chinatown in North America, after San Francisco and New York.

For the most part, this is a real Chinese market and business district, full of stores with hanging ducks, bales of strange dried fish, exotic fruits and Asian remedies. The colors and smells, plus the street signs and the occasional old Chinese-style balcony, can make you believe for a second that you're in Hong Kong.

Chinatown is on the edge of Strathcona, Vancouver's most blighted area along Hastings and Main Sts. Since the recently arrived Hong Kong Chinese live mostly in Richmond, a suburb of Vancouver, the center of Chinese Canadian business and culture has shifted there, at least in part. But Chinatown still throbs with life and remains a safe place to visit if you keep your wits about you.

Parking can be difficult, but Chinatown is an easy walk from downtown; it's also on the No 3, 8, 19 and 22 bus lines and near the Stadium SkyTrain station. The Chinese Cultural Centre of Vancouver (☎ 604-658-8865), 50 E Pender St, leads inexpensive walking tours of the area.

Dr Sun Yat-Sen Classical Chinese Garden

A tranquil oasis amid Chinatown's bustle, this carefully planned garden (☎ 604-689-

7133, 578 Carrall St; admission C$7.50/6/5 adult/senior/student; open 9:30am-7pm in summer (shorter hours in winter) is the only full-scale Ming Dynasty-style garden outside China. Take the guided tour (included with the price of admission) to best understand and appreciate its subtle design, which incorporates the Taoist principles of yin and yang. Tours take place year-round and include a Chinese tea service.

Concerts take place on Friday evening in summer, and each fall and winter the garden hosts the Mid-Autumn Moon Festival and Chinese New Year celebrations. Adjacent to the formal garden, the city's free Dr Sun Yat-Sen Park features a similar design.

Sam Kee Building
Recognized by *Ripley's Believe It or Not!* and the *Guinness Book of World Records* as the World's Narrowest Office Building, the building at the corner of Pender and Carrall Sts is easy to miss, not only due to its narrowness but also because it looks like the front of the larger, attached building behind. Built in 1913, it's only 1.5m (4.9 feet) wide and two stories tall. It results from a grudge: the city, intent on widening Pender St, neglected to pay Kee for this narrow strip of property, so he put up this slim building out of spite.

Science World
A fine place to spend a rainy day, Science World *(☎ 604-443-7443, 1455 Quebec St; adult/senior, student & child C$14.75/9.25; open 10am-6pm Jul & Aug; 10am-5pm weekdays & 10am-6pm weekends Sept-June)* occupies the geodesic dome originally built for Expo '86. The high-tech playground includes interactive exhibits about the forces of nature, a Kidspace gallery, Internet access terminals, a 3D laser theater and a Visual Illusions space that showcases optical effects. The **Alcan OMNIMAX Theatre** features a 28-speaker digital sound system and one of the world's largest domed screens. Joint admission to Science World and the OMNIMAX Theatre is C$19.75/14.25. To get there, take SkyTrain to the Science World-Main St station or Bus No 3, 8 or 19.

EAST VANCOUVER (MAP 4)
Traditionally the working-class and non-British section of Vancouver, the area east of Main Street still attracts many immigrants. Long the center of Vancouver's Italian community, **Commercial Dr**, or 'The Drive' as it's commonly called, remains one of the city's liveliest melting pots. The large lesbian community living here adds to the area's vibrancy, as does a counterculture vibe that thrives with earnest political conversations echoing among the many vegetarian cafes, bookstores, hemp shops and coffeehouses. Don't leave Vancouver without spending some time here.

Playland
Vancouver's amusement park *(☎ 604-253-2311, on the Pacific National Exhibition Park grounds at Cassiar and Hastings Sts; all day passes adult/young children or non-riding adults who accompany children C$22.95/10; open 11am-7pm weekends late Apr–mid-June, 11am-9pm daily mid-June–mid-Aug)* offers such thrills and chills as a classic wooden roller coaster. It's also home to the Hellevator, which shoots up a tower at 75km (246 feet) before sending riders in a free-fall toward the ground. Half of the 25 rides, though, cater to little tykes. Playland is also open during the Pacific National Expo itself, which runs for two weeks in late August and early September. To get there, catch bus No 4, 10 or 16 from downtown.

GRANVILLE ISLAND (MAP 5)
On the southern side of False Creek, under the Granville Bridge, this small, formerly industrial island has turned into a busy blend of businesses, restaurants, galleries and theaters. The center of activity is the **Granville Island Public Market**, a food lover's dream, with dozens of greengrocers, fishmongers, butchers, bakers and cheese shops displaying their wares. It's open 9am to 6pm daily, from mid-May through mid-October, and Tuesday through Sunday the rest of the year.

The market faces a waterfront plaza that's nearly always filled with shoppers, frolicking children, buskers and swarms of pigeons and gulls. Kids will love the free outdoor **Granville Island Water Park**, or the indoor **Kids Only Market**, which lures young visitors with clowns, magicians, face-painters and toy shops.

Granville Island is also an arts center, home to the **Emily Carr Institute of Art & Design** (☎ 604-844-3800, 1299 Johnston St), which holds frequent exhibits in its galleries. Shops on the island include several commercial art galleries and craft studios, interspersed with recreational-equipment shops and ship chandlers. At night, the focus shifts from shopping to the performing arts, as several theater companies and live music clubs open their doors.

The **Granville Island Museums** complex (☎ 604-683-1939, 1502 Duranleau St; admission adult/senior & student/child C$6.50/5/3.50; open 10am-5:30pm) houses three collections under one roof: sport fishing, model ships and model trains. The admission gets you in to all three museums.

The Granville Island Information Centre (☎ 604-666-5784), 1398 Cartwright St, is open 9am to 6pm. Parking can be hellacious on Granville Island. Consider taking the Aquabus or False Creek Ferries (see Getting Around, later in this section) or catching bus No 50 from Gastown or No 51 from Broadway and Granville St.

KITSILANO (MAP 6)

The neighborhood of Kitsilano spreads across the southern shore of English Bay, roughly from Burrard St to the University of British Columbia. During the 1960s and '70s, Kitsilano became a hippie enclave. But everyone and everything grows up; the hippies are now lawyers, and the neighborhood has gone genteel.

Kitsilano – usually referred to simply as 'Kits' – is still a fun area to explore, particularly along W 4th Ave and W Broadway, the primary commercial streets. One thing that hasn't changed in Kitsilano are the beaches. **Kitsilano Beach**, near Vanier Park, and **Jericho Beach**, farther west on W 4th Ave at Jericho Beach Park, remain two of the city's most popular places to gather and to worship the sun.

Vanier Park

Vanier Park, on English Bay south of False Creek and below the Burrard Bridge, boasts several museums and a great beach, along with a swimming pool, tennis courts and other sporting grounds. When the weather's fine, you'll see lots of people strolling, jogging, cycling, walking their dogs or simply sitting and watching the ships moving between English Bay and False Creek. To reach Vanier Park from downtown, catch the No 22 bus or take Aquabus or the False Creek Ferries from downtown or Granville Island.

Vancouver Museum (☎ 604-736-4431, 1100 Chestnut St; adult/senior & student C$8/5.50; open 10am-5pm daily, until 9pm Thur) recounts Vancouver's past and recent history.

Part of the Vancouver Museum complex, **HR MacMillan Space Centre** (☎ 604-738-7827; adult/senior & student/child C$12.75/9.75/8.75; open 10am-5pm daily, closed Mon Sept-June) features regularly changing shows projected onto a 20m (66 foot)-wide dome. Other attractions include a virtual-reality simulator ride and a 'Cosmic Courtyard' of hands-on exhibits that let visitors launch a rocket or morph into a space alien. Evening laser shows (C$8.65) start at 9:30pm Thursday to Saturday, with additional shows at 10:45pm Friday and Saturday. On the same grounds, the **Gordon MacMillan Southam Observatory** (☎ 604-738-2855; admission free; open noon-5pm daily, plus 7pm-11pm weekends) lets you check out space through large telescopes when skies are clear and volunteers available. Call to make sure it's open.

For a glimpse of the city's rich seafaring heritage, stop at the **Vancouver Maritime Museum** (☎ 604-257-8300, 1905 Ogden Ave, adult/senior, student & child C$7/4; open 10am-5pm daily, closed Mon in winter), whose signature exhibit is the St Roch, a 1928 Royal Canadian Mounted Police (RCMP) Arctic patrol sailing ship.

UNIVERSITY OF BRITISH COLUMBIA

Usually just called UBC, this 400-hectare (988-acre) college campus (☎ 604-822-2211) of more than 35,000 students sits at the western-most point of Vancouver. Forest still covers much of the grounds, particularly at Pacific Spirit Regional Park. Bus Nos 4 and 10 run to the university every 10 minutes or so from downtown; the journey takes about 40 minutes.

Housed in a building that in itself is a work of art, the **UBC Museum of Anthropology** (☎ *604-822-3825, 6393 NW Marine Dr; adult/senior/student, C$7/5/4; free 5pm-9pm Tues; open 10am-5pm daily, until 9pm Tues)* contains outstanding art and artifacts that tell the story of BC's First Nations peoples. Included among the works of Haida artist Bill Reid, is his monumental yellow cedar carving of *Raven and the First Men*.

UBC Botanical Gardens (☎ *604-822-3928, 6804 SW Marine Dr, near the cnr of W 16th Ave; adult/senior & student C$4.75/2.50, free in winter; open 10am-6pm, mid-March–mid-Oct, 10am-2:30pm the rest of the year)* cover 28 hectares (69 acres) and include Canada's largest collection of rhododendrons and a 16th-century-style apothecary garden.

QUEEN ELIZABETH PARK
The highest point in Vancouver, Queen Elizabeth Park, at Cambie St and W 33rd Ave, sits atop 150m (492-foot) Little Mountain.

Dome-shaped **Bloedel Conservatory** (☎ *604-257-8570; adult/senior/youth/child C$3.75/2.25/2.85/1.85; open 9am-8pm weekdays, 10am-9pm weekends)* takes in three climate zones and houses 500 species of gorgeous plants, though the 50 species of free-flying tropical birds often steal the show.

To get to the park, take bus No 15 from Burrard or Robson Sts downtown.

ACTIVITIES
'You can ski in the morning and sail in the afternoon' must be the most common Vancouver cliché. But like most clichés, it has an element of truth. You can also bike, scuba dive, swim, skate, surf – and the list goes on.

Bicycling
Stanley Park's 9.5km (5.9-mile) seawall is probably Vancouver's favorite place to cycle. Rental bikes aren't available in the park, but

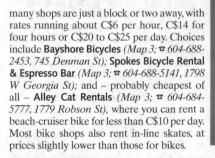

It's Only Natural

No off-the-beaten-path destination, Wreck Beach – Vancouver's only nude sunbathing spot – attracts 100,000 people each year. The three main sections of the 6km (3.7-mile) beach appeal to different crowds. Gay men tend to congregate on the north end; the central section is full of people peddling food and other consumables; and the southern stretch is a throwback to the 1960s, with everyone just hanging loose and having a good time. Bear in mind while you're baring it all, that on this or any other Canadian public beach nude sunbathing is technically illegal – but at Wreck Beach, Vancouver authorities look the other way.

Wreck Beach lies on the west side of the UBC campus; get there by taking NW Marine Dr south past the Rose Garden and the Museum of Anthropology to any of the trails marked No 4, 5 or 6.

many shops are just a block or two away, with rates running about C$6 per hour, C$14 for four hours or C$20 to C$25 per day. Choices include **Bayshore Bicycles** *(Map 3; ☎ 604-688-2453, 745 Denman St);* **Spokes Bicycle Rental & Espresso Bar** *(Map 3; ☎ 604-688-5141, 1798 W Georgia St);* and – probably cheapest of all – **Alley Cat Rentals** *(Map 3; ☎ 604-684-5777, 1779 Robson St),* where you can rent a beach-cruiser bike for less than C$10 per day. Most bike shops also rent in-line skates, at prices slightly lower than those for bikes.

Swimming
Cool off at Second and Third Beaches in Stanley Park, at English Bay and Sunset Beaches downtown, or at Kitsilano and Jericho Beaches on the southern side of English Bay. Kits Beach is the largest and most popular; as many as 10,000 people may hit the sand here on a hot summer day. You can also swim in the **outdoor heated saltwater pool** *(☎ 604-731-0011)* here. Admission to the pool is C$4.

For serious swimmers, the **Vancouver Aquatic Centre** *(Map 3; ☎ 604-665-3424, 1050 Beach Ave)*, at the foot of Thurlow St downtown, offers an indoor heated swimming pool, whirlpool, diving tank, gym and sauna. It's open daily and adult swim lanes are always available. Admission is C$4/ 2.40/3/2 adult/senior/youth/child. You'll find another aquatic center at UBC.

Other Activities
Ecomarine Ocean Kayak Centre *(Map 5; ☎ 604-689-7575, 1668 Duranleau St)*, on Granville Island, rents solo sea kayaks (C$26 for two hours, C$36 for four hours) and double kayaks (C$36 for two hours, C$46 for four hours). Its Jericho Beach location *(Map 6; ☎ 604-222-3565, 1300 Discovery St)*, also rents kayaks and offers three-hour beginning kayaking classes (C$49).

Windsure Windsurfing School *(Map 6; ☎ 604-224-0615, 1300 Discovery St)*, at the Jericho Sailing Centre, rents boards and wetsuits and gives lessons (C$29 and up for a two-hour group lesson).

You'll find the best **scuba diving** off the North Shore: at Cates Park on Deep Cove, up Indian Arm; at Lighthouse Park near West Vancouver; and at Porteau Cove, 26km (16 miles) north of Horseshoe Bay. For equipment, training and trips, stop in at any of the **Diving Locker**'s four Lower Mainland locations, including the shop in Kitsilano *(Map 6; ☎ 604-736-2681, 2745 W 4th Ave)*.

With more than 180 free public **tennis** courts (including some at Stanley Park, Queen Elizabeth Park and Kits Beach Park), Vancouver offers plenty of places to play tennis. City courts are available on a first-come, first-served basis; you can only occupy a court for 30 minutes if someone's waiting.

ORGANIZED TOURS
Gray Line *(☎ 604-879-3363)* specializes in traditional bus sightseeing tours, including the three-and-a-half-hour Deluxe Grand City Tour (adult/senior/child C$45/43/30). Shorter, less-structured trips are also available. The ***Vancouver Trolley Company*** *(☎ 604-801-5515)* offers a bus-slash-tour service with 16 stops throughout the city.

The trip is colored by the bus driver's historical commentary; one-day tickets cost C$24/12 adult/child.

West Coast Sightseeing *(☎ 604-451-1600)* runs the usual city bus tours, but it also offers a four-hour Native Culture Tour that visits various Vancouver museums and sights relating to the First Nations people. The cost is C$49/46/29 adult/senior and student/child. The company also leads city tours in German and Mandarin.

Harbour Cruises *(☎ 604-688-7246)* offers 75-minute cruises (adult/senior and teen/ child C$18/15/6), as well as three-hour sunset dinner cruises (adult/child C$60/50) around False Creek, English Bay and Burrard Inlet. Boats leave from the operator's office, at the north foot of Denman St near Stanley Park.

Harbour Air Seaplanes *(☎ 604-688-1277)* features air tours aboard float planes, departing from its water terminal at the base of Burrard St (one block north of Canada Place). The least expensive flight (C$80) tours the Vancouver area for 20 minutes.

SPECIAL EVENTS
Vancouver loves to party, with big events scheduled nearly every month of the year, beginning with January's Polar Bear Swim *(☎ 604-605-2304)*, a popular and chilly affair that takes place January 1 at English Bay Beach. Sometime in late January or early February, Chinatown hosts a 15-day Chinese New Year celebration *(☎ 604-687-6021)*, with dancers, music, fireworks and food.

Come spring, runners and walkers take to the streets for late April's Vancouver Sun Run *(☎ 604-689-9441)*, one of the world's largest 10km (6.2-mile) races, which winds through downtown before finishing with a big party at BC Place Stadium.

May features two events: the New Music West Festival *(☎ 604-684-9338)*, an international music-industry event in early May; and the Vancouver International Children's Festival *(☎ 604-708-5655)*, a fun, family-oriented performing-arts festival that takes place in Vanier Park late in the month.

In mid-June, the Dragon Boat Festival *(☎ 604-688-2382)*, on False Creek, attracts nearly 2000 competitors from around the world. At the end of the month, big-name stars and local favorites appear at the du-Maurier International Jazz Festival (☎ 604-872-5200), one of the best in Canada.

On July 1, Canada Day celebrations take place at Canada Place (☎ 604-666-8477) and Granville Island (☎ 604-666-5784). At early August's Symphony of Fire (☎ 604-738-4304), an international fireworks extravaganza, countries compete to see who can ignite the biggest bangs off a barge in English Bay. Held the first weekend in August, Pride (☎ 604-687-0955) celebrates Vancouver's gay and lesbian communities. It culminates in a Sunday parade along Denman and Beach Sts, followed by a fair and entertainment at Sunset Beach.

The Pacific National Exposition (PNE; ☎ 604-253-2311), the second-largest fair in Canada, takes place from late August to early September at the Pacific National Exhibition Grounds at Hastings Park in East Vancouver.

The largest spectator sporting event in Canada, the Molson Indy Vancouver (☎ 604-280-4639 for tickets), held in early September, draws 350,000 spectators to watch pro race drivers roar around the streets of downtown Vancouver. In mid-September, the Vancouver Fringe Festival (☎ 604-257-0350) presents drama, musical theater, comedy and dance from around the world. From late September through early October, the Vancouver International Film Festival (☎ 604-685-0260) showcases 300 films from 50 nations.

During the December holiday season, the month-long Christmas at Canada Place (☎ 604-666-8477) features ornate trees, wreaths and holiday window displays.

PLACES TO STAY

Vancouver is not a cheap place to stay during its summer season (May to September). You won't find any place to camp in the city itself (see North Vancouver, Burnaby and Richmond, later in the chapter, for camping possibilities in the suburbs), and you'll have to look far and wide for budget accommodations beyond the hostels. Most

hotel rooms in Vancouver top C$100. The Super, Natural British Columbia reservations service (☎ 604-435-5622, 800-435-5622) can be a great help in finding reasonably priced accommodation. Tourism British Columbia publishes an annual accommodations directory that lists thousands of approved campgrounds, B&Bs, motels and hotels throughout the province. Also check out the website at ⓦ www.hellobc.com.

Rates listed here are peak-season (summer) rack rates, many of which go down dramatically in the off-season. Prices are quoted without taxes, so be prepared for the extra 14% tax (7% GST and 7% PST) – ouch!

Hostels

Most of the good hostels fill up throughout summer and remain quite busy in winter, so it's wise to book ahead. Most have very limited parking, so it's best to arrive without a car.

HI-Vancouver Downtown (Map 3; ☎ 604-684-4565, 888-203-4302, fax 604-684-4540, ⓦ www.hihostels.bc.ca, 1114 Burnaby St, cnr Thurlow St) Dorm beds C$20/24 members/non-members, private rooms (for up to two people) C$55/63. A safe bet for budget travelers of all ages, this low-key, hospitable hostel with an excellent location contains 212 beds, with no more than four in a room. Scheduled activities abound, including a variety of local tours; the hostel also offers a free shuttle service to the bus and train stations, and to the Jericho Beach HI hostel.

Global Village Backpackers (map 3; ☎ 604-682-8226, 888-844-7875, ⓔ gvbp@interlog.com, 1018 Granville St) Dorm beds C$21/24 members/non-members; double private rooms with shared bath C$57/60, or C$62/65 with private bath. Global Village is the newest and hippest hostel in town. Brightly painted and lively, it strikes a nice balance between squeaky clean HI facilities and the grunginess of some other Vancouver hostels. Features include 220 beds, a rooftop patio, nightly pub runs with no-lineup access to some of downtown's hottest clubs, good apartment and job boards, lockers, a bike storage room and a lounge with pool table.

YMCA (Map 3; ☎ 604-681-0221, 955 Burrard St) Singles/doubles C$48/57. All rooms have a shared bath. A handful of family rooms cost about C$80 (women and couples are allowed). Parking costs C$7 per night, and small pets may stay for an extra C$11 per night. Guests can use the Y's gym and pool facilities. A small, inexpensive restaurant off the lobby serves breakfasts and sandwiches.

YWCA (Map 3; ☎ 604-895-5830, 800-663-1424 in Canada, e hotel@ywcavan.org, 733 Beatty St) Singles/doubles C$56/85 and up. Near SkyTrain, BC Place and downtown, the YWCA welcomes everyone – women, men, couples and families. The 155 rooms come in various configurations. Seniors, students and YWCA members can cut about 10% off all room rates. Amenities include in-room refrigerators, common kitchens, TV lounges and a laundry. Parking is C$5 per day.

New Backpackers Hostel (Map 3; ☎ 604-688-0112, 347 W Pender St) Dorm beds C$10, private singles/doubles C$25/30, with shared bath. Also known as Vincent's, this seedy hostel at the edge of Gastown is the cheapest in town, but the place truly is a dive. Trust your instincts here; if you check it out and sense you're better off paying a few more dollars elsewhere, do it.

Cambie International Hostel (Map 4; ☎ 604-684-6466, 877-395-5335, fax 604-687-5618, e info@cambiehostels.com, 300 Cambie St) Dorm beds C$15-20. 'Party here tonight!' screams a billboard on the side of this hostel above the Cambie pub, but it also sums up the vibe at this Gastown-area bunkhouse. Ask about free pick-up from the bus or train station or even from the airport.

HI-Vancouver Jericho Beach (Map 6; ☎ 604-224-3208, 888-203-4303, fax 604-224-4852, e van-jericho@hihostels.bc.ca, w www.hihostels.bc.ca, 1515 Discovery St) Dorm beds members/non-members C$16/20 Oct-May, C$17.50/21 June-Sept; private rooms with shared bath (for one or two people) C$46/55 in Oct-May, C$50/60 June-Sept (plus C$22.50 for a third person). Outdoorsy travelers will like the setting of this giant hostel

close to Jericho Beach Park. With 286 beds, it's the largest in Canada, though there still are never more than four beds to a room. It's about 20 minutes from downtown by southbound bus No 4 on Granville St.

University Housing

When students leave campus for the summer, the University of British Columbia rents out their resident rooms through the **Conference Centre** (☎ 604-822-1010, fax 604-822-1001, e reservation@housing.ubc.ca, w www.conferences.ubc.ca, Gage Towers, 5961 Student Union Blvd). In the hotel-style Gage Building: single with shared bath/double suite with private bath C$37/109 in May & June, C$39/119 in July & Aug. In the hostel-style Vanier Building: single with shared bath/double suite with private bath C$24/59 May-Aug. Self-contained apartments are also available for up to five people. The pleasant campus includes a cafeteria, restaurants, coin laundry, pub and sports facilities.

B&Bs

Vancouver's B&Bs often offer moderate prices, averaging C$75 to C$175 for a double, some with private baths, others with shared baths. If you're looking for information on Vancouver's B&Bs, contact **Old English B&B Registry** (☎ 604-986-5069, fax 986-8810, w www.bandbinn.com, postal address: 1226 Silverwood Crescent, North Vancouver, BC V7P 1J3) or **Town & Country B&B** (☎/fax 604-731-5942, w www.townandcountrybedandbreakfast.com, postal address: PO Box 74542, 2803 W 4th Ave, Vancouver, BC V6K 1K2). The following is just a sampling of the city's many B&Bs.

You'll find two moderately priced B&Bs in the Commercial Dr neighborhood of East Vancouver.

A Place at Penny's (Map 4; ☎ 604-254-2229, 810 Commercial Dr) Studio/1 bedroom C$90/110. Rooms have a private bath, equipped kitchen and a self-catered breakfast of fresh fruit and baked goods. The same innkeeper recently added rooms at similar prices in nearby **Aberdeen Mansion** (Map 4, 1110 Victoria Dr), a building that dates from 1910. Both are near the No 20 bus line.

Windsor Guest House (Map 5; ☎ 604-872-3060, 888-872-3060, fax 604-873-1147, e info@dougwin.com, 325 W 11th Ave) Singles/doubles C$65/75 with shared bath, C$95/105 with private bath. A big Victorian home near Broadway and Cambie St on the West Side, it has a front-porch sitting area. The house's 10 rooms come with free parking.

Douglas Guest House (Map 5; same phone as above, 456 W 13th Ave) Double occupancy C$75-125. A sister of the Windsor, this nearby B&B rents six rooms, two with shared bath and four with private bath, including two suites that can sleep up to five people. The Garden Suite (C$105) comes with its own kitchenette and private entrance.

Shaughnessy Village (Map 5; ☎ 604-736-5511, fax 737-1321, e info@shaughnessyvillage.com, 1125 W 12th Ave) Singles/doubles C$70/80. This high-rise complex bills itself as Canada's largest B&B. Actually an apartment building that just happens to take travelers, it's much safer and a lot more fun than some of the dumpy downtown budget hotels. Expect frumpy decor but amenities galore.

Maple House Bed & Breakfast (Map 6; ☎ 604-739-5833, fax 739-5877, e info@maplehouse.com, 1533 Maple St) Rooms C$120/140 with shared/private bath. Just a five-minute drive from downtown, this spot is close to the beach in Kitsilano.

Mickey's Kits Beach Chalet (Map 6; ☎ 604-739-3342, 888-739-3342, fax 604-739-3342, e mickeys@direct.ca, 2146 W 1st Ave) C$110-150. Some rooms come with private balconies and others with fireplaces.

Motels & Hotels

Downtown (Map 3) Finding a cheap hotel in downtown Vancouver is getting tougher all the time, but you can find a few affordable hotels right downtown, especially along Granville St. The following is a selection of safe, clean hotels offering good value for downtown.

Victorian Hotel (☎ 604-681-6369, 877-681-6369, 514 Homer St) Singles/doubles C$79/89 with shared bath, C$99/109 with private bath. This 27-room European-style pension is a real find in Vancouver. Rooms in this beautifully renovated historic building feature down duvets, some bay windows and kitchenettes. Fenced parking is C$10 per night.

Dufferin Hotel (☎ 604-683-4251, 877-683-5522, fax 604-683-0611, w www.dufferinhotel.com, 900 Seymour St) Singles or doubles C$95. There's free parking and a coffee shop and pub on the premises.

Royal Hotel (☎ 604-685-5335, 877-685-5337, fax 604-685-5351, w www.attheroyal.com, 1025 Granville St) C$109 with shared bath, C$139 with private bath. With a swank blue-and-gold decor, rooms here include a continental breakfast, plus welcoming cocktails in the hotel pub. Both the Dufferin and the Royal pubs serve a primarily gay clientele, though they're straight-friendly too.

Comfort Inn (☎ 604-605-4333, 888-605-5333, fax 604-605-4334, w www.comfortinndowntown.com, 645 Nelson St) Singles/doubles C$129/149. If you're into the club scene, you can also take advantage of the VIP package (C$139 per person), which gets you free VIP admission (and a free drink) at three popular clubs: The Roxy, Babalu and Fred's Uptown Tavern.

Bosman's Motor Hotel (☎ 604-682-3171, 888-267-6267, fax 604-684-4010, e bosmans@bc.sympatico.ca, 1060 Howe St) Singles/doubles C$119/129. Sure, it isn't as hip, but it offers an extremely central location, free parking and an outdoor pool.

Ramada Limited Downtown Vancouver (☎ 604-488-1088, 888-389-5888, fax 604-488-1090, e ramadalimiteddowntown@bc.sympatico.com, 435 W Pender St) Rooms C$159-300. Though recently renovated, the best sight here is the cascading neon waterfall sign outside. Valet parking is C$15 per night.

If you have money to burn, downtown Vancouver offers a number of top-end accommodations.

Crowne Plaza Hotel Georgia (☎ 604-682-5566, 800-663-1111, fax 604-642-5579, e hgsales@hotelgeorgia.bc.ca, 801 W Georgia St) Singles/doubles C$239/259 and up. This hotel oozes with Roaring Twenties ambience.

Wedgewood Hotel (☎ 604-689-7777, 800-663-0666, fax 604-608-5348, e info@wedgewoodhotel.com, 845 Hornby St) Singles/

doubles C$220/240 and up. This business-oriented boutique hotel has 89 rooms, each slightly different. Niceties include balconies, homemade cookies, cordless phones and a health club. Parking is C$15 per day.

Hotel Vancouver (☎ 604-684-3131, 800-441-1414, fax 604-691-1828, 900 W Georgia St, W www.fairmont.com) Singles/doubles C$249/269 and up. You can spot this distinctive city landmark by its green copper roof. The hotel is also noteworthy indoors for its smooth service and refined atmosphere. Guests can enjoy amenities such as the excellent fitness facility and indoor pool, along with superb restaurants and three varieties of afternoon tea: traditional, Asian and West Coast.

Pan Pacific Hotel (☎ 604-662-8111, 800-663-1515 in Canada, 800-937-1515 in the USA, W www.panpac.com, 300–999 Canada Place) Rooms from C$400. Although its regular rates rank among Canada's most expensive, the hotel often offers city-side room discounts for BC residents and for AAA/CAA members.

Four Seasons Hotel (☎ 604-689-9333, 800-268-6282, fax 604-689-3466, 791 W Georgia St) Rooms from C$420. This luxurious hotel sits above the Pacific Centre shopping complex. Find the hotel's reception by taking the escalator to the left of the Buddha statue at the mall level.

West End (Map 3) The West End features the Sylvia Hotel, one of the best values in town, as well as a number of apartment-style hotels whose proximity to Stanley Park, English Bay Beach and Robson St makes them a great base for seeing the sights. Here are a few of the affordable favorites.

Buchan Hotel (☎ 604-685-5354, 800-668-6654, fax 604-685-5367, e BuchanHotel@ bc.sympatico.com, 1906 Haro St) Singles/doubles C$69/79 (with shared bath), or C$85/95 (private bath). You can't get much closer to Stanley Park than this nicely appointed older hotel. There's no parking on the premises.

Sylvia Hotel (☎ 604-681-9321, fax 682-3551, W www.sylviahotel.com, 1154 Gilford St) Rooms C$75-135. Well-loved though slightly faded, the Sylvia enjoys a marvelous location on English Bay close to Stanley Park. Large suites are also available. For bayside views in summer, try to reserve up to a year ahead. Parking is C$7 per day.

Barclay Hotel (☎ 604-688-8850, fax 688-2534, W www.barclayhotel.com, 1348 Robson St) Singles/doubles C$75/95. Right in the thick of things on Robson St, this hotel has small but comfortable rooms. The downstairs lounge serves drinks.

Many former West End apartment buildings have become suite-style properties, with kitchens and a bit of room to spread out. You'll find quite a few along Robson St between Jervis and Nicola Sts.

Tropicana Motor Inn (☎ 604-687-6631, fax 604-687-5724, 1361 Robson St) Rooms C$99-139. The Tropicana may be the best deal, with high-rise one-bedroom suites, free parking and a colorful indoor pool.

Blue Horizon Hotel (☎ 604-688-4461, 800-663-1333, fax 604-688-4461, W www.bluehorizonhotel.com, 1225 Robson St) Standard/upper floor view rooms C$159/199. The large, nicely decorated rooms at this high-rise are all corner suites and most come with great views and balconies.

The West End has its share of higher-end hotels, including a couple of unique places that are worth a look, even if you're not staying the night.

Listel Vancouver (☎ 604-684-8461, 800-663-5491, fax 604-684-7092, e moreinfo@ listel-vancouver.com, 1300 Robson St) Standard/gallery rooms C$240/300. Rooms on the 4th and 5th 'gallery floors' feature original art pieces, though all rooms are modern, large and comfortable.

Pacific Palisades Hotel (☎ 604-688-0461, 800-663-1815, fax 604-688-4374, e reservations@pacificpalisadeshotel.com, 1277 Robson St) Standard rooms/suites C$225/305. This recently redone hotel wins guests over with its offbeat attitude, from the bright retro decor to the unusual mini-bar selections (Clif Bars, Cracker Jacks and travel games). Other amenities include a late-afternoon 'soul flow' reception (a healthier take on 'happy hour') and an on-site health club and pool.

Gastown, Chinatown & East Vancouver (Map 4)
Cheap hotels abound along Pender and Hastings Sts, but many serve as long-term accommodations for the downtrodden and those on low incomes or government assistance. Most travelers will generally want to avoid these places. The following are safe, clean bets for this part of town.

Dominion Hotel (☎ 604-681-6666, 210 Abbot St) Singles/doubles C$50/60 (with shared bath), C$100/110 (private bath). This well-worn but unbeatable value hotel enjoys a good location in Gastown, though you'll want to ask for a room away from the noisy (but fun) Lamplighters Pub on the ground floor.

Waldorf Hotel (☎ 604-253-7141, fax 604-255-8454, e reservations@waldorfhotel com, 1489 E Hastings St) Singles/doubles C$60/70. If you're looking to stay close to Commercial Dr, the Waldorf offers very basic rooms at a good value. Note that if you don't have a major credit card, you'll have to leave a C$150 cash deposit.

Granville Island & West Side (Map 5)
If you're looking to be right in the thick of Granville Island's colorful and bustling atmosphere, the Granville Island Hotel is a treat. Nearby, the Ramada on W Broadway offers easy access to West Side sights and the bridges to downtown.

Granville Island Hotel (☎ 604-683-7373, 800-663-1840, fax 604-683-3061, w www. granvilleislandhotel.com, 1253 Johnston St) Singles/doubles C$219/229. No two rooms are alike at this Granville Island hotel that's close to galleries, night spots and water taxis to downtown.

Ramada Vancouver Centre (☎ 604-872-8661, 800-663-5403, fax 604-872-2270, e ramada@direct.ca, 898 W Broadway) Rooms C$125. On the West Side overlooking downtown, the Ramada rents clean rooms above the Fairview Pub.

PLACES TO EAT
No matter what your tastes, Vancouver offers an excellent selection of fresh food, often served in amazing settings. The city is especially well known for seafood and international cuisine (including sushi, which some think is better here than in Japan) and dim sum, traditional Chinese food served in small portions. Best of all, you'll find a wide range of prices; you can eat very well for a little money – though you can easily spend a lot.

Downtown (Map 3)
If you're on a tight budget, you can always fix your own meals or buy prepared foods at supermarkets, which are everywhere because so many people live in central Vancouver. Shopping center food courts often offer inexpensive eats. Check out the food courts at Waterfront Centre (across from Canada Place) or at Pacific Centre.

White Spot (☎ 604-662-3066, 580 W Georgia St, at Seymour St) Entrees C$7-10. BC's best-known chain serves good salmon burgers and hamburgers with its famous 'triple O' sauce. The menu has a wide range of breakfast favorites, along with a big lunch and dinner menu.

Kitto Japanese House (☎ 604-687-6622, 833 Granville St) Entrees C$6-8. Sometimes described as the McDonald's of Japanese food, Kitto's is good, fast and inexpensive.

Canadian Maple Delights (☎ 604-682-6175, 769 Hornby St) Breakfast C$4-9, lunch C$5-7. This unusual spot specializes in food made with, or complemented by, maple syrup.

Elbow Room (☎ 604-685-3628, 560 Davie St) Breakfast C$3-8, lunch C$7-10. In the Yaletown area, this Vancouver breakfast institution is known for its abusive waiters, though ours was merely surly. At lunch, try the 'You've Got to be F-king Kidding' burger. Go and have fun.

Whether you're looking for a burger and a view, a splendid Italian dinner, or fresh-off-the-boat seafood prepared by star chefs, you'll find plenty of opportunity to eat your heart out downtown.

Allegro (☎ 604-683-8485, 888 Nelson St) Entrees C$12-19. Try this spot for a romantic Northern Italian dinner, where the menu features delicious soups, traditional pastas and pan-seared halibut.

BRITISH COLUMBIA

The Riley (☎ 604-684-3666, 1661 Granville St) Lunch C$8-14, dinner C$8-23. With a waterfront location on False Creek and friendly servers, this is a great spot for pizza and sandwiches at lunch, or dinners such as Malaysian tropical curry (C$14) and caramelized halibut (C$18).

Il Giardino di Umberto (☎ 604-669-2422, 1382 Hornby St) Lunch C$11-16, dinner around C$30. Umberto's Italian restaurants did a lot to put Vancouver on the cuisine map and this, the original restaurant, still offers some of the city's best Tuscan cooking, updated with Canadian delicacies such as berries and wild game.

Five Sails Restaurant (☎ 604-662-8111, 300–999 Canada Place) Entrees C$28-36. Worth the view alone, the Pan Pacific Hotel restaurant is another memorable place to lighten your wallet. The food is delicious but downright pricey. If you're not up for the full meal, consider stopping by earlier in the evening for a cocktail and snack.

C (☎ 604-681-1164, 1600 Howe St) Lunch C$15-20, dinner C$24-40. With its pretty location across False Creek from Granville Island, C is the hottest new seafood restaurant in town. Try the Dim Sum Business Lunch (C$18.50) or, for dinner, the grilled octopus and bacon-wrapped scallops (C$29).

900 West (☎ 604-669-9378, 900 W Georgia St) Lunch C$15-28, dinner C$26-36. This swank place in the Hotel Vancouver features fresh local seafood and a top-notch wine list with about 75 varieties available by the glass.

West End (Map 3)

The West End is one of the best places in Vancouver to get great food at good prices without compromising atmosphere. The people-watching and street life keep even the most mundane meal interesting.

Noodle King Café (☎ 604-683-2913, 1429 Robson St) Entrees C$6-9. Sit at the counter and watch the world go by. The menu features yummy noodle and curry dishes.

Ichibankan (☎ 604-682-6262, 770 Thurlow St) Sushi C$2-5, noodles C$5-7. This place has one of the best sushi bars in Vancouver, along with good noodle dishes.

Stepho's Souvlakia (☎ 604-683-2555, 1124 Davie St) Entrees C$8-12. The nightly lines outside attest to the popularity of this place, which offers great Greek casseroles, souvlaki and meat platters.

Joe's Grill (☎ 604-682-3683, 1031 Davie St) Breakfast C$4-8, lunch & dinner C$7-12. Joe's is a local favorite for good, cheap food morning, noon or night.

Hamburger Mary's (☎ 604-687-1293, 1202 Davie St) Entrees C$7-10. Mary's stays open nearly 'round the clock, but it's at its best on a warm night, when you can sit outside and watch life go by at the Davie-Bute intersection. Look for a good variety of breakfasts, burgers, pasta dishes and salads.

Krishna Pure Vegetarian Restaurant (☎ 604-688-9400, 1726 Davie St) All-you-can-eat buffet lunch/dinner C$6.95/8.95. With a 35-item buffet, Krishna Pure offers one of the city's best buys.

Thai House Restaurant (☎ 604-683-3383, 1116 Robson St) Lunch special C$7, à la carte dishes average C$14. This bustling local favorite serves consistently good food, including traditional combination plates (C$32 for two) or 'Thai fusion' – a blend of curries and seafood into standard favorites.

After walking around the Stanley Park seawall, you'll be ready to find a place where you can flop down and order a beer and a filling meal. You'll feel comfortable dressed up or wearing jeans and a T-shirt at the following casual places.

Musashi Japanese Restaurant (☎ 604-687-0634, 780 Denman St) Sushi plates C$6-12, noodles C$6-8, combination dinners C$14-16. Between Robson and Alberni Sts, this is a good spot to get your sushi fill.

Brass Monkey (☎ 604-685-7626, 1072 Denman St) Entrees C$9-15. This neighborhood favorite serves a killer rock-crab ravioli (C$9.75) and steamed Prince Edward Island mussels (C$9).

Marquee Grill (☎ 604-689-1181, 911 Denman St) Lunch C$7-11, dinner C$18-25. A casually upscale spot in a converted movie theater, the Marquee features live music and good meals plus a wide array of tapas (C$5 to C$11).

The Boathouse (☎ 604-669-7375, 1795 Beach Ave) Lunch C$9-14, dinner C$16-20. The English Bay setting overlooking the beach attracts both visitors and local business types. The bistro downstairs offers such dishes as halibut fish and chips. At the slightly more formal dining room upstairs, fresh fish is available nightly.

Balthazar (☎ 604-689-8822, 1215 Bidwell St) Tapas C$5-12, entrees C$12-24. Filling the space of some interesting restaurants before it, Balthazar ranks as one of the West End's most intriguing newer restaurants. With plenty of hidden corners and alcoves, it's a nice spot for conversation and romance. The Mediterranean and Moroccan menu includes tapas plates and full meals.

The West End has no shortage of great restaurants, many of which feature excellent steaks and seafood all dressed up with Northwest flare.

Joe Fortes (☎ 604-669-1940, 777 Thurlow St) Entrees C$20-25. For steaks, oysters, grilled fish and other staples of traditional Northwest cooking, this is the spot to go. Though Fortes has been slipping in recent years, it still creates wonders with swordfish or tuna.

O'Doul's (☎ 604-661-1400, 1300 Robson St) Breakfast C$6-10, lunch C$6-14, dinner C$18-30. In the Listel Vancouver (see Places to Stay, earlier), O'Doul's menu fuses the cuisine of the Pacific Northwest with the American Deep South in such dishes as jambalaya with saffron risotto. Live jazz accompanies dinner on Friday and Saturday nights.

Raincity Grill (☎ 604-685-7337, 1193 Denman St) Lunch C$10-18, dinner C$14-24. One of the West End's best-known and most popular restaurants, Raincity offers such choices as spaghetti and lamb meatballs and a low-calorie, low-fat 'spa fish.' Dinner entrees include treats like Dungeness crab cakes with black-bean-chorizo-roasted-fennel hash.

Liliget Feast House (☎ 604-681-7044, 1724 Davie St) Entrees C$20-30. Pacific Northwest dining doesn't get much more authentic than Native Indian cuisine, served up at this unique restaurant. Try dishes like venison steak (C$22), arctic caribou tenderloin (C$30) or one of the 'feast' dishes for two (C$49).

Stanley Park

Stanley Park offers three restaurant choices, all of which tend to be pricey but worth the money, considering the setting and scenery.

Prospect Point Café (☎ 604-669-2737, 2099 Beach Ave) Entrees C$17-25. Featuring good views of the Lions Gate Bridge and Burrard Inlet, Prospect Point is best known for its salmon. The cafe also serves lunch and Sunday brunch (11am to 4pm).

Teahouse Restaurant (☎ 604-669-3281, 7501 Stanley Park Dr) Lunch C$12-18, dinner C$17-28. This classic old-school restaurant at Ferguson Point enjoys wonderful views of English Bay and the North Shore. The menu includes seafood, lamb and duck, always cooked to perfection.

The Fish House in Stanley Park (☎ 604-681-7275, 8901 Stanley Park Dr) Lunch C$10-16, dinner C$16-25. Much more lively and hip, the Fish House specializes in oysters and good wine, but people also rave about dinners like the shiitake mushroom-dusted Chilean sea bass (C$23). An early-bird special (5pm to 6pm Sunday to Thursday) lets you pay full price for one entree and get C$15 off a second main dish.

Gastown (Map 4)

Old Spaghetti Factory (☎ 604-684-1288, 53 Water St) Lunch C$7-10, dinner C$8-14. Always popular and lively, the OSF can't be beat for value with its all-inclusive meals and big portions.

Raintree at the Landing (☎ 604-688-5570, 375 Water St) Lunch C$5-13, dinner C$16-25. This spot seems like two restaurants in one: a cool bistro overlooking Water St and a more upscale dining room with views of Burrard Inlet and the North Shore.

Water Street Café (☎ 604-689-2832, 300 Water St) Lunch C$12-15, dinner C$18-25. Housed in one of the few buildings to escape the Great Fire of 1886, this classy cafe offers a chic menu and some outdoor seating right in the center of Gastown.

BRITISH COLUMBIA

Jewel of India (☎ 604-687-5665, 52 Alexander St) Lunch C$7-10, dinner C$10-14. Though a bit off the beaten path, this is a great spot for tandoori dishes, the house specialty. Come for the live sitar music on Friday and Saturday evenings.

Chinatown (Map 4)

Chinatown is jammed with restaurants. These often look like holes in the wall, but open up into grand dining rooms – they're just not geared at tourists.

The Gain Wah (☎ 604-684-1740, 218 Keefer St) Congee from C$3. This spot features 16 different varieties of *congee*, (a rice or noodle soup loaded with goodies).

Hon's Wun- Tun House (☎ 604-688-0871, 108–268 Keefer St) Entrees average C$5. This local favorite operates several locations around town, including this Chinatown location. Expect good value and a huge selection of noodle dishes.

Buddhist Vegetarian Restaurant (☎ 604-683-8816, 137 E Pender St) Entrees C$6-12. This restaurant serves good chow mein and deluxe vegetarian dishes.

Pink Pearl (☎ 604-253-4316, 1132 E Hastings St) Entrees C$8-14. Though it's about eight blocks east of Chinatown, Pink Pearl offers some of the best dim sum in town; come before 3pm for the small plates. Later in the day, the menu shifts to Cantonese specialties.

East Vancouver (Map 4)

Café Deux Soleil (☎ 604-254-1195, 2096 Commercial Dr) Breakfast C$4-7, lunch & dinner C$7-10. Hip and friendly, this popular breakfast spot offers 'kid food' selections (C$2.50) and a play area on the small stage where acoustic musicians entertain on the weekend.

Café du Soleil (☎ 604-254-1145, 1392 Commercial St) Though not to be confused with Café Deux Soleil, the two share common origins, similar menus and prices.

Bukowski's (☎ 604-253-4770, 1447 Commercial Dr) Entrees C$8-15. Named for the curmudgeonly drunkard poet, Bukowski's is a 21st-century hangout for beatniks. The place features a varied menu, plus live jazz

or blues Monday and Thursday nights and spoken-word performances on Tuesday.

WaaZuBee Café (☎ 604-253-5299, 1622 Commercial Dr) Entrees C$8-12. This is a groovy, hip spot, serving great salads, sandwiches and pastas. The coffee here is good as well.

Latin Quarter Restaurant (☎ 604-251-1144, 1305 Commercial Dr) Tapas C$7-10, entrees C$9-14. Ever lively and always fun, the Latin Quarter is a must-stop for delicious tapas. There's live music on weekends.

El Cocal (☎ 604-255-4580, 1037 Commercial Dr) Entrees C$8-12. Specializing in Salvadoran and Brazilian food, the menu here also features more familiar Mexican dishes. Selections include *feijoada* (pork stew) and *mukeka de peixe* (fish stew). El Cocal also hosts an open-mic night for prose writers the second Monday of every month.

Nick's Spaghetti House (☎ 604-254-5633, 631 Commercial Dr) Entrees C$9-15. A few blocks away from the bustle, Nick's is Vancouver's classic and casual authentic Italian joint, serving large portions of old favorites like spaghetti and meat balls and lasagna.

Cannery Seafood Restaurant (☎ 604-254-9606, 2205 Commissioner St) Entrees C$16-22. From Commercial Dr head northeast toward the waterfront to this long-loved restaurant, known for its terrific views, fresh fish and extensive wine list.

Granville Island & West Side (Map 5)

For only-in-Vancouver picnic provisions, head to the *Granville Island Public Market*. But Granville Island also has its share of good sit-down restaurants.

Bridges (☎ 604-687-4400, 1696 Duranleau St) Downstairs pub C$8-18, upstairs restaurant C$23-35. For sipping wine and margaritas, Bridges remains the longtime favorite, with a large outdoor deck and great views. Enjoy pub fare on the downstairs patio overlooking False Creek, or more serious Northwest cuisine in the upstairs dining room.

Cat's Meow (☎ 604-647-2287, 1540 Old Bridge St) Lunch & dinner C$10-15. By day this is a good spot for moderately priced lunches and weekend brunches (design-your-own omelet for C$8.50). By night, it's a happening pub with frequent live music.

One of Vancouver's most interesting fine-dining areas, the Broadway & South Granville neighborhood (between Burrard and Main Sts on Broadway and 4th and 15th Aves on S Granville St) includes many creative upstarts, as well as plenty of proven favorites.

Ouisi (☎ *604-732-7550, 3014 S Granville St)* Lunch C$7-10, dinner C$11-16. This New Orleans-style bistro serves entrees like spicy pecan-crusted catfish with orange chipotle cream. Live jazz acts play several times a week.

Szechuan Chongqing Seafood Restaurant (☎ *604-734-2668, 1668 W Broadway)* Entrees C$15-20. A longtime favorite, the menu here offers a staggering array of choices (nearly 200 dishes), many featuring fresh seafood.

Afghan Horsemen (☎ *604-873-5923, 445 W Broadway)* Entrees C$11-17. With delicious Afghani food, this restaurant has been in business since 1974, which makes it one of the old-timers in this part of town. You can perch at either a standard table or join the communal seating on the floor.

Kitsilano (Map 6)

Naam (☎ *604-738-7151, 2724 W 4th Ave)* Entrees C$7-11. Kitsilano's hippie past lives on at this funky 24-hour restaurant serving delicious vegetarian stir-fries and veggie burger platters. Live, usually acoustic, music plays every evening.

Sophie's Cosmic Cafe (☎ *604-732-6810, 2095 W 4th Ave)* Breakfast C$4-8, lunch & dinner C$8-10. Ask any local where to go for breakfast and they'll send you to Sophie's, where they serve up giant breakfasts and offbeat dishes like a BC oyster burger (C$8).

Topanga Cafe (☎ *604-733-3713, 2904 W 4th Ave)* Entrees C$9-15. This is a great deal for good and hefty Californian-Mexican meals.

Nyala Restaurant (☎ *604-731-7899, 2930 W 4th Ave)* Entrees C$9-13. The richly spiced Ethiopian food here is eaten without

utensils – you use *injera* (flatbread) instead. The service is extraordinarily friendly.

Montri's Thai Restaurant (☎ *604-738-9888, 3629 W Broadway)* Entrees C$10-12. This is widely considered the best Thai place in Vancouver, with superb pad Thai.

Lumiere (☎ *604-739-8185, 2551 W Broadway)* Entrees C$18-35. One of the most highly regarded restaurants in Canada, Lumiere's menu offers French-fusion cooking that brings in the best of world cuisine and then drapes it in wonderful sauces. Menus vary seasonally. Try one of several eight-course tasting menus for C$55 to C$75 (add C$40 for wine).

Queen Elizabeth Park & Around (Map 2)

Seasons in the Park (☎ *604-874-8008, Cambie St at W 33rd Ave)* Lunch C$10-22, dinner C$14-24. Don't overlook this special-occasion restaurant set amid the lovely gardens of Queen Elizabeth Park. Weekend brunch is also available.

Spread out along Main St from E 48th to E 51st Aves, the Punjabi Market area is a great place to go for Indian food.

Zeenaz Restaurant (☎ *604-324-9344, 6460 Main St)* Closed Tues. Vegetarian buffet C$8, with meat C$10. Eat as much as you want at this Indian restaurant.

All India Sweets & Restaurant (☎ *604-327-0891, 6505 Main St)* Buffet C$6. This place gives Zeenaz a run for its money, with a 45-item all-you-can-eat vegetarian buffet.

ENTERTAINMENT

The best source of information on the arts and nightlife is *The Georgia Straight,* published every Thursday, and available online at **w** www.straight.com. *The West Ender* offers good general coverage, too. Both are free and you can pick them up around town.

Tickets for most events are available from TicketMaster (performing arts ☎ 604-280-3311, concerts ☎ 280-4444, sports ☎ 280-4400, **w** www.ticketmaster.ca). For details on upcoming performances and exhibitions, call the Arts Hotline (☎ 604-684-2787) or see the Alliance for Arts and Culture's website at **w** www.allianceforarts.com.

BRITISH COLUMBIA

Bars & Clubs

Downtown (Map 3)

Some of the big downtown nightclubs also double as live-music venues for a wide array of touring acts. Most of the clubs in Vancouver close at 2am (they're not legally allowed to be open later).

Richard's on Richards
(☎ 604-687-6794, 1036 Richards St) Often shortened to 'Dick's on Dicks,' this has been a top dance and live-music club for many years.

Roxy (☎ 604-684-7699, 932 Granville St) The Roxy is another Vancouver standby, playing mostly mainstream rock and Top-40 tunes. There's a similar vibe at the ***Starfish Room*** (☎ 604-682-4171, 1055 Homer St).

Vogue Theatre (☎ 604-331-7900, 918 Granville St) Housed in a converted cinema, the Vogue has canned and live music, and the vibe changes with whatever's playing.

Commodore Ballroom (☎ 604-739-4550, 868 Granville St) With a big bouncy dance floor and good acoustics, the Commodore attracts excellent bands.

Babalu (☎ 604-605-4343, 654 Nelson St) Looking like a salsa movie come to life, this is the city's top Latin venue. Neighboring ***Fred's Uptown Tavern*** (☎ 604-605-4350, 1006 Granville St) is a yuppie haunt. The clothes are casual, and so is the atmosphere.

The Yale (☎ 604-681-9253, 1300 Granville St) Despite its sketchy location, The Yale is one of the best blues bars in the city, featuring nightly live R&B music acts. Musicians from around the world come to here to pay homage to the blues of yesteryear, or to create the blues of today.

Luv-A-Fair (☎ 604-685-3288, 1275 Seymour St) Here you can groove to alternative and industrial dance music spun by DJs, dance on the speakers or wear your shiny new gold pants.

Railway Club (☎ 604-681-1625, 579 Dunsmuir St) The Railway is Vancouver at its best. This is a great place to see local bands, meet local folks and drink local beer. A variety of music plays nightly and good original jazz plays on Saturday afternoon.

Gastown (Map 4)

If you're looking to sip cocktails and boogie down, Gastown's is your best bet to hear live music or new DJs spinning their stuff.

The Purple Onion (☎ 604-602-9442, 15 Water St) A good, fun club, the Purple Onion offers live jazz and blues in one room and DJ dance music in the other.

Lamplighter's Pub (☎ 604-681-6666, 210 Abbott St) This bar in the Dominion Hotel presents Top 40 bands and a Celtic night on Tuesday.

Alibi Room (☎ 604-623-3383, 157 Alexander St) Although the Alibi is tucked well away from the main Gastown scene, it's a well known spot among Vancouver's hippest club-goers, including many from the city's film industry. Expect good food in the upstairs dining room and techno music in the downstairs lounge. Screenplay readings take place the last Sunday of each month.

Gay & Lesbian Venues

Vancouver's large gay population means there's a varied and ever-evolving club scene. For the latest, see the listings in the free weekly *Xtra! West*.

Royal Pub (Map 3; ☎ 604-685-5335, 1025 Granville St) Downtown in the Royal Hotel, is one of the top places to dance and dish, with a Tuesday-night bingo series that raises money for local gay charities. Get there by 7:30pm for a seat.

Numbers (Map 3; ☎ 604-685-4077, 1042 Davie St) This long-time venue is a multi-level men's cruise bar.

Odyssey (Map 3; ☎ 604-689-5256, 1251 Howe St) Odyssey has earned a reputation as the wildest gay dance club, with go-go boys and shower-room viewing.

Lotus Hotel (Map 4; ☎ 604-685-7777, 455 Abbott St) Formerly the Heritage Hotel, the newly renovated Lotus still harbors a variety of queer-friendly (if not exclusively gay) entertainment under one roof. The underground (literally) dance spot *Lotus Sound Lounge* welcomes anyone from straight ravers to flamboyant drag sisters. Upstairs the new *Milk Bar* and *Honey Lounge* are particular faves for FlyGirl! DJ nights.

Brewpubs

Steamworks Brewing Co (Map 4; ☎ 604-689-2739, 375 Water St) Play pool or admire the North Shore views at this Gastown brewpub.

Granville Island Brewery (Map 5; ☎ 604-687-2739, 1441 Cartwright St) This brewery offers free tours and tastings 10am to 4pm daily.

Cinemas

Movie tickets typically cost about C\$9, but most theaters advertise discounted shows all day on Tuesday and until late afternoon on other days. Major first-run multiplex theaters include the downtown *Granville Cineplex Odeon (Map 3; ☎ 604-684-4000, 855 Granville St);* Alliance Atlantis' *Fifth Avenue Cinemas (Map 6; ☎ 604-734-7469, 2110 Burrard St),* in Kitsilano; and the *Cinemark Tinseltown (Map 4; ☎ 604-806-0799, 88 W Pender St),* in the Gastown area. The *Denman Place Discount Cinema (Map 3; ☎ 604-663-2201, 1737 Comox St),* on the West End, shows three films for C\$3 on Tuesday.

Classical Music & Dance

Vancouver Symphony Orchestra (information & tickets ☎ 604-876-3434) The third-largest symphony in Canada performs more than 100 concerts annually at the Orpheum Theatre (Map 3), on Granville St at Smithe St.

Ballet British Columbia (☎ 604-732-5003, tickets ☎ 604-280-3311) Vancouver's top dance troupe takes the stage at the Queen Elizabeth Theatre (Map 3) at 600 Hamilton St from October to May.

Vancouver Opera (☎ 604-683-0222, tickets ☎ 280-3311) The opera stages four annual productions, also at the Queen Elizabeth Theatre.

Theater

All kinds of theater, from mainstream to fringe, are flourishing in Vancouver.

Vancouver Playhouse Theatre Company (☎ 604-873-3311) At the Vancouver Playhouse, this troupe, part of the Queen Elizabeth Theatre complex, presents a six-play season from September to May. The Queen Elizabeth Theatre is itself a key venue for touring Broadway shows and other major productions.

Arts Club Theatre (Map 5; ☎ 604-687-1644, on Granville Island) Michael J Fox and many other Canadian actors got their start on an Arts Club stage. Performances are also held at the *Stanley Theatre (Map 5; 2750 Granville Street).*

Firehall Arts Centre (Map 4; ☎ 604-689-0926, 280 E Cordova St) This small theater puts on plays by Canadian and foreign playwrights, as well as dance presentations.

No one wants to be indoors on fine Vancouver summer evenings, so two theater groups present plays in the city's parks. The annual *Bard on the Beach* festival *(☎ 604-739-0559,* W *www.bardonthebeach.org)* takes place from mid-June through September under an open tent at Vanier Park.

Theatre Under the Stars (☎ 604-687-0174, W *www.tuts.bc.ca)* also stages several Broadway musicals at Stanley Park's Malkin Bowl from mid-July to mid-August each year.

SPECTATOR SPORTS

From September through April, the *Vancouver Canucks (☎ 604-899-4625)* of the National Hockey League play at *GM Place* (Map 3), also the home of the *Vancouver Grizzlies (☎ 604-899-4667)* of the National Basketball Association.

The *BC Lions (☎ 604-589-7627),* Vancouver's Canadian Football League team, play in *BC Place Stadium* (Map 3) from July to September.

The *Vancouver Canadians (☎ 604-872-5232),* a single-A farm team for Major League Baseball's Oakland As, play a short season (June through August) at *Nat Bailey Stadium* (Map 2), 4601 Ontario St, next to Queen Elizabeth Park.

BRITISH COLUMBIA

The *Vancouver 86ers*, a professional soccer team, play May through August at *Swanguard Stadium* (Map 2), at the intersection of Boundary Rd and Kingsway in Burnaby. Tickets for the Grizzlies, Lions, Canucks and 86ers are available through TicketMaster (☎ 604-280-4400).

SHOPPING

Vancouver's central district contains some of the city's most dynamic shopping areas. On *Robson St*, the busiest shopping street in town, you can buy everything from couture to condoms, from Italian newspapers to fresh crab; you'll find lots of souvenir and gift shops here as well. Or you can buy nothing at all and simply enjoy the lively street scene.

The other major downtown shopping destination is *Pacific Centre*, a three-block-long underground shopping mall that runs from Robson to Pender Sts between Granville and Howe Sts. While in the Gastown-Chinatown area, check out the new *International Village* complex *(Map 4; 88 W Pender St)*. It features everything from hip clothing stores to a TNT Supermarket, best described as a traditional Chinese market on steroids. Gastown is also a good place to look for First Nations art.

After Robson St, you won't find a more fun place to shop in Vancouver than *Granville Island.* The stalls at the warehouse-like public market *(Map 5; ☎ 604-666-5784)* overflow with fresh fish, vegetables, meats, cheeses and fresh-baked goods. Merchants also sell fancy jams, syrups and other preserved foods that make good gifts; the fishmongers can pack fish for air shipment. Granville Island is also a good spot to shop for outdoor gear, books, and arts and crafts.

Along W Broadway on the West Side, you'll find one of the best spots in the country to go for outdoor equipment and clothing.

Mountain Equipment Co-op (Map 5; ☎ 604-872-7858, 130 W Broadway) Gearheads, hold on to your hats. You can bet that almost everyone in Vancouver has spent some money at MEC, which has everything from camping, cycling and ski gear to the ubiquitous fleece vest. You have to become a MEC member to buy in the store; lifetime memberships cost C$5 and are available onsite. Shopping at MEC theoretically entitles you to a share in any future company surpluses, but such dividends are few and far between. Still, MEC is a hip, ecologically sensitive company that's worth checking out if you're in the market for outdoor gear.

See the Burnaby section, later in this chapter, for information on the Metrotown complex, Greater Vancouver's biggest shopping destination.

GETTING THERE & AWAY
Air

Vancouver International Airport (YVR) is about 10km (6 miles) south of the city on Sea Island, between Vancouver and the municipality of Richmond. The two recently merged major Canadian airlines – Air Canada and Canadian Airlines (☎ 888-247-2262) – dominate service; commuter subsidiaries fly to the smaller towns in the region. You'll have to pay an airport improvement fee (C$5 to C$15, depending on your destination) at the airport before your flight departs.

The Vancouver area has three seaplane terminals: on the Fraser River, south of the main terminals at Vancouver International Airport; on the harbor near Canada Place; and in New Westminster. There's a helicopter terminal on the harbor near Waterfront Station.

Bus

Buses arrive and depart from Pacific Central Station (also the train station), 1150 Station St. Greyhound buses (☎ 800-661-8747, 604-482-8747) link Vancouver with Seattle and other cities in Canada and the USA. Greyhound does not offer service to Victoria.

The following are sample one-way fares and average travel times from Vancouver to major western Canada destinations: Banff, 14 hours (848km/526 miles) C$105; Calgary, 16 hours (974km/605 miles) C$122; Jasper, 13 hours (1154km/717 miles) C$105; Kamloops, five hours (355km/221 miles) C$49; Kelowna, six hours (395km/245 miles 6) C$54; Prince

George, 12½ hours (778km/483 miles) C$96; Prince Rupert, 25 hours (1502km/933 miles) C$184.

To/From Victoria Pacific Coach Lines (☎ 604-662-8074, 800-661-1725) runs buses to Victoria every hour 5:45am to 8:45pm during July and August and every two hours the rest of the year. The fare, including the ferry, is C$28/54 one-way/roundtrip for adults, C$19/36 for seniors and C$14/27 for children. It's the same price from Vancouver International Airport; buses connect with the airport shuttle bus at Delta Pacific Resort in Richmond.

To/From Seattle Quick Shuttle (☎ 604-940-4428, 800-665-2122, Ⓦ www.quick coach.com) operates a shuttle bus to downtown Seattle for C$34/61 one-way/roundtrip; the bus also makes stops at Bellingham Airport (C$22/40) and Seattle's Sea-Tac Airport (C $44/79). Buses leave from most major hotels in downtown Vancouver. Bigfoot Adventure Shuttle (☎ 604-278-8224, 888-244-6673) also makes the Vancouver-Seattle run for C$32/59, with service between major hostels in each city.

Train
Vancouver is the western terminus for Canada's VIA Rail (☎ 888-842-7245). It's also served by Amtrak (☎ 800-872-7245), which runs an evening train to Seattle (C$35, four hours), with a stop in Bellingham; from Seattle, the train departs at 7:45am.

You'll find the Pacific Central Station just off Main St, at 1150 Station St, between National and Terminal Aves southeast of downtown. The 'left luggage' counter is open 8am to 10pm. Lockers are available for C$2 (small) and C$4 (large).

Car
If you're coming from the USA (Washington State), you'll be on I-5 until the border town of Blaine. At the border is the Peace Arch Provincial and State Park. The first town in BC is White Rock. Hwy 99 veers west, then north to Vancouver. Close to the city, it passes over two arms of the Fraser River and eventually turns into Granville St, one of the main thoroughfares of downtown Vancouver.

Ferry
BC Ferries (☎ 888-223-3779) provides service between the mainland and Vancouver Island. The main route runs from Tsawwassen to Swartz Bay, which is just north of Sidney (1½ hours). Between eight and 15 ferries travel in each direction daily, depending on the day and season. Ferries also go to Nanaimo from Tsawwassen and Horseshoe Bay in West Vancouver. The one-way fare from the mainland to Vancouver Island during peak times is C$9.50/4.75 adult/child, *plus* C$2.50 for a bicycle and C$33.50 for a car.

Sunday afternoon, Friday evening and holidays are the busiest times for Vancouver Island crossings from both terminals, and people who plan to take their cars on the ferry must often wait one or two sailings for their turn. To avoid this, plan to cross at other times or reserve a space for your vehicle by calling ☎ 604-444-2890 or ☎ 888-724-5223 (in BC) or by visiting the website Ⓦ www.bcferries.com/res. BC Ferries also offers service from Tsawwassen to the major Gulf Islands. See the Southern Gulf Islands, in the Vancouver Island chapter, for information on these routes.

GETTING AROUND
BC Transit (☎ 604-953-3333) produces two publications about getting around the city: the *Transit Guide,* a map of Greater Vancouver that shows bus, train and ferry routes, and *Discover Vancouver on Transit,* which lists many of the city's attractions and provides directions on how to get to them (including Victoria). You can buy the former for C$1.50 at newsstands and bookstores; pick up the latter for free at the Visitor Info Centre.

To/From the Airport
There are two ways of getting between the airport and downtown by bus. The mint-green Vancouver Airporter (☎ 604-946-8866, 800-668-3141) stops at Pacific Central

BRITISH COLUMBIA

Station and all major central hotels. Tickets cost C$12 one-way, C$18 roundtrip (with no time limit). You can purchase them from the driver. Buses leave the airport every 30 minutes between 6:15am and 12:15am daily. The trip to downtown takes about an hour, though it's sometimes longer in heavy traffic.

You can also get to/from the airport on BC Transit buses. To get to the airport, take No 8 south on Granville St to 70th Ave. From there, transfer to bus No 100, bound for the airport. From the airport, do the reverse. The total travel time is one hour, and the fare is C$3.50 on weekdays, C$1.75 at night and on weekends. You need to have exact change.

A taxi between downtown Vancouver and the airport costs around C$30.

To/From the Ferry Terminals

To get to Tsawwassen ferry terminal from downtown, take bus No 601 on Howe St to the Ladner Exchange, then bus No 640 to the ferry terminal. Allow about 75 minutes for the trip. To get to the Horseshoe Bay ferry terminal, take bus No 250 or 257 on Georgia St. The trip lasts about an hour, sometimes longer during rush hours.

Bus, SkyTrain & SeaBus

BC Transit (☎ 604-953-3333) offers three modes of public transportation: regular buses, the SkyTrain automated light-rail system and SeaBus ferries to North Vancouver.

The transit system is divided into three zones: the inner zone covers central Vancouver; the next zone includes the suburbs of Richmond, Burnaby, New Westminster, North Vancouver, West Vancouver and Sea Island; the outer zone encompasses Ladner, Tsawwassen, Delta, Surrey, White Rock, Langley, Port Moody and Coquitlam.

On weekdays before 6:30pm, you pay a flat fare of C$1.75/2.50/3.50 for one/two/three zones of travel, whether you ride the regular buses, SkyTrain or SeaBus. (Discount fares, available to children ages five to 13 and seniors 65 and older, are C$1.25/1.75/2.50.) At night and on weekends, all travel is C$1.75 (C$1.25 discount fare). When you pay your fare, you can ask the driver for a free transfer, good for 90 minutes and valid for any other mode of transport used on a single journey.

Day passes, good for unlimited travel, cost C$7; they're available at the Tsawwassen ferry terminal and at London Drugs and convenience stores throughout town. If you're staying a while, you might want to consider purchasing the 10-trip FareSaver Tickets or the monthly FareCards.

The wheelchair-accessible SkyTrain connects downtown Vancouver with Burnaby, New Westminster and Surrey. SeaBus passenger-only catamarans zip back and forth across Burrard Inlet between Waterfront Station downtown and Lonsdale Quay in North Vancouver. For both, try to avoid rush hours, when many commuters crowd aboard.

Car

Vancouver has no expressways. On one hand, this means that the incredible vistas aren't marred by tangled layers of concrete interchanges – a refreshing change from other North American cities. But it also means that everyone must travel surface streets to get through the city. Congestion is a big problem and traffic can back up for blocks during rush hours. Parking is often hard to find in commercial and central residential areas. It's a good idea to park away from the center and catch a bus or SkyTrain downtown; it'll probably be quicker and better for your blood pressure, too.

You'll have your pick of car rental companies in Vancouver. Some offer discount coupons, which are available at various outlets, including the Visitor Info Centre (see Information, at the beginning of this chapter). Check the yellow pages for a complete listing of car rental companies. Some downtown agencies include the following (all of which operate counters at the airport as well):

Avis (☎ 604-606-2872) 757 Hornby St (Map 3)
Budget (☎ 604-668-7000) 1705 Burrard St (Map 6)

Hertz (☎ 604-606-4711) 1128 Seymour St (Map 3)

Lo-Cost (☎ 604-689-9664) 1105 Granville St (Map 3)

National/Tilden (☎ 604-685-6111) 1130 W Georgia St (Map 3)

Rent-A-Wreck (☎ 604-688-0001) 1349 Hornby St (Map 3)

Thrifty (☎ 604-606-1666) 1400 Robson St (Map 3)

Taxi

Unless you're staying at a big hotel, you'll probably have to phone ahead for a cab. Companies include Black Top & Checker Cabs (☎ 604-671-1111, 731-1111 or 681-2181) and Yellow Cab (☎ 604-681-1111, 876-5555 or 255-6262).

Bicycle

Vancouver is a great cycling city. Several secondary-street bikeways run across town, giving people the option of traveling by cycle away from the main arteries. The Adanac Bikeway, for example, runs 5.5km (3.4 miles) from downtown to the eastern city limits; others include the Seaside Bike Route and the Cassiar Bikeway. For more information, call the Bike Hotline (☎ 604-871-6070).

Bikes are allowed on the SeaBus, as well as on the ferries across False Creek. The Bicycling Association of BC publishes a cycling map of the city, which is available at the Visitor Info Centre and most bike shops.

Mini-Ferries

Two companies operate mini-ferry shuttles across False Creek. The False Creek Ferries (☎ 604-684-7781) stop at the Vancouver Aquatic Centre near Sunset Beach; at Granville Island at the Vancouver Maritime Museum by Kitsilano Point; and at Stamp's Landing near the Cambie Bridge. Aquabus (☎ 604-689-5858) travels between Granville Island and downtown docks at the bottom of Howe and the end of Davie St, as well as Stamp's Landing and Science World. The fare is C$2 to C$5, depending on your route. Both day passes and multi-trip tickets are available.

Greater Vancouver (Map 2)

Though Vancouver offers plenty of attractions to occupy visitors, most travelers find no shortage of reasons to explore beyond the city limits. Home to some of the metro area's best-known destinations, the suburbs feature entertainment and recreation opportunities for people of all interests. Whether you head over the bridges to North and West Vancouver on the North Shore, east to Burnaby and New Westminster, south to Richmond and Steveston, or beyond to the Fraser Valley, you're sure to find lots to do.

NORTH VANCOUVER

'North Van'(population 125,220) is home to two of the metro area's biggest attractions: the Capilano Suspension Bridge and Grouse Mountain. Most visitors to Vancouver will want to set aside a half-day or so to cross Burrard Inlet and visit these marquee spots. With the SeaBus terminal at hand, North Van also makes a good base for exploring downtown Vancouver.

Lonsdale Quay Market

At the center of the North Shore SeaBus terminal complex, this lively marketplace (☎ 604-985-6261; open 9:30am-6:30pm, until 9pm Friday) features a lower floor devoted to fresh food and frequent entertainment, and an upstairs area with specialty shops and several sit-down restaurants. A booth in the SeaBus terminal offers information on North Shore attractions. North Vancouver buses leave from this location. To get there, take the SeaBus from Waterfront Station in Vancouver.

Capilano Suspension Bridge

Capilano Suspension Bridge (☎ 604-985-7474, W www.capbridge.com, 3735 Capilano Rd; adult/senior/student/child C$12.75/10.50/8/3.75; open 8am-dusk mid-May–Sept, 9am-5pm Oct–mid-May) Each year about 800,000 people, arriving by the busload,

Spanning the Decades

No Vancouver landmark is both as revered and reviled as the Lions Gate Bridge. This 842m (half-mile) span, rising 60m (196 feet) above the First Narrows and named for the twin mountain peaks north of Vancouver, opened in 1938 as the longest suspension bridge in the British Empire. About 5600 vehicles drove across that first day.

Flash forward 60 years. By 1998, the bridge carried 60,000 vehicles per day. Although its cables and towers remained strong and its lights (added in 1986) dazzling, its decking had deteriorated into a corroded mess. How to fix the problem remains a top political debate. The province finally began replacing the entire bridge surface in the fall of 2000 and, to the chagrin of most locals, the resurfacing continues today.

Despite all the work, the bridge still only contains three lanes. The center lane's direction changes as traffic conditions warrant (though the center lane inevitably seems to be closed to vehicles traveling in your direction). Etiquette dictates you take turns merging on to the Lions Gate Bridge – and once you're up there, enjoy the view, but don't slow down. If you'd like to read a lovely essay, look for Douglas Coupland's 'Lions Gate Bridge, Vancouver, BC, Canada,' included in his book *Postcards from the Dead*.

cross this 140m (459-foot) pedestrian bridge, rising 70m (230 feet) above the Capilano River. Guided tours start every half-hour. Though the site is spectacular, the crowds can be oppressive. Many visitors leave wondering how much more beautiful the place would be if there weren't so many people (for a free, less crowded suspension bridge, see Lynn Canyon Park, below).

From downtown Georgia St, take bus No 246 westbound. Or take SeaBus from Vancouver's Waterfront Station to Lonsdale Quay. From there, take bus No 236 (May to September) or bus No 230 to Lonsdale Ave and 15th St, then bus No 232 to Edgemont Blvd and Capilano Rd, which is a block north of the park. If you're driving from Vancouver, head north over Lions Gate Bridge to Marine Dr in North Vancouver, then turn left (north) onto Capilano Rd.

Capilano Salmon Hatchery

This fish facility (☎ 604-666-1790, 4500 Capilano Rd), north of the suspension bridge, is most interesting from July to November, when you can see adult salmon swim through fish ladders to reach spawning grounds upstream. Bus No 236 runs here from Lonsdale Quay.

Grouse Mountain Resort

Billed as 'the Peak of Vancouver,' this resort (☎ 604-984-0661, W www.grousemtn.com, 6400 Nancy Greene Way) at the northern extension of Capilano Rd, is the city's most convenient ski area, as well as a popular summer destination.

The **Skyride** (adult/senior/student/child C$19/17/12/7) is an aerial tramway that takes people up the mountain for 360-degree views. Activities at the top include hiking, mountain biking, paragliding and helicopter tours. Don't miss the free *Born to Fly* movie in the Theatre in the Sky. The several dining options include *The Observatory* (fine dining), *Bar 98 Bistro* (more casual fare) and *Hiwus Feasthouse* (with First Nations storytelling, music and dancing).

Those who'd rather hike their way to the top can try the **Grouse Grind**, probably the most popular alpine hike in the Vancouver area. The well-traveled (some might say 'trampled') trail follows a steep, 2.9km (1.8-mile) route with an elevation gain of 853m (2798 feet) – the makings for a good cardio workout. Very fit people make it up in about an hour, but 90 minutes is more typical. Wear boots and bug repellent and bring water. It's free to hike up; if you like, you can catch the Skyride down from the top for C$5.

In winter, Grouse Mountain's activities include cross-country skiing, skating and sleigh rides. Don't forget **downhill skiing** *(ski report ☎ 604-986-6262)*. All-day lift tickets are C$29/22/16 adult/senior/teen and include access to 22 ski runs. Open 9am to 10pm December to April. Lessons, rentals and night skiing are also available.

Bus No 236 from Lonsdale Quay runs right to the base of the mountain.

Lynn Canyon Park

It's only a third as long as the Capilano Bridge and not quite so high, but the suspension bridge at Lynn Canyon sees only a fraction of the tourist traffic on the Capilano Bridge. Plus, it's free.

The **Lynn Canyon Park Ecology Centre** *(☎ 604-981-3103, 3663 Park Rd; open 10am-5pm Apr-Oct, noon-4pm weekends only Nov-Mar)* can educate you about the biology of the area through displays, films and slide shows.

To get to the park, take bus No 228 or 229 from Lonsdale Quay and get off at Peters Rd. It's a 15-minute walk from there. If you're driving, cross Second Narrows Bridge, turn right on Lynn Valley Rd, then turn right (east) on Peters Rd, where you'll see signs that point the way.

Mt Seymour Provincial Park

Another quick escape from Vancouver, this park *(☎ 604-924-2200)* features several lakes, hiking trails and many scenic viewpoints. Some areas are very rugged, so visitors on overnight trips should register with park rangers. **Mt Seymour Resorts** *(☎ 604-986-2261)* operates a downhill ski area here in winter. To get to the park from Vancouver, cross the Second Narrows Bridge, turn right (east) on the Mt Seymour Parkway, then north on Mt Seymour Rd.

Places to Stay

Capilano RV Park *(☎ 604-987-4722, 295 Tomahawk Ave)* Tents C$28, RVs C$28-38. Right by the Lions Gate Bridge, this camp-

ground offers a pool, showers and laundry, though beware: it can get crowded.

Globetrotter's Inn *(☎ 604-988-2082, 170 W Esplanade)* Singles/doubles with shared bath C$30/35, double with private bath C$45. Formerly a hostel, Globetrotter's is now a motel-style inn. Though there are no longer dorm rooms here, the rates are still reasonable and there is a communal kitchen for guests. It's just a short walk from the Lonsdale Quay SeaBus terminal.

Canyon Court *(☎ 604-988-3181, 888-988-3181, fax 604-990-1554, e info@canyon court.com, 1748 Capilano Rd)* Singles/doubles C$109. This basic motel, with a free continental breakfast, laundry and a pool is close to Lions Gate Bridge.

The Grouse Inn *(☎ 604-988-7101, 800-779-7888, e admin@grouse-inn.com, 1633 Capilano Rd)* Rooms with/without kitchenettes C$125/138. Nearby, this inn features similar amenities.

Lonsdale Quay Hotel *(☎ 604-986-6111, 800-836-6111, fax 604-986-8782, e sales@lonsdalequayhotel.bc.ca, 123 Carrie Cates Court)* Singles/doubles C$125. This comfortable and friendly hotel right on the waterfront offers great views of Vancouver.

Places to Eat

Grab a quick bite from any of the many food vendors at Lonsdale Quay Market or head upstairs to the sit-down restaurants.

Q Café *(☎ 604-986-6111, also in the upstairs market)* Entrees C$11-20. This upscale option stays casual and features great views of the city.

Sailor Hagar's Brew Pub *(☎ 604-984-7669, 235 W 1st St)* Pub grub C$8-12. Along with excellent beer, Hagar's serves up good burgers and fish-and-chips just a couple of blocks up from the quay.

WEST VANCOUVER

This tony suburb (population 40,900) has earned two spots in the records book: the first is for having the highest per capita income in Canada, and the second (under the category 'dubious distinctions'), for producing Canada's first mall, the Park Royal Shopping

Centre. You might be forgiven for thinking that the only thing West Vancouverites do is make and spend money, but woven into the warm patchwork of wealth are several lovely public parks, beaches and trails.

Lighthouse Park (☎ 604-925-7200) boasts some of Vancouver's largest trees, including a rare stand of original coastal forest. Hiking trails wind through the park. To get there, turn west (left) on Marine Dr after crossing Lions Gate Bridge and drive 9.5km (5.9 miles). Or catch bus No 250 going west on West Georgia St downtown.

Cypress Provincial Park (☎ 604-924-2200, 8km (5 miles) north of West Vancouver off Hwy 99) features trails for hiking and mountain biking, along with several mountain lakes. You can do some downhill skiing at the Cypress Bowl Ski Area (☎ 604-926-5612) or glide along the cross-country trails.

Places to Stay & Eat
Wilderness camping is permitted in Cypress Provincial Park, but there are no facilities.

Park Royal Hotel (☎ 604-926-5511, 877-926-5511, fax 604-926-6082 540 Clyde Ave) Rooms facing street/garden C$159/189. This small 30-room hotel has the feel of an English country inn, complete with pub. In summer, weddings are often held in the garden, so if you're looking for quiet, ask for a room facing the street.

Stands on West Vancouver's Dundarave Pier offer fish and chips and burgers. For something more, try two of the metro area's most noted restaurants.

Salmon House on the Hill (☎ 604-926-3212, 2229 Folkestone Way) Entrees C$19-29. Fresh fish dominates the menu, and the view overlooking Vancouver is tough to beat.

Beach House at Dundarave Pier (☎ 604-922-1414, 150 25th St) Entrees C$16-32. You'll pay a little more for these spectacular views, but the well-prepared seafood, lamb and steaks are worth it. Both places are open for lunch, dinner and Sunday brunch.

HORSESHOE BAY
The small coastal community of Horseshoe Bay marks the end of the North Shore. It's a pretty spot with great views across the bay and up the fjord to distant glaciated peaks, but it's probably best known for its ferry terminal, which services Bowen Island, Nanaimo on Vancouver Island and Langdale on the Sunshine Coast.

Whytecliff Park, at the far end of Marine Dr, attracts scuba divers and hikers. Trails lead to vistas and a gazebo, where you can watch the boat traffic wend its way in and out of Burrard Inlet.

BOWEN ISLAND
If you don't have time to explore the Gulf Islands, consider a trip to Bowen Island (population 3100), less than an hour from downtown Vancouver. A favorite destination for work-weary Lower Mainlanders, Bowen Island offers good visitor amenities and plenty of relaxing activities. You can stroll the island's waterfront boardwalks, rent kayaks right off the ferry dock or take on the 45-minute hike from the ferry dock to Killarney Lake. The island also features several art galleries and creature comforts like aromatherapy, massage and reflexology at the *Cottage (call ☎ 604-947-9161 for an appointment)*.

Places to Stay & Eat
Earthwoods Country Retreat (☎ 604-947-9712, W www.earthwoods.com, 1416 Westside Rd) Rooms/cabins C$60/85. This lovely spot sits on a wooded lot on the west side of the island. Rent your own cabin (with kitchen) or stay at the main house and eat delicious vegetarian food.

Xenia (☎ 604-947-9816, fax 604-947-9076, e xeniatlc@direct.ca) Cabins singles/doubles C$85/110. See a thousand-year-old Douglas fir tree at this soulful retreat center.

Vineyard at Bowen Island (☎ 604-947-0028, e staff@vineyard.bc.ca, 687 Cates Lane) Rooms C$125-225. This four-star B&B on a working vineyard has eight guest rooms with their own entrances. Amenities include a pool and croquet court.

Blue Eyed Mary's/The Breakfast Café (☎ 604-947-2583, 451 Bowen Trunk Rd) Breakfast C$4-11, dinner C$12-20. Breakfast is served Friday through Sunday, and a creative West Coast bistro-style dinner is served Thursday through Sunday.

La Mangerie *(☎ 604-947-2127, Artisan Square off Grafton Rd)* Entrees C$4-10. This is a good stop for quiches, salads and other light fare.

Doc Morgan's Inn *(☎ 604-947-0808, at the Union Steamship Company complex on the boardwalk)* Pub fare C$7-12, dinners C$15-23, Saturday and Sunday brunch C$5-C$11. This lively pub is the beating heart of Bowen Island. Residents and tourists alike stop by for good pub food and friendly conversation.

Getting There & Around

BC Ferries serves Bowen Island from Horseshoe Bay, with about 16 sailings daily in each direction. The roundtrip fare for the 20-minute trip is C$5.75/3 adult/child; cars are C$18.25.

BURNABY

Burnaby, the city immediately east of Vancouver, is probably best known as the home of **Metrotown** *(☎ 604-438-2444)*. Comprised of more than 500 stores, it's BC's biggest shopping complex and the second-largest mall in Canada after the West Edmonton Mall. SkyTrain runs right to the door from downtown Vancouver.

Burnaby (population 180,000) is also home to **Simon Fraser University**, established in 1965. Noted Canadian architect Arthur Erickson designed the university, which sits atop Burnaby Mountain, about 20km/12 miles east of downtown Vancouver.

Near SFU, the lofty **Burnaby Mountain Park** offers some grand views of Greater Vancouver and its mountains and seascapes. Don't miss Kamui Mintara, 'Playground of the Gods,' a sculpture installation by the father-son team of Nuburi and Shusei Toko.

Burnaby Village Museum *(☎ 604-293-6501, Deer Lake Park; admission adult/senior/teen/child C$6.60/4.45/4.55/3.95; open daily late Apr–mid-Sept)* re-creates the atmosphere of a southwestern BC town between 1890 and 1925, with an old schoolhouse, printing shop, drugstore and other

establishments. There's also a large, working steam-train model and a restored 1912 carousel. The 36 wooden horses look almost brand-new, but all were carved between 1912 and 1926. To get to the museum, take bus No 123 east on Hastings St or follow the signs from the Trans-Canada Hwy.

If you're looking to stay in Burnaby, here are a couple of options.

Simon Fraser University *(☎ 604-291-4503,* **W** *www.sfu.ca/conference-accommodation, postal address: Housing & Conference Services, Room 212, McTaggart-Cowan Hall, Burnaby, BC V5A 1S6)* Singles without/with bedding C$19/29. Available May-Aug. These fully furnished university dorm rooms with shared bathrooms make a convenient place to stay.

Holiday Inn Metrotown *(☎ 604-438-1881, 877-323-1177, fax 604-438-1883,* **e** *holiday@direct.ca, 4405 Central Blvd)* Singles/doubles C$169/179. If access to shopping is what you're looking for, this hotel attached to the huge retail complex offers comfortable rooms.

NEW WESTMINSTER

The oldest town in western Canada, New Westminster (population 49,500) was established in 1859 and briefly served as BC's capital city. Once the area's primary seaport, New Westminster still boasts districts with period charm along the Fraser River. The waterfront area at Westminster Quay Public Market & Esplanade is home to the new **Fraser River Discovery Centre** *(☎ 604-521-8401)*, which interprets river history.

It also just happens to share a building with the new **Royal City Star Riverboat Casino**, with 300 slot machines and 30 gaming tables. The New Westminster Visitor Info Centre *(☎ 604-526-1905)*, 790 Quayside Dr, is next door.

If you want to stay overnight, try the ***Inn at Westminster Quay*** *(☎ 604-520-1776, 800-663-2001, fax 604-520-5645, 900 Quayside Dr)*, with singles or doubles for C$170. Built over the water beside the Public Market, this hotel offers a view of Fraser River from every room. Restaurants and nightclubs line Columbia St near the waterfront.

You can reach New Westminster by taking SkyTrain.

RICHMOND

Richmond (population 149,000) has become closely identified with BC's recent influx of Hong Kong Chinese. But don't expect to find the bustling, slightly seedy charm of a Chinatown – everything here is upscale, sanitized and suburban.

For the real Richmond experience, drive along No 3 Rd and look for the many large shopping malls collectively known as **Asia West**. Among them, Yaohan Centre and Parker Place both feature gleaming stores filled with Chinese products and mostly Chinese shoppers, along with excellent Chinese food at very reasonable prices. To reach No 3 Rd in Richmond, take bus No 401, 403, 406 or 407 from Howe St in downtown Vancouver.

Visitors are welcome to view the gardens, murals and shrines of Canada's largest **Buddhist temple** (☎ 604-274-2822, 9160 Steveston Hwy between No 3 and No 4 Rds; admission free; open 9:30am-5pm). Take bus No 403 from Howe St in Vancouver to get there.

Steveston

In the southwest corner of Richmond, the old fishing village of Steveston makes a good day trip from Vancouver. You can smell the salt in the air as you stroll past Steveston's docks, where many anglers hawk fresh catch directly from their boats.

For an interesting activity, stop by the **Gulf of Georgia Cannery National Historic Site** (☎ 604-664-9009, 12138 4th Ave; adult/senior & student/child C$6.50/5/3.25; open 10am-5pm June-Aug, Thur-Mon April, May, Sept & Oct). The cannery dates from 1894 and features exhibits and entertaining tours led by former fisheries workers.

Take bus No 401, 406 or 407 to Steveston from Howe St in downtown Vancouver. If you're driving, take the Steveston Hwy exit west off Hwy 99.

Places to Stay & Eat

The Richmond area is a good place to stay if you want to be near Vancouver International Airport. Many motels and hotels offer free shuttle service.

Richmond RV Park (☎ 604-270-7878, e richmondrv@aol.com, 6200 River Rd) Tent sites/RV hookups C$17/23-26. Sites are available April to October only.

Accent Inn (☎ 604-273-3311, 800-663-0298, fax 604-273-9522, e accent@accentinns.com, 10551 St Edwards Dr) Singles/doubles C$89/99. Amenities include an indoor hot tub and restaurant.

Holiday Inn Express (☎ 604-223-9971, 800-465-4329, fax 604-214-8488, e service@ hi-express.bc.ca, 9351 Bridgeport Rd) Basic rooms at this hotel start at singles/doubles C$109/119.

Delta Vancouver Airport Hotel & Marina (☎ 604-278-1241, 800-268-1133, fax 604-276-1975, w www.deltahotels.com, 3500 Cessna Dr) Rooms from C$150. Try this bustling hotel for a touch more luxury.

Steveston Hotel (☎ 604-277-9511, 12111 3rd Ave) Singles/doubles C$50/55 with shared bath, C$75/85 with private bath, suites C$105-175. The hotel is also home to the Buccaneer Bar & Grill, a good stop for pub grub and beer.

Dave's Fish & Chips (☎ 604-271-7555, 3460 Moncton St) Fish baskets C$6. You can get delicious cod and halibut in the dining room from the take-out window. A second Dave's location on Steveston Landing charges a bit more.

TSAWWASSEN (MAP 1)

Yes, it's best known for the BC Ferries terminal that serves as Vancouver's main gateway to Victoria. But Tsawwassen also fronts on Boundary Bay, where **Centennial Beach Park** ranks among the Greater Vancouver area's best-kept secrets, with long stretches of lovely beach, excellent birdwatching and warm water for swimming at high tide. To get there, take Hwy 17 toward the Tsawwassen ferry terminal, then go south on 56th St to 12th Ave and east to Boundary Bay Rd.

The Great Dividing Line

Just a 30-minute drive from Vancouver, south of Tsawwassen on the Georgia Strait and across Boundary Bay from White Rock, sits a little knob of land called Point Roberts. This 12.5-sq-km (5-sq-mile) peninsula is detached from Washington State by water and land, but because it is on the south side of the 49th parallel, the dividing line between Canada and the USA, it is a US possession.

Even though an exception was made for Vancouver Island in 1846 when it was decided that the border would follow the 49th parallel west to the Pacific Ocean, no such exception was made for Point Roberts. The area falls under Washington State's jurisdiction, and there is an official border crossing open 24 hours. However, the area has been utilized far more by Canadians than by Americans, and over the years Canada has provided most of the services (water, gas, electricity, police etc).

Canadians have owned summer homes here for a long time, mainly to make use of the long stretches of sandy beach and the shallow bay's warm water – the beach at Point Roberts has been ranked one of the top 15 beaches in the USA. You'll find a marina, a small airport, shops, restaurants, two taverns and the 7-hectare (17-acre) Lighthouse Park, with campsites and picnic areas.

At one time, this was little more than a farming community settled by Icelandic immigrants. In time, the fishing and canning industries became the main sources of employment, along with the taverns, which for many years gave Canadians a reason to make the trip from Vancouver.

Starting in the late 1940s, Point Roberts began drawing crowds for cheap beer and music at two of the largest taverns in Washington State (The Reef and Breakers), especially on Sunday, when bars and clubs in BC were closed. In recent years, that attraction has diminished, and now most people come here for the beaches, boating, fishing and, of course, the novelty of being in the USA while still being in Canada. But the bars still do a brisk business, too, with beer gardens that seat several thousand people.

To get to Point Roberts from Vancouver, follow Hwy 99 south, turn south onto Hwy 17 (the road to the BC Ferries terminal at Tsawwassen), and at 56th St (Point Roberts Rd), turn south again.

– Chris Wyness

BRITISH COLUMBIA

Fraser Valley

Heading east, two roads parallel the Fraser River on its final flow to the ocean. The Trans-Canada Hwy (Hwy 1), south of the river, handles most of the traffic and although occasionally scenic, it's mostly a no-nonsense, limited-access freeway. Hwy 7, by contrast, meanders through farmland and small towns north of the Fraser for one of the Lower Mainland's prettiest drives. At Hope, Hwy 1 becomes the slow road, heading north through the Fraser River Canyon. Towns and parks in this section are listed roughly west to east, then north from Hope.

The Fraser Valley takes its name from Simon Fraser, who in 1808 explored the river that now bears his name as well. Most travelers rip through the Fraser Valley, eager to get to Vancouver and points west or east. But some of the valley's small towns, deep canyons, wild rivers and accessible wilderness areas deserve a closer look.

GOLDEN EARS PROVINCIAL PARK

The lovely 55,900-hectare Golden Ears Provincial Park (☎ 604-924-2400) was named for Mt Blanshard's twin peaks, which sometimes seem to glow in the sun. Golden Ears is about an hour's drive from Vancouver via the Lougheed Hwy (Hwy 7).

Alouette Lake, once a Native fishing area, is Golden Ears' centerpiece, with good opportunities for fishing, canoeing and windsurfing.

Alouette and Gold Creek Campgrounds (☎ *604-689-9025, reservations* ☎ *800-689-9025)* Sites C$18.50. Even with about 400 campsites, reservations are a good idea on summer weekends. Backcountry camping is also permitted in the park (C$5 per person).

LANGLEY & AROUND
Your basic sprawling suburb, Langley (population 83,173) nonetheless boasts one cool attraction: the 19-screen *Famous Players Colossus* (☎ 604-513-8747, *200 St at Hwy 1)*. This giant movie theater looks like a spaceship ready to launch.

Fort Langley (population 2578) is a picturesque village whose main attraction is the **Fort Langley National Historic Site** (☎ *604-513-4777, 23433 Mavis Ave just east of Glover Rd, the main street in Fort Langley; adult/senior/child C$4/3/2; open 10am-5pm Mar-Nov)*. It was here on November 19, 1858 that James Douglas read the proclamation that created the colony of British Columbia.

You'll find chain hotels near Hwy 1 in Langley, but for a more memorable stay, go to Fort Langley.

Fort Camping Resorts (☎ *604-888-3678, 9451 Glover Rd)* Campsites from C$18. The campground, on an island in the Fraser River, includes a pool, playground, showers and laundry.

Eagle's Reach Bed & Breakfast (☎ *604-888-4470, 800-393-9888, fax 604-888-4773,* W *www.eaglesreach.net, 24658 87 Ave)* Singles/doubles C$80-105/C$110-135. Amenities include a saltwater indoor pool, fitness room and river and mountain views, along with a three-course breakfast.

East along Hwy 1 brings you to the small farming community of Aldergrove (population 9500), whose best feature is the **Greater Vancouver Zoo** (☎ *604-856-6825, 5048 264 St; adult/senior & child C$12/9; open 9am to dusk)*. The center houses more than 900 animals from about 200 species, including rhinos, lions, tigers, elephants and apes.

Farther east, Abbotsford (population 107,410), the major trade center for the Fraser Valley, attracts visitors for the popular annual **Abbotsford International Air Show** (☎ *604-852-8511,* W *ww.abbotsfordairshow.com)*, which takes place on the second full weekend each August. Adult/child admission is C$20/10.

HARRISON HOT SPRINGS
Set on expansive Harrison Lake, once a shortcut to the Cariboo gold fields, Harrison Hot Springs (population 1060) has been a resort area since the 1880s. It also occupies a prominent place in local mythology: rumor has it that Sasquatch, or bigfoot, lives here. Many visitors to the region have claimed to see the hairy creature stomping around the backcountry.

Area hotels pipe in mineral water from the local springs, but campers or others not sleeping in town can soak their weary bones at the indoor **Harrison Public Pool** (☎ *604-796-2244, 224 Esplanade; adult/child C$7/5; open 9am to 9pm)*. The Visitor Info Centre (☎ 604-796-3425), 499 Hot Springs Rd, is open May through October.

Sasquatch Provincial Park (☎ *604-824-2300, 6km, or 3.7 miles, north of Harrison Hot Springs via Hwy 7)* Sites C$12. The campground contains 177 sites.

Executive Inn (☎ *604-796-5555, 888-265-1155, fax 604-796-3731, 190 Lillooet Ave)* Singles/doubles C$99-149. This basic but clean hotel has a hot tub, sauna and fitness room.

Harrison Hot Springs Resort (☎ *604-796-2244, 800-663-2266, fax 604-796-3682,* e *info@harrisonresort.com, 100 Esplanade)* Rooms C$150 and up. The hotel offers a variety of rooms (and prices), but guests come here for the outdoor and indoor mineral pools. There are also spa services, as well as fine-dining and casual restaurants.

CHILLIWACK & AROUND
Farmland, rivers and lakes surround Chilliwack (population 62,582), on Hwy 1 about 100km (62 miles) east of Vancouver, making the area a big outdoor playground. For information on recreation opportunities, inquire at the Visitor Info Centre (☎ 604-

858-8121), 44150 Luckakuck Way (Hwy 1 exit 116), which is open year-round.

Hyak Wilderness Adventures (☎ *604-734-5718, 800-663-7238*) and **Chilliwack River Rafting** (☎ *604-824-0334, 800-410-7238*) offer **white-water rafting** trips on the Chilliwack River, parts of which can be floated year-round.

Cultus Lake Provincial Park, 8km (5 miles) south of Chilliwack via Vedder Rd, is a good spot for sunbathing, camping and more serene water sports. A pretty cascade of water tumbles over the rocks at the 122m (400-foot) **Bridal Veil Falls**, east of Chilliwack on Hwy 1 exit 135.

HOPE

Established as a Hudson's Bay Company fort, Hope (population 7000) remains a major hub for the Fraser Valley. Hwys 1, 3 and 5 converge here, and a number of reasonably priced restaurants and motels have sprung up near the crossroads. You may recognize Hope from *First Blood,* the first of the 'Rambo' movies, which was partially filmed here in 1981.

Hope's biggest asset is its scenic river setting, with mountain views all around. Ironically, though, city planners established riverside **Centennial Park** near the city center, then planted so many trees and hedges that visitors can see neither the river nor many of the mountain peaks. The Visitor Info Centre (☎ 604-869-2021), 919 Water Ave, is open 9am to 5pm.

From Hope, the toll road Coquihalla Hwy (Hwy 5) heads north to Kamloops. You'll find few service stations along the way, so leave with a full tank. The Crowsnest Hwy (Hwy 3) sweeps south through Manning Provincial Park on its way to the Okanagan Valley. Hwy 1 heads north into the impressive steep-sided scenery of the Fraser River Canyon, with plenty of places to camp, play or simply enjoy the view.

Hell's Gate Airtram (☎ *604-867-9277, 45km, or 28 miles, north of Hope; adult/senior/child C$10/8.50/6.50; open 9am-6pm mid-June–early Sept, slightly shorter hours Apr-May & Oct)* Hell's Gate is a tourist trap to be sure, but fun nonetheless.

Hope offers some camping, and its over-abundance of motel rooms means prices are reasonable.

Telte Yet Campsite (☎ *604-869-9481, 600 Water Ave)* Tent sites C$15. Adjacent to the city's Centennial Park is this facility run by the Stolo First Nations band. Amenities include showers, a self-serve laundry and a small children's play area.

City Centre Motel (☎ *604-869-5411, 455 Wallace St)* Singles/doubles C$40/50. The big rooms have TVs and mini-fridges but no phones. For about the same price, **Lucky Strike Motel** (☎ *604-869-5715, 504 Old Hope Princeton Way)* offers the same amenities plus telephones and clock radios.

Maple Leaf Motor Inn (☎ *604-869-7107, fax 869-7131, 377 Old Hope Princeton Way)* Rooms C$50-55. Here you can rest weary bones in the indoor pool and hot tub.

Home Restaurant (☎ *604-869-5558, 665 Old Hope Princeton Way)* Breakfast/lunch C$5-8, dinner C$7-12. This popular spot features basic home cooking and is popular for breakfast.

Kibo Café (☎ *604-869-7317, 267 King St)* Entrees C$6-13. This smart little place offers Japanese food and outside seating when the weather is nice.

MANNING PROVINCIAL PARK

This 70,000-hectare park (☎ *250-840-8836),* about 30km (19 miles) southeast of Hope via Hwy 3, ranks among BC's most popular and highly developed provincial parks. It provides a habitat for more than 200 species of birds plus abundant mammals; you're almost certain to see black bears (but no grizzlies). Manning also marks the usual end of the 4240km (2629-mile) **Pacific Crest Trail** from Mexico to Canada via the USA's Sierra and Cascade Mountains (see the Activities chapter). In the fall, PCT through-hikers can be found swapping tales inside the Bear's Den pub at the Manning Park Resort.

Interpretive hikes and programs abound. For information, stop at the park visitor center (open 8:30am to 4:30pm mid-June to mid-October; 8:30am to 4pm weekdays the rest of year). You can fly-fish for trout in Lightning, Flash and Strike Lakes or angle for Dolly Varden in the Sumallo River. In winter, Manning features a small downhill ski and snowboard area at Gibson Pass and about 100km (62 miles) of groomed trails for cross-country skiing and snowshoeing.

Plenty of people stay outdoors at the park's four *campgrounds (reservations ☎ 800-689-9025, in Greater Vancouver ☎ 604-689-9025).* Sites are C$12 at Coldspring, Hampton and Mule, and C$18.50 at Lightning Lake.

***Manning Park Resort** (☎ 250-840-8822, 800-330-3321, fax 250-840-8848)* Rooms/cabins/chalets C$109/139-259/259. The resort's rooms are comfy and the cabins and chalets (sleeps six), though placed in an unfortunate parking-lot setting, are nicely furnished inside.

LYTTON

Lytton (population 366) marks the spot where the clear-running Thompson River meets the cloudy Fraser. It's a major outfitting point for **white-water rafting** trips and is the gateway to **Stein Valley Nlaka'pamux Heritage Park**, one of the last major tracts of unlogged wilderness in southwestern BC. The helpful staff at the Visitor Info Centre (☎ 250-455-2523), 400 Fraser St, offers heaps of information on area recreation.

Whistler & the Sunshine Coast

If you're looking for easily accessible adventure, it's hard to beat the regions north of Vancouver. No matter what your outdoor passion, chances are you can pursue it within a few kilometers of the Sea to Sky Hwy or on the lesser-known Sunshine Coast, accessible only by ferry. But these regions also please less-active travelers who desire nothing more than stupendous scenery, memorable lodgings and a few good meals.

Highlights

- Driving the breathtaking Sea to Sky Hwy
- Climbing the imposing Stawamus Chief or bald-eagle watching in Squamish
- Hitting the powdery slopes at Whistler and the Blackcomb Mountains
- Beachcombing along the shore in Gibsons and Sechelt

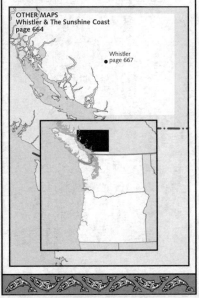

OTHER MAPS
Whistler & The Sunshine Coast
page 664

Whistler
• page 667

Sea to Sky Highway

Hwy 99, nicknamed the Sea to Sky Hwy, offers one of the prettiest drives in BC, with the blue panorama of Howe Sound on the southern portions and mountain scenery that rivals the Rockies stretching north from Squamish. In other words, don't plan on napping in the car.

The free magazine *99 North,* widely available along the route, offers comprehensive coverage of the area's sights and activities. In winter, occasional hazardous conditions force the Sea to Sky Hwy to close north of Squamish. 'The Mountain' radio station (107.1 FM in Squamish, 102.1 FM in Whistler) provides helpful reports on traffic and road conditions.

For information on the BC Parks sites in this region, call ☎ 604-898-3678. For information on the BC Forest Service lands, call the Squamish Forest District (☎ 604-898-2100).

On the way up, you'll pass through **Lion's Bay**, known for having some of Howe Sound's best **scuba diving**. Prime spots include Porteau Cove Marine Park and Bowyer Island. Sea to Sky Ocean Sports (☎ 604-892-3366), 37819 2nd Ave in Squamish, rents equipment and offers lessons and charter trips.

Another small way-station along the Sea to Sky Hwy, **Britannia Beach** contains only one real attraction: the **BC Museum of Mining** *(☎ 604-896-2233, 688-8735),* which tells the story of the Britannia Mine and lets you mine for gold. The museum offers 90-minute tours daily in summer, and Wednesday through Sunday in spring and fall. Admission is C$9.50/7.50 adult/student & child. Gold-panning costs an extra C$3.50 per person, but you're guaranteed to get a few flecks to take home.

SQUAMISH

Located about halfway between Vancouver and Whistler, Squamish (population 15,000)

WHISTLER & THE SUNSHINE COAST

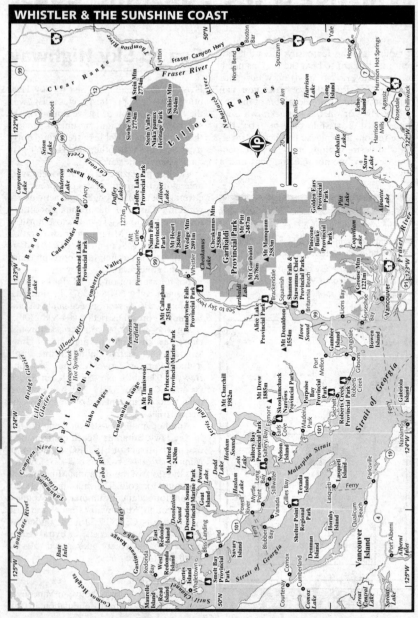

BRITISH COLUMBIA

enjoys an incredible natural setting. The Stawamus Chief looms over town to the southeast, its bulk nearly as great as Gibraltar. Mountains rise in most every other direction, too. A tiny harbor sits snugly between town and the monolith, and another arm of Howe Sound's headwaters – the Squamish River Estuary – cuts inland to the west.

For years, Squamish has primarily served as a forestry hub, but recreation has long been a big draw and general tourism is starting to catch up. A diverse group of visitors passes through this area every year: rock climbers, windsurfers, railroad history buffs and, in winter, birdwatchers eager to see hundreds of bald eagles.

If you're coming from Vancouver, turn left off Hwy 99 at the McDonald's to reach Cleveland Ave and Squamish's small downtown. The well-stocked Visitor Info Centre (☎ 604-892-9244), 37950 Cleveland Ave, is near the far end of the street.

One of the world's largest concentrations of bald eagles congregates in the Brackendale area, 7km (4 miles) north of Squamish, from late October to mid-February each year. As many as 3700 eagles gather along a 15km (9-mile) stretch of the Squamish River to feed on the dead salmon that float downstream after spawning. Seeing this many of these magnificent creatures gathered together is truly an amazing site. The main viewing site is at Eagle Run, beside Government Rd north of Garibaldi Way and south of Depot Rd. Volunteer interpreters often staff the site on Saturday and Sunday afternoons during eagle season. The Brackendale Art Gallery (☎ 604-898-3333), at the corner of Government and Depot Rds, offers helpful information about the eagle migration.

Things to See & Do

At 335m (1165 feet), Shannon Falls ranks among Canada's highest and most beautiful waterfalls. A short hiking trail leads to the falls in the small **Shannon Falls Provincial Park**, along Hwy 99 just south of Squamish. In winter, when the falls freeze, ice climbers pick and pull their way to the top.

The small **Alice Lake Provincial Park** (*BC Parks* ☎ 604-898-3678) makes a nice base

for camping and exploring the area. The 6.5km (4-mile) Four Lakes Trail takes about two hours to trek, but if you only have a half-hour to spare, you can hike to and around Stump Lake, the first lake on the loop. **Sea to Sky Kayaking School** (☎ 604-898-5498) offers rentals and lessons on Alice Lake.

Overlooking Squamish from a height of 652m (2139 feet), the Stawamus Chief is widely considered to be BC's best granite destination for **rock climbing**, with about 200 climbing routes. A few climbing outfitters are based in Squamish, including **Slipstream Rock & Ice** (☎ 604-898-4891, 5010 Cheakamus Valley Rd).

You'll find some awesome **windsurfing** at Squamish Harbour, where winds from the mouth of the Squamish River can push sailboards to speeds as high as 60km/h (37mph). (In fact, Squamish is a Coast Salish word meaning 'Mother of the Winds.') For information on conditions, call the Squamish Windsurfing Society (☎ 604-892-2235).

Mountain biking also draws lots of enthusiasts, who ride on more than 60 trails around Squamish. Stop by **Tantalus Bike Shop** (☎ 604-898-2588, 40446 Government Rd) for bike rentals and trail information.

Places to Stay & Eat

Squamish Hostel (☎ 604-892-9240, 800-449-8614, e hostel@mountain-inter.net, 38490 Buckley Ave) Dorm beds/private rooms C$15/25. Casual and friendly, this outdoorsy hostel organizes rock-climbing and rafting trips. Amenities include bikes to borrow, a small rock climbing wall, fully equipped kitchen, laundry and rooftop deck. It's an easy walk from downtown.

Sunwolf Outdoor Centre (☎ 604-898-1537, fax 898-1634, e sunwolf@mountain-inter.net, 70002 Squamish Valley Rd) Cabins without/with kitchen C$90/100. Stay in one of the riverside cabins and enjoy rafting trips, eagle-viewing floats and guided fishing, hiking and mountain-biking trips.

Howe Sound Inn & Brewing Company (☎ 604-892-2603, 800-919-2537, e hsibrew@howesound.com, 37801 Cleveland Ave)

Rooms C$105. Squamish's most upscale choice features 20 welcoming rooms with wood accents and thick duvets. Amenities include a sauna and outdoor granite climbing wall and two restaurants: a brew pub (entrees C$8-13), and its slightly more upscale cousin, the Red Heather Grill (entrees C$11-18). A telescope on the patio is often trained on climbers making their ways up the Chief.

Getting There & Away

Greyhound (☎ 604-898-3914) serves Squamish from Vancouver for C$8.50/17 one way/roundtrip. Buses arrive and depart from the depot at 40446 Government Rd in Garibaldi Highlands. About six buses daily travel the 56km (35 miles) between Squamish and Vancouver (northbound and southbound). The trip takes one hour and 15 minutes.

BC Rail's Cariboo Prospector (within BC ☎ 800-339-8752, elsewhere ☎ 800-663-8238) offers train service between Vancouver and Squamish (and onward to Whistler, Pemberton and Lillooet), with one train daily in each direction. The trip takes one hour, 20 minutes and the fare from North Vancouver is C$21/42 one way/roundtrip. BC Rail also operates the Royal Hudson Steam Train, a scenic ride from North Vancouver to Squamish, which runs Wednesday through Sunday, June through September; the basic roundtrip fare is C$50/43/13 for adult/senior & teen/child five to 11.

GARIBALDI PROVINCIAL PARK

East of both Squamish and Whistler, 195,000-hectare (482,000-acre) Garibaldi Provincial Park (☎ 604-898-3678) ranks among the Lower Mainland's largest parks. Best known for its superb alpine hiking, Garibaldi includes more than 67km (42 miles) of developed trails that become cross-country ski routes in winter. Throughout the park, you'll find hike-in backcountry campsites (C$3 to C$5 per person).

Garibaldi has five main developed areas, including **Diamond Head**, **Black Tusk/ Garibaldi Lake**, **Cheakamus Lake**, **Singing Pass** and **Wedgemount Lake**. You can't take your dogs to Garibaldi Park, and the park

also restricts the use of mountain bikes to certain trails. For more information, stop by BC Parks' district office at Alice Lake Provincial Park.

WHISTLER

The shorthand name 'Whistler' encompasses both the resort town 123km (76 miles) north of Vancouver and the Whistler-Blackcomb ski resort that brought the town fame. Many people agree that Whistler (population 9000) ranks as the best ski destination in North America. It's a beguiling spot in summer, too, with ample recreation options for every interest and far lower lodging prices than in winter.

Built almost entirely from scratch during the 1970s and '80s, Whistler tries to look much older. The massive hotels recall castles, and even shopping centers feature facades made out of venerable-looking quarried stone. But despite the contrived feel of Whistler Village, the skiers, shoppers and hikers who gather here lend the place a light, relaxing atmosphere.

Orientation

Whistler is divided into four main areas: Whistler Creekside, Whistler Village, Village North and Upper Village. If you're approaching town from the south, you'll enter at Whistler Creekside, the original Whistler base and home to a BC Rail train station.

The other three areas, which lie about 4km (2½ miles) up the highway past Alta Lake, tend to blur into one large village, collectively known to most as Whistler Village, or simply 'the Village.' If you're driving, turn east (right) onto Village Gate Blvd, and follow it to the end. You'll find large parking areas on the other side of Blackcomb Way.

Information

The Whistler Chamber of Commerce (☎ 604-932-5528, fax 932-3755) operates a Visitor Info Centre at Whistler Creekside, at the intersection of Hwy 99 and Cheakamus Lake Rd. It's open 9am to 5pm daily. The center will be moving to Whistler Village in summer 2002. There are also three small

WHISTLER

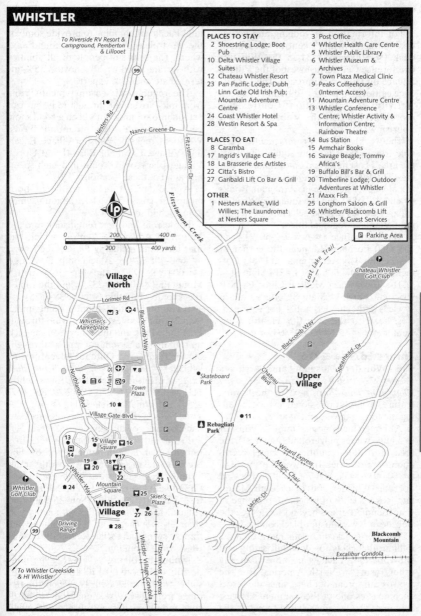

To Riverside RV Resort &
Campground, Pemberton
& Lillooet

PLACES TO STAY
2   Shoestring Lodge; Boot
    Pub
10 Delta Whistler Village
    Suites
12 Chateau Whistler Resort
23 Pan Pacific Lodge; Dubh
    Linn Gate Old Irish Pub;
    Mountain Adventure
    Centre
24 Coast Whistler Hotel
28 Westin Resort & Spa

PLACES TO EAT
8   Caramba
17 Ingrid's Village Café
18 La Brasserie des Artistes
22 Citta's Bistro
27 Garibaldi Lift Co Bar & Grill

OTHER
1   Nesters Market; Wild
    Willies; The Laundromat
    at Nesters Square
3   Post Office
4   Whistler Health Care Centre
5   Whistler Public Library
6   Whistler Museum &
    Archives
7   Town Plaza Medical Clinic
9   Peaks Coffeehouse
    (Internet Access)
11 Mountain Adventure Centre
13 Whistler Conference
    Centre; Whistler Activity &
    Information Centre;
    Rainbow Theatre
14 Bus Station
15 Armchair Books
16 Savage Beagle; Tommy
    Africa's
19 Buffalo Bill's Bar & Grill
20 Timberline Lodge; Outdoor
    Adventures at Whistler
21 Maxx Fish
25 Longhorn Saloon & Grill
26 Whistler/Blackcomb Lift
    Tickets & Guest Services

Parking Area

Nesters Rd

Nancy Greene Dr

Fitzsimmons Dr

Fitzsimmons Creek

0   200   400 m
0   200   400 yards

Village
North

Lorimer Rd

Whistler's
Marketplace

Blackcomb Way

Lost Lake Trail

Chateau Whistler
Golf Club

Skateboard
Park

Chateau Blvd

Upper
Village

Speedhead Dr

Northlands Blvd

Main St

Town
Plaza

Village Gate Blvd

Rebagliati
Park

Wizard Express

Village
Square

Magic Chair

Whistler Way

Mountain
Square

Skier's
Plaza

Whistler
Golf Club

Whistler
Village

Driving
Range

Glacier Dr

Blackcomb
Mountain

Excalibur Gondola

Whistler Village Gondola

Fitzsimmons Express

To Whistler Creekside
& HI Whistler

BRITISH COLUMBIA

summer-only information booths located throughout the Village.

For information on lodging and activities, contact Whistler's central reservation desk (☎ 800-944-7853) in the Whistler Conference Centre, just west of the Village Square on Golfers Approach. The conference center also houses Tourism Whistler's Activity & Information Centre. For more details, visit the website W www .tourismwhistler.com.

The weekly *Pique Newsmagazine,* available free in Whistler and Squamish, offers the area's best news and entertainment listings. The *Whistler Question* is a more traditional weekly newspaper. Armchair Books (☎ 604-932-5557), on the square in Whistler Village, carries a good selection of fiction, nonfiction and regional titles.

The post office (☎ 604-932-5012) is at 106-4360 Lorimer Rd, near the corner of Blackcomb Way. Access email at Peaks Coffeehouse (☎ 604-905-2980), 4314 Main St.

The Town Plaza Medical Clinic (☎ 604-905-7089), 40-4314 Main St, offers walk-in services and extended hours. For emergencies, head to the Whistler Health Care Center (☎ 604-932-4911), 4380 Lorimer Rd.

Things to See & Do

This **Whistler Museum and Archives** *(☎ 604-932-2019, 4329 Main St; C$1, open 10am-4pm Thur-Sun),* next to the library, features exhibits on regional history, including the town's development as a resort.

Although many people think of Whistler as a huge winter playground (and it is!), the area also offers countless summer recreation opportunities. Intrawest Corporation (☎ 604-932-3434, 800-766-0449) owns and operates Whistler and Blackcomb Mountain Resorts, both of which offer a range of year-round programs beyond skiing (see the website W www.whistler-blackcomb.com).

Whistler-Blackcomb sells more than 2.1 million lift tickets for **downhill skiing** and **snowboarding** each year, more than any other resort in North America. But the crowds can spread out here, since the resort encompasses one of the continent's largest ski areas. The usually reliable snowfall, the

vertical drop (1609m/5278 feet on Blackcomb, 1530m/5019 feet on Whistler) and the mild Pacific air combine to provide some of the most pleasant skiing to be found anywhere. The runs suit people of all abilities with terrain rated as 20% novice, 55% intermediate and 25% expert.

The regular ski season typically runs from mid-November through May, but can extend into summer if it's been a good snow year. There are five mountain bases: Whistler Creekside, Whistler Village, Excalibur Village, Excalibur Base II and Upper Village Blackcomb. You'll find high-speed lifts at all of these locations.

A one-day lift ticket usable at both mountains costs C$63/54/32 for adult/senior & teen/child seven to 12.

For lessons and gear rental, look into the **Mountain Adventure Centres**, which has four locations, including Pan Pacific Lodge (☎ 604-905-2295); Blackcomb Daylodge (☎ 604-938-7737); the top of Whistler Mountain (☎ 604-905-2325); and the top of Blackcomb Mountain (☎ 604-938-7425).

If you prefer **cross-country skiing**, more than 28km (18 miles) of trails wind through Lost Lake Park and the valley. You can pick up trail maps and rent equipment throughout the resort area. **Outdoor Adventures At Whistler** *(☎ 604-932-0647, in the Timberline Lodge)* offers **snowshoeing** tours, while **TLH Heliskiing** *(☎ 250-558-5379, 800-667-4854)* and **Whistler Heli-Skiing** *(☎ 604-932-4105, 888-435-4754)* lead helicopter treks to backcountry powder skiing.

From July through September, lifts remain open on both mountains, providing access to 48km (30 miles) of **hiking** trails. Summer sightseeing lift-ticket prices cost C$22/19 adult/senior and teen; children ride free. The lifts run until 8pm in July and August. The Village bustles with activity in summer, too; check out the climbing wall, trapeze swing and social scene at the base of Blackcomb Mountain.

Mountain biking is another popular pursuit, with more than 100km (62 miles) of single track in the area. The opportunities range from easy recreational trails to hardcore mountain descents for experienced cyclists. Call **Intrawest** (☎ 604-932-3434 or 800-766-0449) for information on tours, lessons and rentals. **Wild Willies** (☎ 604-938-8836, 7011 Nesters Rd) rents bikes and gives free bike tours of the valley daily in summer.

Many outfitters offer **horseback riding**, including **Adventures on Horseback** (☎ 604-894-6269) and the **Whistler Outdoor Experience Co** (☎ 604-932-3389).

Special Events

Whistler is the setting for several major winter sports events, including the Winter-Start Festival in early December; the racing series from January through March; the annual Whistler Gay Ski Week in early February; and the TELUS World Ski & Snowboard Festival in mid-April.

In early June, the Whistler Arts Experience festival features workshops, gallery walks and entertainment. A fringe festival, ArtRageous, takes place at the same time. Music festivals happen all summer into early fall; these include the Whistler Roots Weekend in mid-July; the Summit Concert Series, with on-mountain performances during weekends in August; and the Whistler Jazz & Blues Weekend in mid-September. The festivities continue in fall, with such events as the Alpine Wine Festival in early September; Oktoberfest in mid-October; and Cornucopia, a food and wine festival in early November.

Places to Stay

Hotels abound in Whistler, but few of them are cheap. December, February and March are Whistler's peak months – during this time, you need to book hotels well in advance or, if you're on a budget, re-think your timing altogether. Rates quoted below are for the peak winter season; expect much better deals the rest of the year.

Whistler's central reservation service (☎ 604-664-5625, in North America ☎ 800-944-7853, fax 604-938-5758) can book you a room at almost any of the area's hotels, lodges and condominiums. The Visitor Info Center (see Information) can supply you with a list of Whistler B&Bs.

In summer, camping in Whistler is an excellent way to go. In winter, check out one of the hostels or affordable lodges.

Riverside RV Resort & Campground (☎ 604-932-5469, 877-905-5533, fax 604-905-5539, e info@whistlercamping.com, 8018 Mons Rd) Tent sites C$25. Amenities here include a hot tub, laundry, showers and shuttle service to Whistler Village. Ask about cabins, which can sleep up to six people.

HI Whistler (☎ 604-932-5492, fax 932-4687, e whistler@hihostels.bc.ca, 5678 Alta Lake Rd) Dorm beds members/nonmembers C$19.50/23.50. Though rather remote, this small hostel enjoys a beautiful setting on Alta Lake, about a 45-minute walk from Whistler Village.

BRITISH COLUMBIA

Working at Whistler-Blackcomb

Whistler-Blackcomb hires several thousand people each year for seasonal jobs that range from ski-lift operators to food service personnel. October/November and February/March are the peak recruiting times; most jobs go to Canadian residents or people with Canadian working holiday visas, such as Australians and New Zealanders. Hourly wages range from about C$8 to C$12, plus good benefits: A season ski pass to both mountains, 50% food discounts and free ski and snowboard lessons. Anyone who's done it will tell you that working a season at Whistler is unforgettable fun.

However, once you've got a job, the tough part is finding an affordable place to live – housing is often expensive or nonexistent. It's not unusual for five or six people to share a one-bedroom apartment because they can't find (or afford) anything else. The resort makes some rooms available through its Glacier Residence program. Call ☎ 604-938-7500 for information.

For information about job openings and applications, call ☎ 604-938-7366, fax 604-938-7838 or visit the resort's website at w www.whistler-blackcomb.com.

SouthSide Lodge (☎ 604-932-3644, fax 932-0551, e info@snowboardwhistler.com, 2121 Lake Placid Rd) Dorm beds C$25. Convenient to the Creekside area, this lodge offers 30 beds that are grouped five to a room. Each room comes with its own bathroom and shower, cable TV and VCR.

Shoestring Lodge (☎ 604-932-3338, fax 932-8347, e shoe@direct.ca, 7124 Nancy Greene Dr) Dorm beds from C$28, motel-style rooms C$120. A 15-minute walk from the village, this place can get rowdy, with exotic dancers and bands in the on-premises Boot Pub, so ask for a room well down the hall if you want some peace and quiet.

Accommodations in Whistler skyrocket in the peak seasons, when getting a room is tough, let alone an affordable one. Some of the better hotels offer deals throughout the year. It's worthwhile calling to see if any are available while you're in town.

Whistler Resort & Club (☎ 604-932-2343, fax 932-2969, e reserve@rainbowretreats .com, 2129 Lake Placid Rd) Rooms/suites C$120/185. In the Whistler Creekside area, this place suffers from a rather dated 1970s feel but offers some of the lowest prices in Whistler.

Delta Whistler Village Suites (☎ 604-905-3987, 888-299-3987, fax 604-938-6335, e resdwvs@delta-whistler.com, 4308 Main St) Studio suites C$230 and up. With on-site concierge, restaurants and modernized rooms, the Delta makes a good central choice.

Pan Pacific Lodge (☎ 604-905-2999, 888-905-9995, fax 604-905-2995, e whistler@ panpacific-hotel.com, 4320 Sundial Crescent) Rooms from C$260. Rooms here come with fireplaces, kitchens and soaker tubs.

Coast Whistler Hotel (☎ 604-932-2522, 800-663-5644, fax 604-932-6711, e reserve@ direct.ca, 4005 Whistler Way) Rooms from C$280. The small but modern rooms here include the use of a heated pool, whirlpool and fitness center.

Westin Resort & Spa (☎ 604-905-5000, 888-634-5577, fax 604-905-5589, e reservations@westinwhistler.net, 4090 Whistler Way) Rooms from C$320. One of Whistler's newest and biggest hotels, with

419 suite-style rooms, the Westin's amenities include ski-in, ski-out access and a huge health club and spa.

Chateau Whistler Resort (☎ 604-938-8000, 800-441-1414, fax 604-938-2055, 4599 Chateau Blvd) Rooms from C$400. This is Whistler's biggest and fanciest hotel, with 558 rooms, a golf course and spa, as well as ski-in, ski-out access to Blackcomb Mountain.

Places to Eat

With more than 80 restaurants in Whistler, you'll have no trouble finding something good to eat.

Nesters Market (☎ 604-932-3545, 7019 Nesters Rd) This is a reasonably priced store for groceries; there's a laundry here too.

Ingrid's Village Café (☎ 604-932-7000, 4305 Skiers Approach, just off the Village Square) Breakfast & lunch C$4-7. This is a great stop for a hearty breakfast or lunch, which includes sandwiches and several varieties of vegetarian burgers.

La Brasserie des Artistes (☎ 604-932-3569, right on the Village Square). Entrees C$8-12. Serving up good breakfast all day, plus lunch and dinner (burgers and pastas), this is also a good spot to kick back and have a beer, with plenty of outdoor seating on sunny days.

Garibaldi Lift Co Bar & Grill (☎ 604-905-2220, 2320 London Lane) Entrees C$8-14. With huge burgers made to order, tasty margaritas and slopeside views, this is a great spot to hang out after a day on the slopes.

Caramba (☎ 604-938-1879, 12-4314 Main St) Entrees C$11-17. The Mediterranean menu here comes highly recommended by visitors and locals alike. Specialties include pasta, pizza and rotisserie meats.

Citta's Bistro (☎ 604-932-4177, 4217 Village Stroll, on the Village Square) Entrees C$9-20. The lively Citta's (pronounced **chee**-tahs) serves up good, creative food, such as the Cajun Caesar wrap or the Jim Beam-and-garlic steak (C$19).

Dubh Linn Gate Old Irish Pub (☎ 604-905-4047) Lunch C$9-15, dinner C$14-20. You'll find a vibrant social scene at this fun pub in the Pan Pacific Lodge. Specialties include such soups as seafood corn chowder or Guinness-and-crab.

Entertainment
Canada's top ski resort is a partying place. Whether you're kicking off your ski boots, climbing off your mountain bike, or out for an evening on the town, Whistler has it all. Après ski entertainment runs 4pm to 7pm, and many bars and clubs feature live music during those hours.

Longhorn Saloon & Grill *(☎ 604-932-5999, 4290 Mountain Square)* This popular spot right at Whistler base attracts crowds coming off the slopes.

Tommy Africa's *(☎ 604-932-6090)* and the ***Savage Beagle*** *(☎ 604-938-3337)*. These popular bars under the same roof at 4222 Village Square, both draw a younger crowd of mostly 19- to 25-year-olds.

Buffalo Bill's Bar & Grill *(☎ 604-932-6613, 4122 Village Green)* The scene here attracts the 30-and-older set with occasional live music and comedy nights.

Maxx Fish *(☎ 604-932-1904, 4232 Village Stroll)* This is the alternative spot in town. DJs spin a good variety of hip-hop, house and funk music.

Getting There & Around
Most people get to Whistler via ground transportation from Vancouver, which is the only option in winter. But in summer, Whistler Air (☎ 604-932-6615, 888-806-2299) offers scheduled float-plane service between Whistler's Green Lake and Vancouver for C$125 each way.

Greyhound (☎ 604-932-5031, 800-661-8747) offers about six daily trips from Vancouver's Pacific Central Station to Whistler; the fare is C$21/42 one way/roundtrip. Most trips take 2½ hours, but the once-daily, early-morning Ski Express arrives at Whistler Village in two hours. Buses stop at the main bus station, outside the Whistler Conference Centre. Purchase tickets on the bus (cash only) or at Mail Boxes Etc, 4338 Main St in Village North. See the website W www.whistlerbus.com for more details.

Bigfoot Adventure Tours (in Vancouver ☎ 604-278-8224, 888-244-6673) runs a shuttle between Vancouver and Whistler for C$25/50 one way/roundtrip. Other shuttle services (at almost double the price) include Perimeter Whistler Express (☎ 604-266-5386 in Vancouver, 604-905-0041 in Whistler) and Vancouver Whistler Star Express (☎ 604-685-5546 in Vancouver, 604-905-7668 in Whistler).

BC Rail's Cariboo Prospector (within BC ☎ 800-339-8752, elsewhere ☎ 800-663-8238) runs one train daily each morning from North Vancouver to Whistler, with a return run in the evening. The trip takes 2½ hours. The fare (including breakfast or dinner) is C$39/69 one way/roundtrip. Reservations are required.

The Wave (☎ 604-932-4020) offers bus rides around the Whistler area for C$1.50. Buses are equipped with outside ski racks and bicycle racks. Sea to Sky Taxi (☎ 604-932-3333, 938-3333) provides taxi service.

PEMBERTON
Just 32km (20 miles) north of Whistler on Hwy 99, Pemberton (population 855) is somewhat of a bedroom community for people priced out of the ski-town market. For local information, stop at the Visitor Info Centre (☎ 604-894-6175), across from the Petro Canada station.

Area attractions include **Nairn Falls Provincial Park**, about 6km (4 miles) south of Pemberton along Hwy 99. The trail to the namesake falls (3km or 2-mile roundtrip) winds along steep banks overlooking the swift-flowing Green River. Another 4km (2½-mile) roundtrip trail leads to One Mile Lake.

If you're willing to detour from the highway, you'll find adventure aplenty via backcountry roads. After a day of exercise, rest your weary bones at **Meager Creek Hot Springs**, 47km (29 miles) north of Pemberton via the Upper Lillooet River Rd. This world-class soaking site features Japanese-style bathing pools and interpretive trails. Geological hazards occasionally close Meager Creek, so inquire in Pemberton or call the Forest Service (☎ 604-898-2100) before setting out. Admission is C$5 per person.

Birkenhead Lake Provincial Park offers excellent wildlife watching, canoeing and fishing, plus an 85-site campground. It's

55km (34 miles) from Pemberton. Take the turnoff to D'Arcy at Mt Currie, 6km (4 miles) north of Pemberton on Hwy 99. The final 17km (11 miles) to the park are on a gravel road.

The following are some lodging and food options:

Nairn Falls Provincial Park (☎ *604-898-3678*) Tent sites C$12. With 92 campsites, this park usually has plenty of available sites. It's open April to October.

Pemberton Hotel (☎ *604-894-6313, fax 894-6655, 7423 Frontier St*) Rooms with shared bath C$30, private baths start at C$50/60. The Pemberton has 33 comfortable rooms, a lounge and fireside restaurant.

Pony Espresso (☎ *604-894-5700, 1426 Portage Rd*) Sandwiches C$7. This is a funky eatery popular with everyone from Whistler commuters to longtime Pemberton locals.

Greyhound (☎ 604-894-6818, 800-661-8747) operates four daily bus trips from Vancouver's Pacific Central Station to Pemberton. Four buses leave daily going in each direction. The trip takes about 3½ hours, and the one-way fare is C$21.75. BC Rail's Cariboo Prospector (☎ 800-339-8752 within BC, 800-663-8238 outside BC) runs one train daily in each direction. The 3½-hour trip costs C$45/90 one way/roundtrip.

LILLOOET

The 101km (63-mile) stretch of Hwy 99 between Pemberton and Lillooet (population 2058) is a beauty, even more serpentine than the southern stretch of the Sea to Sky Hwy. The route crests near Joffre Lakes Provincial Park, where you can take a short hike to the first lake or follow a much more ambitious trail to the upper backcountry. After that, it's all downhill – at grades up to 17% – past Duffey Lake and along Cayoosh Creek.

Lillooet's mountainous setting belies its semi-arid climate, which sees some of the hottest temperatures in Canada. For local information, stop at the Visitor Info Centre (☎ 250-256-4308), 790 Main St, inside a converted church that also serves as a museum.

The Info Centre can give you more specifics about places to camp in the outlying wilderness, but if you're looking to stay and eat in Lillooet, the following are good choices.

Cayoosh Creek Campground (☎ *250-256-4180, 877-748-2628, fax 250-256-4174,* e *rjansen@lillonet.org*) Sites C$12-18. About 1km south of the Hwy 12 and 99 junction, this woodsy campground offers 48 sites, showers and lots of activities.

Hotel Victoria (☎ *250-256-4112, fax 256-4997, 667 Main St*) Singles/doubles C$70/80. This old hotel features nicely refurbished rooms, many with kitchenettes. In the hotel, the reliable **Vic Café** offers breakfast and lunch, along with email access; later on, the hotel's dining rooms serve both fine-dining cuisine and pizza.

BC Rail's Cariboo Prospector stops at Lillooet once daily in each direction. The fare from North Vancouver is C$75/150 one way/roundtrip. and the trip takes just less than six hours.

Sunshine Coast

Stretching from Langdale to Lund, the Sunshine Coast is a geographical orphan, separated from the rest of the Lower Mainland by the formidable Coast Mountains. The only way to get there is by ferry.

Hwy 101 (the Sunshine Coast Hwy) winds nearly the length of the coast, but the trip is interrupted by water between Earls Cove and Saltery Bay, where BC Ferries bridges the gap. From Saltery Bay, the road continues to Powell River, the region's largest town. Allow at least 90 minutes for the winding 84km (52-mile) drive from Langdale to Earls Cove, then 50 minutes for the ferry crossing to Saltery Bay. From Saltery Bay, it's a 35km (22-mile) drive to Powell River and another 23km (14 miles) from Powell River to Lund. Although you can get from Langdale to Powell River (including the ferry crossing) in about three hours, you'll want to allow more time for sightseeing or other activities en route.

BC Ferries (☎ 888-223-3779) offers about eight daily sailings between Horseshoe Bay and Langdale at the southern end of the Sunshine Coast. The 40-minute trip costs

C\$8/4 adult/child; cars are C\$27.75. This fare essentially covers two ferry trips: either the roundtrip from Horseshoe Bay to Langdale, or the one-way through-trip including Horseshoe Bay to Langdale and Earls Cove to Saltery Bay (the northern Sunshine Coast ferry). Allow 90 minutes for the 84km (52 mile) drive from Langdale to Earls Cove.

Malaspina Coach Lines (☎ 604-886-7742, 877-227-8287) serves the Sunshine Coast (Gibsons, Roberts Creek, Sechelt and Powell River) from Vancouver's Pacific Central Station. The fare to Gibsons, Roberts Creek and Sechelt is approximately C\$20/30 one way/roundtrip. The trip to Powell River costs around C\$30/60. Fares include all ferry costs.

BC Transit's Sunshine Coast Transit System (☎ 604-885-6899) serves the Lower Sunshine Coast from Langdale to Gibsons and Sechelt. For complete information, see the transit schedules at the website w www.suncoastcentral.com.

You can also fly to Powell River from Vancouver with Pacific Coastal Airlines (☎ 800-663-2872). The cost is about C\$100 one way.

GIBSONS

If you want to sample the Sunshine Coast on a day trip from Vancouver, Gibsons makes a fine destination. It's a short (5km) hop from the Langdale Ferry Terminal, which is only a 40-minute ferry ride from Horseshoe Bay. People still know Gibsons as the setting for *The Beachcombers,* a popular CBC series filmed here in the 1970s.

The town of Gibsons (population 4000) is divided into two sections: the visitor-oriented Gibsons Landing and Upper Gibsons, the commercial strip farther up the hill along Hwy 101. The Gibsons Chamber of Commerce operates a tourist information desk (☎ 604-886-2325) outside the Sunnycrest Mall, just off Hwy 101 along the commercial strip; it's open 9am to 5pm daily. The chamber also staffs a seasonal information center at Gibsons Landing; it's open on weekends in June and daily in July and August.

There following are some lodging options:

Lookout B&B (☎ *604-886-1655, fax 886-1655,* e *lookout@sunshine.net, 318 Shoal Lookout)* Singles/doubles C\$75/90. At this spot on Gibsons Bluff, at the far end of the village, you can survey the ocean where Howe Sound and the Georgia Strait meet.

Marina House B&B (☎ *604-886-7888,* e *marinahouse@sunshine.net, 546 Marine Dr)* Singles/doubles C\$95/110. Just 1km north of the village toward Langdale and tucked below the road, rooms here enjoy beach access and wonderful views of Shoal Channel.

Ritz Inn Motor Hotel (☎ *604-886-3343, 800-649-1138, fax 604-886-8189,* e *ritz_inn@ dccnet.com, 505 Gower Point Rd)* Singles/doubles C\$75/85. Each room here has kitchen facilities, but you'll be charged an extra C\$8 if you want to use the kitchen to cook your own meals.

You'll find a good variety of restaurants in Gibsons.

Molly's Reach (☎ *604-886-9710)* Breakfast C\$3-8, lunch C\$6-8, dinner C\$8-20. At the intersection of Marine Dr and Gower Point Rd, popular Molly's features harbor views and lots of *Beachcombers* memorabilia.

Gibsons Fish Market (☎ *604-886-8363, 292 Gower Point Rd)* Entrees C\$5-10. You can buy fresh seafood right off the dock, or visit this salty restaurant, where you can sit at tables to enjoy fish and chips.

The Flying Cow (☎ *604-886-0301, 451 Marine Dr)* Entrees C\$6-10. This makes a good vegetarian choice, with yummy soups (about C\$4) and omelets (C\$7 to C\$8).

ROBERTS CREEK

During the Vietnam War era of the late 1960s and early '70s, many US residents opposed to the conflict headed north to Canada. Quite a few settled in the Roberts Creek area, 7km (4 miles) northwest of Gibsons, and the area retains a strong counterculture feel.

Roberts Creek Rd, off Hwy 101, leads to the anti-commercial center of town, where you'll find a post office, general store, library and several shops and restaurants. But the

BRITISH COLUMBIA

true heart of Roberts Creek (population 2500) is probably its community hall, which frequently hosts concerts, dances and lectures. Check the placards around town to see what's playing.

Roberts Creek has a couple of good camping options and a great retreat-style hostel that delights travelers on any budget.

Head for **Roberts Creek Provincial Park**, just west of town off Hwy 101, for camping or a day at the beach.

Roberts Creek Provincial Park *(☎ 604-898-3678)* Tent sites C$12. This campground has 25 campsites available May through September.

Moon Cradle Backpackers Retreat *(☎ 604-885-0238, 877-350-5862, fax 604-885-6640, e mooncradle@uniserve.com, 3125 Sunshine Coast Hwy)* Dorm beds C$19/23 without/with breakfast, private rooms singles/doubles C$35/45 (members) or C$50/60 (nonmembers). This is the only hostel on the lower Sunshine Coast, and it's a good one. Innkeepers Shaeah Fialkow and Richard Biel, both dedicated environmentalists, have created a welcoming home in the woods. Amenities include a free all-organic continental breakfast, shoulder massage, kitchen access (vegetarian food only) and drum circles and bonfires in summer.

SECHELT

The second-largest town on the Sunshine Coast, Sechelt (**see**-shelt; population 8000) enjoys a waterside setting on a narrow isthmus amid several bays. Parks and beaches abound. This area has long been an important stronghold of the Coast Salish people; in 1986, the Sechelt Band became the first in modern Canada to attain self-government.

Sechelt's downtown area is centered around the intersection of Hwy 101 and Wharf Ave. From here, if you're coming from Roberts Creek, turn right for Porpoise Bay or left for Halfmoon Bay and the Earls Cove ferry.

The Sechelt & District Chamber of Commerce (☎ 604-885-0662) operates a Visitor Info Centre in the Trail Bay Mall, 5755 Cowrie St. The post office (☎ 604-885-2411) is at the corner of Dolphin and Inlet Sts. The Daily Roast coffee shop (☎ 604-885-4345), 5547 Wharf St, offers free email access for patrons. Sechelt Coin Laundry (☎ 604-885-3393), 5660 Dolphin St, is open until 6pm Monday to Saturday; closed Sunday.

With a good kayak launch and a sandy beach, **Porpoise Bay Provincial Park**, northeast of downtown, makes an ideal base camp for paddlers and cyclists exploring the Sunshine Coast. Ask at the Info Centre for cycling, kayaking and diving outfitters.

The Sechelt First Nations band has its headquarters at the **House of Hewhiwus** *(☎ 604-885-8991)*, on the south end of town. This impressive complex includes a theater, a museum and gift shop. Admission to the museum is by donation.

The **Sunshine Coast Arts Centre** *(☎ 604-885-5412)*, at the corner of Trail Ave and Medusa St, displays art in its gallery and holds cultural events in its performance space. Sechelt also hosts the Festival of the Written Arts (☎ 604-885-9631), a major Canadian literary gathering held each August at the Rockwood Centre on Cowrie St.

Ask at the Visitor Info Centre for a list of Sechelt's numerous B&Bs, where rooms cost C$90 to C$120. The following are some other options:

Porpoise Bay Provincial Park *(☎ 604-898-3678, 4km north of Sechelt)* Tent sites C$18.50. This campground features a separate area set aside for hikers and cyclists (C$10), along with regular sites. From July through September, you can reserve a spot by calling ☎ 800-689-9025 (in Greater Vancouver ☎ 604-689-9025).

Driftwood Inn *(☎ 604-885-5811, fax 885-5836, e driftwood-inn@sunshine.net, 5454 Trail Ave)* Singles/doubles C$79/89. Location is key at this inn on the waterfront downtown.

Bella Beach Inn *(☎ 604-885-7191, 800-665-1925, fax 604-885-3794, 4748 Hwy 101)* Singles/doubles C$79/89. At Davis Bay, each room here comes with an ocean view and outside deck.

You'll find three of Sechelt's very best restaurants in a downtown plaza at 5530 Wharf Ave.

Wild Flour Bakery (☎ *604-740-9998*) Stop by for decadent baked goods made with fresh ingredients.

Sun Fish Café (☎ *604-885-0237*) Salads & sandwiches C$7, entrees C$9-17. This bright, friendly restaurant serves up full breakfasts, light lunches and good steaks, as well as seafood and vegetarian dinners.

Old Boot Eatery (☎ *604-885-2727*) Entrees C$9-18. The Old Boot features a wide menu of pasta, pizza, seafood and steaks.

The Wharf (☎ *604-885-7285, 4748 Hwy 101*) Dinner from 5pm daily, open Fri-Wed. Located at the Bella Beach Inn, The Wharf offers both Japanese and Canadian food.

Pebbles (☎ *604-885-5811, 5454 Trail Ave*) Lunch C$4-9, dinner C$15-24. In the Driftwood Inn, this spot features a wide menu with seafood specialties.

POWELL RIVER

Powell River is an industrial mill town anchoring the top of the Sunshine Coast. Most travelers pass through quickly on a circle tour of the Sunshine Coast and Vancouver Island, but those who linger will find low-cost amenities and a good array of recreational opportunities.

Powell River (population 14,000) lies 31km (19 miles) north of the Saltery Bay ferry terminal. Hwy 101 becomes Marine Ave through downtown. The Townsite area north of downtown is home to the huge Pacific Paper mill. From there, Hwy 101 continues until Lund, 23km (14 miles) north.

The Powell River Visitor Info Centre (☎ 604-485-4701), 4690 Marine Ave, stays open year-round. You'll find the post office (☎ 604-485-5552) at 4812 Joyce Ave; there's also a postal services counter, plus ATMs and a grocery store, in the Town Centre Mall, 7100 Alberni St (enter on Joyce Ave). Access email at Armourtech (☎ 604-485-6423), 4717 Marine Ave, or at the Powell River Public Library (☎ 604-485-4796), 4411 Michigan Ave.

You can do laundry at Atwater Laundromat (☎ 604-485-2023), 4454 Willingdon Ave. For medical emergencies, go to Powell River General Hospital (☎ 604-485-3211), 5000 Joyce Ave.

Things to See & Do

Willingdon Beach, west of downtown, is a pleasant place to pass time. Across Willingdon Ave from the beach is the **Powell River Museum** (☎ *604-485-2222; open 9am-5pm daily June-Aug, weekdays only Sept-May*). The museum contains a replica of a shack once occupied by Billy Goat Smith, a hermit who lived (with his goats) in the area in the early 20th century.

If you're looking for maximum adventure, check out the 180km (112 mile) **Sunshine Coast Trail** from Sarah Point (near the town of Lund) to Saltery Bay (31km;19 miles south of Powell River). Hiking the entire trail takes about 12 days and locals recommend you start at the Sarah Point end (which is only accessible by boat). The trail branches out into 27 shorter trails; all are shown on the excellent Powell River Visitor Map (C$2), available at the Visitor Info Centre. The same map details the 57km (35 mile) Powell Forest Canoe Route, which connects 12 lakes via easily portaged trails.

For information on the ample **scuba diving** around Powell River, contact **Don's Dive Shop** (☎ *604-485-6969, 6789 Wharf St*), which leads guided dives and rents gear. **Taw's Cycle & Sports** (☎ *604-485-2555, 4597 Marine Ave*) rents bikes and offers sound advice on local **mountain biking**, camping and hiking. **Powell River Sea Kayak** (☎ *604-485-2144, 6812E Alberni Place*) rents boats and leads a range of **kayaking** tours, from two-hour paddles to multi-day trips, into Desolation Sound.

Places to Stay

Willingdon Beach Campsite (☎ *604-485-2242, 4845 Marine Ave*) Tent sites C$15. Facilities here include showers, laundry and 82 campsites.

Old Courthouse Inn & Hostel (☎ *604-483-4000, 6243 Walnut St*) Dorm beds C$17, shared-bath singles/doubles C$30/40, private-bath C$40/50. The rate includes linens and towels and kitchen access – though there's also a great little cafe on the ground floor. Ask about low-cost pick-ups from the bus or ferry.

Inn at Westview (☎ *604-485-6281, fax 485-2622,* e *theinnatwestview@prcn.org,*

BRITISH COLUMBIA

7050 Alberni St) Singles/doubles C$58/62. Rooms here are basic but come with balconies.

Beacon Bed & Breakfast (☎ *604-485-5563, 877-485-5563, fax 604-485-9450,* e *beacon@aisl.bc.ca, 3750 Marine Ave)* Rooms C$80-140. South of town toward Saltery Bay, this B&B features a waterfront setting and on-site massage therapy.

Coast Town Centre Hotel (☎ *604-485-3000, 800-663-1144, fax 604-485-3031, 4660 Joyce Ave)* Rooms C$99/109. This hotel boasts an exercise room and outdoor hot tub.

Powell Lake is popular for houseboating. Houseboats come equipped with a kitchen (you bring your own food) and bunks that can sleep six people or more. Plan to spend about C$700 (three-day stays) or C$1000 (a week) for a cruiser. Outfitters include **Papa Bear's Vacations** (☎ *604-483-8224, fax 853-3135)* and **Sunquest Houseboat Rentals** (☎ *604-485-4043)*.

Places to Eat

Small Planet Whole Foods (☎ *604-485-9134, 4449 Marine Ave)* This vegetarian deli/cafe offers sandwiches (C$4 to C$5) and desserts (C$1 to C$3).

Captain Billy's Old Fashioned Fish and Chips (☎ *604-485-2252)* Open Apr-Sept. Billy's has been dishing out the fish (C$6.45 for two pieces) near the ferry terminal for more than 25 years.

Little Tea Pot Euro Café (☎ *604-485-5955 Willingdon Ave)* Lunch C$7-9. This funky cafe serves homemade soups (about C$4) and lunch specialties and hosts Sunday-afternoon poetry readings.

Shinglemill Pub (☎ *604-483-2001, 6233 Powell Place)* Entrees C$7-15. This pub serves moderately priced bistro-type food accompanied by great views.

LUND & AROUND

Lund, located at the northern end of Hwy 101, serves as a staging point for trips to **Desolation Sound** and tropical **Savary Island**. Desolation Sound got its name from Captain George Vancouver, who thought the region's seascapes seemed remote and forbidding. With its many sheltered bays, 8256-hectare (20,401-acre) Desolation Sound Provincial Marine Park offers lots of boating, fishing, kayaking and diving opportunities.

Sometimes called 'the Hawaii of the North,' Savary Island features sandy beaches galore and a few visitor accommodations (although most cottages are private retreats). For more information, visit the website w www.savary.bc.ca. For access to the island, call Lund Water Taxi (☎ 604-483-9749), which charges C$6.50/13 one way/roundtrip from Powell River (half-price for children six and under).

Eagle Adventures (☎ *604-483-4033)* offers guided tours to Savary Island and the Copeland Islands, as well as bike, kayak and canoe rentals. **Pristine Charters** (☎ *604-483-4541)* does fishing trips and dining cruises.

The following are some places to stay:

Cedar Lodge B&B Resort (☎ *604-483-4414, 9825 Malaspina Rd)* Standard rooms/suites from C$55/75. This is a good value, with nice European-style pension rooms.

Lund Hotel (☎ *604-414-0474, 1436 Hwy 101)* facing town/waterfront. C$119/129. This hotel was recently refurbished (it reopened in summer 2000).

Desolation Resort (☎ *604-483-3592, fax 483-7942,* e *desolres @prcn.org, 2694 Dawson Rd)* Chalets from C$140. This resort features cedar chalets right on Okeover Inlet. The chalets range in size and price, so call ahead to find out your options.

Vancouver Island

The largest island off the west coast of the Americas, Vancouver Island stretches 450km (279 miles) and has become home to more than 500,000 people, most of whom live along the southeast coast. A mountain range runs down the center of the island, its snowcapped peaks framing forests, lakes and streams. The coastline is rocky and tempestuous in some places, sandy and calm in others. It rains only about 64cm

OTHER MAPS
Vancouver Island
page 678

Southern
Gulf Islands
page 707

Victoria
pages 680-681

Highlights

- Sipping high tea at the Empress and strolling along Victoria's Inner Harbour
- Storm-, wildlife- and whale-watching near Tofino
- Marveling at some of Canada's biggest trees
- Kayaking around one of the Southern Gulf Islands

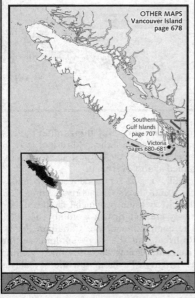

(25 inches) a year in Victoria, but it rains 762cm (300 inches) a year in Port Alberni, just 75km (47 miles) due north. Overall, however, the island enjoys the mildest climate in Canada.

For years, Vancouver Island has been dependent on its natural resources. But in the 1990s, amid falling lumber prices and depleted fishing stocks, many small communities lost much of their livelihood. Towns have had to find ways to adapt, with mixed success. Tourism has proven to be the salvation for many communities, but other areas, surrounded by clear-cuts, have less success luring visitors.

Vancouver Island is a popular destination, and Victoria in particular draws crowds in midsummer, but the island is also a major haven for 'snowbirds,' who travel here in winter to escape colder climes. You can save money and avoid the heaviest crowds by traveling in spring and fall, which are also quite pleasant.

VICTORIA

Victoria, British Columbia's provincial capital, lies at the southeast end of Vancouver Island, 67km (42 miles) southwest of Vancouver. Although bounded on three sides by water, it is sheltered from the Pacific Ocean by the Olympic Peninsula, across the Strait of Juan de Fuca, in Washington State.

Despite its reputation as a genteel city of Anglophiles, Victoria (population 318,000) has attracted a broad range of international settlers who have brought their own cuisine and customs and created a city that is cosmopolitan in its own unique way. Plenty of travelers come to Victoria for its heavily publicized major attractions: the Butchart Gardens, high tea at the Empress, shopping on Government St. But many others use Victoria as a springboard for outdoor adventures, including kayaking the Inner Harbour or hiking the West Coast Trail, a few hours farther afield.

BRITISH COLUMBIA

BRITISH COLUMBIA

VANCOUVER ISLAND

History

James Douglas, a fur trader who later became the governor of Vancouver Island, was dispatched by the Hudson's Bay Company to find a suitable location that could replace Fort Vancouver along the Columbia River, an area that was being overrun with American pioneers who were bent on settling the Oregon territory. In 1842, Douglas strode off the SS *Beaver* at Clover Point, crossed present-day Beacon Hill Park and chose a fort site at what is now Bastion Square, in the heart of present-day Victoria. (Fort Victoria was erected the

following year.) But things didn't really start hopping until the gold rush of 1857; as miners stormed the outpost, the town blossomed almost overnight.

Still, Victoria remained a scruffy, muddy place until the 1860s. Incorporated in 1862, the city became provincial capital of the newly created British Columbia in 1868. The completion of the Canadian Pacific Railroad and the city's sublime setting (Rudyard Kipling once described Victoria as 'Brighton Pavilion with the Himalayas for a backdrop') ensured Victoria's future popularity.

Orientation

The Inner Harbour is Victoria's focal point, surrounded by the Empress Hotel, Parliament Buildings and the Royal British Columbia Museum. From the Inner Harbour, Wharf St leads north to Bastion Square. Two blocks east, Government St attracts lots of tourists.

One block east of Government St, Douglas St is downtown's north-south thoroughfare. Fort St, a one-way street heading east, is another major artery. Following Fort St east up the hill and then along Oak Bay Ave will lead you through the 'tweed curtain' to the wealthier, very British area of Oak Bay, about 3km (2 miles) from downtown.

Both Douglas and Blanshard Sts lead north out of the city – the former to the Trans-Canada Hwy (Hwy 1) and Nanaimo; the latter to the Patricia Bay Hwy (also known as the Pat Bay Hwy and Hwy 17), Sidney and the BC Ferries terminal at Swartz Bay. Hwy 17 also is the route to Butchart Gardens, about 21km (13 miles) north of Victoria. Hwy 1A is an alternate route (via Gorge and Craigflower Rds) to either the Trans-Canada Hwy or Hwy 14, the road to Sooke and Port Renfrew.

The *Official Victoria Free Map* includes discounts to local attractions. AAA/CAA and MapArt both publish good street maps. BC Transit's free *Explore Victoria by Bus* leaflet tells you how to get to attractions by public transportation.

Information

Tourist Offices Near the water at the Inner Harbour, the Visitor Info Centre (☎ 250-953-2033, fax 382-6539, Ⓦ www.tourismvictoria.com), 812 Wharf St, is open 8:30am to 7:30pm June 15 through September 30; 9am to 5pm the rest of the year.

Money ATMs are everywhere, including at major bank branches along Douglas St. For money exchange, try Custom House Currency Exchange (☎ 250-389-6007); its six locations include 815 Wharf St, across from the Visitor Info Centre; the BC Ferries terminal at Swartz Bay; and Victoria International Airport.

You can also change money at American Express (☎ 250-385-8731), 1203 Douglas St. Many downtown businesses accept US and even other foreign currency, but the exchange rate is not usually as favorable as the exchange rate you can get via an ATM withdrawal.

Post & Communications You'll find the main post office (☎ 250-953-1352) at 714 Yates St, between Blanshard and Douglas Sts. Cyber Station of Victoria (☎ 250-386-4687), 1113 Blanshard St, provides Internet access for C$10 per hour; it's open until 10pm Monday to Saturday.

Media The *Times Colonist* is the daily newspaper. The weekly *Monday Magazine* features arts and entertainment news. Tune your radio dial to 90.5 FM for the CBC. Other popular area radio stations include 'The Q' at 100.3 FM and 'The Ocean' at 98.5 FM.

Travel Agencies Travel Cuts has two Victoria locations: downtown at 634 Johnson St (☎ 250-995-8556) and in the University of Victoria student union (☎ 250-721-8634).

Bookstores & Libraries Munro's Books (☎ 250-382-2464), 1108 Government St, is a longstanding independent bookseller and a great place to browse. The local outpost of the megachain Chapters (☎ 250-380-9009), 1212 Douglas St, is open 9am to 11pm daily. Wells Books (☎ 250-360-2929), 824 Fort St, specializes in nautical fare.

You'll find the main branch of the Greater Victoria Public Library (☎ 250-382-7241) at 735 Broughton St.

Universities In the city's northeast section, the University of Victoria campus can be reached via a 20-minute ride from downtown on bus No 14.

Laundry A small coin-op laundry with showers sits right under the main Visitor Info Centre, on the waterfront level. The Laundry (☎ 250-598-7977), 1769 Fort St, also has Internet terminals. A bit closer to

BRITISH COLUMBIA

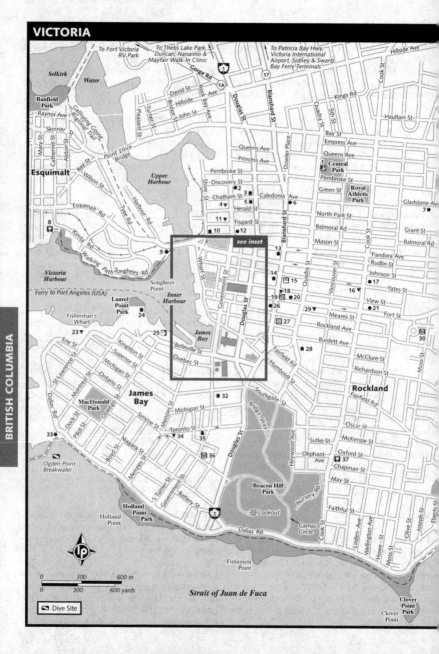

VICTORIA

To Fort Victoria RV Park

To Thetis Lake Park, Duncan, Nanaimo & Mayfair Walk-In Clinic

To Patricia Bay Hwy, Victoria International Airport, Sidney & Swartz Bay Ferry Terminals

Gorge Rd

Hillside Ave

Cook St

Selkirk Water

Banfield Park

Raynor Ave

David St

Hillside

1A

17

Bridge St

John St

Kings Rd

Skinner

Mary St

Catherine St

Alston St

Pleasant St

Turner St

Bay St

Rock Bay Ave

Douglas St

Blanshard St

Government St

5th St

Haultain St

Galloping Goose Regional Trail

Point Ellice Bridge

Bay St

Empress Ave

Esquimalt

Wilson St

Bay St

Queens Ave

Princess Ave

Queens Ave

Central Park

1

Esquimalt Rd

Harbour Rd

Tree Rd

Upper Harbour

Pembroke St

Discovery St

2

Pembroke St

Green St

Royal Athletic Park

Store St

Chatham St

3

Caledonia Ave

Gladstone Ave

Kimta Rd

8

4

5

6

7

Herald St

North Park St

Grant St

9

11

Fisgard St

Balmoral Rd

Balmoral Rd

Walking Path

Songhees Rd

10

12

see inset

Quadra St

Cook St

Mason St

Pandora Ave

Victoria Harbour

Songhees Point

13

Rudlin St

Johnson St

Ferry to Port Angeles (USA)

Inner Harbour

14

15

Blanshard St

Vancouver St

16

17

Yates St

Laurel Point Park

24

Wharf St

Government St

19

18

20

26

29

View St

21

Fort St

Fisherman's Wharf

25

James Bay

Belleville St

Douglas St

27

Meares St

Rockland Ave

23

Kingston St

Superior St

Quebec St

Burdett Ave

28

30

Erie St

Michigan St

Fairfield Rd

McClure St

Moss St

St Lawrence St

Montreal St

Ontario St

Humboldt St

Richardson St

Rockland

Dallas Rd

MacDonald Park

Oswego St

James Bay

Simcoe St

Menzies St

Michigan St

32

Southgate St

Bridge Way

Fairfield Rd

33

Dock St

Pilot St

Boyd St

Niagara St

Toronto St

34

35

Heywood Ave

Oscar St

McKenzie St

Ogden Point Breakwater

Mentes St

S Turtle St

Government St

Battery St

36

Douglas St

Sutlej St

Oliphant Ave

Oxford St

Chapman St

Holland Point Park

Holland Point

Beacon Hill Park

Lookout

Nursery Rd

May St

Cook St

Faithful St

Linden Ave

Wellington Ave

Howe St

Olive St

Joseph St

Eberts St

1

Dallas Rd

Camas Circle

Finlayson Point

LP

0   300   600 m

0   300   600 yards

Dive Site

Strait of Juan de Fuca

Clover Point Park

Clover Point

BRITISH COLUMBIA

VICTORIA

PLACES TO STAY
3 Paul's Motor Inn
5 Traveller's Inn
9 Ocean Pointe Resort;
   Seacoast Expeditions
10 Swans Hotel; Swans
   Brewpub
13 Ocean Island Backpackers
   Inn
14 Dominion Hotel
22 Craigmyle Guest House
24 Laurel Point Inn
28 Abigail's Hotel
32 Birdcage Walk Guest House
35 James Bay Inn
45 HI Victoria Hostel
67 Strathcona Hotel; Sticky
   Wicket Pub; Legends
85 Crystal Court Motel

PLACES TO EAT
4 Herald St Café
11 Don Mee Seafood
   Restaurant
16 Pluto's Mesquite Diner

18 Baan Thai
23 Barb's Place
29 Blue Fox Café
34 The Bent Mast
40 Green Cuisine
42 John's Place
43 Chandler's Seafood
   Restaurant
44 Il Terrazo
49 Wharfside Eatery
50 Suze Lounge & Restaurant
52 Re-Bar
54 Growlie's
59 Camille's Fine Westcoast
   Dining
60 Koto Japanese Restaurant
63 Pagliacci's
72 Sam's Deli
75 Milestone's

OTHER
1 Crystal Pool & Fitness
   Centre
2 Sports Rent
6 Frank White's Scuba Shop

7 Belfry Playhouse
8 Spinnakers Brewpub &
   Restaurant
12 McPherson Playhouse
15 Famous Players Capitol 6
17 Maytag Homestyle Laundry
19 Cyber Station of Victoria
20 Wells Books
21 BC Ferries Information
   Office
25 Inner Harbour Ferry
   Terminal
26 Mocambo Coffee
27 Royal Theatre
30 Art Gallery of Greater
   Victoria
31 Craigdarroch Castle
33 Ogden Point Dive Centre
36 Carr House
37 Flying Beagle Pub
38 E&N Railiner Station
39 Ocean River Sports
41 Travel CUTS
46 Steamers Public House
47 Main Post Office
48 Odeon Theatre
51 Maritime Museum
53 Sasquatch Trading
   Company
55 Chapters
56 American Express
57 Cuda Marine Adventures
58 Victoria Bug Zoo
61 Munro's Books
62 Hermann's Jazz Club
64 Avis
65 SpringTide Whale
   Watching Tours; British
   Colony Adventures
66 Rogers' Chocolates
68 Greater Victoria Public
   Library
69 Custom House Currency
   Exchange
70 Harbour Rentals
71 Canadian Impressions
73 Vic Theatre
74 Visitor Info Centre; Prince
   of Whales
76 Royal London Wax Museum
77 Pacific Undersea Gardens
78 Victoria Harbour Ferry
79 Bus Station
80 National/Tilden
81 Budget
82 Parliament Buildings
83 Royal British Columbia
   Museum
84 Thunderbird Park

BRITISH COLUMBIA

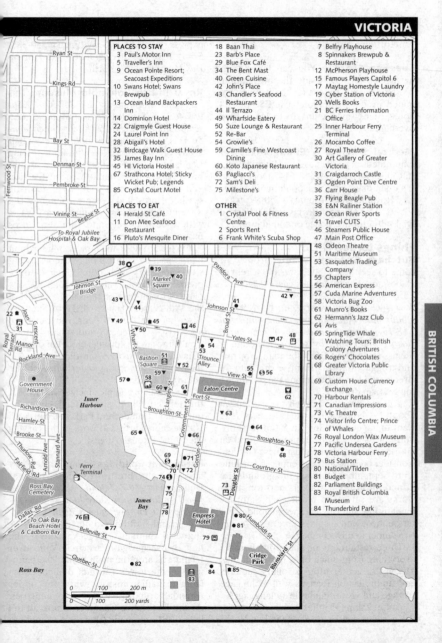

downtown, the Maytag Homestyle Laundry (☎ 250-386-1799), 1309 Cook St, is open 7am to 10pm daily.

Luggage Storage You can leave your luggage in lockers beside the bus station, 700 Douglas St. Tokens for the lockers, obtained inside the station, cost C$2 per 24 hours. Signs say it's unsafe to leave bags overnight.

Medical Services & Emergencies For minor medical needs, head to Mayfair Walk-In Clinic (☎ 250-383-9898), 3147 Douglas St. It's open daily, with no appointment necessary. Royal Jubilee Hospital (☎ 250-595-9200, 595-9212 for emergencies) is at 1900 Fort St. Dial ☎ 911 for fire, police or ambulance.

Things to See & Do

Butchart Gardens Visitors from afar come to see these 20 hectares (49 acres) of elaborate, manicured gardens (☎ 250-652-5256, 866-652-4422, 800 Benvenuto Ave, W www.butchartgardens.com; C$18/9.25/2 adult/youth/child mid-June–Oct, admission C$8-13 rest of the year; open 9am daily, closing times vary by season). Though it seems ironic given BC's abundance of raw and rugged natural beauty, this site in Brentwood Bay ranks among the province's top tourism draws.

You can wander through the gardens in about 1½ hours, but avid gardeners may want to linger much longer. If time is short, don't miss the truly impressive Sunken Gardens and the peaceful Japanese Garden. Consider coming in the evenings from June 15 to September 15, when the grounds are lit and musical entertainers perform. Fireworks are set off to music each Saturday night in July and August. Special holiday entertainment and displays take place every November and December.

Three restaurants on the grounds serve everything from quick bites to fine cuisine. The visitor center offers strollers, cameras and umbrellas on loan, as well as luggage storage and visitor guides in 19 languages.

About 21km (13 miles) north of Victoria, the gardens can be reached via bus No 75 from downtown Victoria, though it's a slow trek. Better to take the C$4.25 one-way express shuttle from Gray Line (☎ 250-388-5248). If you're driving, follow the Patricia Bay Hwy (Hwy 17) north.

Royal British Columbia Museum This acclaimed museum (☎ 250-387-3701, 250-953-4629, 675 Belleville St; C$9 adult, C$6 senior, student & child 6-18 years; open 9am-5pm) is well worth a few hours or even half a day of your time. The 2nd-floor 'Living Land, Living Sea' gallery includes an impressive woolly-mammoth reconstruction and a walk-through exhibit of realistic seashore, forest and river environments. The 'Open Ocean' mimics an undersea voyage, with special effects and film sequences based on actual deep-sea dives.

On the 3rd floor, the First Peoples exhibit hall is packed with carvings, canoes, beadwork, basketry and more. Hushed tones prevail as visitors wander through the displays of totem-pole sections and a model of the 19th-century Haida village of Skedans. Elsewhere on the 3rd floor, you can learn about BC's European and Asian history. You'll find a walk-through model of Captain Vancouver's *Discovery,* an old-time movie theater and a working water wheel in the gold-rush exhibit.

The museum complex includes an IMAX theater, gift shop and cafe. Beside the museum in Thunderbird Park, you can catch Native Indian artists at work in the carving shed June through August.

Parliament Buildings Francis Rattenbury designed the multiturreted Parliament Buildings (☎ 250-387-3046, 501 Belleville St; free 35-minute tours daily June-Sept, weekends only Oct-May; open 8:30am-5:30pm). The grand buildings date from 1898. A statue of Captain George Vancouver, the first British navigator to circle Vancouver Island, sits atop the main dome. The paintings in the lower rotunda depict scenes from Canadian history, while the upper rotunda's art portrays BC's main industries. At the Legislative Chamber, where all the laws of BC are made (there is no Senate in the provincial parliament), you can view the debates from the public gallery when the legislature is in session, the schedule of which varies from year to year. The buildings are spectacular at night, thanks to the glow of more than 3000 lightbulbs.

Pacific Undersea Gardens This popular attraction (*☎ 250-382-5717, 490 Belleville St; C$7.50/6.50/5/3.50 adult/senior/youth/child; open 10am-7pm July & Aug, 10am-5pm Sept-June*) is a sort of natural aquarium. Descend beneath the water's surface to gaze through windows at sea creatures and human divers who interact with them.

Royal London Wax Museum This wax museum (*☎ 250-388-4461, 470 Belleville St; C$8.50/7.50/6.50/4 adult/senior/student/child; open 9:30am-5pm Jan–mid-May, 9am-7:30pm mid-May–Aug, 9:30am-6pm Sept-Dec*) contains more than 300 wax models of historical and contemporary figures.

Bastion Square On the site of old Fort Victoria, between Government and Wharf Sts, Bastion Square once held the courthouse, jail, gallows and a brothel, but the square's old buildings have since become restaurants, nightclubs, boutiques, galleries and offices. You can purchase handcrafted local wares at the ongoing **Bastion Square Festival of the Arts**, held Wednesday to Sunday June through September and Thursday through Sunday in April and May.

The **Maritime Museum** (*☎ 250-385-4222, 28 Bastion Square; C$6/5/3/2 adult/senior/student/child; open 9:30am-4:30pm*) explores all aspects of Vancouver Island's seafaring past and present. Housed in an 1889 building that once served as BC's first provincial law courts, the museum features more than 400 ship models dating back to 1810.

Victoria Bug Zoo Anyone fascinated by creepy crawlers will love this place (*☎ 250-384-2847, 1107 Wharf St; C$6/5/4 adult/senior & student/child; open 9:30am-5:30pm Mon-Sat, 11am-5:30pm Sun*). Even people who loathe bugs may come away with a new appreciation of all kinds of insects, from giant desert hairy scorpions to perpetually pregnant Australian stick insects. You'll see several dozen of the world's most unusual insects and spiders living in a series of Plexiglas tubes. If looking isn't enough, you can touch and even hold many of them! Informative guides tell how the bugs eat, mate, give birth and more.

Chinatown Set on the northern edge of downtown, Victoria's small Chinatown is the oldest in Canada. A selection of mostly inexpensive restaurants and authentic Asian markets line Fisgard St, the main thoroughfare. Look for Fan Tan Alley, supposedly the narrowest passageway in the world. Set between Fisgard St and Pandora Ave, the alley was a good spot to buy opium in the early 19th century. Today, you can visit little shops tucked in the alley's nooks.

Fisherman's Wharf Just west of the Inner Harbour, Fisherman's Wharf bustles with fishing boats and pleasure craft coming and going. Buy fresh seafood from the boats, or stop by Barb's Place for fish and chips (see Places to Eat, later in this section).

Starting from Fisherman's Wharf, the **scenic marine drive** skirts the coast along Dallas Rd and Beach Dr. You'll see several parks and beaches along the way. The Gray Line double-decker bus includes Marine Dr in its tour (see Organized Tours, later in this section). You can also begin the drive at Beacon Hill Park.

Beacon Hill Park South of downtown via Douglas St, this 61-hectare park offers an oasis of trees, gardens, ponds, pathways and playing fields. A tall totem pole here is among the world's highest; you'll also find a 100-year-old cricket pitch, a wildfowl sanctuary and a children's petting zoo. The southern edge overlooks the ocean. Look for a staircase down to the beach off the walking path across Dallas Rd. The park is an easy walk from downtown; you can also take bus No 5.

Carr House This birthplace of BC's best-known painter, Carr House (*☎ 250-383-5843,*

207 Government St; C\$5/4/3 adult/senior/child; open 10am-5pm late May–mid-Oct) features displays on Emily Carr's life and work, including some of her paintings (see the boxed text 'The Life & Work of Emily Carr').

Art Gallery of Greater Victoria About 1km (.62 miles) east of the downtown area, the art gallery *(☎ 250-384-4101, 1040 Moss St; C\$5/3 adult/senior & student; open 10am-5pm Mon-Sat (until 9pm Thur), 1pm-5pm Sun),* just off Fort St, features good collections of Asian art, pre-Columbian Latin American objects and contemporary Canadian paintings.

Craigdarroch Castle This opulent house *(☎ 250-592-5323, 1050 Joan Crescent; C\$8/5.50/2.50 adult/student/child; open 9am-7pm in summer, 10am-4:30pm the rest of the year)* was built in the mid-1880s by coal millionaire Robert Dunsmuir. It later served as a military hospital and college. Now completely restored, the castle boasts exquisite stained glass and a good view from the top floors. Be aware that you'll have to climb 87 steps to get to the top – there is no elevator. Incidentally, the street (Joan Crescent) was named for Dunsmuir's wife.

Victoria Butterfly Gardens Close to Butchart Gardens, this lesser-known attraction *(☎ 250-652-3822, 877-722-0272, 1461 Benvenuto Ave, Ⓦ www.butterflygardens .com; C\$8/7/4.50 adult/senior & student/child; open 9am-5pm Mar-Oct)* features more than 300 free-flying butterflies from 30 species.

Kayaking For canoe or kayak rental, try **Ocean River Sports** *(☎ 250-381-4233, 1437 Store St).* The company offers guided trips, locally and island-wide. Canoe or kayak rentals cost C\$14 per hour or C\$40 per day. **British Colony Adventures** *(☎ 250-216-5646, 950 Wharf St)* leads local guided tours starting at C\$55. **Sports Rent** *(☎ 250-385-7368, 611 Discovery St)* rents canoes and kayaks for about C\$30 per day, but you have to be able to transport them yourself.

Scuba Diving Good shore dives near Victoria include **Saxe Point Park**, off Esquimalt Rd; the **Ogden Point Breakwater**, just south of Beacon Hill Park off Dallas Rd; **10 Mile Point**, northeast of downtown near the University of Victoria on Cadboro Bay; and the entire **Saanich Inlet**, which contains Willis Point Park. **Race Rocks**, 18km (11 miles) southwest of Victoria Harbour, offers superb scenery both above and below the water. Diving charters and dive shops in Victoria provide equipment sales, service, rentals and instruction. Good resources include the downtown location of **Frank White's Scuba Shops** *(☎ 250-385-4713, 1855 Blanshard St)* and Ogden Point Dive Centre *(☎ 250-380-9119, Ⓦ www.divevictoria.com, 199 Dallas Rd).*

Swimming Crystal Pool & Fitness Centre *(☎ 250-361-0732),* 2275 Quadra St, contains a pool, sauna and whirlpool. **Thetis Lake Park**, off the Trans-Canada Hwy northwest of town (about a 20-minute drive), shelters pretty Thetis Lake, a great spot for a dip on a hot day.

Whale Watching About a dozen outfitters offer trips out into Georgia Strait to watch orcas (killer whales) and other marine wildlife. A three-hour excursion costs C\$75 to C\$85 for adults. For information and reservations, browse the brochures at the Visitor Info Centre. Outfitters include **Seacoast Expeditions** *(☎ 250-383-2254, 45 Songhees Rd),* at the Ocean Pointe Resort; **Prince of Whales** *(☎ 250-383-4884, 812 Wharf St),* just below the Info Centre; **Cuda Marine Adventures** *(☎ 250-995-2832),* on the Wharf St pier; and **SpringTide Whale Watching Tours** *(☎ 250-386-6016, 950 Wharf St).*

Windsurfing Board sailing is big in **Cadboro Bay**, near the university, and at **Willows Beach** in Oak Bay. To hop on board, contact **Excel Watersports** *(☎ 250-383-8667, 2001 Douglas St)* for local information.

Organized Tours
Gray Line (☎ 250-388-5248, 700 Douglas St) features many kinds of tours, including its

The Life & Work of Emily Carr

When Emily Carr died in 1945, only 50 mourners attended her funeral. These days, hundreds of people view her art each week at museums in Vancouver and Victoria – fitting vindication for a talent that was just barely recognized during her lifetime in British Columbia.

Carr was born in Victoria in 1871; both her parents died by the time she was 17. She yearned to attend art school in San Francisco, but instead, she became a teacher in early adulthood. It wasn't until 1899, when she accompanied a clergyman to his mission at Ucluelet, on Vancouver Island, that she found her spark as an artist. The Native Indian villages had a profound effect and, inspired by what she saw, Carr began using both the landscape and the Natives as subject matter. She soon realized, however, that she needed to learn technique, so she went to London to study landscape painting.

In 1906, after traveling to Europe, Toronto and the Cariboo region of BC, Carr moved to Vancouver to paint and teach art. She returned to Europe in 1910 for more study in Paris. It was during this time that Carr developed a unique style that combined the use of dark colors, undulating broad brush strokes and the subject matter of British Columbia's coastal forests and Native culture.

Returning to Vancouver in 1912, Carr rented a studio at 1465 W Broadway to exhibit her French paintings; she had another exhibit of 200 paintings in 1913. But her work wasn't taken seriously; some of her paintings were even deemed offensive, resulting in the withdrawal of students from her art classes. A social outcast at 42, she returned to Victoria, living on family property and working as a landlady to make ends meet.

It wasn't until the late 1920s that her scorned 1912 paintings were shown in eastern Canada and finally discovered. She then met the members of the increasingly well-known and influential school of painters called the Group of Seven, and with renewed energy and confidence continued to develop as an artist. Over the next 10 years, she revisited many of her cherished Indian locales and painted some of her most acclaimed art. She also succeeded in capturing the changing face of BC's forests. *Scorned As Timber, Beloved of the Sky* (1935) shows a few solitary trees amid stumps against a billowing background of clouds. *Logger's Culls,* from the same year, shows a field of stumps, but the eye is drawn mainly to the rippling blue sky and lofty clouds.

As Carr's health failed and she became bedridden, she took to writing. Her book *Klee Wyck,* meaning 'laughing one,' the name given to her by the Kwakiutl people, is a collection of stories recalling her life among the Native Indians. *The Book of Small* chronicles her childhood in Victoria, and *The House of All Sorts* describes her years as a landlady.

Her house in Victoria, the Carr House, is open to the public, and her paintings can be viewed at the Vancouver Art Gallery and the Art Gallery of Greater Victoria, as well as at other major museums across Canada.

basic 90-minute double-decker bus trip (C\$18/9 adult/child). ***Tally-Ho Sightseeing*** (☎ *250-383-5067*) offers tours in a large, horse-drawn wagon for C\$14/8.50/6 adult/student/child. If you want to rent an entire small carriage (which seats up to six), you'll pay C\$60 for 30 minutes, C\$85 for 45 minutes, C\$105 for an hour or C\$150 for 90 minutes. ***Victoria Carriage Tours*** (☎ *250-383-2207*) leads tours in horse-drawn carriages

On the Ale Trail

Oh-so-refined Victoria has earned a robust reputation as a serious beer-drinking town. The Victoria Ale Trail tour offers you a prime chance to visit brewpubs and microbreweries, learn about the brewing process, sample finished ales and lagers, and cap it all off with a gourmet dinner of inspired beer-and-food pairings.

The tour takes place one Saturday night per month and costs C$119 per person. Stops include the Harbour Canoe Club, Hugo's Grill & Brew Club, the Lighthouse Brewing Company, Spinnakers Brewpub, the Strathcona Hotel, Buckerfield's Brewery and Vancouver Island Brewery. Special lodging rates are available. For more information, contact First Island Destinations & Travel Ltd (☎ 250-658-5367, W www.firstislandtours.com).

that seat four at similar prices. Both carriage companies board at the corner of Belleville and Menzies Sts, near the Pacific Undersea Gardens.

Victoria Harbour Ferry (☎ 250-708-0201) offers a 45-minute tour for C$12/6 adult/child. Passengers can hop on and off as they like at regular stops such as Fisherman's Wharf and Spinnakers Brewpub.

Places to Stay

You'll have trouble finding reasonably priced rooms from mid-May through September. Make reservations as soon as you know your travel plans. ***Tourism Victoria's room-reservation service*** (☎ 800-663-3883) may be able to help.

Camping The best camping options are a bit of a drive from Victoria, but they're worth the effort.

Goldstream Provincial Park (☎ 250-391-2300, reservations ☎ 800-689-9025) Tent sites C$18.50. Just 19km (12 miles) north of Victoria, this park is a great stop and is considered the best place to camp near Victoria. Best known for its chum-salmon spawning

season (late October through December), there's also good fishing and hiking, along with human- and natural-history exhibits at the park's visitor center.

Thetis Lake Campground (☎ 250-478-3845, fax 478-6151, 1938 W Park Lane) Tent sites C$16. This campground is about a 20-minute drive northwest of the city center on Rural Route 6 off the Trans-Canada Hwy. You can shower and do your laundry, or take a dip in refreshing Thetis Lake. The campground is about 1.5km (1 mile) from the No 50 bus route.

Fort Victoria RV Park (☎ 250-479-8112, fax 479-5806, e info@fortvicrv.com, 340 Island Hwy) Tent/RV sites C$23/28. On Hwy 1A, this nonwoodsy, RV-oriented campground is the closest to town. Bus No 14 or 15 from downtown stops right at the gate.

Hostels Victoria is a hosteller's dream town, with accommodations to suit every age and taste. The only drawback is that places fill up fast in high season; reservations are essential in summer and advised year round.

Ocean Island Backpackers Inn (☎ 250-385-1785, 888-888-4180, fax 250-385-1780, W www.oceanisland.com, 791 Pandora Ave) Dorm rooms C$20 (C$16.75 with a hostel card or student ID), private singles/doubles C$59/69. Full of life and art, this big old building features about 155 beds and spacious kitchen facilities; amenities include Internet access and free morning coffee. Both the young and the young-at-heart will feel right at home.

HI Victoria Hostel (☎ 250-385-4511, 888-883-0099, fax 250-385-3232, e victoria@hihostels.bc.ca, 516 Yates St) Dorm beds C$17/20.50 members/nonmembers, private doubles C$38-45. In a convenient location near the Inner Harbour and all the major sights, the barracks-style dorm rooms fill up quickly in summer. Reservations are a must. In peak season, it's advisable to register before 4pm.

B&Bs Victoria is packed with B&Bs, with rates ranging from about C$50 to C$200. For help finding one, contact ***Victoria Vacationer***

B&B *(☎ 250-382-9469, postal address: 1143 Leonard St, Victoria, BC V8V 2S3)* or inquire at the Visitor Info Centre.

Birdcage Walk Guest House *(☎ 250-389-0804, 877-389-0804, fax 250-389-0348, 505 Government St)* Singles/doubles C$85-105/C$105-125. Convenient to the Inner Harbour, this lovely spot offers five guest rooms with private bathrooms in a historic home for C$100 to C$150. Each room also includes cooking facilities, and some are suitable for small families.

Craigmyle Guest House *(☎ 250-595-5411, 1037 Craigdarroch Rd,* e *craigmyle@home.com).* Singles/doubles C$65/80. This old English inn about 1km east of downtown next to Craigdarroch Castle has quaint rooms with private baths (though they're located across or down the hall). The full English breakfast includes eggs, toast, fruit and coffee.

Motels & Hotels You won't find any budget motels in downtown Victoria in the high season, but a few possibilities lie nearby. The Gorge Rd area, northwest of downtown, features several lower-cost motels, as does Douglas St heading north away from downtown. If you can afford to spend a little extra, the downtown area contains several moderately priced options. Most hotel rooms in Victoria top C$150 May through September, so you'll find the most choices in this category. The rates listed apply to the high season, with better deals abounding the rest of the year; many higher-priced places fall in the mid-range or even budget bracket from October through April.

Paul's Motor Inn *(☎ 250-382-9231, 1900 Douglas St)* Singles/doubles C$65. Walking distance from downtown, Paul's basic amenities include a 24-hour restaurant and free parking.

Crystal Court Motel *(☎ 250-384-0551, fax 384-5125,* e *mbscott@vanisle.net, 701 Belleville St)* Singles/doubles C$75/80. This no-frills motel is one of the best values in downtown Victoria and boasts a good location, across from the bus station.

Traveller's Inn *(☎ 250-381-1000, 1850 Douglas St,* w *www.travellersinn.com)*

Singles/doubles C$79/89. This chain operates six motels in Victoria, including this spot close to downtown at Caledonia Ave. Look for discount coupons, widely available on the ferries, at visitor centers and in the official BC Accommodations guide.

Strathcona Hotel *(☎ 250-383-7137, 800-663-7476, fax 250-383-6893,* e *lou@strathcona hotel.com, 919 Douglas St)* Singles/doubles C$89/99. The Strathcona bustles with several popular bars and a restaurant; ask for a room away from the action. Parking is C$4 per night.

James Bay Inn *(☎ 250-384-7151, 800-836-2649, fax 250-385-2311, 270 Government St)* Singles/doubles C$110/121. A few blocks from the Inner Harbour, this warm and well-kept older hotel is a favorite choice.

Dominion Hotel *(☎ 250-384-4136, 800-663-6101, fax 250-382-6416,* e *dominion@dominion-hotel.com, 759 Yates St)* Singles/doubles C$119/129 (plus C$5 per day for parking). Recently renovated, the Dominion offers charming rooms. The prices simply plummet mid-October through April, when a double room, three-course dinner and continental breakfast for two can cost as little as C$60.

Swans Hotel *(☎ 250-361-3310, 800-668-7926, fax 250-361-3491,* e *reservations@swanshotel.com, 506 Pandora Ave)* Studio suites from C$160, 1-bedroom suites C$180, 2-bedroom suites C$250. This gem of a downtown building right by the waterfront overlooks the Johnson St Bridge and boasts the always fun Swans Pub. Parking is C$8 per day.

Ocean Pointe Resort *(☎ 250-360-2999, 800-667-4677, 45 Songhees Rd)* Rooms C$185-305. Across the Inner Harbour from downtown and the Parliament Buildings, and with tremendous views of both, the Ocean Pointe combines luxury-class rooms with spa and sports facilities. Don't let its location away from downtown hinder you; the Victoria Harbour Ferry floats across the harbor throughout the day (see Getting Around, later in this section).

Oak Bay Beach Hotel *(☎ 250-598-4556, 800-668-7758, 1175 Beach Dr)* Rooms C$198-475. This seaside hotel, 5.6km (3½ miles) from downtown, is perched over excellent views of the beach and ocean. The hotel provides a summer shuttle service into the city center. Ask about the lunchtime boat cruises.

Laurel Point Inn (☎ 250-386-8721, 800-663-7667, e reservations@laurelpoint.com, 680 Montreal St) Rooms from C$190. This longtime Victoria hotel guards the entrance to the Inner Harbour. Amenities include saunas, an indoor pool, balconies and good views.

Abigail's Hotel (☎ 250-388-5363, 800-561-6565, e innkeepeer@abigailshotel.com, 906 McClure St) Rooms C$199-329. If you're looking for a romantic retreat, this Tudor-style mansion's 22 rooms are stocked with fresh flowers and goose-down duvets. Rooms include a three-course breakfast (served in your room, if you like) and evening hors d'oeuvres.

Empress Hotel (☎ 250-348-8111, 800-441-1414, 721 Government St). Rooms C$240-700. This incredible hotel, built in 1908 and surrounded by lovely gardens, is practically synonymous with Victoria. Its 477 rooms and 33 suites attract everyone from honeymooners and bus-tour groups to well-heeled travelers. Rates are all over the map, depending on season and demand. Cheaper rooms face the city; you pay a little extra for a harbor view. The Empress also houses three high-end restaurants: Kipling's, the Bengal Lounge and the formal Empress Room.

Places to Eat

Victoria is a great dining town, with everything from tea rooms and pubs to cutting-edge Pacific Rim cuisine. Prices vary widely, so it's easy to eat cheap at one meal and splurge at the next, if you desire.

Budget Victoria has plenty of options for a meal that's light on the wallet.

Growlie's (☎ 250-383-2654, 615 Yates St) Entrees C$6-10. Growlie's features 10 varieties of eggs Benedict with such toppings as spinach, chicken breast or back bacon.

John's Place (☎ 250-389-0799, 723 Pandora Ave) Breakfast & lunch C$7-10. This often-crowded spot is a favorite for breakfast and lunch.

Blue Fox Café (☎ 250-380-1683, 919 Fort St, No 101) Breakfast C$6-9. Locals argue the Blue Fox gets the top vote for breakfast, with a good menu, sunny staff and (sometimes) fewer crowds than John's.

Sam's Deli (☎ 250-382-8424, 805 Government St) Sandwiches C$6. Despite its proximity to the high-rent district (the Inner Harbour), Sam's offers reasonable prices, with sandwiches big enough for two.

Pluto's Mesquite Diner (☎ 250-385-4747, 1150 Cook St) Breakfast C$6-8, lunch & dinner C$7-11. A few blocks from downtown in a converted gas station, this funky joint serves breakfast until 2pm and a variety of burgers, quesadillas and Mexican platters for lunch and dinner.

Green Cuisine (☎ 250-385-1809, 560 Johnson St) On the courtyard level of Market Square, at the corner of Johnson and Store Sts, this good spot offers a delicious vegetarian buffet, with food priced by weight.

Don Mee Seafood Restaurant (☎ 250-383-1032, 538 Fisgard St) À la carte menu C$7-10. This is the best place in Chinatown for dim sum. The size of this giant restaurant means you rarely have to wait to be seated.

Barb's Place (☎ 250-384-6515, 310 St Lawrence St) Fish & chips C$7. If you're getting the British vibe and have a hankering for fish and chips, look for Barb's, housed in a shack on Fisherman's Wharf.

The Bent Mast (☎ 250-383-6000, 512 Simcoe St) Entrees C$10. While exploring the James Bay neighborhood, look for this neat little spot that's open late every night. Wash the good food down with some BC beers. The Bent Mast features live music most nights, starting at about 9:30pm.

Re-Bar (☎ 250-360-2401, 50 Bastion Square) Entrees C$7-12. Lunch daily, dinner Tues-Sat. With its eclectic international menu, juice bar and onsite bakery, this happening spot makes vegetarians salivate and jump for joy. The food here is simply delicious.

Mid-Range Check out one of the following places if you're feeling a little spendier.

Baan Thai (☎ 250-383-0050, 1117 Blanshard St) Entrees C$8-15. This is the best place in town for authentic Thai cuisine.

Suze Lounge & Restaurant (☎ 250-383-2829, 515 Yates St) Entrees C$10-20. This good spot for drinks and dinner features pizza, pasta and nightly specials of Pacific Northwest cuisine.

Pagliacci's (☎ 250-386-1662, 1011 Broad St) Entrees C$11-20. This wildly popular spot features a clever movie-theme menu, friendly staff and an always upbeat crowd. Live music acts play Sunday through Wednesday evenings.

Milestone's (☎ 250-381-2244, 812 Wharf St) Entrees C$12-18. Right on the harbor below the Visitor Info Centre, Milestone's features a good view of both the Parliament Buildings and the Inner Harbour, along with a good menu and casual atmosphere.

Wharfside Eatery (☎ 250-360-1808, 1208 Wharf St) Entrees C$12-25. The indoor–outdoor patio at the Wharfside makes it a popular spot, though the menu always seems a little pricier than it should be. You can get decent seafood here, along with pizza and burgers.

Top End If you're in for a bit of a splurge, one of these restaurants ought to do the trick.

Il Terrazzo (☎ 250-361-0028, 555 Johnson St) Lunch/dinner C$8-16/15-30. This fabulous place is known for its Italian pastas, grilled meats and tempting pizza. Grab a seat in the courtyard and you might feel you've been transported to Italy.

Herald St Café (☎ 250-381-1441, 546 Herald St) Lunch/dinner C$9-15/16-20. The recipe for success at this popular spot is the mix of elegance and casualness that's often missing at many top-end restaurants. The menu features delicious pastas, grilled meats and vegetarian dishes, great desserts and about 350 wine selections.

Chandler's Seafood Restaurant (☎ 250-385-3474, 1250 Wharf St) Lunch/dinner C$10-13/15-30. This well-established spot specializes in ocean fare, including the mouthwatering Victoria Seafood Platter (C$30).

Koto Japanese Restaurant (☎ 250-382-1514, 510 Fort St) Entrees C$16-26, sushi à la carte. This longtime local favorite features seafood dishes, sushi and a salad bar.

Tea Time, Victoria-Style

Nothing says Victoria like taking afternoon tea at the Empress Hotel (see Places to Stay), where mouthwatering scones, fresh berries in Devonshire cream and decadent pastries are all on the menu. Sittings take place four times daily. If you'd like to indulge, plan to reserve ahead by calling ☎ 250-384-8111 at least several days in advance during the busy season. You'll want to skip the rest of your meals that day, not just because you'll be stuffed, but because this experience doesn't come cheap: C$46 per person (C$23 for children four to 11 years).

Camille's Fine Westcoast Dining (☎ 250-381-3433, 45 Bastion Square) Entrees C$20-30. Dinner only. Camille's is among Victoria's most inventive restaurants. The menu combines seasonally changing Northwest ingredients with eclectic, international cuisine.

Entertainment

Pubs Sitting in a pub with a tasty local brew is a fine way to get a feel for the Anglophilia in Victoria.

Spinnakers Brewpub & Restaurant (☎ 250-386-2739, 308 Catherine St) Serving up some of the best beer in BC, Spinnaker's also has a great deck with views of the Inner Harbour. This pub is definitely worth the trip across the harbor.

Swans Brewpub (☎ 250-361-3310, 506 Pandora Ave) This fun, popular spot takes up half the main floor of Swans Hotel. Visit Thursday for Celtic music.

Sticky Wicket Pub (☎ 250-383-7137, 919 Douglas St) The Sticky Wicket, inside the Strathcona Hotel, offers an extensive selection of international beer on tap, as well as creative food, seating for families and a rooftop patio with beach volleyball courts.

Flying Beagle Pub (☎ 250-382-3301, 301 Cook St) Though a little farther from downtown, this neighborhood pub serves up good grub, accompanied by many beers on tap.

Coffeehouses Caffeine isn't the only stimulant at *Mocambo Coffee* (☎ 250-384-4468, *1028 Blanshard St)*, where philosophy discussions take place at 7pm Tuesdays and poets hold forth at 7:30pm Fridays.

Theater & Performing Arts There are several solid options for live performances.

McPherson Playhouse (☎ 250-386-6121, 3 *Centennial Square)* This is one of Victoria's biggest venues for theater and music shows.

Royal Theatre (☎ 250-386-6121, 805 *Broughton St)* The elegant Royal hosts a range of musical performances, including ballet, dance and concerts – many of which are performed by the resident Victoria Symphony (☎ 250-385-6515) and the Pacific Opera Victoria (☎ 250-386-6121).

Belfry (☎ 250-385-6815, 1291 Gladstone *Ave)*. Northeast of downtown, this small theater puts on great alternative theater.

Live Music Victoria boasts a musically creative community, which means you don't have to go far to hear live music. Check out the calendar in *Monday Magazine* to see what's happening when you visit.

Legends (☎ 250-383-7137, 919 Douglas *St)* This rockin' spot in the Strathcona Hotel features a wide spectrum of live music acts. The cover charge varies.

Steamers Public House (☎ 381-4340, 570 *Yates St)* Steamers is the place to see good local bands. The cover charge and atmosphere change nightly, depending on the band.

Hermann's Jazz Bar (☎ 250-388-9166, *753 View St)* This groovy venue attracts some excellent local and well-heeled jazz musicians. The lively but mellow atmosphere makes this a good place to hear live music and still have a conversation.

Cinemas Admission at commercial cinemas such as the *Famous Players Capitol 6* (☎ 250-384-6811, 805 Yates St) and the *Odeon Theatre* (☎ 250-383-0513, 780 Yates *St)* is typically about C$8 to C$9, reduced to C$5.25 on Tuesday.

Vic Theatre (☎ 250-383-1998, 808 Douglas *St)* This small theater screens classic movies on weekend afternoons for just C$1.

Cinecenta (☎ 250-721-8365) C$7/6/5 adult/student/senior & child; all seats C$4 for weekend matinees. This University of Victoria's movie house features recently released and classic independent films in the Student Union Building.

Shopping

On Government St, the main downtown shopping thoroughfare, an interesting mix of local and chain retailers compete for visitor dollars. Sure, you'll find a fair bit of English fluff and tourist knickknacks, but a few local shops are worthy of your attention.

Rogers' Chocolates (☎ 250-384-7021, 913 *Government St)* Anyone with a sweet tooth should head to this shop for its famously rich chocolate.

Canadian Impressions (☎ 250-383-2641, *811 Government St)* Come here for crafts by local First Nations people.

Sasquatch Trading Company (☎ 250-386-9033, 1233 Government St) This shop has a good selection of hand-knit Cowichan sweaters, unique to BC.

Eaton Centre (☎ 250-382-7141, Government St btwn Fort & View Sts) The mall can be fun to stroll around even if you aren't looking to spend money. The complex includes five floors and 100 shops, plus restaurants, fountains and a rooftop garden.

Getting There & Away

Air Victoria International Airport (YYJ) is in Sidney, about 26km (16 miles) north of the city off the Patricia Bay Hwy (Hwy 17). Air Canada (☎ 888-247-2262, ⓦ www.aircanada .ca) serves Victoria with daily service from Vancouver and Seattle; Horizon Air (☎ 800-547-9308, ⓦ www.horizonair.com) has regular service between Victoria and Seattle; North Vancouver Air (☎ 800-228-6608, ⓦ www.northvanair.com) has flights to Vancouver, Whistler, Tofino, Campbell River and Powell River; and WestJet Airlines (☎ 800-538-5696, ⓦ www.westjet.com) offers flights to Vancouver and other Western Canadian cities.

West Coast Air (☎ 250-388-4521, 800-347-2222, ⓦ www.westcoastair.com) and Harbour Air Seaplanes (☎ 250-384-2215,

800-665-0212, [W] www.harbour-air.com) offer seaplane flights to Vancouver Harbour. Kenmore Air (☎ 425-486-1257, 800-543-9595) offers seaplane flights from Seattle's Lake Union. Helijet Airways (☎ 800-665-4354) flies helicopters from Boeing Field (near Sea-Tac) to Victoria.

Bus The bus station is at 700 Douglas St. Pacific Coach Lines (☎ 250-385-4411, 800-661-1725, [W] www.pacificcoach.com) operates buses to Vancouver every hour between 6am and 6pm (until 9pm on Friday and Sunday) during July and August and every two hours from 6am to 8pm the rest of the year. The fare, which includes the ferry, is C$28/54 one-way/roundtrip for adults and C$14/27 for children ages five to 11. It's the same price to Vancouver International Airport; buses connect with the airport shuttle bus at Delta Pacific Resort, in Richmond.

Laidlaw Coach Lines (☎ 250-385-4411, [W] www.victoriatours.com) covers Vancouver Island. Six or seven buses a day travel to Nanaimo; from there, two buses go on to Tofino, and one or two buses go to Port Hardy.

Although Greyhound has no service on Vancouver Island or from Victoria to the mainland, it does maintain an office (☎ 250-388-5248) in the bus station where you can purchase tickets for buses departing from Vancouver.

Train The Esquimalt & Nanaimo Railiner, or E&N Railiner, operated by VIA Rail (☎ 250-383-4324, 800-561-8630, [W] www.viarail.ca), connects Victoria with points north, including Duncan, Nanaimo, Parksville and Courtenay. There is one train in each direction per day – northbound from Victoria at 8:15am, southbound from Courtenay at 1:30pm. The scenic journey takes about 4½ hours. The *Malahat*, as the train is known, is very popular, so book ahead. Seven-day advance purchases are cheaper.

Full schedules are available on the website or in person at travel agencies or the Visitor Info Centre. The E&N Railiner station, 405 Pandora Ave, is near the corner of Johnson and Wharf Sts. To get there, take bus No 6, 24 or 25.

Ferry BC Ferries (☎ 250-386-3431, 888-223-3779) operates service to the mainland from Swartz Bay, 27 km (17 miles) north of Victoria via Hwy 17. Ferry schedules are widely available around town. BC Ferries' information office, 1112 Fort St, is open 8:30am to 4:30pm weekdays.

The trip between Swartz Bay and Tsawwassen, near Vancouver, takes 95 minutes, with sailings every hour between 7am and 10pm in July and August. (In the off season, sailings begin on odds hours between 7am and 9pm, though check the schedule, because ships do not leave hourly.) The peak-season one-way fare is C$9.50/4.75 adult/child; a car is C$33.50. To reserve a spot for your vehicle, call ☎ 888-724-5223 in BC or 604-444-2890 outside BC, or visit [W] www.bcferries.com.

BC Ferries also operates between Swartz Bay and five of the southern Gulf Islands: Galiano, Mayne, Saturna, Salt Spring and North Pender. Schedules and fares vary by season and destination, with more frequent sailings in July and August.

Three passenger-only ferry services and one car-ferry service serve Washington State from the Inner Harbour ferry terminal at 430 Belleville St. The ferry MV *Coho*, operated by Black Ball Transport (☎ 250-386-2202), sails to Port Angeles, just across the Strait of Juan de Fuca. Fares are calculated in US dollars, but Canadian currency is accepted: the rate is about C$10.35 (US$7.75) for a walk-on passenger. A car and driver cost about C$43 (US$30). The trip takes about 1½ hours. From mid-June through mid-September, four boats a day leave Victoria, departing at 6:10am, 10:30am, 3pm and 7:30pm. During the rest of the year, boats leave at 10:30am and 4pm only.

The passenger-only *Victoria Express* (☎ 250-361-9144) also goes to Port Angeles from the Inner Harbour terminal, departing two to three times daily from late May through September; the fare is about C$17/35 (US$12.50/25) one-way/roundtrip.

BRITISH COLUMBIA

The *Victoria Clipper* fleet, run by Clipper Navigation (☎ 250-382-8100, 800-888-2535, **W** www.victoriaclipper.com), sails year round to Seattle's Pier 69 in water jet–propelled catamarans. The journey takes about three hours; the peak-season one-way/roundtrip fare is C$101/167 for adults, C$55/84 children, C$92/152 seniors. From May to early September, one boat a day stops at San Juan Island en route and takes 5¼ hours to complete the journey, while another high-speed boat crosses in two hours at additional charge.

May through September, the passenger-only *Victoria Star II*, operated by Victoria San Juan Cruises (☎ 800-443-4552), makes a trip to Bellingham and back daily (adult C$75/136, child C$37/68, senior C$67/121; 3 hours).

See the Sidney section, later in this chapter, for information on ferry service to the San Juan Islands in the USA.

Getting Around

To/From the Airport Airporter shuttle buses (☎ 250-386-2525) provide service between the airport and all area hotels and B&Bs. It runs every half-hour from 4:30am to midnight daily and costs C$13/6.50 adult/senior & student. A taxi to the airport from downtown costs about C$40. City bus No 70 passes within 1km of the airport.

Bus BC Transit buses (☎ 250-382-6161) run frequently and cover a wide area. The normal one-way fare is C$1.75 (C$2.50 if you travel into a second zone, such as the suburbs of Colwood or Sidney). Have exact change ready. All-day passes (C$5.50/4 adult/senior & student) are not sold on buses but are available from convenience stores and the Visitor Info Centre.

Bus No 70 goes to the BC Ferries terminal at Swartz Bay; catch it early, as it takes a rather circuitous route. Bus No 75 travels to the Washington State Ferries dock in Sidney. The BC Transit fare from downtown to the ferry docks is C$2.50.

Car Shop around for the best rental prices. All major rental companies have offices at the airport and in and around the downtown area, including Avis (☎ 250-386-8468), 1001 Douglas St; Budget (☎ 250-953-5300), 757 Douglas St; Enterprise (☎ 250-475-6900), 2507 Government St; and National/Tilden (☎ 250-386-1213), 767 Douglas St. Thrifty (☎ 250-383-3659), 625 Frances Ave, has an office right across from the Mayfair Mall on Douglas and Finlayson Sts.

Taxi Call Empress Taxi (☎ 250-381-2222), Victoria Taxi (☎ 250-383-7111) or Blue Bird Cabs (☎ 250-382-3611). Or try two-seat human-powered Kabuki Kabs (☎ 250-385-4243), which cost C$1 per minute.

Bicycle For bike rentals, contact Harbour Rentals (☎ 250-995-1661), 811 Wharf St, which also rents scooters, and Sports Rent (☎ 250-385-7368), 611 Discovery St.

Mini-Ferry Victoria Harbour Ferry provides service to the Empress Hotel, Visitor Info Centre, Ocean Pointe Resort, Fisherman's Wharf, Spinnakers Brewpub and other stops on the Inner Harbour and Gorge waterway. Fares start at C$3/1.50 adult/child under 12; prices vary depending on how far you travel.

SOUTHERN VANCOUVER ISLAND

Beyond Victoria, Southern Vancouver Island's attractions include tide pools, plenty of coastal hiking trails and excellent bicycling routes for outdoor types.

The Saanich Peninsula, north of Victoria on Hwys 17 and 17A, is Southern Vancouver Island's transportation hub, containing Victoria International Airport and ferry connections to the Southern Gulf Islands and the USA's San Juan Islands.

Just north of Victoria on the Island Hwy, the winding, mountainous stretch of highway referred to as 'The Malahat' climbs up Malahat Ridge and offers tremendous views over the Saanich Peninsula and Gulf Islands.

Sidney

At the north end of the Saanich Peninsula, near the airport and ferry terminal, Sidney

Totem Poles

Whether you're in Vancouver, Victoria or anywhere else in BC, you'll most likely be awed by the intricate Native art around you. Though most northwest coastal First Nations group lack formal written history as we know it, centuries of traditions manage to live on. Instead of words on a page or historical documents, the rich Native history has long been retold through the masterful art of carving, drawing and painting.

Carved from a single cedar trunk, totems identify a household's lineage in the same way a family crest might identify a group or clan in England, although the totem pole is more of a historical pictograph depicting the entire ancestry. Like a family crest, totem poles carry a sense of prestige and prosperity.

Despite the saying 'low man on the totem pole,' the most important figures are usually at eye level. Figures at the bottom usually have an integral, grounding function that supports the rest of the pole. Totem figures can represent individuals, spirits, births, deaths, catastrophes or legends.

The carving of totem poles was largely squashed after the Canadian government outlawed the potlatch ceremony in 1884. Most totems only last 60 to 80 years, though some on the Queen Charlotte Islands are more than 100 years old. When a totem falls, tradition says that it should be left there until another is erected in its place.

Today, totem carving is experiencing somewhat of a revival, though the poles are more frequently constructed for nontraditional uses, such as public art. Modern totems commissioned for college campuses, museums and public buildings no longer recount the lineage of any one household but instead stand to honor the First Nations and their outstanding artistry.

(population 11,000) is often seen as a way station to somewhere else. But the town itself features an offshore provincial park and seven bookstores, possibly the most per capita in BC. It's also the northern terminus of the Galloping Goose Trail (see the boxed text on the next page).

Sidney's two visitor information centers (10382 Patricia Bay Hwy; Fifth St S at Lochside Ave) stay open from March to December. Tanners (☎ 250-656-2345, 2436 Beacon Ave) is the biggest of Sidney's bookstores, with an excellent map department and thousands of magazine titles.

Sidney Spit Provincial Marine Park is a great spot for swimming, sunbathing and beachcombing. A passenger ferry (☎ 250-474-5145) runs between the Beacon Ave wharf and Sidney Spit from May 15 to September 30. Ferries depart Sidney on the hour and the park on the half-hour from 9am to 5pm Monday to Thursday and until 6pm Friday to Sunday (till 7pm weekends during July and August). The roundtrip fare is C$9/7/6 adult/senior/child.

The following are some decent ways for you to rest your head.

McDonald Provincial Park (☎ 250-391-2300, near the Swartz Bay ferry terminal) Tent sites C$12. This is a great spot to set up base if you're looking to kayak or take day trips by ferry to the Gulf Islands. The park has beach access, running water and pit toilets.

Sidney Spit Provincial Park (☎ 250-391-2300, accessed by a foot-passenger ferry from Sidney) Tent sites C$12. This park, one of the most beautiful, features white-sand beaches, tidal flats and marshland that teems with marine life. Amenities here include beach access, hiking trails, running water and pit toilets. Get the ferry ($9/6 adult/child roundtrip) from the government pier at the foot of Beacon Ave.

Waterfront Hotel Sidney (☎ 250-656-1131, 888-656-1131, 2537 Beacon Ave) Streetside/waterfront rooms C$80/90. This is a great place from which to explore Sidney. Rooms include a continental breakfast.

Victoria Airport Travelodge (☎ 250-656-1176, 800-578-7878, **w** www.travelodge.com, 2280 Beacon Ave) Singles/doubles from C$89/95. This clean though basic spot is a good place to stay if you're catching an early ferry or flight.

Sooke to Port Renfrew
A scenic 34km (21-mile) drive (or bus ride on No 61) west of Victoria, Sooke (population 11,620) is noted for its natural beauty and good recreational opportunities. If you're traveling west from here, note that there are no gas stations on Hwy 14 between Sooke and Port Renfrew.

The **Sooke Potholes** make a great spot for swimming and picnicking. Look for the turnoff east of town on Hwy 14, then follow the winding road north for several kilometers. The **Sooke Regional Museum** and

The Galloping Goose

Stretching from Swartz Bay to the Sooke area, the 100km (62-mile) Galloping Goose/Peninsula trail system ranks among the best cycling/pedestrian routes in BC.

The Galloping Goose, named for a noisy gas railcar that ran between Victoria and Sooke in the 1920s, is built mostly on abandoned Victoria & Sidney and Canadian National railway beds. Four bus lines along the route – Nos 50 (Goldstream), 61 (Sooke), 70 (Pat Bay Hwy) and 75 (Central Saanich) – are bike-rack equipped. For a brochure with maps or more information, ask at area Visitor Info Centres or call the Capital Region District Parks office at ☎ 250-478-3344. The Greater Victoria Cycling Coalition's website at **w** www.gvcc.bc.ca is a good place to look for regional cycling information.

Sooke Visitor Info Centre (☎ 250-642-6351), both at 2070 Phillips Rd, are open 9am to 5pm.

East Sooke Regional Park offers outstanding hikes, from short strolls to the beach to the 10km (6-mile) Coast Trail. **The Ocean Kayak Institute** (*TOKI; ☎ 250-642-2159, 5449 Sooke Rd*) offers **kayaking** lessons, rentals, guide training and a range of short and multiday tours. For **cycling**, rent bikes at **Sooke Cycle & Surf** (☎ 250-642-3123, 6707 West Coast Rd).

Sooke has more than 60 B&Bs, most costing about C$65 to C$75 a night, including a dozen or so on the Galloping Goose Trail. Stop at the Visitor Info Centre to see the displays many have posted.

Sooke River Flats Campsite (☎ 250-642-6076, up the road from the visitor center) Tent sites C$15. Open Apr-Sept. This 42-site campground is a popular spot for people who've just finished hiking the West Coast or Juan de Fuca Trails.

French Beach Provincial Park (☎ 250-391-2300, reservations ☎ 800-689-9025, in Greater Vancouver ☎ 604-689-9025) Sites C$12. This park, which is 20km (12 miles) west of Sooke and near the town of Jordan River, sits on a wide stretch of beach along the Strait of Juan de Fuca. Amenities are rustic, but people come here for that, as well as for the outdoorsy West Coast experience.

Juan De Fuca Marine Trail
The West Coast Trail (see Pacific Rim National Park Reserve, under Central Vancouver Island, later in this section) is still considered BC's preeminent long-distance coastal hike, but the 47km (29-mile) Juan de Fuca Marine Trail has become a worthy alternative. Unlike the WCT, the Juan de Fuca doesn't require hiking reservations (at least not yet), and it features several access points so you don't have to tramp the whole length.

From east to west, access points from Hwy 14 are at **China Beach**, 63km (39 miles) from Victoria and just west of Jordan River; **Sombrio Beach; Parkinson Creek;** and **Botanical Beach.** There are six established *campsites* en route, with fees of C$5 per person per night (cash only, exact change). Most through-hikers take four days to make the complete trek. The most difficult part of the trail is the stretch from the Bear Beach campsite to China Beach, but any part can be a major slog, with slippery tree roots and mud. For detailed information on planning a trip, contact BC Parks' South Vancouver Island District (☎ 250-391-2300, W www.bcparks.gov .bc.ca). West Coast Trail Express (☎ 250-477-8700, W www.trailbus.com) provides shuttle service between Victoria and the trailheads.

China Beach is an especially nice spot for a day trip along the Juan de Fuca. An easy 15-minute walk from the parking lot leads to a sandy beach and water warm enough for wading. You'll find a waterfall at the western end of the beach.

Port Renfrew

May through September, this sleepy community (population 400) at the end of Hwy 14 hums with activity as hikers prepare to tackle (or arrive to recuperate from) the West Coast Trail. The added popularity of the year-round Juan de Fuca Marine Trail has given Port Renfrew a bit more business in the off season.

For information on the West Coast Trail, see the Pacific Rim National Park Reserve, later in this chapter. Visitors looking for a short hike will enjoy the 2.7km (1.7-mile) loop to Botanical Beach, known especially for its tide pools. (Allow about 90 minutes, and go at low tide.) **Seafoam Kayak Rentals** (*☎ 250-647-0019*), next to Pacheedaht Campground, rents single or double kayaks by the hour or day.

The following are some area accommodations and dining options.

Pacheedaht Campground (*☎ 250-647-0090*) Sites C$5-20. This spot near the WCT trailhead on the Pacheedaht Reserve is popular with hikers.

Port Renfrew Hotel (*☎ 250-647-5541, at Snuggery Cove*) C$30. These simple, two-person rooms share a bath and shower down the hall. There's also a laundry across the street.

Arbutus Beach Lodge (*☎ 250-647-5458*) Rooms C$65-95. This waterfront B&B also

has a hikers' room that sleeps five (C$85 for two, plus C$15 per extra person).

Lighthouse Neighbourhood Pub & Restaurant (*☎ 250-647-5543*) Entrees C$7-12. Look for this red-roofed pub and treat yourself to an incredible post-hike hamburger and beer.

Cowichan Valley

Just over the Malahat from Victoria, this valley is home to the Cowichan, BC's largest aboriginal group, with about 4500 people. The valley is the gateway to Carmanah Walbran Provincial Park, noted for its giant trees. Cowichan means 'land warmed by the sun,' and this area enjoys the highest average annual temperatures in Canada.

Duncan & Around The town of Duncan (population 5330) grabs the moniker 'City of Totems' for its several dozen examples of this West Coast art form on view along its streets.

The Duncan Visitor Info Centre (☎ 250-746-4636, W www.duncancc.bc.ca, 381A Trans-Canada Hwy) is open 9am to 5pm daily, mid-April through mid-October.

Cowichan Native Village (*☎ 250-746-8119, 200 Cowichan Way; C$10/6/4 adult/senior/ child; open 10am-5pm*) is one of Vancouver Island's best First Nations attractions. Call to check upcoming dates for midday salmon barbecues and Coast Salish feasts, which are accompanied by live entertainment.

Cowichan Lake, 22km (14 miles) west of Duncan via Hwy 18, is the largest freshwater lake on Vancouver Island. Back roads along the way parallel the lovely Cowichan River. Outdoor recreation opportunities abound in this area. **Nitinat Lake**, west of Cowichan Lake, is one of the best windsurfing spots on Vancouver Island; for information, visit W www.island.net/~nitinat. Pachena Bay Express (☎ 250-728-1290) runs shuttles to and from Nitinat by reservation only; call for schedules and fares.

Duncan RV Park & Campground (*☎ 250-748-8511, 2950 Boys Rd*) Sites C$13-20. This spot along the river off Hwy 1 makes a convenient stop if you don't want to travel far off the Trans-Canada Hwy.

Chemainus Up island from Duncan, Chemainus (population 4000) wavered on the brink of extinction when its sawmill shut down in 1983, but in a robust effort to save the small town, officials commissioned a large outdoor mural depicting local history. People took notice, and 33 murals now adorn city buildings. Chemainus has since done quite well; there's even a new sawmill, along with many shops and galleries.

The Visitor Info Centre (☎ 250-246-3944, W www.chemainus.com), 9796 Willow St, is open May through August; if it's closed, look for informational exhibits across the street in Waterwheel Park.

BC Ferries provides frequent daily service from Chemainus to nearby **Thetis Island**, known for its warm-water beaches, and **Kuper Island**, a Native Indian reserve with no visitor amenities. The roundtrip fare is C$5/12.75 per passenger/vehicle.

Ladysmith About 17km (11 miles) north of Chemainus, Ladysmith (population 6700) was named one of the prettiest small towns in Canada by *Harrowsmith Country Living* magazine. Its revitalized main street features many restored buildings from the late 19th and early 20th centuries. Ladysmith is also the birthplace of bombshell Pamela Anderson Lee.

The Visitor Info Centre (☎ 250-245-2112, W www.ladysmithcofc.com), 26 Gatacre St, is supplemented in the summer months by an information booth on the Trans-Canada Hwy.

Carmanah Walbran Provincial Park

This 16,450-hectare (40,641-acre) park boasts some of the last remaining old-growth forest on Vancouver Island, including 95m (312-foot) spruce trees and cedars more than 1000 years old. Unfortunately, the park can only be reached via a slow, dusty drive over active logging roads. (It's best to travel on weekends or evenings, when the loggers aren't working.)

From Gordon Bay Provincial Park, which is about 40km (25 miles) off Hwy 1, follow S Shore Rd to the Nitinat Main Rd. Follow Nitinat Main to its junction with Junction South. Turn left onto S Main and continue to the Caycus River Bridge. South of the bridge, stop at the safety checkpoint (it monitors logging-truck traffic). Turn right and follow Rosander Main for 29km (18 miles) to the park. Once you're there, it's a relatively short hike of an hour or so (in good weather) into the tallest trees. Campsites with tent pads, tables and water are provided, but there are no other services nearby. The closest phone and gas station are on the Didtidaht Reserve, 33km (20 miles) away. Before heading out on this road, be sure you have a spare tire – chances are you'll need it.

Nanaimo & Around

The second-largest city (population 73,000) on Vancouver Island, with two BC Ferries terminals, Nanaimo (nah-**nyme**-oh) is a major hub for adventure-seekers traveling west and north to the island's wilderness splendor. Not long ago, Nanaimo was a place to get through quickly; nothing compelling prompted visitors to hang around. But the city has done a superb job of revitalizing its downtown waterfront, adding eateries and pubs around the inner harbor.

A number of First Nations bands once shared the area, which was called 'Sne-Ny-Mos,' a Salish word meaning 'meeting place.' Coal was discovered in 1852, and mining dominated the town for 100 years. Mining has declined in importance, and tourism and forestry now power the area's economy. Nanaimo's Marine Festival and World Championship Bathtub race take place each July.

Orientation Nanaimo's city center lies behind the harbor, with most shops on Commercial St and Terminal Ave. To the south, Nicol St, the southern extension of Terminal Ave, leads to the Trans-Canada Hwy and BC Ferries Duke Point terminal via Hwy 19 E. To the north, Terminal Ave forks – the right fork becomes Stewart Ave (Hwy 1) and leads to the BC Ferries terminal in Departure Bay; the left fork becomes Hwy 19A (known in town as the N Island Hwy), which heads up island to Courtenay, Campbell River and Port Hardy.

Information Far from the city center, Nanaimo's Visitor Info Centre (☎ 250-756-0106, 800-663-7337, fax 250-756-0075, W www.tourismnanaimo.com) is at 2290 Bower Rd, 1km (half a mile) off Hwy 19 at Northfield Rd. It's open 8am to 7pm daily May to September, then 9am to 5pm weekdays and 10am to 4pm weekends October to April. In summer, an information office stays open daily in The Bastion, on the waterfront. You'll find the headquarters of Tourism Vancouver Island (☎ 250-754-3500, fax 754-3599, W www.islands.bc.ca) on the 2nd floor of 335 Wesley St in the Old City Quarter.

Of several good used bookstores along Commercial St, the most interesting is the Literacy Nanaimo Bookstore (☎ 250-754-8982, 22 Commercial St), where profits go to help people learn to read.

Nanaimo Regional General Hospital (☎ 250-754-2121) is at 1200 Dufferin Crescent, northwest of the downtown area. Dial ☎ 911 for police, fire or ambulance.

Things to See & Do Nanaimo's attractions are generally affiliated with the local Native peoples.

Nanaimo District Museum (☎ 250-753-1821, 100 Cameron Rd; C$2/1.75/75¢ adult/senior/child; open 9am-5pm daily mid-May–Sept; closed Mon rest of the year). Overlooking downtown, the museum traces the growth of the city, with exhibits on the First Nations people, the Hudson's Bay Company and coal mining.

The Bastion (Front St at cnr of Bastion St; admission C$1; open 9am-5pm Wed-Sun Jul-Aug), built by the Hudson's Bay Company in 1853 for protection from the local Native peoples, was never used but for the odd firing of a cannon to quell a disturbance. Get there at noon to see and hear the cannon.

About 3km (2 miles) south of Nanaimo on Hwy 1, the small **Petroglyph Provincial Park** features some ancient Native Indian carvings in sandstone. Most are now barely visible, but there are castings from which you can make rubbings.

Set on and around a bridge spanning the Nanaimo River south of town, the **Bungy Zone** (☎ 250-716-7874, 35 Nanaimo River Rd off Hwy 1) offers a full menu of thrills. One jump is C$95, or you can become a lifetime member for C$100 and get jumps for C$25 apiece. You can camp on the premises for C$10 per tent if someone jumps (C$10 per head otherwise). Zone staff will pick you up free from either local BC Ferry terminal if at least one person in your group pays for a full-price jump.

Nanaimo and its nearby islands offer some of the best **scuba diving** in BC. Dive enthusiasts recently sunk the Cape Breton World War II supply ship northwest of Gabriola Island, creating the area's newest and largest artificial reef. For information on dive sites, or for guides, lessons or equipment, visit **Sundown Diving** (☎ 250-753-1880, 888-773-3483, 22 Esplanade).

The **Kayak Shack/Western Wildcat Tours** (☎ 250-753-3234) offers sea kayaking lessons, rentals and tours from its headquarters near the Departure Bay terminal.

Nanaimo's **Parkway Trail** extends 20km (12 miles) along Hwy 19, the city's bypass route, and offers opportunities for cycling, inline skating, jogging and walking.

Places to Stay Budget accommodations tend to fill up and empty out in tune with ferry schedules, especially in summer. If you know you're going to get to Nanaimo at night, try to reserve something ahead of time.

Living Forest Oceanside Campground & RV Park (☎ 250-755-1755, 6 Maki Rd, south of town off Hwy 1). Tent sites/full hookups C$17-20. You can usually find a site at this 193-site campground, which features showers and laundry.

Nicol St Hostel (☎ 250-753-1188, fax 753-1185, e nanaimohostel@home.com, 65 Nicol St) Tent sites/dorm beds/private rooms C$10/15/40. This homey hostel is a five-minute walk from the Harbour Park Mall. Amenities include linens and towels, a coin-operated laundry and kitchen privileges. The backyard features great views, an airy outdoor shower, barbecue facilities and a fun mural created by past guests. Families would feel at home here. Reservations are advised. You should plan to check in between 4pm and 11pm.

Cambie International Hostel, Nanaimo (☎ 250-754-5323, 877-395-5335, e *nanaimo@ cambie hostels.com, 63 Victoria Crescent*) Dorm beds/doubles C$15-20/25. The Cambie enjoys an even more central location, but it can't match the Nicol St Hostel for ambience. Dorm rooms sleep four people, and each room has its own toilet. There are no cooking facilities, but Cambie throws in free breakfast at its downstairs cafe. The pub downstairs is one of Nanaimo's rowdiest, so ask for a room well away from the noise.

Bluebird Motel (☎ 250-753-4151, 995 N Terminal Ave) Singles/doubles C$49/55. A helpful front desk and good-sized rooms await travelers at this motel.

Buccaneer Inn (☎ 250-753-1246, e *info@ thebuccaneerinn.com, 1577 Stewart Ave*) Rooms/suites C$59/99. This is the closest motel to the Departure Bay ferry terminal; some of the comfortable rooms have ocean views. This place is very popular with divers; amenities include a gear-rinse station, dry-gear storage room and access to showers after checkout.

Best Western Dorchester Hotel (☎ 250-754-6835, 800-661-2449, 70 Church St) Streetside/oceanside rooms C$105/120. This refurbished and historic downtown hotel features rooms and suites with harbor views.

Long Lake Inn Resort (☎ 250-758-1144, 800-565-1144, 4700 N Island Hwy) Rooms C$110-150. Just 3km (1.8 miles) north of Nanaimo, this pleasant spot achieves a resort feel, with friendly staff, a swimming beach, a marina and canoe rentals.

Places to Eat There are lots of great places to eat in Nanaimo.

Café Bakery at the Cambie (☎ 250-754-5323, 63 Victoria Crescent) Breakfast C$3. This is Nanaimo's best bet for breakfast, where a mere C$3 gets you bacon, eggs, toast and hash browns. Locals throng here for the freshly baked bread and pastries, including an outstanding version of the town's signature sweet, the Nanaimo bar.

Flo's Diner (☎ 250-753-2148, 187 Commercial St) 'Big-Ass Breakfast' C$7. Flo's

also serves omelets, burgers. In a previous incarnation, Flo's was owned by the father of jazz star (and local-girl-made-good) Diana Krall.

Katerina's Restaurant (☎ 250-754-1351, 15 Front St) Entrees C$10-17. This mid-range restaurant is one of the most romantic spots in town, offering Greek fare and seafood.

Gina's Café (☎ 250-753-5411, 47 Skinner St) Entrees C$9-12. This brightly colored spot is a local favorite for its lively atmosphere and Mexican combination plates.

Green Garden Restaurant (☎ 250-753-2828) Buffet lunch/entrees C$7.50/10. Open until 3am Fri-Sun. Eat your heart out at this smorgasbord restaurant in the Harbour Park Mall.

Lighthouse Bistro (☎ 250-754-3212, 50 Anchor Way) Entrees C$9-30. On the waterfront, the Lighthouse features a white-linen atmosphere and a menu that includes pasta, lamb and schnitzel. The pub upstairs has lower prices and a more casual feel. From either floor, you can watch seaplanes taking off and landing.

Getting There & Away Most flights to Nanaimo are via seaplane, and the terminal is right downtown on the Pioneer Waterfront Plaza. Companies include Baxter Aviation (☎ 250-754-1066) and Harbour Air (☎ 250-714-0900, 800-665-0212). The fare for the Nanaimo-Vancouver run is about C$54 one way, though roundtrip specials as low as C$85 are often available. Nanaimo Collishaw Air Terminal (☎ 250-245-2157) is a 15-minute drive south of town on Hwy 1. Pacific Coastal Airlines (☎ 800-665-1177) offers scheduled flights to and from Vancouver.

If you want to travel by bus, Laidlaw Coach Lines (☎ 250-753-4371) connects Nanaimo with points north and south; the one-way fare to or from Victoria is C$19.25. The station is behind the Howard Johnson Harbourside Hotel, at 1 N Terminal Ave, north of the center at Comox Rd. See the Victoria Getting There & Away section, earlier in this chapter, for more information.

The E&N Railiner (☎ 800-561-8630) passes through once a day in each direction and stops at the station at 321 Selby St. The one-way train fare to Victoria is C$22 ($17 if you book seven days in advance). Tickets can be purchased from the conductor. See the Victoria Getting There & Away section, earlier in this chapter, for more information.

BC Ferries (☎ 888-724-5223 in BC, ☎ 604-444-2890 outside BC, **W** www.bcferries.com) has two Nanaimo terminals with service to the Vancouver area. Sailings from Departure Bay go to Horseshoe Bay. The 39km (24-mile) trip takes 80 to 95 minutes, depending on the ship. Fares and sailings vary seasonally, but in peak season (late June through mid-September), there are about 11 trips each way. Bet on about eight daily peak-season sailings between Duke Point and Tsawwassen. The trip takes two hours. The one-way fares for both routes are the same: C$9.50/4.75/33.50 adult/child/car.

Getting Around BC Transit Bus No 2 goes to the Departure Bay ferry terminal. No city buses run to Duke Point. Local bus fares are C$1.75; day passes cost C$4.50. For more information, call ☎ 250-390-4531 or pick up a transit guide at the tourist office. All buses pass through the Harbour Park Mall, located at Front St and Terminal Ave.

The shuttle company Nanaimo Seaporter (☎ 250-753-2118) provides door-to-door service from hotels to the Departure Bay ferry terminal for C$6.50 and to the Duke Point terminal for C$14; fares are good for either one or two people traveling together.

CENTRAL VANCOUVER ISLAND

Vancouver Island's midsection includes some of its greatest recreational assets: long stretches of sand at Parksville and Qualicum Beach, windswept Pacific Rim National Park, Clayoquot Sound near Tofino and more.

Parksville & Qualicum Beach Area

Parksville (population 10,000), Qualicum Beach (population 7000) and the coast toward Comox have become major vacation destinations, especially for families and the RV set. These towns are also departure points for Tofino and the rest of

the island's west coast via Hwy 4, just south of Parksville, or Hwy 4A from Qualicum Beach.

Look for Visitor Info Centres at 1275 E Island Hwy in Parksville (☎ 250-248-3613) and at 2711 W Island Hwy in Qualicum Beach (☎ 250-752-9532), or visit **W** www .oceansidetourism.com. For information on parks, contact the Strathcona District Office of BC Parks (☎ 250-954-4600), in Rathtrevor Beach Provincial Park (see below).

Just off the east side of Vancouver Island between Qualicum Beach and Courtenay are the southernmost of the so-called Northern Gulf Islands. **Denman Island** and **Hornby Island** offer excellent access to outdoor activities, including camping and kayaking. BC Ferries offers service to both islands from the Buckley Bay terminal, 75km (46 miles) north of Nanaimo. For Denman Island information, call ☎ 250-335-1636 or see the website **W** www.denmanis.bc.ca. For Hornby information, visit **W** www.hornbyisland.com.

The following are some nice places to stay.

Rathtrevor Beach Provincial Park Sites C$12-18.50. Just 3km (2 miles) south of Parksville off Hwy 19, this is the area's most popular campground, with long stretches of sandy beach, flush toilets and showers. You'll also find camping at ***Englishman River Falls Provincial Park***, on Errington Rd, and ***Little Qualicum Falls Provincial Park***, 19km (12 miles) west of Parksville on Hwy 4. Both charge C$15.

Englishman River Motel (☎ 250-248-6532, 762 E Island Hwy, Parksville) Singles/doubles C$60/70. This motel may be well worn, but the prices, the kitchen and the riverside setting still make it a good value.

Paradise Sea Shell Motel (☎ 250-248-6171, 877-337-3529, 411 W Island Hwy, Parksville) Singles/doubles C$60/80. Beach access is just a couple minutes' walk away. Rooms come with a free continental breakfast.

Old Dutch Inn (☎ 250-752-6914, 800-661-0199, 2690 Island Hwy W, Qualicum Beach) Rooms C$80/90. This nice inn across the road from the beach has a restaurant, an indoor pool, a whirlpool and a sauna.

Pacific Shores Nature Resort (☎ 250-468-7121, 800-500-7212, fax 250-469-2001,

W *www.pacific-shores.com, 1-1600 Stroulger Rd, Nanoose Bay)* Rooms/suites & townhouses C$95/120-270. All the rooms here are brightly decorated and well furnished. Canoes, kayaks and mountain bikes are available for rent; other amenities include hot tubs, an indoor pool, a fitness room and a convenience store/deli.

***Tigh Na Mara Resort Hotel* (☎ 250-248-2072, 800-663-7373, 1095 Island Hwy E)** From C$110. Set amid arbutus and fir forests and close to the beach, this resort offers lodge rooms, cottages and condos – plus a fitness room, tennis courts, an indoor pool and watercraft rentals. The world-class restaurant specializes in local fish, produce and wines.

Port Alberni & Around

The gateway to Vancouver Island's west coast, Port Alberni (population 19,500) was built on natural resources. More than 300 commercial fishing boats work out of the area, most catching salmon.

The Alberni Valley Visitor Info Centre (☎ 250-724-6535, fax 724-6560) is at 2533 Redford St. For medical help, go to West Coast General Hospital (☎ 250-723-2135), 3841 8th Ave.

Port Alberni's big draw is **Lady Rose Marine Services** (☎ 250-723-8313, 800-663-7192, *W* *www.ladyrosemarine.com)*, which runs day trips up Barkley Sound to Bamfield, Ucluelet and the Broken Group Islands on the 100-passenger *Lady Rose* and 200-passenger *Frances Barkley.* The Bamfield run takes place 8am to 5:30pm Tuesday, Thursday and Saturday year round, as well as Friday and Sunday during July and August; it costs C$40 roundtrip. There's a coffee shop on board. Bring a sweater or jacket, even if it's warm in Port Alberni.

These working packet freighters make numerous stops en route to deliver mail and supplies, with a 60- to 90-minute layover in Bamfield. Taking a ride on one of them is an enjoyable, scenic way to spend a lazy day, as well as a practical means of returning from the West Coast Trail's north end at Bamfield. From October to May, kayakers and canoeists can request a stop at the Broken Group Islands. The company also makes a separate run to Ucluelet (C$50 roundtrip) and the Broken Group Islands (C$40 roundtrip) on Monday, Wednesday and Friday from June through September. An additional sailing leaves Sunday in July and August. That trip leaves at 8am and returns about 7pm, with a 90-minute stop in Ucluelet.

Laidlaw Coach Lines (☎ 250-724-1266), 4541 Margaret St, runs buses from Nanaimo to Port Alberni ($13.75 one way). From Port Alberni, buses travel to Ucluelet (C$16.50 one way) and Tofino (C$19.25). The West Coast Trail Express bus (☎ 250-477-8700, *W* www.trailbus.com) offers shuttle-bus service to Bamfield and the West Coast Trail trailhead.

***Arrowvale Campground* (☎ 250-723-7948, 5955 Hector Rd)** C$15-20. On the Somass River, 6km (4 miles) west of Port Alberni, Arrowvale offers 45 sites, showers, swimming, a playground, farm tours and laundry facilities.

Stamp River Provincial Park Sites C$12. This small, primitive campground 14.5km (9 miles) west of Port Alberni on Beaver Creek Rd sits near a waterfall. Salmon migrate through here in late August.

***Personal Touch Hostel* (☎ 250-723-2484, 4908 Burde St)** Dorm beds C$15. Though smoky and spartan, this hostel helps fill Port Alberni's need for cheap beds.

***Riverside Lodge* (☎ 250-724-9916, 5065 Roger St)** Singles/doubles from C$63/69. Although this place is convenient to the bus station, the rooms lack phones, but there's a laundry, and the owners are friendly and helpful.

Bamfield

A gateway to the West Coast Trail and a layover point for the *Lady Rose* or *Frances Barkley,* tiny Bamfield (population 520) is divided into Bamfield East – where you'll arrive if you take the 100km (62-mile) drive west from Port Alberni – and Bamfield West, where you'll spend your *Lady Rose* layover on the boardwalk. The Bamfield Chamber of Commerce (☎ 250-728-3006, *W* www.alberni.net/bamcham) maintains a Visitor Info Centre on Grappler Rd, in Bamfield East.

Broken Island Adventures (☎ *250-728-3500, 888-728-6200*) specializes in **scuba diving** throughout Barkley Sound.

The following are a couple of local accommodations.

Pachena Bay Campground (☎ *250-728-1287*) Sites C$25. This First Nations–run campground sits in a splendid setting about 3km (2 miles) from Bamfield East, on Port Alberni Rd.

Bamfield Trails Motel (☎ *250-728-3231*) Rooms C$100-145. Near the dock at Bamfield East, this motel is popular with West Coast Trail hikers. It's just 5km (3 miles) from the trailhead. A shuttle bus runs hikers from the motel or campground for C$5 per person.

Tofino & Around

The most appealing end-of-the-road town on Vancouver Island, Tofino (population 1200) sits on Clayoquot (**clay**-kwot) Sound at the terminus of Hwy 4, 122km (76 miles) west of Port Alberni. Its population doubles in summer as people come to visit nearby Pacific Rim National Park and other natural attractions.

Dotted with islands and rimmed by mountains, Tofino's setting is both serene and spectacular. If you want to see whales, sea lions and other marine creatures, this is a top place to go.

The Visitor Info Centre (☎ 250-725-3414, fax 250-725-3296, ⓦ www.island.net/~tofino), 380 Campbell St, is open 9am to 7pm May to September. Pick up the *Long Beach Maps* brochure, which offers helpful listings for Tofino, Ucluelet and Pacific Rim National Park.

The Sound is a local magazine distributed around Tofino. The post office is on First St. The Tofino Laundromat, 448 Campbell St, is open 9am to 9pm.

Hot Springs Cove One of BC's best daytrip destinations, Hot Springs Cove is the best-known part of Maquinna Provincial Marine Park, 37km (23 miles) north of Tofino. Most sojourners travel by Zodiac boat, watching for whales and other sea critters en route, though seaplane service is available. From the boat landing, you can hike 2km (1.2 miles) over boardwalks to a series of natural hot pools perfect for soaking.

Many outfitters make the run to Hot Springs Cove. ***Remote Passages*** (☎ *250-725-3330, 800-666-9833, 71 Wharf St*) is one of the more ecologically minded companies, with guides well versed in the natural history of Clayoquot Sound. Its six- to seven-hour Hot Springs Explorer trip costs C$89/59 adult/child. Tofino Air Lines (☎ 250-725-4454) flies to Hot Springs Cove, as does Magna Helicopters (☎ 250-726-8946, 877-999-4356).

For overnight stays, there are a few primitive campsites near the hot-springs boat landing. The Hesquiaht First Nation operates ***Hot Springs Lodge*** (☎ *250-670-1106*), in the community of Hot Springs Cove. You can only get to the lodge by water-taxi (roundtrip C$60/40 adult/child).

Meares Island Visible from Tofino, Meares Island is home to the Big Tree Trail, a 400m (¼-mile) boardwalk stroll through old-growth forest, including a red cedar tree that's been standing for 1500 years. The island was the site of a key 1984 antilogging protest that kicked off the modern environmental movement in Clayoquot Sound. **Rainforest Boat Shuttle** (☎ *250-725-3793*) runs a 2½-hour trip to Meares Island for C$20/10 adult/child. **Sea Trek Tours** (☎ *250-725-4412, 800-811-9155, 411-B Campbell St*) operates 90-minute trips that feature a glass-bottom boat ride for C$25/20/15/5 adult/senior & student/child six to 12 years/child two to five years.

Activities Tofino is a swell place to go surfing (pun intended) or to learn how. **Inner Rhythm Surf Camp** (☎ *250-726-2211,* ⓦ *www.innerrhythm.net*) features a variety of adult and youth surf classes and camps, plus food and lodging. **Surf Sister** (☎ *250-725-4456, 877-724-7873*) is BC's only all-female surf school, with two-day courses for C$195, including gear rentals.

Tofino Sea Kayaking Co (☎ *250-725-4222, 800-863-4664, 320 Main St*) offers tours

(C$40 and up), rentals, lessons and a great bookstore called Wildside Booksellers.

Clayoquot Sound features year-round **fishing** for chinook salmon, plus seasonal catches of halibut, steelhead and coho salmon. Guides include **Osray Charters** (☎ 250-725-2133, 888-286-3466, 350 Main St) and **Springtime Charters** (☎ 250-725-2351, 586 Campbell St).

You're likely to see whales on any trip to Hot Springs Cove or Flores Island – or sometimes even from shore in Tofino – but you can also book a trip devoted to **whale watching**. Many local outfitters run two- to three-hour trips (for about C$50 to C$70). Ask at the Info Centre for details.

From mid-October through March, Tofino offers a front seat to watch some of the most spectacular storms on the North American West Coast. Many visitors are content to watch the pounding surf from their hotel rooms, but **Long Beach Nature Tours Company** (☎ 250-726-7099) offers guided hikes to safe viewing spots for C$160 (half-day) or C$320 (full day); rates cover up to five people.

Places to Stay Tofino's budget lodging scene has brightened in recent years, but you still won't find many rooms under C$100 from May through September, so you will want to book way ahead. You'll find several good, albeit pricey, camping choices south of Tofino, all with sites around C$30.

Bella Pacifica Resort & Campground (☎ 250-725-3400), 3km (2 miles) south of Tofino on Pacific Rim Hwy, has both forest and beachfront sites. *Mackenzie Beach Resort* (☎ 250-725-3439, 1101 Pacific Rim Hwy) also has a variety of cottages. *Crystal Cove Beach Resort* (☎ 250-725-4213, 1165 Cedarwood Place) offers tent sites and some log cottages beginning at C$160.

Whalers on the Point Guesthouse (☎ 250-725-3443, fax 725-3463, e info@tofinohostel.com, 81 West St) Dorm beds C$22/24 for HI members/nonmembers. One of the nicest and newest hostels in Canada, Whalers sits right by the ocean in Tofino's west end. Built specifically as a hostel in 1999, this handsome HI affiliate features a

game room, bike rentals, surfboard lockers, a spacious kitchen and dining and lounging areas. Private rooms are also available.

Dolphin Motel (☎ 250-725-3377, fax 725-3374, 1190 Pacific Rim Hwy) 1/2 beds C$79/99. About 3km (2 miles) south of town near Chesterman Beach, this place has rooms that come equipped with refrigerators.

Schooner Motel (☎ 250-725-3478, fax 725-3499, 311–312 Campbell St) Singles/doubles from C$95/125. Located downtown, the Schooner has some rooms overlooking the bay.

Best Western Tin Wis Resort (☎ 250-725-4445, 800-661-9995, fax 250-725-4447, e tinwis@mail.island.net, 1119 Pacific Rim Hwy) Rooms from C$160. Long used as a safe haven for Native fishermen, this lovely resort, owned and operated by the Tla-o-qui-aht First Nation, features 86 oceanfront rooms and an excellent restaurant dedicated to using local ingredients.

Duffin Cove Resort (☎ 250-725-2448, 888-629-2903, e duffin@island.net, 215 Campbell St) Rooms C$165-300. Located on a quiet residential street close to downtown, this motel with 13 rooms makes a nice spot for anyone seeking a little rest and relaxation.

Wickaninnish Inn (☎ 250-725-3100, 800-333-4604, fax 250-725-3110, e wick@wickinn.com) Rooms C$340-420. On Osprey Lane, south of town, the Wickaninnish's exquisite guest rooms feature push-button gas fireplaces, two-person hot tubs and private balconies.

Places to Eat Anywhere you chose to eat in Tofino is usually casual and great for relaxing and people-watching.

Common Loaf Bake Shop (☎ 250-725-3915, 180 First St). This low-key gathering spot serves up tasty homemade muffins, cookies, breads and cakes.

Alley Way Café (☎ 250-725-3105) Entrees C$8. Tucked in the yard behind the corner of First and Campbell Sts, this cafe serves a range of all-day breakfasts, Mexican-style and vegetarian dishes.

Pointe Restaurant (☎ 250-725-3100, at Wickaninnish Inn) Lunch C$10-21, dinner

C$25-40 à la carte. The Pointe ranks among BC's very best, and the views can't be beat. In addition to à la carte menu items, the Wickanninish serves a fixed-price menu nightly. The six-course dinner costs C$57/70 vegetarian/seafood and, for the ultimate in gastronomic indulgence, the nine-course dinner is C$85. Reservations are essential for dinner.

Getting There & Away North Vancouver Air (☎ 800-228-6608) flies to Tofino from Vancouver (C$270 roundtrip). The Tofino Airport is south of town, off the Pacific Rim Hwy. Sound Flight (☎ 800-825-0722) and Northwest Seaplanes (☎ 800-690-0086) run scheduled high-season float-plane service between the Seattle area and Tofino; the fare is about US$225 one way with a seven-day advance purchase.

Laidlaw Coach Lines (☎ 250-725-3431) operates daily bus trips to Tofino's station, at 450 Campbell St, with two runs daily in summer. The one-way fare is C$33 from Nanaimo and C$52.25 from Victoria.

Pacific Rim National Park Reserve

With rain forests of huge cedar and fir trees, and tremendous waves rolling in from across the ocean, Pacific Rim National Park Reserve has become one of BC's top attractions. The 50,000-hectare (123,552-acre) park includes three units: the Long Beach area between Tofino and Ucluelet, the Broken Group Islands in Barkley Sound and the famous West Coast Trail. Stop by the park information center on Hwy 4 just inside the southern boundary. If you drive in, you have to pay a park-use fee at the Wickaninnish Centre or at a trailhead parking lot. The cost is C$3 per vehicle for two hours or C$8 per vehicle per day, good until 11pm. If you plan to stay more than a few days, an annual pass is available for C$42 per vehicle (C$31.50 for seniors). There's no charge to drive through the park to Tofino.

For trips to the Broken Group Islands or the West Coast Trail, get updated, detailed information from Parks Canada (☎ 250-726-7721, fax 726-4720, ✉ pacrim_info@pch

.gc.ca); you can also write to Pacific Rim National Park Reserve, PO Box 280, Ucluelet, BC V0R 3A0; or visit the website at ⓦ http://parkscan.harbour.com/pacrim/.

Long Beach Unit Easily accessed by Hwy 4, the Long Beach Unit attracts the largest number of visitors in the park. Start with a stop at the **Wickaninnish Centre**, with interpretive exhibits on the park's cultural and natural history. The center was named for a chief of the Nuu-chah-nulth tribe, who have lived in the Long Beach area for centuries. Also try one or more of the trails that range in length from 100m to 5km (110 yards to 3 miles).

Green Point Campground (☎ 800-689-9025) Sites C$20. This is the only park-run site; it's 18km (11 miles) from Tofino and 20km (12 miles) from Ucluelet along Hwy 4. The 94 drive-in sites can be reserved up to three months ahead; the 20 walk-in sites (C$14) are first-come, first-served.

Broken Group Islands This unit includes about 100 islands at the entrance to Barkley Sound. **Broken Island Adventures** (☎ 250-728-3500, 888-728-6200) runs **sightseeing trips** from Sechart or Bamfield. The islands are an increasingly popular **kayaking** destination, but visitors must know what they're doing – or sign on with a guided trip.

West Coast Trail The third and most southerly section of the park is the 75km (46½-mile) West Coast Trail, one of Canada's best-known and toughest hiking routes. The trail runs between Pachena Bay (☎ 250-728-3234), near Bamfield on the north end, and Gordon River (☎ 250-647-5434), near Port Renfrew on the south. Hikers must be able to manage rough terrain, rock-face ladders, stream crossings, hand-propelled cable cars and adverse weather conditions. Plan on six to eight days to hike the entire route.

Only 52 people can begin the trail on any given day, 26 in each direction. To apply, call the Super Natural British Columbia Reservation Service (☎ 800-663-6000 in the USA and Canada, ☎ 604-663-6000 in Greater Vancouver, ☎ 250-387-1642 worldwide). The

BRITISH COLUMBIA

nonrefundable reservation fee (C$25 per hiker) includes a trail guide and map. In addition to the reservation fee, you'll pay a C$70-per-person trail use fee, plus two ferry fees totaling C$25, payable when you sign in at the registration center. The trail is open May through September.

A few companies lead guided through-hikes on the West Coast Trail. Parks Canada keeps a list of these companies, it's available in January.

Getting There & Away It takes 90 minutes to drive from Port Alberni to Bamfield (Pachena Bay) on a gravel logging road. It's a two-hour drive on paved Hwy 14 from Victoria to Port Renfrew (Gordon River). West Coast Trail Express (☎ 250-477-8700, W www.trailbus.com) offers roundtrip shuttle-bus service to Bamfield and Port Renfrew from Victoria and Nanaimo. Pachena Bay Express (☎ 250-728-1290) operates shuttle service from Port Alberni to Bamfield and Pachena. Lady Rose Marine Services (see the Port Alberni section, earlier) runs a passenger ferry to and from Bamfield.

Ucluelet

Something of a poor relation to Tofino, Ucluelet (population 1700) doesn't match Tofino's charm, mainly due to the extensive forest clear-cutting that's readily visible from town on clear days. Still, Ucluelet has plenty of visitor services at generally cheaper prices than in Tofino. The Visitor Info Centre (☎ 250-726-4641, fax 726-4611), at the Hwy 4 junction, is open June through August.

Comox Valley

The Comox Valley, on the east coast of Vancouver Island, includes **Courtenay** (population 20,000) and **Comox** (population 12,000). The two towns are important supply hubs for trips to Mt Washington, 32km (20 miles) west of Courtenay, and to Strathcona Provincial Park.

In Courtenay, the Comox Valley Visitor Info Centre (☎ 250-334-3234, 888-357-4471, W www.tourism-comox-valley.bc.ca), 2040 Cliffe Ave, distributes information on both cities and the surrounding area.

Air Canada (☎ 888-247-2262) and Pacific Coastal (☎ 800-663-2872) serve the Comox Valley Regional Airport, in Comox. An advance-purchase roundtrip fare from Vancouver costs about C$160. Island Coach Lines (☎ 250-334-2475) serves Courtenay; the one-way bus fare is C$35 from Victoria and C$17.50 from Nanaimo. Courtenay is also the end of the line for VIA Rail's E&N Railiner (☎ 800-561-8630), 899 Cumberland Ave. The fare from Victoria costs C$40/80 one way/roundtrip.

Known as *the* place to ski on Vancouver Island, **Mt Washington Alpine Resort** (☎ 250-338-1386, W www.mtwashington.ca) stays open year round. From early December to late April, the resort features 50 Alpine ski runs, a snowboard park, cross-country and snow-shoe trails and a snow-tubing park. In summer, Mt Washington has horseback riding, fly-fishing and chair-lift rides for hikers and mountain bikers.

Campbell River

Vancouver Island's northernmost trading center, Campbell River (population 30,700), the self-proclaimed 'Salmon Capital of the World,' is a hot spot for salmon fishing and scuba diving on the sunken HBCS *Columbia*. It also acts as a supply depot for adventures north and west, and as the main departure point for Strathcona Provincial Park. Just a quick ferry hop from Campbell River are the remote **Quadra Island** and **Cortes Island**, often collectively called the 'Discovery Islands' for their location in the Discovery Passage.

For local information or to find out about **diving** and **fishing** outfitters, stop at the Visitor Info Centre (☎ 250-287-4636, fax 286-6490, W www.campbellrivertourism .bc.ca), 1235 Shoppers Row.

Canadian Regional (☎ 888-247-2262) and Pacific Coastal (☎ 800-663-2872) provide scheduled air service to Campbell River from Vancouver for about C$160 roundtrip. Kenmore Air (☎ 800-543-9595) operates float planes from Seattle for about C$360 roundtrip. Air Rainbow (☎ 250-287-8371, 888-287-8366) offers float-plane service from Vancouver for about C$420 roundtrip.

Island Coach Lines (☎ 250-287-7151), on the corner of 13th Ave and Cedar St, runs one daily bus north to Port Hardy (C$52.50 one way) and four buses south to Victoria (C$40).

The following are some local accommodations for every budget.

Elk Falls Provincial Park Sites C$12. This spot, 10km (6 miles) west of Campbell River on Hwy 28, is your best bet for camping near town.

Above Tide Motel (☎ 250-286-6231, 361 Island Hwy) Singles/doubles C$49/59. This is a quiet place to stay south of downtown, with ocean views.

Painter's Lodge Holiday & Fishing Resort (☎ 250-286-1102, 1625 MacDonald Rd) Rooms C$160 and up. Sport fishermen are the main clients at this fancy lodge, which has a restaurant and lots of activities.

Strathcona Provincial Park

By far the largest provincial park on Vancouver Island, 250,000-hectare (618,000-acre) Strathcona Provincial Park (☎ 250-337-2400) is BC's oldest protected area and a hiker's paradise. Campbell River is the main access point, with Hwy 28 cutting across the Buttle Lake district. The park's Forbidden Plateau area is reached via Courtenay, as is the popular Mt Washington alpine resort area, just outside the park. Della Falls, Canada's highest waterfall, also lies within Strathcona, but it's easiest to get to it by way of Port Alberni. Mt Golden Hinde (2200m, or 7217 feet), the highest point on Vancouver Island, occupies the center of the park west of Buttle Lake.

Strathcona runs a variety of programs, including 'Alpine to Ocean Adventures' (C$260 to C$1325), which feature hiking, canoeing and sea-kayaking trips to remote locales. Most visitors stay a week, but you'll find some overnight accommodations, ranging from a double room with shared bath (C$40) to a cabin that sleeps 12 (C$275). The dining-hall meals include both buffet options (breakfast and lunch C$9 each, dinner C$16; half-price for children under 12) and table service. You can rent kayaks and canoes or spend your time sampling the nearby hiking trails. Strathcona Park Lodge also operates a chalet at Mt Washington.

Strathcona has two campgrounds, both in the Buttle Lake area. Backcountry sites throughout the park cost C$3 per person.

Buttle Lake Campground Sites C$15. Both first-come, first-served and reservable sites are available here. The swimming area and the nearby playground make this a good choice for families.

Ralph River Campground (☎ 250-954-4600) Sites C$12. It's first-come, first-served at this campground, located 26km (16 miles) south of the Hwy 28 junction.

Strathcona Park Lodge (☎ 250-286-3122, fax 286-6010, e info@strathcona.bc.ca) Begun in 1959 as an outdoor education center, this family-run business on Hwy 28 maintains teaching as its mission. For most of the year, the lodge welcomes school-children for weeklong introductions to the natural world. In summer, the lodge becomes a base camp for travelers – especially families – eager to experience the outdoors with few distractions.

NORTHERN VANCOUVER ISLAND

Of the half million people who live on Vancouver Island, fewer than 20,000 reside north of Campbell River – even though this region takes up about half the island's land mass.

Port McNeill & Around

About 190km (118 miles) north of Campbell River along Hwy 19, you'll find the small community of **Telegraph Cove**, a major base for wildlife-watching tours. Keep going, and you'll get to Port McNeill (population 2700), a gateway to the nearby island communities of **Alert Bay** (population 600), on Cormorant Island, and **Sointula** (population 635), on Malcolm Island. You'll find the Visitor Info Centre (☎ 250-956-3131, fax 956-4633) at 351 Shelley Crest.

Air Rainbow (☎ 250-956-2020) offers float-plane service to and from Vancouver and Seattle. Laidlaw Coach Lines (☎ 250-949-7532) travels to Port McNeill from Victoria (C$82.50 one-way) and Nanaimo (C$65

BRITISH COLUMBIA

one-way). Rainbow Express Water Taxi Service (☎ 250-956-8294), on Beach Dr, offers kayak support and fishing charters.

Port McNeill makes a good base for **helicopter tours** and **scuba-diving** and **fishing** trips.

The best places to stay in these parts are the cozy B&Bs run by locals.

Tranquil Space B&B *(☎ 250-956-2002, 2702 Brockington Place)* Rooms from C$45. This low-key spot includes a self-catered breakfast.

Seeview B&B *(☎ 250-956-4818, 2291 Quatsino Crescent)* Rooms C$65-95. Slightly more upscale, the Seaview still offers reasonable prices, a full breakfast and a hot tub.

Haida-Way Motor Inn *(☎ 250-956-3373, 1817 Campbell Way)* Singles/doubles C$70/86. This comfortable inn offers free email access in the lobby, and its restaurant serves food all day.

Port Hardy & Around

This small town (population 5300) at the northern end of Vancouver Island is best known as a departure point for BC Ferries trips up the Inside Passage to Prince Rupert.

The area around Port Hardy offers good **salmon fishing**, **scuba diving** and **wildlife-watching**. For a list of outfitters, stop by the Visitor Info Centre (☎ 250-949-7622, fax 949-6653) at 7250 Market St. Pacific Coastal Airlines (☎ 250-949-6353, 800-663-2872) offers air service to Port Hardy from Vancouver, but there are no direct flights from Victoria. The standard adult, one-way fare from Vancouver is C$177, though prices vary by season and advance purchase. Laidlaw Coach Lines (☎ 250-949-7532), on the corner of Market and Hastings Sts, runs one bus a day to Victoria (C$92.50) and Nanaimo (C$75). North Island Transportation, operating out of the same office, runs a shuttle bus to and from the ferry terminal for C$5 one way. The bus will pick you up and drop you off wherever you're staying.

From mid-May to mid-October, BC Ferries sails the *Queen of the North* up the Inside Passage to Prince Rupert on spectac-

ular, 15-hour daylight trips. BC Ferries also runs the Discovery Coast Passage ferries that sail between Port Hardy and Bella Bella, and to Bella Coola, on the west coast of the BC mainland. Reservations are essential for both.

About 70km (40 miles) west of Port Hardy, the remote **Cape Scott Provincial Park** offers pristine beaches, challenging hiking and wilderness camping for those wishing to truly get away from it all.

Port Hardy fills up most nights from June through September with people waiting to catch the ferry, so book ahead.

Campgrounds include ***Wildwood Campsite*** *(☎ 250-949-6753)*, on the ferry terminal road, with sites for C$15; and ***Quatse River Campground*** *(☎ 250-949-2395, 8400 Byng Rd)*, where nice, shady tent sites cost C$16. This spot, 5km (3 miles) from the ferry terminal, has hot showers and a laundry facilities. Fishing opportunities abound here, where a portion of the proceeds goes toward salmon preservation.

This Old House Bed & Breakfast *(☎ 250-949-8372, 8735 Hastings St)* Singles/doubles/triples C$40/70/85. This B&B is handily near the bus depot and restaurants.

Oceanview Bed & Breakfast *(☎ 250-949-8302, 7735 Cedar Place)* Singles/doubles C$75/85. Stay here for lovely sea views, comfortable rooms and a delicious breakfast.

Quarterdeck Inn *(☎ 250-902-0455, 6555 Hardy Bay Rd)* Rooms C$100. This recently built inn offers waterfront views.

SOUTHERN GULF ISLANDS

When Canadians refer to British Columbia as 'lotus land,' the Gulf Islands are often what they have in mind. The mild climate, abundant flora and fauna, relative isolation and natural beauty combine to make the islands an escapist's dream. Indeed, the islands have attracted many retirees, artists and counterculture types who shun the nine-to-five grind of mainland life.

If you actually lived here, you might have to worry about having your well run dry in summer or finding a viable means of making a living. But as a visitor, you'll only encounter the abundant charms that make

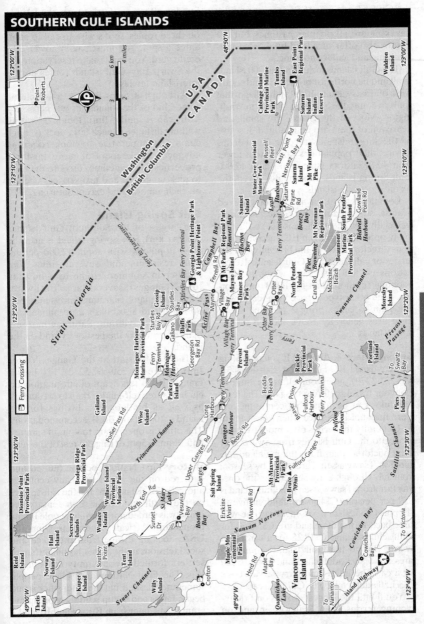

the Gulf Islands one of BC's most popular destinations. Scuba diving, sailing and kayaking are all popular pastimes, but the islands also offer such land-based pleasures as hiking and gallery hopping.

The Gulf Islands include about 200 islands in all and lie northeast of Victoria and southwest of Tsawwassen in an archipelago that spills over into the San Juan Islands, in Washington. Most of the islands are small, and nearly all of them are uninhabited. Just five of the larger islands receive BC Ferries service; their populations range from fewer than 400 (Saturna Island) to about 12,000 (Salt Spring Island). This chapter covers the six most popular islands.

Lodging is tight on all the ferry-served islands, so you must make reservations, especially for the high season. You'll find many options in Tourism BC's accommodations directory; pick up the brochures on the ferries or call Canadian Gulf Islands Reservations (☎ 888-539-2930), which handles bookings for more than 100 B&Bs, inns, cottages and other types of accommodations. If you plan to camp, bring a propane stove, since fires generally aren't allowed on the Gulf Islands.

Getting There & Around If you're visiting the islands via BC Ferries (☎ 250-386-3431, 888-223-3779), give yourself some time to plot your travels before setting out. The ferry schedules can be somewhat confusing, and there may not be service when you want to go. Generally, the ferries offer more frequent service to the Gulf Islands from Swartz Bay (near Victoria) than from the mainland terminal at Tsawwassen. Fares vary by season: from July through early September, the one-way fare from Tsawwassen to a Gulf Island is C$9 per person (C$4.50 for children five to 11), plus C$35.50 for a passenger car; one-way fares back to the mainland are C$5/2.50 for adults/children and C$18.25 for a car. From Swartz Bay to the Gulf Islands, roundtrip fares are C$6/3 adult/child and about C$20 for a car. The interisland ferry service costs C$3/1.50 adult/child, plus C$7 for a car.

You'll find the biggest crowds on Friday-evening ferries from Tsawwassen and on Sunday-afternoon ferries from the islands. You're allowed to reserve vehicular spaces on these routes, so it's wise to call to guarantee a spot. You must pay in advance by credit card. You can't make reservations for the Swartz Bay–Gulf Islands routes, nor for interisland ferries.

Although it helps to have a vehicle on some kind of the islands, it's not necessary. You can usually find lodgings within walking distance of each ferry dock (though again, it's imperative to book rooms in advance). Innkeepers of more far-flung properties will sometimes drive to the dock to pick up guests, and taxi services operate on each major island except Saturna.

Salt Spring Island

The largest of the Southern Gulf Islands (180 sq km), Salt Spring Island is also the most populous, with about 12,000 permanent residents and several times that number in summer. Home to a bustling town (Ganges), several large freshwater lakes and many charming farmsteads, Salt Spring Island also boasts a prominent arts scene and a vibrant Saturday-morning market, probably the best of its kind on the islands.

The helpful staff at the Ganges Visitor Info Centre (☎ 250-537-5252), 121 Lower Ganges Rd, offers heaps of information, including a free self-guided map to art studios, as well as binders with listings for the island's 100 or so B&B accommodations. The office is open 10am to 4pm in summer and 11am to 3pm during the rest of the year.

History First Nations people hunted and gathered on the island for many centuries and called it 'Klaathem' for the salt springs on the north end. In the 19th century, the island was settled not by white people but by pioneering African Americans from the USA. Seeking escape from prejudice and social tensions in the States, a small group of settlers formed a community at Vesuvius Bay. The First Nations and black people sometimes clashed, but the latter stuck it out, began farms and set up schools. More immigrants came later from Britain and Ireland.

Salt Spring Island was BC's major fruit-growing area until the 1930s, when the Okanagan region took over. But the island retains its agricultural heritage today, as local farms produce everything from apples to organic cheese to some of Canada's best lamb and wool. In fact, sheep serve as the unofficial symbol of Salt Spring Island; they graze in pastures, and sheep signposts point the way to local artists' studios.

Ganges All roads on Salt Spring lead to Ganges, the island's main commercial center. Ganges' well-known **Market in the Park** (☎ 250-537-4448) features wares from local artists, craftspeople and farmers. It takes place 8am to 4pm Saturday from April through October. The Salt Spring **Festival of the Arts** (☎ 250-537-4167) takes place each July, when local and touring artists present music, theater and dance performances.

Ruckle Provincial Park (☎ 250-653-4115) ranks among the best parks in the Gulf Islands, with good camping and a beautiful shoreline along Beaver Point. Set on the site of one of the oldest family farms in BC (established in 1872), the park still contains an active farmstead. Ruckle also features some easy hiking trails through forests and along the shore and offers opportunities for fishing, bicycling and boating. **Mt Maxwell Provincial Park** contains one of the Gulf Islands' most accessible viewpoints. It's about 9km (5.6 miles) off the main road, on a route safe for all but large RVs and trailers. Mt Bruce (709m, or 2326 feet) caps the park and offers sweeping views of Salt Spring Island and beyond.

Activities The narrow, winding and steep roads here don't discourage many people from **cycling**. Pick up the *Cycling Map of Salt Spring Island* (C50¢) at the Visitor Info Centre to find the best local routes. Another good publication, *Salt Spring Out of Doors*, costs less than C$5 and includes details on hiking trails, beach-access points, historic sites, berry picking and more. **Salt Spring Kayaking** (☎ *250-653-4222, 2923 Fulford-Ganges Rd*), at Fulford Wharf, rents **bicycles** for C$5/25 per hour/day. It also rents

kayaks for C$12/20 single/double per hour. **Sea Otter Kayaking** (☎ *250-537-5678, 1186 North End Rd*), rents kayaks and offers guided trips that depart from the foot of Rainbow Rd at Ganges Harbour.

If you'd rather have someone else be skipper, **Herberg Charters** (☎ *250-537-9321, 888-293-1603*) features **boat trips** by the hour, day or longer.

Places to Stay Check with the Visitor Info Center for the B&B listings on the island. Motel accommodations are in somewhat limited supply on Salt Spring, but there are a few good choices.

Ruckle Provincial Park (☎ *250-391-2300*) Sites C$12. This beautiful campground offers 70 primitive, mostly walk-in campsites near the ocean on a first-come, first-served basis.

Salt Spring Island Hostel (☎ *250-537-4149, e hostel@saltspring.com, 640 Cusheon Lake Rd*) Beds C$15.50/19.50 members/ nonmembers; tree house C$50/60. Tucked away in the woods, this Hostelling International affiliate offers everything from dorm beds to romantic adults-only rooms in a tree house. Amenities include Internet access, kitchen facilities, communal campfires and a short trail to one of the prettiest waterfalls in the Gulf Islands.

Seabreeze Inn (☎ *250-537-4145, fax 537-4323, e seabreeze@saltspring.com, 101 Bittancourt Rd*) Rooms from C$70. This quiet spot offers rooms overlooking Ganges Harbour.

Salty Springs Spa & Seaside Resort (☎ *250-537-4111, fax 537-2939, 1460 North Beach Rd*) Rooms from C$190. Near Vesuvius Bay, this health-oriented resort features upscale seaside chalets with fireplaces, some with kitchens. The indulgent activities here include massages, body wraps, yoga and more.

Places to Eat There are some pleasant waterfront restaurants in the Ganges area.

Treehouse Café (☎ *250-537-5379, 106 Purvis Lane*) Breakfast & lunch C$3-8. Close to the Ganges waterfront, this hip cafe features outdoor tables and reasonable prices. In July and August, it stays open for dinner as well, with live music some evenings.

Moby's Marine Pub (☎ 250-537-5559, 124 Upper Ganges Rd) Entrees C$7-12. With a lively atmosphere, excellent views of Ganges Harbour and good food, Moby's is a popular island hangout and a great spot for lunch or dinner. On Sunday, come for brunch in the morning or live jazz in the evening.

Alfresco Waterfront Restaurant (☎ 250-537-5979) Entrees C$8-17. In Ganges' Grace Point Square, this restaurant serves everything from good burgers to pasta and seafood, and there's a patio.

Getting There & Away Several seaplane companies serve Salt Spring: Seair (☎ 800-447-3247), Pacific Spirit Air (☎ 800-665-2359) and Harbour Air (☎ 800-665-0212). All offer daily scheduled flights between the Vancouver area and the Gulf Islands. The one-way/roundtrip fare to Ganges is about C$60/120.

Most visitors arrive by boat. Salt Spring has three BC Ferries terminals: at Long Harbour, Fulford Harbour and Vesuvius Bay. Boats sail twice daily between Tsawwassen and Long Harbour (sometimes more in summer). Ferries travel more frequently between Tsawwassen and Swartz Bay, where you can transfer to a boat bound for Salt Spring's Fulford Harbour. Swartz Bay-Fulford ferries run about eight times a day. There are more than a dozen daily sailings between Vesuvius Bay and Crofton, roughly midway between Victoria and Nanaimo.

North & South Pender Islands

Recreation trumps the arts on the Pender Islands – where are actually two islands joined by a short bridge. You may see some artists' studios here, but the more than 1000 islanders prefer to spend their time playing in the glorious natural surroundings. The Penders fall in the geographical center of the Gulf and San Juan Islands – and this, locals would have you believe, makes them the center of the universe. It's an undeniably spectacular place, where the sea, sky and neighboring islands all seem close enough to touch.

If the Visitor Info Centre (☎ 250-629-6541), 2332 Otter Bay Rd, on North Pender, isn't open when you arrive, you'll still find a helpful informational board listing the locations and phone numbers of lodgings and other businesses. You won't find ATMs anywhere on the Penders, so come prepared.

Things to See & Do The Penders have much to offer for the outdoor enthusiast.

Prior Centennial Provincial Park, on North Pender, features a short walking trail and forested campsites that draw many cyclists. It's just a few hundred meters away from **Medicine Beach**, a good sunbathing spot at Bedwell Harbour.

Just over the bridge to South Pender, take the moderately steep, hour-long hike up and down **Mt Norman** (255m, or 836 feet) for some grand views of the San Juan Islands, Vancouver Island and (on a clear day) Washington state's Cascade Mountains.

If you want to lounge on the sand, the nicest beaches include **Hamilton Beach**, in Browning Harbour, on North Pender, and **Mortimer Spit**, on South Pender. Watch for the more or less tame deer around the islands.

Cycling is popular on the Penders, but use caution on the winding, narrow roads. Rent bikes at Otter Bay Marina, Cooper's Landing, Bedwell Harbour Island Resort or the Driftwood Auto Centre (part of the Driftwood Centre).

Kayak Pender Island (☎ 250-629-6939, 2319 MacKinnon Rd), at Otter Bay Marina, on North Pender, offers guided kayaking tours (C$35/30 for adults/children) and lessons (C$50).

Places to Stay Accommodations here are generally pretty affordable.

Prior Centennial Provincial Park (☎ 250-391-2300) Sites C$12. With just 17 campsites, this campground fills up fast. Reserve by calling ☎ 800-689-9025 (in Greater Victoria, ☎ 604-689-9025). Sites also are available at Beaumont Provincial Marine Park, on South Pender, but the park is only reachable by private boat.

Otter Bay Marina (☎ 250-629-3579, 2319 MacKinnon Rd) On North Pender, close to the ferry terminal, this marina rents a dozen large, waterproof tents that sleep up to four people (C$35). They're carpeted, and they come with two cots. A single furnished cabin with cooking facilities can accommodate up to three people for C$75.

Cooper's Landing (☎ 250-629-6133, 888-921-3111, ℮ info@cooperslanding.com, 5734 Canal Rd) Dorm beds C$20/30 members/nonmembers; outside tipi beds C$15; singles/doubles in lodge C$64/85 (shared bath). On the North Pender side, this wonderful HI hostel offers a magical combination of reasonably priced accommodations and abundant recreation. This former scuba-diving lodge still offers trips for experienced divers, along with bike rentals, kayak rentals and lessons, nature tours, and canoe trips. The Mt Norman trailhead is a 10-minute walk away. A sauna or massage might not sound bad after all that activity, so Cooper's Landing offers those, too.

Inn on Pender Island (☎ 250-629-3353, 800-550-1572, 4709 Canal Rd) Singles/doubles C$70/80. This small motel in the woods on North Pender is popular with cyclists. The rooms are simple but comfortable. A few cabins – with private hot tubs or porches with good views – sleep up to three people for C$130. The inn also features a hot tub and room service for the continental breakfast.

Places to Eat The following are some recommendable dining options.

Memories at the Inn (☎ 250-629-3353). Entrees C$7-20. Adjacent to the Inn on Pender Island, Memories serves both excellent pizza and fine-dining fare, such as peel-and-eat prawns steamed in Kokanee beer.

Islanders Restaurant (☎ 250-629-6811, 1325 MacKinnon Rd) Entrees C$10-26. On North Pender, this small and refined restaurant features a range of unusual dishes, from an open-faced shrimp sandwich to wild Arctic musk ox.

Getting There & Around BC Ferries offers transportation from the Penders to Tsawwassen (once or twice daily; reservations are suggested on weekends), Swartz Bay (about seven or eight times Monday to Saturday; four times Sunday), Galiano and Mayne Islands (two to four times daily), Salt Spring Island/Long Harbour (once or twice daily) and Saturna Island (once or twice daily except Sunday).

Since you can find several lodging options close to the ferry dock, a car isn't an absolute necessity. If you have no wheels and your accommodations host can't pick you up, you can always catch a ride with Pender Island Taxi (☎ 250-629-6050).

Saturna Island

The most lightly populated island, Saturna is a bit harder to reach than the other main Gulf Islands. To many people, however, this inaccessibility makes it all the more attractive as a remote and tranquil escape for a few days or more.

For the latest local information, pick up a copy of the annual Saturna Island map brochure on one of the BC Ferries, or see ⓦ www.saturnatourism.bc.ca.

BC Ferries sails to Lyall Harbour on Saturna, but to get there from Tsawwassen, you must either sail through Swartz Bay or transfer at Mayne Island. Either way, plan to spend two to four hours on most of the roundabout voyages, some of which don't dock at Saturna until nearly 10pm. BC Ferries leave Tsawwassen for Saturna via Swartz Bay or Mayne Island twice daily on weekdays and once daily on weekends. You can reserve vehicle space on these ferries by asking for a 'through-fare' if you travel from Tsawwassen to Saturna via Swartz Bay. Ferries sail to Saturna from Swartz Bay four times daily on Saturday and Monday through Thursday, five times on Friday and twice on Sunday, but no vehicle reservations are accepted for the ferry from Swartz Bay.

Saturna, like the other Gulf Islands, has its share of resident artists. See the annual map brochure for a listing of those who invite visitors to their studios, usually by appointment. Gallery Rosa (☎ 250-539-2866), 111 East Point Rd, offers a selection of local works. It's open weekend and holiday afternoons.

BRITISH COLUMBIA

Winter Cove Provincial Marine Park, on the island's north side, features a sandy beach and offers access to fishing, boating and hiking. At the top of **Mt Warburton Pike**, you'll find a wildlife reserve with feral goats and fine views, though you'll also have to look at a mess of telecommunications equipment.

For **swimming**, try Veruna Bay, near Winter Cove; Russell Reef, off the east side of the island; or East Point Regional Park, where you can also experience some of the best **whale watching** in the Southern Gulf Islands. **Saturna Sea Kayaking** (☎ 250-539-5553), in Boot Cove (only a five-minute walk from the ferry), offers kayaking lessons and rentals, along with good paddling advice for Saturna and surrounding islands.

There are no campgrounds on Saturna Island and no more than a dozen places to stay indoors, so it's important to book well ahead for a stay here.

Breezy Bay B&B (☎ 250-539-2937, e *breezybay@gulfislands.com, 131 Payne Rd*) Singles/doubles C$60/70. On a small farm less than 1.5km from the ferry terminal, Breezy Bay's innkeeper Renie Muir takes a special interest in the people and culture of India, and many photos of her travels decorate the walls.

East Point Resort (☎ 250-539-2975) Rooms from C$80. Demanding a seven-day minimum during the high season, this resort offers six cottages on the waterfront, with private sandy-beach access and forested trails.

Saturna Lodge (☎ 250-539-2254, 888-539-8800, fax 250-539-3091, e *saturnalodge@ hotmail.com, 130 Payne Rd*) Rooms C$135-195. Managing to be upscale but unpretentious, this lodge offers rooms that include a gourmet breakfast, access to the hot tub, bicycles, badminton and croquet. There is also fine dining on the premises.

Mayne Island

If you're a geographer or an anthropologist, you won't find a much more interesting spot on the Gulf Islands than Mayne Island. First off, for the natural-history buffs, the bay

fronts on Active Pass, a narrow channel that's the tightest squeeze on the Tsawwassen-Swartz Bay BC Ferries route. The human history of the island is also unique. In the 19th century, gold rushers congregated here, halfway between Vancouver Island and the Fraser River, to fortify themselves for the rest of their trip. Today, Mayne Island has attracted a number of resident artists, musicians and writers, plus plenty of professional people who have set up second (and third) homes on this less-visited island.

On the ferry en route to the island, pick up a free Mayne Island brochure, which contains current listings of places to stay, eat and play, plus a good map. You'll also find an information panel set up just past the Village Bay ferry terminal, on the right-hand side. For more local information, visit the website w www.mayneislandchamber.ca. Note, there are no ATMs on Mayne Island.

Things to See & Do The **Plumper Pass Lock-up** (☎ 250-539-5286), at Miners Bay, once served as a jailhouse for late-19th-century rowdies. Now it's a museum, open 11am to 3pm Friday through Monday late June through early September or by appointment. About two dozen **artists' studios** operate on Mayne, with wildly varying hours. A brochure available across the island lists their addresses and phone numbers. Fernhill Centre, 574 Fernhill Rd (about halfway between Miners Bay and Bennett Bay), includes several galleries and gift shops featuring local works.

The hour-long roundtrip hike to the top of **Mt Parke** will reward you with great 360° views of Active Pass, the Gulf Islands and beyond. The trailhead is at the end of Montrose Dr, near Fernhill Centre.

If you're looking for good **beaches**, head to Dinner Bay Park, on Mayne's south shore; Campbell Bay, on the northeast side; or Georgina Point Heritage Park and Lighthouse Point, at the island's northern tip.

Mayne Island Kayak & Canoe Rentals (☎ 250-539-2667 or 539-0077) offers kayaking instruction and fast-boat pickups at remote locations for people who don't want to paddle back to Mayne. Kayak and canoe rentals are C\$42 per 24-hour period, but rates go down for multiday rentals.

Places to Stay The following are some good places to stay.

Mayne Island Kayak & Canoe Rentals (☎ 250-539-2667, **W** www.maynekayak.com) Tent sites C\$12 per person. At Seal Beach near Miners Bay, this company offers waterfront tent camping, with a hot tub and outdoor showers.

Tinkerers B&B & Till Eulenspiegel Guesthouse B&B (☎ 250-539-2280, **e** tinkerers@gulfnet.pinc.com) Rooms C\$65-95. Along Sunset Place, in Miners Bay, these two accommodations share ownership and an international clientele. The staff speaks Spanish and German, as well as English, and the owners offer language-practicum programs. But if that's not your thing, you can simply laze about the hammock, enjoy the sea views or go for a bike ride.

Root Seller Inn (☎ 250-539-2621) Singles/doubles C\$50/70. A self-catering budget B&B at Miners Bay, this spot attracts cyclists and other active guests.

Springwater Lodge (☎ 250-539-5521, **e** springwaterlodge@netscape.net) Rooms with shared bath C\$40; two-bedroom cabins C\$85. Built on Miners Bay in the 1890s, the Springwater is now possibly the oldest continuously operating hotel in BC, a good place to sleep and an even better place to eat.

Getting There & Away BC Ferries docks at Village Bay, on Mayne Island's west side. Ferries arrive from Tsawwassen about twice daily. Reservations are encouraged all week long, and they're necessary for the Friday-evening and Saturday-morning sailings. Service from Swartz Bay is more frequent, about five or six times daily. Ferries also run between Mayne and Galiano, Salt Spring, Saturna and the Pender Islands.

Galiano Island

Despite its proximity to Tsawwassen (it's the closest of the major Southern Gulf Islands), the dry, long and narrow Galiano Island maintains an uncrowded feel. Only about 1000 people live here, most of them on the southeast side of the island, near Sturdies Bay. Despite the small population, Galiano boasts a thriving community of artists and writers, notably Jane Rule and Audrey Thomas. The island's creative energy inspires residents and tourists alike. Wilderness prevails beyond Sturdies Bay, from the sheer rock cliffs below Bodega Ridge to the many small islands just off Galiano's coast. The island's excellent beaches include the superlative Montague Harbour Provincial Marine Park.

As always, look for the helpful island map brochure on the ferry, or stop by the information shack on your right-hand side as you leave the ferry terminal at Sturdies Bay. For more information, call the Galiano Chamber of Commerce (☎ 250-539-2233), see the island's website at **W** www.galianoisland .com, or write to PO Box 73, Galiano Island, BC V0N 1P0. Galiano Island has no banks or ATMs.

Activities With its sheltered setting, **Montague Harbour Provincial Marine Park** (see Places to Stay, next) is one of the two best provincial parks in the Southern Gulf Islands (the other is Ruckle Provincial Park, on Salt Spring.) A trail leads from the campground along a long stretch of crushed-shell beach where First Nations people once shucked their seafood harvest. Today, it's a superb spot to watch a sunset. Take care not to walk on the sand spits, where rare black oyster-catcher birds lay their eggs April through August.

Bluffs Park boasts great views of Active Pass, along with 5km (3 miles) of hiking paths. You can access the park by rough but passable Bluff Rd, which leads between Burrill and Georgeson Bay Rds. Known for its abundant and colorful bird life, **Bodega Ridge Provincial Park** also contains the highest point on the island, the 382m (1253-foot) Bodega Hill. Kayakers like to camp at **Dionisio Point Provincial Park**, at the island's far northwest end; the park can only be reached by boat or via the hiking trail from Devina Dr.

You'll find good scuba diving around Galiano. For gear and tours, contact

Galiano Island Diving *(☎ 250-539-3109, 1005 Devina Dr).*

Kayaking is terrific off Galiano Island. **Gulf Island Kayaking** *(☎ 250-539-2442),* at Montague Marina, specializes in half-day trips (about C$40) and two- to seven-day camping tours (starting at C$155 without meals, C$245 fully catered). The **Sutil Lodge** *(☎ 888-539-2930; see Places to Stay, below)* provides kayak rentals, lessons, and guided tours starting as low as C$20.

The island's narrow, hilly roads make cycling a challenge, but if you're up for it, rent bikes at **Galiano Bicycle Rental & Repair** *(☎ 250-539-9906, 36 Burrill Rd),* near Sturdies Bay. For something different, try the **scooter** rentals (C$22 per hour) at Montague Marina.

Places to Stay Accommodations on Galiano Island are interesting and diverse.

Montague Harbour Provincial Marine Park *(☎ 250-391-2300, reservations ☎ 800-689-9025, in Greater Vancouver ☎ 604-689-9025)* Sites C$15. About 9.5km (6 miles) from the Sturdies Bay ferry terminal, this park includes 25 primitive drive-in and 15 walk-in campsites.

Glenn Gulch Farm *(☎ 250-539-5218, ℮ ggfarm@island.net, 1721 Porlier Pass Rd).* No hostels grace Galiano, but you can exchange six hours of chores at this working organic farm for basic bed and board. Call ahead or just stop by. Even if you don't stay here, you can drop by the farm to stock up on fresh produce, free-range poultry and pork, cut flowers and more.

Sutil Lodge *(☎ 250-539-2930, 888-539-2930, ℮ reservations@gulfislands.com, 637 Southwind Dr)* Singles/doubles start at C$60/75. Galiano has quite a few B&Bs, including this, one of the oldest, which dates from the 1920s. Since it's near the beach at Montague Harbour, the lodge offers free use of canoes, plus on-site kayak rentals. Ask about spring package deals.

Galiano Lodge *(☎ 250-539-3388, 877-530-3939, ℮ galianolodge@gulfislands.com, 134 Madrona Dr)* Rooms C$75-150. The plush rooms here are among the best deals on Galiano. They all include fireplaces,

patios and a continental breakfast buffet. A few simpler rooms outside the main lodge cost C$50. Just a five-minute walk from the ferry terminal, the lodge offers beach access.

Bodega Resort *(☎ 250-539-2677, 120 Cook Rd)* Doubles from C$80, plus C$20/10 for extra adult/child. The two-story fully furnished log cottages here can sleep up to six people. Two rooms in the main lodge go for C$40 and C$60, including breakfast. Innkeepers Barb Geary and Steve Ocsko are friendly folks; Steve also is a talented stone carver whose works adorn the grounds.

Places to Eat Try one of these places for a unique meal and a fun time.

Max & Moritz Spicy Island Food House *(☎ 250-539-5888)* Entrees C$3-8. Arrive early at the ferry so you can sample this delicious Indonesian and German food – yes,

---

Idyllic Arts Retreats

Galiano Island offers two unusual retreats for travelers hooked on books or cinema. Bibliophiles should enjoy the **Weekends for Readers** (☎ 250-539-2764, **w** www .duthiebooks.com/galiano), hosted by the legendary Celia Duthie, who is now retired from the Vancouver bookstore that bears her name. Held at the Bodega Resort, these weekends allow ample time for avid book lovers to read and talk about beloved (or not-so-beloved) tomes. Each features a noted author, with past guests including mystery writer William Deverell, poet Susan Musgrave and writer/designer Barbara Hodgson. A readers' weekend costs C$300/500 single/double occupancy, with most meals provided.

The **Gulf Islands Film & Television School** (GIFTS; ☎ 250-539-3290, **w** www.youth films.com) bills itself as a 'film, video and animation boot camp.' Mainly, it offers courses for kids ages 10 to 19, but adults can sign up for weeklong programs in drama and documentary filmmaking. Every student leaves with a complete, original video. The cost is C$595, plus C$245 for room and board.

that's right. Dishes include pita breakfast sandwiches, Berliner currywurst and the awesome ayam bumbu kacang, a grilled chicken breast with peanut sauce, rice and veggies. Bring your own plate (or cup, for drinks) and get 25¢ off.

Hummingbird Pub *(☎ 250-539-5472, 47 Sturdies Bay Rd)* Entrees C$7-10. This lively pub features live entertainment on summer weekends and an outdoor picnic and barbecue area.

Getting There & Around BC Ferries serves Sturdies Bay on the island's east side. Boats bound for Galiano leave twice daily from Tsawwassen; reservations are essential for the Friday-evening and Saturday-morning boats. Ferries from Swartz Bay arrive at Galiano four times a day. There's also service between Galiano and Salt Spring, Mayne and the Pender Islands.

Go Galiano Island Shuttle (☎ 250-539-0202) meets the ferries daily in July and August and on weekends in May, June and September. Rides cost C$3 per person between Sturdies Bay and Montague Harbour.

Gabriola Island

Considered the most northerly of the Southern Gulf Islands, Gabriola Island makes a fine trip from Nanaimo for an afternoon or longer. Hundreds of artists live on the island, but it's just as well known for its scenery, recreation and unusual sandstone caves.

The Visitor Info Centre (☎ 250-247-9332, ⓦ www.gabriolaisland.org), 575 North Rd, in the Folklife Village Shopping Centre, is open May through September.

Pacific Spirit Air offers daily seaplane flights from Vancouver to Silva Bay, on the south end of Gabriola. The 12-minute flight costs C$130 roundtrip. BC Ferries travels between Nanaimo and Gabriola Island about 15 times daily. The peak-season roundtrip fare for the 20-minute trip is C$5.25/13.50 per passenger/car. The Nanaimo dock is near the Harbour Park Mall.

The following places to stay are all convenient to Gabriola's ferry terminal.

Gabriola Campground *(☎ 250-247-2079)* Sites C$15. For campers, this spot is convenient to the ferry and has 28 beachside campsites.

Casa Blanca by the Sea *(☎ 250-247-9824, 1707 El Verano Dr)* Singles/doubles C$50/60, suite C$80. This B&B-style inn also has kayak rentals and guided tours starting at C$25.

Surf Lodge *(☎ 250-247-9231, fax 250-247-8336, ⓔ surflod@island.net, 885 Berry Point Rd)* Rooms/cabins C$85-105/95-165. This lodge's Sunset Lounge serves great fish and chips (C$8.75). Bald eagles often perch high in the treetops just outside.

BRITISH COLUMBIA

Thanks

Many thanks to the readers who wrote to us with helpful anecdotes, tips and advice:

Ethan Ashley, Charles Citroen, Kay Cook, Patricia Covey, Bo Dahlborg, Jim Feist, Mike Gorman, Lise Guyot, Martin Hall, Trisha Howell, Mike Jacobs, Jane King, Andreas Lober, Michael Marquardt, Shannon O'Loughlin, David Plourde, Heiko Rupp, Rick Samuels, Sue Sollars, Priscilla Stone, Chris Tudor, Chris Webber, Christine Wegener, Jennifer Whitley, Clive & Joan Wilkinson, Trevor Willson, J Davis Wilson and Jessica Young

Index

Bold indicates maps.

Bold indicates maps.

Bold indicates maps.

Bold indicates maps.

T

U

Boxed Text

MAP LEGEND

ROUTES

City | **Regional**

Freeway	Pedestrian Mall
Tollway	Steps
Primary Road	Tunnel
Secondary Road	Trail
Tertiary Road	Walking Tour
Dirt Road	Path

TRANSPORTATION

Train	Bus Route
Metro	Ferry

HYDROGRAPHY

River; Creek	Spring; Rapids
Canal	Waterfalls
Lake	Glacier

ROUTE SHIELDS

80 Interstate Freeway	F7 US Forest Service Road	95 State Highway
101 US Highway	1 Trans-Canada Highway	G4 County Road

BOUNDARIES

International	County
State	Disputed

AREAS

Beach	Cemetery	Golf Course	Reservation
Building	Forest; Wilderness	Park	Sports Field
Campus	Garden; Zoo	Plaza; Military	Swamp; Mangrove

POPULATION SYMBOLS

○ NATIONAL CAPITAL ... National Capital	● **Large City** ... Large City	● Small City ... Small City
◉ STATE CAPITAL ... State Capital	● **Medium City** ... Medium City	○ Town; Village ... Town; Village

MAP SYMBOLS

■ ... Place to Stay	▼ ... Place to Eat	● ... Point of Interest

Airfield	Church	Museum	Skiing - Downhill
Airport	Cinema	Observatory	Stately Home
Archeological Site; Ruin	Dive Site	Park	Surfing
Bank	Fishing	Parking Area	Synagogue
Baseball Diamond	Footbridge	Pass	Tao Temple
Battlefield	Gas Station	Picnic Area	Taxi
Bike Trail	Hospital	Police Station	Telephone
Border Crossing	Information	Pool	Theater
Buddhist Temple	Internet Access	Post Office	Toilet - Public
Bus Station; Terminal	Lighthouse	Pub; Bar	Tomb
Cable Car; Chairlift	Lookout	RV Park	Trailhead
Campground	Mine	Shelter	Tram Stop
Castle	Mission	Shipwreck	Transportation
Cathedral	Monument	Shopping Mall	Winery
Cave	Mountain	Skiing - Cross Country	Zoo

Note: Not all symbols displayed above appear in this book.

LONELY PLANET OFFICES

Australia
Locked Bag 1, Footscray, Victoria 3011
☎ 03 8379 8000 fax 03 8379 8111
email talk2us@lonelyplanet.com.au

UK
10a Spring Place, London NW5 3BH
☎ 020 7428 4800 fax 020 7428 4828
email go@lonelyplanet.co.uk

USA
150 Linden Street, Oakland, CA 94607
☎ 510 893 8555, TOLL FREE 800 275 8555
fax 510 893 8572
email info@lonelyplanet.com

France
1 rue du Dahomey, 75011 Paris
☎ 01 55 25 33 00 fax 01 55 25 33 01
email bip@lonelyplanet.fr
www.lonelyplanet.fr

World Wide Web: www.lonelyplanet.com *or* AOL keyword: lp
Lonely Planet Images: lpi@lonelyplanet.com.au

PORTLAND

COLUMBIA RIVER GORGE & MT HOOD

OREGON COAST

WILLAMETTE VALLEY

SOUTHERN OREGON

CENTRAL OREGON

Contents

Pacific Northwest
3rd edition – June 2002
First published – October 1995

Published by
Lonely Planet Publications Pty Ltd ABN 36 005 607 983
90 Maribyrnong St, Footscray, Victoria 3011, Australia

Lonely Planet Offices
Australia Locked Bag 1, Footscray, Victoria 3011
USA 150 Linden St, Oakland, CA 94607
UK 10a Spring Place, London NW5 3BH
France 1 rue du Dahomey, 75011 Paris

Photographs
Many of the images in this guide are available for licensing from
Lonely Planet Images.
W www.lonelyplanetimages.com

Front cover photograph
Dead Horse Trail Paradise Area
in Mt Rainier National Park (Richard Cummins)

ISBN 1 86450 377 7

Elevation

14,000 ft
12,000 ft
8000 ft
4000 ft
2000 ft
1000 ft
Sea Level

0 — 25 — 40 — 80 km
0 — 25 — 50 miles

Volcanic Monument
This peak blew its top in 1980; three viewer centers now provide access to the eerie ash-strewn landscapes

Portland
An easygoing city with a great downtown, roses galore and volcanoes right out its back door

Columbia River Gorge
Windsurfing, waterfalls and enchanting forest hikes in a canyon cut through the Cascade Range

Mt Hood
Oregon's highest peak, with year-round skiing and the WPA-era Timberline Lodge

Oregon Coast
There are 300 miles of it, all preserved as public land by a farsighted state government

Ashland
Famous for its Shakespeare festival, b&bs, good restaurants and summertime crowds

Crater Lake National Park
An imposingly blue-green lake in the mouth of an ancient volcano – bring your camera

John Day Fossil Beds National Monument
Miocene-era animal graveyards and some of Oregon's most dramatic scenery

Steens Mountain
A desert mountain range with cliffs dropping 5000ft from alpine meadows into hot borax lakebeds